סידור קורן יחד

The Koren Yachad Siddur

YACHAD

קוֹרֵן ירושלים

OUPRESS

THE LEGACY HERITAGE EDITION

סידור קורן יחד
THE KOREN YACHAD SIDDUR

סידור לימות החול ולשבת

יחד
שבטי
ישראל

TRANSLATION AND COMMENTARY BY

Rabbi Dr. Benjy Leibowitz
and Michael Adler

•

KOREN PUBLISHERS JERUSALEM
OU PRESS

The Koren Yachad Siddur
First Hebrew/English Edition, 2022
Combined American/Canadian Edition

Koren Publishers Jerusalem Ltd.
POB 4044, Jerusalem 91040, ISRAEL
POB 8531, New Milford, CT 06776, USA
www.korenpub.com

OU Press, an imprint of the Orthodox Union
11 Broadway, New York, NY 10004
www.oupress.org

Printed in the PRC

Standard Size, Hardcover, ISBN 978 965 301 986 7

KYSA02

This Siddur is dedicated
in loving memory of

Ida Cabakoff ז״ל

a unique individual
who did not let her special needs define her.

As a young girl, Ida was diagnosed with debilitating tuberculosis of the spine. Despite severe handicaps, including an impaired spine and leg, she lived a full and meaningful life. At a time when people with disabilities were not accommodated, Ida refused to be cowed. She was active and productive, never using her illness as an excuse. She helped raise her young siblings, went on to assist her brother with his dental practice and then worked thirteen-hour days at Bella (her sister) and Harry Wexner's retail business. Remarkably, even with all of her formidable challenges, Ida retained her sunny personality.

Ida Cabakoff surely would be proud that, in her memory, people with special needs will now have a Siddur designed to help them express in prayer their hopes and aspirations.

Lovingly dedicated by Legacy Heritage Fund
July 2019

DEDICATION

The concept of the **Koren Yachad Siddur** started when our son Jacob had his Bar Mitzva and we realized there were no appropriate Siddurim for adults with special needs. Once the idea of producing a Siddur for Yachad was conceived, Jacob made sure it became a reality. Jacob's amazing relationship with *Hashem*, his desire to pray with a congregation, and his boundless determination have been the driving force for this project. So first and foremost, we dedicate this Siddur to our wonderful, tenacious, sweet, and soulful son Jacob, and to his siblings, Shaina and Seth, who have done so much to participate in and support Yachad.

We further dedicate this Siddur to the incredible staff and volunteers at the OU and Yachad for their tireless efforts to create so many opportunities for Jews of all abilities to participate in all aspects of Jewish life. Rabbi Nachman of Breslov would say, "*The day you were born, that is the day on which Hashem declared that the world could not be preserved without you.*" This simple statement underscores the importance of every single person. Yachad, along with its staff and volunteers, is the living embodiment of this principle. Their efforts have enriched the lives of so many people.

Finally, we dedicate this Siddur
to the loving memory of our parents,
חיים יהודה בן דוד ע״ה Allen Gross;
ישראל בן אברהם ע״ה Raymond Goldbaum; and
צביה בת יוסף ע״ה Vicki Goldbaum.

May it be *Hashem*'s will
that every time someone uses this Siddur,
that it provides an *aliya* for all their *neshamot*.

Ethan and Yael Gross

ICONS KEY

Throughout this Siddur, the following icons are used to help you know when to perform the following actions:

- TZITZIT: touch or kiss the tzitzit.
- TALLIT: wrap yourself in the tallit.
- TEFILLIN SHEL YAD: wrap or touch the tefillin on your arm.
- TEFILLIN SHEL ROSH: tighten or touch the tefillin on your head.
- STAND: stand for this section of prayer.
- SIT: sit for this section of prayer.
- BOW: bow when reciting these words.
- COVER EYES: cover your eyes while reciting these words.
- STRIKE CHEST: strike the left side of your chest.
- LEAN HEAD: Lean head on arm while sitting when reciting this paragraph.
- SHABBAT: recite these words on Shabbat.
- SUCCOT/FOUR SPECIES: wave the four species or recite words on Sukkot.
- PESACH: recite these words on Pesach.

COLOR KEY

A stripe in this color on the margin of the page indicates important tefillot.

Throughout this Siddur, the following colors are used to help you follow the tefillot:

- *Text that appears in this color is recited only by the* Leader.
- *Text that appears in this color has* commentary on the bottom of the page.
- *Text that appears with this shaded background is recited on* Aseret Yemei Teshuva.
- *Text that appears with this shaded background is recited on* Rosh Chodesh and Chol HaMoed.
- *Text that appears with this shaded background is recited on* Chanuka and Purim.
- *Text that appears with this shaded background is recited on* Fast Days.

ICON KEY

Throughout this siddur, the following icons are used to help you know when to perform the following actions:

TZITZIT: touch or kiss the tzitzit.

TALLIT: wrap yourself in the tallit.

TEFILLIN SHEL YAD: wrap or touch the tefillin on your arm.

TEFILLIN SHEL ROSH: tighten or touch the tefillin on your head.

STAND: stand for this section of prayer.

SIT: sit for this section of prayer.

BOW: bow while reciting these words.

COVER EYES: cover your eyes while reciting these words.

STRIKE CHEST: strike the left side of your chest.

LEAN HEAD: Lean head on arm, while sitting, when reciting this paragraph.

SHABBAT: recite these words on Shabbat.

SUKKOT/FOUR SPECIES: wave the four species [illegible]

[illegible] these words [illegible]

COLORS

[illegible] on the margin of the page indicates important [illegible]

Throughout [illegible], the following colors are used to help you follow the [illegible]

Text that appears in [illegible] is recited aloud by the Leader.

Text that appears in this color is commentary at the bottom of the page.

[illegible]

[illegible] and [illegible]

[illegible]

[illegible]

CONTENTS

PUBLISHER'S PREFACE

Know that each and every shepherd has his own unique melody.
Know that each and every blade of grass has its own unique song.
And from the singing of the grass, the melody of the shepherd is created.

(*Shirat HaAsavim,* Rabbi Nachman of Breslov, adapted by Naomi Shemer)

We learn the practice of true prayer from Hannah, a marginalized biblical personality brought to the forefront on Rosh HaShana, the epicenter of Jewish prayer. A woman who appealed to God directly, without a mediator, with genuine fervor and sincerity, yet without voice. Her unconventional approach is initially and mistakenly the cause of consternation and rebuke, yet Hannah is now upheld as the epitome of how we should pray, and in the end her "voice" is heard, her prayers answered with favor. In Jewish prayer all voices can make their way heavenward. It is no coincidence that the Hebrew words for "voice" and "all" – קול and כל – are homophones. *Shema koleinu* – hear *our* voice, we pray in the collective, gathering together each individual melody into a powerful chorus.

With this in mind, we are honored to present the new **Koren Yachad Siddur**, a prayer book meticulously and lovingly designed to promote an inclusive and uniting prayer experience.

We are of course deeply indebted to the fantastic team at OU Yachad whose forward-thinking vision and never-ending devotion have brought this project to fruition. Special thanks to Avromie Adler, International Director of Yachad; Dr. Jeffrey Lichtman, International Director Emeritus of Yachad; Michael Adler; and Rabbi Dr. Benjy Leibowitz.

We also thank our friends at the OU Press, in particular Rabbi Simon Posner and Rabbi Eliyahu Krakowski, for their continuing enthusiasm and partnership.

Thank you to my colleagues at Koren – specifically Esther Be'er, Avishai Magence, and Rachel Meghnagi – for bringing the dream to printed reality.

It is our sincere hope that through its unique design elements and the careful consideration evident on each page, this Siddur will enable and enhance the tefilla experience for all, together, Yachad.

Matthew Miller, Publisher
Jerusalem, Menaḥem Av 5779 (August 2019)

FOREWORD

Yachad – יחד – means "together" and signifies the concept of unity. We see the word used numerous times in our daily *tefilla* and throughout *Tanach* in different iterations. Perhaps the most well known is when the Jewish people were at Mount Sinai. The Torah states, "The entire people responded **together** and said, 'Everything that God has spoken we shall do.'" Every Jew responded unanimously and in one voice that they accept the Torah and all its commandments. The commentators teach us that at Mount Sinai every Jew was not only present, but that every Jew was healed of any ailment they may have had. Those that could not previously hear, see or walk were cured and able to fully participate in the receiving of the Torah. Full participation in Jewish life is a core and critical value in Judaism and this has been the impetus for Yachad as an organization, and more specifically for the **Koren Yachad Siddur**. There is no more powerful tool that we the Jewish people have than prayer. Just as every Jew was at Mount Sinai and able to accept the Torah, the goal of this magnificent Siddur is to allow all Jews to connect with God in his/her own special way and to be able to use the powerful tool of prayer.

The visionaries behind this project have been Mr. and Mrs. Ethan and Yael Gross of Detroit, Michigan. A few years back, Ethan came up with the idea of a Yachad Siddur when he realized that his beloved Jacob needed something different, something extra to be able to pray and connect with God. Ethan understood that the Jewish people needs Jacob's prayers. Ethan approached the Yachad leadership with the idea and thus the project was launched. Ethan has remained involved in the development and production of the Siddur since its inception. We are deeply grateful to Ethan and Yael Gross for their partnership and vision.

There are many people that need to come together – *BeYachad* – for a project like this to succeed. First and foremost, I extend thanks to the professional and lay leadership of the Orthodox Union, the parent organization of Yachad. The OU has been behind this Siddur from the beginning, and without the support and encouragement of our leadership, we could not have achieved our goal. I would like to thank our partners at Koren Publishers Jerusalem, especially publisher Matthew Miller, whose patience and sensitivity throughout this project have been monumental.

◂ The expertise

The expertise and professionalism of the entire Koren team, including Avishai Magence, Esther Be'er, Rachel Meghnagi, and Eliyahu Misgav, added immeasurably to the quality of the Siddur. My colleagues at OU Press, Rabbi Simon Posner and Rabbi Eliyahu Krakowski, spent countless hours reviewing, editing, commenting, and working hand in hand with Koren and Yachad to see this project to fruition, and I am grateful for their efforts. My heartfelt appreciation and recognition goes to Dr. Jeffrey Lichtman, International Director Emeritus of Yachad, who for over thirty years pioneered the concept of including individuals with disabilities in all aspects of Jewish life and who was the driving force behind this Siddur since its inception. Dr. Lichtman was not just a willing participant when this idea was first presented to him; he took the lead, and this beautiful Siddur we see today is a testament to his vision and passion for full participation in Jewish life for all Jews. This project could not have been realized without the financial support of our benefactors. In addition to our thanks to Ethan and Yael Gross, we extend sincere gratitude to the Legacy Heritage Foundation for their generosity.

The two individuals most responsible for the pioneering and painstaking work of ensuring that this Siddur can be used by every Jew are my colleagues at Yachad, Michael Adler and Rabbi Dr. Benjy Leibowitz. Navigating in uncharted waters, they created a conceptual translation of the *tefillot* tailored for the Yachad audience, molded the content of the Siddur to suit the needs of that audience, and designed the presentation of the Siddur to maximize its value and usefulness to the broad spectrum of the Yachad audience. Michael and Benjy spearheaded this project from the outset, and over the course of more than three years, reviewed every word, passage, and design element in the Siddur with the goal of making it accessible for all. Their achievement has been extraordinary, and the entire Jewish community owes them a profound debt of gratitude.

Yachad is proud to present this Siddur to the Jewish community. May it be the will of *Hashem* that the **Koren Yachad Siddur** accomplishes what it has set out to do, and in the merit of all Jews being able to pray to and connect with *Hashem* may we see the coming of *Mashiach* and the rebuilding of the *Beit HaMikdash*.

Avromie Adler
International Director Yachad
New York 5779 (2019)

INTRODUCTION

Tefilla, prayer, is referred to in the Talmud as "worship of the heart," suggesting that the supplicant's obligations reach beyond mechanical participation in prayer and instead include concentration, understanding, and a search for meaning. The text of prayer, however, can be difficult to understand and appreciate without proper study; the text, written in an often abstruse and archaic poetic Hebrew, can be difficult to fully grasp for those lacking a strong Hebrew language background. Embedded in the prayer text are a variety of verses from across *Tanach* which require background knowledge to lead to a meaningful prayer experience. Additionally, the prayer text is accompanied by various actions such as bowing, beating our chests, sitting, standing, and taking steps forward and backwards to further aid our concentration and help us experience a palpable encounter with *Hashem*. Lastly, the prayer text often includes fundamental concepts and symbols that are crucial for extracting purpose and meaning from the text. Those who lack fluency in the Hebrew language, are not aware of why we stand, bow, or beat our chests during prayer, or do not have the educational background to fully appreciate fundamental concepts that are embedded in *tefilla* are potentially disadvantaged in the opportunity to forge a meaningful relationship with *Hashem* through the text of *tefilla*. Prayer is a space where every Jew should be able to join family and peers in encountering God, articulating one's needs and wants, and continuing to develop one's relationship with *Hashem*. To accomplish this, prayer must be accessible.

Yachad, a global organization dedicated to addressing the needs of Jewish individuals with disabilities, has embodied the mission of creating acceptance, tolerance and mutual respect for individuals with special needs within the Jewish community since its inception in 1983. The **Koren Yachad Siddur** invites readers of varying levels of skill to join and be included in *tefilla* by addressing the aforementioned difficulties encountered in prayer. First and foremost, this groundbreaking Siddur features easy-to-read conceptual English translation and commentary focused on fundamental concepts of *tefilla* that bring the text alive. While maintaining the traditional Hebrew text, the "conceptual translation" allows English readers to follow along with a smooth and clear English text that highlights and explains fundamental concepts.

◂ This Siddur

This Siddur is designed to enhance ease of navigation through innovative graphic design and formatting elements. Critical sections of prayer are demarcated by gray stripes along the outer margin of each page to allow access to a more concise *tefilla* for those who either struggle to keep pace with the congregation or are pressed for time. Readers simply need to look for the gray stripes for a shortened *tefilla* that includes the critical sections of prayer as noted by the *Mishna Berura*. Color coding is used for a variety of purposes. Color coding in conjunction with the commentary allows readers to quickly identify which words of prayer are the focus of the commentary. The words in the Siddur on which there is commentary are printed in a teal font in both the Hebrew and English texts as well as in the header of the commentary on the bottom of the page. Responsive sections, recited alternately by the congregation and the Leader, are also color-coded to allow readers to clearly discern which words of prayer are to be said by the congregation and which words are to be recited by the Leader. Maroon text signifies text for the Leader only to recite, while the congregational response appears in black. Pastel shading is used to draw attention to portions of *tefilla* recited in connection with holidays, such as *Al HaNisim* on Chanukah and Purim, *Ya'aleh ve'Yavo* on *Chol HaMo'ed*, and the special insertions during *Aseret Yemei Teshuvah*. Icons are strategically placed throughout the Siddur to provide pictorial instruction for actions embedded in the *tefilla*. Lastly, a *Chazarat HaShatz* section is included after each *amida* to help readers follow the Leader's *berachot* and reduce non-linear page-flipping. Each blessing recited by the Leader is condensed into two sentences that highlight the main purpose of the blessing so readers can follow along easily and in a meaningful manner.

With this array of features, we have strived to produce a Siddur that will provide the reader with a text that allows for easy navigation through *tefilla*, an understanding of the concepts presented, an improved connection to the prayer text, and ultimately a *tefilla* that is meaningful and transformative, and which fully embraces *Chazal*'s ideal of *tefilla* being a "worship of the heart."

In producing this pioneering Siddur, we have been ably assisted by many. The Yachad leadership has been unfailingly supportive, and we extend thanks to Dr. Jeffrey Lichtman, International Director Emeritus of

◂ Yachad

Yachad, for his encouragement, direction, and involvement in this project from beginning to end, and to Avromie Adler, International Director of Yachad, for joining the team and overseeing its final stages. Thank you to Ethan and Yael Gross for inspiring the formation of this project and for their financial and consultative support throughout the project. Rabbi Simon Posner and Rabbi Eliyahu Krakowski of OU Press were closely involved in editing, consulting, and guiding us through the publication process of this Siddur. We are grateful to our publishing partner, Koren Publishers Jerusalem, for producing this Siddur with immeasurable flexibility, formatting and reformatting the pages within to reinvent the layout of a traditional Siddur in a fashion that allows for superior accessibility. We are indebted to our families, Shifra Leibowitz, Ayelet, Akiva, and Gavriel Leibowitz, and Neema Adler, for their encouragement and their flexibility in accommodating our early morning and late-night meetings. Finally, we are profoundly grateful to *HaKadosh Baruch Hu* for allowing us to be involved in such an uplifting project. It has certainly inspired us as individuals and improved our concentration in *tefilla,* and it is our hope that this Siddur will have the same impact upon those who use it. May it be *Hashem*'s will that the **Koren Yachad Siddur** allows *tefilla* to be a space for all readers to pray together, *beyachad*.

Rabbi Dr. Benjy Leibowitz and Michael Adler

סידור קורן יחד

THE KOREN YACHAD SIDDUR

סידור לימות החול ולשבת

Shacharit

ON WAKING

מוֹדֶה I am thankful to You, *Hashem,* our King
For waking me up and giving me a new day to live.
By waking me up, You show that You believe in me.

Wash hands and say the following blessings.

בָּרוּךְ Thank You, *Hashem,* our God, King of the world,
for setting us apart as Your special people
by commanding us to wash our hands.

רֵאשִׁית The first step to understanding *Hashem*
is knowing that *Hashem* always watches me.
There is always something
that we can be thankful to *Hashem* for.
Thank You *Hashem,* King of the world,
today and every day, forever.

בָּרוּךְ Thank You, *Hashem,* our God, King of the world
who created us with wisdom
and allows our bodies to work properly.

רַבָּה אֱמוּנָתֶךָ *You believe in me. Hashem* created each of us and allows us to continue living. Every day there are opportunities to serve *Hashem* by doing *mitzvot* and helping others. Before planning what we need to do each day, we take a moment to think about how *Hashem* allowed us to live today because He believes we can do something worthwhile. *Hashem* believes in us, so we must believe in ourselves and act on these opportunities.

שחרית

השכמת הבוקר

men מוֹדֶה/*women* מוֹדָה/ אֲנִי לְפָנֶיךָ מֶלֶךְ חַי וְקַיָּם
שֶׁהֶחֱזַרְתָּ בִּי נִשְׁמָתִי בְּחֶמְלָה
רַבָּה אֱמוּנָתֶךָ.

Wash hands and say the following blessings.

בָּרוּךְ אַתָּה יהוה אֱלֹהֵינוּ מֶלֶךְ הָעוֹלָם
אֲשֶׁר קִדְּשָׁנוּ בְּמִצְוֹתָיו
וְצִוָּנוּ עַל נְטִילַת יָדָיִם.

רֵאשִׁית חָכְמָה יִרְאַת יהוה
שֵׂכֶל טוֹב לְכָל־עֹשֵׂיהֶם
תְּהִלָּתוֹ עֹמֶדֶת לָעַד:
תּוֹרָה צִוָּה־לָנוּ מֹשֶׁה, מוֹרָשָׁה קְהִלַּת יַעֲקֹב:
בָּרוּךְ שֵׁם כְּבוֹד מַלְכוּתוֹ לְעוֹלָם וָעֶד.

בָּרוּךְ אַתָּה יהוה אֱלֹהֵינוּ מֶלֶךְ הָעוֹלָם
אֲשֶׁר יָצַר אֶת הָאָדָם בְּחָכְמָה
וּבָרָא בוֹ נְקָבִים נְקָבִים, חֲלוּלִים חֲלוּלִים.

If one of our inner body parts were to stop working
we would be unable to live and stand before You.
Thank You, *Hashem,* who heals us and keeps us healthy.

אֱלֹהַי *Hashem,* the soul You placed within me is pure.
You created my soul and protect it while it is within me.
One day, You, *Hashem,* will take my soul from me,
and will return it to me in the times of *Mashiach.*
As long as I live I gratefully thank You, *Hashem,*
God of my ancestors, Master of all souls.
Thank You, *Hashem,*
who returns souls to those who pass away.

BLESSING ON TZITZIT

One should hold his TZITZIT *as he recites the following blessing:*

בָּרוּךְ Thank You, *Hashem,* our God, King of the world,
for setting us apart as Your special people
by commanding us to wear *tzitzit.*

וּלְהַחֲזִירָהּ בִּי לֶעָתִיד לָבוֹא *And will return it to me in the times of Mashiach.* Inside every Jewish person is a spark from *Hashem* that we call our *neshama,* our soul. The *neshama* belongs to *Hashem* and we care for it by doing *mitzvot,* staying away from *aveirot,* sins, and by trying to think of *Hashem* at all times. When a person passes away, the body is buried and the *neshama* continues to live. In the time of *Mashiach, Hashem* brings all Jewish people that served Him back to life and returns their *neshamot* to them.

עַל מִצְוַת צִיצִית *To wear tzitzit.* If a man wears clothing that has four corners, he must make sure that tzitzit strings are tied onto each corner. It is recommended that all men wear clothing with four corners and tzitzit so that one can fulfill this special *mitzva.* The tzitzit remind us to keep all of *Hashem's* 613 *mitzvot.*

גָּלוּי וְיָדוּעַ לִפְנֵי כִסֵּא כְבוֹדֶךָ
שֶׁאִם יִפָּתֵחַ אֶחָד מֵהֶם אוֹ יִסָּתֵם אֶחָד מֵהֶם
אִי אֶפְשַׁר לְהִתְקַיֵּם וְלַעֲמֹד לְפָנֶיךָ.
בָּרוּךְ אַתָּה יהוה, רוֹפֵא כָל בָּשָׂר וּמַפְלִיא לַעֲשׂוֹת.

אֱלֹהַי
נְשָׁמָה שֶׁנָּתַתָּ בִּי טְהוֹרָה הִיא.
אַתָּה בְרָאתָהּ, אַתָּה יְצַרְתָּהּ, אַתָּה נְפַחְתָּהּ בִּי
וְאַתָּה מְשַׁמְּרָהּ בְּקִרְבִּי,
וְאַתָּה עָתִיד לִטְּלָהּ מִמֶּנִּי
וּלְהַחֲזִירָהּ בִּי לֶעָתִיד לָבוֹא.
כָּל זְמַן שֶׁהַנְּשָׁמָה בְקִרְבִּי
men מוֹדֶה/ *women* מוֹדָה/ אֲנִי לְפָנֶיךָ
יהוה אֱלֹהַי וֵאלֹהֵי אֲבוֹתַי
רִבּוֹן כָּל הַמַּעֲשִׂים, אֲדוֹן כָּל הַנְּשָׁמוֹת.
בָּרוּךְ אַתָּה יהוה
הַמַּחֲזִיר נְשָׁמוֹת לִפְגָרִים מֵתִים.

לבישת ציצית

One should hold his ציצית *as he recites the following blessing:*

בָּרוּךְ אַתָּה יהוה אֱלֹהֵינוּ מֶלֶךְ הָעוֹלָם
אֲשֶׁר קִדְּשָׁנוּ בְּמִצְוֹתָיו, וְצִוָּנוּ עַל מִצְוַת צִיצִית.

BLESSINGS ON THE TORAH

Before beginning to pray, we engage in a miniature act of study, preceded by the appropriate blessings. The blessings are followed by brief selections from Tanach, Mishna and Gemara, the three foundational texts of Judaism.

בָּרוּךְ Thank You, *Hashem,* our God, King of the world, for setting us apart as Your special people by commanding us to study Your Torah. *Hashem,* please allow me to enjoy the sweet words of Your Torah so that I, my family and friends, and all of the Jewish people can better understand You and how You would like us to live our lives. Thank You, *Hashem,* for allowing the Jewish people to study Your Torah.

בָּרוּךְ Thank You, *Hashem,* our God, King of the world, for choosing us, the Jewish people, from all the other nations of the world, to be Your special people and for giving us Your Torah. Thank You, *Hashem,* for giving us Your Torah.

יְבָרֶכְךָ *Hashem* should bless and protect you.
Hashem should be kind and favorable towards you.
Hashem should grant you peace.

BIRCHOT HATORAH – BLESSINGS ON THE TORAH

We say *berachot* before doing *mitzvot* to help us focus on serving *Hashem.* After reciting the *beracha,* we must do the *mitzva* right away, without interruption. Therefore, just like one should not delay between making a *beracha* and eating, one should not delay between saying Birchot HaTorah and learning Torah. Following these *berachot* are some portions of Torah learning, and one should be careful to learn them without delay.

ברכות התורה

Before beginning to pray, we engage in a miniature act of study, preceded by the appropriate blessings. The blessings are followed by brief selections from תנ״ך, משנה *and* גמרא, *the three foundational texts of Judaism.*

בָּרוּךְ אַתָּה יהוה אֱלֹהֵינוּ מֶלֶךְ הָעוֹלָם
אֲשֶׁר קִדְּשָׁנוּ בְּמִצְוֹתָיו
וְצִוָּנוּ לַעֲסֹק בְּדִבְרֵי תוֹרָה.
וְהַעֲרֶב נָא יהוה אֱלֹהֵינוּ אֶת דִּבְרֵי תוֹרָתְךָ
בְּפִינוּ וּבְפִי עַמְּךָ בֵּית יִשְׂרָאֵל
וְנִהְיֶה אֲנַחְנוּ וְצֶאֱצָאֵינוּ
וְצֶאֱצָאֵי עַמְּךָ בֵּית יִשְׂרָאֵל
כֻּלָּנוּ יוֹדְעֵי שְׁמֶךָ וְלוֹמְדֵי תוֹרָתְךָ לִשְׁמָהּ.
בָּרוּךְ אַתָּה יהוה, הַמְלַמֵּד תּוֹרָה לְעַמּוֹ יִשְׂרָאֵל.

בָּרוּךְ אַתָּה יהוה אֱלֹהֵינוּ מֶלֶךְ הָעוֹלָם
אֲשֶׁר בָּחַר בָּנוּ מִכָּל הָעַמִּים
וְנָתַן לָנוּ אֶת תּוֹרָתוֹ.
בָּרוּךְ אַתָּה יהוה, נוֹתֵן הַתּוֹרָה.

יְבָרֶכְךָ יהוה וְיִשְׁמְרֶךָ:
יָאֵר יהוה פָּנָיו אֵלֶיךָ וִיחֻנֶּךָּ:
יִשָּׂא יהוה פָּנָיו אֵלֶיךָ וְיָשֵׂם לְךָ שָׁלוֹם:

אֵלּוּ Some *mitzvot* do not have a set measure.
There is no limit to:
How much produce you can leave in your field for the poor,
How many new fruits you can bring to Jerusalem for the *Kohen*,
How many *korbanot* you can bring in the *Beit HaMikdash* on *Pesach, Shavuot,* and *Sukkot,*
How many kind acts you can perform, and
How much Torah you can study.

אֵלּוּ A person receives reward
both in this world and the world-to-come
for performing the following *mitzvot*:
Respecting one's mother and father,
Acts of kindness,
Arriving early to the *Beit Midrash* in the morning and at night,
Welcoming guests,
Visiting the sick,
Helping a poor bride,
Taking care of a dead person's needs,
Focusing on prayers, and
Making peace between friends.
The reward for studying Torah is equal
to performing all of these *mitzvot* combined.

אֵלּוּ דְבָרִים שֶׁאֵין לָהֶם שִׁעוּר

הַפֵּאָה

וְהַבִּכּוּרִים

וְהָרֵאָיוֹן

וּגְמִילוּת חֲסָדִים וְתַלְמוּד תּוֹרָה.

אֵלּוּ דְבָרִים שֶׁאָדָם אוֹכֵל פֵּרוֹתֵיהֶם בָּעוֹלָם הַזֶּה

וְהַקֶּרֶן קַיֶּמֶת לוֹ לָעוֹלָם הַבָּא

וְאֵלּוּ הֵן

כִּבּוּד אָב וָאֵם

וּגְמִילוּת חֲסָדִים

וְהַשְׁכָּמַת בֵּית הַמִּדְרָשׁ שַׁחֲרִית וְעַרְבִית

וְהַכְנָסַת אוֹרְחִים

וּבִקּוּר חוֹלִים

וְהַכְנָסַת כַּלָּה

וּלְוָיַת הַמֵּת

וְעִיּוּן תְּפִלָּה

וַהֲבָאַת שָׁלוֹם בֵּין אָדָם לַחֲבֵרוֹ

וְתַלְמוּד תּוֹרָה כְּנֶגֶד כֻּלָּם.

TALLIT

FOR THOSE WHO WEAR A TALLIT:

One should hold the TALLIT above his head while saying this blessing:

בָּרוּךְ Thank You, *Hashem,* our God, King of the world,
for setting us apart as Your special people
by commanding us to wrap ourselves in a *tallit.*

Upon completing the blessing, one should wrap the TALLIT around his body.

TEFILLIN

FOR THOSE WHO WEAR TEFILLIN:

One should place the TEFILLIN SHEL YAD on his arm and say the blessing below before tightening the knot on his upper arm.

בָּרוּךְ Thank You, *Hashem,* our God, King of the world,
for setting us apart as Your special people
by commanding us to put on *tefillin.*

Upon completing the blessing, one should tighten the knot then wrap the TEFILLIN strap around his arm seven times.

Place the box of the TEFILLIN SHEL ROSH at the edge of your hairline, centered between your eyes, and say the blessing below before fixing the TEFILLIN in place:

בָּרוּךְ Thank You, *Hashem,* our God, King of the world,
for setting us apart as Your special people
by commanding us to wear *tefillin.*

The TEFILLIN should be tightened and the straps should hang over your shoulders in front of you. Then say the following:

בָּרוּךְ We bless *Hashem*'s name forever and ever!

Wrap the strap of your TEFILLIN SHEL YAD three times around your middle finger while saying the following three lines:

וְאֵרַשְׂתִּיךְ I will bind you to Me forever,
I will bind you to Me with righteousness,
justice, kindness, and mercy.
I will bind you to Me with trust so that you
will know that I am *Hashem,* your God.

עטיפת טלית

FOR THOSE WHO WEAR A טלית:

One should hold the טלית above his head while saying this blessing:

בָּרוּךְ אַתָּה יהוה אֱלֹהֵינוּ מֶלֶךְ הָעוֹלָם
אֲשֶׁר קִדְּשָׁנוּ בְּמִצְוֹתָיו וְצִוָּנוּ לְהִתְעַטֵּף בַּצִּיצִית.

Upon completing the blessing, one should wrap the טלית around his body.

הנחת תפילין

FOR THOSE WHO WEAR תפילין:

One should place the תפילין של יד on his arm and say the blessing below before tightening the knot on his upper arm.

בָּרוּךְ אַתָּה יהוה אֱלֹהֵינוּ מֶלֶךְ הָעוֹלָם
אֲשֶׁר קִדְּשָׁנוּ בְּמִצְוֹתָיו וְצִוָּנוּ לְהָנִיחַ תְּפִלִּין.

Upon completing the blessing, one should tighten the knot then wrap the תפילין strap around his arm seven times.

Place the box of the תפילין של ראש at the edge of your hairline, centered between your eyes, and say the blessing below before fixing the תפילין in place:

בָּרוּךְ אַתָּה יהוה אֱלֹהֵינוּ מֶלֶךְ הָעוֹלָם
אֲשֶׁר קִדְּשָׁנוּ בְּמִצְוֹתָיו וְצִוָּנוּ עַל מִצְוַת תְּפִלִּין.

The תפילין should be tightened and the straps should hang over your shoulders in front of you. Then say the following:

בָּרוּךְ שֵׁם כְּבוֹד מַלְכוּתוֹ לְעוֹלָם וָעֶד

Wrap the strap of your תפילין של יד three times around your middle finger while saying the following three lines:

וְאֵרַשְׂתִּיךְ לִי לְעוֹלָם
וְאֵרַשְׂתִּיךְ לִי בְּצֶדֶק וּבְמִשְׁפָּט וּבְחֶסֶד וּבְרַחֲמִים:
וְאֵרַשְׂתִּיךְ לִי בֶּאֱמוּנָה, וְיָדַעַתְּ אֶת־יהוה:

PREPARATION FOR PRAYER

On entering the Synagogue:

GREAT
AMOUNTS OF GOOD
can be found in places
set aside for Jews
to pray and study Torah.
Hashem,
I love Your home,
the *Beit HaMikdash.*

I will visit You there,
bend my knee
and bow before You,
Hashem, my Creator.

May my prayers
come before You
at a favorable time
so that You answer me
with kindness.

הכנה לתפילה

On entering the בית כנסת*:*

מַה־טֹּֽבוּ

אֹהָלֶיךָ יַעֲקֹב, מִשְׁכְּנֹתֶיךָ יִשְׂרָאֵל:
וַאֲנִי בְּרֹב חַסְדְּךָ אָבוֹא בֵיתֶךָ
אֶשְׁתַּחֲוֶה אֶל־הֵיכַל־קָדְשְׁךָ
בְּיִרְאָתֶךָ:
יהוה אָהַבְתִּי מְעוֹן בֵּיתֶךָ
וּמְקוֹם מִשְׁכַּן כְּבוֹדֶךָ:

וַאֲנִי אֶשְׁתַּחֲוֶה
וְאֶכְרָעָה
אֶבְרְכָה לִפְנֵי יהוה עֹשִׂי.

וַאֲנִי תְפִלָּתִי־לְךָ יהוה
עֵת רָצוֹן
אֱלֹהִים בְּרָב־חַסְדֶּךָ
עֲנֵנִי בֶּאֱמֶת יִשְׁעֶךָ:

אֲדוֹן עוֹלָם You, *Hashem,* are Master of the world.

You, *Hashem,* existed before the world
was created.

You, *Hashem,* were crowned King
when the world was made.

You, *Hashem,* will still be King
when the world no longer exists.

You, *Hashem,* have always existed,
and You, *Hashem,* will always exist.

You, *Hashem,* rule the world alone.
There is no other God but You.

You, *Hashem,* have unlimited strength.
I turn to You for all my needs.

You, *Hashem,* are always there for me
no matter what challenges I face.

You, *Hashem,* watch over me during the day
and protect me at night.

You, *Hashem,* are always with me,
and You protect me from harm.

It is because of You, *Hashem,*
that I have nothing to fear.

אֲדוֹן עוֹלָם

אֲשֶׁר מָלַךְ בְּטֶרֶם כָּל־יְצִיר נִבְרָא.

לְעֵת נַעֲשָׂה בְחֶפְצוֹ כֹּל אֲזַי מֶלֶךְ שְׁמוֹ נִקְרָא.

וְאַחֲרֵי כִּכְלוֹת הַכֹּל לְבַדּוֹ יִמְלֹךְ נוֹרָא.

וְהוּא הָיָה וְהוּא הֹוֶה וְהוּא יִהְיֶה בְּתִפְאָרָה.

וְהוּא אֶחָד וְאֵין שֵׁנִי לְהַמְשִׁיל לוֹ לְהַחְבִּירָה.

בְּלִי רֵאשִׁית בְּלִי תַכְלִית וְלוֹ הָעֹז וְהַמִּשְׂרָה.

וְהוּא אֵלִי וְחַי גֹּאֲלִי וְצוּר חֶבְלִי בְּעֵת צָרָה.

וְהוּא נִסִּי וּמָנוֹס לִי מְנָת כּוֹסִי בְּיוֹם אֶקְרָא.

בְּיָדוֹ אַפְקִיד רוּחִי בְּעֵת אִישַׁן וְאָעִירָה.

וְעִם רוּחִי גְּוִיָּתִי יהוה לִי וְלֹא אִירָא.

יִגְדַּל *Hashem*, our God, is great and should be praised.

He has always been and will always be our God.

Hashem is the only God. There is none else like Him.

He has no physical body and there is nothing else
that can be compared to Him.

Hashem existed before anything was created.

He shows His kingship over every living creature.

Hashem gave prophets to His Jewish people.

He gave us Moshe, the greatest of all prophets.

Hashem gave the Torah to His Jewish people.

He will never change the laws of His Torah.
His laws are forever.

Hashem knows and studies our deepest secrets
and knows what will happen in the future.

He rewards the good with kindness
and punishes the wicked with evil,
each person according to what he deserves.

Hashem will send *Mashiach* to those waiting
for his arrival.

He will bring the dead back to life.
For this kindness, we forever thank *Hashem*.

יִגְדַּל

אֱלֹהִים חַי וְיִשְׁתַּבַּח, נִמְצָא וְאֵין עֵת אֶל מְצִיאוּתוֹ.

אֶחָד וְאֵין יָחִיד כְּיִחוּדוֹ, נֶעְלָם וְגַם אֵין סוֹף לְאַחְדוּתוֹ.

אֵין לוֹ דְּמוּת הַגּוּף וְאֵינוֹ גוּף, לֹא נַעֲרֹךְ אֵלָיו קְדֻשָּׁתוֹ.

קַדְמוֹן לְכָל דָּבָר אֲשֶׁר נִבְרָא, רִאשׁוֹן וְאֵין רֵאשִׁית לְרֵאשִׁיתוֹ.

הִנּוֹ אֲדוֹן עוֹלָם, וְכָל נוֹצָר יוֹרֶה גְדֻלָּתוֹ וּמַלְכוּתוֹ.

שֶׁפַע נְבוּאָתוֹ נְתָנוֹ אֶל־אַנְשֵׁי סְגֻלָּתוֹ וְתִפְאַרְתּוֹ.

לֹא קָם בְּיִשְׂרָאֵל כְּמֹשֶׁה, עוֹד נָבִיא וּמַבִּיט אֶת תְּמוּנָתוֹ.

תּוֹרַת אֱמֶת נָתַן לְעַמּוֹ אֵל עַל יַד נְבִיאוֹ נֶאֱמַן בֵּיתוֹ.

לֹא יַחֲלִיף הָאֵל וְלֹא יָמִיר דָּתוֹ לְעוֹלָמִים לְזוּלָתוֹ.

צוֹפֶה וְיוֹדֵעַ סְתָרֵינוּ, מַבִּיט לְסוֹף דָּבָר בְּקַדְמָתוֹ.

גּוֹמֵל לְאִישׁ חֶסֶד כְּמִפְעָלוֹ, נוֹתֵן לְרָשָׁע רָע כְּרִשְׁעָתוֹ.

יִשְׁלַח לְקֵץ יָמִין מְשִׁיחֵנוּ לִפְדּוֹת מְחַכֵּי קֵץ יְשׁוּעָתוֹ.

מֵתִים יְחַיֶּה אֵל בְּרֹב חַסְדּוֹ, בָּרוּךְ עֲדֵי עַד שֵׁם תְּהִלָּתוֹ.

MORNING BLESSINGS

Stand while saying the following:

Thank You, *Hashem,* our God,
King of the world
Who allows me to understand
the difference between day and night.

Thank You, *Hashem,* our God,
King of the world
Who made me a Jew.

Thank You, *Hashem,* our God,
King of the world
Who provided me with freedom.

Thank You, *Hashem,* our God, King of the world
Men: Who allows me to do the
special *mitzvot* for men.
Women: Who allows me to do the
special *mitzvot* for women.

Thank You, *Hashem,* our God,
King of the world
Who allows me to see.

Thank You, *Hashem,* our God,
King of the world
Who provides me with clothing.

ברכות השחר

Stand while saying the following:

בָּרוּךְ אַתָּה יהוה אֱלֹהֵינוּ מֶלֶךְ הָעוֹלָם
אֲשֶׁר נָתַן לַשֶּׂכְוִי בִינָה
לְהַבְחִין בֵּין יוֹם וּבֵין לָיְלָה.

בָּרוּךְ אַתָּה יהוה אֱלֹהֵינוּ מֶלֶךְ הָעוֹלָם
שֶׁלֹּא עָשַׂנִי גּוֹי.

בָּרוּךְ אַתָּה יהוה אֱלֹהֵינוּ מֶלֶךְ הָעוֹלָם
שֶׁלֹּא עָשַׂנִי עָבֶד.

בָּרוּךְ אַתָּה יהוה אֱלֹהֵינוּ מֶלֶךְ הָעוֹלָם
men שֶׁלֹּא עָשַׂנִי אִשָּׁה.
women שֶׁעָשַׂנִי כִּרְצוֹנוֹ.

בָּרוּךְ אַתָּה יהוה אֱלֹהֵינוּ מֶלֶךְ הָעוֹלָם
פּוֹקֵחַ עִוְרִים.

בָּרוּךְ אַתָּה יהוה אֱלֹהֵינוּ מֶלֶךְ הָעוֹלָם
מַלְבִּישׁ עֲרֻמִּים.

BIRCHOT HASHACHAR – MORNING BLESSINGS

A *beracha,* blessing, is a way of thanking *Hashem* for all that He does for us, as well as a request that He continue to do those actions for us. When saying a *beracha,* one should speak slowly and carefully, thinking about the meaning of each word.

Thank You, *Hashem*, our God,
King of the world
Who helps me
when I am in difficult situations.

Thank You, *Hashem*, our God,
King of the world
Who allows me to sit and stand.

Thank You, *Hashem*, our God,
King of the world
Who made land and water.

Thank You, *Hashem*, our God,
King of the world
Who gives me everything that I need.

Thank You, *Hashem*, our God,
King of the world
Who helps me travel to where I need to go.

Thank You, *Hashem*, our God,
King of the world
Who gives my mind the strength to focus.

Thank You, *Hashem*, our God,
King of the world
Who crowns me as part of His Jewish people.

Thank You, *Hashem*, our God,
King of the world
Who gives my body strength.

בָּרוּךְ אַתָּה יהוה אֱלֹהֵינוּ מֶלֶךְ הָעוֹלָם
מַתִּיר אֲסוּרִים.

בָּרוּךְ אַתָּה יהוה אֱלֹהֵינוּ מֶלֶךְ הָעוֹלָם
זוֹקֵף כְּפוּפִים.

בָּרוּךְ אַתָּה יהוה אֱלֹהֵינוּ מֶלֶךְ הָעוֹלָם
רוֹקַע הָאָרֶץ עַל הַמָּיִם.

בָּרוּךְ אַתָּה יהוה אֱלֹהֵינוּ מֶלֶךְ הָעוֹלָם
שֶׁעָשָׂה לִי כָּל צָרְכִּי.

בָּרוּךְ אַתָּה יהוה אֱלֹהֵינוּ מֶלֶךְ הָעוֹלָם
הַמֵּכִין מִצְעֲדֵי גָבֶר.

בָּרוּךְ אַתָּה יהוה אֱלֹהֵינוּ מֶלֶךְ הָעוֹלָם
אוֹזֵר יִשְׂרָאֵל בִּגְבוּרָה.

בָּרוּךְ אַתָּה יהוה אֱלֹהֵינוּ מֶלֶךְ הָעוֹלָם
עוֹטֵר יִשְׂרָאֵל בְּתִפְאָרָה.

בָּרוּךְ אַתָּה יהוה אֱלֹהֵינוּ מֶלֶךְ הָעוֹלָם
הַנּוֹתֵן לַיָּעֵף כֹּחַ.

Thank You, *Hashem,* our God, King of the world
Who removes sleep from my eyes
and allows me to be awake.
Hashem, my God and God of my ancestors,
please allow me to study Your Torah
and do Your *mitzvot.*
Please do not place me in a position
where I will make mistakes and sin,
or in a position where I will feel embarrassed
about my religious practices.
Please do not allow my *yetzer hara*
to mislead me,
and keep me away from people
that are bad influences.
Allow me to follow my *yetzer hatov*
and do good actions.
Please show me Your kindness and mercy
today and every other day.
▸ Thank You, *Hashem,*
who shows kindness to His Jewish people.

יֵצֶר הָרָע *Yetzer hara.* Every person has times that he or she wants to do *mitzvot* and other times when he or she wants to do *aveirot.* The want or desire to do good is called our *yetzer hatov* and the desire to sin is called our *yetzer hara.* The *yetzer hara* can be difficult to control. In this *beracha* we ask *Hashem* for help in controlling our *yetzer hara* so that we can stay away from sin and focus on serving *Hashem* better.

בָּרוּךְ אַתָּה יהוה אֱלֹהֵינוּ מֶלֶךְ הָעוֹלָם
הַמַּעֲבִיר שֵׁנָה מֵעֵינַי וּתְנוּמָה מֵעַפְעַפָּי.
וִיהִי רָצוֹן מִלְּפָנֶיךָ
יהוה אֱלֹהֵינוּ וֵאלֹהֵי אֲבוֹתֵינוּ
שֶׁתַּרְגִּילֵנוּ בְּתוֹרָתֶךָ
וְדַבְּקֵנוּ בְּמִצְוֹתֶיךָ
וְאַל תְּבִיאֵנוּ לֹא לִידֵי חֵטְא
וְלֹא לִידֵי עֲבֵרָה וְעָוֹן
וְלֹא לִידֵי נִסָּיוֹן וְלֹא לִידֵי בִזָּיוֹן
וְאַל תַּשְׁלֶט בָּנוּ יֵצֶר הָרָע
וְהַרְחִיקֵנוּ מֵאָדָם רָע וּמֵחָבֵר רָע
וְדַבְּקֵנוּ בְּיֵצֶר הַטּוֹב
וּבְמַעֲשִׂים טוֹבִים
וְכֹף אֶת יִצְרֵנוּ לְהִשְׁתַּעְבֶּד לָךְ
וּתְנֵנוּ הַיּוֹם וּבְכָל יוֹם
לְחֵן וּלְחֶסֶד וּלְרַחֲמִים
בְּעֵינֶיךָ, וּבְעֵינֵי כָל רוֹאֵינוּ
וְתִגְמְלֵנוּ חֲסָדִים טוֹבִים.
◄ בָּרוּךְ אַתָּה יהוה
גּוֹמֵל חֲסָדִים טוֹבִים לְעַמּוֹ יִשְׂרָאֵל.

ACCEPTING THE SOVEREIGNTY OF HEAVEN

לְעוֹלָם A person should always fear God in public
when others are watching,
and in private when one is alone.
One should seek the truth and speak the truth.
One should wake up early in the morning
and say:

רִבּוֹן כָּל הָעוֹלָמִים Master of the world!
We do not pray before You
because we deserve it,
but because we know of Your great kindness.
Compared to You,
what are people?
What have we made of our lives?
What kindness have we done?
What strength do we have?
What can we possibly say before You?
Hashem,
compared to You
the mighty people are weak,
the famous people are not known,
and the wise people are lacking wisdom.

אֲבָל But, as Jews,
we are Your people;
sons of Avraham, Yitzchak and Ya'akov!

קבלת עול מלכות שמים

לְעוֹלָם יְהֵא אָדָם יְרֵא שָׁמַיִם בְּסֵתֶר וּבְגָלוּי
וּמוֹדֶה עַל הָאֱמֶת, וְדוֹבֵר אֱמֶת בִּלְבָבוֹ
וְיַשְׁכֵּם וְיֹאמַר

רִבּוֹן כָּל הָעוֹלָמִים
לֹא עַל־צִדְקוֹתֵינוּ אֲנַחְנוּ מַפִּילִים תַּחֲנוּנֵינוּ לְפָנֶיךָ
כִּי עַל־רַחֲמֶיךָ הָרַבִּים:
מָה אָנוּ, מֶה חַיֵּינוּ, מֶה חַסְדֵּנוּ, מַה צִּדְקוֹתֵינוּ
מַה יְשׁוּעָתֵנוּ, מַה כֹּחֵנוּ, מַה גְּבוּרָתֵנוּ
מַה נֹּאמַר לְפָנֶיךָ, יהוה אֱלֹהֵינוּ וֵאלֹהֵי אֲבוֹתֵינוּ
הֲלֹא כָּל הַגִּבּוֹרִים כְּאַיִן לְפָנֶיךָ, וְאַנְשֵׁי הַשֵּׁם כְּלֹא הָיוּ
וַחֲכָמִים כִּבְלִי מַדָּע, וּנְבוֹנִים כִּבְלִי הַשְׂכֵּל
כִּי רֹב מַעֲשֵׂיהֶם תֹּהוּ, וִימֵי חַיֵּיהֶם הֶבֶל לְפָנֶיךָ
וּמוֹתַר הָאָדָם מִן־הַבְּהֵמָה אָיִן, כִּי הַכֹּל הָבֶל:

אֲבָל אֲנַחְנוּ עַמְּךָ בְּנֵי בְרִיתֶךָ
בְּנֵי אַבְרָהָם אֹהַבְךָ שֶׁנִּשְׁבַּעְתָּ לוֹ בְּהַר הַמּוֹרִיָּה
זֶרַע יִצְחָק יְחִידוֹ שֶׁנֶּעֱקַד עַל גַּבֵּי הַמִּזְבֵּחַ
עֲדַת יַעֲקֹב בִּנְךָ בְּכוֹרֶךָ
שֶׁמֵּאַהֲבָתְךָ שֶׁאָהַבְתָּ אוֹתוֹ, וּמִשִּׂמְחָתְךָ שֶׁשָּׂמַחְתָּ בּוֹ
קָרָאתָ אֶת שְׁמוֹ יִשְׂרָאֵל וִישֻׁרוּן.

לְפִיכָךְ Therefore,
we thank You, praise You,
bless You, and speak of You.
We are fortunate to have
the beautiful Jewish traditions
as part of our lives!

▸ אַשְׁרֵינוּ We are fortunate to be able to come to *shul*
early every morning
and stay late every night
to say:

Say this line out loud:

Listen and understand, Jewish people,
Hashem is our one and only God.

Say this line quietly:

Thank You, *Hashem,* our God.
Your kingdom lasts forever.

אַתָּה הוּא You, *Hashem,*
are all there was
before the world was created,
and You, *Hashem,*
are the main purpose of the world
now that it has been created.
You are the God of this world
and the God of the world-to-come.
▸ Thank You, *Hashem,*
Who brings holiness to the world.

לְפִיכָךְ אֲנַֽחְנוּ חַיָּבִים
לְהוֹדוֹת לְךָ וּלְשַׁבֵּֽחֲךָ וּלְפָאֶרְךָ
וּלְבָרֵךְ וּלְקַדֵּשׁ וְלָתֵת שֶֽׁבַח וְהוֹדָיָה לִשְׁמֶֽךָ.
אַשְׁרֵֽינוּ, מַה טּוֹב חֶלְקֵֽנוּ
וּמַה נָּעִים גּוֹרָלֵֽנוּ, וּמַה יָּפָה יְרֻשָּׁתֵֽנוּ.

◂ אַשְׁרֵֽינוּ, שֶׁאֲנַֽחְנוּ מַשְׁכִּימִים וּמַעֲרִיבִים עֶֽרֶב וָבֹֽקֶר
וְאוֹמְרִים פַּעֲמַֽיִם בְּכָל יוֹם

Say this line out loud:

שְׁמַע יִשְׂרָאֵל, יהוה אֱלֹהֵֽינוּ, יהוה **אֶחָד**:

Say this line quietly:

בָּרוּךְ שֵׁם כְּבוֹד מַלְכוּתוֹ לְעוֹלָם וָעֶד.

אַתָּה הוּא עַד שֶׁלֹּא נִבְרָא הָעוֹלָם
אַתָּה הוּא מִשֶּׁנִּבְרָא הָעוֹלָם.
אַתָּה הוּא בָּעוֹלָם הַזֶּה
וְאַתָּה הוּא לָעוֹלָם הַבָּא.
◂ קַדֵּשׁ אֶת שִׁמְךָ עַל מַקְדִּישֵׁי שְׁמֶֽךָ
וְקַדֵּשׁ אֶת שִׁמְךָ בְּעוֹלָמֶֽךָ
וּבִישׁוּעָתְךָ תָּרוּם וְתַגְבִּֽיהַּ קַרְנֵֽנוּ.
בָּרוּךְ אַתָּה יהוה
הַמְקַדֵּשׁ אֶת שִׁמְךָ בָּרַבִּים.

KORBANOT

TAMID – THE DAILY SACRIFICE

Hashem said to Moshe,
"Command the Jewish people
to bring Me the Daily Sacrifice, twice a day;
once in the morning and once in the afternoon."
The Daily Sacrifice,
prepared and brought by the *Kohanim,*
includes a lamb,
flour, olive oil, and wine.

MISHNAYOT ZEVACHIM

There are several types of sacrifices that are brought to *Hashem,* each designed for a different purpose and occasion. Some sacrifices are *kodshei kodashim,* more holy, while others are *kodashim kalim,* less holy. Sacrifices consisted of animals, birds, flour, or any combination of these items.

Below are some examples of sacrifices that were brought when the *Beit HaMikdash* stood:

A. *Kodshei Kodashim* – More Holy Sacrifices

1. CHATAOT SHEL YOM KIPPUR – *Sin Offerings of Yom Kippur:* These sacrifices were brought on *Yom Kippur* as a form of prayer for forgiveness. One consisted of a bull and was brought by the *Kohen Gadol* prior to beginning the *Yom Kippur* service. A second sin offering sacrifice brought by the *Kohen*

קרבנות

פרשת קרבן התמיד

וַיְדַבֵּר יהוה אֶל־מֹשֶׁה לֵּאמֹר: צַו אֶת־בְּנֵי יִשְׂרָאֵל וְאָמַרְתָּ אֲלֵהֶם, אֶת־קָרְבָּנִי לַחְמִי לְאִשַּׁי, רֵיחַ נִיחֹחִי, תִּשְׁמְרוּ לְהַקְרִיב לִי בְּמוֹעֲדוֹ: וְאָמַרְתָּ לָהֶם, זֶה הָאִשֶּׁה אֲשֶׁר תַּקְרִיבוּ לַיהוה, כְּבָשִׂים בְּנֵי־שָׁנָה תְמִימִם שְׁנַיִם לַיּוֹם, עֹלָה תָמִיד: אֶת־הַכֶּבֶשׂ אֶחָד תַּעֲשֶׂה בַבֹּקֶר, וְאֵת הַכֶּבֶשׂ הַשֵּׁנִי תַּעֲשֶׂה בֵּין הָעַרְבָּיִם: וַעֲשִׂירִית הָאֵיפָה סֹלֶת לְמִנְחָה, בְּלוּלָה בְּשֶׁמֶן כָּתִית רְבִיעִת הַהִין: עֹלַת תָּמִיד, הָעֲשֻׂיָה בְּהַר סִינַי, לְרֵיחַ נִיחֹחַ אִשֶּׁה לַיהוה: וְנִסְכּוֹ רְבִיעִת הַהִין לַכֶּבֶשׂ הָאֶחָד, בַּקֹּדֶשׁ הַסֵּךְ נֶסֶךְ שֵׁכָר לַיהוה: וְאֵת הַכֶּבֶשׂ הַשֵּׁנִי תַּעֲשֶׂה בֵּין הָעַרְבָּיִם, כְּמִנְחַת הַבֹּקֶר וּכְנִסְכּוֹ תַּעֲשֶׂה, אִשֵּׁה רֵיחַ נִיחֹחַ לַיהוה:

דיני זבחים

אֵיזֶהוּ מְקוֹמָן שֶׁל זְבָחִים. קָדְשֵׁי קָדָשִׁים שְׁחִיטָתָן בַּצָּפוֹן. פַּר וְשָׂעִיר שֶׁל יוֹם הַכִּפּוּרִים, שְׁחִיטָתָן בַּצָּפוֹן, וְקִבּוּל דָּמָן בִּכְלֵי שָׁרֵת בַּצָּפוֹן, וְדָמָן טָעוּן הַזָּיָה עַל בֵּין הַבַּדִּים, וְעַל הַפָּרֹכֶת, וְעַל מִזְבַּח הַזָּהָב. מַתָּנָה אַחַת מֵהֶן מְעַכָּבֶת. שְׁיָרֵי הַדָּם הָיָה שׁוֹפֵךְ עַל יְסוֹד מַעֲרָבִי שֶׁל מִזְבֵּחַ הַחִיצוֹן, אִם לֹא נָתַן לֹא עִכֵּב.

פָּרִים הַנִּשְׂרָפִים וּשְׂעִירִים הַנִּשְׂרָפִים, שְׁחִיטָתָן בַּצָּפוֹן, וְקִבּוּל דָּמָן בִּכְלֵי שָׁרֵת בַּצָּפוֹן, וְדָמָן טָעוּן הַזָּיָה עַל הַפָּרֹכֶת וְעַל מִזְבַּח הַזָּהָב. מַתָּנָה אַחַת מֵהֶן מְעַכָּבֶת. שְׁיָרֵי הַדָּם הָיָה שׁוֹפֵךְ עַל יְסוֹד מַעֲרָבִי שֶׁל מִזְבֵּחַ הַחִיצוֹן, אִם לֹא נָתַן לֹא עִכֵּב. אֵלּוּ וָאֵלּוּ נִשְׂרָפִין בְּבֵית הַדָּשֶׁן.

חַטֹּאת הַצִּבּוּר וְהַיָּחִיד. אֵלּוּ הֵן חַטֹּאת הַצִּבּוּר: שְׂעִירֵי רָאשֵׁי חֳדָשִׁים וְשֶׁל מוֹעֲדוֹת. שְׁחִיטָתָן בַּצָּפוֹן, וְקִבּוּל דָּמָן בִּכְלֵי שָׁרֵת בַּצָּפוֹן, וְדָמָן טָעוּן אַרְבַּע מַתָּנוֹת עַל אַרְבַּע קְרָנוֹת. כֵּיצַד, עָלָה בַכֶּבֶשׁ, וּפָנָה לַסּוֹבֵב,

Gadol consisted of a male goat and was brought on behalf of the Jewish nation.

2. OLAH – *Burnt Offering:* This sacrifice was brought every day in the form of the *Korban Tamid*. Also, on many different occasions including *Shabbat, Rosh Chodesh, Pesach, Sukkot,* and *Shavuot* additional burnt offerings were brought. Depending on the occasion, this sacrifice sometimes consisted of lambs, rams, bulls, or combinations of these animals. The Burnt Offering was completely burnt, leaving no meat behind for people to eat. It was completely set aside for *Hashem*.

B. *Kodashim Kalim* – Less Holy Sacrifices

1. TODAH – *Thanksgiving Offering:* This sacrifice was brought by any individual or group to express thanks to *Hashem*. It consisted of either a sheep, goat, cow, or bull. The meat was eaten in Jerusalem and the person who brought this sacrifice could share the meat with friends and family.
2. PESACH – *The Pesach Offering:* This sacrifice was brought on the afternoon before the first night of *Pesach*. Every Jew would join a group which would purchase either a male lamb or goat, and enter the courtyard of the *Beit HaMikdash* to bring their sacrifice. *Kohanim* were present throughout the afternoon to collect the blood of each sacrifice brought. The group would then take the meat of their sacrifice outside of the courtyard and eat it together in Jerusalem.

וּבָא לוֹ לְקֶרֶן דְּרוֹמִית מִזְרָחִית, מִזְרָחִית צְפוֹנִית, צְפוֹנִית מַעֲרָבִית, מַעֲרָבִית דְּרוֹמִית. שְׁיָרֵי הַדָּם הָיָה שׁוֹפֵךְ עַל יְסוֹד דְּרוֹמִי. וְנֶאֱכָלִין לִפְנִים מִן הַקְּלָעִים, לְזִכְרֵי כְהֻנָּה, בְּכָל מַאֲכָל, לְיוֹם וָלַיְלָה עַד חֲצוֹת.

הָעוֹלָה קֹדֶשׁ קָדָשִׁים. שְׁחִיטָתָהּ בַּצָּפוֹן, וְקִבּוּל דָּמָהּ בִּכְלִי שָׁרֵת בַּצָּפוֹן, וְדָמָהּ טָעוּן שְׁתֵּי מַתָּנוֹת שֶׁהֵן אַרְבַּע, וּטְעוּנָה הֶפְשֵׁט וְנִתּוּחַ, וְכָלִיל לָאִשִּׁים.

זִבְחֵי שַׁלְמֵי צִבּוּר וַאֲשָׁמוֹת. אֵלּוּ הֵן אֲשָׁמוֹת: אֲשַׁם גְּזֵלוֹת, אֲשַׁם מְעִילוֹת, אֲשַׁם שִׁפְחָה חֲרוּפָה, אֲשַׁם נָזִיר, אֲשַׁם מְצֹרָע, אָשָׁם תָּלוּי. שְׁחִיטָתָן בַּצָּפוֹן, וְקִבּוּל דָּמָן בִּכְלִי שָׁרֵת בַּצָּפוֹן, וְדָמָן טָעוּן שְׁתֵּי מַתָּנוֹת שֶׁהֵן אַרְבַּע. וְנֶאֱכָלִין לִפְנִים מִן הַקְּלָעִים, לְזִכְרֵי כְהֻנָּה, בְּכָל מַאֲכָל, לְיוֹם וָלַיְלָה עַד חֲצוֹת.

הַתּוֹדָה וְאֵיל נָזִיר קָדָשִׁים קַלִּים. שְׁחִיטָתָן בְּכָל מָקוֹם בָּעֲזָרָה, וְדָמָן טָעוּן שְׁתֵּי מַתָּנוֹת שֶׁהֵן אַרְבַּע, וְנֶאֱכָלִין בְּכָל הָעִיר, לְכָל אָדָם, בְּכָל מַאֲכָל, לְיוֹם וָלַיְלָה עַד חֲצוֹת. הַמּוּרָם מֵהֶם כַּיּוֹצֵא בָהֶם, אֶלָּא שֶׁהַמּוּרָם נֶאֱכָל לַכֹּהֲנִים, לִנְשֵׁיהֶם, וְלִבְנֵיהֶם וּלְעַבְדֵיהֶם.

שְׁלָמִים קָדָשִׁים קַלִּים. שְׁחִיטָתָן בְּכָל מָקוֹם בָּעֲזָרָה, וְדָמָן טָעוּן שְׁתֵּי מַתָּנוֹת שֶׁהֵן אַרְבַּע, וְנֶאֱכָלִין בְּכָל הָעִיר, לְכָל אָדָם, בְּכָל מַאֲכָל, לִשְׁנֵי יָמִים וְלַיְלָה אֶחָד. הַמּוּרָם מֵהֶם כַּיּוֹצֵא בָהֶם, אֶלָּא שֶׁהַמּוּרָם נֶאֱכָל לַכֹּהֲנִים, לִנְשֵׁיהֶם, וְלִבְנֵיהֶם וּלְעַבְדֵיהֶם.

הַבְּכוֹר וְהַמַּעֲשֵׂר וְהַפֶּסַח קָדָשִׁים קַלִּים. שְׁחִיטָתָן בְּכָל מָקוֹם בָּעֲזָרָה, וְדָמָן טָעוּן מַתָּנָה אֶחָת, וּבִלְבָד שֶׁיִּתֵּן כְּנֶגֶד הַיְסוֹד. שִׁנָּה בַאֲכִילָתָן, הַבְּכוֹר נֶאֱכָל לַכֹּהֲנִים וְהַמַּעֲשֵׂר לְכָל אָדָם, וְנֶאֱכָלִין בְּכָל הָעִיר, בְּכָל מַאֲכָל, לִשְׁנֵי יָמִים וְלַיְלָה אֶחָד. הַפֶּסַח אֵינוֹ נֶאֱכָל אֶלָּא בַלַּיְלָה, וְאֵינוֹ נֶאֱכָל אֶלָּא עַד חֲצוֹת, וְאֵינוֹ נֶאֱכָל אֶלָּא לִמְנוּיָיו, וְאֵינוֹ נֶאֱכָל אֶלָּא צָלִי.

RABBI YISHMAEL

רַבִּי יִשְׁמָעֵאל Rabbi Yishmael explains
that there are thirteen rules
which we use
to understand the laws of the Torah.

Below are some examples of rules
that were listed by Rabbi Yishmael.

One of these rules is *Gezeira Shava.*
When the same word appears
in two different areas of the Torah,
Rabbi Yishmael explains
that you can transfer the rules
from one area to the other.

Another rule is about two topics
which are next to each other in the Torah.
In this case, Rabbi Yishmael explains that
we may apply the rules
from one area to the other.
The fact that these two topics
were placed next to each other in the Torah
can teach us that the same laws apply to both.

Another rule is about two *pesukim*
that contradict each other.
Rabbi Yishmael explains
that when there are two *pesukim*
which seem to contradict each other,

ברייתא דרבי ישמעאל

רַבִּי יִשְׁמָעֵאל אוֹמֵר:

בִּשְׁלֹשׁ עֶשְׂרֵה מִדּוֹת הַתּוֹרָה נִדְרֶשֶׁת

מִקַּל וָחֹמֶר

וּמִגְּזֵרָה שָׁוָה

מִבִּנְיַן אָב מִכָּתוּב אֶחָד, וּמִבִּנְיַן אָב מִשְּׁנֵי כְתוּבִים

מִכְּלָל וּפְרָט

מִפְּרָט וּכְלָל

כְּלָל וּפְרָט וּכְלָל, אִי אַתָּה דָן אֶלָּא כְּעֵין הַפְּרָט

מִכְּלָל שֶׁהוּא צָרִיךְ לִפְרָט

וּמִפְּרָט שֶׁהוּא צָרִיךְ לִכְלָל

כָּל דָּבָר שֶׁהָיָה בִּכְלָל, וְיָצָא מִן הַכְּלָל לְלַמֵּד

לֹא לְלַמֵּד עַל עַצְמוֹ יָצָא

אֶלָּא לְלַמֵּד עַל הַכְּלָל כֻּלּוֹ יָצָא

כָּל דָּבָר שֶׁהָיָה בִּכְלָל

וְיָצָא לִטְעֹן טֹעַן אֶחָד שֶׁהוּא כְעִנְיָנוֹ

יָצָא לְהָקֵל וְלֹא לְהַחֲמִיר

כָּל דָּבָר שֶׁהָיָה בִּכְלָל

וְיָצָא לִטְעֹן טֹעַן אַחֵר שֶׁלֹּא כְעִנְיָנוֹ

יָצָא לְהָקֵל וּלְהַחֲמִיר

we must look for a third *pasuk*
to help resolve the contradiction.

- The third *pasuk* will explain how each of
the other *pesukim* only applies in certain cases.

We ask You, *Hashem*, our God and God
of Avraham, Yitzchak, and Yaakov,
to please quickly rebuild the *Beit HaMikdash*
so that we are able to serve You in the best way possible.

KADDISH DERABANAN

The following prayer, said by mourners, requires the presence of a minyan. A transliteration can be found on page 864.

Mourner: יִתְגַּדַּל May *Hashem* be recognized
as great and holy (*Congregation:* Amen)
in the world that He created.
May He establish His kingdom
during my lifetime and the lifetime of all Jews,
quickly and soon.
Let us say: "Amen" (*Congregation:* Amen).

Congregation: May we thank *Hashem* for ever and ever.
Mourner: May we thank *Hashem* for ever and ever.

Mourner: *Hashem* should be thanked, praised,
and honored (*Congregation:* He is blessed).

אָמֵן *Amen.* The word "Amen" means "I agree." We say "Amen" after hearing someone recite a blessing to show that we agree with the blessing. The word also shares the same root-letters as the word *emunah* (אמונה), belief. Every time we say "Amen" to a blessing, we are showing *Hashem* that we agree to the blessing and that we fully believe in *Hashem*.

כָּל דָּבָר שֶׁהָיָה בִּכְלָל, וְיָצָא לָדוּן בַּדָּבָר הֶחָדָשׁ
אִי אַתָּה יָכוֹל לְהַחֲזִירוֹ לִכְלָלוֹ
עַד שֶׁיַּחֲזִירֶנּוּ הַכָּתוּב לִכְלָלוֹ בְּפֵרוּשׁ
דָּבָר הַלָּמֵד מֵעִנְיָנוֹ, וְדָבָר הַלָּמֵד מִסּוֹפוֹ
◂ וְכֵן שְׁנֵי כְתוּבִים הַמַּכְחִישִׁים זֶה אֶת זֶה
עַד שֶׁיָּבוֹא הַכָּתוּב הַשְּׁלִישִׁי וְיַכְרִיעַ בֵּינֵיהֶם.

יְהִי רָצוֹן מִלְּפָנֶיךָ, יהוה אֱלֹהֵינוּ וֵאלֹהֵי אֲבוֹתֵינוּ, שֶׁיִּבָּנֶה בֵּית הַמִּקְדָּשׁ בִּמְהֵרָה בְיָמֵינוּ, וְתֵן חֶלְקֵנוּ בְּתוֹרָתֶךָ, וְשָׁם נַעֲבָדְךָ בְּיִרְאָה כִּימֵי עוֹלָם וּכְשָׁנִים קַדְמוֹנִיּוֹת.

קדיש דרבנן

The following prayer, said by mourners, requires the presence of a מנין.
A transliteration can be found on page 864.

אבל: יִתְגַּדַּל וְיִתְקַדַּשׁ שְׁמֵהּ רַבָּא (קהל: אָמֵן)
בְּעָלְמָא דִּי בְרָא כִרְעוּתֵהּ, וְיַמְלִיךְ מַלְכוּתֵהּ
בְּחַיֵּיכוֹן וּבְיוֹמֵיכוֹן וּבְחַיֵּי דְכָל בֵּית יִשְׂרָאֵל
בַּעֲגָלָא וּבִזְמַן קָרִיב, וְאִמְרוּ אָמֵן. (קהל: אָמֵן)

קהל יְהֵא שְׁמֵהּ רַבָּא מְבָרַךְ לְעָלַם וּלְעָלְמֵי עָלְמַיָּא.
אבל: יְהֵא שְׁמֵהּ רַבָּא מְבָרַךְ לְעָלַם וּלְעָלְמֵי עָלְמַיָּא.

אבל: יִתְבָּרַךְ וְיִשְׁתַּבַּח וְיִתְפָּאַר וְיִתְרוֹמַם וְיִתְנַשֵּׂא
וְיִתְהַדָּר וְיִתְעַלֶּה וְיִתְהַלָּל
שְׁמֵהּ דְּקֻדְשָׁא בְּרִיךְ הוּא (קהל: בְּרִיךְ הוּא)

Hashem is beyond all the blessings,
songs, or praises
that we could offer.
Let us say:
"Amen" (*Congregation:* Amen).

To the Jewish people including:
Teachers,
Students,
Students of students, and
All those that spend time learning Torah,
May *Hashem* provide them with peace,
kindness, mercy, long-life, and food to live.
Let us say:
"Amen." (*Congregation:* Amen.)

May *Hashem* give us, and all Jews,
peace and good life.
Let us all say:
"Amen." (*Congregation:* Amen.)

The mourner takes three steps back before saying this line, bows to the left when saying "May," bows to the right when saying "the One," bows to the middle when saying "make peace for us":

May *Hashem*, the One
who makes peace in heaven,
make peace for us and all Jews.
Let us say:
"Amen." (*Congregation:* Amen.)

On Shabbat, continue Shacharit on page 408.

לְעֵלָּא מִן כָּל בִּרְכָתָא

/ בעשרת ימי תשובה: לְעֵלָּא לְעֵלָּא מִכָּל בִּרְכָתָא/

וְשִׁירָתָא, תֻּשְׁבְּחָתָא וְנֶחֱמָתָא, דַּאֲמִירָן בְּעָלְמָא

וְאִמְרוּ אָמֵן. (קהל: אָמֵן)

עַל יִשְׂרָאֵל וְעַל רַבָּנָן

וְעַל תַּלְמִידֵיהוֹן וְעַל כָּל תַּלְמִידֵי תַלְמִידֵיהוֹן

וְעַל כָּל מָאן דְּעָסְקִין בְּאוֹרַיְתָא

דִּי בְאַתְרָא הָדֵין, וְדִי בְּכָל אֲתַר וַאֲתַר

יְהֵא לְהוֹן וּלְכוֹן שְׁלָמָא רַבָּא

חִנָּא וְחִסְדָּא, וְרַחֲמֵי, וְחַיֵּי אֲרִיכֵי, וּמְזוֹנֵי רְוִיחֵי

וּפֻרְקָנָא מִן קֳדָם אֲבוּהוֹן דִּי בִשְׁמַיָּא

וְאִמְרוּ אָמֵן. (קהל: אָמֵן)

יְהֵא שְׁלָמָא רַבָּא מִן שְׁמַיָּא

וְחַיִּים (טוֹבִים) עָלֵינוּ וְעַל כָּל יִשְׂרָאֵל

וְאִמְרוּ אָמֵן. (קהל: אָמֵן)

The mourner takes three steps back before saying this line, bows to the left when saying עֹשֶׂה*, bows to the right when saying* הוּא*, bows to the middle when saying* יַעֲשֶׂה בְרַחֲמָיו שָׁלוֹם*:*

עֹשֶׂה שָׁלוֹם /בעשרת ימי תשובה: הַשָּׁלוֹם/ בִּמְרוֹמָיו

הוּא יַעֲשֶׂה בְרַחֲמָיו שָׁלוֹם עָלֵינוּ וְעַל כָּל יִשְׂרָאֵל

וְאִמְרוּ אָמֵן. (קהל: אָמֵן)

On שבת*, continue* שחרית *on page 409.*

MIZMOR SHIR

מִזְמוֹר This is a prayer written by King David
in honor of the first use of the *Beit HaMikdash*:
I praise *Hashem* who saves me from my enemies.
Hashem's anger lasts for a moment
but His kindness lasts forever.
In the dark of night I may weep
but *Hashem* brings the morning
filled with light and joy.
Knowing that *Hashem* supports me gives me strength.
Were *Hashem* to hide from me it would be terrifying.
When I cry out for help it is *Hashem* who saves me.
Listen *Hashem* and show kindness to me;
Hashem please help me.
The dust and the dirt
do not have the ability to thank You like I do.
▸ *Hashem,* You have turned my sadness and sorrow
into joy and dancing.
From my soul I will sing to You and not be silent.
Hashem, I will always thank You.

MIZMOR SHIR

King David was the king of the Jewish people in Israel, a mighty warrior, a Torah scholar, and the author of many songs called *Tehillim,* Psalms. Although King David was a wise, strong, and wealthy king, he had many difficulties in his life. King David's songs allowed him to connect to *Hashem* in his most difficult times. Today, when we experience difficulties, we sing the same songs that King David wrote, the *Tehillim,* to connect to *Hashem.*

מזמור לפני פסוקי דזמרה

מִזְמוֹר שִׁיר־חֲנֻכַּת הַבַּיִת לְדָוִד:
אֲרוֹמִמְךָ יהוה כִּי דִלִּיתָנִי, וְלֹא־שִׂמַּחְתָּ אֹיְבַי לִי:
יהוה אֱלֹהָי, שִׁוַּעְתִּי אֵלֶיךָ וַתִּרְפָּאֵנִי:
יהוה, הֶעֱלִיתָ מִן־שְׁאוֹל נַפְשִׁי
חִיִּיתַנִי מִיָּרְדִי־בוֹר:
זַמְּרוּ לַיהוה חֲסִידָיו, וְהוֹדוּ לְזֵכֶר קָדְשׁוֹ:
כִּי רֶגַע בְּאַפּוֹ, חַיִּים בִּרְצוֹנוֹ
בָּעֶרֶב יָלִין בֶּכִי וְלַבֹּקֶר רִנָּה:
וַאֲנִי אָמַרְתִּי בְשַׁלְוִי, בַּל־אֶמּוֹט לְעוֹלָם:
יהוה, בִּרְצוֹנְךָ הֶעֱמַדְתָּה לְהַרְרִי עֹז
הִסְתַּרְתָּ פָנֶיךָ הָיִיתִי נִבְהָל:
אֵלֶיךָ יהוה אֶקְרָא, וְאֶל־אֲדֹנָי אֶתְחַנָּן:
מַה־בֶּצַע בְּדָמִי, בְּרִדְתִּי אֶל שָׁחַת
הֲיוֹדְךָ עָפָר, הֲיַגִּיד אֲמִתֶּךָ:
שְׁמַע־יהוה וְחָנֵּנִי, יהוה הֱיֵה־עֹזֵר לִי:
◂ הָפַכְתָּ מִסְפְּדִי לְמָחוֹל לִי
פִּתַּחְתָּ שַׂקִּי, וַתְּאַזְּרֵנִי שִׂמְחָה:
לְמַעַן יְזַמֶּרְךָ כָבוֹד וְלֹא יִדֹּם
יהוה אֱלֹהַי, לְעוֹלָם אוֹדֶךָּ:

KADDISH YATOM

The following prayer, said by mourners, requires the presence of a minyan. A transliteration can be found on page 865.

Mourner: יִתְגַּדַּל May *Hashem* be recognized
as great and holy (*Congregation:* Amen)
in the world that He created.
May He establish His kingdom
during my lifetime
and the lifetime of all Jews,
quickly and soon.
Let us say: "Amen" (*Congregation:* Amen).

Congregation: May we thank *Hashem* for ever and ever.
Mourner: May we thank *Hashem* for ever and ever.

Mourner: *Hashem* should be thanked, praised,
and honored (*Congregation:* He is blessed).
Hashem is beyond all the blessings,
songs, or praises
that we could offer.
Let us say: "Amen" (*Congregation:* Amen).

May *Hashem* give us, and all Jews,
peace and good life.
Let us say: "Amen." (*Congregation:* Amen).

The mourner takes three steps back before saying this line, bows to the left when saying "May," bows to the right when saying "the One," bows to the middle when saying "make peace for us":

May *Hashem*, the One
who makes peace in heaven,
make peace for us and for all Jews.
Let us say: "Amen." (*Congregation:* Amen).

קדיש יתום

The following prayer, said by mourners, requires the presence of a מנין.
A transliteration can be found on page 865.

אבל: יִתְגַּדַּל וְיִתְקַדַּשׁ שְׁמֵהּ רַבָּא (קהל: אָמֵן)
בְּעָלְמָא דִּי בְרָא כִרְעוּתֵהּ, וְיַמְלִיךְ מַלְכוּתֵהּ
בְּחַיֵּיכוֹן וּבְיוֹמֵיכוֹן וּבְחַיֵּי דְכָל בֵּית יִשְׂרָאֵל
בַּעֲגָלָא וּבִזְמַן קָרִיב, וְאִמְרוּ אָמֵן. (קהל: אָמֵן)

קהל: יְהֵא שְׁמֵהּ רַבָּא מְבָרַךְ לְעָלַם וּלְעָלְמֵי עָלְמַיָּא.
אבל: יְהֵא שְׁמֵהּ רַבָּא מְבָרַךְ לְעָלַם וּלְעָלְמֵי עָלְמַיָּא.

אבל: יִתְבָּרַךְ וְיִשְׁתַּבַּח וְיִתְפָּאַר
וְיִתְרוֹמַם וְיִתְנַשֵּׂא וְיִתְהַדָּר וְיִתְעַלֶּה וְיִתְהַלָּל
שְׁמֵהּ דְּקֻדְשָׁא בְּרִיךְ הוּא (קהל: בְּרִיךְ הוּא)
לְעֵלָּא מִן כָּל בִּרְכָתָא
/בעשרת ימי תשובה: לְעֵלָּא לְעֵלָּא מִכָּל בִּרְכָתָא/
וְשִׁירָתָא, תֻּשְׁבְּחָתָא וְנֶחֱמָתָא
דַּאֲמִירָן בְּעָלְמָא, וְאִמְרוּ אָמֵן. (קהל: אָמֵן)

יְהֵא שְׁלָמָא רַבָּא מִן שְׁמַיָּא
וְחַיִּים, עָלֵינוּ וְעַל כָּל יִשְׂרָאֵל, וְאִמְרוּ אָמֵן. (קהל: אָמֵן)

The mourner takes three steps back before saying this line, bows to the left when saying עֹשֶׂה*, bows to the right when saying* הוּא*, bows to the middle when saying* יַעֲשֶׂה שָׁלוֹם עָלֵינוּ*:*

עֹשֶׂה שָׁלוֹם /בעשרת ימי תשובה: הַשָּׁלוֹם/ בִּמְרוֹמָיו
הוּא יַעֲשֶׂה שָׁלוֹם עָלֵינוּ
וְעַל כָּל יִשְׂרָאֵל, וְאִמְרוּ אָמֵן. (קהל: אָמֵן)

PESUKEI DEZIMRA

Baruch She'amar is the beginning of a long and special beracha in which we praise Hashem. It is important not to speak from this point until the end of Shemoneh Esreh.
Stand while saying this prayer.
Kiss your TZITZIT *when saying the words "worthy of praise."*

WE THANK YOU, *HASHEM*, WHO:

Created the world with His words.
Makes promises and keeps to His word.
Makes rules and follows them.
Shows kindness to the earth.
Shows kindness to all people and animals.
Rewards people who are always thinking about *Hashem*.
Lives forever.
Protects and saves people from difficulties that arise.

בָּרוּךְ שֶׁאָמַר וְהָיָה הָעוֹלָם *We thank You, Hashem, who Created the world with His words.* Using His words alone, *Hashem* created the world in seven days, making something from nothing. Everything in the world exists today because *Hashem* said it should be so, including:

Day 1: Light and darkness,
Day 2: Sky and sea,
Day 3: Land, trees and plants,
Day 4: Stars, sun, and moon,
Day 5: Fish and birds,
Day 6: Animals and people, and
Day 7: Shabbat.

We thank *Hashem* for creating a beautiful world and for continuously caring for all of His creations, including us.

פסוקי דזמרה

בָּרוּךְ שֶׁאָמַר is the beginning of a long and special beracha in which we praise Hashem. It is important not to speak from this point until the end of שמונה עשרה.
Stand while saying this prayer.
Kiss your ציצית when saying the words "מְהֻלָּל בְּתִשְׁבָּחוֹת."

בָּרוּךְ שֶׁאָמַר

וְהָיָה הָעוֹלָם, בָּרוּךְ הוּא.

בָּרוּךְ עוֹשֶׂה בְרֵאשִׁית

בָּרוּךְ אוֹמֵר וְעוֹשֶׂה

בָּרוּךְ גּוֹזֵר וּמְקַיֵּם

בָּרוּךְ מְרַחֵם עַל הָאָרֶץ

בָּרוּךְ מְרַחֵם עַל הַבְּרִיּוֹת

בָּרוּךְ מְשַׁלֵּם שָׂכָר

טוֹב לִירֵאָיו

בָּרוּךְ חַי לָעַד

וְקַיָּם לָנֶצַח

בָּרוּךְ פּוֹדֶה וּמַצִּיל

בָּרוּךְ שְׁמוֹ

We thank You *Hashem*,
our God and King of the world
whom we praise
through our actions and prayers.
▸ Your greatness has no end.
Thank You, *Hashem*, our King
who is worthy of praise.

Sit while saying the following.

הודו Thank *Hashem* and sing out to him!
Tell the world about the miracles He has performed.
Take pride in serving *Hashem*.
Remember His strength and search Him out.
Hashem is always present.
Remember the great miracles *Hashem* has performed
for His Jewish people;
Hashem is God and His laws can be found
across the earth.
Hashem is our God
and has been for thousands of years,
beginning with our ancestors,
Avraham, Yitzchak, and Yaakov.
Since the time of Avraham,
the Jewish people were promised Israel as their land.
Throughout Jewish history,
even when we were a small nation
wandering from one country to the next,
Hashem has protected the Jewish people.

בָּרוּךְ אַתָּה יהוה אֱלֹהֵינוּ מֶלֶךְ הָעוֹלָם
הָאֵל הָאָב הָרַחֲמָן הַמְהֻלָּל בְּפִי עַמּוֹ
מְשֻׁבָּח וּמְפֹאָר בִּלְשׁוֹן חֲסִידָיו וַעֲבָדָיו
וּבְשִׁירֵי דָוִד עַבְדֶּךָ, נְהַלֶּלְךָ יהוה אֱלֹהֵינוּ.
בִּשְׁבָחוֹת וּבִזְמִירוֹת
נְגַדֶּלְךָ וּנְשַׁבֵּחֲךָ וּנְפָאֶרְךָ וְנַזְכִּיר שִׁמְךָ וְנַמְלִיכְךָ
מַלְכֵּנוּ אֱלֹהֵינוּ, ◂ יָחִיד חֵי הָעוֹלָמִים
מֶלֶךְ, מְשֻׁבָּח וּמְפֹאָר עֲדֵי עַד שְׁמוֹ הַגָּדוֹל
בָּרוּךְ אַתָּה יהוה, מֶלֶךְ מְהֻלָּל בַּתִּשְׁבָּחוֹת.

Sit while saying the following.

הוֹדוּ לַיהוה קִרְאוּ בִשְׁמוֹ, הוֹדִיעוּ בָעַמִּים עֲלִילֹתָיו: שִׁירוּ לוֹ, זַמְּרוּ־לוֹ, שִׂיחוּ בְּכָל־נִפְלְאוֹתָיו: הִתְהַלְלוּ בְּשֵׁם קָדְשׁוֹ, יִשְׂמַח לֵב מְבַקְשֵׁי יהוה: דִּרְשׁוּ יהוה וְעֻזּוֹ, בַּקְּשׁוּ פָנָיו תָּמִיד: זִכְרוּ נִפְלְאֹתָיו אֲשֶׁר עָשָׂה, מֹפְתָיו וּמִשְׁפְּטֵי־פִיהוּ: זֶרַע יִשְׂרָאֵל עַבְדּוֹ, בְּנֵי יַעֲקֹב בְּחִירָיו: הוּא יהוה אֱלֹהֵינוּ בְּכָל־הָאָרֶץ מִשְׁפָּטָיו: זִכְרוּ לְעוֹלָם בְּרִיתוֹ, דָּבָר צִוָּה לְאֶלֶף דּוֹר: אֲשֶׁר כָּרַת אֶת־אַבְרָהָם, וּשְׁבוּעָתוֹ לְיִצְחָק: וַיַּעֲמִידֶהָ לְיַעֲקֹב לְחֹק, לְיִשְׂרָאֵל בְּרִית עוֹלָם: לֵאמֹר, לְךָ אֶתֵּן אֶרֶץ־כְּנָעַן, חֶבֶל נַחֲלַתְכֶם: בִּהְיוֹתְכֶם מְתֵי מִסְפָּר, כִּמְעַט וְגָרִים בָּהּ: וַיִּתְהַלְּכוּ מִגּוֹי אֶל־גּוֹי,

Praise, sing, thank, and speak of *Hashem*'s greatness
every day since He is the only God.
▸ *Hashem* is awesome! He is the Creator of heaven.

Hashem is all-powerful and the source of all glory.
Give honor, bring sacrifices,
tremble, and bow before *Hashem* for He is mighty.
Angels in heaven and every being on earth
declares *Hashem* as King.
The fish in the sea, plants in the fields,
and trees in the forest sing to *Hashem* with joy.
Thank *Hashem* for He is good
and His kindness lasts forever.
Hashem, save Your Jewish people from other nations.
Thank *Hashem*, God of the Jewish people,
for ever and ever.

▸ Praise *Hashem*, our holy God, and bow before His throne.
Praise *Hashem*, our holy God, and bow before His holy mountain.

רוֹמְמוּ ה׳ אֱלֹהֵינוּ וְהִשְׁתַּחֲווּ לְהַר קָדְשׁוֹ *Praise Hashem, our holy God, and bow before His holy mountain.* The *Beit HaMikdash* was built on a holy mountain called Har HaMoriah, Mount Moriah, in the center of Yerushalayim. Many important events took place on this mountain before the *Beit HaMikdash* was built. This is the place where Adam was created, where Avraham was ready to bring Yitzchak as a *korban* (*Akeidat Yitzchak*), and where Yaakov had a dream in which he saw angels going up and down a ladder to heaven. When praying, Jews around the world face towards Har HaMoriah, the holy mountain, the most holy spot in the world.

וּמִמַּמְלָכָה אֶל־עַם אַחֵר: לֹא־הִנִּיחַ לְאִישׁ לְעָשְׁקָם, וַיּוֹכַח עֲלֵיהֶם מְלָכִים: אַל־תִּגְּעוּ בִּמְשִׁיחָי, וּבִנְבִיאַי אַל־תָּרֵעוּ: שִׁירוּ לַיהוה כָּל־הָאָרֶץ, בַּשְּׂרוּ מִיּוֹם־אֶל־יוֹם יְשׁוּעָתוֹ: סַפְּרוּ בַגּוֹיִם אֶת־כְּבוֹדוֹ, בְּכָל־הָעַמִּים נִפְלְאֹתָיו: כִּי גָדוֹל יהוה וּמְהֻלָּל מְאֹד, וְנוֹרָא הוּא עַל־כָּל־אֱלֹהִים:
◂ כִּי כָּל־אֱלֹהֵי הָעַמִּים אֱלִילִים, וַיהוה שָׁמַיִם עָשָׂה:

הוֹד וְהָדָר לְפָנָיו, עֹז וְחֶדְוָה בִּמְקֹמוֹ: הָבוּ לַיהוה מִשְׁפְּחוֹת עַמִּים, הָבוּ לַיהוה כָּבוֹד וָעֹז: הָבוּ לַיהוה כְּבוֹד שְׁמוֹ, שְׂאוּ מִנְחָה וּבֹאוּ לְפָנָיו, הִשְׁתַּחֲווּ לַיהוה בְּהַדְרַת־קֹדֶשׁ: חִילוּ מִלְּפָנָיו כָּל־הָאָרֶץ, אַף־תִּכּוֹן תֵּבֵל בַּל־תִּמּוֹט: יִשְׂמְחוּ הַשָּׁמַיִם וְתָגֵל הָאָרֶץ, וְיֹאמְרוּ בַגּוֹיִם יהוה מָלָךְ: יִרְעַם הַיָּם וּמְלוֹאוֹ, יַעֲלֹץ הַשָּׂדֶה וְכָל־אֲשֶׁר־בּוֹ: אָז יְרַנְּנוּ עֲצֵי הַיָּעַר, מִלִּפְנֵי יהוה, כִּי־בָא לִשְׁפּוֹט אֶת־הָאָרֶץ: הוֹדוּ לַיהוה כִּי טוֹב, כִּי לְעוֹלָם חַסְדּוֹ: וְאִמְרוּ, הוֹשִׁיעֵנוּ אֱלֹהֵי יִשְׁעֵנוּ, וְקַבְּצֵנוּ וְהַצִּילֵנוּ מִן־הַגּוֹיִם, לְהֹדוֹת לְשֵׁם קָדְשֶׁךָ, לְהִשְׁתַּבֵּחַ בִּתְהִלָּתֶךָ: בָּרוּךְ יהוה אֱלֹהֵי יִשְׂרָאֵל מִן־הָעוֹלָם וְעַד־הָעֹלָם, וַיֹּאמְרוּ כָל־הָעָם אָמֵן, וְהַלֵּל לַיהוה:

◂ רוֹמְמוּ יהוה אֱלֹהֵינוּ וְהִשְׁתַּחֲווּ לַהֲדֹם רַגְלָיו, קָדוֹשׁ הוּא: רוֹמְמוּ יהוה אֱלֹהֵינוּ וְהִשְׁתַּחֲווּ לְהַר קָדְשׁוֹ, כִּי־קָדוֹשׁ יהוה אֱלֹהֵינוּ:

Hashem, You show kindness
by forgiving our mistakes
instead of destroying the Jewish people in anger.
By protecting me,
You show me Your kindness.
May You protect us with Your love and kindness
as You always have.
Hashem, You are awesome
and You grant strength to Your Jewish people.
You protect Your Jewish people
and take revenge on our enemies.
▸ Praiseworthy is the person who trusts in You, *Hashem.*
May You, *Hashem,* answer and save us
on the day that we call out to You.

Hashem, save Your Jewish people
and care for them forever.
Our hearts are happy when we are close to You
because You are our protector.
We have complete trust in You, *Hashem,* who loves us.
Hashem, please show Your kindness by saving us.
You saved the Jewish people from Egypt
and we ask that You continue to save us now.
We are fortunate to have You, *Hashem,* as our God.
▸ I trust that You, *Hashem,*
will have the kindness to save us,
and I will sing praises to You.

וְהוּא רַחוּם, יְכַפֵּר עָוֹן וְלֹא־יַשְׁחִית, וְהִרְבָּה לְהָשִׁיב אַפּוֹ, וְלֹא־יָעִיר כָּל־חֲמָתוֹ: אַתָּה יהוה לֹא־תִכְלָא רַחֲמֶיךָ מִמֶּנִּי, חַסְדְּךָ וַאֲמִתְּךָ תָּמִיד יִצְּרוּנִי: זְכֹר־רַחֲמֶיךָ יהוה וַחֲסָדֶיךָ, כִּי מֵעוֹלָם הֵמָּה: תְּנוּ עֹז לֵאלֹהִים, עַל־יִשְׂרָאֵל גַּאֲוָתוֹ, וְעֻזּוֹ בַּשְּׁחָקִים: נוֹרָא אֱלֹהִים מִמִּקְדָּשֶׁיךָ, אֵל יִשְׂרָאֵל הוּא נֹתֵן עֹז וְתַעֲצֻמוֹת לָעָם, בָּרוּךְ אֱלֹהִים: אֵל־נְקָמוֹת יהוה, אֵל נְקָמוֹת הוֹפִיעַ: הִנָּשֵׂא שֹׁפֵט הָאָרֶץ, הָשֵׁב גְּמוּל עַל־גֵּאִים: לַיהוה הַיְשׁוּעָה, עַל־עַמְּךָ בִרְכָתֶךָ סֶּלָה: › יהוה צְבָאוֹת עִמָּנוּ, מִשְׂגָּב לָנוּ אֱלֹהֵי יַעֲקֹב סֶלָה: יהוה צְבָאוֹת, אַשְׁרֵי אָדָם בֹּטֵחַ בָּךְ: יהוה הוֹשִׁיעָה, הַמֶּלֶךְ יַעֲנֵנוּ בְיוֹם־קָרְאֵנוּ:

הוֹשִׁיעָה אֶת־עַמֶּךָ, וּבָרֵךְ אֶת־נַחֲלָתֶךָ, וּרְעֵם וְנַשְּׂאֵם עַד־הָעוֹלָם: נַפְשֵׁנוּ חִכְּתָה לַיהוה, עֶזְרֵנוּ וּמָגִנֵּנוּ הוּא: כִּי־בוֹ יִשְׂמַח לִבֵּנוּ, כִּי בְשֵׁם קָדְשׁוֹ בָטָחְנוּ: יְהִי־חַסְדְּךָ יהוה עָלֵינוּ, כַּאֲשֶׁר יִחַלְנוּ לָךְ: הַרְאֵנוּ יהוה חַסְדֶּךָ, וְיֶשְׁעֲךָ תִּתֶּן־לָנוּ: קוּמָה עֶזְרָתָה לָּנוּ, וּפְדֵנוּ לְמַעַן חַסְדֶּךָ: אָנֹכִי יהוה אֱלֹהֶיךָ הַמַּעַלְךָ מֵאֶרֶץ מִצְרָיִם, הַרְחֶב־פִּיךָ וַאֲמַלְאֵהוּ: אַשְׁרֵי הָעָם שֶׁכָּכָה לּוֹ, אַשְׁרֵי הָעָם שֶׁיהוה אֱלֹהָיו: › וַאֲנִי בְּחַסְדְּךָ בָטַחְתִּי, יָגֵל לִבִּי בִּישׁוּעָתֶךָ, אָשִׁירָה לַיהוה, כִּי גָמַל עָלָי:

Stand while saying this section.
This is not said on Erev Pesach, Chol HaMoed Pesach, or Erev Yom Kippur.

מִזְמוֹר Everyone, sing out thanks to *Hashem*. Serve *Hashem* with happiness and come before Him with joy. Know that *Hashem* is God and that He created and formed the Jewish people into His nation. *Hashem* cares for our needs as a shepherd cares for his sheep. Therefore, we come before *Hashem* with praise and thanks.
▸ *Hashem* is good and His kindness lasts forever.

On Hoshana Raba, continue with "A song written by David" on page 418.

Sit while saying the following.

יְהִי כְבוֹד *Hashem,* Your honor lasts forever,
take pride in Your creations.
We praise You, *Hashem,* from sunrise to sunset,
generation to generation, and for ever and ever.
Hashem, You rule over all the nations;
Your throne is in the heavens.
Hashem, Your creation of the earth and heavens
is a sign of Your greatness.
You *Hashem* are the King, You were always the King,
and You will be the King forever.
When other nations make evil plans against us,
Hashem stops them.

מִזְמוֹר לְתוֹדָה *Everyone, sing out thanks to Hashem.* This song was sung in the *Beit HaMikdash* while people sacrificed the *korban todah,* a special sacrifice brought as a thank you to *Hashem* for helping during difficult times. Since the *korban todah* would not have been brought in the *Beit HaMikdash* on the day before *Yom Kippur,* the day before *Pesach,* or *Chol HaMoed Pesach,* we do not say *Mizmor LeTodah* on these days.

Stand while saying this section.
This is not said on ערב יום כיפור *or* ,ערב פסח, חול המועד פסח.

מִזְמוֹר לְתוֹדָה, הָרִיעוּ לַיהוה כָּל־הָאָרֶץ: עִבְדוּ אֶת־יהוה בְּשִׂמְחָה, בֹּאוּ לְפָנָיו בִּרְנָנָה: דְּעוּ כִּי־יהוה הוּא אֱלֹהִים, הוּא עָשָׂנוּ וְלוֹ אֲנַחְנוּ, עַמּוֹ וְצֹאן מַרְעִיתוֹ: בֹּאוּ שְׁעָרָיו בְּתוֹדָה, חֲצֵרֹתָיו בִּתְהִלָּה, הוֹדוּ לוֹ, בָּרְכוּ שְׁמוֹ: ‹ כִּי־טוֹב יהוה, לְעוֹלָם חַסְדּוֹ, וְעַד־דֹּר וָדֹר אֱמוּנָתוֹ:

On הושענא רבה, *continue with* לַמְנַצֵּחַ *on page 419.*

Sit while saying the following.

יְהִי כְבוֹד יהוה לְעוֹלָם, יִשְׂמַח יהוה בְּמַעֲשָׂיו: יְהִי שֵׁם יהוה מְבֹרָךְ, מֵעַתָּה וְעַד־עוֹלָם: מִמִּזְרַח־שֶׁמֶשׁ עַד־מְבוֹאוֹ, מְהֻלָּל שֵׁם יהוה: רָם עַל־כָּל־גּוֹיִם יהוה, עַל הַשָּׁמַיִם כְּבוֹדוֹ: יהוה שִׁמְךָ לְעוֹלָם, יהוה זִכְרְךָ לְדֹר־וָדֹר: יהוה בַּשָּׁמַיִם הֵכִין כִּסְאוֹ, וּמַלְכוּתוֹ בַּכֹּל מָשָׁלָה: יִשְׂמְחוּ הַשָּׁמַיִם וְתָגֵל הָאָרֶץ, וְיֹאמְרוּ בַגּוֹיִם יהוה מָלָךְ: יהוה מֶלֶךְ, יהוה מָלָךְ, יהוה יִמְלֹךְ לְעוֹלָם וָעֶד. יהוה מֶלֶךְ עוֹלָם וָעֶד, אָבְדוּ גוֹיִם מֵאַרְצוֹ: יהוה הֵפִיר עֲצַת־גּוֹיִם, הֵנִיא מַחְשְׁבוֹת עַמִּים: רַבּוֹת מַחֲשָׁבוֹת בְּלֶב־אִישׁ, וַעֲצַת יהוה הִיא תָקוּם: עֲצַת יהוה לְעוֹלָם תַּעֲמֹד, מַחְשְׁבוֹת לִבּוֹ לְדֹר וָדֹר: כִּי הוּא אָמַר וַיֶּהִי, הוּא־צִוָּה וַיַּעֲמֹד: כִּי־בָחַר יהוה בְּצִיּוֹן, אִוָּהּ לְמוֹשָׁב לוֹ: כִּי־יַעֲקֹב

Man is free to think on his own
but it is *Hashem*'s plans that will always last.
Hashem chose Zion as His home.
Israel is *Hashem*'s special treasure.
Hashem chose Yaakov and his descendants,
the Jewish people, to be His special nation.
Hashem will never forget His Jewish people.
Hashem is caring and forgives our sins.
▸ *Hashem,* shows kindness by forgiving our mistakes
rather than destroying us with anger.
Hashem, please save us!
You are our King who answers us when we call out to You.

The line beginning with "Hashem opens His hands" should be said with special concentration. Some have the custom to touch the TEFILLIN SHEL YAD *and the* TEFILLIN SHEL ROSH *at the relevant icons.*

אַשְׁרֵי We are happy with the opportunity to sit and pray.
We are happy that You are our God and that we are Your people.
David HaMelech wrote this song:

א GOD – *Hashem* is our God and King.

ב THANK – We appreciate *Hashem* and we will thank Him every day, forever.

ג GREATNESS – *Hashem*'s greatness is endless.

ד GENERATIONS – We will tell our children about the spectacular actions You have done for us in every generation.

ה MIRACLES – The miracles that *Hashem* performs for His people are glorious.

בָּחַר לוֹ יָהּ, יִשְׂרָאֵל לִסְגֻלָּתוֹ: כִּי לֹא־יִטֹּשׁ יהוה עַמּוֹ, וְנַחֲלָתוֹ לֹא יַעֲזֹב: ◂ וְהוּא רַחוּם, יְכַפֵּר עָוֺן וְלֹא־יַשְׁחִית, וְהִרְבָּה לְהָשִׁיב אַפּוֹ, וְלֹא־יָעִיר כָּל־חֲמָתוֹ: יהוה הוֹשִׁיעָה, הַמֶּלֶךְ יַעֲנֵנוּ בְיוֹם־קָרְאֵנוּ:

The line beginning with פּוֹתֵחַ אֶת יָדֶךָ *should be said with special concentration. Some have the custom to touch the* תפילין של יד *and the* תפילין של ראש *at the relevant icons.*

אַשְׁרֵי יוֹשְׁבֵי בֵיתֶךָ, עוֹד יְהַלְלוּךָ סֶּלָה:
אַשְׁרֵי הָעָם שֶׁכָּכָה לּוֹ, אַשְׁרֵי הָעָם שֶׁיהוה אֱלֹהָיו:
תְּהִלָּה לְדָוִד
אֲרוֹמִמְךָ אֱלוֹהַי הַמֶּלֶךְ, וַאֲבָרְכָה שִׁמְךָ לְעוֹלָם וָעֶד:
בְּכָל־יוֹם אֲבָרְכֶךָּ, וַאֲהַלְלָה שִׁמְךָ לְעוֹלָם וָעֶד:
גָּדוֹל יהוה וּמְהֻלָּל מְאֹד, וְלִגְדֻלָּתוֹ אֵין חֵקֶר:
דּוֹר לְדוֹר יְשַׁבַּח מַעֲשֶׂיךָ, וּגְבוּרֹתֶיךָ יַגִּידוּ:
הֲדַר כְּבוֹד הוֹדֶךָ, וְדִבְרֵי נִפְלְאֹתֶיךָ אָשִׂיחָה:

אַשְׁרֵי *We are happy.* If one says Ashrei three times a day, he or she is promised a place in *Olam Haba,* the world-to-come. Ashrei is special for two reasons:

- Each line of Ashrei begins with a different letter of the Aleph-Bet. This represents the unlimited praise and thanks we feel toward *Hashem.*
- Ashrei contains the line beginning *"Potei'ach et Yadecha,"* which means, "*Hashem* opens His hands and provides us with all of our needs." This teaches us that everything comes from *Hashem.*

We say Ashrei three times a day, twice during Shacharit and once at Mincha, to remind ourselves of these important messages: everything comes from *Hashem* and we cannot thank and praise Him enough.

ו STRENGTH – *Hashem*'s strength is awesome beyond comparison.

ז REMEMBER – We remember the good that *Hashem* does for us.

ח MERCY – *Hashem* is slow to get angry.

ט GOODNESS – *Hashem* is good to all His creations, humans and animals alike.

י KINDNESS – All creations of *Hashem* are thankful for His kindness.

כ HONOR – We give *Hashem* the honor that He deserves.

ל MIGHTY – We inform all people of *Hashem*'s mighty actions.

מ KINGSHIP – *Hashem* has and always will rule the world.

ס HELP – *Hashem* helps us when we need Him.

ע RELY – We rely on *Hashem* to give us the food that we need to live.

פ PROVIDES – *Hashem* opens His hands and provides us with our needs.

צ RIGHTEOUS – Everything *Hashem* does is righteous and with good intentions.

ק CLOSENESS – *Hashem* is close to all those that call out to Him.

ר SAVES – *Hashem* listens to our cries and saves those in need.

ש GUARDS – *Hashem* protects all those who love Him and turn to Him in times of need.

▸ ת PRAISE – For all of these reasons, everyone praises *Hashem* and thanks Him every day.

וֶעֱזוּז נוֹרְאֹתֶיךָ יֹאמֵרוּ, וּגְדוּלָּתְךָ אֲסַפְּרֶנָּה:
זֵכֶר רַב־טוּבְךָ יַבִּיעוּ, וְצִדְקָתְךָ יְרַנֵּנוּ:
חַנּוּן וְרַחוּם יהוה, אֶרֶךְ אַפַּיִם וּגְדָל־חָסֶד:
טוֹב־יהוה לַכֹּל, וְרַחֲמָיו עַל־כָּל־מַעֲשָׂיו:
יוֹדוּךָ יהוה כָּל־מַעֲשֶׂיךָ, וַחֲסִידֶיךָ יְבָרְכוּכָה:
כְּבוֹד מַלְכוּתְךָ יֹאמֵרוּ, וּגְבוּרָתְךָ יְדַבֵּרוּ:
לְהוֹדִיעַ לִבְנֵי הָאָדָם גְּבוּרֹתָיו, וּכְבוֹד הֲדַר מַלְכוּתוֹ:
מַלְכוּתְךָ מַלְכוּת כָּל־עֹלָמִים
וּמֶמְשַׁלְתְּךָ בְּכָל־דּוֹר וָדֹר:
סוֹמֵךְ יהוה לְכָל־הַנֹּפְלִים, וְזוֹקֵף לְכָל־הַכְּפוּפִים:
עֵינֵי־כֹל אֵלֶיךָ יְשַׂבֵּרוּ
וְאַתָּה נוֹתֵן־לָהֶם אֶת־אָכְלָם בְּעִתּוֹ:
פּוֹתֵחַ אֶת־יָדֶךָ, וּמַשְׂבִּיעַ לְכָל־חַי רָצוֹן:
צַדִּיק יהוה בְּכָל־דְּרָכָיו, וְחָסִיד בְּכָל־מַעֲשָׂיו:
קָרוֹב יהוה לְכָל־קֹרְאָיו, לְכֹל אֲשֶׁר יִקְרָאֻהוּ בֶאֱמֶת:
רְצוֹן־יְרֵאָיו יַעֲשֶׂה, וְאֶת־שַׁוְעָתָם יִשְׁמַע, וְיוֹשִׁיעֵם:
שׁוֹמֵר יהוה אֶת־כָּל־אֹהֲבָיו
וְאֵת כָּל־הָרְשָׁעִים יַשְׁמִיד:
◂ תְּהִלַּת יהוה יְדַבֶּר פִּי
וִיבָרֵךְ כָּל־בָּשָׂר שֵׁם קָדְשׁוֹ לְעוֹלָם וָעֶד:
וַאֲנַחְנוּ נְבָרֵךְ יָהּ מֵעַתָּה וְעַד־עוֹלָם, הַלְלוּיָהּ:

הַלְלוּיָהּ Halleluya!
I praise *Hashem*
from the depths of my soul.
I will sing and praise *Hashem*
as long as I live.
Do not put your trust in man.
People do not live forever
and they may not be able to save you
during your time of need.
The person who turns to *Hashem* for help
will be glad.
Hashem created the heaven, earth, and sea,
and all that lives within.
Hashem alone knows truth.
Hashem protects people by:

Helping those who are struggling,
Giving food to those who are hungry,
Giving freedom to captives,
Giving sight to those who cannot see,
Supporting those who need physical help,
Loving the righteous,
Protecting the weak,
Giving strength to orphans and widows, and
Destroying the plans of the wicked.

▸ *Hashem* will rule as King forever
and for all generations.
Halleluya!

הַלְלוּיָהּ

הַלְלִי נַפְשִׁי אֶת־יהוה:

אֲהַלְלָה יהוה בְּחַיָּי, אֲזַמְּרָה לֵאלֹהַי בְּעוֹדִי:

אַל־תִּבְטְחוּ בִנְדִיבִים

בְּבֶן־אָדָם שֶׁאֵין לוֹ תְשׁוּעָה:

תֵּצֵא רוּחוֹ, יָשֻׁב לְאַדְמָתוֹ

בַּיּוֹם הַהוּא אָבְדוּ עֶשְׁתֹּנֹתָיו:

אַשְׁרֵי שֶׁאֵל יַעֲקֹב בְּעֶזְרוֹ, שִׂבְרוֹ עַל־יהוה אֱלֹהָיו:

עֹשֶׂה שָׁמַיִם וָאָרֶץ, אֶת־הַיָּם וְאֶת־כָּל־אֲשֶׁר־בָּם

הַשֹּׁמֵר אֱמֶת לְעוֹלָם:

עֹשֶׂה מִשְׁפָּט לַעֲשׁוּקִים

נֹתֵן לֶחֶם לָרְעֵבִים

יהוה מַתִּיר אֲסוּרִים:

יהוה פֹּקֵחַ עִוְרִים

יהוה זֹקֵף כְּפוּפִים

יהוה אֹהֵב צַדִּיקִים:

יהוה שֹׁמֵר אֶת־גֵּרִים

יָתוֹם וְאַלְמָנָה יְעוֹדֵד

וְדֶרֶךְ רְשָׁעִים יְעַוֵּת:

◂ יִמְלֹךְ יהוה לְעוֹלָם, אֱלֹהַיִךְ צִיּוֹן לְדֹר וָדֹר, הַלְלוּיָהּ:

הַלְלוּיָהּ Halleluya!
It is proper to sing songs to *Hashem* and to praise Him.
Hashem will rebuild Jerusalem and gather in all Jews
that are scattered around the world.
He heals the wounds of the brokenhearted.
He counts each of the stars and gives a name to each one.
Hashem is great and mighty;
His understanding has no limit.
Hashem gives courage to the humble
and casts away the wicked.
Sing out to *Hashem* in thanks and make music for Him.
Hashem covers the sky with clouds,
provides the earth with rain
and causes the hills to sprout grass.
He gives food to the cattle and birds when they cry.
It is not speed or strength that *Hashem* desires from man,
but the service and fear of God.
Praise *Hashem* who protects Jerusalem
and blesses the people within it.
He has brought peace to the land
and provided us with fine foods.

הַלְלוּיָהּ *Halleluya!* Although *Hashem* created the entire world, from the people, animals, and plants that live on Earth to the distant planets, He still pays close attention and has a special bond with each and every creation. Every star that we can see in the dark night sky, and even each star that we cannot see, is noticed by *Hashem* and is given a special name. Similarly, *Hashem* has a special connection with every person as well, and we are fortunate to be able to pray and do *mitzvot* to strengthen our relationship.

הַלְלוּיָהּ
כִּי־טוֹב זַמְּרָה אֱלֹהֵינוּ
כִּי־נָעִים נָאוָה תְהִלָּה:
בּוֹנֵה יְרוּשָׁלַםִ יהוה, נִדְחֵי יִשְׂרָאֵל יְכַנֵּס:
הָרוֹפֵא לִשְׁבוּרֵי לֵב, וּמְחַבֵּשׁ לְעַצְּבוֹתָם:
מוֹנֶה מִסְפָּר לַכּוֹכָבִים, לְכֻלָּם שֵׁמוֹת יִקְרָא:
גָּדוֹל אֲדוֹנֵינוּ וְרַב־כֹּחַ, לִתְבוּנָתוֹ אֵין מִסְפָּר:
מְעוֹדֵד עֲנָוִים יהוה, מַשְׁפִּיל רְשָׁעִים עֲדֵי־אָרֶץ:
עֱנוּ לַיהוה בְּתוֹדָה, זַמְּרוּ לֵאלֹהֵינוּ בְכִנּוֹר:
הַמְכַסֶּה שָׁמַיִם בְּעָבִים, הַמֵּכִין לָאָרֶץ מָטָר
הַמַּצְמִיחַ הָרִים חָצִיר:
נוֹתֵן לִבְהֵמָה לַחְמָהּ, לִבְנֵי עֹרֵב אֲשֶׁר יִקְרָאוּ:
לֹא בִגְבוּרַת הַסּוּס יֶחְפָּץ, לֹא־בְשׁוֹקֵי הָאִישׁ יִרְצֶה:
רוֹצֶה יהוה אֶת־יְרֵאָיו, אֶת־הַמְיַחֲלִים לְחַסְדּוֹ:
שַׁבְּחִי יְרוּשָׁלַםִ אֶת־יהוה, הַלְלִי אֱלֹהַיִךְ צִיּוֹן:
כִּי־חִזַּק בְּרִיחֵי שְׁעָרָיִךְ, בֵּרַךְ בָּנַיִךְ בְּקִרְבֵּךְ:
הַשָּׂם־גְּבוּלֵךְ שָׁלוֹם, חֵלֶב חִטִּים יַשְׂבִּיעֵךְ:
הַשֹּׁלֵחַ אִמְרָתוֹ אָרֶץ, עַד־מְהֵרָה יָרוּץ דְּבָרוֹ:
הַנֹּתֵן שֶׁלֶג כַּצָּמֶר, כְּפוֹר כָּאֵפֶר יְפַזֵּר:
מַשְׁלִיךְ קַרְחוֹ כְפִתִּים
לִפְנֵי קָרָתוֹ מִי יַעֲמֹד:

Hashem placed His commandments on earth
and shared them with the Jewish people.
He has not done this for any other nation;
▸ His laws and commandments are for the Jewish people.
Halleluya!

הַלְלוּיָהּ Halleluya!
Heaven and all of *Hashem*'s heavenly creations
praise Him,
including the:
    Angels,
    Sun, moon, and stars,
    Sky and all that is above it.
The earth and all of *Hashem*'s earthly creations
praise Him,
including the:
    Fish and sea life,
    Mountains, hills, and trees,
    Animals, insects, and birds,
    Kings and nations,
    Princes and judges,
    Young and old,
    Men and women.
▸ Let all of these people, places, and things come together
to praise *Hashem,* the only God.
Hashem's greatness fills the heavens and earth.
Halleluya!

יִשְׁלַח דְּבָרוֹ וְיַמְסֵם, יַשֵּׁב רוּחוֹ יִזְּלוּ־מָיִם:
◂ מַגִּיד דְּבָרָו לְיַעֲקֹב, חֻקָּיו וּמִשְׁפָּטָיו לְיִשְׂרָאֵל:
לֹא עָשָׂה כֵן לְכָל־גּוֹי, וּמִשְׁפָּטִים בַּל־יְדָעוּם, הַלְלוּיָהּ:

הַלְלוּיָהּ, הַלְלוּ אֶת־יהוה מִן־הַשָּׁמַיִם
הַלְלְוּהוּ בַּמְּרוֹמִים:
הַלְלְוּהוּ כָל־מַלְאָכָיו, הַלְלְוּהוּ כָּל־צְבָאָו:
הַלְלְוּהוּ שֶׁמֶשׁ וְיָרֵחַ, הַלְלְוּהוּ כָּל־כּוֹכְבֵי אוֹר:
הַלְלְוּהוּ שְׁמֵי הַשָּׁמָיִם, וְהַמַּיִם אֲשֶׁר מֵעַל הַשָּׁמָיִם:
יְהַלְלוּ אֶת־שֵׁם יהוה, כִּי הוּא צִוָּה וְנִבְרָאוּ:
וַיַּעֲמִידֵם לָעַד לְעוֹלָם, חָק־נָתַן וְלֹא יַעֲבוֹר:
הַלְלוּ אֶת־יהוה מִן־הָאָרֶץ, תַּנִּינִים וְכָל־תְּהֹמוֹת:
אֵשׁ וּבָרָד שֶׁלֶג וְקִיטוֹר, רוּחַ סְעָרָה עֹשָׂה דְבָרוֹ:
הֶהָרִים וְכָל־גְּבָעוֹת, עֵץ פְּרִי וְכָל־אֲרָזִים:
הַחַיָּה וְכָל־בְּהֵמָה, רֶמֶשׂ וְצִפּוֹר כָּנָף:
מַלְכֵי־אֶרֶץ וְכָל־לְאֻמִּים, שָׂרִים וְכָל־שֹׁפְטֵי אָרֶץ:
בַּחוּרִים וְגַם־בְּתוּלוֹת, זְקֵנִים עִם־נְעָרִים:
◂ יְהַלְלוּ אֶת־שֵׁם יהוה, כִּי־נִשְׂגָּב שְׁמוֹ לְבַדּוֹ
הוֹדוֹ עַל־אֶרֶץ וְשָׁמָיִם:
וַיָּרֶם קֶרֶן לְעַמּוֹ, תְּהִלָּה לְכָל־חֲסִידָיו
לִבְנֵי יִשְׂרָאֵל עַם קְרֹבוֹ, הַלְלוּיָהּ:

הַלְלוּיָהּ Halleluya!
Create a new song to sing praises to *Hashem*.
With joy, the Jewish people sing to *Hashem*,
our King and Creator.
Praise *Hashem* with dancing, instruments, and song.
Even as we lie in our beds ready to sleep,
we sing out praise to *Hashem*
▸ for He protects us and punishes our enemies.
Halleluya!

הַלְלוּיָהּ Halleluya!
Praise *Hashem* who rests His Presence
in the *Beit HaMikdash* and the heavens.
Praise *Hashem* for His great and mighty deeds.
Praise *Hashem* with the blast of the shofar,
with many musical instruments,
and through dance.
▸ All those who are living should praise *Hashem*, Halleluya!
All those who are living should praise *Hashem*, Halleluya!

הַלְלוּ־אֵל בְּקָדְשׁוֹ *Praise Hashem who rests His Presence.* The *Beit HaMikdash* was *Hashem*'s home. Today, the *Beit HaMikdash* no longer stands, but every shul represents the *Beit HaMikdash* and serves as *Hashem*'s home. A shul is called a *mikdash me'at*, a small *Beit HaMikdash*, and it is set up similarly. Like the *Beit HaMikdash*, the shul has an *Aron* to hold the Torah, a *Shulchan*, a table to read the Torah from, and a *Ner Tamid*, an everlasting light, which represents the light of the Menorah.

הַלְלוּיָהּ
שִׁירוּ לַיהוה שִׁיר חָדָשׁ
תְּהִלָּתוֹ בִּקְהַל חֲסִידִים:
יִשְׂמַח יִשְׂרָאֵל בְּעֹשָׂיו, בְּנֵי־צִיּוֹן יָגִילוּ בְמַלְכָּם:
יְהַלְלוּ שְׁמוֹ בְמָחוֹל, בְּתֹף וְכִנּוֹר יְזַמְּרוּ־לוֹ:
כִּי־רוֹצֶה יהוה בְּעַמּוֹ, יְפָאֵר עֲנָוִים בִּישׁוּעָה:
יַעְלְזוּ חֲסִידִים בְּכָבוֹד, יְרַנְּנוּ עַל־מִשְׁכְּבוֹתָם:
רוֹמְמוֹת אֵל בִּגְרוֹנָם, וְחֶרֶב פִּיפִיּוֹת בְּיָדָם:
לַעֲשׂוֹת נְקָמָה בַּגּוֹיִם, תּוֹכֵחוֹת בַּלְאֻמִּים:
◂ לֶאְסֹר מַלְכֵיהֶם בְּזִקִּים, וְנִכְבְּדֵיהֶם בְּכַבְלֵי בַרְזֶל:
לַעֲשׂוֹת בָּהֶם מִשְׁפָּט כָּתוּב
הָדָר הוּא לְכָל־חֲסִידָיו, הַלְלוּיָהּ:

הַלְלוּיָהּ, הַלְלוּ־אֵל בְּקָדְשׁוֹ, הַלְלוּהוּ בִּרְקִיעַ עֻזּוֹ:
הַלְלוּהוּ בִגְבוּרֹתָיו, הַלְלוּהוּ כְּרֹב גֻּדְלוֹ:
הַלְלוּהוּ בְּתֵקַע שׁוֹפָר, הַלְלוּהוּ בְּנֵבֶל וְכִנּוֹר:
הַלְלוּהוּ בְתֹף וּמָחוֹל, הַלְלוּהוּ בְּמִנִּים וְעֻגָב:
הַלְלוּהוּ בְצִלְצְלֵי־שָׁמַע, הַלְלוּהוּ בְּצִלְצְלֵי תְרוּעָה:
◂ כֹּל הַנְּשָׁמָה תְּהַלֵּל יָהּ, הַלְלוּיָהּ:
כֹּל הַנְּשָׁמָה תְּהַלֵּל יָהּ, הַלְלוּיָהּ:

בָּרוּךְ *Hashem* is praised forever.
Hashem, from Your holy city of Jerusalem,
You are praised.
Hashem, who does wonders for His people,
You are praised.
▸ *Hashem,* Your name itself is praised.
May the whole world be filled
with Your greatness forever.
Amen and *Amen.*

Stand until after "Let us Thank" (page 76).

וַיְבָרֶךְ King David thanked *Hashem* in front of the entire Jewish people, saying: Thank You *Hashem,* God of the Jewish people. You are our God and You will be our God forever. *Hashem,* You are:

Great,
Strong,
Beautiful, and
Full of glory and splendor.

Hashem, You are ruler of all, and control:

Who is wealthy and who is poor,
Who is strong and who is weak, and
Who is honored and who is not.

For all of this, we thank and praise You, *Hashem. Hashem,* You alone created and gave life to the heavens, earth, and seas, and all that is within them. ▸ You, *Hashem,* are the

בָּרוּךְ יהוה לְעוֹלָם, אָמֵן וְאָמֵן:
בָּרוּךְ יהוה מִצִּיּוֹן, שֹׁכֵן יְרוּשָׁלָםִ, הַלְלוּיָהּ:
בָּרוּךְ יהוה אֱלֹהִים אֱלֹהֵי יִשְׂרָאֵל
עֹשֵׂה נִפְלָאוֹת לְבַדּוֹ:
‹ וּבָרוּךְ שֵׁם כְּבוֹדוֹ לְעוֹלָם
וְיִמָּלֵא כְבוֹדוֹ אֶת־כָּל־הָאָרֶץ
אָמֵן וְאָמֵן:

Stand until after בָּרְכוּ *(page 77).*

וַיְבָרֶךְ דָּוִיד אֶת־יהוה לְעֵינֵי כָּל־הַקָּהָל, וַיֹּאמֶר דָּוִיד, בָּרוּךְ אַתָּה יהוה, אֱלֹהֵי יִשְׂרָאֵל אָבִינוּ, מֵעוֹלָם וְעַד־עוֹלָם: לְךָ יהוה הַגְּדֻלָּה וְהַגְּבוּרָה וְהַתִּפְאֶרֶת וְהַנֵּצַח וְהַהוֹד, כִּי־כֹל בַּשָּׁמַיִם וּבָאָרֶץ, לְךָ יהוה הַמַּמְלָכָה וְהַמִּתְנַשֵּׂא לְכֹל לְרֹאשׁ: וְהָעֹשֶׁר וְהַכָּבוֹד מִלְּפָנֶיךָ, וְאַתָּה מוֹשֵׁל בַּכֹּל, וּבְיָדְךָ כֹּחַ וּגְבוּרָה, וּבְיָדְךָ לְגַדֵּל וּלְחַזֵּק לַכֹּל: וְעַתָּה אֱלֹהֵינוּ מוֹדִים אֲנַחְנוּ לָךְ, וּמְהַלְלִים לְשֵׁם תִּפְאַרְתֶּךָ: אַתָּה־הוּא יהוה לְבַדֶּךָ, אַתָּ עָשִׂיתָ אֶת־הַשָּׁמַיִם, שְׁמֵי הַשָּׁמַיִם וְכָל־צְבָאָם, הָאָרֶץ וְכָל־אֲשֶׁר עָלֶיהָ, הַיַּמִּים וְכָל־אֲשֶׁר בָּהֶם, וְאַתָּה מְחַיֶּה אֶת־כֻּלָּם, וּצְבָא הַשָּׁמַיִם לְךָ מִשְׁתַּחֲוִים: ‹ אַתָּה הוּא יהוה הָאֱלֹהִים

God of Avraham who saved him from Ur Kasdim because he was faithful to You. ◂

וְכָרוֹת עִמּוֹ הַבְּרִית *Hashem,* You made a commitment to Avraham to give the Jewish people the Land of Israel. You fulfilled Your promise, because You are righteous. Our ancestors suffered when they were slaves in Egypt. *Hashem,* You saw their suffering and brought the miracle of the ten plagues against Pharaoh and all the Egyptians. As we escaped from Egypt, You, *Hashem,* heard our cries for help at the Sea of Reeds. *Hashem,* Your actions have made Your name famous throughout the world forever. ▸ You split the sea for the Jewish people, allowing them to walk through on dry land. Then, the Egyptians, who chased after the Jews, had the waters of the sea crash down on them, drowning them like stones.

וַיּוֹשַׁע *Hashem* saved the Jewish people on that day by rescuing them from Egypt. ▸ When the Jewish people saw that the Egyptians had been killed, they realized that *Hashem* saved them. The greatness of *Hashem*'s actions led the Jews to fear *Hashem,* and they had faith in *Hashem* and in Moshe, *Hashem*'s servant.

וְהוֹצֵאתוֹ מֵאוּר כַּשְׂדִּים *Who saved him from Ur Kasdim.* Avraham was born in Ur Kasdim, where everyone served other gods. At a very young age, Avraham found *Hashem* and began to serve Him loyally. When others found out what Avraham was doing they threw him into a large oven filled with fire and told him, "Let your God save you." Avraham walked out of the oven without injury. *Hashem* saved Avraham and showed the people of Ur Kasdim that *Hashem* is real and powerful.

אֲשֶׁר בָּחַרְתָּ בְּאַבְרָם, וְהוֹצֵאתוֹ מֵאוּר כַּשְׂדִּים, וְשַׂמְתָּ שְׁמוֹ אַבְרָהָם: וּמָצָאתָ אֶת־לְבָבוֹ נֶאֱמָן לְפָנֶיךָ, ◂ וְכָרוֹת עִמּוֹ הַבְּרִית לָתֵת אֶת־אֶרֶץ הַכְּנַעֲנִי הַחִתִּי הָאֱמֹרִי וְהַפְּרִזִּי וְהַיְבוּסִי וְהַגִּרְגָּשִׁי, לָתֵת לְזַרְעוֹ, וַתָּקֶם אֶת־דְּבָרֶיךָ, כִּי צַדִּיק אָתָּה: וַתֵּרֶא אֶת־עֳנִי אֲבֹתֵינוּ בְּמִצְרָיִם, וְאֶת־זַעֲקָתָם שָׁמַעְתָּ עַל־יַם־סוּף: וַתִּתֵּן אֹתֹת וּמֹפְתִים בְּפַרְעֹה וּבְכָל־עֲבָדָיו וּבְכָל־עַם אַרְצוֹ, כִּי יָדַעְתָּ כִּי הֵזִידוּ עֲלֵיהֶם, וַתַּעַשׂ־לְךָ שֵׁם כְּהַיּוֹם הַזֶּה: ◂ וְהַיָּם בָּקַעְתָּ לִפְנֵיהֶם, וַיַּעַבְרוּ בְתוֹךְ־הַיָּם בַּיַּבָּשָׁה, וְאֶת־רֹדְפֵיהֶם הִשְׁלַכְתָּ בִמְצוֹלֹת כְּמוֹ־אֶבֶן, בְּמַיִם עַזִּים:

וַיּוֹשַׁע יהוה בַּיּוֹם הַהוּא אֶת־יִשְׂרָאֵל מִיַּד מִצְרָיִם, וַיַּרְא יִשְׂרָאֵל אֶת־מִצְרַיִם מֵת עַל־שְׂפַת הַיָּם: ◂ וַיַּרְא יִשְׂרָאֵל אֶת־הַיָּד הַגְּדֹלָה אֲשֶׁר עָשָׂה יהוה בְּמִצְרַיִם, וַיִּירְאוּ הָעָם אֶת־יהוה, וַיַּאֲמִינוּ בַּיהוה וּבְמֹשֶׁה עַבְדּוֹ:

וַיַּרְא יִשְׂרָאֵל אֶת־הַיָּד הַגְּדֹלָה אֲשֶׁר עָשָׂה ה׳ בְּמִצְרַיִם *When the Jewish people saw that the Egyptians had been killed, they realized that Hashem saved them.* Why did the Jews need to see the Egyptians killed? When the Jews left Egypt, they thought they were free, but when they saw the entire Egyptian army chasing after them they were overcome with fear. Had *Hashem* not allowed the Jewish people to see the Egyptians dead, the Jewish people would have feared that perhaps their enemies were still alive and would continue chasing them. Seeing the Egyptians dead allowed the Jewish people to realize that *Hashem* saved them and that they were finally free.

אָז יָשִׁיר־מֹשֶׁה Then Moshe and the Jewish people sang this song to *Hashem*:

I will sing to *Hashem* for He has shown His greatness.

He threw all of our enemies, Egyptian horses and riders, into the sea.

Hashem gives me strength and protects me.

I will honor *Hashem* by doing His *mitzvot* beautifully, for He is my God.

I will praise Him for He is the God of my father.

Hashem is a warrior; His name alone wins wars.

Pharaoh's chariots and army were cast into the sea, drowning the best of the Egyptian fighters like stones.

Your hand, *Hashem,* is powerful. Your hand alone defeats our enemies.

With a blast of air, You caused the water to split and form solid walls on either side.

The enemies said, "I will chase them into the sea, draw my sword, and destroy the Jewish people."

Then, You caused another wind to blow, broke down the walls of water upon the Egyptians, and drowned them like lead.

Who is like You, *Hashem*? No being is as mighty or could perform such miracles!

You stretched out Your hand causing our enemies to be swallowed by the earth.

With Your great kindness, You then led Your Jewish people to Your Holy place.

אָז יָשִׁיר־מֹשֶׁה וּבְנֵי יִשְׂרָאֵל אֶת־הַשִּׁירָה הַזֹּאת לַיהוה, וַיֹּאמְרוּ
לֵאמֹר, אָשִׁירָה לַיהוה כִּי־גָאֹה גָּאָה, סוּס
וְרֹכְבוֹ רָמָה בַיָּם: עָזִּי וְזִמְרָת יָהּ וַיְהִי־לִי
לִישׁוּעָה, זֶה אֵלִי וְאַנְוֵהוּ, אֱלֹהֵי
אָבִי וַאֲרֹמְמֶנְהוּ: יהוה אִישׁ מִלְחָמָה, יהוה
שְׁמוֹ: מַרְכְּבֹת פַּרְעֹה וְחֵילוֹ יָרָה בַיָּם, וּמִבְחַר
שָׁלִשָׁיו טֻבְּעוּ בְיַם־סוּף: תְּהֹמֹת יְכַסְיֻמוּ, יָרְדוּ בִמְצוֹלֹת כְּמוֹ־
אָבֶן: יְמִינְךָ יהוה נֶאְדָּרִי בַּכֹּחַ, יְמִינְךָ
יהוה תִּרְעַץ אוֹיֵב: וּבְרֹב גְּאוֹנְךָ תַּהֲרֹס
קָמֶיךָ, תְּשַׁלַּח חֲרֹנְךָ יֹאכְלֵמוֹ כַּקַּשׁ: וּבְרוּחַ
אַפֶּיךָ נֶעֶרְמוּ מַיִם, נִצְּבוּ כְמוֹ־נֵד
נֹזְלִים, קָפְאוּ תְהֹמֹת בְּלֶב־יָם: אָמַר
אוֹיֵב אֶרְדֹּף, אַשִּׂיג, אֲחַלֵּק שָׁלָל, תִּמְלָאֵמוֹ
נַפְשִׁי, אָרִיק חַרְבִּי תּוֹרִישֵׁמוֹ יָדִי: נָשַׁפְתָּ
בְרוּחֲךָ כִּסָּמוֹ יָם, צָלְלוּ כַּעוֹפֶרֶת בְּמַיִם
אַדִּירִים: מִי־כָמֹכָה בָּאֵלִם יהוה, מִי
כָּמֹכָה נֶאְדָּר בַּקֹּדֶשׁ, נוֹרָא תְהִלֹּת עֹשֵׂה
פֶלֶא: נָטִיתָ יְמִינְךָ תִּבְלָעֵמוֹ אָרֶץ: נָחִיתָ
בְחַסְדְּךָ עַם־זוּ גָּאָלְתָּ, נֵהַלְתָּ בְעָזְּךָ אֶל־נְוֵה

When the other nations of the world heard of Your great power they became filled with fear:
The Philistines were gripped with terror.
The chiefs of Edom panicked.
The leaders of Moav trembled beyond control.
The people of Canaan fell apart.
You will bring the Jewish people to Your chosen mountain, build the *Beit HaMikdash*, and reign as King forever.

Hashem shall reign as King forever!
Hashem shall reign as King forever!

When Pharaoh's horses, chariots, and riders went into the sea,
Hashem covered them with water while the Jewish people walked through on dry land.

אָז נִבְהֲלוּ אַלּוּפֵי אֱדוֹם *The chiefs of Edom panicked.* Yitzchak had twin sons, Yaakov and Esav, who were the same age but were very different:

- Yaakov was born with smooth skin, while Esav appeared red and had lots of hair.
- Yaakov was a simple man who studied Torah and followed in the ways of *Hashem*, while Esav was a hunter and strong man, who chose not to follow in the ways of *Hashem*.
- Yaakov was given the additional name Yisrael, meaning "you have become great before God," while Esav was nicknamed Edom, which means "red."

The Jewish nation comes from Yaakov and is called Bnei Yisrael, the children of Yisrael, while Esav's children are not Jewish, and their nation is called Edom.

קָדְשֶׁךָ: שָׁמְעוּ עַמִּים יִרְגָּזוּן, חִיל
אָחַז יֹשְׁבֵי פְּלָשֶׁת: אָז נִבְהֲלוּ אַלּוּפֵי
אֱדוֹם, אֵילֵי מוֹאָב יֹאחֲזֵמוֹ רָעַד, נָמֹגוּ
כֹּל יֹשְׁבֵי כְנָעַן: תִּפֹּל עֲלֵיהֶם אֵימָתָה
וָפַחַד, בִּגְדֹל זְרוֹעֲךָ יִדְּמוּ כָּאָבֶן, עַד־
יַעֲבֹר עַמְּךָ יהוה, עַד־יַעֲבֹר עַם־זוּ
קָנִיתָ: תְּבִאֵמוֹ וְתִטָּעֵמוֹ בְּהַר נַחֲלָתְךָ, מָכוֹן
לְשִׁבְתְּךָ פָּעַלְתָּ יהוה, מִקְּדָשׁ אֲדֹנָי כּוֹנְנוּ
יָדֶיךָ: יהוה ׀ יִמְלֹךְ לְעֹלָם וָעֶד:

יהוה יִמְלֹךְ לְעֹלָם וָעֶד.
יהוה מַלְכוּתֵהּ קָאֵם לְעָלַם וּלְעָלְמֵי עָלְמַיָּא.

כִּי
בָא סוּס פַּרְעֹה בְּרִכְבּוֹ וּבְפָרָשָׁיו בַּיָּם, וַיָּשֶׁב יהוה עֲלֵהֶם אֶת־מֵי
הַיָּם, וּבְנֵי יִשְׂרָאֵל הָלְכוּ בַיַּבָּשָׁה בְּתוֹךְ הַיָּם:

▸ כִּי *Hashem* is the King,
He rules over all nations.
We will enter Zion
and destroy our enemies
who are in the land.
Then, on this day,
Hashem will be seen
as the only King
over all the earth!

יִשְׁתַּבַּח We sing praises
to You, *Hashem*,
as You are our King and God.
You rule over the heavens and earth
with great strength and power.
Now and forever,
we owe You
▸ unlimited blessings and thanks.
Thank You, *Hashem*,
our God, King,
and Creator of life.

◂ כִּי לַיהוה הַמְּלוּכָה וּמֹשֵׁל בַּגּוֹיִם:
וְעָלוּ מוֹשִׁעִים בְּהַר צִיּוֹן לִשְׁפֹּט אֶת־הַר עֵשָׂו
וְהָיְתָה לַיהוה הַמְּלוּכָה:
וְהָיָה יהוה לְמֶלֶךְ עַל־כָּל־הָאָרֶץ
בַּיּוֹם הַהוּא יִהְיֶה יהוה אֶחָד וּשְׁמוֹ אֶחָד:

יִשְׁתַּבַּח

שִׁמְךָ לָעַד, מַלְכֵּנוּ
הָאֵל הַמֶּלֶךְ הַגָּדוֹל וְהַקָּדוֹשׁ בַּשָּׁמַיִם וּבָאָרֶץ
כִּי לְךָ נָאֶה, יהוה אֱלֹהֵינוּ וֵאלֹהֵי אֲבוֹתֵינוּ
שִׁיר וּשְׁבָחָה, הַלֵּל וְזִמְרָה
עֹז וּמֶמְשָׁלָה, נֶצַח, גְּדֻלָּה וּגְבוּרָה
תְּהִלָּה וְתִפְאֶרֶת, קְדֻשָּׁה וּמַלְכוּת
◂ בְּרָכוֹת וְהוֹדָאוֹת, מֵעַתָּה וְעַד עוֹלָם.
בָּרוּךְ אַתָּה יהוה
אֵל מֶלֶךְ גָּדוֹל בַּתִּשְׁבָּחוֹת
אֵל הַהוֹדָאוֹת, אֲדוֹן הַנִּפְלָאוֹת
הַבּוֹחֵר בְּשִׁירֵי זִמְרָה
מֶלֶךְ, אֵל, חֵי הָעוֹלָמִים.

Between Rosh HaShana and Yom Kippur, and on Hoshana Raba add the following paragraph.

שִׁיר הַמַּעֲלוֹת From the depths of my soul, I call to You, *Hashem,* when I need You the most. Please hear my cries, *Hashem,* and listen to my requests. You, *Hashem,* forgive our mistakes, so we can be deserving of being helped. I put all my hope in You, *Hashem,* and constantly look forward to the time when You will bring *Mashiach*. *Hashem,* in Your kindness save Your Jewish people.

HALF KADDISH

Leader: יִתְגַּדַּל May *Hashem* be recognized
as great and holy (*Congregation:* Amen)
in the world that He created.
May He establish His kingdom
during my lifetime
and the lifetime of all Jews,
quickly and soon.
Let us say:
"Amen" (*Congregation:* Amen).

Congregation: May we thank *Hashem* for ever and ever.
Leader: May we thank *Hashem* for ever and ever.

Leader: *Hashem* should be thanked, praised,
and honored (*Congregation:* He is blessed).
Hashem is beyond all the blessings,
songs, or praises
that we could offer.
Let us say:
"Amen" (*Congregation:* Amen).

During the עשרת ימי תשובה*, and on* הושענא רבה*,*
add the following paragraph.

שִׁיר הַמַּעֲלוֹת, מִמַּעֲמַקִּים קְרָאתִיךָ יהוה: אֲדֹנָי שִׁמְעָה בְקוֹלִי, תִּהְיֶינָה אָזְנֶיךָ קַשֻּׁבוֹת לְקוֹל תַּחֲנוּנָי: אִם־עֲוֹנוֹת תִּשְׁמָר־יָהּ, אֲדֹנָי מִי יַעֲמֹד: כִּי־עִמְּךָ הַסְּלִיחָה, לְמַעַן תִּוָּרֵא: קִוִּיתִי יהוה קִוְּתָה נַפְשִׁי, וְלִדְבָרוֹ הוֹחָלְתִּי: נַפְשִׁי לַאדֹנָי, מִשֹּׁמְרִים לַבֹּקֶר, שֹׁמְרִים לַבֹּקֶר: יַחֵל יִשְׂרָאֵל אֶל יהוה, כִּי־עִם־יהוה הַחֶסֶד, וְהַרְבֵּה עִמּוֹ פְדוּת: וְהוּא יִפְדֶּה אֶת־יִשְׂרָאֵל, מִכֹּל עֲוֹנֹתָיו:

חצי קדיש

חזן: יִתְגַּדַּל וְיִתְקַדַּשׁ שְׁמֵהּ רַבָּא (קהל: אָמֵן)
בְּעָלְמָא דִּי בְרָא כִרְעוּתֵהּ, וְיַמְלִיךְ מַלְכוּתֵהּ
בְּחַיֵּיכוֹן וּבְיוֹמֵיכוֹן וּבְחַיֵּי דְכָל בֵּית יִשְׂרָאֵל
בַּעֲגָלָא וּבִזְמַן קָרִיב, וְאִמְרוּ אָמֵן. (קהל: אָמֵן)

קהל יְהֵא שְׁמֵהּ רַבָּא מְבָרַךְ לְעָלַם וּלְעָלְמֵי עָלְמַיָּא.
חזן: יְהֵא שְׁמֵהּ רַבָּא מְבָרַךְ לְעָלַם וּלְעָלְמֵי עָלְמַיָּא.

חזן: יִתְבָּרַךְ וְיִשְׁתַּבַּח וְיִתְפָּאַר וְיִתְרוֹמַם וְיִתְנַשֵּׂא
וְיִתְהַדָּר וְיִתְעַלֶּה וְיִתְהַלָּל
שְׁמֵהּ דְּקֻדְשָׁא בְּרִיךְ הוּא (קהל: בְּרִיךְ הוּא)
לְעֵלָּא מִן כָּל בִּרְכָתָא
/בעשרת ימי תשובה: לְעֵלָּא לְעֵלָּא מִכָּל בִּרְכָתָא/
וְשִׁירָתָא, תֻּשְׁבְּחָתָא וְנֶחֱמָתָא
דַּאֲמִירָן בְּעָלְמָא, וְאִמְרוּ אָמֵן. (קהל: אָמֵן)

BLESSINGS OF THE SHEMA

Only say the following introduction when praying with a minyan:

Bow when saying the word "Thank."

Leader: **LET US THANK**
Hashem,
for He deserves thanksgiving.

Congregation: Thank *Hashem* for ever and ever!

Leader: Thank *Hashem* for ever and ever!

Those praying without a minyan begin here:

Sit when saying this section.

בָּרוּךְ Thank You, *Hashem,* our God, King of the world,
Who creates light and darkness,
Makes peace, and creates all.

הַמֵּאִיר לָאָרֶץ With mercy, *Hashem*
sheds light onto the land
and the people who live upon it.
With goodness,
He continues to renew the works of creation every day.
The earth is filled with Your many creations
which are made with great wisdom.
Hashem alone is King
and has been since the beginning of time.
He has been praised, honored,
and elevated since the world began.

קריאת שמע וברכותיה

Only say the following introduction when praying with a מנין:

Bow when saying the word בָּרוּךְ.

חזן: בָּרְכוּ אֶת יהוה הַמְבֹרָךְ.

קהל: בָּרוּךְ יהוה הַמְבֹרָךְ לְעוֹלָם וָעֶד.

חזן: בָּרוּךְ יהוה הַמְבֹרָךְ לְעוֹלָם וָעֶד.

Those praying without a מנין begin here:

Sit when saying this section.

בָּרוּךְ אַתָּה יהוה אֱלֹהֵינוּ מֶלֶךְ הָעוֹלָם
יוֹצֵר אוֹר וּבוֹרֵא חֹשֶׁךְ
עֹשֶׂה שָׁלוֹם וּבוֹרֵא אֶת הַכֹּל.

הַמֵּאִיר לָאָרֶץ וְלַדָּרִים עָלֶיהָ בְּרַחֲמִים
וּבְטוּבוֹ מְחַדֵּשׁ בְּכָל יוֹם תָּמִיד מַעֲשֵׂה בְרֵאשִׁית.
מָה־רַבּוּ מַעֲשֶׂיךָ יהוה, כֻּלָּם בְּחָכְמָה עָשִׂיתָ
מָלְאָה הָאָרֶץ קִנְיָנֶךָ:
הַמֶּלֶךְ הַמְרוֹמָם לְבַדּוֹ מֵאָז
הַמְשֻׁבָּח וְהַמְפֹאָר וְהַמִּתְנַשֵּׂא מִימוֹת עוֹלָם.

With Your great mercy,
Hashem,
take pity on us.
Hashem,
our God,
You are the source
of our strength and protection.

With great knowledge,
Hashem created the sun and stars.
Hashem created angels
who honor Him
by announcing His holiness.
Thank You *Hashem,* our God,
for forming the sun, moon, and stars,
and all of Your excellent creations.
May all Your creations
praise You forever!

תִּתְבָּרַךְ Thank You,
our Protector and King,
for creating holy beings.
May You be praised forever!
Our everlasting King and living God,
You created angels
who announce Your holy words.

אֱלֹהֵי עוֹלָם
בְּרַחֲמֶיךָ הָרַבִּים רַחֵם עָלֵינוּ
אֲדוֹן עֻזֵּנוּ, צוּר מִשְׂגַּבֵּנוּ
מָגֵן יִשְׁעֵנוּ, מִשְׂגָּב בַּעֲדֵנוּ.
אֵל בָּרוּךְ גְּדוֹל דֵּעָה
הֵכִין וּפָעַל זָהֳרֵי חַמָּה
טוֹב יָצַר כָּבוֹד לִשְׁמוֹ
מְאוֹרוֹת נָתַן סְבִיבוֹת עֻזּוֹ
פִּנּוֹת צְבָאָיו קְדוֹשִׁים, רוֹמְמֵי שַׁדַּי
תָּמִיד מְסַפְּרִים כְּבוֹד אֵל וּקְדֻשָּׁתוֹ.
תִּתְבָּרַךְ יהוה אֱלֹהֵינוּ
עַל שֶׁבַח מַעֲשֵׂה יָדֶיךָ.
וְעַל מְאוֹרֵי אוֹר שֶׁעָשִׂיתָ
יְפָאֲרוּךָ סֶּלָה.

תִּתְבָּרַךְ
צוּרֵנוּ מַלְכֵּנוּ וְגוֹאֲלֵנוּ, בּוֹרֵא קְדוֹשִׁים
יִשְׁתַּבַּח שִׁמְךָ לָעַד, מַלְכֵּנוּ, יוֹצֵר מְשָׁרְתִים
וַאֲשֶׁר מְשָׁרְתָיו כֻּלָּם עוֹמְדִים בְּרוּם עוֹלָם
וּמַשְׁמִיעִים בְּיִרְאָה יַחַד בְּקוֹל
דִּבְרֵי אֱלֹהִים חַיִּים וּמֶלֶךְ עוֹלָם.

The angels perform the will
of their Creator, *Hashem,*
with purity, might, appreciation, and devotion.
▸ The angels open their holy and pure mouths
in song to:

Bless,
Praise,
Give honor to, and
Declare the Kingship of –

Hashem, our God,
the great, mighty, awesome, and holy King.
▸ All of the angels accept upon themselves
the responsibility of serving *Hashem.*
They dedicate themselves to *Hashem,*
their Creator,
by praising Him
with pure speech and sweet songs.
Together as one,
all of the angels announce *Hashem*'s holiness
by saying:

Say the following line out loud:
"Holy, holy, holy is *Hashem*:
the world is filled with His honor!"

▸ In response, the angels turn to each other
and enthusiastically praise *Hashem*
by saying:

Say the following line out loud:
"Blessed is the honor of *Hashem*!"

כֻּלָּם אֲהוּבִים, כֻּלָּם בְּרוּרִים, כֻּלָּם גִּבּוֹרִים
וְכֻלָּם עוֹשִׂים בְּאֵימָה וּבְיִרְאָה רְצוֹן קוֹנָם
◂ וְכֻלָּם פּוֹתְחִים אֶת פִּיהֶם בִּקְדֻשָּׁה וּבְטָהֳרָה
בְּשִׁירָה וּבְזִמְרָה
וּמְבָרְכִים וּמְשַׁבְּחִים וּמְפָאֲרִים
וּמַעֲרִיצִים וּמַקְדִּישִׁים וּמַמְלִיכִים ◂
אֶת שֵׁם הָאֵל הַמֶּלֶךְ הַגָּדוֹל, הַגִּבּוֹר וְהַנּוֹרָא
קָדוֹשׁ הוּא.
◂ וְכֻלָּם מְקַבְּלִים עֲלֵיהֶם עֹל מַלְכוּת שָׁמַיִם זֶה מִזֶּה
וְנוֹתְנִים רְשׁוּת זֶה לָזֶה
לְהַקְדִּישׁ לְיוֹצְרָם בְּנַחַת רוּחַ
בְּשָׂפָה בְרוּרָה וּבִנְעִימָה
קְדֻשָּׁה כֻּלָּם כְּאֶחָד
עוֹנִים וְאוֹמְרִים בְּיִרְאָה

Say the following line out loud:

קָדוֹשׁ, קָדוֹשׁ, קָדוֹשׁ יהוה צְבָאוֹת
מְלֹא כָל־הָאָרֶץ כְּבוֹדוֹ:

◂ וְהָאוֹפַנִּים וְחַיּוֹת הַקֹּדֶשׁ
בְּרַעַשׁ גָּדוֹל מִתְנַשְּׂאִים לְעֻמַּת שְׂרָפִים
לְעֻמָּתָם מְשַׁבְּחִים וְאוֹמְרִים

Say the following line out loud:

בָּרוּךְ כְּבוֹד־יהוה מִמְּקוֹמוֹ:

לְאֵל בָּרוּךְ Sing sweet songs of praise
to *Hashem*, our King,
the living God who alone:

Acts with great might,
Creates new things,
Is the Master of war,
Rewards those who act kindly,
Rescues us,
Creates cures,
Deserves praise, and
Performs miracles.

In His greatness,
Hashem renews the works of creation every day.

May You, *Hashem*,
continue to recreate the sun, moon, and stars,
so that we, Your Jewish people,
may enjoy that light.

▸ *Hashem,* please allow that light to shine
on a rebuilt Jerusalem.
Thank You, *Hashem*, who creates the sources of light.

אַהֲבָה רַבָּה You, *Hashem*, have shown us
great love and kindness.
Our Father and King,
remember our ancestors who put their trust in You.
Just as You taught them the laws of Your Torah
and guided them on how to live life,
please teach and guide us as well.

לָאֵל בָּרוּךְ נְעִימוֹת יִתֵּנוּ, לַמֶּלֶךְ אֵל חַי וְקַיָּם
זְמִירוֹת יֹאמֵרוּ וְתִשְׁבָּחוֹת יַשְׁמִיעוּ
כִּי הוּא לְבַדּוֹ
פּוֹעֵל גְּבוּרוֹת
עוֹשֶׂה חֲדָשׁוֹת
בַּעַל מִלְחָמוֹת
זוֹרֵעַ צְדָקוֹת
מַצְמִיחַ יְשׁוּעוֹת
בּוֹרֵא רְפוּאוֹת
נוֹרָא תְהִלּוֹת
אֲדוֹן הַנִּפְלָאוֹת
הַמְחַדֵּשׁ בְּטוּבוֹ בְּכָל יוֹם תָּמִיד מַעֲשֵׂה בְרֵאשִׁית
כָּאָמוּר
לְעֹשֵׂה אוֹרִים גְּדֹלִים, כִּי לְעוֹלָם חַסְדּוֹ:
‹ אוֹר חָדָשׁ עַל צִיּוֹן תָּאִיר וְנִזְכֶּה כֻלָּנוּ מְהֵרָה לְאוֹרוֹ.
בָּרוּךְ אַתָּה יהוה, יוֹצֵר הַמְּאוֹרוֹת.

אַהֲבָה רַבָּה אֲהַבְתָּנוּ, יהוה אֱלֹהֵינוּ
חֶמְלָה גְדוֹלָה וִיתֵרָה חָמַלְתָּ עָלֵינוּ.
אָבִינוּ מַלְכֵּנוּ
בַּעֲבוּר אֲבוֹתֵינוּ שֶׁבָּטְחוּ בְךָ
וַתְּלַמְּדֵם חֻקֵּי חַיִּים, כֵּן תְּחָנֵּנוּ וּתְלַמְּדֵנוּ.

Just as a father shows kindness to a child,
please show kindness to us.
Let our hearts desire to:

Understand,
Listen,
Learn,
Teach,
Keep,
Perform, and
Fulfill,

All the laws of Your Torah with love.
Let our eyes see and understand more of Your Torah,
and let our hearts continue to grow in love
for Your *mitzvot.*
As one nation, let all of our hearts join together
to love You, *Hashem.*
We believe that we will soon rejoice
in being saved by You.

Those wearing TZITZIT *should pick them up in their left hand.*

Today, the Jewish people are scattered
all over the world.
Please bring us back to our land, Israel, peacefully.
▸ As God, You chose us from all the nations of the world,
and we trust that You will save us.
You have brought us close to You
so we can lovingly praise and thank You.
Thank You, *Hashem,*
for showing us love
by choosing us as Your people.

אָבִינוּ, הָאָב הָרַחֲמָן, הַמְרַחֵם
רַחֵם עָלֵינוּ, וְתֵן בְּלִבֵּנוּ
לְהָבִין וּלְהַשְׂכִּיל, לִשְׁמֹעַ
לִלְמֹד וּלְלַמֵּד, לִשְׁמֹר וְלַעֲשׂוֹת, וּלְקַיֵּם
אֶת כָּל דִּבְרֵי תַלְמוּד תּוֹרָתֶךָ בְּאַהֲבָה.
וְהָאֵר עֵינֵינוּ בְּתוֹרָתֶךָ, וְדַבֵּק לִבֵּנוּ בְּמִצְוֹתֶיךָ
וְיַחֵד לְבָבֵנוּ לְאַהֲבָה וּלְיִרְאָה אֶת שְׁמֶךָ
וְלֹא נֵבוֹשׁ לְעוֹלָם וָעֶד.
כִּי בְשֵׁם קָדְשְׁךָ הַגָּדוֹל וְהַנּוֹרָא בָּטָחְנוּ
נָגִילָה וְנִשְׂמְחָה בִּישׁוּעָתֶךָ.

Those wearing ציצית *should pick them up in their left hand.*

וַהֲבִיאֵנוּ לְשָׁלוֹם מֵאַרְבַּע כַּנְפוֹת הָאָרֶץ
וְתוֹלִיכֵנוּ קוֹמְמִיּוּת לְאַרְצֵנוּ.
► כִּי אֵל פּוֹעֵל יְשׁוּעוֹת אָתָּה וּבָנוּ בָחַרְתָּ מִכָּל עַם וְלָשׁוֹן
וְקֵרַבְתָּנוּ לְשִׁמְךָ הַגָּדוֹל סֶלָה, בֶּאֱמֶת
לְהוֹדוֹת לְךָ וּלְיַחֶדְךָ בְּאַהֲבָה.
בָּרוּךְ אַתָּה יהוה, הַבּוֹחֵר בְּעַמּוֹ יִשְׂרָאֵל בְּאַהֲבָה.

הַבּוֹחֵר בְּעַמּוֹ יִשְׂרָאֵל בְּאַהֲבָה *For showing us love by choosing us as Your people.* While *Hashem* loves every Jew individually, he has a special kind of love for us as a nation. *Hashem* loves when Jews pray to Him, but it is even greater when Jews pray in a *minyan*. This adds extra honor to *Hashem*, our King: "*B'rov am hadrat melech*," "a large group brings honor to the king." The more people praying, the greater the honor.

Say this line when praying alone:

God, You are our trustworthy King.

Cover your eyes with your right hand, and say this line aloud:

LISTEN AND UNDERSTAND, JEWISH PEOPLE, *HASHEM* IS OUR ONE AND ONLY GOD.

Say this line quietly:

Thank You, *Hashem*, our God.
Your kingdom lasts forever.

Touch the TEFILLIN SHEL YAD *and the* TEFILLIN SHEL ROSH *at the relevant icons.*

וְאָהַבְתָּ Love *Hashem*, your God,
with all of your heart, soul, and belongings.
Live according to God's words and *mitzvot*.
Think about and recite the Shema
when sitting in your home,
when traveling on the road,
when you go to sleep at night,
and when you first wake up in the morning.
Wear *tefillin* on your arm and head,
and hang a *mezuzah* on your door.

וְאָהַבְתָּ אֵת ה׳ אֱלֹהֶיךָ, בְּכָל־לְבָבְךָ וּבְכָל־נַפְשְׁךָ וּבְכָל־מְאֹדֶךָ *Love Hashem, your God, with all of your heart, soul, and belongings.* We must love *Hashem* with all our:

- HEARTS – We are excited to serve *Hashem* every day!
- SOULS – *Hashem* gave us life and therefore we dedicate ourselves to Him!
- BELONGINGS – Everything we have is a gift from *Hashem* and therefore we are ready to serve Him with everything we own.

Say this line when praying alone:

אֵל מֶלֶךְ נֶאֱמָן

Cover your eyes with your right hand, and say this line aloud:

שְׁמַע יִשְׂרָאֵל, יְהֹוָה אֱלֹהֵינוּ, יְהֹוָה ׀ אֶחָד:

Say this line quietly:

בָּרוּךְ שֵׁם כְּבוֹד מַלְכוּתוֹ לְעוֹלָם וָעֶד.

Touch the תפילין של יד *and the* תפילין של ראש *at the relevant icons.*

וְאָהַבְתָּ אֵת יְהֹוָה אֱלֹהֶיךָ
בְּכָל־לְבָבְךָ וּבְכָל־נַפְשְׁךָ וּבְכָל־מְאֹדֶךָ:
וְהָיוּ הַדְּבָרִים הָאֵלֶּה
אֲשֶׁר אָנֹכִי מְצַוְּךָ הַיּוֹם, עַל־לְבָבֶךָ:
וְשִׁנַּנְתָּם לְבָנֶיךָ וְדִבַּרְתָּ בָּם
בְּשִׁבְתְּךָ בְּבֵיתֶךָ וּבְלֶכְתְּךָ בַדֶּרֶךְ, וּבְשָׁכְבְּךָ וּבְקוּמֶךָ:
וּקְשַׁרְתָּם לְאוֹת עַל־יָדֶךָ
וְהָיוּ לְטֹטָפֹת בֵּין עֵינֶיךָ:
וּכְתַבְתָּם עַל־מְזֻזוֹת בֵּיתֶךָ וּבִשְׁעָרֶיךָ:

שְׁמַע יִשְׂרָאֵל, ה׳ אֱלֹהֵינוּ, ה׳ אֶחָד *Listen and understand, Jewish people, Hashem is our one and only God.* When we say Shema, we cover our eyes and concentrate on *Hashem* and how He alone rules the world. Everything comes from Him and everything is controlled by Him. The "ע" and "ד" in the *pasuk* of Shema are written larger than the other letters. Together, these two letters spell the word עד, witness. When we say Shema and declare out loud that *Hashem* is God, we serve as witnesses that *Hashem* alone is King.

Touch the TEFILLIN SHEL YAD *and the* TEFILLIN SHEL ROSH *at the relevant icons.*

וְהָיָה If you live according to the *mitzvot* of *Hashem,*
loving and serving Him with all your effort,
Hashem will give you reward.
Hashem will bring rain for your plants to grow
and provide you with the food you need to live.
However, if you sin and do not serve *Hashem,*
there will be consequences and punishments;
Hashem might not provide you
with health, money, or other basics you need to live.
Therefore, be careful to follow *Hashem's mitzvot*
and set yourself reminders,
such as wearing *tefillin* on
your arms and head,
and placing *mezuzot* on your doorposts.
If you do this, you will live a long life.

הִשָּׁמְרוּ לָכֶם *However, if you sin.* We read in *Shema* that the reward from *Hashem* for keeping the *mitzvot* is having enough rain to grow the food we need to live. Right after this, *Hashem* tells us what the punishment will be if we do not keep the *mitzvot.* Why do we need both, one right after the other? When people are successful, they have more than enough food to eat, along with many other kinds of riches from their work. This is the exact time when it is easiest to forget that all the success comes only from *Hashem.* Man can be blinded by his own success, thinking everything he has is because of his own work, effort, and ideas. He forgets that everything we have is only because *Hashem* wants us to have it and enjoy it. By placing the punishment for not serving *Hashem* right after the reward, we are being warned not to fall into the trap of thinking that we are in control of our success. By keeping this in mind, we will hopefully never need to experience the punishment described here.

Touch the תפילין של יד *and the* תפילין של ראש *at the relevant icons.*

וְהָיָה אִם־שָׁמֹעַ תִּשְׁמְעוּ אֶל־מִצְוֹתַי
אֲשֶׁר אָנֹכִי מְצַוֶּה אֶתְכֶם הַיּוֹם
לְאַהֲבָה אֶת־יהוה אֱלֹהֵיכֶם וּלְעָבְדוֹ
בְּכָל־לְבַבְכֶם וּבְכָל־נַפְשְׁכֶם:
וְנָתַתִּי מְטַר־אַרְצְכֶם בְּעִתּוֹ, יוֹרֶה וּמַלְקוֹשׁ
וְאָסַפְתָּ דְגָנֶךָ וְתִירֹשְׁךָ וְיִצְהָרֶךָ:
וְנָתַתִּי עֵשֶׂב בְּשָׂדְךָ לִבְהֶמְתֶּךָ, וְאָכַלְתָּ וְשָׂבָעְתָּ:
הִשָּׁמְרוּ לָכֶם פֶּן־יִפְתֶּה לְבַבְכֶם
וְסַרְתֶּם וַעֲבַדְתֶּם אֱלֹהִים אֲחֵרִים וְהִשְׁתַּחֲוִיתֶם לָהֶם:
וְחָרָה אַף־יהוה בָּכֶם, וְעָצַר אֶת־הַשָּׁמַיִם וְלֹא־יִהְיֶה מָטָר
וְהָאֲדָמָה לֹא תִתֵּן אֶת־יְבוּלָהּ
וַאֲבַדְתֶּם מְהֵרָה מֵעַל הָאָרֶץ הַטֹּבָה אֲשֶׁר יהוה נֹתֵן לָכֶם:
וְשַׂמְתֶּם אֶת־דְּבָרַי אֵלֶּה עַל־לְבַבְכֶם וְעַל־נַפְשְׁכֶם
וּקְשַׁרְתֶּם אֹתָם לְאוֹת עַל־יֶדְכֶם
וְהָיוּ לְטוֹטָפֹת בֵּין עֵינֵיכֶם:
וְלִמַּדְתֶּם אֹתָם אֶת־בְּנֵיכֶם לְדַבֵּר בָּם
בְּשִׁבְתְּךָ בְּבֵיתֶךָ וּבְלֶכְתְּךָ בַדֶּרֶךְ, וּבְשָׁכְבְּךָ וּבְקוּמֶךָ:
וּכְתַבְתָּם עַל־מְזוּזוֹת בֵּיתֶךָ וּבִשְׁעָרֶיךָ:
לְמַעַן יִרְבּוּ יְמֵיכֶם וִימֵי בְנֵיכֶם עַל הָאֲדָמָה
אֲשֶׁר נִשְׁבַּע יהוה לַאֲבֹתֵיכֶם לָתֵת לָהֶם
כִּימֵי הַשָּׁמַיִם עַל־הָאָרֶץ:

Place your TZITZIT *in your right hand and kiss them each time you read the word "*TZITZIT.*"*

Look at your TZITZIT *when you read the words "*YOU CAN SEE THEM.*"*

וַיֹּאמֶר *Hashem* told Moshe
that we, the Jewish people,
should have *tzitzit*
on the corners of our clothing.
Each set of *tzitzit* strings
should have a blue string.
The *tzitzit* should be worn
so that you can see them.
They will remind you to focus on God
and His *mitzvot.*
Hashem, the same God
who miraculously saved the Jewish people
from slavery in Egypt,
is your God.

THIS IS TRUE.

The Leader repeats:

▸ *Hashem* is your true God.

אֲנִי ה׳ אֱלֹהֵיכֶם, אֲשֶׁר הוֹצֵאתִי אֶתְכֶם מֵאֶרֶץ מִצְרַיִם לִהְיוֹת לָכֶם לֵאלֹהִים *Hashem, the same God who miraculously saved the Jewish people from slavery in Egypt, is your God.* It is a special *mitzva* to remember that the Jewish people were once slaves in Mitzrayim, Egypt, and that *Hashem* led us out to freedom. We do this *mitzva* by saying this *pasuk* every day. The purpose of this *mitzva* is to remember that while freeing us from Mitzrayim, *Hashem* did many miracles for us which made it clear to everyone, both Jews and non-Jews, that *Hashem* is God over the entire world.

Place your ציצית in your right hand and kiss them each time you read the word ציצית.

Look at your ציצית when you read the words וּרְאִיתֶם אֹתוֹ.

וַיֹּ֥אמֶר יְהֹוָ֖ה אֶל־מֹשֶׁ֥ה לֵּאמֹֽר׃
דַּבֵּ֞ר אֶל־בְּנֵ֤י יִשְׂרָאֵל֙ וְאָמַרְתָּ֣ אֲלֵהֶ֔ם
וְעָשׂ֨וּ לָהֶ֥ם צִיצִ֛ת עַל־כַּנְפֵ֥י בִגְדֵיהֶ֖ם לְדֹרֹתָ֑ם
וְנָֽתְנ֛וּ עַל־צִיצִ֥ת הַכָּנָ֖ף פְּתִ֥יל תְּכֵֽלֶת׃
וְהָיָ֣ה לָכֶם֮ לְצִיצִת֒
וּרְאִיתֶ֣ם אֹת֗וֹ
וּזְכַרְתֶּם֙ אֶת־כָּל־מִצְוֺ֣ת יְהֹוָ֔ה וַעֲשִׂיתֶ֖ם אֹתָ֑ם
וְלֹֽא תָת֜וּרוּ אַחֲרֵ֤י לְבַבְכֶם֙ וְאַחֲרֵ֣י עֵֽינֵיכֶ֔ם
אֲשֶׁר־אַתֶּ֥ם זֹנִ֖ים אַחֲרֵיהֶֽם׃
לְמַ֣עַן תִּזְכְּר֔וּ וַעֲשִׂיתֶ֖ם אֶת־כָּל־מִצְוֺתָ֑י
וִהְיִיתֶ֥ם קְדֹשִׁ֖ים לֵאלֹֽהֵיכֶֽם׃
אֲנִ֞י יְהֹוָ֣ה אֱלֹֽהֵיכֶ֗ם
אֲשֶׁ֨ר הוֹצֵ֤אתִי אֶתְכֶם֙ מֵאֶ֣רֶץ מִצְרַ֔יִם
לִהְי֥וֹת לָכֶ֖ם לֵאלֹהִ֑ים
אֲנִ֖י יְהֹוָ֥ה אֱלֹהֵיכֶֽם׃

אֱמֶת

The חזן repeats:

◂ יְהֹוָה אֱלֹהֵיכֶם אֱמֶת

True and solid, established and lasting, right,
trustworthy, loved, dear, pleasant,
awesome, mighty, perfect, good, and beautiful
is our belief in *Hashem* forever.

True is *Hashem,* our God, King and Protector.
He lives through all generations.
His throne,
Kingship, and trustworthiness are everlasting.

At the icon, kiss the TZITZIT *and release them.*

Hashem's words exist for all time.
Just as the words of Torah
▸ guided our ancestors,
so to do they guide us,
and they will continue to guide our children
and all of their children after them.◂
Our belief in *Hashem*
has lasted since earlier generations
and remained strong
through all generations that followed.
Our belief lasts forever
and does not change.

It is true that You, *Hashem,* are our:
God and God of our ancestors,
▸ King and King of our ancestors,
Protector and Protector of our ancestors,
Creator and Savior,
and Deliverer and Rescuer.
There is no God but You.

וְיַצִּיב, וְנָכוֹן וְקַיָּם, וְיָשָׁר וְנֶאֱמָן
וְאָהוּב וְחָבִיב, וְנֶחְמָד וְנָעִים
וְנוֹרָא וְאַדִּיר, וּמְתֻקָּן וּמְקֻבָּל, וְטוֹב וְיָפֶה
הַדָּבָר הַזֶּה עָלֵינוּ לְעוֹלָם וָעֶד.

אֱמֶת אֱלֹהֵי עוֹלָם מַלְכֵּנוּ
צוּר יַעֲקֹב מָגֵן יִשְׁעֵנוּ
לְדוֹר וָדוֹר הוּא קַיָּם וּשְׁמוֹ קַיָּם
וְכִסְאוֹ נָכוֹן
וּמַלְכוּתוֹ וֶאֱמוּנָתוֹ לָעַד קַיֶּמֶת.

At the icon, kiss the ציצית *and release them.*

וּדְבָרָיו חָיִים וְקַיָּמִים, נֶאֱמָנִים וְנֶחֱמָדִים
לָעַד וּלְעוֹלְמֵי עוֹלָמִים
◂ עַל אֲבוֹתֵינוּ וְעָלֵינוּ, עַל בָּנֵינוּ וְעַל דּוֹרוֹתֵינוּ
וְעַל כָּל דּוֹרוֹת זֶרַע יִשְׂרָאֵל עֲבָדֶיךָ. ◂
עַל הָרִאשׁוֹנִים וְעַל הָאַחֲרוֹנִים
דָּבָר טוֹב וְקַיָּם לְעוֹלָם וָעֶד

אֱמֶת וֶאֱמוּנָה, חֹק וְלֹא יַעֲבֹר.

אֱמֶת שָׁאַתָּה הוּא יהוה אֱלֹהֵינוּ וֵאלֹהֵי אֲבוֹתֵינוּ
◂ מַלְכֵּנוּ מֶלֶךְ אֲבוֹתֵינוּ, גּוֹאֲלֵנוּ גּוֹאֵל אֲבוֹתֵינוּ
יוֹצְרֵנוּ צוּר יְשׁוּעָתֵנוּ, פּוֹדֵנוּ וּמַצִּילֵנוּ מֵעוֹלָם שְׁמֶךָ
אֵין אֱלֹהִים זוּלָתֶךָ.

עֶזְרַת *Hashem*, You have always been there
to help our ancestors,
and You continuously protect
and save their children in every generation.
You exist beyond our universe.
Your justice and righteousness
reach the whole earth.
Praiseworthy is the person
who follows Your *mitzvot*
and listens to the words of Your Torah.

It is true that You are a mighty King
and Master of Your people.

It is true that You are the first and You are the last;
there is no king, protector, or savior besides You.
You, *Hashem*, our God,
saved us from Egypt where we were enslaved.
You split the Reed Sea,
allowed Your beloved Jewish people
to cross on dry land,
and drowned our enemies.
Not even one of our enemies survived.

For this reason, we praise and sing, bless and thank
Hashem, our King, the living God.
Hashem is elevated, great, and awesome.
He lowers those who think too highly of themselves,
and raises those who think lowly of themselves.
He saves those in need, helps the poor,
and answers His people when they cry out to Him.

עֶזְרַת אֲבוֹתֵינוּ אַתָּה הוּא מֵעוֹלָם
מָגֵן וּמוֹשִׁיעַ לִבְנֵיהֶם אַחֲרֵיהֶם בְּכָל דּוֹר וָדוֹר.
בְּרוּם עוֹלָם מוֹשָׁבֶךָ
וּמִשְׁפָּטֶיךָ וְצִדְקָתְךָ עַד אַפְסֵי אָרֶץ.
אַשְׁרֵי אִישׁ שֶׁיִּשְׁמַע לְמִצְוֹתֶיךָ
וְתוֹרָתְךָ וּדְבָרְךָ יָשִׂים עַל לִבּוֹ.
אֱמֶת אַתָּה הוּא אָדוֹן לְעַמֶּךָ, וּמֶלֶךְ גִּבּוֹר לָרִיב רִיבָם.
אֱמֶת אַתָּה הוּא רִאשׁוֹן וְאַתָּה הוּא אַחֲרוֹן
וּמִבַּלְעָדֶיךָ אֵין לָנוּ מֶלֶךְ גּוֹאֵל וּמוֹשִׁיעַ.
מִמִּצְרַיִם גְּאַלְתָּנוּ, יהוה אֱלֹהֵינוּ
וּמִבֵּית עֲבָדִים פְּדִיתָנוּ
כָּל בְּכוֹרֵיהֶם הָרָגְתָּ, וּבְכוֹרְךָ גָּאָלְתָּ
וְיַם סוּף בָּקַעְתָּ, וְזֵדִים טִבַּעְתָּ, וִידִידִים הֶעֱבַרְתָּ
וַיְכַסּוּ־מַיִם צָרֵיהֶם, אֶחָד מֵהֶם לֹא נוֹתָר:

עַל זֹאת שִׁבְּחוּ אֲהוּבִים, וְרוֹמְמוּ אֵל
וְנָתְנוּ יְדִידִים זְמִירוֹת, שִׁירוֹת וְתִשְׁבָּחוֹת
בְּרָכוֹת וְהוֹדָאוֹת לְמֶלֶךְ אֵל חַי וְקַיָּם
רָם וְנִשָּׂא, גָּדוֹל וְנוֹרָא
מַשְׁפִּיל גֵּאִים וּמַגְבִּיהַּ שְׁפָלִים
מוֹצִיא אֲסִירִים, וּפוֹדֶה עֲנָוִים וְעוֹזֵר דַּלִּים
וְעוֹנֶה לְעַמּוֹ בְּעֵת שַׁוְּעָם אֵלָיו.

Stand while saying this section.
Take three steps back.

▸ Praise to *Hashem,* our God, who deserves thanks.
When Moshe and the Jewish people
sang with great joy
they said:
"Who is as strong as You, *Hashem*?
Who is as holy and awesome as You, *Hashem*?"

▸ The Jewish people praised You, *Hashem,*
with a new song at the seashore.
Together, they all gave thanks
and announced You as King,
saying:
"*Hashem* will rule as King for ever and ever."

▸ *Hashem,* fortress of Your Jewish people,
arise and help Your Jewish people.
Deliver us as You promised.
Our savior is *Hashem,*
the source of our holiness.

Thank You, *Hashem,*
for saving the Jewish people.

תְּהִלּוֹת לְאֵל עֶלְיוֹן *Praise to Hashem, our God.* Prior to saying the Amida, one takes three steps forward. These steps help us prepare ourselves as we stand before *Hashem* and make requests from Him. While taking the three steps, one should think about coming before the throne of the greatest King of all kings, *Hashem.*

Stand while saying this section.
Take three steps back.

תְּהִלּוֹת לְאֵל עֶלְיוֹן
בָּרוּךְ הוּא וּמְבֹרָךְ
מֹשֶׁה וּבְנֵי יִשְׂרָאֵל
לְךָ עָנוּ שִׁירָה בְּשִׂמְחָה רַבָּה
וְאָמְרוּ כֻלָּם
מִי־כָמֹֽכָה בָּאֵלִם, יהוה
מִי כָּמֹֽכָה נֶאְדָּר בַּקֹּֽדֶשׁ
נוֹרָא תְהִלֹּת, עֹֽשֵׂה פֶֽלֶא:

שִׁירָה חֲדָשָׁה שִׁבְּחוּ גְאוּלִים
לְשִׁמְךָ עַל שְׂפַת הַיָּם
יַֽחַד כֻּלָּם הוֹדוּ וְהִמְלִֽיכוּ
וְאָמְרוּ
יהוה יִמְלֹךְ לְעֹלָם וָעֶד:

צוּר יִשְׂרָאֵל
קֽוּמָה בְּעֶזְרַת יִשְׂרָאֵל
וּפְדֵה כִנְאֻמֶֽךָ יְהוּדָה וְיִשְׂרָאֵל.
גֹּאֲלֵֽנוּ יהוה צְבָאוֹת שְׁמוֹ, קְדוֹשׁ יִשְׂרָאֵל:
בָּרוּךְ אַתָּה יהוה, גָּאַל יִשְׂרָאֵל.

AMIDA

Take three steps forward then stand with your feet together.

Hashem, open my lips and help my mouth recite Your praise.

ANCESTORS

Bend the knees when saying "We thank," bow when saying "You," and stand straight before saying "Hashem."

בָּרוּךְ We thank You, *Hashem,*
our God, and God of our ancestors,
Avraham, Yitzchak, and Yaakov.
You, *Hashem,* are the great, mighty, awesome, kind,
and all-powerful Creator.
It is because of the greatness of our ancestors,
Avraham, Yitzchak, and Yaakov,
that *Hashem* will bring *Mashiach.*

Between Rosh Hashana and Yom Kippur say:

Give us life in the year to come and write us
in the book of life, *Hashem,* who gives life.

Hashem is our King who helps, guides, and protects us.

Bend the knees when saying "Thank," bow when saying "You," and stand straight before saying "Hashem."

Thank You, *Hashem,*
who protects us in the merit of Avraham.

מֶלֶךְ עוֹזֵר וּמוֹשִׁיעַ וּמָגֵן *Hashem is our King who helps, guides, and protects us.* These words describe three levels of how closely *Hashem* is involved with our lives. *Hashem* "HELPS US" when we ask Him for help, He "SAVES US" even when we are unable to cry out to Him for help, and He "PROTECTS US" by preventing us from even reaching difficult situations that would require help.

עמידה

Take three steps forward then stand with your feet together.

אֲדֹנָי, שְׂפָתַי תִּפְתָּח, וּפִי יַגִּיד תְּהִלָּתֶךָ:

אבות

Bend the knees when saying בָּרוּךְ, *bow when saying* אַתָּה, *and stand straight before saying Hashem's name.*

בָּרוּךְ אַתָּה יהוה
אֱלֹהֵינוּ וֵאלֹהֵי אֲבוֹתֵינוּ
אֱלֹהֵי אַבְרָהָם, אֱלֹהֵי יִצְחָק, וֵאלֹהֵי יַעֲקֹב
הָאֵל הַגָּדוֹל הַגִּבּוֹר וְהַנּוֹרָא, אֵל עֶלְיוֹן
גּוֹמֵל חֲסָדִים טוֹבִים, וְקֹנֵה הַכֹּל
וְזוֹכֵר חַסְדֵי אָבוֹת
וּמֵבִיא גוֹאֵל לִבְנֵי בְנֵיהֶם לְמַעַן שְׁמוֹ בְּאַהֲבָה.

Between ראש השנה *and* יום כיפור *say:*

זָכְרֵנוּ לְחַיִּים, מֶלֶךְ חָפֵץ בַּחַיִּים
וְכָתְבֵנוּ בְּסֵפֶר הַחַיִּים
לְמַעַנְךָ אֱלֹהִים חַיִּים.

מֶלֶךְ עוֹזֵר וּמוֹשִׁיעַ וּמָגֵן.

Bend the knees when saying בָּרוּךְ, *bow when saying* אַתָּה, *and stand straight before saying Hashem's name.*

בָּרוּךְ אַתָּה יהוה, מָגֵן אַבְרָהָם.

HASHEM'S STRENGTH

אַתָּה You, *Hashem,* have unlimited strength.
You save people in their time of need,
and You have the power to bring the dead back to life.

This line is said during the rainy season, from Simchat Torah to Pesach:
(You make the wind blow and cause the rain to fall)

With kindness You provide the living
with the necessities to live,
and with mercy You keep Your promise
of bringing the dead back to life.
For the living, You:
Support those who are falling,
Heal those who are sick, and
Free those who are in challenging situations.
Who is like You, *Hashem,*
and who can compare to You?
You, *Hashem,* are our King
who has the power to cause death and life.

Between Rosh Hashana and Yom Kippur say:
Who is like You, *Hashem,* our caring Father
who remembers His people for good
and gives them life?

We have complete faith
that You will bring us back to life after our passing.
Thank You, *Hashem,*
for bringing the dead back to life.

גבורות

אַתָּה גִּבּוֹר לְעוֹלָם, אֲדֹנָי
מְחַיֵּה מֵתִים אַתָּה, רַב לְהוֹשִׁיעַ

This line is said during the rainy season, from שמחת תורה *to* פסח:

(מַשִּׁיב הָרְוּחַ וּמוֹרִיד הַגֶּשֶׁם)

מְכַלְכֵּל חַיִּים בְּחֶסֶד, מְחַיֵּה מֵתִים בְּרַחֲמִים רַבִּים
סוֹמֵךְ נוֹפְלִים, וְרוֹפֵא חוֹלִים, וּמַתִּיר אֲסוּרִים
וּמְקַיֵּם אֱמוּנָתוֹ לִישֵׁנֵי עָפָר.
מִי כָמְוֹךָ, בַּעַל גְּבוּרוֹת
וּמִי דּוֹמֶה לָּךְ
מֶלֶךְ, מֵמִית וּמְחַיֶּה וּמַצְמִיחַ יְשׁוּעָה.

Between ראש השנה *and* יום כיפור *say:*

מִי כָמְוֹךָ אַב הָרַחֲמִים
זוֹכֵר יְצוּרָיו לְחַיִּים בְּרַחֲמִים.

וְנֶאֱמָן אַתָּה לְהַחֲיוֹת מֵתִים.
בָּרוּךְ אַתָּה יהוה, מְחַיֵּה הַמֵּתִים.

מְחַיֵּה מֵתִים אַתָּה *You have the power to bring the dead back to life.* When *Mashiach* comes, all those who followed the ways of *Hashem* and are no longer living will be brought back to life to continue serving *Hashem*. This miracle of righteous people being brought back to life is called "*Techiyat HaMeitim,*" the "re-awakening of the dead."

HASHEM'S HOLINESS

אַתָּה קָדוֹשׁ *Hashem,*
You are holy and Your name is holy.
The Jewish people, who are holy,
will praise You, *Hashem,* each day.
Thank You, *Hashem,*
the holy God. / *Between Rosh Hashana & Yom Kippur say:* the holy King./

GIVE US WISDOM

אַתָּה חוֹנֵן You, *Hashem,*
give wisdom and understanding to man.
Please continue to give us
wisdom, understanding,
and the ability to properly use our wisdom
in our daily lives.
Thank You, *Hashem,*
for giving us wisdom.

דעת – GIVE US WISDOM

We ask for wisdom as our very first request in the *Amida. Pirkei Avot* (4:1) teaches: "Who is a wise person? Someone who learns from everyone." Although *Hashem* provides us with the ability to learn and understand, we still need to put in our best efforts to try to learn from everyone we meet.

קדושת השם

אַתָּה קָדוֹשׁ וְשִׁמְךָ קָדוֹשׁ
וּקְדוֹשִׁים בְּכָל יוֹם יְהַלְלוּךָ סֶּלָה.
בָּרוּךְ אַתָּה יהוה
הָאֵל הַקָּדוֹשׁ. / *Between* ראש השנה *&* יום כיפור *say* **הַמֶּלֶךְ הַקָּדוֹשׁ.**/

דעת

אַתָּה חוֹנֵן לְאָדָם דַּעַת
וּמְלַמֵּד לֶאֱנוֹשׁ בִּינָה.
חָנֵּנוּ מֵאִתְּךָ דֵּעָה בִּינָה וְהַשְׂכֵּל.
בָּרוּךְ אַתָּה יהוה
חוֹנֵן הַדָּעַת.

קדושת השם – *HASHEM'S* HOLINESS

What does it mean to be holy? The Hebrew word for holy is "*kadosh*," which also means "separate." *Hashem* commanded us, "*Kedoshim tihyu*" – "You shall be holy," to teach us that Jews must separate from all other nations and follow the laws of the Torah. By separating from other nations, we become holy. Similarly, in this blessing, we describe *Hashem* as "holy" to show that He is above and separate from all living beings.

RETURN US TO *HASHEM*

הֲשִׁיבֵנוּ *Hashem,*
we feel distanced from Your Torah
and from serving You properly.
Please accept us and bring us closer to You, *Hashem.*
We feel bad for our mistakes
that distanced us from You.
Thank You, *Hashem*
for wanting us to return to You.

FORGIVE US

*(Lightly hit the left side of your chest
when you say "accidentally" and "purposely.")*

סְלַח *Hashem,*
please forgive us for the sins we have done
accidentally and purposely.
You, *Hashem,* are forgiving and understanding.
Thank You, *Hashem,*
who repeatedly forgives.

סליחה – FORGIVE US

Sometimes we are fully aware of a sin before we do it, but we have a hard time controlling ourselves. Other times we make mistakes without even knowing. *Hashem* forgives anyone who regrets their actions and asks for forgiveness. We must keep both types of sin in mind when saying this blessing.

תשובה

הֲשִׁיבֵנוּ אָבִינוּ לְתוֹרָתֶךָ
וְקָרְבֵנוּ מַלְכֵּנוּ לַעֲבוֹדָתֶךָ
וְהַחֲזִירֵנוּ בִּתְשׁוּבָה שְׁלֵמָה לְפָנֶיךָ.
בָּרוּךְ אַתָּה יהוה
הָרוֹצֶה בִּתְשׁוּבָה.

סליחה

(Lightly hit the left side of your chest when you say חָטָאנוּ *and* פָּשָׁעְנוּ*)*

סְלַח לָנוּ אָבִינוּ כִּי חָטָאנוּ
מְחַל לָנוּ מַלְכֵּנוּ כִּי פָשָׁעְנוּ
כִּי מוֹחֵל וְסוֹלֵחַ אָתָּה.
בָּרוּךְ אַתָּה יהוה
חַנּוּן הַמַּרְבֶּה לִסְלֹחַ.

תשובה – RETURN US TO *HASHEM*

When we sin, we become distanced from *Hashem*. To become closer to *Hashem* we need to go through a process called *teshuva,* which means "returning [to *Hashem*]." To do *teshuva,* a person needs to understand the sin he or she did, feel bad about having done it, and try to avoid doing the sin again in the future. Doing *teshuva* can be difficult, but *Hashem* wants us to be close to Him, and He helps those that ask for help during this blessing.

SAVE US

רְאֵה *Hashem,*
please see our difficulties
and help us face our struggles.
Save us because You have great power.
Thank You, *Hashem,*
who saves the Jewish people.

HEAL US

רְפָאֵנוּ *Hashem,*
if You decide to heal the sick,
they will be healed.
If You decide to save those in need,
they will be saved.
Please allow the sick
to recover completely from all sicknesses,
for You are the true source of healing and saving.
Thank You, *Hashem,*
who heals the Jewish people who are sick.

רפואה – HEAL US

Hashem heals us when we are sick. Although the Torah encourages us to go to doctors when we are sick, doctors only offer advice for how we can get better. We must be careful to follow this advice, but we must also pray to *Hashem* for a quick and healthy recovery, because *Hashem* is the only one who can actually change our health.

גאולה

רְאֵה בְעָנְיֵנוּ, וְרִיבָה רִיבֵנוּ
וּגְאָלֵנוּ מְהֵרָה לְמַעַן שְׁמֶךָ
כִּי גּוֹאֵל חָזָק אָתָּה.
בָּרוּךְ אַתָּה יהוה
גּוֹאֵל יִשְׂרָאֵל.

רפואה

רְפָאֵנוּ יהוה וְנֵרָפֵא
הוֹשִׁיעֵנוּ וְנִוָּשֵׁעָה, כִּי תְהִלָּתֵנוּ אָתָּה
וְהַעֲלֵה רְפוּאָה שְׁלֵמָה לְכָל מַכּוֹתֵינוּ
כִּי אֵל מֶלֶךְ רוֹפֵא נֶאֱמָן וְרַחֲמָן אָתָּה.
בָּרוּךְ אַתָּה יהוה
רוֹפֵא חוֹלֵי עַמּוֹ יִשְׂרָאֵל.

גאולה – SAVE US

When we pray, we are not just praying for ourselves, but for the struggles and challenges that our friends, family, and fellow Jews face as well. When we say, "*Hashem,* please see our difficulties and help us face our struggles," we are not only praying on behalf of ourselves but for the entire Jewish nation. It is important to take a moment before davening to think about our families and friends who are struggling and could use help from *Hashem*.

PROVIDE FOOD FOR US

בָּרֵךְ Bless this year for us *Hashem,*
so that we should always have food to eat.

Say this phrase during the winter season, from December 4th through Pesach.

Provide rain and dew as a blessing

Say this phrase during the summer season, from Chol Hamoed Pesach through Mincha of December 3rd.

Provide blessing

across the earth,
allowing this year to be a great year of food supply.
Thank You, *Hashem,*
for filling our year with blessing.

GATHER US

תְּקַע *Hashem,* blow the great shofar
to announce our freedom from exile.
Make a clear sign so that all Jews know where to gather.
Hashem, help gather all Jews together
from the four corners of the earth.
Thank You, *Hashem,*
who gathers His scattered Jewish people.

קיבוץ גלויות – GATHER US

Every day we long for *Yemot HaMashiach,* the time of *Mashiach,* when *Hashem* will reveal His great power to every living being. When *Mashiach* arrives, every person from every nation will recognize *Hashem,* the *Beit HaMikdash* will be rebuilt, and all Jews will gather in Jerusalem to bring pleasing sacrifices before *Hashem.* Without all of this, the Jewish people live in exile, a state of being without a strong spiritual connection to *Hashem.*

ברכת השנים

בָּרֵךְ עָלֵינוּ יהוה אֱלֹהֵינוּ אֶת הַשָּׁנָה הַזֹּאת
וְאֶת כָּל מִינֵי תְבוּאָתָהּ, לְטוֹבָה

Say this phrase during the winter season,
from December 4th through פסח.

וְתֵן טַל וּמָטָר לִבְרָכָה

Say this phrase during the summer season,
from חול המועד פסח *through* מנחה *of December 3rd.*

וְתֵן בְּרָכָה

עַל פְּנֵי הָאֲדָמָה, וְשַׂבְּעֵנוּ מִטּוּבָהּ
וּבָרֵךְ שְׁנָתֵנוּ כַּשָּׁנִים הַטּוֹבוֹת.
בָּרוּךְ אַתָּה יהוה, מְבָרֵךְ הַשָּׁנִים.

קיבוץ גלויות

תְּקַע בְּשׁוֹפָר גָּדוֹל לְחֵרוּתֵנוּ
וְשָׂא נֵס לְקַבֵּץ גָּלֻיּוֹתֵינוּ
וְקַבְּצֵנוּ יַחַד מֵאַרְבַּע כַּנְפוֹת הָאָרֶץ.
בָּרוּךְ אַתָּה יהוה, מְקַבֵּץ נִדְחֵי עַמּוֹ יִשְׂרָאֵל.

ברכת השנים – PROVIDE FOOD FOR US

In this blessing we pray that we should always have plentiful food to eat. Rain allows food to grow, and rain falls differently in each season. Therefore, our request changes depending on the time of year. During seasons of the year when it usually rains, we ask *Hashem* to provide enough rain for our food to grow, while during times of the year when it usually does not rain, we simply ask *Hashem* for "blessing" in allowing the continued growth of our food.

REESTABLISH JEWISH COURTS

הָשִׁיבָה Bring back our Jewish judges and leaders
as it once was,
And remove the difficulties and frustration we face
as a result of not having their guidance.
Hashem, may You alone rule and judge us
with kindness, mercy, and fairness.
Thank You, *Hashem,*
the King who loves righteousness and fairness.
/*Between Rosh Hashana and Yom Kippur say:* the King of fairness./

THE WICKED

וְלַמַּלְשִׁינִים *Hashem,* please do not assist those
who speak or act with bad intentions towards Jews.
Hashem, soon may all Your enemies be destroyed.
For Jews that turned away from Judaism,
may You quickly help guide them back
towards the ways of *Hashem.*
Thank You, *Hashem,* for destroying our enemies
and for returning Jews that turned away.

ברכת המינים – THE WICKED

The *Amida* is often called "*Shemoneh Esreh,*" meaning "eighteen," because of the original 18 blessings of the *Amida*. Today, however, there are nineteen blessings in the *Amida*. Why was there an extra blessing added?

This blessing for the wicked was added because there was a time when some non-Jews tried to trick the Jewish people into not following halacha, Jewish law. In response, the Jewish Sages wrote this blessing to ask *Hashem* for help in preventing these groups from tricking the Jewish people. Though the name *Shemoneh Esreh* did not change, this additional blessing remains a part of our daily prayers.

השבת המשפט

הָשִׁיבָה שׁוֹפְטֵינוּ כְּבָרִאשׁוֹנָה
וְיוֹעֲצֵינוּ כְּבַתְּחִלָּה
וְהָסֵר מִמֶּנּוּ יָגוֹן וַאֲנָחָה
וּמְלֹךְ עָלֵינוּ אַתָּה יהוה לְבַדְּךָ בְּחֶסֶד וּבְרַחֲמִים
וְצַדְּקֵנוּ בַּמִּשְׁפָּט.
בָּרוּךְ אַתָּה יהוה, מֶלֶךְ אוֹהֵב צְדָקָה וּמִשְׁפָּט.
/ Between ראש השנה & יום כיפור say הַמֶּלֶךְ הַמִּשְׁפָּט./

ברכת המינים

וְלַמַּלְשִׁינִים אַל תְּהִי תִקְוָה
וְכָל הָרִשְׁעָה כְּרֶגַע תֹּאבֵד
וְכָל אוֹיְבֵי עַמְּךָ מְהֵרָה יִכָּרֵתוּ
וְהַזֵּדִים מְהֵרָה תְעַקֵּר וּתְשַׁבֵּר וּתְמַגֵּר וְתַכְנִיעַ
בִּמְהֵרָה בְיָמֵינוּ.
בָּרוּךְ אַתָּה יהוה, שׁוֹבֵר אוֹיְבִים וּמַכְנִיעַ זֵדִים.

השבת המשפט – REESTABLISH JEWISH COURTS

After asking *Hashem* to end our exile in the previous blessing, now we ask *Hashem* to allow us to set up a *Beit Din,* Jewish courts, with wise judges who can guide us in keeping His Torah properly. Nowadays, in addition to following the *Beit Din* we must also follow the laws and courts of whatever country we are in.

THE RIGHTEOUS

עַל *Hashem*, when You think of us,
consider the righteous, humble, elderly,
and wise people within our nation,
and have mercy on us, Your Jewish people, for their sake.
Please give reward
to all those who sincerely believe in You,
and give us the ability to be placed
in this righteous group.
Thank You, *Hashem*,
for supporting righteous people.

REBUILDING JERUSALEM

וְלִירוּשָׁלַיִם *Hashem*, please return to Your city, Jerusalem,
and live there as You once did.
Please rebuild the *Beit HaMikdash* soon,
in our lifetimes, and let it last forever.
Complete this process by appointing a Jewish king
from the family of King David.
Thank You, *Hashem*,
for rebuilding Jerusalem.

בניין ירושלים – REBUILDING JERUSALEM

Even though Jews currently live in Jerusalem, the city is still incomplete. Until the *Beit HaMikdash* is rebuilt, the daily sacrifices are restored, and the land is led by Torah law, sadly, *Hashem* will not fully be present in Jerusalem, and Jerusalem will not be complete. In this blessing, we pray that *Hashem* rebuild Jerusalem by allowing for the construction of the *Beit HaMikdash* so that Jerusalem can be complete, and *Hashem* can continue to be present there as He once was.

על הצדיקים

עַל הַצַּדִּיקִים וְעַל הַחֲסִידִים
וְעַל זִקְנֵי עַמְּךָ בֵּית יִשְׂרָאֵל
וְעַל פְּלֵיטַת סוֹפְרֵיהֶם
וְעַל גֵּרֵי הַצֶּדֶק, וְעָלֵינוּ
יֶהֱמוּ רַחֲמֶיךָ יהוה אֱלֹהֵינוּ
וְתֵן שָׂכָר טוֹב לְכָל הַבּוֹטְחִים בְּשִׁמְךָ בֶּאֱמֶת
וְשִׂים חֶלְקֵנוּ עִמָּהֶם, וּלְעוֹלָם לֹא נֵבוֹשׁ כִּי בְךָ בָטָחְנוּ.
בָּרוּךְ אַתָּה יהוה, מִשְׁעָן וּמִבְטָח לַצַּדִּיקִים.

בניין ירושלים

וְלִירוּשָׁלַיִם עִירְךָ בְּרַחֲמִים תָּשׁוּב
וְתִשְׁכֹּן בְּתוֹכָהּ כַּאֲשֶׁר דִּבַּרְתָּ
וּבְנֵה אוֹתָהּ בְּקָרוֹב בְּיָמֵינוּ בִּנְיַן עוֹלָם
וְכִסֵּא דָוִד מְהֵרָה לְתוֹכָהּ תָּכִין.
בָּרוּךְ אַתָּה יהוה, בּוֹנֵה יְרוּשָׁלָיִם.

על הצדיקים – THE RIGHTEOUS

"Elders" does not necessarily mean people who are old. Rather, it refers to people who are wise, such as our Torah leaders, who have gained much life experience and knowledge. These "elders" are the people we turn to when we have questions or seek advice. When we are unsure what to do, it is important to ask our Torah leaders for advice and follow their directions, as they have a strong sense of how *Hashem* wants us to behave.

KINGDOM OF DAVID

אֶת צֶמַח Please bring *Mashiach,*
who comes from the family of King David,
quickly as we think about
and hope for his arrival every day.
Thank You, *Hashem,*
who brings *Mashiach.*

LISTEN TO OUR PRAYERS

שְׁמַע *Hashem,*
please listen to our voices
and accept our prayers with mercy.
You, *Hashem,* show mercy
by listening to the prayers of the Jewish people.
Please do not let our prayers go unanswered.
Thank You, *Hashem,*
for listening to our prayers.

שומע תפילה – LISTEN TO OUR PRAYERS

Prayer is a conversation with *Hashem.* Sometimes when we speak to our friends we are searching for a response or asking a question. Other times, we simply want somebody to listen to us. In praying to *Hashem,* we are not asking that He respond to us, but that He listen to us and consider our requests. Though He may respond "no," it is important for us to remember that *Hashem* always listens.

מלכות בית דוד

אֶת צֶמַח דָּוִד עַבְדְּךָ מְהֵרָה תַצְמִיחַ
וְקַרְנוֹ תָּרוּם בִּישׁוּעָתֶךָ
כִּי לִישׁוּעָתְךָ קִוִּינוּ כָּל הַיּוֹם.
בָּרוּךְ אַתָּה יהוה, מַצְמִיחַ קֶרֶן יְשׁוּעָה.

שומע תפילה

שְׁמַע קוֹלֵנוּ יהוה אֱלֹהֵינוּ
חוּס וְרַחֵם עָלֵינוּ
וְקַבֵּל בְּרַחֲמִים וּבְרָצוֹן אֶת תְּפִלָּתֵנוּ
כִּי אֵל שׁוֹמֵעַ תְּפִלּוֹת וְתַחֲנוּנִים אָתָּה
וּמִלְּפָנֶיךָ מַלְכֵּנוּ רֵיקָם אַל תְּשִׁיבֵנוּ
כִּי אַתָּה שׁוֹמֵעַ תְּפִלַּת עַמְּךָ יִשְׂרָאֵל בְּרַחֲמִים.
בָּרוּךְ אַתָּה יהוה, שׁוֹמֵעַ תְּפִלָּה.

מלכות בית דוד – KINGDOM OF DAVID

As Jews, we must hope and pray for the coming of *Mashiach* every day. *Hashem* promised that He would send *Mashiach* and we have complete *emunah*, faith, that this will take place. The focus of this blessing is the urgency; we pray that *Hashem* send *Mashiach* soon as we want and need him to come now.

We can help bring *Mashiach* speedily by doing more *mitzvot*, being kind to our family and friends, and by praying to *Hashem* and focusing on the meaning of this *beracha*.

SERVICE IN THE *BEIT HAMIKDASH*

רְצֵה *Hashem,* please accept Your Jewish people
and their prayers.
We eagerly await the rebuilding of the *Beit HaMikdash*
so we can serve You with *korbanot.*
Until the *Beit HaMikdash* is rebuilt,
please accept our prayers with love.

On Rosh Chodesh and Chol HaMo'ed, say:

אֱלֹהֵינוּ Our God, and God of our ancestors, may our prayers:
Rise from our mouths,
Come before You,
Reach You at a desirable time,
Be heard,
And be fulfilled.

Hashem, You remember and know each of our hardships.
You remember:
Our ancestors,
Mashiach,
Your holy city, Jerusalem, and
Your united Jewish people,
for goodness, kindness, mercy, life, and peace
on this day of:

On Rosh Chodesh: *Rosh Chodesh.*
On Pesach: the Holiday of *Matzot.*
On Sukkot: the Holiday of *Sukkot.*

Hashem, on this day please remember us
with good thoughts, consider us for blessing,
and help us with difficult times in our lives.
Be kind and merciful with us, *Hashem,*
as we look towards You as our King.

עבודה

רְצֵה יהוה אֱלֹהֵינוּ בְּעַמְּךָ יִשְׂרָאֵל, וּבִתְפִלָּתָם
וְהָשֵׁב אֶת הָעֲבוֹדָה לִדְבִיר בֵּיתֶךָ
וְאִשֵּׁי יִשְׂרָאֵל וּתְפִלָּתָם בְּאַהֲבָה תְקַבֵּל בְּרָצוֹן
וּתְהִי לְרָצוֹן תָּמִיד עֲבוֹדַת יִשְׂרָאֵל עַמֶּךָ.

On ראש חודש *and* חול המועד*, say:*

אֱלֹהֵינוּ וֵאלֹהֵי אֲבוֹתֵינוּ
יַעֲלֶה וְיָבוֹא וְיַגִּיעַ, וְיֵרָאֶה וְיֵרָצֶה וְיִשָּׁמַע
וְיִפָּקֵד וְיִזָּכֵר זִכְרוֹנֵנוּ וּפִקְדוֹנֵנוּ, וְזִכְרוֹן אֲבוֹתֵינוּ
וְזִכְרוֹן מָשִׁיחַ בֶּן דָּוִד עַבְדֶּךָ
וְזִכְרוֹן יְרוּשָׁלַיִם עִיר קָדְשֶׁךָ
וְזִכְרוֹן כָּל עַמְּךָ בֵּית יִשְׂרָאֵל
לְפָנֶיךָ, לִפְלֵיטָה לְטוֹבָה
לְחֵן וּלְחֶסֶד וּלְרַחֲמִים, לְחַיִּים וּלְשָׁלוֹם
בְּיוֹם

בראש חודש: רֹאשׁ הַחֹדֶשׁ הַזֶּה.

בפסח: חַג הַמַּצּוֹת הַזֶּה.

בסוכות: חַג הַסֻּכּוֹת הַזֶּה.

זָכְרֵנוּ יהוה אֱלֹהֵינוּ בּוֹ לְטוֹבָה, וּפָקְדֵנוּ בוֹ לִבְרָכָה
וְהוֹשִׁיעֵנוּ בוֹ לְחַיִּים.
וּבִדְבַר יְשׁוּעָה וְרַחֲמִים
חוּס וְחָנֵּנוּ וְרַחֵם עָלֵינוּ וְהוֹשִׁיעֵנוּ
כִּי אֵלֶיךָ עֵינֵינוּ, כִּי אֵל מֶלֶךְ חַנּוּן וְרַחוּם אָתָּה.

May we be worthy
to see the rebuilding of the *Beit HaMikdash*.
We thank You, *Hashem*,
for returning Your presence to Zion.

THANK YOU

Bow when saying the words "We thank You."

מוֹדִים We thank You, *Hashem*,
for You are and always will be
our God, and the God of our ancestors.
You give us life
and You always protect us.
We thank and praise You for:
Our lives which are in Your hands,
Our souls which are in Your control,
The miracles You perform for us every day, and
The goodness You show us
at all times, morning, noon, and night.
You, *Hashem*, have unlimited mercy and kindness
and therefore we have always placed our hope in You.

On Chanuka say:

עַל הַנִּסִּים We thank You, *Hashem*, for the miracles, the deliverances, the great strength, and the victories in war that You displayed for us in earlier times and in our times.

בִּימֵי מַתִּתְיָהוּ In the days of Mattityahu, son of Yochanan the *Kohen Gadol*, the Hasmonean, and his sons, the wicked Greeks challenged Your Jewish people trying to make them forget Your Torah and sin. In Your great kindness, You, *Hashem*, supported

וְתֶחֱזֶינָה עֵינֵינוּ בְּשׁוּבְךָ לְצִיּוֹן בְּרַחֲמִים.
בָּרוּךְ אַתָּה יהוה, הַמַּחֲזִיר שְׁכִינָתוֹ לְצִיּוֹן.

הודאה

Bow when saying the words מוֹדִים אֲנַחְנוּ לָךְ שָׁאַתָּה הוּא.

מוֹדִים אֲנַחְנוּ לָךְ
שָׁאַתָּה הוּא יהוה אֱלֹהֵינוּ וֵאלֹהֵי אֲבוֹתֵינוּ לְעוֹלָם וָעֶד.
צוּר חַיֵּינוּ, מָגֵן יִשְׁעֵנוּ, אַתָּה הוּא לְדוֹר וָדוֹר.
נוֹדֶה לְּךָ וּנְסַפֵּר תְּהִלָּתֶךָ
עַל חַיֵּינוּ הַמְּסוּרִים בְּיָדֶךָ
וְעַל נִשְׁמוֹתֵינוּ הַפְּקוּדוֹת לָךְ
וְעַל נִסֶּיךָ שֶׁבְּכָל יוֹם עִמָּנוּ
וְעַל נִפְלְאוֹתֶיךָ וְטוֹבוֹתֶיךָ
שֶׁבְּכָל עֵת, עֶרֶב וָבֹקֶר וְצָהֳרָיִם.
הַטּוֹב, כִּי לֹא כָלוּ רַחֲמֶיךָ
וְהַמְרַחֵם, כִּי לֹא תַמּוּ חֲסָדֶיךָ
מֵעוֹלָם קִוִּינוּ לָךְ.

בחנוכה:

עַל הַנִּסִּים וְעַל הַפֻּרְקָן וְעַל הַגְּבוּרוֹת וְעַל הַתְּשׁוּעוֹת וְעַל הַמִּלְחָמוֹת שֶׁעָשִׂיתָ לַאֲבוֹתֵינוּ בַּיָּמִים הָהֵם בַּזְּמַן הַזֶּה.

בִּימֵי מַתִּתְיָהוּ בֶּן יוֹחָנָן כֹּהֵן גָּדוֹל חַשְׁמוֹנַאי וּבָנָיו, כְּשֶׁעָמְדָה מַלְכוּת יָוָן הָרְשָׁעָה עַל עַמְּךָ יִשְׂרָאֵל לְהַשְׁכִּיחָם תּוֹרָתֶךָ וּלְהַעֲבִירָם מֵחֻקֵּי רְצוֹנֶךָ, וְאַתָּה בְּרַחֲמֶיךָ הָרַבִּים עָמַדְתָּ לָהֶם בְּעֵת צָרָתָם,

us in this difficult time. You allowed for:

The weak Jews to defeat the mighty Greeks,
The few Jews to defeat the many Greeks,
The pure Jews to defeat the impure Greeks,
The righteous Jews to defeat the wicked Greeks, and
The Jews who studied Your Torah to defeat the Greeks who did not.

Hashem, on this day everyone in the world recognized You as You miraculously saved Your Jewish people. Your Jewish people then entered the *Beit HaMikdash* to clean and purify it. They lit candles in the courtyard of the *Beit HaMikdash* and set aside these eight days of *Chanukah* for giving thanks and praising You.

Continue with "For all these reasons."

On Purim say:

עַל הַנִּסִּים We thank You, *Hashem,* for the miracles, the deliverances, the great strength, and the victories in war that You displayed for us in earlier times and in our times.

בִּימֵי מָרְדְּכַי In the days of Mordechai and Esther, the wicked Haman planned to destroy all Jews, men, women, and children, young and old, on the 13th of Adar, and steal their belongings. In Your great mercy, You, *Hashem,* ruined Haman's plans and instead Haman and his sons were hanged on the gallows.

Continue with "For all these reasons."

For all these reasons
we will thank You, *Hashem,* our King, forever.

Between Rosh Hashana & Yom Kippur say:
And write all Your children in the book of good life.

Every living person will recognize and praise You, *Hashem,* for You are the God that helps and saves Your people.

Bend the knees when saying "Thank," bow when saying "You," and stand straight before saying "Hashem."

Thank You, *Hashem,* for You are worthy of being thanked.

רַבְתָּ אֶת רִיבָם, דַּנְתָּ אֶת דִּינָם, נָקַמְתָּ אֶת נִקְמָתָם, מָסַרְתָּ גִּבּוֹרִים בְּיַד חַלָּשִׁים, וְרַבִּים בְּיַד מְעַטִּים, וּטְמֵאִים בְּיַד טְהוֹרִים, וּרְשָׁעִים בְּיַד צַדִּיקִים, וְזֵדִים בְּיַד עוֹסְקֵי תוֹרָתֶךָ, וּלְךָ עָשִׂיתָ שֵׁם גָּדוֹל וְקָדוֹשׁ בְּעוֹלָמֶךָ, וּלְעַמְּךָ יִשְׂרָאֵל עָשִׂיתָ תְּשׁוּעָה גְדוֹלָה וּפֻרְקָן כְּהַיּוֹם הַזֶּה. וְאַחַר כֵּן בָּאוּ בָנֶיךָ לִדְבִיר בֵּיתֶךָ, וּפִנּוּ אֶת הֵיכָלֶךָ, וְטִהֲרוּ אֶת מִקְדָּשֶׁךָ, וְהִדְלִיקוּ נֵרוֹת בְּחַצְרוֹת קָדְשֶׁךָ, וְקָבְעוּ שְׁמוֹנַת יְמֵי חֲנֻכָּה אֵלּוּ, לְהוֹדוֹת וּלְהַלֵּל לְשִׁמְךָ הַגָּדוֹל.

Continue with וְעַל כֻּלָּם.

בפורים:

עַל הַנִּסִּים וְעַל הַפֻּרְקָן וְעַל הַגְּבוּרוֹת וְעַל הַתְּשׁוּעוֹת וְעַל הַמִּלְחָמוֹת שֶׁעָשִׂיתָ לַאֲבוֹתֵינוּ בַּיָּמִים הָהֵם בַּזְּמַן הַזֶּה.

בִּימֵי מָרְדְּכַי וְאֶסְתֵּר בְּשׁוּשַׁן הַבִּירָה, כְּשֶׁעָמַד עֲלֵיהֶם הָמָן הָרָשָׁע, בִּקֵּשׁ לְהַשְׁמִיד לַהֲרֹג וּלְאַבֵּד אֶת־כָּל־הַיְּהוּדִים מִנַּעַר וְעַד־זָקֵן טַף וְנָשִׁים בְּיוֹם אֶחָד, בִּשְׁלוֹשָׁה עָשָׂר לְחֹדֶשׁ שְׁנֵים־עָשָׂר, הוּא־חֹדֶשׁ אֲדָר, וּשְׁלָלָם לָבוֹז: וְאַתָּה בְּרַחֲמֶיךָ הָרַבִּים הֵפַרְתָּ אֶת עֲצָתוֹ, וְקִלְקַלְתָּ אֶת מַחֲשַׁבְתּוֹ, וַהֲשֵׁבוֹתָ לּוֹ גְּמוּלוֹ בְּרֹאשׁוֹ, וְתָלוּ אוֹתוֹ וְאֶת בָּנָיו עַל הָעֵץ.

Continue with וְעַל כֻּלָּם.

וְעַל כֻּלָּם

יִתְבָּרַךְ וְיִתְרוֹמַם שִׁמְךָ מַלְכֵּנוּ תָּמִיד לְעוֹלָם וָעֶד.

Between ראש השנה *&* יום כיפור *say* וּכְתֹב לְחַיִּים טוֹבִים כָּל בְּנֵי בְרִיתֶךָ.

וְכֹל הַחַיִּים יוֹדוּךָ סֶּלָה, וִיהַלְלוּ אֶת שִׁמְךָ בֶּאֱמֶת הָאֵל יְשׁוּעָתֵנוּ וְעֶזְרָתֵנוּ סֶלָה.

Bend the knees when saying בָּרוּךְ, *bow when saying* אַתָּה, *and stand straight before saying Hashem's name.*

ר׳ בָּרוּךְ אַתָּה יהוה, הַטּוֹב שִׁמְךָ וּלְךָ נָאֶה לְהוֹדוֹת.

PEACE

שִׂים שָׁלוֹם *Hashem,*
please provide Your Jewish people
with peace, goodness, blessing, kindness, and mercy.
Bless us, *Hashem,* all as one.
Hashem, You have given us Your Torah of life,
and treated us with kindness, righteousness,
blessing, mercy, and peace.
May it be good in Your eyes, *Hashem,*
to bless Your Jewish people with peace
at every moment of every hour.

Between Rosh Hashana and Yom Kippur continue with "May You remember," below.

Thank You, *Hashem,*
who blesses His Jewish people with peace.

Between Rosh Hashana and Yom Kippur say:
May You remember all of the Jewish people for life,
blessing, peace, and riches
and write us in the book of good life and peace.
Thank You, *Hashem,* who makes peace.

שלום – PEACE

While standing at Mount Sinai, the Jewish people were united, "like one person with one heart." Everyone treated each other with respect. We learn from this that the Torah could not be given until there was peace within the nation. Although studying Torah is extremely important, showing respect towards our families and friends comes before studying Torah – "*derech eretz kadma laTorah.*"

שלום

שִׂים שָׁלוֹם טוֹבָה וּבְרָכָה
חֵן וָחֶסֶד וְרַחֲמִים עָלֵינוּ
וְעַל כָּל יִשְׂרָאֵל עַמֶּךָ.
בָּרְכֵנוּ אָבִינוּ כֻּלָּנוּ כְּאֶחָד בְּאוֹר פָּנֶיךָ
כִּי בְאוֹר פָּנֶיךָ נָתַתָּ לָּנוּ יהוה אֱלֹהֵינוּ
תּוֹרַת חַיִּים וְאַהֲבַת חֶסֶד
וּצְדָקָה וּבְרָכָה
וְרַחֲמִים וְחַיִּים וְשָׁלוֹם.
וְטוֹב בְּעֵינֶיךָ לְבָרֵךְ אֶת עַמְּךָ יִשְׂרָאֵל
בְּכָל עֵת וּבְכָל שָׁעָה בִּשְׁלוֹמֶךָ.

Between ראש השנה *and* יום כיפור *continue with* בְּסֵפֶר חַיִּים, *below.*

בָּרוּךְ אַתָּה יהוה
הַמְבָרֵךְ אֶת עַמּוֹ יִשְׂרָאֵל בַּשָּׁלוֹם.

Between ראש השנה *and* יום כיפור *say:*

בְּסֵפֶר חַיִּים, בְּרָכָה וְשָׁלוֹם, וּפַרְנָסָה טוֹבָה
נִזָּכֵר וְנִכָּתֵב לְפָנֶיךָ
אֲנַחְנוּ וְכָל עַמְּךָ בֵּית יִשְׂרָאֵל
לְחַיִּים טוֹבִים וּלְשָׁלוֹם.
בָּרוּךְ אַתָּה יהוה, עוֹשֵׂה הַשָּׁלוֹם.

CONCLUSION OF AMIDA

אֱלֹהַי *Hashem,* please help me:

Control my mouth from speaking badly
about other people,
Stay silent and not respond if someone speaks badly
about me,
Learn Your Torah, and do Your *mitzvot.*

Hashem, if people plan to do something evil against me,
please stop these plans and protect me.
Even if I am not deserving of being helped,
please act on my behalf
as I represent Your name and Your Torah.
Hashem, please save Your Jewish people
from difficult situations and answer my requests.
May You find my thoughts and prayers favorable.

Take three steps backwards and bow to your left as you say:

You, *Hashem,* make peace in heaven.

Bow to your right as you say:

Please may You bring peace to us

Bow forward as you say:

And all Your Jewish people.

Before taking three steps forward, say the following quietly:

Hashem, our God and God of our ancestors, may You please rebuild the *Beit HaMikdash* soon. *Hashem,* please allow us to learn Your Torah and serve You in the *Beit HaMikdash* as the Jewish people once did.

When praying with a minyan, the Amida is repeated by the Leader (on the next page).

When not praying with a minyan: on days when Tachanun is said, start Tachanun on page 160. On Mondays and Thursdays start Tachanun on page 152. On days when Tachanun is not said continue with Ashrei on page 178.

Between Rosh HaShana and Yom Kippur (but not on Erev Yom Kippur, unless it falls on Friday), and on fast days, say Avinu Malkenu on page 146.

On Rosh Chodesh, Chol HaMoed, and Chanukah, say Hallel on page 720.

סיום העמידה

אֱלֹהַי, נְצֹר לְשׁוֹנִי מֵרָע וּשְׂפָתַי מִדַּבֵּר מִרְמָה
וְלִמְקַלְלַי נַפְשִׁי תִדֹּם, וְנַפְשִׁי כֶּעָפָר לַכֹּל תִּהְיֶה.
פְּתַח לִבִּי בְּתוֹרָתֶךָ, וּבְמִצְוֹתֶיךָ תִּרְדֹּף נַפְשִׁי.
וְכָל הַחוֹשְׁבִים עָלַי רָעָה
מְהֵרָה הָפֵר עֲצָתָם וְקַלְקֵל מַחֲשַׁבְתָּם.
עֲשֵׂה לְמַעַן שְׁמֶךָ, עֲשֵׂה לְמַעַן יְמִינֶךָ
עֲשֵׂה לְמַעַן קְדֻשָּׁתֶךָ, עֲשֵׂה לְמַעַן תּוֹרָתֶךָ.
לְמַעַן יֵחָלְצוּן יְדִידֶיךָ, הוֹשִׁיעָה יְמִינְךָ וַעֲנֵנִי:
יִהְיוּ לְרָצוֹן אִמְרֵי־פִי וְהֶגְיוֹן לִבִּי לְפָנֶיךָ, יהוה צוּרִי וְגֹאֲלִי:

Take three steps backwards and bow to your left as you say:

עֹשֶׂה שָׁלוֹם / *Between* ראש השנה *&* יום כיפור *say* הַשָּׁלוֹם/ בִּמְרוֹמָיו

Bow to your right as you say:

הוּא יַעֲשֶׂה שָׁלוֹם עָלֵינוּ

Bow forward as you say:

וְעַל כָּל יִשְׂרָאֵל, וְאִמְרוּ אָמֵן.

Before taking three steps forward, say the following quietly:

יְהִי רָצוֹן מִלְּפָנֶיךָ יהוה אֱלֹהֵינוּ וֵאלֹהֵי אֲבוֹתֵינוּ. שֶׁיִּבָּנֶה בֵּית הַמִּקְדָּשׁ בִּמְהֵרָה בְיָמֵינוּ, וְתֵן חֶלְקֵנוּ בְּתוֹרָתֶךָ. וְשָׁם נַעֲבָדְךָ בְּיִרְאָה כִּימֵי עוֹלָם וּכְשָׁנִים קַדְמֹנִיּוֹת. וְעָרְבָה לַיהוה מִנְחַת יְהוּדָה וִירוּשָׁלָיִם כִּימֵי עוֹלָם וּכְשָׁנִים קַדְמֹנִיּוֹת:

When praying with a מנין*, the* עמידה *is repeated by the* חזן *(on the next page).*

When not praying with a מנין*: on days when* תחנון *is said, start* תחנון *on page 161. On Mondays and Thursdays start* תחנון *on page 153. On days when* תחנון *is not said, continue with* אַשְׁרֵי *on page 179.*

Between ראש השנה *and* יום כיפור *(but not on* ערב יום כיפור*, unless it falls on Friday), and on fast days, say* אבינו מלכנו *on page 147.*

On ראש חודש*,* חול המועד*, and* חנוכה *say* הלל *on page 721.*

THE LEADER'S REPETITION

Try to focus on each blessing that the Leader reads, by following along and thinking about the sentences below. After each beracha that the Leader recites, answer "Amen."

Hashem, open my lips
and help my mouth recite Your praise.

ANCESTORS

We praise You, *Hashem,*
for protecting, helping, and saving us
as You did for our ancestors,
Avraham, Yitzchak, and Yaakov.
Thank You, *Hashem,*
who protects us in the merit of Avraham.

(*Congregation:* Amen.)

HASHEM'S STRENGTH

We praise You, *Hashem,*
for providing food to those who are hungry,
support to those who are falling,
health to those who are sick,
and help to those who are in challenging situations.
Thank You, *Hashem,*
for bringing the dead back to life. (*Congregation:* Amen.)

חזרת הש"ץ

Try to focus on each blessing that the חזן *reads, by following along and thinking about the sentences below. After each beracha that the* חזן *recites, answer* אָמֵן.

אֲדֹנָי, שְׂפָתַי תִּפְתָּח, וּפִי יַגִּיד תְּהִלָּתֶךָ:

אבות

בָּרוּךְ אַתָּה יהוה, אֱלֹהֵינוּ וֵאלֹהֵי אֲבוֹתֵינוּ
אֱלֹהֵי אַבְרָהָם, אֱלֹהֵי יִצְחָק, וֵאלֹהֵי יַעֲקֹב
הָאֵל הַגָּדוֹל הַגִּבּוֹר וְהַנּוֹרָא, אֵל עֶלְיוֹן
גּוֹמֵל חֲסָדִים טוֹבִים, וְקוֹנֵה הַכֹּל, וְזוֹכֵר חַסְדֵי אָבוֹת
וּמֵבִיא גוֹאֵל לִבְנֵי בְנֵיהֶם לְמַעַן שְׁמוֹ בְּאַהֲבָה.

Between ראש השנה *&* יום כיפור *say* זָכְרֵנוּ לְחַיִּים, מֶלֶךְ חָפֵץ בַּחַיִּים
וְכָתְבֵנוּ בְּסֵפֶר הַחַיִּים, לְמַעַנְךָ אֱלֹהִים חַיִּים.

מֶלֶךְ עוֹזֵר וּמוֹשִׁיעַ וּמָגֵן.

בָּרוּךְ אַתָּה יהוה, מָגֵן אַבְרָהָם. (קהל: **אָמֵן**)

גבורות

אַתָּה גִּבּוֹר לְעוֹלָם, אֲדֹנָי, מְחַיֵּה מֵתִים אַתָּה, רַב לְהוֹשִׁיעַ

This line is said during the rainy season, from שמחת תורה *to* פסח*:*

(מַשִּׁיב הָרְוּחַ וּמוֹרִיד הַגֶּשֶׁם)

מְכַלְכֵּל חַיִּים בְּחֶסֶד, מְחַיֵּה מֵתִים בְּרַחֲמִים רַבִּים
סוֹמֵךְ נוֹפְלִים, וְרוֹפֵא חוֹלִים, וּמַתִּיר אֲסוּרִים
וּמְקַיֵּם אֱמוּנָתוֹ לִישֵׁנֵי עָפָר.
מִי כָמְוֹךָ, בַּעַל גְּבוּרוֹת, וּמִי דּוֹמֶה לָּךְ
מֶלֶךְ, מֵמִית וּמְחַיֶּה וּמַצְמִיחַ יְשׁוּעָה.

Between ראש השנה *&* יום כיפור *say* מִי כָמְוֹךָ אַב הָרַחֲמִים, זוֹכֵר יְצוּרָיו לְחַיִּים בְּרַחֲמִים.

וְנֶאֱמָן אַתָּה לְהַחֲיוֹת מֵתִים.

בָּרוּךְ אַתָּה יהוה, מְחַיֵּה הַמֵּתִים. (קהל: **אָמֵן**)

KEDUSHA

This section of tefillah is said while standing silently with feet together. The sentences are said responsively, Congregation followed by the Leader.

Congregation then Leader: נְקַדֵּשׁ We will announce You, *Hashem*,
as holy in this world,
just as the angels
announce You as holy in heaven.
As Your prophet wrote,
The angels call to one another saying:

(Stand on your toes as you repeat the word "Holy")

Congregation then Leader: Holy, holy, holy, is *Hashem*.
The whole world is filled with Your holiness.

Leader: All the Jewish people and the angels
say in response:

Congregation then Leader: Blessed is *Hashem*'s holiness.

Leader: It is written in *Tehillim*:

Congregation then Leader: *Hashem*, You have ruled over the Jewish
people for generations, and You shall
continue to be our King forever.

Leader: *Hashem*, in every generation we will discuss
Your holiness and greatness. Our mouths
shall never stop speaking of Your praises,
for You, *Hashem*, are a great and holy King.
Thank You, *Hashem*, our holy God.
/*Between Rosh Hashana & Yom Kippur say:* the holy King./

(*Congregation:* Amen.)

קדושה

This section of tefillah is said while standing silently with feet together. The sentences are said responsively, קהל *followed by the* חזן*.*

קהל *then* חזן: נְקַדֵּשׁ אֶת שִׁמְךָ בָּעוֹלָם
כְּשֵׁם שֶׁמַּקְדִּישִׁים אוֹתוֹ בִּשְׁמֵי מָרוֹם
כַּכָּתוּב עַל יַד נְבִיאֶךָ, וְקָרָא זֶה אֶל־זֶה וְאָמַר

(Stand on your toes as you repeat the word קָדוֹשׁ*)*

קהל *then* חזן: קָדוֹשׁ, קָדוֹשׁ, קָדוֹשׁ, יהוה צְבָאוֹת
מְלֹא כָל־הָאָרֶץ כְּבוֹדוֹ:

חזן: לְעֻמָּתָם בָּרוּךְ יֹאמֵרוּ

קהל *then* חזן: בָּרוּךְ כְּבוֹד־יהוה מִמְּקוֹמוֹ:

חזן: וּבְדִבְרֵי קָדְשְׁךָ כָּתוּב לֵאמֹר

קהל *then* חזן: יִמְלֹךְ יהוה לְעוֹלָם
אֱלֹהַיִךְ צִיּוֹן לְדֹר וָדֹר, הַלְלוּיָהּ:

חזן: לְדוֹר וָדוֹר נַגִּיד גָּדְלֶךָ
וּלְנֵצַח נְצָחִים קְדֻשָּׁתְךָ נַקְדִּישׁ
וְשִׁבְחֲךָ אֱלֹהֵינוּ מִפִּינוּ לֹא יָמוּשׁ לְעוֹלָם וָעֶד
כִּי אֵל מֶלֶךְ גָּדוֹל וְקָדוֹשׁ אָתָּה.
בָּרוּךְ אַתָּה יהוה, הָאֵל הַקָּדוֹשׁ.

/ *Between* ראש השנה *&* יום כיפור *say* הַמֶּלֶךְ הַקָּדוֹשׁ. /

(קהל: אָמֵן)

Reminder: Say "Amen" after the Leader recites each beracha.

GIVE US WISDOM

We pray to You, *Hashem*,
that You give us wisdom
and the ability to understand.
Thank You, *Hashem*,
for giving us wisdom. (*Congregation:* Amen.)

RETURN US TO *HASHEM*

We pray to You, *Hashem*,
that You allow us to return to You after we sin.
Thank You, *Hashem*
for wanting us to return to You. (*Congregation:* Amen.)

FORGIVE US

We pray to You, *Hashem*,
that You accept our apologies.
Thank You, *Hashem*,
who repeatedly forgives. (*Congregation:* Amen.)

SAVE US

We pray to You, *Hashem*,
that You protect and save Your Jewish people.
Thank You, *Hashem*,
who saves the Jewish people. (*Congregation:* Amen.)

Reminder: Say אָמֵן *after the* חזן *recites each beracha.*

דעת

אַתָּה חוֹנֵן לְאָדָם דַּעַת
וּמְלַמֵּד לֶאֱנוֹשׁ בִּינָה.
חָנֵּנוּ מֵאִתְּךָ דֵּעָה בִּינָה וְהַשְׂכֵּל.
בָּרוּךְ אַתָּה יהוה, חוֹנֵן הַדָּעַת. (קהל: אָמֵן)

תשובה

הֲשִׁיבֵנוּ אָבִינוּ לְתוֹרָתֶךָ
וְקָרְבֵנוּ מַלְכֵּנוּ לַעֲבוֹדָתֶךָ
וְהַחֲזִירֵנוּ בִּתְשׁוּבָה שְׁלֵמָה לְפָנֶיךָ.
בָּרוּךְ אַתָּה יהוה, הָרוֹצֶה בִּתְשׁוּבָה. (קהל: אָמֵן)

סליחה

סְלַח לָנוּ אָבִינוּ כִּי חָטָאנוּ
מְחַל לָנוּ מַלְכֵּנוּ כִּי פָשָׁעְנוּ
כִּי מוֹחֵל וְסוֹלֵחַ אָתָּה.
בָּרוּךְ אַתָּה יהוה, חַנּוּן הַמַּרְבֶּה לִסְלֹחַ. (קהל: אָמֵן)

גאולה

רְאֵה בְעָנְיֵנוּ, וְרִיבָה רִיבֵנוּ
וּגְאָלֵנוּ מְהֵרָה לְמַעַן שְׁמֶךָ
כִּי גּוֹאֵל חָזָק אָתָּה.
בָּרוּךְ אַתָּה יהוה, גּוֹאֵל יִשְׂרָאֵל. (קהל: אָמֵן)

Reminder: Say "Amen" after the Leader recites each beracha.

On Fast Days the Leader adds:

עֲנֵנוּ Answer us, *Hashem,* on this fast day, because we are in pain. *Hashem,* do not look at our bad actions, turn away from us, or ignore our prayers. Be close to us and comfort us. Even before we call You, answer us, as it says, "Even before they call Me, I will answer them. While they are still speaking, I will hear." Because You, *Hashem,* answer us in our time of pain, and save us from suffering. Thank You, *Hashem,* who answers us in our time of pain. (*Congregation:* Amen.)

HEAL US

We pray to You, *Hashem,*
that You heal the sick.
Thank You, *Hashem,*
who heals the Jewish people who are sick.
(*Congregation:* Amen.)

PROVIDE FOOD FOR US

We pray to You, *Hashem,*
that You will provide us
with the food we need to live.
Thank You, *Hashem,*
for filling our year with blessing. (*Congregation:* Amen.)

Reminder: Say אָמֵן after the חזן recites each beracha.

On Fast Days the חזן adds:

עֲנֵנוּ יהוה עֲנֵנוּ בְּיוֹם צוֹם תַּעֲנִיתֵנוּ, כִּי בְצָרָה גְדוֹלָה אֲנָחְנוּ. אַל תֵּפֶן אֶל רִשְׁעֵנוּ, וְאַל תַּסְתֵּר פָּנֶיךָ מִמֶּנּוּ, וְאַל תִּתְעַלַּם מִתְּחִנָּתֵנוּ. הֱיֵה נָא קָרוֹב לְשַׁוְעָתֵנוּ, יְהִי נָא חַסְדְּךָ לְנַחֲמֵנוּ, טֶרֶם נִקְרָא אֵלֶיךָ עֲנֵנוּ, כַּדָּבָר שֶׁנֶּאֱמַר: וְהָיָה טֶרֶם יִקְרָאוּ וַאֲנִי אֶעֱנֶה, עוֹד הֵם מְדַבְּרִים וַאֲנִי אֶשְׁמָע: כִּי אַתָּה יהוה הָעוֹנֶה בְּעֵת צָרָה, פּוֹדֶה וּמַצִּיל בְּכָל עֵת צָרָה וְצוּקָה. בָּרוּךְ אַתָּה יהוה, הָעוֹנֶה בְּעֵת צָרָה. (קהל: אָמֵן)

רפואה

רְפָאֵנוּ יהוה וְנֵרָפֵא, הוֹשִׁיעֵנוּ וְנִוָּשֵׁעָה, כִּי תְהִלָּתֵנוּ אָתָּה
וְהַעֲלֵה רְפוּאָה שְׁלֵמָה לְכָל מַכּוֹתֵינוּ
כִּי אֵל מֶלֶךְ רוֹפֵא נֶאֱמָן וְרַחֲמָן אָתָּה.
בָּרוּךְ אַתָּה יהוה, רוֹפֵא חוֹלֵי עַמּוֹ יִשְׂרָאֵל. (קהל: אָמֵן)

ברכת השנים

בָּרֵךְ עָלֵינוּ יהוה אֱלֹהֵינוּ אֶת הַשָּׁנָה הַזֹּאת
וְאֶת כָּל מִינֵי תְבוּאָתָהּ, לְטוֹבָה

Say this phrase during the winter season, from December 4th through פסח.

וְתֵן טַל וּמָטָר לִבְרָכָה

Say this phrase during the summer season, from חול המועד פסח through מנחה of December 3rd.

וְתֵן בְּרָכָה

עַל פְּנֵי הָאֲדָמָה, וְשַׂבְּעֵנוּ מִטּוּבָהּ, וּבָרֵךְ שְׁנָתֵנוּ כַּשָּׁנִים הַטּוֹבוֹת.
בָּרוּךְ אַתָּה יהוה, מְבָרֵךְ הַשָּׁנִים. (קהל: אָמֵן)

Reminder: Say "Amen" after the Leader recites each beracha.

GATHER US

We pray to You, *Hashem,*
that You gather Your Jewish people
from across the world
and lead us into freedom from exile.
Thank You, *Hashem,*
who gathers His scattered Jewish people.

(*Congregation:* Amen.)

REESTABLISH JEWISH COURTS

We pray to You, *Hashem,*
that You bring back our Jewish judges
and leaders as it once was.
Thank You, *Hashem,*
the King who loves righteousness and fairness.
/*Between Rosh Hashana and Yom Kippur say:* the King of fairness./

(*Congregation:* Amen.)

THE WICKED

We pray to You, *Hashem,*
that You destroy the wickedness
and evil among Your Jewish people.
Thank You, *Hashem,*
for destroying our enemies
and for returning Jews that turned away.

(*Congregation:* Amen.)

Reminder: Say אָמֵן after the חזן recites each beracha.

קבוץ גלויות

תְּקַע בְּשׁוֹפָר גָּדוֹל לְחֵרוּתֵנוּ
וְשָׂא נֵס לְקַבֵּץ גָּלֻיּוֹתֵינוּ
וְקַבְּצֵנוּ יַחַד מֵאַרְבַּע כַּנְפוֹת הָאָרֶץ.

בָּרוּךְ אַתָּה יהוה, מְקַבֵּץ נִדְחֵי עַמּוֹ יִשְׂרָאֵל. (קהל: **אָמֵן**)

השבת המשפט

הָשִׁיבָה שׁוֹפְטֵינוּ כְּבָרִאשׁוֹנָה
וְיוֹעֲצֵינוּ כְּבַתְּחִלָּה
וְהָסֵר מִמֶּנּוּ יָגוֹן וַאֲנָחָה
וּמְלֹךְ עָלֵינוּ אַתָּה יהוה לְבַדְּךָ בְּחֶסֶד וּבְרַחֲמִים
וְצַדְּקֵנוּ בַּמִּשְׁפָּט.

בָּרוּךְ אַתָּה יהוה, מֶלֶךְ אוֹהֵב צְדָקָה וּמִשְׁפָּט.

/ *Between* ראש השנה *and* יום כיפור *say* **הַמֶּלֶךְ הַמִּשְׁפָּט.** /

(קהל: **אָמֵן**)

ברכת המינים

וְלַמַּלְשִׁינִים אַל תְּהִי תִקְוָה
וְכָל הָרִשְׁעָה כְּרֶגַע תֹּאבֵד
וְכָל אוֹיְבֵי עַמְּךָ מְהֵרָה יִכָּרֵתוּ
וְהַזֵּדִים מְהֵרָה תְעַקֵּר וּתְשַׁבֵּר וּתְמַגֵּר וְתַכְנִיעַ
בִּמְהֵרָה בְיָמֵינוּ.

בָּרוּךְ אַתָּה יהוה, שׁוֹבֵר אוֹיְבִים וּמַכְנִיעַ זֵדִים.

(קהל: **אָמֵן**)

Reminder: Say "Amen" after the Leader recites each beracha.

THE RIGHTEOUS

We pray to You, *Hashem,*
that You reward the righteous, pious, and wise
among Your Jewish people.
Thank You, *Hashem,*
for supporting righteous people. (*Congregation:* Amen.)

REBUILDING JERUSALEM

We pray to You, *Hashem,*
that You rebuild Jerusalem
and Your home, the *Beit HaMikdash.*
Thank You, *Hashem,*
for rebuilding Jerusalem. (*Congregation:* Amen.)

KINGDOM OF DAVID

We pray to You, *Hashem,*
that You soon send *Mashiach*
from the family of King David.
Thank You, *Hashem,*
who brings *Mashiach.* (*Congregation:* Amen.)

LISTEN TO OUR PRAYERS

We pray to You, *Hashem,*
that You have mercy on us
and listen to our prayers.
Thank You, *Hashem,*
for listening to our prayers. (*Congregation:* Amen.)

Reminder: Say אָמֵן after the חזן recites each beracha.

על הצדיקים

עַל הַצַּדִּיקִים וְעַל הַחֲסִידִים, וְעַל זִקְנֵי עַמְּךָ בֵּית יִשְׂרָאֵל
וְעַל פְּלֵיטַת סוֹפְרֵיהֶם, וְעַל גֵּרֵי הַצֶּדֶק, וְעָלֵינוּ
יֶהֱמוּ רַחֲמֶיךָ יהוה אֱלֹהֵינוּ
וְתֵן שָׂכָר טוֹב לְכָל הַבּוֹטְחִים בְּשִׁמְךָ בֶּאֱמֶת
וְשִׂים חֶלְקֵנוּ עִמָּהֶם, וּלְעוֹלָם לֹא נֵבוֹשׁ כִּי בְךָ בָּטָחְנוּ.

בָּרוּךְ אַתָּה יהוה, מִשְׁעָן וּמִבְטָח לַצַּדִּיקִים. (קהל: אָמֵן)

בניין ירושלים

וְלִירוּשָׁלַיִם עִירְךָ בְּרַחֲמִים תָּשׁוּב, וְתִשְׁכֹּן בְּתוֹכָהּ כַּאֲשֶׁר דִּבַּרְתָּ
וּבְנֵה אוֹתָהּ בְּקָרוֹב בְּיָמֵינוּ בִּנְיַן עוֹלָם
וְכִסֵּא דָוִד מְהֵרָה לְתוֹכָהּ תָּכִין.

בָּרוּךְ אַתָּה יהוה, בּוֹנֵה יְרוּשָׁלָיִם. (קהל: אָמֵן)

מלכות בית דוד

אֶת צֶמַח דָּוִד עַבְדְּךָ מְהֵרָה תַצְמִיחַ, וְקַרְנוֹ תָּרוּם בִּישׁוּעָתֶךָ
כִּי לִישׁוּעָתְךָ קִוִּינוּ כָּל הַיּוֹם.

בָּרוּךְ אַתָּה יהוה, מַצְמִיחַ קֶרֶן יְשׁוּעָה. (קהל: אָמֵן)

שומע תפילה

שְׁמַע קוֹלֵנוּ יהוה אֱלֹהֵינוּ
חוּס וְרַחֵם עָלֵינוּ, וְקַבֵּל בְּרַחֲמִים וּבְרָצוֹן אֶת תְּפִלָּתֵנוּ
כִּי אֵל שׁוֹמֵעַ תְּפִלּוֹת וְתַחֲנוּנִים אָתָּה
וּמִלְּפָנֶיךָ מַלְכֵּנוּ רֵיקָם אַל תְּשִׁיבֵנוּ
כִּי אַתָּה שׁוֹמֵעַ תְּפִלַּת עַמְּךָ יִשְׂרָאֵל בְּרַחֲמִים.

בָּרוּךְ אַתָּה יהוה, שׁוֹמֵעַ תְּפִלָּה. (קהל: אָמֵן)

Reminder: Say "Amen" after the Leader recites the beracha.

SERVICE IN THE *BEIT HAMIKDASH*

We pray to You, *Hashem,* that You accept our prayers
as though they are the sacrifices
that were once brought to You
in Your holy *Beit HaMikdash.*

On Rosh Chodesh and Chol HaMo'ed, say:

Our God, and God of our ancestors, may our prayers:
Rise from our mouths, Come before You,
Reach You at a desirable time, Be heard, And be fulfilled.
Hashem, You remember and know each of our hardships.
You remember:
Our ancestors, *Mashiach,* Your holy city, Jerusalem,
and Your united Jewish people,
for goodness, kindness, mercy, life,
and peace on this day of:

On Rosh Chodesh: *Rosh Chodesh.*
On Pesach: the Holiday of *Matzot.*
On Sukkot: the Holiday of *Sukkot.*

Hashem, on this day please remember us
with good thoughts, consider us for blessing,
and help us with difficult times in our lives.
Be kind and merciful with us, *Hashem,*
as we look towards You as our King.

May we be worthy
to see the rebuilding of the *Beit HaMikdash.*
We thank You, *Hashem,*
for returning Your presence to Zion. (*Congregation:* Amen.)

Reminder: Say אָמֵן after the חזן recites the beracha.

עבודה

רְצֵה יהוה אֱלֹהֵינוּ בְּעַמְּךָ יִשְׂרָאֵל, וּבִתְפִלָּתָם
וְהָשֵׁב אֶת הָעֲבוֹדָה לִדְבִיר בֵּיתֶךָ
וְאִשֵּׁי יִשְׂרָאֵל וּתְפִלָּתָם בְּאַהֲבָה תְקַבֵּל בְּרָצוֹן
וּתְהִי לְרָצוֹן תָּמִיד עֲבוֹדַת יִשְׂרָאֵל עַמֶּךָ.

On ראש חודש and חול המועד, say:

אֱלֹהֵינוּ וֵאלֹהֵי אֲבוֹתֵינוּ
יַעֲלֶה וְיָבוֹא וְיַגִּיעַ, וְיֵרָאֶה וְיֵרָצֶה וְיִשָּׁמַע
וְיִפָּקֵד וְיִזָּכֵר זִכְרוֹנֵנוּ וּפִקְדוֹנֵנוּ, וְזִכְרוֹן אֲבוֹתֵינוּ
וְזִכְרוֹן מָשִׁיחַ בֶּן דָּוִד עַבְדֶּךָ
וְזִכְרוֹן יְרוּשָׁלַיִם עִיר קָדְשֶׁךָ
וְזִכְרוֹן כָּל עַמְּךָ בֵּית יִשְׂרָאֵל
לְפָנֶיךָ, לִפְלֵיטָה לְטוֹבָה, לְחֵן וּלְחֶסֶד וּלְרַחֲמִים
לְחַיִּים וּלְשָׁלוֹם, בְּיוֹם

בראש חודש: רֹאשׁ הַחֹדֶשׁ הַזֶּה.
בפסח: חַג הַמַּצּוֹת הַזֶּה.
בסוכות: חַג הַסֻּכּוֹת הַזֶּה.

זָכְרֵנוּ יהוה אֱלֹהֵינוּ בּוֹ לְטוֹבָה, וּפָקְדֵנוּ בוֹ לִבְרָכָה
וְהוֹשִׁיעֵנוּ בוֹ לְחַיִּים.
וּבִדְבַר יְשׁוּעָה וְרַחֲמִים, חוּס וְחָנֵּנוּ וְרַחֵם עָלֵינוּ וְהוֹשִׁיעֵנוּ
כִּי אֵלֶיךָ עֵינֵינוּ, כִּי אֵל מֶלֶךְ חַנּוּן וְרַחוּם אָתָּה.

וְתֶחֱזֶינָה עֵינֵינוּ בְּשׁוּבְךָ לְצִיּוֹן בְּרַחֲמִים.

בָּרוּךְ אַתָּה יהוה, הַמַּחֲזִיר שְׁכִינָתוֹ לְצִיּוֹן. (קהל: אָמֵן)

THANK YOU

While the Leader says this prayer, the Congregation says the prayer on the bottom of this page.

You, *Hashem,* have unlimited mercy and kindness
and therefore we have always placed our hope in You.

The following is said quietly while the Leader says the above. Bow when saying the first sentence below beginning with the words "Thank You, Hashem."

מוֹדִים Thank You, *Hashem,*
our God and God of our ancestors.
You are God of all people,
You created us, and You created the entire world.
Thank You for giving us life
and for providing us with food to eat.
May You continue to give us life and food to eat.
May You gather us from exile
and return us to Your holy places
so we can keep Your laws,
and serve You with a perfect heart.
Thank You *Hashem,*
our God to whom thanksgiving is due.

הודאה – THANK YOU

During the Leader's Repetition, the congregation participates by bowing at the word "*modim*" and saying a prayer called "*Modim DeRabanan.*" This active participation is different than the rest of the Leader's Repetition where the congregation only says "amen" to the *berachot.*

The purpose of *Modim* is to thank *Hashem*. One should say thank you directly, and not through a messenger. Though the Leader represents the congregation, when it comes to thanking *Hashem* for all that He does for us, each member of the congregation should say "thank You" to *Hashem* directly, without relying on the Leader.

הודאה

While the חזן *says this prayer, the* קהל *says the prayer on the bottom of this page.*

מוֹדִים אֲנַחְנוּ לָךְ
שָׁאַתָּה הוּא יהוה אֱלֹהֵינוּ וֵאלֹהֵי אֲבוֹתֵינוּ לְעוֹלָם וָעֶד.
צוּר חַיֵּינוּ, מָגֵן יִשְׁעֵנוּ אַתָּה הוּא לְדוֹר וָדוֹר.
נוֹדֶה לְּךָ וּנְסַפֵּר תְּהִלָּתֶךָ
עַל חַיֵּינוּ הַמְּסוּרִים בְּיָדֶךָ, וְעַל נִשְׁמוֹתֵינוּ הַפְּקוּדוֹת לָךְ
וְעַל נִסֶּיךָ שֶׁבְּכָל יוֹם עִמָּנוּ, וְעַל נִפְלְאוֹתֶיךָ וְטוֹבוֹתֶיךָ
שֶׁבְּכָל עֵת, עֶרֶב וָבֹקֶר וְצָהֳרָיִם.
הַטּוֹב, כִּי לֹא כָלוּ רַחֲמֶיךָ
וְהַמְרַחֵם, כִּי לֹא תַמּוּ חֲסָדֶיךָ, מֵעוֹלָם קִוִּינוּ לָךְ.

The following is said quietly while the חזן *says the above. Bow when saying the first sentence below beginning with the words* מוֹדִים אֲנַחְנוּ לָךְ.

מוֹדִים אֲנַחְנוּ לָךְ
שָׁאַתָּה הוּא יהוה אֱלֹהֵינוּ וֵאלֹהֵי אֲבוֹתֵינוּ
אֱלֹהֵי כָל בָּשָׂר, יוֹצְרֵנוּ, יוֹצֵר בְּרֵאשִׁית.
בְּרָכוֹת וְהוֹדָאוֹת לְשִׁמְךָ הַגָּדוֹל וְהַקָּדוֹשׁ
עַל שֶׁהֶחֱיִיתָנוּ וְקִיַּמְתָּנוּ.
כֵּן תְּחַיֵּנוּ וּתְקַיְּמֵנוּ
וְתֶאֱסֹף גָּלֻיּוֹתֵינוּ לְחַצְרוֹת קָדְשֶׁךָ
לִשְׁמֹר חֻקֶּיךָ וְלַעֲשׂוֹת רְצוֹנֶךָ וּלְעָבְדְּךָ בְּלֵבָב שָׁלֵם
עַל שֶׁאֲנַחְנוּ מוֹדִים לָךְ.
בָּרוּךְ אֵל הַהוֹדָאוֹת.

Reminder: Say "Amen" after the Leader recites the beracha.

On Chanuka say:

We thank You, *Hashem,* for the miracles, the deliverances, the great strength, and the victories in war that You displayed for us in earlier times and in our times.

In the days of Mattityahu, son of Yochanan the *Kohen Gadol,* the Hasmonean, and his sons, the wicked Greeks challenged Your Jewish people trying to make them forget Your Torah and sin. In Your great kindness, You, *Hashem,* supported us in this difficult time. You allowed for: The weak Jews to defeat the mighty Greeks, The few Jews to defeat the many Greeks, The pure Jews to defeat the impure Greeks, The righteous Jews to defeat the wicked Greeks, and The Jews who studied Your Torah to defeat the Greeks who did not. *Hashem,* on this day everyone in the world recognized You as You miraculously saved Your Jewish people. Your Jewish people then entered the *Beit HaMikdash* to clean and purify it. They lit candles in the courtyard of the *Beit HaMikdash* and set aside these eight days of *Chanukah* for giving thanks and praising You.

Continue with "We thank You"

On Purim say:

We thank You, *Hashem,* for the miracles, the deliverances, the great strength, and the victories in war that You displayed for us in earlier times and in our times.

In the days of Mordechai and Esther, the wicked Haman planned to destroy all Jews, men, women, and children, young and old, on the 13th of Adar, and steal their belongings. In Your great mercy, You, *Hashem,* ruined Haman's plans and instead Haman and his sons were hanged on the gallows.

Continue with "We thank You"

We thank You, *Hashem,* for You are good
and all that You do is good.
Thank You, *Hashem,*
for You are worthy of being thanked. (*Congregation:* Amen.)

Reminder: Say אָמֵן after the חזן recites the beracha.

בחנוכה:

עַל הַנִּסִּים וְעַל הַפֻּרְקָן וְעַל הַגְּבוּרוֹת וְעַל הַתְּשׁוּעוֹת וְעַל הַמִּלְחָמוֹת שֶׁעָשִׂיתָ לַאֲבוֹתֵינוּ בַּיָּמִים הָהֵם בַּזְּמַן הַזֶּה.

בִּימֵי מַתִּתְיָהוּ בֶּן יוֹחָנָן כֹּהֵן גָּדוֹל חַשְׁמוֹנַאי וּבָנָיו, כְּשֶׁעָמְדָה מַלְכוּת יָוָן הָרְשָׁעָה עַל עַמְּךָ יִשְׂרָאֵל לְהַשְׁכִּיחָם תּוֹרָתֶךָ וּלְהַעֲבִירָם מֵחֻקֵּי רְצוֹנֶךָ, וְאַתָּה בְּרַחֲמֶיךָ הָרַבִּים עָמַדְתָּ לָהֶם בְּעֵת צָרָתָם, רַבְתָּ אֶת רִיבָם, דַּנְתָּ אֶת דִּינָם, נָקַמְתָּ אֶת נִקְמָתָם, מָסַרְתָּ גִבּוֹרִים בְּיַד חַלָּשִׁים, וְרַבִּים בְּיַד מְעַטִּים, וּטְמֵאִים בְּיַד טְהוֹרִים, וּרְשָׁעִים בְּיַד צַדִּיקִים, וְזֵדִים בְּיַד עוֹסְקֵי תוֹרָתֶךָ, וּלְךָ עָשִׂיתָ שֵׁם גָּדוֹל וְקָדוֹשׁ בְּעוֹלָמֶךָ, וּלְעַמְּךָ יִשְׂרָאֵל עָשִׂיתָ תְּשׁוּעָה גְדוֹלָה וּפֻרְקָן כְּהַיּוֹם הַזֶּה. וְאַחַר כֵּן בָּאוּ בָנֶיךָ לִדְבִיר בֵּיתֶךָ, וּפִנּוּ אֶת הֵיכָלֶךָ, וְטִהֲרוּ אֶת מִקְדָּשֶׁךָ, וְהִדְלִיקוּ נֵרוֹת בְּחַצְרוֹת קָדְשֶׁךָ, וְקָבְעוּ שְׁמוֹנַת יְמֵי חֲנֻכָּה אֵלּוּ, לְהוֹדוֹת וּלְהַלֵּל לְשִׁמְךָ הַגָּדוֹל.

Continue with וְעַל כֻּלָּם.

בפורים:

עַל הַנִּסִּים וְעַל הַפֻּרְקָן וְעַל הַגְּבוּרוֹת וְעַל הַתְּשׁוּעוֹת וְעַל הַמִּלְחָמוֹת שֶׁעָשִׂיתָ לַאֲבוֹתֵינוּ בַּיָּמִים הָהֵם בַּזְּמַן הַזֶּה.

בִּימֵי מָרְדְּכַי וְאֶסְתֵּר בְּשׁוּשַׁן הַבִּירָה, כְּשֶׁעָמַד עֲלֵיהֶם הָמָן הָרָשָׁע, בִּקֵּשׁ לְהַשְׁמִיד לַהֲרֹג וּלְאַבֵּד אֶת־כָּל־הַיְּהוּדִים מִנַּעַר וְעַד־זָקֵן טַף וְנָשִׁים בְּיוֹם אֶחָד, בִּשְׁלוֹשָׁה עָשָׂר לְחֹדֶשׁ שְׁנֵים־עָשָׂר, הוּא־חֹדֶשׁ אֲדָר, וּשְׁלָלָם לָבוֹז: וְאַתָּה בְּרַחֲמֶיךָ הָרַבִּים הֵפַרְתָּ אֶת עֲצָתוֹ, וְקִלְקַלְתָּ אֶת מַחֲשַׁבְתּוֹ, וַהֲשֵׁבוֹתָ לּוֹ גְּמוּלוֹ בְּרֹאשׁוֹ, וְתָלוּ אוֹתוֹ וְאֶת בָּנָיו עַל הָעֵץ.

Continue with וְעַל כֻּלָּם.

וְעַל כֻּלָּם, יִתְבָּרַךְ וְיִתְרוֹמַם שִׁמְךָ מַלְכֵּנוּ תָּמִיד לְעוֹלָם וָעֶד.

Between ראש השנה *&* יום כיפור *say* וּכְתֹב לְחַיִּים טוֹבִים כָּל בְּנֵי בְרִיתֶךָ.

וְכֹל הַחַיִּים יוֹדוּךָ סֶּלָה, וִיהַלְלוּ אֶת שִׁמְךָ בֶּאֱמֶת הָאֵל יְשׁוּעָתֵנוּ וְעֶזְרָתֵנוּ סֶלָה.

בָּרוּךְ אַתָּה יהוה, הַטּוֹב שִׁמְךָ וּלְךָ נָאֶה לְהוֹדוֹת. (קהל: אָמֵן)

BLESSINGS OF THE *KOHANIM*

אֱלֹהֵינוּ *Hashem,* Our God and God of our ancestors, provide us with the three blessings that Aharon the *Kohen* and the *kohanim* his descendants use to bless the Jewish people.

Leader: *Hashem* should bless and protect you.

(*Congregation:* May it be as you say!)

Leader: *Hashem* should be kind and favorable towards you.

(*Congregation:* May it be as you say!)

Leader: *Hashem* should grant you peace.

(*Congregation:* May it be as you say!)

Reminder: Say "Amen" after the Leader recites the beracha.

PEACE

We pray to You, *Hashem,*
that You grant peace to Your Jewish people
at every moment of every hour, forever.

Between Rosh Hashana and Yom Kippur the Leader continues with "May You remember," below.

Thank You, *Hashem,*
who blesses His Jewish people with peace.

(*Congregation:* Amen.)

Between Rosh Hashana and Yom Kippur say:

May You remember all of the Jewish people for life,
blessing, peace, and riches
and write us in the book of good life and peace.
Thank You, *Hashem,* who makes peace. (*Congregation:* Amen.)

On days when Tachanun is said, start Tachanun on page 160. On Mondays and Thursdays start Tachanun on page 152. On days when Tachanun is not said, the Leader says Half Kaddish on page 166.

Between Rosh HaShana and Yom Kippur (but not on Erev Yom Kippur, unless it falls on Friday), and on fast days, say Avinu Malkenu on page 146.

On Rosh Chodesh, Chol HaMoed, and Chanukah, say Hallel on page 720.

ברכת כוהנים

אֱלֹהֵינוּ וֵאלֹהֵי אֲבוֹתֵינוּ, בָּרְכֵנוּ בַּבְּרָכָה הַמְשֻׁלֶּשֶׁת בַּתּוֹרָה, הַכְּתוּבָה עַל יְדֵי מֹשֶׁה עַבְדֶּךָ, הָאֲמוּרָה מִפִּי אַהֲרֹן וּבָנָיו כֹּהֲנִים עַם קְדוֹשֶׁיךָ, כָּאָמוּר

חזן: יְבָרֶכְךָ יהוה וְיִשְׁמְרֶךָ: קהל: כֵּן יְהִי רָצוֹן

חזן: יָאֵר יהוה פָּנָיו אֵלֶיךָ וִיחֻנֶּךָּ: קהל: כֵּן יְהִי רָצוֹן

חזן: יִשָּׂא יהוה פָּנָיו אֵלֶיךָ וְיָשֵׂם לְךָ שָׁלוֹם: קהל: כֵּן יְהִי רָצוֹן

Reminder: Say אָמֵן after the חזן recites the beracha.

שלום

שִׂים שָׁלוֹם טוֹבָה וּבְרָכָה
חֵן וָחֶסֶד וְרַחֲמִים עָלֵינוּ וְעַל כָּל יִשְׂרָאֵל עַמֶּךָ.
בָּרְכֵנוּ אָבִינוּ כֻּלָּנוּ כְּאֶחָד בְּאוֹר פָּנֶיךָ
כִּי בְאוֹר פָּנֶיךָ נָתַתָּ לָּנוּ יהוה אֱלֹהֵינוּ
תּוֹרַת חַיִּים וְאַהֲבַת חֶסֶד, וּצְדָקָה וּבְרָכָה וְרַחֲמִים וְחַיִּים וְשָׁלוֹם.
וְטוֹב בְּעֵינֶיךָ לְבָרֵךְ אֶת עַמְּךָ יִשְׂרָאֵל
בְּכָל עֵת וּבְכָל שָׁעָה בִּשְׁלוֹמֶךָ.

Between ראש השנה and יום כיפור the חזן continues with בְּסֵפֶר חַיִּים, below.

בָּרוּךְ אַתָּה יהוה, הַמְבָרֵךְ אֶת עַמּוֹ יִשְׂרָאֵל בַּשָּׁלוֹם.
(קהל: אָמֵן)

Between ראש השנה and יום כיפור say:

בְּסֵפֶר חַיִּים, בְּרָכָה וְשָׁלוֹם, וּפַרְנָסָה טוֹבָה, נִזָּכֵר וְנִכָּתֵב לְפָנֶיךָ אֲנַחְנוּ וְכָל עַמְּךָ בֵּית יִשְׂרָאֵל לְחַיִּים טוֹבִים וּלְשָׁלוֹם.
בָּרוּךְ אַתָּה יהוה, עוֹשֵׂה הַשָּׁלוֹם. (קהל: אָמֵן)

On days when תחנון is said, start תחנון on page 161. On Mondays and Thursdays start תחנון on page 153. On days when תחנון is not said, the חזן says חצי קדיש on page 167.

Between ראש השנה and יום כיפור (but not on ערב יום כיפור, unless it falls on Friday), and on fast days, say אבינו מלכנו on page 147.

On ראש חודש, חול המועד, and חנוכה, say הלל on page 721.

Between Rosh Hashana and Yom Kippur, and on fast days, say the following.

AVINU MALKENU

The Ark is opened.

אָבִינוּ מַלְכֵּנוּ Our Father and King, we have sinned.

Our Father and King, You are our only King.

Our Father and King, act with us kindly because You are kind.

Our Father and King, bless us with a good year.

/*Between Rosh Hashana and Yom Kippur say:*
bring upon us a good new year./

Our Father and King, cancel all harsh promises that have been made against us.

Our Father and King, cancel the plans of those who hate us.

Our Father and King, do not listen to the advice of our enemies.

Our Father and King, destroy all of our enemies.

Our Father and King, do not allow our enemies to speak badly about us anymore.

Our Father and King, protect Your Jewish people from plague, war, hunger, being taken captive by our enemies, destruction, and sin.

Our Father and King, protect us from illness.

Our Father and King, forgive us for all our sins.

Our Father and King, remove our sins from Your sight.

Our Father and King, please erase our sins with mercy, as if we never committed them.

Between ראש השנה and יום כיפור, and on fast days, say the following.

אבינו מלכנו

The ארון קודש is opened.

אָבִינוּ מַלְכֵּנוּ, חָטָאנוּ לְפָנֶיךָ.

אָבִינוּ מַלְכֵּנוּ, אֵין לָנוּ מֶלֶךְ אֶלָּא אָתָּה.

אָבִינוּ מַלְכֵּנוּ, עֲשֵׂה עִמָּנוּ לְמַעַן שְׁמֶךָ.

אָבִינוּ מַלְכֵּנוּ, בָּרֵךְ / בעשרת ימי תשובה: חַדֵּשׁ/ עָלֵינוּ שָׁנָה טוֹבָה.

אָבִינוּ מַלְכֵּנוּ, בַּטֵּל מֵעָלֵינוּ כָּל גְּזֵרוֹת קָשׁוֹת.

אָבִינוּ מַלְכֵּנוּ, בַּטֵּל מַחְשְׁבוֹת שׂוֹנְאֵינוּ.

אָבִינוּ מַלְכֵּנוּ, הָפֵר עֲצַת אוֹיְבֵינוּ.

אָבִינוּ מַלְכֵּנוּ, כַּלֵּה כָּל צַר וּמַשְׂטִין מֵעָלֵינוּ.

אָבִינוּ מַלְכֵּנוּ, סְתֹם פִּיּוֹת מַשְׂטִינֵנוּ וּמְקַטְרְגֵינוּ.

אָבִינוּ מַלְכֵּנוּ, כַּלֵּה דֶּבֶר וְחֶרֶב וְרָעָב וּשְׁבִי וּמַשְׁחִית
וְעָוֹן וּשְׁמַד מִבְּנֵי בְרִיתֶךָ.

אָבִינוּ מַלְכֵּנוּ, מְנַע מַגֵּפָה מִנַּחֲלָתֶךָ.

אָבִינוּ מַלְכֵּנוּ, סְלַח וּמְחַל לְכָל עֲוֹנוֹתֵינוּ.

אָבִינוּ מַלְכֵּנוּ, מְחֵה וְהַעֲבֵר פְּשָׁעֵינוּ וְחַטֹּאתֵינוּ מִנֶּגֶד עֵינֶיךָ.

אָבִינוּ מַלְכֵּנוּ, מְחֹק בְּרַחֲמֶיךָ הָרַבִּים כָּל שִׁטְרֵי חוֹבוֹתֵינוּ.

The following lines are said
first by the Leader and then by the congregation:

Our Father and King, please accept us because we regret our wrong actions and want to return to You.

Our Father and King, heal the sick members of Your Jewish people.

Our Father and King, tear up the evil plans made against us.

Our Father and King, remember us with kindness.

Between Rosh Hashana and Yom Kippur:

Our Father and King, write us in the book that promises us good life.

Our Father and King, write us in the book that promises we will be saved.

Our Father and King, write us in the book that promises we will have money and food to live.

Our Father and King, write us in the book that recognizes the good actions we have done.

Our Father and King, write us in the book that promises we will be forgiven.

Fast Days:

Our Father and King, remember us and provide us with a good life.

Our Father and King, remember us and save us.

Our Father and King, remember us and provide us with money and food to live.

Our Father and King, remember us and all the good actions we have done.

Our Father and King, remember us and forgive us.

End of responsive reading.

Our Father and King, free us from exile soon.

Our Father and King, support Your Jewish people.

Our Father and King, support *Mashiach,* the savior of the Jewish people.

The following nine sentences are said first by the חזן*, then by the* קהל*:*

אָבִֽינוּ מַלְכֵּֽנוּ, הַחֲזִירֵֽנוּ בִּתְשׁוּבָה שְׁלֵמָה לְפָנֶֽיךָ.

אָבִֽינוּ מַלְכֵּֽנוּ, שְׁלַח רְפוּאָה שְׁלֵמָה לְחוֹלֵי עַמֶּֽךָ.

אָבִֽינוּ מַלְכֵּֽנוּ, קְרַע רֹֽעַ גְּזַר דִּינֵֽנוּ.

אָבִֽינוּ מַלְכֵּֽנוּ, זָכְרֵֽנוּ בְּזִכָּרוֹן טוֹב לְפָנֶֽיךָ.

Between ראש השנה *and* יום כיפור*:*

אָבִֽינוּ מַלְכֵּֽנוּ, כָּתְבֵֽנוּ בְּסֵֽפֶר חַיִּים טוֹבִים.

אָבִֽינוּ מַלְכֵּֽנוּ, כָּתְבֵֽנוּ בְּסֵֽפֶר גְּאֻלָּה וִישׁוּעָה.

אָבִֽינוּ מַלְכֵּֽנוּ, כָּתְבֵֽנוּ בְּסֵֽפֶר פַּרְנָסָה וְכַלְכָּלָה.

אָבִֽינוּ מַלְכֵּֽנוּ, כָּתְבֵֽנוּ בְּסֵֽפֶר זְכֻיּוֹת.

אָבִֽינוּ מַלְכֵּֽנוּ, כָּתְבֵֽנוּ בְּסֵֽפֶר סְלִיחָה וּמְחִילָה.

On Fast Days:

אָבִֽינוּ מַלְכֵּֽנוּ, זָכְרֵֽנוּ לְחַיִּים טוֹבִים.

אָבִֽינוּ מַלְכֵּֽנוּ, זָכְרֵֽנוּ לִגְאֻלָּה וִישׁוּעָה.

אָבִֽינוּ מַלְכֵּֽנוּ, זָכְרֵֽנוּ לְפַרְנָסָה וְכַלְכָּלָה.

אָבִֽינוּ מַלְכֵּֽנוּ, זָכְרֵֽנוּ לִזְכֻיּוֹת.

אָבִֽינוּ מַלְכֵּֽנוּ, זָכְרֵֽנוּ לִסְלִיחָה וּמְחִילָה.

End of responsive reading.

אָבִֽינוּ מַלְכֵּֽנוּ, הַצְמַח לָֽנוּ יְשׁוּעָה בְּקָרוֹב.

אָבִֽינוּ מַלְכֵּֽנוּ, הָרֵם קֶֽרֶן יִשְׂרָאֵל עַמֶּֽךָ.

אָבִֽינוּ מַלְכֵּֽנוּ, הָרֵם קֶֽרֶן מְשִׁיחֶֽךָ.

Our Father and King, give us many blessings.

Our Father and King, allow us to have plentiful amounts of food.

Our Father and King, hear our voices and take pity on us.

Our Father and King, please accept our prayers with mercy.

Our Father and King, open up the gates of heaven to our prayers.

Our Father and King, remember that we are made from dust.

Our Father and King, please do not turn us away from You empty-handed.

Our Father and King, may this time be a time of mercy.

Our Father and King, have pity on us and our children.

Our Father and King, help us because of the many Jews who gave their lives for Your sake.

Our Father and King, help us because of the many Jews who were injured by fire and water for Your sake.

Our Father and King, punish our enemies for harming Your Jewish people.

Our Father and King, act for Your sake if not for ours.

Our Father and King, help us for Your sake and save us.

Our Father and King, help us because You are filled with overflowing mercy.

Our Father and King, help us because You are great, mighty, and fearsome.

▸ Our Father and King, show us mercy and answer us even though we do not deserve it; treat us with charity and kindness, and save us.

The Ark is closed.

אָבִינוּ מַלְכֵּנוּ, מַלֵּא יָדֵינוּ מִבִּרְכוֹתֶיךָ.
אָבִינוּ מַלְכֵּנוּ, מַלֵּא אֲסָמֵינוּ שָׂבָע.
אָבִינוּ מַלְכֵּנוּ, שְׁמַע קוֹלֵנוּ, חוּס וְרַחֵם עָלֵינוּ.
אָבִינוּ מַלְכֵּנוּ, קַבֵּל בְּרַחֲמִים וּבְרָצוֹן אֶת תְּפִלָּתֵנוּ.
אָבִינוּ מַלְכֵּנוּ, פְּתַח שַׁעֲרֵי שָׁמַיִם לִתְפִלָּתֵנוּ.
אָבִינוּ מַלְכֵּנוּ, זְכֹר כִּי עָפָר אֲנָחְנוּ.
אָבִינוּ מַלְכֵּנוּ, נָא אַל תְּשִׁיבֵנוּ רֵיקָם מִלְּפָנֶיךָ.
אָבִינוּ מַלְכֵּנוּ, תְּהֵא הַשָּׁעָה הַזֹּאת שְׁעַת רַחֲמִים וְעֵת רָצוֹן מִלְּפָנֶיךָ.
אָבִינוּ מַלְכֵּנוּ, חֲמֹל עָלֵינוּ וְעַל עוֹלָלֵינוּ וְטַפֵּנוּ.
אָבִינוּ מַלְכֵּנוּ, עֲשֵׂה לְמַעַן הֲרוּגִים עַל שֵׁם קָדְשֶׁךָ.
אָבִינוּ מַלְכֵּנוּ, עֲשֵׂה לְמַעַן טְבוּחִים עַל יִחוּדֶךָ.
אָבִינוּ מַלְכֵּנוּ, עֲשֵׂה לְמַעַן בָּאֵי בָאֵשׁ וּבַמַּיִם עַל קִדּוּשׁ שְׁמֶךָ.
אָבִינוּ מַלְכֵּנוּ, נְקֹם לְעֵינֵינוּ נִקְמַת דַּם עֲבָדֶיךָ הַשָּׁפוּךְ.
אָבִינוּ מַלְכֵּנוּ, עֲשֵׂה לְמַעַנְךָ אִם לֹא לְמַעֲנֵנוּ.
אָבִינוּ מַלְכֵּנוּ, עֲשֵׂה לְמַעַנְךָ וְהוֹשִׁיעֵנוּ.
אָבִינוּ מַלְכֵּנוּ, עֲשֵׂה לְמַעַן רַחֲמֶיךָ הָרַבִּים.
אָבִינוּ מַלְכֵּנוּ, עֲשֵׂה לְמַעַן שִׁמְךָ הַגָּדוֹל הַגִּבּוֹר וְהַנּוֹרָא, שֶׁנִּקְרָא עָלֵינוּ.
◂ אָבִינוּ מַלְכֵּנוּ, חָנֵּנוּ וַעֲנֵנוּ, כִּי אֵין בָּנוּ מַעֲשִׂים
עֲשֵׂה עִמָּנוּ צְדָקָה וָחֶסֶד וְהוֹשִׁיעֵנוּ.

The ארון קודש *is closed.*

TACHANUN

Tachanun is not said on Rosh Chodesh, Chanuka, Purim, Shushan Purim, during Nissan, on Yom HaAtzmaut, Lag BaOmer, Yom Yerushalayim, from Rosh Chodesh Sivan until after Shavuot, Tisha B'Av, Tu B'Av, Erev Rosh HaShana, and from Erev Yom Kippur until the day after Simchat Torah. It is also not said on the morning of a Brit Mila, during the week of Sheva Berachot when a chatan is present, and in a house of mourning.

On Monday and Thursday, begin Tachanun here.
On all other days, begin with "King David once said" on page 160.

The following is said standing.

וְהוּא רַחוּם *Hashem* is forgiving of sins;
He does not destroy the Jewish people
when we make a mistake.
Show us Your kindness and mercy, *Hashem*;
control Your anger and protect us.
Save us from our enemies,
even if we are not deserving,
so we can continue to praise and thank You.
Our Father and King,
remember Your promise to our ancestors
to protect the Jewish people.
Hear our cries in our times of struggle
and answer us when we call out to You.

וְעַתָּה *Hashem*, You saved our ancestors
and took them out of Egypt,
but since then
we have made mistakes and sinned.

סדר תחנון

Tachanun is not said on ראש חודש, חנוכה, פורים, שושן פורים*, during* ניסן*, on* יום העצמאות, לג בעומר, יום ירושלים*, from* ראש חודש סיון *until after* שבועות*,* תשעה באב, טו באב, ערב ראש השנה*, and from* ערב יום הכיפורים *until the day after* שמחת תורה*. It is also not said on the morning of a* ברית מילה*, during the week of* שבע ברכות *when a* חתן *is present, and in a house of mourning.*

On Mondays and Thursdays, begin תחנון *here.*
On all other days begin with וַיֹּאמֶר דָּוִד *on page 161.*

The following is said standing.

וְהוּא רַחוּם, יְכַפֵּר עָוֹן וְלֹא־יַשְׁחִית, וְהִרְבָּה לְהָשִׁיב אַפּוֹ וְלֹא־יָעִיר כָּל־חֲמָתוֹ: אַתָּה יהוה לֹא־תִכְלָא רַחֲמֶיךָ מִמֶּנּוּ, חַסְדְּךָ וַאֲמִתְּךָ תָּמִיד יִצְּרוּנוּ. הוֹשִׁיעֵנוּ יהוה אֱלֹהֵינוּ וְקַבְּצֵנוּ מִן־הַגּוֹיִם, לְהוֹדוֹת לְשֵׁם קָדְשֶׁךָ, לְהִשְׁתַּבֵּחַ בִּתְהִלָּתֶךָ: אִם־עֲוֹנוֹת תִּשְׁמָר־יָהּ, אֲדֹנָי מִי יַעֲמֹד: כִּי־עִמְּךָ הַסְּלִיחָה לְמַעַן תִּוָּרֵא: לֹא כַחֲטָאֵינוּ תַּעֲשֶׂה לָּנוּ, וְלֹא כַעֲוֹנוֹתֵינוּ תִּגְמֹל עָלֵינוּ. אִם־עֲוֹנֵינוּ עָנוּ בָנוּ, יהוה עֲשֵׂה לְמַעַן שְׁמֶךָ: זְכֹר־רַחֲמֶיךָ יהוה וַחֲסָדֶיךָ, כִּי מֵעוֹלָם הֵמָּה: יַעַנְנוּ יהוה בְּיוֹם צָרָה, יְשַׂגְּבֵנוּ שֵׁם אֱלֹהֵי יַעֲקֹב. יהוה הוֹשִׁיעָה, הַמֶּלֶךְ יַעֲנֵנוּ בְיוֹם־קָרְאֵנוּ: אָבִינוּ מַלְכֵּנוּ, חָנֵּנוּ וַעֲנֵנוּ, כִּי אֵין בָּנוּ מַעֲשִׂים, צְדָקָה עֲשֵׂה עִמָּנוּ לְמַעַן שְׁמֶךָ. אֲדוֹנֵינוּ אֱלֹהֵינוּ, שְׁמַע קוֹל תַּחֲנוּנֵינוּ, וּזְכָר לָנוּ אֶת בְּרִית אֲבוֹתֵינוּ וְהוֹשִׁיעֵנוּ לְמַעַן שְׁמֶךָ.

וְעַתָּה אֲדֹנָי אֱלֹהֵינוּ, אֲשֶׁר הוֹצֵאתָ אֶת־עַמְּךָ מֵאֶרֶץ מִצְרַיִם בְּיָד חֲזָקָה וַתַּעַשׂ־לְךָ שֵׁם כַּיּוֹם הַזֶּה, חָטָאנוּ רָשָׁעְנוּ: אֲדֹנָי, כְּכָל־צִדְקֹתֶךָ יָשָׁב־נָא אַפְּךָ וַחֲמָתְךָ, מֵעִירְךָ יְרוּשָׁלַםִ הַר־קָדְשֶׁךָ, כִּי בַחֲטָאֵינוּ וּבַעֲוֹנוֹת אֲבֹתֵינוּ, יְרוּשָׁלַםִ וְעַמְּךָ לְחֶרְפָּה לְכָל־סְבִיבֹתֵינוּ: וְעַתָּה שְׁמַע אֱלֹהֵינוּ אֶל־תְּפִלַּת עַבְדְּךָ וְאֶל־תַּחֲנוּנָיו, וְהָאֵר פָּנֶיךָ עַל־מִקְדָּשְׁךָ הַשָּׁמֵם, לְמַעַן אֲדֹנָי: הַטֵּה אֱלֹהַי אָזְנְךָ

Jerusalem has been destroyed
and we are left with nothing.
Hashem, please turn Your anger away from us
and listen to our prayers and heartfelt cries.

אָבִינוּ *Hashem,*
our merciful Father,
gather all the Jews
from around the world to Israel.
Let all the nations of the world know
that You, *Hashem,* are our God.
Hashem, for Your sake please
do not allow Your nation to be embarrassed
by other nations.
As our Father,
have compassion on Your children and answers us.
Hashem,
You always do wonders for us.

הַבֵּט נָא *Hashem*
we beg of You to show mercy on Your nation.
We rely on You for protection
as the sheep rely on the shepherd.
Please do not act with anger towards us;
answer us in our time of need.
Please forgive us, for we are Your people
and You are a kind and caring King.

אָנָּא *Hashem,*
do not distance Yourself from us

וּשְׁמָע, פְּקַח עֵינֶיךָ וּרְאֵה שֹׁמְמוֹתֵינוּ וְהָעִיר אֲשֶׁר־נִקְרָא שִׁמְךָ עָלֶיהָ, כִּי לֹא עַל־צִדְקֹתֵינוּ אֲנַחְנוּ מַפִּילִים תַּחֲנוּנֵינוּ לְפָנֶיךָ, כִּי עַל־רַחֲמֶיךָ הָרַבִּים: אֲדֹנָי שְׁמָעָה, אֲדֹנָי סְלָחָה, אֲדֹנָי הַקְשִׁיבָה וַעֲשֵׂה אַל־תְּאַחַר, לְמַעַנְךָ אֱלֹהַי, כִּי־שִׁמְךָ נִקְרָא עַל־עִירְךָ וְעַל־עַמֶּךָ:

אָבִינוּ הָאָב הָרַחֲמָן, הַרְאֵנוּ אוֹת לְטוֹבָה וְקַבֵּץ נְפוּצוֹתֵינוּ מֵאַרְבַּע כַּנְפוֹת הָאָרֶץ. יַכִּירוּ וְיֵדְעוּ כָּל הַגּוֹיִם כִּי אַתָּה יהוה אֱלֹהֵינוּ. וְעַתָּה יהוה אָבִינוּ אָתָּה, אֲנַחְנוּ הַחֹמֶר וְאַתָּה יֹצְרֵנוּ וּמַעֲשֵׂה יָדְךָ כֻּלָּנוּ: הוֹשִׁיעֵנוּ לְמַעַן שְׁמֶךָ, צוּרֵנוּ מַלְכֵּנוּ וְגוֹאֲלֵנוּ. חוּסָה יהוה עַל־עַמֶּךָ, וְאַל־תִּתֵּן נַחֲלָתְךָ לְחֶרְפָּה לִמְשָׁל־בָּם גּוֹיִם, לָמָּה יֹאמְרוּ בָעַמִּים אַיֵּה אֱלֹהֵיהֶם: יָדַעְנוּ כִּי חָטָאנוּ וְאֵין מִי יַעֲמֹד בַּעֲדֵנוּ, שִׁמְךָ הַגָּדוֹל יַעֲמָד לָנוּ בְּעֵת צָרָה. יָדַעְנוּ כִּי אֵין בָּנוּ מַעֲשִׂים, צְדָקָה עֲשֵׂה עִמָּנוּ לְמַעַן שְׁמֶךָ. כְּרַחֵם אָב עַל בָּנִים כֵּן תְּרַחֵם יהוה עָלֵינוּ, וְהוֹשִׁיעֵנוּ לְמַעַן שְׁמֶךָ. חֲמֹל עַל עַמֶּךָ, רַחֵם עַל נַחֲלָתֶךָ, חוּסָה נָּא כְּרֹב רַחֲמֶיךָ, חָנֵּנוּ וַעֲנֵנוּ. כִּי לְךָ יהוה הַצְּדָקָה, עֹשֵׂה נִפְלָאוֹת בְּכָל עֵת.

הַבֶּט נָא, רַחֵם נָא עַל עַמְּךָ מְהֵרָה לְמַעַן שְׁמֶךָ בְּרַחֲמֶיךָ הָרַבִּים יהוה אֱלֹהֵינוּ. חוּס וְרַחֵם וְהוֹשִׁיעָה צֹאן מַרְעִיתֶךָ, וְאַל יִמְשָׁל בָּנוּ קֶצֶף, כִּי לְךָ עֵינֵינוּ תְלוּיוֹת. הוֹשִׁיעֵנוּ לְמַעַן שְׁמֶךָ. רַחֵם עָלֵינוּ לְמַעַן בְּרִיתֶךָ. הַבִּיטָה וַעֲנֵנוּ בְּעֵת צָרָה, כִּי לְךָ יהוה הַיְשׁוּעָה. בְּךָ תוֹחַלְתֵּנוּ אֱלוֹהַּ סְלִיחוֹת, אָנָּא סְלַח נָא אֵל טוֹב וְסַלָּח, כִּי אֵל מֶלֶךְ חַנּוּן וְרַחוּם אָתָּה.

אָנָּא מֶלֶךְ חַנּוּן וְרַחוּם, זְכֹר וְהַבֵּט לִבְרִית בֵּין הַבְּתָרִים, וְתֵרָאֶה לְפָנֶיךָ עֲקֵדַת יָחִיד לְמַעַן יִשְׂרָאֵל. אָבִינוּ מַלְכֵּנוּ, חָנֵּנוּ וַעֲנֵנוּ, כִּי

when we are in a time of need.
Rescue us, *Hashem*;
our hope and future is in Your hands.
Please listen to our prayers
and save us.

אֵל רַחוּם *Hashem,*
there is none like You.
You are the only God.
Our Father and King,
our God and Protector,
You are mighty, generous, good,
and slow to anger.
We turn to You
to be forgiven and saved.
Our creator,
please do not forget us
in our time of need.

אֵין כָּמוֹךָ *Hashem,*
You are full of kindness, mercy, and good grace.
Please ignore our weaknesses and mistakes;
instead remember the goodness of our ancestors,
Avraham, Yitzchak, and Yaakov.

שִׁמְךָ הַגָּדוֹל נִקְרָא עָלֵינוּ. עֹשֵׂה נִפְלָאוֹת בְּכָל עֵת, עֲשֵׂה עִמָּנוּ כְּחַסְדֶּךָ. חַנּוּן וְרַחוּם, הַבִּיטָה וַעֲנֵנוּ בְּעֵת צָרָה, כִּי לְךָ יהוה הַיְשׁוּעָה. אָבִינוּ מַלְכֵּנוּ מַחֲסֵנוּ, אַל תַּעַשׂ עִמָּנוּ כְּרֹעַ מַעֲלָלֵינוּ. זְכֹר רַחֲמֶיךָ יהוה וַחֲסָדֶיךָ, וּכְרֹב טוּבְךָ הוֹשִׁיעֵנוּ, וַחֲמָל נָא עָלֵינוּ, כִּי אֵין לָנוּ אֱלוֹהַּ אַחֵר מִבַּלְעָדֶיךָ צוּרֵנוּ. אַל תַּעַזְבֵנוּ יהוה אֱלֹהֵינוּ אַל תִּרְחַק מִמֶּנּוּ. כִּי נַפְשֵׁנוּ קְצָרָה, מֵחֶרֶב וּמִשְּׁבִי וּמִדֶּבֶר וּמִמַּגֵּפָה. וּמִכָּל צָרָה וְיָגוֹן הַצִּילֵנוּ, כִּי לְךָ קִוִּינוּ. וְאַל תַּכְלִימֵנוּ יהוה אֱלֹהֵינוּ, וְהָאֵר פָּנֶיךָ בָּנוּ, וּזְכָר לָנוּ אֶת בְּרִית אֲבוֹתֵינוּ וְהוֹשִׁיעֵנוּ לְמַעַן שְׁמֶךָ. רְאֵה בְצָרוֹתֵינוּ, וּשְׁמַע קוֹל תְּפִלָּתֵנוּ, כִּי אַתָּה שׁוֹמֵעַ תְּפִלַּת כָּל פֶּה.

אֵל רַחוּם וְחַנּוּן, רַחֵם עָלֵינוּ וְעַל כָּל מַעֲשֶׂיךָ, כִּי אֵין כָּמְוֹךָ יהוה אֱלֹהֵינוּ. אָנָּא שָׂא נָא פְשָׁעֵינוּ, אָבִינוּ מַלְכֵּנוּ צוּרֵנוּ וְגוֹאֲלֵנוּ, אֵל חַי וְקַיָּם הַחֲסִין בַּכֹּחַ, חָסִיד וָטוֹב עַל כָּל מַעֲשֶׂיךָ, כִּי אַתָּה הוּא יהוה אֱלֹהֵינוּ. אֵל אֶרֶךְ אַפַּיִם וּמָלֵא רַחֲמִים, עֲשֵׂה עִמָּנוּ כְּרֹב רַחֲמֶיךָ, וְהוֹשִׁיעֵנוּ לְמַעַן שְׁמֶךָ. שְׁמַע מַלְכֵּנוּ תְּפִלָּתֵנוּ, וּמִיַּד אוֹיְבֵינוּ הַצִּילֵנוּ. שְׁמַע מַלְכֵּנוּ תְּפִלָּתֵנוּ, וּמִכָּל צָרָה וְיָגוֹן הַצִּילֵנוּ. אָבִינוּ מַלְכֵּנוּ אַתָּה, וְשִׁמְךָ עָלֵינוּ נִקְרָא. אַל תַּנִּיחֵנוּ, אַל תַּעַזְבֵנוּ אָבִינוּ וְאַל תִּטְּשֵׁנוּ בּוֹרְאֵנוּ וְאַל תִּשְׁכָּחֵנוּ יוֹצְרֵנוּ, כִּי אֵל מֶלֶךְ חַנּוּן וְרַחוּם אָתָּה.

אֵין כָּמְוֹךָ חַנּוּן וְרַחוּם יהוה אֱלֹהֵינוּ, אֵין כָּמְוֹךָ אֵל אֶרֶךְ אַפַּיִם וְרַב חֶסֶד וֶאֱמֶת. הוֹשִׁיעֵנוּ בְּרַחֲמֶיךָ הָרַבִּים, מֵרַעַשׁ וּמֵרֹגֶז הַצִּילֵנוּ. זְכֹר לַעֲבָדֶיךָ לְאַבְרָהָם לְיִצְחָק וּלְיַעֲקֹב, אַל תֵּפֶן אֶל קָשְׁיֵנוּ וְאֶל רִשְׁעֵנוּ וְאֶל חַטָּאתֵנוּ. שׁוּב מֵחֲרוֹן אַפֶּךָ, וְהִנָּחֵם

In Your kindness,
You grant mercy in every generation,
even though it is not deserved.
Please save Your Jewish people,
bring us success,
and answer us when we call.

הַפּוֹתֵחַ *Hashem,*
Your hands are open
to accept our apologies
and to forgive us.
Please remember our ancestors
and save us,
even if we are not worthy.
How long will You let Your Jewish people suffer?
Please quickly act on our behalf
in our time of need.
Show kindness
to Your Jewish people
who say that You, *Hashem,*
are the one and only God.

עַל־הָרָעָה לְעַמֶּךָ: וְהָסֵר מִמֶּנּוּ מַכַּת הַמָּוֶת כִּי רַחוּם אָתָּה, כִּי כֵן דַּרְכֶּךָ, עֹשֶׂה חֶסֶד חִנָּם בְּכָל דּוֹר וָדוֹר. חוּסָה יהוה עַל עַמֶּךָ וְהַצִּילֵנוּ מִזַּעְמֶךָ, וְהָסֵר מִמֶּנּוּ מַכַּת הַמַּגֵּפָה וּגְזֵרָה קָשָׁה, כִּי אַתָּה שׁוֹמֵר יִשְׂרָאֵל. לְךָ אֲדֹנָי הַצְּדָקָה וְלָנוּ בֹּשֶׁת הַפָּנִים: מַה נִּתְאוֹנֵן, מַה נֹּאמַר, מַה נְּדַבֵּר וּמַה נִּצְטַדָּק. נַחְפְּשָׂה דְרָכֵינוּ וְנַחְקֹרָה וְנָשׁוּבָה אֵלֶיךָ, כִּי יְמִינְךָ פְשׁוּטָה לְקַבֵּל שָׁבִים. אָנָּא יהוה הוֹשִׁיעָה נָּא, אָנָּא יהוה הַצְלִיחָה נָא: אָנָּא יהוה עֲנֵנוּ בְיוֹם קָרְאֵנוּ. לְךָ יהוה חִכִּינוּ, לְךָ יהוה קִוִּינוּ, לְךָ יהוה נְיַחֵל. אַל תֶּחֱשֶׁה וּתְעַנֵּנוּ, כִּי נָאֲמוּ גוֹיִם, אָבְדָה תִקְוָתָם. כָּל בֶּרֶךְ וְכָל קוֹמָה, לְךָ לְבַד תִּשְׁתַּחֲוֶה.

הַפּוֹתֵחַ יָד בִּתְשׁוּבָה לְקַבֵּל פּוֹשְׁעִים וְחַטָּאִים, נִבְהֲלָה נַפְשֵׁנוּ מֵרֹב עִצְּבוֹנֵנוּ. אַל תִּשְׁכָּחֵנוּ נֶצַח, קוּמָה וְהוֹשִׁיעֵנוּ כִּי חָסִינוּ בָךְ. אָבִינוּ מַלְכֵּנוּ, אִם אֵין בָּנוּ צְדָקָה וּמַעֲשִׂים טוֹבִים, זְכָר לָנוּ אֶת בְּרִית אֲבוֹתֵינוּ וְעֵדוֹתֵנוּ בְּכָל יוֹם יהוה אֶחָד. הַבִּיטָה בְעָנְיֵנוּ, כִּי רַבּוּ מַכְאוֹבֵינוּ וְצָרוֹת לְבָבֵנוּ. חוּסָה יהוה עָלֵינוּ בְּאֶרֶץ שִׁבְיֵנוּ, וְאַל תִּשְׁפֹּךְ חֲרוֹנְךָ עָלֵינוּ, כִּי אֲנַחְנוּ עַמְּךָ בְּנֵי בְרִיתֶךָ. אֵל, הַבִּיטָה, דַּל כְּבוֹדֵנוּ בַּגּוֹיִם וְשִׁקְּצוּנוּ כְּטֻמְאַת הַנִּדָּה. עַד מָתַי עֻזְּךָ בַּשְּׁבִי, וְתִפְאַרְתְּךָ בְּיַד צָר. עוֹרְרָה גְבוּרָתְךָ וְקִנְאָתְךָ עַל אוֹיְבֶיךָ. הֵם יֵבֹשׁוּ וְיֵחַתּוּ מִגְּבוּרָתָם. וְאַל יִמְעֲטוּ לְפָנֶיךָ תְּלָאוֹתֵינוּ, מַהֵר יְקַדְּמוּנוּ רַחֲמֶיךָ בְּיוֹם צָרָתֵנוּ. וְאִם לֹא לְמַעֲנֵנוּ, לְמַעַנְךָ פְעַל, וְאַל תַּשְׁחִית זֵכֶר שְׁאֵרִיתֵנוּ, וְחֹן אֹם הַמְיַחֲדִים שִׁמְךָ פַּעֲמַיִם בְּכָל יוֹם תָּמִיד בְּאַהֲבָה, וְאוֹמְרִים, שְׁמַע יִשְׂרָאֵל, יהוה אֱלֹהֵינוּ, יהוה אֶחָד:

LOWERING THE HEAD

On Sundays, Tuesdays, Wednesdays and Fridays, begin Tachanun here.
The following is said sitting.
Lean on your left arm while saying the following paragraph.
If you are wearing tefillin on your left arm, lean on your right arm instead.

וַיֹּאמֶר דָּוִד King David once said "I am very troubled.
Let the Jewish people be punished by *Hashem*
rather than by people, for *Hashem* is filled with mercy."

Hashem, You have shown great understanding and kindness.
I have sinned before You.
Please show me Your mercy and accept my prayers.

Hashem, if I am deserving of punishment,
please show me kindness and do so when You are calm.
Hashem, forgive me,
for my body shakes in fear of Your punishment.
Hashem, how long must I wait for forgiveness?
Hashem, save me and allow me to return to You,
for tears drip from my eyes every night as I cry out to You.
For enemies that wish to harm me,
know that *Hashem* has heard my cry
and will accept my prayer for forgiveness.

Sit up at this point.

נפילת אפים – LOWERING THE HEAD

This is the only place in davening where we rest our heads on our arms. After the Jewish people served the *Egel HaZahav,* the Golden Calf, both Moshe and Yehoshua fell on their faces and cried to *Hashem* in prayer. When asking *Hashem* to accept our prayers after we have sinned, we lean our heads on our arms, falling on our faces as Moshe and Yehoshua did. We begin *Tachanun* by praying with our heads on our arms, then we sit up, and finally we stand, to show *Hashem* that we are trying everything in our power to connect with Him.

נפילת אפיים

On Sundays, Tuesdays, Wednesdays and Fridays, begin תחנון *here.*

The following is said sitting.

Lean on your left arm while saying the following paragraph.
If you are wearing תפילין*, on your left arm, lean on your right arm instead.*

וַיֹּאמֶר דָּוִד אֶל־גָּד, צַר־לִי מְאֹד
נִפְּלָה־נָּא בְיַד־יהוה
כִּי רַבִּים רַחֲמָו
וּבְיַד־אָדָם אַל־אֶפֹּלָה:

רַחוּם וְחַנּוּן, חָטָאתִי לְפָנֶיךָ.
יהוה מָלֵא רַחֲמִים, רַחֵם עָלַי וְקַבֵּל תַּחֲנוּנָי.

יהוה, אַל־בְּאַפְּךָ תוֹכִיחֵנִי, וְאַל־בַּחֲמָתְךָ תְיַסְּרֵנִי:
חָנֵּנִי יהוה, כִּי אֻמְלַל אָנִי
רְפָאֵנִי יהוה, כִּי נִבְהֲלוּ עֲצָמָי:
וְנַפְשִׁי נִבְהֲלָה מְאֹד, וְאַתָּ יהוה, עַד־מָתָי:
שׁוּבָה יהוה, חַלְּצָה נַפְשִׁי, הוֹשִׁיעֵנִי לְמַעַן חַסְדֶּךָ:
כִּי אֵין בַּמָּוֶת זִכְרֶךָ, בִּשְׁאוֹל מִי יוֹדֶה־לָּךְ:
יָגַעְתִּי בְּאַנְחָתִי, אַשְׂחֶה בְכָל־לַיְלָה מִטָּתִי
בְּדִמְעָתִי עַרְשִׂי אַמְסֶה:
עָשְׁשָׁה מִכַּעַס עֵינִי, עָתְקָה בְּכָל־צוֹרְרָי:
סוּרוּ מִמֶּנִּי כָּל־פֹּעֲלֵי אָוֶן, כִּי שָׁמַע יהוה קוֹל בִּכְיִי:
שָׁמַע יהוה תְּחִנָּתִי, יהוה תְּפִלָּתִי יִקָּח:
יֵבֹשׁוּ וְיִבָּהֲלוּ מְאֹד כָּל־אֹיְבָי, יָשֻׁבוּ יֵבֹשׁוּ רָגַע:

Sit up at this point.

On Monday and Thursday continue below.
On all other days continue to "Protector of Your Jewish people" on the next page.

יהוה *Hashem,* God of the Jewish people, turn away from Your anger and change the evil plans for Your people.

Hashem, look from above and see that Your Jewish people have become lowly in the eyes of other nations. Despite this we have not forgotten You, *Hashem*. Please do not forget us.

> *Hashem,* God of the Jewish people, turn away from Your anger and change the evil plans for Your people.

Other nations say we should give up hope. *Hashem,* have mercy on Your Jewish people as we believe in You. We are tired but we are not allowed to rest. May Your kindness overcome Your anger, *Hashem,* and may You be kind to Your people.

> *Hashem,* God of the Jewish people, turn away from Your anger and change the evil plans for Your people.

Hashem, show kindness to us, do not allow others to harm us. Do not let other people ask, "Where is *Hashem,* your God?" Quickly, *Hashem,* treat Your people with kindness. May Your kindness overcome Your anger, *Hashem,* and may You be kind to Your people.

> *Hashem,* God of the Jewish people, turn away from Your anger and change the evil plans for Your people.

Listen to our voices and be kind, do not let our enemies defeat us. Remember the promise You made to our ancestors that they will have as many children as the stars in the sky. Now, even though there have been difficult times, we have not forgotten You, *Hashem*. Please do not forget us.

> *Hashem,* God of the Jewish people, turn away from Your anger and change the evil plans for Your people.

On Monday and Thursday continue below.
On all other days continue to שׁוֹמֵר יִשְׂרָאֵל *on the next page.*

יהוה אֱלֹהֵי יִשְׂרָאֵל, שׁוּב מֵחֲרוֹן אַפֶּךָ וְהִנָּחֵם עַל הָרָעָה לְעַמֶּךָ.

הַבֵּט מִשָּׁמַיִם וּרְאֵה כִּי הָיִינוּ לַעַג וָקֶלֶס בַּגּוֹיִם, נֶחְשַׁבְנוּ כַּצֹּאן לַטֶּבַח יוּבָל, לַהֲרֹג וּלְאַבֵּד וּלְמַכָּה וּלְחֶרְפָּה. וּבְכָל זֹאת שִׁמְךָ לֹא שָׁכָחְנוּ, נָא אַל תִּשְׁכָּחֵנוּ.

יהוה אֱלֹהֵי יִשְׂרָאֵל, שׁוּב מֵחֲרוֹן אַפֶּךָ וְהִנָּחֵם עַל הָרָעָה לְעַמֶּךָ.

זָרִים אוֹמְרִים אֵין תּוֹחֶלֶת וְתִקְוָה, חֹן אֹם לְשִׁמְךָ מְקַוֶּה, טָהוֹר יְשׁוּעָתֵנוּ קָרְבָה, יָגַעְנוּ וְלֹא הוּנַח לָנוּ, רַחֲמֶיךָ יִכְבְּשׁוּ אֶת כַּעַסְךָ מֵעָלֵינוּ. אָנָּא שׁוּב מֵחֲרוֹנְךָ וְרַחֵם סְגֻלָּה אֲשֶׁר בָּחָרְתָּ.

יהוה אֱלֹהֵי יִשְׂרָאֵל, שׁוּב מֵחֲרוֹן אַפֶּךָ וְהִנָּחֵם עַל הָרָעָה לְעַמֶּךָ.

חוּסָה יהוה עָלֵינוּ בְּרַחֲמֶיךָ, וְאַל תִּתְּנֵנוּ בִּידֵי אַכְזָרִים. לָמָּה יֹאמְרוּ הַגּוֹיִם אַיֵּה נָא אֱלֹהֵיהֶם, לְמַעַנְךָ עֲשֵׂה עִמָּנוּ חֶסֶד וְאַל תְּאַחַר. אָנָּא שׁוּב מֵחֲרוֹנְךָ וְרַחֵם סְגֻלָּה אֲשֶׁר בָּחָרְתָּ.

יהוה אֱלֹהֵי יִשְׂרָאֵל, שׁוּב מֵחֲרוֹן אַפֶּךָ וְהִנָּחֵם עַל הָרָעָה לְעַמֶּךָ.

קוֹלֵנוּ תִשְׁמַע וְתָחֹן, וְאַל תִּטְּשֵׁנוּ בְּיַד אֹיְבֵינוּ לִמְחוֹת אֶת שְׁמֵנוּ. זְכֹר אֲשֶׁר נִשְׁבַּעְתָּ לַאֲבוֹתֵינוּ כְּכוֹכְבֵי הַשָּׁמַיִם אַרְבֶּה אֶת זַרְעֲכֶם, וְעַתָּה נִשְׁאַרְנוּ מְעַט מֵהַרְבֵּה. וּבְכָל זֹאת שִׁמְךָ לֹא שָׁכָחְנוּ, נָא אַל תִּשְׁכָּחֵנוּ.

יהוה אֱלֹהֵי יִשְׂרָאֵל, שׁוּב מֵחֲרוֹן אַפֶּךָ וְהִנָּחֵם עַל הָרָעָה לְעַמֶּךָ.

עָזְרֵנוּ אֱלֹהֵי יִשְׁעֵנוּ עַל־דְּבַר כְּבוֹד־שְׁמֶךָ, וְהַצִּילֵנוּ וְכַפֵּר עַל־חַטֹּאתֵינוּ לְמַעַן שְׁמֶךָ:

יהוה אֱלֹהֵי יִשְׂרָאֵל, שׁוּב מֵחֲרוֹן אַפֶּךָ וְהִנָּחֵם עַל הָרָעָה לְעַמֶּךָ.

On all days continue here:

שׁוֹמֵר Protector of Your Jewish people,
do not allow Your Jewish people to be destroyed.

Protector of Your special nation,
do not allow Your special nation to be destroyed.

Protector of Your holy nation,
do not allow Your holy nation to be destroyed.

Hashem, in the past
You have shown mercy towards our pleas.

Please once again
show mercy to Your people,
for there is nobody else who can help us but You.

Our Father and King, though we do not deserve it,
please listen to our pleas
with kindness, and save us.

Stand for the following.

וַאֲנַחְנוּ We do not know
what else there is for us to do
but look towards You for help.
The world was created upon Your mercy and kindness.
Hashem, please show Your kindness to us.
When You remember us,
do not think about our sins
and the sins of our ancestors.

On all days continue here:

שׁוֹמֵר יִשְׂרָאֵל, שְׁמֹר שְׁאֵרִית יִשְׂרָאֵל
וְאַל יֹאבַד יִשְׂרָאֵל
הָאוֹמְרִים שְׁמַע יִשְׂרָאֵל.

שׁוֹמֵר גּוֹי אֶחָד, שְׁמֹר שְׁאֵרִית עַם אֶחָד
וְאַל יֹאבַד גּוֹי אֶחָד
הַמְיַחֲדִים שִׁמְךָ, יהוה אֱלֹהֵינוּ יהוה אֶחָד.

שׁוֹמֵר גּוֹי קָדוֹשׁ, שְׁמֹר שְׁאֵרִית עַם קָדוֹשׁ
וְאַל יֹאבַד גּוֹי קָדוֹשׁ
הַמְשַׁלְּשִׁים בְּשָׁלֹשׁ קְדֻשּׁוֹת לְקָדוֹשׁ.

מִתְרַצֶּה בְּרַחֲמִים וּמִתְפַּיֵּס בְּתַחֲנוּנִים
הִתְרַצֵּה וְהִתְפַּיֵּס לְדוֹר עָנִי
כִּי אֵין עוֹזֵר.

אָבִינוּ מַלְכֵּנוּ, חָנֵּנוּ וַעֲנֵנוּ
כִּי אֵין בָּנוּ מַעֲשִׂים
עֲשֵׂה עִמָּנוּ צְדָקָה וָחֶסֶד וְהוֹשִׁיעֵנוּ.

Stand for the following.

וַאֲנַחְנוּ לֹא נֵדַע מַה־נַּעֲשֶׂה, כִּי עָלֶיךָ עֵינֵינוּ:
זְכֹר־רַחֲמֶיךָ יהוה וַחֲסָדֶיךָ, כִּי מֵעוֹלָם הֵמָּה:
יְהִי־חַסְדְּךָ יהוה עָלֵינוּ, כַּאֲשֶׁר יִחַלְנוּ לָךְ:
אַל־תִּזְכָּר־לָנוּ עֲוֹנֹת רִאשֹׁנִים
מַהֵר יְקַדְּמוּנוּ רַחֲמֶיךָ, כִּי דַלּוֹנוּ מְאֹד:

Please be kind to us
and show us Your mercy,
as we are no more than dust before You.
‣ *Hashem*, help us, save us, and forgive our sins,
for Your sake.

HALF KADDISH

Leader: יִתְגַּדַּל May *Hashem* be recognized
as great and holy (*Congregation:* Amen)
in the world that He created.
May He establish His kingdom
during my lifetime
and the lifetime of all Jews,
quickly and soon.
Let us say:
"Amen" (*Congregation:* Amen).

Congregation: May we thank *Hashem* for ever and ever.
Leader: May we thank *Hashem* for ever and ever.

Leader: *Hashem* should be thanked, praised,
and honored (*Congregation:* He is blessed).
Hashem is beyond all the blessings,
songs, or praises
that we could offer.
Let us say:
"Amen" (*Congregation:* Amen).

On Mondays and Thursdays, Rosh Chodesh, Chol HaMo'ed, Chanuka, Purim and Fast Days, the Torah is read when a minyan is present. *On all other days, continue with "We are happy" on page 178.*

חָנֵּנוּ יהוה חָנֵּנוּ, כִּי־רַב שָׂבַעְנוּ בוּז:
בְּרֹגֶז רַחֵם תִּזְכּוֹר:
כִּי־הוּא יָדַע יִצְרֵנוּ, זָכוּר כִּי־עָפָר אֲנָחְנוּ:
◂ עָזְרֵנוּ אֱלֹהֵי יִשְׁעֵנוּ עַל־דְּבַר כְּבוֹד־שְׁמֶךָ
וְהַצִּילֵנוּ וְכַפֵּר עַל־חַטֹּאתֵינוּ לְמַעַן שְׁמֶךָ:

חצי קדיש

חזן: יִתְגַּדַּל וְיִתְקַדַּשׁ שְׁמֵהּ רַבָּא (קהל: אָמֵן)
בְּעָלְמָא דִּי בְרָא כִרְעוּתֵהּ, וְיַמְלִיךְ מַלְכוּתֵהּ
בְּחַיֵּיכוֹן וּבְיוֹמֵיכוֹן וּבְחַיֵּי דְכָל בֵּית יִשְׂרָאֵל
בַּעֲגָלָא וּבִזְמַן קָרִיב, וְאִמְרוּ אָמֵן. (קהל: אָמֵן)

קהל: יְהֵא שְׁמֵהּ רַבָּא מְבָרַךְ לְעָלַם וּלְעָלְמֵי עָלְמַיָּא.
חזן: יְהֵא שְׁמֵהּ רַבָּא מְבָרַךְ לְעָלַם וּלְעָלְמֵי עָלְמַיָּא.

חזן: יִתְבָּרַךְ וְיִשְׁתַּבַּח וְיִתְפָּאַר וְיִתְרוֹמַם וְיִתְנַשֵּׂא
וְיִתְהַדָּר וְיִתְעַלֶּה וְיִתְהַלָּל
שְׁמֵהּ דְּקֻדְשָׁא בְּרִיךְ הוּא (קהל: בְּרִיךְ הוּא)
לְעֵלָּא מִן כָּל בִּרְכָתָא
/בעשרת ימי תשובה: לְעֵלָּא לְעֵלָּא מִכָּל בִּרְכָתָא/
וְשִׁירָתָא, תֻּשְׁבְּחָתָא וְנֶחֱמָתָא
דַּאֲמִירָן בְּעָלְמָא, וְאִמְרוּ אָמֵן. (קהל: אָמֵן)

On Mondays and Thursdays, ראש חודש, חול המועד, חנוכה, פורים *and Fast Days, the* תורה *is read when a* מנין *is present.*
On all other days, continue with אַשְׁרֵי *on page 179.*

TAKING OUT THE TORAH

Stand until the Torah has been put down to be read.
This is not said on Rosh Chodesh, Chol HaMo'ed, and other festive occasions.

אֵל אֶרֶךְ *Hashem,* You are slow to anger
and You are filled with kindness and truth.
Do not punish us while You are angry.
Hashem, show us pity and save us from evil.
You are our Master, and we have sinned.
Hashem, we beg You to forgive us
because You have great mercy.

The Aron Kodesh is opened.

וַיְהִי Every time the *Aron* would travel Moshe would say,
"*Hashem,* may our enemies scatter
and run away from You."
The Torah comes from Zion
and the words of *Hashem* come from Jerusalem.
Thank You, *Hashem,* for giving the Torah
to Your Jewish people.

בְּרִיךְ שְׁמֵהּ We are thankful to You, *Hashem,* Master and King of the World. May You always show kindness towards Your Jewish people, accept our prayers with mercy, and rebuild the *Beit HaMikdash*. Please grant me a long life and provide protection for me, for all that is mine, and for the entire Jewish nation. As King, You feed all and rule over all. You rule over all kings as well. I am a servant to *Hashem,* and I therefore show respect towards the Torah at all times. I don't rely on any man or angel, but on *Hashem* alone for He is the God of love and truth. ▸ *Hashem,* may You open my heart and the hearts of all Your Jewish people to the Torah so that we can have goodness, long life, and peace.

הוצאת ספר תורה

Stand until the Torah has been put down to be read.
This is not said on ראש חודש, חול המועד*, and other festive occasions.*

אֵל אֶרֶךְ אַפַּיִם וְרַב חֶסֶד וֶאֱמֶת
אַל בְּאַפְּךָ תוֹכִיחֵנוּ.
חוּסָה יהוה עַל עַמֶּךָ, וְהוֹשִׁיעֵנוּ מִכָּל רָע.
חָטָאנוּ לְךָ אָדוֹן
סְלַח נָא כְּרֹב רַחֲמֶיךָ אֵל.

The ארון קודש *is opened.*

וַיְהִי בִּנְסֹעַ הָאָרֹן וַיֹּאמֶר מֹשֶׁה, קוּמָה יהוה וְיָפֻצוּ אֹיְבֶיךָ וְיָנֻסוּ מְשַׂנְאֶיךָ מִפָּנֶיךָ: כִּי מִצִּיּוֹן תֵּצֵא תוֹרָה וּדְבַר־יהוה מִירוּשָׁלָיִם: בָּרוּךְ שֶׁנָּתַן תּוֹרָה לְעַמּוֹ יִשְׂרָאֵל בִּקְדֻשָּׁתוֹ.

בְּרִיךְ שְׁמֵהּ דְּמָרֵא עָלְמָא, בְּרִיךְ כִּתְרָךְ וְאַתְרָךְ. יְהֵא רְעוּתָךְ עִם עַמָּךְ יִשְׂרָאֵל לְעָלַם, וּפֻרְקַן יְמִינָךְ אַחֲזֵי לְעַמָּךְ בְּבֵית מַקְדְּשָׁךְ, וּלְאַמְטוּיֵי לַנָא מִטּוּב נְהוֹרָךְ, וּלְקַבֵּל צְלוֹתַנָא בְּרַחֲמִין. יְהֵא רַעֲוָא קֳדָמָךְ דְּתוֹרִיךְ לַן חַיִּין בְּטִיבוּ, וְלֶהֱוֵי אֲנָא פְקִידָא בְּגוֹ צַדִּיקַיָּא, לְמִרְחַם עָלַי וּלְמִנְטַר יָתִי וְיַת כָּל דִּי לִי וְדִי לְעַמָּךְ יִשְׂרָאֵל. אַנְתְּ הוּא זָן לְכֹלָּא וּמְפַרְנֵס לְכֹלָּא, אַנְתְּ הוּא שַׁלִּיט עַל כֹּלָּא, אַנְתְּ הוּא דְּשַׁלִּיט עַל מַלְכַיָּא, וּמַלְכוּתָא דִּילָךְ הִיא. אֲנָא עַבְדָּא דְקֻדְשָׁא בְּרִיךְ הוּא, דְּסָגֵדְנָא קַמֵּהּ וּמִקַּמֵּי דִּיקָר אוֹרַיְתֵהּ בְּכָל עִדָּן וְעִדָּן. לָא עַל אֱנָשׁ רָחִיצְנָא וְלָא עַל בַּר אֱלָהִין סָמִיכְנָא, אֶלָּא בֶּאֱלָהָא דִשְׁמַיָּא, דְּהוּא אֱלָהָא קְשׁוֹט, וְאוֹרַיְתֵהּ קְשׁוֹט, וּנְבִיאוֹהִי קְשׁוֹט, וּמַסְגֵּא לְמֶעְבַּד טַבְוָן וּקְשׁוֹט. ‹ בֵּהּ אֲנָא רָחִיץ, וְלִשְׁמֵהּ קַדִּישָׁא יַקִּירָא אֲנָא אֵמַר תֻּשְׁבְּחָן. יְהֵא רַעֲוָא קֳדָמָךְ דְּתִפְתַּח לִבַּאי בְּאוֹרַיְתָא, וְתַשְׁלִים מִשְׁאֲלִין דְּלִבַּאי וְלִבָּא דְכָל עַמָּךְ יִשְׂרָאֵל לְטָב וּלְחַיִּין וְלִשְׁלָם.

The Leader takes the Torah and says:

גַּדְּלוּ Let us recognize the greatness of *Hashem* and sing praises to Him together.

The Aron Kodesh is closed. The Congregation says:

לְךָ *Hashem,* You are great, powerful, glorious, and majestic! Everything in heaven and earth is Yours, and You are King over all.

רוֹמְמוּ Praise *Hashem,* our God, and bow before Him, for He is holy. Praise, *Hashem,* our God, and bow before His holy mountain, the *Beit HaMikdash,* for *Hashem* is holy.

אַב הָרַחֲמִים May *Hashem,* our Father, have mercy on His people. May He remember our ancestors and rescue us in difficult times. May He answer our requests and save us.

After the gabbai calls the Kohen to the Bima for an Aliya, the congregation says:

"All of you that follow the ways of *Hashem,* your God, are alive today."

Before each Aliya, the person called up says:

Person called up for the Aliya: **בָּרְכוּ Let us thank *Hashem,* for He deserves thanksgiving!**

Congregation: Thank *Hashem* for ever and ever!

Person called up for the Aliya: **Thank *Hashem* for ever and ever!**

Person called up for the Aliya: **Thank You, *Hashem,* our God, King of the world, for choosing us, the Jewish people, from all the other nations of the world, to be Your special people and for giving us Your Torah. Thank You, *Hashem,* for giving us Your Torah.**

After each Aliya, the person called up says:

Person called up for the Aliya: **Thank You, *Hashem,* our God, King of the world, for giving us the Torah. It is filled with truth and provides us with a meaningful life. Thank You, *Hashem,* for giving us Your Torah.**

The חזן *takes the* ספר תורה *and says:*

גַּדְּלוּ לַיהוה אִתִּי וּנְרוֹמְמָה שְׁמוֹ יַחְדָּו:

The ארון קודש *is closed. The* קהל *says:*

לְךָ יהוה הַגְּדֻלָּה וְהַגְּבוּרָה וְהַתִּפְאֶרֶת וְהַנֵּצַח וְהַהוֹד, כִּי־כֹל בַּשָּׁמַיִם וּבָאָרֶץ, לְךָ יהוה הַמַּמְלָכָה וְהַמִּתְנַשֵּׂא לְכֹל לְרֹאשׁ:

רוֹמְמוּ יהוה אֱלֹהֵינוּ וְהִשְׁתַּחֲווּ לַהֲדֹם רַגְלָיו, קָדוֹשׁ הוּא: רוֹמְמוּ יהוה אֱלֹהֵינוּ וְהִשְׁתַּחֲווּ לְהַר קָדְשׁוֹ, כִּי־קָדוֹשׁ יהוה אֱלֹהֵינוּ:

אַב הָרַחֲמִים הוּא יְרַחֵם עַם עֲמוּסִים, וְיִזְכֹּר בְּרִית אֵיתָנִים, וְיַצִּיל נַפְשׁוֹתֵינוּ מִן הַשָּׁעוֹת הָרָעוֹת, וְיִגְעַר בְּיֵצֶר הָרָע מִן הַנְּשׂוּאִים, וְיָחֹן אוֹתָנוּ לִפְלֵיטַת עוֹלָמִים, וִימַלֵּא מִשְׁאֲלוֹתֵינוּ בְּמִדָּה טוֹבָה יְשׁוּעָה וְרַחֲמִים.

After the גבאי *calls the* כהן *to the* בימה *for an* עליה, *the* קהל *says:*

וְאַתֶּם הַדְּבֵקִים בַּיהוה אֱלֹהֵיכֶם חַיִּים כֻּלְּכֶם הַיּוֹם:

Before each עליה, *the person called up says:*

עולה: **בָּרְכוּ אֶת יהוה הַמְבֹרָךְ.**

קהל: בָּרוּךְ יהוה הַמְבֹרָךְ לְעוֹלָם וָעֶד.

עולה: **בָּרוּךְ יהוה הַמְבֹרָךְ לְעוֹלָם וָעֶד.**
בָּרוּךְ אַתָּה יהוה, אֱלֹהֵינוּ מֶלֶךְ הָעוֹלָם
אֲשֶׁר בָּחַר בָּנוּ מִכָּל הָעַמִּים וְנָתַן לָנוּ אֶת תּוֹרָתוֹ.
בָּרוּךְ אַתָּה יהוה, נוֹתֵן הַתּוֹרָה.

After each עליה, *the person called up says:*

עולה: **בָּרוּךְ אַתָּה יהוה אֱלֹהֵינוּ מֶלֶךְ הָעוֹלָם**
אֲשֶׁר נָתַן לָנוּ תּוֹרַת אֱמֶת וְחַיֵּי עוֹלָם נָטַע בְּתוֹכֵנוּ.
בָּרוּךְ אַתָּה יהוה, נוֹתֵן הַתּוֹרָה.

After the three Aliyot have been read the reader says:

HALF KADDISH

Reader: יִתְגַּדַּל May *Hashem* be recognized
as great and holy (*Congregation:* Amen)
in the world that He created.
May He establish His kingdom
during my lifetime
and the lifetime of all Jews,
quickly and soon.
Let us say:
"Amen" (*Congregation:* Amen).

Congregation: May we thank *Hashem* for ever and ever.
Reader: May we thank *Hashem* for ever and ever.

Reader: *Hashem* should be thanked, praised,
and honored (*Congregation:* He is blessed).
Hashem is beyond all the blessings,
songs, or praises
that we could offer.
Let us say:
"Amen" (*Congregation:* Amen).

HAGBAHA AND GELILA

Stand until the Torah has been returned to the Aron.
The following line is said aloud when the Torah is lifted in the air:

וְזֹאת הַתּוֹרָה This is the Torah that Moshe placed
before the Jewish people
as *Hashem* commanded.

After the three עליות *have been read, the* קורא *says:*

חצי קדיש

קורא: יִתְגַּדַּל וְיִתְקַדַּשׁ שְׁמֵהּ רַבָּא (קהל: אָמֵן)
בְּעָלְמָא דִּי בְרָא כִרְעוּתֵהּ
וְיַמְלִיךְ מַלְכוּתֵהּ
בְּחַיֵּיכוֹן וּבְיוֹמֵיכוֹן וּבְחַיֵּי דְכָל בֵּית יִשְׂרָאֵל
בַּעֲגָלָא וּבִזְמַן קָרִיב, וְאִמְרוּ אָמֵן. (קהל: אָמֵן)

קהל יְהֵא שְׁמֵהּ רַבָּא מְבָרַךְ לְעָלַם וּלְעָלְמֵי עָלְמַיָּא.
קורא: יְהֵא שְׁמֵהּ רַבָּא מְבָרַךְ לְעָלַם וּלְעָלְמֵי עָלְמַיָּא.

קורא: יִתְבָּרַךְ וְיִשְׁתַּבַּח וְיִתְפָּאַר וְיִתְרוֹמַם וְיִתְנַשֵּׂא
וְיִתְהַדָּר וְיִתְעַלֶּה וְיִתְהַלָּל
שְׁמֵהּ דְּקֻדְשָׁא בְּרִיךְ הוּא (קהל: בְּרִיךְ הוּא)
לְעֵלָּא מִן כָּל בִּרְכָתָא
/בעשרת ימי תשובה: לְעֵלָּא לְעֵלָּא מִכָּל בִּרְכָתָא/
וְשִׁירָתָא, תֻּשְׁבְּחָתָא וְנֶחֱמָתָא
דַּאֲמִירָן בְּעָלְמָא, וְאִמְרוּ אָמֵן. (קהל: אָמֵן)

הגבהה וגלילה

Stand until the תורה *has been returned to the* ארון קודש*.*
The following line is said aloud when the תורה *is lifted in the air:*

וְזֹאת הַתּוֹרָה אֲשֶׁר־שָׂם מֹשֶׁה לִפְנֵי בְּנֵי יִשְׂרָאֵל:
עַל־פִּי יהוה בְּיַד־מֹשֶׁה:

The Leader reads the following while the Torah is being wrapped:

Leader: May *Hashem,* our Father in heaven,
soon rebuild the *Beit HaMikdash*
and live among us. (*Congregation:* Amen).

Leader: May *Hashem,* our Father in heaven,
take pity on us and protect us
from destruction and plague. (*Congregation:* Amen).

Leader: May *Hashem,* our Father in heaven,
protect our great rabbis, their families,
and all of their students. (*Congregation:* Amen).

Leader: May *Hashem,* our Father in heaven,
allow us to hear the great news
of the Jewish people being saved
and gathered from the four corners
of the world. (*Congregation:* Amen).

Everyone reads the following paragraph together:

May *Hashem* show mercy to all members of our family, the Jewish people, who are struggling or who have been taken captive. *Hashem,* quickly lead these people from difficult times to safety, from darkness to light, and from suffering to freedom.

RETURNING THE TORAH

The Aron Kodesh is opened.

Leader: יְהַלְלוּ Let the Jewish people praise *Hashem*
because He alone is God.

Congregation: *Hashem*'s majesty is found on earth and in heaven.
He honors His Jewish people by raising them up
and bringing them close to Him. Halleluya!

The חזן *reads the following while the* ספר תורה *is being wrapped:*

חזן: יְהִי רָצוֹן מִלִּפְנֵי אָבִינוּ שֶׁבַּשָּׁמַיִם, לְכוֹנֵן אֶת בֵּית חַיֵּינוּ, וּלְהָשִׁיב אֶת שְׁכִינָתוֹ בְּתוֹכֵנוּ, בִּמְהֵרָה בְיָמֵינוּ, וְנֹאמַר אָמֵן. (קהל: אָמֵן)

חזן: יְהִי רָצוֹן מִלִּפְנֵי אָבִינוּ שֶׁבַּשָּׁמַיִם, לְרַחֵם עָלֵינוּ וְעַל פְּלֵיטָתֵנוּ, וְלִמְנֹעַ מַשְׁחִית וּמַגֵּפָה מֵעָלֵינוּ, וּמֵעַל כָּל עַמּוֹ בֵּית יִשְׂרָאֵל, וְנֹאמַר אָמֵן. (קהל: אָמֵן)

חזן: יְהִי רָצוֹן מִלִּפְנֵי אָבִינוּ שֶׁבַּשָּׁמַיִם, לְקַיֵּם בָּנוּ חַכְמֵי יִשְׂרָאֵל, הֵם וּנְשֵׁיהֶם וּבְנֵיהֶם וּבְנוֹתֵיהֶם, וְתַלְמִידֵיהֶם וְתַלְמִידֵי תַלְמִידֵיהֶם, בְּכָל מְקוֹמוֹת מוֹשְׁבוֹתֵיהֶם, וְנֹאמַר אָמֵן. (קהל: אָמֵן)

חזן: יְהִי רָצוֹן מִלִּפְנֵי אָבִינוּ שֶׁבַּשָּׁמַיִם, שֶׁנִּשְׁמַע וְנִתְבַּשֵּׂר בְּשׂוֹרוֹת טוֹבוֹת, יְשׁוּעוֹת וְנֶחָמוֹת, וִיקַבֵּץ נִדָּחֵינוּ מֵאַרְבַּע כַּנְפוֹת הָאָרֶץ, וְנֹאמַר אָמֵן. (קהל: אָמֵן)

Everyone reads the following paragraph together:

אַחֵינוּ כָּל בֵּית יִשְׂרָאֵל, הַנְּתוּנִים בְּצָרָה וּבְשִׁבְיָה, הָעוֹמְדִים בֵּין בַּיָּם וּבֵין בַּיַּבָּשָׁה, הַמָּקוֹם יְרַחֵם עֲלֵיהֶם וְיוֹצִיאֵם מִצָּרָה לִרְוָחָה, וּמֵאֲפֵלָה לְאוֹרָה, וּמִשִּׁעְבּוּד לִגְאֻלָּה, הַשְׁתָּא בַּעֲגָלָא וּבִזְמַן קָרִיב, וְנֹאמַר אָמֵן.

הכנסת ספר תורה

The ארון קודש *is opened.*

חזן: יְהַלְלוּ אֶת־שֵׁם יהוה, כִּי נִשְׂגָּב־שְׁמוֹ, לְבַדּוֹ

קהל: הוֹדוֹ עַל־אֶרֶץ וְשָׁמָיִם: וַיָּרֶם קֶרֶן לְעַמּוֹ, תְּהִלָּה לְכָל־חֲסִידָיו, לִבְנֵי יִשְׂרָאֵל עַם קְרֹבוֹ, הַלְלוּיָהּ:

As the Torah is returned to the Aron Kodesh, say:

לְדָוִד The earth and everything on it belong to *Hashem*. *Hashem* created the world beginning with the waters of the seas and rivers. Who may go to the *Beit HaMikdash* and stand in the presence of *Hashem*'s holiness? One with pure actions and thoughts. This person will receive blessing and kindness from *Hashem*. Who is the King worthy of honor? *Hashem*, Master of the world, is the King worthy of honor!

As the Torah is placed into the Aron Kodesh, say:

וּבְנֻחֹה When the *Aron* would come to rest,
Moshe would say,
"*Hashem*, return to the thousands of people
in Your Jewish nation."
Your *Kohanim* are clothed ready to serve You,
and Your followers sing to You in joy,
awaiting Your arrival.
For the sake of David, do not reject us.
Hashem, You commanded us
not to abandon Your Torah.
It is a tree of life to all those who hold onto it
and a source of happiness for all those who follow it.
Following the Torah is pleasant and it leads to peace.
▸ *Hashem*, bring us back to You
and we will return to You.
Let us live again as we did
in the times of the *Beit HaMikdash*.

The Aron Kodesh is closed.
Sit after the Torah has been returned to the Aron Kodesh.

As the ספר תורה *is returned to the* ארון קודש*, say:*

לְדָוִד מִזְמוֹר, לַיהוה הָאָרֶץ וּמְלוֹאָהּ, תֵּבֵל וְיֹשְׁבֵי בָהּ: כִּי־הוּא עַל־יַמִּים יְסָדָהּ, וְעַל־נְהָרוֹת יְכוֹנְנֶהָ: מִי־יַעֲלֶה בְהַר־יהוה, וּמִי־יָקוּם בִּמְקוֹם קָדְשׁוֹ: נְקִי כַפַּיִם וּבַר־לֵבָב, אֲשֶׁר לֹא־נָשָׂא לַשָּׁוְא נַפְשִׁי וְלֹא נִשְׁבַּע לְמִרְמָה: יִשָּׂא בְרָכָה מֵאֵת יהוה, וּצְדָקָה מֵאֱלֹהֵי יִשְׁעוֹ: זֶה דּוֹר דֹּרְשָׁו, מְבַקְשֵׁי פָנֶיךָ, יַעֲקֹב, סֶלָה: שְׂאוּ שְׁעָרִים רָאשֵׁיכֶם, וְהִנָּשְׂאוּ פִּתְחֵי עוֹלָם, וְיָבוֹא מֶלֶךְ הַכָּבוֹד: מִי זֶה מֶלֶךְ הַכָּבוֹד, יהוה עִזּוּז וְגִבּוֹר, יהוה גִּבּוֹר מִלְחָמָה: שְׂאוּ שְׁעָרִים רָאשֵׁיכֶם, וּשְׂאוּ פִּתְחֵי עוֹלָם, וְיָבֹא מֶלֶךְ הַכָּבוֹד: מִי הוּא זֶה מֶלֶךְ הַכָּבוֹד, יהוה צְבָאוֹת הוּא מֶלֶךְ הַכָּבוֹד, סֶלָה:

As the ספר תורה *is placed into the* ארון קודש*, say:*

וּבְנֻחֹה יֹאמַר, שׁוּבָה יהוה רִבְבוֹת אַלְפֵי יִשְׂרָאֵל:\
קוּמָה יהוה לִמְנוּחָתֶךָ, אַתָּה וַאֲרוֹן עֻזֶּךָ:\
כֹּהֲנֶיךָ יִלְבְּשׁוּ־צֶדֶק, וַחֲסִידֶיךָ יְרַנֵּנוּ:\
בַּעֲבוּר דָּוִד עַבְדֶּךָ אַל־תָּשֵׁב פְּנֵי מְשִׁיחֶךָ:\
כִּי לֶקַח טוֹב נָתַתִּי לָכֶם, תּוֹרָתִי אַל־תַּעֲזֹבוּ:\
עֵץ־חַיִּים הִיא לַמַּחֲזִיקִים בָּהּ, וְתֹמְכֶיהָ מְאֻשָּׁר:\
דְּרָכֶיהָ דַרְכֵי־נֹעַם וְכָל־נְתִיבֹתֶיהָ שָׁלוֹם:\
◂ הֲשִׁיבֵנוּ יהוה אֵלֶיךָ וְנָשׁוּבָה, חַדֵּשׁ יָמֵינוּ כְּקֶדֶם:

The ארון קודש *is closed.*\
Sit after the ספר תורה *has been returned to the* ארון קודש*.*

CONCLUSION OF THE SERVICE

The line beginning with "Hashem opens His hands" should be said with special concentration. Some have the custom to touch the TEFILLIN SHEL YAD *and the* TEFILLIN SHEL ROSH *at the relevant icons.*

אַשְׁרֵי We are happy with the opportunity to sit and pray. We are happy that You are our God and that we are Your people.

David HaMelech wrote this song:

א GOD – *Hashem* is our God and King.

ב THANK – We appreciate *Hashem* and we will thank Him every day, forever.

ג GREATNESS – *Hashem*'s greatness is endless.

ד GENERATIONS – We will tell our children about the spectacular actions You have done for us in every generation.

ה MIRACLES – The miracles that *Hashem* performs for His people are glorious.

ו STRENGTH – *Hashem*'s strength is awesome beyond comparison.

ז REMEMBER – We remember the good that *Hashem* does for us.

ח MERCY – *Hashem* is slow to get angry.

ט GOODNESS – *Hashem* is good to all His creations, humans and animals alike.

י KINDNESS – All creations of *Hashem* are thankful for His kindness.

כ HONOR – We give *Hashem* the honor that He deserves.

ל MIGHTY – We inform all people of *Hashem*'s mighty actions.

מ KINGSHIP – *Hashem* has and always will rule the world.

ס HELP – *Hashem* helps us when we need Him.

סיום התפילה

The line beginning with פּוֹתֵחַ אֶת יָדֶךָ *should be said with special concentration. Some have the custom to touch the* תפילין של יד *and the* תפילין של ראש *at the relevant icons.*

אַשְׁרֵי יוֹשְׁבֵי בֵיתֶךָ, עוֹד יְהַלְלְוּךָ סֶּלָה:
אַשְׁרֵי הָעָם שֶׁכָּכָה לּוֹ, אַשְׁרֵי הָעָם שֶׁיהוה אֱלֹהָיו:
תְּהִלָּה לְדָוִד
אֲרוֹמִמְךָ אֱלוֹהַי הַמֶּלֶךְ, וַאֲבָרְכָה שִׁמְךָ לְעוֹלָם וָעֶד:
בְּכָל־יוֹם אֲבָרְכֶךָּ, וַאֲהַלְלָה שִׁמְךָ לְעוֹלָם וָעֶד:
גָּדוֹל יהוה וּמְהֻלָּל מְאֹד, וְלִגְדֻלָּתוֹ אֵין חֵקֶר:
דּוֹר לְדוֹר יְשַׁבַּח מַעֲשֶׂיךָ, וּגְבוּרֹתֶיךָ יַגִּידוּ:
הֲדַר כְּבוֹד הוֹדֶךָ, וְדִבְרֵי נִפְלְאֹתֶיךָ אָשִֽׂיחָה:
וֶעֱזוּז נוֹרְאֹתֶיךָ יֹאמֵרוּ, וּגְדוּלָּתְךָ אֲסַפְּרֶנָּה:
זֵכֶר רַב־טוּבְךָ יַבִּיעוּ, וְצִדְקָתְךָ יְרַנֵּנוּ:
חַנּוּן וְרַחוּם יהוה, אֶרֶךְ אַפַּיִם וּגְדָל־חָסֶד:
טוֹב־יהוה לַכֹּל, וְרַחֲמָיו עַל־כָּל־מַעֲשָׂיו:
יוֹדְוּךָ יהוה כָּל־מַעֲשֶׂיךָ, וַחֲסִידֶיךָ יְבָרְכוּכָה:
כְּבוֹד מַלְכוּתְךָ יֹאמֵרוּ, וּגְבוּרָתְךָ יְדַבֵּרוּ:
לְהוֹדִיעַ לִבְנֵי הָאָדָם גְּבוּרֹתָיו
וּכְבוֹד הֲדַר מַלְכוּתוֹ:
מַלְכוּתְךָ מַלְכוּת כָּל־עֹלָמִים
וּמֶמְשַׁלְתְּךָ בְּכָל־דּוֹר וָדֹר:
סוֹמֵךְ יהוה לְכָל־הַנֹּפְלִים, וְזוֹקֵף לְכָל־הַכְּפוּפִים:

ע RELY – We rely on *Hashem* to give us the food that we need to live.

פ PROVIDES – *Hashem* opens His hands and provides us with our needs.

צ RIGHTEOUS – Everything *Hashem* does is righteous and with good intentions.

ק CLOSENESS – *Hashem* is close to all those that call out to Him.

ר SAVES – *Hashem* listens to our cries and saves those in need.

ש GUARDS – *Hashem* protects all those who love Him and turn to Him in times of need.

▸ ת PRAISE – For all of these reasons, everyone praises *Hashem* and thanks Him every day.

This is not said on Rosh Chodesh, Chol HaMo'ed, Erev Pesach, Erev Yom Kippur, Chanuka, the 14th and 15th of Adar I, Purim and Shushan Purim, Yom HaAtzma'ut, Yom Yerushalayim, Tisha B'Av, or in a house of mourning, and in Israel on Isru Chag.

לַמְנַצֵּחַ May *Hashem* answer us in our time of need. May He protect us, just as He protected *Yaakov*. May *Hashem*'s help come from the *Beit HaMikdash,* His holiest place. *Hashem,* remember how we served You in the *Beit HaMikdash,* and because of that accept our prayers and save us. May He give you all of your heart's desires and make all your plans succeed. When You save us, we will shout in joy and make Your greatness known. While some people trust in the strength of an army, we put our trust in *Hashem*. Other nations fall and do not last, but the Jewish people will last. ▸ *Hashem,* please save and answer us on the day we call.

יְשַׂגֶּבְךָ שֵׁם אֱלֹהֵי יַעֲקֹב *Just as He protected Yaakov.* When Yaakov left his father's house while fleeing from Esav, he found himself alone and unprotected. *Hashem* came to Yaakov in a dream and promised that He would always protect him. Just as *Hashem* was there to protect Yaakov, we ask *Hashem* to answer and protect us in our times of need.

עֵינֵי־כֹל אֵלֶיךָ יְשַׂבֵּרוּ
וְאַתָּה נוֹתֵן־לָהֶם אֶת־אָכְלָם בְּעִתּוֹ:
פּוֹתֵחַ אֶת־יָדֶךָ, וּמַשְׂבִּיעַ לְכָל־חַי רָצוֹן:
צַדִּיק יהוה בְּכָל־דְּרָכָיו, וְחָסִיד בְּכָל־מַעֲשָׂיו:
קָרוֹב יהוה לְכָל־קֹרְאָיו, לְכֹל אֲשֶׁר יִקְרָאֻהוּ בֶאֱמֶת:
רְצוֹן־יְרֵאָיו יַעֲשֶׂה, וְאֶת־שַׁוְעָתָם יִשְׁמַע, וְיוֹשִׁיעֵם:
שׁוֹמֵר יהוה אֶת־כָּל־אֹהֲבָיו, וְאֵת כָּל־הָרְשָׁעִים יַשְׁמִיד:
› תְּהִלַּת יהוה יְדַבֶּר פִּי
וִיבָרֵךְ כָּל־בָּשָׂר שֵׁם קָדְשׁוֹ לְעוֹלָם וָעֶד:
וַאֲנַחְנוּ נְבָרֵךְ יָהּ מֵעַתָּה וְעַד־עוֹלָם, הַלְלוּיָהּ:

This is not said on ראש חודש, חול המועד, ערב פסח, ערב יום כיפור, חנוכה, *the 14th and 15th of* אדר א׳, פורים *and* פורים שושן, יום העצמאות, יום ירושלים, *or in a house of mourning, and in* ארץ ישראל *on* אסרו חג, תשעה באב.

לַמְנַצֵּחַ מִזְמוֹר לְדָוִד: יַעַנְךָ יהוה בְּיוֹם צָרָה, יְשַׂגֶּבְךָ שֵׁם אֱלֹהֵי יַעֲקֹב: יִשְׁלַח־עֶזְרְךָ מִקֹּדֶשׁ, וּמִצִּיּוֹן יִסְעָדֶךָּ: יִזְכֹּר כָּל־מִנְחֹתֶיךָ, וְעוֹלָתְךָ יְדַשְּׁנֶה סֶלָה: יִתֶּן־לְךָ כִלְבָבֶךָ וְכָל־עֲצָתְךָ יְמַלֵּא: נְרַנְּנָה בִּישׁוּעָתֶךָ, וּבְשֵׁם־אֱלֹהֵינוּ נִדְגֹּל, יְמַלֵּא יהוה כָּל־מִשְׁאֲלוֹתֶיךָ: עַתָּה יָדַעְתִּי כִּי הוֹשִׁיעַ יהוה מְשִׁיחוֹ, יַעֲנֵהוּ מִשְּׁמֵי קָדְשׁוֹ, בִּגְבוּרוֹת יֵשַׁע יְמִינוֹ: אֵלֶּה בָרֶכֶב וְאֵלֶּה בַסּוּסִים, וַאֲנַחְנוּ בְּשֵׁם־יהוה אֱלֹהֵינוּ נַזְכִּיר: הֵמָּה כָּרְעוּ וְנָפָלוּ, וַאֲנַחְנוּ קַמְנוּ וַנִּתְעוֹדָד: › יהוה הוֹשִׁיעָה, הַמֶּלֶךְ יַעֲנֵנוּ בְיוֹם־קָרְאֵנוּ:

וּבָא לְצִיּוֹן *Hashem* said, "*Mashiach* will come to Zion
and redeem those who abandon their sins
and return to *Hashem*."

"From this point and onwards,
all Jews shall learn the words of my Torah
and teach the Torah to their children
and their children's children.
The words of my Torah shall never be forgotten!"

▸ וְאַתָּה קָדוֹשׁ *Hashem*, You are holy and the Jewish people praise You. The angels will call to each other saying:

All say aloud:

"Holy, holy, holy is *Hashem*: the world is filled with His honor."

The angels then say to each other: "Heaven is holy because *Hashem* lives there, and the earth is holy because *Hashem* created it. The entire world is filled with *Hashem*'s holiness."

▸ When a wind lifted the prophet Yechezkel, he heard the angels praising *Hashem*, saying,

All say aloud:

"Blessed is the honor of *Hashem* who lives in heaven!"

When a wind lifted the prophet Yechezkel, he heard the angels praising *Hashem*, saying, "Blessed is the honor of *Hashem* who lives in heaven."

All say aloud:

Hashem shall reign as King forever!

Hashem's kingdom is established forever and ever.

יהוה *Hashem*, God of Avraham, Yitzchak, and Yaakov,

וּבָא לְצִיּוֹן גּוֹאֵל, וּלְשָׁבֵי פֶשַׁע בְּיַעֲקֹב, נְאֻם יהוה:

וַאֲנִי זֹאת בְּרִיתִי אוֹתָם, אָמַר יהוה, רוּחִי אֲשֶׁר עָלֶיךָ וּדְבָרַי אֲשֶׁר־שַׂמְתִּי בְּפִיךָ, לֹא־יָמוּשׁוּ מִפִּיךָ וּמִפִּי זַרְעֲךָ וּמִפִּי זֶרַע זַרְעֲךָ, אָמַר יהוה, מֵעַתָּה וְעַד־עוֹלָם:

◂ וְאַתָּה קָדוֹשׁ יוֹשֵׁב תְּהִלּוֹת יִשְׂרָאֵל:
וְקָרָא זֶה אֶל־זֶה וְאָמַר

All say aloud:

קָדוֹשׁ, קָדוֹשׁ, קָדוֹשׁ, יהוה צְבָאוֹת
מְלֹא כָל־הָאָרֶץ כְּבוֹדוֹ:

וּמְקַבְּלִין דֵּין מִן דֵּין וְאָמְרִין, קַדִּישׁ בִּשְׁמֵי מְרוֹמָא עִלָּאָה בֵּית שְׁכִינְתֵּהּ, קַדִּישׁ עַל אַרְעָא עוֹבַד גְּבוּרְתֵּהּ, קַדִּישׁ לְעָלַם וּלְעָלְמֵי עָלְמַיָּא, יהוה צְבָאוֹת, מַלְיָא כָל אַרְעָא זִיו יְקָרֵהּ.

◂ וַתִּשָּׂאֵנִי רוּחַ, וָאֶשְׁמַע אַחֲרַי קוֹל רַעַשׁ גָּדוֹל

All say aloud:

בָּרוּךְ כְּבוֹד־יהוה מִמְּקוֹמוֹ:

וּנְטָלַתְנִי רוּחָא, וּשְׁמָעִית בַּתְרַי קָל זִיעַ סַגִּיא, דִּמְשַׁבְּחִין וְאָמְרִין, בְּרִיךְ יְקָרָא דַיהוה מֵאֲתַר בֵּית שְׁכִינְתֵּהּ.

All say aloud:

יהוה יִמְלֹךְ לְעֹלָם וָעֶד:

יהוה מַלְכוּתֵהּ קָאֵם לְעָלַם וּלְעָלְמֵי עָלְמַיָּא.

יהוה אֱלֹהֵי אַבְרָהָם יִצְחָק וְיִשְׂרָאֵל אֲבֹתֵינוּ, שָׁמְרָה־זֹּאת לְעוֹלָם לְיֵצֶר מַחְשְׁבוֹת לְבַב עַמֶּךָ, וְהָכֵן לְבָבָם אֵלֶיךָ:

please allow Your Jewish people
to keep these thoughts in mind,
and help direct their hearts towards You.
You are merciful and You show Your kindness
by forgiving our sins.
Your Torah is true and Your righteousness lasts forever.
Please treat us with loyalty and kindness
as You promised our forefathers.
Hashem, You are our protector; You are always with us.
Praiseworthy is the person who trusts in You.
May *Hashem,* the King,
answer us on the day that we call out to Him.

בָּרוּךְ Thank You, *Hashem,* for giving us the Torah,
allowing us to honor You,
and providing us the opportunity
to live on in the world-to-come.
May *Hashem* open our hearts through studying His Torah,
and allow us to serve Him wholeheartedly
with love and fear.

יְהִי רָצוֹן May *Hashem,* our God and God of our ancestors,
allow us to keep His *mitzvot* in this world
so that we can gain the blessings promised to us
in the times of *Mashiach* and in the world-to-come.
I will thank *Hashem* forever. ▸ Trust in *Hashem,*
for *Hashem* is our protector.

On Rosh Chodesh and Chol HaMo'ed, the Leader says Half Kaddish, page 166. The service then continues with Musaf for Rosh Chodesh on page 736, for Chol HaMo'ed on page 766.
On other days the Leader continues with Kaddish Shalem on the next page.

וְהוּא רַחוּם יְכַפֵּר עָוֹן וְלֹא־יַשְׁחִית, וְהִרְבָּה לְהָשִׁיב אַפּוֹ, וְלֹא־יָעִיר כָּל־חֲמָתוֹ: כִּי־אַתָּה אֲדֹנָי טוֹב וְסַלָּח, וְרַב־חֶסֶד לְכָל־קֹרְאֶיךָ: צִדְקָתְךָ צֶדֶק לְעוֹלָם וְתוֹרָתְךָ אֱמֶת: תִּתֵּן אֱמֶת לְיַעֲקֹב, חֶסֶד לְאַבְרָהָם, אֲשֶׁר־נִשְׁבַּעְתָּ לַאֲבֹתֵינוּ מִימֵי קֶדֶם: בָּרוּךְ אֲדֹנָי יוֹם יוֹם יַעֲמָס־לָנוּ, הָאֵל יְשׁוּעָתֵנוּ סֶלָה: יהוה צְבָאוֹת עִמָּנוּ, מִשְׂגָּב לָנוּ אֱלֹהֵי יַעֲקֹב סֶלָה: יהוה צְבָאוֹת, אַשְׁרֵי אָדָם בֹּטֵחַ בָּךְ: יהוה הוֹשִׁיעָה, הַמֶּלֶךְ יַעֲנֵנוּ בְיוֹם־קָרְאֵנוּ:

בָּרוּךְ הוּא אֱלֹהֵינוּ שֶׁבְּרָאָנוּ לִכְבוֹדוֹ, וְהִבְדִּילָנוּ מִן הַתּוֹעִים, וְנָתַן לָנוּ תּוֹרַת אֱמֶת, וְחַיֵּי עוֹלָם נָטַע בְּתוֹכֵנוּ. הוּא יִפְתַּח לִבֵּנוּ בְּתוֹרָתוֹ, וְיָשֵׂם בְּלִבֵּנוּ אַהֲבָתוֹ וְיִרְאָתוֹ וְלַעֲשׂוֹת רְצוֹנוֹ וּלְעָבְדוֹ בְּלֵבָב שָׁלֵם, לְמַעַן לֹא נִיגַע לָרִיק וְלֹא נֵלֵד לַבֶּהָלָה.

יְהִי רָצוֹן מִלְּפָנֶיךָ יהוה אֱלֹהֵינוּ וֵאלֹהֵי אֲבוֹתֵינוּ, שֶׁנִּשְׁמֹר חֻקֶּיךָ בָּעוֹלָם הַזֶּה, וְנִזְכֶּה וְנִחְיֶה וְנִרְאֶה וְנִירַשׁ טוֹבָה וּבְרָכָה, לִשְׁנֵי יְמוֹת הַמָּשִׁיחַ וּלְחַיֵּי הָעוֹלָם הַבָּא. לְמַעַן יְזַמֶּרְךָ כָבוֹד וְלֹא יִדֹּם, יהוה אֱלֹהַי, לְעוֹלָם אוֹדֶךָּ: בָּרוּךְ הַגֶּבֶר אֲשֶׁר יִבְטַח בַּיהוה, וְהָיָה יהוה מִבְטַחוֹ: בִּטְחוּ בַיהוה עֲדֵי־עַד, כִּי בְּיָהּ יהוה צוּר עוֹלָמִים: ‹ וְיִבְטְחוּ בְךָ יוֹדְעֵי שְׁמֶךָ, כִּי לֹא־עָזַבְתָּ דֹרְשֶׁיךָ, יהוה: יהוה חָפֵץ לְמַעַן צִדְקוֹ, יַגְדִּיל תּוֹרָה וְיַאְדִּיר:

On ראש חודש *and* חול המועד, *the* חזן *says* חצי קדיש, *page 167.*
The service then continues with מוסף *for* ראש חודש
on page 737, for חול המועד *on page 767.*

On other days the חזן *continues with* קדיש שלם *on the next page.*

KADDISH SHALEM

Leader: יִתְגַּדַּל May *Hashem* be recognized
as great and holy (*Congregation:* Amen)
in the world that He created.
May He establish His kingdom
during my lifetime and the lifetime of all Jews,
quickly and soon.
Let us say: "Amen" (*Congregation:* Amen).

Congregation: May we thank *Hashem* for ever and ever.
Leader: May we thank *Hashem* for ever and ever.

Leader: *Hashem* should be thanked, praised,
and honored (*Congregation:* He is blessed).
Hashem is beyond all the blessings,
songs, or praises that we could offer.
Let us say: "Amen" (*Congregation:* Amen).

May *Hashem* accept our prayers
and the prayers of all Jews.
Let us say: "Amen." (*Congregation:* Amen).

May *Hashem* give us, and all Jews,
peace and good life.
Let us say: "Amen." (*Congregation:* Amen).

The Leader takes three steps back before saying this line, bows to the left when saying "May," bows to the right when saying "the One," bows to the middle when saying "make peace for us":

May *Hashem,* the One
who makes peace in heaven,
make peace for us and for all Jews.
Let us say: "Amen." (*Congregation:* Amen).

קדיש שלם

חזן: יִתְגַּדַּל וְיִתְקַדַּשׁ שְׁמֵהּ רַבָּא (קהל: אָמֵן)
בְּעָלְמָא דִּי בְרָא כִרְעוּתֵהּ, וְיַמְלִיךְ מַלְכוּתֵהּ
בְּחַיֵּיכוֹן וּבְיוֹמֵיכוֹן וּבְחַיֵּי דְכָל בֵּית יִשְׂרָאֵל
בַּעֲגָלָא וּבִזְמַן קָרִיב, וְאִמְרוּ אָמֵן. (קהל: אָמֵן)

קהל יְהֵא שְׁמֵהּ רַבָּא מְבָרַךְ לְעָלַם וּלְעָלְמֵי עָלְמַיָּא.
חזן: יְהֵא שְׁמֵהּ רַבָּא מְבָרַךְ לְעָלַם וּלְעָלְמֵי עָלְמַיָּא.

חזן: יִתְבָּרַךְ וְיִשְׁתַּבַּח וְיִתְפָּאַר וְיִתְרוֹמַם וְיִתְנַשֵּׂא וְיִתְהַדָּר
וְיִתְעַלֶּה וְיִתְהַלָּל שְׁמֵהּ דְּקֻדְשָׁא בְּרִיךְ הוּא (קהל: בְּרִיךְ הוּא)
לְעֵלָּא מִן כָּל בִּרְכָתָא
/בעשרת ימי תשובה: לְעֵלָּא לְעֵלָּא מִכָּל בִּרְכָתָא/
וְשִׁירָתָא, תֻּשְׁבְּחָתָא וְנֶחֱמָתָא
דַּאֲמִירָן בְּעָלְמָא, וְאִמְרוּ אָמֵן. (קהל: אָמֵן)

תִּתְקַבַּל צְלוֹתְהוֹן וּבָעוּתְהוֹן דְּכָל יִשְׂרָאֵל
קֳדָם אֲבוּהוֹן דִּי בִשְׁמַיָּא, וְאִמְרוּ אָמֵן. (קהל: אָמֵן)

יְהֵא שְׁלָמָא רַבָּא מִן שְׁמַיָּא
וְחַיִּים, עָלֵינוּ וְעַל כָּל יִשְׂרָאֵל, וְאִמְרוּ אָמֵן. (קהל: אָמֵן)

The חזן *takes three steps back before saying this line, bows to the left when saying* עֹשֶׂה*, bows to the right when saying* הוּא*, bows to the middle when saying* יַעֲשֶׂה שָׁלוֹם עָלֵינוּ*:*

עֹשֶׂה שָׁלוֹם /בעשרת ימי תשובה: הַשָּׁלוֹם/ בִּמְרוֹמָיו
הוּא יַעֲשֶׂה שָׁלוֹם
עָלֵינוּ וְעַל כָּל יִשְׂרָאֵל, וְאִמְרוּ אָמֵן. (קהל: אָמֵן)

Stand while saying "It is our role."

עָלֵינוּ It is our role to praise You, *Hashem*,
Master of all and Creator of the world.
You have not made us like other nations of the world,
rather, You set the Jewish people apart
allowing us the opportunity to serve You.
(Other nations pray to gods that do not exist, while)
we bend our knees and bow in prayer
before the King of all kings, *Hashem*,
in order to give thanks.
Hashem created the heavens above and the land below.
Hashem sits on His awesome throne in heaven
as He, alone, is our God and ruler of the world.
We willingly accept Him as our King,
there is none else but Him.
As it says in the Torah,
"Today You should understand that *Hashem* is God
in the heavens above and on the earth below.
There is no other God but You."

עָלֵינוּ *It is our role.* This prayer is repeated three times a day, at the end of Shacharit, Mincha, and Maariv, because it includes an important message to think about throughout the day: *Hashem* alone created the world and is actively involved in ruling it every moment of every day. One day, all people will recognize *Hashem*'s great power, accept Him as King, and give Him great honor. We say *Aleinu* at the end of each prayer, at the beginning of the day, in middle of the day, and at day's end, to remind us that no matter what we are involved with, *Hashem* is in control.

Stand while saying עָלֵינוּ.

עָלֵינוּ לְשַׁבֵּחַ לַאֲדוֹן הַכֹּל
לָתֵת גְּדֻלָּה לְיוֹצֵר בְּרֵאשִׁית
שֶׁלֹּא עָשָׂנוּ כְּגוֹיֵי הָאֲרָצוֹת
וְלֹא שָׂמָנוּ כְּמִשְׁפְּחוֹת הָאֲדָמָה
שֶׁלֹּא שָׂם חֶלְקֵנוּ כָּהֶם, וְגוֹרָלֵנוּ כְּכָל הֲמוֹנָם.
(שֶׁהֵם מִשְׁתַּחֲוִים לְהֶבֶל וָרִיק
וּמִתְפַּלְלִים אֶל אֵל לֹא יוֹשִׁיעַ.)
וַאֲנַחְנוּ כּוֹרְעִים וּמִשְׁתַּחֲוִים וּמוֹדִים
לִפְנֵי מֶלֶךְ מַלְכֵי הַמְּלָכִים, הַקָּדוֹשׁ בָּרוּךְ הוּא
שֶׁהוּא נוֹטֶה שָׁמַיִם וְיוֹסֵד אָרֶץ
וּמוֹשַׁב יְקָרוֹ בַּשָּׁמַיִם מִמַּעַל
וּשְׁכִינַת עֻזּוֹ בְּגָבְהֵי מְרוֹמִים.
הוּא אֱלֹהֵינוּ, אֵין עוֹד.
אֱמֶת מַלְכֵּנוּ, אֶפֶס זוּלָתוֹ
כַּכָּתוּב בְּתוֹרָתוֹ
וְיָדַעְתָּ הַיּוֹם וַהֲשֵׁבֹתָ אֶל־לְבָבֶךָ
כִּי יהוה הוּא הָאֱלֹהִים
בַּשָּׁמַיִם מִמַּעַל וְעַל־הָאָרֶץ מִתָּחַת
אֵין עוֹד:

Hashem,
we hope that all false gods
will be removed from the world
and everyone will soon turn to You alone
as the almighty God of the universe.
All the people of the world
will turn to You
and give honor.
They will accept You as their King,
and You will rule over them soon and forever.
For You are King of the world
and You will remain the ruling King forever.
As it says in Your Torah,
▸ "*Hashem* will be king over all the land.
On that day *Hashem* will be One and His name One."

עַל כֵּן נְקַוֶּה לְּךָ יהוה אֱלֹהֵינוּ
לִרְאוֹת מְהֵרָה בְּתִפְאֶרֶת עֻזֶּךָ
לְהַעֲבִיר גִּלּוּלִים מִן הָאָרֶץ
וְהָאֱלִילִים כָּרוֹת יִכָּרֵתוּן
לְתַקֵּן עוֹלָם בְּמַלְכוּת שַׁדַּי.
וְכָל בְּנֵי בָשָׂר יִקְרְאוּ בִשְׁמֶךָ
לְהַפְנוֹת אֵלֶיךָ כָּל רִשְׁעֵי אָרֶץ.
יַכִּירוּ וְיֵדְעוּ כָּל יוֹשְׁבֵי תֵבֵל
כִּי לְךָ תִּכְרַע כָּל בֶּרֶךְ
תִּשָּׁבַע כָּל לָשׁוֹן.
לְפָנֶיךָ יהוה אֱלֹהֵינוּ יִכְרְעוּ וְיִפֹּלוּ
וְלִכְבוֹד שִׁמְךָ יְקָר יִתֵּנוּ
וִיקַבְּלוּ כֻלָּם אֶת עֹל מַלְכוּתֶךָ
וְתִמְלֹךְ עֲלֵיהֶם מְהֵרָה לְעוֹלָם וָעֶד.
כִּי הַמַּלְכוּת שֶׁלְּךָ הִיא
וּלְעוֹלְמֵי עַד תִּמְלֹךְ בְּכָבוֹד
כַּכָּתוּב בְּתוֹרָתֶךָ
יהוה יִמְלֹךְ לְעֹלָם וָעֶד:
◄ וְנֶאֱמַר, וְהָיָה יהוה לְמֶלֶךְ עַל־כָּל־הָאָרֶץ
בַּיּוֹם הַהוּא יִהְיֶה יהוה אֶחָד וּשְׁמוֹ אֶחָד:

KADDISH YATOM

The following prayer, said by mourners, requires the presence of a minyan. A transliteration can be found on page 865.

Mourner: יִתְגַּדַּל May *Hashem* be recognized
as great and holy (*Congregation:* Amen)
in the world that He created.
May He establish His kingdom
during my lifetime
and the lifetime of all Jews,
quickly and soon.
Let us say: "Amen" (*Congregation:* Amen).

Congregation: May we thank *Hashem* for ever and ever.
Mourner: May we thank *Hashem* for ever and ever.

Mourner: *Hashem* should be thanked, praised,
and honored (*Congregation:* He is blessed).
Hashem is beyond all the blessings,
songs, or praises that we could offer.
Let us say: "Amen" (*Congregation:* Amen).

May *Hashem* give us, and all Jews,
peace and good life.
Let us say: "Amen." (*Congregation:* Amen).

The mourner takes three steps back before saying this line, bows to the left when saying "May," bows to the right when saying "the One," bows to the middle when saying "make peace for us":

May *Hashem,* the One
who makes peace in heaven,
make peace for us and for all Jews.
Let us say: "Amen." (*Congregation:* Amen).

קדיש יתום

The following prayer, said by mourners, requires the presence of a מנין*.*
A transliteration can be found on page 865.

אבל: **יִתְגַּדַּל וְיִתְקַדַּשׁ שְׁמֵהּ רַבָּא** (קהל: **אָמֵן**)
בְּעָלְמָא דִּי בְרָא כִרְעוּתֵהּ, וְיַמְלִיךְ מַלְכוּתֵהּ
בְּחַיֵּיכוֹן וּבְיוֹמֵיכוֹן וּבְחַיֵּי דְכָל בֵּית יִשְׂרָאֵל
בַּעֲגָלָא וּבִזְמַן קָרִיב, וְאִמְרוּ אָמֵן. (קהל: **אָמֵן**)

קהל **יְהֵא שְׁמֵהּ רַבָּא מְבָרַךְ לְעָלַם וּלְעָלְמֵי עָלְמַיָּא.**
אבל: **יְהֵא שְׁמֵהּ רַבָּא מְבָרַךְ לְעָלַם וּלְעָלְמֵי עָלְמַיָּא.**

אבל: **יִתְבָּרַךְ וְיִשְׁתַּבַּח וְיִתְפָּאַר**
וְיִתְרוֹמַם וְיִתְנַשֵּׂא וְיִתְהַדָּר וְיִתְעַלֶּה וְיִתְהַלָּל
שְׁמֵהּ דְּקֻדְשָׁא בְּרִיךְ הוּא (קהל: **בְּרִיךְ הוּא**)
לְעֵלָּא מִן כָּל בִּרְכָתָא
/ בעשרת ימי תשובה: **לְעֵלָּא לְעֵלָּא מִכָּל בִּרְכָתָא**/
וְשִׁירָתָא, תֻּשְׁבְּחָתָא וְנֶחֱמָתָא
דַּאֲמִירָן בְּעָלְמָא, וְאִמְרוּ אָמֵן. (קהל: **אָמֵן**)

יְהֵא שְׁלָמָא רַבָּא מִן שְׁמַיָּא
וְחַיִּים, עָלֵינוּ וְעַל כָּל יִשְׂרָאֵל, וְאִמְרוּ אָמֵן. (קהל: **אָמֵן**)

The mourner takes three steps back before saying this line, bows to the left when saying עֹשֶׂה*, bows to the right when saying* הוּא*, bows to the middle when saying* יַעֲשֶׂה שָׁלוֹם עָלֵינוּ*:*

עֹשֶׂה שָׁלוֹם /בעשרת ימי תשובה: **הַשָּׁלוֹם**/ **בִּמְרוֹמָיו**
הוּא יַעֲשֶׂה שָׁלוֹם עָלֵינוּ
וְעַל כָּל יִשְׂרָאֵל, וְאִמְרוּ אָמֵן. (קהל: **אָמֵן**)

SHIR SHEL YOM

One of the following psalms is said on the appropriate day of the week.

Sunday: Today is the first day of the week.
On this day, the Levi'im said the following
in the *Beit HaMikdash*:

לְדָוִד מִזְמוֹר The earth and everything on it belong to *Hashem*.
Hashem created the world
beginning with the waters of the seas and rivers.
Who may go to the *Beit HaMikdash*
and stand in the presence of *Hashem*'s holiness?
One with pure actions and thoughts.
This person will receive blessing and kindness
from *Hashem*.
Who is the King worthy of honor?
▸ *Hashem*, Master of the world,
is the King worthy of honor!

Kaddish Yatom (page 202)

Monday: Today is the second day of the week.
On this day, the Levi'im said the following
in the *Beit HaMikdash*:

שִׁיר מִזְמוֹר *Hashem* is great! He is praised in Jerusalem,
on His beautiful and holy mountain, Mount Zion.

שֶׁבּוֹ הָיוּ הַלְוִיִּם אוֹמְרִים בְּבֵית הַמִּקְדָּשׁ *The Levi'im said the following in the Beit HaMikdash.* While the *korban tamid,* daily sacrifice, was brought every morning in the *Beit HaMikdash,* the Levi'im would stand on the stairs leading up to the *Beit HaMikdash* with instruments in their hands, and sing these beautiful songs. Every day had its own song, relating to the days of creation. To see the service of *Hashem,* smell the sweet-smelling *korbanot,* and hear the beautiful songs made serving *Hashem* an awe-inspiring experience.

שיר של יום

One of the following psalms is said on the appropriate day of the week.

Sunday הַיּוֹם יוֹם רִאשׁוֹן בְּשַׁבָּת, שֶׁבּוֹ הָיוּ הַלְוִיִּם אוֹמְרִים בְּבֵית הַמִּקְדָּשׁ:

לְדָוִד מִזְמוֹר, לַיהוה הָאָרֶץ וּמְלוֹאָהּ, תֵּבֵל וְיֹשְׁבֵי בָהּ: כִּי־הוּא עַל־יַמִּים יְסָדָהּ, וְעַל־נְהָרוֹת יְכוֹנְנֶהָ: מִי־יַעֲלֶה בְהַר־יהוה, וּמִי־יָקוּם בִּמְקוֹם קָדְשׁוֹ: נְקִי כַפַּיִם וּבַר־לֵבָב, אֲשֶׁר לֹא־נָשָׂא לַשָּׁוְא נַפְשִׁי, וְלֹא נִשְׁבַּע לְמִרְמָה: יִשָּׂא בְרָכָה מֵאֵת יהוה, וּצְדָקָה מֵאֱלֹהֵי יִשְׁעוֹ: זֶה דּוֹר דֹּרְשָׁו, מְבַקְשֵׁי פָנֶיךָ יַעֲקֹב סֶלָה: שְׂאוּ שְׁעָרִים רָאשֵׁיכֶם, וְהִנָּשְׂאוּ פִּתְחֵי עוֹלָם, וְיָבוֹא מֶלֶךְ הַכָּבוֹד: מִי זֶה מֶלֶךְ הַכָּבוֹד, יהוה עִזּוּז וְגִבּוֹר, יהוה גִּבּוֹר מִלְחָמָה: שְׂאוּ שְׁעָרִים רָאשֵׁיכֶם, וּשְׂאוּ פִּתְחֵי עוֹלָם, וְיָבֹא מֶלֶךְ הַכָּבוֹד: ‹ מִי הוּא זֶה מֶלֶךְ הַכָּבוֹד, יהוה צְבָאוֹת הוּא מֶלֶךְ הַכָּבוֹד סֶלָה:

קדיש יתום (*page 203*)

Monday הַיּוֹם יוֹם שֵׁנִי בְּשַׁבָּת, שֶׁבּוֹ הָיוּ הַלְוִיִּם אוֹמְרִים בְּבֵית הַמִּקְדָּשׁ:

שִׁיר מִזְמוֹר לִבְנֵי־קֹרַח: גָּדוֹל יהוה וּמְהֻלָּל מְאֹד, בְּעִיר אֱלֹהֵינוּ, הַר־קָדְשׁוֹ: יְפֵה נוֹף מְשׂוֹשׂ כָּל־הָאָרֶץ, הַר־צִיּוֹן יַרְכְּתֵי צָפוֹן, קִרְיַת מֶלֶךְ רָב: אֱלֹהִים בְּאַרְמְנוֹתֶיהָ נוֹדַע לְמִשְׂגָּב: כִּי־הִנֵּה הַמְּלָכִים נוֹעֲדוּ, עָבְרוּ יַחְדָּו: הֵמָּה רָאוּ כֵּן תָּמָהוּ, נִבְהֲלוּ נֶחְפָּזוּ: רְעָדָה אֲחָזָתַם שָׁם, חִיל כַּיּוֹלֵדָה: בְּרוּחַ קָדִים תְּשַׁבֵּר אֳנִיּוֹת תַּרְשִׁישׁ: כַּאֲשֶׁר שָׁמַעְנוּ כֵּן רָאִינוּ, בְּעִיר־יהוה צְבָאוֹת, בְּעִיר אֱלֹהֵינוּ,

Jerusalem is an amazing sight that brings joy to all the earth.
The kings of many nations joined together
to try to capture Jerusalem,
but they were filled with fear and ran away.
Walk through Jerusalem,
count its towers, note its strong walls,
▸ so that we can share with future generations
that this city is the work of *Hashem*,
who will continue to guide and protect us forever.

Kaddish Yatom (page 202)

Tuesday: Today is the third day of the week.
On this day, the Levi'im said the following
in the *Beit HaMikdash*:

מִזְמוֹר לְאָסָף *Hashem* oversees the judges.
Please, *Hashem* cause all the judges to judge favorably,
help and save those in need
and those without parents.
The judges walk in darkness, not understanding
as the world around them collapses.
▸ Arise, *Hashem*, and judge the nations,
because the world belongs to You. *Kaddish Yatom (page 202)*

Wednesday: Today is the fourth day of the week.
On this day, the Levi'im said the following
in the *Beit HaMikdash*:

אֵל-נְקָמוֹת *Hashem*, arise and judge the world!
How long will You, *Hashem*,
allow the wicked people to be successful?

אֱלֹהִים יְכוֹנְנֶהָ עַד־עוֹלָם סֶלָה: דִּמִּינוּ אֱלֹהִים חַסְדֶּךָ, בְּקֶרֶב הֵיכָלֶךָ: כְּשִׁמְךָ אֱלֹהִים כֵּן תְּהִלָּתְךָ עַל־קַצְוֵי־אֶרֶץ, צֶדֶק מָלְאָה יְמִינֶךָ: יִשְׂמַח הַר־צִיּוֹן, תָּגֵלְנָה בְּנוֹת יְהוּדָה, לְמַעַן מִשְׁפָּטֶיךָ: סֹבּוּ צִיּוֹן וְהַקִּיפוּהָ, סִפְרוּ מִגְדָּלֶיהָ: שִׁיתוּ לִבְּכֶם לְחֵילָה, פַּסְּגוּ אַרְמְנוֹתֶיהָ, לְמַעַן תְּסַפְּרוּ לְדוֹר אַחֲרוֹן: ‹ כִּי זֶה אֱלֹהִים אֱלֹהֵינוּ עוֹלָם וָעֶד, הוּא יְנַהֲגֵנוּ עַל־מוּת:

קדיש יתום (*page 203*)

Tuesday הַיּוֹם יוֹם שְׁלִישִׁי בְּשַׁבָּת, שֶׁבּוֹ הָיוּ הַלְוִיִּם אוֹמְרִים בְּבֵית הַמִּקְדָּשׁ:

מִזְמוֹר לְאָסָף, אֱלֹהִים נִצָּב בַּעֲדַת־אֵל, בְּקֶרֶב אֱלֹהִים יִשְׁפֹּט: עַד־מָתַי תִּשְׁפְּטוּ־עָוֶל, וּפְנֵי רְשָׁעִים תִּשְׂאוּ־סֶלָה: שִׁפְטוּ־דַל וְיָתוֹם, עָנִי וָרָשׁ הַצְדִּיקוּ: פַּלְּטוּ־דַל וְאֶבְיוֹן, מִיַּד רְשָׁעִים הַצִּילוּ: לֹא יָדְעוּ וְלֹא יָבִינוּ, בַּחֲשֵׁכָה יִתְהַלָּכוּ, יִמּוֹטוּ כָּל־מוֹסְדֵי אָרֶץ: אֲנִי־אָמַרְתִּי אֱלֹהִים אַתֶּם, וּבְנֵי עֶלְיוֹן כֻּלְּכֶם: אָכֵן כְּאָדָם תְּמוּתוּן, וּכְאַחַד הַשָּׂרִים תִּפֹּלוּ: ‹ קוּמָה אֱלֹהִים שָׁפְטָה הָאָרֶץ, כִּי־אַתָּה תִנְחַל בְּכָל־הַגּוֹיִם:

קדיש יתום (*page 203*)

Wednesday הַיּוֹם יוֹם רְבִיעִי בְּשַׁבָּת, שֶׁבּוֹ הָיוּ הַלְוִיִּם אוֹמְרִים בְּבֵית הַמִּקְדָּשׁ:

אֵל־נְקָמוֹת יהוה, אֵל נְקָמוֹת הוֹפִיעַ: הִנָּשֵׂא שֹׁפֵט הָאָרֶץ, הָשֵׁב גְּמוּל עַל־גֵּאִים: עַד־מָתַי רְשָׁעִים, יהוה, עַד־מָתַי רְשָׁעִים יַעֲלֹזוּ: יַבִּיעוּ יְדַבְּרוּ עָתָק, יִתְאַמְּרוּ כָּל־פֹּעֲלֵי אָוֶן: עַמְּךָ יהוה יְדַכְּאוּ, וְנַחֲלָתְךָ יְעַנּוּ: אַלְמָנָה וְגֵר יַהֲרֹגוּ,

The wicked people do not take pity
on Your Jewish people;
instead they speak lies and hurt them,
saying, "God will not see."
If only the wicked people knew
that it is *Hashem*
who gives the eye the ability to see
and the ear the ability to hear.
Hashem will not abandon His Jewish people,
but will punish the nations that try to hurt us.

▸ Come and let us sing to *Hashem*
as we call out to our hero to save us.
Let us greet Him with our thanks and praise.
Hashem is the great God
and King over all other powers.

Kaddish Yatom (page 202)

Thursday: Today is the fifth day of the week.
On this day, the Levi'im said the following
in the *Beit HaMikdash*:

לַמְנַצֵּחַ *Hashem* gives us strength.
Sing to *Hashem* with happiness,
and sound the drum, harp, and other instruments!

וִיתוֹמִים יְרַצֵּחוּ: וַיֹּאמְרוּ לֹא יִרְאֶה־יָּהּ, וְלֹא־יָבִין אֱלֹהֵי יַעֲקֹב: בִּינוּ בֹּעֲרִים בָּעָם, וּכְסִילִים מָתַי תַּשְׂכִּילוּ: הֲנֹטַע אֹזֶן הֲלֹא יִשְׁמָע, אִם־יֹצֵר עַיִן הֲלֹא יַבִּיט: הֲיֹסֵר גּוֹיִם הֲלֹא יוֹכִיחַ, הַמְלַמֵּד אָדָם דָּעַת: יהוה יֹדֵעַ מַחְשְׁבוֹת אָדָם, כִּי־הֵמָּה הָבֶל: אַשְׁרֵי הַגֶּבֶר אֲשֶׁר־תְּיַסְּרֶנּוּ יָּהּ, וּמִתּוֹרָתְךָ תְלַמְּדֶנּוּ: לְהַשְׁקִיט לוֹ מִימֵי רָע, עַד יִכָּרֶה לָרָשָׁע שָׁחַת: כִּי לֹא־יִטֹּשׁ יהוה עַמּוֹ, וְנַחֲלָתוֹ לֹא יַעֲזֹב: כִּי־עַד־צֶדֶק יָשׁוּב מִשְׁפָּט, וְאַחֲרָיו כָּל־יִשְׁרֵי־לֵב: מִי־יָקוּם לִי עִם־מְרֵעִים, מִי־יִתְיַצֵּב לִי עִם־פֹּעֲלֵי אָוֶן: לוּלֵי יהוה עֶזְרָתָה לִּי, כִּמְעַט שָׁכְנָה דוּמָה נַפְשִׁי: אִם־אָמַרְתִּי מָטָה רַגְלִי, חַסְדְּךָ יהוה יִסְעָדֵנִי: בְּרֹב שַׂרְעַפַּי בְּקִרְבִּי, תַּנְחוּמֶיךָ יְשַׁעַשְׁעוּ נַפְשִׁי: הַיְחָבְרְךָ כִּסֵּא הַוּוֹת, יֹצֵר עָמָל עֲלֵי־חֹק: יָגוֹדּוּ עַל־נֶפֶשׁ צַדִּיק, וְדָם נָקִי יַרְשִׁיעוּ: וַיְהִי יהוה לִי לְמִשְׂגָּב, וֵאלֹהַי לְצוּר מַחְסִי: וַיָּשֶׁב עֲלֵיהֶם אֶת־אוֹנָם, וּבְרָעָתָם יַצְמִיתֵם, יַצְמִיתֵם יהוה אֱלֹהֵינוּ:

› לְכוּ נְרַנְּנָה לַיהוה, נָרִיעָה לְצוּר יִשְׁעֵנוּ: נְקַדְּמָה פָנָיו בְּתוֹדָה, בִּזְמִרוֹת נָרִיעַ לוֹ: כִּי אֵל גָּדוֹל יהוה, וּמֶלֶךְ גָּדוֹל עַל־כָּל־אֱלֹהִים:

קדיש יתום (*page 203*)

Thursday הַיּוֹם יוֹם חֲמִישִׁי בְּשַׁבָּת, שֶׁבּוֹ הָיוּ הַלְוִיִּם אוֹמְרִים בְּבֵית הַמִּקְדָּשׁ:

לַמְנַצֵּחַ עַל־הַגִּתִּית לְאָסָף: הַרְנִינוּ לֵאלֹהִים עוּזֵּנוּ, הָרִיעוּ לֵאלֹהֵי יַעֲקֹב: שְׂאוּ־זִמְרָה וּתְנוּ־תֹף, כִּנּוֹר נָעִים עִם־נָבֶל:

Hashem freed His Jewish people from slavery in Egypt.
Every Rosh Hashana,
we blow the shofar to remember
that on this day we were freed from work as slaves.
When we felt troubled in Egypt,
we called out to *Hashem* and He answered us.
Do not turn to any other god,
for it is *Hashem* who freed us from Egypt,
and it is *Hashem* who provides for us
when we are in need.
If we follow in the ways of *Hashem*,
Hashem could destroy all of our enemies in one moment.
▸ We only need to open our mouths to *Hashem*,
and He will take care of us.

Kaddish Yatom (page 202)

Friday: Today is the sixth day of the week.
On this day, the Levi'im said the following
in the *Beit HaMikdash*:

יהוה מָלָךְ *Hashem* is King,
dressed in greatness and might!
From His throne He created the world;
Hashem lives forever.
As a river flows so will our enemies come against us,
but You, *Hashem* are mightier
than the many waves of the sea.
▸ We fully believe in You.
Hashem, may Your home, the *Beit HaMikdash*,
stand for a long time.

תִּקְעוּ בַחֹדֶשׁ שׁוֹפָר, בַּכֶּסֶה לְיוֹם חַגֵּנוּ: כִּי חֹק לְיִשְׂרָאֵל הוּא, מִשְׁפָּט לֵאלֹהֵי יַעֲקֹב: עֵדוּת בִּיהוֹסֵף שָׂמוֹ, בְּצֵאתוֹ עַל־אֶרֶץ מִצְרָיִם, שְׂפַת לֹא־יָדַעְתִּי אֶשְׁמָע: הֲסִירוֹתִי מִסֵּבֶל שִׁכְמוֹ, כַּפָּיו מִדּוּד תַּעֲבֹרְנָה: בַּצָּרָה קָרָאתָ וָאֲחַלְּצֶךָּ, אֶעֶנְךָ בְּסֵתֶר רַעַם, אֶבְחָנְךָ עַל־מֵי מְרִיבָה סֶלָה: שְׁמַע עַמִּי וְאָעִידָה בָּךְ, יִשְׂרָאֵל אִם־תִּשְׁמַע־לִי: לֹא־יִהְיֶה בְךָ אֵל זָר, וְלֹא תִשְׁתַּחֲוֶה לְאֵל נֵכָר: אָנֹכִי יהוה אֱלֹהֶיךָ, הַמַּעַלְךָ מֵאֶרֶץ מִצְרָיִם, הַרְחֶב־פִּיךָ וַאֲמַלְאֵהוּ: וְלֹא־שָׁמַע עַמִּי לְקוֹלִי, וְיִשְׂרָאֵל לֹא־אָבָה לִי: וָאֲשַׁלְּחֵהוּ בִּשְׁרִירוּת לִבָּם, יֵלְכוּ בְּמוֹעֲצוֹתֵיהֶם: לוּ עַמִּי שֹׁמֵעַ לִי, יִשְׂרָאֵל בִּדְרָכַי יְהַלֵּכוּ: כִּמְעַט אוֹיְבֵיהֶם אַכְנִיעַ, וְעַל־צָרֵיהֶם אָשִׁיב יָדִי: מְשַׂנְאֵי יהוה יְכַחֲשׁוּ־לוֹ, וִיהִי עִתָּם לְעוֹלָם: ‹ וַיַּאֲכִילֵהוּ מֵחֵלֶב חִטָּה, וּמִצּוּר, דְּבַשׁ אַשְׂבִּיעֶךָ:

קדיש יתום (*page 203*)

Friday הַיּוֹם יוֹם שִׁשִּׁי בְּשַׁבָּת, שֶׁבּוֹ הָיוּ הַלְוִיִּם אוֹמְרִים בְּבֵית הַמִּקְדָּשׁ

יהוה מָלָךְ, גֵּאוּת לָבֵשׁ, לָבֵשׁ יהוה עֹז הִתְאַזָּר, אַף־תִּכּוֹן תֵּבֵל בַּל־תִּמּוֹט: נָכוֹן כִּסְאֲךָ מֵאָז, מֵעוֹלָם אָתָּה: נָשְׂאוּ נְהָרוֹת יהוה, נָשְׂאוּ נְהָרוֹת קוֹלָם, יִשְׂאוּ נְהָרוֹת דָּכְיָם: מִקֹּלוֹת מַיִם רַבִּים, אַדִּירִים מִשְׁבְּרֵי־יָם, אַדִּיר בַּמָּרוֹם יהוה: ‹ עֵדֹתֶיךָ נֶאֶמְנוּ מְאֹד, לְבֵיתְךָ נַאֲוָה־קֹדֶשׁ, יהוה לְאֹרֶךְ יָמִים:

KADDISH YATOM

The following prayer, said by mourners, requires the presence of a minyan. A transliteration can be found on page 865.

Mourner: יִתְגַּדַּל May *Hashem* be recognized
as great and holy (*Congregation:* Amen)
in the world that He created.
May He establish His kingdom
during my lifetime
and the lifetime of all Jews,
quickly and soon.
Let us say: "Amen" (*Congregation:* Amen).

Congregation: May we thank *Hashem* for ever and ever.
Mourner: May we thank *Hashem* for ever and ever.

Mourner: *Hashem* should be thanked, praised,
and honored (*Congregation:* He is blessed).
Hashem is beyond all the blessings,
songs, or praises
that we could offer.
Let us say: "Amen" (*Congregation:* Amen).

May *Hashem* give us, and all Jews,
peace and good life.
Let us say: "Amen." (*Congregation:* Amen).

The mourner takes three steps back before saying this line, bows to the left when saying "May," bows to the right when saying "the One," bows to the middle when saying "make peace for us":

May *Hashem*, the One
who makes peace in heaven,
make peace for us and for all Jews.
Let us say: "Amen." (*Congregation:* Amen).

קדיש יתום

The following prayer, said by mourners, requires the presence of a מנין.
A transliteration can be found on page 865.

אבל: יִתְגַּדַּל וְיִתְקַדַּשׁ שְׁמֵהּ רַבָּא (קהל: אָמֵן)
בְּעָלְמָא דִּי בְרָא כִרְעוּתֵהּ, וְיַמְלִיךְ מַלְכוּתֵהּ
בְּחַיֵּיכוֹן וּבְיוֹמֵיכוֹן וּבְחַיֵּי דְכָל בֵּית יִשְׂרָאֵל
בַּעֲגָלָא וּבִזְמַן קָרִיב, וְאִמְרוּ אָמֵן. (קהל: אָמֵן)

קהל יְהֵא שְׁמֵהּ רַבָּא מְבָרַךְ לְעָלַם וּלְעָלְמֵי עָלְמַיָּא.
אבל: יְהֵא שְׁמֵהּ רַבָּא מְבָרַךְ לְעָלַם וּלְעָלְמֵי עָלְמַיָּא.

אבל: יִתְבָּרַךְ וְיִשְׁתַּבַּח וְיִתְפָּאַר
וְיִתְרוֹמַם וְיִתְנַשֵּׂא וְיִתְהַדָּר וְיִתְעַלֶּה וְיִתְהַלָּל
שְׁמֵהּ דְּקֻדְשָׁא בְּרִיךְ הוּא (קהל: בְּרִיךְ הוּא)
לְעֵלָּא מִן כָּל בִּרְכָתָא
/בעשרת ימי תשובה: לְעֵלָּא לְעֵלָּא מִכָּל בִּרְכָתָא/
וְשִׁירָתָא, תֻּשְׁבְּחָתָא וְנֶחֱמָתָא
דַּאֲמִירָן בְּעָלְמָא, וְאִמְרוּ אָמֵן. (קהל: אָמֵן)

יְהֵא שְׁלָמָא רַבָּא מִן שְׁמַיָּא
וְחַיִּים, עָלֵינוּ וְעַל כָּל יִשְׂרָאֵל, וְאִמְרוּ אָמֵן. (קהל: אָמֵן)

The mourner takes three steps back before saying this line, bows to the left when saying עֹשֶׂה*, bows to the right when saying* הוּא*, bows to the middle when saying* יַעֲשֶׂה שָׁלוֹם עָלֵינוּ*:*

עֹשֶׂה שָׁלוֹם /בעשרת ימי תשובה: הַשָּׁלוֹם/ בִּמְרוֹמָיו
הוּא יַעֲשֶׂה שָׁלוֹם עָלֵינוּ
וְעַל כָּל יִשְׂרָאֵל, וְאִמְרוּ אָמֵן. (קהל: אָמֵן)

On Rosh Chodesh, say the following:

בָּרְכִי נַפְשִׁי I thank You, *Hashem,* my God,
who is truly great.
You created:
Light,
The sky,
Clouds,
Water,
Wind, and
Fire.

All these elements serve as messengers of *Hashem.*
Hashem, You created the earth to last forever
and covered it with water and mountains.
Hashem, You control the water,
providing drink for man and animal.
You provide water for fields
to produce plants.
You make grass grow
for the animals,
and plants grow for man
so that he can produce wine, oil, and bread.
You, *Hashem,* give the birds trees to build their nests.
You give the goats mountains to live on,
and badgers rocks to hide in.
You gave us the moon
for setting the dates of our holidays on the calendar
and the sun to begin and end each day.
Hashem, how many are Your creations?

On ראש חודש*, say the following:*

בָּרְכִי נַפְשִׁי אֶת־יהוה, יהוה אֱלֹהַי גָּדַלְתָּ מְּאֹד, הוֹד
וְהָדָר לָבָשְׁתָּ: עֹטֶה־אוֹר כַּשַּׂלְמָה, נוֹטֶה שָׁמַיִם כַּיְרִיעָה:
הַמְקָרֶה בַמַּיִם עֲלִיּוֹתָיו, הַשָּׂם־עָבִים רְכוּבוֹ, הַמְהַלֵּךְ עַל־
כַּנְפֵי־רוּחַ: עֹשֶׂה מַלְאָכָיו רוּחוֹת, מְשָׁרְתָיו אֵשׁ לֹהֵט: יָסַד־
אֶרֶץ עַל־מְכוֹנֶיהָ, בַּל־תִּמּוֹט עוֹלָם וָעֶד: תְּהוֹם כַּלְּבוּשׁ
כִּסִּיתוֹ, עַל־הָרִים יַעַמְדוּ־מָיִם: מִן־גַּעֲרָתְךָ יְנוּסוּן, מִן־קוֹל
רַעַמְךָ יֵחָפֵזוּן: יַעֲלוּ הָרִים, יֵרְדוּ בְקָעוֹת, אֶל־מְקוֹם זֶה
יָסַדְתָּ לָהֶם: גְּבוּל־שַׂמְתָּ בַּל־יַעֲבֹרוּן, בַּל־יְשׁוּבוּן לְכַסּוֹת
הָאָרֶץ: הַמְשַׁלֵּחַ מַעְיָנִים בַּנְּחָלִים, בֵּין הָרִים יְהַלֵּכוּן:
יַשְׁקוּ כָּל־חַיְתוֹ שָׂדָי, יִשְׁבְּרוּ פְרָאִים צְמָאָם: עֲלֵיהֶם
עוֹף־הַשָּׁמַיִם יִשְׁכּוֹן, מִבֵּין עֳפָאיִם יִתְּנוּ־קוֹל: מַשְׁקֶה
הָרִים מֵעֲלִיּוֹתָיו, מִפְּרִי מַעֲשֶׂיךָ תִּשְׂבַּע הָאָרֶץ: מַצְמִיחַ
חָצִיר לַבְּהֵמָה, וְעֵשֶׂב לַעֲבֹדַת הָאָדָם, לְהוֹצִיא לֶחֶם מִן־
הָאָרֶץ: וְיַיִן יְשַׂמַּח לְבַב־אֱנוֹשׁ, לְהַצְהִיל פָּנִים מִשָּׁמֶן,
וְלֶחֶם לְבַב־אֱנוֹשׁ יִסְעָד: יִשְׂבְּעוּ עֲצֵי יהוה, אַרְזֵי לְבָנוֹן
אֲשֶׁר נָטָע: אֲשֶׁר־שָׁם צִפֳּרִים יְקַנֵּנוּ, חֲסִידָה בְּרוֹשִׁים
בֵּיתָהּ: הָרִים הַגְּבֹהִים לַיְּעֵלִים, סְלָעִים מַחְסֶה לַשְׁפַנִּים:
עָשָׂה יָרֵחַ לְמוֹעֲדִים, שֶׁמֶשׁ יָדַע מְבוֹאוֹ: תָּשֶׁת־חֹשֶׁךְ
וִיהִי לָיְלָה, בּוֹ־תִרְמֹשׂ כָּל־חַיְתוֹ־יָעַר: הַכְּפִירִים שֹׁאֲגִים
לַטָּרֶף, וּלְבַקֵּשׁ מֵאֵל אָכְלָם: תִּזְרַח הַשֶּׁמֶשׁ יֵאָסֵפוּן, וְאֶל־
מְעוֹנֹתָם יִרְבָּצוּן: יֵצֵא אָדָם לְפָעֳלוֹ, וְלַעֲבֹדָתוֹ עֲדֵי־עָרֶב:

You created them all with wisdom.
You created the vast sea
with uncountable numbers of creatures.
Every person and animal on earth
turns to You for the food we need to live.
Only when You, *Hashem,* open Your hand
and provide for us are we given what we need.
Hashem, You created us
and You can also take away our breath.
When You restore Your breath,
everyone will be given new life.
Hashem, may Your glory last forever.
▸I will sing sweet songs of praise to You for as long as I live.
We thank You, *Hashem,* who destroys our enemies
and allows us to live and celebrate.

Kaddish Yatom (page 202)

From the second day of Rosh Chodesh Elul until Shemini Atzeret add the following:

לְדָוִד David HaMelech wrote:
I have no fear because *Hashem* protects me
and brings light to my darkness.
When enemies or even armies attack,
I am not afraid as I trust that *Hashem* will defeat them.
The only thing that I ask of *Hashem*
is to see the *Beit HaMikdash* built
and be able to serve Him there.
Hashem is my protector;
He will take me in and hide me from my enemies.
When I feel safe, I will sing songs of praise to *Hashem.*

מָה־רַבּוּ מַעֲשֶׂיךָ יהוה, כֻּלָּם בְּחָכְמָה עָשִׂיתָ, מָלְאָה הָאָרֶץ קִנְיָנֶךָ: זֶה הַיָּם גָּדוֹל וּרְחַב יָדָיִם, שָׁם־רֶמֶשׂ וְאֵין מִסְפָּר, חַיּוֹת קְטַנּוֹת עִם־גְּדֹלוֹת: שָׁם אֳנִיּוֹת יְהַלֵּכוּן, לִוְיָתָן זֶה־יָצַרְתָּ לְשַׂחֶק־בּוֹ: כֻּלָּם אֵלֶיךָ יְשַׂבֵּרוּן, לָתֵת אָכְלָם בְּעִתּוֹ: תִּתֵּן לָהֶם יִלְקֹטוּן, תִּפְתַּח יָדְךָ יִשְׂבְּעוּן טוֹב: תַּסְתִּיר פָּנֶיךָ יִבָּהֵלוּן, תֹּסֵף רוּחָם יִגְוָעוּן, וְאֶל־עֲפָרָם יְשׁוּבוּן: תְּשַׁלַּח רוּחֲךָ יִבָּרֵאוּן, וּתְחַדֵּשׁ פְּנֵי אֲדָמָה: יְהִי כְבוֹד יהוה לְעוֹלָם, יִשְׂמַח יהוה בְּמַעֲשָׂיו: הַמַּבִּיט לָאָרֶץ וַתִּרְעָד, יִגַּע בֶּהָרִים וְיֶעֱשָׁנוּ: אָשִׁירָה לַיהוה בְּחַיָּי, אֲזַמְּרָה לֵאלֹהַי בְּעוֹדִי: ‹ יֶעֱרַב עָלָיו שִׂיחִי, אָנֹכִי אֶשְׂמַח בַּיהוה: יִתַּמּוּ חַטָּאִים מִן־הָאָרֶץ, וּרְשָׁעִים עוֹד אֵינָם, בָּרְכִי נַפְשִׁי אֶת־יהוה, הַלְלוּיָהּ:

קדיש יתום (*page 203*)

From the second day of ראש חודש אלול *until* שמיני עצרת *add the following:*

לְדָוִד, יהוה אוֹרִי וְיִשְׁעִי, מִמִּי אִירָא, יהוה מָעוֹז־חַיַּי, מִמִּי אֶפְחָד: בִּקְרֹב עָלַי מְרֵעִים לֶאֱכֹל אֶת־בְּשָׂרִי, צָרַי וְאֹיְבַי לִי, הֵמָּה כָשְׁלוּ וְנָפָלוּ: אִם־תַּחֲנֶה עָלַי מַחֲנֶה, לֹא־יִירָא לִבִּי, אִם־תָּקוּם עָלַי מִלְחָמָה, בְּזֹאת אֲנִי בוֹטֵחַ: אַחַת שָׁאַלְתִּי מֵאֵת־יהוה, אוֹתָהּ אֲבַקֵּשׁ, שִׁבְתִּי בְּבֵית־יהוה כָּל־יְמֵי חַיַּי, לַחֲזוֹת בְּנֹעַם־יהוה, וּלְבַקֵּר בְּהֵיכָלוֹ: כִּי יִצְפְּנֵנִי בְּסֻכֹּה בְּיוֹם רָעָה, יַסְתִּרֵנִי בְּסֵתֶר אָהֳלוֹ, בְּצוּר יְרוֹמְמֵנִי: וְעַתָּה יָרוּם רֹאשִׁי עַל אֹיְבַי סְבִיבוֹתַי, וְאֶזְבְּחָה בְאָהֳלוֹ

Hashem, listen to my voice when I call for help
and please answer me.
Do not ignore or hide from me, when You are angry.
My heart knows it is only You to whom I can call for help.
Hashem, help us learn how to make the right choices
and not make mistakes.
▸ I trust in *Hashem,* I hope for His help at all times;
He gives me strength and courage.

Kaddish Yatom (page 202)

On Chanuka insert the following:

מִזְמוֹר This is a prayer written by David HaMelech
in honor of the first use of the *Beit HaMikdash*:
I praise *Hashem* who saves me from my enemies.
Hashem's anger lasts for a moment
but His kindness lasts forever.
In the dark of night I may weep
but *Hashem* brings the morning filled with light and joy.
Knowing that *Hashem* supports me, gives me strength.
Were *Hashem* to hide from me it would be terrifying.
When I cry out for help it is *Hashem* who saves me.
Listen *Hashem* and show kindness to me;
Hashem please help me.
The dust and the dirt
do not have the ability to thank You like I do.
▸ *Hashem,* You have turned my sadness and sorrow
into joy and dancing.
From my soul I will sing to You and not be silent.
Hashem, I will always thank You.

Kaddish Yatom (page 202)

זִבְחֵי תְרוּעָה, אָשִׁירָה וַאֲזַמְּרָה לַיהוה: שְׁמַע־יהוה קוֹלִי אֶקְרָא, וְחָנֵּנִי וַעֲנֵנִי: לְךָ אָמַר לִבִּי בַּקְּשׁוּ פָנָי, אֶת־פָּנֶיךָ יהוה אֲבַקֵּשׁ: אַל־תַּסְתֵּר פָּנֶיךָ מִמֶּנִּי, אַל תַּט־בְּאַף עַבְדֶּךָ, עֶזְרָתִי הָיִיתָ, אַל־תִּטְּשֵׁנִי וְאַל־תַּעַזְבֵנִי, אֱלֹהֵי יִשְׁעִי: כִּי־אָבִי וְאִמִּי עֲזָבוּנִי, וַיהוה יַאַסְפֵנִי: הוֹרֵנִי יהוה דַּרְכֶּךָ, וּנְחֵנִי בְּאֹרַח מִישׁוֹר, לְמַעַן שׁוֹרְרָי: אַל־תִּתְּנֵנִי בְּנֶפֶשׁ צָרָי, כִּי קָמוּ־בִי עֵדֵי־שֶׁקֶר, וִיפֵחַ חָמָס: ‹ לוּלֵא הֶאֱמַנְתִּי לִרְאוֹת בְּטוּב־יהוה בְּאֶרֶץ חַיִּים: קַוֵּה אֶל־יהוה, חֲזַק וְיַאֲמֵץ לִבֶּךָ, וְקַוֵּה אֶל־יהוה:

קדיש יתום (*page 203*)

On חנוכה *insert the following:*

מִזְמוֹר שִׁיר־חֲנֻכַּת הַבַּיִת לְדָוִד: אֲרוֹמִמְךָ יהוה כִּי דִלִּיתָנִי, וְלֹא־שִׂמַּחְתָּ אֹיְבַי לִי: יהוה אֱלֹהָי, שִׁוַּעְתִּי אֵלֶיךָ וַתִּרְפָּאֵנִי: יהוה, הֶעֱלִיתָ מִן־שְׁאוֹל נַפְשִׁי, חִיִּיתַנִי מִיָּרְדִי־בוֹר: זַמְּרוּ לַיהוה חֲסִידָיו, וְהוֹדוּ לְזֵכֶר קָדְשׁוֹ: כִּי רֶגַע בְּאַפּוֹ, חַיִּים בִּרְצוֹנוֹ, בָּעֶרֶב יָלִין בֶּכִי וְלַבֹּקֶר רִנָּה: וַאֲנִי אָמַרְתִּי בְשַׁלְוִי, בַּל־אֶמּוֹט לְעוֹלָם: יהוה, בִּרְצוֹנְךָ הֶעֱמַדְתָּה לְהַרְרִי עֹז, הִסְתַּרְתָּ פָנֶיךָ הָיִיתִי נִבְהָל: אֵלֶיךָ יהוה אֶקְרָא, וְאֶל־אֲדֹנָי אֶתְחַנָּן: מַה־בֶּצַע בְּדָמִי, בְּרִדְתִּי אֶל שָׁחַת, הֲיוֹדְךָ עָפָר, הֲיַגִּיד אֲמִתֶּךָ: שְׁמַע־יהוה וְחָנֵּנִי, יהוה הֱיֵה־עֹזֵר לִי: ‹ הָפַכְתָּ מִסְפְּדִי לְמָחוֹל לִי, פִּתַּחְתָּ שַׂקִּי, וַתְּאַזְּרֵנִי שִׂמְחָה: לְמַעַן יְזַמֶּרְךָ כָבוֹד וְלֹא יִדֹּם, יהוה אֱלֹהַי, לְעוֹלָם אוֹדֶךָּ:

קדיש יתום (*page 203*)

Many congregations say the following paragraphs after tefilla:

שִׁיר לַמַּעֲלוֹת I look to the top of the mountains and ask,
"Where will help come from?"
Help is only from *Hashem*
who made the heavens and earth.
Hashem does not sleep;
He is always there protecting me
and the entire Jewish people.
Hashem always protects us;
the sun will not burn us during the day
and we will not be harmed at night.
Now and forever *Hashem* will protect us,
wherever we are.

שִׁיר הַמַּעֲלוֹת From the depths of my soul,
I call to You, *Hashem,* when I need You the most.
Please hear my cries, *Hashem,* and listen to my requests.
You, *Hashem,* forgive our mistakes,
so we can be deserving of being helped.
I put all my hope in You, *Hashem,*
and constantly look forward to the time
when You will bring *Mashiach.*
Hashem, in Your kindness save Your Jewish people.

אַחֵינוּ May *Hashem* show mercy
to all members of our family, the Jewish people,
who are struggling or who have been taken captive.
Hashem, quickly lead these people
from difficult times to safety, from darkness to light,
and from suffering to freedom.

Many congregations say the following paragraphs after tefilla:

שִׁיר לַמַּעֲלוֹת, אֶשָּׂא עֵינַי אֶל־הֶהָרִים, מֵאַיִן יָבֹא עֶזְרִי: עֶזְרִי מֵעִם יהוה, עֹשֵׂה שָׁמַיִם וָאָרֶץ: אַל־יִתֵּן לַמּוֹט רַגְלֶךָ, אַל־יָנוּם שֹׁמְרֶךָ: הִנֵּה לֹא־יָנוּם וְלֹא יִישָׁן, שׁוֹמֵר יִשְׂרָאֵל: יהוה שֹׁמְרֶךָ, יהוה צִלְּךָ עַל־יַד יְמִינֶךָ: יוֹמָם הַשֶּׁמֶשׁ לֹא־יַכֶּכָּה, וְיָרֵחַ בַּלָּיְלָה: יהוה יִשְׁמָרְךָ מִכָּל־רָע, יִשְׁמֹר אֶת־נַפְשֶׁךָ: יהוה יִשְׁמָר־צֵאתְךָ וּבוֹאֶךָ, מֵעַתָּה וְעַד־עוֹלָם:

שִׁיר הַמַּעֲלוֹת, מִמַּעֲמַקִּים קְרָאתִיךָ יהוה: אֲדֹנָי שִׁמְעָה בְקוֹלִי, תִּהְיֶינָה אָזְנֶיךָ קַשֻּׁבוֹת לְקוֹל תַּחֲנוּנָי: אִם־עֲוֹנוֹת תִּשְׁמָר־יָהּ, אֲדֹנָי מִי יַעֲמֹד: כִּי־עִמְּךָ הַסְּלִיחָה, לְמַעַן תִּוָּרֵא: קִוִּיתִי יהוה קִוְּתָה נַפְשִׁי, וְלִדְבָרוֹ הוֹחָלְתִּי: נַפְשִׁי לַאדֹנָי, מִשֹּׁמְרִים לַבֹּקֶר, שֹׁמְרִים לַבֹּקֶר: יַחֵל יִשְׂרָאֵל אֶל־יהוה, כִּי־עִם־יהוה הַחֶסֶד, וְהַרְבֵּה עִמּוֹ פְדוּת: וְהוּא יִפְדֶּה אֶת־יִשְׂרָאֵל, מִכֹּל עֲוֹנוֹתָיו:

אַחֵינוּ כָּל בֵּית יִשְׂרָאֵל\
הַנְּתוּנִים בְּצָרָה וּבְשִׁבְיָה\
הָעוֹמְדִים בֵּין בַּיָּם וּבֵין בַּיַּבָּשָׁה\
הַמָּקוֹם יְרַחֵם עֲלֵיהֶם וְיוֹצִיאֵם מִצָּרָה לִרְוָחָה\
וּמֵאֲפֵלָה לְאוֹרָה, וּמִשִּׁעְבּוּד לִגְאֻלָּה\
הַשְׁתָּא בַּעֲגָלָא וּבִזְמַן קָרִיב\
וְנֹאמַר אָמֵן.

Mincha

The line beginning with "Hashem opens His hands" should be said with special concentration.

אַשְׁרֵי We are happy with the opportunity to sit and pray. We are happy that You are our God and that we are Your people.

David HaMelech wrote this song:

א GOD – *Hashem* is our God and King.

ב THANK – We appreciate *Hashem* and we will thank Him every day, forever.

ג GREATNESS – *Hashem*'s greatness is endless.

ד GENERATIONS – We will tell our children about the spectacular actions You have done for us in every generation.

ה MIRACLES – The miracles that *Hashem* performs for His people are glorious.

ו STRENGTH – *Hashem*'s strength is awesome beyond comparison.

ז REMEMBER – We remember the good that *Hashem* does for us.

ח MERCY – *Hashem* is slow to get angry.

ט GOODNESS – *Hashem* is good to all His creations, humans and animals alike.

י KINDNESS – All creations of *Hashem* are thankful for His kindness.

כ HONOR – We give *Hashem* the honor that He deserves.

ל MIGHTY – We inform all people of *Hashem*'s mighty actions.

מ KINGSHIP – *Hashem* has and always will rule the world.

מנחה

The line beginning with פּוֹתֵחַ אֶת יָדֶךָ *should be said with special concentration.*

אַשְׁרֵי יוֹשְׁבֵי בֵיתֶךָ, עוֹד יְהַלְלוּךָ סֶּלָה:
אַשְׁרֵי הָעָם שֶׁכָּכָה לּוֹ
אַשְׁרֵי הָעָם שֶׁיהוה אֱלֹהָיו:
תְּהִלָּה לְדָוִד
אֲרוֹמִמְךָ אֱלוֹהַי הַמֶּלֶךְ, וַאֲבָרְכָה שִׁמְךָ לְעוֹלָם וָעֶד:
בְּכָל־יוֹם אֲבָרְכֶךָּ, וַאֲהַלְלָה שִׁמְךָ לְעוֹלָם וָעֶד:
גָּדוֹל יהוה וּמְהֻלָּל מְאֹד, וְלִגְדֻלָּתוֹ אֵין חֵקֶר:
דּוֹר לְדוֹר יְשַׁבַּח מַעֲשֶׂיךָ, וּגְבוּרֹתֶיךָ יַגִּידוּ:
הֲדַר כְּבוֹד הוֹדֶךָ, וְדִבְרֵי נִפְלְאֹתֶיךָ אָשִׂיחָה:
וֶעֱזוּז נוֹרְאֹתֶיךָ יֹאמֵרוּ, וּגְדוּלָּתְךָ אֲסַפְּרֶנָּה:
זֵכֶר רַב־טוּבְךָ יַבִּיעוּ, וְצִדְקָתְךָ יְרַנֵּנוּ:
חַנּוּן וְרַחוּם יהוה, אֶרֶךְ אַפַּיִם וּגְדָל־חָסֶד:
טוֹב־יהוה לַכֹּל, וְרַחֲמָיו עַל־כָּל־מַעֲשָׂיו:
יוֹדוּךָ יהוה כָּל־מַעֲשֶׂיךָ, וַחֲסִידֶיךָ יְבָרְכוּכָה:
כְּבוֹד מַלְכוּתְךָ יֹאמֵרוּ, וּגְבוּרָתְךָ יְדַבֵּרוּ:
לְהוֹדִיעַ לִבְנֵי הָאָדָם גְּבוּרֹתָיו, וּכְבוֹד הֲדַר מַלְכוּתוֹ:
מַלְכוּתְךָ מַלְכוּת כָּל־עֹלָמִים
וּמֶמְשַׁלְתְּךָ בְּכָל־דּוֹר וָדֹר:

ס HELP – *Hashem* helps us when we need Him.

ע RELY – We rely on *Hashem* to give us the food that we need to live.

פ PROVIDES – *Hashem* opens His hands and provides us with our needs.

צ RIGHTEOUS – Everything *Hashem* does is righteous and with good intentions.

ק CLOSENESS – *Hashem* is close to all those that call out to Him.

ר SAVES – *Hashem* listens to our cries and saves those in need.

ש GUARDS – *Hashem* protects all those who love Him and turn to Him in times of need.

▸ ת PRAISE – For all of these reasons, everyone praises *Hashem* and thanks Him every day.

HALF KADDISH

Leader: יִתְגַּדַּל May *Hashem* be recognized
as great and holy (*Congregation:* Amen)
in the world that He created.
May He establish His kingdom
during my lifetime
and the lifetime of all Jews,
quickly and soon.
Let us say:
"Amen" (*Congregation:* Amen).

Congregation: May we thank *Hashem* for ever and ever.
Leader: May we thank *Hashem* for ever and ever.

סוֹמֵךְ יהוה לְכָל־הַנֹּפְלִים, וְזוֹקֵף לְכָל־הַכְּפוּפִים:
עֵינֵי־כֹל אֵלֶיךָ יְשַׂבֵּרוּ
וְאַתָּה נוֹתֵן־לָהֶם אֶת־אָכְלָם בְּעִתּוֹ:
פּוֹתֵחַ אֶת־יָדֶךָ, וּמַשְׂבִּיעַ לְכָל־חַי רָצוֹן:
צַדִּיק יהוה בְּכָל־דְּרָכָיו, וְחָסִיד בְּכָל־מַעֲשָׂיו:
קָרוֹב יהוה לְכָל־קֹרְאָיו, לְכֹל אֲשֶׁר יִקְרָאֻהוּ בֶאֱמֶת:
רְצוֹן־יְרֵאָיו יַעֲשֶׂה, וְאֶת־שַׁוְעָתָם יִשְׁמַע, וְיוֹשִׁיעֵם:
שׁוֹמֵר יהוה אֶת־כָּל־אֹהֲבָיו,
וְאֵת כָּל־הָרְשָׁעִים יַשְׁמִיד:
◂ תְּהִלַּת יהוה יְדַבֶּר פִּי
וִיבָרֵךְ כָּל־בָּשָׂר שֵׁם קָדְשׁוֹ לְעוֹלָם וָעֶד:
וַאֲנַחְנוּ נְבָרֵךְ יָהּ מֵעַתָּה וְעַד־עוֹלָם, הַלְלוּיָהּ:

חצי קדיש

חזן: יִתְגַּדַּל וְיִתְקַדַּשׁ שְׁמֵהּ רַבָּא (קהל: אָמֵן)
בְּעָלְמָא דִּי בְרָא כִרְעוּתֵהּ, וְיַמְלִיךְ מַלְכוּתֵהּ
בְּחַיֵּיכוֹן וּבְיוֹמֵיכוֹן וּבְחַיֵּי דְכָל בֵּית יִשְׂרָאֵל
בַּעֲגָלָא וּבִזְמַן קָרִיב, וְאִמְרוּ אָמֵן. (קהל: אָמֵן)

קהל: יְהֵא שְׁמֵהּ רַבָּא מְבָרַךְ לְעָלַם וּלְעָלְמֵי עָלְמַיָּא.
חזן: יְהֵא שְׁמֵהּ רַבָּא מְבָרַךְ לְעָלַם וּלְעָלְמֵי עָלְמַיָּא.

Leader: *Hashem* should be thanked, praised,
and honored (*Congregation:* He is blessed).
Hashem is beyond all the blessings,
songs, or praises
that we could offer.
Let us say:
"Amen" (*Congregation:* Amen).

On fast days, turn to Taking Out the Torah on page 168.
After the Torah is returned to the Ark, the Leader says Half Kaddish.

AMIDA

Take three steps back then three steps forward
then stand with your feet together.

I will call out to *Hashem*, let us all give praise to Him.
Hashem, open my lips and help my mouth recite Your praise.

ANCESTORS

Bend the knees when saying "We thank," bow when saying "You,"
and stand straight before saying "Hashem."

בָּרוּךְ We thank You, *Hashem*,
our God, and God of our ancestors,
Avraham, Yitzchak, and Yaakov.
You, *Hashem*, are the great, mighty, awesome, kind,
and all-powerful Creator.
It is because of the greatness of our ancestors,
Avraham, Yitzchak, and Yaakov,
that *Hashem* will bring *Mashiach*.

Between Rosh Hashana and Yom Kippur say:
Give us life in the year to come and write us
in the book of life, *Hashem*, who gives life.

חזן: יִתְבָּרַךְ וְיִשְׁתַּבַּח וְיִתְפָּאַר וְיִתְרוֹמַם וְיִתְנַשֵּׂא
וְיִתְהַדָּר וְיִתְעַלֶּה וְיִתְהַלָּל
שְׁמֵהּ דְּקֻדְשָׁא בְּרִיךְ הוּא (קהל: בְּרִיךְ הוּא)
לְעֵלָּא מִן כָּל בִּרְכָתָא
/בעשרת ימי תשובה: לְעֵלָּא לְעֵלָּא מִכָּל בִּרְכָתָא/
וְשִׁירָתָא, תֻּשְׁבְּחָתָא וְנֶחֱמָתָא
דַּאֲמִירָן בְּעָלְמָא, וְאִמְרוּ אָמֵן. (קהל: אָמֵן)

On fast days, turn to הוצאת ספר תורה *on page 169.*
After the תורה *is returned to the* ארון קודש*, the* חזן *says* חצי קדיש.

עמידה

Take three steps back then three steps forward
then stand with your feet together.

כִּי שֵׁם יהוה אֶקְרָא, הָבוּ גֹדֶל לֵאלֹהֵינוּ:
אֲדֹנָי, שְׂפָתַי תִּפְתָּח, וּפִי יַגִּיד תְּהִלָּתֶךָ:

אבות

Bend the knees when saying בָּרוּךְ*, bow when saying* אַתָּה*,*
and stand straight before saying Hashem's name.

בָּרוּךְ אַתָּה יהוה, אֱלֹהֵינוּ וֵאלֹהֵי אֲבוֹתֵינוּ
אֱלֹהֵי אַבְרָהָם, אֱלֹהֵי יִצְחָק, וֵאלֹהֵי יַעֲקֹב
הָאֵל הַגָּדוֹל הַגִּבּוֹר וְהַנּוֹרָא, אֵל עֶלְיוֹן
גּוֹמֵל חֲסָדִים טוֹבִים, וְקוֹנֵה הַכֹּל, וְזוֹכֵר חַסְדֵי אָבוֹת
וּמֵבִיא גוֹאֵל לִבְנֵי בְנֵיהֶם לְמַעַן שְׁמוֹ בְּאַהֲבָה.

Between ראש השנה *and* יום כיפור *say:*

זָכְרֵנוּ לְחַיִּים, מֶלֶךְ חָפֵץ בַּחַיִּים, וְכָתְבֵנוּ בְּסֵפֶר הַחַיִּים
לְמַעַנְךָ אֱלֹהִים חַיִּים.

Hashem is our King who helps, guides, and protects us.

Bend the knees when saying "Thank," bow when saying "You," and stand straight before saying "Hashem."

Thank You, *Hashem*,
who protects us in the merit of Avraham.

HASHEM'S STRENGTH

אַתָּה You, *Hashem*, have unlimited strength.
You save people in their time of need,
and You have the power to bring the dead back to life.

This line is said during the rainy season, from Simchat Torah to Pesach:
(You make the wind blow and cause the rain to fall)

With kindness You provide the living
with the necessities to live,
and with mercy You keep Your promise
of bringing the dead back to life.
For the living, You:
Support those who are falling,
Heal those who are sick, and
Free those who are in challenging situations.
Who is like You, *Hashem*, and who can compare to You?
You, *Hashem*, are our King
who has the power to cause death and life.

Between Rosh Hashana and Yom Kippur say:
Who is like You, *Hashem*, our caring Father
who remembers His people for good and gives them life?

We have complete faith
that You will bring us back to life after our passing.
Thank You, *Hashem*, for bringing the dead back to life.

מֶלֶךְ עוֹזֵר וּמוֹשִׁיעַ וּמָגֵן.

Bend the knees when saying בָּרוּךְ*, bow when saying* אַתָּה*,*
and stand straight before saying Hashem's name.

בָּרוּךְ אַתָּה יהוה, מָגֵן אַבְרָהָם.

גבורות

אַתָּה גִּבּוֹר לְעוֹלָם, אֲדֹנָי
מְחַיֵּה מֵתִים אַתָּה, רַב לְהוֹשִׁיעַ

This line is said during the rainy season, from שמחת תורה *to* פסח*:*

(מַשִּׁיב הָרְוּחַ וּמוֹרִיד הַגֶּשֶׁם)

מְכַלְכֵּל חַיִּים בְּחֶסֶד, מְחַיֵּה מֵתִים בְּרַחֲמִים רַבִּים
סוֹמֵךְ נוֹפְלִים, וְרוֹפֵא חוֹלִים
וּמַתִּיר אֲסוּרִים
וּמְקַיֵּם אֱמוּנָתוֹ לִישֵׁנֵי עָפָר.
מִי כָמוֹךָ, בַּעַל גְּבוּרוֹת
וּמִי דּוֹמֶה לָּךְ
מֶלֶךְ, מֵמִית וּמְחַיֶּה וּמַצְמִיחַ יְשׁוּעָה.

Between ראש השנה *and* יום כיפור *say:*

מִי כָמוֹךָ אַב הָרַחֲמִים
זוֹכֵר יְצוּרָיו לְחַיִּים בְּרַחֲמִים.

וְנֶאֱמָן אַתָּה לְהַחֲיוֹת מֵתִים.
בָּרוּךְ אַתָּה יהוה, מְחַיֵּה הַמֵּתִים.

HASHEM'S HOLINESS

אַתָּה קָדוֹשׁ *Hashem,* You are holy and Your name is holy.
The Jewish people, who are holy,
will praise You, *Hashem,* each day.
Thank You, *Hashem,*
the holy God. / *Between Rosh Hashana & Yom Kippur say:* the holy King./

GIVE US WISDOM

אַתָּה חוֹנֵן You, *Hashem,*
give wisdom and understanding to man.
Please continue to give us wisdom, understanding,
and the ability to properly use our wisdom
in our daily lives.
Thank You, *Hashem,* for giving us wisdom.

RETURN US TO *HASHEM*

הֲשִׁיבֵנוּ *Hashem,* we feel distanced from Your Torah
and from serving You properly.
Please accept us and bring us closer to You, *Hashem.*
We feel bad for our mistakes that distanced us from You.
Thank You, *Hashem,* for wanting us to return to You.

FORGIVE US

*(Lightly hit the left side of your chest
when you say "accidentally" and "purposely.")*
סְלַח *Hashem,* please forgive us for the sins we have done
accidentally and purposely.
You, *Hashem,* are forgiving and understanding.
Thank You, *Hashem,* who repeatedly forgives.

קדושת השם

אַתָּה קָדוֹשׁ וְשִׁמְךָ קָדוֹשׁ
וּקְדוֹשִׁים בְּכָל יוֹם יְהַלְלוּךָ סֶּלָה.
בָּרוּךְ אַתָּה יהוה
הָאֵל הַקָּדוֹשׁ. / *Between* ראש השנה *&* יום כיפור *say* **הַמֶּלֶךְ הַקָּדוֹשׁ.** /

דעת

אַתָּה חוֹנֵן לְאָדָם דַּעַת
וּמְלַמֵּד לֶאֱנוֹשׁ בִּינָה.
חָנֵּנוּ מֵאִתְּךָ דֵּעָה בִּינָה וְהַשְׂכֵּל.
בָּרוּךְ אַתָּה יהוה, חוֹנֵן הַדָּעַת.

תשובה

הֲשִׁיבֵנוּ אָבִינוּ לְתוֹרָתֶךָ, וְקָרְבֵנוּ מַלְכֵּנוּ לַעֲבוֹדָתֶךָ
וְהַחֲזִירֵנוּ בִּתְשׁוּבָה שְׁלֵמָה לְפָנֶיךָ.
בָּרוּךְ אַתָּה יהוה, הָרוֹצֶה בִּתְשׁוּבָה.

סליחה

(Lightly hit the left side of your chest when you say חָטָאנוּ *and* פָּשָׁעְנוּ*)*

סְלַח לָנוּ אָבִינוּ כִּי חָטָאנוּ
מְחַל לָנוּ מַלְכֵּנוּ כִּי פָשָׁעְנוּ
כִּי מוֹחֵל וְסוֹלֵחַ אָתָּה.
בָּרוּךְ אַתָּה יהוה, חַנּוּן הַמַּרְבֶּה לִסְלֹחַ.

SAVE US

רְאֵה *Hashem,* please see our difficulties
and help us face our struggles.
Save us because You have great power.
Thank You, *Hashem,*
who saves the Jewish people.

HEAL US

רְפָאֵנוּ *Hashem,* if You decide to heal the sick,
they will be healed.
If You decide to save those in need, they will be saved.
Please allow the sick
to recover completely from all sicknesses,
for You are the true source of healing and saving.
Thank You, *Hashem,*
who heals the Jewish people who are sick.

PROVIDE FOOD FOR US

בָּרֵךְ Bless this year for us *Hashem,*
so that we should always have food to eat.

Say this phrase during the winter season,
from December 4th through Pesach.
Provide rain and dew as a blessing

Say this phrase during the summer season,
from Chol Hamoed Pesach through Mincha of December 3rd.
Provide blessing

across the earth,
allowing this year to be a great year of food supply.
Thank You, *Hashem,*
for filling our year with blessing.

גאולה

רְאֵה בְעָנְיֵנוּ, וְרִיבָה רִיבֵנוּ
וּגְאָלֵנוּ מְהֵרָה לְמַעַן שְׁמֶךָ, כִּי גּוֹאֵל חָזָק אָתָּה.
בָּרוּךְ אַתָּה יהוה, גּוֹאֵל יִשְׂרָאֵל.

רפואה

רְפָאֵנוּ יהוה וְנֵרָפֵא
הוֹשִׁיעֵנוּ וְנִוָּשֵׁעָה, כִּי תְהִלָּתֵנוּ אָתָּה
וְהַעֲלֵה רְפוּאָה שְׁלֵמָה לְכָל מַכּוֹתֵינוּ
כִּי אֵל מֶלֶךְ רוֹפֵא נֶאֱמָן וְרַחֲמָן אָתָּה.
בָּרוּךְ אַתָּה יהוה, רוֹפֵא חוֹלֵי עַמּוֹ יִשְׂרָאֵל.

ברכת השנים

בָּרֵךְ עָלֵינוּ יהוה אֱלֹהֵינוּ אֶת הַשָּׁנָה הַזֹּאת
וְאֶת כָּל מִינֵי תְבוּאָתָהּ, לְטוֹבָה

Say this phrase during the winter season, from December 4th through פסח.

וְתֵן טַל וּמָטָר לִבְרָכָה

Say this phrase during the summer season, from חול המועד פסח *through* מנחה *of December 3rd.*

וְתֵן בְּרָכָה

עַל פְּנֵי הָאֲדָמָה, וְשַׂבְּעֵנוּ מִטּוּבָהּ
וּבָרֵךְ שְׁנָתֵנוּ כַּשָּׁנִים הַטּוֹבוֹת.
בָּרוּךְ אַתָּה יהוה, מְבָרֵךְ הַשָּׁנִים.

GATHER US

תְּקַע *Hashem,* blow the great shofar
to announce our freedom from exile.
Make a clear sign so that all Jews know where to gather.
Hashem, help gather all Jews together
from the four corners of the earth.
Thank You, *Hashem,*
who gathers His scattered Jewish people.

REESTABLISH JEWISH COURTS

הָשִׁיבָה Bring back our Jewish judges and leaders
as it once was,
And remove the difficulties and frustration we face
as a result of not having their guidance.
Hashem, may You alone rule and judge us
with kindness, mercy, and fairness.
Thank You, *Hashem,*
the King who loves righteousness and fairness.
/*Between Rosh Hashana and Yom Kippur say:* the King of fairness./

THE WICKED

וְלַמַּלְשִׁינִים *Hashem,* please do not assist those
who speak or act with bad intentions towards Jews.
Hashem, soon may all Your enemies be destroyed.
For Jews that turned away from Judaism,
may You quickly help guide them back
towards the ways of *Hashem*.
Thank You, *Hashem,* for destroying our enemies
and for returning Jews that turned away.

קיבוץ גלויות

תְּקַע בְּשׁוֹפָר גָּדוֹל לְחֵרוּתֵנוּ
וְשָׂא נֵס לְקַבֵּץ גָּלֻיּוֹתֵינוּ
וְקַבְּצֵנוּ יַחַד מֵאַרְבַּע כַּנְפוֹת הָאָרֶץ.
בָּרוּךְ אַתָּה יהוה, מְקַבֵּץ נִדְחֵי עַמּוֹ יִשְׂרָאֵל.

השבת המשפט

הָשִׁיבָה שׁוֹפְטֵינוּ כְּבָרִאשׁוֹנָה
וְיוֹעֲצֵינוּ כְּבַתְּחִלָּה
וְהָסֵר מִמֶּנּוּ יָגוֹן וַאֲנָחָה
וּמְלֹךְ עָלֵינוּ אַתָּה יהוה לְבַדְּךָ בְּחֶסֶד וּבְרַחֲמִים
וְצַדְּקֵנוּ בַּמִּשְׁפָּט.
בָּרוּךְ אַתָּה יהוה, מֶלֶךְ אוֹהֵב צְדָקָה וּמִשְׁפָּט.

/ *Between* ראש השנה *and* יום כיפור *say* הַמֶּלֶךְ הַמִּשְׁפָּט. /

ברכת המינים

וְלַמַּלְשִׁינִים אַל תְּהִי תִקְוָה
וְכָל הָרִשְׁעָה כְּרֶגַע תֹּאבֵד
וְכָל אוֹיְבֵי עַמְּךָ מְהֵרָה יִכָּרֵתוּ
וְהַזֵּדִים מְהֵרָה תְעַקֵּר וּתְשַׁבֵּר וּתְמַגֵּר וְתַכְנִיעַ
בִּמְהֵרָה בְיָמֵינוּ.
בָּרוּךְ אַתָּה יהוה, שׁוֹבֵר אוֹיְבִים וּמַכְנִיעַ זֵדִים.

THE RIGHTEOUS

עַל *Hashem,* when You think of us,
consider the righteous, humble, elderly,
and wise people within our nation,
and have mercy on us, Your Jewish people, for their sake.
Please give reward
to all those who sincerely believe in You,
and give us the ability to be placed
in this righteous group.
Thank You, *Hashem,*
for supporting righteous people.

REBUILDING JERUSALEM

וְלִירוּשָׁלַיִם *Hashem,* please return to Your city, Jerusalem,
and live there as You once did.
Please rebuild the *Beit HaMikdash* soon,
in our lifetimes, and let it last forever.
Complete this process by appointing a Jewish king
from the family of King David.
Thank You, *Hashem,*
for rebuilding Jerusalem.

KINGDOM OF DAVID

אֶת צֶמַח Please bring *Mashiach,*
who comes from the family of King David,
quickly as we think about
and hope for his arrival every day.
Thank You, *Hashem,*
who brings *Mashiach.*

על הצדיקים

עַל הַצַּדִּיקִים וְעַל הַחֲסִידִים
וְעַל זִקְנֵי עַמְּךָ בֵּית יִשְׂרָאֵל
וְעַל פְּלֵיטַת סוֹפְרֵיהֶם
וְעַל גֵּרֵי הַצֶּדֶק, וְעָלֵינוּ
יֶהֱמוּ רַחֲמֶיךָ יהוה אֱלֹהֵינוּ
וְתֵן שָׂכָר טוֹב לְכָל הַבּוֹטְחִים בְּשִׁמְךָ בֶּאֱמֶת
וְשִׂים חֶלְקֵנוּ עִמָּהֶם, וּלְעוֹלָם לֹא נֵבוֹשׁ כִּי בְךָ בָטָחְנוּ.
בָּרוּךְ אַתָּה יהוה, מִשְׁעָן וּמִבְטָח לַצַּדִּיקִים.

בניין ירושלים

וְלִירוּשָׁלַיִם עִירְךָ בְּרַחֲמִים תָּשׁוּב
וְתִשְׁכֹּן בְּתוֹכָהּ כַּאֲשֶׁר דִּבַּרְתָּ
וּבְנֵה אוֹתָהּ בְּקָרוֹב בְּיָמֵינוּ בִּנְיַן עוֹלָם
וְכִסֵּא דָוִד מְהֵרָה לְתוֹכָהּ תָּכִין.
בָּרוּךְ אַתָּה יהוה, בּוֹנֵה יְרוּשָׁלָיִם.

מלכות בית דוד

אֶת צֶמַח דָּוִד עַבְדְּךָ מְהֵרָה תַצְמִיחַ
וְקַרְנוֹ תָּרוּם בִּישׁוּעָתֶךָ
כִּי לִישׁוּעָתְךָ קִוִּינוּ כָּל הַיּוֹם.
בָּרוּךְ אַתָּה יהוה, מַצְמִיחַ קֶרֶן יְשׁוּעָה.

LISTEN TO OUR PRAYERS

שְׁמַע *Hashem,*
please listen to our voices
and accept our prayers with mercy.
You, *Hashem,* show mercy
by listening to the prayers of the Jewish people.
Please do not let our prayers go unanswered.

On Fast Days, insert here:

עֲנֵנוּ Answer us, *Hashem,* on this fast day, because we are in pain. *Hashem,* do not look at our bad actions, turn away from us, or ignore our prayers. Be close to us and comfort us. Even before we call You, answer us, as it says, "Even before they call Me, I will answer them. While they are still speaking, I will hear." Because You, *Hashem,* answer us in our time of pain, and save us from suffering.

Thank You, *Hashem,*
for listening to our prayers.

SERVICE IN THE *BEIT HAMIKDASH*

רְצֵה *Hashem,* please accept Your Jewish people
and their prayers.
We eagerly await
the rebuilding of the *Beit HaMikdash*
so we can serve You with *korbanot.*
Until the *Beit HaMikdash* is rebuilt,
please accept our prayers with love.

שומע תפילה

שְׁמַע קוֹלֵנוּ יהוה אֱלֹהֵינוּ
חוּס וְרַחֵם עָלֵינוּ
וְקַבֵּל בְּרַחֲמִים וּבְרָצוֹן אֶת תְּפִלָּתֵנוּ
כִּי אֵל שׁוֹמֵעַ תְּפִלּוֹת וְתַחֲנוּנִים אָתָּה
וּמִלְּפָנֶיךָ מַלְכֵּנוּ רֵיקָם אַל תְּשִׁיבֵנוּ

On Fast Days, insert here:

עֲנֵנוּ יהוה עֲנֵנוּ בְּיוֹם צוֹם תַּעֲנִיתֵנוּ, כִּי בְצָרָה גְדוֹלָה אֲנָחְנוּ. אַל תֵּפֶן אֶל רִשְׁעֵנוּ, וְאַל תַּסְתֵּר פָּנֶיךָ מִמֶּנּוּ, וְאַל תִּתְעַלַּם מִתְּחִנָּתֵנוּ. הֱיֵה נָא קָרוֹב לְשַׁוְעָתֵנוּ, יְהִי נָא חַסְדְּךָ לְנַחֲמֵנוּ, טֶרֶם נִקְרָא אֵלֶיךָ עֲנֵנוּ, כַּדָּבָר שֶׁנֶּאֱמַר: וְהָיָה טֶרֶם יִקְרָאוּ וַאֲנִי אֶעֱנֶה, עוֹד הֵם מְדַבְּרִים וַאֲנִי אֶשְׁמָע: כִּי אַתָּה יהוה הָעוֹנֶה בְּעֵת צָרָה, פּוֹדֶה וּמַצִּיל בְּכָל עֵת צָרָה וְצוּקָה.

כִּי אַתָּה שׁוֹמֵעַ תְּפִלַּת עַמְּךָ יִשְׂרָאֵל בְּרַחֲמִים.
בָּרוּךְ אַתָּה יהוה, שׁוֹמֵעַ תְּפִלָּה.

עבודה

רְצֵה יהוה אֱלֹהֵינוּ בְּעַמְּךָ יִשְׂרָאֵל, וּבִתְפִלָּתָם
וְהָשֵׁב אֶת הָעֲבוֹדָה לִדְבִיר בֵּיתֶךָ
וְאִשֵּׁי יִשְׂרָאֵל וּתְפִלָּתָם בְּאַהֲבָה תְקַבֵּל בְּרָצוֹן
וּתְהִי לְרָצוֹן תָּמִיד עֲבוֹדַת יִשְׂרָאֵל עַמֶּךָ.

On Rosh Chodesh and Chol HaMo'ed, say:

אֱלֹהֵינוּ Our God, and God of our ancestors,
may our prayers:
Rise from our mouths,
Come before You,
Reach You at a desirable time,
Be heard,
And be fulfilled.
Hashem, You remember and know each of our hardships.
You remember:
Our ancestors,
Mashiach,
Your holy city, Jerusalem, and
Your united Jewish people,
for goodness, kindness, mercy, life, and peace
on this day of:
On Rosh Chodesh: *Rosh Chodesh.*
On Pesach: the Holiday of *Matzot.*
On Sukkot: the Holiday of *Sukkot.*
Hashem, on this day please remember us
with good thoughts, consider us for blessing,
and help us with difficult times in our lives.
Be kind and merciful with us, *Hashem,*
as we look towards You as our King.

May we be worthy
to see the rebuilding of the *Beit HaMikdash.*
We thank You, *Hashem,*
for returning Your presence to Zion.

On ראש חודש *and* חול המועד*, say:*

אֱלֹהֵינוּ וֵאלֹהֵי אֲבוֹתֵינוּ
יַעֲלֶה וְיָבוֹא וְיַגִּיעַ, וְיֵרָאֶה וְיֵרָצֶה וְיִשָּׁמַע
וְיִפָּקֵד וְיִזָּכֵר זִכְרוֹנֵנוּ וּפִקְדּוֹנֵנוּ, וְזִכְרוֹן אֲבוֹתֵינוּ
וְזִכְרוֹן מָשִׁיחַ בֶּן דָּוִד עַבְדֶּךָ
וְזִכְרוֹן יְרוּשָׁלַיִם עִיר קָדְשֶׁךָ
וְזִכְרוֹן כָּל עַמְּךָ בֵּית יִשְׂרָאֵל
לְפָנֶיךָ, לִפְלֵיטָה לְטוֹבָה
לְחֵן וּלְחֶסֶד וּלְרַחֲמִים, לְחַיִּים וּלְשָׁלוֹם
בְּיוֹם

בראש חודש: רֹאשׁ הַחֹדֶשׁ הַזֶּה.
בפסח: חַג הַמַּצּוֹת הַזֶּה.
בסוכות: חַג הַסֻּכּוֹת הַזֶּה.

זָכְרֵנוּ יהוה אֱלֹהֵינוּ בּוֹ לְטוֹבָה
וּפָקְדֵנוּ בוֹ לִבְרָכָה
וְהוֹשִׁיעֵנוּ בוֹ לְחַיִּים.
וּבִדְבַר יְשׁוּעָה וְרַחֲמִים
חוּס וְחָנֵּנוּ וְרַחֵם עָלֵינוּ וְהוֹשִׁיעֵנוּ
כִּי אֵלֶיךָ עֵינֵינוּ, כִּי אֵל מֶלֶךְ חַנּוּן וְרַחוּם אָתָּה.

וְתֶחֱזֶינָה עֵינֵינוּ בְּשׁוּבְךָ לְצִיּוֹן בְּרַחֲמִים.
בָּרוּךְ אַתָּה יהוה, הַמַּחֲזִיר שְׁכִינָתוֹ לְצִיּוֹן.

THANK YOU

Bow when saying the words "We thank You."

מוֹדִים We thank You, *Hashem,*
for You are and always will be
our God, and the God of our ancestors.
You give us life
and You always protect us.
We thank and praise You
for:

Our lives which are in Your hands,
Our souls which are in Your control,
The miracles You perform for us every day, and
The goodness You show us
at all times, morning, noon, and night.

You, *Hashem,*
have unlimited mercy and kindness
and therefore
we have always placed our hope in You.

On Chanuka say:

עַל הַנִּסִּים We thank You, *Hashem,* for the miracles, the deliverances, the great strength, and the victories in war that You displayed for us in earlier times and in our times.

בִּימֵי מַתִּתְיָהוּ In the days of Mattityahu, son of Yochanan the *Kohen Gadol,* the Hasmonean, and his sons, the wicked Greeks challenged Your Jewish people trying to make them forget Your Torah and sin. In Your great kindness, You, *Hashem,* supported

הודאה

Bow when saying the words מוֹדִים אֲנַחְנוּ לָךְ שָׁאַתָּה הוּא.

מוֹדִים אֲנַחְנוּ לָךְ
שָׁאַתָּה הוּא יהוה אֱלֹהֵינוּ
וֵאלֹהֵי אֲבוֹתֵינוּ לְעוֹלָם וָעֶד.
צוּר חַיֵּינוּ, מָגֵן יִשְׁעֵנוּ, אַתָּה הוּא לְדוֹר וָדוֹר.
נוֹדֶה לְּךָ וּנְסַפֵּר תְּהִלָּתֶךָ
עַל חַיֵּינוּ הַמְּסוּרִים בְּיָדֶךָ
וְעַל נִשְׁמוֹתֵינוּ הַפְּקוּדוֹת לָךְ
וְעַל נִסֶּיךָ שֶׁבְּכָל יוֹם עִמָּנוּ
וְעַל נִפְלְאוֹתֶיךָ וְטוֹבוֹתֶיךָ
שֶׁבְּכָל עֵת, עֶרֶב וָבֹקֶר וְצָהֳרָיִם.
הַטּוֹב, כִּי לֹא כָלוּ רַחֲמֶיךָ
וְהַמְרַחֵם, כִּי לֹא תַמּוּ חֲסָדֶיךָ
מֵעוֹלָם קִוִּינוּ לָךְ.

בחנוכה:

עַל הַנִּסִּים וְעַל הַפֻּרְקָן וְעַל הַגְּבוּרוֹת וְעַל הַתְּשׁוּעוֹת וְעַל הַמִּלְחָמוֹת שֶׁעָשִׂיתָ לַאֲבוֹתֵינוּ בַּיָּמִים הָהֵם בַּזְּמַן הַזֶּה.

בִּימֵי מַתִּתְיָהוּ בֶּן יוֹחָנָן כֹּהֵן גָּדוֹל חַשְׁמוֹנַאי וּבָנָיו, כְּשֶׁעָמְדָה מַלְכוּת יָוָן הָרְשָׁעָה עַל עַמְּךָ יִשְׂרָאֵל לְהַשְׁכִּיחָם תּוֹרָתֶךָ וּלְהַעֲבִירָם מֵחֻקֵּי רְצוֹנֶךָ, וְאַתָּה בְּרַחֲמֶיךָ הָרַבִּים עָמַדְתָּ לָהֶם בְּעֵת צָרָתָם,

us in this difficult time. You allowed for:

The weak Jews to defeat the mighty Greeks,
The few Jews to defeat the many Greeks,
The pure Jews to defeat the impure Greeks,
The righteous Jews to defeat the wicked Greeks, and
The Jews who studied Your Torah to defeat the Greeks who did not.

Hashem, on this day everyone in the world recognized You as You miraculously saved Your Jewish people. Your Jewish people then entered the *Beit HaMikdash* to clean and purify it. They lit candles in the courtyard of the *Beit HaMikdash* and set aside these eight days of *Chanukah* for giving thanks and praising You.

Continue with "For all these reasons."

On Purim say:

עַל הַנִּסִּים We thank You, *Hashem,* for the miracles, the deliverances, the great strength, and the victories in war that You displayed for us in earlier times and in our times.

בִּימֵי מָרְדְּכַי In the days of Mordechai and Esther, the wicked Haman planned to destroy all Jews, men, women, and children, young and old, on the 13th of Adar, and steal their belongings. In Your great mercy, You, *Hashem,* ruined Haman's plans and instead Haman and his sons were hanged on the gallows.

Continue with "For all these reasons."

For all these reasons
we will thank You, *Hashem,* our King, forever.

Between Rosh Hashana & Yom Kippur say:

And write all Your children in the book of good life.

Every living person will recognize and praise You, *Hashem,* for You are the God that helps and saves Your people.

Bend the knees when saying "Thank," bow when saying "You," and stand straight before saying "Hashem."

Thank You, *Hashem,* for You are worthy of being thanked.

רַבְתָּ אֶת רִיבָם, דַּנְתָּ אֶת דִּינָם, נָקַמְתָּ אֶת נִקְמָתָם, מָסַרְתָּ גִבּוֹרִים בְּיַד חַלָּשִׁים, וְרַבִּים בְּיַד מְעַטִּים, וּטְמֵאִים בְּיַד טְהוֹרִים, וּרְשָׁעִים בְּיַד צַדִּיקִים, וְזֵדִים בְּיַד עוֹסְקֵי תוֹרָתֶךָ, וּלְךָ עָשִׂיתָ שֵׁם גָּדוֹל וְקָדוֹשׁ בְּעוֹלָמֶךָ, וּלְעַמְּךָ יִשְׂרָאֵל עָשִׂיתָ תְּשׁוּעָה גְדוֹלָה וּפֻרְקָן כְּהַיּוֹם הַזֶּה. וְאַחַר כֵּן בָּאוּ בָנֶיךָ לִדְבִיר בֵּיתֶךָ, וּפִנּוּ אֶת הֵיכָלֶךָ, וְטִהֲרוּ אֶת מִקְדָּשֶׁךָ, וְהִדְלִיקוּ נֵרוֹת בְּחַצְרוֹת קָדְשֶׁךָ, וְקָבְעוּ שְׁמוֹנַת יְמֵי חֲנֻכָּה אֵלּוּ, לְהוֹדוֹת וּלְהַלֵּל לְשִׁמְךָ הַגָּדוֹל.

Continue with וְעַל כֻּלָּם.

בפורים:

עַל הַנִּסִּים וְעַל הַפֻּרְקָן וְעַל הַגְּבוּרוֹת וְעַל הַתְּשׁוּעוֹת וְעַל הַמִּלְחָמוֹת שֶׁעָשִׂיתָ לַאֲבוֹתֵינוּ בַּיָּמִים הָהֵם בַּזְּמַן הַזֶּה.

בִּימֵי מָרְדְּכַי וְאֶסְתֵּר בְּשׁוּשַׁן הַבִּירָה, כְּשֶׁעָמַד עֲלֵיהֶם הָמָן הָרָשָׁע, בִּקֵּשׁ לְהַשְׁמִיד לַהֲרֹג וּלְאַבֵּד אֶת־כָּל־הַיְּהוּדִים מִנַּעַר וְעַד־זָקֵן טַף וְנָשִׁים בְּיוֹם אֶחָד, בִּשְׁלוֹשָׁה עָשָׂר לְחֹדֶשׁ שְׁנֵים־עָשָׂר, הוּא־חֹדֶשׁ אֲדָר, וּשְׁלָלָם לָבוֹז: וְאַתָּה בְּרַחֲמֶיךָ הָרַבִּים הֵפַרְתָּ אֶת עֲצָתוֹ, וְקִלְקַלְתָּ אֶת מַחֲשַׁבְתּוֹ, וַהֲשֵׁבוֹתָ לּוֹ גְּמוּלוֹ בְּרֹאשׁוֹ, וְתָלוּ אוֹתוֹ וְאֶת בָּנָיו עַל הָעֵץ.

Continue with וְעַל כֻּלָּם.

וְעַל כֻּלָּם

יִתְבָּרַךְ וְיִתְרוֹמַם שִׁמְךָ מַלְכֵּנוּ תָּמִיד לְעוֹלָם וָעֶד.

Between ראש השנה *&* יום כיפור *say* וּכְתֹב לְחַיִּים טוֹבִים כָּל בְּנֵי בְרִיתֶךָ.

וְכֹל הַחַיִּים יוֹדוּךָ סֶּלָה, וִיהַלְלוּ אֶת שִׁמְךָ בֶּאֱמֶת הָאֵל יְשׁוּעָתֵנוּ וְעֶזְרָתֵנוּ סֶלָה.

Bend the knees when saying בָּרוּךְ, *bow when saying* אַתָּה, *and stand straight before saying Hashem's name.*

בָּרוּךְ אַתָּה יהוה, הַטּוֹב שִׁמְךָ וּלְךָ נָאֶה לְהוֹדוֹת.

PEACE

On all days say "Hashem, You are King."
On fast days say "Hashem, please provide" below.

שָׁלוֹם רָב *Hashem,* You are King and master of peace.
May it be good in Your eyes
to bless Your Jewish people with peace
at all times and at every hour, forever.

On fast days:

שִׂים שָׁלוֹם *Hashem,* please provide Your Jewish people
with peace, goodness, blessing, kindness, and mercy.
Bless us, *Hashem,* all as one.
Hashem, You have given us Your Torah of life,
and treated us with kindness, righteousness,
blessing, mercy, and peace.
May it be good in Your eyes, *Hashem,*
to bless Your Jewish people with peace
at every moment of every hour.

Between Rosh Hashana and Yom Kippur continue
with "May You remember," below.

Thank You, *Hashem,*
who blesses His Jewish people
with peace.

Between Rosh Hashana and Yom Kippur say:

May You remember
all of the Jewish people for life,
blessing, peace, and riches
and write us in the book of good life and peace.
Thank You, *Hashem,*
who makes peace.

שלום

On all days say שָׁלוֹם רָב. *On fast days say* שִׂים שָׁלוֹם *below.*

שָׁלוֹם רָב עַל יִשְׂרָאֵל עַמְּךָ תָּשִׂים לְעוֹלָם
כִּי אַתָּה הוּא מֶלֶךְ אָדוֹן לְכָל הַשָּׁלוֹם.
וְטוֹב בְּעֵינֶיךָ לְבָרֵךְ אֶת עַמְּךָ יִשְׂרָאֵל
בְּכָל עֵת וּבְכָל שָׁעָה בִּשְׁלוֹמֶךָ.

On fast days:

שִׂים שָׁלוֹם טוֹבָה וּבְרָכָה
חֵן וָחֶסֶד וְרַחֲמִים עָלֵינוּ וְעַל כָּל יִשְׂרָאֵל עַמֶּךָ.
בָּרְכֵנוּ אָבִינוּ כֻּלָּנוּ כְּאֶחָד בְּאוֹר פָּנֶיךָ
כִּי בְאוֹר פָּנֶיךָ נָתַתָּ לָּנוּ יהוה אֱלֹהֵינוּ
תּוֹרַת חַיִּים וְאַהֲבַת חֶסֶד
וּצְדָקָה וּבְרָכָה וְרַחֲמִים וְחַיִּים וְשָׁלוֹם.
וְטוֹב בְּעֵינֶיךָ לְבָרֵךְ אֶת עַמְּךָ יִשְׂרָאֵל
בְּכָל עֵת וּבְכָל שָׁעָה בִּשְׁלוֹמֶךָ.

Between ראש השנה *and* יום כיפור *continue with* בְּסֵפֶר חַיִּים, *below.*

בָּרוּךְ אַתָּה יהוה
הַמְבָרֵךְ אֶת עַמּוֹ יִשְׂרָאֵל בַּשָּׁלוֹם.

Between ראש השנה *and* יום כיפור *say:*

בְּסֵפֶר חַיִּים, בְּרָכָה וְשָׁלוֹם, וּפַרְנָסָה טוֹבָה
נִזָּכֵר וְנִכָּתֵב לְפָנֶיךָ, אֲנַחְנוּ וְכָל עַמְּךָ בֵּית יִשְׂרָאֵל
לְחַיִּים טוֹבִים וּלְשָׁלוֹם.
בָּרוּךְ אַתָּה יהוה, עוֹשֵׂה הַשָּׁלוֹם.

CONCLUSION OF AMIDA

אֱלֹהַי *Hashem,* please help me:

Control my mouth from speaking badly
about other people,
Stay silent and not respond if someone speaks badly
about me,
Learn Your Torah, and do Your *mitzvot.*

Hashem, if people plan to do something evil against me,
please stop these plans and protect me.
Even if I am not deserving of being helped,
please act on my behalf
as I represent Your name and Your Torah.
Hashem, please save Your Jewish people
from difficult situations and answer my requests.
May You find my thoughts and prayers favorable.

Take three steps backwards and bow to your left as you say:

You, *Hashem,* make peace in heaven.

Bow to your right as you say:

Please may You bring peace to us

Bow forward as you say:

And all Your Jewish people.

Before taking three steps forward, say the following quietly:

Hashem, our God and God of our ancestors, may You please rebuild the *Beit HaMikdash* soon. *Hashem,* please allow us to learn Your Torah and serve You in the *Beit HaMikdash* as the Jewish people once did.

When praying with a minyan, the Amida is repeated by the Leader (on the next page).

Between Rosh HaShana and Yom Kippur and on fast days, except days when Tachanun is not said, say Avinu Malkenu on page 260.

On days when Tachanun is said, start Tachanun on page 266.
On days when Tachanun is not said, the Leader says the Full Kaddish on page 270.

סיום העמידה

אֱלֹהַי, נְצֹר לְשׁוֹנִי מֵרָע וּשְׂפָתַי מִדַּבֵּר מִרְמָה
וְלִמְקַלְלַי נַפְשִׁי תִדֹּם, וְנַפְשִׁי כֶּעָפָר לַכֹּל תִּהְיֶה.
פְּתַח לִבִּי בְּתוֹרָתֶךָ, וּבְמִצְוֹתֶיךָ תִּרְדֹּף נַפְשִׁי.
וְכָל הַחוֹשְׁבִים עָלַי רָעָה
מְהֵרָה הָפֵר עֲצָתָם וְקַלְקֵל מַחֲשַׁבְתָּם.
עֲשֵׂה לְמַעַן שְׁמֶךָ, עֲשֵׂה לְמַעַן יְמִינֶךָ
עֲשֵׂה לְמַעַן קְדֻשָּׁתֶךָ, עֲשֵׂה לְמַעַן תּוֹרָתֶךָ.
לְמַעַן יֵחָלְצוּן יְדִידֶיךָ, הוֹשִׁיעָה יְמִינְךָ וַעֲנֵנִי:
יִהְיוּ לְרָצוֹן אִמְרֵי־פִי וְהֶגְיוֹן לִבִּי לְפָנֶיךָ, יהוה צוּרִי וְגֹאֲלִי:

Take three steps backwards and bow to your left as you say:

עֹשֶׂה שָׁלוֹם / *Between* ראש השנה *&* יום כיפור *say* הַשָּׁלוֹם/ בִּמְרוֹמָיו

Bow to your right as you say:

הוּא יַעֲשֶׂה שָׁלוֹם עָלֵינוּ

Bow forward as you say:

וְעַל כָּל יִשְׂרָאֵל, וְאִמְרוּ אָמֵן.

Before taking three steps forward, say the following quietly:

יְהִי רָצוֹן מִלְּפָנֶיךָ יהוה אֱלֹהֵינוּ וֵאלֹהֵי אֲבוֹתֵינוּ. שֶׁיִּבָּנֶה בֵּית הַמִּקְדָּשׁ בִּמְהֵרָה בְיָמֵינוּ, וְתֵן חֶלְקֵנוּ בְּתוֹרָתֶךָ. וְשָׁם נַעֲבָדְךָ בְּיִרְאָה כִּימֵי עוֹלָם וּכְשָׁנִים קַדְמֹנִיּוֹת. וְעָרְבָה לַיהוה מִנְחַת יְהוּדָה וִירוּשָׁלָםִ כִּימֵי עוֹלָם וּכְשָׁנִים קַדְמֹנִיּוֹת:

When praying with a מנין, *the* עמידה *is repeated by the* חזן *(on the next page).*

Between ראש השנה *and* יום כיפור *and on fast days,*
except days when תחנון *is not said, say* אבינו מלכנו *on page 261.*

On days when תחנון *is said, start* תחנון *on page 267.*
On days when תחנון *is not said, the* חזן *says* קדיש שלם *on page 271.*

THE LEADER'S REPETITION

Try to focus on each blessing that the Leader reads, by following along and thinking about the sentences below. After each beracha that the Leader recites, answer "Amen."

I will call out to Hashem, let us all give praise to Him.
Hashem, open my lips
and help my mouth recite Your praise.

ANCESTORS

We praise You, *Hashem,*
for protecting, helping, and saving us
as You did for our ancestors,
Avraham, Yitzchak, and Yaakov.
Thank You, *Hashem,*
who protects us in the merit of Avraham.

(*Congregation:* Amen.)

HASHEM'S STRENGTH

We praise You, *Hashem,*
for providing food to those who are hungry,
support to those who are falling,
health to those who are sick,
and help to those who are in challenging situations.
Thank You, *Hashem,*
for bringing the dead back to life. (*Congregation:* Amen.)

חזרת הש״ץ

Try to focus on each blessing that the חזן *reads, by following along and thinking about the sentences below. After each beracha that the* חזן *recites, answer* אָמֵן.

כִּי שֵׁם יהוה אֶקְרָא, הָבוּ גֹדֶל לֵאלֹהֵינוּ:
אֲדֹנָי, שְׂפָתַי תִּפְתָּח, וּפִי יַגִּיד תְּהִלָּתֶךָ:

אבות

בָּרוּךְ אַתָּה יהוה, אֱלֹהֵינוּ וֵאלֹהֵי אֲבוֹתֵינוּ
אֱלֹהֵי אַבְרָהָם, אֱלֹהֵי יִצְחָק, וֵאלֹהֵי יַעֲקֹב
הָאֵל הַגָּדוֹל הַגִּבּוֹר וְהַנּוֹרָא, אֵל עֶלְיוֹן
גּוֹמֵל חֲסָדִים טוֹבִים, וְקוֹנֵה הַכֹּל, וְזוֹכֵר חַסְדֵי אָבוֹת
וּמֵבִיא גוֹאֵל לִבְנֵי בְנֵיהֶם לְמַעַן שְׁמוֹ בְּאַהֲבָה.

Between ראש השנה *&* יום כיפור *say* זָכְרֵנוּ לְחַיִּים, מֶלֶךְ חָפֵץ בַּחַיִּים
וְכָתְבֵנוּ בְּסֵפֶר הַחַיִּים, לְמַעַנְךָ אֱלֹהִים חַיִּים.

מֶלֶךְ עוֹזֵר וּמוֹשִׁיעַ וּמָגֵן.

בָּרוּךְ אַתָּה יהוה, מָגֵן אַבְרָהָם. (קהל: אָמֵן)

גבורות

אַתָּה גִּבּוֹר לְעוֹלָם, אֲדֹנָי, מְחַיֵּה מֵתִים אַתָּה, רַב לְהוֹשִׁיעַ

This line is said during the rainy season, from שמחת תורה *to* פסח*:*

(מַשִּׁיב הָרְוּחַ וּמוֹרִיד הַגֶּשֶׁם)

מְכַלְכֵּל חַיִּים בְּחֶסֶד, מְחַיֵּה מֵתִים בְּרַחֲמִים רַבִּים
סוֹמֵךְ נוֹפְלִים, וְרוֹפֵא חוֹלִים, וּמַתִּיר אֲסוּרִים
וּמְקַיֵּם אֱמוּנָתוֹ לִישֵׁנֵי עָפָר.
מִי כָמְוֹךָ, בַּעַל גְּבוּרוֹת, וּמִי דְּוֹמֶה לָּךְ
מֶלֶךְ, מֵמִית וּמְחַיֶּה וּמַצְמִיחַ יְשׁוּעָה.

Between ראש השנה *&* יום כיפור *say* מִי כָמְוֹךָ אַב הָרַחֲמִים, זוֹכֵר יְצוּרָיו לְחַיִּים בְּרַחֲמִים.

וְנֶאֱמָן אַתָּה לְהַחֲיוֹת מֵתִים.

בָּרוּךְ אַתָּה יהוה, מְחַיֵּה הַמֵּתִים. (קהל: אָמֵן)

KEDUSHA

This section of tefillah is said while standing silently with feet together. The sentences are said responsively, Congregation followed by the Leader.

Congregation then Leader: נְקַדֵּשׁ We will announce You, *Hashem,*
as holy in this world,
just as the angels
announce You as holy in heaven.
As Your prophet wrote,
The angels call to one another saying:

(Stand on your toes as you repeat the word "Holy")

Congregation then Leader: Holy, holy, holy, is *Hashem.*
The whole world is filled with Your holiness.

Leader: All the Jewish people and the angels
say in response:

Congregation then Leader: Blessed is *Hashem*'s holiness.

Leader: It is written in *Tehillim*:

Congregation then Leader: *Hashem,* You have ruled over the Jewish people for generations, and You shall continue to be our King forever.

Leader: *Hashem,* in every generation we will discuss Your holiness and greatness. Our mouths shall never stop speaking of Your praises, for You, *Hashem,* are a great and holy King. Thank You, *Hashem,* our holy God.
/*Between Rosh Hashana & Yom Kippur say:* the holy King./

(*Congregation:* Amen.)

קדושה

This section of tefillah is said while standing silently with feet together. The sentences are said responsively, קהל followed by the חזן.

קהל *then* חזן: נְקַדֵּשׁ אֶת שִׁמְךָ בָּעוֹלָם
כְּשֵׁם שֶׁמַּקְדִּישִׁים אוֹתוֹ בִּשְׁמֵי מָרוֹם
כַּכָּתוּב עַל יַד נְבִיאֶךָ, וְקָרָא זֶה אֶל־זֶה וְאָמַר

(Stand on your toes as you repeat the word קָדוֹשׁ*)*

קהל *then* חזן: קָדוֹשׁ, קָדוֹשׁ, קָדוֹשׁ, יהוה צְבָאוֹת
מְלֹא כָל־הָאָרֶץ כְּבוֹדוֹ:

חזן: לְעֻמָּתָם בָּרוּךְ יֹאמֵרוּ

קהל *then* חזן: בָּרוּךְ כְּבוֹד־יהוה מִמְּקוֹמוֹ:

חזן: וּבְדִבְרֵי קָדְשְׁךָ כָּתוּב לֵאמֹר

קהל *then* חזן: יִמְלֹךְ יהוה לְעוֹלָם
אֱלֹהַיִךְ צִיּוֹן לְדֹר וָדֹר, הַלְלוּיָהּ:

חזן: לְדוֹר וָדוֹר נַגִּיד גָּדְלֶךָ
וּלְנֵצַח נְצָחִים קְדֻשָּׁתְךָ נַקְדִּישׁ
וְשִׁבְחֲךָ אֱלֹהֵינוּ מִפִּינוּ לֹא יָמוּשׁ לְעוֹלָם וָעֶד
כִּי אֵל מֶלֶךְ גָּדוֹל וְקָדוֹשׁ אָתָּה.
בָּרוּךְ אַתָּה יהוה, הָאֵל הַקָּדוֹשׁ.

/*Between* ראש השנה *&* יום כיפור *say* הַמֶּלֶךְ הַקָּדוֹשׁ./

(קהל: אָמֵן)

Reminder: Say "Amen" after the Leader recites each beracha.

GIVE US WISDOM

We pray to You, *Hashem,*
that You give us wisdom
and the ability to understand.
Thank You, *Hashem,*
for giving us wisdom. (*Congregation:* Amen.)

RETURN US TO *HASHEM*

We pray to You, *Hashem,*
that You allow us to return to You after we sin.
Thank You, *Hashem*
for wanting us to return to You. (*Congregation:* Amen.)

FORGIVE US

We pray to You, *Hashem,*
that You accept our apologies.
Thank You, *Hashem,*
who repeatedly forgives. (*Congregation:* Amen.)

SAVE US

We pray to You, *Hashem,*
that You protect and save Your Jewish people.
Thank You, *Hashem,*
who saves the Jewish people. (*Congregation:* Amen.)

Reminder: Say אָמֵן *after the* חזן *recites each beracha.*

דעת

אַתָּה חוֹנֵן לְאָדָם דַּעַת
וּמְלַמֵּד לֶאֱנוֹשׁ בִּינָה.
חָנֵּנוּ מֵאִתְּךָ דֵּעָה בִּינָה וְהַשְׂכֵּל.
בָּרוּךְ אַתָּה יהוה, חוֹנֵן הַדָּעַת. (קהל: אָמֵן)

תשובה

הֲשִׁיבֵנוּ אָבִינוּ לְתוֹרָתֶךָ
וְקָרְבֵנוּ מַלְכֵּנוּ לַעֲבוֹדָתֶךָ
וְהַחֲזִירֵנוּ בִּתְשׁוּבָה שְׁלֵמָה לְפָנֶיךָ.
בָּרוּךְ אַתָּה יהוה, הָרוֹצֶה בִּתְשׁוּבָה. (קהל: אָמֵן)

סליחה

סְלַח לָנוּ אָבִינוּ כִּי חָטָאנוּ
מְחַל לָנוּ מַלְכֵּנוּ כִּי פָשָׁעְנוּ
כִּי מוֹחֵל וְסוֹלֵחַ אָתָּה.
בָּרוּךְ אַתָּה יהוה, חַנּוּן הַמַּרְבֶּה לִסְלֹחַ. (קהל: אָמֵן)

גאולה

רְאֵה בְעָנְיֵנוּ, וְרִיבָה רִיבֵנוּ
וּגְאָלֵנוּ מְהֵרָה לְמַעַן שְׁמֶךָ
כִּי גוֹאֵל חָזָק אָתָּה.
בָּרוּךְ אַתָּה יהוה, גּוֹאֵל יִשְׂרָאֵל. (קהל: אָמֵן)

Reminder: Say "Amen" after the Leader recites each beracha.

On Fast Days the Leader adds:

עֲנֵנוּ Answer us, *Hashem,* on this fast day, because we are in pain. *Hashem,* do not look at our bad actions, turn away from us, or ignore our prayers. Be close to us and comfort us. Even before we call You, answer us, as it says, "Even before they call Me, I will answer them. While they are still speaking, I will hear." Because You, *Hashem,* answer us in our time of pain, and save us from suffering. Thank You, *Hashem,* who answers us in our time of pain. (*Congregation:* Amen.)

HEAL US

We pray to You, *Hashem,*
that You heal the sick.
Thank You, *Hashem,*
who heals the Jewish people who are sick.
(*Congregation:* Amen.)

PROVIDE FOOD FOR US

We pray to You, *Hashem,*
that You will provide us
with the food we need to live.
Thank You, *Hashem,*
for filling our year with blessing. (*Congregation:* Amen.)

Reminder: Say אָמֵן after the חזן recites each beracha.

On Fast Days the חזן adds:

עֲנֵנוּ יהוה עֲנֵנוּ בְּיוֹם צוֹם תַּעֲנִיתֵנוּ, כִּי בְצָרָה גְדוֹלָה אֲנָחְנוּ. אַל תֵּפֶן אֶל רִשְׁעֵנוּ, וְאַל תַּסְתֵּר פָּנֶיךָ מִמֶּנּוּ, וְאַל תִּתְעַלַּם מִתְּחִנָּתֵנוּ. הֱיֵה נָא קָרוֹב לְשַׁוְעָתֵנוּ, יְהִי נָא חַסְדְּךָ לְנַחֲמֵנוּ, טֶרֶם נִקְרָא אֵלֶיךָ עֲנֵנוּ, כַּדָּבָר שֶׁנֶּאֱמַר: וְהָיָה טֶרֶם יִקְרָאוּ וַאֲנִי אֶעֱנֶה, עוֹד הֵם מְדַבְּרִים וַאֲנִי אֶשְׁמָע: כִּי אַתָּה יהוה הָעוֹנֶה בְּעֵת צָרָה, פּוֹדֶה וּמַצִּיל בְּכָל עֵת צָרָה וְצוּקָה. בָּרוּךְ אַתָּה יהוה, הָעוֹנֶה בְּעֵת צָרָה. (קהל: אָמֵן)

רפואה

רְפָאֵנוּ יהוה וְנֵרָפֵא, הוֹשִׁיעֵנוּ וְנִוָּשֵׁעָה, כִּי תְהִלָּתֵנוּ אָתָּה
וְהַעֲלֵה רְפוּאָה שְׁלֵמָה לְכָל מַכּוֹתֵינוּ
כִּי אֵל מֶלֶךְ רוֹפֵא נֶאֱמָן וְרַחֲמָן אָתָּה.
בָּרוּךְ אַתָּה יהוה, רוֹפֵא חוֹלֵי עַמּוֹ יִשְׂרָאֵל. (קהל: אָמֵן)

ברכת השנים

בָּרֵךְ עָלֵינוּ יהוה אֱלֹהֵינוּ אֶת הַשָּׁנָה הַזֹּאת
וְאֶת כָּל מִינֵי תְבוּאָתָהּ, לְטוֹבָה

Say this phrase during the winter season, from December 4th through פסח.

וְתֵן טַל וּמָטָר לִבְרָכָה

Say this phrase during the summer season, from מנחה חול המועד פסח through מנחה of December 3rd.

וְתֵן בְּרָכָה

עַל פְּנֵי הָאֲדָמָה, וְשַׂבְּעֵנוּ מִטּוּבָהּ, וּבָרֵךְ שְׁנָתֵנוּ כַּשָּׁנִים הַטּוֹבוֹת.
בָּרוּךְ אַתָּה יהוה, מְבָרֵךְ הַשָּׁנִים. (קהל: אָמֵן)

Reminder: Say "Amen" after the Leader recites each beracha.

GATHER US

We pray to You, *Hashem,*
that You gather Your Jewish people
from across the world
and lead us into freedom from exile.
Thank You, *Hashem,*
who gathers His scattered Jewish people.

(*Congregation:* Amen.)

REESTABLISH JEWISH COURTS

We pray to You, *Hashem,*
that You bring back our Jewish judges
and leaders as it once was.
Thank You, *Hashem,*
the King who loves righteousness and fairness.
/*Between Rosh Hashana and Yom Kippur say:* the King of fairness./

(*Congregation:* Amen.)

THE WICKED

We pray to You, *Hashem,*
that You destroy the wickedness
and evil among Your Jewish people.
Thank You, *Hashem,*
for destroying our enemies
and for returning Jews that turned away.

(*Congregation:* Amen.)

Reminder: Say אָמֵן after the חזן recites each beracha.

קבוץ גלויות

תְּקַע בְּשׁוֹפָר גָּדוֹל לְחֵרוּתֵֽנוּ

וְשָׂא נֵס לְקַבֵּץ גָּלֻיּוֹתֵֽינוּ

וְקַבְּצֵֽנוּ יַֽחַד מֵאַרְבַּע כַּנְפוֹת הָאָֽרֶץ.

בָּרוּךְ אַתָּה יהוה, מְקַבֵּץ נִדְחֵי עַמּוֹ יִשְׂרָאֵל. (קהל: אָמֵן)

השבת המשפט

הָשִֽׁיבָה שׁוֹפְטֵֽינוּ כְּבָרִאשׁוֹנָה

וְיוֹעֲצֵֽינוּ כְּבַתְּחִלָּה

וְהָסֵר מִמֶּֽנּוּ יָגוֹן וַאֲנָחָה

וּמְלֹךְ עָלֵֽינוּ אַתָּה יהוה לְבַדְּךָ בְּחֶֽסֶד וּבְרַחֲמִים

וְצַדְּקֵֽנוּ בַּמִּשְׁפָּט.

בָּרוּךְ אַתָּה יהוה, מֶֽלֶךְ אוֹהֵב צְדָקָה וּמִשְׁפָּט.

/ *Between* ראש השנה *and* יום כיפור *say* הַמֶּֽלֶךְ הַמִּשְׁפָּט. /

(קהל: אָמֵן)

ברכת המינים

וְלַמַּלְשִׁינִים אַל תְּהִי תִקְוָה

וְכָל הָרִשְׁעָה כְּרֶֽגַע תֹּאבֵד

וְכָל אוֹיְבֵי עַמְּךָ מְהֵרָה יִכָּרֵֽתוּ

וְהַזֵּדִים מְהֵרָה תְעַקֵּר וּתְשַׁבֵּר וּתְמַגֵּר וְתַכְנִֽיעַ

בִּמְהֵרָה בְיָמֵֽינוּ.

בָּרוּךְ אַתָּה יהוה, שׁוֹבֵר אוֹיְבִים וּמַכְנִֽיעַ זֵדִים.

(קהל: אָמֵן)

Reminder: Say "Amen" after the Leader recites each beracha.

THE RIGHTEOUS

We pray to You, *Hashem,*
that You reward the righteous, pious, and wise
among Your Jewish people.
Thank You, *Hashem,*
for supporting righteous people. (*Congregation:* Amen.)

REBUILDING JERUSALEM

We pray to You, *Hashem,*
that You rebuild Jerusalem
and Your home, the *Beit HaMikdash.*
Thank You, *Hashem,*
for rebuilding Jerusalem. (*Congregation:* Amen.)

KINGDOM OF DAVID

We pray to You, *Hashem,*
that You soon send *Mashiach*
from the family of King David.
Thank You, *Hashem,*
who brings *Mashiach.* (*Congregation:* Amen.)

LISTEN TO OUR PRAYERS

We pray to You, *Hashem,*
that You have mercy on us
and listen to our prayers.
Thank You, *Hashem,*
for listening to our prayers. (*Congregation:* Amen.)

Reminder: Say אָמֵן after the חזן recites each beracha.

על הצדיקים

עַל הַצַּדִּיקִים וְעַל הַחֲסִידִים, וְעַל זִקְנֵי עַמְּךָ בֵּית יִשְׂרָאֵל
וְעַל פְּלֵיטַת סוֹפְרֵיהֶם, וְעַל גֵּרֵי הַצֶּדֶק, וְעָלֵינוּ
יֶהֱמוּ רַחֲמֶיךָ יהוה אֱלֹהֵינוּ
וְתֵן שָׂכָר טוֹב לְכָל הַבּוֹטְחִים בְּשִׁמְךָ בֶּאֱמֶת
וְשִׂים חֶלְקֵנוּ עִמָּהֶם, וּלְעוֹלָם לֹא נֵבוֹשׁ כִּי בְךָ בָּטָחְנוּ.
בָּרוּךְ אַתָּה יהוה, מִשְׁעָן וּמִבְטָח לַצַּדִּיקִים. (קהל: אָמֵן)

בניין ירושלים

וְלִירוּשָׁלַיִם עִירְךָ בְּרַחֲמִים תָּשׁוּב, וְתִשְׁכֹּן בְּתוֹכָהּ כַּאֲשֶׁר דִּבַּרְתָּ
וּבְנֵה אוֹתָהּ בְּקָרוֹב בְּיָמֵינוּ בִּנְיַן עוֹלָם
וְכִסֵּא דָוִד מְהֵרָה לְתוֹכָהּ תָּכִין.
בָּרוּךְ אַתָּה יהוה, בּוֹנֵה יְרוּשָׁלָיִם. (קהל: אָמֵן)

מלכות בית דוד

אֶת צֶמַח דָּוִד עַבְדְּךָ מְהֵרָה תַצְמִיחַ, וְקַרְנוֹ תָּרוּם בִּישׁוּעָתֶךָ
כִּי לִישׁוּעָתְךָ קִוִּינוּ כָּל הַיּוֹם.
בָּרוּךְ אַתָּה יהוה, מַצְמִיחַ קֶרֶן יְשׁוּעָה. (קהל: אָמֵן)

שומע תפילה

שְׁמַע קוֹלֵנוּ יהוה אֱלֹהֵינוּ
חוּס וְרַחֵם עָלֵינוּ, וְקַבֵּל בְּרַחֲמִים וּבְרָצוֹן אֶת תְּפִלָּתֵנוּ
כִּי אֵל שׁוֹמֵעַ תְּפִלּוֹת וְתַחֲנוּנִים אָתָּה
וּמִלְּפָנֶיךָ מַלְכֵּנוּ רֵיקָם אַל תְּשִׁיבֵנוּ
כִּי אַתָּה שׁוֹמֵעַ תְּפִלַּת עַמְּךָ יִשְׂרָאֵל בְּרַחֲמִים.
בָּרוּךְ אַתָּה יהוה, שׁוֹמֵעַ תְּפִלָּה. (קהל: אָמֵן)

Reminder: Say "Amen" after the Leader recites the beracha.

SERVICE IN THE *BEIT HAMIKDASH*

We pray to You, *Hashem,* that You accept our prayers
as though they are the sacrifices
that were once brought to You
in Your holy *Beit HaMikdash.*

On Rosh Chodesh and Chol HaMo'ed, say:

Our God, and God of our ancestors, may our prayers:
Rise from our mouths, Come before You,
Reach You at a desirable time, Be heard, And be fulfilled.
Hashem, You remember and know each of our hardships.
You remember:
Our ancestors, *Mashiach,* Your holy city, Jerusalem,
and Your united Jewish people,
for goodness, kindness, mercy, life,
and peace on this day of:

On Rosh Chodesh: *Rosh Chodesh.*
On Pesach: the Holiday of *Matzot.*
On Sukkot: the Holiday of *Sukkot.*

Hashem, on this day please remember us
with good thoughts, consider us for blessing,
and help us with difficult times in our lives.
Be kind and merciful with us, *Hashem,*
as we look towards You as our King.

May we be worthy
to see the rebuilding of the *Beit HaMikdash.*
We thank You, *Hashem,*
for returning Your presence to Zion. (*Congregation:* Amen.)

Reminder: Say אָמֵן after the חזן recites the beracha.

עבודה

רְצֵה יהוה אֱלֹהֵינוּ בְּעַמְּךָ יִשְׂרָאֵל, וּבִתְפִלָּתָם
וְהָשֵׁב אֶת הָעֲבוֹדָה לִדְבִיר בֵּיתֶךָ
וְאִשֵּׁי יִשְׂרָאֵל וּתְפִלָּתָם בְּאַהֲבָה תְקַבֵּל בְּרָצוֹן
וּתְהִי לְרָצוֹן תָּמִיד עֲבוֹדַת יִשְׂרָאֵל עַמֶּךָ.

On ראש חודש and חול המועד, say:

אֱלֹהֵינוּ וֵאלֹהֵי אֲבוֹתֵינוּ
יַעֲלֶה וְיָבוֹא וְיַגִּיעַ, וְיֵרָאֶה וְיֵרָצֶה וְיִשָּׁמַע
וְיִפָּקֵד וְיִזָּכֵר זִכְרוֹנֵנוּ וּפִקְדּוֹנֵנוּ, וְזִכְרוֹן אֲבוֹתֵינוּ
וְזִכְרוֹן מָשִׁיחַ בֶּן דָּוִד עַבְדֶּךָ
וְזִכְרוֹן יְרוּשָׁלַיִם עִיר קָדְשֶׁךָ
וְזִכְרוֹן כָּל עַמְּךָ בֵּית יִשְׂרָאֵל
לְפָנֶיךָ, לִפְלֵיטָה לְטוֹבָה, לְחֵן וּלְחֶסֶד וּלְרַחֲמִים
לְחַיִּים וּלְשָׁלוֹם, בְּיוֹם

בראש חודש: רֹאשׁ הַחֹדֶשׁ הַזֶּה.
בפסח: חַג הַמַּצּוֹת הַזֶּה.
בסוכות: חַג הַסֻּכּוֹת הַזֶּה.

זָכְרֵנוּ יהוה אֱלֹהֵינוּ בּוֹ לְטוֹבָה, וּפָקְדֵנוּ בוֹ לִבְרָכָה
וְהוֹשִׁיעֵנוּ בוֹ לְחַיִּים.
וּבִדְבַר יְשׁוּעָה וְרַחֲמִים, חוּס וְחָנֵּנוּ וְרַחֵם עָלֵינוּ וְהוֹשִׁיעֵנוּ
כִּי אֵלֶיךָ עֵינֵינוּ, כִּי אֵל מֶלֶךְ חַנּוּן וְרַחוּם אָתָּה.

וְתֶחֱזֶינָה עֵינֵינוּ בְּשׁוּבְךָ לְצִיּוֹן בְּרַחֲמִים.

בָּרוּךְ אַתָּה יהוה, הַמַּחֲזִיר שְׁכִינָתוֹ לְצִיּוֹן. (קהל: אָמֵן)

THANK YOU

While the Leader says this prayer, the Congregation says the prayer on the bottom of this page.

You, *Hashem*,
have unlimited mercy and kindness
and therefore
we have always placed our hope in You.

The following is said quietly while the Leader says the above. Bow when saying the first sentence below beginning with the words "Thank You, Hashem."

מוֹדִים Thank You, *Hashem*,
our God and God of our ancestors.
You are God of all people,
You created us,
and You created the entire world.
Thank You for giving us life
and for providing us
with food to eat.
May You continue
to give us life and food to eat.
May You gather us from exile
and return us to Your holy places
so we can keep Your laws,
and serve You
with a perfect heart.
Thank You *Hashem*,
our God
to whom thanksgiving is due.

הודאה

While the חזן *says this prayer, the* קהל *says the prayer on the bottom of this page.*

מוֹדִים אֲנַחְנוּ לָךְ
שָׁאַתָּה הוּא יהוה אֱלֹהֵינוּ וֵאלֹהֵי אֲבוֹתֵינוּ לְעוֹלָם וָעֶד.
צוּר חַיֵּינוּ, מָגֵן יִשְׁעֵנוּ אַתָּה הוּא לְדוֹר וָדוֹר.
נוֹדֶה לְּךָ וּנְסַפֵּר תְּהִלָּתֶךָ
עַל חַיֵּינוּ הַמְּסוּרִים בְּיָדֶךָ, וְעַל נִשְׁמוֹתֵינוּ הַפְּקוּדוֹת לָךְ
וְעַל נִסֶּיךָ שֶׁבְּכָל יוֹם עִמָּנוּ, וְעַל נִפְלְאוֹתֶיךָ וְטוֹבוֹתֶיךָ
שֶׁבְּכָל עֵת, עֶרֶב וָבֹקֶר וְצָהֳרָיִם.
הַטּוֹב, כִּי לֹא כָלוּ רַחֲמֶיךָ
וְהַמְרַחֵם, כִּי לֹא תַמּוּ חֲסָדֶיךָ, מֵעוֹלָם קִוִּינוּ לָךְ.

The following is said quietly while the חזן *says the above. Bow when saying the first sentence below beginning with the words* מוֹדִים אֲנַחְנוּ לָךְ.

מוֹדִים אֲנַחְנוּ לָךְ
שָׁאַתָּה הוּא יהוה אֱלֹהֵינוּ וֵאלֹהֵי אֲבוֹתֵינוּ
אֱלֹהֵי כָל בָּשָׂר, יוֹצְרֵנוּ, יוֹצֵר בְּרֵאשִׁית.
בְּרָכוֹת וְהוֹדָאוֹת לְשִׁמְךָ הַגָּדוֹל וְהַקָּדוֹשׁ
עַל שֶׁהֶחֱיִיתָנוּ וְקִיַּמְתָּנוּ.
כֵּן תְּחַיֵּנוּ וּתְקַיְּמֵנוּ וְתֶאֱסֹף גָּלֻיּוֹתֵינוּ לְחַצְרוֹת קָדְשֶׁךָ
לִשְׁמֹר חֻקֶּיךָ וְלַעֲשׂוֹת רְצוֹנֶךָ וּלְעָבְדְּךָ בְּלֵבָב שָׁלֵם
עַל שֶׁאֲנַחְנוּ מוֹדִים לָךְ.
בָּרוּךְ אֵל הַהוֹדָאוֹת.

Reminder: Say "Amen" after the Leader recites the beracha.

On Chanuka say:

We thank You, *Hashem,* for the miracles, the deliverances, the great strength, and the victories in war that You displayed for us in earlier times and in our times.

In the days of Mattityahu, son of Yochanan the *Kohen Gadol,* the Hasmonean, and his sons, the wicked Greeks challenged Your Jewish people trying to make them forget Your Torah and sin. In Your great kindness, You, *Hashem,* supported us in this difficult time. You allowed for: The weak Jews to defeat the mighty Greeks, The few Jews to defeat the many Greeks, The pure Jews to defeat the impure Greeks, The righteous Jews to defeat the wicked Greeks, and The Jews who studied Your Torah to defeat the Greeks who did not. *Hashem,* on this day everyone in the world recognized You as You miraculously saved Your Jewish people. Your Jewish people then entered the *Beit HaMikdash* to clean and purify it. They lit candles in the courtyard of the *Beit HaMikdash* and set aside these eight days of *Chanukah* for giving thanks and praising You.

Continue with "We thank You"

On Purim say:

We thank You, *Hashem,* for the miracles, the deliverances, the great strength, and the victories in war that You displayed for us in earlier times and in our times.

In the days of Mordechai and Esther, the wicked Haman planned to destroy all Jews, men, women, and children, young and old, on the 13th of Adar, and steal their belongings. In Your great mercy, You, *Hashem,* ruined Haman's plans and instead Haman and his sons were hanged on the gallows.

Continue with "We thank You"

We thank You, *Hashem,* for You are good
and all that You do is good.
Thank You, *Hashem,*
for You are worthy of being thanked. (*Congregation:* Amen.)

Reminder: Say אָמֵן after the חזן recites the beracha.

בחנוכה:

עַל הַנִּסִּים וְעַל הַפֻּרְקָן וְעַל הַגְּבוּרוֹת וְעַל הַתְּשׁוּעוֹת וְעַל הַמִּלְחָמוֹת שֶׁעָשִׂיתָ לַאֲבוֹתֵינוּ בַּיָּמִים הָהֵם בַּזְּמַן הַזֶּה.

בִּימֵי מַתִּתְיָהוּ בֶּן יוֹחָנָן כֹּהֵן גָּדוֹל חַשְׁמוֹנַאי וּבָנָיו, כְּשֶׁעָמְדָה מַלְכוּת יָוָן הָרְשָׁעָה עַל עַמְּךָ יִשְׂרָאֵל לְהַשְׁכִּיחָם תּוֹרָתֶךָ וּלְהַעֲבִירָם מֵחֻקֵּי רְצוֹנֶךָ, וְאַתָּה בְּרַחֲמֶיךָ הָרַבִּים עָמַדְתָּ לָהֶם בְּעֵת צָרָתָם, רַבְתָּ אֶת רִיבָם, דַּנְתָּ אֶת דִּינָם, נָקַמְתָּ אֶת נִקְמָתָם, מָסַרְתָּ גִבּוֹרִים בְּיַד חַלָּשִׁים, וְרַבִּים בְּיַד מְעַטִּים, וּטְמֵאִים בְּיַד טְהוֹרִים, וּרְשָׁעִים בְּיַד צַדִּיקִים, וְזֵדִים בְּיַד עוֹסְקֵי תוֹרָתֶךָ, וּלְךָ עָשִׂיתָ שֵׁם גָּדוֹל וְקָדוֹשׁ בְּעוֹלָמֶךָ, וּלְעַמְּךָ יִשְׂרָאֵל עָשִׂיתָ תְּשׁוּעָה גְדוֹלָה וּפֻרְקָן כְּהַיּוֹם הַזֶּה. וְאַחַר כֵּן בָּאוּ בָנֶיךָ לִדְבִיר בֵּיתֶךָ, וּפִנּוּ אֶת הֵיכָלֶךָ, וְטִהֲרוּ אֶת מִקְדָּשֶׁךָ, וְהִדְלִיקוּ נֵרוֹת בְּחַצְרוֹת קָדְשֶׁךָ, וְקָבְעוּ שְׁמוֹנַת יְמֵי חֲנֻכָּה אֵלּוּ, לְהוֹדוֹת וּלְהַלֵּל לְשִׁמְךָ הַגָּדוֹל.

Continue with וְעַל כֻּלָּם.

בפורים:

עַל הַנִּסִּים וְעַל הַפֻּרְקָן וְעַל הַגְּבוּרוֹת וְעַל הַתְּשׁוּעוֹת וְעַל הַמִּלְחָמוֹת שֶׁעָשִׂיתָ לַאֲבוֹתֵינוּ בַּיָּמִים הָהֵם בַּזְּמַן הַזֶּה.

בִּימֵי מָרְדְּכַי וְאֶסְתֵּר בְּשׁוּשַׁן הַבִּירָה, כְּשֶׁעָמַד עֲלֵיהֶם הָמָן הָרָשָׁע, בִּקֵּשׁ לְהַשְׁמִיד לַהֲרֹג וּלְאַבֵּד אֶת־כָּל־הַיְּהוּדִים מִנַּעַר וְעַד־זָקֵן טַף וְנָשִׁים בְּיוֹם אֶחָד, בִּשְׁלוֹשָׁה עָשָׂר לְחֹדֶשׁ שְׁנֵים־עָשָׂר, הוּא־חֹדֶשׁ אֲדָר, וּשְׁלָלָם לָבוֹז: וְאַתָּה בְּרַחֲמֶיךָ הָרַבִּים הֵפַרְתָּ אֶת עֲצָתוֹ, וְקִלְקַלְתָּ אֶת מַחֲשַׁבְתּוֹ, וַהֲשֵׁבוֹתָ לּוֹ גְּמוּלוֹ בְּרֹאשׁוֹ, וְתָלוּ אוֹתוֹ וְאֶת בָּנָיו עַל הָעֵץ.

Continue with וְעַל כֻּלָּם.

וְעַל כֻּלָּם, יִתְבָּרַךְ וְיִתְרוֹמַם שִׁמְךָ מַלְכֵּנוּ תָּמִיד לְעוֹלָם וָעֶד.

Between ראש השנה *&* יום כיפור *say* וּכְתֹב לְחַיִּים טוֹבִים כָּל בְּנֵי בְרִיתֶךָ.

וְכֹל הַחַיִּים יוֹדוּךָ סֶּלָה, וִיהַלְלוּ אֶת שִׁמְךָ בֶּאֱמֶת הָאֵל יְשׁוּעָתֵנוּ וְעֶזְרָתֵנוּ סֶלָה.

בָּרוּךְ אַתָּה יהוה, הַטּוֹב שִׁמְךָ וּלְךָ נָאֶה לְהוֹדוֹת. (קהל: אָמֵן)

BLESSINGS OF THE *KOHANIM*

The following is said only on public fast days.

Hashem, Our God and God of our ancestors, provide us with the three blessings that Aharon the *Kohen* and the *kohanim* his descendants use to bless the Jewish people.

Leader: *Hashem* should bless and protect you.

(*Congregation:* May it be as you say!)

Leader: *Hashem* should be kind and favorable towards you.

(*Congregation:* May it be as you say!)

Leader: *Hashem* should grant you peace.

(*Congregation:* May it be as you say!)

Reminder: Say "Amen" after the Leader recites the beracha.

PEACE

On all days "Hashem, You are King" is said.
On fast days "Hashem, please provide," below, is said.

We pray to You, *Hashem*,
that You grant peace to Your Jewish people
at every moment of every hour, forever.

On fast days:

Hashem, please provide Your Jewish people with peace, goodness, blessing, kindness, and mercy. Bless us, *Hashem*, all as one. *Hashem*, You have given us Your Torah of life, and treated us with kindness, righteousness, blessing, mercy, and peace. May it be good in Your eyes, *Hashem*, to bless Your Jewish people with peace at every moment of every hour.

Between Rosh Hashana and Yom Kippur the Leader continues with "May You remember," below.

Thank You, *Hashem*,
who blesses His Jewish people with peace.

(*Congregation:* Amen.)

Between Rosh Hashana and Yom Kippur say:

May You remember all of the Jewish people for life, blessing, peace, and riches and write us in the book of good life and peace. Thank You, *Hashem*, who makes peace. (*Congregation:* Amen.)

ברכת כוהנים

The following is said only on public fast days.

אֱלֹהֵינוּ וֵאלֹהֵי אֲבוֹתֵינוּ, בָּרְכֵנוּ בַבְּרָכָה הַמְשֻׁלֶּשֶׁת בַּתּוֹרָה, הַכְּתוּבָה עַל יְדֵי מֹשֶׁה עַבְדֶּךָ, הָאֲמוּרָה מִפִּי אַהֲרֹן וּבָנָיו כֹּהֲנִים עַם קְדוֹשֶׁיךָ, כָּאָמוּר

חזן: יְבָרֶכְךָ יהוה וְיִשְׁמְרֶךָ: קהל: כֵּן יְהִי רָצוֹן

חזן: יָאֵר יהוה פָּנָיו אֵלֶיךָ וִיחֻנֶּךָּ: קהל: כֵּן יְהִי רָצוֹן

חזן: יִשָּׂא יהוה פָּנָיו אֵלֶיךָ וְיָשֵׂם לְךָ שָׁלוֹם: קהל: כֵּן יְהִי רָצוֹן

Reminder: Say אָמֵן *after the* חזן *recites the beracha.*

שלום

On all days שָׁלוֹם רָב *is said. On fast days* שִׂים שָׁלוֹם*, below, is said.*

שָׁלוֹם רָב עַל יִשְׂרָאֵל עַמְּךָ תָּשִׂים לְעוֹלָם
כִּי אַתָּה הוּא מֶלֶךְ אָדוֹן לְכָל הַשָּׁלוֹם.
וְטוֹב בְּעֵינֶיךָ לְבָרֵךְ אֶת עַמְּךָ יִשְׂרָאֵל
בְּכָל עֵת וּבְכָל שָׁעָה בִּשְׁלוֹמֶךָ.

On fast days:

שִׂים שָׁלוֹם טוֹבָה וּבְרָכָה, חֵן וָחֶסֶד וְרַחֲמִים עָלֵינוּ וְעַל כָּל יִשְׂרָאֵל עַמֶּךָ. בָּרְכֵנוּ אָבִינוּ כֻּלָּנוּ כְּאֶחָד בְּאוֹר פָּנֶיךָ, כִּי בְאוֹר פָּנֶיךָ נָתַתָּ לָּנוּ יהוה אֱלֹהֵינוּ, תּוֹרַת חַיִּים וְאַהֲבַת חֶסֶד, וּצְדָקָה וּבְרָכָה וְרַחֲמִים וְחַיִּים וְשָׁלוֹם. וְטוֹב בְּעֵינֶיךָ לְבָרֵךְ אֶת עַמְּךָ יִשְׂרָאֵל, בְּכָל עֵת וּבְכָל שָׁעָה בִּשְׁלוֹמֶךָ.

Between ראש השנה *and* יום כיפור *the* חזן *continues with* בְּסֵפֶר חַיִּים*, below.*

בָּרוּךְ אַתָּה יהוה, הַמְבָרֵךְ אֶת עַמּוֹ יִשְׂרָאֵל בַּשָּׁלוֹם.
(קהל: אָמֵן)

Between ראש השנה *and* יום כיפור *say:*

בְּסֵפֶר חַיִּים, בְּרָכָה וְשָׁלוֹם, וּפַרְנָסָה טוֹבָה, נִזָּכֵר וְנִכָּתֵב לְפָנֶיךָ, אֲנַחְנוּ וְכָל עַמְּךָ בֵּית יִשְׂרָאֵל לְחַיִּים טוֹבִים וּלְשָׁלוֹם. בָּרוּךְ אַתָּה יהוה, עוֹשֵׂה הַשָּׁלוֹם. (קהל: אָמֵן)

Between Rosh Hashana and Yom Kippur, and on fast days, say the following.

On days when Tachanun is said, turn to page 266.

On days when Tachanun is not said, the Leader says Kaddish Shalem on page 270.

AVINU MALKENU

The Ark is opened.

אָבִינוּ מַלְכֵּנוּ Our Father and King, we have sinned.

Our Father and King, You are our only King.

Our Father and King, act with us kindly because You are kind.

Our Father and King, bless us with a good year.

/*Between Rosh Hashana and Yom Kippur say:* bring upon us a good new year./

Our Father and King, cancel all harsh promises that have been made against us.

Our Father and King, cancel the plans of those who hate us.

Our Father and King, do not listen to the advice of our enemies.

Our Father and King, destroy all of our enemies.

Our Father and King, do not allow our enemies to speak badly about us anymore.

Our Father and King, protect Your Jewish people from plague, war, hunger, being taken captive by our enemies, destruction, and sin.

Our Father and King, protect us from illness.

Our Father and King, forgive us for all our sins.

Our Father and King, remove our sins from Your sight.

Our Father and King, please erase our sins with mercy, as if we never committed them.

Between ראש השנה and יום כיפור, and on fast days, say the following.

On days when תחנון is said, turn to page 267.

On days when תחנון is not said, the חזן says קדיש שלם on page 271.

אבינו מלכנו

The ארון קודש is opened.

אָבִינוּ מַלְכֵּנוּ, חָטָאנוּ לְפָנֶיךָ.

אָבִינוּ מַלְכֵּנוּ, אֵין לָנוּ מֶלֶךְ אֶלָּא אָתָּה.

אָבִינוּ מַלְכֵּנוּ, עֲשֵׂה עִמָּנוּ לְמַעַן שְׁמֶךָ.

אָבִינוּ מַלְכֵּנוּ, בָּרֵךְ / בעשרת ימי תשובה: חַדֵּשׁ/ עָלֵינוּ שָׁנָה טוֹבָה.

אָבִינוּ מַלְכֵּנוּ, בַּטֵּל מֵעָלֵינוּ כָּל גְּזֵרוֹת קָשׁוֹת.

אָבִינוּ מַלְכֵּנוּ, בַּטֵּל מַחְשְׁבוֹת שׂוֹנְאֵינוּ.

אָבִינוּ מַלְכֵּנוּ, הָפֵר עֲצַת אוֹיְבֵינוּ.

אָבִינוּ מַלְכֵּנוּ, כַּלֵּה כָּל צַר וּמַשְׂטִין מֵעָלֵינוּ.

אָבִינוּ מַלְכֵּנוּ, סְתֹם פִּיּוֹת מַשְׂטִינֵינוּ וּמְקַטְרְגֵינוּ.

אָבִינוּ מַלְכֵּנוּ, כַּלֵּה דֶּבֶר וְחֶרֶב וְרָעָב וּשְׁבִי וּמַשְׁחִית
וְעָוֹן וּשְׁמַד מִבְּנֵי בְרִיתֶךָ.

אָבִינוּ מַלְכֵּנוּ, מְנַע מַגֵּפָה מִנַּחֲלָתֶךָ.

אָבִינוּ מַלְכֵּנוּ, סְלַח וּמְחַל לְכָל עֲוֹנוֹתֵינוּ.

אָבִינוּ מַלְכֵּנוּ, מְחֵה וְהַעֲבֵר פְּשָׁעֵינוּ וְחַטֹּאתֵינוּ מִנֶּגֶד עֵינֶיךָ.

אָבִינוּ מַלְכֵּנוּ, מְחֹק בְּרַחֲמֶיךָ הָרַבִּים כָּל שִׁטְרֵי חוֹבוֹתֵינוּ.

The following lines are said first by the Leader and then by the congregation:

Our Father and King, please accept us because we regret our wrong actions and want to return to You.

Our Father and King, heal the sick members of Your Jewish people.

Our Father and King, tear up the evil plans made against us.

Our Father and King, remember us with kindness.

Between Rosh Hashana and Yom Kippur:

Our Father and King, write us in the book that promises us good life.

Our Father and King, write us in the book that promises we will be saved.

Our Father and King, write us in the book that promises we will have money and food to live.

Our Father and King, write us in the book that recognizes the good actions we have done.

Our Father and King, write us in the book that promises we will be forgiven.

Fast Days:

Our Father and King, remember us and provide us with a good life.

Our Father and King, remember us and save us.

Our Father and King, remember us and provide us with money and food to live.

Our Father and King, remember us and all the good actions we have done.

Our Father and King, remember us and forgive us.

End of responsive reading.

Our Father and King, free us from exile soon.

Our Father and King, support Your Jewish people.

Our Father and King, support *Mashiach,* the savior of the Jewish people.

The following nine sentences are said first by the חזן*, then by the* קהל*:*

אָבִינוּ מַלְכֵּנוּ, הַחֲזִירֵנוּ בִּתְשׁוּבָה שְׁלֵמָה לְפָנֶיךָ.
אָבִינוּ מַלְכֵּנוּ, שְׁלַח רְפוּאָה שְׁלֵמָה לְחוֹלֵי עַמֶּךָ.
אָבִינוּ מַלְכֵּנוּ, קְרַע רֹעַ גְּזַר דִּינֵנוּ.
אָבִינוּ מַלְכֵּנוּ, זָכְרֵנוּ בְּזִכְרוֹן טוֹב לְפָנֶיךָ.

Between ראש השנה *and* יום כיפור*:*

אָבִינוּ מַלְכֵּנוּ, כָּתְבֵנוּ בְּסֵפֶר חַיִּים טוֹבִים.
אָבִינוּ מַלְכֵּנוּ, כָּתְבֵנוּ בְּסֵפֶר גְּאֻלָּה וִישׁוּעָה.
אָבִינוּ מַלְכֵּנוּ, כָּתְבֵנוּ בְּסֵפֶר פַּרְנָסָה וְכַלְכָּלָה.
אָבִינוּ מַלְכֵּנוּ, כָּתְבֵנוּ בְּסֵפֶר זְכֻיּוֹת.
אָבִינוּ מַלְכֵּנוּ, כָּתְבֵנוּ בְּסֵפֶר סְלִיחָה וּמְחִילָה.

On Fast Days:

אָבִינוּ מַלְכֵּנוּ, זָכְרֵנוּ לְחַיִּים טוֹבִים.
אָבִינוּ מַלְכֵּנוּ, זָכְרֵנוּ לִגְאֻלָּה וִישׁוּעָה.
אָבִינוּ מַלְכֵּנוּ, זָכְרֵנוּ לְפַרְנָסָה וְכַלְכָּלָה.
אָבִינוּ מַלְכֵּנוּ, זָכְרֵנוּ לִזְכֻיּוֹת.
אָבִינוּ מַלְכֵּנוּ, זָכְרֵנוּ לִסְלִיחָה וּמְחִילָה.

End of responsive reading.

אָבִינוּ מַלְכֵּנוּ, הַצְמַח לָנוּ יְשׁוּעָה בְּקָרוֹב.
אָבִינוּ מַלְכֵּנוּ, הָרֵם קֶרֶן יִשְׂרָאֵל עַמֶּךָ.
אָבִינוּ מַלְכֵּנוּ, הָרֵם קֶרֶן מְשִׁיחֶךָ.

Our Father and King, give us many blessings.

Our Father and King, allow us to have plentiful amounts of food.

Our Father and King, hear our voices and take pity on us.

Our Father and King, please accept our prayers with mercy.

Our Father and King, open up the gates of heaven to our prayers.

Our Father and King, remember that we are made from dust.

Our Father and King, please do not turn us away from You empty-handed.

Our Father and King, may this time be a time of mercy.

Our Father and King, have pity on us and our children.

Our Father and King, help us because of the many Jews who gave their lives for Your sake.

Our Father and King, help us because of the many Jews who were injured by fire and water for Your sake.

Our Father and King, punish our enemies for harming Your Jewish people.

Our Father and King, act for Your sake if not for ours.

Our Father and King, help us for Your sake and save us.

Our Father and King, help us because You are filled with overflowing mercy.

Our Father and King, help us because You are great, mighty, and fearsome.

▸ Our Father and King, show us mercy and answer us even though we do not deserve it; treat us with charity and kindness, and save us.

The Ark is closed.

אָבִינוּ מַלְכֵּנוּ, מַלֵּא יָדֵינוּ מִבִּרְכוֹתֶיךָ.
אָבִינוּ מַלְכֵּנוּ, מַלֵּא אֲסָמֵינוּ שָׂבָע.
אָבִינוּ מַלְכֵּנוּ, שְׁמַע קוֹלֵנוּ, חוּס וְרַחֵם עָלֵינוּ.
אָבִינוּ מַלְכֵּנוּ, קַבֵּל בְּרַחֲמִים וּבְרָצוֹן אֶת תְּפִלָּתֵנוּ.
אָבִינוּ מַלְכֵּנוּ, פְּתַח שַׁעֲרֵי שָׁמַיִם לִתְפִלָּתֵנוּ.
אָבִינוּ מַלְכֵּנוּ, זְכֹר כִּי עָפָר אֲנָחְנוּ.
אָבִינוּ מַלְכֵּנוּ, נָא אַל תְּשִׁיבֵנוּ רֵיקָם מִלְּפָנֶיךָ.
אָבִינוּ מַלְכֵּנוּ, תְּהֵא הַשָּׁעָה הַזֹּאת שְׁעַת רַחֲמִים וְעֵת רָצוֹן מִלְּפָנֶיךָ.
אָבִינוּ מַלְכֵּנוּ, חֲמֹל עָלֵינוּ וְעַל עוֹלָלֵינוּ וְטַפֵּנוּ.
אָבִינוּ מַלְכֵּנוּ, עֲשֵׂה לְמַעַן הֲרוּגִים עַל שֵׁם קָדְשֶׁךָ.
אָבִינוּ מַלְכֵּנוּ, עֲשֵׂה לְמַעַן טְבוּחִים עַל יִחוּדֶךָ.
אָבִינוּ מַלְכֵּנוּ, עֲשֵׂה לְמַעַן בָּאֵי בָאֵשׁ וּבַמַּיִם עַל קִדּוּשׁ שְׁמֶךָ.
אָבִינוּ מַלְכֵּנוּ, נְקֹם לְעֵינֵינוּ נִקְמַת דַּם עֲבָדֶיךָ הַשָּׁפוּךְ.
אָבִינוּ מַלְכֵּנוּ, עֲשֵׂה לְמַעַנְךָ אִם לֹא לְמַעֲנֵנוּ.
אָבִינוּ מַלְכֵּנוּ, עֲשֵׂה לְמַעַנְךָ וְהוֹשִׁיעֵנוּ.
אָבִינוּ מַלְכֵּנוּ, עֲשֵׂה לְמַעַן רַחֲמֶיךָ הָרַבִּים.
אָבִינוּ מַלְכֵּנוּ, עֲשֵׂה לְמַעַן שִׁמְךָ הַגָּדוֹל הַגִּבּוֹר וְהַנּוֹרָא, שֶׁנִּקְרָא עָלֵינוּ.
◄ אָבִינוּ מַלְכֵּנוּ, חָנֵּנוּ וַעֲנֵנוּ, כִּי אֵין בָּנוּ מַעֲשִׂים
עֲשֵׂה עִמָּנוּ צְדָקָה וָחֶסֶד וְהוֹשִׁיעֵנוּ.

The ארון קודש *is closed.*

TACHANUN

LOWERING THE HEAD

The following is said sitting.

Lean on your left arm while saying the following paragraph.

וַיֹּאמֶר דָּוִד King David once said
"I am very troubled.
Let the Jewish people be punished by *Hashem*
rather than by people,
for *Hashem* is filled with mercy."

Hashem,
You have shown great understanding and kindness.
I have sinned before You.
Please show me Your mercy and accept my prayers.

Hashem,
if I am deserving of punishment,
please show me kindness
and do so when You are calm.
Hashem, forgive me,
for my body shakes in fear of Your punishment.
Hashem, how long must I wait for forgiveness?
Hashem, save me and allow me to return to You,
for tears drip from my eyes every night
as I cry out to You.
For enemies that wish to harm me,
know that *Hashem* has heard my cry
and will accept my prayer for forgiveness.

Sit up at this point.

סדר תחנון

נפילת אפיים

The following is said sitting.

Lean on your left arm while saying the following paragraph.

וַיֹּאמֶר דָּוִד אֶל־גָּד, צַר־לִי מְאֹד
נִפְּלָה־נָּא בְיַד־יהוה, כִּי רַבִּים רַחֲמָו
וּבְיַד־אָדָם אַל־אֶפֹּלָה:

רַחוּם וְחַנּוּן, חָטָאתִי לְפָנֶיךָ.
יהוה מָלֵא רַחֲמִים, רַחֵם עָלַי וְקַבֵּל תַּחֲנוּנָי.

יהוה, אַל־בְּאַפְּךָ תוֹכִיחֵנִי, וְאַל־בַּחֲמָתְךָ תְיַסְּרֵנִי:
חָנֵּנִי יהוה, כִּי אֻמְלַל אָנִי
רְפָאֵנִי יהוה, כִּי נִבְהֲלוּ עֲצָמָי:
וְנַפְשִׁי נִבְהֲלָה מְאֹד, וְאַתָּ יהוה, עַד־מָתָי:
שׁוּבָה יהוה, חַלְּצָה נַפְשִׁי, הוֹשִׁיעֵנִי לְמַעַן חַסְדֶּךָ:
כִּי אֵין בַּמָּוֶת זִכְרֶךָ, בִּשְׁאוֹל מִי יוֹדֶה־לָּךְ:
יָגַעְתִּי בְּאַנְחָתִי, אַשְׂחֶה בְכָל־לַיְלָה מִטָּתִי
בְּדִמְעָתִי עַרְשִׂי אַמְסֶה:
עָשְׁשָׁה מִכַּעַס עֵינִי, עָתְקָה בְּכָל־צוֹרְרָי:
סוּרוּ מִמֶּנִּי כָּל־פֹּעֲלֵי אָוֶן, כִּי שָׁמַע יהוה קוֹל בִּכְיִי:
שָׁמַע יהוה תְּחִנָּתִי, יהוה תְּפִלָּתִי יִקָּח:
יֵבֹשׁוּ וְיִבָּהֲלוּ מְאֹד כָּל־אֹיְבָי, יָשֻׁבוּ יֵבֹשׁוּ רָגַע:

Sit up at this point.

On all days continue here:

שׁוֹמֵר Protector of Your Jewish people,
do not allow Your Jewish people to be destroyed.

Protector of Your special nation,
do not allow Your special nation to be destroyed.

Protector of Your holy nation,
do not allow Your holy nation to be destroyed.

Hashem, in the past
You have shown mercy towards our pleas.

Please once again
show mercy to Your people,
for there is nobody else who can help us but You.

Our Father and King, though we do not deserve it,
please listen to our pleas
with kindness, and save us.

Stand for the following.

וַאֲנַחְנוּ We do not know what else there is for us to do
but look towards You for help.
The world was created upon Your mercy and kindness.
Hashem, please show Your kindness to us.
When You remember us,
do not think about our sins and the sins of our ancestors.
Please be kind to us and show us Your mercy,
as we are no more than dust before You.
▸ *Hashem,* help us, save us, and forgive our sins,
for Your sake.

On all days continue here:

שׁוֹמֵר יִשְׂרָאֵל, שְׁמֹר שְׁאֵרִית יִשְׂרָאֵל, וְאַל יֹאבַד יִשְׂרָאֵל
הָאוֹמְרִים שְׁמַע יִשְׂרָאֵל.

שׁוֹמֵר גּוֹי אֶחָד, שְׁמֹר שְׁאֵרִית עַם אֶחָד, וְאַל יֹאבַד גּוֹי אֶחָד
הַמְיַחֲדִים שִׁמְךָ, יהוה אֱלֹהֵינוּ יהוה אֶחָד.

שׁוֹמֵר גּוֹי קָדוֹשׁ, שְׁמֹר שְׁאֵרִית עַם קָדוֹשׁ, וְאַל יֹאבַד גּוֹי קָדוֹשׁ
הַמְשַׁלְּשִׁים בְּשָׁלֹשׁ קְדֻשּׁוֹת לְקָדוֹשׁ.

מִתְרַצֶּה בְּרַחֲמִים וּמִתְפַּיֵּס בְּתַחֲנוּנִים
הִתְרַצֵּה וְהִתְפַּיֵּס לְדוֹר עָנִי, כִּי אֵין עוֹזֵר.

אָבִינוּ מַלְכֵּנוּ, חָנֵּנוּ וַעֲנֵנוּ, כִּי אֵין בָּנוּ מַעֲשִׂים
עֲשֵׂה עִמָּנוּ צְדָקָה וָחֶסֶד וְהוֹשִׁיעֵנוּ.

Stand for the following.

וַאֲנַחְנוּ לֹא נֵדַע מַה־נַּעֲשֶׂה, כִּי עָלֶיךָ עֵינֵינוּ:
זְכֹר־רַחֲמֶיךָ יהוה וַחֲסָדֶיךָ, כִּי מֵעוֹלָם הֵמָּה:
יְהִי־חַסְדְּךָ יהוה עָלֵינוּ, כַּאֲשֶׁר יִחַלְנוּ לָךְ:
אַל־תִּזְכָּר־לָנוּ עֲוֹנֹת רִאשֹׁנִים
מַהֵר יְקַדְּמוּנוּ רַחֲמֶיךָ, כִּי דַלּוֹנוּ מְאֹד:
חָנֵּנוּ יהוה חָנֵּנוּ, כִּי־רַב שָׂבַעְנוּ בוּז:
בְּרֹגֶז רַחֵם תִּזְכּוֹר:
כִּי־הוּא יָדַע יִצְרֵנוּ, זָכוּר כִּי־עָפָר אֲנָחְנוּ:
◄ עָזְרֵנוּ אֱלֹהֵי יִשְׁעֵנוּ עַל־דְּבַר כְּבוֹד־שְׁמֶךָ
וְהַצִּילֵנוּ וְכַפֵּר עַל־חַטֹּאתֵינוּ לְמַעַן שְׁמֶךָ:

KADDISH SHALEM

Leader: יִתְגַּדַּל May *Hashem* be recognized
as great and holy (*Congregation:* Amen)
in the world that He created.
May He establish His kingdom
during my lifetime and the lifetime of all Jews,
quickly and soon.
Let us say: "Amen" (*Congregation:* Amen).

Congregation: May we thank *Hashem* for ever and ever.
Leader: May we thank *Hashem* for ever and ever.

Leader: *Hashem* should be thanked, praised,
and honored (*Congregation:* He is blessed).
Hashem is beyond all the blessings,
songs, or praises that we could offer.
Let us say: "Amen" (*Congregation:* Amen).

May *Hashem* accept our prayers
and the prayers of all Jews.
Let us say: "Amen." (*Congregation:* Amen).

May *Hashem* give us, and all Jews,
peace and good life.
Let us say: "Amen." (*Congregation:* Amen).

The Leader takes three steps back before saying this line, bows to the left when saying "May," bows to the right when saying "the One," bows to the middle when saying "make peace for us":

May *Hashem*, the One
who makes peace in heaven,
make peace for us and for all Jews.
Let us say: "Amen." (*Congregation:* Amen).

קדיש שלם

חזן: יִתְגַּדַּל וְיִתְקַדַּשׁ שְׁמֵהּ רַבָּא (קהל: אָמֵן)
בְּעָלְמָא דִּי בְרָא כִרְעוּתֵהּ, וְיַמְלִיךְ מַלְכוּתֵהּ
בְּחַיֵּיכוֹן וּבְיוֹמֵיכוֹן וּבְחַיֵּי דְכָל בֵּית יִשְׂרָאֵל
בַּעֲגָלָא וּבִזְמַן קָרִיב, וְאִמְרוּ אָמֵן. (קהל: אָמֵן)

קהל יְהֵא שְׁמֵהּ רַבָּא מְבָרַךְ לְעָלַם וּלְעָלְמֵי עָלְמַיָּא.
חזן: יְהֵא שְׁמֵהּ רַבָּא מְבָרַךְ לְעָלַם וּלְעָלְמֵי עָלְמַיָּא.

חזן: יִתְבָּרַךְ וְיִשְׁתַּבַּח וְיִתְפָּאַר וְיִתְרוֹמַם וְיִתְנַשֵּׂא וְיִתְהַדָּר
וְיִתְעַלֶּה וְיִתְהַלָּל שְׁמֵהּ דְּקֻדְשָׁא בְּרִיךְ הוּא (קהל: בְּרִיךְ הוּא)
לְעֵלָּא מִן כָּל בִּרְכָתָא
/בעשרת ימי תשובה: לְעֵלָּא לְעֵלָּא מִכָּל בִּרְכָתָא/
וְשִׁירָתָא, תֻּשְׁבְּחָתָא וְנֶחֱמָתָא
דַּאֲמִירָן בְּעָלְמָא, וְאִמְרוּ אָמֵן. (קהל: אָמֵן)

תִּתְקַבַּל צְלוֹתְהוֹן וּבָעוּתְהוֹן דְּכָל יִשְׂרָאֵל
קֳדָם אֲבוּהוֹן דִּי בִשְׁמַיָּא, וְאִמְרוּ אָמֵן. (קהל: אָמֵן)

יְהֵא שְׁלָמָא רַבָּא מִן שְׁמַיָּא
וְחַיִּים, עָלֵינוּ וְעַל כָּל יִשְׂרָאֵל, וְאִמְרוּ אָמֵן. (קהל: אָמֵן)

The חזן takes three steps back before saying this line, bows to the left when saying עֹשֶׂה, bows to the right when saying הוּא, bows to the middle when saying יַעֲשֶׂה שָׁלוֹם עָלֵינוּ:

עֹשֶׂה שָׁלוֹם /בעשרת ימי תשובה: הַשָּׁלוֹם/ בִּמְרוֹמָיו
הוּא יַעֲשֶׂה שָׁלוֹם
עָלֵינוּ וְעַל כָּל יִשְׂרָאֵל, וְאִמְרוּ אָמֵן. (קהל: אָמֵן)

Stand while saying "It is our role."

עָלֵינוּ It is our role
to praise You, *Hashem*,
Master of all
and Creator of the world.
You have not made us
like other nations of the world,
rather, You set the Jewish people apart
allowing us the opportunity to serve You.
(Other nations pray to gods that do not exist, while)
we bend our knees and bow in prayer
before the King of all kings, *Hashem*,
in order to give thanks.
Hashem created the heavens above and the land below.
Hashem sits on His awesome throne in heaven
as He, alone, is our God
and ruler of the world.
We willingly accept Him as our King,
there is none else but Him.
As it says in the Torah,
"Today You should understand
that *Hashem* is God
in the heavens above
and on the earth below.
There is no other God but You."

Stand while saying עָלֵינוּ.

עָלֵינוּ לְשַׁבֵּחַ לַאֲדוֹן הַכֹּל
לָתֵת גְּדֻלָּה לְיוֹצֵר בְּרֵאשִׁית
שֶׁלֹּא עָשָׂנוּ כְּגוֹיֵי הָאֲרָצוֹת
וְלֹא שָׂמָנוּ כְּמִשְׁפְּחוֹת הָאֲדָמָה
שֶׁלֹּא שָׂם חֶלְקֵנוּ כָּהֶם, וְגוֹרָלֵנוּ כְּכָל הֲמוֹנָם.
(שֶׁהֵם מִשְׁתַּחֲוִים לְהֶבֶל וָרִיק
וּמִתְפַּלְלִים אֶל אֵל לֹא יוֹשִׁיעַ.)

וַאֲנַחְנוּ כּוֹרְעִים וּמִשְׁתַּחֲוִים וּמוֹדִים
לִפְנֵי מֶלֶךְ מַלְכֵי הַמְּלָכִים, הַקָּדוֹשׁ בָּרוּךְ הוּא
שֶׁהוּא נוֹטֶה שָׁמַיִם וְיוֹסֵד אָרֶץ
וּמוֹשַׁב יְקָרוֹ בַּשָּׁמַיִם מִמַּעַל
וּשְׁכִינַת עֻזּוֹ בְּגָבְהֵי מְרוֹמִים.
הוּא אֱלֹהֵינוּ, אֵין עוֹד.
אֱמֶת מַלְכֵּנוּ, אֶפֶס זוּלָתוֹ
כַּכָּתוּב בְּתוֹרָתוֹ, וְיָדַעְתָּ הַיּוֹם וַהֲשֵׁבֹתָ אֶל־לְבָבֶךָ
כִּי יהוה הוּא הָאֱלֹהִים
בַּשָּׁמַיִם מִמַּעַל וְעַל־הָאָרֶץ מִתָּחַת
אֵין עוֹד:

Hashem,
we hope that all false gods
will be removed from the world
and everyone will soon turn to You alone
as the almighty God of the universe.
All the people of the world
will turn to You
and give honor.
They will accept You as their King,
and You will rule over them soon and forever.
For You are King of the world
and You will remain the ruling King forever.
As it says in Your Torah,
▸ "*Hashem* will be king over all the land.
On that day *Hashem* will be One and His name One."

KADDISH YATOM

The following prayer, said by mourners, requires the presence of a minyan. A transliteration can be found on *page 865.*

Mourner: יִתְגַּדַּל May *Hashem* be recognized
as great and holy (*Congregation:* Amen)
in the world that He created.
May He establish His kingdom
during my lifetime
and the lifetime of all Jews,
quickly and soon.
Let us say:
"Amen" (*Congregation:* Amen).

עַל כֵּן נְקַוֶּה לְּךָ יהוה אֱלֹהֵינוּ
לִרְאוֹת מְהֵרָה בְּתִפְאֶרֶת עֻזֶּךָ
לְהַעֲבִיר גִּלּוּלִים מִן הָאָרֶץ, וְהָאֱלִילִים כָּרוֹת יִכָּרֵתוּן
לְתַקֵּן עוֹלָם בְּמַלְכוּת שַׁדַּי.
וְכָל בְּנֵי בָשָׂר יִקְרְאוּ בִשְׁמֶךָ
לְהַפְנוֹת אֵלֶיךָ כָּל רִשְׁעֵי אָרֶץ.
יַכִּירוּ וְיֵדְעוּ כָּל יוֹשְׁבֵי תֵבֵל
כִּי לְךָ תִּכְרַע כָּל בֶּרֶךְ, תִּשָּׁבַע כָּל לָשׁוֹן.
לְפָנֶיךָ יהוה אֱלֹהֵינוּ יִכְרְעוּ וְיִפֹּלוּ, וְלִכְבוֹד שִׁמְךָ יְקָר יִתֵּנוּ
וִיקַבְּלוּ כֻלָּם אֶת עֹל מַלְכוּתֶךָ
וְתִמְלֹךְ עֲלֵיהֶם מְהֵרָה לְעוֹלָם וָעֶד.
כִּי הַמַּלְכוּת שֶׁלְּךָ הִיא וּלְעוֹלְמֵי עַד תִּמְלֹךְ בְּכָבוֹד
כַּכָּתוּב בְּתוֹרָתֶךָ, יהוה יִמְלֹךְ לְעֹלָם וָעֶד:
◄ וְנֶאֱמַר, וְהָיָה יהוה לְמֶלֶךְ עַל־כָּל־הָאָרֶץ
בַּיּוֹם הַהוּא יִהְיֶה יהוה אֶחָד וּשְׁמוֹ אֶחָד:

קדיש יתום

The following prayer, said by mourners, requires the presence of a מנין.
A transliteration can be found on page 865.

אבל: יִתְגַּדַּל וְיִתְקַדַּשׁ שְׁמֵהּ רַבָּא (קהל: אָמֵן)
בְּעָלְמָא דִּי בְרָא כִרְעוּתֵהּ, וְיַמְלִיךְ מַלְכוּתֵהּ
בְּחַיֵּיכוֹן וּבְיוֹמֵיכוֹן וּבְחַיֵּי דְכָל בֵּית יִשְׂרָאֵל
בַּעֲגָלָא וּבִזְמַן קָרִיב, וְאִמְרוּ אָמֵן. (קהל: אָמֵן)

Congregation: May we thank *Hashem* for ever and ever.

Mourner: May we thank *Hashem* for ever and ever.

Mourner: *Hashem* should be thanked, praised,
and honored (*Congregation:* He is blessed).
Hashem is beyond all the blessings,
songs, or praises that we could offer.
Let us say:
"Amen" (*Congregation:* Amen).

May *Hashem* give us, and all Jews,
peace and good life.
Let us say:
"Amen." (*Congregation:* Amen).

The mourner takes three steps back before saying this line, bows to the left when saying "May," bows to the right when saying "the One," bows to the middle when saying "make peace for us":

May *Hashem*, the One
who makes peace in heaven,
make peace for us and for all Jews.
Let us say:
"Amen." (*Congregation:* Amen).

קהל יְהֵא שְׁמֵהּ רַבָּא מְבָרַךְ לְעָלַם וּלְעָלְמֵי עָלְמַיָּא.

אבל: יְהֵא שְׁמֵהּ רַבָּא מְבָרַךְ לְעָלַם וּלְעָלְמֵי עָלְמַיָּא.

אבל: יִתְבָּרַךְ וְיִשְׁתַּבַּח וְיִתְפָּאַר
וְיִתְרוֹמַם וְיִתְנַשֵּׂא וְיִתְהַדָּר וְיִתְעַלֶּה וְיִתְהַלָּל
שְׁמֵהּ דְּקֻדְשָׁא בְּרִיךְ הוּא (קהל: בְּרִיךְ הוּא)
לְעֵלָּא מִן כָּל בִּרְכָתָא
/בעשרת ימי תשובה: לְעֵלָּא לְעֵלָּא מִכָּל בִּרְכָתָא/
וְשִׁירָתָא, תֻּשְׁבְּחָתָא וְנֶחֱמָתָא
דַּאֲמִירָן בְּעָלְמָא, וְאִמְרוּ אָמֵן. (קהל: אָמֵן)

יְהֵא שְׁלָמָא רַבָּא מִן שְׁמַיָּא
וְחַיִּים, עָלֵינוּ וְעַל כָּל יִשְׂרָאֵל, וְאִמְרוּ אָמֵן. (קהל: אָמֵן)

The mourner takes three steps back before saying this line, bows to the left when saying עֹשֶׂה*, bows to the right when saying* הוּא*, bows to the middle when saying* יַעֲשֶׂה שָׁלוֹם עָלֵינוּ*:*

עֹשֶׂה שָׁלוֹם /בעשרת ימי תשובה: הַשָּׁלוֹם/ בִּמְרוֹמָיו
הוּא יַעֲשֶׂה שָׁלוֹם עָלֵינוּ
וְעַל כָּל יִשְׂרָאֵל, וְאִמְרוּ אָמֵן. (קהל: אָמֵן)

Ma'ariv for Weekdays

Only say the following introduction when praying with a minyan:

Stand when saying the following.

וְהוּא רַחוּם *Hashem* shows kindness
by forgiving our mistakes
rather than destroying us with anger.
Hashem, please save us!
You are our King who answers us
when we call out to You.

Bow when saying the word "Thank."

Leader: **LET US THANK**
Hashem,
for He deserves thanksgiving.

Congregation: Thank *Hashem* for ever and ever!

Leader: Thank *Hashem* for ever and ever!

Those praying without a minyan begin here:
Sit while saying the following.

בָּרוּךְ We thank You,
Hashem, King of the universe,
Who, with His words, brings night.

מעריב לחול

Only say the following introduction when praying with a מנין:

Stand when saying the following.

וְהוּא רַחוּם, יְכַפֵּר עָוֹן וְלֹא־יַשְׁחִית
וְהִרְבָּה לְהָשִׁיב אַפּוֹ, וְלֹא־יָעִיר כָּל־חֲמָתוֹ:
יהוה הוֹשִׁיעָה, הַמֶּלֶךְ יַעֲנֵנוּ בְיוֹם־קָרְאֵנוּ:

Bow when saying the word בָּרוּךְ.

חזן: **בָּרְכוּ**
אֶת יהוה הַמְבֹרָךְ.

קהל: בָּרוּךְ יהוה הַמְבֹרָךְ לְעוֹלָם וָעֶד.

חזן: בָּרוּךְ יהוה הַמְבֹרָךְ לְעוֹלָם וָעֶד.

Those praying without a מנין *begin here:*
Sit while saying the following.

בָּרוּךְ אַתָּה יהוה אֱלֹהֵינוּ מֶלֶךְ הָעוֹלָם
אֲשֶׁר בִּדְבָרוֹ מַעֲרִיב עֲרָבִים

With great wisdom *Hashem* creates:
Time and seasons,
Stars and their placement in the sky,
Day and night, and
Light and dark.
▸ It is *Hashem* who oversees all.
May You, *Hashem,* continue to always rule over us.
Thank You, *Hashem,* who brings night.

אַהֲבַת עוֹלָם *Hashem,* You have shown great love
to Your Jewish people,
by teaching us Your Torah and *mitzvot.*
Therefore, *Hashem,* we will speak about Your *mitzvot*
and enjoy the words of Your Torah
when we go to sleep and when we wake.
Torah and *mitzvot* are the basis of our lives;
▸ we will think about them day and night.
Hashem, may You never lessen Your love
for the Jewish people.
Thank You, *Hashem,* who loves His Jewish people.

וּבָהֶם נֶהְגֶּה יוֹמָם וָלָיְלָה *We will think about them day and night.* We connect to *Hashem* by learning Torah and doing *mitzvot.* Since we were created to serve *Hashem* and connect with Him, we must make Torah and *mitzvot* a central part of our lives by partaking in these holy actions every day and night.

בְּחָכְמָה פּוֹתֵחַ שְׁעָרִים
וּבִתְבוּנָה מְשַׁנֶּה עִתִּים
וּמַחֲלִיף אֶת הַזְּמַנִּים
וּמְסַדֵּר אֶת הַכּוֹכָבִים בְּמִשְׁמְרוֹתֵיהֶם בָּרָקִיעַ כִּרְצוֹנוֹ.
בּוֹרֵא יוֹם וָלָיְלָה
גּוֹלֵל אוֹר מִפְּנֵי חֹשֶׁךְ וְחֹשֶׁךְ מִפְּנֵי אוֹר
◂ וּמַעֲבִיר יוֹם וּמֵבִיא לָיְלָה
וּמַבְדִּיל בֵּין יוֹם וּבֵין לָיְלָה
יהוה צְבָאוֹת שְׁמוֹ.
אֵל חַי וְקַיָּם תָּמִיד, יִמְלֹךְ עָלֵינוּ לְעוֹלָם וָעֶד.
בָּרוּךְ אַתָּה יהוה, הַמַּעֲרִיב עֲרָבִים.

אַהֲבַת עוֹלָם בֵּית יִשְׂרָאֵל עַמְּךָ אָהָבְתָּ
תּוֹרָה וּמִצְוֹת, חֻקִּים וּמִשְׁפָּטִים, אוֹתָנוּ לִמַּדְתָּ
עַל כֵּן יהוה אֱלֹהֵינוּ בְּשָׁכְבֵנוּ וּבְקוּמֵנוּ נָשִׂיחַ בְּחֻקֶּיךָ
וְנִשְׂמַח בְּדִבְרֵי תוֹרָתֶךָ וּבְמִצְוֹתֶיךָ לְעוֹלָם וָעֶד
◂ כִּי הֵם חַיֵּינוּ וְאֹרֶךְ יָמֵינוּ
וּבָהֶם נֶהְגֶּה יוֹמָם וָלָיְלָה.
וְאַהֲבָתְךָ אַל תָּסִיר מִמֶּנּוּ לְעוֹלָמִים.
בָּרוּךְ אַתָּה יהוה, אוֹהֵב עַמּוֹ יִשְׂרָאֵל.

Say this line when praying alone:

God, You are our trustworthy King.

Cover your eyes with your right hand, and say this line aloud:

LISTEN AND UNDERSTAND, JEWISH PEOPLE,
HASHEM IS OUR ONE AND ONLY GOD.

Say this line quietly:

Thank You, *Hashem,* our God.
Your kingdom lasts forever.

וְאָהַבְתָּ Love *Hashem,* your God,
with all of your heart, soul, and belongings.
Live according to God's words and *mitzvot.*
Think about and recite the Shema
when sitting in your home,
when traveling on the road,
when you go to sleep at night,
and when you first wake up in the morning.
Wear *tefillin* on your arm and head,
and hang a *mezuzah* on your door.

וְהָיָה If you live
according to the *mitzvot* of *Hashem,*
loving and serving Him
with all your effort,
Hashem will give you reward.
Hashem will bring rain for your plants to grow
and provide you with the food you need to live.

Say this line when praying alone:

אֵל מֶלֶךְ נֶאֱמָן

Cover your eyes with your right hand, and say this line aloud:

שְׁמַע יִשְׂרָאֵל, יהוה אֱלֹהֵינוּ, יהוה ׀ אֶחָד:

Say this line quietly:

בָּרוּךְ שֵׁם כְּבוֹד מַלְכוּתוֹ לְעוֹלָם וָעֶד.

וְאָהַבְתָּ אֵת יהוה אֱלֹהֶיךָ
בְּכָל־לְבָבְךָ וּבְכָל־נַפְשְׁךָ וּבְכָל־מְאֹדֶךָ:
וְהָיוּ הַדְּבָרִים הָאֵלֶּה, אֲשֶׁר אָנֹכִי מְצַוְּךָ הַיּוֹם, עַל־לְבָבֶךָ:
וְשִׁנַּנְתָּם לְבָנֶיךָ וְדִבַּרְתָּ בָּם
בְּשִׁבְתְּךָ בְּבֵיתֶךָ וּבְלֶכְתְּךָ בַדֶּרֶךְ, וּבְשָׁכְבְּךָ וּבְקוּמֶךָ:
וּקְשַׁרְתָּם לְאוֹת עַל־יָדֶךָ, וְהָיוּ לְטֹטָפֹת בֵּין עֵינֶיךָ:
וּכְתַבְתָּם עַל־מְזֻזוֹת בֵּיתֶךָ וּבִשְׁעָרֶיךָ:

וְהָיָה אִם־שָׁמֹעַ תִּשְׁמְעוּ אֶל־מִצְוֺתַי
אֲשֶׁר אָנֹכִי מְצַוֶּה אֶתְכֶם הַיּוֹם
לְאַהֲבָה אֶת־יהוה אֱלֹהֵיכֶם וּלְעָבְדוֹ
בְּכָל־לְבַבְכֶם וּבְכָל־נַפְשְׁכֶם:
וְנָתַתִּי מְטַר־אַרְצְכֶם בְּעִתּוֹ, יוֹרֶה וּמַלְקוֹשׁ
וְאָסַפְתָּ דְגָנֶךָ וְתִירֹשְׁךָ וְיִצְהָרֶךָ:
וְנָתַתִּי עֵשֶׂב בְּשָׂדְךָ לִבְהֶמְתֶּךָ, וְאָכַלְתָּ וְשָׂבָעְתָּ:

However, if you sin
and do not serve *Hashem*,
there will be consequences and punishments;
Hashem might not provide you
with health, money,
or other basics you need to live.
Therefore,
be careful to follow *Hashem*'s *mitzvot*
and set yourself reminders,
such as wearing *tefillin* on
your arms and head,
and placing *mezuzot* on your doorposts.
If you do this,
you will live a long life.

וַיֹּאמֶר *Hashem* told Moshe
that we, the Jewish people,
should have *tzitzit*
on the corners of our clothing.
Each set of *tzitzit* strings
should have a blue string.
The *tzitzit* should be worn
so that you can see them.
They will remind you to focus on God
and His *mitzvot*.

הִשָּׁמְרוּ לָכֶם פֶּן־יִפְתֶּה לְבַבְכֶם
וְסַרְתֶּם וַעֲבַדְתֶּם אֱלֹהִים אֲחֵרִים וְהִשְׁתַּחֲוִיתֶם לָהֶם:
וְחָרָה אַף־יהוה בָּכֶם, וְעָצַר אֶת־הַשָּׁמַיִם וְלֹא־יִהְיֶה מָטָר
וְהָאֲדָמָה לֹא תִתֵּן אֶת־יְבוּלָהּ
וַאֲבַדְתֶּם מְהֵרָה מֵעַל הָאָרֶץ הַטֹּבָה אֲשֶׁר יהוה נֹתֵן לָכֶם:
וְשַׂמְתֶּם אֶת־דְּבָרַי אֵלֶּה עַל־לְבַבְכֶם וְעַל־נַפְשְׁכֶם
וּקְשַׁרְתֶּם אֹתָם לְאוֹת עַל־יֶדְכֶם
וְהָיוּ לְטוֹטָפֹת בֵּין עֵינֵיכֶם:
וְלִמַּדְתֶּם אֹתָם אֶת־בְּנֵיכֶם לְדַבֵּר בָּם
בְּשִׁבְתְּךָ בְּבֵיתֶךָ וּבְלֶכְתְּךָ בַדֶּרֶךְ, וּבְשָׁכְבְּךָ וּבְקוּמֶךָ:
וּכְתַבְתָּם עַל־מְזוּזוֹת בֵּיתֶךָ וּבִשְׁעָרֶיךָ:
לְמַעַן יִרְבּוּ יְמֵיכֶם וִימֵי בְנֵיכֶם עַל הָאֲדָמָה
אֲשֶׁר נִשְׁבַּע יהוה לַאֲבֹתֵיכֶם לָתֵת לָהֶם
כִּימֵי הַשָּׁמַיִם עַל־הָאָרֶץ:

וַיֹּאמֶר יהוה אֶל־מֹשֶׁה לֵּאמֹר:
דַּבֵּר אֶל־בְּנֵי יִשְׂרָאֵל וְאָמַרְתָּ אֲלֵהֶם
וְעָשׂוּ לָהֶם צִיצִת עַל־כַּנְפֵי בִגְדֵיהֶם לְדֹרֹתָם
וְנָתְנוּ עַל־צִיצִת הַכָּנָף פְּתִיל תְּכֵלֶת:
וְהָיָה לָכֶם לְצִיצִת, וּרְאִיתֶם אֹתוֹ
וּזְכַרְתֶּם אֶת־כָּל־מִצְוֹת יהוה וַעֲשִׂיתֶם אֹתָם

Hashem, the same God
who miraculously saved the Jewish people
from slavery in Egypt,
is your God.

THIS IS TRUE.

The Leader repeats:

▸ *Hashem* is your true God.

We have complete faith that:

Hashem is our God,
There is none else but Him, and
We, the Jewish nation, are His people.

Hashem is our King who:

Saves us from our enemies,
Does great actions
beyond our understanding,
Performs miracles
that are too many to count,
Protects us from getting hurt,

וְלֹא תָתֽוּרוּ אַחֲרֵי לְבַבְכֶם וְאַחֲרֵי עֵינֵיכֶם
אֲשֶׁר־אַתֶּם זֹנִים אַחֲרֵיהֶם:
לְמַעַן תִּזְכְּרוּ וַעֲשִׂיתֶם אֶת־כָּל־מִצְוֺתָי
וִהְיִיתֶם קְדֹשִׁים לֵאלֹהֵיכֶם:
אֲנִי יהוה אֱלֹהֵיכֶם, אֲשֶׁר הוֹצֵאתִי אֶתְכֶם מֵאֶרֶץ מִצְרַיִם
לִהְיוֹת לָכֶם לֵאלֹהִים
אֲנִי יהוה אֱלֹהֵיכֶם:

אֱמֶת

The חזן *repeats:*

› יהוה אֱלֹהֵיכֶם אֱמֶת

וֶאֱמוּנָה כָּל זֹאת וְקַיָּם עָלֵינוּ
כִּי הוּא יהוה אֱלֹהֵינוּ וְאֵין זוּלָתוֹ
וַאֲנַחְנוּ יִשְׂרָאֵל עַמּוֹ.
הַפּוֹדֵנוּ מִיַּד מְלָכִים
מַלְכֵּנוּ הַגּוֹאֲלֵנוּ מִכַּף כָּל הֶעָרִיצִים.
הָאֵל הַנִּפְרָע לָנוּ מִצָּרֵינוּ
וְהַמְשַׁלֵּם גְּמוּל לְכָל אוֹיְבֵי נַפְשֵׁנוּ.
הָעוֹשֶׂה גְדוֹלוֹת עַד אֵין חֵקֶר
וְנִפְלָאוֹת עַד אֵין מִסְפָּר
הַשָּׂם נַפְשֵׁנוּ בַּחַיִּים, וְלֹא־נָתַן לַמּוֹט רַגְלֵנוּ:

Led us to victory over our enemies,
Performed miracles on our behalf and
fought our war against Pharaoh,
Took the lives of the first born Egyptians,
Brought the Jewish people out of Egypt and
into freedom forever,
Split the Reed Sea, and
led His Jewish people through it, and
Saved the Jewish people by bringing the water
crashing down upon our enemies.

When the Jewish people saw these miracles
they praised, thanked, ▸ and accepted You,
Hashem, as their only Ruler.
Moshe and all of the Jewish people
sang praise to You *Hashem*
and cried out:

Say the following two sentences out loud:

"Who is as strong as You, *Hashem*?
Who is as holy and awesome as You, *Hashem*?"

▸ When You, *Hashem*, split the sea,
Moshe and Your Jewish people knew
that You were King and said, "This is my God."
They then said:

Say the following sentence out loud:

"*Hashem* will rule as King for ever and ever."

▸ The Torah writes:
"*Hashem*, You have saved the Jewish people
from a stronger nation."
Thank You, *Hashem*, who saves the Jewish people.

הַמַּדְרִיכֵנוּ עַל בָּמוֹת אוֹיְבֵינוּ
וַיָּרֶם קַרְנֵנוּ עַל כָּל שׂוֹנְאֵינוּ.
הָעוֹשֶׂה לָּנוּ נִסִּים וּנְקָמָה בְּפַרְעֹה
אוֹתוֹת וּמוֹפְתִים בְּאַדְמַת בְּנֵי חָם.
הַמַּכֶּה בְעֶבְרָתוֹ כָּל בְּכוֹרֵי מִצְרָיִם
וַיּוֹצֵא אֶת עַמּוֹ יִשְׂרָאֵל מִתּוֹכָם לְחֵרוּת עוֹלָם.
הַמַּעֲבִיר בָּנָיו בֵּין גִּזְרֵי יַם סוּף
אֶת רוֹדְפֵיהֶם וְאֶת שׂוֹנְאֵיהֶם בִּתְהוֹמוֹת טִבַּע
וְרָאוּ בָנָיו גְּבוּרָתוֹ, שִׁבְּחוּ וְהוֹדוּ לִשְׁמוֹ
◂ וּמַלְכוּתוֹ בְּרָצוֹן קִבְּלוּ עֲלֵיהֶם.
מֹשֶׁה וּבְנֵי יִשְׂרָאֵל, לְךָ עָנוּ שִׁירָה בְּשִׂמְחָה רַבָּה
וְאָמְרוּ כֻלָּם

Say the following two sentences out loud:

מִי־כָמֹכָה בָּאֵלִם יהוה
מִי כָּמֹכָה נֶאְדָּר בַּקֹּדֶשׁ
נוֹרָא תְהִלֹּת עֹשֵׂה פֶלֶא:

◂ מַלְכוּתְךָ רָאוּ בָנֶיךָ, בּוֹקֵעַ יָם לִפְנֵי מֹשֶׁה
זֶה אֵלִי עָנוּ, וְאָמְרוּ

Say the following sentence out loud:

יהוה יִמְלֹךְ לְעֹלָם וָעֶד:

◂ וְנֶאֱמַר

כִּי־פָדָה יהוה אֶת־יַעֲקֹב, וּגְאָלוֹ מִיַּד חָזָק מִמֶּנּוּ:
בָּרוּךְ אַתָּה יהוה, גָּאַל יִשְׂרָאֵל.

הַשְׁכִּיבֵנוּ *Hashem,* please allow us
to lie down at night in peace
and awake in the morning with life.
With peace, protect us, direct us, and save us.
Protect us and remove our:
Enemies,
Hunger,
Sorrow, and
All those who are against us.
You, *Hashem,* our God, are a kind and merciful King.
▸ Guard us when in public and in private,
For life and peace, from now and forever.
Thank You, *Hashem,*
who forever guards His Jewish people.

בָּרוּךְ *Hashem* is praised forever.
Hashem, from Your holy city of Jerusalem,
You are praised.
Hashem, who does wonders for His people,
You are praised.
Hashem, Your name itself is praised.
May the whole world be filled
with Your greatness forever. *Amen* and *Amen.*
Hashem, Your honor lasts forever,
take pride in Your creations.
We praise You, *Hashem,* for ever and ever.
Hashem will not forget His Jewish people,
He promised to make us His nation.
Seeing the miracles of the world,
the Jewish people declared *Hashem* is God.

הַשְׁכִּיבֵנוּ יהוה אֱלֹהֵינוּ לְשָׁלוֹם
וְהַעֲמִידֵנוּ מַלְכֵּנוּ לְחַיִּים
וּפְרֹשׂ עָלֵינוּ סֻכַּת שְׁלוֹמֶךָ, וְתַקְּנֵנוּ בְּעֵצָה טוֹבָה מִלְּפָנֶיךָ
וְהוֹשִׁיעֵנוּ לְמַעַן שְׁמֶךָ.
וְהָגֵן בַּעֲדֵנוּ, וְהָסֵר מֵעָלֵינוּ אוֹיֵב, דֶּבֶר וְחֶרֶב וְרָעָב וְיָגוֹן
וְהָסֵר שָׂטָן מִלְּפָנֵינוּ וּמֵאַחֲרֵינוּ, וּבְצֵל כְּנָפֶיךָ תַּסְתִּירֵנוּ
כִּי אֵל שׁוֹמְרֵנוּ וּמַצִּילֵנוּ אָתָּה
כִּי אֵל מֶלֶךְ חַנּוּן וְרַחוּם אָתָּה.
◂ וּשְׁמֹר צֵאתֵנוּ וּבוֹאֵנוּ לְחַיִּים וּלְשָׁלוֹם מֵעַתָּה וְעַד עוֹלָם.
בָּרוּךְ אַתָּה יהוה, שׁוֹמֵר עַמּוֹ יִשְׂרָאֵל לָעַד.

בָּרוּךְ יהוה לְעוֹלָם, אָמֵן וְאָמֵן:
בָּרוּךְ יהוה מִצִּיּוֹן, שֹׁכֵן יְרוּשָׁלָםִ, הַלְלוּיָהּ:
בָּרוּךְ יהוה אֱלֹהִים אֱלֹהֵי יִשְׂרָאֵל, עֹשֵׂה נִפְלָאוֹת לְבַדּוֹ:
וּבָרוּךְ שֵׁם כְּבוֹדוֹ לְעוֹלָם
וְיִמָּלֵא כְבוֹדוֹ אֶת־כָּל־הָאָרֶץ, אָמֵן וְאָמֵן:
יְהִי כְבוֹד יהוה לְעוֹלָם, יִשְׂמַח יהוה בְּמַעֲשָׂיו:
יְהִי שֵׁם יהוה מְבֹרָךְ מֵעַתָּה וְעַד־עוֹלָם:
כִּי לֹא־יִטֹּשׁ יהוה אֶת־עַמּוֹ בַּעֲבוּר שְׁמוֹ הַגָּדוֹל
כִּי הוֹאִיל יהוה לַעֲשׂוֹת אֶתְכֶם לוֹ לְעָם:
וַיַּרְא כָּל־הָעָם וַיִּפְּלוּ עַל־פְּנֵיהֶם
וַיֹּאמְרוּ, יהוה הוּא הָאֱלֹהִים, יהוה הוּא הָאֱלֹהִים:

Hashem will be king
over all the land.
On that day
Hashem will be One and His name One.
We have complete trust in You, *Hashem*,
who loves us.
Please save us *Hashem*, our God,
and rescue us from our enemies
so we can thank and serve You.
All the nations of the world
will bow before You, *Hashem*,
and honor You,
because You are great
and perform miracles.
We are Your people
and we will thank You forever,
for every generation.

בָּרוּךְ We thank *Hashem*
in the morning when we wake up,
and at night when we go to sleep,
for it is *Hashem* who gives us life.
Hashem, unite and rule over us
for ever and ever.

יִרְאוּ May we have the opportunity
to see and celebrate the rebuilding
of the *Beit HaMikdash*.

וְהָיָה יהוה לְמֶלֶךְ עַל־כָּל־הָאָרֶץ
בַּיּוֹם הַהוּא יִהְיֶה יהוה אֶחָד וּשְׁמוֹ אֶחָד:
יְהִי־חַסְדְּךָ יהוה עָלֵינוּ, כַּאֲשֶׁר יִחַלְנוּ לָךְ:
הוֹשִׁיעֵנוּ יהוה אֱלֹהֵינוּ, וְקַבְּצֵנוּ מִן־הַגּוֹיִם
לְהוֹדוֹת לְשֵׁם קָדְשֶׁךָ, לְהִשְׁתַּבֵּחַ בִּתְהִלָּתֶךָ:
כָּל־גּוֹיִם אֲשֶׁר עָשִׂיתָ, יָבוֹאוּ וְיִשְׁתַּחֲווּ לְפָנֶיךָ, אֲדֹנָי
וִיכַבְּדוּ לִשְׁמֶךָ:
כִּי־גָדוֹל אַתָּה וְעֹשֵׂה נִפְלָאוֹת, אַתָּה אֱלֹהִים לְבַדֶּךָ:
וַאֲנַחְנוּ עַמְּךָ וְצֹאן מַרְעִיתֶךָ, נוֹדֶה לְּךָ לְעוֹלָם
לְדוֹר וָדֹר נְסַפֵּר תְּהִלָּתֶךָ:

בָּרוּךְ יהוה בַּיּוֹם, בָּרוּךְ יהוה בַּלָּיְלָה
בָּרוּךְ יהוה בְּשָׁכְבֵנוּ, בָּרוּךְ יהוה בְּקוּמֵנוּ.
כִּי בְיָדְךָ נַפְשׁוֹת הַחַיִּים וְהַמֵּתִים.
אֲשֶׁר בְּיָדוֹ נֶפֶשׁ כָּל־חָי, וְרוּחַ כָּל־בְּשַׂר־אִישׁ:
בְּיָדְךָ אַפְקִיד רוּחִי, פָּדִיתָה אוֹתִי יהוה אֵל אֱמֶת:
אֱלֹהֵינוּ שֶׁבַּשָּׁמַיִם, יַחֵד שִׁמְךָ וְקַיֵּם מַלְכוּתְךָ תָּמִיד
וּמְלֹךְ עָלֵינוּ לְעוֹלָם וָעֶד.

יִרְאוּ עֵינֵינוּ וְיִשְׂמַח לִבֵּנוּ
וְתָגֵל נַפְשֵׁנוּ בִּישׁוּעָתְךָ בֶּאֱמֶת
בֶּאֱמֹר לְצִיּוֹן מָלַךְ אֱלֹהָיִךְ.

You *Hashem* are the King,
You were always the King,
and You will be the King forever.
▸ *Hashem,* You have ruled forever and You will always rule,
there is no King other than You.
Thank You, *Hashem,* who will rule over us
and all of His creations forever.

HALF KADDISH

Leader: יִתְגַּדַּל May *Hashem* be recognized
as great and holy (*Congregation:* Amen)
in the world that He created.
May He establish His kingdom
during my lifetime
and the lifetime of all Jews,
quickly and soon.
Let us say:
"Amen" (*Congregation:* Amen).

Congregation: May we thank *Hashem* for ever and ever.
Leader: May we thank *Hashem* for ever and ever.

Leader: *Hashem* should be thanked, praised,
and honored (*Congregation:* He is blessed).
Hashem is beyond all the blessings,
songs, or praises
that we could offer.
Let us say:
"Amen" (*Congregation:* Amen).

יהוה מֶלֶךְ, יהוה מָלָךְ, יהוה יִמְלֹךְ לְעֹלָם וָעֶד.

‹ כִּי הַמַּלְכוּת שֶׁלְּךָ הִיא, וּלְעוֹלְמֵי עַד תִּמְלֹךְ בְּכָבוֹד
כִּי אֵין לָנוּ מֶלֶךְ אֶלָּא אָתָּה.
בָּרוּךְ אַתָּה יהוה
הַמֶּלֶךְ בִּכְבוֹדוֹ תָּמִיד, יִמְלֹךְ עָלֵינוּ לְעוֹלָם וָעֶד
וְעַל כָּל מַעֲשָׂיו.

חצי קדיש

חזן: יִתְגַּדַּל וְיִתְקַדַּשׁ שְׁמֵהּ רַבָּא (קהל: אָמֵן)
בְּעָלְמָא דִּי בְרָא כִרְעוּתֵהּ, וְיַמְלִיךְ מַלְכוּתֵהּ
בְּחַיֵּיכוֹן וּבְיוֹמֵיכוֹן וּבְחַיֵּי דְכָל בֵּית יִשְׂרָאֵל
בַּעֲגָלָא וּבִזְמַן קָרִיב, וְאִמְרוּ אָמֵן. (קהל: אָמֵן)

קהל יְהֵא שְׁמֵהּ רַבָּא מְבָרַךְ לְעָלַם וּלְעָלְמֵי עָלְמַיָּא.

חזן: יְהֵא שְׁמֵהּ רַבָּא מְבָרַךְ לְעָלַם וּלְעָלְמֵי עָלְמַיָּא.

חזן: יִתְבָּרַךְ וְיִשְׁתַּבַּח וְיִתְפָּאַר וְיִתְרוֹמַם וְיִתְנַשֵּׂא
וְיִתְהַדָּר וְיִתְעַלֶּה וְיִתְהַלָּל
שְׁמֵהּ דְּקֻדְשָׁא בְּרִיךְ הוּא (קהל: בְּרִיךְ הוּא)
לְעֵלָּא מִן כָּל בִּרְכָתָא
/בעשרת ימי תשובה: לְעֵלָּא לְעֵלָּא מִכָּל בִּרְכָתָא/
וְשִׁירָתָא, תֻּשְׁבְּחָתָא וְנֶחֱמָתָא
דַּאֲמִירָן בְּעָלְמָא, וְאִמְרוּ אָמֵן. (קהל: אָמֵן)

AMIDA

Take three steps back then three steps forward then stand with your feet together.

Hashem, open my lips and help my mouth recite Your praise.

ANCESTORS

Bend the knees when saying "We thank," bow when saying "You," and stand straight before saying "Hashem."

בָּרוּךְ We thank You, *Hashem,*
our God, and God of our ancestors,
Avraham, Yitzchak, and Yaakov.
You, *Hashem,* are the great, mighty, awesome, kind,
and all-powerful Creator.
It is because of the greatness of our ancestors,
Avraham, Yitzchak, and Yaakov,
that *Hashem* will bring *Mashiach.*

Between Rosh Hashana and Yom Kippur say:

Give us life in the year to come
and write us in the book of life, *Hashem,*
who gives life.

Hashem is our King who helps, guides, and protects us.

Bend the knees when saying "Thank," bow when saying "You," and stand straight before saying "Hashem."

Thank You, *Hashem,*
who protects us in the merit of Avraham.

HASHEM'S STRENGTH

אַתָּה You, *Hashem,* have unlimited strength.
You save people in their time of need,
and You have the power to bring the dead back to life.

עמידה

Take three steps back then three steps forward then stand with your feet together.

אֲדֹנָי, שְׂפָתַי תִּפְתָּח, וּפִי יַגִּיד תְּהִלָּתֶךָ:

אבות

Bend the knees when saying בָּרוּךְ*, bow when saying* אַתָּה*, and stand straight before saying Hashem's name.*

בָּרוּךְ אַתָּה יהוה, אֱלֹהֵינוּ וֵאלֹהֵי אֲבוֹתֵינוּ
אֱלֹהֵי אַבְרָהָם, אֱלֹהֵי יִצְחָק, וֵאלֹהֵי יַעֲקֹב
הָאֵל הַגָּדוֹל הַגִּבּוֹר וְהַנּוֹרָא, אֵל עֶלְיוֹן
גּוֹמֵל חֲסָדִים טוֹבִים, וְקוֹנֵה הַכֹּל
וְזוֹכֵר חַסְדֵי אָבוֹת
וּמֵבִיא גוֹאֵל לִבְנֵי בְנֵיהֶם לְמַעַן שְׁמוֹ בְּאַהֲבָה.

Between ראש השנה *and* יום כיפור *say:*

זָכְרֵנוּ לְחַיִּים, מֶלֶךְ חָפֵץ בַּחַיִּים
וְכָתְבֵנוּ בְּסֵפֶר הַחַיִּים
לְמַעַנְךָ אֱלֹהִים חַיִּים.

מֶלֶךְ עוֹזֵר וּמוֹשִׁיעַ וּמָגֵן.

Bend the knees when saying בָּרוּךְ*, bow when saying* אַתָּה*, and stand straight before saying Hashem's name.*

בָּרוּךְ אַתָּה יהוה, מָגֵן אַבְרָהָם.

גבורות

אַתָּה גִּבּוֹר לְעוֹלָם, אֲדֹנָי
מְחַיֵּה מֵתִים אַתָּה, רַב לְהוֹשִׁיעַ

This line is said during the rainy season, from Simchat Torah to Pesach:
(You make the wind blow and cause the rain to fall)

With kindness You provide the living
with the necessities to live,
and with mercy You keep Your promise
of bringing the dead back to life.
For the living, You:
Support those who are falling,
Heal those who are sick, and
Free those who are in challenging situations.
Who is like You, *Hashem,*
and who can compare to You?
You, *Hashem,* are our King
who has the power to cause death and life.

Between Rosh Hashana and Yom Kippur say:
Who is like You, *Hashem,* our caring Father
who remembers His people for good and gives them life?

We have complete faith
that You will bring us back to life after our passing.
Thank You, *Hashem,* for bringing the dead back to life.

HASHEM'S HOLINESS

אַתָּה קָדוֹשׁ *Hashem,* You are holy and Your name is holy.
The Jewish people, who are holy,
will praise You, *Hashem,* each day.
Thank You, *Hashem,*
the holy God. /*Between Rosh Hashana & Yom Kippur say:* the holy King./

This line is said during the rainy season, from שמחת תורה *to* פסח*:*

(מַשִּׁיב הָרְוּחַ וּמוֹרִיד הַגֶּֽשֶׁם)

מְכַלְכֵּל חַיִּים בְּחֶסֶד, מְחַיֵּה מֵתִים בְּרַחֲמִים רַבִּים
סוֹמֵךְ נוֹפְלִים
וְרוֹפֵא חוֹלִים
וּמַתִּיר אֲסוּרִים
וּמְקַיֵּם אֱמוּנָתוֹ לִישֵׁנֵי עָפָר.
מִי כָמְוֹךָ, בַּֽעַל גְּבוּרוֹת
וּמִי דּֽוֹמֶה לָּךְ
מֶֽלֶךְ, מֵמִית וּמְחַיֶּה וּמַצְמִֽיחַ יְשׁוּעָה.

Between ראש השנה *and* יום כיפור *say:*

מִי כָמְוֹךָ אַב הָרַחֲמִים
זוֹכֵר יְצוּרָיו לְחַיִּים בְּרַחֲמִים.

וְנֶאֱמָן אַתָּה לְהַחֲיוֹת מֵתִים.
בָּרוּךְ אַתָּה יהוה, מְחַיֵּה הַמֵּתִים.

קדושת השם

אַתָּה קָדוֹשׁ וְשִׁמְךָ קָדוֹשׁ
וּקְדוֹשִׁים בְּכָל יוֹם יְהַלְלְוּךָ סֶּֽלָה.
בָּרוּךְ אַתָּה יהוה
הָאֵל הַקָּדוֹשׁ. / *Between* ראש השנה & יום כיפור *say* הַמֶּֽלֶךְ הַקָּדוֹשׁ. /

GIVE US WISDOM

אַתָּה חוֹנֵן You, *Hashem*,
give wisdom and understanding to man.

On Motza'ei Shabbat and Motza'ei Yom Tov add:

אַתָּה חוֹנַנְתָּנוּ You, *Hashem*, gave us Your precious Torah and allowed us to perform Your *mitzvot*. You made clear the differences between:

Holy and non-holy,
Light and darkness,
Israel and other nations, and
Shabbat, the seventh day, and the six days of work.

Hashem, our Father and King, allow this coming week to bring us peace. Please free us from sin and allow us to draw closer to You. And...

Please continue to give us wisdom, understanding,
and the ability to properly use our wisdom
in our daily lives.
Thank You, *Hashem*, for giving us wisdom.

RETURN US TO *HASHEM*

הֲשִׁיבֵנוּ *Hashem*, we feel distanced from Your Torah
and from serving You properly.
Please accept us and bring us closer to You, *Hashem*.
We feel bad for our mistakes that distanced us from You.
Thank You, *Hashem*, for wanting us to return to You.

FORGIVE US

(Lightly hit the left side of your chest when you say "accidentally" and "purposely.")

סְלַח *Hashem*, please forgive us for the sins we have done
accidentally and purposely.
You, *Hashem*, are forgiving and understanding.
Thank You, *Hashem*, who repeatedly forgives.

דעת

אַתָּה חוֹנֵן לְאָדָם דַּעַת, וּמְלַמֵּד לֶאֱנוֹשׁ בִּינָה.

On מוצאי יום טוב *and* מוצאי שבת *add:*

אַתָּה חוֹנַנְתָּנוּ לְמַדַּע תּוֹרָתֶךָ, וַתְּלַמְּדֵנוּ לַעֲשׂוֹת חֻקֵּי רְצוֹנֶךָ
וַתַּבְדֵּל יהוה אֱלֹהֵינוּ בֵּין קֹדֶשׁ לְחֹל
בֵּין אוֹר לְחֹשֶׁךְ
בֵּין יִשְׂרָאֵל לָעַמִּים
בֵּין יוֹם הַשְּׁבִיעִי לְשֵׁשֶׁת יְמֵי הַמַּעֲשֶׂה.
אָבִינוּ מַלְכֵּנוּ, הָחֵל עָלֵינוּ הַיָּמִים הַבָּאִים לִקְרָאתֵנוּ לְשָׁלוֹם,
חֲשׂוּכִים מִכָּל חֵטְא וּמְנֻקִּים מִכָּל עָוֹן וּמְדֻבָּקִים בְּיִרְאָתֶךָ. וְ

חָנֵּנוּ מֵאִתְּךָ דֵּעָה בִּינָה וְהַשְׂכֵּל.
בָּרוּךְ אַתָּה יהוה, חוֹנֵן הַדָּעַת.

תשובה

הֲשִׁיבֵנוּ אָבִינוּ לְתוֹרָתֶךָ, וְקָרְבֵנוּ מַלְכֵּנוּ לַעֲבוֹדָתֶךָ
וְהַחֲזִירֵנוּ בִּתְשׁוּבָה שְׁלֵמָה לְפָנֶיךָ.
בָּרוּךְ אַתָּה יהוה, הָרוֹצֶה בִּתְשׁוּבָה.

סליחה

(Lightly hit the left side of your chest when you say חָטָאנוּ *and* פָּשָׁעְנוּ*)*

סְלַח לָנוּ אָבִינוּ כִּי חָטָאנוּ
מְחַל לָנוּ מַלְכֵּנוּ כִּי פָשָׁעְנוּ
כִּי מוֹחֵל וְסוֹלֵחַ אָתָּה.
בָּרוּךְ אַתָּה יהוה, חַנּוּן הַמַּרְבֶּה לִסְלֹחַ.

SAVE US

רְאֵה *Hashem*, please see our difficulties
and help us face our struggles.
Save us because You have great power.
Thank You, *Hashem*,
who saves the Jewish people.

HEAL US

רְפָאֵנוּ *Hashem*, if You decide to heal the sick,
they will be healed.
If You decide to save those in need, they will be saved.
Please allow the sick
to recover completely from all sicknesses,
for You are the true source of healing and saving.
Thank You, *Hashem*,
who heals the Jewish people who are sick.

PROVIDE FOOD FOR US

בָּרֵךְ Bless this year for us *Hashem*,
so that we should always have food to eat.

> *Say this phrase during the winter season, from December 4th through Pesach.*
>
> Provide rain and dew as a blessing
>
> *Say this phrase during the summer season, from Chol Hamoed Pesach through Mincha of December 3rd.*
>
> Provide blessing

across the earth,
allowing this year to be a great year of food supply.
Thank You, *Hashem*,
for filling our year with blessing.

גאולה

רְאֵה בְעָנְיֵנוּ, וְרִיבָה רִיבֵנוּ
וּגְאָלֵנוּ מְהֵרָה לְמַעַן שְׁמֶךָ, כִּי גּוֹאֵל חָזָק אָתָּה.
בָּרוּךְ אַתָּה יהוה, גּוֹאֵל יִשְׂרָאֵל.

רפואה

רְפָאֵנוּ יהוה וְנֵרָפֵא
הוֹשִׁיעֵנוּ וְנִוָּשֵׁעָה, כִּי תְהִלָּתֵנוּ אָתָּה
וְהַעֲלֵה רְפוּאָה שְׁלֵמָה לְכָל מַכּוֹתֵינוּ
כִּי אֵל מֶלֶךְ רוֹפֵא נֶאֱמָן וְרַחֲמָן אָתָּה.
בָּרוּךְ אַתָּה יהוה, רוֹפֵא חוֹלֵי עַמּוֹ יִשְׂרָאֵל.

ברכת השנים

בָּרֵךְ עָלֵינוּ יהוה אֱלֹהֵינוּ אֶת הַשָּׁנָה הַזֹּאת
וְאֶת כָּל מִינֵי תְבוּאָתָהּ, לְטוֹבָה

Say this phrase during the winter season, from December 4th through פסח*.*

וְתֵן טַל וּמָטָר לִבְרָכָה

Say this phrase during the summer season, from חול המועד פסח *through* מנחה *of December 3rd.*

וְתֵן בְּרָכָה

עַל פְּנֵי הָאֲדָמָה, וְשַׂבְּעֵנוּ מִטּוּבָהּ
וּבָרֵךְ שְׁנָתֵנוּ כַּשָּׁנִים הַטּוֹבוֹת.
בָּרוּךְ אַתָּה יהוה, מְבָרֵךְ הַשָּׁנִים.

GATHER US

תְּקַע *Hashem,* blow the great shofar
to announce our freedom from exile.
Make a clear sign so that all Jews know where to gather.
Hashem, help gather all Jews together
from the four corners of the earth.
Thank You, *Hashem,*
who gathers His scattered Jewish people.

REESTABLISH JEWISH COURTS

הָשִׁיבָה Bring back our Jewish judges and leaders
as it once was,
And remove the difficulties and frustration we face
as a result of not having their guidance.
Hashem, may You alone rule and judge us
with kindness, mercy, and fairness.
Thank You, *Hashem,*
the King who loves righteousness and fairness.
/*Between Rosh Hashana and Yom Kippur say:* the King of fairness./

THE WICKED

וְלַמַּלְשִׁינִים *Hashem,* please do not assist those
who speak or act with bad intentions towards Jews.
Hashem, soon may all Your enemies be destroyed.
For Jews that turned away from Judaism,
may You quickly help guide them back
towards the ways of *Hashem.*
Thank You, *Hashem,* for destroying our enemies
and for returning Jews that turned away.

קיבוץ גלויות

תְּקַע בְּשׁוֹפָר גָּדוֹל לְחֵרוּתֵנוּ
וְשָׂא נֵס לְקַבֵּץ גָּלֻיּוֹתֵינוּ
וְקַבְּצֵנוּ יַחַד מֵאַרְבַּע כַּנְפוֹת הָאָרֶץ.
בָּרוּךְ אַתָּה יהוה, מְקַבֵּץ נִדְחֵי עַמּוֹ יִשְׂרָאֵל.

השבת המשפט

הָשִׁיבָה שׁוֹפְטֵינוּ כְּבָרִאשׁוֹנָה
וְיוֹעֲצֵינוּ כְּבַתְּחִלָּה
וְהָסֵר מִמֶּנּוּ יָגוֹן וַאֲנָחָה
וּמְלֹךְ עָלֵינוּ אַתָּה יהוה לְבַדְּךָ בְּחֶסֶד וּבְרַחֲמִים
וְצַדְּקֵנוּ בַּמִּשְׁפָּט.
בָּרוּךְ אַתָּה יהוה, מֶלֶךְ אוֹהֵב צְדָקָה וּמִשְׁפָּט.

/ *Between* ראש השנה *and* יום כיפור *say* הַמֶּלֶךְ הַמִּשְׁפָּט./

ברכת המינים

וְלַמַּלְשִׁינִים אַל תְּהִי תִקְוָה
וְכָל הָרִשְׁעָה כְּרֶגַע תֹּאבֵד
וְכָל אוֹיְבֵי עַמְּךָ מְהֵרָה יִכָּרֵתוּ
וְהַזֵּדִים מְהֵרָה תְעַקֵּר וּתְשַׁבֵּר וּתְמַגֵּר וְתַכְנִיעַ
בִּמְהֵרָה בְיָמֵינוּ.
בָּרוּךְ אַתָּה יהוה, שׁוֹבֵר אוֹיְבִים וּמַכְנִיעַ זֵדִים.

THE RIGHTEOUS

עַל *Hashem,* when You think of us,
consider the righteous, humble, elderly,
and wise people within our nation,
and have mercy on us, Your Jewish people, for their sake.
Please give reward
to all those who sincerely believe in You,
and give us the ability to be placed
in this righteous group.
Thank You, *Hashem,*
for supporting righteous people.

REBUILDING JERUSALEM

וְלִירוּשָׁלַיִם *Hashem,* please return to Your city, Jerusalem,
and live there as You once did.
Please rebuild the *Beit HaMikdash* soon,
in our lifetimes, and let it last forever.
Complete this process by appointing a Jewish king
from the family of King David.
Thank You, *Hashem,*
for rebuilding Jerusalem.

KINGDOM OF DAVID

אֶת צֶמַח Please bring *Mashiach,*
who comes from the family of King David,
quickly as we think about
and hope for his arrival every day.
Thank You, *Hashem,*
who brings *Mashiach.*

על הצדיקים

עַל הַצַּדִּיקִים וְעַל הַחֲסִידִים
וְעַל זִקְנֵי עַמְּךָ בֵּית יִשְׂרָאֵל
וְעַל פְּלֵיטַת סוֹפְרֵיהֶם
וְעַל גֵּרֵי הַצֶּדֶק, וְעָלֵינוּ
יֶהֱמוּ רַחֲמֶיךָ יהוה אֱלֹהֵינוּ
וְתֵן שָׂכָר טוֹב לְכָל הַבּוֹטְחִים בְּשִׁמְךָ בֶּאֱמֶת
וְשִׂים חֶלְקֵנוּ עִמָּהֶם, וּלְעוֹלָם לֹא נֵבוֹשׁ כִּי בְךָ בָּטָחְנוּ.
בָּרוּךְ אַתָּה יהוה, מִשְׁעָן וּמִבְטָח לַצַּדִּיקִים.

בניין ירושלים

וְלִירוּשָׁלַיִם עִירְךָ בְּרַחֲמִים תָּשׁוּב
וְתִשְׁכֹּן בְּתוֹכָהּ כַּאֲשֶׁר דִּבַּרְתָּ
וּבְנֵה אוֹתָהּ בְּקָרוֹב בְּיָמֵינוּ בִּנְיַן עוֹלָם
וְכִסֵּא דָוִד מְהֵרָה לְתוֹכָהּ תָּכִין.
בָּרוּךְ אַתָּה יהוה, בּוֹנֵה יְרוּשָׁלָיִם.

מלכות בית דוד

אֶת צֶמַח דָּוִד עַבְדְּךָ מְהֵרָה תַצְמִיחַ
וְקַרְנוֹ תָּרוּם בִּישׁוּעָתֶךָ
כִּי לִישׁוּעָתְךָ קִוִּינוּ כָּל הַיּוֹם.
בָּרוּךְ אַתָּה יהוה, מַצְמִיחַ קֶרֶן יְשׁוּעָה.

LISTEN TO OUR PRAYERS

שְׁמַע *Hashem,* please listen to our voices
and accept our prayers with mercy.
You, *Hashem,* show mercy
by listening to the prayers of the Jewish people.
Please do not let our prayers go unanswered.
Thank You, *Hashem,* for listening to our prayers.

SERVICE IN THE *BEIT HAMIKDASH*

רְצֵה *Hashem,* please accept Your Jewish people
and their prayers.
We eagerly await the rebuilding of the *Beit HaMikdash*
so we can serve You with *korbanot.*
Until the *Beit HaMikdash* is rebuilt,
please accept our prayers with love.

On Rosh Chodesh and Chol HaMo'ed, say:

אֱלֹהֵינוּ Our God, and God of our ancestors, may our prayers:
Rise from our mouths,
Come before You,
Reach You at a desirable time,
Be heard,
And be fulfilled.
Hashem, You remember and know each of our hardships.
You remember:
Our ancestors,
Mashiach,
Your holy city, Jerusalem, and
Your united Jewish people,
for goodness, kindness, mercy, life, and peace

שומע תפילה

שְׁמַע קוֹלֵנוּ יהוה אֱלֹהֵינוּ
חוּס וְרַחֵם עָלֵינוּ, וְקַבֵּל בְּרַחֲמִים וּבְרָצוֹן אֶת תְּפִלָּתֵנוּ
כִּי אֵל שׁוֹמֵעַ תְּפִלּוֹת וְתַחֲנוּנִים אָתָּה
וּמִלְּפָנֶיךָ מַלְכֵּנוּ רֵיקָם אַל תְּשִׁיבֵנוּ
כִּי אַתָּה שׁוֹמֵעַ תְּפִלַּת עַמְּךָ יִשְׂרָאֵל בְּרַחֲמִים.
בָּרוּךְ אַתָּה יהוה, שׁוֹמֵעַ תְּפִלָּה.

עבודה

רְצֵה יהוה אֱלֹהֵינוּ בְּעַמְּךָ יִשְׂרָאֵל, וּבִתְפִלָּתָם
וְהָשֵׁב אֶת הָעֲבוֹדָה לִדְבִיר בֵּיתֶךָ
וְאִשֵּׁי יִשְׂרָאֵל וּתְפִלָּתָם בְּאַהֲבָה תְקַבֵּל בְּרָצוֹן
וּתְהִי לְרָצוֹן תָּמִיד עֲבוֹדַת יִשְׂרָאֵל עַמֶּךָ.

On ראש חודש *and* חול המועד*, say:*

אֱלֹהֵינוּ וֵאלֹהֵי אֲבוֹתֵינוּ
יַעֲלֶה וְיָבוֹא וְיַגִּיעַ, וְיֵרָאֶה וְיֵרָצֶה וְיִשָּׁמַע
וְיִפָּקֵד וְיִזָּכֵר זִכְרוֹנֵנוּ וּפִקְדוֹנֵנוּ, וְזִכְרוֹן אֲבוֹתֵינוּ
וְזִכְרוֹן מָשִׁיחַ בֶּן דָּוִד עַבְדֶּךָ
וְזִכְרוֹן יְרוּשָׁלַיִם עִיר קָדְשֶׁךָ
וְזִכְרוֹן כָּל עַמְּךָ בֵּית יִשְׂרָאֵל
לְפָנֶיךָ, לִפְלֵיטָה לְטוֹבָה
לְחֵן וּלְחֶסֶד וּלְרַחֲמִים, לְחַיִּים וּלְשָׁלוֹם

on this day of:
On Rosh Chodesh: *Rosh Chodesh.*
On Pesach: the Holiday of *Matzot.*
On Sukkot: the Holiday of *Sukkot.*
Hashem, on this day please remember us
with good thoughts, consider us for blessing,
and help us with difficult times in our lives.
Be kind and merciful with us, *Hashem,*
as we look towards You as our King.

May we be worthy
to see the rebuilding of the *Beit HaMikdash.*
We thank You, *Hashem,*
for returning Your presence to Zion.

THANK YOU

Bow when saying the words "We thank You."

מוֹדִים We thank You, *Hashem,*
for You are and always will be
our God, and the God of our ancestors.
You give us life
and You always protect us.
We thank and praise You
for:
Our lives which are in Your hands,
Our souls which are in Your control,
The miracles You perform for us every day, and
The goodness You show us
at all times, morning, noon, and night.

בְּיוֹם

בראש חודש: רֹאשׁ הַחֹדֶשׁ הַזֶּה.

בפסח: חַג הַמַּצּוֹת הַזֶּה.

בסוכות: חַג הַסֻּכּוֹת הַזֶּה.

זָכְרֵנוּ יהוה אֱלֹהֵינוּ בּוֹ לְטוֹבָה, וּפָקְדֵנוּ בוֹ לִבְרָכָה
וְהוֹשִׁיעֵנוּ בוֹ לְחַיִּים.

וּבִדְבַר יְשׁוּעָה וְרַחֲמִים, חוּס וְחָנֵּנוּ וְרַחֵם עָלֵינוּ וְהוֹשִׁיעֵנוּ
כִּי אֵלֶיךָ עֵינֵינוּ, כִּי אֵל מֶלֶךְ חַנּוּן וְרַחוּם אָתָּה.

וְתֶחֱזֶינָה עֵינֵינוּ בְּשׁוּבְךָ לְצִיּוֹן בְּרַחֲמִים.
בָּרוּךְ אַתָּה יהוה, הַמַּחֲזִיר שְׁכִינָתוֹ לְצִיּוֹן.

הודאה

Bow when saying the words מוֹדִים אֲנַחְנוּ לָךְ שָׁאַתָּה הוּא.

מוֹדִים אֲנַחְנוּ לָךְ
שָׁאַתָּה הוּא יהוה אֱלֹהֵינוּ וֵאלֹהֵי אֲבוֹתֵינוּ לְעוֹלָם וָעֶד.
צוּר חַיֵּינוּ, מָגֵן יִשְׁעֵנוּ, אַתָּה הוּא לְדוֹר וָדוֹר.
נוֹדֶה לְּךָ וּנְסַפֵּר תְּהִלָּתֶךָ
עַל חַיֵּינוּ הַמְּסוּרִים בְּיָדֶךָ
וְעַל נִשְׁמוֹתֵינוּ הַפְּקוּדוֹת לָךְ
וְעַל נִסֶּיךָ שֶׁבְּכָל יוֹם עִמָּנוּ
וְעַל נִפְלְאוֹתֶיךָ וְטוֹבוֹתֶיךָ
שֶׁבְּכָל עֵת, עֶרֶב וָבֹקֶר וְצָהֳרָיִם.

You, *Hashem,* have unlimited mercy and kindness and therefore we have always placed our hope in You.

On Chanuka say:

עַל הַנִּסִּים We thank You, *Hashem,* for the miracles, the deliverances, the great strength, and the victories in war that You displayed for us in earlier times and in our times.

בִּימֵי מַתִּתְיָהוּ In the days of Mattityahu, son of Yochanan the *Kohen Gadol,* the Hasmonean, and his sons, the wicked Greeks challenged Your Jewish people trying to make them forget Your Torah and sin. In Your great kindness, You, *Hashem,* supported us in this difficult time. You allowed for:

The weak Jews to defeat the mighty Greeks,
The few Jews to defeat the many Greeks,
The pure Jews to defeat the impure Greeks,
The righteous Jews to defeat the wicked Greeks, and
The Jews who studied Your Torah to defeat the Greeks who did not.

Hashem, on this day everyone in the world recognized You as You miraculously saved Your Jewish people. Your Jewish people then entered the *Beit HaMikdash* to clean and purify it. They lit candles in the courtyard of the *Beit HaMikdash* and set aside these eight days of *Chanukah* for giving thanks and praising You.

Continue with "For all these reasons."

On Purim say:

עַל הַנִּסִּים We thank You, *Hashem,* for the miracles, the deliverances, the great strength, and the victories in war that You displayed for us in earlier times and in our times.

בִּימֵי מָרְדְּכַי In the days of Mordechai and Esther, the wicked Haman planned to destroy all Jews, men, women, and children, young and old, on the 13th of Adar, and steal their belongings.

הַטּוֹב, כִּי לֹא כָלוּ רַחֲמֶיךָ
וְהַמְרַחֵם, כִּי לֹא תַמּוּ חֲסָדֶיךָ
מֵעוֹלָם קִוִּינוּ לָךְ.

בחנוכה:

עַל הַנִּסִּים וְעַל הַפֻּרְקָן וְעַל הַגְּבוּרוֹת וְעַל הַתְּשׁוּעוֹת וְעַל הַמִּלְחָמוֹת שֶׁעָשִׂיתָ לַאֲבוֹתֵינוּ בַּיָּמִים הָהֵם בַּזְּמַן הַזֶּה.

בִּימֵי מַתִּתְיָהוּ בֶּן יוֹחָנָן כֹּהֵן גָּדוֹל חַשְׁמוֹנַאי וּבָנָיו, כְּשֶׁעָמְדָה מַלְכוּת יָוָן הָרְשָׁעָה עַל עַמְּךָ יִשְׂרָאֵל לְהַשְׁכִּיחָם תּוֹרָתֶךָ וּלְהַעֲבִירָם מֵחֻקֵּי רְצוֹנֶךָ, וְאַתָּה בְּרַחֲמֶיךָ הָרַבִּים עָמַדְתָּ לָהֶם בְּעֵת צָרָתָם, רַבְתָּ אֶת רִיבָם, דַּנְתָּ אֶת דִּינָם, נָקַמְתָּ אֶת נִקְמָתָם, מָסַרְתָּ גִבּוֹרִים בְּיַד חַלָּשִׁים, וְרַבִּים בְּיַד מְעַטִּים, וּטְמֵאִים בְּיַד טְהוֹרִים, וּרְשָׁעִים בְּיַד צַדִּיקִים, וְזֵדִים בְּיַד עוֹסְקֵי תוֹרָתֶךָ, וּלְךָ עָשִׂיתָ שֵׁם גָּדוֹל וְקָדוֹשׁ בְּעוֹלָמֶךָ, וּלְעַמְּךָ יִשְׂרָאֵל עָשִׂיתָ תְּשׁוּעָה גְדוֹלָה וּפֻרְקָן כְּהַיּוֹם הַזֶּה. וְאַחַר כֵּן בָּאוּ בָנֶיךָ לִדְבִיר בֵּיתֶךָ, וּפִנּוּ אֶת הֵיכָלֶךָ, וְטִהֲרוּ אֶת מִקְדָּשֶׁךָ, וְהִדְלִיקוּ נֵרוֹת בְּחַצְרוֹת קָדְשֶׁךָ, וְקָבְעוּ שְׁמוֹנַת יְמֵי חֲנֻכָּה אֵלּוּ, לְהוֹדוֹת וּלְהַלֵּל לְשִׁמְךָ הַגָּדוֹל.

Continue with וְעַל כֻּלָּם.

בפורים:

עַל הַנִּסִּים וְעַל הַפֻּרְקָן וְעַל הַגְּבוּרוֹת וְעַל הַתְּשׁוּעוֹת וְעַל הַמִּלְחָמוֹת שֶׁעָשִׂיתָ לַאֲבוֹתֵינוּ בַּיָּמִים הָהֵם בַּזְּמַן הַזֶּה.

בִּימֵי מָרְדְּכַי וְאֶסְתֵּר בְּשׁוּשַׁן הַבִּירָה, כְּשֶׁעָמַד עֲלֵיהֶם הָמָן הָרָשָׁע, בִּקֵּשׁ לְהַשְׁמִיד לַהֲרֹג וּלְאַבֵּד אֶת־כָּל־הַיְּהוּדִים מִנַּעַר וְעַד־זָקֵן טַף וְנָשִׁים בְּיוֹם אֶחָד, בִּשְׁלוֹשָׁה עָשָׂר לְחֹדֶשׁ

In Your great mercy, You, *Hashem*, ruined Haman's plans and instead Haman and his sons were hanged on the gallows.

Continue with "For all these reasons."

For all these reasons
we will thank You, *Hashem*, our King, forever.

Between Rosh Hashana & Yom Kippur say:

And write all Your children in the book of good life.

Every living person will recognize and praise You, *Hashem*,
for You are the God that helps and saves Your people.

Bend the knees when saying "Thank," bow when saying "You," and stand straight before saying "Hashem."

Thank You, *Hashem*,
for You are worthy of being thanked.

PEACE

שָׁלוֹם רָב *Hashem*, You are King and master of peace.
May it be good in Your eyes
to bless Your Jewish people with peace
at all times and at every hour, forever.

Between Rosh Hashana and Yom Kippur continue with "May You remember," below.

Thank You, *Hashem*,
who blesses His Jewish people with peace.

Between Rosh Hashana and Yom Kippur say:

May You remember
all of the Jewish people for life,
blessing, peace, and riches
and write us in the book of good life and peace.
Thank You, *Hashem*,
who makes peace.

שְׁנֵים־עָשָׂר, הוּא־חֹדֶשׁ אֲדָר, וּשְׁלָלָם לָבוֹז: וְאַתָּה בְּרַחֲמֶיךָ הָרַבִּים הֵפַרְתָּ אֶת עֲצָתוֹ, וְקִלְקַלְתָּ אֶת מַחֲשַׁבְתּוֹ, וַהֲשֵׁבוֹתָ לּוֹ גְּמוּלוֹ בְּרֹאשׁוֹ, וְתָלוּ אוֹתוֹ וְאֶת בָּנָיו עַל הָעֵץ.

Continue with וְעַל כֻּלָּם.

וְעַל כֻּלָּם

יִתְבָּרַךְ וְיִתְרוֹמַם שִׁמְךָ מַלְכֵּנוּ תָּמִיד לְעוֹלָם וָעֶד.

Between ראש השנה *&* יום כיפור *say* וּכְתֹב לְחַיִּים טוֹבִים כָּל בְּנֵי בְרִיתֶךָ.

וְכֹל הַחַיִּים יוֹדְוּךָ סֶּלָה, וִיהַלְלוּ אֶת שִׁמְךָ בֶּאֱמֶת
הָאֵל יְשׁוּעָתֵנוּ וְעֶזְרָתֵנוּ סֶלָה.

Bend the knees when saying בָּרוּךְ*, bow when saying* אַתָּה*,*
and stand straight before saying Hashem's name.

בָּרוּךְ אַתָּה יהוה, הַטּוֹב שִׁמְךָ וּלְךָ נָאֶה לְהוֹדוֹת.

שלום

שָׁלוֹם רָב עַל יִשְׂרָאֵל עַמְּךָ תָּשִׂים לְעוֹלָם
כִּי אַתָּה הוּא מֶלֶךְ אָדוֹן לְכָל הַשָּׁלוֹם.
וְטוֹב בְּעֵינֶיךָ לְבָרֵךְ אֶת עַמְּךָ יִשְׂרָאֵל
בְּכָל עֵת וּבְכָל שָׁעָה בִּשְׁלוֹמֶךָ.

Between ראש השנה *and* יום כיפור *continue with* בְּסֵפֶר חַיִּים*, below.*

בָּרוּךְ אַתָּה יהוה, הַמְבָרֵךְ אֶת עַמּוֹ יִשְׂרָאֵל בַּשָּׁלוֹם.

Between ראש השנה *and* יום כיפור *say:*

בְּסֵפֶר חַיִּים, בְּרָכָה וְשָׁלוֹם, וּפַרְנָסָה טוֹבָה, נִזָּכֵר וְנִכָּתֵב לְפָנֶיךָ
אֲנַחְנוּ וְכָל עַמְּךָ בֵּית יִשְׂרָאֵל, לְחַיִּים טוֹבִים וּלְשָׁלוֹם.
בָּרוּךְ אַתָּה יהוה, עוֹשֵׂה הַשָּׁלוֹם.

CONCLUSION OF AMIDA

אֱלֹהַי *Hashem,* please help me:

Control my mouth from speaking badly
about other people,
Stay silent and not respond if someone speaks badly
about me,
Learn Your Torah, and do Your *mitzvot.*

Hashem, if people plan to do something evil against me,
please stop these plans and protect me.
Even if I am not deserving of being helped,
please act on my behalf
as I represent Your name and Your Torah.
Hashem, please save Your Jewish people
from difficult situations and answer my requests.
May You find my thoughts and prayers favorable.

Take three steps backwards and bow to your left as you say

You, *Hashem,* make peace in heaven.

Bow to your right as you say:

Please may You bring peace to us

Bow forward as you say:

And all Your Jewish people.

Before taking three steps forward, say the following quietly:

Hashem, our God and God of our ancestors, may You please rebuild the *Beit HaMikdash* soon. *Hashem,* please allow us to learn Your Torah and serve You in the *Beit HaMikdash* as the Jewish people once did.

On Motza'ei Shabbat (except when Yom Tov or Erev Pesach falls in the following week), the Leader continues with Half Kaddish on page 294, then "May Hashem act kindly" on page 688.

On Motza'ei Shabbat when Yom Tov falls in the following week, and on other evenings the Leader says Kaddish Shalem.

סיום העמידה

אֱלֹהַי, נְצֹר לְשׁוֹנִי מֵרָע וּשְׂפָתַי מִדַּבֵּר מִרְמָה
וְלִמְקַלְלַי נַפְשִׁי תִדֹּם, וְנַפְשִׁי כֶּעָפָר לַכֹּל תִּהְיֶה.
פְּתַח לִבִּי בְּתוֹרָתֶךָ, וּבְמִצְוֹתֶיךָ תִּרְדֹּף נַפְשִׁי.
וְכָל הַחוֹשְׁבִים עָלַי רָעָה
מְהֵרָה הָפֵר עֲצָתָם וְקַלְקֵל מַחֲשַׁבְתָּם.
עֲשֵׂה לְמַעַן שְׁמֶךָ, עֲשֵׂה לְמַעַן יְמִינֶךָ
עֲשֵׂה לְמַעַן קְדֻשָּׁתֶךָ, עֲשֵׂה לְמַעַן תּוֹרָתֶךָ.
לְמַעַן יֵחָלְצוּן יְדִידֶיךָ, הוֹשִׁיעָה יְמִינְךָ וַעֲנֵנִי:
יִהְיוּ לְרָצוֹן אִמְרֵי־פִי וְהֶגְיוֹן לִבִּי לְפָנֶיךָ, יהוה צוּרִי וְגֹאֲלִי:

Take three steps backwards and bow to your left as you say

עֹשֶׂה שָׁלוֹם / *Between* ראש השנה & יום כיפור *say* הַשָּׁלוֹם/ בִּמְרוֹמָיו

Bow to your right as you say:

הוּא יַעֲשֶׂה שָׁלוֹם עָלֵינוּ

Bow forward as you say:

וְעַל כָּל יִשְׂרָאֵל, וְאִמְרוּ אָמֵן.

Before taking three steps forward, say the following quietly:

יְהִי רָצוֹן מִלְּפָנֶיךָ יהוה אֱלֹהֵינוּ וֵאלֹהֵי אֲבוֹתֵינוּ. שֶׁיִּבָּנֶה בֵּית הַמִּקְדָּשׁ בִּמְהֵרָה בְיָמֵינוּ, וְתֵן חֶלְקֵנוּ בְּתוֹרָתֶךָ. וְשָׁם נַעֲבָדְךָ בְּיִרְאָה כִּימֵי עוֹלָם וּכְשָׁנִים קַדְמֹנִיּוֹת. וְעָרְבָה לַיהוה מִנְחַת יְהוּדָה וִירוּשָׁלָיִם כִּימֵי עוֹלָם וּכְשָׁנִים קַדְמֹנִיּוֹת:

On מוצאי שבת *(except when* יום טוב *or* ערב פסח *falls in the following week), the* חזן *continues with* חצי קדיש *on page 295, then* וִיהִי נֹעַם *on page 689.*

On מוצאי שבת *when* יום טוב *falls in the following week, and on other evenings the* חזן *says* קדיש שלם.

KADDISH SHALEM

Leader: יִתְגַּדַּל May *Hashem* be recognized
as great and holy (*Congregation:* Amen)
in the world that He created.
May He establish His kingdom
during my lifetime and the lifetime of all Jews,
quickly and soon.
Let us say: "Amen" (*Congregation:* Amen).

Congregation: May we thank *Hashem* for ever and ever.
Leader: May we thank *Hashem* for ever and ever.

Leader: *Hashem* should be thanked, praised,
and honored (*Congregation:* He is blessed).
Hashem is beyond all the blessings,
songs, or praises that we could offer.
Let us say: "Amen" (*Congregation:* Amen).

May *Hashem* accept our prayers
and the prayers of all Jews.
Let us say: "Amen." (*Congregation:* Amen).

May *Hashem* give us, and all Jews,
peace and good life.
Let us say: "Amen." (*Congregation:* Amen).

The Leader takes three steps back before saying this line, bows to the left when saying "May," bows to the right when saying "the One," bows to the middle when saying "make peace for us":

May *Hashem*, the One
who makes peace in heaven,
make peace for us and for all Jews.
Let us say: "Amen." (*Congregation:* Amen).

קדיש שלם

חזן: יִתְגַּדַּל וְיִתְקַדַּשׁ שְׁמֵהּ רַבָּא (קהל: אָמֵן)
בְּעָלְמָא דִּי בְרָא כִרְעוּתֵהּ, וְיַמְלִיךְ מַלְכוּתֵהּ
בְּחַיֵּיכוֹן וּבְיוֹמֵיכוֹן וּבְחַיֵּי דְכָל בֵּית יִשְׂרָאֵל
בַּעֲגָלָא וּבִזְמַן קָרִיב, וְאִמְרוּ אָמֵן. (קהל: אָמֵן)

קהל יְהֵא שְׁמֵהּ רַבָּא מְבָרַךְ לְעָלַם וּלְעָלְמֵי עָלְמַיָּא.
חזן: יְהֵא שְׁמֵהּ רַבָּא מְבָרַךְ לְעָלַם וּלְעָלְמֵי עָלְמַיָּא.

חזן: יִתְבָּרַךְ וְיִשְׁתַּבַּח וְיִתְפָּאַר וְיִתְרוֹמַם וְיִתְנַשֵּׂא וְיִתְהַדָּר
וְיִתְעַלֶּה וְיִתְהַלָּל שְׁמֵהּ דְּקֻדְשָׁא בְּרִיךְ הוּא (קהל: בְּרִיךְ הוּא)
לְעֵלָּא מִן כָּל בִּרְכָתָא

/בעשרת ימי תשובה: לְעֵלָּא לְעֵלָּא מִכָּל בִּרְכָתָא/

וְשִׁירָתָא, תֻּשְׁבְּחָתָא וְנֶחֱמָתָא
דַּאֲמִירָן בְּעָלְמָא, וְאִמְרוּ אָמֵן. (קהל: אָמֵן)

תִּתְקַבַּל צְלוֹתְהוֹן וּבָעוּתְהוֹן דְּכָל יִשְׂרָאֵל
קֳדָם אֲבוּהוֹן דִּי בִשְׁמַיָּא, וְאִמְרוּ אָמֵן. (קהל: אָמֵן)

יְהֵא שְׁלָמָא רַבָּא מִן שְׁמַיָּא
וְחַיִּים, עָלֵינוּ וְעַל כָּל יִשְׂרָאֵל, וְאִמְרוּ אָמֵן. (קהל: אָמֵן)

The חזן *takes three steps back before saying this line, bows to the left when saying* עֹשֶׂה*, bows to the right when saying* הוּא*, bows to the middle when saying* יַעֲשֶׂה שָׁלוֹם עָלֵינוּ*:*

עֹשֶׂה שָׁלוֹם /בעשרת ימי תשובה: הַשָּׁלוֹם/ בִּמְרוֹמָיו
הוּא יַעֲשֶׂה שָׁלוֹם
עָלֵינוּ וְעַל כָּל יִשְׂרָאֵל, וְאִמְרוּ אָמֵן. (קהל: אָמֵן)

From the second night of Pesach until the night before Shavuot, the Omer is counted here *(page 328).*

On Purim, Megillat Esther is read; on Tisha B'Av, Megillat Eicha is read.

Stand while saying "It is our role."

עָלֵינוּ It is our role
to praise You, *Hashem,*
Master of all
and Creator of the world.
You have not made us
like other nations of the world,
rather, You set the Jewish people apart
allowing us the opportunity to serve You.
(Other nations pray to gods that do not exist,
while)
we bend our knees and bow in prayer
before the King of all kings, *Hashem,*
in order to give thanks.
Hashem created the heavens above and the land below.
Hashem sits on His awesome throne in heaven
as He, alone, is our God
and ruler of the world.
We willingly accept Him as our King,
there is none else but Him.
As it says in the Torah,
"Today You should understand
that *Hashem* is God
in the heavens above and on the earth below.
There is no other God but You."

From the second night of פסח *until the night before* שבועות*, the* עומר *is counted here* *(page 329).*

On פורים*,* מגילת אסתר *is read; on* תשעה באב*,* מגילת איכה *is read.*

Stand while saying עָלֵינוּ*.*

עָלֵינוּ לְשַׁבֵּחַ לַאֲדוֹן הַכֹּל
לָתֵת גְּדֻלָּה לְיוֹצֵר בְּרֵאשִׁית
שֶׁלֹּא עָשָׂנוּ כְּגוֹיֵי הָאֲרָצוֹת
וְלֹא שָׂמָנוּ כְּמִשְׁפְּחוֹת הָאֲדָמָה
שֶׁלֹּא שָׂם חֶלְקֵנוּ כָּהֶם, וְגוֹרָלֵנוּ כְּכָל הֲמוֹנָם.
(שֶׁהֵם מִשְׁתַּחֲוִים לְהֶבֶל וָרִיק
וּמִתְפַּלְּלִים אֶל אֵל לֹא יוֹשִׁיעַ.)
וַאֲנַחְנוּ כּוֹרְעִים וּמִשְׁתַּחֲוִים וּמוֹדִים
לִפְנֵי מֶלֶךְ מַלְכֵי הַמְּלָכִים, הַקָּדוֹשׁ בָּרוּךְ הוּא
שֶׁהוּא נוֹטֶה שָׁמַיִם וְיוֹסֵד אָרֶץ
וּמוֹשַׁב יְקָרוֹ בַּשָּׁמַיִם מִמַּעַל
וּשְׁכִינַת עֻזּוֹ בְּגָבְהֵי מְרוֹמִים.
הוּא אֱלֹהֵינוּ, אֵין עוֹד.
אֱמֶת מַלְכֵּנוּ, אֶפֶס זוּלָתוֹ
כַּכָּתוּב בְּתוֹרָתוֹ, וְיָדַעְתָּ הַיּוֹם וַהֲשֵׁבֹתָ אֶל־לְבָבֶךָ
כִּי יהוה הוּא הָאֱלֹהִים
בַּשָּׁמַיִם מִמַּעַל וְעַל־הָאָרֶץ מִתָּחַת, אֵין עוֹד:

Hashem,
we hope that all false gods
will be removed from the world
and everyone will soon turn to You alone
as the almighty God of the universe.
All the people of the world
will turn to You
and give honor.
They will accept You as their King,
and You will rule over them soon and forever.
For You are King of the world
and You will remain the ruling King forever.
As it says in Your Torah,
▸ "*Hashem* will be king over all the land.
On that day *Hashem* will be One and His name One."

KADDISH YATOM

The following prayer, said by mourners, requires the presence of a minyan. A transliteration can be found on page 865.

Mourner: יִתְגַּדַּל May *Hashem* be recognized
as great and holy (*Congregation:* Amen)
in the world that He created.
May He establish His kingdom
during my lifetime
and the lifetime of all Jews,
quickly and soon.
Let us say:
"Amen" (*Congregation:* Amen).

עַל כֵּן נְקַוֶּה לְּךָ יהוה אֱלֹהֵינוּ
לִרְאוֹת מְהֵרָה בְּתִפְאֶרֶת עֻזֶּךָ
לְהַעֲבִיר גִּלּוּלִים מִן הָאָרֶץ, וְהָאֱלִילִים כָּרוֹת יִכָּרֵתוּן
לְתַקֵּן עוֹלָם בְּמַלְכוּת שַׁדַּי.
וְכָל בְּנֵי בָשָׂר יִקְרְאוּ בִשְׁמֶךָ
לְהַפְנוֹת אֵלֶיךָ כָּל רִשְׁעֵי אָרֶץ.
יַכִּירוּ וְיֵדְעוּ כָּל יוֹשְׁבֵי תֵבֵל
כִּי לְךָ תִּכְרַע כָּל בֶּרֶךְ, תִּשָּׁבַע כָּל לָשׁוֹן.
לְפָנֶיךָ יהוה אֱלֹהֵינוּ יִכְרְעוּ וְיִפֹּלוּ, וְלִכְבוֹד שִׁמְךָ יְקָר יִתֵּנוּ
וִיקַבְּלוּ כֻלָּם אֶת עֹל מַלְכוּתֶךָ
וְתִמְלֹךְ עֲלֵיהֶם מְהֵרָה לְעוֹלָם וָעֶד.
כִּי הַמַּלְכוּת שֶׁלְּךָ הִיא וּלְעוֹלְמֵי עַד תִּמְלֹךְ בְּכָבוֹד
כַּכָּתוּב בְּתוֹרָתֶךָ, יהוה יִמְלֹךְ לְעֹלָם וָעֶד:
◄ וְנֶאֱמַר, וְהָיָה יהוה לְמֶלֶךְ עַל־כָּל־הָאָרֶץ
בַּיּוֹם הַהוּא יִהְיֶה יהוה אֶחָד וּשְׁמוֹ אֶחָד:

קדיש יתום

The following prayer, said by mourners, requires the presence of a מנין.
A transliteration can be found on page 865.

אבל: **יִתְגַּדַּל וְיִתְקַדַּשׁ שְׁמֵהּ רַבָּא** (קהל: אָמֵן)
בְּעָלְמָא דִּי בְרָא כִרְעוּתֵהּ, וְיַמְלִיךְ מַלְכוּתֵהּ
בְּחַיֵּיכוֹן וּבְיוֹמֵיכוֹן וּבְחַיֵּי דְכָל בֵּית יִשְׂרָאֵל
בַּעֲגָלָא וּבִזְמַן קָרִיב, וְאִמְרוּ אָמֵן. (קהל: אָמֵן)

Congregation: May we thank *Hashem* for ever and ever.
Mourner: May we thank *Hashem* for ever and ever.

Mourner: *Hashem* should be thanked, praised,
and honored (*Congregation:* He is blessed).
Hashem is beyond all the blessings,
songs, or praises that we could offer.
Let us say:
"Amen" (*Congregation:* Amen).

May *Hashem* give us, and all Jews,
peace and good life.
Let us say:
"Amen." (*Congregation:* Amen).

The mourner takes three steps back before saying this line, bows to the left when saying "May," bows to the right when saying "the One," bows to the middle when saying "make peace for us":

May *Hashem,* the One
who makes peace in heaven,
make peace for us and for all Jews.
Let us say:
"Amen." (*Congregation:* Amen).

From the second day of Rosh Chodesh Elul until Shemini Atzeret add the following:

לְדָוִד David HaMelech wrote:
I have no fear because *Hashem* protects me
and brings light to my darkness.
When enemies or even armies attack,

קהל: יְהֵא שְׁמֵהּ רַבָּא מְבָרַךְ לְעָלַם וּלְעָלְמֵי עָלְמַיָּא.
אבל: יְהֵא שְׁמֵהּ רַבָּא מְבָרַךְ לְעָלַם וּלְעָלְמֵי עָלְמַיָּא.

אבל: יִתְבָּרַךְ וְיִשְׁתַּבַּח וְיִתְפָּאַר
וְיִתְרוֹמַם וְיִתְנַשֵּׂא וְיִתְהַדָּר וְיִתְעַלֶּה וְיִתְהַלָּל
שְׁמֵהּ דְּקֻדְשָׁא בְּרִיךְ הוּא (קהל: בְּרִיךְ הוּא)
לְעֵלָּא מִן כָּל בִּרְכָתָא
/בעשרת ימי תשובה: לְעֵלָּא לְעֵלָּא מִכָּל בִּרְכָתָא/
וְשִׁירָתָא, תֻּשְׁבְּחָתָא וְנֶחֱמָתָא
דַּאֲמִירָן בְּעָלְמָא, וְאִמְרוּ אָמֵן. (קהל: אָמֵן)

יְהֵא שְׁלָמָא רַבָּא מִן שְׁמַיָּא
וְחַיִּים, עָלֵינוּ וְעַל כָּל יִשְׂרָאֵל, וְאִמְרוּ אָמֵן. (קהל: אָמֵן)

The mourner takes three steps back before saying this line, bows to the left when saying עֹשֶׂה, *bows to the right when saying* הוּא, *bows to the middle when saying* יַעֲשֶׂה שָׁלוֹם עָלֵינוּ:

עֹשֶׂה שָׁלוֹם /בעשרת ימי תשובה: הַשָּׁלוֹם/ בִּמְרוֹמָיו
הוּא יַעֲשֶׂה שָׁלוֹם עָלֵינוּ
וְעַל כָּל יִשְׂרָאֵל, וְאִמְרוּ אָמֵן. (קהל: אָמֵן)

From the second day of ראש חודש אלול *until* שמיני עצרת *add the following:*

לְדָוִד, יהוה אוֹרִי וְיִשְׁעִי, מִמִּי אִירָא
יהוה מָעוֹז־חַיַּי, מִמִּי אֶפְחָד:
בִּקְרֹב עָלַי מְרֵעִים לֶאֱכֹל אֶת־בְּשָׂרִי
צָרַי וְאֹיְבַי לִי, הֵמָּה כָשְׁלוּ וְנָפָלוּ:

I am not afraid
as I trust that *Hashem* will defeat them.
The only thing that I ask of *Hashem*
is to see the *Beit HaMikdash* built
and be able to serve Him there.
Hashem is my protector;
He will take me in
and hide me from my enemies.
When I feel safe,
I will sing songs of praise to *Hashem.*
Hashem,
listen to my voice
when I call for help
and please answer me.
Do not ignore or hide from me,
when You are angry.
My heart knows
it is only You to whom I can call for help.
Hashem,
help us learn how to make the right choices
and not make mistakes.
▸ I trust in *Hashem,*
I hope for His help
at all times;
He gives me strength and courage.

Kaddish Yatom (page 322)

אִם־תַּחֲנֶה עָלַי מַחֲנֶה, לֹא־יִירָא לִבִּי
אִם־תָּקוּם עָלַי מִלְחָמָה, בְּזֹאת אֲנִי בוֹטֵחַ:
אַחַת שָׁאַלְתִּי מֵאֵת־יהוה, אוֹתָהּ אֲבַקֵּשׁ
שִׁבְתִּי בְּבֵית־יהוה כָּל־יְמֵי חַיַּי
לַחֲזוֹת בְּנֹעַם־יהוה, וּלְבַקֵּר בְּהֵיכָלוֹ:
כִּי יִצְפְּנֵנִי בְּסֻכֹּה בְּיוֹם רָעָה
יַסְתִּרֵנִי בְּסֵתֶר אָהֳלוֹ, בְּצוּר יְרוֹמְמֵנִי:
וְעַתָּה יָרוּם רֹאשִׁי עַל אֹיְבַי סְבִיבוֹתַי
וְאֶזְבְּחָה בְאָהֳלוֹ זִבְחֵי תְרוּעָה
אָשִׁירָה וַאֲזַמְּרָה לַיהוה:
שְׁמַע־יהוה קוֹלִי אֶקְרָא, וְחָנֵּנִי וַעֲנֵנִי:
לְךָ אָמַר לִבִּי בַּקְּשׁוּ פָנָי, אֶת־פָּנֶיךָ יהוה אֲבַקֵּשׁ:
אַל־תַּסְתֵּר פָּנֶיךָ מִמֶּנִּי, אַל תַּט־בְּאַף עַבְדֶּךָ
עֶזְרָתִי הָיִיתָ, אַל־תִּטְּשֵׁנִי וְאַל־תַּעַזְבֵנִי, אֱלֹהֵי יִשְׁעִי:
כִּי־אָבִי וְאִמִּי עֲזָבוּנִי, וַיהוה יַאַסְפֵנִי:
הוֹרֵנִי יהוה דַּרְכֶּךָ, וּנְחֵנִי בְּאֹרַח מִישׁוֹר, לְמַעַן שׁוֹרְרָי:
אַל־תִּתְּנֵנִי בְּנֶפֶשׁ צָרָי, כִּי קָמוּ־בִי עֵדֵי־שֶׁקֶר, וִיפֵחַ חָמָס:
◂ לוּלֵא הֶאֱמַנְתִּי לִרְאוֹת בְּטוּב־יהוה בְּאֶרֶץ חַיִּים:
קַוֵּה אֶל־יהוה, חֲזַק וְיַאֲמֵץ לִבֶּךָ, וְקַוֵּה אֶל־יהוה:

קדיש יתום (*page 323*)

COUNTING OF THE OMER

From the second night of Pesach through the night before Shavuot we count the Omer.

בָּרוּךְ Thank, You, *Hashem,* King of the world,
for setting us apart as Your special people
by commanding us to count the *Omer*.

DATE	COUNTING THE OMER
16 Nisan	1. Today is the first day of the Omer.
17 Nisan	2. Today is the second day of the Omer.
18 Nisan	3. Today is the third day of the Omer.
19 Nisan	4. Today is the fourth day of the Omer.
20 Nisan	5. Today is the fifth day of the Omer.
21 Nisan	6. Today is the sixth day of the Omer.
22 Nisan	7. Today is the seventh day, making one week of the Omer.
23 Nisan	8. Today is the eighth day, making one week and one day of the Omer.
24 Nisan	9. Today is the ninth day, making one week and two days of the Omer.
25 Nisan	10. Today is the tenth day, making one week and three days of the Omer.

סדר ספירת העומר

From the second night of פסח *through the night before* שבועות *we count the* עומר.

בָּרוּךְ אַתָּה יהוה אֱלֹהֵינוּ מֶלֶךְ הָעוֹלָם אֲשֶׁר קִדְּשָׁנוּ בְּמִצְוֹתָיו וְצִוָּנוּ עַל סְפִירַת הָעֹמֶר.

COUNTING THE OMER	DATE
1. הַיּוֹם יוֹם אֶחָד בָּעֹמֶר.	טז בניסן
2. הַיּוֹם שְׁנֵי יָמִים בָּעֹמֶר.	יז בניסן
3. הַיּוֹם שְׁלֹשָׁה יָמִים בָּעֹמֶר.	יח בניסן
4. הַיּוֹם אַרְבָּעָה יָמִים בָּעֹמֶר.	יט בניסן
5. הַיּוֹם חֲמִשָּׁה יָמִים בָּעֹמֶר.	כ בניסן
6. הַיּוֹם שִׁשָּׁה יָמִים בָּעֹמֶר.	כא בניסן
7. הַיּוֹם שִׁבְעָה יָמִים שֶׁהֵם שָׁבוּעַ אֶחָד בָּעֹמֶר.	כב בניסן
8. הַיּוֹם שְׁמוֹנָה יָמִים שֶׁהֵם שָׁבוּעַ אֶחָד וְיוֹם אֶחָד בָּעֹמֶר.	כג בניסן
9. הַיּוֹם תִּשְׁעָה יָמִים שֶׁהֵם שָׁבוּעַ אֶחָד וּשְׁנֵי יָמִים בָּעֹמֶר.	כד בניסן
10. הַיּוֹם עֲשָׂרָה יָמִים שֶׁהֵם שָׁבוּעַ אֶחָד וּשְׁלֹשָׁה יָמִים בָּעֹמֶר.	כה בניסן

DATE	COUNTING THE OMER
26 Nisan	11. Today is the eleventh day, making one week and four days of the Omer.
27 Nisan	12. Today is the twelfth day, making one week and five days of the Omer.
28 Nisan	13. Today is the thirteenth day, making one week and six days of the Omer.
29 Nisan	14. Today is the fourteenth day, making two weeks of the Omer.
30 Nisan, 1st day Rosh Chodesh	15. Today is the fifteenth day, making two weeks and one day of the Omer.
1 Iyar, 2nd day Rosh Chodesh	16. Today is the sixteenth day, making two weeks and two days of the Omer.
2 Iyar	17. Today is the seventeenth day, making two weeks and three days of the Omer.
3 Iyar	18. Today is the eighteenth day, making two weeks and four days of the Omer.
4 Iyar	19. Today is the nineteenth day, making two weeks and five days of the Omer.
5 Iyar, Yom HaAtzma'ut	20. Today is the twentieth day, making two weeks and six days of the Omer.
6 Iyar	21. Today is the twenty-first day, making three weeks of the Omer.

COUNTING THE OMER	DATE
11. הַיּוֹם אַחַד עָשָׂר יוֹם שֶׁהֵם שָׁבוּעַ אֶחָד וְאַרְבָּעָה יָמִים בָּעֹמֶר.	כו בניסן
12. הַיּוֹם שְׁנֵים עָשָׂר יוֹם שֶׁהֵם שָׁבוּעַ אֶחָד וַחֲמִשָּׁה יָמִים בָּעֹמֶר.	כז בניסן
13. הַיּוֹם שְׁלֹשָׁה עָשָׂר יוֹם שֶׁהֵם שָׁבוּעַ אֶחָד וְשִׁשָּׁה יָמִים בָּעֹמֶר.	כח בניסן
14. הַיּוֹם אַרְבָּעָה עָשָׂר יוֹם שֶׁהֵם שְׁנֵי שָׁבוּעוֹת בָּעֹמֶר.	כט בניסן
15. הַיּוֹם חֲמִשָּׁה עָשָׂר יוֹם שֶׁהֵם שְׁנֵי שָׁבוּעוֹת וְיוֹם אֶחָד בָּעֹמֶר.	ל בניסן, א׳ דראש חודש
16. הַיּוֹם שִׁשָּׁה עָשָׂר יוֹם שֶׁהֵם שְׁנֵי שָׁבוּעוֹת וּשְׁנֵי יָמִים בָּעֹמֶר.	א באייר, ב׳ דראש חודש
17. הַיּוֹם שִׁבְעָה עָשָׂר יוֹם שֶׁהֵם שְׁנֵי שָׁבוּעוֹת וּשְׁלֹשָׁה יָמִים בָּעֹמֶר.	ב באייר
18. הַיּוֹם שְׁמוֹנָה עָשָׂר יוֹם שֶׁהֵם שְׁנֵי שָׁבוּעוֹת וְאַרְבָּעָה יָמִים בָּעֹמֶר.	ג באייר
19. הַיּוֹם תִּשְׁעָה עָשָׂר יוֹם שֶׁהֵם שְׁנֵי שָׁבוּעוֹת וַחֲמִשָּׁה יָמִים בָּעֹמֶר.	ד באייר
20. הַיּוֹם עֶשְׂרִים יוֹם שֶׁהֵם שְׁנֵי שָׁבוּעוֹת וְשִׁשָּׁה יָמִים בָּעֹמֶר.	ה באייר, יום העצמאות
21. הַיּוֹם אֶחָד וְעֶשְׂרִים יוֹם שֶׁהֵם שְׁלֹשָׁה שָׁבוּעוֹת בָּעֹמֶר.	ו באייר

DATE	COUNTING THE OMER
7 Iyar	22. Today is the twenty-second day, making three weeks and one day of the Omer.
8 Iyar	23. Today is the twenty-third day, making three weeks and two days of the Omer.
9 Iyar	24. Today is the twenty-fourth day, making three weeks and three days of the Omer.
10 Iyar	25. Today is the twenty-fifth day, making three weeks and four days of the Omer.
11 Iyar	26. Today is the twenty-sixth day, making three weeks and five days of the Omer.
12 Iyar	27. Today is the twenty-seventh day, making three weeks and six days of the Omer.
13 Iyar	28. Today is the twenty-eighth day, making four weeks of the Omer.
14 Iyar	29. Today is the twenty-ninth day, making four weeks and one day of the Omer.
15 Iyar	30. Today is the thirtieth day, making four weeks and two days of the Omer.
16 Iyar	31. Today is the thirty-first day, making four weeks and three days of the Omer.
17 Iyar	32. Today is the thirty-second day, making four weeks and four days of the Omer.

COUNTING THE OMER	DATE
22. הַיּוֹם שְׁנַיִם וְעֶשְׂרִים יוֹם שֶׁהֵם שְׁלֹשָׁה שָׁבוּעוֹת וְיוֹם אֶחָד בָּעֹמֶר.	ז באייר
23. הַיּוֹם שְׁלֹשָׁה וְעֶשְׂרִים יוֹם שֶׁהֵם שְׁלֹשָׁה שָׁבוּעוֹת וּשְׁנֵי יָמִים בָּעֹמֶר.	ח באייר
24. הַיּוֹם אַרְבָּעָה וְעֶשְׂרִים יוֹם שֶׁהֵם שְׁלֹשָׁה שָׁבוּעוֹת וּשְׁלֹשָׁה יָמִים בָּעֹמֶר.	ט באייר
25. הַיּוֹם חֲמִשָּׁה וְעֶשְׂרִים יוֹם שֶׁהֵם שְׁלֹשָׁה שָׁבוּעוֹת וְאַרְבָּעָה יָמִים בָּעֹמֶר.	י באייר
26. הַיּוֹם שִׁשָּׁה וְעֶשְׂרִים יוֹם שֶׁהֵם שְׁלֹשָׁה שָׁבוּעוֹת וַחֲמִשָּׁה יָמִים בָּעֹמֶר.	יא באייר
27. הַיּוֹם שִׁבְעָה וְעֶשְׂרִים יוֹם שֶׁהֵם שְׁלֹשָׁה שָׁבוּעוֹת וְשִׁשָּׁה יָמִים בָּעֹמֶר.	יב באייר
28. הַיּוֹם שְׁמוֹנָה וְעֶשְׂרִים יוֹם שֶׁהֵם אַרְבָּעָה שָׁבוּעוֹת בָּעֹמֶר.	יג באייר
29. הַיּוֹם תִּשְׁעָה וְעֶשְׂרִים יוֹם שֶׁהֵם אַרְבָּעָה שָׁבוּעוֹת וְיוֹם אֶחָד בָּעֹמֶר.	יד באייר
30. הַיּוֹם שְׁלֹשִׁים יוֹם שֶׁהֵם אַרְבָּעָה שָׁבוּעוֹת וּשְׁנֵי יָמִים בָּעֹמֶר.	טו באייר
31. הַיּוֹם אֶחָד וּשְׁלֹשִׁים יוֹם שֶׁהֵם אַרְבָּעָה שָׁבוּעוֹת וּשְׁלֹשָׁה יָמִים בָּעֹמֶר.	טז באייר
32. הַיּוֹם שְׁנַיִם וּשְׁלֹשִׁים יוֹם שֶׁהֵם אַרְבָּעָה שָׁבוּעוֹת וְאַרְבָּעָה יָמִים בָּעֹמֶר.	יז באייר

DATE	COUNTING THE OMER
18 Iyar, Lag BaOmer	33. Today is the thirty-third day, making four weeks and five days of the Omer.
19 Iyar	34. Today is the thirty-fourth day, making four weeks and six days of the Omer.
20 Iyar	35. Today is the thirty-fifth day, making five weeks of the Omer.
21 Iyar	36. Today is the thirty-sixth day, making five weeks and one day of the Omer.
22 Iyar	37. Today is the thirty-seventh day, making five weeks and two days of the Omer.
23 Iyar	38. Today is the thirty-eighth day, making five weeks and three days of the Omer.
24 Iyar	39. Today is the thirty-ninth day, making five weeks and four days of the Omer.
25 Iyar	40. Today is the fortieth day, making five weeks and five days of the Omer.
26 Iyar	41. Today is the forty-first day, making five weeks and six days of the Omer.
27 Iyar	42. Today is the forty-second day, making six weeks of the Omer.
28 Iyar, Yom Yerushalayim	43. Today is the forty-third day, making six weeks and one day of the Omer.

COUNTING THE OMER	DATE
33. הַיּוֹם שְׁלֹשָׁה וּשְׁלֹשִׁים יוֹם שֶׁהֵם אַרְבָּעָה שָׁבוּעוֹת וַחֲמִשָּׁה יָמִים בָּעֹמֶר.	יח באייר, לג בעומר
34. הַיּוֹם אַרְבָּעָה וּשְׁלֹשִׁים יוֹם שֶׁהֵם אַרְבָּעָה שָׁבוּעוֹת וְשִׁשָּׁה יָמִים בָּעֹמֶר.	יט באייר
35. הַיּוֹם חֲמִשָּׁה וּשְׁלֹשִׁים יוֹם שֶׁהֵם חֲמִשָּׁה שָׁבוּעוֹת בָּעֹמֶר.	כ באייר
36. הַיּוֹם שִׁשָּׁה וּשְׁלֹשִׁים יוֹם שֶׁהֵם חֲמִשָּׁה שָׁבוּעוֹת וְיוֹם אֶחָד בָּעֹמֶר.	כא באייר
37. הַיּוֹם שִׁבְעָה וּשְׁלֹשִׁים יוֹם שֶׁהֵם חֲמִשָּׁה שָׁבוּעוֹת וּשְׁנֵי יָמִים בָּעֹמֶר.	כב באייר
38. הַיּוֹם שְׁמוֹנָה וּשְׁלֹשִׁים יוֹם שֶׁהֵם חֲמִשָּׁה שָׁבוּעוֹת וּשְׁלֹשָׁה יָמִים בָּעֹמֶר.	כג באייר
39. הַיּוֹם תִּשְׁעָה וּשְׁלֹשִׁים יוֹם שֶׁהֵם חֲמִשָּׁה שָׁבוּעוֹת וְאַרְבָּעָה יָמִים בָּעֹמֶר.	כד באייר
40. הַיּוֹם אַרְבָּעִים יוֹם שֶׁהֵם חֲמִשָּׁה שָׁבוּעוֹת וַחֲמִשָּׁה יָמִים בָּעֹמֶר.	כה באייר
41. הַיּוֹם אֶחָד וְאַרְבָּעִים יוֹם שֶׁהֵם חֲמִשָּׁה שָׁבוּעוֹת וְשִׁשָּׁה יָמִים בָּעֹמֶר.	כו באייר
42. הַיּוֹם שְׁנַיִם וְאַרְבָּעִים יוֹם שֶׁהֵם שִׁשָּׁה שָׁבוּעוֹת בָּעֹמֶר.	כז באייר
43. הַיּוֹם שְׁלֹשָׁה וְאַרְבָּעִים יוֹם שֶׁהֵם שִׁשָּׁה שָׁבוּעוֹת וְיוֹם אֶחָד בָּעֹמֶר.	כח באייר, יום ירושלים

DATE	COUNTING THE OMER
29 Iyar	44. Today is the forty-fourth day, making six weeks and two days of the Omer.
1 Sivan, Rosh Chodesh	45. Today is the forty-fifth day, making six weeks and three days of the Omer.
2 Sivan	46. Today is the forty-sixth day, making six weeks and four days of the Omer.
3 Sivan	47. Today is the forty-seventh day, making six weeks and five days of the Omer.
4 Sivan	48. Today is the forty-eighth day, making six weeks and six days of the Omer.
5 Sivan, Erev Shavuot	49. Today is the forty-ninth day, making seven weeks of the Omer.

הָרַחֲמָן *Hashem,*
please be kind
and rebuild the *Beit HaMikdash* quickly,
Amen.

The service continues with Aleinu on page 320.

COUNTING THE OMER	DATE
44. הַיּוֹם אַרְבָּעָה וְאַרְבָּעִים יוֹם שֶׁהֵם שִׁשָּׁה שָׁבוּעוֹת וּשְׁנֵי יָמִים בָּעְֹמֶר.	כט באייר
45. הַיּוֹם חֲמִשָּׁה וְאַרְבָּעִים יוֹם שֶׁהֵם שִׁשָּׁה שָׁבוּעוֹת וּשְׁלֹשָׁה יָמִים בָּעְֹמֶר.	א בסיון, ראש חודש
46. הַיּוֹם שִׁשָּׁה וְאַרְבָּעִים יוֹם שֶׁהֵם שִׁשָּׁה שָׁבוּעוֹת וְאַרְבָּעָה יָמִים בָּעְֹמֶר.	ב בסיון
47. הַיּוֹם שִׁבְעָה וְאַרְבָּעִים יוֹם שֶׁהֵם שִׁשָּׁה שָׁבוּעוֹת וַחֲמִשָּׁה יָמִים בָּעְֹמֶר.	ג בסיון
48. הַיּוֹם שְׁמוֹנָה וְאַרְבָּעִים יוֹם שֶׁהֵם שִׁשָּׁה שָׁבוּעוֹת וְשִׁשָּׁה יָמִים בָּעְֹמֶר.	ד בסיון
49. הַיּוֹם תִּשְׁעָה וְאַרְבָּעִים יוֹם שֶׁהֵם שִׁבְעָה שָׁבוּעוֹת בָּעְֹמֶר.	ה בסיון, ערב שבועות

הָרַחֲמָן הוּא יַחֲזִיר לָֽנוּ עֲבוֹדַת בֵּית הַמִּקְדָּשׁ
לִמְקוֹמָהּ בִּמְהֵרָה בְיָמֵֽינוּ
אָמֵן סֶֽלָה.

The service continues with עָלֵֽינוּ *on page 321.*

Erev Shabbat

The service starts with Mincha for Weekdays on page 212.
Most congregations sing "From the depths of our souls" before the Kabbalat Shabbat service.
On Yom Tov or Motza'ei Yom Tov falling on Shabbat, or on Shabbat Chol HaMo'ed, the service begins with Psalm 92 on page 352.

יְדִיד From the depths of our souls we love You, *Hashem,*
and ask that You bring us close to serve You.
We will run as fast as a deer to bow before You.
Your love for us is sweeter than the sweetest honey.

הָדוּר *Hashem,* beautiful and mighty, our souls long for You.
Please show us the warmth of Your love so we will be strong
and serve You forever with great strength.

וָתִיק *Hashem,* You have ruled forever. Please be kind to Your children and show us Your strength.
Hashem, please hurry to show us Your love
and do not hide from us.

הִגָּלֵה *Hashem,* allow the world to be filled with peace and joy under Your kingship.
The time has come for You, *Hashem,*
to show us Your love as You have in the past.

ערב שבת

The service starts with מנחה לחול *on page 213.*
Most congregations sing יְדִיד נֶפֶשׁ *at this point before* קבלת שבת*.*
On יום טוב *or* מוצאי יום טוב *falling on* שבת*, or on* שבת חול המועד*,*
the service begins with מִזְמוֹר שִׁיר *on page 353.*

יְדִיד נֶפֶשׁ, אָב הָרַחֲמָן, מְשֹׁךְ עַבְדְּךָ אֶל רְצוֹנֶךָ
יָרוּץ עַבְדְּךָ כְּמוֹ אַיָּל, יִשְׁתַּחֲוֶה מוּל הֲדָרֶךָ
כִּי יֶעֱרַב לוֹ יְדִידוּתָךְ, מִנֹּפֶת צוּף וְכָל טָעַם.

הָדוּר, נָאֶה, זִיו הָעוֹלָם, נַפְשִׁי חוֹלַת אַהֲבָתֶךָ
אָנָּא, אֵל נָא, רְפָא נָא לָהּ, בְּהַרְאוֹת לָהּ נֹעַם זִיוָךְ
אָז תִּתְחַזֵּק וְתִתְרַפֵּא, וְהָיְתָה לָךְ שִׁפְחַת עוֹלָם.

וָתִיק, יֶהֱמוּ רַחֲמֶיךָ, וְחוּס נָא עַל בֵּן אוֹהֲבָךְ
כִּי זֶה כַּמֶּה נִכְסֹף נִכְסַף לִרְאוֹת בְּתִפְאֶרֶת עֻזָּךְ
אָנָּא, אֵלִי, מַחְמַד לִבִּי, חוּשָׁה נָּא, וְאַל תִּתְעַלָּם.

הִגָּלֶה נָא וּפְרֹשׂ, חָבִיב, עָלַי אֶת סֻכַּת שְׁלוֹמָךְ
תָּאִיר אֶרֶץ מִכְּבוֹדָךְ, נָגִילָה וְנִשְׂמְחָה בָךְ.
מַהֵר, אָהוּב, כִּי בָא מוֹעֵד, וְחָנֵּנִי כִּימֵי עוֹלָם.

Kabbalat Shabbat

לְכוּ נְרַנְּנָה Come, let us sing and shout to *Hashem* with joy
because He saves us.
We will thank *Hashem* through song
for He is a great God and King.
His hands control the earth,
from the lowest lands to the tops of the mountains.
Hashem created the sea and the land.
Let us show our appreciation to *Hashem,* our Creator,
by bowing before Him.
Hashem is our God and we are His people.
If we will listen to *Hashem,* He will watch over us
as a shepherd cares for his sheep.
When our ancestors wandered the desert,
they challenged You, *Hashem,*
because they did not understand Your actions.
▸ For forty years they angered You,
and You did not allow them to enter the Land of Israel.

שִׁירוּ Let everyone sing a new song of thanks to *Hashem.*
Sing a song to *Hashem* and speak of His miracles every day.

לְכוּ נְרַנְּנָה *Come, let us sing.* The word "come" in this section, is an invitation to other Jews to join us in welcoming Shabbat together. We ask the chazzan and all those praying alongside us to leave behind the events of their busy week and instead join together in focusing on accepting a holy and meaningful Shabbat. This invitation is to remind ourselves and others that we are about to stand before *Hashem* on a holy day and should do so with a focused mind and heart.

קבלת שבת

לְכוּ נְרַנְּנָה לַיהוה, נָרִיעָה לְצוּר יִשְׁעֵנוּ: נְקַדְּמָה פָנָיו בְּתוֹדָה, בִּזְמִרוֹת נָרִיעַ לוֹ: כִּי אֵל גָּדוֹל יהוה, וּמֶלֶךְ גָּדוֹל עַל־כָּל־אֱלֹהִים: אֲשֶׁר בְּיָדוֹ מֶחְקְרֵי־אָרֶץ, וְתוֹעֲפוֹת הָרִים לוֹ: אֲשֶׁר־לוֹ הַיָּם וְהוּא עָשָׂהוּ, וְיַבֶּשֶׁת יָדָיו יָצָרוּ: בֹּאוּ נִשְׁתַּחֲוֶה וְנִכְרָעָה, נִבְרְכָה לִפְנֵי־יהוה עֹשֵׂנוּ: כִּי הוּא אֱלֹהֵינוּ, וַאֲנַחְנוּ עַם מַרְעִיתוֹ וְצֹאן יָדוֹ, הַיּוֹם אִם־בְּקֹלוֹ תִשְׁמָעוּ: אַל־תַּקְשׁוּ לְבַבְכֶם כִּמְרִיבָה, כְּיוֹם מַסָּה בַּמִּדְבָּר: אֲשֶׁר נִסּוּנִי אֲבוֹתֵיכֶם, בְּחָנוּנִי גַּם רָאוּ פָעֳלִי: ◂ אַרְבָּעִים שָׁנָה אָקוּט בְּדוֹר, וָאֹמַר עַם תֹּעֵי לֵבָב הֵם, וְהֵם לֹא־יָדְעוּ דְרָכָי: אֲשֶׁר־נִשְׁבַּעְתִּי בְאַפִּי, אִם־יְבֹאוּן אֶל מְנוּחָתִי:

שִׁירוּ לַיהוה שִׁיר חָדָשׁ, שִׁירוּ לַיהוה כָּל־הָאָרֶץ: שִׁירוּ לַיהוה, בָּרְכוּ שְׁמוֹ, בַּשְּׂרוּ מִיּוֹם־לְיוֹם יְשׁוּעָתוֹ: סַפְּרוּ

KABBALAT SHABBAT

This section of special prayers is called *Kabbalat Shabbat*, welcoming Shabbat. We sing *Kabbalat Shabbat* late Friday afternoon as we prepare ourselves for the holy Shabbat that is arriving soon. It contains six sections of *Tehillim*, one for each of the six days that *Hashem* created the world, and a beautiful song called "*Lecha Dodi*" about Shabbat, the special day of rest that we look forward to each week.

Tell all the people of the world
about the wonders that *Hashem* does.
Hashem is worthy of praise; even the angels fear Him.
The gods of other nations are not real;
Hashem alone created heaven.
Hashem is the source of strength and beauty.
Tell the other nations to fear *Hashem,*
the King who created and runs the whole world.
Give honor to *Hashem* and bring *korbanot,* sacrifices,
to Him in the *Beit HaMikdash.*
Bow down before *Hashem* and fear Him.
Let the other nations know *Hashem* is King
and He judges everyone fairly.
▸ The heaven and earth, sea and fields,
and trees of the forest are all filled with happiness
because *Hashem* continues to judge the world fairly.

יהוה מָלָךְ The whole world is happy
because *Hashem* is King.
He rules the world with fairness and justice.
Hashem will destroy His enemies with fire.
Anyone who sees His lightning light up the world
shakes in fear.
The heavens will testify to *Hashem*'s fairness
and all people will see *Hashem*'s greatness.
Those who worship idols will be embarrassed
by their mistakes and turn to *Hashem.*
Then, the Jewish people will be happy because *Hashem,*
our King, will be known as the ruler over earth.
▸ Whoever loves *Hashem* should hate evil;

בַגּוֹיִם כְּבוֹדוֹ, בְּכָל־הָעַמִּים נִפְלְאוֹתָיו: כִּי גָדוֹל יהוה וּמְהֻלָּל מְאֹד, נוֹרָא הוּא עַל־כָּל־אֱלֹהִים: כִּי כָּל־אֱלֹהֵי הָעַמִּים אֱלִילִים, וַיהוה שָׁמַיִם עָשָׂה: הוֹד־וְהָדָר לְפָנָיו, עֹז וְתִפְאֶרֶת בְּמִקְדָּשׁוֹ: הָבוּ לַיהוה מִשְׁפְּחוֹת עַמִּים, הָבוּ לַיהוה כָּבוֹד וָעֹז: הָבוּ לַיהוה כְּבוֹד שְׁמוֹ, שְׂאוּ־מִנְחָה וּבֹאוּ לְחַצְרוֹתָיו: הִשְׁתַּחֲווּ לַיהוה בְּהַדְרַת־קֹדֶשׁ, חִילוּ מִפָּנָיו כָּל־הָאָרֶץ: אִמְרוּ בַגּוֹיִם יהוה מָלָךְ, אַף־תִּכּוֹן תֵּבֵל בַּל־תִּמּוֹט, יָדִין עַמִּים בְּמֵישָׁרִים: › יִשְׂמְחוּ הַשָּׁמַיִם וְתָגֵל הָאָרֶץ, יִרְעַם הַיָּם וּמְלֹאוֹ: יַעֲלֹז שָׂדַי וְכָל־אֲשֶׁר־בּוֹ, אָז יְרַנְּנוּ כָּל־עֲצֵי־יָעַר: לִפְנֵי יהוה כִּי בָא, כִּי בָא לִשְׁפֹּט הָאָרֶץ, יִשְׁפֹּט־תֵּבֵל בְּצֶדֶק, וְעַמִּים בֶּאֱמוּנָתוֹ:

יהוה מָלָךְ תָּגֵל הָאָרֶץ, יִשְׂמְחוּ אִיִּים רַבִּים: עָנָן וַעֲרָפֶל סְבִיבָיו, צֶדֶק וּמִשְׁפָּט מְכוֹן כִּסְאוֹ: אֵשׁ לְפָנָיו תֵּלֵךְ, וּתְלַהֵט סָבִיב צָרָיו: הֵאִירוּ בְרָקָיו תֵּבֵל, רָאֲתָה וַתָּחֵל הָאָרֶץ: הָרִים כַּדּוֹנַג נָמַסּוּ מִלִּפְנֵי יהוה, מִלִּפְנֵי אֲדוֹן כָּל־הָאָרֶץ: הִגִּידוּ הַשָּׁמַיִם צִדְקוֹ, וְרָאוּ כָל־הָעַמִּים כְּבוֹדוֹ: יֵבֹשׁוּ כָּל־עֹבְדֵי פֶסֶל הַמִּתְהַלְלִים בָּאֱלִילִים, הִשְׁתַּחֲווּ־לוֹ כָּל־אֱלֹהִים: שָׁמְעָה וַתִּשְׂמַח צִיּוֹן, וַתָּגֵלְנָה בְּנוֹת יְהוּדָה, לְמַעַן מִשְׁפָּטֶיךָ יהוה: כִּי־אַתָּה יהוה עֶלְיוֹן עַל־כָּל־הָאָרֶץ, מְאֹד נַעֲלֵיתָ עַל־כָּל־אֱלֹהִים: › אֹהֲבֵי יהוה שִׂנְאוּ

Hashem protects those who serve Him from the wicked.
Thank *Hashem* and rejoice
that He is good to the Jewish people.

מִזְמוֹר Sing to *Hashem* for all the wonders
He has performed.
Hashem has revealed His fairness to the world.
He always treats His Jewish people with love.
Shout with joy, sing songs of praise,
and play music to *Hashem*
with harps, trumpets, and the *shofar*.
‣ The seas, rivers, mountains, lands, and people
sing to *Hashem*, who judges the world with fairness.

יהוה מָלָךְ *Hashem* rules over the world;
all nations should fear Him.
When *Hashem* returns His presence to Jerusalem,
all the nations of the world will recognize His greatness.
They will praise Him
because He is awesome, holy, mighty, and a fair ruler.
We bow before *Hashem*, our holy God.
Moshe, Aharon, and Shmuel,
leaders of the Jewish people,
were answered by *Hashem*
when they called out to Him.
‣ *Hashem* spoke to the Jewish people
and they observed His commandments.
Hashem, although you punished the Jewish people
for their wrongdoings,

רָע, שֹׁמֵר נַפְשׁוֹת חֲסִידָיו, מִיַּד רְשָׁעִים יַצִּילֵם: אוֹר זָרֻעַ לַצַּדִּיק, וּלְיִשְׁרֵי־לֵב שִׂמְחָה: שִׂמְחוּ צַדִּיקִים בַּיהוה, וְהוֹדוּ לְזֵכֶר קָדְשׁוֹ:

מִזְמוֹר, שִׁירוּ לַיהוה שִׁיר חָדָשׁ כִּי־נִפְלָאוֹת עָשָׂה, הוֹשִׁיעָה־לּוֹ יְמִינוֹ וּזְרוֹעַ קָדְשׁוֹ: הוֹדִיעַ יהוה יְשׁוּעָתוֹ, לְעֵינֵי הַגּוֹיִם גִּלָּה צִדְקָתוֹ: זָכַר חַסְדּוֹ וֶאֱמוּנָתוֹ לְבֵית יִשְׂרָאֵל, רָאוּ כָל־אַפְסֵי־אָרֶץ אֵת יְשׁוּעַת אֱלֹהֵינוּ: הָרִיעוּ לַיהוה כָּל־הָאָרֶץ, פִּצְחוּ וְרַנְּנוּ וְזַמֵּרוּ: זַמְּרוּ לַיהוה בְּכִנּוֹר, בְּכִנּוֹר וְקוֹל זִמְרָה: בַּחֲצֹצְרוֹת וְקוֹל שׁוֹפָר, הָרִיעוּ לִפְנֵי הַמֶּלֶךְ יהוה: ‹ יִרְעַם הַיָּם וּמְלֹאוֹ, תֵּבֵל וְיֹשְׁבֵי בָהּ: נְהָרוֹת יִמְחֲאוּ־כָף, יַחַד הָרִים יְרַנֵּנוּ: לִפְנֵי יהוה כִּי בָא לִשְׁפֹּט הָאָרֶץ, יִשְׁפֹּט־תֵּבֵל בְּצֶדֶק, וְעַמִּים בְּמֵישָׁרִים:

יהוה מָלָךְ יִרְגְּזוּ עַמִּים, יֹשֵׁב כְּרוּבִים תָּנוּט הָאָרֶץ: יהוה בְּצִיּוֹן גָּדוֹל, וְרָם הוּא עַל־כָּל־הָעַמִּים: יוֹדוּ שִׁמְךָ גָּדוֹל וְנוֹרָא קָדוֹשׁ הוּא: וְעֹז מֶלֶךְ מִשְׁפָּט אָהֵב, אַתָּה כּוֹנַנְתָּ מֵישָׁרִים, מִשְׁפָּט וּצְדָקָה בְּיַעֲקֹב אַתָּה עָשִׂיתָ: רוֹמְמוּ יהוה אֱלֹהֵינוּ, וְהִשְׁתַּחֲווּ לַהֲדֹם רַגְלָיו, קָדוֹשׁ הוּא: מֹשֶׁה וְאַהֲרֹן בְּכֹהֲנָיו, וּשְׁמוּאֵל בְּקֹרְאֵי שְׁמוֹ, קֹרְאִים אֶל־יהוה וְהוּא יַעֲנֵם: ‹ בְּעַמּוּד עָנָן יְדַבֵּר אֲלֵיהֶם, שָׁמְרוּ עֵדֹתָיו וְחֹק נָתַן־לָמוֹ: יהוה אֱלֹהֵינוּ אַתָּה עֲנִיתָם, אֵל נֹשֵׂא

You also answered their prayers
and forgave them.
We praise and bow down to You, *Hashem,* our holy God.

Stand while saying this paragraph.

מִזְמוֹר לְדָוִד Give honor and bow to *Hashem*
for He is holy.
The voice of *Hashem* can be heard like thunder.
The voice of *Hashem* is filled with power,
beauty, and might.
The voice of *Hashem* can break mighty trees
and make the desert shake.
▸ *Hashem* was God during the floods of Noach.
Hashem is King and rules forever.
Hashem will give His Jewish people strength and peace.

אָנָּא Please, *Hashem,* with the power of Your right hand
let Your Jewish people be free.
Accept Your Jewish people's prayers, and give us strength.
Hashem, please use Your strength
to protect those who serve You.
Always bless and show mercy
to Your Jewish people.
Hashem, You are holy;
please guide Your nation.
You, and only You, *Hashem,* turn to Your Jewish people.
Listen and accept our cries
because You know our inner thoughts.
Thank You, *Hashem,* our God,
Your kingdom lasts forever.

הָיִיתָ לָהֶם, וְנֹקֵם עַל־עֲלִילוֹתָם: רוֹמְמוּ יהוה אֱלֹהֵינוּ, וְהִשְׁתַּחֲווּ לְהַר קָדְשׁוֹ, כִּי־קָדוֹשׁ יהוה אֱלֹהֵינוּ:

Stand while saying this paragraph.

מִזְמוֹר לְדָוִד, הָבוּ לַיהוה בְּנֵי אֵלִים, הָבוּ לַיהוה כָּבוֹד וָעֹז: הָבוּ לַיהוה כְּבוֹד שְׁמוֹ, הִשְׁתַּחֲווּ לַיהוה בְּהַדְרַת־קֹדֶשׁ: קוֹל יהוה עַל הַמָּיִם, אֵל־הַכָּבוֹד הִרְעִים, יהוה עַל־מַיִם רַבִּים: קוֹל־יהוה בַּכֹּחַ, קוֹל יהוה בֶּהָדָר: קוֹל יהוה שֹׁבֵר אֲרָזִים, וַיְשַׁבֵּר יהוה אֶת־אַרְזֵי הַלְּבָנוֹן: וַיַּרְקִידֵם כְּמוֹ־עֵגֶל, לְבָנוֹן וְשִׂרְיוֹן כְּמוֹ בֶן־רְאֵמִים: קוֹל־יהוה חֹצֵב לַהֲבוֹת אֵשׁ: קוֹל יהוה יָחִיל מִדְבָּר, יָחִיל יהוה מִדְבַּר קָדֵשׁ: › קוֹל יהוה יְחוֹלֵל אַיָּלוֹת וַיֶּחֱשֹׂף יְעָרוֹת, וּבְהֵיכָלוֹ, כֻּלּוֹ אֹמֵר כָּבוֹד: יהוה לַמַּבּוּל יָשָׁב, וַיֵּשֶׁב יהוה מֶלֶךְ לְעוֹלָם: יהוה עֹז לְעַמּוֹ יִתֵּן, יהוה יְבָרֵךְ אֶת־עַמּוֹ בַשָּׁלוֹם:

אָנָּא, בְּכֹחַ גְּדֻלַּת יְמִינְךָ, תַּתִּיר צְרוּרָה.
קַבֵּל רִנַּת עַמְּךָ, שַׂגְּבֵנוּ, טַהֲרֵנוּ, נוֹרָא.
נָא גִבּוֹר, דּוֹרְשֵׁי יִחוּדְךָ כְּבָבַת שָׁמְרֵם.
בָּרְכֵם, טַהֲרֵם, רַחֲמֵם, צִדְקָתְךָ תָּמִיד גָּמְלֵם.
חֲסִין קָדוֹשׁ, בְּרֹב טוּבְךָ נַהֵל עֲדָתֶךָ.
יָחִיד גֵּאֶה, לְעַמְּךָ פְּנֵה, זוֹכְרֵי קְדֻשָּׁתֶךָ.
שַׁוְעָתֵנוּ קַבֵּל וּשְׁמַע צַעֲקָתֵנוּ, יוֹדֵעַ תַּעֲלוּמוֹת.
בָּרוּךְ שֵׁם כְּבוֹד מַלְכוּתוֹ לְעוֹלָם וָעֶד.

Come, *Hashem,* and let us welcome the Shabbat
as a groom greets his bride.

Come, *Hashem,* and let us welcome the Shabbat
as a groom greets his bride.

The words "Guard" and "Remember"
were said at once at Har Sinai;
Hashem, our God, miraculously allowed us
to hear them together.
Hashem is One, He alone is God,
And He is filled with honor, majesty, and praise.

Come, *Hashem,* and let us welcome the Shabbat
as a groom greets his bride.

Come let us go welcome the Shabbat,
For it is a source of blessing.
From the beginning of time, Shabbat was honored.
Shabbat was the end of creation,
but it was *Hashem*'s first thought.

Come, *Hashem,* and let us welcome the Shabbat
as a groom greets his bride.

People of Jerusalem, our King's royal city,
Stand up and leave behind your sadness.
You have lived with tears for too long.
Hashem will show you great mercy.

Come, *Hashem,* and let us welcome the Shabbat
as a groom greets his bride.

לְכָה דוֹדִי לִקְרַאת כַּלָּה, פְּנֵי שַׁבָּת נְקַבְּלָה.

לְכָה דוֹדִי לִקְרַאת כַּלָּה, פְּנֵי שַׁבָּת נְקַבְּלָה.

שָׁמוֹר וְזָכוֹר בְּדִבּוּר אֶחָד
הִשְׁמִיעָנוּ אֵל הַמְיֻחָד
יהוה אֶחָד וּשְׁמוֹ אֶחָד
לְשֵׁם וּלְתִפְאֶרֶת וְלִתְהִלָּה.

לְכָה דוֹדִי לִקְרַאת כַּלָּה, פְּנֵי שַׁבָּת נְקַבְּלָה.

לִקְרַאת שַׁבָּת לְכוּ וְנֵלְכָה
כִּי הִיא מְקוֹר הַבְּרָכָה
מֵרֹאשׁ מִקֶּדֶם נְסוּכָה
סוֹף מַעֲשֶׂה בְּמַחֲשָׁבָה תְּחִלָּה.

לְכָה דוֹדִי לִקְרַאת כַּלָּה, פְּנֵי שַׁבָּת נְקַבְּלָה.

מִקְדַּשׁ מֶלֶךְ עִיר מְלוּכָה
קוּמִי צְאִי מִתּוֹךְ הַהֲפֵכָה
רַב לָךְ שֶׁבֶת בְּעֵמֶק הַבָּכָא
וְהוּא יַחֲמֹל עָלַיִךְ חֶמְלָה.

לְכָה דוֹדִי לִקְרַאת כַּלָּה, פְּנֵי שַׁבָּת נְקַבְּלָה.

Shake yourselves off and arise from the dust.
My Jewish people, dress yourselves
in your nicest clothing,
Because we will be brought near and redeemed
Through *Mashiach,* the son of Yishai.

Come, *Hashem,* and let us welcome the Shabbat
as a groom greets his bride.

Wake up, wake up,
The light of *Hashem* is shining on you.
Awaken and praise *Hashem* through song,
For His honor is within you.

Come, *Hashem,* and let us welcome the Shabbat
as a groom greets his bride.

Do not be ashamed or confused.
There is no reason for sadness or mourning.
Now is the time to support others,
And know the *Beit HaMikdash*
will soon be rebuilt.

Come, *Hashem,* and let us welcome the Shabbat
as a groom greets his bride.

Those who made you sad will be saddened,
And those who took Jerusalem will be sent away.
Hashem will rejoice with you,
As a groom rejoices with his bride.

Come, *Hashem,* and let us welcome the Shabbat
as a groom greets his bride.

הִתְנַעֲרִי, מֵעָפָר קוּמִי
לִבְשִׁי בִּגְדֵי תִפְאַרְתֵּךְ עַמִּי
עַל יַד בֶּן יִשַׁי בֵּית הַלַּחְמִי
קָרְבָה אֶל נַפְשִׁי, גְּאָלָהּ.
לְכָה דוֹדִי לִקְרַאת כַּלָּה, פְּנֵי שַׁבָּת נְקַבְּלָה.

הִתְעוֹרְרִי הִתְעוֹרְרִי
כִּי בָא אוֹרֵךְ קוּמִי אוֹרִי
עוּרִי עוּרִי, שִׁיר דַּבֵּרִי
כְּבוֹד יהוה עָלַיִךְ נִגְלָה.
לְכָה דוֹדִי לִקְרַאת כַּלָּה, פְּנֵי שַׁבָּת נְקַבְּלָה.

לֹא תֵבֹשִׁי וְלֹא תִכָּלְמִי
מַה תִּשְׁתּוֹחֲחִי וּמַה תֶּהֱמִי
בָּךְ יֶחֱסוּ עֲנִיֵּי עַמִּי
וְנִבְנְתָה עִיר עַל תִּלָּהּ.
לְכָה דוֹדִי לִקְרַאת כַּלָּה, פְּנֵי שַׁבָּת נְקַבְּלָה.

וְהָיוּ לִמְשִׁסָּה שֹׁאסָיִךְ
וְרָחֲקוּ כָּל מְבַלְּעָיִךְ
יָשִׂישׂ עָלַיִךְ אֱלֹהָיִךְ
כִּמְשׂוֹשׂ חָתָן עַל כַּלָּה.
לְכָה דוֹדִי לִקְרַאת כַּלָּה, פְּנֵי שַׁבָּת נְקַבְּלָה.

Whether you turn left or right, Always think of *Hashem*.
We will be redeemed by *Mashiach*,
a descendant of Peretz,
Then we will celebrate and be glad.

Come, *Hashem*, and let us welcome the Shabbat
as a groom greets his bride.

Stand and face the back of the shul. Bow towards the back of the shul while saying the words "Enter like a bride!" and then turn to face the front of the shul.

Come in peace, O Shabbat, our crown,
Come with joy and celebration.
Enter among Your Jewish people.
Enter like a bride! Enter like a bride!

Come, *Hashem*, and let us welcome the Shabbat
as a groom grets his bride.

On Yom Tov, Motza'ei Yom Tov or Shabbat Chol HaMo'ed,
Kabbalat Shabbat begins here.

מִזְמוֹר שִׁיר A song for Shabbat.
It is good to thank *Hashem* and sing songs to Him.
We sing about *Hashem*'s kindness in the morning
and we are thankful for His protection at night.
We use musical instruments to thank *Hashem;*
we sing out to Him with great joy.
We cannot understand how great and wise *Hashem* is.

בּוֹאִי כַלָּה *Enter like a bride.* Just as we stand when a bride walks down the aisle at her wedding, when we say "Enter like a bride," everyone in the shul stands, turns towards the back of the shul, and bows to welcome in Shabbat.

יָמִין וּשְׂמֹאל תִּפְרֹֽצִי
וְאֶת יהוה תַּעֲרִֽיצִי
עַל יַד אִישׁ בֶּן פַּרְצִי
וְנִשְׂמְחָה וְנָגִֽילָה.
לְכָה דוֹדִי לִקְרַאת כַּלָּה, פְּנֵי שַׁבָּת נְקַבְּלָה.

Stand and face the back of the בית כנסת*. Bow towards the back of the shul while saying the words* בּוֹאִי כַלָּה *and then turn to face the front of the* בית כנסת*.*

בּוֹאִי בְשָׁלוֹם עֲטֶרֶת בַּעְלָהּ
גַּם בְּשִׂמְחָה וּבְצָהֳלָה
תּוֹךְ אֱמוּנֵי עַם סְגֻלָּה
בּוֹאִי כַלָּה, בּוֹאִי כַלָּה.
לְכָה דוֹדִי לִקְרַאת כַּלָּה, פְּנֵי שַׁבָּת נְקַבְּלָה.

On קבלת שבת, שבת חול המועד *or* יום טוב, מוצאי יום טוב *begins here.*

מִזְמוֹר שִׁיר לְיוֹם הַשַּׁבָּת:
טוֹב לְהֹדוֹת לַיהוה, וּלְזַמֵּר לְשִׁמְךָ עֶלְיוֹן:
לְהַגִּיד בַּבֹּקֶר חַסְדֶּךָ, וֶאֱמוּנָתְךָ בַּלֵּילוֹת:
עֲלֵי־עָשׂוֹר וַעֲלֵי־נָבֶל, עֲלֵי הִגָּיוֹן בְּכִנּוֹר:
כִּי שִׂמַּחְתַּנִי יהוה בְּפָעֳלֶךָ, בְּמַעֲשֵׂי יָדֶיךָ אֲרַנֵּן:
מַה־גָּדְלוּ מַעֲשֶׂיךָ יהוה, מְאֹד עָמְקוּ מַחְשְׁבֹתֶיךָ:
אִישׁ־בַּעַר לֹא יֵדָע, וּכְסִיל לֹא־יָבִין אֶת־זֹאת:

Even when it appears
that evil people are successful,
Hashem will not allow
their success to last forever.
All of *Hashem's* enemies
will one day be defeated and scattered;
Hashem will lift up His Jewish people.
▸ The righteous will be fruitful
like a date tree and strong like a cedar tree.
Like a tree planted in *Hashem*'s garden,
the righteous will continue to have success
even in old age,
and will remain full of strength.
Hashem is fair;
He is perfect in His ways.

יהוה מָלָךְ *Hashem* is King,
dressed in greatness and might!
He created the world;
Hashem lives forever.
As a river flows
so will our enemies come against us,
▸ but You, *Hashem*, are mightier
than the many waves of the sea.
We fully believe in Your promises.
Hashem,
may the *Beit HaMikdash* stand
for a long time.

בִּפְרֹחַ רְשָׁעִים כְּמוֹ עֵשֶׂב, וַיָּצִיצוּ כָּל־פֹּעֲלֵי אָוֶן
לְהִשָּׁמְדָם עֲדֵי־עַד:
וְאַתָּה מָרוֹם לְעֹלָם יהוה:
כִּי הִנֵּה אֹיְבֶיךָ יהוה, כִּי־הִנֵּה אֹיְבֶיךָ יֹאבֵדוּ
יִתְפָּרְדוּ כָּל־פֹּעֲלֵי אָוֶן:
וַתָּרֶם כִּרְאֵים קַרְנִי, בַּלֹּתִי בְּשֶׁמֶן רַעֲנָן:
וַתַּבֵּט עֵינִי בְּשׁוּרָי, בַּקָּמִים עָלַי מְרֵעִים תִּשְׁמַעְנָה אָזְנָי:
◂ צַדִּיק כַּתָּמָר יִפְרָח, כְּאֶרֶז בַּלְּבָנוֹן יִשְׂגֶּה:
שְׁתוּלִים בְּבֵית יהוה, בְּחַצְרוֹת אֱלֹהֵינוּ יַפְרִיחוּ:
עוֹד יְנוּבוּן בְּשֵׂיבָה, דְּשֵׁנִים וְרַעֲנַנִּים יִהְיוּ:
לְהַגִּיד כִּי־יָשָׁר יהוה, צוּרִי, וְלֹא־עַוְלָתָה בּוֹ:

יהוה מָלָךְ, גֵּאוּת לָבֵשׁ
לָבֵשׁ יהוה עֹז הִתְאַזָּר, אַף־תִּכּוֹן תֵּבֵל בַּל־תִּמּוֹט:
נָכוֹן כִּסְאֲךָ מֵאָז, מֵעוֹלָם אָתָּה:
נָשְׂאוּ נְהָרוֹת יהוה, נָשְׂאוּ נְהָרוֹת קוֹלָם
יִשְׂאוּ נְהָרוֹת דָּכְיָם:
◂ מִקֹּלוֹת מַיִם רַבִּים, אַדִּירִים מִשְׁבְּרֵי־יָם
אַדִּיר בַּמָּרוֹם יהוה:
עֵדֹתֶיךָ נֶאֶמְנוּ מְאֹד, לְבֵיתְךָ נַאֲוָה־קֹדֶשׁ
יהוה לְאֹרֶךְ יָמִים:

KADDISH YATOM

The following prayer, said by mourners, requires the presence of a minyan. A transliteration can be found on page 865.

Mourner: יִתְגַּדַּל May *Hashem* be recognized
as great and holy (*Congregation:* Amen)
in the world that He created.
May He establish His kingdom
during my lifetime
and the lifetime of all Jews,
quickly and soon.
Let us say: "Amen" (*Congregation:* Amen).

Congregation: May we thank *Hashem* for ever and ever.
Mourner: May we thank *Hashem* for ever and ever.

Mourner: *Hashem* should be thanked, praised,
and honored (*Congregation:* He is blessed).
Hashem is beyond all the blessings,
songs, or praises that we could offer.
Let us say: "Amen" (*Congregation:* Amen).

May *Hashem* give us, and all Jews,
peace and good life.
Let us say: "Amen." (*Congregation:* Amen).

The mourner takes three steps back before saying this line, bows to the left when saying "May," bows to the right when saying "the One," bows to the middle when saying "make peace for us":

May *Hashem*, the One
who makes peace in heaven,
make peace for us and for all Jews.
Let us say: "Amen." (*Congregation:* Amen).

קדיש יתום

The following prayer, said by mourners, requires the presence of a מנין.
A transliteration can be found on page 865.

אבל: יִתְגַּדַּל וְיִתְקַדַּשׁ שְׁמֵהּ רַבָּא (קהל: אָמֵן)
בְּעָלְמָא דִּי בְרָא כִרְעוּתֵהּ, וְיַמְלִיךְ מַלְכוּתֵהּ
בְּחַיֵּיכוֹן וּבְיוֹמֵיכוֹן וּבְחַיֵּי דְכָל בֵּית יִשְׂרָאֵל
בַּעֲגָלָא וּבִזְמַן קָרִיב, וְאִמְרוּ אָמֵן. (קהל: אָמֵן)

קהל יְהֵא שְׁמֵהּ רַבָּא מְבָרַךְ לְעָלַם וּלְעָלְמֵי עָלְמַיָּא.
אבל: יְהֵא שְׁמֵהּ רַבָּא מְבָרַךְ לְעָלַם וּלְעָלְמֵי עָלְמַיָּא.

אבל: יִתְבָּרַךְ וְיִשְׁתַּבַּח וְיִתְפָּאַר
וְיִתְרוֹמַם וְיִתְנַשֵּׂא וְיִתְהַדָּר וְיִתְעַלֶּה וְיִתְהַלָּל
שְׁמֵהּ דְּקֻדְשָׁא בְּרִיךְ הוּא (קהל: בְּרִיךְ הוּא)
לְעֵלָּא מִן כָּל בִּרְכָתָא
/בשבת שובה: לְעֵלָּא לְעֵלָּא מִכָּל בִּרְכָתָא/
וְשִׁירָתָא, תֻּשְׁבְּחָתָא וְנֶחֱמָתָא
דַּאֲמִירָן בְּעָלְמָא, וְאִמְרוּ אָמֵן. (קהל: אָמֵן)

יְהֵא שְׁלָמָא רַבָּא מִן שְׁמַיָּא
וְחַיִּים, עָלֵינוּ וְעַל כָּל יִשְׂרָאֵל, וְאִמְרוּ אָמֵן. (קהל: אָמֵן)

The mourner takes three steps back before saying this line, bows to the left when saying עֹשֶׂה, *bows to the right when saying* הוּא, *bows to the middle when saying* יַעֲשֶׂה שָׁלוֹם עָלֵינוּ:

עֹשֶׂה שָׁלוֹם /בשבת שובה: הַשָּׁלוֹם/ בִּמְרוֹמָיו
הוּא יַעֲשֶׂה שָׁלוֹם עָלֵינוּ
וְעַל כָּל יִשְׂרָאֵל, וְאִמְרוּ אָמֵן. (קהל: אָמֵן)

The following is not said on Yom Tov, Shabbat Chol HaMo'ed or Motza'ei Yom Tov.

בַּמֶּה מַדְלִיקִין When it comes to lighting the Shabbat candles there are many laws to keep in mind.

Some kinds of oils and wicks can be used
and others cannot.
The wicks used for the Shabbat lights
should not be made from something
that causes the light to flicker.
Instead, we should use wicks that burn steadily.

The oil used for the Shabbat lights
must burn easily.
Oils that do not burn easily
may not be used.

You may not put out a fire on Shabbat
unless your safety is at risk.

בַּמֶּה מַדְלִיקִין *Bameh Madlikin* is the second chapter of Mishnayot Shabbat. This chapter focuses on preparations for Shabbat, especially the rules about lighting Shabbat candles. After welcoming Shabbat with Kabbalat Shabbat, we take a few moments to think about all the preparations that went into entering this holy day, to help us appreciate the day of rest. Keeping the rules of Shabbat allows us to focus on connecting with our family and with *Hashem*.

The following is not said on מוצאי יום טוב *or* יום טוב, שבת חול המועד.

א בַּמֶּה מַדְלִיקִין וּבַמָּה אֵין מַדְלִיקִין. אֵין מַדְלִיקִין לֹא בְלֶכֶשׁ, וְלֹא בְחֹסֶן, וְלֹא בְכַלָּךְ, וְלֹא בִּפְתִילַת הָאִידָן, וְלֹא בִּפְתִילַת הַמִּדְבָּר, וְלֹא בִירוֹקָה שֶׁעַל פְּנֵי הַמָּיִם. וְלֹא בְזֶפֶת וְלֹא בְשַׁעֲוָה וְלֹא בְּשֶׁמֶן קִיק וְלֹא בְּשֶׁמֶן שְׂרֵפָה וְלֹא בְאַלְיָה וְלֹא בְחֵלֶב. נַחוּם הַמָּדִי אוֹמֵר: מַדְלִיקִין בְּחֵלֶב מְבֻשָּׁל, וַחֲכָמִים אוֹמְרִים: אֶחָד מְבֻשָּׁל וְאֶחָד שֶׁאֵינוֹ מְבֻשָּׁל, אֵין מַדְלִיקִין בּוֹ.

ב אֵין מַדְלִיקִין בְּשֶׁמֶן שְׂרֵפָה בְּיוֹם טוֹב. רַבִּי יִשְׁמָעֵאל אוֹמֵר: אֵין מַדְלִיקִין בְּעִטְרָן מִפְּנֵי כְבוֹד הַשַּׁבָּת. וַחֲכָמִים מַתִּירִין בְּכָל הַשְּׁמָנִים, בְּשֶׁמֶן שֻׁמְשְׁמִין, בְּשֶׁמֶן אֱגוֹזִים, בְּשֶׁמֶן צְנוֹנוֹת, בְּשֶׁמֶן דָּגִים, בְּשֶׁמֶן פַּקֻּעוֹת, בְּעִטְרָן וּבְנֵפְט. רַבִּי טַרְפוֹן אוֹמֵר: אֵין מַדְלִיקִין אֶלָּא בְּשֶׁמֶן זַיִת בִּלְבָד.

ג כָּל הַיּוֹצֵא מִן הָעֵץ אֵין מַדְלִיקִין בּוֹ, אֶלָּא פִשְׁתָּן. וְכָל הַיּוֹצֵא מִן הָעֵץ אֵינוֹ מִטַּמֵּא טֻמְאַת אֹהָלִים, אֶלָּא פִשְׁתָּן. פְּתִילַת הַבֶּגֶד שֶׁקִּפְּלָהּ וְלֹא הִבְהֲבָהּ, רַבִּי אֱלִיעֶזֶר אוֹמֵר: טְמֵאָה הִיא, וְאֵין מַדְלִיקִין בָּהּ. רַבִּי עֲקִיבָא אוֹמֵר: טְהוֹרָה הִיא, וּמַדְלִיקִין בָּהּ.

ד לֹא יִקֹּב אָדָם שְׁפוֹפֶרֶת שֶׁל בֵּיצָה וִימַלְּאֶנָּה שֶׁמֶן וְיִתְּנֶנָּה עַל פִּי הַנֵּר, בִּשְׁבִיל שֶׁתְּהֵא מְנַטֶּפֶת, וַאֲפִילוּ הִיא שֶׁל חֶרֶס. וְרַבִּי יְהוּדָה מַתִּיר. אֲבָל אִם חִבְּרָהּ הַיּוֹצֵר מִתְּחִלָּה מֻתָּר, מִפְּנֵי שֶׁהוּא כְּלִי אֶחָד. לֹא יְמַלֵּא אָדָם אֶת הַקְּעָרָה שֶׁמֶן וְיִתְּנֶנָּה בְּצַד הַנֵּר וְיִתֵּן רֹאשׁ הַפְּתִילָה בְּתוֹכָהּ, בִּשְׁבִיל שֶׁתְּהֵא שׁוֹאֶבֶת. וְרַבִּי יְהוּדָה מַתִּיר.

ה הַמְכַבֶּה אֶת הַנֵּר מִפְּנֵי שֶׁהוּא מִתְיָרֵא מִפְּנֵי גוֹיִם, מִפְּנֵי לִסְטִים, מִפְּנֵי רוּחַ רָעָה, אוֹ בִּשְׁבִיל הַחוֹלֶה שֶׁיִּישַׁן, פָּטוּר. כְּחָס עַל הַנֵּר, כְּחָס עַל הַשֶּׁמֶן, כְּחָס עַל הַפְּתִילָה, חַיָּב. רַבִּי יוֹסֵי פּוֹטֵר בְּכֻלָּן חוּץ מִן הַפְּתִילָה, מִפְּנֵי שֶׁהוּא עוֹשָׂה פֶּחָם.

Before Shabbat it is important to make sure that the following things are taken care of:

If you baked your own bread,
a portion, called the *challah*, is set aside to be burnt.

The *eruv* is set up properly so that one can carry on Shabbat.

The candles are lit before Shabbat begins.

You should check your pockets before Shabbat to make sure that you are only carrying items which you are permitted to carry on Shabbat.

Those who study and love Torah bring peace to the world.

▸ *Hashem* will give His people strength and peace.

KADDISH DERABANAN

The following prayer, said by mourners, requires the presence of a minyan. A transliteration can be found on page 864.

Mourner: יִתְגַּדַּל May *Hashem* be recognized
as great and holy (*Congregation:* Amen)
in the world that He created.
May He establish His kingdom
during my lifetime and the lifetime of all Jews,
quickly and soon.
Let us say: "Amen" (*Congregation:* Amen).

Congregation: May we thank *Hashem* for ever and ever.

Mourner: May we thank *Hashem* for ever and ever.

וּמְעָרְבִין *The Eruv.* There are many actions we cannot do on Shabbat as they are considered "work." One of these actions is carrying items in outdoor public areas. However, we are allowed to carry items in a private area. Many Jewish neighborhoods tie an *eruv*, a string hanging around the edges of a community, as a sign that the enclosed area is a shared and private space. With an *eruv*, one is allowed to carry in these communities.

ו עַל שָׁלֹשׁ עֲבֵרוֹת נָשִׁים מֵתוֹת בִּשְׁעַת לֵדָתָן, עַל שֶׁאֵינָן זְהִירוֹת בַּנִּדָּה, בַּחַלָּה וּבְהַדְלָקַת הַנֵּר.

ז שְׁלֹשָׁה דְבָרִים צָרִיךְ אָדָם לוֹמַר בְּתוֹךְ בֵּיתוֹ עֶרֶב שַׁבָּת עִם חֲשֵׁכָה: עִשַּׂרְתֶּם, עֵרַבְתֶּם, הַדְלִיקוּ אֶת הַנֵּר. סָפֵק חֲשֵׁכָה סָפֵק אֵינָהּ חֲשֵׁכָה, אֵין מְעַשְּׂרִין אֶת הַוַּדַּאי, וְאֵין מַטְבִּילִין אֶת הַכֵּלִים, וְאֵין מַדְלִיקִין אֶת הַנֵּרוֹת. אֲבָל מְעַשְּׂרִין אֶת הַדְּמַאי, וּמְעָרְבִין וְטוֹמְנִין אֶת הַחַמִּין.

תַּנְיָא, אָמַר רַבִּי חֲנִינָא: חַיָּב אָדָם לְמַשְׁמֵשׁ בְּגָדָיו בְּעֶרֶב שַׁבָּת עִם חֲשֵׁכָה, שֶׁמָּא יִשְׁכַּח וְיֵצֵא. אָמַר רַב יוֹסֵף: הִלְכְתָא רַבְּתָא לְשַׁבְּתָא.

אָמַר רַבִּי אֶלְעָזָר, אָמַר רַבִּי חֲנִינָא: תַּלְמִידֵי חֲכָמִים מַרְבִּים שָׁלוֹם בָּעוֹלָם, שֶׁנֶּאֱמַר: וְכָל־בָּנַיִךְ לִמּוּדֵי יהוה, וְרַב שְׁלוֹם בָּנָיִךְ: אַל תִּקְרֵי בָּנָיִךְ, אֶלָּא בּוֹנָיִךְ. שָׁלוֹם רָב לְאֹהֲבֵי תוֹרָתֶךָ, וְאֵין־לָמוֹ מִכְשׁוֹל: יְהִי־שָׁלוֹם בְּחֵילֵךְ, שַׁלְוָה בְּאַרְמְנוֹתָיִךְ: לְמַעַן אַחַי וְרֵעָי אֲדַבְּרָה־נָּא שָׁלוֹם בָּךְ: לְמַעַן בֵּית־יהוה אֱלֹהֵינוּ אֲבַקְשָׁה טוֹב לָךְ: ◂ יהוה עֹז לְעַמּוֹ יִתֵּן, יהוה יְבָרֵךְ אֶת־עַמּוֹ בַשָּׁלוֹם:

קדיש דרבנן

The following prayer, said by mourners, requires the presence of a מנין.
A transliteration can be found on page 864.

אבל: יִתְגַּדַּל וְיִתְקַדַּשׁ שְׁמֵהּ רַבָּא (קהל: אָמֵן)
בְּעָלְמָא דִּי בְרָא כִרְעוּתֵהּ, וְיַמְלִיךְ מַלְכוּתֵהּ
בְּחַיֵּיכוֹן וּבְיוֹמֵיכוֹן וּבְחַיֵּי דְכָל בֵּית יִשְׂרָאֵל
בַּעֲגָלָא וּבִזְמַן קָרִיב, וְאִמְרוּ אָמֵן. (קהל: אָמֵן)

קהל יְהֵא שְׁמֵהּ רַבָּא מְבָרַךְ לְעָלַם וּלְעָלְמֵי עָלְמַיָּא.
אבל: יְהֵא שְׁמֵהּ רַבָּא מְבָרַךְ לְעָלַם וּלְעָלְמֵי עָלְמַיָּא.

Mourner: *Hashem* should be thanked, praised,
and honored (*Congregation:* He is blessed).
Hashem is beyond all the blessings,
songs, or praises
that we could offer.
Let us say:
"Amen" (*Congregation:* Amen).

To the Jewish people including:
Teachers,
Students,
Students of students, and
All those that spend time learning Torah,
May *Hashem* provide them with peace,
kindness, mercy, long-life, and food to live.
Let us say:
"Amen." (*Congregation:* Amen.)

May *Hashem* give us, and all Jews,
peace and good life.
Let us all say:
"Amen." (*Congregation:* Amen.)

The mourner takes three steps back before saying this line, bows to the left when saying "May," bows to the right when saying "the One," bows to the middle when saying "make peace for us":

May *Hashem*, the One
who makes peace in heaven,
make peace for us and all Jews.
Let us say:
"Amen." (*Congregation:* Amen.)

אבל: יִתְבָּרַךְ וְיִשְׁתַּבַּח וְיִתְפָּאַר וְיִתְרוֹמַם וְיִתְנַשֵּׂא
וְיִתְהַדָּר וְיִתְעַלֶּה וְיִתְהַלָּל
שְׁמֵהּ דְּקֻדְשָׁא בְּרִיךְ הוּא (קהל: בְּרִיךְ הוּא)
לְעֵלָּא מִן כָּל בִּרְכָתָא /בשבת שובה: לְעֵלָּא לְעֵלָּא מִכָּל בִּרְכָתָא/
וְשִׁירָתָא, תֻּשְׁבְּחָתָא וְנֶחֱמָתָא, דַּאֲמִירָן בְּעָלְמָא
וְאִמְרוּ אָמֵן. (קהל: אָמֵן)

עַל יִשְׂרָאֵל וְעַל רַבָּנָן
וְעַל תַּלְמִידֵיהוֹן וְעַל כָּל תַּלְמִידֵי תַלְמִידֵיהוֹן
וְעַל כָּל מָאן דְּעָסְקִין בְּאוֹרַיְתָא
דִּי בְּאַתְרָא הָדֵין, וְדִי בְּכָל אֲתַר וַאֲתַר
יְהֵא לְהוֹן וּלְכוֹן שְׁלָמָא רַבָּא
חִנָּא וְחִסְדָּא, וְרַחֲמֵי, וְחַיֵּי אֲרִיכֵי, וּמְזוֹנֵי רְוִיחֵי
וּפֻרְקָנָא מִן קֳדָם אֲבוּהוֹן דִּי בִשְׁמַיָּא
וְאִמְרוּ אָמֵן. (קהל: אָמֵן)

יְהֵא שְׁלָמָא רַבָּא מִן שְׁמַיָּא
וְחַיִּים (טוֹבִים) עָלֵינוּ וְעַל כָּל יִשְׂרָאֵל
וְאִמְרוּ אָמֵן. (קהל: אָמֵן)

The mourner takes three steps back before saying this line, bows to the left when saying עֹשֶׂה*, bows to the right when saying* הוּא*, bows to the middle when saying* יַעֲשֶׂה בְרַחֲמָיו שָׁלוֹם*:*

עֹשֶׂה שָׁלוֹם /בשבת שובה: הַשָּׁלוֹם/ בִּמְרוֹמָיו
הוּא יַעֲשֶׂה בְרַחֲמָיו שָׁלוֹם עָלֵינוּ וְעַל כָּל יִשְׂרָאֵל
וְאִמְרוּ אָמֵן. (קהל: אָמֵן)

Ma'ariv for Shabbat

BLESSINGS OF THE SHEMA

Bow when saying the word "Thank."

Leader: **LET US THANK**
Hashem,
for He deserves thanksgiving.

Congregation: Thank *Hashem* for ever and ever!

Leader: Thank *Hashem* for ever and ever!

Those praying without a minyan begin here:
Sit while saying the following.

בָּרוּךְ We thank You,
Hashem, King of the universe,
Who, with His words, brings night.
With great wisdom *Hashem* creates:
Time and seasons,
Stars and their placement in the sky,
Day and night, and
Light and dark.
▸ It is *Hashem* who oversees all.
May You, *Hashem,* continue to always rule over us.
Thank You, *Hashem,*
who brings night.

מעריב לשבת

קריאת שמע וברכותיה

Bow when saying the word בָּרוּךְ.

חזן: **בָּרְכוּ**
אֶת יהוה הַמְבֹרָךְ.

קהל: בָּרוּךְ יהוה הַמְבֹרָךְ לְעוֹלָם וָעֶד.

חזן: **בָּרוּךְ יהוה הַמְבֹרָךְ לְעוֹלָם וָעֶד.**

Those praying without a מנין *begin here:*
Sit while saying the following.

בָּרוּךְ אַתָּה יהוה אֱלֹהֵינוּ מֶלֶךְ הָעוֹלָם
אֲשֶׁר בִּדְבָרוֹ מַעֲרִיב עֲרָבִים
בְּחָכְמָה פּוֹתֵחַ שְׁעָרִים
וּבִתְבוּנָה מְשַׁנֶּה עִתִּים וּמַחֲלִיף אֶת הַזְּמַנִּים
וּמְסַדֵּר אֶת הַכּוֹכָבִים בְּמִשְׁמְרוֹתֵיהֶם בָּרָקִיעַ כִּרְצוֹנוֹ.
בּוֹרֵא יוֹם וָלָיְלָה, גּוֹלֵל אוֹר מִפְּנֵי חֹשֶׁךְ וְחֹשֶׁךְ מִפְּנֵי אוֹר
◂ וּמַעֲבִיר יוֹם וּמֵבִיא לָיְלָה, וּמַבְדִּיל בֵּין יוֹם וּבֵין לָיְלָה
יהוה צְבָאוֹת שְׁמוֹ.
אֵל חַי וְקַיָּם תָּמִיד, יִמְלֹךְ עָלֵינוּ לְעוֹלָם וָעֶד.
בָּרוּךְ אַתָּה יהוה, הַמַּעֲרִיב עֲרָבִים.

אַהֲבַת עוֹלָם *Hashem,* You have shown great love
to Your Jewish people,
by teaching us Your Torah and *mitzvot.*
Therefore, *Hashem,* we will speak about Your *mitzvot*
and enjoy the words of Your Torah
when we go to sleep and when we wake.
Torah and *mitzvot* are the basis of our lives;
▸ we will think about them day and night.
Hashem, may You never lessen Your love
for the Jewish people.
Thank You, *Hashem,* who loves His Jewish people.

Say this line when praying alone:

God, You are our trustworthy King.

Cover your eyes with your right hand, and say this line aloud:

LISTEN AND UNDERSTAND, JEWISH PEOPLE,
HASHEM IS OUR ONE AND ONLY GOD.

Say this line quietly:

Thank You, *Hashem,* our God. Your kingdom lasts forever.

וְאָהַבְתָּ Love *Hashem,* your God,
with all of your heart, soul, and belongings.
Live according to God's words and *mitzvot.*
Think about and recite the Shema
when sitting in your home,
when traveling on the road,
when you go to sleep at night,
and when you first wake up in the morning.
Wear *tefillin* on your arm and head,
and hang a *mezuzah* on your door.

אַהֲבַת עוֹלָם בֵּית יִשְׂרָאֵל עַמְּךָ אָהָבְתָּ
תּוֹרָה וּמִצְוֹת, חֻקִּים וּמִשְׁפָּטִים, אוֹתָנוּ לִמַּדְתָּ
עַל כֵּן יהוה אֱלֹהֵינוּ בְּשָׁכְבֵנוּ וּבְקוּמֵנוּ נָשִׂיחַ בְּחֻקֶּיךָ
וְנִשְׂמַח בְּדִבְרֵי תוֹרָתֶךָ וּבְמִצְוֹתֶיךָ לְעוֹלָם וָעֶד
◄ כִּי הֵם חַיֵּינוּ וְאֹרֶךְ יָמֵינוּ
וּבָהֶם נֶהְגֶּה יוֹמָם וָלָיְלָה.
וְאַהֲבָתְךָ אַל תָּסִיר מִמֶּנּוּ לְעוֹלָמִים.
בָּרוּךְ אַתָּה יהוה, אוֹהֵב עַמּוֹ יִשְׂרָאֵל.

Say this line when praying alone:

אֵל מֶלֶךְ נֶאֱמָן

Cover your eyes with your right hand, and say this line aloud:

שְׁמַע יִשְׂרָאֵל, יהוה אֱלֹהֵינוּ, יהוה ׀ אֶחָד:

Say this line quietly:

בָּרוּךְ שֵׁם כְּבוֹד מַלְכוּתוֹ לְעוֹלָם וָעֶד.

וְאָהַבְתָּ אֵת יהוה אֱלֹהֶיךָ
בְּכָל־לְבָבְךָ וּבְכָל־נַפְשְׁךָ וּבְכָל־מְאֹדֶךָ:
וְהָיוּ הַדְּבָרִים הָאֵלֶּה, אֲשֶׁר אָנֹכִי מְצַוְּךָ הַיּוֹם, עַל־לְבָבֶךָ:
וְשִׁנַּנְתָּם לְבָנֶיךָ וְדִבַּרְתָּ בָּם
בְּשִׁבְתְּךָ בְּבֵיתֶךָ וּבְלֶכְתְּךָ בַדֶּרֶךְ, וּבְשָׁכְבְּךָ וּבְקוּמֶךָ:
וּקְשַׁרְתָּם לְאוֹת עַל־יָדֶךָ, וְהָיוּ לְטֹטָפֹת בֵּין עֵינֶיךָ:
וּכְתַבְתָּם עַל־מְזֻזוֹת בֵּיתֶךָ וּבִשְׁעָרֶיךָ:

וְהָיָה If you live
according to the *mitzvot* of *Hashem*,
loving and serving Him
with all your effort,
Hashem will give you reward.
Hashem will bring rain
for your plants to grow
and provide you with the food
you need to live.
However, if you sin
and do not serve *Hashem*,
there will be consequences and punishments;
Hashem might not provide you
with health, money,
or other basics you need to live.
Therefore,
be careful to follow *Hashem*'s *mitzvot*
and set yourself reminders,
such as wearing *tefillin* on
your arms and head,
and placing *mezuzot* on your doorposts.
If you do this,
you will live a long life.

וְהָיָה אִם־שָׁמֹעַ תִּשְׁמְעוּ אֶל־מִצְוֺתַי
אֲשֶׁר אָנֹכִי מְצַוֶּה אֶתְכֶם הַיּוֹם
לְאַהֲבָה אֶת־יהוה אֱלֹהֵיכֶם וּלְעָבְדוֹ
בְּכָל־לְבַבְכֶם וּבְכָל־נַפְשְׁכֶם:
וְנָתַתִּי מְטַר־אַרְצְכֶם בְּעִתּוֹ, יוֹרֶה וּמַלְקוֹשׁ
וְאָסַפְתָּ דְגָנֶךָ וְתִירֹשְׁךָ וְיִצְהָרֶךָ:
וְנָתַתִּי עֵשֶׂב בְּשָׂדְךָ לִבְהֶמְתֶּךָ, וְאָכַלְתָּ וְשָׂבָעְתָּ:
הִשָּׁמְרוּ לָכֶם פֶּן־יִפְתֶּה לְבַבְכֶם
וְסַרְתֶּם וַעֲבַדְתֶּם אֱלֹהִים אֲחֵרִים וְהִשְׁתַּחֲוִיתֶם לָהֶם:
וְחָרָה אַף־יהוה בָּכֶם, וְעָצַר אֶת־הַשָּׁמַיִם וְלֹא־יִהְיֶה מָטָר
וְהָאֲדָמָה לֹא תִתֵּן אֶת־יְבוּלָהּ
וַאֲבַדְתֶּם מְהֵרָה מֵעַל הָאָרֶץ הַטֹּבָה אֲשֶׁר יהוה נֹתֵן לָכֶם:
וְשַׂמְתֶּם אֶת־דְּבָרַי אֵלֶּה עַל־לְבַבְכֶם וְעַל־נַפְשְׁכֶם
וּקְשַׁרְתֶּם אֹתָם לְאוֹת עַל־יֶדְכֶם
וְהָיוּ לְטוֹטָפֹת בֵּין עֵינֵיכֶם:
וְלִמַּדְתֶּם אֹתָם אֶת־בְּנֵיכֶם לְדַבֵּר בָּם
בְּשִׁבְתְּךָ בְּבֵיתֶךָ וּבְלֶכְתְּךָ בַדֶּרֶךְ, וּבְשָׁכְבְּךָ וּבְקוּמֶךָ:
וּכְתַבְתָּם עַל־מְזוּזוֹת בֵּיתֶךָ וּבִשְׁעָרֶיךָ:
לְמַעַן יִרְבּוּ יְמֵיכֶם וִימֵי בְנֵיכֶם עַל הָאֲדָמָה
אֲשֶׁר נִשְׁבַּע יהוה לַאֲבֹתֵיכֶם לָתֵת לָהֶם
כִּימֵי הַשָּׁמַיִם עַל־הָאָרֶץ:

וַיֹּאמֶר *Hashem* told Moshe
that we, the Jewish people,
should have *tzitzit*
on the corners of our clothing.
Each set of *tzitzit* strings
should have a blue string.
The *tzitzit* should be worn
so that you can see them.
They will remind you
to focus on God
and His *mitzvot*.
Hashem, the same God
who miraculously
saved the Jewish people
from slavery in Egypt,
is your God.

THIS IS TRUE.

The Leader repeats:

▸ *Hashem* is your true God.

We have complete faith that:

Hashem is our God,
There is none else but Him, and
We, the Jewish nation, are His people.

וַיֹּאמֶר יְהוָה אֶל־מֹשֶׁה לֵּאמֹר:
דַּבֵּר אֶל־בְּנֵי יִשְׂרָאֵל וְאָמַרְתָּ אֲלֵהֶם
וְעָשׂוּ לָהֶם צִיצִת עַל־כַּנְפֵי בִגְדֵיהֶם לְדֹרֹתָם
וְנָתְנוּ עַל־צִיצִת הַכָּנָף פְּתִיל תְּכֵלֶת:
וְהָיָה לָכֶם לְצִיצִת, וּרְאִיתֶם אֹתוֹ
וּזְכַרְתֶּם אֶת־כָּל־מִצְוֺת יְהוָה וַעֲשִׂיתֶם אֹתָם
וְלֹא תָתֻרוּ אַחֲרֵי לְבַבְכֶם וְאַחֲרֵי עֵינֵיכֶם
אֲשֶׁר־אַתֶּם זֹנִים אַחֲרֵיהֶם:
לְמַעַן תִּזְכְּרוּ וַעֲשִׂיתֶם אֶת־כָּל־מִצְוֺתָי
וִהְיִיתֶם קְדֹשִׁים לֵאלֹהֵיכֶם:
אֲנִי יְהוָה אֱלֹהֵיכֶם, אֲשֶׁר הוֹצֵאתִי אֶתְכֶם מֵאֶרֶץ מִצְרַיִם
לִהְיוֹת לָכֶם לֵאלֹהִים
אֲנִי יְהוָה אֱלֹהֵיכֶם:

אֱמֶת

The חזן *repeats:*

◂ יְהוָה אֱלֹהֵיכֶם אֱמֶת

וֶאֱמוּנָה כָּל זֹאת וְקַיָּם עָלֵינוּ
כִּי הוּא יְהוָה אֱלֹהֵינוּ וְאֵין זוּלָתוֹ
וַאֲנַחְנוּ יִשְׂרָאֵל עַמּוֹ.

Hashem is our King who:

Saves us from our enemies,
Does great actions
beyond our understanding,
Performs miracles
that are too many to count,
Protects us from getting hurt,
Led us to victory over our enemies,
Performed miracles on our behalf and
fought our war against Pharaoh,
Took the lives of the first born Egyptians,
Brought the Jewish people
out of Egypt and
into freedom forever,
Split the Reed Sea, and
led His Jewish people through it, and
Saved the Jewish people by bringing the water
crashing down upon our enemies.

When the Jewish people saw these miracles
they praised, thanked,
▸ and accepted You, *Hashem*, as their only Ruler.
Moshe and all of the Jewish people
sang praise to You *Hashem*
and cried out:

Say the following two sentences out loud:

"Who is as strong as You, *Hashem*?
Who is as holy
and awesome as You, *Hashem*?"

הַפּוֹדֵנוּ מִיַּד מְלָכִים
מַלְכֵּנוּ הַגּוֹאֲלֵנוּ מִכַּף כָּל הֶעָרִיצִים.
הָאֵל הַנִּפְרָע לָנוּ מִצָּרֵינוּ
וְהַמְשַׁלֵּם גְּמוּל לְכָל אוֹיְבֵי נַפְשֵׁנוּ.
הָעוֹשֶׂה גְדוֹלוֹת עַד אֵין חֵקֶר, וְנִפְלָאוֹת עַד אֵין מִסְפָּר
הַשָּׂם נַפְשֵׁנוּ בַּחַיִּים, וְלֹא־נָתַן לַמּוֹט רַגְלֵנוּ:
הַמַּדְרִיכֵנוּ עַל בָּמוֹת אוֹיְבֵינוּ
וַיָּרֶם קַרְנֵנוּ עַל כָּל שׂוֹנְאֵינוּ.
הָעוֹשֶׂה לָּנוּ נִסִּים וּנְקָמָה בְּפַרְעֹה
אוֹתוֹת וּמוֹפְתִים בְּאַדְמַת בְּנֵי חָם.
הַמַּכֶּה בְעֶבְרָתוֹ כָּל בְּכוֹרֵי מִצְרָיִם
וַיּוֹצֵא אֶת עַמּוֹ יִשְׂרָאֵל מִתּוֹכָם לְחֵרוּת עוֹלָם.
הַמַּעֲבִיר בָּנָיו בֵּין גִּזְרֵי יַם סוּף
אֶת רוֹדְפֵיהֶם וְאֶת שׂוֹנְאֵיהֶם בִּתְהוֹמוֹת טִבַּע
וְרָאוּ בָנָיו גְּבוּרָתוֹ, שִׁבְּחוּ וְהוֹדוּ לִשְׁמוֹ
◂ וּמַלְכוּתוֹ בְּרָצוֹן קִבְּלוּ עֲלֵיהֶם.
מֹשֶׁה וּבְנֵי יִשְׂרָאֵל, לְךָ עָנוּ שִׁירָה בְּשִׂמְחָה רַבָּה
וְאָמְרוּ כֻלָּם

Say the following two sentences out loud:

מִי־כָמֹכָה בָּאֵלִם יהוה
מִי כָּמֹכָה נֶאְדָּר בַּקֹּדֶשׁ
נוֹרָא תְהִלֹּת עֹשֵׂה פֶלֶא:

▸ When You, *Hashem,* split the sea,
Moshe and Your Jewish people knew
that You were King and said, "This is my God."
They then said:

Say the following sentence out loud:
"*Hashem* will rule as King for ever and ever."

▸ The Torah writes:
"*Hashem,* You have saved the Jewish people
from a stronger nation."

Thank You, *Hashem,*
who saves the Jewish people.

הַשְׁכִּיבֵנוּ *Hashem,* please allow us
to lie down at night in peace
and awake in the morning with life.
With peace, protect us, direct us, and save us.
Protect us and remove our:

Enemies,
Hunger,
Sorrow, and
All those who are against us.

You, *Hashem,* our God, are a kind and merciful King.
▸ Protect us when in public and in private
and allow us to live peacefully,
for now and forever.
Thank You, *Hashem,*
for providing peace to us, Your Jewish people,
and to Jerusalem.

◂ מַלְכוּתְךָ רָאוּ בָנֶיךָ, בּוֹקֵעַ יָם לִפְנֵי מֹשֶׁה
זֶה אֵלִי עָנוּ, וְאָמְרוּ

Say the following sentence out loud:

יהוה יִמְלֹךְ לְעֹלָם וָעֶד:

◂ וְנֶאֱמַר

כִּי־פָדָה יהוה אֶת־יַעֲקֹב, וּגְאָלוֹ מִיַּד חָזָק מִמֶּנּוּ:
בָּרוּךְ אַתָּה יהוה, גָּאַל יִשְׂרָאֵל.

הַשְׁכִּיבֵנוּ יהוה אֱלֹהֵינוּ לְשָׁלוֹם
וְהַעֲמִידֵנוּ מַלְכֵּנוּ לְחַיִּים
וּפְרֹשׂ עָלֵינוּ סֻכַּת שְׁלוֹמֶךָ, וְתַקְּנֵנוּ בְּעֵצָה טוֹבָה מִלְּפָנֶיךָ
וְהוֹשִׁיעֵנוּ לְמַעַן שְׁמֶךָ.
וְהָגֵן בַּעֲדֵנוּ
וְהָסֵר מֵעָלֵינוּ אוֹיֵב, דֶּבֶר וְחֶרֶב וְרָעָב וְיָגוֹן
וְהָסֵר שָׂטָן מִלְּפָנֵינוּ וּמֵאַחֲרֵינוּ, וּבְצֵל כְּנָפֶיךָ תַּסְתִּירֵנוּ
כִּי אֵל שׁוֹמְרֵנוּ וּמַצִּילֵנוּ אָתָּה
כִּי אֵל מֶלֶךְ חַנּוּן וְרַחוּם אָתָּה.
◂ וּשְׁמֹר צֵאתֵנוּ וּבוֹאֵנוּ לְחַיִּים וּלְשָׁלוֹם מֵעַתָּה וְעַד עוֹלָם.
וּפְרֹשׂ עָלֵינוּ סֻכַּת שְׁלוֹמֶךָ.
בָּרוּךְ אַתָּה יהוה
הַפּוֹרֵשׂ סֻכַּת שָׁלוֹם עָלֵינוּ וְעַל כָּל עַמּוֹ יִשְׂרָאֵל
וְעַל יְרוּשָׁלָיִם.

On Shabbat, the congregation stands and, together with the Leader, says:

The Jewish people must observe Shabbat as the day that represents the agreement between *Hashem* and the Jewish people forever. Shabbat will always remind us that *Hashem* created heaven and earth in six days and rested on the seventh day.

HALF KADDISH

Leader: יִתְגַּדַּל May *Hashem* be recognized
as great and holy (*Congregation:* Amen)
in the world that He created.
May He establish His kingdom
during my lifetime and the lifetime of all Jews,
quickly and soon.
Let us say: "Amen" (*Congregation:* Amen).

Congregation: May we thank *Hashem* for ever and ever.
Leader: May we thank *Hashem* for ever and ever.

Leader: *Hashem* should be thanked, praised,
and honored (*Congregation:* He is blessed).
Hashem is beyond all the blessings,
songs, or praises that we could offer.
Let us say: "Amen" (*Congregation:* Amen).

לַעֲשׂוֹת אֶת־הַשַּׁבָּת לְדֹרֹתָם בְּרִית עוֹלָם *Shabbat as the day that represents the agreement between Hashem and the Jewish people forever.* Resting from work on Shabbat is our way of showing *Hashem* that we believe He created the world in six days and rested on the seventh day, Shabbat. We agree to keep Shabbat, as a weekly reminder that *Hashem*, our God, created the world. In return, *Hashem* agrees to watch and protect His people. As we accept Shabbat upon ourselves and begin the first *Amida* of the holy day, we take a moment to remember the great privilege and responsibility of resting from work on Shabbat.

On שבת*, the* קהל *stands and, together with the* חזן*, says:*

וְשָׁמְרוּ בְנֵי־יִשְׂרָאֵל אֶת־הַשַּׁבָּת, לַעֲשׂוֹת אֶת־הַשַּׁבָּת לְדֹרֹתָם בְּרִית עוֹלָם: בֵּינִי וּבֵין בְּנֵי יִשְׂרָאֵל, אוֹת הִוא לְעֹלָם, כִּי־שֵׁשֶׁת יָמִים עָשָׂה יהוה אֶת־הַשָּׁמַיִם וְאֶת־הָאָרֶץ, וּבַיּוֹם הַשְּׁבִיעִי שָׁבַת וַיִּנָּפַשׁ:

חצי קדיש

חזן: יִתְגַּדַּל וְיִתְקַדַּשׁ שְׁמֵהּ רַבָּא (קהל: אָמֵן)
בְּעָלְמָא דִּי בְרָא כִרְעוּתֵהּ, וְיַמְלִיךְ מַלְכוּתֵהּ
בְּחַיֵּיכוֹן וּבְיוֹמֵיכוֹן וּבְחַיֵּי דְכָל בֵּית יִשְׂרָאֵל
בַּעֲגָלָא וּבִזְמַן קָרִיב
וְאִמְרוּ אָמֵן. (קהל: אָמֵן)

קהל יְהֵא שְׁמֵהּ רַבָּא מְבָרַךְ לְעָלַם וּלְעָלְמֵי עָלְמַיָּא.
חזן: יְהֵא שְׁמֵהּ רַבָּא מְבָרַךְ לְעָלַם וּלְעָלְמֵי עָלְמַיָּא.

חזן: יִתְבָּרַךְ וְיִשְׁתַּבַּח וְיִתְפָּאַר וְיִתְרוֹמַם וְיִתְנַשֵּׂא
וְיִתְהַדָּר וְיִתְעַלֶּה וְיִתְהַלָּל
שְׁמֵהּ דְּקֻדְשָׁא בְּרִיךְ הוּא (קהל: בְּרִיךְ הוּא)
לְעֵלָּא מִן כָּל בִּרְכָתָא
/בשבת שובה: לְעֵלָּא לְעֵלָּא מִכָּל בִּרְכָתָא/
וְשִׁירָתָא, תֻּשְׁבְּחָתָא וְנֶחֱמָתָא
דַּאֲמִירָן בְּעָלְמָא
וְאִמְרוּ אָמֵן. (קהל: אָמֵן)

AMIDA

Take three steps back then three steps forward then stand with your feet together.

Hashem, open my lips and help my mouth recite Your praise.

ANCESTORS

Bend the knees when saying "We thank," bow when saying "You," and stand straight before saying "Hashem."

בָּרוּךְ We thank You, *Hashem,*
our God, and God of our ancestors,
Avraham, Yitzchak, and Yaakov.
You, *Hashem,* are the great, mighty, awesome, kind,
and all-powerful Creator.
It is because of the greatness of our ancestors,
Avraham, Yitzchak, and Yaakov,
that *Hashem* will bring *Mashiach.*

Between Rosh Hashana and Yom Kippur say:
Give us life in the year to come
and write us in the book of life, *Hashem,* who gives life.

Hashem is our King who helps, guides, and protects us.

Bend the knees when saying "Thank," bow when saying "You," and stand straight before saying "Hashem."

Thank You, *Hashem,*
who protects us in the merit of Avraham.

HASHEM'S STRENGTH

אַתָּה You, *Hashem,* have unlimited strength.
You save people in their time of need,
and You have the power to bring the dead back to life.

עמידה

Take three steps back then three steps forward then stand with your feet together.

אֲדֹנָי, שְׂפָתַי תִּפְתָּח, וּפִי יַגִּיד תְּהִלָּתֶךָ:

אבות

Bend the knees when saying בָּרוּךְ*, bow when saying* אַתָּה*, and stand straight before saying Hashem's name.*

בָּרוּךְ אַתָּה יהוה, אֱלֹהֵינוּ וֵאלֹהֵי אֲבוֹתֵינוּ
אֱלֹהֵי אַבְרָהָם, אֱלֹהֵי יִצְחָק, וֵאלֹהֵי יַעֲקֹב
הָאֵל הַגָּדוֹל הַגִּבּוֹר וְהַנּוֹרָא, אֵל עֶלְיוֹן
גּוֹמֵל חֲסָדִים טוֹבִים, וְקֹנֵה הַכֹּל
וְזוֹכֵר חַסְדֵי אָבוֹת
וּמֵבִיא גוֹאֵל לִבְנֵי בְנֵיהֶם לְמַעַן שְׁמוֹ בְּאַהֲבָה.

On שבת שובה *say:*

זָכְרֵנוּ לְחַיִּים, מֶלֶךְ חָפֵץ בַּחַיִּים
וְכָתְבֵנוּ בְּסֵפֶר הַחַיִּים, לְמַעַנְךָ אֱלֹהִים חַיִּים.

מֶלֶךְ עוֹזֵר וּמוֹשִׁיעַ וּמָגֵן.

Bend the knees when saying בָּרוּךְ*, bow when saying* אַתָּה*, and stand straight before saying Hashem's name.*

בָּרוּךְ אַתָּה יהוה, מָגֵן אַבְרָהָם.

גבורות

אַתָּה גִּבּוֹר לְעוֹלָם, אֲדֹנָי
מְחַיֵּה מֵתִים אַתָּה, רַב לְהוֹשִׁיעַ

This line is said during the rainy season, from Simchat Torah to Pesach:

(You make the wind blow and cause the rain to fall)

With kindness You provide the living
with the necessities to live,
and with mercy You keep Your promise
of bringing the dead back to life.
For the living, You:
Support those who are falling,
Heal those who are sick, and
Free those who are in challenging situations.
Who is like You, *Hashem*,
and who can compare to You?
You, *Hashem*, are our King
who has the power to cause death and life.

Between Rosh Hashana and Yom Kippur say:

Who is like You, *Hashem*, our caring Father
who remembers His people for good and gives them life?

We have complete faith
that You will bring us back to life after our passing.
Thank You, *Hashem*, for bringing the dead back to life.

HASHEM'S HOLINESS

אַתָּה קָדוֹשׁ *Hashem*, You are holy and Your name is holy.
The Jewish people, who are holy,
will praise You, *Hashem*, each day.
Thank You, *Hashem*,
the holy God. / *Between Rosh Hashana & Yom Kippur say:* the holy King./

This line is said during the rainy season, from שמחת תורה *to* פסח:

(מַשִּׁיב הָרְוּחַ וּמוֹרִיד הַגֶּשֶׁם)

מְכַלְכֵּל חַיִּים בְּחֶסֶד, מְחַיֵּה מֵתִים בְּרַחֲמִים רַבִּים
סוֹמֵךְ נוֹפְלִים
וְרוֹפֵא חוֹלִים
וּמַתִּיר אֲסוּרִים
וּמְקַיֵּם אֱמוּנָתוֹ לִישֵׁנֵי עָפָר.
מִי כָמְוֹךָ, בַּעַל גְּבוּרוֹת
וּמִי דּוֹמֶה לָּךְ
מֶלֶךְ, מֵמִית וּמְחַיֶּה וּמַצְמִיחַ יְשׁוּעָה.

On שבת שובה *say:*

מִי כָמְוֹךָ אַב הָרַחֲמִים
זוֹכֵר יְצוּרָיו לְחַיִּים בְּרַחֲמִים.

וְנֶאֱמָן אַתָּה לְהַחֲיוֹת מֵתִים.
בָּרוּךְ אַתָּה יהוה, מְחַיֵּה הַמֵּתִים.

קדושת השם

אַתָּה קָדוֹשׁ וְשִׁמְךָ קָדוֹשׁ
וּקְדוֹשִׁים בְּכָל יוֹם יְהַלְלְוּךָ סֶּלָה.
בָּרוּךְ אַתָּה יהוה
הָאֵל הַקָּדוֹשׁ. / *On* שבת שובה *say* הַמֶּלֶךְ הַקָּדוֹשׁ./

HOLINESS OF SHABBAT

Hashem, You completed the creation
of heaven and earth on this day,
therefore the seventh day is holy.
You blessed this day and made this time holy,
as You wrote in Your Torah:

The creation of heaven and earth
was completed on the seventh day.
On this day, *Hashem* rested
from all the work He had done.
Hashem blessed the seventh day
and made it holy,
because on this day He rested from His work.

Hashem, our God and God of our ancestors,
we rest from work today for Your sake.
Allow us to become holy
through keeping Your *mitzvot*
and studying Your Torah.
Be good to us, save us, and
purify our hearts to serve You sincerely.

וְטַהֵר לִבֵּנוּ לְעָבְדְּךָ בֶּאֱמֶת *Purify our hearts to serve You sincerely.* Having a pure heart means ridding ourselves of thoughts and desires that distract us from serving *Hashem*. When our hearts are pure, it is easy to see how *Hashem* is involved with our lives every moment of the day. However, getting to the level of having a pure heart is difficult. Therefore, we try our best by doing *mitzvot* and davening with concentration, and we ask *Hashem* to assist us.

קדושת היום

אַתָּה קִדַּשְׁתָּ אֶת יוֹם הַשְּׁבִיעִי לִשְׁמֶךָ

תַּכְלִית מַעֲשֵׂה שָׁמַיִם וָאָרֶץ

וּבֵרַכְתּוֹ מִכָּל הַיָּמִים, וְקִדַּשְׁתּוֹ מִכָּל הַזְּמַנִּים

וְכֵן כָּתוּב בְּתוֹרָתֶךָ

וַיְכֻלּוּ הַשָּׁמַיִם וְהָאָרֶץ וְכָל־צְבָאָם:

וַיְכַל אֱלֹהִים בַּיּוֹם הַשְּׁבִיעִי מְלַאכְתּוֹ אֲשֶׁר עָשָׂה

וַיִּשְׁבֹּת בַּיּוֹם הַשְּׁבִיעִי מִכָּל־מְלַאכְתּוֹ אֲשֶׁר עָשָׂה:

וַיְבָרֶךְ אֱלֹהִים אֶת־יוֹם הַשְּׁבִיעִי, וַיְקַדֵּשׁ אֹתוֹ

כִּי בוֹ שָׁבַת מִכָּל־מְלַאכְתּוֹ

אֲשֶׁר־בָּרָא אֱלֹהִים לַעֲשׂוֹת:

אֱלֹהֵינוּ וֵאלֹהֵי אֲבוֹתֵינוּ, רְצֵה בִמְנוּחָתֵנוּ.

קַדְּשֵׁנוּ בְּמִצְוֹתֶיךָ, וְתֵן חֶלְקֵנוּ בְּתוֹרָתֶךָ

שַׂבְּעֵנוּ מִטּוּבֶךָ, וְשַׂמְּחֵנוּ בִּישׁוּעָתֶךָ

וְטַהֵר לִבֵּנוּ לְעָבְדְּךָ בֶּאֱמֶת.

וּבֵרַכְתּוֹ מִכָּל הַיָּמִים, וְקִדַּשְׁתּוֹ מִכָּל הַזְּמַנִּים *You blessed this day and made this time holy.* Every Shabbat, *Hashem* joins us to spend the day together with us. We do not do work or do any actions that are similar to work. Rather, Shabbat is a time to spend with our families, a time to focus on prayer and Torah study, and a time to relax and enjoy the beautiful world that *Hashem* created for us. The holiness of Shabbat comes from our ability to reconnect with *Hashem*, our creator and provider of life; There is no greater way to spend our time!

Hashem, our God, show us Your love
and allow us to observe Your holy Shabbat
so that Your Jewish people can rest.
Thank You, *Hashem*, for making Shabbat holy.

SERVICE IN THE *BEIT HAMIKDASH*

רְצֵה *Hashem*, please accept Your Jewish people
and their prayers.
We eagerly await the rebuilding of the *Beit HaMikdash*
so we can serve You with *korbanot*.
Until the *Beit HaMikdash* is rebuilt,
please accept our prayers with love.

On Rosh Chodesh and Chol HaMo'ed, say:

אֱלֹהֵינוּ Our God, and God of our ancestors, may our prayers:
Rise from our mouths,
Come before You,
Reach You at a desirable time,
Be heard,
And be fulfilled.
Hashem, You remember and know each of our hardships.
You remember:
Our ancestors,
Mashiach,
Your holy city, Jerusalem, and
Your united Jewish people,
for goodness, kindness, mercy, life, and peace
on this day of:
On Rosh Chodesh: *Rosh Chodesh*.
On Pesach: the Holiday of *Matzot*.
On Sukkot: the Holiday of *Sukkot*.

וְהַנְחִילֵנוּ, יהוה אֱלֹהֵינוּ, בְּאַהֲבָה וּבְרָצוֹן שַׁבַּת קָדְשֶׁךָ
וְיָנוּחוּ בָהּ יִשְׂרָאֵל מְקַדְּשֵׁי שְׁמֶךָ.
בָּרוּךְ אַתָּה יהוה, מְקַדֵּשׁ הַשַּׁבָּת.

עבודה

רְצֵה יהוה אֱלֹהֵינוּ בְּעַמְּךָ יִשְׂרָאֵל, וּבִתְפִלָּתָם
וְהָשֵׁב אֶת הָעֲבוֹדָה לִדְבִיר בֵּיתֶךָ
וְאִשֵּׁי יִשְׂרָאֵל וּתְפִלָּתָם בְּאַהֲבָה תְקַבֵּל בְּרָצוֹן
וּתְהִי לְרָצוֹן תָּמִיד עֲבוֹדַת יִשְׂרָאֵל עַמֶּךָ.

On ראש חודש *and* חול המועד*, say:*

אֱלֹהֵינוּ וֵאלֹהֵי אֲבוֹתֵינוּ
יַעֲלֶה וְיָבוֹא וְיַגִּיעַ, וְיֵרָאֶה וְיֵרָצֶה וְיִשָּׁמַע
וְיִפָּקֵד וְיִזָּכֵר זִכְרוֹנֵנוּ וּפִקְדוֹנֵנוּ, וְזִכְרוֹן אֲבוֹתֵינוּ
וְזִכְרוֹן מָשִׁיחַ בֶּן דָּוִד עַבְדֶּךָ
וְזִכְרוֹן יְרוּשָׁלַיִם עִיר קָדְשֶׁךָ
וְזִכְרוֹן כָּל עַמְּךָ בֵּית יִשְׂרָאֵל
לְפָנֶיךָ, לִפְלֵיטָה לְטוֹבָה
לְחֵן וּלְחֶסֶד וּלְרַחֲמִים
לְחַיִּים וּלְשָׁלוֹם
בְּיוֹם

בראש חודש: רֹאשׁ הַחֹדֶשׁ הַזֶּה.
בפסח: חַג הַמַּצּוֹת הַזֶּה.
בסוכות: חַג הַסֻּכּוֹת הַזֶּה.

Hashem, on this day please remember us
with good thoughts, consider us for blessing,
and help us with difficult times in our lives.
Be kind and merciful with us, *Hashem,*
as we look towards You as our King.

May we be worthy
to see the rebuilding of the *Beit HaMikdash.*
We thank You, *Hashem,*
for returning Your presence to Zion.

THANK YOU

Bow when saying the words "We thank You."

מוֹדִים We thank You, *Hashem,*
for You are and always will be
our God, and the God of our ancestors.
You give us life
and You always protect us.
We thank and praise You
for:
Our lives which are in Your hands,
Our souls which are in Your control,
The miracles You perform for us every day, and
The goodness You show us
at all times, morning, noon, and night.
You, *Hashem,*
have unlimited mercy and kindness
and therefore we have always placed our hope in You.

זָכְרֵנוּ יהוה אֱלֹהֵינוּ בּוֹ לְטוֹבָה, וּפָקְדֵנוּ בוֹ לִבְרָכָה
וְהוֹשִׁיעֵנוּ בוֹ לְחַיִּים.
וּבִדְבַר יְשׁוּעָה וְרַחֲמִים, חוּס וְחָנֵּנוּ וְרַחֵם עָלֵינוּ וְהוֹשִׁיעֵנוּ
כִּי אֵלֶיךָ עֵינֵינוּ, כִּי אֵל מֶלֶךְ חַנּוּן וְרַחוּם אָתָּה.

וְתֶחֱזֶינָה עֵינֵינוּ בְּשׁוּבְךָ לְצִיּוֹן בְּרַחֲמִים.
בָּרוּךְ אַתָּה יהוה, הַמַּחֲזִיר שְׁכִינָתוֹ לְצִיּוֹן.

הודאה

Bow when saying the words מוֹדִים אֲנַחְנוּ לָךְ שָׁאַתָּה הוּא.

מוֹדִים אֲנַחְנוּ לָךְ
שָׁאַתָּה הוּא יהוה אֱלֹהֵינוּ וֵאלֹהֵי אֲבוֹתֵינוּ לְעוֹלָם וָעֶד.
צוּר חַיֵּינוּ, מָגֵן יִשְׁעֵנוּ, אַתָּה הוּא לְדוֹר וָדוֹר.
נוֹדֶה לְּךָ וּנְסַפֵּר תְּהִלָּתֶךָ
עַל חַיֵּינוּ הַמְּסוּרִים בְּיָדֶךָ
וְעַל נִשְׁמוֹתֵינוּ הַפְּקוּדוֹת לָךְ
וְעַל נִסֶּיךָ שֶׁבְּכָל יוֹם עִמָּנוּ
וְעַל נִפְלְאוֹתֶיךָ וְטוֹבוֹתֶיךָ
שֶׁבְּכָל עֵת, עֶרֶב וָבֹקֶר וְצָהֳרָיִם.
הַטּוֹב, כִּי לֹא כָלוּ רַחֲמֶיךָ
וְהַמְרַחֵם, כִּי לֹא תַמּוּ חֲסָדֶיךָ
מֵעוֹלָם קִוִּינוּ לָךְ.

On Chanuka say:

עַל הַנִּסִּים We thank You, *Hashem,* for the miracles, the deliverances, the great strength, and the victories in war that You displayed for us in earlier times and in our times.

בִּימֵי מַתִּתְיָהוּ In the days of Mattityahu, son of Yochanan the *Kohen Gadol,* the Hasmonean, and his sons, the wicked Greeks challenged Your Jewish people trying to make them forget Your Torah and sin. In Your great kindness, You, *Hashem,* supported us in this difficult time. You allowed for:

The weak Jews to defeat the mighty Greeks,
The few Jews to defeat the many Greeks,
The pure Jews to defeat the impure Greeks,
The righteous Jews to defeat the wicked Greeks, and
The Jews who studied Your Torah to defeat the Greeks who did not.

Hashem, on this day everyone in the world recognized You as You miraculously saved Your Jewish people. Your Jewish people then entered the *Beit HaMikdash* to clean and purify it. They lit candles in the courtyard of the *Beit HaMikdash* and set aside these eight days of *Chanukah* for giving thanks and praising You.

Continue with "For all these reasons."

For all these reasons
we will thank You, *Hashem,* our King, forever.

Between Rosh Hashana & Yom Kippur say:

And write all Your children in the book of good life.

Every living person will recognize and praise You, *Hashem,*
for You are the God that helps and saves Your people.

Bend the knees when saying "Thank," bow when saying "You," and stand straight before saying "Hashem."

Thank You, *Hashem,*
for You are worthy of being thanked.

בחנוכה:

עַל הַנִּסִּים וְעַל הַפֻּרְקָן וְעַל הַגְּבוּרוֹת וְעַל הַתְּשׁוּעוֹת וְעַל הַמִּלְחָמוֹת שֶׁעָשִׂיתָ לַאֲבוֹתֵינוּ בַּיָּמִים הָהֵם בַּזְּמַן הַזֶּה.

בִּימֵי מַתִּתְיָהוּ בֶּן יוֹחָנָן כֹּהֵן גָּדוֹל חַשְׁמוֹנָאִי וּבָנָיו, כְּשֶׁעָמְדָה מַלְכוּת יָוָן הָרְשָׁעָה עַל עַמְּךָ יִשְׂרָאֵל לְהַשְׁכִּיחָם תּוֹרָתֶךָ וּלְהַעֲבִירָם מֵחֻקֵּי רְצוֹנֶךָ, וְאַתָּה בְּרַחֲמֶיךָ הָרַבִּים עָמַדְתָּ לָהֶם בְּעֵת צָרָתָם, רַבְתָּ אֶת רִיבָם, דַּנְתָּ אֶת דִּינָם, נָקַמְתָּ אֶת נִקְמָתָם, מָסַרְתָּ גִּבּוֹרִים בְּיַד חַלָּשִׁים, וְרַבִּים בְּיַד מְעַטִּים, וּטְמֵאִים בְּיַד טְהוֹרִים, וּרְשָׁעִים בְּיַד צַדִּיקִים, וְזֵדִים בְּיַד עוֹסְקֵי תוֹרָתֶךָ, וּלְךָ עָשִׂיתָ שֵׁם גָּדוֹל וְקָדוֹשׁ בְּעוֹלָמֶךָ, וּלְעַמְּךָ יִשְׂרָאֵל עָשִׂיתָ תְּשׁוּעָה גְדוֹלָה וּפֻרְקָן כְּהַיּוֹם הַזֶּה. וְאַחַר כֵּן בָּאוּ בָנֶיךָ לִדְבִיר בֵּיתֶךָ, וּפִנּוּ אֶת הֵיכָלֶךָ, וְטִהֲרוּ אֶת מִקְדָּשֶׁךָ, וְהִדְלִיקוּ נֵרוֹת בְּחַצְרוֹת קָדְשֶׁךָ, וְקָבְעוּ שְׁמוֹנַת יְמֵי חֲנֻכָּה אֵלּוּ, לְהוֹדוֹת וּלְהַלֵּל לְשִׁמְךָ הַגָּדוֹל.

Continue with וְעַל כֻּלָּם.

וְעַל כֻּלָּם

יִתְבָּרַךְ וְיִתְרוֹמַם שִׁמְךָ מַלְכֵּנוּ תָּמִיד לְעוֹלָם וָעֶד.

On שבת שובה *say* וּכְתֹב לְחַיִּים טוֹבִים כָּל בְּנֵי בְרִיתֶךָ.

וְכֹל הַחַיִּים יוֹדוּךָ סֶּלָה, וִיהַלְלוּ אֶת שִׁמְךָ בֶּאֱמֶת הָאֵל יְשׁוּעָתֵנוּ וְעֶזְרָתֵנוּ סֶלָה.

Bend the knees when saying בָּרוּךְ, *bow when saying* אַתָּה, *and stand straight before saying Hashem's name.*

בָּרוּךְ אַתָּה יהוה

הַטּוֹב שִׁמְךָ וּלְךָ נָאֶה לְהוֹדוֹת.

PEACE

שָׁלוֹם רָב *Hashem,* You are King and master of peace.
May it be good in Your eyes
to bless Your Jewish people with peace
at all times and at every hour, forever.

Between Rosh Hashana and Yom Kippur continue with "May You remember," below.

Thank You, *Hashem,*
who blesses His Jewish people with peace.

Between Rosh Hashana and Yom Kippur say:

May You remember all of the Jewish people for life,
blessing, peace, and riches
and write us in the book of good life and peace.
Thank You, *Hashem,* who makes peace.

CONCLUSION OF AMIDA

אֱלֹהַי *Hashem,* please help me:
Control my mouth from speaking badly
about other people,
Stay silent and not respond if someone speaks badly
about me,
Learn Your Torah, and do Your *mitzvot.*
Hashem, if people plan to do something evil against me,
please stop these plans and protect me.
Even if I am not deserving of being helped,
please act on my behalf
as I represent Your name and Your Torah.
Hashem, please save Your Jewish people
from difficult situations and answer my requests.
May You find my thoughts and prayers favorable.

שלום

שָׁלוֹם רָב עַל יִשְׂרָאֵל עַמְּךָ תָּשִׂים לְעוֹלָם
כִּי אַתָּה הוּא מֶלֶךְ אָדוֹן לְכָל הַשָּׁלוֹם.
וְטוֹב בְּעֵינֶיךָ לְבָרֵךְ אֶת עַמְּךָ יִשְׂרָאֵל
בְּכָל עֵת וּבְכָל שָׁעָה בִּשְׁלוֹמֶךָ.

On שבת שובה *continue with* בְּסֵֽפֶר חַיִּים*, below.*

בָּרוּךְ אַתָּה יהוה, הַמְבָרֵךְ אֶת עַמּוֹ יִשְׂרָאֵל בַּשָּׁלוֹם.

On שבת שובה *say:*

בְּסֵֽפֶר חַיִּים, בְּרָכָה וְשָׁלוֹם, וּפַרְנָסָה טוֹבָה
נִזָּכֵר וְנִכָּתֵב לְפָנֶֽיךָ, אֲנַֽחְנוּ וְכָל עַמְּךָ בֵּית יִשְׂרָאֵל
לְחַיִּים טוֹבִים וּלְשָׁלוֹם.
בָּרוּךְ אַתָּה יהוה, עוֹשֵׂה הַשָּׁלוֹם.

סיום העמידה

אֱלֹהַי, נְצֹר לְשׁוֹנִי מֵרָע וּשְׂפָתַי מִדַּבֵּר מִרְמָה
וְלִמְקַלְלַי נַפְשִׁי תִדֹּם, וְנַפְשִׁי כֶּעָפָר לַכֹּל תִּהְיֶה.
פְּתַח לִבִּי בְּתוֹרָתֶֽךָ, וּבְמִצְוֹתֶֽיךָ תִּרְדֹּף נַפְשִׁי.
וְכָל הַחוֹשְׁבִים עָלַי רָעָה
מְהֵרָה הָפֵר עֲצָתָם וְקַלְקֵל מַחֲשַׁבְתָּם.
עֲשֵׂה לְמַֽעַן שְׁמֶֽךָ, עֲשֵׂה לְמַֽעַן יְמִינֶֽךָ
עֲשֵׂה לְמַֽעַן קְדֻשָּׁתֶֽךָ, עֲשֵׂה לְמַֽעַן תּוֹרָתֶֽךָ.
לְמַֽעַן יֵחָלְצוּן יְדִידֶֽיךָ, הוֹשִֽׁיעָה יְמִינְךָ וַעֲנֵֽנִי:
יִהְיוּ לְרָצוֹן אִמְרֵי־פִי וְהֶגְיוֹן לִבִּי לְפָנֶֽיךָ, יהוה צוּרִי וְגֹאֲלִי:

Take three steps backwards and bow to your left as you say:

You, *Hashem,* make peace in heaven.

Bow to your right as you say:

Please may You bring peace to us

Bow forward as you say:

And all Your Jewish people.

Before taking three steps forward, say the following quietly:

Hashem, our God and God of our ancestors, may You please rebuild the *Beit HaMikdash* soon. *Hashem,* please allow us to learn Your Torah and serve You in the *Beit HaMikdash* as the Jewish people once did.

All stand and say:

The creation of heaven and earth
was completed on the seventh day.
On this day, *Hashem* rested from all the work
He had done.
Hashem blessed the seventh day and made it holy,
because on this day
He rested from His work.

The following until "For making Shabbat holy" on the next page, is omitted when praying with an occasional minyan or alone.

The Leader continues:

Thank You, *Hashem,* our God,
and God of our ancestors,
Avraham, Yitzchak, and Yaakov,
for You are the great, mighty, and awesome God
who created heaven and earth.

Take three steps backwards and bow to your left as you say:

עֹשֶׂה שָׁלוֹם / *On* שבת שובה *say* הַשָּׁלוֹם/ בִּמְרוֹמָיו

Bow to your right as you say:

הוּא יַעֲשֶׂה שָׁלוֹם עָלֵינוּ

Bow forward as you say:

וְעַל כָּל יִשְׂרָאֵל, וְאִמְרוּ אָמֵן.

Before taking three steps forward, say the following quietly:

יְהִי רָצוֹן מִלְּפָנֶיךָ יהוה אֱלֹהֵינוּ וֵאלֹהֵי אֲבוֹתֵינוּ. שֶׁיִּבָּנֶה בֵּית הַמִּקְדָּשׁ בִּמְהֵרָה בְיָמֵינוּ, וְתֵן חֶלְקֵנוּ בְּתוֹרָתֶךָ. וְשָׁם נַעֲבָדְךָ בְּיִרְאָה כִּימֵי עוֹלָם וּכְשָׁנִים קַדְמֹנִיּוֹת. וְעָרְבָה לַיהוה מִנְחַת יְהוּדָה וִירוּשָׁלָםִ כִּימֵי עוֹלָם וּכְשָׁנִים קַדְמֹנִיּוֹת:

All stand and say:

וַיְכֻלּוּ הַשָּׁמַיִם וְהָאָרֶץ וְכָל־צְבָאָם:
וַיְכַל אֱלֹהִים בַּיּוֹם הַשְּׁבִיעִי מְלַאכְתּוֹ אֲשֶׁר עָשָׂה
וַיִּשְׁבֹּת בַּיּוֹם הַשְּׁבִיעִי מִכָּל־מְלַאכְתּוֹ אֲשֶׁר עָשָׂה:
וַיְבָרֶךְ אֱלֹהִים אֶת־יוֹם הַשְּׁבִיעִי, וַיְקַדֵּשׁ אֹתוֹ
כִּי בוֹ שָׁבַת מִכָּל־מְלַאכְתּוֹ
אֲשֶׁר־בָּרָא אֱלֹהִים, לַעֲשׂוֹת:

The following until מְקַדֵּשׁ הַשַּׁבָּת *on the next page,*
is omitted when praying with an occasional מנין *or alone.*

The חזן *continues:*

בָּרוּךְ אַתָּה יהוה, אֱלֹהֵינוּ וֵאלֹהֵי אֲבוֹתֵינוּ
אֱלֹהֵי אַבְרָהָם, אֱלֹהֵי יִצְחָק, וֵאלֹהֵי יַעֲקֹב
הָאֵל הַגָּדוֹל הַגִּבּוֹר וְהַנּוֹרָא, אֵל עֶלְיוֹן, קֹנֵה שָׁמַיִם וָאָרֶץ.

The congregation then the Leader:

Hashem,
You protected our ancestors,
and You will one day bring the dead back to life.
There is nobody like You, *Hashem,* our holy God,
who shows love to His Jewish people
by giving them rest on Shabbat.
For this reason,
we come before *Hashem* to pray
and give thanks every day.
Hashem deserves our thanks for He brings peace,
gives holiness to Shabbat,
and provides a day of rest for His Jewish people
so they can remember the creation of the world.

The Leader continues:

Hashem, our God and God of our ancestors,
we rest from work today for Your sake.
Allow us to become holy
through keeping Your *mitzvot*
and studying Your Torah.
Be good to us, save us, and purify our hearts
to serve you sincerely.
Hashem, our God, show us Your love
and allow us to observe Your holy Shabbat
so that Your Jewish people can rest.
Thank You, *Hashem,* for making Shabbat holy.

The קהל *then the* חזן:

מָגֵן אָבוֹת בִּדְבָרוֹ
מְחַיֵּה מֵתִים בְּמַאֲמָרוֹ
הָאֵל / בשבת שובה: הַמֶּלֶךְ / הַקָּדוֹשׁ שֶׁאֵין כָּמְוֹהוּ
הַמֵּנִיחַ לְעַמּוֹ בְּיוֹם שַׁבַּת קָדְשׁוֹ
כִּי בָם רָצָה לְהָנִיחַ לָהֶם
לְפָנָיו נַעֲבֹד בְּיִרְאָה וָפַחַד
וְנוֹדֶה לִשְׁמוֹ בְּכָל יוֹם תָּמִיד, מֵעֵין הַבְּרָכוֹת
אֵל הַהוֹדָאוֹת, אֲדוֹן הַשָּׁלוֹם
מְקַדֵּשׁ הַשַּׁבָּת וּמְבָרֵךְ שְׁבִיעִי
וּמֵנִיחַ בִּקְדֻשָּׁה לְעַם מְדֻשְּׁנֵי עֹנֶג
זֵכֶר לְמַעֲשֵׂה בְרֵאשִׁית.

The חזן *continues:*

אֱלֹהֵינוּ וֵאלֹהֵי אֲבוֹתֵינוּ, רְצֵה בִמְנוּחָתֵנוּ.
קַדְּשֵׁנוּ בְּמִצְוֹתֶיךָ וְתֵן חֶלְקֵנוּ בְּתוֹרָתֶךָ
שַׂבְּעֵנוּ מִטּוּבֶךָ וְשַׂמְּחֵנוּ בִּישׁוּעָתֶךָ
וְטַהֵר לִבֵּנוּ לְעָבְדְּךָ בֶּאֱמֶת.
וְהַנְחִילֵנוּ יהוה אֱלֹהֵינוּ בְּאַהֲבָה וּבְרָצוֹן שַׁבַּת קָדְשֶׁךָ
וְיָנְוּחוּ בָהּ יִשְׂרָאֵל מְקַדְּשֵׁי שְׁמֶךָ.
בָּרוּךְ אַתָּה יהוה, מְקַדֵּשׁ הַשַּׁבָּת.

KADDISH SHALEM

Leader: יִתְגַּדַּל May *Hashem* be recognized
as great and holy (*Congregation:* Amen)
in the world that He created.
May He establish His kingdom
during my lifetime and the lifetime of all Jews,
quickly and soon.
Let us say: "Amen" (*Congregation:* Amen).

Congregation: May we thank *Hashem* for ever and ever.
Leader: May we thank *Hashem* for ever and ever.

Leader: *Hashem* should be thanked, praised,
and honored (*Congregation:* He is blessed).
Hashem is beyond all the blessings,
songs, or praises that we could offer.
Let us say: "Amen" (*Congregation:* Amen).

May *Hashem* accept our prayers
and the prayers of all Jews.
Let us say: "Amen." (*Congregation:* Amen).

May *Hashem* give us, and all Jews,
peace and good life.
Let us say: "Amen." (*Congregation:* Amen).

The Leader takes three steps back before saying this line, bows to the left when saying "May," bows to the right when saying "the One," bows to the middle when saying "make peace for us":

May *Hashem,* the One
who makes peace in heaven,
make peace for us and for all Jews.
Let us say: "Amen." (*Congregation:* Amen).

קדיש שלם

חזן: יִתְגַּדַּל וְיִתְקַדַּשׁ שְׁמֵהּ רַבָּא (קהל: אָמֵן)
בְּעָלְמָא דִּי בְרָא כִרְעוּתֵהּ, וְיַמְלִיךְ מַלְכוּתֵהּ
בְּחַיֵּיכוֹן וּבְיוֹמֵיכוֹן וּבְחַיֵּי דְכָל בֵּית יִשְׂרָאֵל
בַּעֲגָלָא וּבִזְמַן קָרִיב, וְאִמְרוּ אָמֵן. (קהל: אָמֵן)

קהל יְהֵא שְׁמֵהּ רַבָּא מְבָרַךְ לְעָלַם וּלְעָלְמֵי עָלְמַיָּא.
חזן: יְהֵא שְׁמֵהּ רַבָּא מְבָרַךְ לְעָלַם וּלְעָלְמֵי עָלְמַיָּא.

חזן: יִתְבָּרַךְ וְיִשְׁתַּבַּח וְיִתְפָּאַר וְיִתְרוֹמַם וְיִתְנַשֵּׂא וְיִתְהַדָּר
וְיִתְעַלֶּה וְיִתְהַלָּל שְׁמֵהּ דְּקֻדְשָׁא בְּרִיךְ הוּא (קהל: בְּרִיךְ הוּא)
לְעֵלָּא מִן כָּל בִּרְכָתָא
/בשבת שובה: לְעֵלָּא לְעֵלָּא מִכָּל בִּרְכָתָא/
וְשִׁירָתָא, תֻּשְׁבְּחָתָא וְנֶחֱמָתָא
דַּאֲמִירָן בְּעָלְמָא, וְאִמְרוּ אָמֵן. (קהל: אָמֵן)

תִּתְקַבַּל צְלוֹתְהוֹן וּבָעוּתְהוֹן דְּכָל יִשְׂרָאֵל
קֳדָם אֲבוּהוֹן דִּי בִשְׁמַיָּא, וְאִמְרוּ אָמֵן. (קהל: אָמֵן)

יְהֵא שְׁלָמָא רַבָּא מִן שְׁמַיָּא
וְחַיִּים, עָלֵינוּ וְעַל כָּל יִשְׂרָאֵל, וְאִמְרוּ אָמֵן. (קהל: אָמֵן)

The חזן takes three steps back before saying this line, bows to the left when saying עֹשֶׂה, bows to the right when saying הוּא, bows to the middle when saying יַעֲשֶׂה שָׁלוֹם עָלֵינוּ:

עֹשֶׂה שָׁלוֹם /בשבת שובה: הַשָּׁלוֹם/ בִּמְרוֹמָיו
הוּא יַעֲשֶׂה שָׁלוֹם
עָלֵינוּ וְעַל כָּל יִשְׂרָאֵל, וְאִמְרוּ אָמֵן. (קהל: אָמֵן)

From the second night of Pesach through the night before Shavuot, the Omer is counted (page 328).

(page 328)

Stand while saying "It is our role."

עָלֵינוּ It is our role
to praise You, *Hashem*,
Master of all
and Creator of the world.
You have not made us
like other nations of the world,
rather, You set the Jewish people apart
allowing us the opportunity to serve You.
(Other nations pray to gods that do not exist,
while)
we bend our knees and bow in prayer
before the King of all kings, *Hashem*,
in order to give thanks.
Hashem created the heavens above and the land below.
Hashem sits on His awesome throne in heaven
as He, alone, is our God
and ruler of the world.
We willingly accept Him as our King,
there is none else but Him.
As it says in the Torah,
"Today You should understand
that *Hashem* is God
in the heavens above and on the earth below.
There is no other God but You."

From the second night of פסח *through the night before* שבועות*,*
the עומר *is counted (page 329).*

Stand while saying עָלֵינוּ.

עָלֵינוּ לְשַׁבֵּחַ לַאֲדוֹן הַכֹּל
לָתֵת גְּדֻלָּה לְיוֹצֵר בְּרֵאשִׁית
שֶׁלֹּא עָשָׂנוּ כְּגוֹיֵי הָאֲרָצוֹת
וְלֹא שָׂמָנוּ כְּמִשְׁפְּחוֹת הָאֲדָמָה
שֶׁלֹּא שָׂם חֶלְקֵנוּ כָּהֶם, וְגוֹרָלֵנוּ כְּכָל הֲמוֹנָם.
(שֶׁהֵם מִשְׁתַּחֲוִים לְהֶבֶל וָרִיק
וּמִתְפַּלְלִים אֶל אֵל לֹא יוֹשִׁיעַ.)

וַאֲנַחְנוּ כּוֹרְעִים וּמִשְׁתַּחֲוִים וּמוֹדִים
לִפְנֵי מֶלֶךְ מַלְכֵי הַמְּלָכִים, הַקָּדוֹשׁ בָּרוּךְ הוּא
שֶׁהוּא נוֹטֶה שָׁמַיִם וְיוֹסֵד אָרֶץ
וּמוֹשַׁב יְקָרוֹ בַּשָּׁמַיִם מִמַּעַל
וּשְׁכִינַת עֻזּוֹ בְּגָבְהֵי מְרוֹמִים.
הוּא אֱלֹהֵינוּ, אֵין עוֹד.
אֱמֶת מַלְכֵּנוּ, אֶפֶס זוּלָתוֹ
כַּכָּתוּב בְּתוֹרָתוֹ, וְיָדַעְתָּ הַיּוֹם וַהֲשֵׁבֹתָ אֶל־לְבָבֶךָ
כִּי יהוה הוּא הָאֱלֹהִים
בַּשָּׁמַיִם מִמַּעַל וְעַל־הָאָרֶץ מִתָּחַת, אֵין עוֹד:

Hashem,
we hope that all false gods
will be removed from the world
and everyone will soon turn to You alone
as the almighty God of the universe.
All the people of the world
will turn to You
and give honor.
They will accept You as their King,
and You will rule over them
soon and forever.
For You are King of the world
and You will remain the ruling King forever.
As it says in Your Torah,
▸ "*Hashem* will be king over all the land.
On that day *Hashem* will be One and His name One."

KADDISH YATOM

The following prayer, said by mourners, requires the presence of a minyan. A transliteration can be found on page 865.

Mourner: יִתְגַּדַּל May *Hashem* be recognized
as great and holy (*Congregation:* Amen)
in the world that He created.
May He establish His kingdom
during my lifetime
and the lifetime of all Jews,
quickly and soon.
Let us say:
"Amen" (*Congregation:* Amen).

עַל כֵּן נְקַוֶּה לְּךָ יהוה אֱלֹהֵינוּ
לִרְאוֹת מְהֵרָה בְּתִפְאֶרֶת עֻזֶּךָ
לְהַעֲבִיר גִּלּוּלִים מִן הָאָרֶץ, וְהָאֱלִילִים כָּרוֹת יִכָּרֵתוּן
לְתַקֵּן עוֹלָם בְּמַלְכוּת שַׁדַּי.
וְכָל בְּנֵי בָשָׂר יִקְרְאוּ בִשְׁמֶךָ
לְהַפְנוֹת אֵלֶיךָ כָּל רִשְׁעֵי אָרֶץ.
יַכִּירוּ וְיֵדְעוּ כָּל יוֹשְׁבֵי תֵבֵל
כִּי לְךָ תִּכְרַע כָּל בֶּרֶךְ, תִּשָּׁבַע כָּל לָשׁוֹן.
לְפָנֶיךָ יהוה אֱלֹהֵינוּ יִכְרְעוּ וְיִפֹּלוּ, וְלִכְבוֹד שִׁמְךָ יְקָר יִתֵּנוּ
וִיקַבְּלוּ כֻלָּם אֶת עֹל מַלְכוּתֶךָ
וְתִמְלֹךְ עֲלֵיהֶם מְהֵרָה לְעוֹלָם וָעֶד.
כִּי הַמַּלְכוּת שֶׁלְּךָ הִיא וּלְעוֹלְמֵי עַד תִּמְלֹךְ בְּכָבוֹד
כַּכָּתוּב בְּתוֹרָתֶךָ, יהוה יִמְלֹךְ לְעֹלָם וָעֶד:
◄ וְנֶאֱמַר, וְהָיָה יהוה לְמֶלֶךְ עַל־כָּל־הָאָרֶץ
בַּיּוֹם הַהוּא יִהְיֶה יהוה אֶחָד וּשְׁמוֹ אֶחָד:

קדיש יתום

The following prayer, said by mourners, requires the presence of a מנין.
A transliteration can be found on page 865.

אבל: יִתְגַּדַּל וְיִתְקַדַּשׁ שְׁמֵהּ רַבָּא (קהל: אָמֵן)
בְּעָלְמָא דִּי בְרָא כִרְעוּתֵהּ, וְיַמְלִיךְ מַלְכוּתֵהּ
בְּחַיֵּיכוֹן וּבְיוֹמֵיכוֹן וּבְחַיֵּי דְכָל בֵּית יִשְׂרָאֵל
בַּעֲגָלָא וּבִזְמַן קָרִיב, וְאִמְרוּ אָמֵן. (קהל: אָמֵן)

Congregation: May we thank *Hashem* for ever and ever.
Mourner: May we thank *Hashem* for ever and ever.

Mourner: *Hashem* should be thanked, praised,
and honored (*Congregation:* He is blessed).
Hashem is beyond all the blessings,
songs, or praises that we could offer.
Let us say:
"Amen" (*Congregation:* Amen).

May *Hashem* give us, and all Jews,
peace and good life.
Let us say:
"Amen." (*Congregation:* Amen).

The mourner takes three steps back before saying this line, bows to the left when saying "May," bows to the right when saying "the One," bows to the middle when saying "make peace for us":

May *Hashem,* the One
who makes peace in heaven,
make peace for us and for all Jews.
Let us say:
"Amen." (*Congregation:* Amen).

From the second day of Rosh Chodesh Elul until Shemini Atzeret add the following:

לְדָוִד David HaMelech wrote:
I have no fear because *Hashem* protects me
and brings light to my darkness.
When enemies or even armies attack,

קהל יְהֵא שְׁמֵהּ רַבָּא מְבָרַךְ לְעָלַם וּלְעָלְמֵי עָלְמַיָּא.

אבל: יְהֵא שְׁמֵהּ רַבָּא מְבָרַךְ לְעָלַם וּלְעָלְמֵי עָלְמַיָּא.

אבל: יִתְבָּרַךְ וְיִשְׁתַּבַּח וְיִתְפָּאַר

וְיִתְרוֹמַם וְיִתְנַשֵּׂא וְיִתְהַדָּר וְיִתְעַלֶּה וְיִתְהַלָּל

שְׁמֵהּ דְּקֻדְשָׁא בְּרִיךְ הוּא (קהל: בְּרִיךְ הוּא)

לְעֵלָּא מִן כָּל בִּרְכָתָא

/בשבת שובה: לְעֵלָּא לְעֵלָּא מִכָּל בִּרְכָתָא/

וְשִׁירָתָא, תֻּשְׁבְּחָתָא וְנֶחֱמָתָא

דַּאֲמִירָן בְּעָלְמָא, וְאִמְרוּ אָמֵן. (קהל: אָמֵן)

יְהֵא שְׁלָמָא רַבָּא מִן שְׁמַיָּא

וְחַיִּים, עָלֵינוּ וְעַל כָּל יִשְׂרָאֵל, וְאִמְרוּ אָמֵן. (קהל: אָמֵן)

The mourner takes three steps back before saying this line, bows to the left when saying עֹשֶׂה*, bows to the right when saying* הוּא*, bows to the middle when saying* יַעֲשֶׂה שָׁלוֹם עָלֵינוּ*:*

עֹשֶׂה שָׁלוֹם /בשבת שובה: הַשָּׁלוֹם/ בִּמְרוֹמָיו

הוּא יַעֲשֶׂה שָׁלוֹם עָלֵינוּ

וְעַל כָּל יִשְׂרָאֵל, וְאִמְרוּ אָמֵן. (קהל: אָמֵן)

From the second day of ראש חודש אלול *until* שמיני עצרת *add the following:*

לְדָוִד, יהוה אוֹרִי וְיִשְׁעִי, מִמִּי אִירָא

יהוה מָעוֹז־חַיַּי, מִמִּי אֶפְחָד:

בִּקְרֹב עָלַי מְרֵעִים לֶאֱכֹל אֶת־בְּשָׂרִי

צָרַי וְאֹיְבַי לִי, הֵמָּה כָשְׁלוּ וְנָפָלוּ:

I am not afraid
as I trust that *Hashem* will defeat them.
The only thing that I ask of *Hashem*
is to see the *Beit HaMikdash* built
and be able to serve Him there.
Hashem is my protector;
He will take me in
and hide me from my enemies.
When I feel safe,
I will sing songs of praise to *Hashem.*
Hashem,
listen to my voice
when I call for help
and please answer me.
Do not ignore or hide from me,
when You are angry.
My heart knows
it is only You to whom I can call for help.
Hashem,
help us learn how to make the right choices
and not make mistakes.
▸ I trust in *Hashem,*
I hope for His help
at all times;
He gives me strength and courage.

Kaddish Yatom (page 400)

אִם־תַּחֲנֶה עָלַי מַחֲנֶה, לֹא־יִירָא לִבִּי
אִם־תָּקוּם עָלַי מִלְחָמָה, בְּזֹאת אֲנִי בוֹטֵחַ:
אַחַת שָׁאַלְתִּי מֵאֵת־יהוה, אוֹתָהּ אֲבַקֵּשׁ
שִׁבְתִּי בְּבֵית־יהוה כָּל־יְמֵי חַיַּי
לַחֲזוֹת בְּנֹעַם־יהוה, וּלְבַקֵּר בְּהֵיכָלוֹ:
כִּי יִצְפְּנֵנִי בְּסֻכֹּה בְּיוֹם רָעָה
יַסְתִּרֵנִי בְּסֵתֶר אָהֳלוֹ, בְּצוּר יְרוֹמְמֵנִי:
וְעַתָּה יָרוּם רֹאשִׁי עַל אֹיְבַי סְבִיבוֹתַי
וְאֶזְבְּחָה בְאָהֳלוֹ זִבְחֵי תְרוּעָה
אָשִׁירָה וַאֲזַמְּרָה לַיהוה:
שְׁמַע־יהוה קוֹלִי אֶקְרָא, וְחָנֵּנִי וַעֲנֵנִי:
לְךָ אָמַר לִבִּי בַּקְּשׁוּ פָנָי, אֶת־פָּנֶיךָ יהוה אֲבַקֵּשׁ:
אַל־תַּסְתֵּר פָּנֶיךָ מִמֶּנִּי, אַל תַּט־בְּאַף עַבְדֶּךָ
עֶזְרָתִי הָיִיתָ, אַל־תִּטְּשֵׁנִי וְאַל־תַּעַזְבֵנִי, אֱלֹהֵי יִשְׁעִי:
כִּי־אָבִי וְאִמִּי עֲזָבוּנִי, וַיהוה יַאַסְפֵנִי:
הוֹרֵנִי יהוה דַּרְכֶּךָ, וּנְחֵנִי בְּאֹרַח מִישׁוֹר, לְמַעַן שׁוֹרְרָי:
אַל־תִּתְּנֵנִי בְּנֶפֶשׁ צָרָי, כִּי קָמוּ־בִי עֵדֵי־שֶׁקֶר, וִיפֵחַ חָמָס:
◂ לוּלֵא הֶאֱמַנְתִּי לִרְאוֹת בְּטוּב־יהוה בְּאֶרֶץ חַיִּים:
קַוֵּה אֶל־יהוה, חֲזַק וְיַאֲמֵץ לִבֶּךָ, וְקַוֵּה אֶל־יהוה:

קדיש יתום (*page 401*)

יִגְדַּל *Hashem*, our God, is great and should be praised.

He has always been and will always be our God.

Hashem is the only God. There is none else like Him.

He has no physical body and there is nothing else
that can be compared to Him.

Hashem existed before anything was created.

He shows His kingship over every living creature.

Hashem gave prophets to His Jewish people.

He gave us Moshe, the greatest of all prophets.

Hashem gave the Torah to His Jewish people.

He will never change the laws of His Torah.
His laws are forever.

Hashem knows and studies our deepest secrets
and knows what will happen in the future.

He rewards the good with kindness
and punishes the wicked with evil,
each person according to what he deserves.

Hashem will send *Mashiach* to those waiting
for his arrival.

He will bring the dead back to life.
For this kindness, we forever thank *Hashem*.

יִגְדַּל

אֱלֹהִים חַי וְיִשְׁתַּבַּח, נִמְצָא וְאֵין עֵת אֶל מְצִיאוּתוֹ.

אֶחָד וְאֵין יָחִיד כְּיִחוּדוֹ, נֶעְלָם וְגַם אֵין סוֹף לְאַחְדוּתוֹ.

אֵין לוֹ דְּמוּת הַגּוּף וְאֵינוֹ גוּף, לֹא נַעֲרֹךְ אֵלָיו קְדֻשָּׁתוֹ.

קַדְמוֹן לְכָל דָּבָר אֲשֶׁר נִבְרָא, רִאשׁוֹן וְאֵין רֵאשִׁית לְרֵאשִׁיתוֹ.

הִנּוֹ אֲדוֹן עוֹלָם, וְכָל נוֹצָר יוֹרֶה גְדֻלָּתוֹ וּמַלְכוּתוֹ.

שֶׁפַע נְבוּאָתוֹ נְתָנוֹ אֶל־אַנְשֵׁי סְגֻלָּתוֹ וְתִפְאַרְתּוֹ.

לֹא קָם בְּיִשְׂרָאֵל כְּמֹשֶׁה, עוֹד נָבִיא וּמַבִּיט אֶת תְּמוּנָתוֹ.

תּוֹרַת אֱמֶת נָתַן לְעַמּוֹ אֵל עַל יַד נְבִיאוֹ נֶאֱמַן בֵּיתוֹ.

לֹא יַחֲלִיף הָאֵל וְלֹא יָמִיר דָּתוֹ לְעוֹלָמִים לְזוּלָתוֹ.

צוֹפֶה וְיוֹדֵעַ סְתָרֵינוּ, מַבִּיט לְסוֹף דָּבָר בְּקַדְמָתוֹ.

גּוֹמֵל לְאִישׁ חֶסֶד כְּמִפְעָלוֹ, נוֹתֵן לְרָשָׁע רָע כְּרִשְׁעָתוֹ.

יִשְׁלַח לְקֵץ יָמִין מְשִׁיחֵנוּ לִפְדּוֹת מְחַכֵּי קֵץ יְשׁוּעָתוֹ.

מֵתִים יְחַיֶּה אֵל בְּרֹב חַסְדּוֹ, בָּרוּךְ עֲדֵי עַד שֵׁם תְּהִלָּתוֹ.

MIZMOR SHIR

Begin with the Modeh Ani on pages 2–36.

מִזְמוֹר This is a prayer
written by King David
in honor of the first use of the *Beit HaMikdash*:
I praise *Hashem*
who saves me from my enemies.
Hashem's anger lasts for a moment
but His kindness lasts forever.
In the dark of night I may weep
but *Hashem* brings the morning
filled with light and joy.
Knowing that *Hashem* supports me
gives me strength.
Were *Hashem* to hide from me
it would be terrifying.
When I cry out for help
it is *Hashem* who saves me.
Listen *Hashem* and show kindness to me;
Hashem please help me.
The dust and the dirt
do not have the ability to thank You like I do.
▸ *Hashem,* You have turned my sadness and sorrow
into joy and dancing.
From my soul I will sing to You
and not be silent.
Hashem,
I will always thank You.

מזמור לפני פסוקי דזמרה

Begin with מוֹדֶה אֲנִי *on pages 3–37.*

מִזְמוֹר שִׁיר־חֲנֻכַּת הַבַּיִת לְדָוִד:
אֲרוֹמִמְךָ יהוה כִּי דִלִּיתָנִי, וְלֹא־שִׂמַּחְתָּ אֹיְבַי לִי:
יהוה אֱלֹהָי, שִׁוַּעְתִּי אֵלֶיךָ וַתִּרְפָּאֵנִי:
יהוה, הֶעֱלִיתָ מִן־שְׁאוֹל נַפְשִׁי
חִיִּיתַנִי מִיָּרְדִי־בוֹר:
זַמְּרוּ לַיהוה חֲסִידָיו, וְהוֹדוּ לְזֵכֶר קָדְשׁוֹ:
כִּי רֶגַע בְּאַפּוֹ, חַיִּים בִּרְצוֹנוֹ
בָּעֶרֶב יָלִין בֶּכִי וְלַבֹּקֶר רִנָּה:
וַאֲנִי אָמַרְתִּי בְשַׁלְוִי, בַּל־אֶמּוֹט לְעוֹלָם:
יהוה, בִּרְצוֹנְךָ הֶעֱמַדְתָּה לְהַרְרִי עֹז
הִסְתַּרְתָּ פָנֶיךָ הָיִיתִי נִבְהָל:
אֵלֶיךָ יהוה אֶקְרָא, וְאֶל־אֲדֹנָי אֶתְחַנָּן:
מַה־בֶּצַע בְּדָמִי, בְּרִדְתִּי אֶל שָׁחַת
הֲיוֹדְךָ עָפָר, הֲיַגִּיד אֲמִתֶּךָ:
שְׁמַע־יהוה וְחָנֵּנִי, יהוה הֱיֵה־עֹזֵר לִי:
◂ הָפַכְתָּ מִסְפְּדִי לְמָחוֹל לִי
פִּתַּחְתָּ שַׂקִּי, וַתְּאַזְּרֵנִי שִׂמְחָה:
לְמַעַן יְזַמֶּרְךָ כָבוֹד וְלֹא יִדֹּם
יהוה אֱלֹהַי, לְעוֹלָם אוֹדֶךָּ:

KADDISH YATOM

The following prayer, said by mourners, requires the presence of a minyan. A transliteration can be found on page 865.

Mourner: יִתְגַּדַּל May *Hashem* be recognized
as great and holy (*Congregation:* Amen)
in the world that He created.
May He establish His kingdom
during my lifetime
and the lifetime of all Jews,
quickly and soon.
Let us say: "Amen" (*Congregation:* Amen).

Congregation: May we thank *Hashem* for ever and ever.
Mourner: May we thank *Hashem* for ever and ever.

Mourner: *Hashem* should be thanked, praised,
and honored (*Congregation:* He is blessed).
Hashem is beyond all the blessings,
songs, or praises
that we could offer.
Let us say: "Amen" (*Congregation:* Amen).

May *Hashem* give us, and all Jews,
peace and good life.
Let us say: "Amen." (*Congregation:* Amen).

The mourner takes three steps back before saying this line, bows to the left when saying "May," bows to the right when saying "the One," bows to the middle when saying "make peace for us":

May *Hashem*, the One
who makes peace in heaven,
make peace for us and for all Jews.
Let us say: "Amen." (*Congregation:* Amen).

קדיש יתום

The following prayer, said by mourners, requires the presence of a מנין*.*
A transliteration can be found on page 865.

A transliteration can be found on page 865.

אבל: **יִתְגַּדַּל וְיִתְקַדַּשׁ שְׁמֵהּ רַבָּא** (קהל: **אָמֵן**)
בְּעָלְמָא דִּי בְרָא כִרְעוּתֵהּ, וְיַמְלִיךְ מַלְכוּתֵהּ
בְּחַיֵּיכוֹן וּבְיוֹמֵיכוֹן וּבְחַיֵּי דְכָל בֵּית יִשְׂרָאֵל
בַּעֲגָלָא וּבִזְמַן קָרִיב, וְאִמְרוּ אָמֵן. (קהל: **אָמֵן**)

קהל **יְהֵא שְׁמֵהּ רַבָּא מְבָרַךְ לְעָלַם וּלְעָלְמֵי עָלְמַיָּא.**
אבל: **יְהֵא שְׁמֵהּ רַבָּא מְבָרַךְ לְעָלַם וּלְעָלְמֵי עָלְמַיָּא.**

אבל: **יִתְבָּרַךְ וְיִשְׁתַּבַּח וְיִתְפָּאַר**
וְיִתְרוֹמַם וְיִתְנַשֵּׂא וְיִתְהַדָּר וְיִתְעַלֶּה וְיִתְהַלָּל
שְׁמֵהּ דְּקֻדְשָׁא בְּרִיךְ הוּא (קהל: **בְּרִיךְ הוּא**)
לְעֵלָּא מִן כָּל בִּרְכָתָא
/בשבת שובה: **לְעֵלָּא לְעֵלָּא מִכָּל בִּרְכָתָא**/
וְשִׁירָתָא, תֻּשְׁבְּחָתָא וְנֶחֱמָתָא
דַּאֲמִירָן בְּעָלְמָא, וְאִמְרוּ אָמֵן. (קהל: **אָמֵן**)

יְהֵא שְׁלָמָא רַבָּא מִן שְׁמַיָּא
וְחַיִּים, עָלֵינוּ וְעַל כָּל יִשְׂרָאֵל, וְאִמְרוּ אָמֵן. (קהל: **אָמֵן**)

The mourner takes three steps back before saying this line, bows to the left when saying עֹשֶׂה*, bows to the right when saying* הוּא*, bows to the middle when saying* יַעֲשֶׂה שָׁלוֹם עָלֵינוּ*:*

עֹשֶׂה שָׁלוֹם /בשבת שובה: **הַשָּׁלוֹם**/ **בִּמְרוֹמָיו**
הוּא יַעֲשֶׂה שָׁלוֹם עָלֵינוּ
וְעַל כָּל יִשְׂרָאֵל, וְאִמְרוּ אָמֵן. (קהל: **אָמֵן**)

PESUKEI DEZIMRA

Baruch She'amar is the beginning of a long and special beracha in which we praise Hashem. It is important not to speak from this point until the end of Shemoneh Esreh.
Stand while saying this prayer.
Kiss your TZITZIT *when saying the words "worthy of praise."*

WE THANK YOU, *HASHEM*, WHO:

Created the world
with His words.
Makes promises
and keeps to His word.
Makes rules
and follows them.
Shows kindness
to the earth.
Shows kindness
to all people and animals.
Rewards people
who are always thinking about *Hashem*.
Lives forever.
Protects and saves people
from difficulties that arise.

We thank You *Hashem*,
our God and King of the world
whom we praise
through our actions and prayers.

פסוקי דזמרה

בָּרוּךְ שֶׁאָמַר is the beginning of a long and special beracha in which we praise Hashem. It is important not to speak from this point until the end of שמונה עשרה.
Stand while saying this prayer.
Kiss your ציצית when saying the words "מְהֻלָּל בְּתִשְׁבָּחוֹת."

בָּרוּךְ שֶׁאָמַר

וְהָיָה הָעוֹלָם, בָּרוּךְ הוּא.

בָּרוּךְ עוֹשֶׂה בְרֵאשִׁית

בָּרוּךְ אוֹמֵר וְעוֹשֶׂה

בָּרוּךְ גּוֹזֵר וּמְקַיֵּם

בָּרוּךְ מְרַחֵם עַל הָאָרֶץ

בָּרוּךְ מְרַחֵם עַל הַבְּרִיּוֹת

בָּרוּךְ מְשַׁלֵּם שָׂכָר טוֹב לִירֵאָיו

בָּרוּךְ חַי לָעַד וְקַיָּם לָנֶצַח

בָּרוּךְ פּוֹדֶה וּמַצִּיל

בָּרוּךְ שְׁמוֹ

בָּרוּךְ אַתָּה יהוה אֱלֹהֵינוּ מֶלֶךְ הָעוֹלָם, הָאֵל הָאָב הָרַחֲמָן הַמְהֻלָּל בְּפִי עַמּוֹ, מְשֻׁבָּח וּמְפֹאָר בִּלְשׁוֹן חֲסִידָיו וַעֲבָדָיו, וּבְשִׁירֵי דָוִד עַבְדֶּךָ, נְהַלֶּלְךָ יהוה אֱלֹהֵינוּ. בִּשְׁבָחוֹת וּבִזְמִירוֹת, נְגַדֶּלְךָ וּנְשַׁבֵּחֲךָ וּנְפָאֶרְךָ וְנַזְכִּיר

▸ Your greatness has no end.
Thank You, *Hashem*, our King
who is worthy of praise.

Sit while saying the following.

הודו Thank *Hashem* and sing out to him!
Tell the world about the miracles He has performed.
Take pride in serving *Hashem*.
Remember His strength and search Him out.
Hashem is always present.
Remember the great miracles *Hashem* has performed
for His Jewish people;
Hashem is God and His laws can be found
across the earth.
Hashem is our God
and has been for thousands of years,
beginning with our ancestors,
Avraham, Yitzchak, and Yaakov.
Since the time of Avraham,
the Jewish people were promised Israel as their land.
Throughout Jewish history,
even when we were a small nation
wandering from one country to the next,
Hashem has protected the Jewish people.
Praise, sing, thank, and speak of *Hashem*'s greatness
every day since He is the only God.
▸ *Hashem* is awesome!
He is the Creator of heaven.

שִׁמְךָ וְנַמְלִיכְךָ, מַלְכֵּנוּ אֱלֹהֵינוּ, ◂ יָחִיד חֵי הָעוֹלָמִים, מֶלֶךְ, מְשֻׁבָּח וּמְפֹאָר עֲדֵי עַד שְׁמוֹ הַגָּדוֹל, בָּרוּךְ אַתָּה יהוה, מֶלֶךְ מְהֻלָּל בַּתִּשְׁבָּחוֹת.

Sit while saying the following.

הוֹדוּ לַיהוה קִרְאוּ בִשְׁמוֹ, הוֹדִיעוּ בָעַמִּים עֲלִילֹתָיו: שִׁירוּ לוֹ, זַמְּרוּ־לוֹ, שִׂיחוּ בְּכָל־נִפְלְאוֹתָיו: הִתְהַלְלוּ בְּשֵׁם קָדְשׁוֹ, יִשְׂמַח לֵב מְבַקְשֵׁי יהוה: דִּרְשׁוּ יהוה וְעֻזּוֹ, בַּקְּשׁוּ פָנָיו תָּמִיד: זִכְרוּ נִפְלְאֹתָיו אֲשֶׁר עָשָׂה, מֹפְתָיו וּמִשְׁפְּטֵי־פִיהוּ: זֶרַע יִשְׂרָאֵל עַבְדּוֹ, בְּנֵי יַעֲקֹב בְּחִירָיו: הוּא יהוה אֱלֹהֵינוּ בְּכָל־הָאָרֶץ מִשְׁפָּטָיו: זִכְרוּ לְעוֹלָם בְּרִיתוֹ, דָּבָר צִוָּה לְאֶלֶף דּוֹר: אֲשֶׁר כָּרַת אֶת־אַבְרָהָם, וּשְׁבוּעָתוֹ לְיִצְחָק: וַיַּעֲמִידֶהָ לְיַעֲקֹב לְחֹק, לְיִשְׂרָאֵל בְּרִית עוֹלָם: לֵאמֹר, לְךָ אֶתֵּן אֶרֶץ־כְּנָעַן, חֶבֶל נַחֲלַתְכֶם: בִּהְיוֹתְכֶם מְתֵי מִסְפָּר, כִּמְעַט וְגָרִים בָּהּ: וַיִּתְהַלְּכוּ מִגּוֹי אֶל־גּוֹי, וּמִמַּמְלָכָה אֶל־עַם אַחֵר: לֹא־הִנִּיחַ לְאִישׁ לְעָשְׁקָם, וַיּוֹכַח עֲלֵיהֶם מְלָכִים: אַל־תִּגְּעוּ בִּמְשִׁיחָי, וּבִנְבִיאַי אַל־תָּרֵעוּ: שִׁירוּ לַיהוה כָּל־הָאָרֶץ, בַּשְּׂרוּ מִיּוֹם־אֶל־יוֹם יְשׁוּעָתוֹ: סַפְּרוּ בַגּוֹיִם אֶת־כְּבוֹדוֹ, בְּכָל־הָעַמִּים נִפְלְאֹתָיו: כִּי גָדוֹל יהוה וּמְהֻלָּל מְאֹד, וְנוֹרָא הוּא עַל־כָּל־אֱלֹהִים: ◂ כִּי כָּל־אֱלֹהֵי הָעַמִּים אֱלִילִים, וַיהוה שָׁמַיִם עָשָׂה:

Hashem is all-powerful
and the source of all glory.
Give honor, bring sacrifices,
tremble, and bow before *Hashem* for He is mighty.
Angels in heaven and every being on earth
declares *Hashem* as King.
The fish in the sea,
plants in the fields,
and trees in the forest
sing to *Hashem* with joy.
Thank *Hashem* for He is good
and His kindness lasts forever.
Hashem, save Your Jewish people
from other nations.
Thank *Hashem,* God of the Jewish people,
for ever and ever.

▸ Praise *Hashem,* our holy God,
and bow before His throne.
Praise *Hashem,* our holy God,
and bow before His holy mountain.

Hashem, You show kindness
by forgiving our mistakes
instead of destroying the Jewish people in anger.
By protecting me,
You show me Your kindness.
May You protect us with Your love and kindness
as You always have.

הוֹד וְהָדָר לְפָנָיו, עֹז וְחֶדְוָה בִּמְקֹמוֹ: הָבוּ לַיהוה מִשְׁפְּחוֹת עַמִּים, הָבוּ לַיהוה כָּבוֹד וָעֹז: הָבוּ לַיהוה כְּבוֹד שְׁמוֹ, שְׂאוּ מִנְחָה וּבֹאוּ לְפָנָיו, הִשְׁתַּחֲווּ לַיהוה בְּהַדְרַת־קֹדֶשׁ: חִילוּ מִלְּפָנָיו כָּל־הָאָרֶץ, אַף־תִּכּוֹן תֵּבֵל בַּל־תִּמּוֹט: יִשְׂמְחוּ הַשָּׁמַיִם וְתָגֵל הָאָרֶץ, וְיֹאמְרוּ בַגּוֹיִם יהוה מָלָךְ: יִרְעַם הַיָּם וּמְלוֹאוֹ, יַעֲלֹץ הַשָּׂדֶה וְכָל־אֲשֶׁר־בּוֹ: אָז יְרַנְּנוּ עֲצֵי הַיָּעַר, מִלִּפְנֵי יהוה, כִּי־בָא לִשְׁפּוֹט אֶת־הָאָרֶץ: הוֹדוּ לַיהוה כִּי טוֹב, כִּי לְעוֹלָם חַסְדּוֹ: וְאִמְרוּ, הוֹשִׁיעֵנוּ אֱלֹהֵי יִשְׁעֵנוּ, וְקַבְּצֵנוּ וְהַצִּילֵנוּ מִן־הַגּוֹיִם, לְהֹדוֹת לְשֵׁם קָדְשֶׁךָ, לְהִשְׁתַּבֵּחַ בִּתְהִלָּתֶךָ: בָּרוּךְ יהוה אֱלֹהֵי יִשְׂרָאֵל מִן־הָעוֹלָם וְעַד־הָעֹלָם, וַיֹּאמְרוּ כָל־הָעָם אָמֵן, וְהַלֵּל לַיהוה:

› רוֹמְמוּ יהוה אֱלֹהֵינוּ וְהִשְׁתַּחֲווּ לַהֲדֹם רַגְלָיו, קָדוֹשׁ הוּא: רוֹמְמוּ יהוה אֱלֹהֵינוּ וְהִשְׁתַּחֲווּ לְהַר קָדְשׁוֹ, כִּי־קָדוֹשׁ יהוה אֱלֹהֵינוּ:

וְהוּא רַחוּם, יְכַפֵּר עָוֹן וְלֹא־יַשְׁחִית, וְהִרְבָּה לְהָשִׁיב אַפּוֹ, וְלֹא־יָעִיר כָּל־חֲמָתוֹ: אַתָּה יהוה לֹא־תִכְלָא רַחֲמֶיךָ מִמֶּנִּי, חַסְדְּךָ וַאֲמִתְּךָ תָּמִיד יִצְּרוּנִי: זְכֹר־רַחֲמֶיךָ יהוה וַחֲסָדֶיךָ, כִּי מֵעוֹלָם הֵמָּה: תְּנוּ עֹז לֵאלֹהִים, עַל־יִשְׂרָאֵל גַּאֲוָתוֹ, וְעֻזּוֹ בַּשְּׁחָקִים: נוֹרָא אֱלֹהִים מִמִּקְדָּשֶׁיךָ, אֵל יִשְׂרָאֵל הוּא נֹתֵן עֹז וְתַעֲצֻמוֹת לָעָם, בָּרוּךְ אֱלֹהִים:

Hashem, You are awesome
and You grant strength to Your Jewish people.
You protect Your Jewish people
and take revenge on our enemies.
▸ Praiseworthy is the person who trusts in You, *Hashem.*
May You, *Hashem,* answer and save us
on the day that we call out to You.

Hashem, save Your Jewish people
and care for them forever.
Our hearts are happy when we are close to You
because You are our protector.
We have complete trust in You, *Hashem,* who loves us.
Hashem, please show Your kindness by saving us.
You saved the Jewish people from Egypt
and we ask that You continue to save us now.
We are fortunate to have You, *Hashem,* as our God.
▸ I trust that You, *Hashem,*
will have the kindness to save us,
and I will sing praises to You.

לַמְנַצֵּחַ A song written by David.
Every day and night,
the heavens show the greatness of *Hashem.*
His continuous miracles are beyond words.
The sun comes out every morning
with great energy,

אֵל־נְקָמוֹת יהוה, אֵל נְקָמוֹת הוֹפִיעַ: הִנָּשֵׂא שֹׁפֵט הָאָרֶץ, הָשֵׁב גְּמוּל עַל־גֵּאִים: לַיהוה הַיְשׁוּעָה, עַל־עַמְּךָ בִרְכָתֶךָ סֶּלָה: ‹ יהוה צְבָאוֹת עִמָּנוּ, מִשְׂגָּב לָנוּ אֱלֹהֵי יַעֲקֹב סֶלָה: יהוה צְבָאוֹת, אַשְׁרֵי אָדָם בֹּטֵחַ בָּךְ: יהוה הוֹשִׁיעָה, הַמֶּלֶךְ יַעֲנֵנוּ בְיוֹם־קָרְאֵנוּ:

הוֹשִׁיעָה אֶת־עַמֶּךָ, וּבָרֵךְ אֶת־נַחֲלָתֶךָ, וּרְעֵם וְנַשְּׂאֵם עַד־הָעוֹלָם: נַפְשֵׁנוּ חִכְּתָה לַיהוה, עֶזְרֵנוּ וּמָגִנֵּנוּ הוּא: כִּי־בוֹ יִשְׂמַח לִבֵּנוּ, כִּי בְשֵׁם קָדְשׁוֹ בָטָחְנוּ: יְהִי־חַסְדְּךָ יהוה עָלֵינוּ, כַּאֲשֶׁר יִחַלְנוּ לָךְ: הַרְאֵנוּ יהוה חַסְדֶּךָ, וְיֶשְׁעֲךָ תִּתֶּן־לָנוּ: קוּמָה עֶזְרָתָה לָּנוּ, וּפְדֵנוּ לְמַעַן חַסְדֶּךָ: אָנֹכִי יהוה אֱלֹהֶיךָ הַמַּעַלְךָ מֵאֶרֶץ מִצְרָיִם, הַרְחֶב־פִּיךָ וַאֲמַלְאֵהוּ: אַשְׁרֵי הָעָם שֶׁכָּכָה לּוֹ, אַשְׁרֵי הָעָם שֶׁיהוה אֱלֹהָיו: ‹ וַאֲנִי בְּחַסְדְּךָ בָטַחְתִּי, יָגֵל לִבִּי בִּישׁוּעָתֶךָ, אָשִׁירָה לַיהוה, כִּי גָמַל עָלָי:

לַמְנַצֵּחַ מִזְמוֹר לְדָוִד:
הַשָּׁמַיִם מְסַפְּרִים כְּבוֹד־אֵל, וּמַעֲשֵׂה יָדָיו מַגִּיד הָרָקִיעַ:
יוֹם לְיוֹם יַבִּיעַ אֹמֶר, וְלַיְלָה לְּלַיְלָה יְחַוֶּה־דָּעַת:
אֵין־אֹמֶר וְאֵין דְּבָרִים, בְּלִי נִשְׁמָע קוֹלָם:
בְּכָל־הָאָרֶץ יָצָא קַוָּם, וּבִקְצֵה תֵבֵל מִלֵּיהֶם
לַשֶּׁמֶשׁ שָׂם־אֹהֶל בָּהֶם:

like a groom celebrating his wedding
and like a runner at the start of a race.
Hashem's Torah is complete;
peace and wisdom will be enjoyed by those who study it.
Hashem's laws are fair; keeping them brings happiness.
Hashem's *mitzvot* are more valuable than gold
and sweeter than honey.
Your servants, the Jewish people,
are careful in observing Your *mitzvot*,
which brings them great reward.
Yet, sometimes we make mistakes;
▸ please, *Hashem*, forgive us for mistakes that we have made.
May You find my thoughts and prayers favorable.

לְדָוִד While running away from Avimelech,
King David said the following prayer:
I will always thank *Hashem*.
Let everyone recognize the greatness of *Hashem*
and sing praises to Him together.

לְדָוִד, בְּשַׁנּוֹתוֹ אֶת־טַעְמוֹ לִפְנֵי אֲבִימֶלֶךְ *While running away from Avimelech, King David said the following prayer.* Before David became king, he spent much of his life running and hiding from others who wanted to harm him. These experiences led him to write *Tehillim*, a series of songs such as this one, which Jewish people still read today when calling out to *Hashem*.

Avimelech was the king of the Philistines, an enemy of the Jewish people. While running for his life, David hid in the land of the Philistines and was seen by Avimelech. Although Avimelech could have killed David, *Hashem* did a miracle that caused Avimelech to spare his life instead. David appeared as though he lost his mind, and Avimelech, feeling sympathy towards David, forced him to leave rather than taking his life.

וְהוּא כְּחָתָן יֹצֵא מֵחֻפָּתוֹ, יָשִׂישׂ כְּגִבּוֹר לָרוּץ אֹרַח:
מִקְצֵה הַשָּׁמַיִם מוֹצָאוֹ, וּתְקוּפָתוֹ עַל־קְצוֹתָם
וְאֵין נִסְתָּר מֵחַמָּתוֹ:
תּוֹרַת יהוה תְּמִימָה, מְשִׁיבַת נָפֶשׁ
עֵדוּת יהוה נֶאֱמָנָה, מַחְכִּימַת פֶּתִי:
פִּקּוּדֵי יהוה יְשָׁרִים, מְשַׂמְּחֵי־לֵב
מִצְוַת יהוה בָּרָה, מְאִירַת עֵינָיִם:
יִרְאַת יהוה טְהוֹרָה, עוֹמֶדֶת לָעַד
מִשְׁפְּטֵי־יהוה אֱמֶת, צָדְקוּ יַחְדָּו:
הַנֶּחֱמָדִים מִזָּהָב וּמִפַּז רָב, וּמְתוּקִים מִדְּבַשׁ וְנֹפֶת צוּפִים:
גַּם־עַבְדְּךָ נִזְהָר בָּהֶם, בְּשָׁמְרָם עֵקֶב רָב:
שְׁגִיאוֹת מִי־יָבִין, מִנִּסְתָּרוֹת נַקֵּנִי:
גַּם מִזֵּדִים חֲשֹׂךְ עַבְדֶּךָ, אַל־יִמְשְׁלוּ־בִי אָז אֵיתָם
וְנִקֵּיתִי מִפֶּשַׁע רָב:
◂ יִהְיוּ לְרָצוֹן אִמְרֵי־פִי וְהֶגְיוֹן לִבִּי לְפָנֶיךָ
יהוה, צוּרִי וְגֹאֲלִי:

לְדָוִד, בְּשַׁנּוֹתוֹ אֶת־טַעְמוֹ לִפְנֵי אֲבִימֶלֶךְ
וַיְגָרְשֵׁהוּ וַיֵּלַךְ:
אֲבָרְכָה אֶת־יהוה בְּכָל־עֵת, תָּמִיד תְּהִלָּתוֹ בְּפִי:
בַּיהוה תִּתְהַלֵּל נַפְשִׁי, יִשְׁמְעוּ עֲנָוִים וְיִשְׂמָחוּ:
גַּדְּלוּ לַיהוה אִתִּי, וּנְרוֹמְמָה שְׁמוֹ יַחְדָּו:

I looked for *Hashem*
and He allowed Himself to be found; my fears were eased.
Those who look to *Hashem* are not sad.
The poor call to *Hashem,* and He answers all their needs.
Hashem's angels are sent to those who serve Him.
The more one learns about the ways of *Hashem,*
the more one sees His goodness.
Those who fear *Hashem* have everything they need.
Those who speak nicely,
and do not say bad things about others,
will be rewarded with a long life.
One should do good, stay far away from bad,
and help make peace with others.
When the righteous call out to *Hashem,*
He listens to their cries and helps them.
Hashem sees those who do evil and acts against them.
Even during difficult times,
know that *Hashem* is still close
and answers those who call out to Him.
▸ *Hashem* protects all those who serve Him.

כִּי־אֵין מַחְסוֹר לִירֵאָיו *Those who fear Hashem have everything they need.* Jews are commanded to both love and fear *Hashem*. We have great love toward *Hashem* as He created us, provides for us, and allows us to live lives filled with happiness and joy. We fear *Hashem* because He oversees all of our actions and thoughts and delivers both reward and punishment for those that are deserving. When we think about *Hashem*'s greatness we are overcome by mixed feelings of love and fear; we appreciate all the kind actions *Hashem* does for us, but we also think about the extent of *Hashem*'s great power and how He can change our lives at any moment.

דָּרַשְׁתִּי אֶת־יהוה וְעָנָנִי, וּמִכָּל־מְגוּרוֹתַי הִצִּילָנִי:
הִבִּיטוּ אֵלָיו וְנָהָרוּ, וּפְנֵיהֶם אַל־יֶחְפָּרוּ:
זֶה עָנִי קָרָא, וַיהוה שָׁמֵעַ, וּמִכָּל־צָרוֹתָיו הוֹשִׁיעוֹ:
חֹנֶה מַלְאַךְ־יהוה סָבִיב לִירֵאָיו, וַיְחַלְּצֵם:
טַעֲמוּ וּרְאוּ כִּי־טוֹב יהוה
אַשְׁרֵי הַגֶּבֶר יֶחֱסֶה־בּוֹ:
יְראוּ אֶת־יהוה קְדֹשָׁיו, כִּי־אֵין מַחְסוֹר לִירֵאָיו:
כְּפִירִים רָשׁוּ וְרָעֵבוּ
וְדֹרְשֵׁי יהוה לֹא־יַחְסְרוּ כָל־טוֹב:
לְכוּ־בָנִים שִׁמְעוּ־לִי, יִרְאַת יהוה אֲלַמֶּדְכֶם:
מִי־הָאִישׁ הֶחָפֵץ חַיִּים, אֹהֵב יָמִים לִרְאוֹת טוֹב:
נְצֹר לְשׁוֹנְךָ מֵרָע, וּשְׂפָתֶיךָ מִדַּבֵּר מִרְמָה:
סוּר מֵרָע וַעֲשֵׂה־טוֹב, בַּקֵּשׁ שָׁלוֹם וְרָדְפֵהוּ:
עֵינֵי יהוה אֶל־צַדִּיקִים, וְאָזְנָיו אֶל־שַׁוְעָתָם:
פְּנֵי יהוה בְּעֹשֵׂי רָע, לְהַכְרִית מֵאֶרֶץ זִכְרָם:
צָעֲקוּ וַיהוה שָׁמֵעַ, וּמִכָּל־צָרוֹתָם הִצִּילָם:
קָרוֹב יהוה לְנִשְׁבְּרֵי־לֵב, וְאֶת־דַּכְּאֵי־רוּחַ יוֹשִׁיעַ:
רַבּוֹת רָעוֹת צַדִּיק, וּמִכֻּלָּם יַצִּילֶנּוּ יהוה:
שֹׁמֵר כָּל־עַצְמוֹתָיו, אַחַת מֵהֵנָּה לֹא נִשְׁבָּרָה:
תְּמוֹתֵת רָשָׁע רָעָה, וְשֹׂנְאֵי צַדִּיק יֶאְשָׁמוּ:
◂ פּוֹדֶה יהוה נֶפֶשׁ עֲבָדָיו, וְלֹא יֶאְשְׁמוּ כָּל־הַחֹסִים בּוֹ:

תְּפִלָּה לְמֹשֶׁה A prayer written by Moshe.
Hashem,
in every generation You protect us.
You were God
before there were mountains or land,
and You will be God forever.
A thousand years is like a day to You;
every morning is a new beginning.
We stay away from sins
as we fear Your anger.
Man's life is short,
and it flies by quickly.
Hashem,
please return to us
and be merciful as we are Your servants.
Please provide for our needs in the morning
so we can spend our day thanking You with song.
Let us have days filled with joy
and not punishment.

תְּפִלָּה לְמֹשֶׁה אִישׁ־הָאֱלֹהִים

אֲדֹנָי, מָעוֹן אַתָּה הָיִיתָ לָּנוּ בְּדֹר וָדֹר:

בְּטֶרֶם הָרִים יֻלָּדוּ, וַתְּחוֹלֵל אֶרֶץ וְתֵבֵל

וּמֵעוֹלָם עַד־עוֹלָם אַתָּה אֵל:

תָּשֵׁב אֱנוֹשׁ עַד־דַּכָּא, וַתֹּאמֶר שׁוּבוּ בְנֵי־אָדָם:

כִּי אֶלֶף שָׁנִים בְּעֵינֶיךָ, כְּיוֹם אֶתְמוֹל כִּי יַעֲבֹר

וְאַשְׁמוּרָה בַלָּיְלָה:

זְרַמְתָּם, שֵׁנָה יִהְיוּ, בַּבֹּקֶר כֶּחָצִיר יַחֲלֹף:

בַּבֹּקֶר יָצִיץ וְחָלָף, לָעֶרֶב יְמוֹלֵל וְיָבֵשׁ:

כִּי־כָלִינוּ בְאַפֶּךָ, וּבַחֲמָתְךָ נִבְהָלְנוּ:

שַׁתָּ עֲוֹנֹתֵינוּ לְנֶגְדֶּךָ, עֲלֻמֵנוּ לִמְאוֹר פָּנֶיךָ:

כִּי כָל־יָמֵינוּ פָּנוּ בְעֶבְרָתֶךָ, כִּלִּינוּ שָׁנֵינוּ כְמוֹ־הֶגֶה:

יְמֵי־שְׁנוֹתֵינוּ בָהֶם שִׁבְעִים שָׁנָה

וְאִם בִּגְבוּרֹת שְׁמוֹנִים שָׁנָה, וְרָהְבָּם עָמָל וָאָוֶן

כִּי־גָז חִישׁ וַנָּעֻפָה:

מִי־יוֹדֵעַ עֹז אַפֶּךָ, וּכְיִרְאָתְךָ עֶבְרָתֶךָ:

לִמְנוֹת יָמֵינוּ כֵּן הוֹדַע, וְנָבִא לְבַב חָכְמָה:

שׁוּבָה יהוה עַד־מָתָי, וְהִנָּחֵם עַל־עֲבָדֶיךָ:

שַׂבְּעֵנוּ בַבֹּקֶר חַסְדֶּךָ, וּנְרַנְּנָה וְנִשְׂמְחָה בְּכָל־יָמֵינוּ:

שַׂמְּחֵנוּ כִּימוֹת עִנִּיתָנוּ, שְׁנוֹת רָאִינוּ רָעָה:

יֵרָאֶה אֶל־עֲבָדֶיךָ פָעֳלֶךָ, וַהֲדָרְךָ עַל־בְּנֵיהֶם:

▸ May *Hashem* act kindly to us
and allow us to benefit
from the work of our hands.

יֹשֵׁב בְּסֵתֶר Those who seek *Hashem*'s shelter
will be protected by Him.
Hashem will save you
from a trap and from disease.
He will give you shelter and shield you.
Do not fear the dark of night,
an attack during the day, or a plague.
Those around you who do not fear *Hashem*
might be harmed, but you will be protected,
because *Hashem* is our protector.
Hashem will send His angels to protect you
wherever you go;
they will lift you up
so that you will not stumble.
Those close to *Hashem* will be protected
from a snake or lion attack.
When you call to *Hashem*
He will answer you
and be with you in your time of need.
▸ *Hashem* will give those who are close to Him
long life filled with His protection.
Hashem will give those who are close to Him
long life filled with His protection.

◂ וִיהִי נֹעַם אֲדֹנָי אֱלֹהֵינוּ עָלֵינוּ
וּמַעֲשֵׂה יָדֵינוּ כּוֹנְנָה עָלֵינוּ, וּמַעֲשֵׂה יָדֵינוּ כּוֹנְנֵהוּ:

יֹשֵׁב בְּסֵתֶר עֶלְיוֹן, בְּצֵל שַׁדַּי יִתְלוֹנָן:
אֹמַר לַיהוה מַחְסִי וּמְצוּדָתִי, אֱלֹהַי אֶבְטַח־בּוֹ:
כִּי הוּא יַצִּילְךָ מִפַּח יָקוּשׁ, מִדֶּבֶר הַוּוֹת:
בְּאֶבְרָתוֹ יָסֶךְ לָךְ, וְתַחַת־כְּנָפָיו תֶּחְסֶה
צִנָּה וְסֹחֵרָה אֲמִתּוֹ:
לֹא־תִירָא מִפַּחַד לָיְלָה, מֵחֵץ יָעוּף יוֹמָם:
מִדֶּבֶר בָּאֹפֶל יַהֲלֹךְ, מִקֶּטֶב יָשׁוּד צָהֳרָיִם:
יִפֹּל מִצִּדְּךָ אֶלֶף, וּרְבָבָה מִימִינֶךָ, אֵלֶיךָ לֹא יִגָּשׁ:
רַק בְּעֵינֶיךָ תַבִּיט, וְשִׁלֻּמַת רְשָׁעִים תִּרְאֶה:
כִּי־אַתָּה יהוה מַחְסִי, עֶלְיוֹן שַׂמְתָּ מְעוֹנֶךָ:
לֹא־תְאֻנֶּה אֵלֶיךָ רָעָה, וְנֶגַע לֹא־יִקְרַב בְּאָהֳלֶךָ:
כִּי מַלְאָכָיו יְצַוֶּה־לָּךְ, לִשְׁמָרְךָ בְּכָל־דְּרָכֶיךָ:
עַל־כַּפַּיִם יִשָּׂאוּנְךָ, פֶּן־תִּגֹּף בָּאֶבֶן רַגְלֶךָ:
עַל־שַׁחַל וָפֶתֶן תִּדְרֹךְ, תִּרְמֹס כְּפִיר וְתַנִּין:
כִּי בִי חָשַׁק וַאֲפַלְּטֵהוּ, אֲשַׂגְּבֵהוּ כִּי־יָדַע שְׁמִי:
יִקְרָאֵנִי וְאֶעֱנֵהוּ, עִמּוֹ אָנֹכִי בְצָרָה, אֲחַלְּצֵהוּ וַאֲכַבְּדֵהוּ:
◂ אֹרֶךְ יָמִים אַשְׂבִּיעֵהוּ, וְאַרְאֵהוּ בִּישׁוּעָתִי:
אֹרֶךְ יָמִים אַשְׂבִּיעֵהוּ, וְאַרְאֵהוּ בִּישׁוּעָתִי:

הַלְלוּיָהּ Sing praises to *Hashem*
and call out to Him,
because He chose us,
the children of Yaakov as a nation.
Hashem's power is greater
than anything else in the world.
He controls the earth, seas, and sky.
He decides when to bring clouds, lightning,
rain, and wind.
When *Hashem* took the Jews out of Egypt
he killed all the firstborn Egyptian males,
and their animals, so we could escape.
Hashem brought many plagues upon the Egyptians
as a sign to let us go.
Hashem destroyed many kings and nations
to give the Jewish people the Land of Israel,
the land of our people forever.
Hashem has mercy when He judges His Jewish people.
Other nations worship idols of silver and gold.
These man-made idols have mouths but cannot speak,
have eyes but cannot see,
and have ears but cannot hear.

הַלְלוּיָהּ, הַלְלוּ אֶת־שֵׁם יהוה, הַלְלוּ עַבְדֵי יהוה:
שֶׁעֹמְדִים בְּבֵית יהוה, בְּחַצְרוֹת בֵּית אֱלֹהֵינוּ:
הַלְלוּיָהּ כִּי־טוֹב יהוה, זַמְּרוּ לִשְׁמוֹ כִּי נָעִים:
כִּי־יַעֲקֹב בָּחַר לוֹ יָהּ, יִשְׂרָאֵל לִסְגֻלָּתוֹ:
כִּי אֲנִי יָדַעְתִּי כִּי־גָדוֹל יהוה, וַאֲדֹנֵינוּ מִכָּל־אֱלֹהִים:
כֹּל אֲשֶׁר־חָפֵץ יהוה עָשָׂה
בַּשָּׁמַיִם וּבָאָרֶץ, בַּיַּמִּים וְכָל־תְּהֹמוֹת:
מַעֲלֶה נְשִׂאִים מִקְצֵה הָאָרֶץ
בְּרָקִים לַמָּטָר עָשָׂה, מוֹצֵא־רוּחַ מֵאוֹצְרוֹתָיו:
שֶׁהִכָּה בְּכוֹרֵי מִצְרָיִם, מֵאָדָם עַד־בְּהֵמָה:
שָׁלַח אוֹתֹת וּמֹפְתִים בְּתוֹכֵכִי מִצְרָיִם
בְּפַרְעֹה וּבְכָל־עֲבָדָיו:
שֶׁהִכָּה גּוֹיִם רַבִּים, וְהָרַג מְלָכִים עֲצוּמִים:
לְסִיחוֹן מֶלֶךְ הָאֱמֹרִי, וּלְעוֹג מֶלֶךְ הַבָּשָׁן
וּלְכֹל מַמְלְכוֹת כְּנָעַן:
וְנָתַן אַרְצָם נַחֲלָה, נַחֲלָה לְיִשְׂרָאֵל עַמּוֹ:
יהוה שִׁמְךָ לְעוֹלָם, יהוה זִכְרְךָ לְדֹר־וָדֹר:
כִּי־יָדִין יהוה עַמּוֹ, וְעַל־עֲבָדָיו יִתְנֶחָם:
עֲצַבֵּי הַגּוֹיִם כֶּסֶף וְזָהָב, מַעֲשֵׂה יְדֵי אָדָם:
פֶּה־לָהֶם וְלֹא יְדַבֵּרוּ, עֵינַיִם לָהֶם וְלֹא יִרְאוּ:
אָזְנַיִם לָהֶם וְלֹא יַאֲזִינוּ, אַף אֵין־יֶשׁ־רוּחַ בְּפִיהֶם:

▸ All Jews who fear *Hashem* –
Kohanim, Levi'im, and Yisraelim –
thank *Hashem*, Halleluya!

Stand for the following.

הוֹדוּ Thank *Hashem* who is good –
His kindness lasts forever.
Thank *Hashem* who is God of the angels –
His kindness lasts forever.
Thank *Hashem* who is God of the sun, moon, and stars –
His kindness lasts forever.
Thank *Hashem* who alone makes great miracles –
His kindness lasts forever.
Thank *Hashem* who made the skies and heaven –
His kindness lasts forever.
Thank *Hashem* who separated land from water –
His kindness lasts forever.
Thank *Hashem* who created light –
His kindness lasts forever.
Thank *Hashem* who made the sun shine during the day –
His kindness lasts forever.
Thank *Hashem* who made the moon and stars shine at night –
His kindness lasts forever.
Thank *Hashem* who killed the firstborn Egyptians –
His kindness lasts forever.
Thank *Hashem* who brought the Jewish people out of Egypt –
His kindness lasts forever.
Thank *Hashem* who saved His people with a strong hand –
His kindness lasts forever.

כְּמוֹהֶם יִהְיוּ עֹשֵׂיהֶם, כֹּל אֲשֶׁר־בֹּטֵחַ בָּהֶם:

◂ בֵּית יִשְׂרָאֵל בָּרְכוּ אֶת־יהוה

בֵּית אַהֲרֹן בָּרְכוּ אֶת־יהוה:

בֵּית הַלֵּוִי בָּרְכוּ אֶת־יהוה

יִרְאֵי יהוה בָּרְכוּ אֶת־יהוה:

בָּרוּךְ יהוה מִצִּיּוֹן, שֹׁכֵן יְרוּשָׁלָםִ, הַלְלוּיָהּ:

Stand for the following.

הוֹדוּ לַיהוה כִּי־טוֹב כִּי לְעוֹלָם חַסְדּוֹ:

הוֹדוּ לֵאלֹהֵי הָאֱלֹהִים כִּי לְעוֹלָם חַסְדּוֹ:

הוֹדוּ לַאֲדֹנֵי הָאֲדֹנִים כִּי לְעוֹלָם חַסְדּוֹ:

לְעֹשֵׂה נִפְלָאוֹת גְּדֹלוֹת לְבַדּוֹ כִּי לְעוֹלָם חַסְדּוֹ:

לְעֹשֵׂה הַשָּׁמַיִם בִּתְבוּנָה כִּי לְעוֹלָם חַסְדּוֹ:

לְרֹקַע הָאָרֶץ עַל־הַמָּיִם כִּי לְעוֹלָם חַסְדּוֹ:

לְעֹשֵׂה אוֹרִים גְּדֹלִים כִּי לְעוֹלָם חַסְדּוֹ:

אֶת־הַשֶּׁמֶשׁ לְמֶמְשֶׁלֶת בַּיּוֹם כִּי לְעוֹלָם חַסְדּוֹ:

אֶת־הַיָּרֵחַ וְכוֹכָבִים

לְמֶמְשְׁלוֹת בַּלָּיְלָה כִּי לְעוֹלָם חַסְדּוֹ:

לְמַכֵּה מִצְרַיִם בִּבְכוֹרֵיהֶם כִּי לְעוֹלָם חַסְדּוֹ:

וַיּוֹצֵא יִשְׂרָאֵל מִתּוֹכָם כִּי לְעוֹלָם חַסְדּוֹ:

בְּיָד חֲזָקָה וּבִזְרוֹעַ נְטוּיָה כִּי לְעוֹלָם חַסְדּוֹ:

Thank *Hashem* who split the Reed Sea –
His kindness lasts forever.
Thank *Hashem* who led the Jewish people through the sea on dry land – His kindness lasts forever.
Thank *Hashem* who drowned Pharaoh and his army in the sea – His kindness lasts forever.
Thank *Hashem* who led the Jewish people through the desert – His kindness lasts forever.
Thank *Hashem* who defeated strong enemy kings –
His kindness lasts forever.
Thank *Hashem* who killed the mighty enemy kings who tried to overpower us – His kindness lasts forever.
Thank *Hashem* who defeated Sichon, the king of the Amorites – His kindness lasts forever.
Thank *Hashem* who defeated Og, the king of Bashan –
His kindness lasts forever.
Thank *Hashem* who gave us Israel as our home –
His kindness lasts forever.
Thank *Hashem* who made this land our home forever –
His kindness lasts forever.
Thank *Hashem* who remembered us when we were lowly slaves – His kindness lasts forever.
Thank *Hashem* who rescued us from our cruel masters –
His kindness lasts forever.
▸ Thank *Hashem* who gives food to everyone –
His kindness lasts forever.
Thank *Hashem* who is the God over the heavens –
His kindness lasts forever.

לְגֹזֵר יַם־סוּף לִגְזָרִים כִּי לְעוֹלָם חַסְדּוֹ:
וְהֶעֱבִיר יִשְׂרָאֵל בְּתוֹכוֹ כִּי לְעוֹלָם חַסְדּוֹ:
וְנִעֵר פַּרְעֹה וְחֵילוֹ בְיַם־סוּף כִּי לְעוֹלָם חַסְדּוֹ:
לְמוֹלִיךְ עַמּוֹ בַּמִּדְבָּר כִּי לְעוֹלָם חַסְדּוֹ:
לְמַכֵּה מְלָכִים גְּדֹלִים כִּי לְעוֹלָם חַסְדּוֹ:
וַיַּהֲרֹג מְלָכִים אַדִּירִים כִּי לְעוֹלָם חַסְדּוֹ:
לְסִיחוֹן מֶלֶךְ הָאֱמֹרִי כִּי לְעוֹלָם חַסְדּוֹ:
וּלְעוֹג מֶלֶךְ הַבָּשָׁן כִּי לְעוֹלָם חַסְדּוֹ:
וְנָתַן אַרְצָם לְנַחֲלָה כִּי לְעוֹלָם חַסְדּוֹ:
נַחֲלָה לְיִשְׂרָאֵל עַבְדּוֹ כִּי לְעוֹלָם חַסְדּוֹ:
שֶׁבְּשִׁפְלֵנוּ זָכַר לָנוּ כִּי לְעוֹלָם חַסְדּוֹ:
וַיִּפְרְקֵנוּ מִצָּרֵינוּ כִּי לְעוֹלָם חַסְדּוֹ:
◂ נֹתֵן לֶחֶם לְכָל־בָּשָׂר כִּי לְעוֹלָם חַסְדּוֹ:
הוֹדוּ לְאֵל הַשָּׁמָיִם כִּי לְעוֹלָם חַסְדּוֹ:

Sit for the following.

רַנְּנוּ Sing joyfully to *Hashem*
for He is deserving of praise.
Use musical instruments
to give thanks to *Hashem*.
Hashem loves those who are good;
His kindness fills the world.
Hashem created the heavens with His words
and the stars with His breath.
When creating the world,
Hashem separated the water from the land.
The earth should fear *Hashem*,
for *Hashem* created the whole world with His words.
Hashem prevents nations from opposing His will;
He does not allow them to succeed.
Hashem's plans last forever.
The Jewish people are happy
because *Hashem* chose them as His people.
Hashem sees everyone's actions;
He understands their thoughts.
Hashem can defeat any army or king.
Do not rely on the strength of an army;
only *Hashem* has the power to save.
Hashem watches over those who fear Him,
and rescues them in their time of need.

Sit for the following.

רַנְּנוּ צַדִּיקִים בַּיהוה, לַיְשָׁרִים נָאוָה תְהִלָּה:
הוֹדוּ לַיהוה בְּכִנּוֹר, בְּנֵבֶל עָשׂוֹר זַמְּרוּ־לוֹ:
שִׁירוּ־לוֹ שִׁיר חָדָשׁ, הֵיטִיבוּ נַגֵּן בִּתְרוּעָה:
כִּי־יָשָׁר דְּבַר־יהוה, וְכָל־מַעֲשֵׂהוּ בֶּאֱמוּנָה:
אֹהֵב צְדָקָה וּמִשְׁפָּט, חֶסֶד יהוה מָלְאָה הָאָרֶץ:
בִּדְבַר יהוה שָׁמַיִם נַעֲשׂוּ, וּבְרוּחַ פִּיו כָּל־צְבָאָם:
כֹּנֵס כַּנֵּד מֵי הַיָּם, נֹתֵן בְּאוֹצָרוֹת תְּהוֹמוֹת:
יִירְאוּ מֵיהוה כָּל־הָאָרֶץ, מִמֶּנּוּ יָגוּרוּ כָּל־יֹשְׁבֵי תֵבֵל:
כִּי הוּא אָמַר וַיֶּהִי, הוּא־צִוָּה וַיַּעֲמֹד:
יהוה הֵפִיר עֲצַת־גּוֹיִם, הֵנִיא מַחְשְׁבוֹת עַמִּים:
עֲצַת יהוה לְעוֹלָם תַּעֲמֹד, מַחְשְׁבוֹת לִבּוֹ לְדֹר וָדֹר:
אַשְׁרֵי הַגּוֹי אֲשֶׁר־יהוה אֱלֹהָיו, הָעָם בָּחַר לְנַחֲלָה לוֹ:
מִשָּׁמַיִם הִבִּיט יהוה, רָאָה אֶת־כָּל־בְּנֵי הָאָדָם:
מִמְּכוֹן־שִׁבְתּוֹ הִשְׁגִּיחַ, אֶל כָּל־יֹשְׁבֵי הָאָרֶץ:
הַיֹּצֵר יַחַד לִבָּם, הַמֵּבִין אֶל־כָּל־מַעֲשֵׂיהֶם:
אֵין־הַמֶּלֶךְ נוֹשָׁע בְּרָב־חָיִל, גִּבּוֹר לֹא־יִנָּצֵל בְּרָב־כֹּחַ:
שֶׁקֶר הַסּוּס לִתְשׁוּעָה, וּבְרֹב חֵילוֹ לֹא יְמַלֵּט:
הִנֵּה עֵין יהוה אֶל־יְרֵאָיו, לַמְיַחֲלִים לְחַסְדּוֹ:
לְהַצִּיל מִמָּוֶת נַפְשָׁם, וּלְחַיּוֹתָם בָּרָעָב:
נַפְשֵׁנוּ חִכְּתָה לַיהוה, עֶזְרֵנוּ וּמָגִנֵּנוּ הוּא:

▸ We are filled with joy
because we put our trust in *Hashem*.
Hashem,
please always show Your kindness to us.

מִזְמוֹר A song for Shabbat.
It is good to thank *Hashem*
and sing songs to Him.
We sing about *Hashem*'s kindness in the morning
and we are thankful for His protection at night.
We use musical instruments to thank *Hashem*;
we sing out to Him with great joy.
We cannot understand how great and wise *Hashem* is.
Even when it appears that evil people are successful,
Hashem will not allow their success to last forever.
All of *Hashem*'s enemies
will one day be defeated and scattered;
Hashem will lift up His Jewish people.
▸ The righteous will be fruitful like a date tree
and strong like a cedar tree.
Like a tree planted in *Hashem*'s garden,
the righteous will continue to have success
even in old age,
and will remain full of strength.
Hashem is fair;
He is perfect in His ways.

◂ כִּי־בוֹ יִשְׂמַח לִבֵּנוּ, כִּי בְשֵׁם קָדְשׁוֹ בָטָחְנוּ:
יְהִי־חַסְדְּךָ יהוה עָלֵינוּ, כַּאֲשֶׁר יִחַלְנוּ לָךְ:

מִזְמוֹר שִׁיר לְיוֹם הַשַּׁבָּת:
טוֹב לְהֹדוֹת לַיהוה, וּלְזַמֵּר לְשִׁמְךָ עֶלְיוֹן:
לְהַגִּיד בַּבֹּקֶר חַסְדֶּךָ, וֶאֱמוּנָתְךָ בַּלֵּילוֹת:
עֲלֵי־עָשׂוֹר וַעֲלֵי־נָבֶל, עֲלֵי הִגָּיוֹן בְּכִנּוֹר:
כִּי שִׂמַּחְתַּנִי יהוה בְּפָעֳלֶךָ, בְּמַעֲשֵׂי יָדֶיךָ אֲרַנֵּן:
מַה־גָּדְלוּ מַעֲשֶׂיךָ יהוה, מְאֹד עָמְקוּ מַחְשְׁבֹתֶיךָ:
אִישׁ־בַּעַר לֹא יֵדָע, וּכְסִיל לֹא־יָבִין אֶת־זֹאת:
בִּפְרֹחַ רְשָׁעִים כְּמוֹ עֵשֶׂב, וַיָּצִיצוּ כָּל־פֹּעֲלֵי אָוֶן
לְהִשָּׁמְדָם עֲדֵי־עַד:
וְאַתָּה מָרוֹם לְעֹלָם יהוה:
כִּי הִנֵּה אֹיְבֶיךָ יהוה, כִּי־הִנֵּה אֹיְבֶיךָ יֹאבֵדוּ
יִתְפָּרְדוּ כָּל־פֹּעֲלֵי אָוֶן:
וַתָּרֶם כִּרְאֵים קַרְנִי, בַּלֹּתִי בְּשֶׁמֶן רַעֲנָן:
וַתַּבֵּט עֵינִי בְּשׁוּרָי, בַּקָּמִים עָלַי מְרֵעִים תִּשְׁמַעְנָה אָזְנָי:
◂ צַדִּיק כַּתָּמָר יִפְרָח, כְּאֶרֶז בַּלְּבָנוֹן יִשְׂגֶּה:
שְׁתוּלִים בְּבֵית יהוה, בְּחַצְרוֹת אֱלֹהֵינוּ יַפְרִיחוּ:
עוֹד יְנוּבוּן בְּשֵׂיבָה, דְּשֵׁנִים וְרַעֲנַנִּים יִהְיוּ:
לְהַגִּיד כִּי־יָשָׁר יהוה, צוּרִי, וְלֹא־עַוְלָתָה בּוֹ:

יהוה מָלָךְ *Hashem* is King,
dressed in greatness and might!
He created the world;
Hashem lives forever.
As a river flows so will our enemies come against us,
▸ but You, *Hashem,*
are mightier than the many waves of the sea.
We fully believe in Your promises.
Hashem, may the *Beit HaMikdash* stand for a long time.

On Hoshana Raba, continue with the weekday service, from "Hashem, Your honor" on page 50.

יְהִי כְבוֹד *Hashem,* Your honor lasts forever,
take pride in Your creations.
We praise You, *Hashem,* from sunrise to sunset,
generation to generation, and for ever and ever.
Hashem, You rule over all the nations;
Your throne is in the heavens.
Hashem, Your creation of the earth and heavens
is a sign of Your greatness.
You *Hashem* are the King, You were always the King,
and You will be the King forever.
When other nations make evil plans against us,
Hashem stops them.
Man is free to think on his own
but it is *Hashem*'s plans that will always last.
Hashem chose Zion as His home.
Israel is *Hashem*'s special treasure.
Hashem chose Yaakov and his descendants,
the Jewish people, to be His special nation.

יהוה מָלָךְ, גֵּאוּת לָבֵשׁ
לָבֵשׁ יהוה עֹז הִתְאַזָּר, אַף־תִּכּוֹן תֵּבֵל בַּל־תִּמּוֹט:
נָכוֹן כִּסְאֲךָ מֵאָז, מֵעוֹלָם אָתָּה:
נָשְׂאוּ נְהָרוֹת יהוה, נָשְׂאוּ נְהָרוֹת קוֹלָם
יִשְׂאוּ נְהָרוֹת דָּכְיָם:
◂ מִקֹּלוֹת מַיִם רַבִּים, אַדִּירִים מִשְׁבְּרֵי־יָם
אַדִּיר בַּמָּרוֹם יהוה:
עֵדֹתֶיךָ נֶאֶמְנוּ מְאֹד לְבֵיתְךָ נַאֲוָה־קֹדֶשׁ
יהוה לְאֹרֶךְ יָמִים:

On הושענא רבה*, continue with* יְהִי כְבוֹד *on page 51.*

יְהִי כְבוֹד יהוה לְעוֹלָם, יִשְׂמַח יהוה בְּמַעֲשָׂיו: יְהִי שֵׁם יהוה מְבֹרָךְ, מֵעַתָּה וְעַד־עוֹלָם: מִמִּזְרַח־שֶׁמֶשׁ עַד־מְבוֹאוֹ, מְהֻלָּל שֵׁם יהוה: רָם עַל־כָּל־גּוֹיִם יהוה, עַל הַשָּׁמַיִם כְּבוֹדוֹ: יהוה שִׁמְךָ לְעוֹלָם, יהוה זִכְרְךָ לְדֹר־וָדֹר: יהוה בַּשָּׁמַיִם הֵכִין כִּסְאוֹ, וּמַלְכוּתוֹ בַּכֹּל מָשָׁלָה: יִשְׂמְחוּ הַשָּׁמַיִם וְתָגֵל הָאָרֶץ, וְיֹאמְרוּ בַגּוֹיִם יהוה מָלָךְ: יהוה מֶלֶךְ, יהוה מָלָךְ, יהוה יִמְלֹךְ לְעוֹלָם וָעֶד. יהוה מֶלֶךְ עוֹלָם וָעֶד, אָבְדוּ גוֹיִם מֵאַרְצוֹ: יהוה הֵפִיר עֲצַת־גּוֹיִם, הֵנִיא מַחְשְׁבוֹת עַמִּים: רַבּוֹת מַחֲשָׁבוֹת בְּלֶב־אִישׁ, וַעֲצַת יהוה הִיא תָקוּם: עֲצַת יהוה לְעוֹלָם תַּעֲמֹד, מַחְשְׁבוֹת לִבּוֹ לְדֹר וָדֹר: כִּי הוּא אָמַר וַיֶּהִי, הוּא־צִוָּה

Hashem will never forget His Jewish people.
Hashem is caring and forgives our sins.
▸ *Hashem,* shows kindness by forgiving our mistakes rather than destroying us with anger.
Hashem, please save us!
You are our King who answers us when we call out to You.

The line beginning with "Hashem opens His hands" should be said with special concentration.

אַשְׁרֵי We are happy with the opportunity to sit and pray. We are happy that You are our God and that we are Your people.
David HaMelech wrote this song:

א GOD – *Hashem* is our God and King.

ב THANK – We appreciate *Hashem* and we will thank Him every day, forever.

ג GREATNESS – *Hashem*'s greatness is endless.

ד GENERATIONS – We will tell our children about the spectacular actions You have done for us in every generation.

ה MIRACLES – The miracles that *Hashem* performs for His people are glorious.

ו STRENGTH – *Hashem*'s strength is awesome beyond comparison.

ז REMEMBER – We remember the good that *Hashem* does for us.

ח MERCY – *Hashem* is slow to get angry.

ט GOODNESS – *Hashem* is good to all His creations, humans and animals alike.

וַיְעַמֵּד: כִּי־בָחַר יהוה בְּצִיּוֹן, אִוָּהּ לְמוֹשָׁב לוֹ: כִּי־יַעֲקֹב בָּחַר לוֹ יָהּ, יִשְׂרָאֵל לִסְגֻלָּתוֹ: כִּי לֹא־יִטֹּשׁ יהוה עַמּוֹ, וְנַחֲלָתוֹ לֹא יַעֲזֹב: ‹ וְהוּא רַחוּם, יְכַפֵּר עָוֹן וְלֹא־יַשְׁחִית, וְהִרְבָּה לְהָשִׁיב אַפּוֹ, וְלֹא־יָעִיר כָּל־חֲמָתוֹ: יהוה הוֹשִׁיעָה, הַמֶּלֶךְ יַעֲנֵנוּ בְיוֹם־קָרְאֵנוּ:

The line beginning with פּוֹתֵחַ אֶת יָדֶךָ *should be said with special concentration.*

אַשְׁרֵי יוֹשְׁבֵי בֵיתֶךָ, עוֹד יְהַלְלוּךָ סֶּלָה:
אַשְׁרֵי הָעָם שֶׁכָּכָה לּוֹ, אַשְׁרֵי הָעָם שֶׁיהוה אֱלֹהָיו:
תְּהִלָּה לְדָוִד
אֲרוֹמִמְךָ אֱלוֹהַי הַמֶּלֶךְ
וַאֲבָרְכָה שִׁמְךָ לְעוֹלָם וָעֶד:
בְּכָל־יוֹם אֲבָרְכֶךָּ
וַאֲהַלְלָה שִׁמְךָ לְעוֹלָם וָעֶד:
גָּדוֹל יהוה וּמְהֻלָּל מְאֹד, וְלִגְדֻלָּתוֹ אֵין חֵקֶר:
דּוֹר לְדוֹר יְשַׁבַּח מַעֲשֶׂיךָ, וּגְבוּרֹתֶיךָ יַגִּידוּ:
הֲדַר כְּבוֹד הוֹדֶךָ, וְדִבְרֵי נִפְלְאֹתֶיךָ אָשִׂיחָה:
וֶעֱזוּז נוֹרְאֹתֶיךָ יֹאמֵרוּ, וּגְדוּלָּתְךָ אֲסַפְּרֶנָּה:
זֵכֶר רַב־טוּבְךָ יַבִּיעוּ, וְצִדְקָתְךָ יְרַנֵּנוּ:
חַנּוּן וְרַחוּם יהוה, אֶרֶךְ אַפַּיִם וּגְדָל־חָסֶד:
טוֹב־יהוה לַכֹּל, וְרַחֲמָיו עַל־כָּל־מַעֲשָׂיו:

י KINDNESS – All creations of *Hashem* are thankful for His kindness.

כ HONOR – We give *Hashem* the honor that He deserves.

ל MIGHTY – We inform all people of *Hashem*'s mighty actions.

מ KINGSHIP – *Hashem* has and always will rule the world.

ס HELP – *Hashem* helps us when we need Him.

ע RELY – We rely on *Hashem* to give us the food that we need to live.

פ PROVIDES – *Hashem* opens His hands and provides us with our needs.

צ RIGHTEOUS – Everything *Hashem* does is righteous and with good intentions.

ק CLOSENESS – *Hashem* is close to all those that call out to Him.

ר SAVES – *Hashem* listens to our cries and saves those in need.

ש GUARDS – *Hashem* protects all those who love Him and turn to Him in times of need.

▸ ת PRAISE – For all of these reasons, everyone praises *Hashem* and thanks Him every day.

הַלְלוּיָהּ Halleluya!
I praise *Hashem* from the depths of my soul.
I will sing and praise *Hashem*
as long as I live.
Do not put your trust in man.

יוֹדוּךָ יהוה כָּל־מַעֲשֶׂיךָ, וַחֲסִידֶיךָ יְבָרְכוּכָה:
כְּבוֹד מַלְכוּתְךָ יֹאמֵרוּ, וּגְבוּרָתְךָ יְדַבֵּרוּ:
לְהוֹדִיעַ לִבְנֵי הָאָדָם גְּבוּרֹתָיו, וּכְבוֹד הֲדַר מַלְכוּתוֹ:
מַלְכוּתְךָ מַלְכוּת כָּל־עֹלָמִים
וּמֶמְשַׁלְתְּךָ בְּכָל־דּוֹר וָדֹר:
סוֹמֵךְ יהוה לְכָל־הַנֹּפְלִים, וְזוֹקֵף לְכָל־הַכְּפוּפִים:
עֵינֵי־כֹל אֵלֶיךָ יְשַׂבֵּרוּ
וְאַתָּה נוֹתֵן־לָהֶם אֶת־אָכְלָם בְּעִתּוֹ:
פּוֹתֵחַ אֶת־יָדֶךָ, וּמַשְׂבִּיעַ לְכָל־חַי רָצוֹן:
צַדִּיק יהוה בְּכָל־דְּרָכָיו, וְחָסִיד בְּכָל־מַעֲשָׂיו:
קָרוֹב יהוה לְכָל־קֹרְאָיו, לְכֹל אֲשֶׁר יִקְרָאֻהוּ בֶאֱמֶת:
רְצוֹן־יְרֵאָיו יַעֲשֶׂה, וְאֶת־שַׁוְעָתָם יִשְׁמַע, וְיוֹשִׁיעֵם:
שׁוֹמֵר יהוה אֶת־כָּל־אֹהֲבָיו, וְאֵת כָּל־הָרְשָׁעִים יַשְׁמִיד:
◂ תְּהִלַּת יהוה יְדַבֶּר פִּי
וִיבָרֵךְ כָּל־בָּשָׂר שֵׁם קָדְשׁוֹ לְעוֹלָם וָעֶד:
וַאֲנַחְנוּ נְבָרֵךְ יָהּ מֵעַתָּה וְעַד־עוֹלָם, הַלְלוּיָהּ:

הַלְלוּיָהּ, הַלְלִי נַפְשִׁי אֶת־יהוה:
אֲהַלְלָה יהוה בְּחַיָּי, אֲזַמְּרָה לֵאלֹהַי בְּעוֹדִי:
אַל־תִּבְטְחוּ בִנְדִיבִים, בְּבֶן־אָדָם שֶׁאֵין לוֹ תְשׁוּעָה:

People do not live forever
and they may not be able to save you
during your time of need.
The person who turns to *Hashem* for help will be glad.
Hashem created the heaven, earth, and sea,
and all that lives within.
Hashem alone knows truth.
Hashem protects people by:

Helping those who are struggling,
Giving food to those who are hungry,
Giving freedom to captives,
Giving sight to those who cannot see,
Supporting those who need physical help,
Loving the righteous,
Protecting the weak,
Giving strength to orphans and widows, and
Destroying the plans of the wicked.

▸ *Hashem* will rule as King forever and for all generations.
Halleluya!

הַלְלוּיָהּ Halleluya!
It is proper to sing songs to *Hashem* and to praise Him.
Hashem will rebuild Jerusalem and gather in all Jews
that are scattered around the world.
He heals the wounds of the brokenhearted.
He counts each of the stars and gives a name to each one.
Hashem is great and mighty;
His understanding has no limit.

תֵּצֵא רוּחוֹ, יָשֻׁב לְאַדְמָתוֹ, בַּיּוֹם הַהוּא אָבְדוּ עֶשְׁתֹּנֹתָיו:
אַשְׁרֵי שֶׁאֵל יַעֲקֹב בְּעֶזְרוֹ, שִׂבְרוֹ עַל־יהוה אֱלֹהָיו:
עֹשֶׂה שָׁמַיִם וָאָרֶץ, אֶת־הַיָּם וְאֶת־כָּל־אֲשֶׁר־בָּם
הַשֹּׁמֵר אֱמֶת לְעוֹלָם:

עֹשֶׂה מִשְׁפָּט לָעֲשׁוּקִים
נֹתֵן לֶחֶם לָרְעֵבִים
יהוה מַתִּיר אֲסוּרִים:
יהוה פֹּקֵחַ עִוְרִים
יהוה זֹקֵף כְּפוּפִים
יהוה אֹהֵב צַדִּיקִים:
יהוה שֹׁמֵר אֶת־גֵּרִים
יָתוֹם וְאַלְמָנָה יְעוֹדֵד
וְדֶרֶךְ רְשָׁעִים יְעַוֵּת:

◂ יִמְלֹךְ יהוה לְעוֹלָם, אֱלֹהַיִךְ צִיּוֹן לְדֹר וָדֹר, הַלְלוּיָהּ:

הַלְלוּיָהּ
כִּי־טוֹב זַמְּרָה אֱלֹהֵינוּ, כִּי־נָעִים נָאוָה תְהִלָּה:
בּוֹנֵה יְרוּשָׁלַםִ יהוה, נִדְחֵי יִשְׂרָאֵל יְכַנֵּס:
הָרוֹפֵא לִשְׁבוּרֵי לֵב, וּמְחַבֵּשׁ לְעַצְּבוֹתָם:
מוֹנֶה מִסְפָּר לַכּוֹכָבִים, לְכֻלָּם שֵׁמוֹת יִקְרָא:
גָּדוֹל אֲדוֹנֵינוּ וְרַב־כֹּחַ, לִתְבוּנָתוֹ אֵין מִסְפָּר:

Hashem gives courage to the humble
and casts away the wicked.
Sing out to *Hashem* in thanks
and make music for Him.
Hashem covers the sky with clouds,
provides the earth with rain
and causes the hills to sprout grass.
He gives food to the cattle
and birds when they cry.
It is not speed or strength that *Hashem* desires from man,
but the service and fear of God.
Praise *Hashem* who protects Jerusalem
and blesses the people within it.
He has brought peace to the land
and provided us with fine foods.
Hashem placed His commandments on earth
and shared them with the Jewish people.
He has not done this for any other nation;
▸ His laws and commandments are for the Jewish people.
Halleluya!

הַלְלוּיָהּ Halleluya!
Heaven and all of *Hashem*'s heavenly creations
praise Him,
including the:
Angels,
Sun, moon, and stars,
Sky and all that is above it.

מְעוֹדֵד עֲנָוִים יהוה, מַשְׁפִּיל רְשָׁעִים עֲדֵי־אָרֶץ:
עֱנוּ לַיהוה בְּתוֹדָה, זַמְּרוּ לֵאלֹהֵינוּ בְכִנּוֹר:
הַמְכַסֶּה שָׁמַיִם בְּעָבִים, הַמֵּכִין לָאָרֶץ מָטָר
הַמַּצְמִיחַ הָרִים חָצִיר:
נוֹתֵן לִבְהֵמָה לַחְמָהּ, לִבְנֵי עֹרֵב אֲשֶׁר יִקְרָאוּ:
לֹא בִגְבוּרַת הַסּוּס יֶחְפָּץ, לֹא־בְשׁוֹקֵי הָאִישׁ יִרְצֶה:
רוֹצֶה יהוה אֶת־יְרֵאָיו, אֶת־הַמְיַחֲלִים לְחַסְדּוֹ:
שַׁבְּחִי יְרוּשָׁלַםִ אֶת־יהוה, הַלְלִי אֱלֹהַיִךְ צִיּוֹן:
כִּי־חִזַּק בְּרִיחֵי שְׁעָרָיִךְ, בֵּרַךְ בָּנַיִךְ בְּקִרְבֵּךְ:
הַשָּׂם־גְּבוּלֵךְ שָׁלוֹם, חֵלֶב חִטִּים יַשְׂבִּיעֵךְ:
הַשֹּׁלֵחַ אִמְרָתוֹ אָרֶץ, עַד־מְהֵרָה יָרוּץ דְּבָרוֹ:
הַנֹּתֵן שֶׁלֶג כַּצָּמֶר, כְּפוֹר כָּאֵפֶר יְפַזֵּר:
מַשְׁלִיךְ קַרְחוֹ כְפִתִּים, לִפְנֵי קָרָתוֹ מִי יַעֲמֹד:
יִשְׁלַח דְּבָרוֹ וְיַמְסֵם, יַשֵּׁב רוּחוֹ יִזְּלוּ־מָיִם:
◂ מַגִּיד דְּבָרָו לְיַעֲקֹב, חֻקָּיו וּמִשְׁפָּטָיו לְיִשְׂרָאֵל:
לֹא עָשָׂה כֵן לְכָל־גּוֹי, וּמִשְׁפָּטִים בַּל־יְדָעוּם, הַלְלוּיָהּ:

הַלְלוּיָהּ, הַלְלוּ אֶת־יהוה מִן־הַשָּׁמַיִם, הַלְלוּהוּ בַּמְּרוֹמִים:
הַלְלוּהוּ כָל־מַלְאָכָיו, הַלְלוּהוּ כָּל־צְבָאָו:
הַלְלוּהוּ שֶׁמֶשׁ וְיָרֵחַ, הַלְלוּהוּ כָּל־כּוֹכְבֵי אוֹר:
הַלְלוּהוּ שְׁמֵי הַשָּׁמָיִם, וְהַמַּיִם אֲשֶׁר מֵעַל הַשָּׁמָיִם:

The earth and all of *Hashem*'s earthly creations
praise Him,
including the:
Fish and sea life,
Mountains, hills, and trees,
Animals, insects, and birds,
Kings and nations,
Princes and judges,
Young and old,
Men and women.

▸ Let all of these people, places, and things
come together
to praise *Hashem,* the only God.
Hashem's greatness fills the heavens and earth.
Halleluya!

הַלְלוּיָהּ Halleluya!
Create a new song to sing praises to *Hashem.*
With joy, the Jewish people sing to *Hashem,*
our King and Creator.
Praise *Hashem*
with dancing, instruments, and song.
Even as we lie in our beds ready to sleep,
we sing out praise to *Hashem*

יְהַלְלוּ אֶת־שֵׁם יהוה, כִּי הוּא צִוָּה וְנִבְרָאוּ:
וַיַּעֲמִידֵם לָעַד לְעוֹלָם, חָק־נָתַן וְלֹא יַעֲבוֹר:
הַלְלוּ אֶת־יהוה מִן־הָאָרֶץ, תַּנִּינִים וְכׇל־תְּהֹמוֹת:
אֵשׁ וּבָרָד שֶׁלֶג וְקִיטוֹר, רוּחַ סְעָרָה עֹשָׂה דְבָרוֹ:
הֶהָרִים וְכׇל־גְּבָעוֹת, עֵץ פְּרִי וְכׇל־אֲרָזִים:
הַחַיָּה וְכׇל־בְּהֵמָה, רֶמֶשׂ וְצִפּוֹר כָּנָף:
מַלְכֵי־אֶרֶץ וְכׇל־לְאֻמִּים, שָׂרִים וְכׇל־שֹׁפְטֵי אָרֶץ:
בַּחוּרִים וְגַם־בְּתוּלוֹת, זְקֵנִים עִם־נְעָרִים:
◂ יְהַלְלוּ אֶת־שֵׁם יהוה, כִּי־נִשְׂגָּב שְׁמוֹ לְבַדּוֹ
הוֹדוֹ עַל־אֶרֶץ וְשָׁמָיִם:
וַיָּרֶם קֶרֶן לְעַמּוֹ, תְּהִלָּה לְכׇל־חֲסִידָיו
לִבְנֵי יִשְׂרָאֵל עַם קְרֹבוֹ, הַלְלוּיָהּ:

הַלְלוּיָהּ
שִׁירוּ לַיהוה שִׁיר חָדָשׁ, תְּהִלָּתוֹ בִּקְהַל חֲסִידִים:
יִשְׂמַח יִשְׂרָאֵל בְּעֹשָׂיו, בְּנֵי־צִיּוֹן יָגִילוּ בְמַלְכָּם:
יְהַלְלוּ שְׁמוֹ בְמָחוֹל, בְּתֹף וְכִנּוֹר יְזַמְּרוּ־לוֹ:
כִּי־רוֹצֶה יהוה בְּעַמּוֹ, יְפָאֵר עֲנָוִים בִּישׁוּעָה:
יַעְלְזוּ חֲסִידִים בְּכָבוֹד, יְרַנְּנוּ עַל־מִשְׁכְּבוֹתָם:
רוֹמְמוֹת אֵל בִּגְרוֹנָם, וְחֶרֶב פִּיפִיּוֹת בְּיָדָם:

▸ for He protects us
and punishes our enemies.
Halleluya!

הַלְלוּיָהּ Halleluya!
Praise *Hashem* who rests His Presence
in the *Beit HaMikdash* and the heavens.
Praise *Hashem* for His great and mighty deeds.
Praise *Hashem* with the blast of the shofar,
with many musical instruments,
and through dance.
▸ All those who are living
should praise *Hashem,* Halleluya!
All those who are living
should praise *Hashem,* Halleluya!

בָּרוּךְ *Hashem* is praised forever.
Hashem, from Your holy city of Jerusalem,
You are praised.
Hashem, who does wonders for His people,
You are praised.
▸ *Hashem,* Your name itself is praised.
May the whole world be filled
with Your greatness forever.
Amen and *Amen.*

לַעֲשׂוֹת נְקָמָה בַּגּוֹיִם, תּוֹכֵחוֹת בַּלְאֻמִּים:
◂ לֶאְסֹר מַלְכֵיהֶם בְּזִקִּים, וְנִכְבְּדֵיהֶם בְּכַבְלֵי בַרְזֶל:
לַעֲשׂוֹת בָּהֶם מִשְׁפָּט כָּתוּב
הָדָר הוּא לְכָל־חֲסִידָיו, הַלְלוּיָהּ:

הַלְלוּיָהּ, הַלְלוּ־אֵל בְּקָדְשׁוֹ, הַלְלוּהוּ בִּרְקִיעַ עֻזּוֹ:
הַלְלוּהוּ בִגְבוּרֹתָיו, הַלְלוּהוּ כְּרֹב גֻּדְלוֹ:
הַלְלוּהוּ בְּתֵקַע שׁוֹפָר, הַלְלוּהוּ בְּנֵבֶל וְכִנּוֹר:
הַלְלוּהוּ בְתֹף וּמָחוֹל, הַלְלוּהוּ בְּמִנִּים וְעוּגָב:
הַלְלוּהוּ בְצִלְצְלֵי־שָׁמַע, הַלְלוּהוּ בְּצִלְצְלֵי תְרוּעָה:
◂ כֹּל הַנְּשָׁמָה תְּהַלֵּל יָהּ, הַלְלוּיָהּ:
כֹּל הַנְּשָׁמָה תְּהַלֵּל יָהּ, הַלְלוּיָהּ:

בָּרוּךְ יהוה לְעוֹלָם, אָמֵן וְאָמֵן:
בָּרוּךְ יהוה מִצִּיּוֹן, שֹׁכֵן יְרוּשָׁלָםִ, הַלְלוּיָהּ:
בָּרוּךְ יהוה אֱלֹהִים אֱלֹהֵי יִשְׂרָאֵל
עֹשֵׂה נִפְלָאוֹת לְבַדּוֹ:
◂ וּבָרוּךְ שֵׁם כְּבוֹדוֹ לְעוֹלָם
וְיִמָּלֵא כְבוֹדוֹ אֶת־כָּל־הָאָרֶץ
אָמֵן וְאָמֵן:

Stand until "The soul" on *(page 458)*.

וַיְבָרֶךְ King David thanked *Hashem* in front of the entire Jewish people, saying: Thank You *Hashem*, God of the Jewish people. You are our God and You will be our God forever. *Hashem*, You are:

Great,
Strong,
Beautiful, and
Full of glory and splendor.

Hashem, You are ruler of all, and control:

Who is wealthy and who is poor,
Who is strong and who is weak, and
Who is honored and who is not.

For all of this, we thank and praise You, *Hashem*. *Hashem*, You alone created and gave life to the heavens, earth, and seas, and all that is within them. ▸ You, *Hashem*, are the God of Avraham who saved him from Ur Kasdim because he was faithful to You. ◂

וְכָרוֹת עִמּוֹ הַבְּרִית *Hashem*, You made a commitment to Avraham to give the Jewish people the Land of Israel. You fulfilled Your promise, because You are righteous. Our ancestors suffered when they were slaves in Egypt. *Hashem*, You saw their suffering and brought the miracle of the ten plagues against Pharaoh and all the Egyptians. As we escaped from Egypt, You, *Hashem*, heard our cries for help at the Sea of Reeds. *Hashem*, Your actions have made Your name famous throughout the world forever. ▸ You split the sea for the Jewish people, allowing them to walk through on dry land. Then, the Egyptians, who chased after the Jews, had the waters of the sea crash down on them, drowning them like stones.

Stand until נִשְׁמַת *on (page 459).*

וַיְבָרֶךְ דָּוִיד אֶת־יהוה לְעֵינֵי כָּל־הַקָּהָל, וַיֹּאמֶר דָּוִיד, בָּרוּךְ אַתָּה יהוה, אֱלֹהֵי יִשְׂרָאֵל אָבִינוּ, מֵעוֹלָם וְעַד־עוֹלָם: לְךָ יהוה הַגְּדֻלָּה וְהַגְּבוּרָה וְהַתִּפְאֶרֶת וְהַנֵּצַח וְהַהוֹד, כִּי־כֹל בַּשָּׁמַיִם וּבָאָרֶץ, לְךָ יהוה הַמַּמְלָכָה וְהַמִּתְנַשֵּׂא לְכֹל לְרֹאשׁ: וְהָעֹשֶׁר וְהַכָּבוֹד מִלְּפָנֶיךָ, וְאַתָּה מוֹשֵׁל בַּכֹּל, וּבְיָדְךָ כֹּחַ וּגְבוּרָה, וּבְיָדְךָ לְגַדֵּל וּלְחַזֵּק לַכֹּל: וְעַתָּה אֱלֹהֵינוּ מוֹדִים אֲנַחְנוּ לָךְ, וּמְהַלְלִים לְשֵׁם תִּפְאַרְתֶּךָ: אַתָּה־הוּא יהוה לְבַדֶּךָ, אַתָּ עָשִׂיתָ אֶת־הַשָּׁמַיִם, שְׁמֵי הַשָּׁמַיִם וְכָל־צְבָאָם, הָאָרֶץ וְכָל־אֲשֶׁר עָלֶיהָ, הַיַּמִּים וְכָל־אֲשֶׁר בָּהֶם, וְאַתָּה מְחַיֶּה אֶת־כֻּלָּם, וּצְבָא הַשָּׁמַיִם לְךָ מִשְׁתַּחֲוִים: ◂ אַתָּה הוּא יהוה הָאֱלֹהִים אֲשֶׁר בָּחַרְתָּ בְּאַבְרָם, וְהוֹצֵאתוֹ מֵאוּר כַּשְׂדִּים, וְשַׂמְתָּ שְׁמוֹ אַבְרָהָם: וּמָצָאתָ אֶת־לְבָבוֹ נֶאֱמָן לְפָנֶיךָ, ◂ וְכָרוֹת עִמּוֹ הַבְּרִית לָתֵת אֶת־אֶרֶץ הַכְּנַעֲנִי הַחִתִּי הָאֱמֹרִי וְהַפְּרִזִּי וְהַיְבוּסִי וְהַגִּרְגָּשִׁי, לָתֵת לְזַרְעוֹ, וַתָּקֶם אֶת־דְּבָרֶיךָ, כִּי צַדִּיק אָתָּה: וַתֵּרֶא אֶת־עֳנִי אֲבֹתֵינוּ בְּמִצְרָיִם, וְאֶת־זַעֲקָתָם שָׁמַעְתָּ עַל־יַם־סוּף: וַתִּתֵּן אֹתֹת וּמֹפְתִים בְּפַרְעֹה וּבְכָל־עֲבָדָיו וּבְכָל־עַם אַרְצוֹ, כִּי יָדַעְתָּ כִּי הֵזִידוּ עֲלֵיהֶם, וַתַּעַשׂ־לְךָ שֵׁם כְּהַיּוֹם הַזֶּה: ◂ וְהַיָּם בָּקַעְתָּ לִפְנֵיהֶם, וַיַּעַבְרוּ בְתוֹךְ־הַיָּם בַּיַּבָּשָׁה, וְאֶת־רֹדְפֵיהֶם הִשְׁלַכְתָּ בִמְצוֹלֹת כְּמוֹ־אֶבֶן, בְּמַיִם עַזִּים:

וַיּוֹשַׁע *Hashem* saved the Jewish people on that day by rescuing them from Egypt. ▸ When the Jewish people saw that the Egyptians had been killed, they realized that *Hashem* saved them. The greatness of *Hashem*'s actions led the Jews to fear *Hashem,* and they had faith in *Hashem* and in Moshe, *Hashem*'s servant.

אָז יָשִׁיר־מֹשֶׁה Then Moshe and the Jewish people sang this song to *Hashem*:

I will sing to *Hashem* for He has shown His greatness.
He threw all of our enemies, Egyptian horses and riders,
 into the sea.
Hashem gives me strength and protects me.
I will honor *Hashem*by doing His m*itzvot* beautifully,
 for He is my God.
I will praise Him for He is the God of my father.
Hashem is a warrior; His name alone wins wars.
Pharaoh's chariots and army were cast into the sea, drowning
 the best of the Egyptian fighters like stones.
Your hand, *Hashem,* is powerful. Your hand alone defeats
 our enemies.
With a blast of air, You caused the water to split and form
 solid walls on either side.
The enemies said, "I will chase them into the sea, draw
 my sword, and destroy the Jewish people."
Then, You caused another wind to blow, broke down the
 walls of water upon the Egyptians, and drowned
 them like lead.
Who is like You, *Hashem*? No being is as mighty or could
 perform such miracles!

וַיּוֹשַׁע יהוה בַּיּוֹם הַהוּא אֶת־יִשְׂרָאֵל מִיַּד מִצְרָיִם, וַיַּרְא יִשְׂרָאֵל אֶת־מִצְרַיִם מֵת עַל־שְׂפַת הַיָּם: ◂ וַיַּרְא יִשְׂרָאֵל אֶת־הַיָּד הַגְּדֹלָה אֲשֶׁר עָשָׂה יהוה בְּמִצְרַיִם, וַיִּירְאוּ הָעָם אֶת־יהוה, וַיַּאֲמִינוּ בַּיהוה וּבְמֹשֶׁה עַבְדּוֹ:

אָז יָשִׁיר־מֹשֶׁה וּבְנֵי יִשְׂרָאֵל אֶת־הַשִּׁירָה הַזֹּאת לַיהוה, וַיֹּאמְרוּ
לֵאמֹר, אָשִׁירָה לַיהוה כִּי־גָאֹה גָּאָה, סוּס
וְרֹכְבוֹ רָמָה בַיָּם: עָזִּי וְזִמְרָת יָהּ וַיְהִי־לִי
לִישׁוּעָה, זֶה אֵלִי וְאַנְוֵהוּ, אֱלֹהֵי
אָבִי וַאֲרֹמְמֶנְהוּ: יהוה אִישׁ מִלְחָמָה, יהוה
שְׁמוֹ: מַרְכְּבֹת פַּרְעֹה וְחֵילוֹ יָרָה בַיָּם, וּמִבְחַר
שָׁלִשָׁיו טֻבְּעוּ בְיַם־סוּף: תְּהֹמֹת יְכַסְיֻמוּ, יָרְדוּ בִמְצוֹלֹת כְּמוֹ־
אָבֶן: יְמִינְךָ יהוה נֶאְדָּרִי בַּכֹּחַ, יְמִינְךָ
יהוה תִּרְעַץ אוֹיֵב: וּבְרֹב גְּאוֹנְךָ תַּהֲרֹס
קָמֶיךָ, תְּשַׁלַּח חֲרֹנְךָ יֹאכְלֵמוֹ כַּקַּשׁ: וּבְרוּחַ
אַפֶּיךָ נֶעֶרְמוּ מַיִם, נִצְּבוּ כְמוֹ־נֵד
נֹזְלִים, קָפְאוּ תְהֹמֹת בְּלֶב־יָם: אָמַר
אוֹיֵב אֶרְדֹּף, אַשִּׂיג, אֲחַלֵּק שָׁלָל, תִּמְלָאֵמוֹ
נַפְשִׁי, אָרִיק חַרְבִּי תּוֹרִישֵׁמוֹ יָדִי: נָשַׁפְתָּ
בְרוּחֲךָ כִּסָּמוֹ יָם, צָלֲלוּ כַּעוֹפֶרֶת בְּמַיִם
אַדִּירִים: מִי־כָמֹכָה בָּאֵלִם יהוה, מִי
כָּמֹכָה נֶאְדָּר בַּקֹּדֶשׁ, נוֹרָא תְהִלֹּת עֹשֵׂה

You stretched out Your hand causing our enemies to be swallowed by the earth.
With Your great kindness, You then led Your Jewish people to Your Holy place.
When the other nations of the world heard of Your great power they became filled with fear:
The Philistines were gripped with terror.
The chiefs of Edom panicked.
The leaders of Moav trembled beyond control.
The people of Canaan fell apart.
You will bring the Jewish people to Your chosen mountain, build the *Beit HaMikdash*, and reign as King forever.

Hashem shall reign as King forever!
Hashem shall reign as King forever!

When Pharaoh's horses, chariots, and riders went into the sea,
Hashem covered them with water while the Jewish people walked through on dry land.

▸ כִּי *Hashem* is the King,
He rules over all nations.
We will enter Zion and destroy our enemies who are in the land.
Then, on this day,
Hashem will be seen as the only King over all the earth!

פֶלֶא׃ נָטִיתָ יְמִינְךָ תִּבְלָעֵמוֹ אָרֶץ׃ נָחִיתָ
בְחַסְדְּךָ עַם־זוּ גָּאָלְתָּ, נֵהַלְתָּ בְעָזְּךָ אֶל־נְוֵה
קָדְשֶׁךָ׃ שָׁמְעוּ עַמִּים יִרְגָּזוּן, חִיל
אָחַז יֹשְׁבֵי פְּלָשֶׁת׃ אָז נִבְהֲלוּ אַלּוּפֵי
אֱדוֹם, אֵילֵי מוֹאָב יֹאחֲזֵמוֹ רָעַד, נָמֹגוּ
כֹּל יֹשְׁבֵי כְנָעַן׃ תִּפֹּל עֲלֵיהֶם אֵימָתָה
וָפַחַד, בִּגְדֹל זְרוֹעֲךָ יִדְּמוּ כָּאָבֶן, עַד־
יַעֲבֹר עַמְּךָ יהוה, עַד־יַעֲבֹר עַם־זוּ
קָנִיתָ׃ תְּבִאֵמוֹ וְתִטָּעֵמוֹ בְּהַר נַחֲלָתְךָ, מָכוֹן
לְשִׁבְתְּךָ פָּעַלְתָּ יהוה, מִקְּדָשׁ אֲדֹנָי כּוֹנְנוּ
יָדֶיךָ׃ יהוה ׀ יִמְלֹךְ לְעֹלָם וָעֶד׃

יהוה יִמְלֹךְ לְעֹלָם וָעֶד.
יהוה מַלְכוּתֵהּ קָאֵם לְעָלַם וּלְעָלְמֵי עָלְמַיָּא.

כִּי
בָא סוּס פַּרְעֹה בְּרִכְבּוֹ וּבְפָרָשָׁיו בַּיָּם, וַיָּשֶׁב יהוה עֲלֵהֶם אֶת־מֵי
הַיָּם, וּבְנֵי יִשְׂרָאֵל הָלְכוּ בַיַּבָּשָׁה בְּתוֹךְ הַיָּם׃

◂ כִּי לַיהוה הַמְּלוּכָה וּמֹשֵׁל בַּגּוֹיִם׃
וְעָלוּ מוֹשִׁעִים בְּהַר צִיּוֹן לִשְׁפֹּט אֶת־הַר עֵשָׂו
וְהָיְתָה לַיהוה הַמְּלוּכָה׃
וְהָיָה יהוה לְמֶלֶךְ עַל־כָּל־הָאָרֶץ
בַּיּוֹם הַהוּא יִהְיֶה יהוה אֶחָד וּשְׁמוֹ אֶחָד׃

Sit for the following.

THE SOUL

of every living being thanks You, *Hashem,* our God.
For ever and ever You are God;
without You we would have no king or savior.
You rescue us when we are in trouble
and are kind to us in our time of need.
Hashem,
You are God over every living being.
You guide the world with kindness.
Hashem does not sleep or rest;
He is always there to help us with our needs.
We give all of our thanks to *Hashem* alone.
Even if we had:

Mouths as full of song as the sea is full of water,
Tongues as quick as the waves of the sea,
Lips with endless praise like the endless skies,
Eyes as bright as the sun and moon,
Hands that spread as wide as an eagle's wings, and
Feet as fast as a deer,

Sit for the following.

נִשְׁמַת

כָּל חַי תְּבָרֵךְ אֶת שִׁמְךָ, יהוה אֱלֹהֵינוּ
וְרוּחַ כָּל בָּשָׂר תְּפָאֵר וּתְרוֹמֵם זִכְרְךָ מַלְכֵּנוּ תָּמִיד.
מִן הָעוֹלָם וְעַד הָעוֹלָם אַתָּה אֵל
וּמִבַּלְעָדֶיךָ אֵין לָנוּ מֶלֶךְ גּוֹאֵל וּמוֹשִׁיעַ
פּוֹדֶה וּמַצִּיל וּמְפַרְנֵס וּמְרַחֵם
בְּכָל עֵת צָרָה וְצוּקָה אֵין לָנוּ מֶלֶךְ אֶלָּא אָתָּה.
אֱלֹהֵי הָרִאשׁוֹנִים וְהָאַחֲרוֹנִים, אֱלוֹהַּ כָּל בְּרִיּוֹת
אֲדוֹן כָּל תּוֹלָדוֹת, הַמְהֻלָּל בְּרֹב הַתִּשְׁבָּחוֹת
הַמְנַהֵג עוֹלָמוֹ בְּחֶסֶד וּבְרִיּוֹתָיו בְּרַחֲמִים.
וַיהוה לֹא יָנוּם וְלֹא יִישָׁן
הַמְעוֹרֵר יְשֵׁנִים וְהַמֵּקִיץ נִרְדָּמִים
וְהַמֵּשִׂיחַ אִלְּמִים וְהַמַּתִּיר אֲסוּרִים
וְהַסּוֹמֵךְ נוֹפְלִים וְהַזּוֹקֵף כְּפוּפִים.
לְךָ לְבַדְּךָ אֲנַחְנוּ מוֹדִים.
אִלּוּ פִינוּ מָלֵא שִׁירָה כַּיָּם, וּלְשׁוֹנֵנוּ רִנָּה כַּהֲמוֹן גַּלָּיו
וְשִׂפְתוֹתֵינוּ שֶׁבַח כְּמֶרְחֲבֵי רָקִיעַ
וְעֵינֵינוּ מְאִירוֹת כַּשֶּׁמֶשׁ וְכַיָּרֵחַ
וְיָדֵינוּ פְרוּשׂוֹת כְּנִשְׁרֵי שָׁמָיִם
וְרַגְלֵינוּ קַלּוֹת כָּאַיָּלוֹת

We could still not thank You enough, *Hashem*.
Hashem, our God and God of our ancestors,
we thank You for the thousands of kindnesses
You did for us.
You took our ancestors out of slavery in Egypt.
You provided us with food,
gave us everything we need,
and saved us from plagues
and from our enemies.
Hashem,
You have always loved us
and never turned away from Your Jewish people.
Every part of our body turns to thank You.
Every mouth and tongue will thank You,
Every knee will bend to serve You,
Every heart will fear You, and
Every being will sing praises to You.

אֵין אֲנַחְנוּ מַסְפִּיקִים לְהוֹדוֹת לְךָ
יהוה אֱלֹהֵינוּ וֵאלֹהֵי אֲבוֹתֵינוּ
וּלְבָרֵךְ אֶת שְׁמֶךָ עַל אַחַת מֵאֶלֶף אֶלֶף אַלְפֵי אֲלָפִים
וְרִבֵּי רְבָבוֹת פְּעָמִים הַטּוֹבוֹת
שֶׁעָשִׂיתָ עִם אֲבוֹתֵינוּ וְעִמָּנוּ.
מִמִּצְרַיִם גְּאַלְתָּנוּ, יהוה אֱלֹהֵינוּ, וּמִבֵּית עֲבָדִים פְּדִיתָנוּ
בְּרָעָב זַנְתָּנוּ וּבְשָׂבָע כִּלְכַּלְתָּנוּ
מֵחֶרֶב הִצַּלְתָּנוּ וּמִדֶּבֶר מִלַּטְתָּנוּ
וּמֵחֳלָיִים רָעִים וְנֶאֱמָנִים דִּלִּיתָנוּ.
עַד הֵנָּה עֲזָרוּנוּ רַחֲמֶיךָ, וְלֹא עֲזָבוּנוּ חֲסָדֶיךָ
וְאַל תִּטְּשֵׁנוּ, יהוה אֱלֹהֵינוּ, לָנֶצַח.
עַל כֵּן אֵבָרִים שֶׁפִּלַּגְתָּ בָּנוּ
וְרוּחַ וּנְשָׁמָה שֶׁנָּפַחְתָּ בְּאַפֵּינוּ, וְלָשׁוֹן אֲשֶׁר שַׂמְתָּ בְּפִינוּ
הֵן הֵם יוֹדוּ וִיבָרְכוּ וִישַׁבְּחוּ וִיפָאֲרוּ
וִירוֹמְמוּ וְיַעֲרִיצוּ וְיַקְדִּישׁוּ וְיַמְלִיכוּ אֶת שִׁמְךָ מַלְכֵּנוּ
כִּי כָל פֶּה לְךָ יוֹדֶה וְכָל לָשׁוֹן לְךָ תִשָּׁבַע
וְכָל בֶּרֶךְ לְךָ תִכְרַע וְכָל קוֹמָה לְפָנֶיךָ תִשְׁתַּחֲוֶה
וְכָל לְבָבוֹת יִירָאוּךָ וְכָל קֶרֶב וּכְלָיוֹת יְזַמְּרוּ לִשְׁמֶךָ
כַּדָּבָר שֶׁכָּתוּב
כָּל עַצְמֹתַי תֹּאמַרְנָה יהוה מִי כָמוֹךָ
מַצִּיל עָנִי מֵחָזָק מִמֶּנּוּ, וְעָנִי וְאֶבְיוֹן מִגֹּזְלוֹ:

No one can be compared to *Hashem*,
the most mighty and awesome God,
who created heaven and earth.
▸ Like King David,
we will praise and thank You,
Hashem, our God,
with our entire body.
Hashem, our God,
all power belongs to You.

הָאֵל You are great and mighty beyond comparison.
Your actions are awesome
and can only be done by You.
You sit as King on Your holy throne,
high above all else.

On Shabbat the Leader begins here:

שׁוֹכֵן עַד ***HASHEM*** **IS HOLY,**
worthy of praise,
and rules forever.
The righteous sing praises to You, *Hashem*.
▸ Your righteous Jews
use their mouths, tongues, and words
to enthusiastically praise and thank You.
The most holy people will honor You.

מִי יִדְמֶה לָּךְ וּמִי יִשְׁוֶה לָּךְ וּמִי יַעֲרָךְ לָךְ.
הָאֵל הַגָּדוֹל, הַגִּבּוֹר וְהַנּוֹרָא, אֵל עֶלְיוֹן
קֹנֵה שָׁמַיִם וָאָרֶץ.

◂ נְהַלֶּלְךָ וּנְשַׁבֵּחֲךָ וּנְפָאֶרְךָ וּנְבָרֵךְ אֶת שֵׁם קָדְשֶׁךָ, כָּאָמוּר
לְדָוִד, בָּרְכִי נַפְשִׁי אֶת־יהוה
וְכָל־קְרָבַי אֶת־שֵׁם קָדְשׁוֹ:

הָאֵל בְּתַעֲצוּמוֹת עֻזֶּךָ
הַגָּדוֹל בִּכְבוֹד שְׁמֶךָ
הַגִּבּוֹר לָנֶצַח וְהַנּוֹרָא בְּנוֹרְאוֹתֶיךָ
הַמֶּלֶךְ הַיּוֹשֵׁב עַל כִּסֵּא
רָם וְנִשָּׂא

On שבת the חזן begins here:

שׁוֹכֵן עַד

מָרוֹם וְקָדוֹשׁ שְׁמוֹ
וְכָתוּב
רַנְּנוּ צַדִּיקִים בַּיהוה, לַיְשָׁרִים נָאוָה תְהִלָּה:

◂ בְּפִי יְשָׁרִים תִּתְהַלָּל
וּבְדִבְרֵי צַדִּיקִים תִּתְבָּרַךְ
וּבִלְשׁוֹן חֲסִידִים תִּתְרוֹמָם
וּבְקֶרֶב קְדוֹשִׁים תִּתְקַדָּשׁ

וּבְמַקְהֲלוֹת Tens of thousands of Your Jewish people
will gather to sing praises to You, *Hashem*, our King.
Hashem,
Our God and God of ancestors,
▸ it is our job
to thank, praise, and honor You
with unlimited words and song
like King David Your loyal servant.

Stand until after "Let us thank" on page 468.

יִשְׁתַּבַּח We sing praises
to You, *Hashem*,
as You are our King and God.
You rule over the heavens and earth
with great strength and power.
Now and forever,
we owe You
▸ unlimited blessings and thanks.
Thank You, *Hashem*,
our God, King,
and Creator of life.

וּבְמַקְהֲלוֹת רִבְבוֹת עַמְּךָ בֵּית יִשְׂרָאֵל
בְּרִנָּה יִתְפָּאַר שִׁמְךָ מַלְכֵּנוּ בְּכָל דּוֹר וָדוֹר
◂ שֶׁכֵּן חוֹבַת כָּל הַיְצוּרִים
לְפָנֶיךָ יהוה אֱלֹהֵינוּ וֵאלֹהֵי אֲבוֹתֵינוּ
לְהוֹדוֹת, לְהַלֵּל, לְשַׁבֵּחַ, לְפָאֵר, לְרוֹמֵם
לְהַדֵּר, לְבָרֵךְ, לְעַלֵּה וּלְקַלֵּס
עַל כָּל דִּבְרֵי שִׁירוֹת וְתִשְׁבְּחוֹת
דָּוִד בֶּן יִשַׁי, עַבְדְּךָ מְשִׁיחֶךָ.

Stand until after בָּרְכוּ *on page 469.*

יִשְׁתַּבַּח

שִׁמְךָ לָעַד, מַלְכֵּנוּ
הָאֵל הַמֶּלֶךְ הַגָּדוֹל וְהַקָּדוֹשׁ בַּשָּׁמַיִם וּבָאָרֶץ
כִּי לְךָ נָאֶה, יהוה אֱלֹהֵינוּ וֵאלֹהֵי אֲבוֹתֵינוּ
שִׁיר וּשְׁבָחָה, הַלֵּל וְזִמְרָה
עֹז וּמֶמְשָׁלָה, נֶצַח, גְּדֻלָּה וּגְבוּרָה
תְּהִלָּה וְתִפְאֶרֶת, קְדֻשָּׁה וּמַלְכוּת
◂ בְּרָכוֹת וְהוֹדָאוֹת, מֵעַתָּה וְעַד עוֹלָם.
בָּרוּךְ אַתָּה יהוה, אֵל מֶלֶךְ גָּדוֹל בַּתִּשְׁבָּחוֹת
אֵל הַהוֹדָאוֹת, אֲדוֹן הַנִּפְלָאוֹת
הַבּוֹחֵר בְּשִׁירֵי זִמְרָה, מֶלֶךְ, אֵל, חֵי הָעוֹלָמִים.

Between Rosh HaShana and Yom Kippur, add the following paragraph.

שִׁיר הַמַּעֲלוֹת From the depths of my soul, I call to You, *Hashem,* when I need You the most. Please hear my cries, *Hashem,* and listen to my requests. You, *Hashem,* forgive our mistakes, so we can be deserving of being helped. I put all my hope in You, *Hashem,* and constantly look forward to the time when You will bring *Mashiach*. *Hashem,* in Your kindness save Your Jewish people.

HALF KADDISH

Leader: יִתְגַּדַּל May *Hashem* be recognized
as great and holy (*Congregation:* Amen)
in the world that He created.
May He establish His kingdom
during my lifetime
and the lifetime of all Jews,
quickly and soon.
Let us say:
"Amen" (*Congregation:* Amen).

Congregation: May we thank *Hashem* for ever and ever.
Leader: May we thank *Hashem* for ever and ever.

Leader: *Hashem* should be thanked, praised,
and honored (*Congregation:* He is blessed).
Hashem is beyond all the blessings,
songs, or praises
that we could offer.
Let us say:
"Amen" (*Congregation:* Amen).

During the עשרת ימי תשובה*, add the following paragraph.*

שִׁיר הַמַּעֲלוֹת, מִמַּעֲמַקִּים קְרָאתִיךָ יהוה: אֲדֹנָי שִׁמְעָה בְקוֹלִי, תִּהְיֶינָה אָזְנֶיךָ קַשֻּׁבוֹת לְקוֹל תַּחֲנוּנָי: אִם־עֲוֹנוֹת תִּשְׁמָר־יָהּ, אֲדֹנָי מִי יַעֲמֹד: כִּי־עִמְּךָ הַסְּלִיחָה, לְמַעַן תִּוָּרֵא: קִוִּיתִי יהוה קִוְּתָה נַפְשִׁי, וְלִדְבָרוֹ הוֹחָלְתִּי: נַפְשִׁי לַאדֹנָי, מִשֹּׁמְרִים לַבֹּקֶר, שֹׁמְרִים לַבֹּקֶר: יַחֵל יִשְׂרָאֵל אֶל יהוה, כִּי־עִם־יהוה הַחֶסֶד, וְהַרְבֵּה עִמּוֹ פְדוּת: וְהוּא יִפְדֶּה אֶת־יִשְׂרָאֵל, מִכֹּל עֲוֹנוֹתָיו:

חצי קדיש

חזן: יִתְגַּדַּל וְיִתְקַדַּשׁ שְׁמֵהּ רַבָּא (קהל: אָמֵן)
בְּעָלְמָא דִּי בְרָא כִרְעוּתֵהּ, וְיַמְלִיךְ מַלְכוּתֵהּ
בְּחַיֵּיכוֹן וּבְיוֹמֵיכוֹן וּבְחַיֵּי דְכָל בֵּית יִשְׂרָאֵל
בַּעֲגָלָא וּבִזְמַן קָרִיב, וְאִמְרוּ אָמֵן. (קהל: אָמֵן)

קהל יְהֵא שְׁמֵהּ רַבָּא מְבָרַךְ לְעָלַם וּלְעָלְמֵי עָלְמַיָּא.
חזן: יְהֵא שְׁמֵהּ רַבָּא מְבָרַךְ לְעָלַם וּלְעָלְמֵי עָלְמַיָּא.

חזן: יִתְבָּרַךְ וְיִשְׁתַּבַּח וְיִתְפָּאַר וְיִתְרוֹמַם וְיִתְנַשֵּׂא
וְיִתְהַדָּר וְיִתְעַלֶּה וְיִתְהַלָּל
שְׁמֵהּ דְּקֻדְשָׁא בְּרִיךְ הוּא (קהל: בְּרִיךְ הוּא)
לְעֵלָּא מִן כָּל בִּרְכָתָא
/בשבת שובה: לְעֵלָּא לְעֵלָּא מִכָּל בִּרְכָתָא/
וְשִׁירָתָא, תֻּשְׁבְּחָתָא וְנֶחֱמָתָא
דַּאֲמִירָן בְּעָלְמָא, וְאִמְרוּ אָמֵן. (קהל: אָמֵן)

BLESSINGS OF THE SHEMA

Only say the following introduction when praying with a minyan:
Bow when saying the word "Thank."

Leader: **LET US THANK**
Hashem, for He deserves thanksgiving.

Congregation: Thank *Hashem* for ever and ever!

Leader: Thank *Hashem* for ever and ever!

Those praying without a minyan begin here:
Sit when saying this section.

בָּרוּךְ Thank You, *Hashem,* our God, King of the world,
Who creates light and darkness,
Makes peace, and creates all.

הַכֹּל יוֹדוּךָ Everyone and everything will thank
and praise You, *Hashem.*
They will all say that there is nothing
as holy as *Hashem.*
Everyone and everything celebrates
that You created the world and everything in it.
Every day, You allow the light of dawn to shine on earth.

הַכֹּל יוֹדוּךָ וְהַכֹּל יְשַׁבְּחוּךָ *Everyone and everything will thank and praise You, Hashem. Hashem* created the entire world from nothing. He created darkness and light, land and water, mountains and grass, trees and plants, animals and people.
Therefore, every person, being, and creation owes gratitude to *Hashem.*

קריאת שמע וברכותיה

Only say the following introduction when praying with a מנין*:*

Bow when saying the word בָּרוּךְ*.*

חזן: **בָּרְכוּ**

אֶת יהוה הַמְבֹרָךְ.

קהל: בָּרוּךְ יהוה הַמְבֹרָךְ לְעוֹלָם וָעֶד.

חזן: **בָּרוּךְ יהוה הַמְבֹרָךְ לְעוֹלָם וָעֶד.**

Those praying without a מנין *begin here:*

Sit when saying this section.

בָּרוּךְ אַתָּה יהוה אֱלֹהֵינוּ מֶלֶךְ הָעוֹלָם
יוֹצֵר אוֹר וּבוֹרֵא חֹשֶׁךְ
עֹשֶׂה שָׁלוֹם וּבוֹרֵא אֶת הַכֹּל.

הַכֹּל יוֹדְוּךָ וְהַכֹּל יְשַׁבְּחְוּךָ
וְהַכֹּל יֹאמְרוּ אֵין קָדוֹשׁ כַּיהוה
הַכֹּל יְרוֹמְמְוּךָ סֶּלָה, יוֹצֵר הַכֹּל.
הָאֵל הַפּוֹתֵחַ בְּכָל יוֹם דַּלְתוֹת שַׁעֲרֵי מִזְרָח
וּבוֹקֵעַ חַלּוֹנֵי רָקִיעַ

You bring out the sun and moon
to give light to the whole world that You created.
With kindness, *Hashem* recreates the world every day.
Hashem has been praised as King
since the beginning of time.
Hashem, You will always be God.
Have mercy on us, protect us, and keep us safe.
You, *Hashem*, are the only God
and there would be nothing in the world without You.

▸ Nothing can be compared to You,
Hashem, in this world or the World-to-come.
No other god will bring our redemption
in the days of *Mashiach*.
Only You, *Hashem*, will bring the dead back to life.

א אֵל אָדוֹן *Hashem* is God over all creations.
ב He is thanked by all.
ג His greatness and goodness fill the world.
ד He knows everything.

אֵין כְּעֶרְכְּךָ, יהוה אֱלֹהֵינוּ, בָּעוֹלָם הַזֶּה, וְאֵין זוּלָתְךָ, מַלְכֵּנוּ, לְחַיֵּי הָעוֹלָם הַבָּא
Nothing can be compared to You, Hashem, in this world or the World-to-come. *Hashem* rewards those who make good decisions when faced with challenges. In this world, "*olam hazeh*," we live lives filled with challenges and decisions every day. For example, when we are tired and in bed, we must decide whether we will get up and pray. However, in the World-to-come, "*olam haba*," *Hashem* will be understood by all. Then, doing *mitzvot* and praying will be less of a challenge, as it is easier to serve the King when He sits before you. We try our best to make good decisions in *olam hazeh* with the hope that we will be rewarded in *olam haba*.

מוֹצִיא חַמָּה מִמְּקוֹמָהּ וּלְבָנָה מִמְּכוֹן שִׁבְתָּהּ
וּמֵאִיר לָעוֹלָם כֻּלּוֹ וּלְיוֹשְׁבָיו שֶׁבָּרָא בְּמִדַּת הָרַחֲמִים.
הַמֵּאִיר לָאָרֶץ וְלַדָּרִים עָלֶיהָ בְּרַחֲמִים
וּבְטוּבוֹ מְחַדֵּשׁ בְּכָל יוֹם תָּמִיד מַעֲשֵׂה בְרֵאשִׁית.
הַמֶּלֶךְ הַמְרוֹמָם לְבַדּוֹ מֵאָז
הַמְשֻׁבָּח וְהַמְפֹאָר וְהַמִּתְנַשֵּׂא מִימוֹת עוֹלָם.
אֱלֹהֵי עוֹלָם, בְּרַחֲמֶיךָ הָרַבִּים רַחֵם עָלֵינוּ
אֲדוֹן עֻזֵּנוּ, צוּר מִשְׂגַּבֵּנוּ, מָגֵן יִשְׁעֵנוּ, מִשְׂגָּב בַּעֲדֵנוּ.

אֵין כְּעֶרְכֶּךָ
וְאֵין זוּלָתֶךָ
אֶפֶס בִּלְתֶּךָ
וּמִי דּוֹמֶה לָּךְ.

◂ אֵין כְּעֶרְכְּךָ, יהוה אֱלֹהֵינוּ, בָּעוֹלָם הַזֶּה
וְאֵין זוּלָתְךָ, מַלְכֵּנוּ, לְחַיֵּי הָעוֹלָם הַבָּא
אֶפֶס בִּלְתְּךָ, גּוֹאֲלֵנוּ, לִימוֹת הַמָּשִׁיחַ
וְאֵין דּוֹמֶה לְּךָ, מוֹשִׁיעֵנוּ, לִתְחִיַּת הַמֵּתִים.

אֵל אָדוֹן עַל כָּל הַמַּעֲשִׂים
בָּרוּךְ וּמְבֹרָךְ בְּפִי כָּל נְשָׁמָה
גָּדְלוֹ וְטוּבוֹ מָלֵא עוֹלָם
דַּעַת וּתְבוּנָה סוֹבְבִים אוֹתוֹ.

ה *Hashem* is above the holy angels.
ו He is honored.
ז *Hashem* judges fairly and with merit.
ח *Hashem* rules from His throne with kindness.

ט *Hashem* created the stars for good.
י Only *Hashem* has
the knowledge and understanding
to have made them.
כ He gives the stars the strength to shine
throughout the world.
ל The stars provide light in the dark of night.

מ The shining stars bring honor to *Hashem*.
נ The light of the stars is beautiful
throughout the world.
ש The stars are happy
when they leave in the morning
and when they return at night.
ע The stars fulfill the will of *Hashem*.

פ The stars beautify and honor *Hashem*.
צ With song, they celebrate *Hashem* being King.
ק He created the sun and gave it light.
ר He formed the moon.

ש All the angels praise *Hashem*.
ת They call *Hashem* great and holy.

הַמִּתְגָּאֶה עַל חַיּוֹת הַקֹּדֶשׁ
וְנֶהְדָּר בְּכָבוֹד עַל הַמֶּרְכָּבָה
זְכוּת וּמִישׁוֹר לִפְנֵי כִסְאוֹ
חֶסֶד וְרַחֲמִים לִפְנֵי כְבוֹדוֹ.

טוֹבִים מְאוֹרוֹת שֶׁבָּרָא אֱלֹהֵינוּ
יְצָרָם בְּדַעַת בְּבִינָה וּבְהַשְׂכֵּל
כֹּחַ וּגְבוּרָה נָתַן בָּהֶם
לִהְיוֹת מוֹשְׁלִים בְּקֶרֶב תֵּבֵל.

מְלֵאִים זִיו וּמְפִיקִים נֹגַהּ
נָאֶה זִיוָם בְּכָל הָעוֹלָם
שְׂמֵחִים בְּצֵאתָם וְשָׂשִׂים בְּבוֹאָם
עוֹשִׂים בְּאֵימָה רְצוֹן קוֹנָם.

פְּאֵר וְכָבוֹד נוֹתְנִים לִשְׁמוֹ
צָהֳלָה וְרִנָּה לְזֵכֶר מַלְכוּתוֹ
קָרָא לַשֶּׁמֶשׁ וַיִּזְרַח אוֹר
רָאָה וְהִתְקִין צוּרַת הַלְּבָנָה.

שֶׁבַח נוֹתְנִים לוֹ כָּל צְבָא מָרוֹם
תִּפְאֶרֶת וּגְדֻלָּה, שְׂרָפִים וְאוֹפַנִּים
וְחַיּוֹת הַקֹּדֶשׁ.

לָאֵל After creating the world in six days,
Hashem rested on His throne on the seventh day.
Hashem declared the seventh day holy and
set it aside as a day of enjoyment.
We praise and thank *Hashem* in joy,
because He rested on the seventh day.
Hashem gave us a day of rest,
and therefore all that He created
should thank, praise, and honor Him.
The name of *Hashem* is holy;
His greatness is known and remembered
in the heavens and earth.
You are deserving of thanks,
Hashem, our savior, and creator of light.

תִּתְבָּרַךְ Thank You, our Protector and King,
for creating holy beings.
May You be praised forever!
Our everlasting King and living God,
You created angels
who announce Your holy words.

עֹנֶג קָרָא לְיוֹם הַשַּׁבָּת *Set it aside as a day of enjoyment.* We honor Shabbat by doing actions that show *Kavod*, honor toward Shabbat, and activities that involve *Oneg*, enjoyment of Shabbat. Honoring Shabbat includes wearing nice clothing, setting a table nicely, and preparing all week long. *Oneg Shabbat* includes eating tasty foods, resting, and spending time studying Torah. Both honoring and enjoying Shabbat make the day special and meaningful.

לָאֵל אֲשֶׁר שָׁבַת מִכָּל הַמַּעֲשִׂים
בַּיּוֹם הַשְּׁבִיעִי נִתְעַלָּה וְיָשַׁב עַל כִּסֵּא כְבוֹדוֹ.
תִּפְאֶרֶת עָטָה לְיוֹם הַמְּנוּחָה, עֹנֶג קָרָא לְיוֹם הַשַּׁבָּת.
זֶה שֶׁבַח שֶׁלַּיּוֹם הַשְּׁבִיעִי שֶׁבּוֹ שָׁבַת אֵל מִכָּל מְלַאכְתּוֹ
וְיוֹם הַשְּׁבִיעִי מְשַׁבֵּחַ וְאוֹמֵר
מִזְמוֹר שִׁיר לְיוֹם הַשַּׁבָּת, טוֹב לְהֹדוֹת לַיהוה:
לְפִיכָךְ יְפָאֲרוּ וִיבָרְכוּ לָאֵל כָּל יְצוּרָיו
שֶׁבַח יְקָר וּגְדֻלָּה יִתְּנוּ לָאֵל מֶלֶךְ יוֹצֵר כֹּל
הַמַּנְחִיל מְנוּחָה לְעַמּוֹ יִשְׂרָאֵל בִּקְדֻשָּׁתוֹ
בְּיוֹם שַׁבַּת קֹדֶשׁ.
שִׁמְךָ יהוה אֱלֹהֵינוּ יִתְקַדַּשׁ, וְזִכְרְךָ מַלְכֵּנוּ יִתְפָּאַר
בַּשָּׁמַיִם מִמַּעַל וְעַל הָאָרֶץ מִתָּחַת.
תִּתְבָּרַךְ מוֹשִׁיעֵנוּ עַל שֶׁבַח מַעֲשֵׂה יָדֶיךָ
וְעַל מְאוֹרֵי אוֹר שֶׁעָשִׂיתָ, יְפָאֲרוּךָ סֶּלָה.

תִּתְבָּרַךְ
צוּרֵנוּ מַלְכֵּנוּ וְגוֹאֲלֵנוּ, בּוֹרֵא קְדוֹשִׁים
יִשְׁתַּבַּח שִׁמְךָ לָעַד, מַלְכֵּנוּ, יוֹצֵר מְשָׁרְתִים
וַאֲשֶׁר מְשָׁרְתָיו כֻּלָּם עוֹמְדִים בְּרוּם עוֹלָם
וּמַשְׁמִיעִים בְּיִרְאָה יַחַד בְּקוֹל
דִּבְרֵי אֱלֹהִים חַיִּים וּמֶלֶךְ עוֹלָם.

The angels perform the will of their Creator, *Hashem,*
with purity, might, appreciation, and devotion.
▸ The angels open their holy and pure mouths
in song to:

Bless,
Praise,
Give honor to, and
Declare the Kingship of –

Hashem, our God,
the great, mighty, awesome, and holy King.
▸ All of the angels accept upon themselves
the responsibility of serving *Hashem.*
They dedicate themselves to *Hashem,*
their Creator,
by praising Him
with pure speech and sweet songs.
Together as one,
all of the angels announce *Hashem*'s holiness
by saying:

Say the following line out loud:
"Holy, holy, holy is *Hashem*:
the world is filled with His honor!"

▸ In response, the angels turn to each other
and enthusiastically praise *Hashem*
by saying:

Say the following line out loud:
"Blessed is the honor of *Hashem*!"

כֻּלָּם אֲהוּבִים, כֻּלָּם בְּרוּרִים, כֻּלָּם גִּבּוֹרִים
וְכֻלָּם עוֹשִׂים בְּאֵימָה וּבְיִרְאָה רְצוֹן קוֹנָם
◂ וְכֻלָּם פּוֹתְחִים אֶת פִּיהֶם בִּקְדֻשָּׁה וּבְטָהֳרָה
בְּשִׁירָה וּבְזִמְרָה
וּמְבָרְכִים וּמְשַׁבְּחִים וּמְפָאֲרִים
וּמַעֲרִיצִים וּמַקְדִּישִׁים וּמַמְלִיכִים ◂
אֶת שֵׁם הָאֵל הַמֶּלֶךְ הַגָּדוֹל, הַגִּבּוֹר וְהַנּוֹרָא
קָדוֹשׁ הוּא.
◂ וְכֻלָּם מְקַבְּלִים עֲלֵיהֶם עֹל מַלְכוּת שָׁמַיִם זֶה מִזֶּה
וְנוֹתְנִים רְשׁוּת זֶה לָזֶה לְהַקְדִּישׁ לְיוֹצְרָם בְּנַחַת רוּחַ
בְּשָׂפָה בְרוּרָה וּבִנְעִימָה
קְדֻשָּׁה כֻּלָּם כְּאֶחָד
עוֹנִים וְאוֹמְרִים בְּיִרְאָה

Say the following line out loud:

קָדוֹשׁ, קָדוֹשׁ, קָדוֹשׁ יהוה צְבָאוֹת
מְלֹא כָל־הָאָרֶץ כְּבוֹדוֹ:

◂ וְהָאוֹפַנִּים וְחַיּוֹת הַקֹּדֶשׁ
בְּרַעַשׁ גָּדוֹל מִתְנַשְּׂאִים לְעֻמַּת שְׂרָפִים
לְעֻמָּתָם מְשַׁבְּחִים וְאוֹמְרִים

Say the following line out loud:

בָּרוּךְ כְּבוֹד־יהוה מִמְּקוֹמוֹ:

לְאֵל בָּרוּךְ Sing sweet songs of praise
to *Hashem*, our King,
the living God who alone:

Acts with great might,
Creates new things,
Is the Master of war,
Rewards those who act kindly,
Rescues us,
Creates cures,
Deserves praise, and
Performs miracles.

In His greatness,
Hashem renews the works of creation every day.

May You, *Hashem*,
continue to recreate the sun, moon, and stars,
so that we, Your Jewish people,
may enjoy that light.

▸ *Hashem*, please allow that light to shine
on a rebuilt Jerusalem.
Thank You, *Hashem*, who creates the sources of light.

הַמְחַדֵּשׁ בְּטוּבוֹ בְּכָל יוֹם תָּמִיד מַעֲשֵׂה בְרֵאשִׁית *Hashem renews the works of creation every day.* Everything in the world that *Hashem* created is re-created every day. For example, *Hashem* takes away our souls when we sleep and returns them to us when we wake up, making us like new. When we wake up, it is as if we are new people and therefore we should try to achieve new levels. Similarly, every creation that *Hashem* formed has a renewed purpose each and every day.

לָאֵל בָּרוּךְ נְעִימוֹת יִתֵּנוּ
לַמֶּלֶךְ אֵל חַי וְקַיָּם
זְמִירוֹת יֹאמֵרוּ
וְתִשְׁבָּחוֹת יַשְׁמִיעוּ
כִּי הוּא לְבַדּוֹ
פּוֹעֵל גְּבוּרוֹת
עוֹשֶׂה חֲדָשׁוֹת
בַּעַל מִלְחָמוֹת
זוֹרֵעַ צְדָקוֹת
מַצְמִיחַ יְשׁוּעוֹת
בּוֹרֵא רְפוּאוֹת
נוֹרָא תְהִלּוֹת
אֲדוֹן הַנִּפְלָאוֹת

הַמְחַדֵּשׁ בְּטוּבוֹ בְּכָל יוֹם תָּמִיד מַעֲשֵׂה בְרֵאשִׁית

כָּאָמוּר
לְעֹשֵׂה אוֹרִים גְּדֹלִים
כִּי לְעוֹלָם חַסְדּוֹ:

‹ אוֹר חָדָשׁ עַל צִיּוֹן תָּאִיר
וְנִזְכֶּה כֻלָּנוּ מְהֵרָה לְאוֹרוֹ.
בָּרוּךְ אַתָּה יהוה, יוֹצֵר הַמְּאוֹרוֹת.

אַהֲבָה רַבָּה You, *Hashem*, have shown us
great love and kindness.
Our Father and King,
remember our ancestors who put their trust in You.
Just as You taught them the laws of Your Torah
and guided them on how to live life,
please teach and guide us as well.
Just as a father shows kindness to a child,
please show kindness to us.
Let our hearts desire to:
Understand,
Listen,
Learn,
Teach,
Keep,
Perform, and
Fulfill,
All the laws of Your Torah with love.
Let our eyes see and understand more of Your Torah,
and let our hearts continue to grow in love
for Your *mitzvot*.
As one nation, let all of our hearts join together
to love You, *Hashem*.
We believe that we will soon rejoice in being saved by You.

Those wearing TZITZIT *should pick them up in their left hand.*

Today, the Jewish people are scattered
all over the world.
Please bring us back to our land, Israel, peacefully.

אַהֲבָה רַבָּה אֲהַבְתָּנוּ, יהוה אֱלֹהֵינוּ
חֶמְלָה גְדוֹלָה וִיתֵרָה חָמַלְתָּ עָלֵינוּ.
אָבִינוּ מַלְכֵּנוּ
בַּעֲבוּר אֲבוֹתֵינוּ שֶׁבָּטְחוּ בְךָ
וַתְּלַמְּדֵם חֻקֵּי חַיִּים
כֵּן תְּחָנֵּנוּ וּתְלַמְּדֵנוּ.
אָבִינוּ, הָאָב הָרַחֲמָן, הַמְרַחֵם
רַחֵם עָלֵינוּ, וְתֵן בְּלִבֵּנוּ
לְהָבִין וּלְהַשְׂכִּיל, לִשְׁמֹעַ
לִלְמֹד וּלְלַמֵּד
לִשְׁמֹר וְלַעֲשׂוֹת, וּלְקַיֵּם
אֶת כָּל דִּבְרֵי תַלְמוּד תּוֹרָתֶךָ בְּאַהֲבָה.
וְהָאֵר עֵינֵינוּ בְּתוֹרָתֶךָ
וְדַבֵּק לִבֵּנוּ בְּמִצְוֹתֶיךָ
וְיַחֵד לְבָבֵנוּ לְאַהֲבָה וּלְיִרְאָה אֶת שְׁמֶךָ
וְלֹא נֵבוֹשׁ לְעוֹלָם וָעֶד.
כִּי בְשֵׁם קָדְשְׁךָ הַגָּדוֹל וְהַנּוֹרָא בָּטָחְנוּ
נָגִילָה וְנִשְׂמְחָה בִּישׁוּעָתֶךָ.

Those wearing ציצית *should pick them up in their left hand.*

וַהֲבִיאֵנוּ לְשָׁלוֹם מֵאַרְבַּע כַּנְפוֹת הָאָרֶץ
וְתוֹלִיכֵנוּ קוֹמְמִיּוּת לְאַרְצֵנוּ.

▸ As God, You chose us from all the nations of the world,
and we trust that You will save us.
You have brought us close to You
so we can lovingly praise and thank You.
Thank You, *Hashem*,
for showing us love
by choosing us as Your people.

Say this line when praying alone:

God, You are our trustworthy King.

Cover your eyes with your right hand, and say this line aloud:

LISTEN AND UNDERSTAND, JEWISH PEOPLE,
HASHEM IS OUR ONE AND ONLY GOD.

Say this line quietly:

Thank You, *Hashem*, our God.
Your kingdom lasts forever.

וְאָהַבְתָּ Love *Hashem*, your God,
with all of your heart, soul, and belongings.
Live according to God's words and *mitzvot*.
Think about and recite the Shema
when sitting in your home,
when traveling on the road,
when you go to sleep at night,
and when you first wake up in the morning.
Wear *tefillin* on your arm and head,
and hang a *mezuzah* on your door.

◂ כִּי אֵל פּוֹעֵל יְשׁוּעוֹת אָתָּה
וּבָנוּ בָחַרְתָּ מִכָּל עַם וְלָשׁוֹן
וְקֵרַבְתָּנוּ לְשִׁמְךָ הַגָּדוֹל סֶלָה, בֶּאֱמֶת
לְהוֹדוֹת לְךָ וּלְיַחֶדְךָ בְּאַהֲבָה.
בָּרוּךְ אַתָּה יהוה, הַבּוֹחֵר בְּעַמּוֹ יִשְׂרָאֵל בְּאַהֲבָה.

Say this line when praying alone:

אֵל מֶלֶךְ נֶאֱמָן

Cover your eyes with your right hand, and say this line aloud:

שְׁמַע יִשְׂרָאֵל, יהוה אֱלֹהֵינוּ, יהוה ׀ אֶחָד:

Say this line quietly:

בָּרוּךְ שֵׁם כְּבוֹד מַלְכוּתוֹ לְעוֹלָם וָעֶד.

וְאָהַבְתָּ אֵת יהוה אֱלֹהֶיךָ
בְּכָל־לְבָבְךָ וּבְכָל־נַפְשְׁךָ וּבְכָל־מְאֹדֶךָ:
וְהָיוּ הַדְּבָרִים הָאֵלֶּה
אֲשֶׁר אָנֹכִי מְצַוְּךָ הַיּוֹם, עַל־לְבָבֶךָ:
וְשִׁנַּנְתָּם לְבָנֶיךָ וְדִבַּרְתָּ בָּם
בְּשִׁבְתְּךָ בְּבֵיתֶךָ וּבְלֶכְתְּךָ בַדֶּרֶךְ, וּבְשָׁכְבְּךָ וּבְקוּמֶךָ:
וּקְשַׁרְתָּם לְאוֹת עַל־יָדֶךָ
וְהָיוּ לְטֹטָפֹת בֵּין עֵינֶיךָ:
וּכְתַבְתָּם עַל־מְזֻזוֹת בֵּיתֶךָ וּבִשְׁעָרֶיךָ:

וְהָיָה If you live according to the *mitzvot* of *Hashem,*
loving and serving Him with all your effort,
Hashem will give you reward.
Hashem will bring rain for your plants to grow
and provide you with the food you need to live.
However, if you sin
and do not serve *Hashem,*
there will be consequences and punishments;
Hashem might not provide you
with health, money,
or other basics you need to live.
Therefore,
be careful to follow *Hashem*'s *mitzvot*
and set yourself reminders,
such as wearing *tefillin* on your arms and head,
and placing *mezuzot* on your doorposts.
If you do this,
you will live a long life.

וְהָיָה אִם־שָׁמֹעַ תִּשְׁמְעוּ אֶל־מִצְוֹתַי
אֲשֶׁר אָנֹכִי מְצַוֶּה אֶתְכֶם הַיּוֹם
לְאַהֲבָה אֶת־יהוה אֱלֹהֵיכֶם וּלְעָבְדוֹ
בְּכָל־לְבַבְכֶם וּבְכָל־נַפְשְׁכֶם:
וְנָתַתִּי מְטַר־אַרְצְכֶם בְּעִתּוֹ, יוֹרֶה וּמַלְקוֹשׁ
וְאָסַפְתָּ דְגָנֶךָ וְתִירֹשְׁךָ וְיִצְהָרֶךָ:
וְנָתַתִּי עֵשֶׂב בְּשָׂדְךָ לִבְהֶמְתֶּךָ, וְאָכַלְתָּ וְשָׂבָעְתָּ:
הִשָּׁמְרוּ לָכֶם פֶּן־יִפְתֶּה לְבַבְכֶם
וְסַרְתֶּם וַעֲבַדְתֶּם אֱלֹהִים אֲחֵרִים וְהִשְׁתַּחֲוִיתֶם לָהֶם:
וְחָרָה אַף־יהוה בָּכֶם, וְעָצַר אֶת־הַשָּׁמַיִם וְלֹא־יִהְיֶה מָטָר
וְהָאֲדָמָה לֹא תִתֵּן אֶת־יְבוּלָהּ
וַאֲבַדְתֶּם מְהֵרָה מֵעַל הָאָרֶץ הַטֹּבָה אֲשֶׁר יהוה נֹתֵן לָכֶם:
וְשַׂמְתֶּם אֶת־דְּבָרַי אֵלֶּה עַל־לְבַבְכֶם וְעַל־נַפְשְׁכֶם
וּקְשַׁרְתֶּם אֹתָם לְאוֹת עַל־יֶדְכֶם
וְהָיוּ לְטוֹטָפֹת בֵּין עֵינֵיכֶם:
וְלִמַּדְתֶּם אֹתָם אֶת־בְּנֵיכֶם לְדַבֵּר בָּם
בְּשִׁבְתְּךָ בְּבֵיתֶךָ וּבְלֶכְתְּךָ בַדֶּרֶךְ, וּבְשָׁכְבְּךָ וּבְקוּמֶךָ:
וּכְתַבְתָּם עַל־מְזוּזוֹת בֵּיתֶךָ וּבִשְׁעָרֶיךָ:
לְמַעַן יִרְבּוּ יְמֵיכֶם וִימֵי בְנֵיכֶם עַל הָאֲדָמָה
אֲשֶׁר נִשְׁבַּע יהוה לַאֲבֹתֵיכֶם לָתֵת לָהֶם
כִּימֵי הַשָּׁמַיִם עַל־הָאָרֶץ:

Place your TZITZIT in your right hand and kiss them each time you read the word "TZITZIT."

Look at your TZITZIT when you read the words "YOU CAN SEE THEM."

וַיֹּאמֶר *Hashem* told Moshe
that we, the Jewish people,
should have *tzitzit*
on the corners of our clothing.
Each set of *tzitzit* strings
should have a blue string.
The *tzitzit* should be worn
so that you can see them.
They will remind you to focus on God
and His *mitzvot*.
Hashem, the same God
who miraculously saved the Jewish people
from slavery in Egypt,
is your God.

THIS IS TRUE.

The Leader repeats:

‣ *Hashem* is your true God.

Place your ציצית *in your right hand and kiss them each time you read the word* ציצית.
Look at your ציצית *when you read the words* וּרְאִיתֶם אֹתוֹ.

וַיֹּ֥אמֶר יְהֹוָ֖ה אֶל־מֹשֶׁ֥ה לֵּאמֹֽר׃
דַּבֵּ֞ר אֶל־בְּנֵ֤י יִשְׂרָאֵל֙ וְאָמַרְתָּ֣ אֲלֵהֶ֔ם
וְעָשׂ֨וּ לָהֶ֥ם צִיצִ֛ת עַל־כַּנְפֵ֥י בִגְדֵיהֶ֖ם לְדֹרֹתָ֑ם
וְנָ֥תְנ֛וּ עַל־צִיצִ֥ת הַכָּנָ֖ף פְּתִ֥יל תְּכֵֽלֶת׃
וְהָיָ֣ה לָכֶם֮ לְצִיצִת֒
וּרְאִיתֶ֣ם אֹת֗וֹ
וּזְכַרְתֶּם֙ אֶת־כָּל־מִצְוֺ֣ת יְהֹוָ֔ה וַעֲשִׂיתֶ֖ם אֹתָ֑ם
וְלֹֽא־תָת֜וּרוּ אַחֲרֵ֤י לְבַבְכֶם֙ וְאַחֲרֵ֣י עֵֽינֵיכֶ֔ם
אֲשֶׁר־אַתֶּ֥ם זֹנִ֖ים אַחֲרֵיהֶֽם׃
לְמַ֣עַן תִּזְכְּר֔וּ וַעֲשִׂיתֶ֖ם אֶת־כָּל־מִצְוֺתָ֑י
וִהְיִיתֶ֥ם קְדֹשִׁ֖ים לֵאלֹהֵיכֶֽם׃
אֲנִ֞י יְהֹוָ֣ה אֱלֹהֵיכֶ֗ם
אֲשֶׁ֨ר הוֹצֵ֤אתִי אֶתְכֶם֙ מֵאֶ֣רֶץ מִצְרַ֔יִם
לִהְי֥וֹת לָכֶ֖ם לֵאלֹהִ֑ים
אֲנִ֖י יְהֹוָ֥ה אֱלֹהֵיכֶֽם׃

אֱמֶת

The חזן *repeats:*

◂ **יהוה אֱלֹהֵיכֶם אֱמֶת**

True and solid, established and lasting, right,
trustworthy, loved, dear, pleasant,
awesome, mighty, perfect, good, and beautiful
is our belief in *Hashem* forever.

True is *Hashem,* our God, King and Protector.
He lives through all generations.
His throne,
Kingship, and trustworthiness are everlasting.

At the icon, kiss the TZITZIT *and release them.*

Hashem's words exist for all time.
Just as the words of Torah
▸ guided our ancestors,
so to do they guide us,
and they will continue to guide our children
and all of their children after them. ◂
Our belief in *Hashem*
has lasted since earlier generations
and remained strong
through all generations that followed.
Our belief lasts forever
and does not change.

It is true that You, *Hashem,* are our:
God and God of our ancestors,
▸ King and King of our ancestors,
Protector and Protector of our ancestors,
Creator and Savior,
and Deliverer and Rescuer.
There is no God but You.

וְיַצִּיב, וְנָכוֹן וְקַיָּם, וְיָשָׁר וְנֶאֱמָן
וְאָהוּב וְחָבִיב, וְנֶחְמָד וְנָעִים
וְנוֹרָא וְאַדִּיר, וּמְתֻקָּן וּמְקֻבָּל, וְטוֹב וְיָפֶה
הַדָּבָר הַזֶּה עָלֵינוּ לְעוֹלָם וָעֶד.

אֱמֶת אֱלֹהֵי עוֹלָם מַלְכֵּנוּ
צוּר יַעֲקֹב מָגֵן יִשְׁעֵנוּ
לְדוֹר וָדוֹר הוּא קַיָּם וּשְׁמוֹ קַיָּם
וְכִסְאוֹ נָכוֹן
וּמַלְכוּתוֹ וֶאֱמוּנָתוֹ לָעַד קַיָּמֶת.

At the icon, kiss the ציצית and release them.

וּדְבָרָיו חַיִּים וְקַיָּמִים, נֶאֱמָנִים וְנֶחֱמָדִים
לָעַד וּלְעוֹלְמֵי עוֹלָמִים
◂ עַל אֲבוֹתֵינוּ וְעָלֵינוּ, עַל בָּנֵינוּ וְעַל דּוֹרוֹתֵינוּ
וְעַל כָּל דּוֹרוֹת זֶרַע יִשְׂרָאֵל עֲבָדֶיךָ. ▸
עַל הָרִאשׁוֹנִים וְעַל הָאַחֲרוֹנִים
דָּבָר טוֹב וְקַיָּם לְעוֹלָם וָעֶד

אֱמֶת וֶאֱמוּנָה, חֹק וְלֹא יַעֲבֹר.

אֱמֶת שָׁאַתָּה הוּא יהוה אֱלֹהֵינוּ וֵאלֹהֵי אֲבוֹתֵינוּ
◂ מַלְכֵּנוּ מֶלֶךְ אֲבוֹתֵינוּ, גּוֹאֲלֵנוּ גּוֹאֵל אֲבוֹתֵינוּ
יוֹצְרֵנוּ צוּר יְשׁוּעָתֵנוּ, פּוֹדֵנוּ וּמַצִּילֵנוּ מֵעוֹלָם שְׁמֶךָ
אֵין אֱלֹהִים זוּלָתֶךָ.

עֶזְרַת *Hashem,*
You have always been there
to help our ancestors,
and You continuously protect
and save their children
in every generation.
You exist beyond our universe.
Your justice and righteousness
reach the whole earth.
Praiseworthy is the person
who follows Your *mitzvot*
and listens to the words of Your Torah.

It is true that You are a mighty King
and Master of Your people.

It is true that You are the first
and You are the last;
there is no king, protector, or savior
besides You.
You, *Hashem*, our God,
saved us from Egypt
where we were enslaved.
You split the Reed Sea,
allowed Your beloved Jewish people
to cross on dry land,
and drowned our enemies.
Not even one of our enemies survived.

עֶזְרַת אֲבוֹתֵינוּ אַתָּה הוּא מֵעוֹלָם
מָגֵן וּמוֹשִׁיעַ לִבְנֵיהֶם אַחֲרֵיהֶם בְּכָל דּוֹר וָדוֹר.
בְּרוּם עוֹלָם מוֹשָׁבֶךָ
וּמִשְׁפָּטֶיךָ וְצִדְקָתְךָ עַד אַפְסֵי אָרֶץ.
אַשְׁרֵי אִישׁ שֶׁיִּשְׁמַע לְמִצְוֹתֶיךָ
וְתוֹרָתְךָ וּדְבָרְךָ יָשִׂים עַל לִבּוֹ.

אֱמֶת אַתָּה הוּא אָדוֹן לְעַמֶּךָ
וּמֶלֶךְ גִּבּוֹר לָרִיב רִיבָם.

אֱמֶת אַתָּה הוּא רִאשׁוֹן
וְאַתָּה הוּא אַחֲרוֹן
וּמִבַּלְעָדֶיךָ אֵין לָנוּ מֶלֶךְ גּוֹאֵל וּמוֹשִׁיעַ.
מִמִּצְרַיִם גְּאַלְתָּנוּ, יהוה אֱלֹהֵינוּ
וּמִבֵּית עֲבָדִים פְּדִיתָנוּ
כָּל בְּכוֹרֵיהֶם הָרַגְתָּ, וּבְכוֹרְךָ גָּאָלְתָּ
וְיַם סוּף בָּקַעְתָּ
וְזֵדִים טִבַּעְתָּ
וִידִידִים הֶעֱבַרְתָּ
וַיְכַסּוּ־מַיִם צָרֵיהֶם
אֶחָד מֵהֶם לֹא נוֹתָר:

For this reason, we praise and sing, bless and thank
Hashem, our King, the living God.
Hashem is elevated, great, and awesome.
He lowers those who think too highly of themselves,
and raises those who think lowly of themselves.
He saves those in need, helps the poor,
and answers His people when they cry out to Him.

Stand while saying this section. Take three steps back.

‣ Praise to *Hashem*, our God, who deserves thanks.
When Moshe and the Jewish people
sang with great joy
they said:
"Who is as strong as You, *Hashem*?
Who is as holy and awesome as You, *Hashem*?"

‣ The Jewish people praised You, *Hashem*,
with a new song at the seashore.
Together, they all gave thanks
and announced You as King,
saying:
"*Hashem* will rule as King for ever and ever."

‣ *Hashem*, fortress of Your Jewish people,
arise and help Your Jewish people.
Deliver us as You promised.
Our savior is *Hashem*,
the source of our holiness.

Thank You, *Hashem*,
for saving the Jewish people.

עַל זֹאת שִׁבְּחוּ אֲהוּבִים, וְרוֹמְמוּ אֵל
וְנָתְנוּ יְדִידִים זְמִירוֹת, שִׁירוֹת וְתִשְׁבָּחוֹת
בְּרָכוֹת וְהוֹדָאוֹת לְמֶלֶךְ אֵל חַי וְקַיָּם
רָם וְנִשָּׂא, גָּדוֹל וְנוֹרָא
מַשְׁפִּיל גֵּאִים וּמַגְבִּיהַּ שְׁפָלִים
מוֹצִיא אֲסִירִים, וּפוֹדֶה עֲנָוִים וְעוֹזֵר דַּלִּים
וְעוֹנֶה לְעַמּוֹ בְּעֵת שַׁוְּעָם אֵלָיו.

Stand while saying this section. Take three steps back.

‹ תְּהִלּוֹת לְאֵל עֶלְיוֹן, בָּרוּךְ הוּא וּמְבֹרָךְ
מֹשֶׁה וּבְנֵי יִשְׂרָאֵל, לְךָ עָנוּ שִׁירָה בְּשִׂמְחָה רַבָּה
וְאָמְרוּ כֻלָּם

מִי־כָמֹכָה בָּאֵלִם, יהוה
מִי כָּמֹכָה נֶאְדָּר בַּקֹּדֶשׁ
נוֹרָא תְהִלֹּת, עֹשֵׂה פֶלֶא:

‹ שִׁירָה חֲדָשָׁה שִׁבְּחוּ גְאוּלִים לְשִׁמְךָ עַל שְׂפַת הַיָּם
יַחַד כֻּלָּם הוֹדוּ וְהִמְלִיכוּ, וְאָמְרוּ

יהוה יִמְלֹךְ לְעֹלָם וָעֶד:

‹ צוּר יִשְׂרָאֵל, קוּמָה בְּעֶזְרַת יִשְׂרָאֵל
וּפְדֵה כִנְאֻמֶךָ יְהוּדָה וְיִשְׂרָאֵל.

גֹּאֲלֵנוּ יהוה צְבָאוֹת שְׁמוֹ, קְדוֹשׁ יִשְׂרָאֵל:

בָּרוּךְ אַתָּה יהוה, גָּאַל יִשְׂרָאֵל.

AMIDA

Take three steps forward
then stand with your feet together.

Hashem, open my lips and help my mouth recite Your praise.

ANCESTORS

Bend the knees when saying "We thank," bow when saying "You," and stand straight before saying "Hashem."

בָּרוּךְ We thank You, *Hashem,*
our God, and God of our ancestors,
Avraham, Yitzchak, and Yaakov.
You, *Hashem,*
are the great, mighty, awesome, kind,
and all-powerful Creator.
It is because of the greatness of our ancestors,
Avraham, Yitzchak, and Yaakov,
that *Hashem* will bring *Mashiach.*

Between Rosh Hashana and Yom Kippur say:
Give us life in the year to come
and write us in the book of life,
Hashem, who gives life.

Hashem is our King
who helps, guides, and protects us.

Bend the knees when saying "Thank," bow when saying "You," and stand straight before saying "Hashem."

Thank You, *Hashem,*
who protects us in the merit of Avraham.

עמידה

Take three steps forward then stand with your feet together.

אֲדֹנָי, שְׂפָתַי תִּפְתָּח, וּפִי יַגִּיד תְּהִלָּתֶךָ:

אבות

Bend the knees when saying בָּרוּךְ, *bow when saying* אַתָּה, *and stand straight before saying Hashem's name.*

בָּרוּךְ אַתָּה יהוה
אֱלֹהֵינוּ וֵאלֹהֵי אֲבוֹתֵינוּ
אֱלֹהֵי אַבְרָהָם, אֱלֹהֵי יִצְחָק, וֵאלֹהֵי יַעֲקֹב
הָאֵל הַגָּדוֹל הַגִּבּוֹר וְהַנּוֹרָא, אֵל עֶלְיוֹן
גּוֹמֵל חֲסָדִים טוֹבִים, וְקוֹנֵה הַכֹּל
וְזוֹכֵר חַסְדֵי אָבוֹת
וּמֵבִיא גוֹאֵל לִבְנֵי בְנֵיהֶם לְמַעַן שְׁמוֹ בְּאַהֲבָה.

On שבת שובה *say:*

זָכְרֵנוּ לְחַיִּים, מֶלֶךְ חָפֵץ בַּחַיִּים
וְכָתְבֵנוּ בְּסֵפֶר הַחַיִּים
לְמַעַנְךָ אֱלֹהִים חַיִּים.

מֶלֶךְ עוֹזֵר וּמוֹשִׁיעַ וּמָגֵן.

Bend the knees when saying בָּרוּךְ, *bow when saying* אַתָּה, *and stand straight before saying Hashem's name.*

בָּרוּךְ אַתָּה יהוה, מָגֵן אַבְרָהָם.

HASHEM'S STRENGTH

אַתָּה You, *Hashem*, have unlimited strength.
You save people in their time of need,
and You have the power to bring the dead back to life.

This line is said during the rainy season, from Simchat Torah to Pesach:
(You make the wind blow and cause the rain to fall)

With kindness You provide the living
with the necessities to live,
and with mercy You keep Your promise
of bringing the dead back to life.
For the living, You:
Support those who are falling,
Heal those who are sick, and
Free those who are in challenging situations.
Who is like You, *Hashem*, and who can compare to You?
You, *Hashem*, are our King
who has the power to cause death and life.

Between Rosh Hashana and Yom Kippur say:
Who is like You, *Hashem*, our caring Father
who remembers His people for good
and gives them life?

We have complete faith
that You will bring us back to life after our passing.
Thank You, *Hashem*,
for bringing the dead back to life.

גבורות

אַתָּה גִּבּוֹר לְעוֹלָם, אֲדֹנָי
מְחַיֵּה מֵתִים אַתָּה, רַב לְהוֹשִׁיעַ

This line is said during the rainy season, from שמחת תורה *to* פסח*:*

(מַשִּׁיב הָרְוּחַ וּמוֹרִיד הַגֶּשֶׁם)

מְכַלְכֵּל חַיִּים בְּחֶסֶד
מְחַיֵּה מֵתִים בְּרַחֲמִים רַבִּים
סוֹמֵךְ נוֹפְלִים
וְרוֹפֵא חוֹלִים
וּמַתִּיר אֲסוּרִים
וּמְקַיֵּם אֱמוּנָתוֹ לִישֵׁנֵי עָפָר.
מִי כָמְוֹךָ, בַּעַל גְּבוּרוֹת
וּמִי דְּוֹמֶה לָּךְ
מֶלֶךְ, מֵמִית וּמְחַיֶּה וּמַצְמְיחַ יְשׁוּעָה.

On שבת שובה *say:*

מִי כָמְוֹךָ אַב הָרַחֲמִים
זוֹכֵר יְצוּרָיו לְחַיִּים בְּרַחֲמִים.

וְנֶאֱמָן אַתָּה לְהַחֲיוֹת מֵתִים.
בָּרוּךְ אַתָּה יהוה, מְחַיֵּה הַמֵּתִים.

HASHEM'S HOLINESS

אַתָּה קָדוֹשׁ *Hashem,*
You are holy
and Your name is holy.
The Jewish people, who are holy,
will praise You, *Hashem,* each day.
Thank You, *Hashem,*
the holy God. / *Between Rosh Hashana & Yom Kippur say:* the holy King./

HOLINESS OF THE DAY

יִשְׂמַח מֹשֶׁה Moshe,
a loyal servant of *Hashem,*
celebrated the gift of Shabbat
that he was given
when he was standing on Har Sinai.
Hashem placed a crown on Moshe's head
and gave him the two stone *luchot,*
which include the *mitzva* to keep Shabbat.

וּשְׁנֵי לוּחוֹת אֲבָנִים הוֹרִיד בְּיָדוֹ *And gave him the two stone luchot.* After forty days and forty nights on Har Sinai, Moshe climbed down the mountain with the *luchot* in his hands. The *luchot* were two large stones that contained the *Aseret HaDibrot,* the Ten Commandments, including the *mitzva* of keeping Shabbat. The *luchot,* however, should not be confused with the Torah. The Torah is made up of five books—Bereishit, Shemot, Vayikra, Bamidbar, and Devarim—and contains 613 *mitzvot.* The *Aseret HaDibrot* are ten important *mitzvot* that *Hashem* taught to the Jewish people Himself. These *mitzvot* represent all of the other *mitzvot* in the Torah.

קדושת השם

אַתָּה קָדוֹשׁ וְשִׁמְךָ קָדוֹשׁ
וּקְדוֹשִׁים בְּכָל יוֹם יְהַלְלוּךָ סֶּלָה.
בָּרוּךְ אַתָּה יהוה
הָאֵל הַקָּדוֹשׁ. / *On* שבת שובה *say* הַמֶּלֶךְ הַקָּדוֹשׁ./

קדושת היום

יִשְׂמַח מֹשֶׁה בְּמַתְּנַת חֶלְקוֹ
כִּי עֶבֶד נֶאֱמָן קָרָאתָ לּוֹ
כְּלִיל תִּפְאֶרֶת בְּרֹאשׁוֹ נָתַתָּ לּוֹ
בְּעָמְדוֹ לְפָנֶיךָ עַל הַר סִינַי
וּשְׁנֵי לוּחוֹת אֲבָנִים הוֹרִיד בְּיָדוֹ
וְכָתוּב בָּהֶם שְׁמִירַת שַׁבָּת
וְכֵן כָּתוּב בְּתוֹרָתֶךָ

כְּלִיל תִּפְאֶרֶת בְּרֹאשׁוֹ נָתַתָּ לּוֹ *Hashem placed a crown on Moshe's head.* Wearing a crown is a symbol of leadership. The Mishnah says there are three crowns: the crown of Torah, the crown of *Kohanim*, and the crown of kings, but the crown of Torah is different from other crowns. Kings receive their crowns by being born the children of kings, and *Kohanim* receive their crowns by being born the children of *Kohanim*. However, the crown of Torah is not given at birth; the crown of Torah must be earned. Moshe Rabbeinu wore the first crown of Torah, or the first symbol of Torah leadership, when he received the *luchot* on Har Sinai. Every Jew can wear the crown of Torah and be a Torah leader by studying and teaching Torah to others.

וְשָׁמְרוּ The Jewish people must observe Shabbat
as the day represents the agreement
between *Hashem* and the Jewish people for all time.
Shabbat will always remind us
that *Hashem* created heaven and earth in six days
and rested on the seventh day.

וְלֹא נְתַתּוֹ *Hashem,*
You did not give the gift of Shabbat
to idol worshipers or to the other nations of the world.
With love, You gave Shabbat to Your Jewish people,
the children of Yaakov.
Those who keep Shabbat will find joy and happiness
in Your most holy and special day.
Keeping Shabbat reminds us
that *Hashem* created the world.

אֱלֹהֵינוּ *Hashem,*
our God and God of our ancestors,
we rest from work today for Your sake.
Allow us to become holy through keeping Your *mitzvot*
and studying Your Torah.
Be good to us, save us, and purify our hearts
to serve You sincerely.
Hashem, our God,
show us Your love
and allow us to observe Your holy Shabbat
so that Your Jewish people can rest.
Thank You, *Hashem,* for making Shabbat holy.

וְשָׁמְרוּ בְנֵי־יִשְׂרָאֵל אֶת־הַשַּׁבָּת
לַעֲשׂוֹת אֶת־הַשַּׁבָּת לְדֹרֹתָם בְּרִית עוֹלָם:
בֵּינִי וּבֵין בְּנֵי יִשְׂרָאֵל אוֹת הִוא לְעֹלָם
כִּי־שֵׁשֶׁת יָמִים עָשָׂה יהוה אֶת־הַשָּׁמַיִם וְאֶת־הָאָרֶץ
וּבַיּוֹם הַשְּׁבִיעִי שָׁבַת וַיִּנָּפַשׁ:

וְלֹא נְתַתּוֹ, יהוה אֱלֹהֵינוּ, לְגוֹיֵי הָאֲרָצוֹת
וְלֹא הִנְחַלְתּוֹ, מַלְכֵּנוּ, לְעוֹבְדֵי פְסִילִים
וְגַם בִּמְנוּחָתוֹ לֹא יִשְׁכְּנוּ עֲרֵלִים
כִּי לְיִשְׂרָאֵל עַמְּךָ נְתַתּוֹ בְּאַהֲבָה
לְזֶרַע יַעֲקֹב אֲשֶׁר בָּם בָּחָרְתָּ.
עַם מְקַדְּשֵׁי שְׁבִיעִי
כֻּלָּם יִשְׂבְּעוּ וְיִתְעַנְּגוּ מִטּוּבֶךָ, וּבַשְּׁבִיעִי רָצִיתָ בּוֹ וְקִדַּשְׁתּוֹ
חֶמְדַּת יָמִים אוֹתוֹ קָרָאתָ, זֵכֶר לְמַעֲשֵׂה בְרֵאשִׁית.

אֱלֹהֵינוּ וֵאלֹהֵי אֲבוֹתֵינוּ, רְצֵה בִמְנוּחָתֵנוּ
קַדְּשֵׁנוּ בְּמִצְוֹתֶיךָ וְתֵן חֶלְקֵנוּ בְּתוֹרָתֶךָ
שַׂבְּעֵנוּ מִטּוּבֶךָ וְשַׂמְּחֵנוּ בִּישׁוּעָתֶךָ
וְטַהֵר לִבֵּנוּ לְעָבְדְּךָ בֶּאֱמֶת
וְהַנְחִילֵנוּ, יהוה אֱלֹהֵינוּ, בְּאַהֲבָה וּבְרָצוֹן שַׁבַּת קָדְשֶׁךָ
וְיָנוּחוּ בוֹ יִשְׂרָאֵל מְקַדְּשֵׁי שְׁמֶךָ.
בָּרוּךְ אַתָּה יהוה, מְקַדֵּשׁ הַשַּׁבָּת.

SERVICE IN THE *BEIT HAMIKDASH*

רְצֵה *Hashem,* please accept Your Jewish people
and their prayers.
We eagerly await the rebuilding of the *Beit HaMikdash*
so we can serve You with *korbanot.*
Until the *Beit HaMikdash* is rebuilt,
please accept our prayers with love.

On Rosh Chodesh and Chol HaMo'ed, say:

אֱלֹהֵינוּ Our God, and God of our ancestors, may our prayers:
Rise from our mouths,
Come before You,
Reach You at a desirable time,
Be heard,
And be fulfilled.
Hashem, You remember and know each of our hardships.
You remember:
Our ancestors,
Mashiach,
Your holy city, Jerusalem, and
Your united Jewish people,
for goodness, kindness, mercy, life, and peace
on this day of:
On Rosh Chodesh: *Rosh Chodesh.*
On Pesach: the Holiday of *Matzot.*
On Sukkot: the Holiday of *Sukkot.*

Hashem, on this day please remember us
with good thoughts, consider us for blessing,
and help us with difficult times in our lives.
Be kind and merciful with us, *Hashem,*
as we look towards You as our King.

עבודה

רְצֵה יהוה אֱלֹהֵינוּ בְּעַמְּךָ יִשְׂרָאֵל, וּבִתְפִלָּתָם
וְהָשֵׁב אֶת הָעֲבוֹדָה לִדְבִיר בֵּיתֶךָ
וְאִשֵּׁי יִשְׂרָאֵל וּתְפִלָּתָם בְּאַהֲבָה תְקַבֵּל בְּרָצוֹן
וּתְהִי לְרָצוֹן תָּמִיד עֲבוֹדַת יִשְׂרָאֵל עַמֶּךָ.

On ראש חודש *and* חול המועד*, say:*

אֱלֹהֵינוּ וֵאלֹהֵי אֲבוֹתֵינוּ
יַעֲלֶה וְיָבוֹא וְיַגִּיעַ, וְיֵרָאֶה וְיֵרָצֶה וְיִשָּׁמַע
וְיִפָּקֵד וְיִזָּכֵר זִכְרוֹנֵנוּ וּפִקְדוֹנֵנוּ, וְזִכְרוֹן אֲבוֹתֵינוּ
וְזִכְרוֹן מָשִׁיחַ בֶּן דָּוִד עַבְדֶּךָ
וְזִכְרוֹן יְרוּשָׁלַיִם עִיר קָדְשֶׁךָ
וְזִכְרוֹן כָּל עַמְּךָ בֵּית יִשְׂרָאֵל
לְפָנֶיךָ, לִפְלֵיטָה לְטוֹבָה
לְחֵן וּלְחֶסֶד וּלְרַחֲמִים, לְחַיִּים וּלְשָׁלוֹם
בְּיוֹם

בראש חודש: רֹאשׁ הַחֹדֶשׁ הַזֶּה.

בפסח: חַג הַמַּצּוֹת הַזֶּה.

בסוכות: חַג הַסֻּכּוֹת הַזֶּה.

זָכְרֵנוּ יהוה אֱלֹהֵינוּ בּוֹ לְטוֹבָה, וּפָקְדֵנוּ בוֹ לִבְרָכָה
וְהוֹשִׁיעֵנוּ בוֹ לְחַיִּים.
וּבִדְבַר יְשׁוּעָה וְרַחֲמִים
חוּס וְחָנֵּנוּ וְרַחֵם עָלֵינוּ וְהוֹשִׁיעֵנוּ
כִּי אֵלֶיךָ עֵינֵינוּ, כִּי אֵל מֶלֶךְ חַנּוּן וְרַחוּם אָתָּה.

May we be worthy
to see the rebuilding of the *Beit HaMikdash*.
We thank You, *Hashem*,
for returning Your presence to Zion.

THANK YOU

Bow when saying the words "We thank You."

מוֹדִים We thank You, *Hashem*,
for You are and always will be
our God, and the God of our ancestors.
You give us life
and You always protect us.
We thank and praise You for:
Our lives which are in Your hands,
Our souls which are in Your control,
The miracles You perform for us every day, and
The goodness You show us
at all times, morning, noon, and night.
You, *Hashem*, have unlimited mercy and kindness
and therefore we have always placed our hope in You.

On Chanuka say:

עַל הַנִּסִּים We thank You, *Hashem*, for the miracles, the deliverances, the great strength, and the victories in war that You displayed for us in earlier times and in our times.

בִּימֵי מַתִּתְיָהוּ In the days of Mattityahu, son of Yochanan the *Kohen Gadol*, the Hasmonean, and his sons, the wicked Greeks challenged Your Jewish people trying to make them forget Your Torah and sin. In Your great kindness, You, *Hashem*, supported

וְתֶחֱזֶינָה עֵינֵינוּ בְּשׁוּבְךָ לְצִיּוֹן בְּרַחֲמִים.
בָּרוּךְ אַתָּה יהוה, הַמַּחֲזִיר שְׁכִינָתוֹ לְצִיּוֹן.

הודאה

Bow when saying the words מוֹדִים אֲנַחְנוּ לָךְ שָׁאַתָּה הוּא.

מוֹדִים אֲנַחְנוּ לָךְ

שָׁאַתָּה הוּא יהוה אֱלֹהֵינוּ וֵאלֹהֵי אֲבוֹתֵינוּ לְעוֹלָם וָעֶד.
צוּר חַיֵּינוּ, מָגֵן יִשְׁעֵנוּ, אַתָּה הוּא לְדוֹר וָדוֹר.
נוֹדֶה לְּךָ וּנְסַפֵּר תְּהִלָּתֶךָ
עַל חַיֵּינוּ הַמְּסוּרִים בְּיָדֶךָ
וְעַל נִשְׁמוֹתֵינוּ הַפְּקוּדוֹת לָךְ
וְעַל נִסֶּיךָ שֶׁבְּכָל יוֹם עִמָּנוּ
וְעַל נִפְלְאוֹתֶיךָ וְטוֹבוֹתֶיךָ
שֶׁבְּכָל עֵת, עֶרֶב וָבֹקֶר וְצָהֳרָיִם.
הַטּוֹב, כִּי לֹא כָלוּ רַחֲמֶיךָ
וְהַמְרַחֵם, כִּי לֹא תַמּוּ חֲסָדֶיךָ
מֵעוֹלָם קִוִּינוּ לָךְ.

בחנוכה:

עַל הַנִּסִּים וְעַל הַפֻּרְקָן וְעַל הַגְּבוּרוֹת וְעַל הַתְּשׁוּעוֹת וְעַל הַמִּלְחָמוֹת שֶׁעָשִׂיתָ לַאֲבוֹתֵינוּ בַּיָּמִים הָהֵם בַּזְּמַן הַזֶּה.

בִּימֵי מַתִּתְיָהוּ בֶּן יוֹחָנָן כֹּהֵן גָּדוֹל חַשְׁמוֹנַאי וּבָנָיו, כְּשֶׁעָמְדָה מַלְכוּת יָוָן הָרְשָׁעָה עַל עַמְּךָ יִשְׂרָאֵל לְהַשְׁכִּיחָם תּוֹרָתֶךָ וּלְהַעֲבִירָם מֵחֻקֵּי רְצוֹנֶךָ, וְאַתָּה בְּרַחֲמֶיךָ הָרַבִּים עָמַדְתָּ לָהֶם בְּעֵת צָרָתָם,

us in this difficult time. You allowed for:

The weak Jews to defeat the mighty Greeks,
The few Jews to defeat the many Greeks,
The pure Jews to defeat the impure Greeks,
The righteous Jews to defeat the wicked Greeks, and
The Jews who studied Your Torah to defeat the Greeks who did not.

Hashem, on this day everyone in the world recognized You as You miraculously saved Your Jewish people. Your Jewish people then entered the *Beit HaMikdash* to clean and purify it. They lit candles in the courtyard of the *Beit HaMikdash* and set aside these eight days of *Chanukah* for giving thanks and praising You.

Continue with "For all these reasons."

For all these reasons
we will thank You, *Hashem,* our King, forever.

Between Rosh Hashana & Yom Kippur say:
And write all Your children in the book of good life.

Every living person
will recognize and praise You, *Hashem,*
for You are the God that helps and saves Your people.

Bend the knees when saying "Thank," bow when saying "You," and stand straight before saying "Hashem."

Thank You, *Hashem,*
for You are worthy of being thanked.

PEACE

שִׂים שָׁלוֹם *Hashem,*
please provide Your Jewish people
with peace, goodness, blessing, kindness, and mercy.

וְרַבְתָּ אֶת רִיבָם, דַּנְתָּ אֶת דִּינָם, נָקַמְתָּ אֶת נִקְמָתָם, מָסַרְתָּ גִּבּוֹרִים בְּיַד חַלָּשִׁים, וְרַבִּים בְּיַד מְעַטִּים, וּטְמֵאִים בְּיַד טְהוֹרִים, וּרְשָׁעִים בְּיַד צַדִּיקִים, וְזֵדִים בְּיַד עוֹסְקֵי תוֹרָתֶךָ, וּלְךָ עָשִׂיתָ שֵׁם גָּדוֹל וְקָדוֹשׁ בְּעוֹלָמֶךָ, וּלְעַמְּךָ יִשְׂרָאֵל עָשִׂיתָ תְּשׁוּעָה גְדוֹלָה וּפֻרְקָן כְּהַיּוֹם הַזֶּה. וְאַחַר כֵּן בָּאוּ בָנֶיךָ לִדְבִיר בֵּיתֶךָ, וּפִנּוּ אֶת הֵיכָלֶךָ, וְטִהֲרוּ אֶת מִקְדָּשֶׁךָ, וְהִדְלִיקוּ נֵרוֹת בְּחַצְרוֹת קָדְשֶׁךָ, וְקָבְעוּ שְׁמוֹנַת יְמֵי חֲנֻכָּה אֵלּוּ, לְהוֹדוֹת וּלְהַלֵּל לְשִׁמְךָ הַגָּדוֹל.

Continue with וְעַל כֻּלָּם.

וְעַל כֻּלָּם
יִתְבָּרַךְ וְיִתְרוֹמַם שִׁמְךָ מַלְכֵּנוּ תָּמִיד לְעוֹלָם וָעֶד.

On שבת שובה *say* **וּכְתֹב לְחַיִּים טוֹבִים כָּל בְּנֵי בְרִיתֶךָ.**

וְכֹל הַחַיִּים יוֹדוּךָ סֶּלָה
וִיהַלְלוּ אֶת שִׁמְךָ בֶּאֱמֶת
הָאֵל יְשׁוּעָתֵנוּ וְעֶזְרָתֵנוּ סֶלָה.

Bend the knees when saying בָּרוּךְ*, bow when saying* אַתָּה*,*
and stand straight before saying Hashem's name.

בָּרוּךְ אַתָּה יהוה, הַטּוֹב שִׁמְךָ וּלְךָ נָאֶה לְהוֹדוֹת.

שלום

שִׂים שָׁלוֹם טוֹבָה וּבְרָכָה
חֵן וָחֶסֶד וְרַחֲמִים עָלֵינוּ
וְעַל כָּל יִשְׂרָאֵל עַמֶּךָ.

Bless us, *Hashem,* all as one.
Hashem,
You have given us Your Torah of life,
and treated us with kindness, righteousness,
blessing, mercy, and peace.
May it be good in Your eyes, *Hashem,*
to bless Your Jewish people with peace
at every moment of every hour.

Between Rosh Hashana and Yom Kippur continue with "May You remember," below.

Thank You, *Hashem,*
who blesses His Jewish people with peace.

Between Rosh Hashana and Yom Kippur say:
May You remember all of the Jewish people for life,
blessing, peace, and riches
and write us in the book of good life and peace.
Thank You, *Hashem,*
who makes peace.

CONCLUSION OF AMIDA

אֱלֹהַי *Hashem,* please help me:
Control my mouth from speaking badly
about other people,
Stay silent and not respond if someone speaks badly
about me,
Learn Your Torah,
and do Your *mitzvot.*

בָּרְכֵנוּ אָבִינוּ כֻּלָּנוּ כְּאֶחָד בְּאוֹר פָּנֶיךָ
כִּי בְאוֹר פָּנֶיךָ נָתַתָּ לָּנוּ יהוה אֱלֹהֵינוּ
תּוֹרַת חַיִּים וְאַהֲבַת חֶסֶד
וּצְדָקָה וּבְרָכָה וְרַחֲמִים
וְחַיִּים וְשָׁלוֹם.
וְטוֹב בְּעֵינֶיךָ לְבָרֵךְ אֶת עַמְּךָ יִשְׂרָאֵל
בְּכָל עֵת וּבְכָל שָׁעָה בִּשְׁלוֹמֶךָ.

On שבת שובה *continue with* בְּסֵפֶר חַיִּים*, below.*

בָּרוּךְ אַתָּה יהוה
הַמְבָרֵךְ אֶת עַמּוֹ יִשְׂרָאֵל בַּשָּׁלוֹם.

On שבת שובה *say:*

בְּסֵפֶר חַיִּים, בְּרָכָה וְשָׁלוֹם, וּפַרְנָסָה טוֹבָה
נִזָּכֵר וְנִכָּתֵב לְפָנֶיךָ
אֲנַחְנוּ וְכָל עַמְּךָ בֵּית יִשְׂרָאֵל
לְחַיִּים טוֹבִים וּלְשָׁלוֹם.
בָּרוּךְ אַתָּה יהוה, עוֹשֵׂה הַשָּׁלוֹם.

סיום העמידה

אֱלֹהַי, נְצֹר לְשׁוֹנִי מֵרָע וּשְׂפָתַי מִדַּבֵּר מִרְמָה
וְלִמְקַלְלַי נַפְשִׁי תִדֹּם, וְנַפְשִׁי כֶּעָפָר לַכֹּל תִּהְיֶה.
פְּתַח לִבִּי בְּתוֹרָתֶךָ, וּבְמִצְוֹתֶיךָ תִּרְדֹּף נַפְשִׁי.

Hashem,
if people plan to do something evil against me,
please stop these plans and protect me.
Even if I am not deserving of being helped,
please act on my behalf
as I represent Your name and Your Torah.
Hashem,
please save Your Jewish people
from difficult situations and answer my requests.
May You find my thoughts and prayers favorable.

Take three steps backwards and bow to your left as you say:

You, *Hashem,* make peace in heaven.

Bow to your right as you say:

Please may You bring peace to us

Bow forward as you say:

And all Your Jewish people.

Before taking three steps forward, say the following quietly:

Hashem, our God and God of our ancestors, may You please rebuild the *Beit HaMikdash* soon. *Hashem,* please allow us to learn Your Torah and serve You in the *Beit HaMikdash* as the Jewish people once did.

When praying with a minyan, the Amida is repeated by the Leader *(on the next page).*

When not praying with a minyan, continue with Av HaRachamim on page 560.
On Rosh Chodesh, Chol HaMo'ed and Chanuka,
the service continues with Hallel on page 720.

וְכָל הַחוֹשְׁבִים עָלַי רָעָה
מְהֵרָה הָפֵר עֲצָתָם וְקַלְקֵל מַחֲשַׁבְתָּם.
עֲשֵׂה לְמַעַן שְׁמֶךָ, עֲשֵׂה לְמַעַן יְמִינֶךָ
עֲשֵׂה לְמַעַן קְדֻשָּׁתֶךָ, עֲשֵׂה לְמַעַן תּוֹרָתֶךָ.
לְמַעַן יֵחָלְצוּן יְדִידֶיךָ, הוֹשִׁיעָה יְמִינְךָ וַעֲנֵנִי:
יִהְיוּ לְרָצוֹן אִמְרֵי־פִי וְהֶגְיוֹן לִבִּי לְפָנֶיךָ, יהוה צוּרִי וְגוֹאֲלִי:

Take three steps backwards and bow to your left as you say:

עֹשֶׂה שָׁלוֹם / *On* שבת שובה *say* הַשָּׁלוֹם/ בִּמְרוֹמָיו

Bow to your right as you say:

הוּא יַעֲשֶׂה שָׁלוֹם עָלֵינוּ

Bow forward as you say:

וְעַל כָּל יִשְׂרָאֵל, וְאִמְרוּ אָמֵן.

Before taking three steps forward, say the following quietly:

יְהִי רָצוֹן מִלְּפָנֶיךָ יהוה אֱלֹהֵינוּ וֵאלֹהֵי אֲבוֹתֵינוּ. שֶׁיִּבָּנֶה בֵּית הַמִּקְדָּשׁ בִּמְהֵרָה בְיָמֵינוּ, וְתֵן חֶלְקֵנוּ בְּתוֹרָתֶךָ. וְשָׁם נַעֲבָדְךָ בְּיִרְאָה כִּימֵי עוֹלָם וּכְשָׁנִים קַדְמֹנִיּוֹת. וְעָרְבָה לַיהוה מִנְחַת יְהוּדָה וִירוּשָׁלָםִ כִּימֵי עוֹלָם וּכְשָׁנִים קַדְמֹנִיּוֹת:

When praying with a מנין*, the* עמידה *is repeated by the* חזן
(on the next page).

When not praying with a מנין*, continue with* אַב הָרַחֲמִים *on page 561.*
On ראש חודש*,* חול המועד*, and* חנוכה*,*
the service continues with הלל *on page 721.*

THE LEADER'S REPETITION

Try to focus on each blessing that the Leader reads, by following along and thinking about the sentences below. After each beracha that the Leader recites, answer "Amen."

Hashem, open my lips
and help my mouth recite Your praise.

ANCESTORS

We praise You, *Hashem,*
for protecting, helping, and saving us
as You did for our ancestors,
Avraham, Yitzchak, and Yaakov.
Thank You, *Hashem,*
who protects us in the merit of Avraham.

(*Congregation:* Amen.)

HASHEM'S STRENGTH

We praise You, *Hashem,*
for providing food to those who are hungry,
support to those who are falling,
health to those who are sick,
and help to those who are in challenging situations.
Thank You, *Hashem,*
for bringing the dead back to life. (*Congregation:* Amen.)

חזרת הש״ץ

Try to focus on each blessing that the חזן *reads, by following along and thinking about the sentences below. After each beracha that the* חזן *recites, answer* אָמֵן*.*

אֲדֹנָי, שְׂפָתַי תִּפְתָּח, וּפִי יַגִּיד תְּהִלָּתֶךָ:

אבות

בָּרוּךְ אַתָּה יהוה, אֱלֹהֵינוּ וֵאלֹהֵי אֲבוֹתֵינוּ
אֱלֹהֵי אַבְרָהָם, אֱלֹהֵי יִצְחָק, וֵאלֹהֵי יַעֲקֹב
הָאֵל הַגָּדוֹל הַגִּבּוֹר וְהַנּוֹרָא, אֵל עֶלְיוֹן
גּוֹמֵל חֲסָדִים טוֹבִים, וְקֹנֵה הַכֹּל, וְזוֹכֵר חַסְדֵי אָבוֹת
וּמֵבִיא גוֹאֵל לִבְנֵי בְנֵיהֶם לְמַעַן שְׁמוֹ בְּאַהֲבָה.

On שבת שובה *say* זָכְרֵנוּ לְחַיִּים, מֶלֶךְ חָפֵץ בַּחַיִּים
וְכָתְבֵנוּ בְּסֵפֶר הַחַיִּים, לְמַעַנְךָ אֱלֹהִים חַיִּים.

מֶלֶךְ עוֹזֵר וּמוֹשִׁיעַ וּמָגֵן.

בָּרוּךְ אַתָּה יהוה, מָגֵן אַבְרָהָם. (קהל: אָמֵן)

גבורות

אַתָּה גִּבּוֹר לְעוֹלָם, אֲדֹנָי, מְחַיֵּה מֵתִים אַתָּה, רַב לְהוֹשִׁיעַ

This line is said during the rainy season, from שמחת תורה *to* פסח*:*

(מַשִּׁיב הָרְוּחַ וּמוֹרִיד הַגֶּשֶׁם)

מְכַלְכֵּל חַיִּים בְּחֶסֶד, מְחַיֵּה מֵתִים בְּרַחֲמִים רַבִּים
סוֹמֵךְ נוֹפְלִים, וְרוֹפֵא חוֹלִים, וּמַתִּיר אֲסוּרִים
וּמְקַיֵּם אֱמוּנָתוֹ לִישֵׁנֵי עָפָר.
מִי כָמְוֹךָ, בַּעַל גְּבוּרוֹת, וּמִי דּוֹמֶה לָּךְ
מֶלֶךְ, מֵמִית וּמְחַיֶּה וּמַצְמִיחַ יְשׁוּעָה.

On שבת שובה *say* מִי כָמְוֹךָ אַב הָרַחֲמִים, זוֹכֵר יְצוּרָיו לְחַיִּים בְּרַחֲמִים.

וְנֶאֱמָן אַתָּה לְהַחֲיוֹת מֵתִים.

בָּרוּךְ אַתָּה יהוה, מְחַיֵּה הַמֵּתִים. (קהל: אָמֵן)

KEDUSHA

*This section of tefillah is said while standing silently with feet together.
The sentences are said responsively,
Congregation followed by the Leader.*

Congregation then Leader: נְקַדֵּשׁ We will announce You, *Hashem*,
as holy in this world,
just as the angels
announce You as holy in heaven.
As Your prophet wrote,
The angels call to one another saying:

(Stand on your toes as you repeat the word "Holy")

Congregation then Leader: Holy, holy, holy, is *Hashem*.
The whole world is filled with Your holiness.

Leader: With a loud and strong voice
the angels will rise up and say:

Congregation then Leader: Blessed is *Hashem*'s holiness.

Leader: *Hashem*, our King,
may You soon rule over Your Jewish people
from Your home in Jerusalem
forever and ever.
May You be praised and honored
in Jerusalem, Your holy city,
for all future generations.
May our eyes
have the opportunity to see
Your kingdom in Jerusalem
as our ancestors have described it.

קדושה

This section of tefillah is said while standing silently with feet together.
The sentences are said responsively,
קהל followed by the חזן.

קהל then חזן: נְקַדֵּשׁ אֶת שִׁמְךָ בָּעוֹלָם
כְּשֵׁם שֶׁמַּקְדִּישִׁים אוֹתוֹ בִּשְׁמֵי מָרוֹם
כַּכָּתוּב עַל יַד נְבִיאֶךָ, וְקָרָא זֶה אֶל־זֶה וְאָמַר

(Stand on your toes as you repeat the word קָדוֹשׁ)

קהל then חזן: קָדוֹשׁ, קָדוֹשׁ, קָדוֹשׁ, יהוה צְבָאוֹת
מְלֹא כָל־הָאָרֶץ כְּבוֹדוֹ:

חזן: אָז בְּקוֹל רַעַשׁ גָּדוֹל אַדִּיר וְחָזָק, מַשְׁמִיעִים קוֹל
מִתְנַשְּׂאִים לְעֻמַּת שְׂרָפִים, לְעֻמָּתָם בָּרוּךְ יֹאמֵרוּ

קהל then חזן: בָּרוּךְ כְּבוֹד־יהוה מִמְּקוֹמוֹ:

חזן: מִמְּקוֹמְךָ מַלְכֵּנוּ תוֹפִיעַ וְתִמְלֹךְ עָלֵינוּ
כִּי מְחַכִּים אֲנַחְנוּ לָךְ
מָתַי תִּמְלֹךְ בְּצִיּוֹן
בְּקָרוֹב בְּיָמֵינוּ לְעוֹלָם וָעֶד תִּשְׁכֹּן
תִּתְגַּדַּל וְתִתְקַדַּשׁ בְּתוֹךְ יְרוּשָׁלַיִם עִירְךָ
לְדוֹר וָדוֹר וּלְנֵצַח נְצָחִים.
וְעֵינֵינוּ תִרְאֶינָה מַלְכוּתֶךָ
כַּדָּבָר הָאָמוּר בְּשִׁירֵי עֻזֶּךָ
עַל יְדֵי דָוִד מְשִׁיחַ צִדְקֶךָ

Congregation then Leader: *Hashem,*
You have ruled over the Jewish people
for generations,
and You shall continue
to be our King forever.

Leader: *Hashem,*
in every generation we will discuss
Your holiness and greatness.
Our mouths shall never stop speaking
of Your praises,
for You, *Hashem,* are a great and holy King.
Thank You, *Hashem,* our holy God.
/ *Between Rosh Hashana & Yom Kippur say:* the holy King./
(*Congregation:* Amen.)

HOLINESS OF THE DAY

Moshe brought down
the two stone *Luchot*
which had the commandment
to keep Shabbat written on them.

Keeping Shabbat
will always remind us
that *Hashem* created
heaven and earth in six days
and rested on the seventh day.

then קהל חזן: יִמְלֹךְ יהוה לְעוֹלָם
אֱלֹהַיִךְ צִיּוֹן לְדֹר וָדֹר, הַלְלוּיָהּ:

חזן: לְדוֹר וָדוֹר נַגִּיד גָּדְלֶךָ
וּלְנֵצַח נְצָחִים קְדֻשָּׁתְךָ נַקְדִּישׁ
וְשִׁבְחֲךָ אֱלֹהֵינוּ מִפִּינוּ לֹא יָמוּשׁ לְעוֹלָם וָעֶד
כִּי אֵל מֶלֶךְ גָּדוֹל וְקָדוֹשׁ אָתָּה.
בָּרוּךְ אַתָּה יהוה, הָאֵל הַקָּדוֹשׁ.
/*On* שבת שובה *say* הַמֶּלֶךְ הַקָּדוֹשׁ./

(קהל: אָמֵן)

קדושת היום
יִשְׂמַח מֹשֶׁה בְּמַתְּנַת חֶלְקוֹ
כִּי עֶבֶד נֶאֱמָן קָרָאתָ לוֹ
כְּלִיל תִּפְאֶרֶת בְּרֹאשׁוֹ נָתַתָּ לוֹ
בְּעָמְדוֹ לְפָנֶיךָ עַל הַר סִינַי
וּשְׁנֵי לוּחוֹת אֲבָנִים הוֹרִיד בְּיָדוֹ
וְכָתוּב בָּהֶם שְׁמִירַת שַׁבָּת
וְכֵן כָּתוּב בְּתוֹרָתֶךָ

וְשָׁמְרוּ בְנֵי־יִשְׂרָאֵל אֶת־הַשַּׁבָּת
לַעֲשׂוֹת אֶת־הַשַּׁבָּת לְדֹרֹתָם בְּרִית עוֹלָם:
בֵּינִי וּבֵין בְּנֵי יִשְׂרָאֵל אוֹת הִוא לְעֹלָם
כִּי־שֵׁשֶׁת יָמִים עָשָׂה יהוה אֶת־הַשָּׁמַיִם וְאֶת־הָאָרֶץ
וּבַיּוֹם הַשְּׁבִיעִי שָׁבַת וַיִּנָּפַשׁ:

Reminder: Say "Amen" after the Leader recites each beracha.

Those who keep Shabbat
will find joy and happiness
in Your most holy and special day.

Hashem, our God,
continue to show us Your love
and allow us to observe Your holy Shabbat
so that Your Jewish people can rest.
Thank You, *Hashem*, for making Shabbat holy.

(*Congregation:* Amen.)

SERVICE IN THE *BEIT HAMIKDASH*

We pray to You, *Hashem*,
that You accept our prayers
as though they are the sacrifices
that were once brought to You
in Your holy *Beit HaMikdash*.

Reminder: Say אָמֵן after the חזן recites the beracha.

וְלֹא נְתַתּוֹ, יהוה אֱלֹהֵינוּ, לְגוֹיֵי הָאֲרָצוֹת
וְלֹא הִנְחַלְתּוֹ, מַלְכֵּנוּ, לְעוֹבְדֵי פְסִילִים
וְגַם בִּמְנוּחָתוֹ לֹא יִשְׁכְּנוּ עֲרֵלִים
כִּי לְיִשְׂרָאֵל עַמְּךָ נְתַתּוֹ בְּאַהֲבָה
לְזֶרַע יַעֲקֹב אֲשֶׁר בָּם בָּחָרְתָּ.
עַם מְקַדְּשֵׁי שְׁבִיעִי
כֻּלָּם יִשְׂבְּעוּ וְיִתְעַנְּגוּ מִטּוּבֶךָ
וּבַשְּׁבִיעִי רָצִיתָ בּוֹ וְקִדַּשְׁתּוֹ
חֶמְדַּת יָמִים אוֹתוֹ קָרָאתָ
זֵכֶר לְמַעֲשֵׂה בְרֵאשִׁית.

אֱלֹהֵינוּ וֵאלֹהֵי אֲבוֹתֵינוּ, רְצֵה בִמְנוּחָתֵנוּ
קַדְּשֵׁנוּ בְּמִצְוֹתֶיךָ וְתֵן חֶלְקֵנוּ בְּתוֹרָתֶךָ
שַׂבְּעֵנוּ מִטּוּבֶךָ וְשַׂמְּחֵנוּ בִּישׁוּעָתֶךָ
וְטַהֵר לִבֵּנוּ לְעָבְדְּךָ בֶּאֱמֶת
וְהַנְחִילֵנוּ, יהוה אֱלֹהֵינוּ, בְּאַהֲבָה וּבְרָצוֹן שַׁבַּת קָדְשֶׁךָ
וְיָנוּחוּ בוֹ יִשְׂרָאֵל מְקַדְּשֵׁי שְׁמֶךָ.

בָּרוּךְ אַתָּה יהוה, מְקַדֵּשׁ הַשַּׁבָּת. (קהל: אָמֵן)

עבודה

רְצֵה יהוה אֱלֹהֵינוּ בְּעַמְּךָ יִשְׂרָאֵל, וּבִתְפִלָּתָם
וְהָשֵׁב אֶת הָעֲבוֹדָה לִדְבִיר בֵּיתֶךָ
וְאִשֵּׁי יִשְׂרָאֵל וּתְפִלָּתָם בְּאַהֲבָה תְקַבֵּל בְּרָצוֹן
וּתְהִי לְרָצוֹן תָּמִיד עֲבוֹדַת יִשְׂרָאֵל עַמֶּךָ.

Reminder: Say "Amen" after the Leader recites the beracha.

On Rosh Chodesh and Chol HaMo'ed, say:

Our God, and God of our ancestors,
may our prayers:
Rise from our mouths, Come before You,
Reach You at a desirable time, Be heard, And be fulfilled.
Hashem,
You remember and know each of our hardships.
You remember:
Our ancestors, *Mashiach,*
Your holy city, Jerusalem,
and Your united Jewish people,
for goodness, kindness, mercy, life,
and peace on this day of:

On Rosh Chodesh: *Rosh Chodesh.*
On Pesach: the Holiday of *Matzot.*
On Sukkot: the Holiday of *Sukkot.*

Hashem, on this day please remember us
with good thoughts,
consider us for blessing,
and help us with difficult times in our lives.
Be kind and merciful with us,
Hashem,
as we look towards You as our King.

May we be worthy
to see the rebuilding of the *Beit HaMikdash.*
We thank You, *Hashem,*
for returning Your presence to Zion. (*Congregation:* Amen.)

Reminder: Say אָמֵן after the חזן recites the beracha.

On ראש חודש *and* חול המועד*, say:*

אֱלֹהֵינוּ וֵאלֹהֵי אֲבוֹתֵינוּ
יַעֲלֶה וְיָבוֹא וְיַגִּיעַ, וְיֵרָאֶה וְיֵרָצֶה וְיִשָּׁמַע
וְיִפָּקֵד וְיִזָּכֵר זִכְרוֹנֵנוּ וּפִקְדוֹנֵנוּ, וְזִכְרוֹן אֲבוֹתֵינוּ
וְזִכְרוֹן מָשִׁיחַ בֶּן דָּוִד עַבְדֶּךָ
וְזִכְרוֹן יְרוּשָׁלַיִם עִיר קָדְשֶׁךָ
וְזִכְרוֹן כָּל עַמְּךָ בֵּית יִשְׂרָאֵל
לְפָנֶיךָ, לִפְלֵיטָה לְטוֹבָה
לְחֵן וּלְחֶסֶד וּלְרַחֲמִים
לְחַיִּים וּלְשָׁלוֹם, בְּיוֹם

בראש חודש: רֹאשׁ הַחֹדֶשׁ הַזֶּה.
בפסח: חַג הַמַּצּוֹת הַזֶּה.
בסוכות: חַג הַסֻּכּוֹת הַזֶּה.

זָכְרֵנוּ יהוה אֱלֹהֵינוּ בּוֹ לְטוֹבָה
וּפָקְדֵנוּ בוֹ לִבְרָכָה
וְהוֹשִׁיעֵנוּ בוֹ לְחַיִּים.
וּבִדְבַר יְשׁוּעָה וְרַחֲמִים
חוּס וְחָנֵּנוּ וְרַחֵם עָלֵינוּ וְהוֹשִׁיעֵנוּ
כִּי אֵלֶיךָ עֵינֵינוּ
כִּי אֵל מֶלֶךְ חַנּוּן וְרַחוּם אָתָּה.

וְתֶחֱזֶינָה עֵינֵינוּ בְּשׁוּבְךָ לְצִיּוֹן בְּרַחֲמִים.

בָּרוּךְ אַתָּה יהוה, הַמַּחֲזִיר שְׁכִינָתוֹ לְצִיּוֹן. (קהל: אָמֵן)

THANK YOU

While the Leader says this prayer, the Congregation says the prayer on the bottom of this page.

You, *Hashem*,
have unlimited mercy and kindness
and therefore
we have always placed our hope in You.

The following is said quietly while the Leader says the above. Bow when saying the first sentence below beginning with the words "Thank You, Hashem."

מוֹדִים Thank You, *Hashem*,
our God and God of our ancestors.
You are God of all people,
You created us,
and You created the entire world.
Thank You for giving us life
and for providing us with food to eat.
May You continue to give us life and food to eat.
May You gather us from exile
and return us to Your holy places
so we can keep Your laws,
and serve You with a perfect heart.
Thank You *Hashem*,
our God to whom thanksgiving is due.

הודאה

While the חזן *says this prayer, the* קהל *says the prayer on the bottom of this page.*

מוֹדִים אֲנַחְנוּ לָךְ
שָׁאַתָּה הוּא יהוה אֱלֹהֵינוּ וֵאלֹהֵי אֲבוֹתֵינוּ לְעוֹלָם וָעֶד.
צוּר חַיֵּינוּ, מָגֵן יִשְׁעֵנוּ אַתָּה הוּא לְדוֹר וָדוֹר.
נוֹדֶה לְּךָ וּנְסַפֵּר תְּהִלָּתֶךָ
עַל חַיֵּינוּ הַמְּסוּרִים בְּיָדֶךָ, וְעַל נִשְׁמוֹתֵינוּ הַפְּקוּדוֹת לָךְ
וְעַל נִסֶּיךָ שֶׁבְּכָל יוֹם עִמָּנוּ, וְעַל נִפְלְאוֹתֶיךָ וְטוֹבוֹתֶיךָ
שֶׁבְּכָל עֵת, עֶרֶב וָבֹקֶר וְצָהֳרָיִם.
הַטּוֹב, כִּי לֹא כָלוּ רַחֲמֶיךָ
וְהַמְרַחֵם, כִּי לֹא תַמּוּ חֲסָדֶיךָ, מֵעוֹלָם קִוִּינוּ לָךְ.

The following is said quietly while the חזן *says the above. Bow when saying the first sentence below beginning with the words* מוֹדִים אֲנַחְנוּ לָךְ.

מוֹדִים אֲנַחְנוּ לָךְ
שָׁאַתָּה הוּא יהוה אֱלֹהֵינוּ וֵאלֹהֵי אֲבוֹתֵינוּ
אֱלֹהֵי כָל בָּשָׂר, יוֹצְרֵנוּ, יוֹצֵר בְּרֵאשִׁית.
בְּרָכוֹת וְהוֹדָאוֹת לְשִׁמְךָ הַגָּדוֹל וְהַקָּדוֹשׁ
עַל שֶׁהֶחֱיִיתָנוּ וְקִיַּמְתָּנוּ.
כֵּן תְּחַיֵּנוּ וּתְקַיְּמֵנוּ, וְתֶאֱסֹף גָּלֻיּוֹתֵינוּ לְחַצְרוֹת קָדְשֶׁךָ
לִשְׁמֹר חֻקֶּיךָ וְלַעֲשׂוֹת רְצוֹנֶךָ וּלְעָבְדְּךָ בְּלֵבָב שָׁלֵם
עַל שֶׁאֲנַחְנוּ מוֹדִים לָךְ.
בָּרוּךְ אֵל הַהוֹדָאוֹת.

Reminder: Say "Amen" after the Leader recites the beracha.

On Chanuka say:

We thank You, *Hashem,* for the miracles, the deliverances, the great strength, and the victories in war that You displayed for us in earlier times and in our times.

In the days of Mattityahu, son of Yochanan the *Kohen Gadol,* the Hasmonean, and his sons, the wicked Greeks challenged Your Jewish people trying to make them forget Your Torah and sin. In Your great kindness, You, *Hashem,* supported us in this difficult time. You allowed for: The weak Jews to defeat the mighty Greeks, The few Jews to defeat the many Greeks, The pure Jews to defeat the impure Greeks, The righteous Jews to defeat the wicked Greeks, and The Jews who studied Your Torah to defeat the Greeks who did not. *Hashem,* on this day everyone in the world recognized You as You miraculously saved Your Jewish people. Your Jewish people then entered the *Beit HaMikdash* to clean and purify it. They lit candles in the courtyard of the *Beit HaMikdash* and set aside these eight days of *Chanukah* for giving thanks and praising You.

Continue with "We thank You"

We thank You, *Hashem,* for You are good
and all that You do is good.
Thank You, *Hashem,* for You are worthy of being thanked.

(*Congregation:* Amen.)

BLESSINGS OF THE *KOHANIM*

אֱלֹהֵינוּ *Hashem,* Our God and God of our ancestors, provide us with the three blessings that Aharon the *Kohen* and the *kohanim* his descendants use to bless the Jewish people.

Leader: *Hashem* should bless and protect you.

(*Congregation:* May it be as you say!)

Leader: *Hashem* should be kind and favorable towards you.

(*Congregation:* May it be as you say!)

Leader: *Hashem* should grant you peace.

(*Congregation:* May it be as you say!)

Reminder: Say אָמֵן after the חזן recites the beracha.

בחנוכה:

עַל הַנִּסִּים וְעַל הַפֻּרְקָן וְעַל הַגְּבוּרוֹת וְעַל הַתְּשׁוּעוֹת וְעַל הַמִּלְחָמוֹת שֶׁעָשִׂיתָ לַאֲבוֹתֵינוּ בַּיָּמִים הָהֵם בַּזְּמַן הַזֶּה.

בִּימֵי מַתִּתְיָהוּ בֶּן יוֹחָנָן כֹּהֵן גָּדוֹל חַשְׁמוֹנַאי וּבָנָיו, כְּשֶׁעָמְדָה מַלְכוּת יָוָן הָרְשָׁעָה עַל עַמְּךָ יִשְׂרָאֵל לְהַשְׁכִּיחָם תּוֹרָתֶךָ וּלְהַעֲבִירָם מֵחֻקֵּי רְצוֹנֶךָ, וְאַתָּה בְּרַחֲמֶיךָ הָרַבִּים עָמַדְתָּ לָהֶם בְּעֵת צָרָתָם, רַבְתָּ אֶת רִיבָם, דַּנְתָּ אֶת דִּינָם, נָקַמְתָּ אֶת נִקְמָתָם, מָסַרְתָּ גִבּוֹרִים בְּיַד חַלָּשִׁים, וְרַבִּים בְּיַד מְעַטִּים, וּטְמֵאִים בְּיַד טְהוֹרִים, וּרְשָׁעִים בְּיַד צַדִּיקִים, וְזֵדִים בְּיַד עוֹסְקֵי תוֹרָתֶךָ, וּלְךָ עָשִׂיתָ שֵׁם גָּדוֹל וְקָדוֹשׁ בְּעוֹלָמֶךָ, וּלְעַמְּךָ יִשְׂרָאֵל עָשִׂיתָ תְּשׁוּעָה גְדוֹלָה וּפֻרְקָן כְּהַיּוֹם הַזֶּה. וְאַחַר כֵּן בָּאוּ בָנֶיךָ לִדְבִיר בֵּיתֶךָ, וּפִנּוּ אֶת הֵיכָלֶךָ, וְטִהֲרוּ אֶת מִקְדָּשֶׁךָ, וְהִדְלִיקוּ נֵרוֹת בְּחַצְרוֹת קָדְשֶׁךָ, וְקָבְעוּ שְׁמוֹנַת יְמֵי חֲנֻכָּה אֵלּוּ, לְהוֹדוֹת וּלְהַלֵּל לְשִׁמְךָ הַגָּדוֹל.

Continue with וְעַל כֻּלָּם.

וְעַל כֻּלָּם, יִתְבָּרַךְ וְיִתְרוֹמַם שִׁמְךָ מַלְכֵּנוּ תָּמִיד לְעוֹלָם וָעֶד.

On שבת שובה *say* וּכְתֹב לְחַיִּים טוֹבִים כָּל בְּנֵי בְרִיתֶךָ.

וְכֹל הַחַיִּים יוֹדוּךָ סֶּלָה, וִיהַלְלוּ אֶת שִׁמְךָ בֶּאֱמֶת הָאֵל יְשׁוּעָתֵנוּ וְעֶזְרָתֵנוּ סֶלָה.

בָּרוּךְ אַתָּה יהוה, הַטּוֹב שִׁמְךָ וּלְךָ נָאֶה לְהוֹדוֹת. (קהל: אָמֵן)

ברכת כוהנים

אֱלֹהֵינוּ וֵאלֹהֵי אֲבוֹתֵינוּ, בָּרְכֵנוּ בַּבְּרָכָה הַמְשֻׁלֶּשֶׁת בַּתּוֹרָה, הַכְּתוּבָה עַל יְדֵי מֹשֶׁה עַבְדֶּךָ, הָאֲמוּרָה מִפִּי אַהֲרֹן וּבָנָיו כֹּהֲנִים עַם קְדוֹשֶׁיךָ, כָּאָמוּר

חזן: יְבָרֶכְךָ יהוה וְיִשְׁמְרֶךָ: קהל: כֵּן יְהִי רָצוֹן

חזן: יָאֵר יהוה פָּנָיו אֵלֶיךָ וִיחֻנֶּךָּ: קהל: כֵּן יְהִי רָצוֹן

חזן: יִשָּׂא יהוה פָּנָיו אֵלֶיךָ וְיָשֵׂם לְךָ שָׁלוֹם: קהל: כֵּן יְהִי רָצוֹן

Reminder: Say "Amen" after the Leader recites the beracha.

PEACE

We pray to You, *Hashem*,
that You grant peace
to Your Jewish people
at every moment of every hour,
forever.

Between Rosh Hashana and Yom Kippur the Leader continues with "May You remember," below.

Thank You, *Hashem*,
who blesses His Jewish people with peace.

(*Congregation:* Amen.)

Between Rosh Hashana and Yom Kippur say:

May You remember
all of the Jewish people for life,
blessing, peace, and riches
and write us in the book of good life and peace.
Thank You, *Hashem*, who makes peace.

(*Congregation:* Amen.)

On Rosh Chodesh, Chol HaMo'ed and Chanuka, the service continues with Hallel on page 720.

Reminder: Say אָמֵן *after the* חזן *recites the beracha.*

שלום

שִׂים שָׁלוֹם טוֹבָה וּבְרָכָה
חֵן וָחֶסֶד וְרַחֲמִים עָלֵינוּ
וְעַל כָּל יִשְׂרָאֵל עַמֶּךָ.
בָּרְכֵנוּ אָבִינוּ כֻּלָּנוּ כְּאֶחָד בְּאוֹר פָּנֶיךָ
כִּי בְאוֹר פָּנֶיךָ נָתַתָּ לָּנוּ יהוה אֱלֹהֵינוּ
תּוֹרַת חַיִּים וְאַהֲבַת חֶסֶד
וּצְדָקָה וּבְרָכָה וְרַחֲמִים
וְחַיִּים וְשָׁלוֹם.
וְטוֹב בְּעֵינֶיךָ לְבָרֵךְ אֶת עַמְּךָ יִשְׂרָאֵל
בְּכָל עֵת וּבְכָל שָׁעָה בִּשְׁלוֹמֶךָ.

On שבת שובה *the* חזן *continues with* בְּסֵפֶר חַיִּים*, below.*

בָּרוּךְ אַתָּה יהוה, הַמְבָרֵךְ אֶת עַמּוֹ יִשְׂרָאֵל בַּשָּׁלוֹם.
(קהל: **אָמֵן**)

On שבת שובה *say:*

בְּסֵפֶר חַיִּים, בְּרָכָה וְשָׁלוֹם, וּפַרְנָסָה טוֹבָה
נִזָּכֵר וְנִכָּתֵב לְפָנֶיךָ
אֲנַחְנוּ וְכָל עַמְּךָ בֵּית יִשְׂרָאֵל לְחַיִּים טוֹבִים וּלְשָׁלוֹם.
בָּרוּךְ אַתָּה יהוה, עוֹשֵׂה הַשָּׁלוֹם. (קהל: **אָמֵן**)

On ראש חודש, חול המועד *and* חנוכה*,*
the service continues with הלל *on page 721.*

KADDISH SHALEM

Leader: יִתְגַּדַּל May *Hashem* be recognized
as great and holy (*Congregation:* Amen)
in the world that He created.
May He establish His kingdom
during my lifetime and the lifetime of all Jews,
quickly and soon.
Let us say: "Amen" (*Congregation:* Amen).

Congregation: May we thank *Hashem* for ever and ever.
Leader: May we thank *Hashem* for ever and ever.

Leader: *Hashem* should be thanked, praised,
and honored (*Congregation:* He is blessed).
Hashem is beyond all the blessings,
songs, or praises that we could offer.
Let us say: "Amen" (*Congregation:* Amen).

May *Hashem* accept our prayers
and the prayers of all Jews.
Let us say: "Amen." (*Congregation:* Amen).

May *Hashem* give us, and all Jews,
peace and good life.
Let us say: "Amen." (*Congregation:* Amen).

The Leader takes three steps back before saying this line, bows to the left when saying "May," bows to the right when saying "the One," bows to the middle when saying "make peace for us":

May *Hashem*, the One
who makes peace in heaven,
make peace for us and for all Jews.
Let us say: "Amen." (*Congregation:* Amen).

קדיש שלם

חזן: יִתְגַּדַּל וְיִתְקַדַּשׁ שְׁמֵהּ רַבָּא (קהל: אָמֵן)
בְּעָלְמָא דִּי בְרָא כִרְעוּתֵהּ, וְיַמְלִיךְ מַלְכוּתֵהּ
בְּחַיֵּיכוֹן וּבְיוֹמֵיכוֹן וּבְחַיֵּי דְכָל בֵּית יִשְׂרָאֵל
בַּעֲגָלָא וּבִזְמַן קָרִיב, וְאִמְרוּ אָמֵן. (קהל: אָמֵן)

קהל יְהֵא שְׁמֵהּ רַבָּא מְבָרַךְ לְעָלַם וּלְעָלְמֵי עָלְמַיָּא.
חזן: יְהֵא שְׁמֵהּ רַבָּא מְבָרַךְ לְעָלַם וּלְעָלְמֵי עָלְמַיָּא.

חזן: יִתְבָּרַךְ וְיִשְׁתַּבַּח וְיִתְפָּאַר וְיִתְרוֹמַם וְיִתְנַשֵּׂא וְיִתְהַדָּר
וְיִתְעַלֶּה וְיִתְהַלָּל שְׁמֵהּ דְּקֻדְשָׁא בְּרִיךְ הוּא (קהל: בְּרִיךְ הוּא)
לְעֵלָּא מִן כָּל בִּרְכָתָא
/בשבת שובה: לְעֵלָּא לְעֵלָּא מִכָּל בִּרְכָתָא/
וְשִׁירָתָא, תֻּשְׁבְּחָתָא וְנֶחֱמָתָא
דַּאֲמִירָן בְּעָלְמָא, וְאִמְרוּ אָמֵן. (קהל: אָמֵן)

תִּתְקַבַּל צְלוֹתְהוֹן וּבָעוּתְהוֹן דְּכָל יִשְׂרָאֵל
קֳדָם אֲבוּהוֹן דִּי בִשְׁמַיָּא, וְאִמְרוּ אָמֵן. (קהל: אָמֵן)

יְהֵא שְׁלָמָא רַבָּא מִן שְׁמַיָּא
וְחַיִּים, עָלֵינוּ וְעַל כָּל יִשְׂרָאֵל, וְאִמְרוּ אָמֵן. (קהל: אָמֵן)

The חזן *takes three steps back before saying this line, bows to the left when saying* עֹשֶׂה, *bows to the right when saying* הוּא, *bows to the middle when saying* יַעֲשֶׂה שָׁלוֹם עָלֵינוּ:

עֹשֶׂה שָׁלוֹם /בשבת שובה: הַשָּׁלוֹם/ בִּמְרוֹמָיו
הוּא יַעֲשֶׂה שָׁלוֹם
עָלֵינוּ וְעַל כָּל יִשְׂרָאֵל, וְאִמְרוּ אָמֵן. (קהל: אָמֵן)

TAKING OUT THE TORAH FROM THE ARK

אֵין־כָּמוֹךָ *Hashem,*
You created everything;
there is nothing like You.
You will rule forever in every generation.

יהוה *Hashem,*
You are our King, were always our King,
and always will be our King.
Please give strength, blessing, and peace
to Your Jewish people.

אַב הָרַחֲמִים *Hashem,*
have mercy on Your Jewish people and rebuild Jerusalem.
Hashem, You are the King, who rules over all,
we only trust in You.

The Aron Kodesh is opened and the congregation stands.

וַיְהִי Every time the *Aron* would travel
Moshe would say,
"*Hashem,* may our enemies scatter
and run away from You."
The Torah comes from Zion
and the words of *Hashem* come from Jerusalem.
Thank You, *Hashem,* for giving the Torah
to Your Jewish people.

On Shabbat, continue with "We are thankful" on page 534.

הוצאת ספר תורה

אֵין־כָּמְוֹךָ בָאֱלֹהִים, אֲדֹנָי, וְאֵין כְּמַעֲשֶׂיךָ:
מַלְכוּתְךָ מַלְכוּת כָּל־עֹלָמִים
וּמֶמְשַׁלְתְּךָ בְּכָל־דּוֹר וָדֹר:

יהוה מֶלֶךְ, יהוה מָלָךְ, יהוה יִמְלֹךְ לְעֹלָם וָעֶד.
יהוה עֹז לְעַמּוֹ יִתֵּן
יהוה יְבָרֵךְ אֶת־עַמּוֹ בַשָּׁלוֹם:

אַב הָרַחֲמִים
הֵיטִיבָה בִרְצוֹנְךָ אֶת־צִיּוֹן
תִּבְנֶה חוֹמוֹת יְרוּשָׁלָיִם:
כִּי בְךָ לְבַד בָּטָחְנוּ
מֶלֶךְ אֵל רָם וְנִשָּׂא, אֲדוֹן עוֹלָמִים.

The ארון קודש *is opened and the* קהל *stands.*

וַיְהִי בִּנְסֹעַ הָאָרֹן וַיֹּאמֶר מֹשֶׁה
קוּמָה יהוה וְיָפֻצוּ אֹיְבֶיךָ וְיָנֻסוּ מְשַׂנְאֶיךָ מִפָּנֶיךָ:
כִּי מִצִּיּוֹן תֵּצֵא תוֹרָה וּדְבַר־יהוה מִירוּשָׁלָיִם:
בָּרוּךְ שֶׁנָּתַן תּוֹרָה לְעַמּוֹ יִשְׂרָאֵל בִּקְדֻשָּׁתוֹ.

On שבת, *continue with* בְּרִיךְ שְׁמֵהּ *on page 535.*

On Hoshana Raba say the following verses three times:

יהוה *Hashem,* You are a God of mercy and kindness.
You do not become angry easily,
You remember our good actions for many years,
and You forgive us when we sin.

On Hoshana Raba continue:

רִבּוֹנוֹ שֶׁל עוֹלָם *Hashem,* Master of the world, please allow me and all of my family to follow Your ways and act properly. Please forgive me and my family for any sins we may have done. Cleanse us as though we never sinned, and remember us only for the good actions we have done. Please give us a good life of peace, money to spend, food to eat, clothes to wear, and a lifetime to dedicate to studying Torah and keeping *mitzvot.* Please allow us to learn Your Torah so that we can deepen our wisdom and understanding. Please heal our pains and allow us to be successful at work. Please protect us from the evil wishes of other people and allow only good things to happen to us. Amen, may it be Your will.

יִהְיוּ לְרָצוֹן May You find
my thoughts and prayers favorable.

Say the following verse three times:

וַאֲנִי May my prayers
come before You
at a favorable time
so that You answer me with kindness.

On הושענא רבה *say the following verses three times:*

יהוה, יהוה, אֵל רַחוּם וְחַנּוּן
אֶרֶךְ אַפַּיִם וְרַב־חֶסֶד וֶאֱמֶת:
נֹצֵר חֶסֶד לָאֲלָפִים, נֹשֵׂא עָוֹן וָפֶשַׁע וְחַטָּאָה, וְנַקֵּה:

On הושענא רבה *continue:*

רִבּוֹנוֹ שֶׁל עוֹלָם, מַלֵּא מִשְׁאֲלוֹתַי לְטוֹבָה, וְהָפֵק רְצוֹנִי וְתֵן שְׁאֵלָתִי, וּמְחוֹל לִי עַל כָּל עֲוֹנוֹתַי וְעַל כָּל עֲוֹנוֹת אַנְשֵׁי בֵיתִי, מְחִילָה בְּחֶסֶד מְחִילָה בְּרַחֲמִים, וְטַהֲרֵנוּ מֵחֲטָאֵינוּ וּמֵעֲוֹנוֹתֵינוּ וּמִפְּשָׁעֵינוּ, וְזָכְרֵנוּ בְּזִכָּרוֹן טוֹב לְפָנֶיךָ, וּפָקְדֵנוּ בִּפְקֻדַּת יְשׁוּעָה וְרַחֲמִים. וְזָכְרֵנוּ לְחַיִּים טוֹבִים וּלְשָׁלוֹם, וּפַרְנָסָה וְכַלְכָּלָה, וְלֶחֶם לֶאֱכֹל וּבֶגֶד לִלְבֹּשׁ, וְעֹשֶׁר וְכָבוֹד, וְאֹרֶךְ יָמִים לַהֲגוֹת בְּתוֹרָתֶךָ וּלְקַיֵּם מִצְוֹתֶיהָ, וְשֵׂכֶל וּבִינָה לְהָבִין וּלְהַשְׂכִּיל עִמְקֵי סוֹדוֹתֶיהָ. וְהָפֵק רְפוּאָה לְכָל מַכְאוֹבֵינוּ, וּבָרֵךְ כָּל מַעֲשֵׂה יָדֵינוּ, וּגְזֹר עָלֵינוּ גְּזֵרוֹת טוֹבוֹת יְשׁוּעוֹת וְנֶחָמוֹת, וּבַטֵּל מֵעָלֵינוּ כָּל גְּזֵרוֹת קָשׁוֹת וְרָעוֹת, וְתֵן בְּלֵב הַמַּלְכוּת וְיוֹעֲצֶיהָ וְשָׂרֶיהָ עָלֵינוּ לְטוֹבָה. אָמֵן וְכֵן יְהִי רָצוֹן.

יִהְיוּ לְרָצוֹן אִמְרֵי־פִי וְהֶגְיוֹן לִבִּי לְפָנֶיךָ
יהוה צוּרִי וְגֹאֲלִי:

Say the following verse three times:

וַאֲנִי תְפִלָּתִי־לְךָ יהוה, עֵת רָצוֹן
אֱלֹהִים בְּרָב־חַסְדֶּךָ
עֲנֵנִי בֶּאֱמֶת יִשְׁעֶךָ:

On Shabbat and on Hoshana Raba:

בְּרִיךְ שְׁמֵהּ We are thankful to You, *Hashem,*
Master and King of the World.
May You always show kindness towards Your Jewish people,
accept our prayers with mercy,
and rebuild the *Beit HaMikdash.*
Please grant me a long life and provide protection for me,
for all that is mine, and for the entire Jewish nation.
As King, You feed all and rule over all.
You rule over all kings as well.
I am a servant to *Hashem,*
and I therefore show respect towards the Torah at all times.
I don't rely on any man or angel, but on *Hashem* alone
for He is the God of love and truth.
‣ *Hashem,* may You open my heart
and the hearts of all Your Jewish people to the Torah
so that we can have goodness, long life, and peace.

Leader then congregation:

שְׁמַע Listen and understand my Jewish people:
Hashem is our one and only God.

Leader then congregation:

אֶחָד *Hashem* is our one and only God;
His name is holy (*On Hoshana Raba:* and awesome).

Leader then congregation:

גַּדְּלוּ Let us recognize the greatness of *Hashem*
and sing praises to Him together.

On שבת *and on* הושענא רבה:

בְּרִיךְ שְׁמֵהּ דְּמָרֵא עָלְמָא, בְּרִיךְ כִּתְרָךְ וְאַתְרָךְ. יְהֵא רְעוּתָךְ עִם עַמָּךְ יִשְׂרָאֵל לְעָלַם, וּפֻרְקַן יְמִינָךְ אַחֲזִי לְעַמָּךְ בְּבֵית מַקְדְּשָׁךְ, וּלְאַמְטוּיֵי לָנָא מִטּוּב נְהוֹרָךְ, וּלְקַבֵּל צְלוֹתַנָא בְּרַחֲמִין. יְהֵא רַעֲוָא קֳדָמָךְ דְּתוֹרִיךְ לַן חַיִּין בְּטִיבוּ, וְלֶהֱוֵי אֲנָא פְקִידָא בְּגוֹ צַדִּיקַיָּא, לְמִרְחַם עֲלַי וּלְמִנְטַר יָתִי וְיָת כָּל דִּי לִי וְדִי לְעַמָּךְ יִשְׂרָאֵל. אַנְתְּ הוּא זָן לְכֹלָּא וּמְפַרְנֵס לְכֹלָּא, אַנְתְּ הוּא שַׁלִּיט עַל כֹּלָּא, אַנְתְּ הוּא דְּשַׁלִּיט עַל מַלְכַיָּא, וּמַלְכוּתָא דִּילָךְ הִיא. אֲנָא עַבְדָּא דְקֻדְשָׁא בְּרִיךְ הוּא, דְּסָגֵדְנָא קַמֵּהּ וּמִקַּמֵּי דִּיקַר אוֹרַיְתֵהּ בְּכָל עִדָּן וְעִדָּן. לָא עַל אֱנָשׁ רְחִיצְנָא וְלָא עַל בַּר אֱלָהִין סָמֵיכְנָא, אֶלָּא בֵּאלָהָא דִשְׁמַיָּא, דְּהוּא אֱלָהָא קְשׁוֹט, וְאוֹרַיְתֵהּ קְשׁוֹט, וּנְבִיאוֹהִי קְשׁוֹט, וּמַסְגֵּא לְמֶעְבַּד טַבְוָן וּקְשׁוֹט. ‹ בֵּהּ אֲנָא רָחִיץ, וְלִשְׁמֵהּ קַדִּישָׁא יַקִּירָא אֲנָא אֵמַר תֻּשְׁבְּחָן. יְהֵא רַעֲוָא קֳדָמָךְ דְּתִפְתַּח לִבַּאי בְּאוֹרַיְתָא, וְתַשְׁלִים מִשְׁאֲלִין דְּלִבַּאי וְלִבָּא דְכָל עַמָּךְ יִשְׂרָאֵל לְטָב וּלְחַיִּין וְלִשְׁלָם.

The חזן *then* קהל:

שְׁמַע יִשְׂרָאֵל, יהוה אֱלֹהֵינוּ, יהוה אֶחָד:

חזן *then* קהל:

אֶחָד אֱלֹהֵינוּ, גָּדוֹל אֲדוֹנֵינוּ

קָדוֹשׁ (בהושענא רבה: וְנוֹרָא) שְׁמוֹ.

חזן *then* קהל:

גַּדְּלוּ לַיהוה אִתִּי וּנְרוֹמְמָה שְׁמוֹ יַחְדָּו:

The Aron Kodesh is closed. The Congregation says:

לְךָ *Hashem,*
You are great, powerful, glorious, and majestic!
Everything in heaven and earth is Yours,
and You are King over all.

רוֹמְמוּ Praise *Hashem,* our God,
and bow before Him,
for He is holy.
Praise, *Hashem,* our God,
and bow before His holy mountain,
the *Beit HaMikdash,*
for *Hashem* is holy.

עַל הַכֹּל May *Hashem,* the King of kings,
be praised and honored
in this world and the world-to-come.
He is the Master of all beings
and the God of all souls.
Let us sing to *Hashem*
whose throne is in heaven.

אַב הָרַחֲמִים May *Hashem,* our Father,
have mercy on His people.
May He remember our ancestors
and rescue us in difficult times.
May He answer our requests
and save us.

The ארון קודש *is closed. The* קהל *says:*

לְךָ יהוה הַגְּדֻלָּה וְהַגְּבוּרָה וְהַתִּפְאֶרֶת וְהַנֵּצַח וְהַהוֹד, כִּי־כֹל בַּשָּׁמַיִם וּבָאָרֶץ, לְךָ יהוה הַמַּמְלָכָה וְהַמִּתְנַשֵּׂא לְכֹל לְרֹאשׁ:

רוֹמְמוּ יהוה אֱלֹהֵינוּ וְהִשְׁתַּחֲווּ לַהֲדֹם רַגְלָיו, קָדוֹשׁ הוּא: רוֹמְמוּ יהוה אֱלֹהֵינוּ וְהִשְׁתַּחֲווּ לְהַר קָדְשׁוֹ, כִּי־קָדוֹשׁ יהוה אֱלֹהֵינוּ:

עַל הַכֹּל יִתְגַּדַּל וְיִתְקַדַּשׁ וְיִשְׁתַּבַּח וְיִתְפָּאַר וְיִתְרוֹמַם וְיִתְנַשֵּׂא שְׁמוֹ שֶׁל מֶלֶךְ מַלְכֵי הַמְּלָכִים הַקָּדוֹשׁ בָּרוּךְ הוּא בָּעוֹלָמוֹת שֶׁבָּרָא, הָעוֹלָם הַזֶּה וְהָעוֹלָם הַבָּא, כִּרְצוֹנוֹ וְכִרְצוֹן יְרֵאָיו וְכִרְצוֹן כָּל בֵּית יִשְׂרָאֵל. צוּר הָעוֹלָמִים, אֲדוֹן כָּל הַבְּרִיּוֹת, אֱלוֹהַּ כָּל הַנְּפָשׁוֹת, הַיּוֹשֵׁב בְּמֶרְחֲבֵי מָרוֹם, הַשּׁוֹכֵן בִּשְׁמֵי שְׁמֵי קֶדֶם, קְדֻשָּׁתוֹ עַל הַחַיּוֹת, וּקְדֻשָּׁתוֹ עַל כִּסֵּא הַכָּבוֹד. וּבְכֵן יִתְקַדַּשׁ שִׁמְךָ בָּנוּ יהוה אֱלֹהֵינוּ לְעֵינֵי כָּל חָי, וְנֹאמַר לְפָנָיו שִׁיר חָדָשׁ, כַּכָּתוּב: שִׁירוּ לֵאלֹהִים זַמְּרוּ שְׁמוֹ, סֹלּוּ לָרֹכֵב בָּעֲרָבוֹת, בְּיָהּ שְׁמוֹ, וְעִלְזוּ לְפָנָיו: וְנִרְאֵהוּ עַיִן בְּעַיִן בְּשׁוּבוֹ אֶל נָוֵהוּ, כַּכָּתוּב: כִּי עַיִן בְּעַיִן יִרְאוּ בְּשׁוּב יהוה צִיּוֹן: וְנֶאֱמַר: וְנִגְלָה כְּבוֹד יהוה, וְרָאוּ כָל־בָּשָׂר יַחְדָּו כִּי פִּי יהוה דִּבֵּר:

אַב הָרַחֲמִים הוּא יְרַחֵם עַם עֲמוּסִים, וְיִזְכֹּר בְּרִית אֵיתָנִים, וְיַצִּיל נַפְשׁוֹתֵינוּ מִן הַשָּׁעוֹת הָרָעוֹת, וְיִגְעַר בְּיֵצֶר הָרָע מִן הַנְּשׂוּאִים, וְיָחֹן אוֹתָנוּ לִפְלֵיטַת עוֹלָמִים, וִימַלֵּא מִשְׁאֲלוֹתֵינוּ בְּמִדָּה טוֹבָה יְשׁוּעָה וְרַחֲמִים.

The Gabbai recites the following:

וְיַעֲזֹר וְיָגֵן *Hashem* helps, protects, and saves everyone who turns to Him. To this we all say Amen. We all recognize that *Hashem* is great and we honor His Torah. We call to the Torah (*name*) son of (*father's name*) for the first Aliya, Kohen. We thank *Hashem* who gave His Jewish people the Torah.

Congregation responds:

You who are close to *Hashem* your God are alive today.

Gabbai responds:

You who are close to *Hashem* your God are alive today.

Person called up for the Aliya:

בָּרְכוּ Let us thank *Hashem*, for He deserves thanksgiving!

Congregation:

Thank *Hashem* for ever and ever!

Person called up for the Aliya:

Thank *Hashem* for ever and ever!

Person called up for the Aliya:

Thank You, *Hashem*, our God, King of the world,
for choosing us, the Jewish people,
from all the other nations of the world,
to be Your special people and for giving us Your Torah.
Thank You, *Hashem*, for giving us Your Torah.

After each Aliya the person called up says:

Thank You, *Hashem*, our God, King of the world,
for giving us the Torah.
It is filled with truth
and provides us with a meaningful life.
Thank You, *Hashem*, for giving us Your Torah.

The גבאי *recites the following:*

וְיַעֲזֹר וְיָגֵן וְיוֹשִׁיעַ לְכָל הַחוֹסִים בּוֹ, וְנֹאמַר אָמֵן. הַכֹּל הָבוּ גֹדֶל לֵאלֹהֵינוּ וּתְנוּ כָבוֹד לַתּוֹרָה. כֹּהֵן קְרַב, יַעֲמֹד (פלוני בֶּן פלוני) הַכֹּהֵן. בָּרוּךְ שֶׁנָּתַן תּוֹרָה לְעַמּוֹ יִשְׂרָאֵל בִּקְדֻשָּׁתוֹ.

The קהל *responds:*

וְאַתֶּם הַדְּבֵקִים בַּיהוה אֱלֹהֵיכֶם חַיִּים כֻּלְּכֶם הַיּוֹם:

The גבאי *responds:*

וְאַתֶּם הַדְּבֵקִים בַּיהוה אֱלֹהֵיכֶם חַיִּים כֻּלְּכֶם הַיּוֹם:

Person called up for the עליה*:*

בָּרְכוּ אֶת יהוה הַמְבֹרָךְ.

קהל*:*

בָּרוּךְ יהוה הַמְבֹרָךְ לְעוֹלָם וָעֶד.

Person called up for the עליה*:*

בָּרוּךְ יהוה הַמְבֹרָךְ לְעוֹלָם וָעֶד.

Person called up for the עליה*:*

בָּרוּךְ אַתָּה יהוה אֱלֹהֵינוּ מֶלֶךְ הָעוֹלָם
אֲשֶׁר בָּחַר בָּנוּ מִכָּל הָעַמִּים, וְנָתַן לָנוּ אֶת תּוֹרָתוֹ.
בָּרוּךְ אַתָּה יהוה, נוֹתֵן הַתּוֹרָה.

After the עליה *the person called up says:*

בָּרוּךְ אַתָּה יהוה אֱלֹהֵינוּ מֶלֶךְ הָעוֹלָם
אֲשֶׁר נָתַן לָנוּ תּוֹרַת אֱמֶת, וְחַיֵּי עוֹלָם נָטַע בְּתוֹכֵנוּ.
בָּרוּךְ אַתָּה יהוה, נוֹתֵן הַתּוֹרָה.

After seven Aliyot have been read the reader says:

HALF KADDISH

Reader: יִתְגַּדַּל May *Hashem* be recognized
as great and holy (*Congregation:* Amen)
in the world that He created.
May He establish His kingdom
during my lifetime and the lifetime of all Jews,
quickly and soon.
Let us say: "Amen" (*Congregation:* Amen).

Congregation: May we thank *Hashem* for ever and ever.
Reader: May we thank *Hashem* for ever and ever.

Reader: *Hashem* should be thanked, praised,
and honored (*Congregation:* He is blessed).
Hashem is beyond all the blessings,
songs, or praises
that we could offer.
Let us say:
"Amen" (*Congregation:* Amen).

After Kaddish, one more person is called up for Maftir.

HAGBAHA AND GELILA

After the Maftir is read,
the Torah scroll is lifted and the congregation says:

וְזֹאת הַתּוֹרָה This is the Torah
that Moses placed before the Jewish people
as *Hashem* commanded.

The Torah scroll is bound and covered.

After seven עליות *have been read, the* קורא *says:*

חצי קדיש

קורא: יִתְגַּדַּל וְיִתְקַדַּשׁ שְׁמֵהּ רַבָּא (קהל: אָמֵן)
בְּעָלְמָא דִּי בְרָא כִרְעוּתֵהּ, וְיַמְלִיךְ מַלְכוּתֵהּ
בְּחַיֵּיכוֹן וּבְיוֹמֵיכוֹן וּבְחַיֵּי דְכָל בֵּית יִשְׂרָאֵל
בַּעֲגָלָא וּבִזְמַן קָרִיב, וְאִמְרוּ אָמֵן. (קהל: אָמֵן)

קהל יְהֵא שְׁמֵהּ רַבָּא מְבָרַךְ לְעָלַם וּלְעָלְמֵי עָלְמַיָּא.
קורא: יְהֵא שְׁמֵהּ רַבָּא מְבָרַךְ לְעָלַם וּלְעָלְמֵי עָלְמַיָּא.

קורא: יִתְבָּרַךְ וְיִשְׁתַּבַּח וְיִתְפָּאַר וְיִתְרוֹמַם וְיִתְנַשֵּׂא
וְיִתְהַדָּר וְיִתְעַלֶּה וְיִתְהַלָּל
שְׁמֵהּ דְּקֻדְשָׁא בְּרִיךְ הוּא (קהל: בְּרִיךְ הוּא)
לְעֵלָּא מִן כָּל בִּרְכָתָא
/בשבת שובה: לְעֵלָּא לְעֵלָּא מִכָּל בִּרְכָתָא/
וְשִׁירָתָא, תֻּשְׁבְּחָתָא וְנֶחֱמָתָא
דַּאֲמִירָן בְּעָלְמָא, וְאִמְרוּ אָמֵן. (קהל: אָמֵן)

After קדיש*, one more person is called up for* מפטיר.

הגבהה וגלילה

After the מפטיר *is read, the* ספר תורה *is lifted and the* קהל *says:*

וְזֹאת הַתּוֹרָה אֲשֶׁר־שָׂם מֹשֶׁה לִפְנֵי בְּנֵי יִשְׂרָאֵל:
עַל־פִּי יהוה בְּיַד מֹשֶׁה:

The ספר תורה *is bound and covered.*

BIRCHOT HA'HAFTARAH

After Hagbaha and Gelila, the person called up for Maftir says the following before the Haftarah:

בָּרוּךְ Thank You, *Hashem,* our God, King of the world,
for choosing good prophets, *Nevi'im,*
who delivered truthful messages.
Thank You, *Hashem,* for choosing the Torah,
Moshe, the Jewish people, and the holy *Nevi'im.*

After the Haftarah, the person called up for Maftir says the following:

בָּרוּךְ Thank You, *Hashem,* our God, King of the world,
who is always fair, keeps His promises,
and speaks only true and holy words.
You are our trustworthy King.
Thank You, *Hashem,*
for being trustworthy in keeping His word.

רַחֵם Be kind to Jerusalem as it is the center of our life,
and may You bring comfort to all those who are sad.
We thank You *Hashem* who will bring joy back
to Jerusalem and all of its people.

שַׂמְּחֵנוּ *Hashem,* may You bring us joy in our hearts
by having Eliyahu come soon
and allow the Kingdom of David to rule again.
May no stranger sit in the throne of David
and rule over the Jewish people,
as You promised David
that he would forever rule over the Jewish people.
Thank You, *Hashem,* who defends David.

ברכות ההפטרה

After הגבהה *and* גלילה*, the person called up for* מפטיר *says the following before the* הפטרה*:*

בָּרוּךְ אַתָּה יהוה אֱלֹהֵינוּ מֶלֶךְ הָעוֹלָם אֲשֶׁר בָּחַר בִּנְבִיאִים טוֹבִים, וְרָצָה בְדִבְרֵיהֶם הַנֶּאֱמָרִים בֶּאֱמֶת. בָּרוּךְ אַתָּה יהוה, הַבּוֹחֵר בַּתּוֹרָה וּבְמֹשֶׁה עַבְדּוֹ וּבְיִשְׂרָאֵל עַמּוֹ וּבִנְבִיאֵי הָאֱמֶת וָצֶדֶק.

After the הפטרה*, the person called up for* מפטיר *says the following:*

בָּרוּךְ אַתָּה יהוה אֱלֹהֵינוּ מֶלֶךְ הָעוֹלָם, צוּר כָּל הָעוֹלָמִים, צַדִּיק בְּכָל הַדּוֹרוֹת, הָאֵל הַנֶּאֱמָן, הָאוֹמֵר וְעוֹשֶׂה, הַמְדַבֵּר וּמְקַיֵּם, שֶׁכָּל דְּבָרָיו אֱמֶת וָצֶדֶק. נֶאֱמָן אַתָּה הוּא יהוה אֱלֹהֵינוּ וְנֶאֱמָנִים דְּבָרֶיךָ, וְדָבָר אֶחָד מִדְּבָרֶיךָ אָחוֹר לֹא יָשׁוּב רֵיקָם, כִּי אֵל מֶלֶךְ נֶאֱמָן (וְרַחֲמָן) אָתָּה. בָּרוּךְ אַתָּה יהוה, הָאֵל הַנֶּאֱמָן בְּכָל דְּבָרָיו.

רַחֵם עַל צִיּוֹן כִּי הִיא בֵּית חַיֵּינוּ, וְלַעֲלוּבַת נֶפֶשׁ תּוֹשִׁיעַ בִּמְהֵרָה בְיָמֵינוּ. בָּרוּךְ אַתָּה יהוה, מְשַׂמֵּחַ צִיּוֹן בְּבָנֶיהָ.

שַׂמְּחֵנוּ יהוה אֱלֹהֵינוּ בְּאֵלִיָּהוּ הַנָּבִיא עַבְדֶּךָ, וּבְמַלְכוּת בֵּית דָּוִד מְשִׁיחֶךָ, בִּמְהֵרָה יָבוֹא וְיָגֵל לִבֵּנוּ. עַל כִּסְאוֹ לֹא יֵשֶׁב זָר, וְלֹא יִנְחֲלוּ עוֹד אֲחֵרִים אֶת כְּבוֹדוֹ, כִּי בְשֵׁם קָדְשְׁךָ נִשְׁבַּעְתָּ לּוֹ שֶׁלֹּא יִכְבֶּה נֵרוֹ לְעוֹלָם וָעֶד. בָּרוּךְ אַתָּה יהוה, מָגֵן דָּוִד.

On Shabbat, including Shabbat Chol HaMo'ed Pesach, say:

עַל הַתּוֹרָה We thank You *Hashem* for the:

Torah,

Korbanot in the Temple,

Nevi'im, and

The day of Shabbat that You gave us for rest.

May we continue to thank You forever and ever
and praise You.

Thank You, *Hashem,* for making Shabbat holy.

On Shabbat Chol HaMo'ed Sukkot, say:

עַל הַתּוֹרָה We thank You *Hashem* for the:

Torah, *Korbanot* in the Temple, Nevi'im,

The day of Shabbat that You gave us for rest, and

The day of *Sukkot* that You gave us for happiness.

May we continue to thank You forever and ever and praise You.

Thank You, *Hashem,* for making Shabbat and the Festivals holy.

The following three paragraphs are only said when praying with a minyan.

יְקוּם פֻּרְקָן *Hashem,* who rules from heaven,
may You please provide all our holy teachers,
rabbis, leaders, and judges, as well as their students:

kindness,

love,

long life,

food to eat,

good health, and

children who will learn Torah.

Hashem, King over the universe,
bless them and give them long life.
May they all be saved from troubles and illness.
We all say Amen.

On שבת*, including* שבת חול המועד פסח*, say:*

עַל הַתּוֹרָה וְעַל הָעֲבוֹדָה וְעַל הַנְּבִיאִים וְעַל יוֹם הַשַּׁבָּת הַזֶּה, שֶׁנָּתַתָּ לָּנוּ יהוה אֱלֹהֵינוּ לִקְדֻשָּׁה וְלִמְנוּחָה, לְכָבוֹד וּלְתִפְאָרֶת. עַל הַכֹּל יהוה אֱלֹהֵינוּ אֲנַחְנוּ מוֹדִים לָךְ וּמְבָרְכִים אוֹתָךְ, יִתְבָּרַךְ שִׁמְךָ בְּפִי כָּל חַי תָּמִיד לְעוֹלָם וָעֶד. בָּרוּךְ אַתָּה יהוה, מְקַדֵּשׁ הַשַּׁבָּת.

On שבת חול המועד סוכות*, say:*

עַל הַתּוֹרָה וְעַל הָעֲבוֹדָה וְעַל הַנְּבִיאִים וְעַל יוֹם הַשַּׁבָּת הַזֶּה, וְעַל יוֹם חַג הַסֻּכּוֹת הַזֶּה, שֶׁנָּתַתָּ לָּנוּ, יהוה אֱלֹהֵינוּ, לִקְדֻשָּׁה וְלִמְנוּחָה, לְשָׂשׂוֹן וּלְשִׂמְחָה, לְכָבוֹד וּלְתִפְאָרֶת. עַל הַכֹּל יהוה אֱלֹהֵינוּ אֲנַחְנוּ מוֹדִים לָךְ וּמְבָרְכִים אוֹתָךְ. יִתְבָּרַךְ שִׁמְךָ בְּפִי כָּל חַי תָּמִיד לְעוֹלָם וָעֶד. בָּרוּךְ אַתָּה יהוה, מְקַדֵּשׁ הַשַּׁבָּת וְיִשְׂרָאֵל וְהַזְּמַנִּים.

The following three paragraphs are only said when praying with a minyan.

יְקוּם פֻּרְקָן מִן שְׁמַיָּא, חִנָּא וְחִסְדָּא וְרַחֲמֵי וְחַיֵּי אֲרִיכֵי וּמְזוֹנֵי רְוִיחֵי, וְסִיַּעְתָּא דִשְׁמַיָּא, וּבַרְיוּת גּוּפָא וּנְהוֹרָא מְעַלְּיָא, זַרְעָא חַיָּא וְקַיָּמָא, זַרְעָא דִּי לָא יִפְסֻק וְדִי לָא יִבְטֻל מִפִּתְגָּמֵי אוֹרַיְתָא, לְמָרָנָן וְרַבָּנָן חֲבוּרָתָא קַדִּישָׁתָא דִּי בְּאַרְעָא דְיִשְׂרָאֵל וְדִי בְּבָבֶל, לְרֵישֵׁי כַלָּה, וּלְרֵישֵׁי גַלְוָתָא, וּלְרֵישֵׁי מְתִיבָתָא, וּלְדַיָּנֵי דְבָבָא, לְכָל תַּלְמִידֵיהוֹן, וּלְכָל תַּלְמִידֵי תַלְמִידֵיהוֹן, וּלְכָל מָאן דְּעָסְקִין בְּאוֹרַיְתָא. מַלְכָּא דְעָלְמָא יְבָרֵךְ יָתְהוֹן, יַפֵּשׁ חַיֵּיהוֹן וְיַסְגֵּא יוֹמֵיהוֹן, וְיִתֵּן אַרְכָא לִשְׁנֵיהוֹן, וְיִתְפָּרְקוּן וְיִשְׁתֵּיזְבוּן מִן כָּל עָקָא

יְקוּם פֻּרְקָן *Hashem* who rules from heaven,
may You please give:
kindness,
love,
long life,
food to eat,
good health, and
children who will learn Torah
to this entire shul; all men, women, and children.
Hashem, King over the universe,
bless them and give them long life.
May they all be saved from troubles and illness.
We all say Amen.

מִי שֶׁבֵּרַךְ *Hashem* who blessed our ancestors,
Avraham, Yitzchak, and Yaakov, bless everyone
in this shul and all the other shuls in the world;
all of the men and women, sons and daughters,
and everything that is theirs.
May You bless the people who create shuls
and all those that come to daven in them.
May You bless those who donate the candle and wine
for Kiddush and Havdalah,
food for guests, *tzedakah* for the poor,
and those that take care of the community's needs.
Hashem, please reward all of these people,
heal their sicknesses, and forgive them for their sins.
May they be blessed with success for all their work,
along with all of the Jewish people.
We all say Amen.

וּמִן כָּל מַרְעִין בִּישִׁין. מָרַן דִּי בִשְׁמַיָּא יְהֵא בְסַעְדְּהוֹן כָּל זְמַן וְעִדָּן, וְנֹאמַר אָמֵן.

יְקוּם פֻּרְקָן מִן שְׁמַיָּא, חִנָּא וְחִסְדָּא וְרַחֲמֵי וְחַיֵּי אֲרִיכֵי וּמְזוֹנֵי רְוִיחֵי, וְסִיַּעְתָּא דִשְׁמַיָּא, וּבַרְיוּת גּוּפָא וּנְהוֹרָא מְעַלְיָא, זַרְעָא חַיָּא וְקַיָּמָא, זַרְעָא דִּי לָא יִפְסֻק וְדִי לָא יִבְטֻל מִפִּתְגָּמֵי אוֹרַיְתָא, לְכָל קְהָלָא קַדִּישָׁא הָדֵין, רַבְרְבַיָּא עִם זְעֵרַיָּא, טַפְלָא וּנְשַׁיָּא. מַלְכָּא דְעָלְמָא יְבָרֵךְ יָתְכוֹן, יַפֵּשׁ חַיֵּיכוֹן וְיַסְגֵּא יוֹמֵיכוֹן, וְיִתֵּן אַרְכָא לִשְׁנֵיכוֹן, וְתִתְפָּרְקוּן וְתִשְׁתֵּיזְבוּן מִן כָּל עָקָא וּמִן כָּל מַרְעִין בִּישִׁין. מָרַן דִּי בִשְׁמַיָּא יְהֵא בְסַעְדְּכוֹן כָּל זְמַן וְעִדָּן, וְנֹאמַר אָמֵן.

מִי שֶׁבֵּרַךְ אֲבוֹתֵינוּ אַבְרָהָם יִצְחָק וְיַעֲקֹב, הוּא יְבָרֵךְ אֶת כָּל הַקָּהָל הַקָּדוֹשׁ הַזֶּה עִם כָּל קְהִלּוֹת הַקֹּדֶשׁ, הֵם וּנְשֵׁיהֶם וּבְנֵיהֶם וּבְנוֹתֵיהֶם וְכָל אֲשֶׁר לָהֶם, וּמִי שֶׁמְּיַחֲדִים בָּתֵּי כְנֵסִיּוֹת לִתְפִלָּה, וּמִי שֶׁבָּאִים בְּתוֹכָם לְהִתְפַּלֵּל, וּמִי שֶׁנּוֹתְנִים נֵר לַמָּאוֹר וְיַיִן לְקִדּוּשׁ וּלְהַבְדָּלָה וּפַת לָאוֹרְחִים וּצְדָקָה לָעֲנִיִּים, וְכָל מִי שֶׁעוֹסְקִים בְּצָרְכֵי צִבּוּר בֶּאֱמוּנָה. הַקָּדוֹשׁ בָּרוּךְ הוּא יְשַׁלֵּם שְׂכָרָם, וְיָסִיר מֵהֶם כָּל מַחֲלָה, וְיִרְפָּא לְכָל גּוּפָם, וְיִסְלַח לְכָל עֲוֹנָם, וְיִשְׁלַח בְּרָכָה וְהַצְלָחָה בְּכָל מַעֲשֵׂי יְדֵיהֶם עִם כָּל יִשְׂרָאֵל אֲחֵיהֶם, וְנֹאמַר אָמֵן.

PRAYER FOR THE WELFARE OF THE AMERICAN GOVERNMENT

The Leader says the following:

הַנּוֹתֵן *Hashem,*
You are able to save and You give control
to kings and princes.
Please protect, guard, help, and uplift
the President, Vice President,
and all officials of America.
May You, *Hashem,* the King of kings,
guide these leaders to be kind to us
and all the Jewish people.
Please allow us to live in safety
and may *Mashiach* come to save us.
Let us say: Amen.

PRAYER FOR THE SAFETY OF THE AMERICAN ARMY

The Leader says the following:

אַדִּיר *Hashem,* our God and King,
please bless the soldiers of the American army
who risk their lives for peace.
Protect, guide, and give them strength and courage
to overcome their enemies.
May their enemies run from them
and may American soldiers
rejoice in Your saving them.
Please bring them back to their homes safely.
Let all people know that You are King of the world.
Let us say: Amen.

תפילה לשלום המלכות

The חזן *says the following:*

הַנּוֹתֵן תְּשׁוּעָה לַמְּלָכִים וּמֶמְשָׁלָה לַנְּסִיכִים, מַלְכוּתוֹ מַלְכוּת כָּל עוֹלָמִים, הַפּוֹצֶה אֶת דָּוִד עַבְדּוֹ מֵחֶרֶב רָעָה, הַנּוֹתֵן בַּיָּם דֶּרֶךְ וּבְמַיִם עַזִּים נְתִיבָה, הוּא יְבָרֵךְ וְיִשְׁמֹר וְיִנְצֹר וְיַעֲזֹר וִירוֹמֵם וִיגַדֵּל וִינַשֵּׂא לְמַעְלָה אֶת הַנָּשִׂיא וְאֵת מִשְׁנֵהוּ וְאֶת כָּל שָׂרֵי הָאָרֶץ הַזֹּאת. מֶלֶךְ מַלְכֵי הַמְּלָכִים, בְּרַחֲמָיו יִתֵּן בְּלִבָּם וּבְלֵב כָּל יוֹעֲצֵיהֶם וְשָׂרֵיהֶם לַעֲשׂוֹת טוֹבָה עִמָּנוּ וְעִם כָּל יִשְׂרָאֵל. בִּימֵיהֶם וּבְיָמֵינוּ תִּוָּשַׁע יְהוּדָה, וְיִשְׂרָאֵל יִשְׁכֹּן לָבֶטַח, וּבָא לְצִיּוֹן גּוֹאֵל. וְכֵן יְהִי רָצוֹן, וְנֹאמַר אָמֵן.

תפילה לשלום חיילי צבא ארצות הברית

The חזן *says the following:*

אַדִּיר בַּמָּרוֹם שׁוֹכֵן בִּגְבוּרָה, מֶלֶךְ שֶׁהַשָּׁלוֹם שֶׁלּוֹ, הַשְׁקִיפָה מִמְּעוֹן קָדְשְׁךָ, וּבָרֵךְ אֶת חַיָּלֵי צְבָא אַרְצוֹת הַבְּרִית, הַמְחָרְפִים נַפְשָׁם בְּלֶכְתָּם לָשִׂים שָׁלוֹם בָּאָרֶץ. הֱיֵה נָא לָהֶם מַחֲסֶה וּמָעוֹז, וְאַל תִּתֵּן לַמּוֹט רַגְלָם, חַזֵּק יְדֵיהֶם וְאַמֵּץ רוּחָם לְהָפֵר עֲצַת אוֹיֵב וּלְהַעֲבִיר מֶמְשֶׁלֶת זָדוֹן, יָפֽוּצוּ אוֹיְבֵיהֶם וְיָנֽוּסוּ מְשַׂנְאֵיהֶם מִפְּנֵיהֶם, וְיִשְׂמְחוּ בִּישׁוּעָתֶךָ. הֲשִׁיבֵם בְּשָׁלוֹם אֶל בֵּיתָם, כַּכָּתוּב בְּדִבְרֵי קָדְשֶׁךָ: יהוה יִשְׁמָרְךָ מִכָּל־רָע, יִשְׁמֹר אֶת־נַפְשֶׁךָ: יהוה יִשְׁמָר־צֵאתְךָ וּבוֹאֶךָ, מֵעַתָּה וְעַד־עוֹלָם: וְקַיֵּם בָּנוּ מִקְרָא שֶׁכָּתוּב: לֹא־יִשָּׂא גוֹי אֶל־גּוֹי חֶרֶב, וְלֹא־יִלְמְדוּ עוֹד מִלְחָמָה: וְיֵדְעוּ כָּל יוֹשְׁבֵי תֵבֵל כִּי לְךָ מְלוּכָה יָאֲתָה, וְשִׁמְךָ נוֹרָא עַל כָּל מַה שֶּׁבָּרָאתָ. וְנֹאמַר אָמֵן.

PRAYER FOR THE WELFARE OF CANADIAN GOVERNMENT

The Leader says the following:

הַנּוֹתֵן *Hashem,*
You are able to save and give control
to kings and princes.
Please protect, guard, help, and uplift
the Prime Minister
and all officials of Canada.
May You, *Hashem,* the King of kings,
guide these leaders to be kind to us
and all the Jewish people.
Please allow us to live in safety
and may *Mashiach* come to save us.
Let us say: Amen.

PRAYER FOR THE SAFETY OF THE CANADIAN ARMY

The Leader says the following:

אַדִּיר *Hashem,* our God and King,
please bless the soldiers of the Canadian army
who risk their lives for peace.
Protect, guide, and give them strength and courage
to overcome their enemies.
May their enemies run from them
and may Canadian soldiers
rejoice in Your saving them.
Please bring them back to their homes safely.
Let all people know that You are King of the world.
Let us say: Amen.

תפילה לשלום המלכות

The חזן *says the following:*

הַנּוֹתֵן תְּשׁוּעָה לַמְּלָכִים וּמֶמְשָׁלָה לַנְּסִיכִים, מַלְכוּתוֹ מַלְכוּת כָּל עוֹלָמִים, הַפּוֹצֶה אֶת דָּוִד עַבְדּוֹ מֵחֶרֶב רָעָה, הַנּוֹתֵן בַּיָּם דֶּרֶךְ וּבְמַיִם עַזִּים נְתִיבָה, הוּא יְבָרֵךְ וְיִשְׁמֹר וְיִנְצֹר וְיַעֲזֹר וִירוֹמֵם וִיגַדֵּל וִינַשֵּׂא לְמַעְלָה אֶת רֹאשׁ הַמֶּמְשָׁלָה וְאֶת כָּל שָׂרֵי הָאָרֶץ הַזֹּאת. מֶלֶךְ מַלְכֵי הַמְּלָכִים, בְּרַחֲמָיו יִתֵּן בְּלִבָּם וּבְלֵב כָּל יוֹעֲצֵיהֶם וְשָׂרֵיהֶם לַעֲשׂוֹת טוֹבָה עִמָּנוּ וְעִם כָּל יִשְׂרָאֵל. בִּימֵיהֶם וּבְיָמֵינוּ תִּוָּשַׁע יְהוּדָה, וְיִשְׂרָאֵל יִשְׁכֹּן לָבֶטַח, וּבָא לְצִיּוֹן גּוֹאֵל. וְכֵן יְהִי רָצוֹן, וְנֹאמַר אָמֵן.

תפילה לשלום חיילי צבא קנדה

The חזן *says the following:*

אַדִּיר בַּמָּרוֹם שׁוֹכֵן בִּגְבוּרָה, מֶלֶךְ שֶׁהַשָּׁלוֹם שֶׁלּוֹ, הַשְׁקִיפָה מִמְּעוֹן קָדְשְׁךָ, וּבָרֵךְ אֶת חַיָּלֵי צְבָא קָנָדָה, הַמְחָרְפִים נַפְשָׁם בְּלֶכְתָּם לָשִׂים שָׁלוֹם בָּאָרֶץ. הֱיֵה נָא לָהֶם מַחֲסֶה וּמָעוֹז, וְאַל תִּתֵּן לַמּוֹט רַגְלָם, חַזֵּק יְדֵיהֶם וְאַמֵּץ רוּחָם לְהָפֵר עֲצַת אוֹיֵב וּלְהַעֲבִיר מֶמְשֶׁלֶת זָדוֹן, יָפֻוצוּ אוֹיְבֵיהֶם וְיָנוּסוּ מְשַׂנְאֵיהֶם מִפְּנֵיהֶם, וְיִשְׂמְחוּ בִּישׁוּעָתֶךָ. הֲשִׁיבֵם בְּשָׁלוֹם אֶל בֵּיתָם, כַּכָּתוּב בְּדִבְרֵי קָדְשֶׁךָ: יהוה יִשְׁמָרְךָ מִכָּל־רָע, יִשְׁמֹר אֶת־נַפְשֶׁךָ: יהוה יִשְׁמָר־צֵאתְךָ וּבוֹאֶךָ, מֵעַתָּה וְעַד־עוֹלָם: וְקַיֵּם בָּנוּ מִקְרָא שֶׁכָּתוּב: לֹא־יִשָּׂא גוֹי אֶל־גּוֹי חֶרֶב, וְלֹא־יִלְמְדוּ עוֹד מִלְחָמָה: וְיֵדְעוּ כָּל יוֹשְׁבֵי תֵבֵל כִּי לְךָ מְלוּכָה יָאֲתָה, וְשִׁמְךָ נוֹרָא עַל כָּל מַה שֶּׁבָּרָאתָ. וְנֹאמַר אָמֵן.

PRAYER FOR THE STATE OF ISRAEL

The Leader says the following:

אָבִינוּ *Hashem,*
our Father in heaven and savior,
bless the State of Israel
and begin our redemption.
Protect Israel with Your kindness
and provide it with peace.
Guide the leaders, ministers, and government
in advising Israel.

Provide Israel's soldiers
with the strength to defend the land
and to lead the country to victory.
Bring peace to Israel and happiness
to those who live there.

For those living outside of Israel,
we remember our land
and we pray that we will soon be led to Israel.
Hashem,
unite our hearts to love and respect You,
and to keep all the *mitzvot* of Your Torah.
Please send *Mashiach* to redeem us.
Hashem, God of Israel, is King
and rules over all.
Amen *selah.*

תפילה לשלום מדינת ישראל

The חזן *says the following:*

אָבִינוּ שֶׁבַּשָּׁמַיִם, צוּר יִשְׂרָאֵל וְגוֹאֲלוֹ, בָּרֵךְ אֶת מְדִינַת יִשְׂרָאֵל, רֵאשִׁית צְמִיחַת גְּאֻלָּתֵנוּ. הָגֵן עָלֶיהָ בְּאֶבְרַת חַסְדֶּךָ וּפְרֹשׂ עָלֶיהָ סֻכַּת שְׁלוֹמֶךָ, וּשְׁלַח אוֹרְךָ וַאֲמִתְּךָ לְרָאשֶׁיהָ, שָׂרֶיהָ וְיוֹעֲצֶיהָ, וְתַקְּנֵם בְּעֵצָה טוֹבָה מִלְּפָנֶיךָ.

חַזֵּק אֶת יְדֵי מְגִנֵּי אֶרֶץ קָדְשֵׁנוּ, וְהַנְחִילֵם אֱלֹהֵינוּ יְשׁוּעָה וַעֲטֶרֶת נִצָּחוֹן תְּעַטְּרֵם, וְנָתַתָּ שָׁלוֹם בָּאָרֶץ וְשִׂמְחַת עוֹלָם לְיוֹשְׁבֶיהָ.

וְאֶת אַחֵינוּ כָּל בֵּית יִשְׂרָאֵל, פְּקָד נָא בְּכָל אַרְצוֹת פְּזוּרֵינוּ, וְתוֹלִיכֵנוּ מְהֵרָה קוֹמְמִיּוּת לְצִיּוֹן עִירֶךָ וְלִירוּשָׁלַיִם מִשְׁכַּן שְׁמֶךָ, כַּכָּתוּב בְּתוֹרַת מֹשֶׁה עַבְדֶּךָ: אִם־יִהְיֶה נִדַּחֲךָ בִּקְצֵה הַשָּׁמָיִם, מִשָּׁם יְקַבֶּצְךָ יהוה אֱלֹהֶיךָ וּמִשָּׁם יִקָּחֶךָ: וֶהֱבִיאֲךָ יהוה אֱלֹהֶיךָ אֶל־הָאָרֶץ אֲשֶׁר־יָרְשׁוּ אֲבֹתֶיךָ וִירִשְׁתָּהּ, וְהֵיטִבְךָ וְהִרְבְּךָ מֵאֲבֹתֶיךָ: וּמָל יהוה אֱלֹהֶיךָ אֶת־לְבָבְךָ וְאֶת־לְבַב זַרְעֶךָ, לְאַהֲבָה אֶת־יהוה אֱלֹהֶיךָ בְּכָל־לְבָבְךָ וּבְכָל־נַפְשְׁךָ, לְמַעַן חַיֶּיךָ:

וְיַחֵד לְבָבֵנוּ לְאַהֲבָה וּלְיִרְאָה אֶת שְׁמֶךָ, וְלִשְׁמֹר אֶת כָּל דִּבְרֵי תוֹרָתֶךָ, וּשְׁלַח לָנוּ מְהֵרָה בֶּן דָּוִד מְשִׁיחַ צִדְקֶךָ, לִפְדּוֹת מְחַכֵּי קֵץ יְשׁוּעָתֶךָ.

וְהוֹפַע בַּהֲדַר גְּאוֹן עֻזֶּךָ עַל כָּל יוֹשְׁבֵי תֵבֵל אַרְצֶךָ וְיֹאמַר כֹּל אֲשֶׁר נְשָׁמָה בְאַפּוֹ, יהוה אֱלֹהֵי יִשְׂרָאֵל מֶלֶךְ וּמַלְכוּתוֹ בַּכֹּל מָשָׁלָה, אָמֵן סֶלָה.

PRAYER FOR THE ISRAELI ARMY

The Leader says the following:

מִי שֶׁבֵּרַךְ *Hashem,*
just as You blessed our ancestors,
Avraham, Yitzchak, and Yaakov,
please bless the soldiers in the Israeli Defense Forces
who guard and protect all borders of our land, Israel.
May those who rise against Israel be defeated.
Hashem,
please protect the soldiers in the IDF
from all trouble, distress, and sickness,
and bless them with success.
Hashem, please join the soldiers in battle
and fight alongside them.
Let us say: Amen.

PRAYER FOR CAPTIVES

The Leader says the following:

מִי שֶׁבֵּרַךְ *Hashem,*
just as You blessed our ancestors,
Avraham, Yitzchak, Yaakov,
Yosef, Moshe, Aharon, David and Shlomo,
please bless and protect the soldiers
in the Israeli Defense Forces who are missing
or held captive by our enemies.
May *Hashem* show His mercy toward them,
speedily save them from their troubles,
and allow them to rejoin their families.
Let us say: Amen.

מי שברך לחיילי צה״ל

The חזן *says the following prayer:*

מִי שֶׁבֵּרַךְ אֲבוֹתֵינוּ אַבְרָהָם יִצְחָק וְיַעֲקֹב הוּא יְבָרֵךְ אֶת חַיָּלֵי צְבָא הַהֲגָנָה לְיִשְׂרָאֵל וְאַנְשֵׁי כֹּחוֹת הַבִּטָּחוֹן, הָעוֹמְדִים עַל מִשְׁמַר אַרְצֵנוּ וְעָרֵי אֱלֹהֵינוּ, מִגְּבוּל הַלְּבָנוֹן וְעַד מִדְבַּר מִצְרַיִם וּמִן הַיָּם הַגָּדוֹל עַד לְבוֹא הָעֲרָבָה וּבְכָל מָקוֹם שֶׁהֵם, בַּיַּבָּשָׁה, בָּאֲוִיר וּבַיָּם. יִתֵּן יהוה אֶת אוֹיְבֵינוּ הַקָּמִים עָלֵינוּ נִגָּפִים לִפְנֵיהֶם. הַקָּדוֹשׁ בָּרוּךְ הוּא יִשְׁמֹר וְיַצִּיל אֶת חַיָּלֵינוּ מִכָּל צָרָה וְצוּקָה וּמִכָּל נֶגַע וּמַחֲלָה, וְיִשְׁלַח בְּרָכָה וְהַצְלָחָה בְּכָל מַעֲשֵׂי יְדֵיהֶם. יַדְבֵּר שׂוֹנְאֵינוּ תַּחְתֵּיהֶם וִיעַטְּרֵם בְּכֶתֶר יְשׁוּעָה וּבַעֲטֶרֶת נִצָּחוֹן. וִיקֻיַּם בָּהֶם הַכָּתוּב: כִּי יהוה אֱלֹהֵיכֶם הַהֹלֵךְ עִמָּכֶם לְהִלָּחֵם לָכֶם עִם־אֹיְבֵיכֶם לְהוֹשִׁיעַ אֶתְכֶם: וְנֹאמַר אָמֵן.

מי שברך לשבויים

If Israeli soldiers or civilians are being held in captivity, the חזן *says the following:*

מִי שֶׁבֵּרַךְ אֲבוֹתֵינוּ אַבְרָהָם יִצְחָק וְיַעֲקֹב, יוֹסֵף מֹשֶׁה וְאַהֲרֹן, דָּוִד וּשְׁלֹמֹה, הוּא יְבָרֵךְ וְיִשְׁמֹר וְיִנְצֹר אֶת נֶעְדְּרֵי צְבָא הַהֲגָנָה לְיִשְׂרָאֵל וּשְׁבוּיָו, וְאֶת כָּל אַחֵינוּ הַנְּתוּנִים בְּצָרָה וּבְשִׁבְיָה, בַּעֲבוּר שֶׁכָּל הַקָּהָל הַקָּדוֹשׁ הַזֶּה מִתְפַּלֵּל בַּעֲבוּרָם. הַקָּדוֹשׁ בָּרוּךְ הוּא יִמָּלֵא רַחֲמִים עֲלֵיהֶם, וְיוֹצִיאֵם מֵחֹשֶׁךְ וְצַלְמָוֶת, וּמוֹסְרוֹתֵיהֶם יְנַתֵּק, וּמִמְּצוּקוֹתֵיהֶם יוֹשִׁיעֵם, וִישִׁיבֵם מְהֵרָה לְחֵיק מִשְׁפְּחוֹתֵיהֶם. יוֹדוּ לַיהוה חַסְדּוֹ וְנִפְלְאוֹתָיו לִבְנֵי אָדָם: וִיקֻיַּם בָּהֶם מִקְרָא שֶׁכָּתוּב: וּפְדוּיֵי יהוה יְשֻׁבוּן, וּבָאוּ צִיּוֹן בְּרִנָּה, וְשִׂמְחַת עוֹלָם עַל־רֹאשָׁם, שָׂשׂוֹן וְשִׂמְחָה יַשִּׂיגוּ, וְנָסוּ יָגוֹן וַאֲנָחָה: וְנֹאמַר אָמֵן.

BLESSING THE NEW MONTH

On the Shabbat before Rosh Chodesh, we say the following. On all other weeks continue with Av Harachamim on page 560.

יְהִי רָצוֹן *Hashem,* our God and God of our ancestors,
may You allow the upcoming new month
to be a month filled with good and blessings.
Give Your Jewish people a long life
filled with:

peace,
goodness,
blessing,
wealth,
health,
fear of sin,
no embarrassment,
honor,
love of Torah, and
our requests being answered for our good.

Amen.

ברכת החודש – BLESSING THE NEW MONTH

The moon goes through many changes during the Hebrew month. On the first day of the month, Rosh Chodesh, the moon appears small and can sometimes be difficult to see. Each night the moon gets bigger, until the 15th of the month when it is a full moon. Then, as the month continues, the moon gets smaller until it can barely even be seen. At this point it becomes Rosh Chodesh again and another new month begins. Just as the moon is constantly changing and "renewing" itself each month, the Jewish people should think on Rosh Chodesh about how they can "renew" themselves and serve *Hashem* better. As the new month comes closer and we begin to think about how we will renew ourselves, we ask *Hashem* for a month filled with blessings.

ברכת החודש

On the שבת before ראש חודש, we say the following. On all other weeks continue with אַב הָרַחֲמִים *on page 561.*

יְהִי רָצוֹן מִלְּפָנֶיךָ
יהוה אֱלֹהֵינוּ וֵאלֹהֵי אֲבוֹתֵינוּ
שֶׁתְּחַדֵּשׁ עָלֵינוּ
אֶת הַחֹדֶשׁ הַזֶּה לְטוֹבָה וְלִבְרָכָה.
וְתִתֶּן לָנוּ חַיִּים אֲרוּכִים
חַיִּים שֶׁל שָׁלוֹם
חַיִּים שֶׁל טוֹבָה
חַיִּים שֶׁל בְּרָכָה
חַיִּים שֶׁל פַּרְנָסָה
חַיִּים שֶׁל חִלּוּץ עֲצָמוֹת
חַיִּים שֶׁיֵּשׁ בָּהֶם
יִרְאַת שָׁמַיִם וְיִרְאַת חֵטְא
חַיִּים שֶׁאֵין בָּהֶם
בּוּשָׁה וּכְלִמָּה
חַיִּים שֶׁל עֹשֶׁר וְכָבוֹד
חַיִּים שֶׁתְּהֵא בָנוּ אַהֲבַת תּוֹרָה
וְיִרְאַת שָׁמַיִם
חַיִּים שֶׁיִּמָּלְאוּ מִשְׁאֲלוֹת לִבֵּנוּ לְטוֹבָה
אָמֵן סֶלָה.

The new moon is announced, then the Leader takes the Torah scroll in his right arm and says:

מִי שֶׁעָשָׂה May He who performed miracles
for our ancestors
and redeemed them from slavery to freedom,
redeem us soon,
and gather in our dispersed people
from the four quarters of the earth,
so that all Israel may be united in friendship,
and let us say: Amen.

The Leader, then the congregation:

The new month (*say the name of the upcoming new month [see list below]*)
will start on (*say the day of the week the new month will start*).
May this month be good for all the Jewish people.

The congregation and Leader continue:

יְחַדְּשֵׁהוּ *Hashem,* may You give us this month:
life and peace,
happiness and joy,
comfort from sadness, and
the coming of *Mashiach.*
We all say Amen.

LIST OF DAYS OF THE WEEK:

Sunday	*Yom Rishon*	Wednesday	*Yom Revi'i*
Monday	*Yom Sheini*	Thursday	*Yom Chamishi*
Tuesday	*Yom Shelishi*	Friday	*Yom Shishi*
Saturday	*Shabbat Kodesh*		

The מולד *is announced, then the* חזן *takes the* ספר תורה
in his right arm and says:

מִי שֶׁעָשָׂה נִסִּים לַאֲבוֹתֵינוּ
וְגָאַל אוֹתָם מֵעַבְדוּת לְחֵרוּת
הוּא יִגְאַל אוֹתָנוּ בְּקָרוֹב
וִיקַבֵּץ נִדָּחֵינוּ מֵאַרְבַּע כַּנְפוֹת הָאָרֶץ
חֲבֵרִים כָּל יִשְׂרָאֵל וְנֹאמַר אָמֵן.

The חזן*, then the* קהל*:*

רֹאשׁ חֹדֶשׁ *month* **יִהְיֶה בְּיוֹם** *day* (***וּבְיוֹם** *day*)
הַבָּא עָלֵינוּ וְעַל כָּל יִשְׂרָאֵל לְטוֹבָה.

**if the second day falls on Sunday, then substitute:* וּלְמָחֳרָתוֹ בְּיוֹם

The קהל *and* חזן *continue:*

יְחַדְּשֵׁהוּ הַקָּדוֹשׁ בָּרוּךְ הוּא
עָלֵינוּ וְעַל כָּל עַמּוֹ בֵּית יִשְׂרָאֵל
לְחַיִּים וּלְשָׁלוֹם
לְשָׂשׂוֹן וּלְשִׂמְחָה
לִישׁוּעָה וּלְנֶחָמָה
וְנֹאמַר אָמֵן.

MONTHS:

Nissan	*Tammuz*	*Tishrei*	*Tevet*
Iyar	*Av*	*Cheshvan*	*Shevat*
Sivan	*Elul*	*Kislev*	*Adar*

The following is omitted on days when Tachanun is not said. It is also omitted on a Shabbat before Rosh Chodesh (except for the Shabbat before Rosh Chodesh Iyar and Rosh Chodesh Sivan) and on Shabbat Shekalim, Zachor, Para and HaChodesh.

אַב הָרַחֲמִים *Hashem,*
our Father in heaven,
may You please remember with kindness
all the holy Jewish communities
which were destroyed
by our enemies while honoring You.
They served You, *Hashem,*
with the speed of eagles
and the strength of lions.
May You remember their good actions
and punish our enemies
as You promised in the Torah.

אַשְׁרֵי We are happy with the opportunity
to sit and pray.
We are happy that You are our God
and that we are Your people.
David HaMelech wrote this song:

א GOD – *Hashem* is our God and King.

ב THANK – We appreciate *Hashem* and we will thank Him every day, forever.

ג GREATNESS – *Hashem*'s greatness is endless.

ד GENERATIONS – We will tell our children about the spectacular actions You have done for us in every generation.

The following is omitted on days when תחנון *is not said. It is also omitted on* שבת מברכים *(except for the* שבת *before* ראש חודש אייר *and* ראש חודש סיון*) and on the "*ארבע פרשיות*," שקלים, זכור, פרה and* החודש.

אַב הָרַחֲמִים שׁוֹכֵן מְרוֹמִים, בְּרַחֲמָיו הָעֲצוּמִים הוּא יִפְקֹד בְּרַחֲמִים הַחֲסִידִים וְהַיְשָׁרִים וְהַתְּמִימִים, קְהִלּוֹת הַקֹּדֶשׁ שֶׁמָּסְרוּ נַפְשָׁם עַל קְדֻשַּׁת הַשֵּׁם, הַנֶּאֱהָבִים וְהַנְּעִימִים בְּחַיֵּיהֶם, וּבְמוֹתָם לֹא נִפְרָדוּ, מִנְּשָׁרִים קַלּוּ וּמֵאֲרָיוֹת גָּבֵרוּ לַעֲשׂוֹת רְצוֹן קוֹנָם וְחֵפֶץ צוּרָם. יִזְכְּרֵם אֱלֹהֵינוּ לְטוֹבָה עִם שְׁאָר צַדִּיקֵי עוֹלָם, וְיִנְקֹם לְעֵינֵינוּ נִקְמַת דַּם עֲבָדָיו הַשָּׁפוּךְ, כַּכָּתוּב בְּתוֹרַת מֹשֶׁה אִישׁ הָאֱלֹהִים: הַרְנִינוּ גוֹיִם עַמּוֹ, כִּי דַם־עֲבָדָיו יִקּוֹם, וְנָקָם יָשִׁיב לְצָרָיו, וְכִפֶּר אַדְמָתוֹ עַמּוֹ: וְעַל יְדֵי עֲבָדֶיךָ הַנְּבִיאִים כָּתוּב לֵאמֹר: וְנִקֵּיתִי, דָּמָם לֹא־נִקֵּיתִי, וַיהוה שֹׁכֵן בְּצִיּוֹן: וּבְכִתְבֵי הַקֹּדֶשׁ נֶאֱמַר: לָמָּה יֹאמְרוּ הַגּוֹיִם אַיֵּה אֱלֹהֵיהֶם, יִוָּדַע בַּגּוֹיִם לְעֵינֵינוּ נִקְמַת דַּם־עֲבָדֶיךָ הַשָּׁפוּךְ: וְאוֹמֵר: כִּי־דֹרֵשׁ דָּמִים אוֹתָם זָכָר, לֹא־שָׁכַח צַעֲקַת עֲנָוִים: וְאוֹמֵר: יָדִין בַּגּוֹיִם מָלֵא גְוִיּוֹת, מָחַץ רֹאשׁ עַל־אֶרֶץ רַבָּה: מִנַּחַל בַּדֶּרֶךְ יִשְׁתֶּה, עַל־כֵּן יָרִים רֹאשׁ:

אַשְׁרֵי יוֹשְׁבֵי בֵיתֶךָ, עוֹד יְהַלְלוּךָ סֶּלָה:
אַשְׁרֵי הָעָם שֶׁכָּכָה לּוֹ, אַשְׁרֵי הָעָם שֶׁיהוה אֱלֹהָיו:
תְּהִלָּה לְדָוִד

אֲרוֹמִמְךָ אֱלוֹהַי הַמֶּלֶךְ, וַאֲבָרְכָה שִׁמְךָ לְעוֹלָם וָעֶד:
בְּכָל־יוֹם אֲבָרְכֶךָּ, וַאֲהַלְלָה שִׁמְךָ לְעוֹלָם וָעֶד:
גָּדוֹל יהוה וּמְהֻלָּל מְאֹד, וְלִגְדֻלָּתוֹ אֵין חֵקֶר:
דּוֹר לְדוֹר יְשַׁבַּח מַעֲשֶׂיךָ, וּגְבוּרֹתֶיךָ יַגִּידוּ:

- ה MIRACLES – The miracles that *Hashem* performs for His people are glorious.
- ו STRENGTH – *Hashem*'s strength is awesome beyond comparison.
- ז REMEMBER – We remember the good that *Hashem* does for us.
- ח MERCY – *Hashem* is slow to get angry.
- ט GOODNESS – *Hashem* is good to all His creations, humans and animals alike.
- י KINDNESS – All creations of *Hashem* are thankful for His kindness.
- כ HONOR – We give *Hashem* the honor that He deserves.
- ל MIGHTY – We inform all people of *Hashem*'s mighty actions.
- מ KINGSHIP – *Hashem* has and always will rule the world.
- ס HELP – *Hashem* helps us when we need Him.
- ע RELY – We rely on *Hashem* to give us the food that we need to live.
- פ PROVIDES – *Hashem* opens His hands and provides us with our needs.
- צ RIGHTEOUS – Everything *Hashem* does is righteous and with good intentions.
- ק CLOSENESS – *Hashem* is close to all those that call out to Him.
- ר SAVES – *Hashem* listens to our cries and saves those in need.
- ש GUARDS – *Hashem* protects all those who love Him and turn to Him in times of need.
- ▸ ת PRAISE – For all of these reasons, everyone praises *Hashem* and thanks Him every day.

הֲדַר כְּבוֹד הוֹדֶךָ, וְדִבְרֵי נִפְלְאֹתֶיךָ אָשִֽׂיחָה:

וֶעֱזוּז נוֹרְאֹתֶיךָ יֹאמֵרוּ, וּגְדוּלָּתְךָ אֲסַפְּרֶֽנָּה:

זֵכֶר רַב־טוּבְךָ יַבִּיעוּ, וְצִדְקָתְךָ יְרַנֵּֽנוּ:

חַנּוּן וְרַחוּם יהוה, אֶֽרֶךְ אַפַּיִם וּגְדָל־חָֽסֶד:

טוֹב־יהוה לַכֹּל, וְרַחֲמָיו עַל־כָּל־מַעֲשָׂיו:

יוֹדוּךָ יהוה כָּל־מַעֲשֶׂיךָ, וַחֲסִידֶיךָ יְבָרְכֽוּכָה:

כְּבוֹד מַלְכוּתְךָ יֹאמֵרוּ, וּגְבוּרָתְךָ יְדַבֵּֽרוּ:

לְהוֹדִיעַ לִבְנֵי הָאָדָם גְּבוּרֹתָיו, וּכְבוֹד הֲדַר מַלְכוּתוֹ:

מַלְכוּתְךָ מַלְכוּת כָּל־עֹלָמִים
וּמֶמְשַׁלְתְּךָ בְּכָל־דּוֹר וָדֹר:

סוֹמֵךְ יהוה לְכָל־הַנֹּפְלִים, וְזוֹקֵף לְכָל־הַכְּפוּפִים:

עֵינֵי־כֹל אֵלֶיךָ יְשַׂבֵּֽרוּ
וְאַתָּה נוֹתֵן־לָהֶם אֶת־אָכְלָם בְּעִתּוֹ:

פּוֹתֵחַ אֶת־יָדֶךָ, וּמַשְׂבִּיעַ לְכָל־חַי רָצוֹן:

צַדִּיק יהוה בְּכָל־דְּרָכָיו, וְחָסִיד בְּכָל־מַעֲשָׂיו:

קָרוֹב יהוה לְכָל־קֹרְאָיו, לְכֹל אֲשֶׁר יִקְרָאֻהוּ בֶאֱמֶת:

רְצוֹן־יְרֵאָיו יַעֲשֶׂה, וְאֶת־שַׁוְעָתָם יִשְׁמַע, וְיוֹשִׁיעֵם:

שׁוֹמֵר יהוה אֶת־כָּל־אֹהֲבָיו, וְאֵת כָּל־הָרְשָׁעִים יַשְׁמִיד:

◂ תְּהִלַּת יהוה יְדַבֶּר פִּי
וִיבָרֵךְ כָּל־בָּשָׂר שֵׁם קָדְשׁוֹ לְעוֹלָם וָעֶד:

וַאֲנַֽחְנוּ נְבָרֵךְ יָהּ מֵעַתָּה וְעַד־עוֹלָם, הַֽלְלוּיָהּ:

RETURNING THE TORAH

The Aron Kodesh is opened.
The Leader says:

יְהַלְלוּ Let the Jewish people praise *Hashem*
because He alone is God.

The congregation says:

Hashem's majesty is found on earth and in heaven.
He honors His Jewish people
by raising them up
and bringing them close to Him.
Halleluya!

The congregation says:

מִזְמוֹר לְדָוִד Give honor and bow to *Hashem*
for He is holy.
The voice of *Hashem*
can be heard like thunder across the waters.
The voice of *Hashem*
is filled with power, beauty, and might.
The voice of *Hashem*
can break mighty trees and make the desert shake.
Hashem was God during the floods of Noach.
Hashem is King and rules forever.
Hashem will give His Jewish people strength and peace.

As the Torah is placed into the Aron Kodesh, all say:

וּבְנֻחֹה When the *Aron* would come to rest,
Moshe would say,
"*Hashem*, return to the thousands of people
in Your Jewish nation."

הכנסת ספר תורה

The ארון קודש *is opened. All stand.*
The חזן *says:*

יְהַלְלוּ אֶת־שֵׁם יהוה, כִּי־נִשְׂגָּב שְׁמוֹ, לְבַדּוֹ

The קהל *says:*

הוֹדוֹ עַל־אֶרֶץ וְשָׁמָיִם:
וַיָּרֶם קֶרֶן לְעַמּוֹ, תְּהִלָּה לְכָל־חֲסִידָיו
לִבְנֵי יִשְׂרָאֵל עַם קְרֹבוֹ, הַלְלוּיָהּ:

The קהל *says:*

מִזְמוֹר לְדָוִד, הָבוּ לַיהוה בְּנֵי אֵלִים, הָבוּ לַיהוה כָּבוֹד וָעֹז: הָבוּ לַיהוה כְּבוֹד שְׁמוֹ, הִשְׁתַּחֲווּ לַיהוה בְּהַדְרַת־קֹדֶשׁ: קוֹל יהוה עַל־הַמָּיִם, אֵל־הַכָּבוֹד הִרְעִים, יהוה עַל־מַיִם רַבִּים: קוֹל־יהוה בַּכֹּחַ, קוֹל יהוה בֶּהָדָר: קוֹל יהוה שֹׁבֵר אֲרָזִים, וַיְשַׁבֵּר יהוה אֶת־אַרְזֵי הַלְּבָנוֹן: וַיַּרְקִידֵם כְּמוֹ־עֵגֶל, לְבָנוֹן וְשִׂרְיוֹן כְּמוֹ בֶן־רְאֵמִים: קוֹל־יהוה חֹצֵב לַהֲבוֹת אֵשׁ: קוֹל יהוה יָחִיל מִדְבָּר, יָחִיל יהוה מִדְבַּר קָדֵשׁ: קוֹל יהוה יְחוֹלֵל אַיָּלוֹת וַיֶּחֱשֹׂף יְעָרוֹת, וּבְהֵיכָלוֹ, כֻּלּוֹ אֹמֵר כָּבוֹד: יהוה לַמַּבּוּל יָשָׁב, וַיֵּשֶׁב יהוה מֶלֶךְ לְעוֹלָם: יהוה עֹז לְעַמּוֹ יִתֵּן, יהוה יְבָרֵךְ אֶת־עַמּוֹ בַשָּׁלוֹם:

As the ספר תורה *is placed into the* ארון קודש*, all say:*

וּבְנֻחֹה יֹאמַר, שׁוּבָה יהוה רִבְבוֹת אַלְפֵי יִשְׂרָאֵל:
קוּמָה יהוה לִמְנוּחָתֶךָ, אַתָּה וַאֲרוֹן עֻזֶּךָ:

Your *Kohanim* are clothed ready to serve You,
and Your followers sing to You in joy,
awaiting Your arrival.
For the sake of David, do not reject us.
Hashem, You commanded us not to abandon Your Torah.
It is a tree of life to all those who hold onto it
and a source of happiness for all those who follow it.
Following the Torah is pleasant and it leads to peace.
▸ *Hashem,* bring us back to You and we will return to You.
Let us live again as we did
in the times of the *Beit HaMikdash.*

The Aron Kodesh is closed.

HALF KADDISH

Leader: יִתְגַּדַּל May *Hashem* be recognized
as great and holy (*Congregation:* Amen)
in the world that He created.
May He establish His kingdom
during my lifetime and the lifetime of all Jews,
quickly and soon.
Let us say: "Amen" (*Congregation:* Amen).

Congregation: May we thank *Hashem* for ever and ever.
Leader: May we thank *Hashem* for ever and ever.

Leader: *Hashem* should be thanked, praised,
and honored (*Congregation:* He is blessed).
Hashem is beyond all the blessings,
songs, or praises that we could offer.
Let us say: "Amen" (*Congregation:* Amen).

כֹּהֲנֶיךָ יִלְבְּשׁוּ־צֶדֶק, וַחֲסִידֶיךָ יְרַנֵּנוּ:
בַּעֲבוּר דָּוִד עַבְדֶּךָ אַל־תָּשֵׁב פְּנֵי מְשִׁיחֶךָ:
כִּי לֶקַח טוֹב נָתַתִּי לָכֶם, תּוֹרָתִי אַל־תַּעֲזֹבוּ:
עֵץ־חַיִּים הִיא לַמַּחֲזִיקִים בָּהּ, וְתֹמְכֶיהָ מְאֻשָּׁר:
דְּרָכֶיהָ דַרְכֵי־נֹעַם וְכָל־נְתִיבוֹתֶיהָ שָׁלוֹם:
◂ הֲשִׁיבֵנוּ יהוה אֵלֶיךָ וְנָשׁוּבָה, חַדֵּשׁ יָמֵינוּ כְּקֶדֶם:

The ארון קודש *is closed.*

חצי קדיש

חזן: יִתְגַּדַּל וְיִתְקַדַּשׁ שְׁמֵהּ רַבָּא (קהל: אָמֵן)
בְּעָלְמָא דִּי בְרָא כִרְעוּתֵהּ, וְיַמְלִיךְ מַלְכוּתֵהּ
בְּחַיֵּיכוֹן וּבְיוֹמֵיכוֹן וּבְחַיֵּי דְכָל בֵּית יִשְׂרָאֵל
בַּעֲגָלָא וּבִזְמַן קָרִיב, וְאִמְרוּ אָמֵן. (קהל: אָמֵן)

קהל: יְהֵא שְׁמֵהּ רַבָּא מְבָרַךְ לְעָלַם וּלְעָלְמֵי עָלְמַיָּא.
חזן: יְהֵא שְׁמֵהּ רַבָּא מְבָרַךְ לְעָלַם וּלְעָלְמֵי עָלְמַיָּא.

חזן: יִתְבָּרַךְ וְיִשְׁתַּבַּח וְיִתְפָּאַר וְיִתְרוֹמַם וְיִתְנַשֵּׂא
וְיִתְהַדָּר וְיִתְעַלֶּה וְיִתְהַלָּל
שְׁמֵהּ דְּקֻדְשָׁא בְּרִיךְ הוּא (קהל: בְּרִיךְ הוּא)
לְעֵלָּא מִן כָּל בִּרְכָתָא
/בשבת שובה: לְעֵלָּא לְעֵלָּא מִכָּל בִּרְכָתָא/
וְשִׁירָתָא, תֻּשְׁבְּחָתָא וְנֶחֱמָתָא
דַּאֲמִירָן בְּעָלְמָא, וְאִמְרוּ אָמֵן. (קהל: אָמֵן)

Musaf for Shabbat

On Shabbat Chol HaMo'ed say the Musaf for Festivals on page 766.

AMIDA

Take three steps forward then stand with your feet together.

I will call out to *Hashem*, let us all give praise to Him.
Hashem, open my lips and help my mouth recite Your praise.

ANCESTORS

Bend the knees when saying "We thank," bow when saying "You," and stand straight before saying "Hashem."

בָּרוּךְ We thank You, *Hashem*,
our God, and God of our ancestors,
Avraham, Yitzchak, and Yaakov.
You, *Hashem*, are the great, mighty, awesome, kind,
and all-powerful Creator.
It is because of the greatness of our ancestors,
Avraham, Yitzchak, and Yaakov,
that *Hashem* will bring *Mashiach*.

Between Rosh Hashana and Yom Kippur say:

Give us life in the year to come
and write us in the book of life,
Hashem, who gives life.

Hashem is our King
who helps, guides, and protects us.

Bend the knees when saying "Thank," bow when saying "You," and stand straight before saying "Hashem."

Thank You, *Hashem*,
who protects us in the merit of Avraham.

מוסף לשבת

On שבת חול המועד *say the* מוסף לשלוש רגלים *on page 767.*

עמידה

Take three steps forward then stand with your feet together.

כִּי שֵׁם יהוה אֶקְרָא, הָבוּ גֹדֶל לֵאלֹהֵינוּ:
אֲדֹנָי, שְׂפָתַי תִּפְתָּח, וּפִי יַגִּיד תְּהִלָּתֶךָ:

אבות

Bend the knees when saying בָּרוּךְ, *bow when saying* אַתָּה,
and stand straight before saying Hashem's name.

בָּרוּךְ אַתָּה יהוה
אֱלֹהֵינוּ וֵאלֹהֵי אֲבוֹתֵינוּ
אֱלֹהֵי אַבְרָהָם, אֱלֹהֵי יִצְחָק, וֵאלֹהֵי יַעֲקֹב
הָאֵל הַגָּדוֹל הַגִּבּוֹר וְהַנּוֹרָא, אֵל עֶלְיוֹן
גּוֹמֵל חֲסָדִים טוֹבִים, וְקוֹנֵה הַכֹּל
וְזוֹכֵר חַסְדֵי אָבוֹת
וּמֵבִיא גוֹאֵל לִבְנֵי בְנֵיהֶם לְמַעַן שְׁמוֹ בְּאַהֲבָה.

On שבת שובה *say:*

זָכְרֵנוּ לְחַיִּים, מֶלֶךְ חָפֵץ בַּחַיִּים
וְכָתְבֵנוּ בְּסֵפֶר הַחַיִּים
לְמַעַנְךָ אֱלֹהִים חַיִּים.

מֶלֶךְ עוֹזֵר וּמוֹשִׁיעַ וּמָגֵן.

Bend the knees when saying בָּרוּךְ, *bow when saying* אַתָּה,
and stand straight before saying Hashem's name.

בָּרוּךְ אַתָּה יהוה, מָגֵן אַבְרָהָם.

HASHEM'S STRENGTH

אַתָּה You, *Hashem,* have unlimited strength.
You save people in their time of need,
and You have the power to bring the dead back to life.

This line is said during the rainy season, from Simchat Torah to Pesach:
(You make the wind blow and cause the rain to fall)

With kindness You provide the living
with the necessities to live, and with mercy
You keep Your promise of bringing the dead back to life.
For the living, You:
Support those who are falling,
Heal those who are sick, and
Free those who are in challenging situations.
Who is like You, *Hashem,* and who can compare to You?
You, *Hashem,* are our King
who has the power to cause death and life.

Between Rosh Hashana and Yom Kippur say:
Who is like You, *Hashem,* our caring Father
who remembers His people for good and gives them life?

We have complete faith
that You will bring us back to life after our passing.
Thank You, *Hashem,* for bringing the dead back to life.

HASHEM'S HOLINESS

אַתָּה קָדוֹשׁ *Hashem,* You are holy and Your name is holy.
The Jewish people, who are holy,
will praise You, *Hashem,* each day.
Thank You, *Hashem,*
the holy God. / *Between Rosh Hashana & Yom Kippur say:* the holy King./

גבורות

אַתָּה גִּבּוֹר לְעוֹלָם, אֲדֹנָי
מְחַיֵּה מֵתִים אַתָּה, רַב לְהוֹשִׁיעַ

This line is said during the rainy season, from שמחת תורה *to* פסח:

(מַשִּׁיב הָרְוּחַ וּמוֹרִיד הַגֶּֽשֶׁם)

מְכַלְכֵּל חַיִּים בְּחֶסֶד, מְחַיֵּה מֵתִים בְּרַחֲמִים רַבִּים
סוֹמֵךְ נוֹפְלִים, וְרוֹפֵא חוֹלִים, וּמַתִּיר אֲסוּרִים
וּמְקַיֵּם אֱמוּנָתוֹ לִישֵׁנֵי עָפָר.
מִי כָמְוֹךָ, בַּעַל גְּבוּרוֹת, וּמִי דּוֹמֶה לָּךְ
מֶלֶךְ, מֵמִית וּמְחַיֶּה וּמַצְמִיחַ יְשׁוּעָה.

On שבת שובה *say:*

מִי כָמְוֹךָ אַב הָרַחֲמִים
זוֹכֵר יְצוּרָיו לְחַיִּים בְּרַחֲמִים.

וְנֶאֱמָן אַתָּה לְהַחֲיוֹת מֵתִים.
בָּרוּךְ אַתָּה יהוה, מְחַיֵּה הַמֵּתִים.

קדושת השם

אַתָּה קָדוֹשׁ וְשִׁמְךָ קָדוֹשׁ
וּקְדוֹשִׁים בְּכָל יוֹם יְהַלְלְוּךָ סֶּלָה.
בָּרוּךְ אַתָּה יהוה
הָאֵל הַקָּדוֹשׁ. / *On* שבת שובה *say* הַמֶּלֶךְ הַקָּדוֹשׁ./

If Rosh Chodesh falls on Shabbat, turn to page 598.

KEDUSHAS HA'YOM

תִּכַּנְתָּ שַׁבָּת *Hashem,* You created Shabbat,
and You accepted the *korbanot* brought on Shabbat
in the *Beit HaMikdash.*
You taught us the laws of *korbanot* and how to offer them.
Those who enjoy Shabbat
are honored in this world and in the world-to-come.
The laws of Shabbat were taught before
the Jewish people received the Torah.
After we were given the Torah,
Hashem taught us about the *korbanot.*

יְהִי רָצוֹן *Hashem,* our God and God of our ancestors,
may You lead Your Jewish people back to our land, Israel.

אָז מִסִּינַי נִצְטַוּוּ עָלֶיהָ *The laws of Shabbat were taught before the Jewish People received the Torah.* After crossing the Yam Suf, the Reed Sea, the Jewish people traveled through the desert for several weeks before arriving at Har Sinai to receive the Torah. Before arriving at Har Sinai, the Jewish people were introduced to the *mitzva* of Shabbat. The reason why learning about Shabbat came before the rest of the Torah is because Shabbat serves as a very important reminder that:

Hashem created the entire world from nothing in six days and rested on the seventh day;

Hashem is God and everything exists only because He allows it; and

Hashem is our source of life and we live to serve Him.

The Jewish people were taught about Shabbat before the rest of the Torah because Shabbat reminds us *why* Torah is so important.

If ראש חודש *falls on* שבת*, turn to page 599.*

קדושת היום

תִּכַּנְתָּ שַׁבָּת

רָצִיתָ קָרְבְּנוֹתֶיהָ

צִוִּיתָ פֵּרוּשֶׁיהָ עִם סִדּוּרֵי נְסָכֶיהָ

מְעַנְּגֶיהָ לְעוֹלָם כָּבוֹד יִנְחָלוּ

טוֹעֲמֶיהָ חַיִּים זָכוּ

וְגַם הָאוֹהֲבִים דְּבָרֶיהָ גְּדֻלָּה בָּחָרוּ.

אָז מִסִּינַי נִצְטַוּוּ עָלֶיהָ

וַתְּצַוֵּנוּ יהוה אֱלֹהֵינוּ

לְהַקְרִיב בָּהּ קָרְבַּן מוּסַף שַׁבָּת כָּרָאוּי.

יְהִי רָצוֹן מִלְּפָנֶיךָ

יהוה אֱלֹהֵינוּ וֵאלֹהֵי אֲבוֹתֵינוּ

שֶׁתַּעֲלֵנוּ בְשִׂמְחָה לְאַרְצֵנוּ

וְתִטָּעֵנוּ בִּגְבוּלֵנוּ

וְשָׁם נַעֲשֶׂה לְפָנֶיךָ

אֶת קָרְבְּנוֹת חוֹבוֹתֵינוּ

תְּמִידִים כְּסִדְרָם

וּמוּסָפִים כְּהִלְכָתָם.

וְאֶת מוּסַף There we will bring the regular daily
and special *musaf korbanot.*
We will bring the *korban musaf* of Shabbat with love,
as You commanded us in Your Torah:

> וּבְיוֹם הַשַּׁבָּת "On the Shabbat day,
> bring two perfect lambs that are a year old
> together with flour and oil as a *korban*
> that is burnt before *Hashem.*"

יִשְׂמְחוּ Those who keep and enjoy Shabbat
bring holiness to the seventh day
and will be overjoyed.
Hashem,
You chose the seventh day and made it holy,
calling it the "most special of days,"
as it is a reminder of the creation of the world.

אֱלֹהֵינוּ *Hashem,* our God and God of our ancestors,
we rest from work today for Your sake.
Allow us to become holy through keeping Your *mitzvot*
and studying Your Torah.
Be good to us, save us, and purify our hearts
to serve you sincerely.
Hashem, our God,
show us Your love
and allow us to observe Your holy Shabbat
so that Your Jewish people can rest.
Thank You, *Hashem,* for making Shabbat holy.

וְאֶת מוּסַף יוֹם הַשַּׁבָּת הַזֶּה
נַעֲשֶׂה וְנַקְרִיב לְפָנֶיךָ בְּאַהֲבָה כְּמִצְוַת רְצוֹנֶךָ
כְּמוֹ שֶׁכָּתַבְתָּ עָלֵינוּ בְּתוֹרָתֶךָ
עַל יְדֵי מֹשֶׁה עַבְדֶּךָ מִפִּי כְבוֹדֶךָ
כָּאָמוּר

וּבְיוֹם הַשַּׁבָּת שְׁנֵי־כְבָשִׂים בְּנֵי־שָׁנָה תְּמִימִם
וּשְׁנֵי עֶשְׂרֹנִים סֹלֶת מִנְחָה בְּלוּלָה בַשֶּׁמֶן וְנִסְכּוֹ:
עֹלַת שַׁבַּת בְּשַׁבַּתּוֹ, עַל־עֹלַת הַתָּמִיד וְנִסְכָּהּ:

יִשְׂמְחוּ בְמַלְכוּתְךָ שׁוֹמְרֵי שַׁבָּת וְקוֹרְאֵי עֹנֶג
עַם מְקַדְּשֵׁי שְׁבִיעִי
כֻּלָּם יִשְׂבְּעוּ וְיִתְעַנְּגוּ מִטּוּבֶךָ
וּבַשְּׁבִיעִי רָצִיתָ בּוֹ וְקִדַּשְׁתּוֹ
חֶמְדַּת יָמִים אוֹתוֹ קָרָאתָ, זֵכֶר לְמַעֲשֵׂה בְרֵאשִׁית.

אֱלֹהֵינוּ וֵאלֹהֵי אֲבוֹתֵינוּ, רְצֵה בִמְנוּחָתֵנוּ
קַדְּשֵׁנוּ בְּמִצְוֹתֶיךָ וְתֵן חֶלְקֵנוּ בְּתוֹרָתֶךָ
שַׂבְּעֵנוּ מִטּוּבֶךָ, וְשַׂמְּחֵנוּ בִּישׁוּעָתֶךָ
וְטַהֵר לִבֵּנוּ לְעָבְדְּךָ בֶּאֱמֶת
וְהַנְחִילֵנוּ יהוה אֱלֹהֵינוּ בְּאַהֲבָה וּבְרָצוֹן שַׁבַּת קָדְשֶׁךָ
וְיָנוּחוּ בוֹ יִשְׂרָאֵל מְקַדְּשֵׁי שְׁמֶךָ.
בָּרוּךְ אַתָּה יהוה, מְקַדֵּשׁ הַשַּׁבָּת.

SERVICE IN THE *BEIT HAMIKDASH*

רְצֵה *Hashem,* please accept Your Jewish people
and their prayers.
We eagerly await the rebuilding of the *Beit HaMikdash*
so we can serve You with *korbanot.*
Until the *Beit HaMikdash* is rebuilt,
please accept our prayers with love.
May we be worthy
to see the rebuilding of the *Beit HaMikdash.*
We thank You, *Hashem,*
for returning Your presence to Zion.

THANK YOU

Bow when saying the words "We thank You."

מוֹדִים We thank You, *Hashem,*
for You are and always will be
our God, and the God of our ancestors.
You give us life
and You always protect us.
We thank and praise You for:
Our lives which are in Your hands,
Our souls which are in Your control,
The miracles You perform for us every day, and
The goodness You show us
at all times, morning, noon, and night.
You, *Hashem,* have unlimited mercy and kindness
and therefore we have always placed our hope in You.

עבודה

רְצֵה יהוה אֱלֹהֵינוּ בְּעַמְּךָ יִשְׂרָאֵל, וּבִתְפִלָּתָם
וְהָשֵׁב אֶת הָעֲבוֹדָה לִדְבִיר בֵּיתֶךָ
וְאִשֵּׁי יִשְׂרָאֵל וּתְפִלָּתָם בְּאַהֲבָה תְקַבֵּל בְּרָצוֹן
וּתְהִי לְרָצוֹן תָּמִיד עֲבוֹדַת יִשְׂרָאֵל עַמֶּךָ.
וְתֶחֱזֶינָה עֵינֵינוּ בְּשׁוּבְךָ לְצִיּוֹן בְּרַחֲמִים.
בָּרוּךְ אַתָּה יהוה, הַמַּחֲזִיר שְׁכִינָתוֹ לְצִיּוֹן.

הודאה

Bow when saying the words מוֹדִים אֲנַחְנוּ לָךְ שָׁאַתָּה הוּא

מוֹדִים אֲנַחְנוּ לָךְ
שָׁאַתָּה הוּא יהוה אֱלֹהֵינוּ וֵאלֹהֵי אֲבוֹתֵינוּ לְעוֹלָם וָעֶד.
צוּר חַיֵּינוּ, מָגֵן יִשְׁעֵנוּ, אַתָּה הוּא לְדוֹר וָדוֹר.
נוֹדֶה לְּךָ וּנְסַפֵּר תְּהִלָּתֶךָ
עַל חַיֵּינוּ הַמְּסוּרִים בְּיָדֶךָ
וְעַל נִשְׁמוֹתֵינוּ הַפְּקוּדוֹת לָךְ
וְעַל נִסֶּיךָ שֶׁבְּכָל יוֹם עִמָּנוּ
וְעַל נִפְלְאוֹתֶיךָ וְטוֹבוֹתֶיךָ
שֶׁבְּכָל עֵת, עֶרֶב וָבֹקֶר וְצָהֳרָיִם.
הַטּוֹב, כִּי לֹא כָלוּ רַחֲמֶיךָ
וְהַמְרַחֵם, כִּי לֹא תַמּוּ חֲסָדֶיךָ
מֵעוֹלָם קִוִּינוּ לָךְ.

On Chanuka say:

עַל הַנִּסִּים We thank You, *Hashem,* for the miracles, the deliverances, the great strength, and the victories in war that You displayed for us in earlier times and in our times.

בִּימֵי מַתִּתְיָהוּ In the days of Mattityahu, son of Yochanan the *Kohen Gadol,* the Hasmonean, and his sons, the wicked Greeks challenged Your Jewish people trying to make them forget Your Torah and sin. In Your great kindness, You, *Hashem,* supported us in this difficult time. You allowed for:

The weak Jews to defeat the mighty Greeks,
The few Jews to defeat the many Greeks,
The pure Jews to defeat the impure Greeks,
The righteous Jews to defeat the wicked Greeks, and
The Jews who studied Your Torah to defeat the Greeks who did not.

Hashem, on this day everyone in the world recognized You as You miraculously saved Your Jewish people. Your Jewish people then entered the *Beit HaMikdash* to clean and purify it. They lit candles in the courtyard of the *Beit HaMikdash* and set aside these eight days of *Chanukah* for giving thanks and praising You.

Continue with "For all these reasons."

For all these reasons
we will thank You, *Hashem,* our King, forever.

Between Rosh Hashana & Yom Kippur say:

And write all Your children in the book of good life.

Every living person will recognize and praise You, *Hashem,*
for You are the God that helps and saves Your people.

Bend the knees when saying "Thank," bow when saying "You,"
and stand straight before saying "Hashem."

Thank You, *Hashem,*
for You are worthy of being thanked.

בחנוכה:

עַל הַנִּסִּים וְעַל הַפֻּרְקָן וְעַל הַגְּבוּרוֹת וְעַל הַתְּשׁוּעוֹת וְעַל הַמִּלְחָמוֹת שֶׁעָשִׂיתָ לַאֲבוֹתֵינוּ בַּיָּמִים הָהֵם בַּזְּמַן הַזֶּה.

בִּימֵי מַתִּתְיָהוּ בֶּן יוֹחָנָן כֹּהֵן גָּדוֹל חַשְׁמוֹנַאי וּבָנָיו, כְּשֶׁעָמְדָה מַלְכוּת יָוָן הָרְשָׁעָה עַל עַמְּךָ יִשְׂרָאֵל לְהַשְׁכִּיחָם תּוֹרָתֶךָ וּלְהַעֲבִירָם מֵחֻקֵּי רְצוֹנֶךָ, וְאַתָּה בְּרַחֲמֶיךָ הָרַבִּים עָמַדְתָּ לָהֶם בְּעֵת צָרָתָם, רַבְתָּ אֶת רִיבָם, דַּנְתָּ אֶת דִּינָם, נָקַמְתָּ אֶת נִקְמָתָם, מָסַרְתָּ גִבּוֹרִים בְּיַד חַלָּשִׁים, וְרַבִּים בְּיַד מְעַטִּים, וּטְמֵאִים בְּיַד טְהוֹרִים, וּרְשָׁעִים בְּיַד צַדִּיקִים, וְזֵדִים בְּיַד עוֹסְקֵי תוֹרָתֶךָ, וּלְךָ עָשִׂיתָ שֵׁם גָּדוֹל וְקָדוֹשׁ בְּעוֹלָמֶךָ, וּלְעַמְּךָ יִשְׂרָאֵל עָשִׂיתָ תְּשׁוּעָה גְדוֹלָה וּפֻרְקָן כְּהַיּוֹם הַזֶּה. וְאַחַר כֵּן בָּאוּ בָנֶיךָ לִדְבִיר בֵּיתֶךָ, וּפִנּוּ אֶת הֵיכָלֶךָ, וְטִהֲרוּ אֶת מִקְדָּשֶׁךָ, וְהִדְלִיקוּ נֵרוֹת בְּחַצְרוֹת קָדְשֶׁךָ, וְקָבְעוּ שְׁמוֹנַת יְמֵי חֲנֻכָּה אֵלּוּ, לְהוֹדוֹת וּלְהַלֵּל לְשִׁמְךָ הַגָּדוֹל.

Continue with וְעַל כֻּלָּם.

וְעַל כֻּלָּם
יִתְבָּרַךְ וְיִתְרוֹמַם שִׁמְךָ מַלְכֵּנוּ תָּמִיד לְעוֹלָם וָעֶד.

On שבת שובה *say* וּכְתֹב לְחַיִּים טוֹבִים כָּל בְּנֵי בְרִיתֶךָ.

וְכֹל הַחַיִּים יוֹדוּךָ סֶּלָה, וִיהַלְלוּ אֶת שִׁמְךָ בֶּאֱמֶת הָאֵל יְשׁוּעָתֵנוּ וְעֶזְרָתֵנוּ סֶלָה.

Bend the knees when saying בָּרוּךְ*, bow when saying* אַתָּה*,*
and stand straight before saying Hashem's name.

בָּרוּךְ אַתָּה יהוה
הַטּוֹב שִׁמְךָ וּלְךָ נָאֶה לְהוֹדוֹת.

PEACE

שִׂים שָׁלוֹם *Hashem,*
please provide Your Jewish people
with peace, goodness,
blessing, kindness, and mercy.
Bless us, *Hashem,* all as one.
Hashem,
You have given us Your Torah of life,
and treated us with kindness, righteousness,
blessing, mercy, and peace.
May it be good in Your eyes, *Hashem,*
to bless Your Jewish people with peace
at every moment of every hour.

Between Rosh Hashana and Yom Kippur continue with "May You remember," below.

Thank You, *Hashem,*
who blesses His Jewish people with peace.

Between Rosh Hashana and Yom Kippur say:

May You remember all of the Jewish people for life,
blessing, peace, and riches
and write us in the book of good life and peace.
Thank You, *Hashem,*
who makes peace.

שלום

שִׂים שָׁלוֹם טוֹבָה וּבְרָכָה
חֵן וָחֶסֶד וְרַחֲמִים עָלֵינוּ
וְעַל כָּל יִשְׂרָאֵל עַמֶּךָ.
בָּרְכֵנוּ אָבִינוּ כֻּלָּנוּ כְּאֶחָד בְּאוֹר פָּנֶיךָ
כִּי בְאוֹר פָּנֶיךָ נָתַתָּ לָּנוּ יהוה אֱלֹהֵינוּ
תּוֹרַת חַיִּים וְאַהֲבַת חֶסֶד
וּצְדָקָה וּבְרָכָה וְרַחֲמִים
וְחַיִּים וְשָׁלוֹם.
וְטוֹב בְּעֵינֶיךָ לְבָרֵךְ אֶת עַמְּךָ יִשְׂרָאֵל
בְּכָל עֵת וּבְכָל שָׁעָה בִּשְׁלוֹמֶךָ.

On שבת שובה *continue with* בְּסֵפֶר חַיִּים*, below.*

בָּרוּךְ אַתָּה יהוה
הַמְבָרֵךְ אֶת עַמּוֹ יִשְׂרָאֵל בַּשָּׁלוֹם.

On שבת שובה *say:*

בְּסֵפֶר חַיִּים, בְּרָכָה וְשָׁלוֹם, וּפַרְנָסָה טוֹבָה
נִזָּכֵר וְנִכָּתֵב לְפָנֶיךָ
אֲנַחְנוּ וְכָל עַמְּךָ בֵּית יִשְׂרָאֵל
לְחַיִּים טוֹבִים וּלְשָׁלוֹם.
בָּרוּךְ אַתָּה יהוה, עוֹשֵׂה הַשָּׁלוֹם.

CONCLUSION OF AMIDA

אֱלֹהַי *Hashem,* please help me:
Control my mouth from speaking badly
about other people,
Stay silent and not respond if someone speaks badly
about me,
Learn Your Torah, and do Your *mitzvot.*
Hashem, if people plan to do something evil against me,
please stop these plans and protect me.
Even if I am not deserving of being helped,
please act on my behalf
as I represent Your name and Your Torah.
Hashem, please save Your Jewish people
from difficult situations and answer my requests.
May You find my thoughts and prayers favorable.

Take three steps backwards and bow to your left as you say:

You, *Hashem,* make peace in heaven.

Bow to your right as you say:

Please may You bring peace to us

Bow forward as you say:

And all Your Jewish people.

Before taking three steps forward, say the following quietly:

Hashem, our God and God of our ancestors, may You please rebuild the *Beit HaMikdash* soon. *Hashem,* please allow us to learn Your Torah and serve You in the *Beit HaMikdash* as the Jewish people once did.

When praying with a minyan, the Amida is repeated by the Leader (on the next page). When not praying with a minyan, continue with "There is no one like You" (page 610).

סיום העמידה

אֱלֹהַי, נְצֹר לְשׁוֹנִי מֵרָע וּשְׂפָתַי מִדַּבֵּר מִרְמָה
וְלִמְקַלְלַי נַפְשִׁי תִדֹּם, וְנַפְשִׁי כֶּעָפָר לַכֹּל תִּהְיֶה.
פְּתַח לִבִּי בְּתוֹרָתֶךָ, וּבְמִצְוֹתֶיךָ תִּרְדֹּף נַפְשִׁי.
וְכָל הַחוֹשְׁבִים עָלַי רָעָה
מְהֵרָה הָפֵר עֲצָתָם וְקַלְקֵל מַחֲשַׁבְתָּם.
עֲשֵׂה לְמַעַן שְׁמֶךָ, עֲשֵׂה לְמַעַן יְמִינֶךָ
עֲשֵׂה לְמַעַן קְדֻשָּׁתֶךָ, עֲשֵׂה לְמַעַן תּוֹרָתֶךָ.
לְמַעַן יֵחָלְצוּן יְדִידֶיךָ, הוֹשִׁיעָה יְמִינְךָ וַעֲנֵנִי:
יִהְיוּ לְרָצוֹן אִמְרֵי־פִי וְהֶגְיוֹן לִבִּי לְפָנֶיךָ, יהוה צוּרִי וְגֹאֲלִי:

Take three steps backwards and bow to your left as you say:

עֹשֶׂה שָׁלוֹם / *On* שבת שובה *say* הַשָּׁלוֹם / בִּמְרוֹמָיו

Bow to your right as you say:

הוּא יַעֲשֶׂה שָׁלוֹם עָלֵינוּ

Bow forward as you say:

וְעַל כָּל יִשְׂרָאֵל, וְאִמְרוּ אָמֵן.

Before taking three steps forward, say the following quietly:

יְהִי רָצוֹן מִלְּפָנֶיךָ יהוה אֱלֹהֵינוּ וֵאלֹהֵי אֲבוֹתֵינוּ. שֶׁיִּבָּנֶה בֵּית הַמִּקְדָּשׁ בִּמְהֵרָה בְיָמֵינוּ, וְתֵן חֶלְקֵנוּ בְּתוֹרָתֶךָ. וְשָׁם נַעֲבָדְךָ בְּיִרְאָה כִּימֵי עוֹלָם וּכְשָׁנִים קַדְמֹנִיּוֹת. וְעָרְבָה לַיהוה מִנְחַת יְהוּדָה וִירוּשָׁלָיִם כִּימֵי עוֹלָם וּכְשָׁנִים קַדְמֹנִיּוֹת:

When praying with a מנין*, the* עמידה *is repeated by the* חזן *(on the next page).*
When not praying with a מנין*, continue with* אֵין כֵּאלֹהֵינוּ *(page 611).*

THE LEADER'S REPETITION

Try to focus on each blessing that the Leader reads, by following along and thinking about the sentences below. After each beracha that the Leader recites, answer "Amen."

I will call out to *Hashem*, let us all give praise to Him.
Hashem, open my lips
and help my mouth recite Your praise.

ANCESTORS

We praise You, *Hashem*,
for protecting, helping, and saving us
as You did for our ancestors,
Avraham, Yitzchak, and Yaakov.
Thank You, *Hashem*,
who protects us in the merit of Avraham.

(*Congregation:* Amen.)

HASHEM'S STRENGTH

We praise You, *Hashem*,
for providing food to those who are hungry,
support to those who are falling,
health to those who are sick,
and help to those who are in challenging situations.
Thank You, *Hashem*,
for bringing the dead back to life. (*Congregation:* Amen.)

חזרת הש״ץ

Try to focus on each blessing that the חזן *reads, by following along and thinking about the sentences below. After each beracha that the* חזן *recites, answer* אָמֵן.

כִּי שֵׁם יהוה אֶקְרָא, הָבוּ גֹדֶל לֵאלֹהֵינוּ:

אֲדֹנָי, שְׂפָתַי תִּפְתָּח, וּפִי יַגִּיד תְּהִלָּתֶךָ:

אבות

בָּרוּךְ אַתָּה יהוה, אֱלֹהֵינוּ וֵאלֹהֵי אֲבוֹתֵינוּ
אֱלֹהֵי אַבְרָהָם, אֱלֹהֵי יִצְחָק, וֵאלֹהֵי יַעֲקֹב
הָאֵל הַגָּדוֹל הַגִּבּוֹר וְהַנּוֹרָא, אֵל עֶלְיוֹן
גּוֹמֵל חֲסָדִים טוֹבִים, וְקוֹנֵה הַכֹּל, וְזוֹכֵר חַסְדֵי אָבוֹת
וּמֵבִיא גוֹאֵל לִבְנֵי בְנֵיהֶם לְמַעַן שְׁמוֹ בְּאַהֲבָה.

On שבת שובה *say* זָכְרֵנוּ לְחַיִּים, מֶלֶךְ חָפֵץ בַּחַיִּים
וְכָתְבֵנוּ בְּסֵפֶר הַחַיִּים, לְמַעַנְךָ אֱלֹהִים חַיִּים.

מֶלֶךְ עוֹזֵר וּמוֹשִׁיעַ וּמָגֵן.

בָּרוּךְ אַתָּה יהוה, מָגֵן אַבְרָהָם. (קהל: אָמֵן)

גבורות

אַתָּה גִּבּוֹר לְעוֹלָם, אֲדֹנָי, מְחַיֵּה מֵתִים אַתָּה, רַב לְהוֹשִׁיעַ

This line is said during the rainy season, from שמחת תורה *to* פסח*:*

(מַשִּׁיב הָרְוּחַ וּמוֹרִיד הַגֶּשֶׁם)

מְכַלְכֵּל חַיִּים בְּחֶסֶד, מְחַיֵּה מֵתִים בְּרַחֲמִים רַבִּים
סוֹמֵךְ נוֹפְלִים, וְרוֹפֵא חוֹלִים, וּמַתִּיר אֲסוּרִים
וּמְקַיֵּם אֱמוּנָתוֹ לִישֵׁנֵי עָפָר.
מִי כָמְוֹךָ, בַּעַל גְּבוּרוֹת, וּמִי דּוֹמֶה לָּךְ
מֶלֶךְ, מֵמִית וּמְחַיֶּה וּמַצְמִיחַ יְשׁוּעָה.

On שבת שובה *say* מִי כָמְוֹךָ אַב הָרַחֲמִים, זוֹכֵר יְצוּרָיו לְחַיִּים בְּרַחֲמִים.

וְנֶאֱמָן אַתָּה לְהַחֲיוֹת מֵתִים.

בָּרוּךְ אַתָּה יהוה, מְחַיֵּה הַמֵּתִים. (קהל: אָמֵן)

KEDUSHA

This section of tefillah is said while standing silently with feet together. The sentences are said responsively, Congregation followed by the Leader.

Congregation then Leader: נַעֲרִיצְךָ We will announce You, *Hashem*,
as holy in this world,
just as the angels announce
You as holy in heaven.
As Your prophet wrote,
The angels call to one another saying:

(Stand on your toes as you repeat the word "Holy")

Congregation then Leader: Holy, holy, holy, is *Hashem*.
The whole world is filled with Your holiness.

Leader: The angels then turn to each other and ask,
Where can we find *Hashem*'s honor?
The angels respond:

Congregation then Leader: Blessed is *Hashem*'s honor.

Leader: May *Hashem* act with mercy
and be kind to His people who say Shema
with love twice a day,
every morning and night, saying:

Congregation then Leader: Listen and understand, Jewish people,
Hashem is our one and only God.

Leader: He is our God, Father, King, and Savior.
With His mercy, He will publicly announce
that He is our God.

קדושה

This section of tefillah is said while standing silently with feet together. The sentences are said responsively, קהל *followed by the* חזן*.*

קהל *then* חזן: נַעֲרִיצְךָ וְנַקְדִּישְׁךָ כְּסוֹד שִׂיחַ שַׂרְפֵי קֹדֶשׁ
הַמַּקְדִּישִׁים שִׁמְךָ בַּקֹּדֶשׁ, כַּכָּתוּב עַל יַד נְבִיאֶךָ:
וְקָרָא זֶה אֶל־זֶה וְאָמַר

(Stand on your toes as you repeat the word קָדוֹשׁ*)*

קהל *then* חזן: קָדוֹשׁ, קָדוֹשׁ, קָדוֹשׁ, יהוה צְבָאוֹת
מְלֹא כָל הָאָרֶץ כְּבוֹדוֹ:

חזן: כְּבוֹדוֹ מָלֵא עוֹלָם, מְשָׁרְתָיו שׁוֹאֲלִים זֶה לָזֶה
אַיֵּה מְקוֹם כְּבוֹדוֹ
לְעֻמָּתָם בָּרוּךְ יֹאמֵרוּ

קהל *then* חזן: ·בָּרוּךְ כְּבוֹד־יהוה מִמְּקוֹמוֹ:

חזן: מִמְּקוֹמוֹ הוּא יִפֶן בְּרַחֲמִים
וְיָחֹן עַם הַמְיַחֲדִים שְׁמוֹ, עֶרֶב וָבֹקֶר בְּכָל יוֹם תָּמִיד
פַּעֲמַיִם בְּאַהֲבָה שְׁמַע אוֹמְרִים

קהל *then* חזן: שְׁמַע יִשְׂרָאֵל, יהוה אֱלֹהֵינוּ, יהוה אֶחָד:

חזן: הוּא אֱלֹהֵינוּ, הוּא אָבִינוּ
הוּא מַלְכֵּנוּ, הוּא מוֹשִׁיעֵנוּ
וְהוּא יַשְׁמִיעֵנוּ בְּרַחֲמָיו שֵׁנִית לְעֵינֵי כָּל חָי
לִהְיוֹת לָכֶם לֵאלֹהִים
אֲנִי יהוה אֱלֹהֵיכֶם:

Leader: It is written in Tanach:

Congregation then Leader: *Hashem,* You have ruled
over the Jewish people for generations,
and You shall continue to be our King forever.

Leader: *Hashem,* in every generation
we will discuss Your holiness and greatness.
Our mouths shall never stop speaking
of Your praises,
for You, *Hashem,* are a great and holy King.
Thank You, *Hashem,* our holy God.
/ *Between Rosh Hashana & Yom Kippur say:* the holy King./

(*Congregation:* Amen.)

If Rosh Chodesh falls on Shabbat, turn to page 604 and continue with Chazarat Hashatz for Shabbat Rosh Chodesh.

KEDUSHAT HA'YOM

We thank You, *Hashem,*
for creating Shabbat as a day for us to rest
and for allowing us
to bring You the *korban musaf* of Shabbat.

וּבְדִבְרֵי קָדְשְׁךָ כָּתוּב לֵאמֹר *It is written in Tanach.* Tanach, written in Hebrew as תנ"ך, is an acronym for (ת)Torah, (נ)Nevi'im, and (ך)Ketuvim. The Torah was presented to the Jewish people on Har Sinai by Moshe and came directly from *Hashem.* Nevi'im are the stories of the many prophets, messengers of *Hashem,* who lived after Moshe. Ketuvim means "writings," and this section of Tanach includes all of the songs, stories, and megillot written by the prophets.

חזן: וּבְדִבְרֵי קָדְשְׁךָ כָּתוּב לֵאמֹר

then קהל חזן: יִמְלֹךְ יהוה לְעוֹלָם, אֱלֹהַיִךְ צִיּוֹן לְדֹר וָדֹר הַלְלוּיָהּ:

חזן: לְדוֹר וָדוֹר נַגִּיד גָּדְלֶךָ

וּלְנֵצַח נְצָחִים קְדֻשָּׁתְךָ נַקְדִּישׁ

וְשִׁבְחֲךָ אֱלֹהֵינוּ מִפִּינוּ לֹא יָמוּשׁ לְעוֹלָם וָעֶד

כִּי אֵל מֶלֶךְ גָּדוֹל וְקָדוֹשׁ אָתָּה.

בָּרוּךְ אַתָּה יהוה, הָאֵל הַקָּדוֹשׁ.

/ On שבת שובה say הַמֶּלֶךְ הַקָּדוֹשׁ./

(קהל: אָמֵן)

If ראש חודש *falls on* שבת*, turn to page 605 and continue with* חזרת הש״ץ *for* שבת ראש חודש.

קדושת היום

תִּכַּנְתָּ שַׁבָּת, רָצִיתָ קָרְבְּנוֹתֶיהָ, צִוִּיתָ פֵּרוּשֶׁיהָ עִם סִדּוּרֵי נְסָכֶיהָ

מְעַנְּגֶיהָ לְעוֹלָם כָּבוֹד יִנְחָלוּ, טוֹעֲמֶיהָ חַיִּים זָכוּ

וְגַם הָאוֹהֲבִים דְּבָרֶיהָ גְּדֻלָּה בָּחָרוּ.

אָז מִסִּינַי נִצְטַוּוּ עָלֶיהָ

וַתְּצַוֵּנוּ יהוה אֱלֹהֵינוּ לְהַקְרִיב בָּהּ קָרְבַּן מוּסַף שַׁבָּת כָּרָאוּי.

יְהִי רָצוֹן מִלְּפָנֶיךָ, יהוה אֱלֹהֵינוּ וֵאלֹהֵי אֲבוֹתֵינוּ

שֶׁתַּעֲלֵנוּ בְשִׂמְחָה לְאַרְצֵנוּ וְתִטָּעֵנוּ בִּגְבוּלֵנוּ

וְשָׁם נַעֲשֶׂה לְפָנֶיךָ אֶת קָרְבְּנוֹת חוֹבוֹתֵינוּ

תְּמִידִים כְּסִדְרָם וּמוּסָפִים כְּהִלְכָתָם.

וְאֶת מוּסַף יוֹם הַשַּׁבָּת הַזֶּה

נַעֲשֶׂה וְנַקְרִיב לְפָנֶיךָ בְּאַהֲבָה כְּמִצְוַת רְצוֹנֶךָ

Those who keep and enjoy Shabbat
bring holiness to the seventh day
and will be overjoyed.
Hashem, You chose the seventh day and made it holy,
calling it the "most special of days,"
as it is a reminder of the creation of the world.

Reminder: Say "Amen" after the Leader recites each berachot.

Hashem, our God and God of our ancestors,
we rest from work today for Your sake.
Allow us to become holy through keeping Your *mitzvot*
and studying Your Torah.
Be good to us, save us, and purify our hearts
to serve you sincerely.
Hashem, our God, show us Your love
and allow us to observe Your holy Shabbat
so that Your Jewish people can rest.
Thank You, *Hashem,* for making Shabbat holy.
(*Congregation:* Amen.)

SERVICE IN THE *BEIT HAMIKDASH*

We pray to You, *Hashem,* that You accept our prayers
as though they are the sacrifices
that were once brought to You
in Your holy *Beit HaMikdash.*
May we be worthy
to see the rebuilding of the *Beit HaMikdash.*
We thank You, *Hashem,*
for returning Your presence to Zion. (*Congregation:* Amen.)

כְּמוֹ שֶׁכָּתַבְתָּ עָלֵינוּ בְּתוֹרָתֶךָ, עַל יְדֵי מֹשֶׁה עַבְדֶּךָ מִפִּי כְבוֹדֶךָ כָּאָמוּר

וּבְיוֹם הַשַּׁבָּת שְׁנֵי־כְבָשִׂים בְּנֵי־שָׁנָה תְּמִימִם
וּשְׁנֵי עֶשְׂרֹנִים סֹלֶת מִנְחָה בְּלוּלָה בַשֶּׁמֶן וְנִסְכּוֹ:
עֹלַת שַׁבַּת בְּשַׁבַּתּוֹ, עַל־עֹלַת הַתָּמִיד וְנִסְכָּהּ:

יִשְׂמְחוּ בְמַלְכוּתְךָ שׁוֹמְרֵי שַׁבָּת וְקוֹרְאֵי עֹנֶג, עַם מְקַדְּשֵׁי שְׁבִיעִי כֻּלָּם יִשְׂבְּעוּ וְיִתְעַנְּגוּ מִטּוּבֶךָ, וּבַשְּׁבִיעִי רָצִיתָ בּוֹ וְקִדַּשְׁתּוֹ חֶמְדַּת יָמִים אוֹתוֹ קָרָאתָ, זֵכֶר לְמַעֲשֵׂה בְרֵאשִׁית.

Reminder: Say אָמֵן *after the* חזן *recites the berachot.*

אֱלֹהֵינוּ וֵאלֹהֵי אֲבוֹתֵינוּ, רְצֵה בִמְנוּחָתֵנוּ
קַדְּשֵׁנוּ בְּמִצְוֹתֶיךָ וְתֵן חֶלְקֵנוּ בְּתוֹרָתֶךָ
שַׂבְּעֵנוּ מִטּוּבֶךָ, וְשַׂמְּחֵנוּ בִּישׁוּעָתֶךָ
וְטַהֵר לִבֵּנוּ לְעָבְדְּךָ בֶּאֱמֶת
וְהַנְחִילֵנוּ יהוה אֱלֹהֵינוּ בְּאַהֲבָה וּבְרָצוֹן שַׁבַּת קָדְשֶׁךָ
וְיָנוּחוּ בוֹ יִשְׂרָאֵל מְקַדְּשֵׁי שְׁמֶךָ.
בָּרוּךְ אַתָּה יהוה, מְקַדֵּשׁ הַשַּׁבָּת. (קהל: **אָמֵן**)

עבודה

רְצֵה יהוה אֱלֹהֵינוּ בְּעַמְּךָ יִשְׂרָאֵל, וּבִתְפִלָּתָם
וְהָשֵׁב אֶת הָעֲבוֹדָה לִדְבִיר בֵּיתֶךָ
וְאִשֵּׁי יִשְׂרָאֵל וּתְפִלָּתָם בְּאַהֲבָה תְקַבֵּל בְּרָצוֹן
וּתְהִי לְרָצוֹן תָּמִיד עֲבוֹדַת יִשְׂרָאֵל עַמֶּךָ.
וְתֶחֱזֶינָה עֵינֵינוּ בְּשׁוּבְךָ לְצִיּוֹן בְּרַחֲמִים.
בָּרוּךְ אַתָּה יהוה, הַמַּחֲזִיר שְׁכִינָתוֹ לְצִיּוֹן. (קהל: **אָמֵן**)

THANK YOU

While the Leader says this prayer, the Congregation says the prayer on the bottom of this page.

You, *Hashem*,
have unlimited mercy and kindness
and therefore
we have always placed our hope in You.

The following is said quietly while the Leader says the above. Bow when saying the first sentence below beginning with the words "Thank You, Hashem."

מוֹדִים Thank You, *Hashem*,
our God and God of our ancestors.
You are God of all people,
You created us,
and You created the entire world.
Thank You for giving us life
and for providing us with food to eat.
May You continue to give us life and food to eat.
May You gather us from exile
and return us to Your holy places
so we can keep Your laws,
and serve You with a perfect heart.
Thank You *Hashem*,
our God to whom thanksgiving is due.

הודאה

While the חזן *says this prayer, the* קהל *says the prayer on the bottom of this page.*

מוֹדִים אֲנַחְנוּ לָךְ
שָׁאַתָּה הוּא יהוה אֱלֹהֵינוּ וֵאלֹהֵי אֲבוֹתֵינוּ לְעוֹלָם וָעֶד.
צוּר חַיֵּינוּ, מָגֵן יִשְׁעֵנוּ אַתָּה הוּא לְדוֹר וָדוֹר.
נוֹדֶה לְּךָ וּנְסַפֵּר תְּהִלָּתֶךָ
עַל חַיֵּינוּ הַמְּסוּרִים בְּיָדֶךָ, וְעַל נִשְׁמוֹתֵינוּ הַפְּקוּדוֹת לָךְ
וְעַל נִסֶּיךָ שֶׁבְּכָל יוֹם עִמָּנוּ, וְעַל נִפְלְאוֹתֶיךָ וְטוֹבוֹתֶיךָ
שֶׁבְּכָל עֵת, עֶרֶב וָבֹקֶר וְצָהֳרָיִם.
הַטּוֹב, כִּי לֹא כָלוּ רַחֲמֶיךָ
וְהַמְרַחֵם, כִּי לֹא תַמּוּ חֲסָדֶיךָ, מֵעוֹלָם קִוִּינוּ לָךְ.

The following is said quietly while the חזן *says the above. Bow when saying the first sentence below beginning with the words* מוֹדִים אֲנַחְנוּ לָךְ.

מוֹדִים אֲנַחְנוּ לָךְ
שָׁאַתָּה הוּא יהוה אֱלֹהֵינוּ וֵאלֹהֵי אֲבוֹתֵינוּ
אֱלֹהֵי כָל בָּשָׂר, יוֹצְרֵנוּ, יוֹצֵר בְּרֵאשִׁית.
בְּרָכוֹת וְהוֹדָאוֹת לְשִׁמְךָ הַגָּדוֹל וְהַקָּדוֹשׁ
עַל שֶׁהֶחֱיִיתָנוּ וְקִיַּמְתָּנוּ.
כֵּן תְּחַיֵּנוּ וּתְקַיְּמֵנוּ, וְתֶאֱסֹף גָּלֻיּוֹתֵינוּ לְחַצְרוֹת קָדְשֶׁךָ
לִשְׁמֹר חֻקֶּיךָ וְלַעֲשׂוֹת רְצוֹנֶךָ וּלְעָבְדְּךָ בְּלֵבָב שָׁלֵם
עַל שֶׁאֲנַחְנוּ מוֹדִים לָךְ.
בָּרוּךְ אֵל הַהוֹדָאוֹת.

Reminder: Say "Amen" after the Leader recites the beracha.

On Chanuka say:

We thank You, *Hashem,* for the miracles, the deliverances, the great strength, and the victories in war that You displayed for us in earlier times and in our times.

In the days of Mattityahu, son of Yochanan the *Kohen Gadol,* the Hasmonean, and his sons, the wicked Greeks challenged Your Jewish people trying to make them forget Your Torah and sin. In Your great kindness, You, *Hashem,* supported us in this difficult time. You allowed for: The weak Jews to defeat the mighty Greeks, The few Jews to defeat the many Greeks, The pure Jews to defeat the impure Greeks, The righteous Jews to defeat the wicked Greeks, and The Jews who studied Your Torah to defeat the Greeks who did not. *Hashem,* on this day everyone in the world recognized You as You miraculously saved Your Jewish people. Your Jewish people then entered the *Beit HaMikdash* to clean and purify it. They lit candles in the courtyard of the *Beit HaMikdash* and set aside these eight days of *Chanukah* for giving thanks and praising You.

Continue with "We thank You"

We thank You, *Hashem,* for You are good
and all that You do is good.
Thank You, *Hashem,* for You are worthy of being thanked.

(*Congregation:* Amen.)

BLESSINGS OF THE *KOHANIM*

אֱלֹהֵינוּ *Hashem,* Our God and God of our ancestors, provide us with the three blessings that Aharon the *Kohen* and the *kohanim* his descendants use to bless the Jewish people.

Leader: *Hashem* should bless and protect you.

(*Congregation:* May it be as you say!)

Leader: *Hashem* should be kind and favorable towards you.

(*Congregation:* May it be as you say!)

Leader: *Hashem* should grant you peace.

(*Congregation:* May it be as you say!)

Reminder: Say אָמֵן *after the* חזן *recites the beracha.*

בחנוכה:

עַל הַנִּסִּים וְעַל הַפֻּרְקָן וְעַל הַגְּבוּרוֹת וְעַל הַתְּשׁוּעוֹת וְעַל הַמִּלְחָמוֹת שֶׁעָשִׂיתָ לַאֲבוֹתֵינוּ בַּיָּמִים הָהֵם בַּזְּמַן הַזֶּה.

בִּימֵי מַתִּתְיָהוּ בֶּן יוֹחָנָן כֹּהֵן גָּדוֹל חַשְׁמוֹנַאי וּבָנָיו, כְּשֶׁעָמְדָה מַלְכוּת יָוָן הָרְשָׁעָה עַל עַמְּךָ יִשְׂרָאֵל לְהַשְׁכִּיחָם תּוֹרָתֶךָ וּלְהַעֲבִירָם מֵחֻקֵּי רְצוֹנֶךָ, וְאַתָּה בְּרַחֲמֶיךָ הָרַבִּים עָמַדְתָּ לָהֶם בְּעֵת צָרָתָם, רַבְתָּ אֶת רִיבָם, דַּנְתָּ אֶת דִּינָם, נָקַמְתָּ אֶת נִקְמָתָם, מָסַרְתָּ גִבּוֹרִים בְּיַד חַלָּשִׁים, וְרַבִּים בְּיַד מְעַטִּים, וּטְמֵאִים בְּיַד טְהוֹרִים, וּרְשָׁעִים בְּיַד צַדִּיקִים, וְזֵדִים בְּיַד עוֹסְקֵי תוֹרָתֶךָ, וּלְךָ עָשִׂיתָ שֵׁם גָּדוֹל וְקָדוֹשׁ בְּעוֹלָמֶךָ, וּלְעַמְּךָ יִשְׂרָאֵל עָשִׂיתָ תְּשׁוּעָה גְדוֹלָה וּפֻרְקָן כְּהַיּוֹם הַזֶּה. וְאַחַר כֵּן בָּאוּ בָנֶיךָ לִדְבִיר בֵּיתֶךָ, וּפִנּוּ אֶת הֵיכָלֶךָ, וְטִהֲרוּ אֶת מִקְדָּשֶׁךָ, וְהִדְלִיקוּ נֵרוֹת בְּחַצְרוֹת קָדְשֶׁךָ, וְקָבְעוּ שְׁמוֹנַת יְמֵי חֲנֻכָּה אֵלּוּ, לְהוֹדוֹת וּלְהַלֵּל לְשִׁמְךָ הַגָּדוֹל.

Continue with וְעַל כֻּלָּם.

וְעַל כֻּלָּם, יִתְבָּרַךְ וְיִתְרוֹמַם שִׁמְךָ מַלְכֵּנוּ תָּמִיד לְעוֹלָם וָעֶד.

On שבת שובה *say* וּכְתֹב לְחַיִּים טוֹבִים כָּל בְּנֵי בְרִיתֶךָ.

וְכֹל הַחַיִּים יוֹדוּךָ סֶּלָה, וִיהַלְלוּ אֶת שִׁמְךָ בֶּאֱמֶת הָאֵל יְשׁוּעָתֵנוּ וְעֶזְרָתֵנוּ סֶלָה.

בָּרוּךְ אַתָּה יהוה, הַטּוֹב שִׁמְךָ וּלְךָ נָאֶה לְהוֹדוֹת. (קהל: אָמֵן)

ברכת כוהנים

אֱלֹהֵינוּ וֵאלֹהֵי אֲבוֹתֵינוּ, בָּרְכֵנוּ בַּבְּרָכָה הַמְשֻׁלֶּשֶׁת בַּתּוֹרָה, הַכְּתוּבָה עַל יְדֵי מֹשֶׁה עַבְדֶּךָ, הָאֲמוּרָה מִפִּי אַהֲרֹן וּבָנָיו כֹּהֲנִים עַם קְדוֹשֶׁיךָ, כָּאָמוּר

חזן: יְבָרֶכְךָ יהוה וְיִשְׁמְרֶךָ: קהל: כֵּן יְהִי רָצוֹן

חזן: יָאֵר יהוה פָּנָיו אֵלֶיךָ וִיחֻנֶּךָּ: קהל: כֵּן יְהִי רָצוֹן

חזן: יִשָּׂא יהוה פָּנָיו אֵלֶיךָ וְיָשֵׂם לְךָ שָׁלוֹם: קהל: כֵּן יְהִי רָצוֹן

Reminder: Say "Amen" after the Leader recites the beracha.

PEACE

that You grant peace
to Your Jewish people
at every moment of every hour,
forever.

Between Rosh Hashana and Yom Kippur the Leader continues with "May You remember," below.

Thank You, *Hashem*,
who blesses His Jewish people with peace.

(*Congregation:* Amen.)

Between Rosh Hashana and Yom Kippur say:

May You remember
all of the Jewish people for life,
blessing, peace, and riches
and write us in the book of good life and peace.
Thank You, *Hashem*, who makes peace.

(*Congregation:* Amen.)

The service continues with Kaddish Shalem on page 608.

Reminder: Say אָמֵן after the חזן recites the beracha.

שלום

שִׂים שָׁלוֹם טוֹבָה וּבְרָכָה
חֵן וָחֶסֶד וְרַחֲמִים עָלֵינוּ
וְעַל כָּל יִשְׂרָאֵל עַמֶּךָ.
בָּרְכֵנוּ אָבִינוּ כֻּלָּנוּ כְּאֶחָד בְּאוֹר פָּנֶיךָ
כִּי בְאוֹר פָּנֶיךָ נָתַתָּ לָּנוּ יהוה אֱלֹהֵינוּ
תּוֹרַת חַיִּים וְאַהֲבַת חֶסֶד
וּצְדָקָה וּבְרָכָה וְרַחֲמִים
וְחַיִּים וְשָׁלוֹם.
וְטוֹב בְּעֵינֶיךָ לְבָרֵךְ אֶת עַמְּךָ יִשְׂרָאֵל
בְּכָל עֵת וּבְכָל שָׁעָה בִּשְׁלוֹמֶךָ.

On שבת שובה the חזן continues with בְּסֵפֶר חַיִּים, below.

בָּרוּךְ אַתָּה יהוה, הַמְבָרֵךְ אֶת עַמּוֹ יִשְׂרָאֵל בַּשָּׁלוֹם.
(קהל: אָמֵן)

On שבת שובה say:

בְּסֵפֶר חַיִּים, בְּרָכָה וְשָׁלוֹם, וּפַרְנָסָה טוֹבָה
נִזָּכֵר וְנִכָּתֵב לְפָנֶיךָ
אֲנַחְנוּ וְכָל עַמְּךָ בֵּית יִשְׂרָאֵל לְחַיִּים טוֹבִים וּלְשָׁלוֹם.
בָּרוּךְ אַתָּה יהוה, עוֹשֶׂה הַשָּׁלוֹם. (קהל: אָמֵן)

The service continues with קדיש שלם on page 609.

On Rosh Chodesh the Amida continues here:

MUSAF FOR SHABBAT ROSH CHODESH

אַתָּה יָצַרְתָּ Long ago, You, *Hashem*, created the world
and rested on Shabbat, the seventh day.
You loved Your Jewish people
and chose us from all other nations.
You made us holy by allowing us to keep Your *mitzvot*,
and You brought us close so we could serve You.
You lovingly gave Your people Shabbat as a day of rest,
and Rosh Chodesh, the new month,
as a day for forgiveness.
Sadly, our ancestors sinned
and You destroyed the *Beit HaMikdash*;
we can no longer bring *korbanot*, sacrifices,
as You want us to.

אַתָּה יָצַרְתָּ עוֹלָמְךָ מִקֶּדֶם, כִּלִּיתָ מְלַאכְתְּךָ בַּיּוֹם הַשְּׁבִיעִי *Long ago, You, Hashem, created the world and rested on Shabbat, the seventh day.* We are well aware that *Hashem* created the world long ago. Why do we highlight this idea specifically in Musaf of Shabbat Rosh Chodesh, a *tefillah* which we do not say often? There was a time when people thought that the sun, moon, and other natural creations had their own powers, and therefore prayed to them. Although on Rosh Chodesh we celebrate the moon's renewal and the beginning of a new month, we are careful not to pray to the moon itself. On Shabbat, the day which reminds us that *Hashem* created the entire world, including the sun, moon, and stars, we mention that *Hashem* created the world and existed before the world. Shabbat Rosh Chodesh is an appropriate time to remind ourselves of this important message.

On ראש חודש the עמידה continues here:

בשבת ראש חודש:

אַתָּה יָצַרְתָּ עוֹלָמְךָ מִקֶּדֶם
כִּלִּיתָ מְלַאכְתְּךָ בַּיּוֹם הַשְּׁבִיעִי
אָהַבְתָּ אוֹתָנוּ וְרָצִיתָ בָּנוּ
וְרוֹמַמְתָּנוּ מִכָּל הַלְּשׁוֹנוֹת
וְקִדַּשְׁתָּנוּ בְּמִצְוֹתֶיךָ
וְקֵרַבְתָּנוּ מַלְכֵּנוּ לַעֲבוֹדָתֶךָ
וְשִׁמְךָ הַגָּדוֹל וְהַקָּדוֹשׁ עָלֵינוּ קָרָאתָ.
וַתִּתֶּן לָנוּ יהוה אֱלֹהֵינוּ בְּאַהֲבָה
שַׁבָּתוֹת לִמְנוּחָה
וְרָאשֵׁי חֳדָשִׁים לְכַפָּרָה.
וּלְפִי שֶׁחָטָאנוּ לְפָנֶיךָ אֲנַחְנוּ וַאֲבוֹתֵינוּ
חָרְבָה עִירֵנוּ
וְשָׁמֵם בֵּית מִקְדָּשֵׁנוּ
וְגָלָה יְקָרֵנוּ
וְנֻטַּל כָּבוֹד מִבֵּית חַיֵּינוּ
וְאֵין אֲנַחְנוּ יְכוֹלִים לַעֲשׂוֹת חוֹבוֹתֵינוּ בְּבֵית בְּחִירָתֶךָ
בַּבַּיִת הַגָּדוֹל וְהַקָּדוֹשׁ שֶׁנִּקְרָא שִׁמְךָ עָלָיו
מִפְּנֵי הַיָּד שֶׁנִּשְׁתַּלְּחָה בְּמִקְדָּשֶׁךָ.

יְהִי רָצוֹן *Hashem,* our God and God of our ancestors,
may it be Your will,
that You lead us back to our land with joy
and allow us to bring *korbanot* to You.
With love we will again bring the special Shabbos
and Rosh Chodesh *korbanot*
as You commanded us in the Torah.

וּבְיוֹם הַשַּׁבָּת On Shabbos we will bring
two perfect young lambs,
together with flour, oil, and wine.
We will burn this *korban*
in addition to the regular daily *korbanot.*

וּבְרָאשֵׁי חָדְשֵׁיכֶם On Rosh Chodesh we will also bring:
Two bulls,
One ram, and
Seven perfect lambs
As a special *korban.*
Along with each bull, ram, and lamb
we will also bring flour and wine *korbanot.*

יִשְׂמְחוּ Those who keep and celebrate Shabbat
will find joy in Your kingship.
Those who make Shabbat holy
will be given what they need and enjoy Your goodness.
Shabbat is Your favorite
and most holy day,
the day You created the world.

יְהִי רָצוֹן מִלְּפָנֶיךָ, יהוה אֱלֹהֵינוּ וֵאלֹהֵי אֲבוֹתֵינוּ
שֶׁתַּעֲלֵנוּ בְשִׂמְחָה לְאַרְצֵנוּ וְתִטָּעֵנוּ בִּגְבוּלֵנוּ
וְשָׁם נַעֲשֶׂה לְפָנֶיךָ אֶת קָרְבְּנוֹת חוֹבוֹתֵינוּ
תְּמִידִים כְּסִדְרָם וּמוּסָפִים כְּהִלְכָתָם.
וְאֶת מוּסְפֵי יוֹם הַשַּׁבָּת הַזֶּה וְיוֹם רֹאשׁ הַחֹדֶשׁ הַזֶּה
נַעֲשֶׂה וְנַקְרִיב לְפָנֶיךָ בְּאַהֲבָה כְּמִצְוַת רְצוֹנֶךָ
כְּמוֹ שֶׁכָּתַבְתָּ עָלֵינוּ בְּתוֹרָתֶךָ עַל יְדֵי מֹשֶׁה עַבְדֶּךָ
מִפִּי כְבוֹדֶךָ, כָּאָמוּר

וּבְיוֹם הַשַּׁבָּת שְׁנֵי־כְבָשִׂים בְּנֵי־שָׁנָה תְּמִימִם
וּשְׁנֵי עֶשְׂרֹנִים סֹלֶת מִנְחָה בְּלוּלָה בַשֶּׁמֶן וְנִסְכּוֹ:
עֹלַת שַׁבַּת בְּשַׁבַּתּוֹ, עַל־עֹלַת הַתָּמִיד וְנִסְכָּהּ:

וּבְרָאשֵׁי חָדְשֵׁיכֶם תַּקְרִיבוּ עֹלָה לַיהוה, פָּרִים בְּנֵי־בָקָר
שְׁנַיִם, וְאַיִל אֶחָד, כְּבָשִׂים בְּנֵי־שָׁנָה שִׁבְעָה, תְּמִימִם:

וּמִנְחָתָם וְנִסְכֵּיהֶם כִּמְדֻבָּר, שְׁלֹשָׁה עֶשְׂרֹנִים לַפָּר
וּשְׁנֵי עֶשְׂרֹנִים לָאַיִל, וְעִשָּׂרוֹן לַכֶּבֶשׂ, וְיַיִן כְּנִסְכּוֹ
וְשָׂעִיר לְכַפֵּר, וּשְׁנֵי תְמִידִים כְּהִלְכָתָם.

יִשְׂמְחוּ בְמַלְכוּתְךָ שׁוֹמְרֵי שַׁבָּת וְקוֹרְאֵי עֹנֶג
עַם מְקַדְּשֵׁי שְׁבִיעִי, כֻּלָּם יִשְׂבְּעוּ וְיִתְעַנְּגוּ מִטּוּבֶךָ
וּבַשְּׁבִיעִי רָצִיתָ בּוֹ וְקִדַּשְׁתּוֹ
חֶמְדַּת יָמִים אוֹתוֹ קָרָאתָ, זֵכֶר לְמַעֲשֵׂה בְרֵאשִׁית.

אֱלֹהֵינוּ *Hashem,*
our God and God of our ancestors,
may You be pleased with our resting on Shabbat.
May You please fill Rosh Chodesh, the new month,
with:

Goodness and blessings,
Joy and happiness,
Comfort and protection,
Support for what we need,
Life and peace, and
Forgiveness.

For You have chosen the Jewish people
from all the other nations
and given them the *mitzva* of Rosh Chodesh.
Thank You, *Hashem,*
for making Shabbat,
the Jewish people,
and the new month holy.

For the completion of the Amida, turn to page 576
and continue with "Hashem, please accept Your Jewish people."

אֱלֹהֵינוּ וֵאלֹהֵי אֲבוֹתֵינוּ
רְצֵה בִמְנוּחָתֵנוּ
וְחַדֵּשׁ עָלֵינוּ בְּיוֹם הַשַּׁבָּת הַזֶּה אֶת הַחֹדֶשׁ הַזֶּה
לְטוֹבָה וְלִבְרָכָה
לְשָׂשׂוֹן וּלְשִׂמְחָה
לִישׁוּעָה וּלְנֶחָמָה
לְפַרְנָסָה וּלְכַלְכָּלָה
לְחַיִּים וּלְשָׁלוֹם
לִמְחִילַת חֵטְא וְלִסְלִיחַת עָוֹן
(*From* מרחשון *to* אדר שני *in a Jewish leap year* וּלְכַפָּרַת פָּשַׁע)
כִּי בְעַמְּךָ יִשְׂרָאֵל בָּחַרְתָּ מִכָּל הָאֻמּוֹת
וְשַׁבַּת קָדְשְׁךָ לָהֶם הוֹדַעְתָּ
וְחֻקֵּי רָאשֵׁי חֳדָשִׁים לָהֶם קָבָעְתָּ.
בָּרוּךְ אַתָּה יהוה
מְקַדֵּשׁ הַשַּׁבָּת וְיִשְׂרָאֵל וְרָאשֵׁי חֳדָשִׁים.

For the completion of the עמידה *turn to page 577*
and continue with רְצֵה.

SHABBAT ROSH CHODESH CHAZARAT HASHATZ

Hashem, creator of the world,
You lovingly gave us Shabbat a day of rest,
and Rosh Chodesh, the new month,
as a day for forgiveness.

Hashem, our God and God of our ancestors,
may it be Your will
that You lead us back to our land with joy
and allow us to bring *Korbanot* to You.

חזרת הש״ץ בשבת ראש חודש:

אַתָּה יָצַרְתָּ עוֹלָמְךָ מִקֶּדֶם, כִּלִּיתָ מְלַאכְתְּךָ בַּיּוֹם הַשְּׁבִיעִי
אָהַבְתָּ אוֹתָנוּ וְרָצִיתָ בָּנוּ, וְרוֹמַמְתָּנוּ מִכָּל הַלְּשׁוֹנוֹת
וְקִדַּשְׁתָּנוּ בְּמִצְוֹתֶיךָ, וְקֵרַבְתָּנוּ מַלְכֵּנוּ לַעֲבוֹדָתֶךָ
וְשִׁמְךָ הַגָּדוֹל וְהַקָּדוֹשׁ עָלֵינוּ קָרָאתָ.
וַתִּתֶּן לָנוּ יהוה אֱלֹהֵינוּ בְּאַהֲבָה
שַׁבָּתוֹת לִמְנוּחָה וְרָאשֵׁי חֳדָשִׁים לְכַפָּרָה.
וּלְפִי שֶׁחָטָאנוּ לְפָנֶיךָ אֲנַחְנוּ וַאֲבוֹתֵינוּ
חָרְבָה עִירֵנוּ, וְשָׁמֵם בֵּית מִקְדָּשֵׁנוּ
וְגָלָה יְקָרֵנוּ, וְנֻטַּל כָּבוֹד מִבֵּית חַיֵּינוּ
וְאֵין אֲנַחְנוּ יְכוֹלִים לַעֲשׂוֹת חוֹבוֹתֵינוּ בְּבֵית בְּחִירָתֶךָ
בַּבַּיִת הַגָּדוֹל וְהַקָּדוֹשׁ שֶׁנִּקְרָא שִׁמְךָ עָלָיו, מִפְּנֵי הַיָּד
שֶׁנִּשְׁתַּלְּחָה בְּמִקְדָּשֶׁךָ.

יְהִי רָצוֹן מִלְּפָנֶיךָ, יהוה אֱלֹהֵינוּ וֵאלֹהֵי אֲבוֹתֵינוּ
שֶׁתַּעֲלֵנוּ בְשִׂמְחָה לְאַרְצֵנוּ וְתִטָּעֵנוּ בִּגְבוּלֵנוּ
וְשָׁם נַעֲשֶׂה לְפָנֶיךָ אֶת קָרְבְּנוֹת חוֹבוֹתֵינוּ
תְּמִידִים כְּסִדְרָם וּמוּסָפִים כְּהִלְכָתָם.
וְאֶת מוּסְפֵי יוֹם הַשַּׁבָּת הַזֶּה וְיוֹם רֹאשׁ הַחֹדֶשׁ הַזֶּה
נַעֲשֶׂה וְנַקְרִיב לְפָנֶיךָ בְּאַהֲבָה כְּמִצְוַת רְצוֹנֶךָ
כְּמוֹ שֶׁכָּתַבְתָּ עָלֵינוּ בְּתוֹרָתֶךָ עַל יְדֵי מֹשֶׁה עַבְדֶּךָ מִפִּי כְבוֹדֶךָ,
כָּאָמוּר

וּבְיוֹם הַשַּׁבָּת שְׁנֵי־כְבָשִׂים בְּנֵי־שָׁנָה תְּמִימִם, וּשְׁנֵי עֶשְׂרֹנִים סֹלֶת מִנְחָה בְּלוּלָה בַשֶּׁמֶן וְנִסְכּוֹ: עֹלַת שַׁבַּת בְּשַׁבַּתּוֹ, עַל־עֹלַת הַתָּמִיד וְנִסְכָּהּ:

Reminder: Say "Amen" after the Leader recites each beracha.

Those who make Shabbat holy
will be given what they need
and enjoy Your goodness.

Hashem, our God, and God of our ancestors,
may You please fill the new month
with goodness for Your Jewish people.
Thank You, *Hashem*,
for making the Jewish people,
Shabbat, and the new month holy. (*Congregation:* Amen.)

For the completion of Chazarat Hashatz, turn to page 590 and continue with Service in the Beit HaMikdash.

Reminder: Say אָמֵן *after the* חזן *recites the beracha.*

וּבְרָאשֵׁי חָדְשֵׁיכֶם תַּקְרִיבוּ עֹלָה לַיהוה, פָּרִים בְּנֵי־בָקָר שְׁנַיִם, וְאַיִל אֶחָד, כְּבָשִׂים בְּנֵי־שָׁנָה שִׁבְעָה, תְּמִימִם:

וּמִנְחָתָם וְנִסְכֵּיהֶם כִּמְדֻבָּר, שְׁלֹשָׁה עֶשְׂרֹנִים לַפָּר, וּשְׁנֵי עֶשְׂרֹנִים לָאָיִל, וְעִשָּׂרוֹן לַכֶּבֶשׂ, וְיַיִן כְּנִסְכּוֹ, וְשָׂעִיר לְכַפֵּר, וּשְׁנֵי תְמִידִים כְּהִלְכָתָם.

יִשְׂמְחוּ בְמַלְכוּתְךָ שׁוֹמְרֵי שַׁבָּת וְקוֹרְאֵי עֹנֶג
עַם מְקַדְּשֵׁי שְׁבִיעִי, כֻּלָּם יִשְׂבְּעוּ וְיִתְעַנְּגוּ מִטּוּבֶךָ
וּבַשְּׁבִיעִי רָצִיתָ בּוֹ וְקִדַּשְׁתּוֹ
חֶמְדַּת יָמִים אוֹתוֹ קָרָאתָ, זֵכֶר לְמַעֲשֵׂה בְרֵאשִׁית.

אֱלֹהֵינוּ וֵאלֹהֵי אֲבוֹתֵינוּ, רְצֵה בִמְנוּחָתֵנוּ
וְחַדֵּשׁ עָלֵינוּ בְּיוֹם הַשַּׁבָּת הַזֶּה אֶת הַחֹדֶשׁ הַזֶּה
לְטוֹבָה וְלִבְרָכָה, לְשָׂשׂוֹן וּלְשִׂמְחָה, לִישׁוּעָה וּלְנֶחָמָה
לְפַרְנָסָה וּלְכַלְכָּלָה, לְחַיִּים וּלְשָׁלוֹם
לִמְחִילַת חֵטְא וְלִסְלִיחַת עָוֹן
(*From* מרחשון *to* אדר שני *in a Jewish leap year* וּלְכַפָּרַת פָּשַׁע)
כִּי בְעַמְּךָ יִשְׂרָאֵל בָּחַרְתָּ מִכָּל הָאֻמּוֹת
וְשַׁבַּת קָדְשְׁךָ לָהֶם הוֹדַעְתָּ וְחֻקֵּי רָאשֵׁי חֳדָשִׁים לָהֶם קָבָעְתָּ.

בָּרוּךְ אַתָּה יהוה
מְקַדֵּשׁ הַשַּׁבָּת וְיִשְׂרָאֵל וְרָאשֵׁי חֳדָשִׁים. (קהל: אָמֵן)

For the completion of חזרת הש״ץ*, turn to page 591 and continue with* רְצֵה.

KADDISH SHALEM

Leader: יִתְגַּדַּל May *Hashem* be recognized
as great and holy (*Congregation:* Amen)
in the world that He created.
May He establish His kingdom
during my lifetime and the lifetime of all Jews,
quickly and soon.
Let us say: "Amen" (*Congregation:* Amen).

Congregation: May we thank *Hashem* for ever and ever.
Leader: May we thank *Hashem* for ever and ever.

Leader: *Hashem* should be thanked, praised,
and honored (*Congregation:* He is blessed).
Hashem is beyond all the blessings,
songs, or praises that we could offer.
Let us say: "Amen" (*Congregation:* Amen).

May *Hashem* accept our prayers
and the prayers of all Jews.
Let us say: "Amen." (*Congregation:* Amen).

May *Hashem* give us, and all Jews,
peace and good life.
Let us say: "Amen." (*Congregation:* Amen).

The Leader takes three steps back before saying this line, bows to the left when saying "May," bows to the right when saying "the One," bows to the middle when saying "make peace for us":

May *Hashem,* the One
who makes peace in heaven,
make peace for us and for all Jews.
Let us say: "Amen." (*Congregation:* Amen).

קדיש שלם

חזן: יִתְגַּדַּל וְיִתְקַדַּשׁ שְׁמֵהּ רַבָּא (קהל: אָמֵן)
בְּעָלְמָא דִּי בְרָא כִרְעוּתֵהּ, וְיַמְלִיךְ מַלְכוּתֵהּ
בְּחַיֵּיכוֹן וּבְיוֹמֵיכוֹן וּבְחַיֵּי דְכָל בֵּית יִשְׂרָאֵל
בַּעֲגָלָא וּבִזְמַן קָרִיב, וְאִמְרוּ אָמֵן. (קהל: אָמֵן)

קהל יְהֵא שְׁמֵהּ רַבָּא מְבָרַךְ לְעָלַם וּלְעָלְמֵי עָלְמַיָּא.
חזן: יְהֵא שְׁמֵהּ רַבָּא מְבָרַךְ לְעָלַם וּלְעָלְמֵי עָלְמַיָּא.

חזן: יִתְבָּרַךְ וְיִשְׁתַּבַּח וְיִתְפָּאַר וְיִתְרוֹמַם וְיִתְנַשֵּׂא וְיִתְהַדָּר
וְיִתְעַלֶּה וְיִתְהַלָּל שְׁמֵהּ דְּקֻדְשָׁא בְּרִיךְ הוּא (קהל: בְּרִיךְ הוּא)
לְעֵלָּא מִן כָּל בִּרְכָתָא
/בשבת שובה: לְעֵלָּא לְעֵלָּא מִכָּל בִּרְכָתָא/
וְשִׁירָתָא, תֻּשְׁבְּחָתָא וְנֶחֱמָתָא
דַּאֲמִירָן בְּעָלְמָא, וְאִמְרוּ אָמֵן. (קהל: אָמֵן)

תִּתְקַבַּל צְלוֹתְהוֹן וּבָעוּתְהוֹן דְּכָל יִשְׂרָאֵל
קֳדָם אֲבוּהוֹן דִּי בִשְׁמַיָּא, וְאִמְרוּ אָמֵן. (קהל: אָמֵן)

יְהֵא שְׁלָמָא רַבָּא מִן שְׁמַיָּא
וְחַיִּים, עָלֵינוּ וְעַל כָּל יִשְׂרָאֵל, וְאִמְרוּ אָמֵן. (קהל: אָמֵן)

The חזן *takes three steps back before saying this line, bows to the left when saying* עֹשֶׂה*, bows to the right when saying* הוּא*, bows to the middle when saying* יַעֲשֶׂה שָׁלוֹם עָלֵינוּ*:*

עֹשֶׂה שָׁלוֹם /בשבת שובה: הַשָּׁלוֹם/ בִּמְרוֹמָיו
הוּא יַעֲשֶׂה שָׁלוֹם
עָלֵינוּ וְעַל כָּל יִשְׂרָאֵל, וְאִמְרוּ אָמֵן. (קהל: אָמֵן)

אֵין כֵּאלֹהֵינוּ There is no one like You, *Hashem,* our God.
There is no one like You, *Hashem,* our Master.
There is no one like You, *Hashem,* our King.
There is no one like You, *Hashem,* who saves us.

Who is like You, *Hashem,* our God?
Who is like You, *Hashem,* our Master?
Who is like You, *Hashem,* our King?
Who is like You, *Hashem,* who saves us?

We will thank You, *Hashem,* our God.
We will thank You, *Hashem,* our Master.
We will thank You, *Hashem,* our King.
We will thank You, *Hashem,* who saves us.

We will bless You, *Hashem,* our God.
We will bless You, *Hashem,* our Master.
We will bless You, *Hashem,* our King.
We will bless You, *Hashem,* who saves us.

You, *Hashem,* are our God.
You, *Hashem,* are our Master.
You, *Hashem,* are our King.
You, *Hashem,* will save us.

פִּטּוּם הַקְּטֹרֶת Our ancestors brought the *Ketoret,*
the sweet smelling sacrifice to You, *Hashem.*
The *Ketoret* has spices, herbs, and wine.
It is not allowed to have honey in it.
No ingredient can be left out.

אֵין כֵּאלֹהֵֽינוּ אֵין כַּאדוֹנֵֽינוּ
אֵין כְּמַלְכֵּֽנוּ אֵין כְּמוֹשִׁיעֵֽנוּ.

מִי כֵאלֹהֵֽינוּ מִי כַאדוֹנֵֽינוּ
מִי כְמַלְכֵּֽנוּ מִי כְמוֹשִׁיעֵֽנוּ.

נוֹדֶה לֵאלֹהֵֽינוּ נוֹדֶה לַאדוֹנֵֽינוּ
נוֹדֶה לְמַלְכֵּֽנוּ נוֹדֶה לְמוֹשִׁיעֵֽנוּ.

בָּרוּךְ אֱלֹהֵֽינוּ בָּרוּךְ אֲדוֹנֵֽינוּ
בָּרוּךְ מַלְכֵּֽנוּ בָּרוּךְ מוֹשִׁיעֵֽנוּ.

אַתָּה הוּא אֱלֹהֵֽינוּ אַתָּה הוּא אֲדוֹנֵֽינוּ
אַתָּה הוּא מַלְכֵּֽנוּ אַתָּה הוּא מוֹשִׁיעֵֽנוּ.
אַתָּה הוּא
שֶׁהִקְטִֽירוּ אֲבוֹתֵֽינוּ לְפָנֶֽיךָ אֶת קְטֹֽרֶת הַסַּמִּים.

פִּטּוּם הַקְּטֹֽרֶת. הַצֳּרִי, וְהַצִּפֹּֽרֶן, וְהַחֶלְבְּנָה, וְהַלְּבוֹנָה מִשְׁקַל שִׁבְעִים שִׁבְעִים מָנֶה, מֹר, וּקְצִיעָה, שִׁבֹּֽלֶת נֵרְדְּ, וְכַרְכֹּם מִשְׁקַל שִׁשָּׁה עָשָׂר שִׁשָּׁה עָשָׂר מָנֶה, הַקֹּשְׁטְ שְׁנֵים עָשָׂר, קִלּוּפָה שְׁלֹשָׁה, וְקִנָּמוֹן תִּשְׁעָה, בֹּרִית כַּרְשִׁינָה תִּשְׁעָה קַבִּין, יֵין קַפְרִיסִין סְאִין תְּלָת וְקַבִּין תְּלָתָא, וְאִם אֵין לוֹ יֵין קַפְרִיסִין, מֵבִיא חֲמַר חִוַּרְיָן עַתִּיק. מֶֽלַח סְדוֹמִית רֹֽבַע, מַעֲלֶה עָשָׁן כָּל שֶׁהוּא. רַבִּי נָתָן הַבַּבְלִי אוֹמֵר: אַף כִּפַּת הַיַּרְדֵּן כָּל שֶׁהוּא, וְאִם נָתַן בָּהּ דְּבַשׁ פְּסָלָהּ, וְאִם חִסַּר אַחַת מִכָּל סַמָּנֶֽיהָ, חַיָּב מִיתָה.

רַבָּן שִׁמְעוֹן Rabbi Shimon also explains
some of the ingredients
used in the sacrifices.

הַשִּׁיר Each day of the week
the Levi'im would sing
a special song in the *Beit HaMikdash*.

On Sunday they would sing –
The whole earth, every person and everything on it,
belongs to *Hashem*.

On Monday they would sing –
Hashem is great
and He should be praised in the *Beit HaMikdash*.

On Tuesday they would sing –
Hashem is the judge over all judges.

On Wednesday they would sing –
Hashem, take revenge on those who deserve it.

On Thursday they would sing –
We sing songs of joy to *Hashem* our God.

On Friday they would sing –
Hashem, the Ruler, is filled with strength;
no one can change His creations.

On Shabbat they would sing –
The song of Shabbat;
a song about the times of *Mashiach*
when we will be able to rest peacefully.

רַבָּן שִׁמְעוֹן בֶּן גַּמְלִיאֵל אוֹמֵר: הַצֳּרִי אֵינוֹ אֶלָּא שְׂרָף הַנּוֹטֵף מֵעֲצֵי הַקְּטָף. בֹּרִית כַּרְשִׁינָה שֶׁשָּׁפִין בָּהּ אֶת הַצִּפֹּרֶן כְּדֵי שֶׁתְּהֵא נָאָה, יֵין קַפְרִיסִין שֶׁשּׁוֹרִין בּוֹ אֶת הַצִּפֹּרֶן כְּדֵי שֶׁתְּהֵא עַזָּה, וַהֲלֹא מֵי רַגְלַיִם יָפִין לָהּ, אֶלָּא שֶׁאֵין מַכְנִיסִין מֵי רַגְלַיִם בַּמִּקְדָּשׁ מִפְּנֵי הַכָּבוֹד.

הַשִּׁיר שֶׁהַלְוִיִּם הָיוּ אוֹמְרִים בְּבֵית הַמִּקְדָּשׁ:

בַּיּוֹם הָרִאשׁוֹן הָיוּ אוֹמְרִים

לַיהוה הָאָרֶץ וּמְלוֹאָהּ, תֵּבֵל וְיֹשְׁבֵי בָהּ:

בַּשֵּׁנִי הָיוּ אוֹמְרִים

גָּדוֹל יהוה וּמְהֻלָּל מְאֹד, בְּעִיר אֱלֹהֵינוּ הַר־קָדְשׁוֹ:

בַּשְּׁלִישִׁי הָיוּ אוֹמְרִים

אֱלֹהִים נִצָּב בַּעֲדַת־אֵל, בְּקֶרֶב אֱלֹהִים יִשְׁפֹּט:

בָּרְבִיעִי הָיוּ אוֹמְרִים

אֵל־נְקָמוֹת יהוה, אֵל נְקָמוֹת הוֹפִיעַ:

בַּחֲמִישִׁי הָיוּ אוֹמְרִים

הַרְנִינוּ לֵאלֹהִים עוּזֵּנוּ, הָרִיעוּ לֵאלֹהֵי יַעֲקֹב:

בַּשִּׁשִּׁי הָיוּ אוֹמְרִים

יהוה מָלָךְ גֵּאוּת לָבֵשׁ

לָבֵשׁ יהוה עֹז הִתְאַזָּר, אַף־תִּכּוֹן תֵּבֵל בַּל־תִּמּוֹט:

בַּשַּׁבָּת הָיוּ אוֹמְרִים

מִזְמוֹר שִׁיר לְיוֹם הַשַּׁבָּת:

מִזְמוֹר שִׁיר לֶעָתִיד לָבוֹא

לְיוֹם שֶׁכֻּלּוֹ שַׁבָּת וּמְנוּחָה לְחַיֵּי הָעוֹלָמִים.

תָּנָא דְבֵי אֵלִיָּהוּ The school of Eliyahu taught
that anyone who studies Torah every day
will go to *Olam Haba*, Heaven.

אָמַר רַבִּי אֶלְעָזָר Rabbi Elazar said
in the name of Rabbi Chanina
that Torah scholars bring peace to the world.
Whoever loves the Torah will have peace;
nothing will hurt them.
May there be peace in Your city, *Hashem*,
and peace for all Jewish people.
‣ *Hashem* will give His Jewish people strength
and bless us with peace.

KADDISH DERABANAN

The following prayer, said by mourners, requires the presence of a minyan. A transliteration can be found on page 864.

Mourner: יִתְגַּדַּל May *Hashem* be recognized
as great and holy (*Congregation:* Amen)
in the world that He created.
May He establish His kingdom
during my lifetime and the lifetime of all Jews,
quickly and soon.
Let us say: "Amen" (*Congregation:* Amen).

Congregation: May we thank *Hashem* for ever and ever.
Mourner: May we thank *Hashem* for ever and ever.

Mourner: *Hashem* should be thanked, praised,
and honored (*Congregation:* He is blessed).

תָּנָא דְבֵי אֵלִיָּהוּ: כָּל הַשּׁוֹנֶה הֲלָכוֹת בְּכָל יוֹם, מֻבְטָח לוֹ שֶׁהוּא בֶּן עוֹלָם הַבָּא, שֶׁנֶּאֱמַר, הֲלִיכוֹת עוֹלָם לוֹ: אַל תִּקְרֵי הֲלִיכוֹת אֶלָּא הֲלָכוֹת.

אָמַר רַבִּי אֶלְעָזָר, אָמַר רַבִּי חֲנִינָא: תַּלְמִידֵי חֲכָמִים מַרְבִּים שָׁלוֹם בָּעוֹלָם, שֶׁנֶּאֱמַר, וְכָל־בָּנַיִךְ לִמּוּדֵי יהוה, וְרַב שְׁלוֹם בָּנָיִךְ: אַל תִּקְרֵי בָּנָיִךְ, אֶלָּא בּוֹנָיִךְ. שָׁלוֹם רָב לְאֹהֲבֵי תוֹרָתֶךָ, וְאֵין־לָמוֹ מִכְשׁוֹל: יְהִי־שָׁלוֹם בְּחֵילֵךְ, שַׁלְוָה בְּאַרְמְנוֹתָיִךְ: לְמַעַן אַחַי וְרֵעָי אֲדַבְּרָה־נָּא שָׁלוֹם בָּךְ: לְמַעַן בֵּית־יהוה אֱלֹהֵינוּ אֲבַקְשָׁה טוֹב לָךְ: ◂ יהוה עֹז לְעַמּוֹ יִתֵּן, יהוה יְבָרֵךְ אֶת־עַמּוֹ בַשָּׁלוֹם:

קדיש דרבנן

The following prayer, said by mourners, requires the presence of a מנין*.*
A transliteration can be found on page 864.

אבל: יִתְגַּדַּל וְיִתְקַדַּשׁ שְׁמֵהּ רַבָּא (קהל: אָמֵן)
בְּעָלְמָא דִּי בְרָא כִרְעוּתֵהּ, וְיַמְלִיךְ מַלְכוּתֵהּ
בְּחַיֵּיכוֹן וּבְיוֹמֵיכוֹן וּבְחַיֵּי דְכָל בֵּית יִשְׂרָאֵל
בַּעֲגָלָא וּבִזְמַן קָרִיב, וְאִמְרוּ אָמֵן. (קהל: אָמֵן)

קהל: יְהֵא שְׁמֵהּ רַבָּא מְבָרַךְ לְעָלַם וּלְעָלְמֵי עָלְמַיָּא.
אבל: יְהֵא שְׁמֵהּ רַבָּא מְבָרַךְ לְעָלַם וּלְעָלְמֵי עָלְמַיָּא.

אבל: יִתְבָּרַךְ וְיִשְׁתַּבַּח וְיִתְפָּאַר וְיִתְרוֹמַם וְיִתְנַשֵּׂא
וְיִתְהַדָּר וְיִתְעַלֶּה וְיִתְהַלָּל
שְׁמֵהּ דְּקֻדְשָׁא בְּרִיךְ הוּא (קהל: בְּרִיךְ הוּא)

Hashem is beyond all the blessings,
songs, or praises
that we could offer.
Let us say:
"Amen" (*Congregation:* Amen).

To the Jewish people including:
Teachers,
Students,
Students of students, and
All those that spend time learning Torah,
May *Hashem* provide them with peace,
kindness, mercy, long-life, and food to live.
Let us say:
"Amen." (*Congregation:* Amen.)

May *Hashem* give us, and all Jews,
peace and good life.
Let us all say:
"Amen." (*Congregation:* Amen.)

The mourner takes three steps back before saying this line, bows to the left when saying "May," bows to the right when saying "the One," bows to the middle when saying "make peace for us":

May *Hashem*, the One
who makes peace in heaven,
make peace for us and all Jews.
Let us say:
"Amen." (*Congregation:* Amen.)

לְעֵלָּא מִן כָּל בִּרְכָתָא
/ בשבת שובה: לְעֵלָּא לְעֵלָּא מִכָּל בִּרְכָתָא/
וְשִׁירָתָא, תֻּשְׁבְּחָתָא וְנֶחֱמָתָא, דַּאֲמִירָן בְּעָלְמָא
וְאִמְרוּ אָמֵן. (קהל: אָמֵן)

עַל יִשְׂרָאֵל וְעַל רַבָּנָן
וְעַל תַּלְמִידֵיהוֹן וְעַל כָּל תַּלְמִידֵי תַלְמִידֵיהוֹן
וְעַל כָּל מָאן דְּעָסְקִין בְּאוֹרַיְתָא
דִּי בְּאַתְרָא הָדֵין, וְדִי בְּכָל אֲתַר וַאֲתַר
יְהֵא לְהוֹן וּלְכוֹן שְׁלָמָא רַבָּא
חִנָּא וְחִסְדָּא, וְרַחֲמֵי, וְחַיֵּי אֲרִיכֵי, וּמְזוֹנֵי רְוִיחֵי
וּפֻרְקָנָא מִן קֳדָם אֲבוּהוֹן דִּי בִשְׁמַיָּא
וְאִמְרוּ אָמֵן. (קהל: אָמֵן)

יְהֵא שְׁלָמָא רַבָּא מִן שְׁמַיָּא
וְחַיִּים (טוֹבִים) עָלֵינוּ וְעַל כָּל יִשְׂרָאֵל
וְאִמְרוּ אָמֵן. (קהל: אָמֵן)

The mourner takes three steps back before saying this line, bows to the left when saying עֹשֶׂה, *bows to the right when saying* הוּא, *bows to the middle when saying* יַעֲשֶׂה בְרַחֲמָיו שָׁלוֹם:

עֹשֶׂה שָׁלוֹם /בשבת שובה: הַשָּׁלוֹם/ בִּמְרוֹמָיו
הוּא יַעֲשֶׂה בְרַחֲמָיו שָׁלוֹם עָלֵינוּ וְעַל כָּל יִשְׂרָאֵל
וְאִמְרוּ אָמֵן. (קהל: אָמֵן)

Stand while saying "It is our role."

עָלֵינוּ It is our role to praise You, *Hashem*,
Master of all and Creator of the world.
You have not made us like other nations of the world,
rather, You set the Jewish people apart
allowing us the opportunity to serve You.
(Other nations pray to gods that do not exist, while)
we bend our knees and bow in prayer
before the King of all kings, *Hashem*,
in order to give thanks.
Hashem created the heavens above and the land below.
Hashem sits on His awesome throne in heaven
as He, alone, is our God and ruler of the world.
We willingly accept Him as our King,
there is none else but Him.
As it says in the Torah,
"Today You should understand that *Hashem* is God
in the heavens above and on the earth below.
There is no other God but You."

Stand while saying עָלֵינוּ.

עָלֵינוּ לְשַׁבֵּחַ לַאֲדוֹן הַכֹּל
לָתֵת גְּדֻלָּה לְיוֹצֵר בְּרֵאשִׁית
שֶׁלֹּא עָשָׂנוּ כְּגוֹיֵי הָאֲרָצוֹת
וְלֹא שָׂמָנוּ כְּמִשְׁפְּחוֹת הָאֲדָמָה
שֶׁלֹּא שָׂם חֶלְקֵנוּ כָּהֶם, וְגוֹרָלֵנוּ כְּכָל הֲמוֹנָם.
(שֶׁהֵם מִשְׁתַּחֲוִים לְהֶבֶל וָרִיק
וּמִתְפַּלְּלִים אֶל אֵל לֹא יוֹשִׁיעַ.)

וַאֲנַחְנוּ כּוֹרְעִים וּמִשְׁתַּחֲוִים וּמוֹדִים
לִפְנֵי מֶלֶךְ מַלְכֵי הַמְּלָכִים, הַקָּדוֹשׁ בָּרוּךְ הוּא
שֶׁהוּא נוֹטֶה שָׁמַיִם וְיוֹסֵד אָרֶץ
וּמוֹשַׁב יְקָרוֹ בַּשָּׁמַיִם מִמַּעַל
וּשְׁכִינַת עֻזּוֹ בְּגָבְהֵי מְרוֹמִים.
הוּא אֱלֹהֵינוּ, אֵין עוֹד.
אֱמֶת מַלְכֵּנוּ, אֶפֶס זוּלָתוֹ
כַּכָּתוּב בְּתוֹרָתוֹ
וְיָדַעְתָּ הַיּוֹם וַהֲשֵׁבֹתָ אֶל־לְבָבֶךָ
כִּי יהוה הוּא הָאֱלֹהִים
בַּשָּׁמַיִם מִמַּעַל וְעַל־הָאָרֶץ מִתָּחַת
אֵין עוֹד:

Hashem,
we hope that all false gods
will be removed from the world
and everyone will soon turn to You alone
as the almighty God of the universe.
All the people of the world
will turn to You
and give honor.
They will accept You as their King,
and You will rule over them soon and forever.
For You are King of the world
and You will remain the ruling King forever.
As it says in Your Torah,
▸ "*Hashem* will be king over all the land.
On that day *Hashem* will be One and His name One."

עַל כֵּן נְקַוֶּה לְּךָ יהוה אֱלֹהֵינוּ
לִרְאוֹת מְהֵרָה בְּתִפְאֶרֶת עֻזֶּךָ
לְהַעֲבִיר גִּלּוּלִים מִן הָאָרֶץ
וְהָאֱלִילִים כָּרוֹת יִכָּרֵתוּן
לְתַקֵּן עוֹלָם בְּמַלְכוּת שַׁדַּי.
וְכָל בְּנֵי בָשָׂר יִקְרְאוּ בִשְׁמֶךָ
לְהַפְנוֹת אֵלֶיךָ כָּל רִשְׁעֵי אָרֶץ.
יַכִּירוּ וְיֵדְעוּ כָּל יוֹשְׁבֵי תֵבֵל
כִּי לְךָ תִּכְרַע כָּל בֶּרֶךְ
תִּשָּׁבַע כָּל לָשׁוֹן.
לְפָנֶיךָ יהוה אֱלֹהֵינוּ יִכְרְעוּ וְיִפֹּלוּ
וְלִכְבוֹד שִׁמְךָ יְקָר יִתֵּנוּ
וִיקַבְּלוּ כֻלָּם אֶת עֹל מַלְכוּתֶךָ
וְתִמְלֹךְ עֲלֵיהֶם מְהֵרָה לְעוֹלָם וָעֶד.
כִּי הַמַּלְכוּת שֶׁלְּךָ הִיא
וּלְעוֹלְמֵי עַד תִּמְלֹךְ בְּכָבוֹד
כַּכָּתוּב בְּתוֹרָתֶךָ
יהוה יִמְלֹךְ לְעֹלָם וָעֶד:
◂ וְנֶאֱמַר, וְהָיָה יהוה לְמֶלֶךְ עַל־כָּל־הָאָרֶץ
בַּיּוֹם הַהוּא יִהְיֶה יהוה אֶחָד וּשְׁמוֹ אֶחָד:

KADDISH YATOM

The following prayer, said by mourners, requires the presence of a minyan. A transliteration can be found on page 865.

Mourner: יִתְגַּדַּל May *Hashem* be recognized
as great and holy (*Congregation:* Amen)
in the world that He created.
May He establish His kingdom
during my lifetime
and the lifetime of all Jews,
quickly and soon.
Let us say: "Amen" (*Congregation:* Amen).

Congregation: May we thank *Hashem* for ever and ever.
Mourner: May we thank *Hashem* for ever and ever.

Mourner: *Hashem* should be thanked, praised,
and honored (*Congregation:* He is blessed).
Hashem is beyond all the blessings,
songs, or praises
that we could offer.
Let us say: "Amen" (*Congregation:* Amen).

May *Hashem* give us, and all Jews,
peace and good life.
Let us say: "Amen." (*Congregation:* Amen).

The mourner takes three steps back before saying this line, bows to the left when saying "May," bows to the right when saying "the One," bows to the middle when saying "make peace for us":

May *Hashem*, the One
who makes peace in heaven,
make peace for us and for all Jews.
Let us say: "Amen." (*Congregation:* Amen).

קדיש יתום

The following prayer, said by mourners, requires the presence of a מנין.
A transliteration can be found on page 865.

אבל: יִתְגַּדַּל וְיִתְקַדַּשׁ שְׁמֵהּ רַבָּא (קהל: אָמֵן)
בְּעָלְמָא דִּי בְרָא כִרְעוּתֵהּ, וְיַמְלִיךְ מַלְכוּתֵהּ
בְּחַיֵּיכוֹן וּבְיוֹמֵיכוֹן וּבְחַיֵּי דְכָל בֵּית יִשְׂרָאֵל
בַּעֲגָלָא וּבִזְמַן קָרִיב, וְאִמְרוּ אָמֵן. (קהל: אָמֵן)

קהל יְהֵא שְׁמֵהּ רַבָּא מְבָרַךְ לְעָלַם וּלְעָלְמֵי עָלְמַיָּא.
אבל: יְהֵא שְׁמֵהּ רַבָּא מְבָרַךְ לְעָלַם וּלְעָלְמֵי עָלְמַיָּא.

אבל: יִתְבָּרַךְ וְיִשְׁתַּבַּח וְיִתְפָּאַר
וְיִתְרוֹמַם וְיִתְנַשֵּׂא וְיִתְהַדָּר וְיִתְעַלֶּה וְיִתְהַלָּל
שְׁמֵהּ דְּקֻדְשָׁא בְּרִיךְ הוּא (קהל: בְּרִיךְ הוּא)
לְעֵלָּא מִן כָּל בִּרְכָתָא
/בשבת שובה: לְעֵלָּא לְעֵלָּא מִכָּל בִּרְכָתָא/
וְשִׁירָתָא, תֻּשְׁבְּחָתָא וְנֶחֱמָתָא
דַּאֲמִירָן בְּעָלְמָא, וְאִמְרוּ אָמֵן. (קהל: אָמֵן)

יְהֵא שְׁלָמָא רַבָּא מִן שְׁמַיָּא
וְחַיִּים, עָלֵינוּ וְעַל כָּל יִשְׂרָאֵל, וְאִמְרוּ אָמֵן. (קהל: אָמֵן)

The mourner takes three steps back before saying this line,
bows to the left when saying עֹשֶׂה, *bows to the right when saying* הוּא,
bows to the middle when saying יַעֲשֶׂה שָׁלוֹם עָלֵינוּ:

עֹשֶׂה שָׁלוֹם /בשבת שובה: הַשָּׁלוֹם/ בִּמְרוֹמָיו
הוּא יַעֲשֶׂה שָׁלוֹם עָלֵינוּ
וְעַל כָּל יִשְׂרָאֵל, וְאִמְרוּ אָמֵן. (קהל: אָמֵן)

ANIM ZEMIROT

The Aron Kodesh is opened and all stand.

Leader: I will sing sweet songs to You, *Hashem*, because my soul wants to be close to You.

Congregation: My soul searches for Your protection and to better understand You.

Leader: The more I speak about Your honor, *Hashem*, the more I want to be close to You.

Congregation: Therefore, I will continue to sing songs that honor You.

Leader: I will sing about Your honor even though I cannot see You.

Congregation: I will describe You based on Your prophets' words.

Leader: Your prophets told stories of Your greatness and Your many great miracles.

Congregation: They told of Your actions and not how You look.

Leader: Through the many prophets we can only imagine You.

Congregation: The ways they described You throughout history show the many different aspects of *Hashem*.

Leader: *Hashem* is described as old and wise regarding judgement, and young and strong regarding war.

Congregation: A strong right arm that led His nation to win wars.

Leader: The light of the shining sun reflects *Hashem*'s presence; we can see Him through the morning dew.

Congregation: We hope that *Hashem* will crown us with His beauty.

Leader: His head is like pure beaten gold.

Congregation: His Jewish people have crowned Him with honor and beauty.

שיר הכבוד

The ארון קודש *is opened and all stand.*

חזן: אַנְעִים זְמִירוֹת וְשִׁירִים אֶאֱרֹג, כִּי אֵלֶיךָ נַפְשִׁי תַעֲרֹג.

קהל: נַפְשִׁי חִמְּדָה בְּצֵל יָדֶךָ, לָדַעַת כָּל רָז סוֹדֶךָ.

חזן: מִדֵּי דַבְּרִי בִּכְבוֹדֶךָ, הוֹמֶה לִבִּי אֶל דּוֹדֶיךָ.

קהל: עַל כֵּן אֲדַבֵּר בְּךָ נִכְבָּדוֹת, וְשִׁמְךָ אֲכַבֵּד בְּשִׁירֵי יְדִידוֹת.

חזן: אֲסַפְּרָה כְבוֹדְךָ וְלֹא רְאִיתִיךָ, אֲדַמְּךָ אֲכַנְּךָ
וְלֹא יְדַעְתִּיךָ.

קהל: בְּיַד נְבִיאֶיךָ בְּסוֹד עֲבָדֶיךָ, דִּמִּיתָ הֲדַר כְּבוֹד הוֹדֶךָ.

חזן: גְּדֻלָּתְךָ וּגְבוּרָתֶךָ, כִּנּוּ לְתֹקֶף פְּעֻלָּתֶךָ.

קהל: דִּמּוּ אוֹתְךָ וְלֹא כְּפִי יֶשְׁךָ, וַיְשַׁוּוּךָ לְפִי מַעֲשֶׂיךָ.

חזן: הִמְשִׁילְוּךָ בְּרֹב חֶזְיוֹנוֹת, הִנְּךָ אֶחָד בְּכָל דִּמְיוֹנוֹת.

קהל: וַיֶּחֱזוּ בְךָ זִקְנָה וּבַחֲרוּת, וּשְׂעַר רֹאשְׁךָ בְּשֵׂיבָה וְשַׁחֲרוּת.

חזן: זִקְנָה בְּיוֹם דִּין וּבַחֲרוּת בְּיוֹם קְרָב, כְּאִישׁ מִלְחָמוֹת
יָדָיו לוֹ רָב.

קהל: חָבַשׁ כּוֹבַע יְשׁוּעָה בְּרֹאשׁוֹ, הוֹשִׁיעָה לּוֹ יְמִינוֹ וּזְרוֹעַ קָדְשׁוֹ.

חזן: טַלְלֵי אוֹרוֹת רֹאשׁוֹ נִמְלָא, קְוֻצּוֹתָיו רְסִיסֵי לָיְלָה.

קהל: יִתְפָּאֵר בִּי כִּי חָפֵץ בִּי, וְהוּא יִהְיֶה לִּי לַעֲטֶרֶת צְבִי.

חזן: כֶּתֶם טָהוֹר פָּז דְּמוּת רֹאשׁוֹ, וְחַק עַל מֵצַח
כְּבוֹד שֵׁם קָדְשׁוֹ.

קהל: לְחֵן וּלְכָבוֹד צְבִי תִפְאָרָה, אֻמָּתוֹ לוֹ עִטְּרָה עֲטָרָה.

Leader: *Hashem* is like a child whose hair flows down in perfect curls; He stays young forever.

Congregation: Anywhere He chooses to be becomes elevated.

Leader: May *Hashem* treat us like His crown, considering us a sign of beauty and majesty.

Congregation: He created us, helped us, and elevated us; we were precious in His eyes.

Leader: We honor *Hashem* and *Hashem* honors us. *Hashem* always feels near to us.

Congregation: He will destroy our enemies.

Leader: When Moshe asked to see *Hashem,* He showed Moshe the knot of His tefillin.

Congregation: *Hashem* is proud of His people and raises the lowly and humble to great heights.

Leader: Seek Your people that seek You.

Congregation: Please listen to our songs and accept them.

Leader: May our praise be like a crown upon Your head.

Congregation: Listen to the poor man's song.

Leader: *Hashem,* our creator and God, allow us plentiful blessing.

Congregation: Please accept our prayers of thanksgiving.

Leader: Please hear our prayers as though they are sweet songs.

The Aron Kodesh is closed.

Hashem, You are great, powerful, glorious, and majestic! Everything in heaven and earth belongs to You; You are King over all. Praise *Hashem,* our God, and bow before Him, for He is holy. Praise, *Hashem,* our God, and bow before His holy mountain, the *Beit HaMikdash,* for *Hashem* is holy. ▸ *Hashem* does many miracles; there is no limit to His praise.

Mourner's Kaddish (page 622)

חזן: **מַחְלְפוֹת רֹאשׁוֹ כְּבִימֵי בְחוּרוֹת, קְוֻצּוֹתָיו תַּלְתַּלִּים שְׁחוֹרוֹת.**

קהל: נְוֵה הַצֶּדֶק צְבִי תִפְאַרְתּוֹ, יַעֲלֶה נָּא עַל רֹאשׁ שִׂמְחָתוֹ.

חזן: **סְגֻלָּתוֹ תְּהִי בְיָדוֹ עֲטֶרֶת, וּצְנִיף מְלוּכָה צְבִי תִפְאֶרֶת.**

קהל: עֲמוּסִים נְשָׂאָם, עֲטֶרֶת עִנְּדָם, מֵאֲשֶׁר יָקְרוּ בְעֵינָיו כִּבְּדָם.

חזן: **פְּאֵרוֹ עָלַי וּפְאֵרִי עָלָיו, וְקָרוֹב אֵלַי בְּקָרְאִי אֵלָיו.**

קהל: צַח וְאָדֹם לִלְבוּשׁוֹ אָדֹם, פּוּרָה בְדָרְכוֹ בְּבוֹאוֹ מֵאֱדוֹם.

חזן: **קֶשֶׁר תְּפִלִּין הֶרְאָה לֶעָנָו, תְּמוּנַת יהוה לְנֶגֶד עֵינָיו.**

קהל: רוֹצֶה בְעַמּוֹ עֲנָוִים יְפָאֵר, יוֹשֵׁב תְּהִלּוֹת בָּם לְהִתְפָּאֵר.

חזן: **רֹאשׁ דְּבָרְךָ אֱמֶת קוֹרֵא מֵרֹאשׁ דּוֹר וָדוֹר עַם דּוֹרֶשְׁךָ דְּרֹשׁ.**

קהל: שִׁית הֲמוֹן שִׁירַי נָא עָלֶיךָ, וְרִנָּתִי תִּקְרַב אֵלֶיךָ.

חזן: **תְּהִלָּתִי תְּהִי לְרֹאשְׁךָ עֲטֶרֶת, וּתְפִלָּתִי תִּכּוֹן קְטֹרֶת.**

קהל: תִּיקַר שִׁירַת רָשׁ בְּעֵינֶיךָ, כַּשִּׁיר יוּשַׁר עַל קָרְבָּנֶיךָ.

חזן: **בִּרְכָתִי תַעֲלֶה לְרֹאשׁ מַשְׁבִּיר, מְחוֹלֵל וּמוֹלִיד צַדִּיק כַּבִּיר.**

קהל: וּבְבִרְכָתִי תְנַעֲנַע לִי רֹאשׁ, וְאוֹתָהּ קַח לְךָ כִּבְשָׂמִים רֹאשׁ.

חזן: **יֶעֱרַב נָא שִׂיחִי עָלֶיךָ, כִּי נַפְשִׁי תַעֲרֹג אֵלֶיךָ.**

The ארון קודש is closed.

לְךָ יהוה הַגְּדֻלָּה וְהַגְּבוּרָה וְהַתִּפְאֶרֶת וְהַנֵּצַח וְהַהוֹד, כִּי־כֹל בַּשָּׁמַיִם וּבָאָרֶץ, לְךָ יהוה הַמַּמְלָכָה וְהַמִּתְנַשֵּׂא לְכֹל לְרֹאשׁ: ‹ מִי יְמַלֵּל גְּבוּרוֹת יהוה, יַשְׁמִיעַ כָּל־תְּהִלָּתוֹ:

קדיש יתום (page 623)

Today is the holy Shabbat.
On this day, the Levi'im sang
the following in the *Beit HaMikdash*:

A song for Shabbat.
It is good to thank *Hashem*
and sing songs to Him.
We sing about *Hashem*'s kindness in the morning
and we are thankful for His protection at night.
We use musical instruments to thank *Hashem;*
we sing out to Him with great joy.
We cannot understand how great and wise *Hashem* is.
Even when it appears that evil people are successful,
Hashem will not allow their success to last forever.
All of *Hashem's* enemies
will one day be defeated and scattered;
Hashem will lift up His Jewish people.
The righteous will be fruitful like a date tree
and strong like a cedar tree.
Like a tree planted in *Hashem*'s garden,
the righteous will continue to have success
even in old age,
and will remain full of strength.
Hashem is fair;
He is perfect in His ways.

Mourner's Kaddish (page 622)

הַיּוֹם יוֹם שַׁבַּת קֹדֶשׁ שֶׁבּוֹ הָיוּ הַלְוִיִּם אוֹמְרִים בְּבֵית הַמִּקְדָּשׁ:

מִזְמוֹר שִׁיר לְיוֹם הַשַּׁבָּת:
טוֹב לְהֹדוֹת לַיהוה, וּלְזַמֵּר לְשִׁמְךָ עֶלְיוֹן:
לְהַגִּיד בַּבֹּקֶר חַסְדֶּךָ, וֶאֱמוּנָתְךָ בַּלֵּילוֹת:
עֲלֵי־עָשׂוֹר וַעֲלֵי־נָבֶל, עֲלֵי הִגָּיוֹן בְּכִנּוֹר:
כִּי שִׂמַּחְתַּנִי יהוה בְּפָעֳלֶךָ, בְּמַעֲשֵׂי יָדֶיךָ אֲרַנֵּן:
מַה־גָּדְלוּ מַעֲשֶׂיךָ יהוה, מְאֹד עָמְקוּ מַחְשְׁבֹתֶיךָ:
אִישׁ־בַּעַר לֹא יֵדָע, וּכְסִיל לֹא־יָבִין אֶת־זֹאת:
בִּפְרֹחַ רְשָׁעִים כְּמוֹ עֵשֶׂב, וַיָּצִיצוּ כָּל־פֹּעֲלֵי אָוֶן
לְהִשָּׁמְדָם עֲדֵי־עַד:
וְאַתָּה מָרוֹם לְעֹלָם יהוה:
כִּי הִנֵּה אֹיְבֶיךָ יהוה, כִּי־הִנֵּה אֹיְבֶיךָ יֹאבֵדוּ
יִתְפָּרְדוּ כָּל־פֹּעֲלֵי אָוֶן:
וַתָּרֶם כִּרְאֵים קַרְנִי, בַּלֹּתִי בְּשֶׁמֶן רַעֲנָן:
וַתַּבֵּט עֵינִי בְּשׁוּרָי, בַּקָּמִים עָלַי מְרֵעִים תִּשְׁמַעְנָה אָזְנָי:
צַדִּיק כַּתָּמָר יִפְרָח, כְּאֶרֶז בַּלְּבָנוֹן יִשְׂגֶּה:
שְׁתוּלִים בְּבֵית יהוה, בְּחַצְרוֹת אֱלֹהֵינוּ יַפְרִיחוּ:
◄ עוֹד יְנוּבוּן בְּשֵׂיבָה, דְּשֵׁנִים וְרַעֲנַנִּים יִהְיוּ:
לְהַגִּיד כִּי־יָשָׁר יהוה, צוּרִי, וְלֹא־עַוְלָתָה בּוֹ:

קדיש יתום (*page 623*)

On Rosh Chodesh, say Barechi Nafshi on page 204 followed by Mourner's Kaddish.
On Chanuka, many congregations add Psalm 30
on page 208 followed by Mourner's Kaddish.

From the second day of Rosh Chodesh Elul until Shemini Atzeret
add the following:

לְדָוִד David HaMelech wrote:
I have no fear because *Hashem* protects me
and brings light to my darkness.
When enemies or even armies attack,
I am not afraid
as I trust that *Hashem* will defeat them.
The only thing that I ask of *Hashem*
is to see the *Beit HaMikdash* built
and be able to serve Him there.
Hashem is my protector;
He will take me in and hide me from my enemies.
When I feel safe, I will sing songs of praise to *Hashem.*
Hashem,
listen to my voice when I call for help
and please answer me.
Do not ignore or hide from me, when You are angry.
My heart knows it is only You to whom I can call for help.
Hashem,
help us learn how to make the right choices
and not make mistakes.
▸ I trust in *Hashem,* I hope for His help at all times;
He gives me strength and courage.

Kaddish Yatom (page 622)

On ראש חודש, *say* בָּרְכִי נַפְשִׁי *on page 205 followed by* קדיש יתום.
On חנוכה, *many congregations add* מִזְמוֹר שִׁיר־חֲנֻכַּת הַבַּיִת *on page 209 followed by* קדיש יתום.

From the second day of ראש חודש אלול *until* שמיני עצרת *add the following:*

לְדָוִד, יהוה אוֹרִי וְיִשְׁעִי, מִמִּי אִירָא, יהוה מָעוֹז־חַיַּי, מִמִּי אֶפְחָד: בִּקְרֹב עָלַי מְרֵעִים לֶאֱכֹל אֶת־בְּשָׂרִי, צָרַי וְאֹיְבַי לִי, הֵמָּה כָשְׁלוּ וְנָפָלוּ: אִם־תַּחֲנֶה עָלַי מַחֲנֶה, לֹא־יִירָא לִבִּי, אִם־תָּקוּם עָלַי מִלְחָמָה, בְּזֹאת אֲנִי בוֹטֵחַ: אַחַת שָׁאַלְתִּי מֵאֵת־יהוה, אוֹתָהּ אֲבַקֵּשׁ, שִׁבְתִּי בְּבֵית־יהוה כָּל־יְמֵי חַיַּי, לַחֲזוֹת בְּנֹעַם־יהוה, וּלְבַקֵּר בְּהֵיכָלוֹ: כִּי יִצְפְּנֵנִי בְּסֻכֹּה בְּיוֹם רָעָה, יַסְתִּרֵנִי בְּסֵתֶר אָהֳלוֹ, בְּצוּר יְרוֹמְמֵנִי: וְעַתָּה יָרוּם רֹאשִׁי עַל אֹיְבַי סְבִיבוֹתַי, וְאֶזְבְּחָה בְאָהֳלוֹ זִבְחֵי תְרוּעָה, אָשִׁירָה וַאֲזַמְּרָה לַיהוה: שְׁמַע־יהוה קוֹלִי אֶקְרָא, וְחָנֵּנִי וַעֲנֵנִי: לְךָ אָמַר לִבִּי בַּקְּשׁוּ פָנָי, אֶת־פָּנֶיךָ יהוה אֲבַקֵּשׁ: אַל־תַּסְתֵּר פָּנֶיךָ מִמֶּנִּי, אַל תַּט־בְּאַף עַבְדֶּךָ, עֶזְרָתִי הָיִיתָ, אַל־תִּטְּשֵׁנִי וְאַל־תַּעַזְבֵנִי, אֱלֹהֵי יִשְׁעִי: כִּי־אָבִי וְאִמִּי עֲזָבוּנִי, וַיהוה יַאַסְפֵנִי: הוֹרֵנִי יהוה דַּרְכֶּךָ, וּנְחֵנִי בְּאֹרַח מִישׁוֹר, לְמַעַן שׁוֹרְרָי: אַל־תִּתְּנֵנִי בְּנֶפֶשׁ צָרָי, כִּי קָמוּ־בִי עֵדֵי־שֶׁקֶר, וִיפֵחַ חָמָס: ‹ לוּלֵא הֶאֱמַנְתִּי לִרְאוֹת בְּטוּב־יהוה בְּאֶרֶץ חַיִּים: קַוֵּה אֶל־יהוה, חֲזַק וְיַאֲמֵץ לִבֶּךָ, וְקַוֵּה אֶל־יהוה:

קדיש יתום (*page 623*)

אֲדוֹן עוֹלָם You, *Hashem,* are Master of the world.

You, *Hashem,* existed before the world
was created.

You, *Hashem,* were crowned King
when the world was made.

You, *Hashem,* will still be King
when the world no longer exists.

You, *Hashem,* have always existed,
and You, *Hashem,* will always exist.

You, *Hashem,* rule the world alone.
There is no other God but You.

You, *Hashem,* have unlimited strength.
I turn to You for all my needs.

You, *Hashem,* are always there for me
no matter what challenges I face.

You, *Hashem,* watch over me during the day
and protect me at night.

You, *Hashem,* are always with me,
and You protect me from harm.

It is because of You, *Hashem,*
that I have nothing to fear.

אֲדוֹן עוֹלָם

אֲשֶׁר מָלַךְ בְּטֶרֶם כָּל־יְצִיר נִבְרָא.

לְעֵת נַעֲשָׂה בְחֶפְצוֹ כֹּל אֲזַי מֶלֶךְ שְׁמוֹ נִקְרָא.

וְאַחֲרֵי כִּכְלוֹת הַכֹּל לְבַדּוֹ יִמְלֹךְ נוֹרָא.

וְהוּא הָיָה וְהוּא הֹוֶה וְהוּא יִהְיֶה בְּתִפְאָרָה.

וְהוּא אֶחָד וְאֵין שֵׁנִי לְהַמְשִׁיל לוֹ לְהַחְבִּירָה.

בְּלִי רֵאשִׁית בְּלִי תַכְלִית וְלוֹ הָעֹז וְהַמִּשְׂרָה.

וְהוּא אֵלִי וְחַי גּוֹאֲלִי וְצוּר חֶבְלִי בְּעֵת צָרָה.

וְהוּא נִסִּי וּמָנוֹס לִי מְנָת כּוֹסִי בְּיוֹם אֶקְרָא.

בְּיָדוֹ אַפְקִיד רוּחִי בְּעֵת אִישַׁן וְאָעִירָה.

וְעִם רוּחִי גְּוִיָּתִי יהוה לִי וְלֹא אִירָא.

Mincha for Shabbat

אַשְׁרֵי We are happy with the opportunity to sit and pray. We are happy that You are our God and that we are Your people.

David HaMelech wrote this song:

א GOD – *Hashem* is our God and King.

ב THANK – We appreciate *Hashem* and we will thank Him every day, forever.

ג GREATNESS – *Hashem*'s greatness is endless.

ד GENERATIONS – We will tell our children about the spectacular actions You have done for us in every generation.

ה MIRACLES – The miracles that *Hashem* performs for His people are glorious.

ו STRENGTH – *Hashem*'s strength is awesome beyond comparison.

ז REMEMBER – We remember the good that *Hashem* does for us.

ח MERCY – *Hashem* is slow to get angry.

ט GOODNESS – *Hashem* is good to all His creations, humans and animals alike.

י KINDNESS – All creations of *Hashem* are thankful for His kindness.

כ HONOR – We give *Hashem* the honor that He deserves.

ל MIGHTY – We inform all people of *Hashem*'s mighty actions.

מ KINGSHIP – *Hashem* has and always will rule the world.

ס HELP – *Hashem* helps us when we need Him.

ע RELY – We rely on *Hashem* to give us the food that we need to live.

מנחה לשבת

אַשְׁרֵי יוֹשְׁבֵי בֵיתֶךָ, עוֹד יְהַלְלוּךָ סֶּלָה:
אַשְׁרֵי הָעָם שֶׁכָּכָה לוֹ, אַשְׁרֵי הָעָם שֶׁיהוה אֱלֹהָיו:
תְּהִלָּה לְדָוִד

אֲרוֹמִמְךָ אֱלוֹהַי הַמֶּלֶךְ, וַאֲבָרְכָה שִׁמְךָ לְעוֹלָם וָעֶד:
בְּכָל־יוֹם אֲבָרְכֶךָּ, וַאֲהַלְלָה שִׁמְךָ לְעוֹלָם וָעֶד:
גָּדוֹל יהוה וּמְהֻלָּל מְאֹד, וְלִגְדֻלָּתוֹ אֵין חֵקֶר:
דּוֹר לְדוֹר יְשַׁבַּח מַעֲשֶׂיךָ, וּגְבוּרֹתֶיךָ יַגִּידוּ:
הֲדַר כְּבוֹד הוֹדֶךָ, וְדִבְרֵי נִפְלְאֹתֶיךָ אָשִׂיחָה:
וֶעֱזוּז נוֹרְאֹתֶיךָ יֹאמֵרוּ, וּגְדוּלָּתְךָ אֲסַפְּרֶנָּה:
זֵכֶר רַב־טוּבְךָ יַבִּיעוּ, וְצִדְקָתְךָ יְרַנֵּנוּ:
חַנּוּן וְרַחוּם יהוה, אֶרֶךְ אַפַּיִם וּגְדָל־חָסֶד:
טוֹב־יהוה לַכֹּל, וְרַחֲמָיו עַל־כָּל־מַעֲשָׂיו:
יוֹדוּךָ יהוה כָּל־מַעֲשֶׂיךָ, וַחֲסִידֶיךָ יְבָרְכוּכָה:
כְּבוֹד מַלְכוּתְךָ יֹאמֵרוּ, וּגְבוּרָתְךָ יְדַבֵּרוּ:
לְהוֹדִיעַ לִבְנֵי הָאָדָם גְּבוּרֹתָיו, וּכְבוֹד הֲדַר מַלְכוּתוֹ:
מַלְכוּתְךָ מַלְכוּת כָּל־עֹלָמִים,
וּמֶמְשַׁלְתְּךָ בְּכָל־דּוֹר וָדֹר:
סוֹמֵךְ יהוה לְכָל־הַנֹּפְלִים, וְזוֹקֵף לְכָל־הַכְּפוּפִים:
עֵינֵי־כֹל אֵלֶיךָ יְשַׂבֵּרוּ
וְאַתָּה נוֹתֵן־לָהֶם אֶת־אָכְלָם בְּעִתּוֹ:

פ PROVIDES – *Hashem* opens His hands and provides us with our needs.

צ RIGHTEOUS – Everything *Hashem* does is righteous and with good intentions.

ק CLOSENESS – *Hashem* is close to all those that call out to Him.

ר SAVES – *Hashem* listens to our cries and saves those in need.

ש GUARDS – *Hashem* protects all those who love Him and turn to Him in times of need.

▸ ת PRAISE – For all of these reasons, everyone praises *Hashem* and thanks Him every day.

וּבָא לְצִיּוֹן *Hashem* said, "*Mashiach* will come to Zion
and redeem those who abandon their sins
and return to *Hashem*."

"From this point and onwards,
all Jews shall learn the words of my Torah
and teach the Torah to their children
and their children's children.
The words of my Torah shall never be forgotten!"

▸ **וְאַתָּה קָדוֹשׁ** *Hashem,* You are holy and the Jewish people praise You. The angels will call to each other saying:

All say aloud:

"Holy, holy, holy is *Hashem*: the world is filled with His honor."

The angels then say to each other: "Heaven is holy because *Hashem* lives there, and the earth is holy because *Hashem* created it. The entire world is filled with *Hashem*'s holiness."

פּוֹתֵחַ אֶת־יָדֶךָ, וּמַשְׂבִּיעַ לְכָל־חַי רָצוֹן:
צַדִּיק יהוה בְּכָל־דְּרָכָיו, וְחָסִיד בְּכָל־מַעֲשָׂיו:
קָרוֹב יהוה לְכָל־קֹרְאָיו, לְכֹל אֲשֶׁר יִקְרָאֻהוּ בֶאֱמֶת:
רְצוֹן־יְרֵאָיו יַעֲשֶׂה, וְאֶת־שַׁוְעָתָם יִשְׁמַע, וְיוֹשִׁיעֵם:
שׁוֹמֵר יהוה אֶת־כָּל־אֹהֲבָיו
וְאֵת כָּל־הָרְשָׁעִים יַשְׁמִיד:
◂ תְּהִלַּת יהוה יְדַבֶּר פִּי
וִיבָרֵךְ כָּל־בָּשָׂר שֵׁם קָדְשׁוֹ לְעוֹלָם וָעֶד:
וַאֲנַחְנוּ נְבָרֵךְ יָהּ מֵעַתָּה וְעַד־עוֹלָם, הַלְלוּיָהּ:

וּבָא לְצִיּוֹן גּוֹאֵל, וּלְשָׁבֵי פֶשַׁע בְּיַעֲקֹב, נְאֻם יהוה:
וַאֲנִי זֹאת בְּרִיתִי אוֹתָם, אָמַר יהוה, רוּחִי אֲשֶׁר עָלֶיךָ וּדְבָרַי אֲשֶׁר־שַׂמְתִּי בְּפִיךָ, לֹא־יָמוּשׁוּ מִפִּיךָ וּמִפִּי זַרְעֲךָ וּמִפִּי זֶרַע זַרְעֲךָ, אָמַר יהוה, מֵעַתָּה וְעַד־עוֹלָם:

◂ וְאַתָּה קָדוֹשׁ יוֹשֵׁב תְּהִלּוֹת יִשְׂרָאֵל:
וְקָרָא זֶה אֶל־זֶה וְאָמַר

All say aloud:

קָדוֹשׁ, קָדוֹשׁ, קָדוֹשׁ, יהוה צְבָאוֹת
מְלֹא כָל־הָאָרֶץ כְּבוֹדוֹ:

וּמְקַבְּלִין דֵּין מִן דֵּין וְאָמְרִין, קַדִּישׁ בִּשְׁמֵי מְרוֹמָא עִלָּאָה בֵּית שְׁכִינְתֵהּ, קַדִּישׁ עַל אַרְעָא עוֹבַד גְּבוּרְתֵהּ, קַדִּישׁ לְעָלַם וּלְעָלְמֵי עָלְמַיָּא, יהוה צְבָאוֹת, מַלְיָא כָל אַרְעָא זִיו יְקָרֵהּ.

▸ When a wind lifted the prophet Yechezkel, he heard the angels praising *Hashem*, saying,

All say aloud:

"Blessed is the honor of *Hashem* who lives in heaven!"

When a wind lifted the prophet Yechezkel, he heard the angels praising *Hashem*, saying, "Blessed is the honor of *Hashem* who lives in heaven."

All say aloud:

Hashem shall reign as King forever!

Hashem's kingdom is established forever and ever.

יהוה *Hashem*, God of Avraham, Yitzchak, and Yaakov,
please allow Your Jewish people
to keep these thoughts in mind,
and help direct their hearts towards You.
You are merciful and You show Your kindness
by forgiving our sins.
Your Torah is true and Your righteousness lasts forever.
Please treat us with loyalty and kindness
as You promised our forefathers.
Hashem, You are our protector; You are always with us.
Praiseworthy is the person who trusts in You.
May *Hashem*, the King,
answer us on the day that we call out to Him.

בָּרוּךְ Thank You, *Hashem*, for giving us the Torah,
allowing us to honor You, and providing us the opportunity
to live on in the world-to-come.
May *Hashem* open our hearts through studying His Torah,
and allow us to serve Him wholeheartedly
with love and fear.

◂ וַתִּשָּׂאֵנִי רְוּחַ, וָאֶשְׁמַע אַחֲרַי קוֹל רַעַשׁ גָּדוֹל

All say aloud:

בָּרוּךְ כְּבוֹד־יהוה מִמְּקוֹמוֹ:

וּנְטָלַתְנִי רוּחָא, וּשְׁמָעִית בַּתְרַי קָל זִיעַ סַגִּיא, דִּמְשַׁבְּחִין
וְאָמְרִין, בְּרִיךְ יְקָרָא דַיהוה מֵאֲתַר בֵּית שְׁכִינְתֵהּ.

All say aloud:

יהוה יִמְלֹךְ לְעֹלָם וָעֶד:

יהוה מַלְכוּתֵהּ קָאֵם לְעָלַם וּלְעָלְמֵי עָלְמַיָּא.

יהוה אֱלֹהֵי אַבְרָהָם יִצְחָק וְיִשְׂרָאֵל אֲבֹתֵינוּ, שָׁמְרָה־זֹּאת לְעוֹלָם לְיֵצֶר מַחְשְׁבוֹת לְבַב עַמֶּךָ, וְהָכֵן לְבָבָם אֵלֶיךָ: וְהוּא רַחוּם יְכַפֵּר עָוֹן וְלֹא־יַשְׁחִית, וְהִרְבָּה לְהָשִׁיב אַפּוֹ, וְלֹא־יָעִיר כָּל־חֲמָתוֹ: כִּי־אַתָּה אֲדֹנָי טוֹב וְסַלָּח, וְרַב־חֶסֶד לְכָל־קֹרְאֶיךָ: צִדְקָתְךָ צֶדֶק לְעוֹלָם וְתוֹרָתְךָ אֱמֶת: תִּתֵּן אֱמֶת לְיַעֲקֹב, חֶסֶד לְאַבְרָהָם, אֲשֶׁר־נִשְׁבַּעְתָּ לַאֲבֹתֵינוּ מִימֵי קֶדֶם: בָּרוּךְ אֲדֹנָי יוֹם יוֹם יַעֲמָס־לָנוּ, הָאֵל יְשׁוּעָתֵנוּ סֶלָה: יהוה צְבָאוֹת עִמָּנוּ, מִשְׂגָּב לָנוּ אֱלֹהֵי יַעֲקֹב סֶלָה: יהוה צְבָאוֹת, אַשְׁרֵי אָדָם בֹּטֵחַ בָּךְ: יהוה הוֹשִׁיעָה, הַמֶּלֶךְ יַעֲנֵנוּ בְיוֹם־קָרְאֵנוּ:

בָּרוּךְ הוּא אֱלֹהֵינוּ שֶׁבְּרָאָנוּ לִכְבוֹדוֹ, וְהִבְדִּילָנוּ מִן הַתּוֹעִים, וְנָתַן לָנוּ תּוֹרַת אֱמֶת, וְחַיֵּי עוֹלָם נָטַע בְּתוֹכֵנוּ. הוּא יִפְתַּח לִבֵּנוּ בְּתוֹרָתוֹ, וְיָשֵׂם בְּלִבֵּנוּ אַהֲבָתוֹ וְיִרְאָתוֹ וְלַעֲשׂוֹת רְצוֹנוֹ וּלְעָבְדוֹ בְּלֵבָב שָׁלֵם, לְמַעַן לֹא נִיגַע לָרִיק וְלֹא נֵלֵד לַבֶּהָלָה.

יְהִי רָצוֹן May *Hashem*,
our God and God of our ancestors,
allow us to keep His *mitzvot* in this world
so that we can gain the blessings promised to us
in the times of *Mashiach* and in the world-to-come.
I will thank *Hashem* forever.
▸ Trust in *Hashem*,
for *Hashem* is our protector.

When not praying with a minyan, continue with the Amida on page 650.

HALF KADDISH

Leader: יִתְגַּדַּל May *Hashem* be recognized
as great and holy (*Congregation:* Amen)
in the world that He created.
May He establish His kingdom
during my lifetime
and the lifetime of all Jews,
quickly and soon.
Let us say:
"Amen" (*Congregation:* Amen).

Congregation: May we thank *Hashem* for ever and ever.
Leader: May we thank *Hashem* for ever and ever.

Leader: *Hashem* should be thanked, praised,
and honored (*Congregation:* He is blessed).
Hashem is beyond all the blessings,
songs, or praises that we could offer.
Let us say:
"Amen" (*Congregation:* Amen).

יְהִי רָצוֹן מִלְּפָנֶיךָ יהוה אֱלֹהֵינוּ וֵאלֹהֵי אֲבוֹתֵינוּ, שֶׁנִּשְׁמֹר חֻקֶּיךָ בָּעוֹלָם הַזֶּה, וְנִזְכֶּה וְנִחְיֶה וְנִרְאֶה וְנִירַשׁ טוֹבָה וּבְרָכָה, לִשְׁנֵי יְמוֹת הַמָּשִׁיחַ וּלְחַיֵּי הָעוֹלָם הַבָּא. לְמַעַן יְזַמֶּרְךָ כָבוֹד וְלֹא יִדֹּם, יהוה אֱלֹהַי, לְעוֹלָם אוֹדֶךָּ: בָּרוּךְ הַגֶּבֶר אֲשֶׁר יִבְטַח בַּיהוה, וְהָיָה יהוה מִבְטַחוֹ: בִּטְחוּ בַיהוה עֲדֵי־עַד, כִּי בְּיָהּ יהוה צוּר עוֹלָמִים: ‹ וְיִבְטְחוּ בְךָ יוֹדְעֵי שְׁמֶךָ, כִּי לֹא־עָזַבְתָּ דֹרְשֶׁיךָ, יהוה: יהוה חָפֵץ לְמַעַן צִדְקוֹ, יַגְדִּיל תּוֹרָה וְיַאְדִּיר:

When not praying with a מנין, continue with the עמידה on page 651.

חצי קדיש

חזן: יִתְגַּדַּל וְיִתְקַדַּשׁ שְׁמֵהּ רַבָּא (קהל: אָמֵן)
בְּעָלְמָא דִּי בְרָא כִרְעוּתֵהּ, וְיַמְלִיךְ מַלְכוּתֵהּ
בְּחַיֵּיכוֹן וּבְיוֹמֵיכוֹן וּבְחַיֵּי דְכָל בֵּית יִשְׂרָאֵל
בַּעֲגָלָא וּבִזְמַן קָרִיב, וְאִמְרוּ אָמֵן. (קהל: אָמֵן)

קהל: יְהֵא שְׁמֵהּ רַבָּא מְבָרַךְ לְעָלַם וּלְעָלְמֵי עָלְמַיָּא.
חזן: יְהֵא שְׁמֵהּ רַבָּא מְבָרַךְ לְעָלַם וּלְעָלְמֵי עָלְמַיָּא.

חזן: יִתְבָּרַךְ וְיִשְׁתַּבַּח וְיִתְפָּאַר וְיִתְרוֹמַם וְיִתְנַשֵּׂא
וְיִתְהַדָּר וְיִתְעַלֶּה וְיִתְהַלָּל
שְׁמֵהּ דְּקֻדְשָׁא בְּרִיךְ הוּא (קהל: בְּרִיךְ הוּא)
לְעֵלָּא מִן כָּל בִּרְכָתָא
/בשבת שובה: לְעֵלָּא לְעֵלָּא מִכָּל בִּרְכָתָא/
וְשִׁירָתָא, תֻּשְׁבְּחָתָא וְנֶחֱמָתָא
דַּאֲמִירָן בְּעָלְמָא, וְאִמְרוּ אָמֵן. (קהל: אָמֵן)

וַאֲנִי May my prayers come before You, *Hashem,* at a time that You want them. *Hashem,* show me Your great love by answering and saving me.

The Aron Kodesh is opened and the congregation stands. All say:

וַיְהִי Every time the *Aron* would travel
Moshe would say,
"*Hashem,* may our enemies scatter and run away from You."
The Torah comes from Zion
and the words of *Hashem* come from Jerusalem.
Thank You, *Hashem,* for giving the Torah
to Your Jewish people.

בְּרִיךְ שְׁמֵהּ We are thankful to You, *Hashem,* Master and King of the World. May You always show kindness towards Your Jewish people, accept our prayers with mercy, and rebuild the *Beit HaMikdash.* Please grant me a long life and provide protection for me, for all that is mine, and for the entire Jewish nation. As King, You feed all and rule over all. You rule over all kings as well. I am a servant to *Hashem,* and I therefore show respect towards the Torah at all times. I don't rely on any man or angel, but on *Hashem* alone for He is the God of love and truth. ▸ *Hashem,* may You open my heart and the hearts of all Your Jewish people to the Torah so that we can have goodness, long life, and peace.

Leader then congregation:

גַּדְּלוּ Let us recognize the greatness of *Hashem* and sing praises to Him together.

The Aron Kodesh is closed. The congregation says:

לְךָ *Hashem,* You are great, powerful, glorious, and majestic! Everything in heaven and earth is Yours, and You are King over all.

וַאֲנִי תְפִלָּתִי־לְךָ יהוה, עֵת רָצוֹן, אֱלֹהִים בְּרָב־חַסְדֶּךָ עֲנֵנִי בֶּאֱמֶת יִשְׁעֶךָ:

The ארון קודש *is opened and the* קהל *stands. All say:*

וַיְהִי בִּנְסֹעַ הָאָרֹן וַיֹּאמֶר מֹשֶׁה
קוּמָה יהוה וְיָפֻצוּ אֹיְבֶיךָ וְיָנֻסוּ מְשַׂנְאֶיךָ מִפָּנֶיךָ:
כִּי מִצִּיּוֹן תֵּצֵא תוֹרָה וּדְבַר־יהוה מִירוּשָׁלָםִ:
בָּרוּךְ שֶׁנָּתַן תּוֹרָה לְעַמּוֹ יִשְׂרָאֵל בִּקְדֻשָּׁתוֹ.

בְּרִיךְ שְׁמֵהּ דְּמָרֵא עָלְמָא, בְּרִיךְ כִּתְרָךְ וְאַתְרָךְ. יְהֵא רְעוּתָךְ עִם עַמָּךְ יִשְׂרָאֵל לְעָלַם, וּפֻרְקַן יְמִינָךְ אַחֲזִי לְעַמָּךְ בְּבֵית מַקְדְּשָׁךְ, וּלְאַמְטוּיֵי לַנָא מִטּוּב נְהוֹרָךְ, וּלְקַבֵּל צְלוֹתַנָא בְּרַחֲמִין. יְהֵא רַעֲוָא קֳדָמָךְ דְּתוֹרִיךְ לַן חַיִּין בְּטִיבוּ, וְלֶהֱוֵי אֲנָא פְקִידָא בְּגוֹ צַדִּיקַיָּא, לְמִרְחַם עָלַי וּלְמִנְטַר יָתִי וְיַת כָּל דִּי לִי וְדִי לְעַמָּךְ יִשְׂרָאֵל. אַנְתְּ הוּא זָן לְכֹלָּא וּמְפַרְנֵס לְכֹלָּא, אַנְתְּ הוּא שַׁלִּיט עַל כֹּלָּא, אַנְתְּ הוּא דְּשַׁלִּיט עַל מַלְכַיָּא, וּמַלְכוּתָא דִּילָךְ הִיא. אֲנָא עַבְדָּא דְקֻדְשָׁא בְּרִיךְ הוּא, דְּסָגֵדְנָא קַמֵּהּ וּמִקַּמֵּי דִּיקָר אוֹרַיְתֵהּ בְּכָל עִדָּן וְעִדָּן. לָא עַל אֱנָשׁ רָחִיצְנָא וְלָא עַל בַּר אֱלָהִין סָמִיכְנָא, אֶלָּא בֶּאֱלָהָא דִשְׁמַיָּא, דְּהוּא אֱלָהָא קְשׁוֹט, וְאוֹרַיְתֵהּ קְשׁוֹט, וּנְבִיאוֹהִי קְשׁוֹט, וּמַסְגֵּא לְמֶעְבַּד טַבְוָן וּקְשׁוֹט. ‹ בֵּהּ אֲנָא רָחִיץ, וְלִשְׁמֵהּ קַדִּישָׁא יַקִּירָא אֲנָא אֵמַר תֻּשְׁבְּחָן. יְהֵא רַעֲוָא קֳדָמָךְ דְּתִפְתַּח לִבַּאי בְּאוֹרַיְתָא, וְתַשְׁלִים מִשְׁאֲלִין דְּלִבַּאי וְלִבָּא דְכָל עַמָּךְ יִשְׂרָאֵל לְטָב וּלְחַיִּין וְלִשְׁלָם.

חזן *then* קהל*:*

גַּדְּלוּ לַיהוה אִתִּי וּנְרוֹמְמָה שְׁמוֹ יַחְדָּו:

The ארון קודש *is closed. The* קהל *says:*

לְךָ יהוה הַגְּדֻלָּה וְהַגְּבוּרָה וְהַתִּפְאֶרֶת וְהַנֵּצַח וְהַהוֹד, כִּי־כֹל בַּשָּׁמַיִם וּבָאָרֶץ, לְךָ יהוה הַמַּמְלָכָה וְהַמִּתְנַשֵּׂא לְכֹל לְרֹאשׁ:

רוֹמְמוּ Praise *Hashem,* our God, and bow before Him, for He is holy. Praise, *Hashem,* our God, and bow before His holy mountain, the *Beit HaMikdash,* for *Hashem* is holy.

אַב הָרַחֲמִים May *Hashem,* our Father, have mercy on His people. May He remember our ancestors and rescue us in difficult times. May He answer our requests and save us.

After the gabbai calls the Kohen to the Bima for an Aliya, the congregation says:

וְאַתֶּם "All of you that follow the ways of *Hashem,* your God, are alive today."

Person called up for the Aliya:

Let us thank *Hashem,* for He deserves thanksgiving!

Congregation:

Thank *Hashem* for ever and ever!

Person called up for the Aliya:

Thank *Hashem* for ever and ever!

Person called up for the Aliya:

Thank You, *Hashem,* our God, King of the world,
for choosing us, the Jewish people,
from all the other nations of the world,
to be Your special people and for giving us Your Torah.
Thank You, *Hashem,* for giving us Your Torah.

After each Aliya the person called up says:

Thank You, *Hashem,* our God, King of the world,
for giving us the Torah.
It is filled with truth
and provides us with a meaningful life.
Thank You, *Hashem,* for giving us Your Torah.

רוֹמְמוּ יהוה אֱלֹהֵינוּ וְהִשְׁתַּחֲווּ לַהֲדֹם רַגְלָיו, קָדוֹשׁ הוּא: רוֹמְמוּ יהוה אֱלֹהֵינוּ וְהִשְׁתַּחֲווּ לְהַר קָדְשׁוֹ, כִּי־קָדוֹשׁ יהוה אֱלֹהֵינוּ:

אַב הָרַחֲמִים הוּא יְרַחֵם עַם עֲמוּסִים, וְיִזְכֹּר בְּרִית אֵיתָנִים, וְיַצִּיל נַפְשׁוֹתֵינוּ מִן הַשָּׁעוֹת הָרָעוֹת, וְיִגְעַר בְּיֵצֶר הָרָע מִן הַנְּשׂוּאִים, וְיָחֹן אוֹתָנוּ לִפְלֵיטַת עוֹלָמִים, וִימַלֵּא מִשְׁאֲלוֹתֵינוּ בְּמִדָּה טוֹבָה יְשׁוּעָה וְרַחֲמִים.

After the גבאי *calls the* כהן *to the* בימה *for an* עליה*, the* קהל *says:*

וְאַתֶּם הַדְּבֵקִים בַּיהוה אֱלֹהֵיכֶם חַיִּים כֻּלְּכֶם הַיּוֹם:

Person called up for the עליה*:*

בָּרְכוּ אֶת יהוה הַמְבֹרָךְ.

קהל*:*

בָּרוּךְ יהוה הַמְבֹרָךְ לְעוֹלָם וָעֶד.

Person called up for the עליה*:*

בָּרוּךְ יהוה הַמְבֹרָךְ לְעוֹלָם וָעֶד.

Person called up for the עליה*:*

בָּרוּךְ אַתָּה יהוה אֱלֹהֵינוּ מֶלֶךְ הָעוֹלָם
אֲשֶׁר בָּחַר בָּנוּ מִכָּל הָעַמִּים וְנָתַן לָנוּ אֶת תּוֹרָתוֹ.
בָּרוּךְ אַתָּה יהוה, נוֹתֵן הַתּוֹרָה.

After the עליה *the person called up says:*

בָּרוּךְ אַתָּה יהוה אֱלֹהֵינוּ מֶלֶךְ הָעוֹלָם
אֲשֶׁר נָתַן לָנוּ תּוֹרַת אֱמֶת וְחַיֵּי עוֹלָם נָטַע בְּתוֹכֵנוּ.
בָּרוּךְ אַתָּה יהוה, נוֹתֵן הַתּוֹרָה.

HAGBAHA AND GELILA

וְזֹאת הַתּוֹרָה This is the Torah
that Moses placed before the Jewish people
as *Hashem* commanded.

The Torah scroll is bound and covered.

RETURNING THE TORAH

The Aron Kodesh is opened.

Leader: יְהַלְלוּ Let the Jewish people praise *Hashem*
because He alone is God.

Congregation: *Hashem*'s majesty is found
on earth and in heaven.
He honors His Jewish people
by raising them up
and bringing them close to Him. Halleluya!

As the Torah is returned to the Aron Kodesh, say:

לְדָוִד The earth and everything on it belong to *Hashem*.
Hashem created the world beginning
with the waters of the seas and rivers.
Who may go to the *Beit HaMikdash*
and stand in the presence of *Hashem*'s holiness?
One with pure actions and thoughts.
This person will receive blessing and kindness
from *Hashem*.
Who is the King worthy of honor?
Hashem, Master of the world,
is the King worthy of honor!

הגבהה וגלילה

וְזֹאת הַתּוֹרָה אֲשֶׁר־שָׂם מֹשֶׁה לִפְנֵי בְּנֵי יִשְׂרָאֵל:
עַל־פִּי יהוה בְּיַד מֹשֶׁה:

The ספר תורה is bound and covered.

הכנסת ספר תורה

The ארון קודש is opened.

חזן: יְהַלְלוּ אֶת־שֵׁם יהוה, כִּי נִשְׂגָּב־שְׁמוֹ, לְבַדּוֹ

קהל: הוֹדוֹ עַל־אֶרֶץ וְשָׁמָיִם: וַיָּרֶם קֶרֶן לְעַמּוֹ, תְּהִלָּה לְכָל־חֲסִידָיו, לִבְנֵי יִשְׂרָאֵל עַם קְרֹבוֹ, הַלְלוּיָהּ:

As the ספר תורה is returned to the ארון קודש, say:

לְדָוִד מִזְמוֹר, לַיהוה הָאָרֶץ וּמְלוֹאָהּ, תֵּבֵל וְיֹשְׁבֵי בָהּ: כִּי־הוּא עַל־יַמִּים יְסָדָהּ, וְעַל־נְהָרוֹת יְכוֹנְנֶהָ: מִי־יַעֲלֶה בְהַר־יהוה, וּמִי־יָקוּם בִּמְקוֹם קָדְשׁוֹ: נְקִי כַפַּיִם וּבַר־לֵבָב, אֲשֶׁר לֹא־נָשָׂא לַשָּׁוְא נַפְשִׁי וְלֹא נִשְׁבַּע לְמִרְמָה: יִשָּׂא בְרָכָה מֵאֵת יהוה, וּצְדָקָה מֵאֱלֹהֵי יִשְׁעוֹ: זֶה דּוֹר דֹּרְשָׁו, מְבַקְשֵׁי פָנֶיךָ, יַעֲקֹב, סֶלָה: שְׂאוּ שְׁעָרִים רָאשֵׁיכֶם, וְהִנָּשְׂאוּ פִּתְחֵי עוֹלָם, וְיָבוֹא מֶלֶךְ הַכָּבוֹד: מִי זֶה מֶלֶךְ הַכָּבוֹד, יהוה עִזּוּז וְגִבּוֹר, יהוה גִּבּוֹר מִלְחָמָה: שְׂאוּ שְׁעָרִים רָאשֵׁיכֶם, וּשְׂאוּ פִּתְחֵי עוֹלָם, וְיָבֹא מֶלֶךְ הַכָּבוֹד: מִי הוּא זֶה מֶלֶךְ הַכָּבוֹד, יהוה צְבָאוֹת הוּא מֶלֶךְ הַכָּבוֹד, סֶלָה:

As the Torah is placed into the Aron Kodesh, say:

וּבְנֻחֹה When the *Aron* would come to rest, Moshe would say, "*Hashem*, return to the thousands of people in Your Jewish nation." Your *Kohanim* are clothed ready to serve You, and Your followers sing to You in joy, awaiting Your arrival. For the sake of David, do not reject us. *Hashem*, You commanded us not to abandon Your Torah. It is a tree of life to all those who hold onto it and a source of happiness for all those who follow it. Following the Torah is pleasant and it leads to peace. ▸ *Hashem*, bring us back to You and we will return to You. Let us live again as we did in the times of the *Beit HaMikdash*.

The Aron Kodesh is closed.

HALF KADDISH

Leader: יִתְגַּדַּל May *Hashem* be recognized
as great and holy (*Congregation:* Amen)
in the world that He created.
May He establish His kingdom
during my lifetime and the lifetime of all Jews,
quickly and soon.
Let us say: "Amen" (*Congregation:* Amen).

Congregation: May we thank *Hashem* for ever and ever.
Leader: May we thank *Hashem* for ever and ever.

Leader: *Hashem* should be thanked, praised,
and honored (*Congregation:* He is blessed).
Hashem is beyond all the blessings,
songs, or praises that we could offer.
Let us say: "Amen" (*Congregation:* Amen).

As the ספר תורה *is placed into the* ארון קודש*, say:*

וּבְנֻחֹה יֹאמַר, שׁוּבָה יהוה רִבְבוֹת אַלְפֵי יִשְׂרָאֵל: קוּמָה יהוה לִמְנוּחָתֶךָ, אַתָּה וַאֲרוֹן עֻזֶּךָ: כֹּהֲנֶיךָ יִלְבְּשׁוּ־צֶדֶק, וַחֲסִידֶיךָ יְרַנֵּנוּ: בַּעֲבוּר דָּוִד עַבְדֶּךָ אַל־תָּשֵׁב פְּנֵי מְשִׁיחֶךָ: כִּי לֶקַח טוֹב נָתַתִּי לָכֶם, תּוֹרָתִי אַל־תַּעֲזֹבוּ: עֵץ־חַיִּים הִיא לַמַּחֲזִיקִים בָּהּ, וְתֹמְכֶיהָ מְאֻשָּׁר: דְּרָכֶיהָ דַרְכֵי־נֹעַם וְכָל־נְתִיבוֹתֶיהָ שָׁלוֹם: ◂ הֲשִׁיבֵנוּ יהוה אֵלֶיךָ וְנָשׁוּבָה, חַדֵּשׁ יָמֵינוּ כְּקֶדֶם:

The ארון קודש *is closed.*

חצי קדיש

חזן: יִתְגַּדַּל וְיִתְקַדַּשׁ שְׁמֵהּ רַבָּא (קהל: אָמֵן)
בְּעָלְמָא דִּי בְרָא כִרְעוּתֵהּ, וְיַמְלִיךְ מַלְכוּתֵהּ
בְּחַיֵּיכוֹן וּבְיוֹמֵיכוֹן וּבְחַיֵּי דְכָל בֵּית יִשְׂרָאֵל
בַּעֲגָלָא וּבִזְמַן קָרִיב, וְאִמְרוּ אָמֵן. (קהל: אָמֵן)

קהל יְהֵא שְׁמֵהּ רַבָּא מְבָרַךְ לְעָלַם וּלְעָלְמֵי עָלְמַיָּא.
חזן: יְהֵא שְׁמֵהּ רַבָּא מְבָרַךְ לְעָלַם וּלְעָלְמֵי עָלְמַיָּא.

חזן: יִתְבָּרַךְ וְיִשְׁתַּבַּח וְיִתְפָּאַר וְיִתְרוֹמַם וְיִתְנַשֵּׂא
וְיִתְהַדָּר וְיִתְעַלֶּה וְיִתְהַלָּל
שְׁמֵהּ דְּקֻדְשָׁא בְּרִיךְ הוּא (קהל: בְּרִיךְ הוּא)
לְעֵלָּא מִן כָּל בִּרְכָתָא / בשבת שובה: לְעֵלָּא לְעֵלָּא מִכָּל בִּרְכָתָא/
וְשִׁירָתָא, תֻּשְׁבְּחָתָא וְנֶחֱמָתָא
דַּאֲמִירָן בְּעָלְמָא, וְאִמְרוּ אָמֵן. (קהל: אָמֵן)

AMIDA

Take three steps back then three steps forward then stand with your feet together.

I will call out to *Hashem,* let us all give praise to Him.

Hashem, open my lips and help my mouth recite Your praise.

ANCESTORS

Bend the knees when saying "We thank," bow when saying "You," and stand straight before saying "Hashem."

בָּרוּךְ We thank You, *Hashem,*
our God, and God of our ancestors,
Avraham, Yitzchak, and Yaakov.
You, *Hashem,* are the great, mighty, awesome, kind,
and all-powerful Creator.
It is because of the greatness of our ancestors,
Avraham, Yitzchak, and Yaakov,
that *Hashem* will bring *Mashiach.*

Between Rosh Hashana and Yom Kippur say:

Give us life in the year to come
and write us in the book of life, *Hashem,* who gives life.

Hashem is our King who helps, guides, and protects us.

Bend the knees when saying "Thank," bow when saying "You," and stand straight before saying "Hashem."

Thank You, *Hashem,*
who protects us in the merit of Avraham.

HASHEM'S STRENGTH

אַתָּה You, *Hashem,* have unlimited strength.
You save people in their time of need,
and You have the power to bring the dead back to life.

עמידה

Take three steps back then three steps forward then stand with your feet together.

כִּי שֵׁם יהוה אֶקְרָא, הָבוּ גֹדֶל לֵאלֹהֵינוּ:
אֲדֹנָי, שְׂפָתַי תִּפְתָּח, וּפִי יַגִּיד תְּהִלָּתֶךָ:

אבות

Bend the knees when saying בָּרוּךְ, *bow when saying* אַתָּה, *and stand straight before saying Hashem's name.*

בָּרוּךְ אַתָּה יהוה, אֱלֹהֵינוּ וֵאלֹהֵי אֲבוֹתֵינוּ
אֱלֹהֵי אַבְרָהָם, אֱלֹהֵי יִצְחָק, וֵאלֹהֵי יַעֲקֹב
הָאֵל הַגָּדוֹל הַגִּבּוֹר וְהַנּוֹרָא, אֵל עֶלְיוֹן
גּוֹמֵל חֲסָדִים טוֹבִים, וְקוֹנֵה הַכֹּל
וְזוֹכֵר חַסְדֵי אָבוֹת
וּמֵבִיא גוֹאֵל לִבְנֵי בְנֵיהֶם לְמַעַן שְׁמוֹ בְּאַהֲבָה.

On שבת שובה *say:*

זָכְרֵנוּ לְחַיִּים, מֶלֶךְ חָפֵץ בַּחַיִּים
וְכָתְבֵנוּ בְּסֵפֶר הַחַיִּים, לְמַעַנְךָ אֱלֹהִים חַיִּים.

מֶלֶךְ עוֹזֵר וּמוֹשִׁיעַ וּמָגֵן.

Bend the knees when saying בָּרוּךְ, *bow when saying* אַתָּה, *and stand straight before saying Hashem's name.*

בָּרוּךְ אַתָּה יהוה, מָגֵן אַבְרָהָם.

גבורות

אַתָּה גִּבּוֹר לְעוֹלָם, אֲדֹנָי
מְחַיֵּה מֵתִים אַתָּה, רַב לְהוֹשִׁיעַ

This line is said during the rainy season, from Simchat Torah to Pesach:

(You make the wind blow and cause the rain to fall)

With kindness You provide the living
with the necessities to live,
and with mercy You keep Your promise
of bringing the dead back to life.
For the living, You:

Support those who are falling,
Heal those who are sick, and
Free those who are in challenging situations.

Who is like You, *Hashem,*
and who can compare to You?
You, *Hashem,* are our King
who has the power to cause death and life.

Between Rosh Hashana and Yom Kippur say:

Who is like You, *Hashem,* our caring Father
who remembers His people for good and gives them life?

We have complete faith
that You will bring us back to life after our passing.
Thank You, *Hashem,* for bringing the dead back to life.

HASHEM'S HOLINESS

אַתָּה קָדוֹשׁ *Hashem,* You are holy and Your name is holy.
The Jewish people, who are holy,
will praise You, *Hashem,* each day.
Thank You, *Hashem,*
the holy God. /*Between Rosh Hashana & Yom Kippur say:* the holy King./

This line is said during the rainy season, from שמחת תורה *to* פסח*:*

(מַשִּׁיב הָרְוּחַ וּמוֹרִיד הַגֶּשֶׁם)

מְכַלְכֵּל חַיִּים בְּחֶסֶד, מְחַיֵּה מֵתִים בְּרַחֲמִים רַבִּים
סוֹמֵךְ נוֹפְלִים
וְרוֹפֵא חוֹלִים
וּמַתִּיר אֲסוּרִים
וּמְקַיֵּם אֱמוּנָתוֹ לִישֵׁנֵי עָפָר.
מִי כָמְוֹךָ, בַּעַל גְּבוּרוֹת
וּמִי דְּוֹמֶה לָּךְ
מֶלֶךְ, מֵמִית וּמְחַיֶּה וּמַצְמְיחַ יְשׁוּעָה.

On שבת שובה *say:*

מִי כָמְוֹךָ אַב הָרַחֲמִים
זוֹכֵר יְצוּרָיו לְחַיִּים בְּרַחֲמִים.

וְנֶאֱמָן אַתָּה לְהַחֲיוֹת מֵתִים.
בָּרוּךְ אַתָּה יהוה, מְחַיֵּה הַמֵּתִים.

קדושת השם

אַתָּה קָדוֹשׁ וְשִׁמְךָ קָדוֹשׁ
וּקְדוֹשִׁים בְּכָל יוֹם יְהַלְלְוּךָ סֶּלָה.
בָּרוּךְ אַתָּה יהוה
הָאֵל הַקָּדוֹשׁ. / *On* שבת שובה *say* הַמֶּלֶךְ הַקָּדוֹשׁ./

HOLINESS OF SHABBAT

אַתָּה אֶחָד *Hashem,*
You are the only God
and there is no nation that serves You
as Your Jewish people.
In Your greatness,
You gave us this holy day of rest.
Avraham, Yitzchak, and Yaakov
will be happy to know
that their children, the Jewish people,
continue to rest on Shabbat.
Shabbat allows us
to further our love and devotion to *Hashem,*
and appreciate the kindness that *Hashem* gives to us.
Shabbat allows us to experience
peace, calmness, and a renewed trust in *Hashem;*
it is a day of complete rest.
Hashem,
may Your Jewish people know
that we were given this day of rest to honor You.

אֱלֹהֵינוּ *Hashem,*
our God and God of our ancestors,
we rest from work today for Your sake.
Allow us to become holy
through keeping Your *mitzvot*
and studying Your Torah.
Be good to us, save us, and purify our hearts
to serve You sincerely.

קדושת היום

אַתָּה אֶחָד וְשִׁמְךָ אֶחָד
וּמִי כְּעַמְּךָ יִשְׂרָאֵל גּוֹי אֶחָד בָּאָרֶץ.
תִּפְאֶרֶת גְּדֻלָּה וַעֲטֶרֶת יְשׁוּעָה
יוֹם מְנוּחָה וּקְדֻשָּׁה לְעַמְּךָ נָתָתָּ.
אַבְרָהָם יָגֵל, יִצְחָק יְרַנֵּן, יַעֲקֹב וּבָנָיו יָנְוּחוּ בוֹ
מְנוּחַת אַהֲבָה וּנְדָבָה, מְנוּחַת אֱמֶת וֶאֱמוּנָה
מְנוּחַת שָׁלוֹם וְשַׁלְוָה וְהַשְׁקֵט וָבֶטַח
מְנוּחָה שְׁלֵמָה שֶׁאַתָּה רוֹצֶה בָּהּ.
יַכִּירוּ בָנֶיךָ וְיֵדְעוּ, כִּי מֵאִתְּךָ הִיא מְנוּחָתָם
וְעַל מְנוּחָתָם יַקְדִּישׁוּ אֶת שְׁמֶךָ.

אֱלֹהֵינוּ וֵאלֹהֵי אֲבוֹתֵינוּ, רְצֵה בִמְנוּחָתֵנוּ
קַדְּשֵׁנוּ בְּמִצְוֹתֶיךָ וְתֵן חֶלְקֵנוּ בְּתוֹרָתֶךָ
שַׂבְּעֵנוּ מִטּוּבֶךָ וְשַׂמְּחֵנוּ בִּישׁוּעָתֶךָ
וְטַהֵר לִבֵּנוּ לְעָבְדְּךָ בֶּאֱמֶת.

אַתָּה אֶחָד שִׁמְךָ אֶחָד וּמִי כְּעַמְּךָ יִשְׂרָאֵל גּוֹי אֶחָד בָּאָרֶץ *Hashem, You are the only God and there is no nation that serves You as Your Jewish people.* Why do we begin the Amida of Shabbat *Mincha* with a reminder that we, the Jewish people, serve *Hashem,* the only God? Is this not obvious? Shabbat *Mincha* is special because it focuses on the future, when *Mashiach* will come, and everyone in the world will know that *Hashem* is the only God. Until that time it is only the Jewish people that serve *Hashem,* which is why we are rewarded with the special day of Shabbat to rest and become closer to Him.

Hashem, our God, show us Your love
and allow us to observe Your holy Shabbat
so that Your Jewish people can rest.
Thank You, *Hashem,* for making Shabbat holy.

SERVICE IN THE *BEIT HAMIKDASH*

רְצֵה *Hashem,* please accept Your Jewish people
and their prayers.
We eagerly await the rebuilding of the *Beit HaMikdash*
so we can serve You with *korbanot.*
Until the *Beit HaMikdash* is rebuilt,
please accept our prayers with love.

On Rosh Chodesh and Chol HaMo'ed, say:

אֱלֹהֵינוּ Our God, and God of our ancestors, may our prayers:
Rise from our mouths,
Come before You,
Reach You at a desirable time,
Be heard,
And be fulfilled.
Hashem, You remember and know each of our hardships.
You remember:
Our ancestors,
Mashiach,
Your holy city, Jerusalem, and
Your united Jewish people,
for goodness, kindness, mercy, life, and peace
on this day of:
On Rosh Chodesh: *Rosh Chodesh.*
On Pesach: the Holiday of *Matzot.*
On Sukkot: the Holiday of *Sukkot.*

וְהַנְחִילֵנוּ יהוה אֱלֹהֵינוּ בְּאַהֲבָה וּבְרָצוֹן שַׁבְּתוֹת קָדְשֶׁךָ
וְיָנְוּחוּ בָם יִשְׂרָאֵל מְקַדְּשֵׁי שְׁמֶךָ.
בָּרוּךְ אַתָּה יהוה, מְקַדֵּשׁ הַשַּׁבָּת.

עבודה

רְצֵה יהוה אֱלֹהֵינוּ בְּעַמְּךָ יִשְׂרָאֵל, וּבִתְפִלָּתָם
וְהָשֵׁב אֶת הָעֲבוֹדָה לִדְבִיר בֵּיתֶךָ
וְאִשֵּׁי יִשְׂרָאֵל וּתְפִלָּתָם בְּאַהֲבָה תְקַבֵּל בְּרָצוֹן
וּתְהִי לְרָצוֹן תָּמִיד עֲבוֹדַת יִשְׂרָאֵל עַמֶּךָ.

On ראש חודש *and* חול המועד*, say:*

אֱלֹהֵינוּ וֵאלֹהֵי אֲבוֹתֵינוּ
יַעֲלֶה וְיָבוֹא וְיַגִּיעַ, וְיֵרָאֶה וְיֵרָצֶה וְיִשָּׁמַע
וְיִפָּקֵד וְיִזָּכֵר זִכְרוֹנֵנוּ וּפִקְדּוֹנֵנוּ, וְזִכְרוֹן אֲבוֹתֵינוּ
וְזִכְרוֹן מָשִׁיחַ בֶּן דָּוִד עַבְדֶּךָ
וְזִכְרוֹן יְרוּשָׁלַיִם עִיר קָדְשֶׁךָ
וְזִכְרוֹן כָּל עַמְּךָ בֵּית יִשְׂרָאֵל
לְפָנֶיךָ, לִפְלֵיטָה לְטוֹבָה
לְחֵן וּלְחֶסֶד וּלְרַחֲמִים
לְחַיִּים וּלְשָׁלוֹם
בְּיוֹם

בראש חודש: רֹאשׁ הַחֹדֶשׁ הַזֶּה.
בפסח: חַג הַמַּצּוֹת הַזֶּה.
בסוכות: חַג הַסֻּכּוֹת הַזֶּה.

Hashem, on this day please remember us
with good thoughts, consider us for blessing,
and help us with difficult times in our lives.
Be kind and merciful with us, *Hashem,*
as we look towards You as our King.

May we be worthy
to see the rebuilding of the *Beit HaMikdash.*
We thank You, *Hashem,*
for returning Your presence to Zion.

THANK YOU

Bow when saying the words "We thank You."

מוֹדִים We thank You, *Hashem,*
for You are and always will be
our God, and the God of our ancestors.
You give us life
and You always protect us.
We thank and praise You
for:
Our lives which are in Your hands,
Our souls which are in Your control,
The miracles You perform for us every day, and
The goodness You show us
at all times, morning, noon, and night.
You, *Hashem,*
have unlimited mercy and kindness
and therefore we have always placed our hope in You.

זָכְרֵנוּ יהוה אֱלֹהֵינוּ בּוֹ לְטוֹבָה, וּפָקְדֵנוּ בוֹ לִבְרָכָה
וְהוֹשִׁיעֵנוּ בוֹ לְחַיִּים.
וּבִדְבַר יְשׁוּעָה וְרַחֲמִים, חוּס וְחָנֵּנוּ וְרַחֵם עָלֵינוּ וְהוֹשִׁיעֵנוּ
כִּי אֵלֶיךָ עֵינֵינוּ, כִּי אֵל מֶלֶךְ חַנּוּן וְרַחוּם אָתָּה.

וְתֶחֱזֶינָה עֵינֵינוּ בְּשׁוּבְךָ לְצִיּוֹן בְּרַחֲמִים.
בָּרוּךְ אַתָּה יהוה, הַמַּחֲזִיר שְׁכִינָתוֹ לְצִיּוֹן.

הודאה

Bow when saying the words מוֹדִים אֲנַחְנוּ לָךְ שָׁאַתָּה הוּא.

מוֹדִים אֲנַחְנוּ לָךְ
שָׁאַתָּה הוּא יהוה אֱלֹהֵינוּ וֵאלֹהֵי אֲבוֹתֵינוּ לְעוֹלָם וָעֶד.
צוּר חַיֵּינוּ, מָגֵן יִשְׁעֵנוּ, אַתָּה הוּא לְדוֹר וָדוֹר.
נוֹדֶה לְּךָ וּנְסַפֵּר תְּהִלָּתֶךָ
עַל חַיֵּינוּ הַמְּסוּרִים בְּיָדֶךָ
וְעַל נִשְׁמוֹתֵינוּ הַפְּקוּדוֹת לָךְ
וְעַל נִסֶּיךָ שֶׁבְּכָל יוֹם עִמָּנוּ
וְעַל נִפְלְאוֹתֶיךָ וְטוֹבוֹתֶיךָ
שֶׁבְּכָל עֵת, עֶרֶב וָבֹקֶר וְצָהֳרָיִם.
הַטּוֹב, כִּי לֹא כָלוּ רַחֲמֶיךָ
וְהַמְרַחֵם, כִּי לֹא תַמּוּ חֲסָדֶיךָ
מֵעוֹלָם קִוִּינוּ לָךְ.

On Chanuka say:

עַל הַנִּסִּים We thank You, *Hashem,* for the miracles, the deliverances, the great strength, and the victories in war that You displayed for us in earlier times and in our times.

בִּימֵי מַתִּתְיָהוּ In the days of Mattityahu, son of Yochanan the *Kohen Gadol,* the Hasmonean, and his sons, the wicked Greeks challenged Your Jewish people trying to make them forget Your Torah and sin. In Your great kindness, You, *Hashem,* supported us in this difficult time. You allowed for:

The weak Jews to defeat the mighty Greeks,
The few Jews to defeat the many Greeks,
The pure Jews to defeat the impure Greeks,
The righteous Jews to defeat the wicked Greeks, and
The Jews who studied Your Torah to defeat the Greeks who did not.

Hashem, on this day everyone in the world recognized You as You miraculously saved Your Jewish people. Your Jewish people then entered the *Beit HaMikdash* to clean and purify it. They lit candles in the courtyard of the *Beit HaMikdash* and set aside these eight days of *Chanukah* for giving thanks and praising You.

Continue with "For all these reasons."

For all these reasons
we will thank You, *Hashem,* our King, forever.

Between Rosh Hashana & Yom Kippur say:

And write all Your children in the book of good life.

Every living person will recognize and praise You, *Hashem,*
for You are the God that helps and saves Your people.

Bend the knees when saying "Thank," bow when saying "You," and stand straight before saying "Hashem."

Thank You, *Hashem,*
for You are worthy of being thanked.

בחנוכה:

עַל הַנִּסִּים וְעַל הַפֻּרְקָן וְעַל הַגְּבוּרוֹת וְעַל הַתְּשׁוּעוֹת וְעַל הַמִּלְחָמוֹת שֶׁעָשִׂיתָ לַאֲבוֹתֵינוּ בַּיָּמִים הָהֵם בַּזְּמַן הַזֶּה.

בִּימֵי מַתִּתְיָהוּ בֶּן יוֹחָנָן כֹּהֵן גָּדוֹל חַשְׁמוֹנַאי וּבָנָיו, כְּשֶׁעָמְדָה מַלְכוּת יָוָן הָרְשָׁעָה עַל עַמְּךָ יִשְׂרָאֵל לְהַשְׁכִּיחָם תּוֹרָתֶךָ וּלְהַעֲבִירָם מֵחֻקֵּי רְצוֹנֶךָ, וְאַתָּה בְּרַחֲמֶיךָ הָרַבִּים עָמַדְתָּ לָהֶם בְּעֵת צָרָתָם, רַבְתָּ אֶת רִיבָם, דַּנְתָּ אֶת דִּינָם, נָקַמְתָּ אֶת נִקְמָתָם, מָסַרְתָּ גִּבּוֹרִים בְּיַד חַלָּשִׁים, וְרַבִּים בְּיַד מְעַטִּים, וּטְמֵאִים בְּיַד טְהוֹרִים, וּרְשָׁעִים בְּיַד צַדִּיקִים, וְזֵדִים בְּיַד עוֹסְקֵי תוֹרָתֶךָ, וּלְךָ עָשִׂיתָ שֵׁם גָּדוֹל וְקָדוֹשׁ בְּעוֹלָמֶךָ, וּלְעַמְּךָ יִשְׂרָאֵל עָשִׂיתָ תְּשׁוּעָה גְדוֹלָה וּפֻרְקָן כְּהַיּוֹם הַזֶּה. וְאַחַר כֵּן בָּאוּ בָנֶיךָ לִדְבִיר בֵּיתֶךָ, וּפִנּוּ אֶת הֵיכָלֶךָ, וְטִהֲרוּ אֶת מִקְדָּשֶׁךָ, וְהִדְלִיקוּ נֵרוֹת בְּחַצְרוֹת קָדְשֶׁךָ, וְקָבְעוּ שְׁמוֹנַת יְמֵי חֲנֻכָּה אֵלּוּ, לְהוֹדוֹת וּלְהַלֵּל לְשִׁמְךָ הַגָּדוֹל.

Continue with וְעַל כֻּלָּם.

וְעַל כֻּלָּם
יִתְבָּרַךְ וְיִתְרוֹמַם שִׁמְךָ מַלְכֵּנוּ תָּמִיד לְעוֹלָם וָעֶד.

On שבת שובה *say* וּכְתֹב לְחַיִּים טוֹבִים כָּל בְּנֵי בְרִיתֶךָ.

וְכֹל הַחַיִּים יוֹדוּךָ סֶּלָה, וִיהַלְלוּ אֶת שִׁמְךָ בֶּאֱמֶת הָאֵל יְשׁוּעָתֵנוּ וְעֶזְרָתֵנוּ סֶלָה.

Bend the knees when saying בָּרוּךְ, *bow when saying* אַתָּה, *and stand straight before saying Hashem's name.*

בָּרוּךְ אַתָּה יהוה
הַטּוֹב שִׁמְךָ וּלְךָ נָאֶה לְהוֹדוֹת.

PEACE

שָׁלוֹם רָב *Hashem,* You are King and master of peace.
May it be good in Your eyes
to bless Your Jewish people with peace
at all times and at every hour, forever.

Between Rosh Hashana and Yom Kippur continue with "May You remember," below.

Thank You, *Hashem,*
who blesses His Jewish people with peace.

Between Rosh Hashana and Yom Kippur say:

May You remember all of the Jewish people for life,
blessing, peace, and riches
and write us in the book of good life and peace.
Thank You, *Hashem,*
who makes peace.

CONCLUSION OF AMIDA

אֱלֹהַי *Hashem,* please help me:
Control my mouth from speaking badly
about other people,
Stay silent and not respond if someone speaks badly
about me,
Learn Your Torah, and do Your *mitzvot.*
Hashem, if people plan to do something evil against me,
please stop these plans and protect me.
Even if I am not deserving of being helped,
please act on my behalf
as I represent Your name and Your Torah.

שלום

שָׁלוֹם רָב עַל יִשְׂרָאֵל עַמְּךָ תָּשִׂים לְעוֹלָם
כִּי אַתָּה הוּא מֶלֶךְ אָדוֹן לְכָל הַשָּׁלוֹם.
וְטוֹב בְּעֵינֶיךָ לְבָרֵךְ אֶת עַמְּךָ יִשְׂרָאֵל
בְּכָל עֵת וּבְכָל שָׁעָה בִּשְׁלוֹמֶךָ.

On שבת שובה continue with בְּסֵפֶר חַיִּים, below.

בָּרוּךְ אַתָּה יהוה
הַמְבָרֵךְ אֶת עַמּוֹ יִשְׂרָאֵל בַּשָּׁלוֹם.

On שבת שובה say:

בְּסֵפֶר חַיִּים, בְּרָכָה וְשָׁלוֹם, וּפַרְנָסָה טוֹבָה
נִזָּכֵר וְנִכָּתֵב לְפָנֶיךָ, אֲנַחְנוּ וְכָל עַמְּךָ בֵּית יִשְׂרָאֵל
לְחַיִּים טוֹבִים וּלְשָׁלוֹם.
בָּרוּךְ אַתָּה יהוה, עוֹשֵׂה הַשָּׁלוֹם.

סיום העמידה

אֱלֹהַי, נְצֹר לְשׁוֹנִי מֵרָע וּשְׂפָתַי מִדַּבֵּר מִרְמָה
וְלִמְקַלְלַי נַפְשִׁי תִדֹּם, וְנַפְשִׁי כֶּעָפָר לַכֹּל תִּהְיֶה.
פְּתַח לִבִּי בְּתוֹרָתֶךָ, וּבְמִצְוֹתֶיךָ תִּרְדֹּף נַפְשִׁי.
וְכָל הַחוֹשְׁבִים עָלַי רָעָה
מְהֵרָה הָפֵר עֲצָתָם וְקַלְקֵל מַחֲשַׁבְתָּם.
עֲשֵׂה לְמַעַן שְׁמֶךָ, עֲשֵׂה לְמַעַן יְמִינֶךָ
עֲשֵׂה לְמַעַן קְדֻשָּׁתֶךָ, עֲשֵׂה לְמַעַן תּוֹרָתֶךָ.

Hashem, please save Your Jewish people
from difficult situations
and answer my requests.
May You find my thoughts and prayers favorable.

Take three steps backwards and bow to your left as you say:

You, *Hashem,* make peace in heaven.

Bow to your right as you say:

Please may You bring peace to us

Bow forward as you say:

And all Your Jewish people.

Before taking three steps forward, say the following quietly:

Hashem, our God and God of our ancestors,
may You please rebuild the *Beit HaMikdash* soon.
Hashem, please allow us to learn Your Torah
and serve You in the *Beit HaMikdash*
as the Jewish people once did.

לְמַעַן יֵחָלְצוּן יְדִידֶיךָ, הוֹשִׁיעָה יְמִינְךָ וַעֲנֵנִי:
יִהְיוּ לְרָצוֹן אִמְרֵי־פִי וְהֶגְיוֹן לִבִּי לְפָנֶיךָ, יהוה צוּרִי וְגֹאֲלִי:

Take three steps backwards and bow to your left as you say:

עֹשֶׂה שָׁלוֹם / *On* שבת שובה *say* הַשָּׁלוֹם/ בִּמְרוֹמָיו

Bow to your right as you say:

הוּא יַעֲשֶׂה שָׁלוֹם עָלֵינוּ

Bow forward as you say:

וְעַל כָּל יִשְׂרָאֵל, וְאִמְרוּ אָמֵן.

Before taking three steps forward, say the following quietly:

יְהִי רָצוֹן מִלְּפָנֶיךָ יהוה אֱלֹהֵינוּ וֵאלֹהֵי אֲבוֹתֵינוּ.
שֶׁיִּבָּנֶה בֵּית הַמִּקְדָּשׁ בִּמְהֵרָה בְיָמֵינוּ
וְתֵן חֶלְקֵנוּ בְּתוֹרָתֶךָ.
וְשָׁם נַעֲבָדְךָ בְּיִרְאָה כִּימֵי עוֹלָם וּכְשָׁנִים קַדְמֹנִיּוֹת.
וְעָרְבָה לַיהוה מִנְחַת יְהוּדָה וִירוּשָׁלָםִ כִּימֵי עוֹלָם וּכְשָׁנִים קַדְמֹנִיּוֹת:

THE LEADER'S REPETITION

Try to focus on each blessing that the Leader reads, by following along and thinking about the sentences below. After each beracha that the Leader recites, answer "Amen."

I will call out to *Hashem,* let us all give praise to Him.
Hashem, open my lips
and help my mouth recite Your praise.

ANCESTORS

We praise You, *Hashem,*
for protecting, helping, and saving us
as You did for our ancestors,
Avraham, Yitzchak, and Yaakov.
Thank You, *Hashem,*
who protects us in the merit of Avraham.

(*Congregation:* Amen.)

HASHEM'S STRENGTH

We praise You, *Hashem,*
for providing food to those who are hungry,
support to those who are falling,
health to those who are sick,
and help to those who are in challenging situations.
Thank You, *Hashem,*
for bringing the dead back to life. (*Congregation:* Amen.)

חזרת הש״ץ

Try to focus on each blessing that the חזן *reads, by following along and thinking about the sentences below. After each beracha that the* חזן *recites, answer* אָמֵן.

כִּי שֵׁם יהוה אֶקְרָא, הָבוּ גֹדֶל לֵאלֹהֵינוּ:
אֲדֹנָי, שְׂפָתַי תִּפְתָּח, וּפִי יַגִּיד תְּהִלָּתֶךָ:

אבות

בָּרוּךְ אַתָּה יהוה, אֱלֹהֵינוּ וֵאלֹהֵי אֲבוֹתֵינוּ
אֱלֹהֵי אַבְרָהָם, אֱלֹהֵי יִצְחָק, וֵאלֹהֵי יַעֲקֹב
הָאֵל הַגָּדוֹל הַגִּבּוֹר וְהַנּוֹרָא, אֵל עֶלְיוֹן
גּוֹמֵל חֲסָדִים טוֹבִים, וְקוֹנֵה הַכֹּל, וְזוֹכֵר חַסְדֵי אָבוֹת
וּמֵבִיא גוֹאֵל לִבְנֵי בְנֵיהֶם לְמַעַן שְׁמוֹ בְּאַהֲבָה.

On שבת שובה *say* זָכְרֵנוּ לְחַיִּים, מֶלֶךְ חָפֵץ בַּחַיִּים
וְכָתְבֵנוּ בְּסֵפֶר הַחַיִּים, לְמַעַנְךָ אֱלֹהִים חַיִּים.

מֶלֶךְ עוֹזֵר וּמוֹשִׁיעַ וּמָגֵן.
בָּרוּךְ אַתָּה יהוה, מָגֵן אַבְרָהָם. (קהל: אָמֵן)

גבורות

אַתָּה גִּבּוֹר לְעוֹלָם, אֲדֹנָי, מְחַיֵּה מֵתִים אַתָּה, רַב לְהוֹשִׁיעַ

This line is said during the rainy season, from שמחת תורה *to* פסח*:*

(מַשִּׁיב הָרוּחַ וּמוֹרִיד הַגֶּשֶׁם)

מְכַלְכֵּל חַיִּים בְּחֶסֶד, מְחַיֵּה מֵתִים בְּרַחֲמִים רַבִּים
סוֹמֵךְ נוֹפְלִים, וְרוֹפֵא חוֹלִים, וּמַתִּיר אֲסוּרִים
וּמְקַיֵּם אֱמוּנָתוֹ לִישֵׁנֵי עָפָר.
מִי כָמוֹךָ, בַּעַל גְּבוּרוֹת, וּמִי דּוֹמֶה לָּךְ
מֶלֶךְ, מֵמִית וּמְחַיֶּה וּמַצְמִיחַ יְשׁוּעָה.

On שבת שובה *say* מִי כָמוֹךָ אַב הָרַחֲמִים, זוֹכֵר יְצוּרָיו לְחַיִּים בְּרַחֲמִים.

וְנֶאֱמָן אַתָּה לְהַחֲיוֹת מֵתִים.
בָּרוּךְ אַתָּה יהוה, מְחַיֵּה הַמֵּתִים. (קהל: אָמֵן)

KEDUSHA

This section of tefillah is said while standing silently with feet together. The sentences are said responsively, Congregation followed by the Leader.

Congregation then Leader: נְקַדֵּשׁ We will announce You, *Hashem*,
as holy in this world,
just as the angels
announce You as holy in heaven.
As Your prophet wrote,
The angels call to one another saying:

(Stand on your toes as you repeat the word "Holy")

Congregation then Leader: Holy, holy, holy, is *Hashem*.
The whole world is filled with Your holiness.

Leader: All the Jewish people and the angels
say in response:

Congregation then Leader: Blessed is *Hashem*'s holiness.

Leader: It is written in *Tehillim*:

Congregation then Leader: *Hashem*, You have ruled over the Jewish
people for generations, and You shall
continue to be our King forever.

Leader: *Hashem*, in every generation we will discuss
Your holiness and greatness. Our mouths
shall never stop speaking of Your praises,
for You, *Hashem*, are a great and holy King.
Thank You, *Hashem*, our holy God.
/ *Between Rosh Hashana & Yom Kippur say:* the holy King./

(*Congregation:* Amen.)

קדושה

This section of tefillah is said while standing silently with feet together.
The sentences are said responsively,
קהל followed by the חזן.

קהל then חזן: נְקַדֵּשׁ אֶת שִׁמְךָ בָּעוֹלָם
כְּשֵׁם שֶׁמַּקְדִּישִׁים אוֹתוֹ בִּשְׁמֵי מָרוֹם
כַּכָּתוּב עַל יַד נְבִיאֶךָ, וְקָרָא זֶה אֶל־זֶה וְאָמַר

(Stand on your toes as you repeat the word קָדוֹשׁ)

קהל then חזן: קָדוֹשׁ, קָדוֹשׁ, קָדוֹשׁ, יהוה צְבָאוֹת
מְלֹא כָל־הָאָרֶץ כְּבוֹדוֹ:

חזן: לְעֻמָּתָם בָּרוּךְ יֹאמֵרוּ

קהל then חזן: בָּרוּךְ כְּבוֹד־יהוה מִמְּקוֹמוֹ:

חזן: וּבְדִבְרֵי קָדְשְׁךָ כָּתוּב לֵאמֹר

קהל then חזן: יִמְלֹךְ יהוה לְעוֹלָם
אֱלֹהַיִךְ צִיּוֹן לְדֹר וָדֹר, הַלְלוּיָהּ:

חזן: לְדוֹר וָדוֹר נַגִּיד גָּדְלֶךָ
וּלְנֵצַח נְצָחִים קְדֻשָּׁתְךָ נַקְדִּישׁ
וְשִׁבְחֲךָ אֱלֹהֵינוּ מִפִּינוּ לֹא יָמוּשׁ לְעוֹלָם וָעֶד
כִּי אֵל מֶלֶךְ גָּדוֹל וְקָדוֹשׁ אָתָּה.
בָּרוּךְ אַתָּה יהוה, הָאֵל הַקָּדוֹשׁ.
/ *On* שבת שובה *say* הַמֶּלֶךְ הַקָּדוֹשׁ./

(קהל: אָמֵן)

Reminder: Say "Amen" after the Leader recites the beracha.

HOLINESS OF THE DAY

Thank You, *Hashem,*
for giving us Shabbat,
a holy day of complete rest.
Shabbat allows us to experience
peace, calmness, and renewed trust in You.
Thank You, *Hashem,*
for making Shabbat holy. (*Congregation:* Amen.)

SERVICE IN THE *BEIT HAMIKDASH*

We pray to You, *Hashem,*
that You accept our prayers
as though they are the sacrifices
that were once brought to You
in Your holy *Beit HaMikdash.*

Reminder: Say אָמֵן *after the* חזן *recites the beracha.*

קדושת היום

אַתָּה אֶחָד וְשִׁמְךָ אֶחָד
וּמִי כְּעַמְּךָ יִשְׂרָאֵל גּוֹי אֶחָד בָּאָרֶץ.
תִּפְאֶרֶת גְּדֻלָּה וַעֲטֶרֶת יְשׁוּעָה
יוֹם מְנוּחָה וּקְדֻשָּׁה לְעַמְּךָ נָתָתָּ.
אַבְרָהָם יָגֵל, יִצְחָק יְרַנֵּן, יַעֲקֹב וּבָנָיו יָנוּחוּ בוֹ
מְנוּחַת אַהֲבָה וּנְדָבָה, מְנוּחַת אֱמֶת וֶאֱמוּנָה
מְנוּחַת שָׁלוֹם וְשַׁלְוָה וְהַשְׁקֵט וָבֶטַח
מְנוּחָה שְׁלֵמָה שֶׁאַתָּה רוֹצֶה בָּהּ.
יַכִּירוּ בָנֶיךָ וְיֵדְעוּ, כִּי מֵאִתְּךָ הִיא מְנוּחָתָם
וְעַל מְנוּחָתָם יַקְדִּישׁוּ אֶת שְׁמֶךָ.

אֱלֹהֵינוּ וֵאלֹהֵי אֲבוֹתֵינוּ, רְצֵה בִמְנוּחָתֵנוּ
קַדְּשֵׁנוּ בְּמִצְוֹתֶיךָ וְתֵן חֶלְקֵנוּ בְּתוֹרָתֶךָ
שַׂבְּעֵנוּ מִטּוּבֶךָ וְשַׂמְּחֵנוּ בִּישׁוּעָתֶךָ
וְטַהֵר לִבֵּנוּ לְעָבְדְּךָ בֶּאֱמֶת.
וְהַנְחִילֵנוּ יהוה אֱלֹהֵינוּ בְּאַהֲבָה וּבְרָצוֹן שַׁבְּתוֹת קָדְשֶׁךָ
וְיָנוּחוּ בָם יִשְׂרָאֵל מְקַדְּשֵׁי שְׁמֶךָ.
בָּרוּךְ אַתָּה יהוה, מְקַדֵּשׁ הַשַּׁבָּת. (קהל: אָמֵן)

עבודה

רְצֵה יהוה אֱלֹהֵינוּ בְּעַמְּךָ יִשְׂרָאֵל, וּבִתְפִלָּתָם
וְהָשֵׁב אֶת הָעֲבוֹדָה לִדְבִיר בֵּיתֶךָ
וְאִשֵּׁי יִשְׂרָאֵל וּתְפִלָּתָם בְּאַהֲבָה תְקַבֵּל בְּרָצוֹן
וּתְהִי לְרָצוֹן תָּמִיד עֲבוֹדַת יִשְׂרָאֵל עַמֶּךָ.

Reminder: Say "Amen" after the Leader recites the beracha.

On Rosh Chodesh and Chol HaMo'ed, say:

Our God, and God of our ancestors,
may our prayers:
Rise from our mouths, Come before You,
Reach You at a desirable time, Be heard, And be fulfilled.
Hashem,
You remember and know each of our hardships.
You remember:
Our ancestors, *Mashiach,*
Your holy city, Jerusalem,
and Your united Jewish people,
for goodness, kindness, mercy, life,
and peace on this day of:

On Rosh Chodesh: *Rosh Chodesh.*
On Pesach: the Holiday of *Matzot.*
On Sukkot: the Holiday of *Sukkot.*

Hashem, on this day please remember us
with good thoughts,
consider us for blessing,
and help us with difficult times in our lives.
Be kind and merciful with us,
Hashem,
as we look towards You as our King.

May we be worthy
to see the rebuilding of the *Beit HaMikdash.*
We thank You, *Hashem,*
for returning Your presence to Zion. (*Congregation:* Amen.)

Reminder: Say אָמֵן *after the* חזן *recites the beracha.*

On ראש חודש *and* חול המועד*, say:*

אֱלֹהֵֽינוּ וֵאלֹהֵי אֲבוֹתֵֽינוּ
יַעֲלֶה וְיָבוֹא וְיַגִּֽיעַ, וְיֵרָאֶה וְיֵרָצֶה וְיִשָּׁמַע
וְיִפָּקֵד וְיִזָּכֵר זִכְרוֹנֵֽנוּ וּפִקְדוֹנֵֽנוּ, וְזִכְרוֹן אֲבוֹתֵֽינוּ
וְזִכְרוֹן מָשִֽׁיחַ בֶּן דָּוִד עַבְדֶּֽךָ
וְזִכְרוֹן יְרוּשָׁלַֽיִם עִיר קָדְשֶֽׁךָ
וְזִכְרוֹן כָּל עַמְּךָ בֵּית יִשְׂרָאֵל
לְפָנֶֽיךָ, לִפְלֵיטָה לְטוֹבָה
לְחֵן וּלְחֶֽסֶד וּלְרַחֲמִים
לְחַיִּים וּלְשָׁלוֹם, בְּיוֹם

בראש חודש: רֹאשׁ הַחֹֽדֶשׁ הַזֶּה.

בפסח: חַג הַמַּצּוֹת הַזֶּה.

בסוכות: חַג הַסֻּכּוֹת הַזֶּה.

זָכְרֵֽנוּ יהוה אֱלֹהֵֽינוּ בּוֹ לְטוֹבָה
וּפָקְדֵֽנוּ בוֹ לִבְרָכָה
וְהוֹשִׁיעֵֽנוּ בוֹ לְחַיִּים.
וּבִדְבַר יְשׁוּעָה וְרַחֲמִים
חוּס וְחָנֵּֽנוּ וְרַחֵם עָלֵֽינוּ וְהוֹשִׁיעֵֽנוּ
כִּי אֵלֶֽיךָ עֵינֵֽינוּ
כִּי אֵל מֶֽלֶךְ חַנּוּן וְרַחוּם אָֽתָּה.

וְתֶחֱזֶֽינָה עֵינֵֽינוּ בְּשׁוּבְךָ לְצִיּוֹן בְּרַחֲמִים.

בָּרוּךְ אַתָּה יהוה, הַמַּחֲזִיר שְׁכִינָתוֹ לְצִיּוֹן. (קהל: **אָמֵן**)

THANK YOU

While the Leader says this prayer, the Congregation says the prayer on the bottom of this page.

You, *Hashem,*
have unlimited mercy and kindness
and therefore
we have always placed our hope in You.

The following is said quietly while the Leader says the above. Bow when saying the first sentence below beginning with the words "Thank You, Hashem."

מוֹדִים Thank You, *Hashem,*
our God and God of our ancestors.
You are God of all people,
You created us,
and You created the entire world.
Thank You for giving us life
and for providing us with food to eat.
May You continue to give us life and food to eat.
May You gather us from exile
and return us to Your holy places
so we can keep Your laws,
and serve You with a perfect heart.
Thank You *Hashem,*
our God to whom thanksgiving is due.

הודאה

While the חזן *says this prayer, the* קהל *says the prayer on the bottom of this page.*

מוֹדִים אֲנַחְנוּ לָךְ
שָׁאַתָּה הוּא יהוה אֱלֹהֵינוּ וֵאלֹהֵי אֲבוֹתֵינוּ לְעוֹלָם וָעֶד.
צוּר חַיֵּינוּ, מָגֵן יִשְׁעֵנוּ אַתָּה הוּא לְדוֹר וָדוֹר.
נוֹדֶה לְּךָ וּנְסַפֵּר תְּהִלָּתֶךָ
עַל חַיֵּינוּ הַמְּסוּרִים בְּיָדֶךָ, וְעַל נִשְׁמוֹתֵינוּ הַפְּקוּדוֹת לָךְ
וְעַל נִסֶּיךָ שֶׁבְּכָל יוֹם עִמָּנוּ, וְעַל נִפְלְאוֹתֶיךָ וְטוֹבוֹתֶיךָ
שֶׁבְּכָל עֵת, עֶרֶב וָבֹקֶר וְצָהֳרָיִם.
הַטּוֹב, כִּי לֹא כָלוּ רַחֲמֶיךָ
וְהַמְרַחֵם, כִּי לֹא תַמּוּ חֲסָדֶיךָ, מֵעוֹלָם קִוִּינוּ לָךְ.

The following is said quietly while the חזן *says the above. Bow when saying the first sentence below beginning with the words* מוֹדִים אֲנַחְנוּ לָךְ.

מוֹדִים אֲנַחְנוּ לָךְ
שָׁאַתָּה הוּא יהוה אֱלֹהֵינוּ וֵאלֹהֵי אֲבוֹתֵינוּ
אֱלֹהֵי כָל בָּשָׂר, יוֹצְרֵנוּ, יוֹצֵר בְּרֵאשִׁית.
בְּרָכוֹת וְהוֹדָאוֹת לְשִׁמְךָ הַגָּדוֹל וְהַקָּדוֹשׁ
עַל שֶׁהֶחֱיִיתָנוּ וְקִיַּמְתָּנוּ.
כֵּן תְּחַיֵּנוּ וּתְקַיְּמֵנוּ, וְתֶאֱסֹף גָּלֻיּוֹתֵינוּ לְחַצְרוֹת קָדְשֶׁךָ
לִשְׁמֹר חֻקֶּיךָ וְלַעֲשׂוֹת רְצוֹנֶךָ וּלְעָבְדְּךָ בְּלֵבָב שָׁלֵם
עַל שֶׁאֲנַחְנוּ מוֹדִים לָךְ.
בָּרוּךְ אֵל הַהוֹדָאוֹת.

Reminder: Say "Amen" after the Leader recites the beracha.

On Chanuka say:

We thank You, *Hashem,* for the miracles, the deliverances, the great strength, and the victories in war that You displayed for us in earlier times and in our times.

In the days of Mattityahu, son of Yochanan the *Kohen Gadol,* the Hasmonean, and his sons, the wicked Greeks challenged Your Jewish people trying to make them forget Your Torah and sin. In Your great kindness, You, *Hashem,* supported us in this difficult time. You allowed for: The weak Jews to defeat the mighty Greeks, The few Jews to defeat the many Greeks, The pure Jews to defeat the impure Greeks, The righteous Jews to defeat the wicked Greeks, and The Jews who studied Your Torah to defeat the Greeks who did not. *Hashem,* on this day everyone in the world recognized You as You miraculously saved Your Jewish people. Your Jewish people then entered the *Beit HaMikdash* to clean and purify it. They lit candles in the courtyard of the *Beit HaMikdash* and set aside these eight days of *Chanukah* for giving thanks and praising You.

Continue with "We thank You"

We thank You, *Hashem,*
for You are good
and all that You do is good.
Thank You, *Hashem,*
for You are worthy of being thanked. (*Congregation:* Amen.)

PEACE

We pray to You, *Hashem,*
that You grant peace
to Your Jewish people
at every moment of every hour, forever.

Reminder: Say אָמֵן *after the* חזן *recites the beracha.*

בחנוכה:

עַל הַנִּסִּים וְעַל הַפֻּרְקָן וְעַל הַגְּבוּרוֹת וְעַל הַתְּשׁוּעוֹת וְעַל הַמִּלְחָמוֹת שֶׁעָשִׂיתָ לַאֲבוֹתֵינוּ בַּיָּמִים הָהֵם בַּזְּמַן הַזֶּה.

בִּימֵי מַתִּתְיָהוּ בֶּן יוֹחָנָן כֹּהֵן גָּדוֹל חַשְׁמוֹנַאי וּבָנָיו, כְּשֶׁעָמְדָה מַלְכוּת יָוָן הָרְשָׁעָה עַל עַמְּךָ יִשְׂרָאֵל לְהַשְׁכִּיחָם תּוֹרָתֶךָ וּלְהַעֲבִירָם מֵחֻקֵּי רְצוֹנֶךָ, וְאַתָּה בְּרַחֲמֶיךָ הָרַבִּים עָמַדְתָּ לָהֶם בְּעֵת צָרָתָם, רַבְתָּ אֶת רִיבָם, דַּנְתָּ אֶת דִּינָם, נָקַמְתָּ אֶת נִקְמָתָם, מָסַרְתָּ גִבּוֹרִים בְּיַד חַלָּשִׁים, וְרַבִּים בְּיַד מְעַטִּים, וּטְמֵאִים בְּיַד טְהוֹרִים, וּרְשָׁעִים בְּיַד צַדִּיקִים, וְזֵדִים בְּיַד עוֹסְקֵי תוֹרָתֶךָ, וּלְךָ עָשִׂיתָ שֵׁם גָּדוֹל וְקָדוֹשׁ בְּעוֹלָמֶךָ, וּלְעַמְּךָ יִשְׂרָאֵל עָשִׂיתָ תְּשׁוּעָה גְדוֹלָה וּפֻרְקָן כְּהַיּוֹם הַזֶּה. וְאַחַר כֵּן בָּאוּ בָנֶיךָ לִדְבִיר בֵּיתֶךָ, וּפִנּוּ אֶת הֵיכָלֶךָ, וְטִהֲרוּ אֶת מִקְדָּשֶׁךָ, וְהִדְלִיקוּ נֵרוֹת בְּחַצְרוֹת קָדְשֶׁךָ, וְקָבְעוּ שְׁמוֹנַת יְמֵי חֲנֻכָּה אֵלּוּ, לְהוֹדוֹת וּלְהַלֵּל לְשִׁמְךָ הַגָּדוֹל.

Continue with וְעַל כֻּלָּם.

וְעַל כֻּלָּם, יִתְבָּרַךְ וְיִתְרוֹמַם שִׁמְךָ מַלְכֵּנוּ תָּמִיד לְעוֹלָם וָעֶד.

On שבת שובה *say* וּכְתֹב לְחַיִּים טוֹבִים כָּל בְּנֵי בְרִיתֶךָ.

וְכֹל הַחַיִּים יוֹדוּךָ סֶּלָה, וִיהַלְלוּ אֶת שִׁמְךָ בֶּאֱמֶת
הָאֵל יְשׁוּעָתֵנוּ וְעֶזְרָתֵנוּ סֶלָה.
בָּרוּךְ אַתָּה יהוה, הַטּוֹב שִׁמְךָ וּלְךָ נָאֶה לְהוֹדוֹת. (קהל: אָמֵן)

שלום

שָׁלוֹם רָב עַל יִשְׂרָאֵל עַמְּךָ תָּשִׂים לְעוֹלָם
כִּי אַתָּה הוּא מֶלֶךְ אָדוֹן לְכָל הַשָּׁלוֹם.
וְטוֹב בְּעֵינֶיךָ לְבָרֵךְ אֶת עַמְּךָ יִשְׂרָאֵל
בְּכָל עֵת וּבְכָל שָׁעָה בִּשְׁלוֹמֶךָ.

Reminder: Say "Amen" after the Leader recites the beracha.

Between Rosh Hashana and Yom Kippur the Leader continues with "May You remember," below.

Thank You, *Hashem*,
who blesses His Jewish people with peace.
(*Congregation:* Amen.)

Between Rosh Hashana and Yom Kippur say:

May You remember all of the Jewish people for life,
blessing, peace, and riches
and write us in the book of good life and peace.
Thank You, *Hashem*, who makes peace. (*Congregation:* Amen.)

The following is omitted on days when Tachanun is not said.

צִדְקָתְךָ Your Torah and judgements are based on truth.
Who can compare to You, our God?
Like the mighty mountains
that reach the highest heights, *Hashem*,
Your goodness has no limit.
You save man and animal with Your goodness.

צִדְקָתְךָ צֶדֶק לְעוֹלָם וְתוֹרָתְךָ אֱמֶת *Your Torah and judgements are based on truth.* Isn't it obvious that *Hashem*'s Torah and judgements are based on truth? This sentence is teaching us a deep message: Even in hard times, or when we feel that we do not have what we need or deserve, everything comes from *Hashem*. *Hashem* knows what is best and gives us exactly what we need. This is what it means to judge truthfully. Knowing this is the ultimate truth and will allow us to see *Hashem*'s truth everywhere.

Reminder: Say אָמֵן after the חזן recites the beracha.

On שבת שובה say the חזן continues with בְּסֵפֶר חַיִּים, below.

בָּרוּךְ אַתָּה יהוה, הַמְבָרֵךְ אֶת עַמּוֹ יִשְׂרָאֵל בַּשָּׁלוֹם.
(קהל: אָמֵן)

On שבת שובה say:

בְּסֵפֶר חַיִּים, בְּרָכָה וְשָׁלוֹם, וּפַרְנָסָה טוֹבָה
נִזָּכֵר וְנִכָּתֵב לְפָנֶיךָ
אֲנַחְנוּ וְכָל עַמְּךָ בֵּית יִשְׂרָאֵל
לְחַיִּים טוֹבִים וּלְשָׁלוֹם.
בָּרוּךְ אַתָּה יהוה, עוֹשֶׂה הַשָּׁלוֹם. (קהל: אָמֵן)

The following is omitted on days when תחנון is not said.

צִדְקָתְךָ צֶדֶק לְעוֹלָם
וְתוֹרָתְךָ אֱמֶת:

וְצִדְקָתְךָ אֱלֹהִים עַד־מָרוֹם
אֲשֶׁר־עָשִׂיתָ גְדֹלוֹת
אֱלֹהִים, מִי כָמוֹךָ:

צִדְקָתְךָ כְּהַרְרֵי־אֵל
מִשְׁפָּטֶיךָ תְּהוֹם רַבָּה
אָדָם וּבְהֵמָה תוֹשִׁיעַ יהוה:

KADDISH SHALEM

Leader: יִתְגַּדַּל May *Hashem* be recognized
as great and holy (*Congregation:* Amen)
in the world that He created.
May He establish His kingdom
during my lifetime and the lifetime of all Jews,
quickly and soon.
Let us say: "Amen" (*Congregation:* Amen).

Congregation: May we thank *Hashem* for ever and ever.
Leader: May we thank *Hashem* for ever and ever.

Leader: *Hashem* should be thanked, praised,
and honored (*Congregation:* He is blessed).
Hashem is beyond all the blessings,
songs, or praises that we could offer.
Let us say: "Amen" (*Congregation:* Amen).

May *Hashem* accept our prayers
and the prayers of all Jews.
Let us say: "Amen." (*Congregation:* Amen).

May *Hashem* give us, and all Jews,
peace and good life.
Let us say: "Amen." (*Congregation:* Amen).

The Leader takes three steps back before saying this line, bows to the left when saying "May," bows to the right when saying "the One," bows to the middle when saying "make peace for us":

May *Hashem*, the One
who makes peace in heaven,
make peace for us and for all Jews.
Let us say: "Amen." (*Congregation:* Amen).

קדיש שלם

חזן: יִתְגַּדַּל וְיִתְקַדַּשׁ שְׁמֵהּ רַבָּא (קהל: אָמֵן)
בְּעָלְמָא דִּי בְרָא כִרְעוּתֵהּ, וְיַמְלִיךְ מַלְכוּתֵהּ
בְּחַיֵּיכוֹן וּבְיוֹמֵיכוֹן וּבְחַיֵּי דְכָל בֵּית יִשְׂרָאֵל
בַּעֲגָלָא וּבִזְמַן קָרִיב, וְאִמְרוּ אָמֵן. (קהל: אָמֵן)

קהל יְהֵא שְׁמֵהּ רַבָּא מְבָרַךְ לְעָלַם וּלְעָלְמֵי עָלְמַיָּא.
חזן: יְהֵא שְׁמֵהּ רַבָּא מְבָרַךְ לְעָלַם וּלְעָלְמֵי עָלְמַיָּא.

חזן: יִתְבָּרַךְ וְיִשְׁתַּבַּח וְיִתְפָּאַר וְיִתְרוֹמַם וְיִתְנַשֵּׂא וְיִתְהַדָּר
וְיִתְעַלֶּה וְיִתְהַלָּל שְׁמֵהּ דְּקֻדְשָׁא בְּרִיךְ הוּא (קהל: בְּרִיךְ הוּא)
לְעֵלָּא מִן כָּל בִּרְכָתָא
/בשבת שובה: לְעֵלָּא לְעֵלָּא מִכָּל בִּרְכָתָא/
וְשִׁירָתָא, תֻּשְׁבְּחָתָא וְנֶחֱמָתָא
דַּאֲמִירָן בְּעָלְמָא, וְאִמְרוּ אָמֵן. (קהל: אָמֵן)

תִּתְקַבַּל צְלוֹתְהוֹן וּבָעוּתְהוֹן דְּכָל יִשְׂרָאֵל
קֳדָם אֲבוּהוֹן דִּי בִשְׁמַיָּא, וְאִמְרוּ אָמֵן. (קהל: אָמֵן)

יְהֵא שְׁלָמָא רַבָּא מִן שְׁמַיָּא
וְחַיִּים, עָלֵינוּ וְעַל כָּל יִשְׂרָאֵל, וְאִמְרוּ אָמֵן. (קהל: אָמֵן)

The חזן takes three steps back before saying this line, bows to the left when saying עֹשֶׂה, bows to the right when saying הוּא, bows to the middle when saying יַעֲשֶׂה שָׁלוֹם עָלֵינוּ:

עֹשֶׂה שָׁלוֹם /בשבת שובה: הַשָּׁלוֹם/ בִּמְרוֹמָיו
הוּא יַעֲשֶׂה שָׁלוֹם
עָלֵינוּ וְעַל כָּל יִשְׂרָאֵל, וְאִמְרוּ אָמֵן. (קהל: אָמֵן)

Stand while saying "It is our role."

עָלֵינוּ It is our role to praise You, *Hashem*,
Master of all and Creator of the world.
You have not made us like other nations of the world,
rather, You set the Jewish people apart
allowing us the opportunity to serve You.
(Other nations pray to gods that do not exist, while)
we bend our knees and bow in prayer
before the King of all kings, *Hashem*,
in order to give thanks.
Hashem created the heavens above and the land below.
Hashem sits on His awesome throne in heaven
as He, alone, is our God and ruler of the world.
We willingly accept Him as our King,
there is none else but Him.
As it says in the Torah,
"Today You should understand that *Hashem* is God
in the heavens above and on the earth below.
There is no other God but You."

Stand while saying עָלֵינוּ

עָלֵינוּ לְשַׁבֵּחַ לַאֲדוֹן הַכֹּל
לָתֵת גְּדֻלָּה לְיוֹצֵר בְּרֵאשִׁית
שֶׁלֹּא עָשָׂנוּ כְּגוֹיֵי הָאֲרָצוֹת
וְלֹא שָׂמָנוּ כְּמִשְׁפְּחוֹת הָאֲדָמָה
שֶׁלֹּא שָׂם חֶלְקֵנוּ כָּהֶם, וְגוֹרָלֵנוּ כְּכָל הֲמוֹנָם.
(שֶׁהֵם מִשְׁתַּחֲוִים לְהֶבֶל וָרִיק
וּמִתְפַּלְלִים אֶל אֵל לֹא יוֹשִׁיעַ.)
וַאֲנַחְנוּ כּוֹרְעִים וּמִשְׁתַּחֲוִים וּמוֹדִים
לִפְנֵי מֶלֶךְ מַלְכֵי הַמְּלָכִים, הַקָּדוֹשׁ בָּרוּךְ הוּא
שֶׁהוּא נוֹטֶה שָׁמַיִם וְיוֹסֵד אָרֶץ
וּמוֹשַׁב יְקָרוֹ בַּשָּׁמַיִם מִמַּעַל
וּשְׁכִינַת עֻזּוֹ בְּגָבְהֵי מְרוֹמִים.
הוּא אֱלֹהֵינוּ, אֵין עוֹד.
אֱמֶת מַלְכֵּנוּ, אֶפֶס זוּלָתוֹ
כַּכָּתוּב בְּתוֹרָתוֹ
וְיָדַעְתָּ הַיּוֹם וַהֲשֵׁבֹתָ אֶל־לְבָבֶךָ
כִּי יהוה הוּא הָאֱלֹהִים
בַּשָּׁמַיִם מִמַּעַל וְעַל־הָאָרֶץ מִתָּחַת
אֵין עוֹד:

Hashem,
we hope that all false gods
will be removed from the world
and everyone will soon turn to You alone
as the almighty God of the universe.
All the people of the world
will turn to You
and give honor.
They will accept You as their King,
and You will rule over them soon and forever.
For You are King of the world
and You will remain the ruling King forever.
As it says in Your Torah,
▸ "*Hashem* will be king over all the land.
On that day *Hashem* will be One and His name One."

עַל כֵּן נְקַוֶּה לְּךָ יהוה אֱלֹהֵינוּ
לִרְאוֹת מְהֵרָה בְּתִפְאֶרֶת עֻזֶּךָ
לְהַעֲבִיר גִּלּוּלִים מִן הָאָרֶץ
וְהָאֱלִילִים כָּרוֹת יִכָּרֵתוּן
לְתַקֵּן עוֹלָם בְּמַלְכוּת שַׁדַּי.
וְכָל בְּנֵי בָשָׂר יִקְרְאוּ בִשְׁמֶךָ
לְהַפְנוֹת אֵלֶיךָ כָּל רִשְׁעֵי אָרֶץ.
יַכִּירוּ וְיֵדְעוּ כָּל יוֹשְׁבֵי תֵבֵל
כִּי לְךָ תִּכְרַע כָּל בֶּרֶךְ
תִּשָּׁבַע כָּל לָשׁוֹן.
לְפָנֶיךָ יהוה אֱלֹהֵינוּ יִכְרְעוּ וְיִפֹּלוּ
וְלִכְבוֹד שִׁמְךָ יְקָר יִתֵּנוּ
וִיקַבְּלוּ כֻלָּם אֶת עֹל מַלְכוּתֶךָ
וְתִמְלֹךְ עֲלֵיהֶם מְהֵרָה לְעוֹלָם וָעֶד.
כִּי הַמַּלְכוּת שֶׁלְּךָ הִיא
וּלְעוֹלְמֵי עַד תִּמְלֹךְ בְּכָבוֹד
כַּכָּתוּב בְּתוֹרָתֶךָ
יהוה יִמְלֹךְ לְעֹלָם וָעֶד:
◄ וְנֶאֱמַר, וְהָיָה יהוה לְמֶלֶךְ עַל־כָּל־הָאָרֶץ
בַּיּוֹם הַהוּא יִהְיֶה יהוה אֶחָד וּשְׁמוֹ אֶחָד:

KADDISH YATOM

The following prayer, said by mourners, requires the presence of a minyan. A transliteration can be found on page 865.

Mourner: יִתְגַּדַּל May *Hashem* be recognized
as great and holy (*Congregation:* Amen)
in the world that He created.
May He establish His kingdom
during my lifetime
and the lifetime of all Jews,
quickly and soon.
Let us say: "Amen" (*Congregation:* Amen).

Congregation: May we thank *Hashem* for ever and ever.
Mourner: May we thank *Hashem* for ever and ever.

Mourner: *Hashem* should be thanked, praised,
and honored (*Congregation:* He is blessed).
Hashem is beyond all the blessings,
songs, or praises
that we could offer.
Let us say: "Amen" (*Congregation:* Amen).

May *Hashem* give us, and all Jews,
peace and good life.
Let us say: "Amen." (*Congregation:* Amen).

The mourner takes three steps back before saying this line, bows to the left when saying "May," bows to the right when saying "the One," bows to the middle when saying "make peace for us":

May *Hashem*, the One
who makes peace in heaven,
make peace for us and for all Jews.
Let us say: "Amen." (*Congregation:* Amen).

קדיש יתום

The following prayer, said by mourners, requires the presence of a מנין*.*
A transliteration can be found on page 865.

אבל: יִתְגַּדַּל וְיִתְקַדַּשׁ שְׁמֵהּ רַבָּא (קהל: אָמֵן)
בְּעָלְמָא דִּי בְרָא כִרְעוּתֵהּ, וְיַמְלִיךְ מַלְכוּתֵהּ
בְּחַיֵּיכוֹן וּבְיוֹמֵיכוֹן וּבְחַיֵּי דְכָל בֵּית יִשְׂרָאֵל
בַּעֲגָלָא וּבִזְמַן קָרִיב, וְאִמְרוּ אָמֵן. (קהל: אָמֵן)

קהל יְהֵא שְׁמֵהּ רַבָּא מְבָרַךְ לְעָלַם וּלְעָלְמֵי עָלְמַיָּא.
אבל: יְהֵא שְׁמֵהּ רַבָּא מְבָרַךְ לְעָלַם וּלְעָלְמֵי עָלְמַיָּא.

אבל: יִתְבָּרַךְ וְיִשְׁתַּבַּח וְיִתְפָּאַר
וְיִתְרוֹמַם וְיִתְנַשֵּׂא וְיִתְהַדָּר וְיִתְעַלֶּה וְיִתְהַלָּל
שְׁמֵהּ דְּקֻדְשָׁא בְּרִיךְ הוּא (קהל: בְּרִיךְ הוּא)
לְעֵלָּא מִן כָּל בִּרְכָתָא
/בשבת שובה: לְעֵלָּא לְעֵלָּא מִכָּל בִּרְכָתָא/
וְשִׁירָתָא, תֻּשְׁבְּחָתָא וְנֶחֱמָתָא
דַּאֲמִירָן בְּעָלְמָא, וְאִמְרוּ אָמֵן. (קהל: אָמֵן)

יְהֵא שְׁלָמָא רַבָּא מִן שְׁמַיָּא
וְחַיִּים, עָלֵינוּ וְעַל כָּל יִשְׂרָאֵל, וְאִמְרוּ אָמֵן. (קהל: אָמֵן)

The mourner takes three steps back before saying this line, bows to the left when saying עֹשֶׂה*, bows to the right when saying* הוּא*, bows to the middle when saying* יַעֲשֶׂה שָׁלוֹם עָלֵינוּ*:*

עֹשֶׂה שָׁלוֹם /בשבת שובה: הַשָּׁלוֹם/ בִּמְרוֹמָיו
הוּא יַעֲשֶׂה שָׁלוֹם עָלֵינוּ
וְעַל כָּל יִשְׂרָאֵל, וְאִמְרוּ אָמֵן. (קהל: אָמֵן)

Ma'ariv for Motza'ei Shabbat

The service begins with Ma'ariv for Weekdays on page 278. After the Amida, the Leader says Half Kaddish and the congregation continues below:

וִיהִי נֹעַם May *Hashem* act kindly to us
and allow us to benefit from the work of our hands.

יֹשֵׁב Those who seek *Hashem*'s shelter
will be protected by Him.
Hashem will save you from a trap and from disease.
He will give you shelter and shield you.
Do not fear the dark of night,
an attack during the day, or a plague.
Those around you who do not fear *Hashem*
might be harmed, but you will be protected,
because Hashe*m* is our protector.
Hashem will send His angels to protect you
wherever you go;
they will lift you up so that you will not stumble.
Those close to *Hashem* will be protected
from a snake or lion attack.
When you call to *Hashem* He will answer you
and be with you in your time of need.
▸ *Hashem* will give those who are close to Him
long life filled with His protection.
Hashem will give those who are close to Him
long life filled with His protection.

מעריב למוצאי שבת

The service begins with מעריב לחול *on page 279.*
After the עמידה, *the* חזן *says* חצי קדיש *and the* קהל *continues below:*

וִיהִי נֹעַם אֲדֹנָי אֱלֹהֵינוּ עָלֵינוּ וּמַעֲשֵׂה יָדֵינוּ כּוֹנְנָה עָלֵינוּ
וּמַעֲשֵׂה יָדֵינוּ כּוֹנְנֵהוּ:

יֹשֵׁב בְּסֵתֶר עֶלְיוֹן, בְּצֵל שַׁדַּי יִתְלוֹנָן: אֹמַר לַיהוה מַחְסִי
וּמְצוּדָתִי, אֱלֹהַי אֶבְטַח־בּוֹ: כִּי הוּא יַצִּילְךָ מִפַּח יָקוּשׁ,
מִדֶּבֶר הַוּוֹת: בְּאֶבְרָתוֹ יָסֶךְ לָךְ, וְתַחַת־כְּנָפָיו תֶּחְסֶה, צִנָּה
וְסֹחֵרָה אֲמִתּוֹ: לֹא־תִירָא מִפַּחַד לָיְלָה, מֵחֵץ יָעוּף יוֹמָם:
מִדֶּבֶר בָּאֹפֶל יַהֲלֹךְ, מִקֶּטֶב יָשׁוּד צָהֳרָיִם: יִפֹּל מִצִּדְּךָ
אֶלֶף, וּרְבָבָה מִימִינֶךָ, אֵלֶיךָ לֹא יִגָּשׁ: רַק בְּעֵינֶיךָ תַבִּיט,
וְשִׁלֻּמַת רְשָׁעִים תִּרְאֶה: כִּי־אַתָּה יהוה מַחְסִי, עֶלְיוֹן שַׂמְתָּ
מְעוֹנֶךָ: לֹא־תְאֻנֶּה אֵלֶיךָ רָעָה, וְנֶגַע לֹא־יִקְרַב בְּאָהֳלֶךָ:
כִּי מַלְאָכָיו יְצַוֶּה־לָּךְ, לִשְׁמָרְךָ בְּכָל־דְּרָכֶיךָ: עַל־כַּפַּיִם
יִשָּׂאוּנְךָ, פֶּן־תִּגֹּף בָּאֶבֶן רַגְלֶךָ: עַל־שַׁחַל וָפֶתֶן תִּדְרֹךְ,
תִּרְמֹס כְּפִיר וְתַנִּין: כִּי בִי חָשַׁק וַאֲפַלְּטֵהוּ, אֲשַׂגְּבֵהוּ כִּי־
יָדַע שְׁמִי: יִקְרָאֵנִי וְאֶעֱנֵהוּ, עִמּוֹ אָנֹכִי בְצָרָה, אֲחַלְּצֵהוּ
וַאֲכַבְּדֵהוּ: ◂ אֹרֶךְ יָמִים אַשְׂבִּיעֵהוּ, וְאַרְאֵהוּ בִּישׁוּעָתִי:
אֹרֶךְ יָמִים אַשְׂבִּיעֵהוּ, וְאַרְאֵהוּ בִּישׁוּעָתִי:

▸ וְאַתָּה קָדוֹשׁ *Hashem,*
You are holy
and the Jewish people praise You.
The angels will call to each other
saying:

All say aloud:

"Holy, holy, holy is *Hashem*:
the world is filled with His honor."

The angels then say to each other:
"Heaven is holy because *Hashem* lives there,
and the earth is holy because *Hashem* created it.
The entire world is filled with *Hashem*'s holiness."

▸ When a wind lifted the prophet Yechezkel,
he heard the angels praising *Hashem*,
saying,

All say aloud:

"Blessed is the honor of *Hashem*
who lives in heaven!"

When a wind lifted the prophet Yechezkel,
he heard the angels praising *Hashem*, saying,
"Blessed is the honor of *Hashem* who lives in heaven."

All say aloud:

Hashem shall reign as King forever!

Hashem's kingdom is established forever and ever.

◂ וְאַתָּה קָדוֹשׁ יוֹשֵׁב תְּהִלּוֹת יִשְׂרָאֵל:
וְקָרָא זֶה אֶל־זֶה וְאָמַר

All say aloud:

קָדוֹשׁ, קָדוֹשׁ, קָדוֹשׁ, יהוה צְבָאוֹת
מְלֹא כָל־הָאָרֶץ כְּבוֹדוֹ:

וּמְקַבְּלִין דֵּין מִן דֵּין וְאָמְרִין
קַדִּישׁ בִּשְׁמֵי מְרוֹמָא עִלָּאָה בֵּית שְׁכִינְתֵּהּ
קַדִּישׁ עַל אַרְעָא עוֹבַד גְּבוּרְתֵּהּ
קַדִּישׁ לְעָלַם וּלְעָלְמֵי עָלְמַיָּא, יהוה צְבָאוֹת
מַלְיָא כָל אַרְעָא זִיו יְקָרֵהּ.

◂ וַתִּשָּׂאֵנִי רוּחַ, וָאֶשְׁמַע אַחֲרַי קוֹל רַעַשׁ גָּדוֹל

All say aloud:

בָּרוּךְ כְּבוֹד־יהוה מִמְּקוֹמוֹ:

וּנְטָלַתְנִי רוּחָא, וּשְׁמָעִית בַּתְרַי קָל זִיעַ סַגִּיא
דִּמְשַׁבְּחִין וְאָמְרִין
בְּרִיךְ יְקָרָא דַיהוה מֵאֲתַר בֵּית שְׁכִינְתֵּהּ.

All say aloud:

יהוה יִמְלֹךְ לְעֹלָם וָעֶד:

יהוה מַלְכוּתֵהּ קָאֵם לְעָלַם וּלְעָלְמֵי עָלְמַיָּא.

יהוה *Hashem,* God of Avraham, Yitzchak, and Yaakov,
please allow Your Jewish people
to keep these thoughts in mind,
and help direct their hearts towards You.
You are merciful and You show Your kindness
by forgiving our sins.
Your Torah is true and Your righteousness lasts forever.
Please treat us with loyalty and kindness
as You promised our forefathers.
Hashem, You are our protector; You are always with us.
Praiseworthy is the person who trusts in You.
May *Hashem,* the King,
answer us on the day that we call out to Him.

בָּרוּךְ Thank You, *Hashem,* for giving us the Torah,
allowing us to honor You, and providing us the
opportunity
to live on in the world-to-come.
May *Hashem* open our hearts through studying His Torah,
and allow us to serve Him wholeheartedly
with love and fear.

יְהִי רָצוֹן May *Hashem,*
our God and God of our ancestors,
allow us to keep His *mitzvot* in this world
so that we can gain the blessings promised to us
in the times of *Mashiach* and in the world-to-come.
I will thank *Hashem* forever.
‣ Trust in *Hashem,*
for *Hashem* is our protector.

יהוה אֱלֹהֵי אַבְרָהָם יִצְחָק וְיִשְׂרָאֵל אֲבֹתֵינוּ, שָׁמְרָה־זֹּאת לְעוֹלָם לְיֵצֶר מַחְשְׁבוֹת לְבַב עַמֶּךָ, וְהָכֵן לְבָבָם אֵלֶיךָ: וְהוּא רַחוּם יְכַפֵּר עָוֹן וְלֹא־יַשְׁחִית, וְהִרְבָּה לְהָשִׁיב אַפּוֹ, וְלֹא־יָעִיר כָּל־חֲמָתוֹ: כִּי־אַתָּה אֲדֹנָי טוֹב וְסַלָּח, וְרַב־חֶסֶד לְכָל־קֹרְאֶיךָ: צִדְקָתְךָ צֶדֶק לְעוֹלָם וְתוֹרָתְךָ אֱמֶת: תִּתֵּן אֱמֶת לְיַעֲקֹב, חֶסֶד לְאַבְרָהָם, אֲשֶׁר־נִשְׁבַּעְתָּ לַאֲבֹתֵינוּ מִימֵי קֶדֶם: בָּרוּךְ אֲדֹנָי יוֹם יוֹם יַעֲמָס־לָנוּ, הָאֵל יְשׁוּעָתֵנוּ סֶלָה: יהוה צְבָאוֹת עִמָּנוּ, מִשְׂגָּב לָנוּ אֱלֹהֵי יַעֲקֹב סֶלָה: יהוה צְבָאוֹת, אַשְׁרֵי אָדָם בֹּטֵחַ בָּךְ: יהוה הוֹשִׁיעָה, הַמֶּלֶךְ יַעֲנֵנוּ בְיוֹם־קָרְאֵנוּ:

בָּרוּךְ הוּא אֱלֹהֵינוּ שֶׁבְּרָאָנוּ לִכְבוֹדוֹ, וְהִבְדִּילָנוּ מִן הַתּוֹעִים, וְנָתַן לָנוּ תּוֹרַת אֱמֶת, וְחַיֵּי עוֹלָם נָטַע בְּתוֹכֵנוּ. הוּא יִפְתַּח לִבֵּנוּ בְּתוֹרָתוֹ, וְיָשֵׂם בְּלִבֵּנוּ אַהֲבָתוֹ וְיִרְאָתוֹ וְלַעֲשׂוֹת רְצוֹנוֹ וּלְעָבְדוֹ בְּלֵבָב שָׁלֵם, לְמַעַן לֹא נִיגַע לָרִיק וְלֹא נֵלֵד לַבֶּהָלָה.

יְהִי רָצוֹן מִלְּפָנֶיךָ יהוה אֱלֹהֵינוּ וֵאלֹהֵי אֲבוֹתֵינוּ, שֶׁנִּשְׁמֹר חֻקֶּיךָ בָּעוֹלָם הַזֶּה, וְנִזְכֶּה וְנִחְיֶה וְנִרְאֶה וְנִירַשׁ טוֹבָה וּבְרָכָה, לִשְׁנֵי יְמוֹת הַמָּשִׁיחַ וּלְחַיֵּי הָעוֹלָם הַבָּא. לְמַעַן יְזַמֶּרְךָ כָבוֹד וְלֹא יִדֹּם, יהוה אֱלֹהַי, לְעוֹלָם אוֹדֶךָּ: בָּרוּךְ הַגֶּבֶר אֲשֶׁר יִבְטַח בַּיהוה, וְהָיָה יהוה מִבְטַחוֹ: בִּטְחוּ בַיהוה עֲדֵי־עַד, כִּי בְּיָהּ יהוה צוּר עוֹלָמִים: ‹ וְיִבְטְחוּ בְךָ יוֹדְעֵי שְׁמֶךָ, כִּי לֹא־עָזַבְתָּ דֹרְשֶׁיךָ, יהוה: יהוה חָפֵץ לְמַעַן צִדְקוֹ, יַגְדִּיל תּוֹרָה וְיַאְדִּיר:

KADDISH SHALEM

Leader: יִתְגַּדַּל May *Hashem* be recognized
as great and holy (*Congregation:* Amen)
in the world that He created.
May He establish His kingdom
during my lifetime and the lifetime of all Jews,
quickly and soon.
Let us say: "Amen" (*Congregation:* Amen).

Congregation: May we thank *Hashem* for ever and ever.
Leader: May we thank *Hashem* for ever and ever.

Leader: *Hashem* should be thanked, praised,
and honored (*Congregation:* He is blessed).
Hashem is beyond all the blessings,
songs, or praises that we could offer.
Let us say: "Amen" (*Congregation:* Amen).

May *Hashem* accept our prayers
and the prayers of all Jews.
Let us say: "Amen." (*Congregation:* Amen).

May *Hashem* give us, and all Jews,
peace and good life.
Let us say: "Amen." (*Congregation:* Amen).

The Leader takes three steps back before saying this line, bows to the left when saying "May," bows to the right when saying "the One," bows to the middle when saying "make peace for us":

May *Hashem*, the One
who makes peace in heaven,
make peace for us and for all Jews.
Let us say: "Amen." (*Congregation:* Amen).

קדיש שלם

חזן: יִתְגַּדַּל וְיִתְקַדַּשׁ שְׁמֵהּ רַבָּא (קהל: אָמֵן)
בְּעָלְמָא דִּי בְרָא כִרְעוּתֵהּ, וְיַמְלִיךְ מַלְכוּתֵהּ
בְּחַיֵּיכוֹן וּבְיוֹמֵיכוֹן וּבְחַיֵּי דְכָל בֵּית יִשְׂרָאֵל
בַּעֲגָלָא וּבִזְמַן קָרִיב, וְאִמְרוּ אָמֵן. (קהל: אָמֵן)

קהל יְהֵא שְׁמֵהּ רַבָּא מְבָרַךְ לְעָלַם וּלְעָלְמֵי עָלְמַיָּא.
חזן: יְהֵא שְׁמֵהּ רַבָּא מְבָרַךְ לְעָלַם וּלְעָלְמֵי עָלְמַיָּא.

חזן: יִתְבָּרַךְ וְיִשְׁתַּבַּח וְיִתְפָּאַר וְיִתְרוֹמַם וְיִתְנַשֵּׂא וְיִתְהַדָּר
וְיִתְעַלֶּה וְיִתְהַלָּל שְׁמֵהּ דְּקֻדְשָׁא בְּרִיךְ הוּא (קהל: בְּרִיךְ הוּא)
לְעֵלָּא מִן כָּל בִּרְכָתָא
/בעשרת ימי תשובה: לְעֵלָּא לְעֵלָּא מִכָּל בִּרְכָתָא/
וְשִׁירָתָא, תֻּשְׁבְּחָתָא וְנֶחֱמָתָא
דַּאֲמִירָן בְּעָלְמָא, וְאִמְרוּ אָמֵן. (קהל: אָמֵן)

תִּתְקַבַּל צְלוֹתְהוֹן וּבָעוּתְהוֹן דְּכָל יִשְׂרָאֵל
קֳדָם אֲבוּהוֹן דִּי בִשְׁמַיָּא, וְאִמְרוּ אָמֵן. (קהל: אָמֵן)

יְהֵא שְׁלָמָא רַבָּא מִן שְׁמַיָּא
וְחַיִּים, עָלֵינוּ וְעַל כָּל יִשְׂרָאֵל, וְאִמְרוּ אָמֵן. (קהל: אָמֵן)

The חזן *takes three steps back before saying this line, bows to the left when saying* עֹשֶׂה*, bows to the right when saying* הוּא*, bows to the middle when saying* יַעֲשֶׂה שָׁלוֹם עָלֵינוּ*:*

עֹשֶׂה שָׁלוֹם /בעשרת ימי תשובה: הַשָּׁלוֹם/ בִּמְרוֹמָיו
הוּא יַעֲשֶׂה שָׁלוֹם
עָלֵינוּ וְעַל כָּל יִשְׂרָאֵל, וְאִמְרוּ אָמֵן. (קהל: אָמֵן)

Between Pesach and Shavuot the Omer is counted at this point on page 328.
On Chanuka, the candles are lit at this point.

Stand while saying "It is our role."

עָלֵינוּ It is our role to praise You, *Hashem*,
Master of all and Creator of the world.
You have not made us like other nations of the world,
rather, You set the Jewish people apart
allowing us the opportunity to serve You.
(Other nations pray to gods that do not exist,
while)
we bend our knees and bow in prayer
before the King of all kings, *Hashem*,
in order to give thanks.
Hashem created the heavens above and the land below.
Hashem sits on His awesome throne in heaven
as He, alone, is our God and ruler of the world.
We willingly accept Him as our King,
there is none else but Him.
As it says in the Torah,
"Today You should understand that *Hashem* is God
in the heavens above and on the earth below.
There is no other God but You."

Between פסח and שבועות the עומר is counted at this point on page 329.
On חנוכה, the candles are lit at this point.

Stand while saying עָלֵינוּ.

עָלֵינוּ לְשַׁבֵּחַ לַאֲדוֹן הַכֹּל
לָתֵת גְּדֻלָּה לְיוֹצֵר בְּרֵאשִׁית
שֶׁלֹּא עָשָׂנוּ כְּגוֹיֵי הָאֲרָצוֹת
וְלֹא שָׂמָנוּ כְּמִשְׁפְּחוֹת הָאֲדָמָה
שֶׁלֹּא שָׂם חֶלְקֵנוּ כָּהֶם, וְגוֹרָלֵנוּ כְּכָל הֲמוֹנָם.
(שֶׁהֵם מִשְׁתַּחֲוִים לְהֶבֶל וָרִיק
וּמִתְפַּלְּלִים אֶל אֵל לֹא יוֹשִׁיעַ.)

וַאֲנַחְנוּ כּוֹרְעִים וּמִשְׁתַּחֲוִים וּמוֹדִים
לִפְנֵי מֶלֶךְ מַלְכֵי הַמְּלָכִים, הַקָּדוֹשׁ בָּרוּךְ הוּא
שֶׁהוּא נוֹטֶה שָׁמַיִם וְיוֹסֵד אָרֶץ
וּמוֹשַׁב יְקָרוֹ בַּשָּׁמַיִם מִמַּעַל
וּשְׁכִינַת עֻזּוֹ בְּגָבְהֵי מְרוֹמִים.
הוּא אֱלֹהֵינוּ, אֵין עוֹד.
אֱמֶת מַלְכֵּנוּ, אֶפֶס זוּלָתוֹ
כַּכָּתוּב בְּתוֹרָתוֹ, וְיָדַעְתָּ הַיּוֹם וַהֲשֵׁבֹתָ אֶל־לְבָבֶךָ
כִּי יהוה הוּא הָאֱלֹהִים
בַּשָּׁמַיִם מִמַּעַל וְעַל־הָאָרֶץ מִתָּחַת
אֵין עוֹד:

Hashem,
we hope that all false gods
will be removed from the world
and everyone will soon turn to You alone
as the almighty God of the universe.
All the people of the world
will turn to You
and give honor.
They will accept You as their King,
and You will rule over them soon and forever.
For You are King of the world
and You will remain the ruling King forever.
As it says in Your Torah,
▸ "*Hashem* will be king over all the land.
On that day *Hashem* will be One and His name One."

עַל כֵּן נְקַוֶּה לְּךָ יהוה אֱלֹהֵינוּ
לִרְאוֹת מְהֵרָה בְּתִפְאֶרֶת עֻזֶּךָ
לְהַעֲבִיר גִּלּוּלִים מִן הָאָרֶץ
וְהָאֱלִילִים כָּרוֹת יִכָּרֵתוּן
לְתַקֵּן עוֹלָם בְּמַלְכוּת שַׁדַּי.
וְכָל בְּנֵי בָשָׂר יִקְרְאוּ בִשְׁמֶךָ
לְהַפְנוֹת אֵלֶיךָ כָּל רִשְׁעֵי אָרֶץ.
יַכִּירוּ וְיֵדְעוּ כָּל יוֹשְׁבֵי תֵבֵל
כִּי לְךָ תִּכְרַע כָּל בֶּרֶךְ
תִּשָּׁבַע כָּל לָשׁוֹן.
לְפָנֶיךָ יהוה אֱלֹהֵינוּ יִכְרְעוּ וְיִפֹּלוּ
וְלִכְבוֹד שִׁמְךָ יְקָר יִתֵּנוּ
וִיקַבְּלוּ כֻלָּם אֶת עֹל מַלְכוּתֶךָ
וְתִמְלֹךְ עֲלֵיהֶם מְהֵרָה לְעוֹלָם וָעֶד.
כִּי הַמַּלְכוּת שֶׁלְּךָ הִיא
וּלְעוֹלְמֵי עַד תִּמְלֹךְ בְּכָבוֹד
כַּכָּתוּב בְּתוֹרָתֶךָ
יהוה יִמְלֹךְ לְעֹלָם וָעֶד:
◂ וְנֶאֱמַר, וְהָיָה יהוה לְמֶלֶךְ עַל־כָּל־הָאָרֶץ
בַּיּוֹם הַהוּא יִהְיֶה יהוה אֶחָד וּשְׁמוֹ אֶחָד:

KADDISH YATOM

The following prayer, said by mourners, requires the presence of a minyan. A transliteration can be found on page 865.

Mourner: יִתְגַּדַּל May *Hashem* be recognized
as great and holy (*Congregation:* Amen)
in the world that He created.
May He establish His kingdom
during my lifetime
and the lifetime of all Jews,
quickly and soon.
Let us say: "Amen" (*Congregation:* Amen).

Congregation: May we thank *Hashem* for ever and ever.
Mourner: May we thank *Hashem* for ever and ever.

Mourner: *Hashem* should be thanked, praised,
and honored (*Congregation:* He is blessed).
Hashem is beyond all the blessings,
songs, or praises
that we could offer.
Let us say: "Amen" (*Congregation:* Amen).

May *Hashem* give us, and all Jews,
peace and good life.
Let us say: "Amen." (*Congregation:* Amen).

The mourner takes three steps back before saying this line, bows to the left when saying "May," bows to the right when saying "the One," bows to the middle when saying "make peace for us":

May *Hashem*, the One
who makes peace in heaven,
make peace for us and for all Jews.
Let us say: "Amen." (*Congregation:* Amen).

קדיש יתום

The following prayer, said by mourners, requires the presence of a מנין.
A transliteration can be found on page 865.

אבל: יִתְגַּדַּל וְיִתְקַדַּשׁ שְׁמֵהּ רַבָּא (קהל: אָמֵן)
בְּעָלְמָא דִּי בְרָא כִרְעוּתֵהּ, וְיַמְלִיךְ מַלְכוּתֵהּ
בְּחַיֵּיכוֹן וּבְיוֹמֵיכוֹן וּבְחַיֵּי דְכָל בֵּית יִשְׂרָאֵל
בַּעֲגָלָא וּבִזְמַן קָרִיב, וְאִמְרוּ אָמֵן. (קהל: אָמֵן)

קהל יְהֵא שְׁמֵהּ רַבָּא מְבָרַךְ לְעָלַם וּלְעָלְמֵי עָלְמַיָּא.
אבל: יְהֵא שְׁמֵהּ רַבָּא מְבָרַךְ לְעָלַם וּלְעָלְמֵי עָלְמַיָּא.

אבל: יִתְבָּרַךְ וְיִשְׁתַּבַּח וְיִתְפָּאַר
וְיִתְרוֹמַם וְיִתְנַשֵּׂא וְיִתְהַדָּר וְיִתְעַלֶּה וְיִתְהַלָּל
שְׁמֵהּ דְּקֻדְשָׁא בְּרִיךְ הוּא (קהל: בְּרִיךְ הוּא)
לְעֵלָּא מִן כָּל בִּרְכָתָא
/בעשרת ימי תשובה: לְעֵלָּא לְעֵלָּא מִכָּל בִּרְכָתָא/
וְשִׁירָתָא, תֻּשְׁבְּחָתָא וְנֶחֱמָתָא
דַּאֲמִירָן בְּעָלְמָא, וְאִמְרוּ אָמֵן. (קהל: אָמֵן)

יְהֵא שְׁלָמָא רַבָּא מִן שְׁמַיָּא
וְחַיִּים, עָלֵינוּ וְעַל כָּל יִשְׂרָאֵל, וְאִמְרוּ אָמֵן. (קהל: אָמֵן)

The mourner takes three steps back before saying this line, bows to the left when saying עֹשֶׂה*, bows to the right when saying* הוּא*, bows to the middle when saying* יַעֲשֶׂה שָׁלוֹם עָלֵינוּ:

עֹשֶׂה שָׁלוֹם /בעשרת ימי תשובה: הַשָּׁלוֹם/ בִּמְרוֹמָיו
הוּא יַעֲשֶׂה שָׁלוֹם עָלֵינוּ
וְעַל כָּל יִשְׂרָאֵל, וְאִמְרוּ אָמֵן. (קהל: אָמֵן)

From the second day of Rosh Chodesh Elul until Shemini Atzeret add the following:

לְדָוִד David HaMelech wrote:
I have no fear because *Hashem* protects me
and brings light to my darkness.
When enemies or even armies attack,
I am not afraid
as I trust that *Hashem* will defeat them.
The only thing that I ask of *Hashem*
is to see the *Beit HaMikdash* built
and be able to serve Him there.
Hashem is my protector;
He will take me in and hide me from my enemies.
When I feel safe, I will sing songs of praise to *Hashem.*
Hashem, listen to my voice when I call for help
and please answer me.
Do not ignore or hide from me, when You are angry.
My heart knows
it is only You to whom I can call for help.
Hashem, help us learn how to make the right choices
and not make mistakes.
▸ I trust in *Hashem,*
I hope for His help at all times;
He gives me strength and courage.

Kaddish Yatom (previous page)

From the second day of ראש חודש אלול *until* שמיני עצרת *add the following:*

לְדָוִד, יהוה אוֹרִי וְיִשְׁעִי, מִמִּי אִירָא, יהוה מָעוֹז־חַיַּי, מִמִּי אֶפְחָד: בִּקְרֹב עָלַי מְרֵעִים לֶאֱכֹל אֶת־בְּשָׂרִי, צָרַי וְאֹיְבַי לִי, הֵמָּה כָשְׁלוּ וְנָפָלוּ: אִם־תַּחֲנֶה עָלַי מַחֲנֶה, לֹא־יִירָא לִבִּי, אִם־תָּקוּם עָלַי מִלְחָמָה, בְּזֹאת אֲנִי בוֹטֵחַ: אַחַת שָׁאַלְתִּי מֵאֵת־יהוה, אוֹתָהּ אֲבַקֵּשׁ, שִׁבְתִּי בְּבֵית־יהוה כָּל־יְמֵי חַיַּי, לַחֲזוֹת בְּנֹעַם־יהוה, וּלְבַקֵּר בְּהֵיכָלוֹ: כִּי יִצְפְּנֵנִי בְּסֻכֹּה בְּיוֹם רָעָה, יַסְתִּרֵנִי בְּסֵתֶר אָהֳלוֹ, בְּצוּר יְרוֹמְמֵנִי: וְעַתָּה יָרוּם רֹאשִׁי עַל אֹיְבַי סְבִיבוֹתַי, וְאֶזְבְּחָה בְאָהֳלוֹ זִבְחֵי תְרוּעָה, אָשִׁירָה וַאֲזַמְּרָה לַיהוה: שְׁמַע־יהוה קוֹלִי אֶקְרָא, וְחָנֵּנִי וַעֲנֵנִי: לְךָ אָמַר לִבִּי בַּקְּשׁוּ פָנָי, אֶת־פָּנֶיךָ יהוה אֲבַקֵּשׁ: אַל־תַּסְתֵּר פָּנֶיךָ מִמֶּנִּי, אַל תַּט־בְּאַף עַבְדֶּךָ, עֶזְרָתִי הָיִיתָ, אַל־תִּטְּשֵׁנִי וְאַל־תַּעַזְבֵנִי, אֱלֹהֵי יִשְׁעִי: כִּי־אָבִי וְאִמִּי עֲזָבוּנִי, וַיהוה יַאַסְפֵנִי: הוֹרֵנִי יהוה דַּרְכֶּךָ, וּנְחֵנִי בְּאֹרַח מִישׁוֹר, לְמַעַן שׁוֹרְרָי: אַל־תִּתְּנֵנִי בְּנֶפֶשׁ צָרָי, כִּי קָמוּ־בִי עֵדֵי־שֶׁקֶר, וִיפֵחַ חָמָס: ‹ לוּלֵא הֶאֱמַנְתִּי לִרְאוֹת בְּטוּב־יהוה בְּאֶרֶץ חַיִּים: קַוֵּה אֶל־יהוה, חֲזַק וְיַאֲמֵץ לִבֶּךָ, וְקַוֵּה אֶל־יהוה:

קדיש יתום (*previous page*)

KIDDUSH LEVANA

Kiddush Levana is said between the third day and the middle day of each Hebrew month. If possible, it should be said on Motza'ei Shabbat, under the open sky, and with a minyan.

הַלְלוּיָהּ Halleluya!
Heaven and all of *Hashem*'s heavenly creations praise Him, including the:
Angels,
Sun, moon, and stars,
Sky and all that is above it.
The earth and all of *Hashem*'s earthly creations praise Him.

כִּי־אֶרְאֶה *Hashem*,
when I see the heaven, moon, and stars
that You created,
I am amazed that You care about man.

Look at the moon, then say:

בָּרוּךְ Thank You, *Hashem*,
our God, King of the world
who created the heavens with His words.
You gave nature laws and set times to fulfill Your will.
You renew the moon each month.
The moon grows from small to full,
as a crown for Your Jewish people.
Like the moon we also grow
and thank *Hashem*, our Creator.
We thank You, *Hashem*,
who gives us new months.

קידוש לבנה

קידוש לבנה is said between the third day and the middle day of each Hebrew month. If possible, it should be said on מוצאי שבת, under the open sky, and with a מנין.

הַלְלוּיָהּ, הַלְלוּ אֶת־יהוה מִן־הַשָּׁמַיִם
הַלְלוּהוּ בַּמְּרוֹמִים:
הַלְלוּהוּ כָל־מַלְאָכָיו, הַלְלוּהוּ כָּל־צְבָאָו:
הַלְלוּהוּ שֶׁמֶשׁ וְיָרֵחַ, הַלְלוּהוּ כָּל־כּוֹכְבֵי אוֹר:
הַלְלוּהוּ שְׁמֵי הַשָּׁמָיִם, וְהַמַּיִם אֲשֶׁר מֵעַל הַשָּׁמָיִם:
יְהַלְלוּ אֶת־שֵׁם יהוה, כִּי הוּא צִוָּה וְנִבְרָאוּ:
וַיַּעֲמִידֵם לָעַד לְעוֹלָם, חָק־נָתַן וְלֹא יַעֲבוֹר:

כִּי־אֶרְאֶה שָׁמֶיךָ מַעֲשֵׂה אֶצְבְּעֹתֶיךָ
יָרֵחַ וְכוֹכָבִים אֲשֶׁר כּוֹנָנְתָּה:
מָה־אֱנוֹשׁ כִּי־תִזְכְּרֶנּוּ, וּבֶן־אָדָם כִּי תִפְקְדֶנּוּ:

Look at the moon, then say:

בָּרוּךְ אַתָּה יהוה אֱלֹהֵינוּ מֶלֶךְ הָעוֹלָם, אֲשֶׁר בְּמַאֲמָרוֹ בָּרָא שְׁחָקִים, וּבְרוּחַ פִּיו כָּל צְבָאָם, חֹק וּזְמַן נָתַן לָהֶם שֶׁלֹּא יְשַׁנּוּ אֶת תַּפְקִידָם. שָׂשִׂים וּשְׂמֵחִים לַעֲשׂוֹת רְצוֹן קוֹנָם, פּוֹעֵל אֱמֶת שֶׁפְּעֻלָּתוֹ אֱמֶת. וְלַלְּבָנָה אָמַר שֶׁתִּתְחַדֵּשׁ, עֲטֶרֶת תִּפְאֶרֶת לַעֲמוּסֵי בָטֶן, שֶׁהֵם עֲתִידִים לְהִתְחַדֵּשׁ כְּמוֹתָהּ וּלְפָאֵר לְיוֹצְרָם עַל שֵׁם כְּבוֹד מַלְכוּתוֹ.
בָּרוּךְ אַתָּה יהוה, מְחַדֵּשׁ חֳדָשִׁים.

בָּרוּךְ We thank the One who formed the moon, who made the moon, who owns the moon, and who created the moon.

We thank the One who formed the moon, who made the moon, who owns the moon, and who created the moon.

We thank the One who formed the moon, who made the moon, who owns the moon, and who created the moon.

While standing on toes.

כְּשֵׁם Just as I try to reach the moon while I dance but will never be able to, so too may our enemies never be able to reach us.

Just as I try to reach the moon while I dance but will never be able to, so too may our enemies never be able to reach us.

Just as I try to reach the moon while I dance but will never be able to, so too may our enemies never be able to reach us.

תִּפֹּל May our enemies fear Your great strength and stay away from us.

May our enemies fear Your great strength and stay away from us.

May our enemies fear Your great strength and stay away from us.

כָּאָבֶן May our enemies be still like rocks, overcome with fear of Your greatness.

May our enemies be still like rocks, overcome with fear of Your greatness.

May our enemies be still like rocks, overcome with fear of Your greatness.

דָּוִד David, the king of the Jewish people, rules and will rule forever.

David, the king of the Jewish people, rules and will rule forever.

David, the king of the Jewish people, rules and will rule forever.

בָּרוּךְ יוֹצְרֵךְ, בָּרוּךְ עוֹשֵׂךְ, בָּרוּךְ קוֹנֵךְ, בָּרוּךְ בּוֹרְאֵךְ.
בָּרוּךְ יוֹצְרֵךְ, בָּרוּךְ עוֹשֵׂךְ, בָּרוּךְ קוֹנֵךְ, בָּרוּךְ בּוֹרְאֵךְ.
בָּרוּךְ יוֹצְרֵךְ, בָּרוּךְ עוֹשֵׂךְ, בָּרוּךְ קוֹנֵךְ, בָּרוּךְ בּוֹרְאֵךְ.

While standing on toes.

כְּשֵׁם שֶׁאֲנִי רוֹקֵד כְּנֶגְדֵּךְ וְאֵינִי יָכוֹל לִנְגֹּעַ בָּךְ
כָּךְ לֹא יוּכְלוּ כָּל אוֹיְבַי לִנְגֹּעַ בִּי לְרָעָה.
כְּשֵׁם שֶׁאֲנִי רוֹקֵד כְּנֶגְדֵּךְ וְאֵינִי יָכוֹל לִנְגֹּעַ בָּךְ
כָּךְ לֹא יוּכְלוּ כָּל אוֹיְבַי לִנְגֹּעַ בִּי לְרָעָה.
כְּשֵׁם שֶׁאֲנִי רוֹקֵד כְּנֶגְדֵּךְ וְאֵינִי יָכוֹל לִנְגֹּעַ בָּךְ
כָּךְ לֹא יוּכְלוּ כָּל אוֹיְבַי לִנְגֹּעַ בִּי לְרָעָה.

תִּפֹּל עֲלֵיהֶם אֵימָתָה וָפַחַד, בִּגְדֹל זְרוֹעֲךָ יִדְּמוּ כָּאָבֶן:
תִּפֹּל עֲלֵיהֶם אֵימָתָה וָפַחַד, בִּגְדֹל זְרוֹעֲךָ יִדְּמוּ כָּאָבֶן:
תִּפֹּל עֲלֵיהֶם אֵימָתָה וָפַחַד, בִּגְדֹל זְרוֹעֲךָ יִדְּמוּ כָּאָבֶן:

כָּאָבֶן יִדְּמוּ זְרוֹעֲךָ בִּגְדֹל, וָפַחַד אֵימָתָה עֲלֵיהֶם תִּפֹּל.
כָּאָבֶן יִדְּמוּ זְרוֹעֲךָ בִּגְדֹל, וָפַחַד אֵימָתָה עֲלֵיהֶם תִּפֹּל.
כָּאָבֶן יִדְּמוּ זְרוֹעֲךָ בִּגְדֹל, וָפַחַד אֵימָתָה עֲלֵיהֶם תִּפֹּל.

דָּוִד מֶלֶךְ יִשְׂרָאֵל חַי וְקַיָּם.
דָּוִד מֶלֶךְ יִשְׂרָאֵל חַי וְקַיָּם.
דָּוִד מֶלֶךְ יִשְׂרָאֵל חַי וְקַיָּם.

Say to three people:

Peace should be with you.

Three people say back to you:

May you have peace.

סִימָן טוֹב May there be a good sign for us
and all the Jewish people, Amen.
May there be a good sign for us
and all the Jewish people, Amen.
May there be a good sign for us
and all the Jewish people, Amen.

קוֹל דּוֹדִי As a deer that jumps over mountains and hills,
the voice that announces *Mashiach* will come suddenly.
We are constantly looking out the window,
waiting for the voice to arrive.

שִׁיר לַמַּעֲלוֹת I look to the top of the mountains and ask,
"Where will help come from?"
Help is only from *Hashem* who made the heavens and earth.
Hashem does not sleep; He is always there protecting me
and the entire Jewish people.
Hashem always protects us;
the sun will not burn us during the day
and we will not be harmed at night.
Now and forever *Hashem* will protect us, wherever we are.

הַלְלוּיָהּ Halleluya!
Praise *Hashem* who rests his Presence
in the *Beit HaMikdash* and the heavens.
Praise *Hashem* for His great and mighty deeds.

Say to three people:

שָׁלוֹם עֲלֵיכֶם.

Three people say back to you:

עֲלֵיכֶם שָׁלוֹם.

סִימָן טוֹב וּמַזָּל טוֹב יְהֵא לָנוּ וּלְכָל יִשְׂרָאֵל, אָמֵן.
סִימָן טוֹב וּמַזָּל טוֹב יְהֵא לָנוּ וּלְכָל יִשְׂרָאֵל, אָמֵן.
סִימָן טוֹב וּמַזָּל טוֹב יְהֵא לָנוּ וּלְכָל יִשְׂרָאֵל, אָמֵן.

קוֹל דּוֹדִי הִנֵּה־זֶה בָּא, מְדַלֵּג עַל־הֶהָרִים, מְקַפֵּץ עַל־הַגְּבָעוֹת: דּוֹמֶה דוֹדִי לִצְבִי אוֹ לְעֹפֶר הָאַיָּלִים, הִנֵּה־זֶה עוֹמֵד אַחַר כָּתְלֵנוּ, מַשְׁגִּיחַ מִן־הַחַלֹּנוֹת, מֵצִיץ מִן־הַחֲרַכִּים:

שִׁיר לַמַּעֲלוֹת, אֶשָּׂא עֵינַי אֶל־הֶהָרִים, מֵאַיִן יָבֹא עֶזְרִי: עֶזְרִי מֵעִם יהוה, עֹשֵׂה שָׁמַיִם וָאָרֶץ: אַל־יִתֵּן לַמּוֹט רַגְלֶךָ, אַל־יָנוּם שֹׁמְרֶךָ: הִנֵּה לֹא־יָנוּם וְלֹא יִישָׁן, שׁוֹמֵר יִשְׂרָאֵל: יהוה שֹׁמְרֶךָ, יהוה צִלְּךָ עַל־יַד יְמִינֶךָ: יוֹמָם הַשֶּׁמֶשׁ לֹא־יַכֶּכָּה, וְיָרֵחַ בַּלָּיְלָה: יהוה יִשְׁמָרְךָ מִכָּל־רָע, יִשְׁמֹר אֶת־נַפְשֶׁךָ: יהוה יִשְׁמָר־צֵאתְךָ וּבוֹאֶךָ, מֵעַתָּה וְעַד־עוֹלָם:

הַלְלוּיָהּ, הַלְלוּ־אֵל בְּקָדְשׁוֹ, הַלְלוּהוּ בִּרְקִיעַ עֻזּוֹ: הַלְלוּהוּ בִגְבוּרֹתָיו, הַלְלוּהוּ כְּרֹב גֻּדְלוֹ: הַלְלוּהוּ בְּתֵקַע שׁוֹפָר,

Praise *Hashem* with the blast of the shofar,
with many musical instruments, and through dance.
All those who are living should praise *Hashem*, Halleluya!

תָּנָא Rabbi Yishmael taught that the Jewish people would be fortunate to greet *Hashem*, our Father in heaven, even once a month. Abbayei said: Therefore, since in Kiddush Levana we are greeting *Hashem*, we must stand while saying it. Who must stand? All those whose ancestors came out of the desert and relied on *Hashem*.

וִיהִי *Hashem*, our God, and God of our ancestors, may it be Your will to increase the light of the moon so that it is as bright as the light of the sun, as it was during the seven days of creation. May You bring *Mashiach* so that the Jewish people return to their greatness, like the light of the moon.

לַמְנַצֵּחַ We sing to *Hashem* that He may be kind and bless us, shining His light on us. May You rescue us and make Yourself known to all the nations of the world; they will all praise You. You judge all fairly and therefore everyone will sing songs to You, *Hashem*, as they will know that You are God. *Hashem*, our God, while all the people of the world fear you, You bless us, Your Jewish people.

וִיהִי אוֹר הַלְּבָנָה כְּאוֹר הַחַמָּה וּכְאוֹר שִׁבְעַת יְמֵי בְרֵאשִׁית *May it be Your will to increase the light of the moon so that it is as bright as the light of the sun, as it was during the seven days of creation.* When *Hashem* created the world, the sun and the moon were the same size. The moon complained to *Hashem* that it was equal to the sun; the moon wanted to be bigger. In response, *Hashem* punished the moon by making it smaller than the sun. We ask *Hashem* to allow the Jewish people to return to the time where there was unity across *Hashem*'s creations.

הַלְלְוּהוּ בְּנֵבֶל וְכִנּוֹר: הַלְלְוּהוּ בְתֹף וּמָחוֹל, הַלְלְוּהוּ בְּמִנִּים וְעֻגָב: הַלְלְוּהוּ בְצִלְצְלֵי־שָׁמַע, הַלְלְוּהוּ בְּצִלְצְלֵי תְרוּעָה: כֹּל הַנְּשָׁמָה תְּהַלֵּל יָהּ, הַלְלוּיָהּ:

תָּנָא דְבֵי רַבִּי יִשְׁמָעֵאל: אִלְמָלֵי לֹא זָכוּ יִשְׂרָאֵל אֶלָּא לְהַקְבִּיל פְּנֵי אֲבִיהֶם שֶׁבַּשָּׁמַיִם פַּעַם אַחַת בַּחֹדֶשׁ, דַּיָּם. אָמַר אַבַּיֵי: הִלְכָּךְ צָרִיךְ לְמֵימְרָא מְעֻמָּד. מִי זֹאת עֹלָה מִן־הַמִּדְבָּר, מִתְרַפֶּקֶת עַל־דּוֹדָהּ:

וִיהִי רָצוֹן מִלְּפָנֶיךָ יהוה אֱלֹהַי וֵאלֹהֵי אֲבוֹתַי, לְמַלֹּאת פְּגִימַת הַלְּבָנָה וְלֹא יִהְיֶה בָּהּ שׁוּם מִעוּט. וִיהִי אוֹר הַלְּבָנָה כְּאוֹר הַחַמָּה וּכְאוֹר שִׁבְעַת יְמֵי בְרֵאשִׁית, כְּמוֹ שֶׁהָיְתָה קֹדֶם מִעוּטָהּ, שֶׁנֶּאֱמַר: אֶת־שְׁנֵי הַמְּאֹרֹת הַגְּדֹלִים: וְיִתְקַיֵּם בָּנוּ מִקְרָא שֶׁכָּתוּב: וּבִקְשׁוּ אֶת־יהוה אֱלֹהֵיהֶם וְאֵת דָּוִיד מַלְכָּם: אָמֵן.

לַמְנַצֵּחַ בִּנְגִינֹת, מִזְמוֹר שִׁיר: אֱלֹהִים יְחָנֵּנוּ וִיבָרְכֵנוּ, יָאֵר פָּנָיו אִתָּנוּ סֶלָה: לָדַעַת בָּאָרֶץ דַּרְכֶּךָ, בְּכָל־גּוֹיִם יְשׁוּעָתֶךָ: יוֹדוּךָ עַמִּים אֱלֹהִים, יוֹדוּךָ עַמִּים כֻּלָּם: יִשְׂמְחוּ וִירַנְּנוּ לְאֻמִּים, כִּי־תִשְׁפֹּט עַמִּים מִישֹׁר, וּלְאֻמִּים בָּאָרֶץ תַּנְחֵם סֶלָה: יוֹדוּךָ עַמִּים אֱלֹהִים, יוֹדוּךָ עַמִּים כֻּלָּם: אֶרֶץ נָתְנָה יְבוּלָהּ, יְבָרְכֵנוּ אֱלֹהִים אֱלֹהֵינוּ: יְבָרְכֵנוּ אֱלֹהִים, וְיִירְאוּ אוֹתוֹ כָּל־אַפְסֵי־אָרֶץ:

Stand while saying "It is our role."

עָלֵינוּ It is our role to praise You, *Hashem*,
Master of all and Creator of the world.
You have not made us like other nations of the world,
rather, You set the Jewish people apart
allowing us the opportunity to serve You.
(Other nations pray to gods that do not exist,
while)
we bend our knees and bow in prayer
before the King of all kings, *Hashem*,
in order to give thanks.
Hashem created the heavens above and the land below.
Hashem sits on His awesome throne in heaven
as He, alone, is our God and ruler of the world.
We willingly accept Him as our King,
there is none else but Him.
As it says in the Torah,
"Today You should understand that *Hashem* is God
in the heavens above and on the earth below.
There is no other God but You."

Stand while saying עָלֵינוּ.

עָלֵינוּ לְשַׁבֵּחַ לַאֲדוֹן הַכֹּל
לָתֵת גְּדֻלָּה לְיוֹצֵר בְּרֵאשִׁית
שֶׁלֹּא עָשָׂנוּ כְּגוֹיֵי הָאֲרָצוֹת
וְלֹא שָׂמָנוּ כְּמִשְׁפְּחוֹת הָאֲדָמָה
שֶׁלֹּא שָׂם חֶלְקֵנוּ כָּהֶם, וְגוֹרָלֵנוּ כְּכָל הֲמוֹנָם.
(שֶׁהֵם מִשְׁתַּחֲוִים לְהֶבֶל וָרִיק
וּמִתְפַּלְלִים אֶל אֵל לֹא יוֹשִׁיעַ.)
וַאֲנַחְנוּ כּוֹרְעִים וּמִשְׁתַּחֲוִים וּמוֹדִים
לִפְנֵי מֶלֶךְ מַלְכֵי הַמְּלָכִים, הַקָּדוֹשׁ בָּרוּךְ הוּא
שֶׁהוּא נוֹטֶה שָׁמַיִם וְיוֹסֵד אָרֶץ
וּמוֹשַׁב יְקָרוֹ בַּשָּׁמַיִם מִמַּעַל
וּשְׁכִינַת עֻזּוֹ בְּגָבְהֵי מְרוֹמִים.
הוּא אֱלֹהֵינוּ, אֵין עוֹד.
אֱמֶת מַלְכֵּנוּ, אֶפֶס זוּלָתוֹ
כַּכָּתוּב בְּתוֹרָתוֹ
וְיָדַעְתָּ הַיּוֹם וַהֲשֵׁבֹתָ אֶל־לְבָבֶךָ
כִּי יהוה הוּא הָאֱלֹהִים
בַּשָּׁמַיִם מִמַּעַל וְעַל־הָאָרֶץ מִתָּחַת
אֵין עוֹד:

Hashem,
we hope that all false gods
will be removed from the world
and everyone will soon turn to You alone
as the almighty God of the universe.
All the people of the world
will turn to You
and give honor.
They will accept You as their King,
and You will rule over them
soon and forever.
For You are King of the world
and You will remain the ruling King forever.
As it says in Your Torah,
▸ "*Hashem* will be king over all the land.
On that day *Hashem* will be One and His name One."

עַל כֵּן נְקַוֶּה לְּךָ יהוה אֱלֹהֵינוּ
לִרְאוֹת מְהֵרָה בְּתִפְאֶרֶת עֻזֶּךָ
לְהַעֲבִיר גִּלּוּלִים מִן הָאָרֶץ
וְהָאֱלִילִים כָּרוֹת יִכָּרֵתוּן
לְתַקֵּן עוֹלָם בְּמַלְכוּת שַׁדַּי.
וְכָל בְּנֵי בָשָׂר יִקְרְאוּ בִשְׁמֶךָ
לְהַפְנוֹת אֵלֶיךָ כָּל רִשְׁעֵי אָרֶץ.
יַכִּירוּ וְיֵדְעוּ כָּל יוֹשְׁבֵי תֵבֵל
כִּי לְךָ תִּכְרַע כָּל בֶּרֶךְ
תִּשָּׁבַע כָּל לָשׁוֹן.
לְפָנֶיךָ יהוה אֱלֹהֵינוּ יִכְרְעוּ וְיִפֹּלוּ
וְלִכְבוֹד שִׁמְךָ יְקָר יִתֵּנוּ
וִיקַבְּלוּ כֻלָּם אֶת עֹל מַלְכוּתֶךָ
וְתִמְלֹךְ עֲלֵיהֶם מְהֵרָה לְעוֹלָם וָעֶד.
כִּי הַמַּלְכוּת שֶׁלְּךָ הִיא
וּלְעוֹלְמֵי עַד תִּמְלֹךְ בְּכָבוֹד
כַּכָּתוּב בְּתוֹרָתֶךָ
יהוה יִמְלֹךְ לְעֹלָם וָעֶד:
◂ וְנֶאֱמַר, וְהָיָה יהוה לְמֶלֶךְ עַל־כָּל־הָאָרֶץ
בַּיּוֹם הַהוּא יִהְיֶה יהוה אֶחָד וּשְׁמוֹ אֶחָד:

KADDISH YATOM

The following prayer, said by mourners, requires the presence of a minyan. A transliteration can be found on page 865.

Mourner: יִתְגַּדַּל May *Hashem* be recognized
as great and holy (*Congregation:* Amen)
in the world that He created.
May He establish His kingdom
during my lifetime
and the lifetime of all Jews,
quickly and soon.
Let us say: "Amen" (*Congregation:* Amen).

Congregation: May we thank *Hashem* for ever and ever.
Mourner: May we thank *Hashem* for ever and ever.

Mourner: *Hashem* should be thanked, praised,
and honored (*Congregation:* He is blessed).
Hashem is beyond all the blessings,
songs, or praises
that we could offer.
Let us say: "Amen" (*Congregation:* Amen).

May *Hashem* give us, and all Jews,
peace and good life.
Let us say: "Amen." (*Congregation:* Amen).

The mourner takes three steps back before saying this line, bows to the left when saying "May," bows to the right when saying "the One," bows to the middle when saying "make peace for us":

May *Hashem,* the One
who makes peace in heaven,
make peace for us and for all Jews.
Let us say: "Amen." (*Congregation:* Amen).

קדיש יתום

The following prayer, said by mourners, requires the presence of a מנין.
A transliteration can be found on page 865.

אבל: יִתְגַּדַּל וְיִתְקַדַּשׁ שְׁמֵהּ רַבָּא (קהל: אָמֵן)
בְּעָלְמָא דִּי בְרָא כִרְעוּתֵהּ, וְיַמְלִיךְ מַלְכוּתֵהּ
בְּחַיֵּיכוֹן וּבְיוֹמֵיכוֹן וּבְחַיֵּי דְכָל בֵּית יִשְׂרָאֵל
בַּעֲגָלָא וּבִזְמַן קָרִיב, וְאִמְרוּ אָמֵן. (קהל: אָמֵן)

קהל יְהֵא שְׁמֵהּ רַבָּא מְבָרַךְ לְעָלַם וּלְעָלְמֵי עָלְמַיָּא.
אבל: יְהֵא שְׁמֵהּ רַבָּא מְבָרַךְ לְעָלַם וּלְעָלְמֵי עָלְמַיָּא.

אבל: יִתְבָּרַךְ וְיִשְׁתַּבַּח וְיִתְפָּאַר
וְיִתְרוֹמַם וְיִתְנַשֵּׂא וְיִתְהַדָּר וְיִתְעַלֶּה וְיִתְהַלָּל
שְׁמֵהּ דְּקֻדְשָׁא בְּרִיךְ הוּא (קהל: בְּרִיךְ הוּא)
לְעֵלָּא מִן כָּל בִּרְכָתָא
/בעשרת ימי תשובה: לְעֵלָּא לְעֵלָּא מִכָּל בִּרְכָתָא/
וְשִׁירָתָא, תֻּשְׁבְּחָתָא וְנֶחֱמָתָא
דַּאֲמִירָן בְּעָלְמָא, וְאִמְרוּ אָמֵן. (קהל: אָמֵן)

יְהֵא שְׁלָמָא רַבָּא מִן שְׁמַיָּא
וְחַיִּים, עָלֵינוּ וְעַל כָּל יִשְׂרָאֵל, וְאִמְרוּ אָמֵן. (קהל: אָמֵן)

The mourner takes three steps back before saying this line, bows to the left when saying עֹשֶׂה, *bows to the right when saying* הוּא, *bows to the middle when saying* יַעֲשֶׂה שָׁלוֹם עָלֵינוּ:

עֹשֶׂה שָׁלוֹם /בעשרת ימי תשובה: הַשָּׁלוֹם/ בִּמְרוֹמָיו
הוּא יַעֲשֶׂה שָׁלוֹם עָלֵינוּ
וְעַל כָּל יִשְׂרָאֵל, וְאִמְרוּ אָמֵן. (קהל: אָמֵן)

Blessing on Taking the Lulav

On Sukkot, except on Shabbat, the lulav and etrog are taken before Hallel.

Some say the following:

יְהִי רָצוֹן *Hashem,* our God and God of our ancestors,
please consider this *mitzva* of waving the four species –
the lulav, etrog, hadasim, and aravot –
as if it was performed
with all of the intentions and meaning that You intended,
and provide blessing to us.

The lulav is taken in the right hand, with the myrtle leaves on the right, willow leaves on the left. The etrog is taken in the left hand, with its pointed end toward the floor. Then say the following blessing:

בָּרוּךְ Thank You, *Hashem,* our God, King of the world,
for setting us apart as Your special people
by commanding us to take the lulav.

On the first day the lulav is taken, add:

בָּרוּךְ Thank You, *Hashem,* our God, King of the world,
who has kept us alive and provided for our needs
until this time.

Invert the etrog, so that its pointed end is facing up. Face the front of the synagogue and wave the lulav and etrog in the following sequence, three times in each direction: ahead, right, back, left, up, down. Continue to hold the lulav and etrog during Hallel.

עַל נְטִילַת לוּלָב *By commanding us to take the lulav.* On *Sukkot* there is a *mitzva* to take and shake the *Arba Minim,* the four species: lulav, etrog, hadasim, and aravot. Since we generally say a *beracha* before completing a *mitzva,* we (1) lift the etrog upside down when first holding the *Arba Minim* together; (2) say the *beracha* of *al netilat lulav*; (3) turn the etrog over so it faces the right way with the point directed upward; and (4) only then do we shake the lulav.

סדר נטילת לולב

On סוכות, except on שבת, the לולב and אתרוג are taken before הלל.

Some say the following:

יְהִי רָצוֹן מִלְּפָנֶיךָ יהוה אֱלֹהַי וֵאלֹהֵי אֲבוֹתַי, בִּפְרִי עֵץ הָדָר וְכַפֹּת תְּמָרִים וַעֲנַף עֵץ עָבוֹת וְעַרְבֵי נַחַל, אוֹתִיּוֹת שִׁמְךָ הַמְיֻחָד תְּקָרֵב אֶחָד אֶל אֶחָד וְהָיוּ לַאֲחָדִים בְּיָדִי, וְלֵידַע אֵיךְ שִׁמְךָ נִקְרָא עָלַי וְיִירְאוּ מִגֶּשֶׁת אֵלָי. וּבְנַעֲנוּעִי אוֹתָם תַּשְׁפִּיעַ שֶׁפַע בְּרָכוֹת מִדַּעַת עֶלְיוֹן לִנְוֵה אַפִּרְיוֹן לִמְכוֹן בֵּית אֱלֹהֵינוּ, וּתְהֵא חֲשׁוּבָה לְפָנֶיךָ מִצְוַת אַרְבָּעָה מִינִים אֵלּוּ כְּאִלּוּ קִיַּמְתִּיהָ בְּכָל פְּרָטוֹתֶיהָ וְשָׁרָשֶׁיהָ וְתַרְיַ״ג מִצְוֹת הַתְּלוּיוֹת בָּהּ, כִּי כַוָּנָתִי לְיַחֲדָא שְׁמָא דְקֻדְשָׁא בְּרִיךְ הוּא וּשְׁכִינְתֵהּ בִּדְחִילוּ וּרְחִימוּ, לְיַחֵד שֵׁם י״ה בו״ה בְּיִחוּדָא שְׁלִים בְּשֵׁם כָּל יִשְׂרָאֵל, אָמֵן. בָּרוּךְ יהוה לְעוֹלָם, אָמֵן וְאָמֵן:

The לולב is taken in the right hand, with the הדסים on the right, ערבות on the left. The אתרוג is taken in the left hand, with its pointed end toward the floor. Then say the following blessing:

בָּרוּךְ אַתָּה יהוה אֱלֹהֵינוּ מֶלֶךְ הָעוֹלָם
אֲשֶׁר קִדְּשָׁנוּ בְּמִצְוֹתָיו וְצִוָּנוּ עַל נְטִילַת לוּלָב.

On the first day the לולב is taken, add:

בָּרוּךְ אַתָּה יהוה אֱלֹהֵינוּ מֶלֶךְ הָעוֹלָם
שֶׁהֶחֱיָנוּ וְקִיְּמָנוּ וְהִגִּיעָנוּ לַזְּמַן הַזֶּה.

Invert the אתרוג, so that its pointed end is facing up. Face the front of the בית כנסת and wave the לולב and אתרוג in the following sequence, three times in each direction: ahead, right, back, left, up, down. Continue to hold the לולב and אתרוג during הלל.

Hallel

On the first two days of Pesach, Shavuot, the entire festival of Sukkot, Shemini Atzeret, Simchat Torah and Chanuka, Full Hallel is said. On Rosh Chodesh and the last six days of Pesach, Half Hallel is said. Customs vary regarding the first two nights of Pesach, Yom HaAtzma'ut and Yom Yerushalayim.

בָּרוּךְ Thank You, *Hashem*, our God, King of the world,
for setting us apart as Your special people
by commanding us to say *Hallel*.

הַלְלוּיָהּ Halleluya!
Your servants, the Jewish people,
praise You, *Hashem*, from sunrise to sunset;
May You be thanked now and forever.
You are above the nations of the world
and Your honor is known in heaven,
yet You pay attention to the lowly beings on earth.
▸ *Hashem*,
You raise the poor and needy from their lowly places
and make them equal to princes.
You make the childless woman a happy mother of children.
Halleluya!

בְּצֵאת When the Jewish people left Egypt,
they became *Hashem*'s nation.
Both the Sea of Reeds and the Jordan River split
when the Jews passed through them.
The mountains jumped for joy
when the Torah was given at Mount Sinai.
▸ What caused the sea and river to split,
and what caused the mountains to jump for joy?

סדר הלל

On the first two days of פסח, שבועות, *the entire festival of* סוכות,
שמיני עצרת, שמחת תורה *and* חנוכה, הלל שלם *is said.*
On ראש חודש *and the last six days of* פסח, הלל בדילוג *is said.*
Customs vary regarding the first two nights of פסח, יום העצמאות *and* יום ירושלים.

בָּרוּךְ אַתָּה יהוה אֱלֹהֵינוּ מֶלֶךְ הָעוֹלָם
אֲשֶׁר קִדְּשָׁנוּ בְּמִצְוֹתָיו וְצִוָּנוּ לִקְרֹא אֶת הַהַלֵּל.

הַלְלוּיָהּ, הַלְלוּ עַבְדֵי יהוה, הַלְלוּ אֶת־שֵׁם יהוה:
יְהִי שֵׁם יהוה מְבֹרָךְ, מֵעַתָּה וְעַד־עוֹלָם:
מִמִּזְרַח־שֶׁמֶשׁ עַד־מְבוֹאוֹ, מְהֻלָּל שֵׁם יהוה:
רָם עַל־כָּל־גּוֹיִם יהוה, עַל הַשָּׁמַיִם כְּבוֹדוֹ:
מִי כַּיהוה אֱלֹהֵינוּ, הַמַּגְבִּיהִי לָשָׁבֶת:
הַמַּשְׁפִּילִי לִרְאוֹת, בַּשָּׁמַיִם וּבָאָרֶץ:
◂ מְקִימִי מֵעָפָר דָּל, מֵאַשְׁפֹּת יָרִים אֶבְיוֹן:
לְהוֹשִׁיבִי עִם־נְדִיבִים, עִם נְדִיבֵי עַמּוֹ:
מוֹשִׁיבִי עֲקֶרֶת הַבַּיִת, אֵם־הַבָּנִים שְׂמֵחָה, הַלְלוּיָהּ:

בְּצֵאת יִשְׂרָאֵל מִמִּצְרָיִם, בֵּית יַעֲקֹב מֵעַם לֹעֵז:
הָיְתָה יְהוּדָה לְקָדְשׁוֹ, יִשְׂרָאֵל מַמְשְׁלוֹתָיו:
הַיָּם רָאָה וַיָּנֹס, הַיַּרְדֵּן יִסֹּב לְאָחוֹר:
הֶהָרִים רָקְדוּ כְאֵילִים, גְּבָעוֹת כִּבְנֵי־צֹאן:
◂ מַה־לְּךָ הַיָּם כִּי תָנוּס, הַיַּרְדֵּן תִּסֹּב לְאָחוֹר:
הֶהָרִים תִּרְקְדוּ כְאֵילִים, גְּבָעוֹת כִּבְנֵי־צֹאן:

Hashem, the Creator of earth,
who turned a rock into flowing water.

This is not said on Rosh Chodesh (except on Chanuka) and the last six days of Pesach:

לֹא לָנוּ We, the Jewish people,
are not deserving but You, *Hashem,*
save us because of Your honor and kindness.
When the other nations ask,
"Where is *Hashem* their God?"
we know that *Hashem* is in the heavens.
He does anything He wants.
However, their idols are made by man out of gold and silver.
The idols have:

Mouths, but cannot speak;
Ears, but cannot hear;
Noses, but cannot smell;
Hands, but cannot feel;
Feet, but cannot walk; and
Throats, but cannot make a sound.

All those who pray to idols will become like idols,
they will not be able to do anything.
▸ The Jewish people should trust in *Hashem,*
because He is the One who can provide help and protection.
The *Kohanim* and those who fear *Hashem*
should trust in Him.
Only *Hashem* can provide help and protection.

יהוה *Hashem* remembers us and blesses the Jewish people;
the *Kohanim* and all those that fear *Hashem,*
simple and great people alike.
Hashem,
please provide us and our children
with more food and comfort on earth.

מִלִּפְנֵי אָדוֹן חְוּלִי אָרֶץ, מִלִּפְנֵי אֱלוֹהַ יַעֲקֹב:
הַהֹפְכִי הַצּוּר אֲגַם־מָיִם, חַלָּמִישׁ לְמַעְיְנוֹ־מָיִם:

This is not said on ראש חודש *(except on* חנוכה*) and the last six days of* פסח*:*

לֹא לָנוּ יהוה לֹא לָנוּ, כִּי־לְשִׁמְךָ תֵּן כָּבוֹד, עַל־חַסְדְּךָ עַל־אֲמִתֶּךָ:
לָמָּה יֹאמְרוּ הַגּוֹיִם אַיֵּה־נָא אֱלֹהֵיהֶם:
וֵאלֹהֵינוּ בַשָּׁמָיִם, כֹּל אֲשֶׁר־חָפֵץ עָשָׂה:
עֲצַבֵּיהֶם כֶּסֶף וְזָהָב, מַעֲשֵׂה יְדֵי אָדָם:
פֶּה־לָהֶם וְלֹא יְדַבֵּרוּ, עֵינַיִם לָהֶם וְלֹא יִרְאוּ:
אָזְנַיִם לָהֶם וְלֹא יִשְׁמָעוּ, אַף לָהֶם וְלֹא יְרִיחוּן:
יְדֵיהֶם וְלֹא יְמִישׁוּן, רַגְלֵיהֶם וְלֹא יְהַלֵּכוּ, לֹא־יֶהְגּוּ בִּגְרוֹנָם:
כְּמוֹהֶם יִהְיוּ עֹשֵׂיהֶם, כֹּל אֲשֶׁר־בֹּטֵחַ בָּהֶם:
◂ יִשְׂרָאֵל בְּטַח בַּיהוה, עֶזְרָם וּמָגִנָּם הוּא:
בֵּית אַהֲרֹן בִּטְחוּ בַיהוה, עֶזְרָם וּמָגִנָּם הוּא:
יִרְאֵי יהוה בִּטְחוּ בַיהוה, עֶזְרָם וּמָגִנָּם הוּא:

יהוה זְכָרָנוּ יְבָרֵךְ
יְבָרֵךְ אֶת־בֵּית יִשְׂרָאֵל, יְבָרֵךְ אֶת־בֵּית אַהֲרֹן:
יְבָרֵךְ יִרְאֵי יהוה, הַקְּטַנִּים עִם־הַגְּדֹלִים:
יֹסֵף יהוה עֲלֵיכֶם, עֲלֵיכֶם וְעַל־בְּנֵיכֶם:
בְּרוּכִים אַתֶּם לַיהוה, עֹשֵׂה שָׁמַיִם וָאָרֶץ:

הַהֹפְכִי הַצּוּר אֲגַם־מָיִם *Who turned a rock into flowing water.* While traveling through the desert after leaving Egypt, the Jewish people became very thirsty and complained to Moshe, their leader, that they had nothing to drink. Moshe hit a rock and *Hashem* performed a miracle that caused water to flow from it for the Jews to drink. *Hashem* controls everything in the world and can do any type of miracle, even making water flow from a rock.

▸ The heaven is Yours,
but You created the earth for us humans.
Thank You *Hashem* now and forever. Halleluya!

This is not said on Rosh Chodesh (except on Chanuka) and the last six days of Pesach:

אָהַבְתִּי I love *Hashem*;
He listens to my voice and requests whenever I call.
When I am in pain or trouble
I call out to *Hashem* to save me;
He is kind and merciful.
I feel at peace because *Hashem* has been good to me.
Hashem has saved me from death,
my eyes from tears, and my feet from tripping.
▸ I will walk before *Hashem* in Israel,
the land chosen by *Hashem*.
I do not believe in man
but I believe in You, *Hashem*.

מָה־אָשִׁיב How can I repay *Hashem*
for all the kindness He did for me?
I will lift my cup to thank *Hashem*
and keep the promises I made to Him.
Hashem, I am Your servant
just as my parents were Your servants;
You free me.
▸ One day I will bring a thanksgiving sacrifice to You,

כּוֹס־יְשׁוּעוֹת אֶשָּׂא *I will lift my cup to thank Hashem.* A man's cup represents his possessions, everything that he owns in this world. When we say "I will lift my cup to thank *Hashem*" in this *tefillah*, we are showing *Hashem* that we are willing to give everything we own to thank Him.

◂ הַשָּׁמַיִם שָׁמַיִם לַיהוה, וְהָאָרֶץ נָתַן לִבְנֵי־אָדָם:
לֹא הַמֵּתִים יְהַלְלוּ־יָהּ, וְלֹא כָּל־יֹרְדֵי דוּמָה:
וַאֲנַחְנוּ נְבָרֵךְ יָהּ, מֵעַתָּה וְעַד־עוֹלָם, הַלְלוּיָהּ:

This is not said on ראש חודש *(except on* חנוכה*) and the last six days of* פסח*:*

אָהַבְתִּי, כִּי־יִשְׁמַע יהוה, אֶת־קוֹלִי תַּחֲנוּנָי:
כִּי־הִטָּה אָזְנוֹ לִי, וּבְיָמַי אֶקְרָא:
אֲפָפוּנִי חֶבְלֵי־מָוֶת, וּמְצָרֵי שְׁאוֹל מְצָאוּנִי, צָרָה וְיָגוֹן אֶמְצָא:
וּבְשֵׁם־יהוה אֶקְרָא, אָנָּה יהוה מַלְּטָה נַפְשִׁי:
חַנּוּן יהוה וְצַדִּיק, וֵאלֹהֵינוּ מְרַחֵם:
שֹׁמֵר פְּתָאיִם יהוה, דַּלּוֹתִי וְלִי יְהוֹשִׁיעַ:
שׁוּבִי נַפְשִׁי לִמְנוּחָיְכִי, כִּי־יהוה גָּמַל עָלָיְכִי:
כִּי חִלַּצְתָּ נַפְשִׁי מִמָּוֶת, אֶת־עֵינִי מִן־דִּמְעָה, אֶת־רַגְלִי מִדֶּחִי:
◂ אֶתְהַלֵּךְ לִפְנֵי יהוה, בְּאַרְצוֹת הַחַיִּים:
הֶאֱמַנְתִּי כִּי אֲדַבֵּר, אֲנִי עָנִיתִי מְאֹד:
אֲנִי אָמַרְתִּי בְחָפְזִי, כָּל־הָאָדָם כֹּזֵב:

מָה־אָשִׁיב לַיהוה, כָּל־תַּגְמוּלוֹהִי עָלָי:
כּוֹס־יְשׁוּעוֹת אֶשָּׂא, וּבְשֵׁם יהוה אֶקְרָא:
נְדָרַי לַיהוה אֲשַׁלֵּם, נֶגְדָה־נָּא לְכָל־עַמּוֹ:
יָקָר בְּעֵינֵי יהוה, הַמָּוְתָה לַחֲסִידָיו:
אָנָּה יהוה כִּי־אֲנִי עַבְדֶּךָ
אֲנִי־עַבְדְּךָ בֶּן־אֲמָתֶךָ, פִּתַּחְתָּ לְמוֹסֵרָי:
◂ לְךָ־אֶזְבַּח זֶבַח תּוֹדָה, וּבְשֵׁם יהוה אֶקְרָא:

Hashem, before all Your Jewish people in Jerusalem. Halleluya!

הַלְלוּ All the nations of the world,
including the Jewish people,
praise *Hashem* because He shows incredible kindness to us
and He can be trusted forever. Halleluya!

The following lines are said by the Leader. After the Leader says each line, the congregation says "His kindness is forever," followed by the next line.

*On Sukkot, the lulav and etrog are waved when the verse "*HODU*" is said. The instructions for waving the lulav and etrog are:*
HODU – *wave forward;* LAHASHEM – *no waving;* KI – *wave to the right;*
TOV – *wave backward;* KI – *wave to the left;* LE'OLAM – *wave upward*
CHASDO – *wave downward.*

הוֹדוּ Thank *Hashem* because He is good
His kindness is forever.

Thank *Hashem* because He is good His kindness is forever.
Let all of Israel say His kindness is forever.

Let all of Israel say
His kindness is forever.

Thank *Hashem* because He is good His kindness is forever.
Let all *Kohanim*, the sons of Aharon, say His kindness is forever.

Let all *Kohanim*, the sons of Aharon, say
His kindness is forever.

Thank *Hashem* because He is good His kindness is forever.
Let all those who fear *Hashem* say His kindness is forever.

Let all those who fear *Hashem* say
His kindness is forever.

Thank *Hashem* because He is good His kindness is forever.

נְדָרַי לַיהוה אֲשַׁלֵּם, נֶגְדָה־נָּא לְכָל־עַמּוֹ:
בְּחַצְרוֹת בֵּית יהוה, בְּתוֹכֵכִי יְרוּשָׁלָםִ, הַלְלוּיָהּ:

הַלְלוּ אֶת־יהוה כָּל־גּוֹיִם, שַׁבְּחוּהוּ כָּל־הָאֻמִּים:
כִּי גָבַר עָלֵינוּ חַסְדּוֹ, וֶאֱמֶת־יהוה לְעוֹלָם, הַלְלוּיָהּ:

The following lines are said by the חזן*. After the* חזן *says each line, the congregation says* הוֹדוּ לַיהוה כִּי־טוֹב, כִּי לְעוֹלָם חַסְדּוֹ*, followed by the next line.*

On סוכות*, the* לולב *and* אתרוג *are waved when the verse* הוֹדוּ *is said. The instructions for waving the* לולב *and* אתרוג *are:*
הוֹדוּ *– wave forward;* לַיהוה *– no waving;* כִּי *– wave to the right;*
טוֹב *– wave backward;* כִּי *– wave to the left;* לְעוֹלָם *– wave upward*
חַסְדּוֹ *– wave downward.*

הוֹדוּ לַיהוה כִּי־טוֹב כִּי לְעוֹלָם חַסְדּוֹ:
הוֹדוּ לַיהוה כִּי־טוֹב כִּי לְעוֹלָם חַסְדּוֹ:
יֹאמַר־נָא יִשְׂרָאֵל כִּי לְעוֹלָם חַסְדּוֹ:

יֹאמַר־נָא יִשְׂרָאֵל כִּי לְעוֹלָם חַסְדּוֹ:
הוֹדוּ לַיהוה כִּי־טוֹב כִּי לְעוֹלָם חַסְדּוֹ:
יֹאמְרוּ־נָא בֵית־אַהֲרֹן כִּי לְעוֹלָם חַסְדּוֹ:

יֹאמְרוּ־נָא בֵית־אַהֲרֹן כִּי לְעוֹלָם חַסְדּוֹ:
הוֹדוּ לַיהוה כִּי־טוֹב כִּי לְעוֹלָם חַסְדּוֹ:
יֹאמְרוּ־נָא יִרְאֵי יהוה כִּי לְעוֹלָם חַסְדּוֹ:

יֹאמְרוּ־נָא יִרְאֵי יהוה כִּי לְעוֹלָם חַסְדּוֹ:
הוֹדוּ לַיהוה כִּי־טוֹב כִּי לְעוֹלָם חַסְדּוֹ:

מִן־הַמֵּצַר I call out to *Hashem* during my difficult times; He answers, helps, and sets me free. Because *Hashem* is with me I have nothing to fear. It is better to trust in *Hashem* than in man because only *Hashem* can cause our enemies to fall. It is better to trust in *Hashem* than in powerful people. When nations surrounded the Jewish people like fire surrounds and burns wood, *Hashem* protects us and causes our enemies to run away. *Hashem* gives me strength. The righteous sing out to *Hashem* about the great miracles He did for the Jewish people. We pray to *Hashem* that He will bring us close to Him so we can better understand, appreciate, and thank *Hashem.* ▸ *Hashem,* open up the gates that allow us to step closer to You. The gates to *Hashem* are opened only for those that are righteous.

אוֹדְךָ I will thank You, *Hashem,*
because I know You will answer and save me.

I will thank You, *Hashem,* because I know You will answer and save me.

אֶבֶן The Jewish people were rejected by other nations
and will be recognized by the whole world
when *Mashiach* comes.

The Jewish people were rejected by other nations
and will be recognized by the whole world when *Mashiach* comes.

מֵאֵת Everything comes from *Hashem*; we are always amazed.

Everything comes from *Hashem*; we are always amazed.

זֶה־הַיּוֹם We rejoice today because we understand
that everything in this world happens for a reason.

We rejoice today because we understand
that everything in this world happens for a reason.

מִן־הַמֵּצַר קָרָאתִי יָּהּ, עָנָנִי בַמֶּרְחָב יָהּ: יהוה לִי לֹא אִירָא, מַה־יַּעֲשֶׂה לִי אָדָם: יהוה לִי בְּעֹזְרָי, וַאֲנִי אֶרְאֶה בְשֹׂנְאָי: טוֹב לַחֲסוֹת בַּיהוה, מִבְּטֹחַ בָּאָדָם: טוֹב לַחֲסוֹת בַּיהוה, מִבְּטֹחַ בִּנְדִיבִים: כָּל־גּוֹיִם סְבָבוּנִי, בְּשֵׁם יהוה כִּי אֲמִילַם: סַבּוּנִי גַם־סְבָבוּנִי, בְּשֵׁם יהוה כִּי אֲמִילַם: סַבּוּנִי כִדְבֹרִים, דֹּעֲכוּ כְּאֵשׁ קוֹצִים, בְּשֵׁם יהוה כִּי אֲמִילַם: דָּחֹה דְחִיתַנִי לִנְפֹּל, וַיהוה עֲזָרָנִי: עָזִּי וְזִמְרָת יָהּ, וַיְהִי־לִי לִישׁוּעָה: קוֹל רִנָּה וִישׁוּעָה בְּאָהֳלֵי צַדִּיקִים, יְמִין יהוה עֹשָׂה חָיִל: יְמִין יהוה רוֹמֵמָה, יְמִין יהוה עֹשָׂה חָיִל: לֹא־אָמוּת כִּי־אֶחְיֶה, וַאֲסַפֵּר מַעֲשֵׂי יָהּ: יַסֹּר יִסְּרַנִּי יָּהּ, וְלַמָּוֶת לֹא נְתָנָנִי: ◂ פִּתְחוּ־לִי שַׁעֲרֵי־צֶדֶק, אָבֹא־בָם אוֹדֶה יָהּ: זֶה־הַשַּׁעַר לַיהוה, צַדִּיקִים יָבֹאוּ בוֹ:

אוֹדְךָ כִּי עֲנִיתָנִי, וַתְּהִי־לִי לִישׁוּעָה:
אוֹדְךָ כִּי עֲנִיתָנִי, וַתְּהִי־לִי לִישׁוּעָה:

אֶבֶן מָאֲסוּ הַבּוֹנִים, הָיְתָה לְרֹאשׁ פִּנָּה:
אֶבֶן מָאֲסוּ הַבּוֹנִים, הָיְתָה לְרֹאשׁ פִּנָּה:

מֵאֵת יהוה הָיְתָה זֹּאת, הִיא נִפְלָאת בְּעֵינֵינוּ:
מֵאֵת יהוה הָיְתָה זֹּאת, הִיא נִפְלָאת בְּעֵינֵינוּ:

זֶה־הַיּוֹם עָשָׂה יהוה, נָגִילָה וְנִשְׂמְחָה בוֹ:
זֶה־הַיּוֹם עָשָׂה יהוה, נָגִילָה וְנִשְׂמְחָה בוֹ:

On Sukkot, the lulav and etrog are waved while saying the first two lines.
The instructions for waving the lulav and etrog are:
ANA – *wave forward and to the right;*
HASHEM – *No waving*
HOSHIA – *wave backward and to the left;*
NA – *wave upward and downward.*

Leader followed by congregation:

אָנָּא *Hashem,* please save us!
Hashem, please save us!

Leader followed by congregation:

Hashem, please save us!
Hashem, please save us!

Leader followed by congregation:

Hashem, please allow us to be successful!
Hashem, please allow us to be successful!

Leader followed by congregation:

Hashem, please allow us to be successful!
Hashem, please allow us to be successful!

בָּרוּךְ The person who acts with *Hashem* in mind is blessed.

The person who acts with *Hashem* in mind is blessed.

אֵל *Hashem,* our God, will free us from exile and allow us to bring *korbanot.*

Hashem, our God, will free us from exile and allow us to bring *korbanot.*

On סוכות*, the* לולב *and* אתרוג *are waved while saying the first two lines.*
The instructions for waving the לולב *and* אתרוג *are:*
אָנָּא *– wave forward and to the right;* ה׳ *– No waving*
הוֹשִׁיעָה *– wave backward and to the left;* נָּא *– wave upward and downward.*

חזן *followed by* קהל*:*

אָנָּא יהוה הוֹשִׁיעָה נָּא:

אָנָּא יהוה הוֹשִׁיעָה נָּא:

חזן *followed by* קהל*:*

אָנָּא יהוה הוֹשִׁיעָה נָּא:

אָנָּא יהוה הוֹשִׁיעָה נָּא:

חזן *followed by* קהל*:*

אָנָּא יהוה הַצְלִיחָה נָא:

אָנָּא יהוה הַצְלִיחָה נָא:

חזן *followed by* קהל*:*

אָנָּא יהוה הַצְלִיחָה נָא:

אָנָּא יהוה הַצְלִיחָה נָא:

בָּרוּךְ הַבָּא בְּשֵׁם יהוה
בֵּרַכְנוּכֶם מִבֵּית יהוה:
בָּרוּךְ הַבָּא בְּשֵׁם יהוה, בֵּרַכְנוּכֶם מִבֵּית יהוה:

אֵל יהוה וַיָּאֶר לָנוּ
אִסְרוּ־חַג בַּעֲבֹתִים עַד־קַרְנוֹת הַמִּזְבֵּחַ:
אֵל יהוה וַיָּאֶר לָנוּ, אִסְרוּ־חַג בַּעֲבֹתִים עַד־קַרְנוֹת הַמִּזְבֵּחַ:

אֵלִי You are my God;
I will thank and praise You.

You are my God;
I will thank and praise You.

On Sukkot, the lulav and etrog are waved, while saying this verse.
HODU – *wave forward;* LAHASHEM – *no waving;*
KI – *wave to the right;* TOV – *wave backward;*
KI – *wave to the left;* LE'OLAM – *wave upward*
CHASDO – *wave downward.*

הוֹדוּ Thank *Hashem* because He is good;
His kindness is forever.

Thank *Hashem* because He is good;
His kindness is forever.

יְהַלְלוּךָ All of Your creations will praise You.
Your Jewish people who always loyally serve You
will joyously thank, bless, praise,
honor, and sanctify You
as we declare You King.
▸ It is proper to thank and praise You, *Hashem*,
because You are God forever.
Thank You, *Hashem*,
our King who deserves praise.

On Sukkot some say at this point Hoshanot on page 806.

On weekday Chanuka (except Rosh Chodesh Tevet),
Yom HaAtzma'ut and Yom Yerushalayim,
the service continues with Half Kaddish on page 166.

אֵלִי אַתָּה וְאוֹדֶךָּ, אֱלֹהַי אֲרוֹמְמֶךָּ:

אֵלִי אַתָּה וְאוֹדֶךָּ, אֱלֹהַי אֲרוֹמְמֶךָּ:

On סוכות*, the* לולב *and* אתרוג *are waved while saying this verse.*
הודו *– wave forward;* לַיהוה *– no waving;* כִּי *– wave to the right;*
טוֹב *– wave backward;* כִּי *– wave to the left;* לְעוֹלָם *– wave upward*
חַסְדּוֹ *– wave downward.*

הוֹדוּ לַיהוה כִּי־טוֹב, כִּי לְעוֹלָם חַסְדּוֹ:

הוֹדוּ לַיהוה כִּי־טוֹב, כִּי לְעוֹלָם חַסְדּוֹ:

יְהַלְלְוּךָ יהוה אֱלֹהֵינוּ כָּל מַעֲשֶׂיךָ
וַחֲסִידֶיךָ צַדִּיקִים עוֹשֵׂי רְצוֹנֶךָ
וְכָל עַמְּךָ בֵּית יִשְׂרָאֵל בְּרִנָּה
יוֹדוּ וִיבָרְכוּ וִישַׁבְּחוּ וִיפָאֲרוּ
וִירוֹמְמוּ וְיַעֲרִיצוּ וְיַקְדִּישׁוּ וְיַמְלִיכוּ
אֶת שִׁמְךָ מַלְכֵּנוּ
◂ כִּי לְךָ טוֹב לְהוֹדוֹת וּלְשִׁמְךָ נָאֶה לְזַמֵּר
כִּי מֵעוֹלָם וְעַד עוֹלָם אַתָּה אֵל.
בָּרוּךְ אַתָּה יהוה
מֶלֶךְ מְהֻלָּל בַּתִּשְׁבָּחוֹת.

On סוכות *some say at this point* הושענות *on page 806.*

On weekday חנוכה *(except* ראש חודש טבת*),* יום העצמאות *and* יום ירושלים*,*
the service continues with חצי קדיש *on page 167.*

KADDISH SHALEM

Leader: יִתְגַּדַּל May *Hashem* be recognized
as great and holy (*Congregation:* Amen)
in the world that He created.
May He establish His kingdom during my lifetime
and the lifetime of all Jews, quickly and soon.
Let us say: "Amen" (*Congregation:* Amen).

Congregation: May we thank *Hashem* for ever and ever.
Leader: May we thank *Hashem* for ever and ever.

Leader: *Hashem* should be thanked, praised,
and honored (*Congregation:* He is blessed).
Hashem is beyond all the blessings,
songs, or praises that we could offer.
Let us say: "Amen" (*Congregation:* Amen).

May *Hashem* accept our prayers
and the prayers of all Jews.
Let us say: "Amen." (*Congregation:* Amen).

May *Hashem* give us, and all Jews, peace and good life.
Let us say: "Amen." (*Congregation:* Amen).

The Leader takes three steps back before saying this line, bows to the left when saying "May," bows to the right when saying "the One," bows to the middle when saying "make peace for us":
May *Hashem*, the One who makes peace in heaven,
make peace for us and for all Jews.
Let us say: "Amen." (*Congregation:* Amen).

On Rosh Chodesh and Chol HaMo'ed, the service continues with the Reading of the Torah on page 168.

Shabbat, and Hoshana Raba, the service continues with the Reading of the Torah on page 530.

On Shabbat Chol HaMo'ed, the appropriate megilla is read before the Torah Reading. In the event that the first day of Yom Tov falls on Shabbat, the megilla is instead read on the last day of Pesach or on Shemini Atzeret.

קדיש שלם

חזן: יִתְגַּדַּל וְיִתְקַדַּשׁ שְׁמֵהּ רַבָּא (קהל: אָמֵן)
בְּעָלְמָא דִּי בְרָא כִרְעוּתֵהּ, וְיַמְלִיךְ מַלְכוּתֵהּ
בְּחַיֵּיכוֹן וּבְיוֹמֵיכוֹן וּבְחַיֵּי דְכָל בֵּית יִשְׂרָאֵל
בַּעֲגָלָא וּבִזְמַן קָרִיב, וְאִמְרוּ אָמֵן. (קהל: אָמֵן)

קהל יְהֵא שְׁמֵהּ רַבָּא מְבָרַךְ לְעָלַם וּלְעָלְמֵי עָלְמַיָּא.
חזן: יְהֵא שְׁמֵהּ רַבָּא מְבָרַךְ לְעָלַם וּלְעָלְמֵי עָלְמַיָּא.

חזן: יִתְבָּרַךְ וְיִשְׁתַּבַּח וְיִתְפָּאַר וְיִתְרוֹמַם וְיִתְנַשֵּׂא וְיִתְהַדָּר
וְיִתְעַלֶּה וְיִתְהַלָּל שְׁמֵהּ דְּקֻדְשָׁא בְּרִיךְ הוּא (קהל: בְּרִיךְ הוּא)
לְעֵלָּא מִן כָּל בִּרְכָתָא וְשִׁירָתָא, תֻּשְׁבְּחָתָא וְנֶחֱמָתָא
דַּאֲמִירָן בְּעָלְמָא, וְאִמְרוּ אָמֵן. (קהל: אָמֵן)

תִּתְקַבַּל צְלוֹתְהוֹן וּבָעוּתְהוֹן דְּכָל יִשְׂרָאֵל
קֳדָם אֲבוּהוֹן דִּי בִשְׁמַיָּא, וְאִמְרוּ אָמֵן. (קהל: אָמֵן)

יְהֵא שְׁלָמָא רַבָּא מִן שְׁמַיָּא
וְחַיִּים, עָלֵינוּ וְעַל כָּל יִשְׂרָאֵל, וְאִמְרוּ אָמֵן. (קהל: אָמֵן)

The חזן *takes three steps back before saying this line,*
bows to the left when saying עֹשֶׂה, *bows to the right when saying* הוּא,
bows to the middle when saying יַעֲשֶׂה שָׁלוֹם עָלֵינוּ:

עֹשֶׂה שָׁלוֹם בִּמְרוֹמָיו, הוּא יַעֲשֶׂה שָׁלוֹם עָלֵינוּ
וְעַל כָּל יִשְׂרָאֵל, וְאִמְרוּ אָמֵן. (קהל: אָמֵן)

On ראש חודש *and* חול המועד, *the service continues with* קריאת התורה *on page 169.*
On שבת, *and* הושענא רבה *the service continues with* קריאת התורה *on page 531.*
On שבת חול המועד, *the appropriate* מגילה *is read before* קריאת התורה.
In the event that the first day of יום טוב *falls on* שבת, *the* מגילה *is instead read on the last day of* פסח *or on* שמיני עצרת.

Weekday Rosh Chodesh Musaf

AMIDA

Take three steps back then three steps forward then stand with your feet together.

I will call out to *Hashem,* let us all give praise to Him.
Hashem, open my lips and help my mouth recite Your praise.

ANCESTORS

Bend the knees when saying "We thank," bow when saying "You," and stand straight before saying "Hashem."

בָּרוּךְ We thank You, *Hashem,*
our God, and God of our ancestors,
Avraham, Yitzchak, and Yaakov.
You, *Hashem,* are the great, mighty, awesome, kind,
and all-powerful Creator.
It is because of the greatness of our ancestors,
Avraham, Yitzchak, and Yaakov,
that *Hashem* will bring *Mashiach.*
Hashem is our King who helps, guides, and protects us.

Bend the knees when saying "Thank," bow when saying "You," and stand straight before saying "Hashem."

Thank You, *Hashem,*
who protects us in the merit of Avraham.

HASHEM'S STRENGTH

אַתָּה You, *Hashem,* have unlimited strength.
You save people in their time of need,
and You have the power to bring the dead back to life.

This line is said during the rainy season, from Simchat Torah to Pesach:

(You make the wind blow and cause the rain to fall)

מוסף לראש חודש

עמידה

Take three steps back then three steps forward then stand with your feet together.

כִּי שֵׁם יהוה אֶקְרָא, הָבוּ גֹדֶל לֵאלֹהֵינוּ:
אֲדֹנָי, שְׂפָתַי תִּפְתָּח, וּפִי יַגִּיד תְּהִלָּתֶךָ:

אבות

Bend the knees when saying בָּרוּךְ, *bow when saying* אַתָּה, *and stand straight before saying Hashem's name.*

בָּרוּךְ אַתָּה יהוה, אֱלֹהֵינוּ וֵאלֹהֵי אֲבוֹתֵינוּ
אֱלֹהֵי אַבְרָהָם, אֱלֹהֵי יִצְחָק, וֵאלֹהֵי יַעֲקֹב
הָאֵל הַגָּדוֹל הַגִּבּוֹר וְהַנּוֹרָא, אֵל עֶלְיוֹן
גּוֹמֵל חֲסָדִים טוֹבִים, וְקוֹנֵה הַכֹּל, וְזוֹכֵר חַסְדֵי אָבוֹת
וּמֵבִיא גוֹאֵל לִבְנֵי בְנֵיהֶם לְמַעַן שְׁמוֹ בְּאַהֲבָה.
מֶלֶךְ עוֹזֵר וּמוֹשִׁיעַ וּמָגֵן.

Bend the knees when saying בָּרוּךְ, *bow when saying* אַתָּה, *and stand straight before saying Hashem's name.*

בָּרוּךְ אַתָּה יהוה, מָגֵן אַבְרָהָם.

גבורות

אַתָּה גִּבּוֹר לְעוֹלָם, אֲדֹנָי
מְחַיֵּה מֵתִים אַתָּה, רַב לְהוֹשִׁיעַ

This line is said during the rainy season, from שמחת תורה *to* פסח:

(מַשִּׁיב הָרוּחַ וּמוֹרִיד הַגֶּשֶׁם)

With kindness You provide the living
with the necessities to live,
and with mercy You keep Your promise
of bringing the dead back to life.
For the living, You:
Support those who are falling,
Heal those who are sick, and
Free those who are in challenging situations.
Who is like You, *Hashem,* and who can compare to You?
You, *Hashem,* are our King
who has the power to cause death and life.
We have complete faith
that You will bring us back to life after our passing.
Thank You, *Hashem,* for bringing the dead back to life.

HASHEM'S HOLINESS

אַתָּה קָדוֹשׁ *Hashem,*
You are holy and Your name is holy.
The Jewish people, who are holy,
will praise You, *Hashem,* each day.
Thank You, *Hashem,* the holy God.

HOLINESS OF ROSH CHODESH

רָאשֵׁי חֳדָשִׁים *Hashem* gave the Jewish people
Rosh Chodesh, the new month,
as a time for forgiveness for us and all future generations.

מְכַלְכֵּל חַיִּים בְּחֶסֶד, מְחַיֵּה מֵתִים בְּרַחֲמִים רַבִּים
סוֹמֵךְ נוֹפְלִים, וְרוֹפֵא חוֹלִים, וּמַתִּיר אֲסוּרִים
וּמְקַיֵּם אֱמוּנָתוֹ לִישֵׁנֵי עָפָר.
מִי כָמוֹךָ, בַּעַל גְּבוּרוֹת
וּמִי דּוֹמֶה לָּךְ
מֶלֶךְ, מֵמִית וּמְחַיֶּה וּמַצְמִיחַ יְשׁוּעָה.
וְנֶאֱמָן אַתָּה לְהַחֲיוֹת מֵתִים.
בָּרוּךְ אַתָּה יהוה, מְחַיֵּה הַמֵּתִים.

קדושת השם

אַתָּה קָדוֹשׁ וְשִׁמְךָ קָדוֹשׁ
וּקְדוֹשִׁים בְּכָל יוֹם יְהַלְלוּךָ סֶּלָה.
בָּרוּךְ אַתָּה יהוה, הָאֵל הַקָּדוֹשׁ.

קדושת היום

רָאשֵׁי חֳדָשִׁים לְעַמְּךָ נָתַתָּ
זְמַן כַּפָּרָה לְכָל תּוֹלְדוֹתָם
בִּהְיוֹתָם מַקְרִיבִים לְפָנֶיךָ זִבְחֵי רָצוֹן
וּשְׂעִירֵי חַטָּאת לְכַפֵּר בַּעֲדָם.
זִכָּרוֹן לְכֻלָּם יִהְיוּ
וּתְשׁוּעַת נַפְשָׁם מִיַּד שׂוֹנֵא.

In the *Beit HaMikdash*
we brought many *korbanot,*
including the Rosh Chodesh *korban*
for forgiveness.
Hashem,
may You please rebuild the *Beit HaMikdash* soon
so that we can once again bring
the *korban* of Rosh Chodesh.
May we be able to celebrate in the *Beit HaMikdash*
and sing the songs of David there.
Hashem,
please remember the promises
You made to our ancestors
and show Your Jewish people love forever.

וַהֲבִיאֵנוּ May You please bring us
back to Your city, Yerushalayim,
and to Your *Beit HaMikdash*
with joy and song.

וְאֶת There, we will bring all the *korbanot,*
including the *korban* of Rosh Chodesh
which is:

Two bulls,
One ram, and
Seven perfect lambs
As a special *korban.*

מִזְבֵּחַ חָדָשׁ בְּצִיּוֹן תָּכִין
וְעוֹלַת רֹאשׁ חֹדֶשׁ נַעֲלֶה עָלָיו
וּשְׂעִירֵי עִזִּים נַעֲשֶׂה בְרָצוֹן
וּבַעֲבוֹדַת בֵּית הַמִּקְדָּשׁ נִשְׂמַח כֻּלָּנוּ
וּבְשִׁירֵי דָוִד עַבְדְּךָ הַנִּשְׁמָעִים בְּעִירֶךָ
הָאֲמוּרִים לִפְנֵי מִזְבְּחֶךָ.
אַהֲבַת עוֹלָם תָּבִיא לָהֶם, וּבְרִית אָבוֹת לַבָּנִים תִּזְכֹּר.

וַהֲבִיאֵנוּ לְצִיּוֹן עִירְךָ בְּרִנָּה
וְלִירוּשָׁלַיִם בֵּית מִקְדָּשְׁךָ בְּשִׂמְחַת עוֹלָם
וְשָׁם נַעֲשֶׂה לְפָנֶיךָ אֶת קָרְבְּנוֹת חוֹבוֹתֵינוּ
תְּמִידִים כְּסִדְרָם וּמוּסָפִים כְּהִלְכָתָם.

וְאֶת מוּסַף יוֹם רֹאשׁ הַחֹדֶשׁ הַזֶּה
נַעֲשֶׂה וְנַקְרִיב לְפָנֶיךָ בְּאַהֲבָה כְּמִצְוַת רְצוֹנֶךָ
כְּמוֹ שֶׁכָּתַבְתָּ עָלֵינוּ בְּתוֹרָתֶךָ
עַל יְדֵי מֹשֶׁה עַבְדֶּךָ מִפִּי כְבוֹדֶךָ
כָּאָמוּר
וּבְרָאשֵׁי חָדְשֵׁיכֶם תַּקְרִיבוּ עֹלָה לַיהוה
פָּרִים בְּנֵי־בָקָר שְׁנַיִם וְאַיִל אֶחָד
כְּבָשִׂים בְּנֵי־שָׁנָה שִׁבְעָה, תְּמִימִם:

Along with each bull, ram, and lamb
we will also bring flour and wine *korbanot*.
On Rosh Chodesh we also bring
a special goat sacrifice for forgiveness
and the two daily *korbanot*
brought in the *Beit HaMikdash*.

אֱלֹהֵינוּ *Hashem*, our God, and God of our ancestors,
may You please fill the new month with:
Goodness and blessings,
Joy and happiness,
Comfort and protection,
Support for what we need,
Life and peace, and
Forgiveness.
For You have chosen the Jewish people
from all the other nations
and given them the mitzva of Rosh Chodesh.
Thank You, *Hashem*,
for making the Jewish people and the new month holy.

בָּרוּךְ אַתָּה יהוה, מְקַדֵּשׁ יִשְׂרָאֵל וְרָאשֵׁי חֳדָשִׁים *Thank You, Hashem, for making the Jewish people and the new month holy.* Why do we mention the Jewish people before the new moon? The *mitzva* of making the new month holy was given to the Jewish people. Without the Jewish people, there would be nobody to bless the new month and make it holy. Therefore, we mention the Jewish people first as they are necessary to celebrate and thank *Hashem* for the new month.

וּמִנְחָתָם וְנִסְכֵּיהֶם כִּמְדֻבָּר
שְׁלֹשָׁה עֶשְׂרֹנִים לַפָּר
וּשְׁנֵי עֶשְׂרֹנִים לָאָיִל
וְעִשָּׂרוֹן לַכֶּבֶשׂ
וְיַיִן כְּנִסְכּוֹ
וְשָׂעִיר לְכַפֵּר
וּשְׁנֵי תְמִידִים כְּהִלְכָתָם.

אֱלֹהֵינוּ וֵאלֹהֵי אֲבוֹתֵינוּ
חַדֵּשׁ עָלֵינוּ אֶת הַחֹדֶשׁ הַזֶּה
לְטוֹבָה וְלִבְרָכָה
לְשָׂשׂוֹן וּלְשִׂמְחָה
לִישׁוּעָה וּלְנֶחָמָה
לְפַרְנָסָה וּלְכַלְכָּלָה
לְחַיִּים וּלְשָׁלוֹם
לִמְחִילַת חֵטְא וְלִסְלִיחַת עָוֹן
(*From* מרחשון *to* אדר שני *in a Jewish leap year* וּלְכַפָּרַת פָּשַׁע)
כִּי בְעַמְּךָ יִשְׂרָאֵל בָּחַרְתָּ מִכָּל הָאֻמּוֹת
וְחֻקֵּי רָאשֵׁי חֳדָשִׁים לָהֶם קָבָעְתָּ.
בָּרוּךְ אַתָּה יהוה, מְקַדֵּשׁ יִשְׂרָאֵל וְרָאשֵׁי חֳדָשִׁים.

SERVICE IN THE *BEIT HAMIKDASH*

רְצֵה *Hashem,* please accept Your Jewish people
and their prayers.
We eagerly await the rebuilding of the *Beit HaMikdash*
so we can serve You with *korbanot.*
Until the *Beit HaMikdash* is rebuilt,
please accept our prayers with love.
May we be worthy
to see the rebuilding of the *Beit HaMikdash.*
We thank You, *Hashem,*
for returning Your presence to Zion.

THANK YOU

Bow when saying the words "We thank You."

מוֹדִים We thank You, *Hashem,*
for You are and always will be
our God, and the God of our ancestors.
You give us life
and You always protect us.
We thank and praise You
for:
Our lives which are in Your hands,
Our souls which are in Your control,
The miracles You perform for us every day, and
The goodness You show us
at all times, morning, noon, and night.
You, *Hashem,*
have unlimited mercy and kindness
and therefore we have always placed our hope in You.

עבודה

רְצֵה יהוה אֱלֹהֵינוּ בְּעַמְּךָ יִשְׂרָאֵל, וּבִתְפִלָּתָם
וְהָשֵׁב אֶת הָעֲבוֹדָה לִדְבִיר בֵּיתֶךָ
וְאִשֵּׁי יִשְׂרָאֵל וּתְפִלָּתָם בְּאַהֲבָה תְקַבֵּל בְּרָצוֹן
וּתְהִי לְרָצוֹן תָּמִיד עֲבוֹדַת יִשְׂרָאֵל עַמֶּךָ.
וְתֶחֱזֶינָה עֵינֵינוּ בְּשׁוּבְךָ לְצִיּוֹן בְּרַחֲמִים.
בָּרוּךְ אַתָּה יהוה, הַמַּחֲזִיר שְׁכִינָתוֹ לְצִיּוֹן.

הודאה

Bow when saying the words מוֹדִים אֲנַחְנוּ לָךְ שָׁאַתָּה הוּא.

מוֹדִים אֲנַחְנוּ לָךְ
שָׁאַתָּה הוּא יהוה אֱלֹהֵינוּ
וֵאלֹהֵי אֲבוֹתֵינוּ לְעוֹלָם וָעֶד.
צוּר חַיֵּינוּ, מָגֵן יִשְׁעֵנוּ, אַתָּה הוּא לְדוֹר וָדוֹר.
נוֹדֶה לְּךָ וּנְסַפֵּר תְּהִלָּתֶךָ
עַל חַיֵּינוּ הַמְּסוּרִים בְּיָדֶךָ
וְעַל נִשְׁמוֹתֵינוּ הַפְּקוּדוֹת לָךְ
וְעַל נִסֶּיךָ שֶׁבְּכָל יוֹם עִמָּנוּ
וְעַל נִפְלְאוֹתֶיךָ וְטוֹבוֹתֶיךָ
שֶׁבְּכָל עֵת, עֶרֶב וָבֹקֶר וְצָהֳרָיִם.
הַטּוֹב, כִּי לֹא כָלוּ רַחֲמֶיךָ
וְהַמְרַחֵם, כִּי לֹא תַמּוּ חֲסָדֶיךָ
מֵעוֹלָם קִוִּינוּ לָךְ.

On Chanuka say:

עַל הַנִּסִּים We thank You, *Hashem,* for the miracles, the deliverances, the great strength, and the victories in war that You displayed for us in earlier times and in our times.

בִּימֵי מַתִּתְיָהוּ In the days of Mattityahu, son of Yochanan the *Kohen Gadol,* the Hasmonean, and his sons, the wicked Greeks challenged Your Jewish people trying to make them forget Your Torah and sin. In Your great kindness, You, *Hashem,* supported us in this difficult time. You allowed for:

The weak Jews to defeat the mighty Greeks,
The few Jews to defeat the many Greeks,
The pure Jews to defeat the impure Greeks,
The righteous Jews to defeat the wicked Greeks, and
The Jews who studied Your Torah to defeat the Greeks who did not.

Hashem, on this day everyone in the world recognized You as You miraculously saved Your Jewish people. Your Jewish people then entered the *Beit HaMikdash* to clean and purify it. They lit candles in the courtyard of the *Beit HaMikdash* and set aside these eight days of *Chanukah* for giving thanks and praising You.

Continue with "For all these reasons."

For all these reasons
we will thank You, *Hashem,* our King, forever.
Every living person will recognize and praise You, *Hashem,*
for You are the God that helps and saves Your people.

Bend the knees when saying "Thank," bow when saying "You," and stand straight before saying "Hashem."

Thank You, *Hashem,* for You are worthy of being thanked.

בחנוכה:

עַל הַנִּסִּים וְעַל הַפֻּרְקָן וְעַל הַגְּבוּרוֹת וְעַל הַתְּשׁוּעוֹת וְעַל הַמִּלְחָמוֹת שֶׁעָשִׂיתָ לַאֲבוֹתֵינוּ בַּיָּמִים הָהֵם בַּזְּמַן הַזֶּה.

בִּימֵי מַתִּתְיָהוּ בֶּן יוֹחָנָן כֹּהֵן גָּדוֹל חַשְׁמוֹנַאי וּבָנָיו, כְּשֶׁעָמְדָה מַלְכוּת יָוָן הָרְשָׁעָה עַל עַמְּךָ יִשְׂרָאֵל לְהַשְׁכִּיחָם תּוֹרָתֶךָ וּלְהַעֲבִירָם מֵחֻקֵּי רְצוֹנֶךָ, וְאַתָּה בְּרַחֲמֶיךָ הָרַבִּים עָמַדְתָּ לָהֶם בְּעֵת צָרָתָם, רַבְתָּ אֶת רִיבָם, דַּנְתָּ אֶת דִּינָם, נָקַמְתָּ אֶת נִקְמָתָם, מָסַרְתָּ גִבּוֹרִים בְּיַד חַלָּשִׁים, וְרַבִּים בְּיַד מְעַטִּים, וּטְמֵאִים בְּיַד טְהוֹרִים, וּרְשָׁעִים בְּיַד צַדִּיקִים, וְזֵדִים בְּיַד עוֹסְקֵי תוֹרָתֶךָ, וּלְךָ עָשִׂיתָ שֵׁם גָּדוֹל וְקָדוֹשׁ בְּעוֹלָמֶךָ, וּלְעַמְּךָ יִשְׂרָאֵל עָשִׂיתָ תְּשׁוּעָה גְדוֹלָה וּפֻרְקָן כְּהַיּוֹם הַזֶּה. וְאַחַר כֵּן בָּאוּ בָנֶיךָ לִדְבִיר בֵּיתֶךָ, וּפִנּוּ אֶת הֵיכָלֶךָ, וְטִהֲרוּ אֶת מִקְדָּשֶׁךָ, וְהִדְלִיקוּ נֵרוֹת בְּחַצְרוֹת קָדְשֶׁךָ, וְקָבְעוּ שְׁמוֹנַת יְמֵי חֲנֻכָּה אֵלּוּ, לְהוֹדוֹת וּלְהַלֵּל לְשִׁמְךָ הַגָּדוֹל.

Continue with וְעַל כֻּלָּם.

וְעַל כֻּלָּם
יִתְבָּרַךְ וְיִתְרוֹמַם שִׁמְךָ מַלְכֵּנוּ תָּמִיד לְעוֹלָם וָעֶד.
וְכֹל הַחַיִּים יוֹדוּךָ סֶּלָה, וִיהַלְלוּ אֶת שִׁמְךָ בֶּאֱמֶת הָאֵל יְשׁוּעָתֵנוּ וְעֶזְרָתֵנוּ סֶלָה.

Bend the knees when saying בָּרוּךְ*, bow when saying* אַתָּה*, and stand straight before saying Hashem's name.*

בָּרוּךְ אַתָּה יהוה, הַטּוֹב שִׁמְךָ וּלְךָ נָאֶה לְהוֹדוֹת.

PEACE

שִׂים שָׁלוֹם *Hashem,*
please provide Your Jewish people
with peace, goodness,
blessing, kindness, and mercy.
Bless us, *Hashem,* all as one.
Hashem,
You have given us Your Torah of life,
and treated us with kindness, righteousness,
blessing, mercy, and peace.
May it be good in Your eyes, *Hashem,*
to bless Your Jewish people with peace
at every moment of every hour.
Thank You, *Hashem,*
who blesses His Jewish people with peace.

CONCLUSION OF AMIDA

אֱלֹהַי *Hashem,* please help me:
Control my mouth from speaking badly
about other people,
Stay silent and not respond
if someone speaks badly about me,
Learn Your Torah, and do Your *mitzvot.*
Hashem,
if people plan to do something evil against me,
please stop these plans and protect me.

שלום

שִׂים שָׁלוֹם טוֹבָה וּבְרָכָה
חֵן וָחֶסֶד וְרַחֲמִים עָלֵינוּ
וְעַל כָּל יִשְׂרָאֵל עַמֶּךָ.
בָּרְכֵנוּ אָבִינוּ כֻּלָּנוּ כְּאֶחָד בְּאוֹר פָּנֶיךָ
כִּי בְאוֹר פָּנֶיךָ נָתַתָּ לָּנוּ יהוה אֱלֹהֵינוּ
תּוֹרַת חַיִּים וְאַהֲבַת חֶסֶד
וּצְדָקָה וּבְרָכָה וְרַחֲמִים
וְחַיִּים וְשָׁלוֹם.
וְטוֹב בְּעֵינֶיךָ לְבָרֵךְ אֶת עַמְּךָ יִשְׂרָאֵל
בְּכָל עֵת וּבְכָל שָׁעָה בִּשְׁלוֹמֶךָ.
בָּרוּךְ אַתָּה יהוה
הַמְבָרֵךְ אֶת עַמּוֹ יִשְׂרָאֵל בַּשָּׁלוֹם.

סיום העמידה

אֱלֹהַי, נְצֹר לְשׁוֹנִי מֵרָע וּשְׂפָתַי מִדַּבֵּר מִרְמָה
וְלִמְקַלְלַי נַפְשִׁי תִדֹּם, וְנַפְשִׁי כֶּעָפָר לַכֹּל תִּהְיֶה.
פְּתַח לִבִּי בְּתוֹרָתֶךָ, וּבְמִצְוֹתֶיךָ תִּרְדֹּף נַפְשִׁי.
וְכָל הַחוֹשְׁבִים עָלַי רָעָה
מְהֵרָה הָפֵר עֲצָתָם וְקַלְקֵל מַחֲשַׁבְתָּם.

Even if I am not deserving of being helped,
please act on my behalf
as I represent Your name and Your Torah.
Hashem, please save Your Jewish people
from difficult situations and answer my requests.
May You find my thoughts and prayers favorable.

Take three steps backwards and bow to your left as you say:

You, *Hashem,* make peace in heaven.

Bow to your right as you say:

Please may You bring peace to us

Bow forward as you say:

And all Your Jewish people.

Before taking three steps forward, say the following quietly:

Hashem, our God and God of our ancestors, may You please rebuild the *Beit HaMikdash* soon. *Hashem,* please allow us to learn Your Torah and serve You in the *Beit HaMikdash* as the Jewish people once did.

עֲשֵׂה לְמַעַן שְׁמֶךָ, עֲשֵׂה לְמַעַן יְמִינֶךָ
עֲשֵׂה לְמַעַן קְדֻשָּׁתֶךָ, עֲשֵׂה לְמַעַן תּוֹרָתֶךָ.
לְמַעַן יֵחָלְצוּן יְדִידֶיךָ, הוֹשִׁיעָה יְמִינְךָ וַעֲנֵנִי:
יִהְיוּ לְרָצוֹן אִמְרֵי־פִי וְהֶגְיוֹן לִבִּי לְפָנֶיךָ, יהוה צוּרִי וְגֹאֲלִי:

Take three steps backwards and bow to your left as you say:

עֹשֶׂה שָׁלוֹם בִּמְרוֹמָיו

Bow to your right as you say:

הוּא יַעֲשֶׂה שָׁלוֹם עָלֵינוּ

Bow forward as you say:

וְעַל כָּל יִשְׂרָאֵל, וְאִמְרוּ אָמֵן.

Before taking three steps forward, say the following quietly:

יְהִי רָצוֹן מִלְּפָנֶיךָ יהוה אֱלֹהֵינוּ וֵאלֹהֵי אֲבוֹתֵינוּ. שֶׁיִּבָּנֶה בֵּית הַמִּקְדָּשׁ בִּמְהֵרָה בְיָמֵינוּ, וְתֵן חֶלְקֵנוּ בְּתוֹרָתֶךָ. וְשָׁם נַעֲבָדְךָ בְּיִרְאָה כִּימֵי עוֹלָם וּכְשָׁנִים קַדְמֹנִיּוֹת. וְעָרְבָה לַיהוה מִנְחַת יְהוּדָה וִירוּשָׁלָיִם כִּימֵי עוֹלָם וּכְשָׁנִים קַדְמֹנִיּוֹת:

THE LEADER'S REPETITION

Try to focus on each blessing that the Leader reads, by following along and thinking about the sentences below. After each beracha that the Leader recites, answer "Amen."

I will call out to *Hashem*, let us all give praise to Him.
Hashem, open my lips
and help my mouth recite Your praise.

ANCESTORS

We praise You, *Hashem,*
for protecting, helping, and saving us
as You did for our ancestors,
Avraham, Yitzchak, and Yaakov.
Thank You, *Hashem,*
who protects us in the merit of Avraham.

(*Congregation:* Amen.)

HASHEM'S STRENGTH

We praise You, *Hashem,*
for providing food to those who are hungry,
support to those who are falling,
health to those who are sick,
and help to those who are in challenging situations.
Thank You, *Hashem,*
for bringing the dead back to life. (*Congregation:* Amen.)

חזרת הש"ץ

Try to focus on each blessing that the חזן *reads,*
by following along and thinking about the sentences below.
After each beracha that the חזן *recites, answer* אָמֵן.

כִּי שֵׁם יהוה אֶקְרָא, הָבוּ גֹדֶל לֵאלֹהֵינוּ:
אֲדֹנָי, שְׂפָתַי תִּפְתָּח, וּפִי יַגִּיד תְּהִלָּתֶךָ:

אבות

בָּרוּךְ אַתָּה יהוה, אֱלֹהֵינוּ וֵאלֹהֵי אֲבוֹתֵינוּ
אֱלֹהֵי אַבְרָהָם, אֱלֹהֵי יִצְחָק, וֵאלֹהֵי יַעֲקֹב
הָאֵל הַגָּדוֹל הַגִּבּוֹר וְהַנּוֹרָא, אֵל עֶלְיוֹן
גּוֹמֵל חֲסָדִים טוֹבִים, וְקוֹנֵה הַכֹּל, וְזוֹכֵר חַסְדֵי אָבוֹת
וּמֵבִיא גוֹאֵל לִבְנֵי בְנֵיהֶם לְמַעַן שְׁמוֹ בְּאַהֲבָה.
מֶלֶךְ עוֹזֵר וּמוֹשִׁיעַ וּמָגֵן.
בָּרוּךְ אַתָּה יהוה, מָגֵן אַבְרָהָם. (קהל: אָמֵן)

גבורות

אַתָּה גִּבּוֹר לְעוֹלָם, אֲדֹנָי, מְחַיֵּה מֵתִים אַתָּה, רַב לְהוֹשִׁיעַ

This line is said during the rainy season, from שמחת תורה *to* פסח*:*

(מַשִּׁיב הָרְוּחַ וּמוֹרִיד הַגֶּשֶׁם)

מְכַלְכֵּל חַיִּים בְּחֶסֶד, מְחַיֵּה מֵתִים בְּרַחֲמִים רַבִּים
סוֹמֵךְ נוֹפְלִים, וְרוֹפֵא חוֹלִים, וּמַתִּיר אֲסוּרִים
וּמְקַיֵּם אֱמוּנָתוֹ לִישֵׁנֵי עָפָר.
מִי כָמְוֹךָ, בַּעַל גְּבוּרוֹת, וּמִי דְּוֹמֶה לָּךְ
מֶלֶךְ, מֵמִית וּמְחַיֶּה וּמַצְמִיחַ יְשׁוּעָה.
וְנֶאֱמָן אַתָּה לְהַחֲיוֹת מֵתִים.
בָּרוּךְ אַתָּה יהוה, מְחַיֵּה הַמֵּתִים. (קהל: אָמֵן)

KEDUSHA

This section of tefillah is said while standing silently with feet together. The sentences are said responsively, Congregation followed by the Leader.

Congregation then Leader: נְקַדֵּשׁ We will announce You, *Hashem*,
as holy in this world,
just as the angels
announce You as holy in heaven.
As Your prophet wrote,
The angels call to one another saying:

(Stand on your toes as you repeat the word "Holy")

Congregation then Leader: Holy, holy, holy, is *Hashem*.
The whole world is filled with Your holiness.

Leader: All the Jewish people and the angels
say in response:

Congregation then Leader: Blessed is *Hashem*'s holiness.

Leader: It is written in *Tehillim*:

Congregation then Leader: *Hashem*, You have ruled over the Jewish people for generations, and You shall continue to be our King forever.

Leader: *Hashem*, in every generation
we will discuss Your holiness and greatness.
Our mouths shall never stop
speaking of Your praises,
for You, *Hashem*, are a great and holy King.
Thank You, *Hashem*, our holy God.

(*Congregation:* Amen.)

קדושה

This section of tefillah is said while standing silently with feet together. The sentences are said responsively, קהל followed by the חזן.

קהל *then* חזן: נְקַדֵּשׁ אֶת שִׁמְךָ בָּעוֹלָם
כְּשֵׁם שֶׁמַּקְדִּישִׁים אוֹתוֹ בִּשְׁמֵי מָרוֹם
כַּכָּתוּב עַל יַד נְבִיאֶךָ
וְקָרָא זֶה אֶל־זֶה וְאָמַר

(Stand on your toes as you repeat the word קָדוֹשׁ*)*

קהל *then* חזן: קָדוֹשׁ, קָדוֹשׁ, קָדוֹשׁ, יהוה צְבָאוֹת
מְלֹא כָל־הָאָרֶץ כְּבוֹדוֹ:

חזן: לְעֻמָּתָם בָּרוּךְ יֹאמֵרוּ

קהל *then* חזן: בָּרוּךְ כְּבוֹד־יהוה מִמְּקוֹמוֹ:

חזן: וּבְדִבְרֵי קָדְשְׁךָ כָּתוּב לֵאמֹר

קהל *then* חזן: יִמְלֹךְ יהוה לְעוֹלָם
אֱלֹהַיִךְ צִיּוֹן לְדֹר וָדֹר, הַלְלוּיָהּ:

חזן: לְדוֹר וָדוֹר נַגִּיד גָּדְלֶךָ
וּלְנֵצַח נְצָחִים קְדֻשָּׁתְךָ נַקְדִּישׁ
וְשִׁבְחֲךָ אֱלֹהֵינוּ מִפִּינוּ לֹא יָמוּשׁ לְעוֹלָם וָעֶד
כִּי אֵל מֶלֶךְ גָּדוֹל וְקָדוֹשׁ אָתָּה.
בָּרוּךְ אַתָּה יהוה, הָאֵל הַקָּדוֹשׁ.

(קהל: אָמֵן)

KEDUSHAT HAYOM

Hashem gave the Jewish people
Rosh Chodesh, the new month,
as a time for forgiveness for us,
and all future generations
and we pray that we will be able to bring
korbanot once again
in the *Beit HaMikdash* on this special day.

רָאשֵׁי חֳדָשִׁים *Rosh Chodesh.* The *mitzva* of Rosh Chodesh is special because it was the first *mitzva* that *Hashem* gave to the Jewish people. Rosh Chodesh was honored with being the first *mitzva* because it celebrates the moon going from its smallest point and beginning to get bigger and bigger, until it becomes a full moon. *Hashem* thought this was a very important message for the Jewish people. There will be times where everything is going well and we are a strong nation and other times which will be harder. It is important for us to remember that these are all from *Hashem*.

קדושת היום

רָאשֵׁי חֳדָשִׁים לְעַמְּךָ נָתַתָּ, זְמַן כַּפָּרָה לְכָל תּוֹלְדוֹתָם
בִּהְיוֹתָם מַקְרִיבִים לְפָנֶיךָ זִבְחֵי רָצוֹן
וּשְׂעִירֵי חַטָּאת לְכַפֵּר בַּעֲדָם.
זִכָּרוֹן לְכֻלָּם יִהְיוּ, וּתְשׁוּעַת נַפְשָׁם מִיַּד שׂוֹנֵא.
מִזְבֵּחַ חָדָשׁ בְּצִיּוֹן תָּכִין, וְעוֹלַת רֹאשׁ חֹדֶשׁ נַעֲלֶה עָלָיו
וּשְׂעִירֵי עִזִּים נַעֲשֶׂה בְרָצוֹן
וּבַעֲבוֹדַת בֵּית הַמִּקְדָּשׁ נִשְׂמַח כֻּלָּנוּ
וּבְשִׁירֵי דָוִד עַבְדְּךָ הַנִּשְׁמָעִים בְּעִירֶךָ
הָאֲמוּרִים לִפְנֵי מִזְבְּחֶךָ.
אַהֲבַת עוֹלָם תָּבִיא לָהֶם, וּבְרִית אָבוֹת לַבָּנִים תִּזְכֹּר.

וַהֲבִיאֵנוּ לְצִיּוֹן עִירְךָ בְּרִנָּה
וְלִירוּשָׁלַיִם בֵּית מִקְדָּשְׁךָ בְּשִׂמְחַת עוֹלָם
וְשָׁם נַעֲשֶׂה לְפָנֶיךָ אֶת קָרְבְּנוֹת חוֹבוֹתֵינוּ
תְּמִידִים כְּסִדְרָם וּמוּסָפִים כְּהִלְכָתָם.

וְאֶת מוּסַף יוֹם רֹאשׁ הַחֹדֶשׁ הַזֶּה
נַעֲשֶׂה וְנַקְרִיב לְפָנֶיךָ בְּאַהֲבָה כְּמִצְוַת רְצוֹנֶךָ
כְּמוֹ שֶׁכָּתַבְתָּ עָלֵינוּ בְּתוֹרָתֶךָ
עַל יְדֵי מֹשֶׁה עַבְדֶּךָ מִפִּי כְבוֹדֶךָ
כָּאָמוּר

וּבְרָאשֵׁי חָדְשֵׁיכֶם תַּקְרִיבוּ עֹלָה לַיהוה
פָּרִים בְּנֵי־בָקָר שְׁנַיִם וְאַיִל אֶחָד
כְּבָשִׂים בְּנֵי־שָׁנָה שִׁבְעָה, תְּמִימִם:

Reminder: Say "Amen" after the Leader recites each beracha.

Hashem,
our God, and God of our ancestors,
may You please fill the new month
with only good things
for Your Jewish people.

Thank You, *Hashem,*
for making the Jewish people
and the new month holy.

SERVICE IN THE *BEIT HAMIKDASH*

We pray to You, *Hashem,*
that You accept our prayers
as though they are the sacrifices
that were once brought to You
in Your holy *Beit HaMikdash.*
May we be worthy
to see the rebuilding of the *Beit HaMikdash.*
We thank You, *Hashem,*
for returning Your presence to Zion. (*Congregation:* Amen.)

Reminder: Say אָמֵן after the חזן recites each beracha.

וּמִנְחָתָם וְנִסְכֵּיהֶם כִּמְדֻבָּר
שְׁלֹשָׁה עֶשְׂרֹנִים לַפָּר, וּשְׁנֵי עֶשְׂרֹנִים לָאָיִל
וְעִשָּׂרוֹן לַכֶּבֶשׂ, וְיַיִן כְּנִסְכּוֹ, וְשָׂעִיר לְכַפֵּר
וּשְׁנֵי תְמִידִים כְּהִלְכָתָם.

אֱלֹהֵינוּ וֵאלֹהֵי אֲבוֹתֵינוּ
חַדֵּשׁ עָלֵינוּ אֶת הַחֹדֶשׁ הַזֶּה לְטוֹבָה וְלִבְרָכָה
לְשָׂשׂוֹן וּלְשִׂמְחָה, לִישׁוּעָה וּלְנֶחָמָה
לְפַרְנָסָה וּלְכַלְכָּלָה, לְחַיִּים וּלְשָׁלוֹם
לִמְחִילַת חֵטְא וְלִסְלִיחַת עָוֹן
(*From* מרחשון *to* אדר שני *in a Jewish leap year* וּלְכַפָּרַת פָּשַׁע)
כִּי בְעַמְּךָ יִשְׂרָאֵל בָּחַרְתָּ מִכָּל הָאֻמּוֹת
וְחֻקֵּי רָאשֵׁי חֳדָשִׁים לָהֶם קָבָעְתָּ.
בָּרוּךְ אַתָּה יהוה, מְקַדֵּשׁ יִשְׂרָאֵל וְרָאשֵׁי חֳדָשִׁים.
(קהל: **אָמֵן**)

עבודה

רְצֵה יהוה אֱלֹהֵינוּ בְּעַמְּךָ יִשְׂרָאֵל, וּבִתְפִלָּתָם
וְהָשֵׁב אֶת הָעֲבוֹדָה לִדְבִיר בֵּיתֶךָ
וְאִשֵּׁי יִשְׂרָאֵל וּתְפִלָּתָם בְּאַהֲבָה תְקַבֵּל בְּרָצוֹן
וּתְהִי לְרָצוֹן תָּמִיד עֲבוֹדַת יִשְׂרָאֵל עַמֶּךָ.
וְתֶחֱזֶינָה עֵינֵינוּ בְּשׁוּבְךָ לְצִיּוֹן בְּרַחֲמִים.
בָּרוּךְ אַתָּה יהוה, הַמַּחֲזִיר שְׁכִינָתוֹ לְצִיּוֹן. (קהל: **אָמֵן**)

THANK YOU

While the Leader says this prayer, the Congregation says the prayer on the bottom of this page.

You, *Hashem,*
have unlimited mercy and kindness
and therefore we have always placed our hope in You.

The following is said quietly while the Leader says the above. Bow when saying the first sentence below beginning with the words "Thank You, Hashem."

מוֹדִים Thank You, *Hashem,*
our God and God of our ancestors.
You are God of all people,
You created us,
and You created the entire world.
Thank You for giving us life
and for providing us with food to eat.
May You continue to give us life and food to eat.
May You gather us from exile
and return us to Your holy places
so we can keep Your laws,
and serve You with a perfect heart.
Thank You *Hashem,*
our God to whom thanksgiving is due.

הודאה

While the חזן *says this prayer, the* קהל *says the prayer on the bottom of this page.*

מוֹדִים אֲנַחְנוּ לָךְ

שָׁאַתָּה הוּא יהוה אֱלֹהֵינוּ וֵאלֹהֵי אֲבוֹתֵינוּ לְעוֹלָם וָעֶד.

צוּר חַיֵּינוּ, מָגֵן יִשְׁעֵנוּ אַתָּה הוּא לְדוֹר וָדוֹר.

נוֹדֶה לְּךָ וּנְסַפֵּר תְּהִלָּתֶךָ

עַל חַיֵּינוּ הַמְּסוּרִים בְּיָדֶךָ, וְעַל נִשְׁמוֹתֵינוּ הַפְּקוּדוֹת לָךְ

וְעַל נִסֶּיךָ שֶׁבְּכָל יוֹם עִמָּנוּ, וְעַל נִפְלְאוֹתֶיךָ וְטוֹבוֹתֶיךָ

שֶׁבְּכָל עֵת, עֶרֶב וָבֹקֶר וְצָהֳרָיִם.

הַטּוֹב, כִּי לֹא כָלוּ רַחֲמֶיךָ

וְהַמְרַחֵם, כִּי לֹא תַמּוּ חֲסָדֶיךָ, מֵעוֹלָם קִוִּינוּ לָךְ.

The following is said quietly while the חזן *says the above.*
Bow when saying the first sentence below beginning with the words מוֹדִים אֲנַחְנוּ לָךְ.

מוֹדִים אֲנַחְנוּ לָךְ

שָׁאַתָּה הוּא יהוה אֱלֹהֵינוּ וֵאלֹהֵי אֲבוֹתֵינוּ

אֱלֹהֵי כָל בָּשָׂר, יוֹצְרֵנוּ, יוֹצֵר בְּרֵאשִׁית.

בְּרָכוֹת וְהוֹדָאוֹת לְשִׁמְךָ הַגָּדוֹל וְהַקָּדוֹשׁ

עַל שֶׁהֶחֱיִיתָנוּ וְקִיַּמְתָּנוּ.

כֵּן תְּחַיֵּנוּ וּתְקַיְּמֵנוּ

וְתֶאֱסֹף גָּלֻיּוֹתֵינוּ לְחַצְרוֹת קָדְשֶׁךָ

לִשְׁמֹר חֻקֶּיךָ וְלַעֲשׂוֹת רְצוֹנֶךָ וּלְעָבְדְּךָ בְּלֵבָב שָׁלֵם

עַל שֶׁאֲנַחְנוּ מוֹדִים לָךְ.

בָּרוּךְ אֵל הַהוֹדָאוֹת.

Reminder: Say "Amen" after the Leader recites the beracha.

On Chanuka say:

We thank You, *Hashem,* for the miracles, the deliverances, the great strength, and the victories in war that You displayed for us in earlier times and in our times.

In the days of Mattityahu, son of Yochanan the *Kohen Gadol,* the Hasmonean, and his sons, the wicked Greeks challenged Your Jewish people trying to make them forget Your Torah and sin. In Your great kindness, You, *Hashem,* supported us in this difficult time. You allowed for: The weak Jews to defeat the mighty Greeks, The few Jews to defeat the many Greeks, The pure Jews to defeat the impure Greeks, The righteous Jews to defeat the wicked Greeks, and The Jews who studied Your Torah to defeat the Greeks who did not. *Hashem,* on this day everyone in the world recognized You as You miraculously saved Your Jewish people. Your Jewish people then entered the *Beit HaMikdash* to clean and purify it. They lit candles in the courtyard of the *Beit HaMikdash* and set aside these eight days of *Chanukah* for giving thanks and praising You.

Continue with "We thank You"

We thank You, *Hashem,* for You are good
and all that You do is good.
Thank You, *Hashem,* for You are worthy of being thanked.

(*Congregation:* Amen.)

BLESSINGS OF THE *KOHANIM*

אֱלֹהֵינוּ *Hashem,* Our God and God of our ancestors, provide us with the three blessings that Aharon the *Kohen* and the *kohanim* his descendants use to bless the Jewish people.

Leader: *Hashem* should bless and protect you.

(*Congregation:* May it be as you say!)

Leader: *Hashem* should be kind and favorable towards you.

(*Congregation:* May it be as you say!)

Leader: *Hashem* should grant you peace.

(*Congregation:* May it be as you say!)

Reminder: Say אָמֵן after the חזן recites the beracha.

בחנוכה:

עַל הַנִּסִּים וְעַל הַפֻּרְקָן וְעַל הַגְּבוּרוֹת וְעַל הַתְּשׁוּעוֹת וְעַל הַמִּלְחָמוֹת שֶׁעָשִׂיתָ לַאֲבוֹתֵינוּ בַּיָּמִים הָהֵם בַּזְּמַן הַזֶּה.

בִּימֵי מַתִּתְיָהוּ בֶּן יוֹחָנָן כֹּהֵן גָּדוֹל חַשְׁמוֹנַאי וּבָנָיו, כְּשֶׁעָמְדָה מַלְכוּת יָוָן הָרְשָׁעָה עַל עַמְּךָ יִשְׂרָאֵל לְהַשְׁכִּיחָם תּוֹרָתֶךָ וּלְהַעֲבִירָם מֵחֻקֵּי רְצוֹנֶךָ, וְאַתָּה בְּרַחֲמֶיךָ הָרַבִּים עָמַדְתָּ לָהֶם בְּעֵת צָרָתָם, רַבְתָּ אֶת רִיבָם, דַּנְתָּ אֶת דִּינָם, נָקַמְתָּ אֶת נִקְמָתָם, מָסַרְתָּ גִבּוֹרִים בְּיַד חַלָּשִׁים, וְרַבִּים בְּיַד מְעַטִּים, וּטְמֵאִים בְּיַד טְהוֹרִים, וּרְשָׁעִים בְּיַד צַדִּיקִים, וְזֵדִים בְּיַד עוֹסְקֵי תוֹרָתֶךָ, וּלְךָ עָשִׂיתָ שֵׁם גָּדוֹל וְקָדוֹשׁ בְּעוֹלָמֶךָ, וּלְעַמְּךָ יִשְׂרָאֵל עָשִׂיתָ תְּשׁוּעָה גְדוֹלָה וּפֻרְקָן כְּהַיּוֹם הַזֶּה. וְאַחַר כֵּן בָּאוּ בָנֶיךָ לִדְבִיר בֵּיתֶךָ, וּפִנּוּ אֶת הֵיכָלֶךָ, וְטִהֲרוּ אֶת מִקְדָּשֶׁךָ, וְהִדְלִיקוּ נֵרוֹת בְּחַצְרוֹת קָדְשֶׁךָ, וְקָבְעוּ שְׁמוֹנַת יְמֵי חֲנֻכָּה אֵלּוּ, לְהוֹדוֹת וּלְהַלֵּל לְשִׁמְךָ הַגָּדוֹל.

Continue with וְעַל כֻּלָּם.

וְעַל כֻּלָּם, יִתְבָּרַךְ וְיִתְרוֹמַם שִׁמְךָ מַלְכֵּנוּ תָּמִיד לְעוֹלָם וָעֶד.
וְכֹל הַחַיִּים יוֹדוּךָ סֶּלָה, וִיהַלְלוּ אֶת שִׁמְךָ בֶּאֱמֶת
הָאֵל יְשׁוּעָתֵנוּ וְעֶזְרָתֵנוּ סֶלָה.

בָּרוּךְ אַתָּה יהוה, הַטּוֹב שִׁמְךָ וּלְךָ נָאֶה לְהוֹדוֹת.

(קהל: **אָמֵן**)

ברכת כוהנים

אֱלֹהֵינוּ וֵאלֹהֵי אֲבוֹתֵינוּ, בָּרְכֵנוּ בַבְּרָכָה הַמְשֻׁלֶּשֶׁת בַּתּוֹרָה, הַכְּתוּבָה עַל יְדֵי מֹשֶׁה עַבְדֶּךָ, הָאֲמוּרָה מִפִּי אַהֲרֹן וּבָנָיו כֹּהֲנִים עַם קְדוֹשֶׁיךָ, כָּאָמוּר

חזן: **יְבָרֶכְךָ יהוה וְיִשְׁמְרֶךָ:** קהל: **כֵּן יְהִי רָצוֹן**

חזן: **יָאֵר יהוה פָּנָיו אֵלֶיךָ וִיחֻנֶּךָּ:** קהל: **כֵּן יְהִי רָצוֹן**

חזן: **יִשָּׂא יהוה פָּנָיו אֵלֶיךָ וְיָשֵׂם לְךָ שָׁלוֹם:** קהל: **כֵּן יְהִי רָצוֹן**

Reminder: Say "Amen" after the Leader recites the beracha.

PEACE

We pray to You, *Hashem*,
that You grant peace to Your Jewish people
at every moment of every hour, forever.
Thank You, *Hashem*,
who blesses His Jewish people with peace.
(*Congregation:* Amen.)

After the Leader's Repetition,
the service continues with Full Kaddish (page 186),
followed by Aleinu (page 188).

Reminder: Say אָמֵן after the חזן recites the beracha.

שלום

שִׂים שָׁלוֹם טוֹבָה וּבְרָכָה
חֵן וָחֶסֶד וְרַחֲמִים עָלֵינוּ
וְעַל כָּל יִשְׂרָאֵל עַמֶּךָ.
בָּרְכֵנוּ אָבִינוּ כֻּלָּנוּ כְּאֶחָד בְּאוֹר פָּנֶיךָ
כִּי בְאוֹר פָּנֶיךָ נָתַתָּ לָּנוּ יהוה אֱלֹהֵינוּ
תּוֹרַת חַיִּים וְאַהֲבַת חֶסֶד
וּצְדָקָה וּבְרָכָה וְרַחֲמִים וְחַיִּים וְשָׁלוֹם.
וְטוֹב בְּעֵינֶיךָ לְבָרֵךְ אֶת עַמְּךָ יִשְׂרָאֵל
בְּכָל עֵת וּבְכָל שָׁעָה בִּשְׁלוֹמֶךָ.

בָּרוּךְ אַתָּה יהוה, הַמְבָרֵךְ אֶת עַמּוֹ יִשְׂרָאֵל בַּשָּׁלוֹם.

(קהל: **אָמֵן**)

After the חזרת הש״ץ, the service continues with קדיש שלם (page 187), followed by עָלֵינוּ (page 189).

Musaf for Chol HaMo'ed

The following Amida is said on Chol HaMo'ed (including Shabbat Chol HaMo'ed).

AMIDA

Take three steps back then three steps forward then stand with your feet together.

I will call out to *Hashem*, let us all give praise to Him.

Hashem, open my lips and help my mouth recite Your praise.

ANCESTORS

Bend the knees when saying "We thank," bow when saying "You," and stand straight before saying "Hashem."

בָּרוּךְ We thank You, *Hashem*,
our God, and God of our ancestors,
Avraham, Yitzchak, and Yaakov.
You, *Hashem*, are the great, mighty, awesome, kind,
and all-powerful Creator.
It is because of the greatness of our ancestors,
Avraham, Yitzchak, and Yaakov,
that *Hashem* will bring *Mashiach*.
Hashem is our King who helps, guides, and protects us.

Bend the knees when saying "Thank," bow when saying "You," and stand straight before saying "Hashem."

Thank You, *Hashem*,
who protects us in the merit of Avraham.

HASHEM'S STRENGTH

אַתָּה You, *Hashem*, have unlimited strength.
You save people in their time of need,
and You have the power to bring the dead back to life.
With kindness You provide the living
with the necessities to live,

מוסף לחול המועד

The following עמידה *is said on* חול המועד *(including* שבת חול המועד*).*

עמידה

Take three steps back then three steps forward then stand with your feet together.

כִּי שֵׁם יהוה אֶקְרָא, הָבוּ גֹדֶל לֵאלֹהֵינוּ:
אֲדֹנָי, שְׂפָתַי תִּפְתָּח, וּפִי יַגִּיד תְּהִלָּתֶךָ:

אבות

Bend the knees when saying בָּרוּךְ*, bow when saying* אַתָּה*, and stand straight before saying Hashem's name.*

בָּרוּךְ אַתָּה יהוה, אֱלֹהֵינוּ וֵאלֹהֵי אֲבוֹתֵינוּ
אֱלֹהֵי אַבְרָהָם, אֱלֹהֵי יִצְחָק, וֵאלֹהֵי יַעֲקֹב
הָאֵל הַגָּדוֹל הַגִּבּוֹר וְהַנּוֹרָא, אֵל עֶלְיוֹן
גּוֹמֵל חֲסָדִים טוֹבִים, וְקוֹנֵה הַכֹּל, וְזוֹכֵר חַסְדֵי אָבוֹת
וּמֵבִיא גוֹאֵל לִבְנֵי בְנֵיהֶם לְמַעַן שְׁמוֹ בְּאַהֲבָה.
מֶלֶךְ עוֹזֵר וּמוֹשִׁיעַ וּמָגֵן.

Bend the knees when saying בָּרוּךְ*, bow when saying* אַתָּה*, and stand straight before saying Hashem's name.*

בָּרוּךְ אַתָּה יהוה, מָגֵן אַבְרָהָם.

גבורות

אַתָּה גִּבּוֹר לְעוֹלָם, אֲדֹנָי
מְחַיֵּה מֵתִים אַתָּה, רַב לְהוֹשִׁיעַ
מְכַלְכֵּל חַיִּים בְּחֶסֶד, מְחַיֵּה מֵתִים בְּרַחֲמִים רַבִּים

and with mercy You keep Your promise
of bringing the dead back to life.
For the living, You:

Support those who are falling,
Heal those who are sick, and
Free those who are in challenging situations.

Who is like You, *Hashem*, and who can compare to You?
You, *Hashem*, are our King
who has the power to cause death and life.
We have complete faith
that You will bring us back to life after our passing.
Thank You, *Hashem*, for bringing the dead back to life.

HASHEM'S HOLINESS

אַתָּה קָדוֹשׁ *Hashem*, You are holy and Your name is holy.
The Jewish people, who are holy,
will praise You, *Hashem*, each day.
Thank You, *Hashem*, the holy God.

HOLINESS OF FESTIVAL

אַתָּה בְחַרְתָּנוּ You, *Hashem*, chose Your Jewish people
from all the other nations and:

Loved us,
Favored us,
Placed us above the other nations,
Made us holy by allowing us to do Your *mitzvot*,
Brought us close to serve You, and
Linked Your great and holy name to us.

סוֹמֵךְ נוֹפְלִים, וְרוֹפֵא חוֹלִים, וּמַתִּיר אֲסוּרִים
וּמְקַיֵּם אֱמוּנָתוֹ לִישֵׁנֵי עָפָר.
מִי כָמְוֹךָ, בַּעַל גְּבוּרוֹת, וּמִי דּוֹמֶה לָּךְ
מֶלֶךְ, מֵמִית וּמְחַיֶּה וּמַצְמִיחַ יְשׁוּעָה.
וְנֶאֱמָן אַתָּה לְהַחֲיוֹת מֵתִים.
בָּרוּךְ אַתָּה יהוה, מְחַיֵּה הַמֵּתִים.

קדושת השם

אַתָּה קָדוֹשׁ וְשִׁמְךָ קָדוֹשׁ
וּקְדוֹשִׁים בְּכָל יוֹם יְהַלְלוּךָ סֶּלָה.
בָּרוּךְ אַתָּה יהוה, הָאֵל הַקָּדוֹשׁ.

קדושת היום

אַתָּה בְחַרְתָּנוּ מִכָּל הָעַמִּים
אָהַבְתָּ אוֹתָנוּ וְרָצִיתָ בָּנוּ, וְרוֹמַמְתָּנוּ מִכָּל הַלְּשׁוֹנוֹת
וְקִדַּשְׁתָּנוּ בְּמִצְוֹתֶיךָ, וְקֵרַבְתָּנוּ מַלְכֵּנוּ לַעֲבוֹדָתֶךָ
וְשִׁמְךָ הַגָּדוֹל וְהַקָּדוֹשׁ עָלֵינוּ קָרָאתָ.

וְשִׁמְךָ הַגָּדוֹל וְהַקָּדוֹשׁ עָלֵינוּ קָרָאתָ *Linked Your great and holy name to us.* By choosing the Jewish people as His nation, *Hashem* linked His name with the Jewish people. This means that as Jews, any time a person sees us, the person will think of *Hashem*, our God. We are honored to be linked to *Hashem*, but we must always remember that it is a big responsibility as well. Each Jew must act appropriately and kindly towards others because our actions represent not only ourselves, but also the Jewish people and *Hashem*.

וַתִּתֶּן לָנוּ With love,
Hashem, our God,
You also gave us holidays to celebrate
with joy and happiness,

(*On Shabbat say:* this day of Shabbat and)

On Pesach say: this Yom Tov of *Matzot,*
the time we were freed from slavery.

On Sukkot say: this Yom Tov of *Sukkot,*
the time of great celebration.

You gave us this holiday
with (*On Shabbat say:* love and) holiness,
for us to remember leaving Egypt.

וּמִפְּנֵי חֲטָאֵינוּ Because the Jewish people sinned,
we were forced to leave our land, Israel,
and we were no longer able to bow before You
and serve You in Your chosen house,
the *Beit HaMikdash.*
Hashem,
our God and God of our ancestors,
may You please have mercy on us
and rebuild the *Beit HaMikdash* soon.
Our Father and King,
please may You soon show us Your kingdom
for all to see
and gather all Jews together
from around the world.

וַתִּתֶּן לָנוּ יהוה אֱלֹהֵינוּ בְּאַהֲבָה

(בשבת: שַׁבָּתוֹת לִמְנוּחָה וּ) מוֹעֲדִים לְשִׂמְחָה

חַגִּים וּזְמַנִּים לְשָׂשׂוֹן, אֶת יוֹם

(בשבת: הַשַּׁבָּת הַזֶּה וְאֶת יוֹם)

בפסח: חַג הַמַּצּוֹת הַזֶּה, זְמַן חֵרוּתֵנוּ

בסוכות: חַג הַסֻּכּוֹת הַזֶּה, זְמַן שִׂמְחָתֵנוּ

(בשבת: בְּאַהֲבָה) מִקְרָא קֹדֶשׁ, זֵכֶר לִיצִיאַת מִצְרָיִם.

וּמִפְּנֵי חֲטָאֵינוּ גָּלִינוּ מֵאַרְצֵנוּ, וְנִתְרַחַקְנוּ מֵעַל אַדְמָתֵנוּ
וְאֵין אֲנַחְנוּ יְכוֹלִים לַעֲלוֹת וְלֵרָאוֹת וּלְהִשְׁתַּחֲווֹת לְפָנֶיךָ
וְלַעֲשׂוֹת חוֹבוֹתֵינוּ בְּבֵית בְּחִירָתֶךָ
בַּבַּיִת הַגָּדוֹל וְהַקָּדוֹשׁ שֶׁנִּקְרָא שִׁמְךָ עָלָיו
מִפְּנֵי הַיָּד שֶׁנִּשְׁתַּלְּחָה בְּמִקְדָּשֶׁךָ.
יְהִי רָצוֹן מִלְּפָנֶיךָ יהוה אֱלֹהֵינוּ וֵאלֹהֵי אֲבוֹתֵינוּ
מֶלֶךְ רַחֲמָן
שֶׁתָּשׁוּב וּתְרַחֵם עָלֵינוּ וְעַל מִקְדָּשְׁךָ בְּרַחֲמֶיךָ הָרַבִּים
וְתִבְנֵהוּ מְהֵרָה וּתְגַדֵּל כְּבוֹדוֹ.
אָבִינוּ מַלְכֵּנוּ, גַּלֵּה כְּבוֹד מַלְכוּתְךָ עָלֵינוּ מְהֵרָה
וְהוֹפַע וְהִנָּשֵׂא עָלֵינוּ לְעֵינֵי כָּל חָי
וְקָרֵב פְּזוּרֵינוּ מִבֵּין הַגּוֹיִם
וּנְפוּצוֹתֵינוּ כַּנֵּס מִיַּרְכְּתֵי אָרֶץ.

וַהֲבִיאֵנוּ With great song and joy, *Hashem*,
please bring us to Your *Beit HaMikdash*
which You will build in Yerushalayim.
There, we will serve You by preparing
the regular and special *Yom Tov korbanot*,
as Jewish law requires.
And the special *korban*
for the *Yom Tov* of:

On Pesach say: *Matzot*,

On Sukkot say: *Sukkot*,

we will prepare and bring before You
with love as You commanded us in Your Torah,
saying:

On Shabbat add:

וּבְיוֹם הַשַּׁבָּת "On the Shabbat day,
bring two perfect lambs that are a year old,
together with flour and oil,
as a *korban* that is burnt before *Hashem*."

On Chol HaMoed Pesach say:

וְהִקְרַבְתֶּם Bring a *korban olah* to *Hashem* with the following animals:

- 2 bulls,
- 1 ram, and
- 7 lambs that are a year old.

Additionally, bring a *korban mincha* as well as a special wine *korban* for each animal, a male goat for forgiveness, and the two daily *korbanot tamid*.

On weekdays, continue with "Hashem, our God" on page 780.
On Shabbat, continue with "Those who keep" at the top of page 780.

וַהֲבִיאֵנוּ לְצִיּוֹן עִירְךָ בְּרִנָּה
וְלִירוּשָׁלַיִם בֵּית מִקְדָּשְׁךָ בְּשִׂמְחַת עוֹלָם
וְשָׁם נַעֲשֶׂה לְפָנֶיךָ אֶת קָרְבְּנוֹת חוֹבוֹתֵינוּ
תְּמִידִים כְּסִדְרָם וּמוּסָפִים כְּהִלְכָתָם
וְאֶת מוּסַף יוֹם / בשבת: וְאֶת מוּסְפֵי יוֹם הַשַּׁבָּת הַזֶּה וְיוֹם/

בפסח: חַג הַמַּצּוֹת הַזֶּה

בסוכות: חַג הַסֻּכּוֹת הַזֶּה

נַעֲשֶׂה וְנַקְרִיב לְפָנֶיךָ בְּאַהֲבָה כְּמִצְוַת רְצוֹנֶךָ
כְּמוֹ שֶׁכָּתַבְתָּ עָלֵינוּ בְּתוֹרָתֶךָ
עַל יְדֵי מֹשֶׁה עַבְדֶּךָ מִפִּי כְבוֹדֶךָ, כָּאָמוּר

On שבת *add:*

וּבְיוֹם הַשַּׁבָּת, שְׁנֵי־כְבָשִׂים בְּנֵי־שָׁנָה תְּמִימִם
וּשְׁנֵי עֶשְׂרֹנִים סֹלֶת מִנְחָה בְּלוּלָה בַשֶּׁמֶן וְנִסְכּוֹ:
עֹלַת שַׁבַּת בְּשַׁבַּתּוֹ, עַל־עֹלַת הַתָּמִיד וְנִסְכָּהּ:

On חול המועד פסח *say:*

וְהִקְרַבְתֶּם אִשֶּׁה עֹלָה לַיהוה, פָּרִים בְּנֵי־בָקָר שְׁנַיִם וְאַיִל אֶחָד, וְשִׁבְעָה כְבָשִׂים בְּנֵי שָׁנָה, תְּמִימִם יִהְיוּ לָכֶם:
וּמִנְחָתָם וְנִסְכֵּיהֶם כִּמְדֻבָּר, שְׁלֹשָׁה עֶשְׂרֹנִים לַפָּר וּשְׁנֵי עֶשְׂרֹנִים לָאָיִל, וְעִשָּׂרוֹן לַכֶּבֶשׂ, וְיַיִן כְּנִסְכּוֹ, וְשָׂעִיר לְכַפֵּר, וּשְׁנֵי תְמִידִים כְּהִלְכָתָם.

On weekdays, continue with אֱלֹהֵינוּ וֵאלֹהֵי אֲבוֹתֵינוּ *on page 781.*
On שבת*, continue with* יִשְׂמְחוּ בְמַלְכוּתְךָ *at the top of page 781.*

On the first day of Chol HaMoed Sukkot say:

וּבַיּוֹם On the second day of *Sukkot* you should bring a *korban olah* to *Hashem* with the following animals:

- 12 bulls,
- 2 rams, and
- 14 lambs that are a year old.

Additionally, bring a *korban mincha* as well as a special wine *korban* for each animal, a male goat for forgiveness, and the two daily *korbanot tamid.*

On the third day of *Sukkot* you should bring a *korban olah* to *Hashem* with the following animals:

- 11 bulls,
- 2 rams, and
- 14 lambs that are a year old.

Additionally, bring a *korban mincha* as well as a special wine *korban* for each animal, a male goat for forgiveness, and the two daily *korbanot tamid.*

On weekdays, continue with "Hashem, our God" on page 780.
On Shabbat, continue with "Those who keep" at the top of page 780.

On the first day of חול המועד סוכות*, say:*

וּבַיּוֹם הַשֵּׁנִי, פָּרִים בְּנֵי־בָקָר שְׁנֵים עָשָׂר, אֵילִם שְׁנָיִם, כְּבָשִׂים בְּנֵי־שָׁנָה אַרְבָּעָה עָשָׂר, תְּמִימִם:
וּמִנְחָתָם וְנִסְכֵּיהֶם כִּמְדֻבָּר, שְׁלֹשָׁה עֶשְׂרֹנִים לַפָּר, וּשְׁנֵי עֶשְׂרֹנִים לָאָיִל, וְעִשָּׂרוֹן לַכֶּבֶשׂ, וְיַיִן כְּנִסְכּוֹ, וְשָׂעִיר לְכַפֵּר, וּשְׁנֵי תְמִידִים כְּהִלְכָתָם.

וּבַיּוֹם הַשְּׁלִישִׁי, פָּרִים עַשְׁתֵּי־עָשָׂר, אֵילִם שְׁנָיִם, כְּבָשִׂים בְּנֵי־שָׁנָה אַרְבָּעָה עָשָׂר, תְּמִימִם:
וּמִנְחָתָם וְנִסְכֵּיהֶם כִּמְדֻבָּר, שְׁלֹשָׁה עֶשְׂרֹנִים לַפָּר, וּשְׁנֵי עֶשְׂרֹנִים לָאָיִל, וְעִשָּׂרוֹן לַכֶּבֶשׂ, וְיַיִן כְּנִסְכּוֹ, וְשָׂעִיר לְכַפֵּר, וּשְׁנֵי תְמִידִים כְּהִלְכָתָם.

On weekdays, continue with אֱלֹהֵינוּ וֵאלֹהֵי אֲבוֹתֵינוּ *on page 781.*
On שבת*, continue with* יִשְׂמְחוּ בְמַלְכוּתְךָ *at the top of page 781.*

וּבַיּוֹם הַשֵּׁנִי *On the second day.* Unlike *Chol HaMoed Pesach,* where each day's *korban* is the same, on *Chol HaMoed Sukkot* the *korban* for each day is slightly different: On each day, one less bull is brought than the day before. There was a time when Jews living outside of Israel did not know when Yom Tov began and therefore celebrated an extra day of Yom Tov, "just in case." Today, when the Jewish calendar is known around the world, Jews living outside of Israel continue to add an additional day of Yom Tov. As a result, on *Sukkot* we mention the two possible sets of *korbanot* that could have been brought each day.

On the second day of Chol HaMoed Sukkot say:

וּבַיּוֹם On the third day of *Sukkot* you should bring a *korban olah* to *Hashem* with the following animals:

- 11 bulls,
- 2 rams, and
- 14 lambs that are a year old.

Additionally, bring a *korban mincha* as well as a special wine *korban* for each animal, a male goat for forgiveness, and the two daily *korbanot tamid.*

On the fourth day of *Sukkot* you should bring a *korban olah* to *Hashem* with the following animals:

- 10 bulls,
- 2 rams, and
- 14 lambs that are a year old.

Additionally, bring a *korban mincha* as well as a special wine *korban* for each animal, a male goat for forgiveness, and the two daily *korbanot tamid.*

On weekdays, continue with "Hashem, our God" on page 780.
On Shabbat, continue with "Those who keep" at the top of page 780.

On the third day of Chol HaMoed Sukkot say:

וּבַיּוֹם On the fourth day of *Sukkot* you should bring a *korban olah* to *Hashem* with the following animals:

- 10 bulls,
- 2 rams, and
- 14 lambs that are each less than a year old.

Additionally, bring a *korban mincha* as well as a special wine *korban* for each animal, a male goat for forgiveness, and the two daily *korbanot tamid.*

On the second day of חול המועד סוכות*, say:*

וּבַיּוֹם הַשְּׁלִישִׁי, פָּרִים עַשְׁתֵּי־עָשָׂר, אֵילִם שְׁנָיִם, כְּבָשִׂים בְּנֵי־שָׁנָה אַרְבָּעָה עָשָׂר, תְּמִימִם:

וּמִנְחָתָם וְנִסְכֵּיהֶם כִּמְדֻבָּר, שְׁלֹשָׁה עֶשְׂרֹנִים לַפָּר, וּשְׁנֵי עֶשְׂרֹנִים לָאָיִל, וְעִשָּׂרוֹן לַכֶּבֶשׂ, וְיַיִן כְּנִסְכּוֹ, וְשָׂעִיר לְכַפֵּר, וּשְׁנֵי תְמִידִים כְּהִלְכָתָם.

וּבַיּוֹם הָרְבִיעִי, פָּרִים עֲשָׂרָה, אֵילִם שְׁנָיִם, כְּבָשִׂים בְּנֵי־שָׁנָה אַרְבָּעָה עָשָׂר, תְּמִימִם:

וּמִנְחָתָם וְנִסְכֵּיהֶם כִּמְדֻבָּר, שְׁלֹשָׁה עֶשְׂרֹנִים לַפָּר, וּשְׁנֵי עֶשְׂרֹנִים לָאָיִל, וְעִשָּׂרוֹן לַכֶּבֶשׂ, וְיַיִן כְּנִסְכּוֹ, וְשָׂעִיר לְכַפֵּר, וּשְׁנֵי תְמִידִים כְּהִלְכָתָם.

On weekdays, continue with אֱלֹהֵינוּ וֵאלֹהֵי אֲבוֹתֵינוּ *on page 781.*
On שבת*, continue with* יִשְׂמְחוּ בְמַלְכוּתְךָ *at the top of page 781.*

On the third day of חול המועד סוכות*, say:*

וּבַיּוֹם הָרְבִיעִי, פָּרִים עֲשָׂרָה, אֵילִם שְׁנָיִם, כְּבָשִׂים בְּנֵי־שָׁנָה אַרְבָּעָה עָשָׂר, תְּמִימִם:

וּמִנְחָתָם וְנִסְכֵּיהֶם כִּמְדֻבָּר, שְׁלֹשָׁה עֶשְׂרֹנִים לַפָּר, וּשְׁנֵי עֶשְׂרֹנִים לָאָיִל, וְעִשָּׂרוֹן לַכֶּבֶשׂ, וְיַיִן כְּנִסְכּוֹ, וְשָׂעִיר לְכַפֵּר, וּשְׁנֵי תְמִידִים כְּהִלְכָתָם.

On the fifth day of *Sukkot* you should bring a *korban olah* to *Hashem* with the following animals:

- 9 bulls,
- 2 rams, and
- 14 lambs that are a year old.

Additionally, bring a *korban mincha* as well as a special wine *korban* for each animal, a male goat for forgiveness, and the two daily *korbanot tamid.*

On weekdays, continue with אֱלֹהֵינוּ וֵאלֹהֵי אֲבוֹתֵינוּ *on the next page.*
On שבת*, continue with* יִשְׂמְחוּ בְמַלְכוּתְךָ *on the next page.*

On the fourth day of Chol HaMoed Sukkot say:

וּבַיּוֹם On the fifth day of *Sukkot* you should bring a *korban olah* to *Hashem* with the following animals:

- 9 bulls,
- 2 rams, and
- 14 lambs that are a year old.

Additionally, bring a *korban mincha* as well as a special wine *korban* for each animal, a male goat for forgiveness, and the two daily *korbanot tamid.*

On the sixth day of *Sukkot* you should bring a *korban olah* to *Hashem* with the following animals:

- 8 bulls,
- 2 rams, and
- 14 lambs that are a year old.

Additionally, bring a *korban mincha* as well as a special wine *korban* for each animal, a male goat for forgiveness, and the two daily *korbanot tamid.*

On weekdays, continue with אֱלֹהֵינוּ וֵאלֹהֵי אֲבוֹתֵינוּ *on the next page.*
On שבת*, continue with* יִשְׂמְחוּ בְמַלְכוּתְךָ *on the next page.*

וּבַיּוֹם הַחֲמִישִׁי, פָּרִים תִּשְׁעָה, אֵילִם שְׁנָיִם, כְּבָשִׂים בְּנֵי־שָׁנָה אַרְבָּעָה עָשָׂר, תְּמִימִם:
וּמִנְחָתָם וְנִסְכֵּיהֶם כִּמְדֻבָּר, שְׁלֹשָׁה עֶשְׂרֹנִים לַפָּר, וּשְׁנֵי עֶשְׂרֹנִים לָאָיִל, וְעִשָּׂרוֹן לַכֶּבֶשׂ, וְיַיִן כְּנִסְכּוֹ, וְשָׂעִיר לְכַפֵּר, וּשְׁנֵי תְמִידִים כְּהִלְכָתָם.

On weekdays, continue with אֱלֹהֵינוּ וֵאלֹהֵי אֲבוֹתֵינוּ *on the next page.*
On שבת, *continue with* יִשְׂמְחוּ בְמַלְכוּתְךָ *on the next page.*

On the fourth day of חול המועד סוכות, *say:*

וּבַיּוֹם הַחֲמִישִׁי, פָּרִים תִּשְׁעָה, אֵילִם שְׁנָיִם, כְּבָשִׂים בְּנֵי־שָׁנָה אַרְבָּעָה עָשָׂר, תְּמִימִם:
וּמִנְחָתָם וְנִסְכֵּיהֶם כִּמְדֻבָּר, שְׁלֹשָׁה עֶשְׂרֹנִים לַפָּר, וּשְׁנֵי עֶשְׂרֹנִים לָאָיִל, וְעִשָּׂרוֹן לַכֶּבֶשׂ, וְיַיִן כְּנִסְכּוֹ, וְשָׂעִיר לְכַפֵּר, וּשְׁנֵי תְמִידִים כְּהִלְכָתָם.

וּבַיּוֹם הַשִּׁשִּׁי, פָּרִים שְׁמֹנָה, אֵילִם שְׁנָיִם, כְּבָשִׂים בְּנֵי־שָׁנָה אַרְבָּעָה עָשָׂר, תְּמִימִם:
וּמִנְחָתָם וְנִסְכֵּיהֶם כִּמְדֻבָּר, שְׁלֹשָׁה עֶשְׂרֹנִים לַפָּר, וּשְׁנֵי עֶשְׂרֹנִים לָאָיִל, וְעִשָּׂרוֹן לַכֶּבֶשׂ, וְיַיִן כְּנִסְכּוֹ, וְשָׂעִיר לְכַפֵּר, וּשְׁנֵי תְמִידִים כְּהִלְכָתָם.

On weekdays, continue with אֱלֹהֵינוּ וֵאלֹהֵי אֲבוֹתֵינוּ *on the next page.*
On שבת, *continue with* יִשְׂמְחוּ בְמַלְכוּתְךָ *on the next page.*

On the fifth day of Chol HaMoed Sukkot, Hoshana Rabba, say:

וּבַיּוֹם On the sixth day of *Sukkot* you should bring a *korban olah* to *Hashem* with the following animals:

- 8 bulls,
- 2 rams, and
- 14 lambs that are a year old.

Additionally, bring a *korban mincha* as well as a special wine *korban* for each animal, a male goat for forgiveness, and the two daily *korbanot tamid.*

On the seventh day of *Sukkot* you should bring a *korban olah* to *Hashem* with the following animals:

- 7 bulls,
- 2 rams, and
- 14 lambs that are a year old.

Additionally, bring a *korban mincha* as well as a special wine *korban* for each animal, a male goat for forgiveness, and the two daily *korbanot tamid.*

Continue with אֱלֹהֵינוּ וֵאלֹהֵי אֲבוֹתֵינוּ *below.*

On Shabbat add:

יִשְׂמְחוּ Those who keep and enjoy Shabbat bring holiness to the seventh day and will be overjoyed. *Hashem,* You chose the seventh day and made it holy, calling it the most special of days, as it is a reminder of the creation of the world.

אֱלֹהֵינוּ *Hashem,* our God and God of our ancestors,
You are our King;
please show us mercy and respond to our call.
Remember all the good our ancestors did
and allow the *Beit HaMikdash* to be rebuilt.
Let us see the rebuilding of the *Beit HaMikdash,*
the *Kohanim* return to their service,
the *Levi'im* return to their song and music,
and the rest of the Jewish people return to their homes in Israel.

On the fifth day of חול המועד סוכות, הושענא רבה*, say:*

וּבַיּוֹם הַשִּׁשִּׁי, פָּרִים שְׁמֹנָה, אֵילִם שְׁנָיִם, כְּבָשִׂים בְּנֵי־שָׁנָה אַרְבָּעָה עָשָׂר, תְּמִימִם: וּמִנְחָתָם וְנִסְכֵּיהֶם כִּמְדֻבָּר, שְׁלֹשָׁה עֶשְׂרֹנִים לַפָּר, וּשְׁנֵי עֶשְׂרֹנִים לָאָיִל, וְעִשָּׂרוֹן לַכֶּבֶשׂ, וְיַיִן כְּנִסְכּוֹ, וְשָׂעִיר לְכַפֵּר, וּשְׁנֵי תְמִידִים כְּהִלְכָתָם.

וּבַיּוֹם הַשְּׁבִיעִי, פָּרִים שִׁבְעָה, אֵילִם שְׁנָיִם, כְּבָשִׂים בְּנֵי־שָׁנָה אַרְבָּעָה עָשָׂר, תְּמִימִם: וּמִנְחָתָם וְנִסְכֵּיהֶם כִּמְדֻבָּר, שְׁלֹשָׁה עֶשְׂרֹנִים לַפָּר, וּשְׁנֵי עֶשְׂרֹנִים לָאָיִל, וְעִשָּׂרוֹן לַכֶּבֶשׂ, וְיַיִן כְּנִסְכּוֹ, וְשָׂעִיר לְכַפֵּר, וּשְׁנֵי תְמִידִים כְּהִלְכָתָם.

Continue with אֱלֹהֵינוּ וֵאלֹהֵי אֲבוֹתֵינוּ *below.*

On שבת *say:*

יִשְׂמְחוּ בְמַלְכוּתְךָ שׁוֹמְרֵי שַׁבָּת וְקוֹרְאֵי עֹנֶג.
עַם מְקַדְּשֵׁי שְׁבִיעִי כֻּלָּם יִשְׂבְּעוּ וְיִתְעַנְּגוּ מִטּוּבֶךָ
וּבַשְּׁבִיעִי רָצִיתָ בּוֹ וְקִדַּשְׁתּוֹ
חֶמְדַּת יָמִים אוֹתוֹ קָרָאתָ, זֵכֶר לְמַעֲשֵׂה בְרֵאשִׁית.

אֱלֹהֵינוּ וֵאלֹהֵי אֲבוֹתֵינוּ
מֶלֶךְ רַחֲמָן רַחֵם עָלֵינוּ, טוֹב וּמֵטִיב הִדָּרֶשׁ לָנוּ
שׁוּבָה אֵלֵינוּ בַּהֲמוֹן רַחֲמֶיךָ, בִּגְלַל אָבוֹת שֶׁעָשׂוּ רְצוֹנֶךָ.
בְּנֵה בֵיתְךָ כְּבַתְּחִלָּה, וְכוֹנֵן מִקְדָּשְׁךָ עַל מְכוֹנוֹ
וְהַרְאֵנוּ בְּבִנְיָנוֹ, וְשַׂמְּחֵנוּ בְּתִקּוּנוֹ
וְהָשֵׁב כֹּהֲנִים לַעֲבוֹדָתָם, וּלְוִיִּם לְשִׁירָם וּלְזִמְרָם
וְהָשֵׁב יִשְׂרָאֵל לִנְוֵיהֶם.

וְשָׁם נַעֲלֶה We will appear and bow before You
in the *Beit HaMikdash* on the three holidays,
Pesach, Shavuot, and *Sukkot,* as it is written in Your Torah:
"All men should appear before *Hashem,* your God,
three times a year – on *Pesach, Shavuot,* and *Sukkot.*
Each person should bring a gift for a *korban* to *Hashem.*"

וְהַשִּׂיאֵנוּ *Hashem,* on this holiday please bless us with
long life, peace, joy and happiness as You promised us.
(*On Shabbat say:* *Hashem,* our God and God of our ancestors,
we rest today for Your sake.)
Allow us to become holy through keeping Your *mitzvot*
and studying Your Torah.
Be good to us, save us, and purify our hearts
to serve You sincerely.
Hashem, our God, (*On Shabbat say:* show us Your love and)
allow us to observe (*On Shabbat say:* Shabbat and)
Your holy festivals with joy.
Let the Jewish people who make Your name holy
celebrate You.
Thank You, *Hashem,* for making (*On Shabbat say:* Shabbat,)
the Jewish people and the holidays holy.

בְּשָׁלֹשׁ פַּעֲמֵי רְגָלֵינוּ *Three holidays.* Through the year the Jewish people celebrate many holidays, yet here the Torah only writes about three of them: *Pesach, Shavuot,* and *Sukkot.* These three holidays are referred to as the *shalosh regalim,* and when the *Beit HaMikdash* is standing, every Jewish man is commanded to travel to the *Beit HaMikdash* on these holidays to bring *korbanot.* Every Shabbat we invite *Hashem* into our homes, but on the *shalosh regalim, Hashem* invites us into His home, the *Beit HaMikdash.*

וְשָׁם נַעֲלֶה וְנֵרָאֶה וְנִשְׁתַּחֲוֶה לְפָנֶיךָ
בְּשָׁלֹשׁ פַּעֲמֵי רְגָלֵינוּ, כַּכָּתוּב בְּתוֹרָתֶךָ
שָׁלוֹשׁ פְּעָמִים בַּשָּׁנָה יֵרָאֶה כָל־זְכוּרְךָ
אֶת־פְּנֵי יהוה אֱלֹהֶיךָ, בַּמָּקוֹם אֲשֶׁר יִבְחָר
בְּחַג הַמַּצּוֹת, וּבְחַג הַשָּׁבֻעוֹת, וּבְחַג הַסֻּכּוֹת
וְלֹא יֵרָאֶה אֶת־פְּנֵי יהוה רֵיקָם:
אִישׁ כְּמַתְּנַת יָדוֹ
כְּבִרְכַּת יהוה אֱלֹהֶיךָ אֲשֶׁר נָתַן־לָךְ:

וְהַשִּׂיאֵנוּ יהוה אֱלֹהֵינוּ אֶת בִּרְכַּת מוֹעֲדֶיךָ
לְחַיִּים וּלְשָׁלוֹם, לְשִׂמְחָה וּלְשָׂשׂוֹן
כַּאֲשֶׁר רָצִיתָ וְאָמַרְתָּ לְבָרְכֵנוּ.
(בשבת: אֱלֹהֵינוּ וֵאלֹהֵי אֲבוֹתֵינוּ, רְצֵה בִמְנוּחָתֵנוּ)
קַדְּשֵׁנוּ בְּמִצְוֹתֶיךָ, וְתֵן חֶלְקֵנוּ בְּתוֹרָתֶךָ
שַׂבְּעֵנוּ מִטּוּבֶךָ, וְשַׂמְּחֵנוּ בִּישׁוּעָתֶךָ
וְטַהֵר לִבֵּנוּ לְעָבְדְּךָ בֶּאֱמֶת
וְהַנְחִילֵנוּ יהוה אֱלֹהֵינוּ (בשבת: בְּאַהֲבָה וּבְרָצוֹן)
בְּשִׂמְחָה וּבְשָׂשׂוֹן (בשבת: שַׁבָּת וּ) מוֹעֲדֵי קָדְשֶׁךָ
וְיִשְׂמְחוּ בְךָ יִשְׂרָאֵל מְקַדְּשֵׁי שְׁמֶךָ.
בָּרוּךְ אַתָּה יהוה
מְקַדֵּשׁ (בשבת: הַשַּׁבָּת וְ) יִשְׂרָאֵל וְהַזְּמַנִּים.

SERVICE IN THE *BEIT HAMIKDASH*

רְצֵה *Hashem,* please accept Your Jewish people
and their prayers.
We eagerly await the rebuilding of the *Beit HaMikdash*
so we can serve You with *korbanot.*
Until the *Beit HaMikdash* is rebuilt,
please accept our prayers with love.
May we be worthy
to see the rebuilding of the *Beit HaMikdash.*
We thank You, *Hashem,*
for returning Your presence to Zion.

THANK YOU

Bow when saying the words "We thank You."

מוֹדִים We thank You, *Hashem,*
for You are and always will be
our God, and the God of our ancestors.
You give us life and You always protect us.
We thank and praise You
for:

Our lives which are in Your hands,
Our souls which are in Your control,
The miracles You perform for us every day, and
The goodness You show us
at all times, morning, noon, and night.

You, *Hashem,*
have unlimited mercy and kindness
and therefore we have always placed our hope in You.

עבודה

רְצֵה יהוה אֱלֹהֵינוּ בְּעַמְּךָ יִשְׂרָאֵל, וּבִתְפִלָּתָם
וְהָשֵׁב אֶת הָעֲבוֹדָה לִדְבִיר בֵּיתֶךָ
וְאִשֵּׁי יִשְׂרָאֵל וּתְפִלָּתָם בְּאַהֲבָה תְקַבֵּל בְּרָצוֹן
וּתְהִי לְרָצוֹן תָּמִיד עֲבוֹדַת יִשְׂרָאֵל עַמֶּךָ.
וְתֶחֱזֶינָה עֵינֵינוּ בְּשׁוּבְךָ לְצִיּוֹן בְּרַחֲמִים.
בָּרוּךְ אַתָּה יהוה, הַמַּחֲזִיר שְׁכִינָתוֹ לְצִיּוֹן.

הודאה

Bow when saying the words מוֹדִים אֲנַחְנוּ לָךְ שָׁאַתָּה הוּא.

מוֹדִים אֲנַחְנוּ לָךְ
שָׁאַתָּה הוּא יהוה אֱלֹהֵינוּ וֵאלֹהֵי אֲבוֹתֵינוּ לְעוֹלָם וָעֶד.
צוּר חַיֵּינוּ, מָגֵן יִשְׁעֵנוּ, אַתָּה הוּא לְדוֹר וָדוֹר.
נוֹדֶה לְּךָ וּנְסַפֵּר תְּהִלָּתֶךָ
עַל חַיֵּינוּ הַמְּסוּרִים בְּיָדֶךָ
וְעַל נִשְׁמוֹתֵינוּ הַפְּקוּדוֹת לָךְ
וְעַל נִסֶּיךָ שֶׁבְּכָל יוֹם עִמָּנוּ
וְעַל נִפְלְאוֹתֶיךָ וְטוֹבוֹתֶיךָ
שֶׁבְּכָל עֵת, עֶרֶב וָבֹקֶר וְצָהֳרָיִם.
הַטּוֹב, כִּי לֹא כָלוּ רַחֲמֶיךָ
וְהַמְרַחֵם, כִּי לֹא תַמּוּ חֲסָדֶיךָ
מֵעוֹלָם קִוִּינוּ לָךְ.

For all these reasons
we will thank You, *Hashem,* our King, forever.
Every living person will recognize and praise You,
Hashem,
for You are the God
that helps and saves Your people.

Bend the knees when saying "Thank," bow when saying "You," and stand straight before saying "Hashem."

Thank You, *Hashem,*
for You are worthy of being thanked.

PEACE

שִׂים שָׁלוֹם *Hashem,*
please provide Your Jewish people
with peace, goodness,
blessing, kindness, and mercy.
Bless us, *Hashem,* all as one.
Hashem,
You have given us Your Torah of life,
and treated us with kindness, righteousness,
blessing, mercy, and peace.
May it be good in Your eyes, *Hashem,*
to bless Your Jewish people with peace
at every moment of every hour.
Thank You, *Hashem,*
who blesses His Jewish people with peace.

וְעַל כֻּלָּם
יִתְבָּרַךְ וְיִתְרוֹמַם שִׁמְךָ מַלְכֵּנוּ תָּמִיד לְעוֹלָם וָעֶד.
וְכֹל הַחַיִּים יוֹדוּךָ סֶּלָה, וִיהַלְלוּ אֶת שִׁמְךָ בֶּאֱמֶת
הָאֵל יְשׁוּעָתֵנוּ וְעֶזְרָתֵנוּ סֶלָה.

Bend the knees when saying בָּרוּךְ, *bow when saying* אַתָּה, *and stand straight before saying Hashem's name.*

בָּרוּךְ אַתָּה יהוה, הַטּוֹב שִׁמְךָ וּלְךָ נָאֶה לְהוֹדוֹת.

שלום

שִׂים שָׁלוֹם טוֹבָה וּבְרָכָה
חֵן וָחֶסֶד וְרַחֲמִים עָלֵינוּ
וְעַל כָּל יִשְׂרָאֵל עַמֶּךָ.
בָּרְכֵנוּ אָבִינוּ כֻּלָּנוּ כְּאֶחָד בְּאוֹר פָּנֶיךָ
כִּי בְאוֹר פָּנֶיךָ נָתַתָּ לָּנוּ יהוה אֱלֹהֵינוּ
תּוֹרַת חַיִּים וְאַהֲבַת חֶסֶד
וּצְדָקָה וּבְרָכָה וְרַחֲמִים
וְחַיִּים וְשָׁלוֹם.
וְטוֹב בְּעֵינֶיךָ לְבָרֵךְ אֶת עַמְּךָ יִשְׂרָאֵל
בְּכָל עֵת וּבְכָל שָׁעָה בִּשְׁלוֹמֶךָ.
בָּרוּךְ אַתָּה יהוה
הַמְבָרֵךְ אֶת עַמּוֹ יִשְׂרָאֵל בַּשָּׁלוֹם.

CONCLUSION OF AMIDA

אֱלֹהַי *Hashem*, please help me:
Control my mouth from speaking badly
about other people,
Stay silent and not respond
if someone speaks badly about me,
Learn Your Torah, and do Your *mitzvot*.

Hashem, if people plan to do something evil against me,
please stop these plans and protect me.
Even if I am not deserving of being helped,
please act on my behalf
as I represent Your name and Your Torah.
Hashem, please save Your Jewish people
from difficult situations and answer my requests.
May You find my thoughts and prayers favorable.

Take three steps backwards and bow to your left as you say:

You, *Hashem*, make peace in heaven.

Bow to your right as you say:

Please may You bring peace to us

Bow forward as you say:

And all Your Jewish people.

Before taking three steps forward, say the following quietly:

Hashem, our God and God of our ancestors, may You please rebuild the *Beit HaMikdash* soon. *Hashem*, please allow us to learn Your Torah and serve You in the *Beit HaMikdash* as the Jewish people once did.

When praying with a minyan, the Amida is repeated by the Leader (on the next page).

When not praying with a minyan: On Sukkot, continue with Hoshanot (page 806). On Pesach, on Shabbat continue with "There is no one like You, Hashem" (page 610); during the week, continue with Aleinu (page 188).

סיום העמידה

אֱלֹהַי, נְצֹר לְשׁוֹנִי מֵרָע וּשְׂפָתַי מִדַּבֵּר מִרְמָה
וְלִמְקַלְלַי נַפְשִׁי תִדֹּם, וְנַפְשִׁי כֶּעָפָר לַכֹּל תִּהְיֶה.
פְּתַח לִבִּי בְּתוֹרָתֶךָ, וּבְמִצְוֹתֶיךָ תִּרְדֹּף נַפְשִׁי.
וְכָל הַחוֹשְׁבִים עָלַי רָעָה
מְהֵרָה הָפֵר עֲצָתָם וְקַלְקֵל מַחֲשַׁבְתָּם.
עֲשֵׂה לְמַעַן שְׁמֶךָ, עֲשֵׂה לְמַעַן יְמִינֶךָ
עֲשֵׂה לְמַעַן קְדֻשָּׁתֶךָ, עֲשֵׂה לְמַעַן תּוֹרָתֶךָ.
לְמַעַן יֵחָלְצוּן יְדִידֶיךָ, הוֹשִׁיעָה יְמִינְךָ וַעֲנֵנִי:
יִהְיוּ לְרָצוֹן אִמְרֵי־פִי וְהֶגְיוֹן לִבִּי לְפָנֶיךָ, יהוה צוּרִי וְגֹאֲלִי:

Take three steps backwards and bow to your left as you say:

עֹשֶׂה שָׁלוֹם בִּמְרוֹמָיו

Bow to your right as you say:

הוּא יַעֲשֶׂה שָׁלוֹם עָלֵינוּ

Bow forward as you say:

וְעַל כָּל יִשְׂרָאֵל, וְאִמְרוּ אָמֵן.

Before taking three steps forward, say the following quietly:

יְהִי רָצוֹן מִלְּפָנֶיךָ יהוה אֱלֹהֵינוּ וֵאלֹהֵי אֲבוֹתֵינוּ. שֶׁיִּבָּנֶה בֵּית הַמִּקְדָּשׁ בִּמְהֵרָה בְיָמֵינוּ, וְתֵן חֶלְקֵנוּ בְּתוֹרָתֶךָ. וְשָׁם נַעֲבָדְךָ בְּיִרְאָה כִּימֵי עוֹלָם וּכְשָׁנִים קַדְמֹנִיּוֹת. וְעָרְבָה לַיהוה מִנְחַת יְהוּדָה וִירוּשָׁלָיִם כִּימֵי עוֹלָם וּכְשָׁנִים קַדְמֹנִיּוֹת:

When praying with a מנין, *the* עמידה *is repeated by the* חזן *(on the next page).*

When not praying with a מנין: *On* סוכות, *continue with* הושענות *(page 806).*
On פסח, *on* שבת *continue with* אֵין כֵּאלֹהֵינוּ *(page 611);*
during the week, continue with עָלֵינוּ *(page 189).*

THE LEADER'S REPETITION

Try to focus on each blessing that the Leader reads, by following along and thinking about the sentences below. After each beracha that the Leader recites, answer "Amen."

I will call out to *Hashem,* let us all give praise to Him.
Hashem, open my lips
and help my mouth recite Your praise.

ANCESTORS

We praise You, *Hashem,*
for protecting, helping, and saving us
as You did for our ancestors,
Avraham, Yitzchak, and Yaakov.
Thank You, *Hashem,*
who protects us in the merit of Avraham.

(*Congregation:* Amen.)

HASHEM'S STRENGTH

We praise You, *Hashem,*
for providing food to those who are hungry,
support to those who are falling,
health to those who are sick,
and help to those who are in challenging situations.
Thank You, *Hashem,*
for bringing the dead back to life. (*Congregation:* Amen.)

חזרת הש״ץ

Try to focus on each blessing that the חזן *reads,*
by following along and thinking about the sentences below.
After each beracha that the חזן *recites, answer* אָמֵן*.*

כִּי שֵׁם יהוה אֶקְרָא, הָבוּ גֹדֶל לֵאלֹהֵינוּ:
אֲדֹנָי, שְׂפָתַי תִּפְתָּח, וּפִי יַגִּיד תְּהִלָּתֶךָ:

אבות

בָּרוּךְ אַתָּה יהוה, אֱלֹהֵינוּ וֵאלֹהֵי אֲבוֹתֵינוּ
אֱלֹהֵי אַבְרָהָם, אֱלֹהֵי יִצְחָק, וֵאלֹהֵי יַעֲקֹב
הָאֵל הַגָּדוֹל הַגִּבּוֹר וְהַנּוֹרָא, אֵל עֶלְיוֹן
גּוֹמֵל חֲסָדִים טוֹבִים, וְקוֹנֵה הַכֹּל
וְזוֹכֵר חַסְדֵי אָבוֹת
וּמֵבִיא גוֹאֵל לִבְנֵי בְנֵיהֶם לְמַעַן שְׁמוֹ בְּאַהֲבָה.
מֶלֶךְ עוֹזֵר וּמוֹשִׁיעַ וּמָגֵן.
בָּרוּךְ אַתָּה יהוה, מָגֵן אַבְרָהָם. (קהל: אָמֵן)

גבורות

אַתָּה גִּבּוֹר לְעוֹלָם, אֲדֹנָי
מְחַיֵּה מֵתִים אַתָּה, רַב לְהוֹשִׁיעַ
מְכַלְכֵּל חַיִּים בְּחֶסֶד, מְחַיֵּה מֵתִים בְּרַחֲמִים רַבִּים
סוֹמֵךְ נוֹפְלִים, וְרוֹפֵא חוֹלִים, וּמַתִּיר אֲסוּרִים
וּמְקַיֵּם אֱמוּנָתוֹ לִישֵׁנֵי עָפָר.
מִי כָמְוֹךָ, בַּעַל גְּבוּרוֹת, וּמִי דּוֹמֶה לָּךְ
מֶלֶךְ, מֵמִית וּמְחַיֶּה וּמַצְמִיחַ יְשׁוּעָה.
וְנֶאֱמָן אַתָּה לְהַחֲיוֹת מֵתִים.
בָּרוּךְ אַתָּה יהוה, מְחַיֵּה הַמֵּתִים. (קהל: אָמֵן)

KEDUSHA

This section of tefillah is said while standing silently with feet together. The sentences are said responsively, Congregation followed by the Leader.

Congregation then Leader: נְקַדֵּשׁ We will announce You, *Hashem*,
as holy in this world,
just as the angels
announce You as holy in heaven.
As Your prophet wrote,
The angels call to one another saying:

(Stand on your toes as you repeat the word "Holy")

Congregation then Leader: Holy, holy, holy, is *Hashem*.
The whole world is filled with Your holiness.

Leader: All the Jewish people and the angels
say in response:

Congregation then Leader: Blessed is *Hashem*'s holiness.

Leader: It is written in *Tehillim*:

Congregation then Leader: *Hashem*, You have ruled over the Jewish
people for generations, and You shall
continue to be our King forever.

Leader: *Hashem*, in every generation
we will discuss Your holiness and greatness.
Our mouths shall never stop
speaking of Your praises,
for You, *Hashem*, are a great and holy King.
Thank You, *Hashem*, our holy God.

(*Congregation:* Amen.)

קדושה

This section of tefillah is said while standing silently with feet together. The sentences are said responsively, קהל followed by the חזן.

קהל then חזן: נְקַדֵּשׁ אֶת שִׁמְךָ בָּעוֹלָם
כְּשֵׁם שֶׁמַּקְדִּישִׁים אוֹתוֹ בִּשְׁמֵי מָרוֹם
כַּכָּתוּב עַל יַד נְבִיאֶךָ
וְקָרָא זֶה אֶל־זֶה וְאָמַר

(Stand on your toes as you repeat the word קָדוֹשׁ)

קהל then חזן: קָדוֹשׁ, קָדוֹשׁ, קָדוֹשׁ, יהוה צְבָאוֹת
מְלֹא כָל־הָאָרֶץ כְּבוֹדוֹ:

חזן: לְעֻמָּתָם בָּרוּךְ יֹאמֵרוּ

קהל then חזן: בָּרוּךְ כְּבוֹד־יהוה מִמְּקוֹמוֹ:

חזן: וּבְדִבְרֵי קָדְשְׁךָ כָּתוּב לֵאמֹר

קהל then חזן: יִמְלֹךְ יהוה לְעוֹלָם
אֱלֹהַיִךְ צִיּוֹן לְדֹר וָדֹר, הַלְלוּיָהּ:

חזן: לְדוֹר וָדוֹר נַגִּיד גָּדְלֶךָ
וּלְנֵצַח נְצָחִים קְדֻשָּׁתְךָ נַקְדִּישׁ
וְשִׁבְחֲךָ אֱלֹהֵינוּ מִפִּינוּ לֹא יָמוּשׁ לְעוֹלָם וָעֶד
כִּי אֵל מֶלֶךְ גָּדוֹל וְקָדוֹשׁ אָתָּה.
בָּרוּךְ אַתָּה יהוה, הָאֵל הַקָּדוֹשׁ.

(קהל: אָמֵן)

KEDUSHAT HAYOM

Hashem,
You gave us holidays
to celebrate with joy and happiness
for us to remember leaving Egypt.

קדושת היום

אַתָּה בְחַרְתָּֽנוּ מִכָּל הָעַמִּים
אָהַבְתָּ אוֹתָֽנוּ וְרָצִֽיתָ בָּֽנוּ
וְרוֹמַמְתָּֽנוּ מִכָּל הַלְּשׁוֹנוֹת
וְקִדַּשְׁתָּֽנוּ בְּמִצְוֹתֶֽיךָ
וְקֵרַבְתָּֽנוּ מַלְכֵּֽנוּ לַעֲבוֹדָתֶֽךָ
וְשִׁמְךָ הַגָּדוֹל וְהַקָּדוֹשׁ עָלֵֽינוּ קָרָֽאתָ.

On שבת, add the words in parentheses:

וַתִּתֶּן לָֽנוּ יהוה אֱלֹהֵֽינוּ בְּאַהֲבָה
(שַׁבָּתוֹת לִמְנוּחָה וּ) מוֹעֲדִים לְשִׂמְחָה
חַגִּים וּזְמַנִּים לְשָׂשׂוֹן
אֶת יוֹם (הַשַּׁבָּת הַזֶּה וְאֶת יוֹם)
בפסח: חַג הַמַּצּוֹת הַזֶּה, זְמַן חֵרוּתֵֽנוּ
בסוכות: חַג הַסֻּכּוֹת הַזֶּה, זְמַן שִׂמְחָתֵֽנוּ
(בְּאַהֲבָה) מִקְרָא קֹֽדֶשׁ, זֵֽכֶר לִיצִיאַת מִצְרָֽיִם.

וּמִפְּנֵי חֲטָאֵֽינוּ גָּלִֽינוּ מֵאַרְצֵֽנוּ, וְנִתְרַחַֽקְנוּ מֵעַל אַדְמָתֵֽנוּ
וְאֵין אֲנַֽחְנוּ יְכוֹלִים לַעֲלוֹת וְלֵרָאוֹת וּלְהִשְׁתַּחֲווֹת לְפָנֶֽיךָ
וְלַעֲשׂוֹת חוֹבוֹתֵֽינוּ בְּבֵית בְּחִירָתֶֽךָ
בַּבַּֽיִת הַגָּדוֹל וְהַקָּדוֹשׁ שֶׁנִּקְרָא שִׁמְךָ עָלָיו
מִפְּנֵי הַיָּד שֶׁנִּשְׁתַּלְּחָה בְּמִקְדָּשֶֽׁךָ.
יְהִי רָצוֹן מִלְּפָנֶֽיךָ יהוה אֱלֹהֵֽינוּ וֵאלֹהֵי אֲבוֹתֵֽינוּ
מֶֽלֶךְ רַחֲמָן
שֶׁתָּשׁוּב וּתְרַחֵם עָלֵֽינוּ וְעַל מִקְדָּשְׁךָ בְּרַחֲמֶֽיךָ הָרַבִּים
וְתִבְנֵֽהוּ מְהֵרָה וּתְגַדֵּל כְּבוֹדוֹ.

אָבִינוּ מַלְכֵּנוּ, גַּלֵּה כְּבוֹד מַלְכוּתְךָ עָלֵינוּ מְהֵרָה
וְהוֹפַע וְהִנָּשֵׂא עָלֵינוּ לְעֵינֵי כָּל חָי
וְקָרֵב פְּזוּרֵינוּ מִבֵּין הַגּוֹיִם
וּנְפוּצוֹתֵינוּ כַּנֵּס מִיַּרְכְּתֵי אָרֶץ.
וַהֲבִיאֵנוּ לְצִיּוֹן עִירְךָ בְּרִנָּה
וְלִירוּשָׁלַיִם בֵּית מִקְדָּשְׁךָ בְּשִׂמְחַת עוֹלָם
וְשָׁם נַעֲשֶׂה לְפָנֶיךָ אֶת קָרְבְּנוֹת חוֹבוֹתֵינוּ
תְּמִידִים כְּסִדְרָם וּמוּסָפִים כְּהִלְכָתָם
וְאֶת מוּסַף יוֹם / שבת: וְאֶת מוּסְפֵי יוֹם הַשַּׁבָּת הַזֶּה וְיוֹם/

בפסח: חַג הַמַּצּוֹת הַזֶּה

בסוכות: חַג הַסֻּכּוֹת הַזֶּה

נַעֲשֶׂה וְנַקְרִיב לְפָנֶיךָ בְּאַהֲבָה כְּמִצְוַת רְצוֹנֶךָ
כְּמוֹ שֶׁכָּתַבְתָּ עָלֵינוּ בְּתוֹרָתֶךָ
עַל יְדֵי מֹשֶׁה עַבְדֶּךָ מִפִּי כְבוֹדֶךָ, כָּאָמוּר

On שבת add:

וּבְיוֹם הַשַּׁבָּת, שְׁנֵי־כְבָשִׂים בְּנֵי־שָׁנָה תְּמִימִם, וּשְׁנֵי עֶשְׂרֹנִים סֹלֶת מִנְחָה בְּלוּלָה בַשֶּׁמֶן וְנִסְכּוֹ: עֹלַת שַׁבַּת בְּשַׁבַּתּוֹ, עַל־עֹלַת הַתָּמִיד וְנִסְכָּהּ:

On חול המועד פסח say:

וְהִקְרַבְתֶּם אִשֶּׁה עֹלָה לַיהוה, פָּרִים בְּנֵי־בָקָר שְׁנַיִם וְאַיִל אֶחָד, וְשִׁבְעָה כְבָשִׂים בְּנֵי שָׁנָה, תְּמִימִם יִהְיוּ לָכֶם: וּמִנְחָתָם וְנִסְכֵּיהֶם כִּמְדֻבָּר, שְׁלֹשָׁה עֶשְׂרֹנִים לַפָּר וּשְׁנֵי עֶשְׂרֹנִים לָאָיִל, וְעִשָּׂרוֹן לַכֶּבֶשׂ, וְיַיִן כְּנִסְכּוֹ, וְשָׂעִיר לְכַפֵּר, וּשְׁנֵי תְמִידִים כְּהִלְכָתָם.

On weekdays, continue with אֱלֹהֵינוּ וֵאלֹהֵי אֲבוֹתֵינוּ *on page 799.*
On שבת*, continue with* יִשְׂמְחוּ בְמַלְכוּתְךָ *on page 799.*

On the first day of חול המועד סוכות*, say the following two paragraphs:*

וּבַיּוֹם הַשֵּׁנִי, פָּרִים בְּנֵי־בָקָר שְׁנֵים עָשָׂר, אֵילִם שְׁנָיִם, כְּבָשִׂים בְּנֵי־שָׁנָה אַרְבָּעָה עָשָׂר, תְּמִימִם: וּמִנְחָתָם וְנִסְכֵּיהֶם כִּמְדֻבָּר, שְׁלֹשָׁה עֶשְׂרֹנִים לַפָּר, וּשְׁנֵי עֶשְׂרֹנִים לָאַיִל, וְעִשָּׂרוֹן לַכֶּבֶשׂ, וְיַיִן כְּנִסְכּוֹ, וְשָׂעִיר לְכַפֵּר, וּשְׁנֵי תְמִידִים כְּהִלְכָתָם.

וּבַיּוֹם הַשְּׁלִישִׁי, פָּרִים עַשְׁתֵּי־עָשָׂר, אֵילִם שְׁנָיִם, כְּבָשִׂים בְּנֵי־שָׁנָה אַרְבָּעָה עָשָׂר, תְּמִימִם: וּמִנְחָתָם וְנִסְכֵּיהֶם כִּמְדֻבָּר, שְׁלֹשָׁה עֶשְׂרֹנִים לַפָּר, וּשְׁנֵי עֶשְׂרֹנִים לָאַיִל, וְעִשָּׂרוֹן לַכֶּבֶשׂ, וְיַיִן כְּנִסְכּוֹ, וְשָׂעִיר לְכַפֵּר, וּשְׁנֵי תְמִידִים כְּהִלְכָתָם.

On weekdays, continue with אֱלֹהֵינוּ וֵאלֹהֵי אֲבוֹתֵינוּ *on page 799.*
On שבת*, continue with* יִשְׂמְחוּ בְמַלְכוּתְךָ *on page 799.*

On the second day of חול המועד סוכות*, say the following two paragraphs:*

וּבַיּוֹם הַשְּׁלִישִׁי, פָּרִים עַשְׁתֵּי־עָשָׂר, אֵילִם שְׁנָיִם, כְּבָשִׂים בְּנֵי־שָׁנָה אַרְבָּעָה עָשָׂר, תְּמִימִם: וּמִנְחָתָם וְנִסְכֵּיהֶם כִּמְדֻבָּר, שְׁלֹשָׁה עֶשְׂרֹנִים לַפָּר, וּשְׁנֵי עֶשְׂרֹנִים לָאַיִל, וְעִשָּׂרוֹן לַכֶּבֶשׂ, וְיַיִן כְּנִסְכּוֹ, וְשָׂעִיר לְכַפֵּר, וּשְׁנֵי תְמִידִים כְּהִלְכָתָם.

וּבַיּוֹם הָרְבִיעִי, פָּרִים עֲשָׂרָה, אֵילִם שְׁנָיִם, כְּבָשִׂים בְּנֵי־שָׁנָה אַרְבָּעָה עָשָׂר, תְּמִימִם: וּמִנְחָתָם וְנִסְכֵּיהֶם כִּמְדֻבָּר, שְׁלֹשָׁה עֶשְׂרֹנִים לַפָּר, וּשְׁנֵי עֶשְׂרֹנִים לָאַיִל, וְעִשָּׂרוֹן לַכֶּבֶשׂ, וְיַיִן כְּנִסְכּוֹ, וְשָׂעִיר לְכַפֵּר, וּשְׁנֵי תְמִידִים כְּהִלְכָתָם.

On weekdays, continue with אֱלֹהֵינוּ וֵאלֹהֵי אֲבוֹתֵינוּ *on page 799.*
On שבת*, continue with* יִשְׂמְחוּ בְמַלְכוּתְךָ *on page 799.*

On the third day of חול המועד סוכות*, say the following two paragraphs:*

וּבַיּוֹם הָרְבִיעִי, פָּרִים עֲשָׂרָה, אֵילִם שְׁנָיִם, כְּבָשִׂים בְּנֵי־שָׁנָה אַרְבָּעָה עָשָׂר, תְּמִימִם: וּמִנְחָתָם וְנִסְכֵּיהֶם כִּמְדֻבָּר, שְׁלֹשָׁה עֶשְׂרֹנִים לַפָּר, וּשְׁנֵי עֶשְׂרֹנִים לָאַיִל, וְעִשָּׂרוֹן לַכֶּבֶשׂ, וְיַיִן כְּנִסְכּוֹ, וְשָׂעִיר לְכַפֵּר, וּשְׁנֵי תְמִידִים כְּהִלְכָתָם.

וּבַיּוֹם הַחֲמִישִׁי, פָּרִים תִּשְׁעָה, אֵילִם שְׁנָיִם, כְּבָשִׂים בְּנֵי־שָׁנָה אַרְבָּעָה עָשָׂר, תְּמִימִם: וּמִנְחָתָם וְנִסְכֵּיהֶם כִּמְדֻבָּר, שְׁלֹשָׁה עֶשְׂרֹנִים לַפָּר, וּשְׁנֵי עֶשְׂרֹנִים לָאַיִל, וְעִשָּׂרוֹן לַכֶּבֶשׂ, וְיַיִן כְּנִסְכּוֹ, וְשָׂעִיר לְכַפֵּר, וּשְׁנֵי תְמִידִים כְּהִלְכָתָם.

On weekdays, continue with אֱלֹהֵינוּ וֵאלֹהֵי אֲבוֹתֵינוּ *on page 799.*
On שבת*, continue with* יִשְׂמְחוּ בְמַלְכוּתְךָ *on page 799.*

May You please
rebuild the *Beit HaMikdash* soon
and gather all Jews together
from around the world
so we can serve You
with the regular *korbanot*
and special *Yom Tov korbanot.*
Please return the *Kohanim* to their service,
the *Levi'im* to their song and music,
and the rest of the Jewish people
to their homes in Israel.

On the fourth day of חול המועד סוכות*, say the following two paragraphs:*

וּבַיּוֹם הַחֲמִישִׁי, פָּרִים תִּשְׁעָה, אֵילִם שְׁנָיִם, כְּבָשִׂים בְּנֵי־שָׁנָה אַרְבָּעָה עָשָׂר, תְּמִימִם: וּמִנְחָתָם וְנִסְכֵּיהֶם כִּמְדֻבָּר, שְׁלֹשָׁה עֶשְׂרֹנִים לַפָּר, וּשְׁנֵי עֶשְׂרֹנִים לָאָיִל, וְעִשָּׂרוֹן לַכֶּבֶשׂ, וְיַיִן כְּנִסְכּוֹ, וְשָׂעִיר לְכַפֵּר, וּשְׁנֵי תְמִידִים כְּהִלְכָתָם.

וּבַיּוֹם הַשִּׁשִּׁי, פָּרִים שְׁמֹנָה, אֵילִם שְׁנָיִם, כְּבָשִׂים בְּנֵי־שָׁנָה אַרְבָּעָה עָשָׂר, תְּמִימִם: וּמִנְחָתָם וְנִסְכֵּיהֶם כִּמְדֻבָּר, שְׁלֹשָׁה עֶשְׂרֹנִים לַפָּר, וּשְׁנֵי עֶשְׂרֹנִים לָאָיִל, וְעִשָּׂרוֹן לַכֶּבֶשׂ, וְיַיִן כְּנִסְכּוֹ, וְשָׂעִיר לְכַפֵּר, וּשְׁנֵי תְמִידִים כְּהִלְכָתָם.

On weekdays, continue with אֱלֹהֵינוּ וֵאלֹהֵי אֲבוֹתֵינוּ *below.*
On שבת*, continue with* יִשְׂמְחוּ בְמַלְכוּתְךָ *below.*

On הושענא רבה*, say the following two paragraphs:*

וּבַיּוֹם הַשִּׁשִּׁי, פָּרִים שְׁמֹנָה, אֵילִם שְׁנָיִם, כְּבָשִׂים בְּנֵי־שָׁנָה אַרְבָּעָה עָשָׂר, תְּמִימִם: וּמִנְחָתָם וְנִסְכֵּיהֶם כִּמְדֻבָּר, שְׁלֹשָׁה עֶשְׂרֹנִים לַפָּר, וּשְׁנֵי עֶשְׂרֹנִים לָאָיִל, וְעִשָּׂרוֹן לַכֶּבֶשׂ, וְיַיִן כְּנִסְכּוֹ, וְשָׂעִיר לְכַפֵּר, וּשְׁנֵי תְמִידִים כְּהִלְכָתָם.

וּבַיּוֹם הַשְּׁבִיעִי, פָּרִים שִׁבְעָה, אֵילִם שְׁנָיִם, כְּבָשִׂים בְּנֵי־שָׁנָה אַרְבָּעָה עָשָׂר, תְּמִימִם: וּמִנְחָתָם וְנִסְכֵּיהֶם כִּמְדֻבָּר, שְׁלֹשָׁה עֶשְׂרֹנִים לַפָּר, וּשְׁנֵי עֶשְׂרֹנִים לָאָיִל, וְעִשָּׂרוֹן לַכֶּבֶשׂ, וְיַיִן כְּנִסְכּוֹ, וְשָׂעִיר לְכַפֵּר, וּשְׁנֵי תְמִידִים כְּהִלְכָתָם.

Continue with אֱלֹהֵינוּ וֵאלֹהֵי אֲבוֹתֵינוּ *below.*

On שבת *say:*

יִשְׂמְחוּ בְמַלְכוּתְךָ שׁוֹמְרֵי שַׁבָּת וְקוֹרְאֵי עֹנֶג. עַם מְקַדְּשֵׁי שְׁבִיעִי כֻּלָּם יִשְׂבְּעוּ וְיִתְעַנְּגוּ מִטּוּבֶךָ, וּבַשְּׁבִיעִי רָצִיתָ בּוֹ וְקִדַּשְׁתּוֹ, חֶמְדַּת יָמִים אוֹתוֹ קָרָאתָ, זֵכֶר לְמַעֲשֵׂה בְרֵאשִׁית.

אֱלֹהֵינוּ וֵאלֹהֵי אֲבוֹתֵינוּ
מֶלֶךְ רַחֲמָן רַחֵם עָלֵינוּ, טוֹב וּמֵטִיב הִדָּרֶשׁ לָנוּ
שׁוּבָה אֵלֵינוּ בַּהֲמוֹן רַחֲמֶיךָ, בִּגְלַל אָבוֹת שֶׁעָשׂוּ רְצוֹנֶךָ.
בְּנֵה בֵיתְךָ כְּבַתְּחִלָּה, וְכוֹנֵן מִקְדָּשְׁךָ עַל מְכוֹנוֹ
וְהַרְאֵנוּ בְּבִנְיָנוֹ, וְשַׂמְּחֵנוּ בְּתִקּוּנוֹ
וְהָשֵׁב כֹּהֲנִים לַעֲבוֹדָתָם, וּלְוִיִּם לְשִׁירָם וּלְזִמְרָם
וְהָשֵׁב יִשְׂרָאֵל לִנְוֵיהֶם.

Reminder: Say "Amen" after the Leader recites each beracha.

Thank You, *Hashem,*
for making (*On Shabbat say:* Shabbat,)
the Jewish people and the holidays holy.
(*Congregation:* Amen.)

SERVICE IN THE *BEIT HAMIKDASH*

We pray to You, *Hashem,*
that You accept our prayers
as though they are the sacrifices
that were once brought to You
in Your holy *Beit HaMikdash.*
May we be worthy
to see the rebuilding of the *Beit HaMikdash.*
We thank You, *Hashem,*
for returning Your presence to Zion. (*Congregation:* Amen.)

Reminder: Say אָמֵן after the חזן recites each beracha.

וְשָׁם נַעֲלֶה וְנֵרָאֶה וְנִשְׁתַּחֲוֶה לְפָנֶיךָ בְּשָׁלֹשׁ פַּעֲמֵי רְגָלֵינוּ
כַּכָּתוּב בְּתוֹרָתֶךָ
שָׁלוֹשׁ פְּעָמִים בַּשָּׁנָה יֵרָאֶה כׇל־זְכוּרְךָ אֶת־פְּנֵי יהוה אֱלֹהֶיךָ
בַּמָּקוֹם אֲשֶׁר יִבְחָר, בְּחַג הַמַּצּוֹת, וּבְחַג הַשָּׁבֻעוֹת, וּבְחַג הַסֻּכּוֹת
וְלֹא יֵרָאֶה אֶת־פְּנֵי יהוה רֵיקָם:
אִישׁ כְּמַתְּנַת יָדוֹ, כְּבִרְכַּת יהוה אֱלֹהֶיךָ אֲשֶׁר נָתַן־לָךְ:

On שבת add the words in parentheses:

וְהַשִּׂיאֵנוּ יהוה אֱלֹהֵינוּ אֶת בִּרְכַּת מוֹעֲדֶיךָ
לְחַיִּים וּלְשָׁלוֹם, לְשִׂמְחָה וּלְשָׂשׂוֹן, כַּאֲשֶׁר רָצִיתָ וְאָמַרְתָּ לְבָרְכֵנוּ.
(אֱלֹהֵינוּ וֵאלֹהֵי אֲבוֹתֵינוּ, רְצֵה בִמְנוּחָתֵנוּ)
קַדְּשֵׁנוּ בְּמִצְוֹתֶיךָ, וְתֵן חֶלְקֵנוּ בְּתוֹרָתֶךָ
שַׂבְּעֵנוּ מִטּוּבֶךָ, וְשַׂמְּחֵנוּ בִּישׁוּעָתֶךָ
וְטַהֵר לִבֵּנוּ לְעׇבְדְּךָ בֶּאֱמֶת
וְהַנְחִילֵנוּ יהוה אֱלֹהֵינוּ (בְּאַהֲבָה וּבְרָצוֹן), בְּשִׂמְחָה וּבְשָׂשׂוֹן
(שַׁבָּת וּ) מוֹעֲדֵי קׇדְשֶׁךָ, וְיִשְׂמְחוּ בְךָ יִשְׂרָאֵל מְקַדְּשֵׁי שְׁמֶךָ.
בָּרוּךְ אַתָּה יהוה, מְקַדֵּשׁ (הַשַּׁבָּת וְ) יִשְׂרָאֵל וְהַזְּמַנִּים.
(קהל: אָמֵן)

עבודה

רְצֵה יהוה אֱלֹהֵינוּ בְּעַמְּךָ יִשְׂרָאֵל, וּבִתְפִלָּתָם
וְהָשֵׁב אֶת הָעֲבוֹדָה לִדְבִיר בֵּיתֶךָ
וְאִשֵּׁי יִשְׂרָאֵל וּתְפִלָּתָם בְּאַהֲבָה תְקַבֵּל בְּרָצוֹן
וּתְהִי לְרָצוֹן תָּמִיד עֲבוֹדַת יִשְׂרָאֵל עַמֶּךָ.
וְתֶחֱזֶינָה עֵינֵינוּ בְּשׁוּבְךָ לְצִיּוֹן בְּרַחֲמִים.
בָּרוּךְ אַתָּה יהוה, הַמַּחֲזִיר שְׁכִינָתוֹ לְצִיּוֹן. (קהל: אָמֵן)

THANK YOU

While the Leader says this prayer, the Congregation says the prayer on the bottom of this page.

You, *Hashem,*
have unlimited mercy and kindness
and therefore we have always placed our hope in You.

The following is said quietly while the Leader says the above. Bow when saying the first sentence below beginning with the words "Thank You, Hashem."

מוֹדִים Thank You, *Hashem,*
our God and God of our ancestors.
You are God of all people,
You created us,
and You created the entire world.
Thank You for giving us life
and for providing us with food to eat.
May You continue to give us life and food to eat.
May You gather us from exile
and return us to Your holy places
so we can keep Your laws,
and serve You with a perfect heart.
Thank You *Hashem,*
our God to whom thanksgiving is due.

הודאה

While the חזן *says this prayer, the* קהל *says the prayer on the bottom of this page.*

מוֹדִים אֲנַחְנוּ לָךְ
שָׁאַתָּה הוּא יהוה אֱלֹהֵינוּ וֵאלֹהֵי אֲבוֹתֵינוּ לְעוֹלָם וָעֶד.
צוּר חַיֵּינוּ, מָגֵן יִשְׁעֵנוּ אַתָּה הוּא לְדוֹר וָדוֹר.
נוֹדֶה לְּךָ וּנְסַפֵּר תְּהִלָּתֶךָ
עַל חַיֵּינוּ הַמְּסוּרִים בְּיָדֶךָ, וְעַל נִשְׁמוֹתֵינוּ הַפְּקוּדוֹת לָךְ
וְעַל נִסֶּיךָ שֶׁבְּכָל יוֹם עִמָּנוּ, וְעַל נִפְלְאוֹתֶיךָ וְטוֹבוֹתֶיךָ
שֶׁבְּכָל עֵת, עֶרֶב וָבֹקֶר וְצָהֳרָיִם.
הַטּוֹב, כִּי לֹא כָלוּ רַחֲמֶיךָ
וְהַמְרַחֵם, כִּי לֹא תַמּוּ חֲסָדֶיךָ, מֵעוֹלָם קִוִּינוּ לָךְ.

The following is said quietly while the חזן *says the above. Bow when saying the first sentence below beginning with the words* מוֹדִים אֲנַחְנוּ לָךְ.

מוֹדִים אֲנַחְנוּ לָךְ
שָׁאַתָּה הוּא יהוה אֱלֹהֵינוּ וֵאלֹהֵי אֲבוֹתֵינוּ
אֱלֹהֵי כָל בָּשָׂר, יוֹצְרֵנוּ, יוֹצֵר בְּרֵאשִׁית.
בְּרָכוֹת וְהוֹדָאוֹת לְשִׁמְךָ הַגָּדוֹל וְהַקָּדוֹשׁ
עַל שֶׁהֶחֱיִיתָנוּ וְקִיַּמְתָּנוּ.
כֵּן תְּחַיֵּנוּ וּתְקַיְּמֵנוּ
וְתֶאֱסֹף גָּלֻיּוֹתֵינוּ לְחַצְרוֹת קָדְשֶׁךָ
לִשְׁמֹר חֻקֶּיךָ וְלַעֲשׂוֹת רְצוֹנֶךָ וּלְעָבְדְּךָ בְּלֵבָב שָׁלֵם
עַל שֶׁאֲנַחְנוּ מוֹדִים לָךְ.
בָּרוּךְ אֵל הַהוֹדָאוֹת.

Reminder: Say "Amen" after the Leader recites each beracha.

We thank You, *Hashem,* for You are good
and all that You do is good.
Thank You, *Hashem,*
for You are worthy of being thanked. (*Congregation:* Amen.)

BLESSINGS OF THE *KOHANIM*

אֱלֹהֵינוּ *Hashem,* Our God and God of our ancestors, provide us with the three blessings that Aharon the *Kohen* and the *kohanim* his descendants use to bless the Jewish people.

Leader: *Hashem* should bless and protect you.
(*Congregation:* May it be as you say!)

Leader: *Hashem* should be kind and favorable towards you.
(*Congregation:* May it be as you say!)

Leader: *Hashem* should grant you peace.
(*Congregation:* May it be as you say!)

PEACE

We pray to You, *Hashem,*
that You grant peace to Your Jewish people
at every moment of every hour, forever.
Thank You, *Hashem,*
who blesses His Jewish people with peace.
(*Congregation:* Amen.)

On Chol HaMo'ed Sukkot, Hoshanot (page 806) are said at this point.

On Shabbat Chol HaMo'ed Pesach, Full Kaddish (page 608) is said and the service continues with "There is no one like You, Hashem" on page 610. On Chol HaMo'ed Pesach, Full Kaddish (page 186) is said and the service continues with Aleinu (page 188).

Reminder: Say אָמֵן *after the* חזן *recites each beracha.*

וְעַל כֻּלָּם, יִתְבָּרַךְ וְיִתְרוֹמַם שִׁמְךָ מַלְכֵּנוּ תָּמִיד לְעוֹלָם וָעֶד.
וְכֹל הַחַיִּים יוֹדְוּךָ סֶּלָה, וִיהַלְלוּ אֶת שִׁמְךָ בֶּאֱמֶת
הָאֵל יְשׁוּעָתֵנוּ וְעֶזְרָתֵנוּ סֶלָה.
בָּרוּךְ אַתָּה יהוה, הַטּוֹב שִׁמְךָ וּלְךָ נָאֶה לְהוֹדוֹת. (קהל: אָמֵן)

ברכת כוהנים

אֱלֹהֵינוּ וֵאלֹהֵי אֲבוֹתֵינוּ, בָּרְכֵנוּ בַּבְּרָכָה הַמְשֻׁלֶּשֶׁת בַּתּוֹרָה, הַכְּתוּבָה עַל יְדֵי מֹשֶׁה עַבְדֶּךָ, הָאֲמוּרָה מִפִּי אַהֲרֹן וּבָנָיו כֹּהֲנִים עַם קְדוֹשֶׁיךָ, כָּאָמוּר

חזן: **יְבָרֶכְךָ יהוה וְיִשְׁמְרֶךָ:** קהל: כֵּן יְהִי רָצוֹן
חזן: **יָאֵר יהוה פָּנָיו אֵלֶיךָ וִיחֻנֶּךָּ:** קהל: כֵּן יְהִי רָצוֹן
חזן: **יִשָּׂא יהוה פָּנָיו אֵלֶיךָ וְיָשֵׂם לְךָ שָׁלוֹם:** קהל: כֵּן יְהִי רָצוֹן

שלום

שִׂים שָׁלוֹם טוֹבָה וּבְרָכָה
חֵן וָחֶסֶד וְרַחֲמִים עָלֵינוּ וְעַל כָּל יִשְׂרָאֵל עַמֶּךָ.
בָּרְכֵנוּ אָבִינוּ כֻּלָּנוּ כְּאֶחָד בְּאוֹר פָּנֶיךָ
כִּי בְאוֹר פָּנֶיךָ נָתַתָּ לָּנוּ יהוה אֱלֹהֵינוּ
תּוֹרַת חַיִּים וְאַהֲבַת חֶסֶד, וּצְדָקָה וּבְרָכָה וְרַחֲמִים וְחַיִּים וְשָׁלוֹם.
וְטוֹב בְּעֵינֶיךָ לְבָרֵךְ אֶת עַמְּךָ יִשְׂרָאֵל בְּכָל עֵת וּבְכָל שָׁעָה בִּשְׁלוֹמֶךָ.
בָּרוּךְ אַתָּה יהוה, הַמְבָרֵךְ אֶת עַמּוֹ יִשְׂרָאֵל בַּשָּׁלוֹם.
(קהל: אָמֵן)

On חול המועד סוכות, הושענות *(page 806) are said at this point.*

On שבת חול המועד פסח, קדיש שלם *(page 609) is said and the service continues with* אֵין כֵּאלֹהֵינוּ *on page 611. On* חול המועד פסח, קדיש שלם *(page 187) is said and the service continues with* עָלֵינוּ *(page 189).*

הושענות

Hoshanot are said after the Leader's Repetition of the Amida of Musaf (and in some congregations after Hallel) on every day of Sukkot.

On weekdays, the Ark is opened, and a Torah scroll is taken to the Bima. Members of the congregation who have a Lulav and Etrog make a circuit around the Bima and say Hoshanot. Mourners do not participate in the circuit.

At the conclusion of the Hoshanot, the Torah scroll is returned to the Ark, which is then closed.

On Shabbat, turn to page 811. On Hoshana Raba, turn to page 815.

If first day of Sukkot falls on	On first day of Chol HaMo'ed	On second day of Chol HaMo'ed	On third day of Chol HaMo'ed	On fouth day of Chol HaMo'ed
Monday	אֶעֱרֹךְ שׁוּעִי	אוֹם אֲנִי חוֹמָה	אֵל לְמוֹשָׁעוֹת	אוֹם נְצוּרָה
Tuesday	אֶעֱרֹךְ שׁוּעִי	אֵל לְמוֹשָׁעוֹת	אוֹם נְצוּרָה	אָדוֹן הַמּוֹשִׁיעַ
Thursday	אוֹם נְצוּרָה	אֶעֱרֹךְ שׁוּעִי	אֵל לְמוֹשָׁעוֹת	אָדוֹן הַמּוֹשִׁיעַ
שבת	אֶעֱרֹךְ שׁוּעִי	אֶבֶן שְׁתִיָּה	אֵל לְמוֹשָׁעוֹת	אָדוֹן הַמּוֹשִׁיעַ

Please save us for Your sake, Hashem, our God. Please save us!

Leader then Congregation:

הוֹשַׁע נָא לְמַעַנְךָ אֱלֹהֵינוּ הוֹשַׁע נָא.

הוֹשַׁע נָא לְמַעַנְךָ אֱלֹהֵינוּ הוֹשַׁע נָא.

Please save us for Your sake, Hashem, our Creator. Please save us!

Leader then Congregation:

הוֹשַׁע נָא לְמַעַנְךָ בּוֹרְאֵנוּ הוֹשַׁע נָא.

הוֹשַׁע נָא לְמַעַנְךָ בּוֹרְאֵנוּ הוֹשַׁע נָא.

Please save us for Your sake, Hashem, our Savior. Please save us!
Leader then Congregation:

הוֹשַׁע נָא לְמַעַנְךָ גּוֹאֲלֵנוּ הוֹשַׁע נָא.
הוֹשַׁע נָא לְמַעַנְךָ גּוֹאֲלֵנוּ הוֹשַׁע נָא.

Please save us for Your sake, Hashem, our God who looks out for us. Please save us!
Leader then Congregation:

הוֹשַׁע נָא לְמַעַנְךָ דּוֹרְשֵׁנוּ הוֹשַׁע נָא.
הוֹשַׁע נָא לְמַעַנְךָ דּוֹרְשֵׁנוּ הוֹשַׁע נָא.

PLEASE SAVE US. On Yom Kippur I prayed to You, Hashem, to be saved. Now, please remember those prayers, forgive my sins, and turn my pain into happiness. Hashem, You have saved us before, please save us now.

הוֹשַׁע נָא

אֶעֱרֹךְ שׁוּעִי. בְּבֵית שַׁוְעִי. גִּלִּיתִי בַצּוֹם פִּשְׁעִי. דְּרַשְׁתִּיךָ בּוֹ לְהוֹשִׁיעִי. הַקְשִׁיבָה לְקוֹל שַׁוְעִי. וְקוּמָה וְהוֹשִׁיעִי. זְכֹר וְרַחֵם מוֹשִׁיעִי. חַי כֵּן תְּשַׁעַשְׁעִי. טוֹב בְּאֶנְקַ שְׁעִי. יוּחַשׁ מוֹשִׁיעִי. כַּלֵּה מַרְשִׁיעִי. לְבַל עוֹד יַרְשִׁיעִי. מַהֵר אֱלֹהֵי יִשְׁעִי. נֶצַח לְהוֹשִׁיעִי. שָׂא נָא עֲוֹן רִשְׁעִי. עֲבֹר עַל פִּשְׁעִי. פְּנֵה נָא לְהוֹשִׁיעִי. צוּר צַדִּיק מוֹשִׁיעִי. קַבֵּל נָא שַׁוְעִי. רוֹמֵם קֶרֶן יִשְׁעִי. שַׁדַּי מוֹשִׁיעִי. תּוֹפִיעַ וְתוֹשִׁיעִי. הוֹשַׁע נָא.

Continue with אֲנִי וָהוֹ הוֹשִׁיעָה נָּא *on page 820.*

PLEASE SAVE US. Hashem, Your Jewish people have suffered terrible pains and exiles. Please end our exile so Your beautiful Jewish people can be saved. You have saved us before; please save us now.

הוֹשַׁע נָא

אֹם אֲנִי חוֹמָה. בָּרָה כַּחַמָּה. גּוֹלָה וְסוּרָה. דָּמְתָה לְתָמָר. הַהֲרוּגָה

עָלֶיךָ. וְנֶחֱשֶׁבֶת כְּצֹאן טִבְחָה. זְרוּיָה בֵּין מַכְעִיסֶיהָ. חֲבוּקָה וּדְבוּקָה בָּךְ. טוֹעֶנֶת עֻלָּךְ. יְחִידָה לְיַחֲדָךְ. כְּבוּשָׁה בַגּוֹלָה. לוֹמֶדֶת יִרְאָתָךְ. מְרוּטַת לֶחִי. נְתוּנָה לְמַכִּים. סוֹבֶלֶת סִבְלָךְ. עֲנִיָּה סוֹעֲרָה. פְּדוּיַת טוֹבִיָּה. צֹאן קָדָשִׁים. קְהִלּוֹת יַעֲקֹב. רְשׁוּמִים בִּשְׁמֶךָ. שׁוֹאֲגִים הוֹשַׁע נָא. תְּמוּכִים עָלֶיךָ. הוֹשַׁע נָא.

Continue with אֲנִי וָהוֹ הוֹשִׁיעָה נָּא *on the next page.*

PLEASE SAVE US. Hashem, save us as You promised. Listen to the calls and prayers of those who want to be saved by You. Please quickly send us leaders who will guide us through our difficulties.

הוֹשַׁע נָא

אֵל לְמוֹשָׁעוֹת. בְּאַרְבַּע שְׁבוּעוֹת. גָּשִׁים בְּשַׁוְעוֹת. דּוֹפְקֵי עֶרֶךְ שׁוּעוֹת. הוֹגֵי שַׁעֲשׁוּעוֹת. וְחִידוֹת מִשְׁתַּעַשְׁעוֹת. זוֹעֲקִים לְהִשָּׁעוֹת. חוֹכֵי יְשׁוּעוֹת. טְפוּלִים בְּךָ שְׁעוֹת. יוֹדְעֵי בִין שָׁעוֹת. כּוֹרְעֶיךָ בְּשַׁוְעוֹת. לְהָבִין שְׁמוּעוֹת. מִפִּיךָ נִשְׁמָעוֹת. נוֹתֵן תְּשׁוּעוֹת. סְפוּרוֹת מַשְׁמָעוֹת. עֵדוֹת מַשְׁמִיעוֹת. פּוֹעֵל יְשׁוּעוֹת. צַדִּיק נוֹשָׁעוֹת. קִרְיַת תְּשׁוּעוֹת. רֶגֶשׁ תְּשׁוּאוֹת. שָׁלֹשׁ שָׁעוֹת. תָּחִישׁ לִתְשׁוּעוֹת. הוֹשַׁע נָא.

Continue with אֲנִי וָהוֹ הוֹשִׁיעָה נָּא *on the next page.*

PLEASE SAVE US. Hashem, there is no savior other than You; You save all no matter how far they may have separated from You. Hashem, please control nature for our good; provide us with crops, rain, and food, and save those who want to be near You.

הוֹשַׁע נָא

אָדוֹן הַמּוֹשִׁיעַ. בִּלְתְּךָ אֵין לְהוֹשִׁיעַ. גִּבּוֹר וְרַב לְהוֹשִׁיעַ. דַּלּוֹתִי וְלִי יְהוֹשִׁיעַ. הָאֵל הַמּוֹשִׁיעַ. וּמַצִּיל וּמוֹשִׁיעַ. זוֹעֲקֶיךָ תּוֹשִׁיעַ. חוֹכֶיךָ הוֹשִׁיעַ. טְלָאֶיךָ תַּשְׂבִּיעַ. יְבוּל לְהַשְׁפִּיעַ. כָּל שִׂיחַ תַּדְשֵׁא

וְתוֹשִׁיעַ. לְגֵיא כָּל תַּרְשִׁיעַ. מְגָדִים תַּמְתִּיק וְתוֹשִׁיעַ. נְשִׂיאִים לְהַסִּיעַ. שְׂעִירִים לְהָנִיעַ. עֲנָנִים מִלְּהַמְנִיעַ. פּוֹתֵחַ יָד וּמַשְׂבִּיעַ. צְמֵאֶיךָ תַּשְׂבִּיעַ. קוֹרְאֶיךָ תּוֹשִׁיעַ. רְחוּמֶיךָ תּוֹשִׁיעַ. שׁוֹחֲרֶיךָ הוֹשִׁיעַ. תְּמִימֶיךָ תּוֹשִׁיעַ. הוֹשַׁע נָא.

Continue with אֲנִי וָהוֹ הוֹשִׁיעָה נָּא *below.*

HASHEM, PLEASE SAVE US. Hashem, throughout history You have saved those who have served You. Just as You have always saved the Jewish people, please save us now.

אֲנִי וָהוֹ הוֹשִׁיעָה נָּא.

כְּהוֹשַׁעְתָּ אֵלִים בְּלוּד עִמָּךְ.
בְּצֵאתְךָ לְיֵשַׁע עַמָּךְ. כֵּן הוֹשַׁע נָא.
כְּהוֹשַׁעְתָּ גּוֹי וֵאלֹהִים.
דְּרוּשִׁים לְיֵשַׁע אֱלֹהִים. כֵּן הוֹשַׁע נָא.
כְּהוֹשַׁעְתָּ הֲמוֹן צְבָאוֹת.
וְעִמָּם מַלְאֲכֵי צְבָאוֹת. כֵּן הוֹשַׁע נָא.
כְּהוֹשַׁעְתָּ זַכִּים מִבֵּית עֲבָדִים.
חַנּוּן בְּיָדָם מַעֲבִידִים. כֵּן הוֹשַׁע נָא.
כְּהוֹשַׁעְתָּ טְבוּעִים בְּצוּל גְּזָרִים.
יְקָרְךָ עִמָּם מַעֲבִירִים. כֵּן הוֹשַׁע נָא.
כְּהוֹשַׁעְתָּ כַּנָּה מְשׁוֹרֶרֶת וַיּוֹשַׁע.
לְגוֹחָה מְצֻיֶּנֶת וַיִּוָּשַׁע. כֵּן הוֹשַׁע נָא.
כְּהוֹשַׁעְתָּ מַאֲמַר וְהוֹצֵאתִי אֶתְכֶם.
נָקוּב וְהוּצֵאתִי אִתְּכֶם. כֵּן הוֹשַׁע נָא.

כְּהוֹשַׁעְתָּ סוֹבְבֵי מִזְבֵּחַ.

עוֹמְסֵי עֲרָבָה לְהַקִּיף מִזְבֵּחַ. כֵּן הוֹשַׁע נָא.

כְּהוֹשַׁעְתָּ פִּלְאֵי אָרוֹן כְּהֻפְשַׁע.

צִעֵר פְּלֶשֶׁת בַּחֲרוֹן אַף, וְנוֹשַׁע. כֵּן הוֹשַׁע נָא.

כְּהוֹשַׁעְתָּ קְהִלּוֹת בָּבֶלָה שִׁלַּחְתָּ.

רַחוּם לְמַעֲנָם שֻׁלַּחְתָּ. כֵּן הוֹשַׁע נָא.

כְּהוֹשַׁעְתָּ שְׁבוּת שִׁבְטֵי יַעֲקֹב.

תָּשׁוּב וְתָשִׁיב שְׁבוּת אָהֳלֵי יַעֲקֹב. וְהוֹשִׁיעָה נָּא.

כְּהוֹשַׁעְתָּ שׁוֹמְרֵי מִצְוֹת וְחוֹכֵי יְשׁוּעוֹת.

אֵל לְמוֹשָׁעוֹת. וְהוֹשִׁיעָה נָּא.

אֲנִי וָהוּ הוֹשִׁיעָה נָּא.

The Torah scroll is returned to the Ark.

Hashem, save Your Jewish people. May the words of my prayers come close to You, Hashem, and may You provide for our needs every day. May the whole world know that Hashem is God and there are no other gods.

הוֹשִׁיעָה אֶת־עַמֶּךָ, וּבָרֵךְ אֶת־נַחֲלָתֶךָ, וּרְעֵם וְנַשְּׂאֵם עַד־הָעוֹלָם: וְיִהְיוּ דְבָרַי אֵלֶּה, אֲשֶׁר הִתְחַנַּנְתִּי לִפְנֵי יהוה, קְרֹבִים אֶל־יהוה אֱלֹהֵינוּ יוֹמָם וָלָיְלָה, לַעֲשׂוֹת מִשְׁפַּט עַבְדּוֹ וּמִשְׁפַּט עַמּוֹ יִשְׂרָאֵל, דְּבַר־יוֹם בְּיוֹמוֹ: לְמַעַן דַּעַת כָּל־עַמֵּי הָאָרֶץ כִּי יהוה הוּא הָאֱלֹהִים, אֵין עוֹד:

The Ark is closed.

The Leader continues the service with Kaddish Shalem on page 187.

הושענות לשבת

The Ark is opened but no Torah scrolls are taken out.
The congregation does not walk around the Bima.

Please save us for Your sake, Hashem, our God. Please save us!
Leader then Congregation:

הוֹשַׁע נָא לְמַעַנְךָ אֱלֹהֵינוּ הוֹשַׁע נָא.
הוֹשַׁע נָא לְמַעַנְךָ אֱלֹהֵינוּ הוֹשַׁע נָא.

Please save us for Your sake, Hashem, our Creator. Please save us!
Leader then Congregation:

הוֹשַׁע נָא לְמַעַנְךָ בּוֹרְאֵנוּ הוֹשַׁע נָא.
הוֹשַׁע נָא לְמַעַנְךָ בּוֹרְאֵנוּ הוֹשַׁע נָא.

Please save us for Your sake, Hashem, our Savior. Please save us!
Leader then Congregation:

הוֹשַׁע נָא לְמַעַנְךָ גּוֹאֲלֵנוּ הוֹשַׁע נָא.
הוֹשַׁע נָא לְמַעַנְךָ גּוֹאֲלֵנוּ הוֹשַׁע נָא.

Please save us for Your sake, Hashem, our God who looks out for us. Please save us!
Leader then Congregation:

הוֹשַׁע נָא לְמַעַנְךָ דּוֹרְשֵׁנוּ הוֹשַׁע נָא.
הוֹשַׁע נָא לְמַעַנְךָ דּוֹרְשֵׁנוּ הוֹשַׁע נָא.

PLEASE SAVE US. *All week long we work and patiently wait for Shabbat. We take great joy in following the mitzvot and laws of Shabbat such as resting, eating special foods, and wearing special clothes.*

הוֹשַׁע נָא

אֹם נְצוּרָה כְּבָבַת. בּוֹנֶנֶת בְּדָת נֶפֶשׁ מְשִׁיבַת. גּוֹמֶרֶת הִלְכוֹת שַׁבָּת.

דּוֹרֶשֶׁת מַשְׂאַת שַׁבָּת. הַקּוֹבַעַת אַלְפַּיִם תְּחוּם שַׁבָּת. וּמְשִׁיבַת רֶגֶל מִשַּׁבָּת. זָכוֹר וְשָׁמוֹר מְקַיֶּמֶת בַּשַּׁבָּת. חָשָׁה לְמַהֵר בִּיאַת שַׁבָּת. טוֹרַחַת כֹּל מִשִּׁשָּׁה לַשַּׁבָּת. יוֹשֶׁבֶת וּמַמְתֶּנֶת עַד כְּלוֹת שַׁבָּת. כָּבוֹד וָעֹנֶג קוֹרְאָה לַשַּׁבָּת. לְבוּשׁ וּכְסוּת מְחַלֶּפֶת בַּשַּׁבָּת. מַאֲכָל וּמִשְׁתֶּה מְכִינָה לַשַּׁבָּת. נֹעַם מְגָדִים מְנַעֶמֶת לַשַּׁבָּת. סְעוּדוֹת שָׁלֹשׁ מְקַיֶּמֶת בַּשַּׁבָּת. עַל שְׁתֵּי כִכָּרוֹת בּוֹצַעַת בַּשַּׁבָּת. פּוֹרֶטֶת אַרְבַּע רְשֻׁיּוֹת שַׁבָּת. צִוּוּי הַדְלָקַת נֵר מַדְלֶקֶת בַּשַּׁבָּת. קִדּוּשׁ הַיּוֹם מְקַדֶּשֶׁת בַּשַּׁבָּת. רֶנֶן שֶׁבַע מְפַלֶּלֶת בַּשַּׁבָּת. שִׁבְעָה בַדָּת קוֹרְאָה בַּשַּׁבָּת. תַּנְחִילֶנָּה לְיוֹם שֶׁכֻּלּוֹ שַׁבָּת. הוֹשַׁע נָא.

HASHEM, PLEASE SAVE US. Throughout history, You, Hashem, have always saved Your Jewish people who have kept Shabbat. So too, please save us now, Hashem.

אֲנִי וָהוּ הוֹשִׁיעָה נָּא.

כְּהוֹשַׁעְתָּ אָדָם יְצִיר כַּפֶּיךָ לְגוֹנְנָה.
בְּשַׁבַּת קֹדֶשׁ הִמְצֵאתוֹ כֹּפֶר וַחֲנִינָה. כֵּן הוֹשַׁע נָא.

כְּהוֹשַׁעְתָּ גּוֹי מְצֻיָּן מְקַוִּים חֹפֶשׁ.
דֵּעָה כִּוְּנוּ לָבוֹר שְׁבִיעִי לְנֹפֶשׁ. כֵּן הוֹשַׁע נָא.

כְּהוֹשַׁעְתָּ הָעָם נָהַגְתָּ כַּצֹּאן לְהַנְחוֹת.
וְחֹק שַׂמְתָּ בְּמָרָה עַל מֵי מְנוּחוֹת. כֵּן הוֹשַׁע נָא.

כְּהוֹשַׁעְתָּ זְבוּדֶיךָ בְּמִדְבַּר סִין בַּמַּחֲנֶה.
חָכְמוּ וְלָקְטוּ בַּשִּׁשִּׁי לֶחֶם מִשְׁנֶה. כֵּן הוֹשַׁע נָא.

כְּהוֹשַׁעְתָּ טְפוּלֶיךָ הוֹרוּ הֲכָנָה בְּמַדָּעָם.
יָשַׁר כֹּחָם, וְהוֹדָה לָמוֹ רוֹעָם. כֵּן הוֹשַׁע נָא.

כְּהוֹשַֽׁעְתָּ כְּלְכְּלוֹ בְּעֹנֶג מָן הַמְּשֻׁמָּר.
לֹא הָפַךְ עֵינוֹ וְרֵיחוֹ לֹא נָמָר. כֵּן הוֹשַֽׁע נָא.
כְּהוֹשַֽׁעְתָּ מִשְׁפְּטֵי מַשָּׂאוֹת שַׁבָּת גְּמָרוּ.
נָחוּ וְשָׁבְתוּ, רְשֻׁיּוֹת וּתְחוּמִים שָׁמָרוּ. כֵּן הוֹשַֽׁע נָא.
כְּהוֹשַֽׁעְתָּ סִינַי הָשְׁמְעוּ בְּדִבּוּר רְבִיעִי.
עִנְיַן זָכוֹר וְשָׁמוֹר לְקַדֵּשׁ שְׁבִיעִי. כֵּן הוֹשַֽׁע נָא.
כְּהוֹשַֽׁעְתָּ פְּקְדוּ יְרִיחוֹ שֶׁבַע לְהַקֵּף.
צָרוּ עַד רִדְתָּהּ בַּשַּׁבָּת לְתַקֵּף. כֵּן הוֹשַֽׁע נָא.
כְּהוֹשַֽׁעְתָּ קֹהֶלֶת וְעַמּוֹ בְּבֵית עוֹלָמִים.
רִצּוּךְ בְּחָגְגָם שִׁבְעָה וְשִׁבְעָה יָמִים. כֵּן הוֹשַֽׁע נָא.
כְּהוֹשַֽׁעְתָּ שָׁבִים עוֹלֵי גוֹלָה לְפִדְיוֹם.
תּוֹרָתְךָ בְּקָרְאָם בֶּחָג יוֹם יוֹם. כֵּן הוֹשַֽׁע נָא.
כְּהוֹשַֽׁעְתָּ מְשַׂמְּחֶיךָ בְּבִנְיַן שֵׁנִי הַמְחֻדָּשׁ.
נוֹטְלִין לוּלָב כָּל שִׁבְעָה בַּמִּקְדָּשׁ. כֵּן הוֹשַֽׁע נָא.
כְּהוֹשַֽׁעְתָּ חִבּוּט עֲרָבָה שַׁבָּת מַדְחִים.
מֻרְבִּיּוֹת מוֹצָא לִיסוֹד מִזְבֵּחַ מַנִּיחִים. כֵּן הוֹשַֽׁע נָא.
כְּהוֹשַֽׁעְתָּ בְּרֵכוֹת וַאֲרֻכּוֹת וּגְבוֹהוֹת מְעַלְּסִים.
בִּפְטִירָתָן יֹפִי לְךָ מִזְבֵּחַ מְקַלְּסִים. כֵּן הוֹשַֽׁע נָא.
כְּהוֹשַֽׁעְתָּ מוֹדִים וּמְיַחֲלִים וְלֹא מְשַׁנִּים.
כֻּלָּנוּ אָנוּ לְיָהּ וְעֵינֵינוּ לְיָהּ שׁוֹנִים. כֵּן הוֹשַֽׁע נָא.
כְּהוֹשַֽׁעְתָּ יֶקֶב מַחֲצָבֶיךָ סוֹבְבִים בְּרַעֲנָנָה.
רוֹנְנִים אֲנִי וָהוּ הוֹשִׁיעָה נָּא. כֵּן הוֹשַֽׁע נָא.
כְּהוֹשַֽׁעְתָּ חֵיל זְרִיזִים מְשָׁרְתִים בִּמְנוּחָה.
קָרְבַּן שַׁבָּת כָּפוּל, עוֹלָה וּמִנְחָה. כֵּן הוֹשַֽׁע נָא.

כְּהוֹשַׁעְתָּ לְוִיֶּיךָ עַל דּוּכָנָם לְהַרְבַּת.
אוֹמְרִים מִזְמוֹר שִׁיר לְיוֹם הַשַּׁבָּת. כֵּן הוֹשַׁע נָא.
כְּהוֹשַׁעְתָּ נְחוּמֶיךָ בְּמִצְוֹתֶיךָ תָּמִיד יִשְׁתַּעְשְׁעוּן.
וּרְצֵם וְהַחֲלִיצֵם בְּשׁוּבָה וָנַחַת יִוָּשֵׁעוּן. כֵּן הוֹשַׁע נָא.
כְּהוֹשַׁעְתָּ שְׁבוּת שִׁבְטֵי יַעֲקֹב.
תָּשׁוּב וְתָשִׁיב שְׁבוּת אָהֳלֵי יַעֲקֹב. וְהוֹשִׁיעָה נָּא.
כְּהוֹשַׁעְתָּ שׁוֹמְרֵי מִצְוֹת וְחוֹכֵי יְשׁוּעוֹת.
אֵל לְמוֹשָׁעוֹת. וְהוֹשִׁיעָה נָּא.

אֲנִי וָהוּ הוֹשִׁיעָה נָּא.

Hashem, save Your Jewish people. May the words of my prayers come close to You, Hashem, and may You provide for our needs every day. May the whole world know that Hashem is God and there are no other gods.

הוֹשִׁיעָה אֶת־עַמֶּךָ, וּבָרֵךְ אֶת־נַחֲלָתֶךָ, וּרְעֵם וְנַשְּׂאֵם עַד־הָעוֹלָם: וְיִהְיוּ דְבָרַי אֵלֶּה, אֲשֶׁר הִתְחַנַּנְתִּי לִפְנֵי יהוה, קְרֹבִים אֶל־יהוה אֱלֹהֵינוּ יוֹמָם וָלָיְלָה, לַעֲשׂוֹת מִשְׁפַּט עַבְדּוֹ וּמִשְׁפַּט עַמּוֹ יִשְׂרָאֵל, דְּבַר־יוֹם בְּיוֹמוֹ: לְמַעַן דַּעַת כָּל־עַמֵּי הָאָרֶץ כִּי יהוה הוּא הָאֱלֹהִים, אֵין עוֹד:

The Ark is closed.

The Leader continues the service with Kaddish Shalem on *page 609.*

הושענות להושענא רבה

All of the Torah scrolls are held on the Bima. Members of the congregation who have a Lulav and Etrog circle the Bima seven times while the Hoshanot are read. After finishing the first circuit, say כִּי־אָמַרְתִּי *and immediately proceed to make another circuit, saying* אֶבֶן שְׁתִיָּה*, etc.*

Please save us for Your sake, Hashem, our God. Please save us!

Leader then Congregation:

הוֹשַׁע נָא לְמַעַנְךָ אֱלֹהֵינוּ הוֹשַׁע נָא.

הוֹשַׁע נָא לְמַעַנְךָ אֱלֹהֵינוּ הוֹשַׁע נָא.

Please save us for Your sake, Hashem, our Creator. Please save us!

Leader then Congregation:

הוֹשַׁע נָא לְמַעַנְךָ בּוֹרְאֵנוּ הוֹשַׁע נָא.

הוֹשַׁע נָא לְמַעַנְךָ בּוֹרְאֵנוּ הוֹשַׁע נָא.

Please save us for Your sake, Hashem, our Savior. Please save us!

Leader then Congregation:

הוֹשַׁע נָא לְמַעַנְךָ גּוֹאֲלֵנוּ הוֹשַׁע נָא.

הוֹשַׁע נָא לְמַעַנְךָ גּוֹאֲלֵנוּ הוֹשַׁע נָא.

Please save us for Your sake, Hashem, our God who looks out for us. Please save us!

Leader then Congregation:

הוֹשַׁע נָא לְמַעַנְךָ דּוֹרְשֵׁנוּ הוֹשַׁע נָא.

הוֹשַׁע נָא לְמַעַנְךָ דּוֹרְשֵׁנוּ הוֹשַׁע נָא.

PLEASE SAVE US. *Hashem, You are a great, kind, powerful King. We cannot begin to list or fully know how great You are.*

הוֹשַׁע נָא

First הקפה*:*

לְמַעַן אֲמִתָּךְ. לְמַעַן בְּרִיתָךְ. לְמַעַן גָּדְלָךְ וְתִפְאַרְתָּךְ. לְמַעַן דָּתָךְ. לְמַעַן הוֹדָךְ. לְמַעַן וִעוּדָךְ. לְמַעַן זִכְרָךְ. לְמַעַן חַסְדָּךְ. לְמַעַן טוּבָךְ. לְמַעַן יִחוּדָךְ. לְמַעַן כְּבוֹדָךְ. לְמַעַן לִמּוּדָךְ. לְמַעַן מַלְכוּתָךְ. לְמַעַן נִצְחָךְ. לְמַעַן סוֹדָךְ. לְמַעַן עֻזָּךְ. לְמַעַן פְּאֵרָךְ. לְמַעַן צִדְקָתָךְ. לְמַעַן קְדֻשָּׁתָךְ. לְמַעַן רַחֲמֶיךָ הָרַבִּים. לְמַעַן שְׁכִינָתָךְ. לְמַעַן תְּהִלָּתָךְ. הוֹשַׁע נָא.

After circling the בימה *the first time, say:*

כִּי־אָמַרְתִּי עוֹלָם חֶסֶד יִבָּנֶה:

PLEASE SAVE US. *Hashem, You gave us the Beit HaMikdash and the holy city of Jerusalem to serve You, in which we felt Your presence. Hashem, please rebuild the Beit HaMikdash so we can serve You there again with love.*

הוֹשַׁע נָא

Second הקפה*:*

אֶבֶן שְׁתִיָּה. בֵּית הַבְּחִירָה. גֹּרֶן אָרְנָן. דְּבִיר הַמֻּצְנָע. הַר הַמּוֹרִיָּה. וְהַר יֵרָאֶה. זְבוּל תִּפְאַרְתֶּךָ. חָנָה דָוִד. טוֹב הַלְּבָנוֹן. יְפֵה נוֹף מְשׂוֹשׂ כָּל הָאָרֶץ. כְּלִילַת יֹפִי. לִינַת הַצֶּדֶק. מָכוֹן לְשִׁבְתֶּךָ. נָוֶה שַׁאֲנָן. סֻכַּת שָׁלֵם. עֲלִיַּת שְׁבָטִים. פִּנַּת יִקְרַת. צִיּוֹן הַמְצֻיֶּנֶת. קֹדֶשׁ הַקֳּדָשִׁים. רָצוּף אַהֲבָה. שְׁכִינַת כְּבוֹדֶךָ. תֵּל תַּלְפִּיּוֹת. הוֹשַׁע נָא.

After circling the בימה *the second time, say:*

לְךָ זְרוֹעַ עִם־גְּבוּרָה

תָּעֹז יָדְךָ תָּרוּם יְמִינֶךָ:

PLEASE SAVE US. Hashem, Your Jewish people have suffered terrible pains and exiles. Please end our exile so Your beautiful Jewish people can be saved. You have saved us before; please save us now.

הוֹשַׁע נָא

Third הקפה*:*

אֹם אֲנִי חוֹמָה. בָּרָה כַּחַמָּה. גּוֹלָה וְסוּרָה. דָּמְתָה לְתָמָר. הַהֲרוּגָה עָלֶיךָ. וְנֶחְשֶׁבֶת כְּצֹאן טִבְחָה. זְרוּיָה בֵּין מַכְעִיסֶיהָ. חֲבוּקָה וּדְבוּקָה בָךְ. טוֹעֶנֶת עֻלָּךְ. יְחִידָה לְיַחֲדָךְ. כְּבוּשָׁה בַגּוֹלָה. לוֹמֶדֶת יִרְאָתָךְ. מְרוּטַת לֶחִי. נְתוּנָה לְמַכִּים. סוֹבֶלֶת סִבְלָךְ. עֲנִיָּה סוֹעֲרָה. פְּדוּיַת טוֹבִיָּה. צֹאן קָדָשִׁים. קְהִלּוֹת יַעֲקֹב. רְשׁוּמִים בִּשְׁמֶךָ. שׁוֹאֲגִים הוֹשַׁע נָא. תְּמוּכִים עָלֶיךָ. הוֹשַׁע נָא.

After circling the בימה *the third time, say:*

תִּתֵּן אֱמֶת לְיַעֲקֹב, חֶסֶד לְאַבְרָהָם:

PLEASE SAVE US. Hashem, there is no savior other than You; You save all no matter how far they may have separated from You. Hashem, please control nature for our good; provide us with crops, rain, and food, and save those who want to be near You.

הוֹשַׁע נָא

Fourth הקפה*:*

אָדוֹן הַמּוֹשִׁיעַ. בִּלְתְּךָ אֵין לְהוֹשִׁיעַ. גִּבּוֹר וְרַב לְהוֹשִׁיעַ. דַּלּוֹתִי וְלִי יְהוֹשִׁיעַ. הָאֵל הַמּוֹשִׁיעַ. וּמַצִּיל וּמוֹשִׁיעַ. זוֹעֲקֶיךָ תּוֹשִׁיעַ. חוֹכֶיךָ הוֹשִׁיעַ. טְלָאֶיךָ תַּשְׂבִּיעַ. יְבוּל לְהַשְׁפִּיעַ. כָּל שִׂיחַ תַּדְשֵׁא וְתוֹשִׁיעַ. לְגֵיא בַּל תַּרְשִׁיעַ. מְגָדִים תַּמְתִּיק וְתוֹשִׁיעַ. נְשִׂיאִים לְהַסִּיעַ. שְׂעִירִים לְהָנִיעַ. עֲנָנִים מִלְּהַמְנִיעַ. פּוֹתֵחַ יָד וּמַשְׂבִּיעַ. צְמֵאֶיךָ תַּשְׂבִּיעַ. קוֹרְאֶיךָ תּוֹשִׁיעַ. רְחוּמֶיךָ תּוֹשִׁיעַ. שׁוֹחֲרֶיךָ הוֹשִׁיעַ. תְּמִימֶיךָ תּוֹשִׁיעַ. הוֹשַׁע נָא.

After circling the בימה *the fourth time, say:*

נְעִמוֹת בִּימִינְךָ נֶצַח:

PLEASE SAVE US. Hashem, You create people and animals, each one different from the other. Hashem, You created nature and allow plants to grow and water to flow across the earth. Hashem, Your powers and holiness are above all.

הוֹשַׁע נָא

Fifth הקפה:

אָדָם וּבְהֵמָה. בָּשָׂר וְרוּחַ וּנְשָׁמָה. גִּיד וְעֶצֶם וְקָרְמָה. דְּמוּת וְצֶלֶם וְרִקְמָה. הוֹד לַהֶבֶל דָּמָה. וְנִמְשַׁל כַּבְּהֵמוֹת נִדְמָה. זִיו וְתֹאַר וְקוֹמָה. חִדּוּשׁ פְּנֵי אֲדָמָה. טִיעַת עֲצֵי נְשַׁמָּה. יְקָבִים וְקָמָה. כְּרָמִים וְשִׁקְמָה. לְתֵבֵל הַמְּסֻיָּמָה. מִטְרוֹת עֹז לְסַמְּמָה. נְשִׁיָּה לְקַיְּמָה. שִׂיחִים לְקוֹמְמָה. עֲדָנִים לְעָצְמָה. פְּרָחִים לְהַעֲצִימָה. צְמָחִים לְגָשְׁמָה. קָרִים לְזָרְמָה. רְבִיבִים לְשַׁלְּמָה. שְׁתִיָּה לְרוֹמְמָה. תְּלוּיָה עַל בְּלִימָה. הוֹשַׁע נָא.

After circling the בימה *the fifth time, say:*

יהוה אֲדֹנֵינוּ מָה־אַדִּיר שִׁמְךָ בְּכָל־הָאָרֶץ אֲשֶׁר־תְּנָה הוֹדְךָ עַל־הַשָּׁמָיִם׃

PLEASE SAVE US. Hashem, please allow our produce to grow quickly and easily, like it used to, so we can do Your mitzvot. Save all of our crops and animals from any disease or misfortune. Hashem, You are holy and kind to Your Jewish people.

הוֹשַׁע נָא

Sixth הקפה:

אֲדָמָה מֵאֶרֶר. בְּהֵמָה מִמְּשַׁכֶּלֶת. גֹּרֶן מִגָּזָם. דָּגָן מִדַּלֶּקֶת. הוֹן מִמְּאֵרָה. וְאֹכֶל מִמְּהוּמָה. זַיִת מִנֶּשֶׁל. חִטָּה מֵחָגָב. טֶרֶף מִגּוֹבַי. יֶקֶב מִיֶּלֶק. כֶּרֶם מִתּוֹלַעַת. לֶקֶשׁ מֵאַרְבֶּה. מֶגֶד מִצְּלָצַל. נֶפֶשׁ מִבֶּהָלָה. שֹׂבַע מִסָּלְעָם. עֲדָרִים מִדַּלּוּת. פֵּרוֹת מִשִּׁדָּפוֹן. צֹאן

מִצְמִיתוּת. קָצִיר מִקְלָלָה. רֹב מֵרָזוֹן. שִׁבֹּלֶת מִצְּנָמוֹן. תְּבוּאָה מֵחָסִיל. הוֹשַׁע נָא.

After circling the בימה *the sixth time, say:*

צַדִּיק יהוה בְּכָל־דְּרָכָיו, וְחָסִיד בְּכָל־מַעֲשָׂיו:

PLEASE SAVE US. Hashem, throughout Jewish history our ancestors and leaders have done great things to show how much they love You and want to serve You. Please remember all of our ancestors and leaders and continue to save the Jewish people as You always have.

הוֹשַׁע נָא

Seventh הקפה*:*

לְמַעַן אֵיתָן הַנִּזְרָק בְּלַהַב אֵשׁ.
לְמַעַן בֵּן הַנֶּעֱקַד עַל עֵצִים וָאֵשׁ.
לְמַעַן גִּבּוֹר הַנֶּאֱבַק עִם שַׂר אֵשׁ.
לְמַעַן דְּגָלִים נָחִיתָ בְּאוֹר וַעֲנַן אֵשׁ.
לְמַעַן הֹעֲלָה לַמָּרוֹם, וְנִתְעַלָּה כְּמַלְאֲכֵי אֵשׁ.
לְמַעַן וְהוּא לָךְ כְּסֶגֶן בְּאֶרְאֶלֵּי אֵשׁ.
לְמַעַן זֶבֶד דִּבְּרוֹת הַנְּתוּנוֹת מֵאֵשׁ.
לְמַעַן חִפּוּי יְרִיעוֹת וַעֲנַן אֵשׁ.
לְמַעַן טֶכֶס הַר יָרַדְתָּ עָלָיו בָּאֵשׁ.
לְמַעַן יְדִידוּת בַּיִת אֲשֶׁר אָהַבְתָּ מִשְּׁמֵי אֵשׁ.
לְמַעַן כָּמַהּ עַד שָׁקְעָה הָאֵשׁ.
לְמַעַן לָקַח מַחְתַּת אֵשׁ וְהֵסִיר חֲרוֹן אֵשׁ.
לְמַעַן מְקַנֵּא קִנְאָה גְדוֹלָה בָּאֵשׁ.
לְמַעַן נָף יָדוֹ וְיָרְדוּ אַבְנֵי אֵשׁ.

לְמַעַן שָׂם טְלֵה חָלָב כְּלִיל אֵשׁ.
לְמַעַן עָמַד בַּגֹּרֶן וְנִתְרַצָּה בָאֵשׁ.
לְמַעַן פִּלֵּל בָּעֲזָרָה וְיָרְדָה הָאֵשׁ.
לְמַעַן צִיר עָלָה וְנִתְעַלָּה בְּרֶכֶב וְסוּסֵי אֵשׁ.
לְמַעַן קְדוֹשִׁים מֻשְׁלָכִים בָּאֵשׁ.
לְמַעַן רִבּוֹ רִבְבָן חָז וְנַהֲרֵי אֵשׁ.
לְמַעַן שְׁמְמוֹת עִירָךְ הַשְּׂרוּפָה בָאֵשׁ.
לְמַעַן תּוֹלְדוֹת אַלּוּפֵי יְהוּדָה, תָּשִׂים כְּכִיּוֹר אֵשׁ. הוֹשַׁע נָא.

Hashem, You are great and strong. Everything on earth belongs to You. When You bring Mashiach, all nations will recognize that You rule over all.

After circling the בימה *the seventh time, say:*

לְךָ יהוה הַגְּדֻלָּה וְהַגְּבוּרָה וְהַתִּפְאֶרֶת וְהַנֵּצַח וְהַהוֹד, כִּי־כֹל בַּשָּׁמַיִם וּבָאָרֶץ, לְךָ יהוה הַמַּמְלָכָה וְהַמִּתְנַשֵּׂא לְכֹל לְרֹאשׁ: וְהָיָה יהוה לְמֶלֶךְ עַל־כָּל־הָאָרֶץ, בַּיּוֹם הַהוּא יִהְיֶה יהוה אֶחָד וּשְׁמוֹ אֶחָד: וּבְתוֹרָתְךָ כָּתוּב לֵאמֹר: שְׁמַע יִשְׂרָאֵל, יהוה אֱלֹהֵינוּ, יהוה אֶחָד: בָּרוּךְ שֵׁם כְּבוֹד מַלְכוּתוֹ לְעוֹלָם וָעֶד.

HASHEM, PLEASE SAVE US! *Hashem, throughout history You have saved those who have served You. Just as You have always saved the Jewish people, please save us now.*

אֲנִי וָהוֹ הוֹשִׁיעָה נָּא.

כְּהוֹשַׁעְתָּ אֵלִים בְּלוּד עִמָּךְ.
בְּצֵאתְךָ לְיֵשַׁע עַמָּךְ. — כֵּן הוֹשַׁע נָא.

כְּהוֹשַׁעְתָּ גּוֹי וֵאלֹהִים.
דְּרוּשִׁים לְיֵשַׁע אֱלֹהִים. — כֵּן הוֹשַׁע נָא.

כְּהוֹשַֽׁעְתָּ הֲמוֹן צְבָאוֹת.
וְעִמָּם מַלְאֲכֵי צְבָאוֹת. כֵּן הוֹשַׁע נָא.

כְּהוֹשַֽׁעְתָּ זַכִּים מִבֵּית עֲבָדִים.
חַנּוּן בְּיָדָם מַעֲבִידִים. כֵּן הוֹשַׁע נָא.

כְּהוֹשַֽׁעְתָּ טְבוּעִים בְּצוּל גְּזָרִים.
יְקָרְךָ עִמָּם מַעֲבִירִים. כֵּן הוֹשַׁע נָא.

כְּהוֹשַֽׁעְתָּ כַּנָּה מְשׁוֹרֶרֶת וַיּֽוֹשַׁע.
לְגוֹחָהּ מְצַיֶּנֶת וַיִּוָּשַׁע. כֵּן הוֹשַׁע נָא.

כְּהוֹשַֽׁעְתָּ מַאֲמַר וְהוֹצֵאתִי אֶתְכֶם.
נָקוּב וְהוּצֵאתִי אִתְּכֶם. כֵּן הוֹשַׁע נָא.

כְּהוֹשַֽׁעְתָּ סוֹבְבֵי מִזְבֵּֽחַ.
עוֹמְסֵי עֲרָבָה לְהַקִּיף מִזְבֵּֽחַ. כֵּן הוֹשַׁע נָא.

כְּהוֹשַֽׁעְתָּ פִּלְאֵי אָרוֹן כְּהֻפְשַׁע.
צִעֵר פְּלֶֽשֶׁת בַּחֲרוֹן אַף, וְנוֹשַׁע. כֵּן הוֹשַׁע נָא.

כְּהוֹשַֽׁעְתָּ קְהִלּוֹת בָּבֶֽלָה שִׁלַּֽחְתָּ.
רַחוּם לְמַעֲנָם שֻׁלַּֽחְתָּ. כֵּן הוֹשַׁע נָא.

כְּהוֹשַֽׁעְתָּ שְׁבוּת שִׁבְטֵי יַעֲקֹב.
תָּשׁוּב וְתָשִׁיב שְׁבוּת אָהֳלֵי יַעֲקֹב. וְהוֹשִֽׁיעָה נָּא.

כְּהוֹשַֽׁעְתָּ שׁוֹמְרֵי מִצְוֹת וְחוֹכֵי יְשׁוּעוֹת.
אֵל לְמוֹשָׁעוֹת. וְהוֹשִֽׁיעָה נָּא.

אֲנִי וָהוֹ הוֹשִֽׁיעָה נָּא.

Hashem, please remove sickness and pain from Your Jewish people and bring us to the Beit HaMikdash where we will serve You beautifully with joy.

תִּתְּנֵנוּ לְשֵׁם וְלִתְהִלָּה.
תְּשִׁיבֵנוּ אֶל הַחֶבֶל וְאֶל הַנַּחֲלָה.
תְּרוֹמְמֵנוּ לְמַעְלָה לְמָעְלָה.
תְּקַבְּצֵנוּ לְבֵית הַתְּפִלָּה.
תַּצִּיבֵנוּ כְּעֵץ עַל פַּלְגֵי מַיִם שְׁתוּלָה.
תִּפְדֵּנוּ מִכָּל נֶגַע וּמַחֲלָה.
תְּעַטְּרֵנוּ בְּאַהֲבָה כְּלוּלָה.
תְּשַׂמְּחֵנוּ בְּבֵית הַתְּפִלָּה.
תְּנַהֲלֵנוּ עַל מֵי מְנוּחוֹת סֶלָה.
תְּמַלְּאֵנוּ חָכְמָה וְשִׂכְלָה.
תַּלְבִּישֵׁנוּ עֹז וּגְדֻלָּה.
תַּכְתִּירֵנוּ בְּכֶתֶר כְּלוּלָה.
תְּיַשְּׁרֵנוּ בְּאֹרַח סְלוּלָה.
תִּטָּעֵנוּ בְּיֹשֶׁר מְסִלָּה.
תְּחָנֵּנוּ בְּרַחֲמִים וּבְחֶמְלָה.
תַּזְכִּירֵנוּ בְּמִי זֹאת עוֹלָה.
תּוֹשִׁיעֵנוּ לְקֵץ הַגְּאֻלָּה.
תְּהַדְּרֵנוּ בְּזִיו הַמְּלֻלָה.
תַּדְבִּיקֵנוּ כְּאֵזוֹר חֲתוּלָה.
תְּגַדְּלֵנוּ בְּיָד הַגְּדוֹלָה.
תְּבִיאֵנוּ לְבֵיתְךָ בְּרִנָּה וְצָהֳלָה.
תְּאַדְּרֵנוּ בְּיֶשַׁע וְגִילָה.
תְּאַמְּצֵנוּ בְּרֶוַח וְהַצָּלָה.

תְּלַבְּבֵנוּ בְּבִנְיַן עִירְךָ כְּבַתְּחִלָּה.
תְּעוֹרְרֵנוּ לְצִיּוֹן בְּשִׁכְלוּלָהּ.
תְּזַכֵּנוּ בְּנִבְנְתָה הָעִיר עַל תִּלָּהּ.
תַּרְבִּיצֵנוּ בְּשָׂשׂוֹן וְגִילָה.
תְּחַזְּקֵנוּ אֱלֹהֵי יַעֲקֹב סֶלָה.

הוֹשַׁע נָא.

PLEASE SAVE US! Hashem, please answer us as You always have answered our ancestors, and provide the rain that we need for plants to grow and for us to drink. Please destroy our enemies and save us now.

Leader then congregation:

אָנָּא, הוֹשִׁיעָה נָּא.

אָנָּא אֱזוֹן חִין תְּאֵבֵי יִשְׁעָךְ.
בְּעַרְבֵי נַחַל לְשַׁעְשְׁעָךְ. וְהוֹשִׁיעָה נָּא.

אָנָּא גְּאַל כַּנַּת נִטְעָךְ.
דוּמָה בְּטַאטְאָךְ. וְהוֹשִׁיעָה נָּא.

אָנָּא הַבֵּט לַבְּרִית טִבְעָךְ.
וּמַחֲשַׁכֵּי אֶרֶץ בְּהַטְבִּיעָךְ. וְהוֹשִׁיעָה נָּא.

אָנָּא זְכָר לָנוּ אָב יְדָעָךְ.
חַסְדְּךָ לָמוֹ בְּהוֹדִיעָךְ. וְהוֹשִׁיעָה נָּא.

אָנָּא טְהוֹרֵי לֵב בְּהַפְלִיאָךְ.
יוֹדֵעַ כִּי הוּא פִּלְאָךְ. וְהוֹשִׁיעָה נָּא.

אָנָּא כַּבִּיר כֹּחַ תֶּן לָנוּ יִשְׁעָךְ.
לַאֲבוֹתֵינוּ כְּהִשָּׁבְעָךְ. וְהוֹשִׁיעָה נָּא.

אָנָּא מַלֵּא מִשְׁאֲלוֹת עַם מְשַׁוְּעָךְ.
נֶעֱקַד בְּהַר מוֹר כְּמוֹ שִׁוְּעָךְ. — וְהוֹשִׁיעָה נָּא.

אָנָּא סַגֵּב אֶשְׁלֵי נִטְעָךְ.
עֲרִיצִים בַּהֲנִיעָךְ. — וְהוֹשִׁיעָה נָּא.

אָנָּא פְּתַח לָנוּ אוֹצְרוֹת רִבְעָךְ.
צִיָּה מֵהֶם בְּהַרְבִּיעָךְ. — וְהוֹשִׁיעָה נָּא.

אָנָּא קוֹרְאֶיךָ אֶרֶץ בְּרוֹעֲעָךְ.
רְעֵם בְּטוּב מִרְעָךְ. — וְהוֹשִׁיעָה נָּא.

אָנָּא שְׁעָרֶיךָ תַּעַל מִמְּשׁוֹאָךְ.
תֵּל תַּלְפִּיּוֹת בְּהַשִּׂיאָךְ. — וְהוֹשִׁיעָה נָּא.

HASHEM, PLEASE SAVE US NOW! Hashem, we have become distant from You like a lost flock of sheep, and our enemies plan to harm us. Now, in our time of need, please help and save us.

Leader then congregation:

אָנָּא, אֵל נָא, הוֹשַׁע נָא וְהוֹשִׁיעָה נָּא.

אֵל נָא תָּעִינוּ כְּשֶׂה אוֹבֵד
שְׁמֵנוּ מִסִּפְרְךָ אַל תְּאַבֵּד — הוֹשַׁע נָא וְהוֹשִׁיעָה נָּא.

אֵל נָא רְעֵה אֶת צֹאן הַהֲרֵגָה
קְצוּפָה, וְעָלֶיךָ הֲרוּגָה — הוֹשַׁע נָא וְהוֹשִׁיעָה נָּא.

אֵל נָא צֹאנְךָ וְצֹאן מַרְעִיתֶךָ
פְּעֻלָּתְךָ וְרַעְיָתֶךָ — הוֹשַׁע נָא וְהוֹשִׁיעָה נָּא.

אֵל נָא עֲנִיֵּי הַצֹּאן
שִׂיחָם עֲנֵה בְּעֵת רָצוֹן — הוֹשַׁע נָא וְהוֹשִׁיעָה נָּא.

אֵל נָא נוֹשְׂאֵי לְךָ עַיִן
מִתְקוֹמְמֶיךָ יִהְיוּ כְּאַיִן הוֹשַׁע נָא וְהוֹשִׁיעָה נָּא.
אֵל נָא לְמְנַסְּכֵי לְךָ מַיִם
כְּמִמַּעַיְנֵי הַיְשׁוּעָה יִשְׁאֲבוּן מַיִם הוֹשַׁע נָא וְהוֹשִׁיעָה נָּא.
אֵל נָא יַעֲלוּ לְצִיּוֹן מוֹשִׁיעִים
טְפוּלִים בְּךָ וּבִשְׁמְךָ נוֹשָׁעִים הוֹשַׁע נָא וְהוֹשִׁיעָה נָּא.
אֵל נָא חֲמוּץ בְּגָדִים
זְעֹם לְנַעֵר כָּל בּוֹגְדִים הוֹשַׁע נָא וְהוֹשִׁיעָה נָּא.
אֵל נָא וְזָכוֹר תִּזְכֹּר
הַנְּכוּרִים בְּלֶתֶךְ וָכֹר הוֹשַׁע נָא וְהוֹשִׁיעָה נָּא.
אֵל נָא דּוֹרְשֶׁיךָ בְּעַנְפֵי עֲרָבוֹת
גְּעִים שְׁעֵה מֵעֲרָבוֹת הוֹשַׁע נָא וְהוֹשִׁיעָה נָּא.
אֵל נָא בָּרֵךְ בְּעִטּוּר שָׁנָה
אֲמָרֵי רְצֵה בְּפִלּוּלִי בְּיוֹם הוֹשַׁעְנָא
הוֹשַׁע נָא וְהוֹשִׁיעָה נָּא.

HASHEM, PLEASE SAVE US NOW! YOU ARE OUR FATHER. Throughout history, the Jewish people have had great ancestors, leaders, and prophets who loved You, Hashem, as much as possible. Each of these great people had an experience in their lives involving water. We remember these events today as we ask You, Hashem, for the water we need to live.

Leader then congregation:

אָנָּא, אֵל נָא, הוֹשַׁע נָא וְהוֹשִׁיעָה נָּא, אָבִינוּ אָתָּה.

לְמַעַן תָּמִים בְּדוֹרוֹתָיו, הַנִּמְלָט בְּרֹב צִדְקוֹתָיו
מֻצָּל מִשֶּׁטֶף בְּבוֹא מַבּוּל מָיִם.
לְאֹם אֲנִי חוֹמָה הוֹשַׁע נָא וְהוֹשִׁיעָה נָּא, אָבִינוּ אָתָּה.

לְמַעַן שָׁלֵם בְּכָל מַעֲשִׂים, הַמְנֻסֶּה בַּעֲשָׂרָה נִסִּים
כְּשָׂר מַלְאָכִים, נָם יֻקַּח נָא מְעַט מַיִם.
לְבָרָה כַּחַמָּה הוֹשַׁע נָא וְהוֹשִׁיעָה נָּא, אָבִינוּ אָתָּה.

לְמַעַן רַךְ וְיָחִיד נֶחֱנַט פְּרִי לְמֵאָה, זָעַק אַיֵּה הַשֶּׂה לְעֹלָה
בִּשְּׂרוּהוּ עֲבָדָיו מָצָאנוּ מָיִם.
לְגוֹלָה וְסוּרָה הוֹשַׁע נָא וְהוֹשִׁיעָה נָּא, אָבִינוּ אָתָּה.

לְמַעַן קָדַם שְׂאֵת בְּרָכָה, הַנִּשְׂטָם וּלְשִׁמְךָ חִכָּה
מְיַחֵם בְּמַקְלוֹת בְּשִׁקְתוֹת הַמָּיִם.
לְדָמְתָה לְתָמָר הוֹשַׁע נָא וְהוֹשִׁיעָה נָּא, אָבִינוּ אָתָּה.

לְמַעַן צָדַק הֱיוֹת לְךָ לְכֹהֵן, כְּחָתָן פְּאֵר יְכַהֵן
מְנֻסֶּה בְּמַסָּה בְּמֵי מְרִיבַת מָיִם.
לְהָהָר הַטּוֹב הוֹשַׁע נָא וְהוֹשִׁיעָה נָּא, אָבִינוּ אָתָּה.

לְמַעַן פְּאֵר הֱיוֹת גְּבִיר לְאֶחָיו, יְהוּדָה אֲשֶׁר גָּבַר בְּאֶחָיו
מִסְפַּר רֹבַע מִדָּלְיָו יִזַּל מַיִם.
לֹא לָנוּ כִּי אִם לְמַעַנְךָ הוֹשַׁע נָא וְהוֹשִׁיעָה נָּא, אָבִינוּ אָתָּה.

לְמַעַן עָנָו מִכֹּל וְנֶאֱמָן, אֲשֶׁר בְּצִדְקוֹ כִּלְכֵּל הַמָּן
מָשׁוּךְ לְגוֹאֵל וּמָשׁוּי מִמַּיִם.
לְזֹאת הַנִּשְׁקָפָה הוֹשַׁע נָא וְהוֹשִׁיעָה נָּא, אָבִינוּ אָתָּה.

לְמַעַן שַׁמָּתוֹ כְּמַלְאֲכֵי מְרוֹמִים, הַלּוֹבֵשׁ אוּרִים וְתֻמִּים
מְצֻוֶּה לָבוֹא בְּמִקְדָּשׁ בְּקִדּוּשׁ יָדַיִם וְרַגְלַיִם וּרְחִיצַת מַיִם.
לְחוֹלַת אַהֲבָה הוֹשַׁע נָא וְהוֹשִׁיעָה נָּא, אָבִינוּ אָתָּה.

לְמַעַן נְבִיאָה מְחוֹלַת מַחֲנַיִם, לִכְמֵהֵי לֵב הוּשְׂמָה עֵינַיִם
לְרַגְלָהּ רָצָה עֲלוֹת וְיָרֶדֶת בְּאֵר מַיִם.
לְטוֹבוּ אֹהָלָיו הוֹשַׁע נָא וְהוֹשִׁיעָה נָּא, אָבִינוּ אָתָּה.

לְמַעַן מְשָׁרֵת לֹא מָשׁ מֵאֹהֶל, וְרוּחַ הַקֹּדֶשׁ עָלָיו אֹהֵל
בְּעָבְרוֹ בַּיַּרְדֵּן נִכְרְתוּ הַמַּיִם.
לְיָפָה וּבָרָה הוֹשַׁע נָא וְהוֹשִׁיעָה נָּא, אָבִינוּ אָתָּה.

לְמַעַן לָמַד רְאוֹת לְטוֹבָה אוֹת, זָעַק אַיֵּה נִפְלָאוֹת
מִצָּה טַל מִגִּזָּה מְלֹא הַסֵּפֶל מָיִם.
לְכַלַּת לְבָנוֹן הוֹשַׁע נָא וְהוֹשִׁיעָה נָּא, אָבִינוּ אָתָּה.

לְמַעַן כְּלוּלֵי עֲשׂוֹת מִלְחַמְתֶּךָ, אֲשֶׁר בְּיָדָם תַּתָּה יְשׁוּעָתֶךָ
צְרוּפֵי מִגּוֹי בְּלָקְקָם בְּיָדָם מָיִם.
לְלֹא בָגְדוּ בָךְ הוֹשַׁע נָא וְהוֹשִׁיעָה נָּא, אָבִינוּ אָתָּה.

לְמַעַן יָחִיד צוֹרְרִים דָּשׁ, אֲשֶׁר מֵרֶחֶם לְנָזִיר הֻקְדָּשׁ
מִמַּכְתֵּשׁ לֶחִי הִבְקַעְתָּ לּוֹ מָיִם.
לְמַעַן שֵׁם קָדְשֶׁךָ הוֹשַׁע נָא וְהוֹשִׁיעָה נָּא, אָבִינוּ אָתָּה.

לְמַעַן טוֹב הוֹלֵךְ וְגָדֵל, אֲשֶׁר מֵעֹשֶׁק עֵדָה חִדֵּל
בְּשׁוּב עַם מֵחֵטְא צִוָּה שְׁאֹב מָיִם.
לְנָאוָה כִּירוּשָׁלָיִם הוֹשַׁע נָא וְהוֹשִׁיעָה נָּא, אָבִינוּ אָתָּה.

לְמַעַן חִכָּךְ מְכַרְכֵּר בְּשִׁיר, הַמְלַמֵּד תּוֹרָה בְּכָל כְּלֵי שִׁיר
מְנַסֵּךְ לְפָנֶיךָ כְּתָאֵב שְׁתוֹת מָיִם.
לְשָׂמוּ בְךָ סִבְרָם הוֹשַׁע נָא וְהוֹשִׁיעָה נָּא, אָבִינוּ אָתָּה.

לְמַעַן זָךְ עָלָה בַּסְּעָרָה, הַמְקַנֵּא וּמֵשִׁיב עֶבְרָה
לִפְלוּלוֹ יָרְדָה אֵשׁ וְלִחֲכָה עָפָר וּמַיִם.
לְעֵינֶיהָ בְּרֵכוֹת הוֹשַׁע נָא וְהוֹשִׁיעָה נָּא, אָבִינוּ אָתָּה.

לְמַעַן וְשֵׁרֵת בֶּאֱמֶת לְרַבּוֹ, פִּי שְׁנַיִם בְּרוּחוֹ נֶאֱצַל בּוֹ
בְּקַחְתּוֹ מְנַגֵּן נִתְמַלְּאוּ גֵּבִים מָיִם.
לְפָצוּ מִי כָמֹכָה הוֹשַׁע נָא וְהוֹשִׁיעָה נָּא, אָבִינוּ אָתָּה.

לְמַעַן הִרְהֵר עֲשׂוֹת רְצוֹנֶךָ, הַמַּכְרִיז תְּשׁוּבָה לְצֹאנֶךָ
אָז בְּבוֹא מְחָרֵף סָתַם עֵינוֹת מָיִם.
לְצִיּוֹן מִכְלַל יֹפִי הוֹשַׁע נָא וְהוֹשִׁיעָה נָּא, אָבִינוּ אָתָּה.

לְמַעַן דְּרָשׁוּךָ בְּתוֹךְ הַגּוֹלָה, וְסוֹדְךָ לָמוֹ נִגְלָה
בְּלִי לְהִתְגָּאֵל דָּרְשׁוּ זֵרְעוֹנִים וּמַיִם.
לְקוֹרְאֶיךָ בַּצַּר הוֹשַׁע נָא וְהוֹשִׁיעָה נָּא, אָבִינוּ אָתָּה.

לְמַעַן גָּמַר חָכְמָה וּבִינָה, סוֹפֵר מָהִיר מְפַלֵּשׁ אֲמָנָה
מְחַכְּמֵנוּ אֲמָרִים הַמְּשׁוּלִים בְּרַחֲבֵי מָיִם.
לְרַבָּתִי עָם הוֹשַׁע נָא וְהוֹשִׁיעָה נָּא, אָבִינוּ אָתָּה.

לְמַעַן בָּאֵי לְךָ הַיּוֹם בְּכָל לֵב, שׁוֹפְכִים לְךָ שִׂיחַ בְּלֹא לֵב וָלֵב
שׁוֹאֲלִים מִמְּךָ עֹז מִטְרוֹת מָיִם.
לְשׁוֹרְרוּ בַיָּם הוֹשַׁע נָא וְהוֹשִׁיעָה נָּא, אָבִינוּ אָתָּה.

לְמַעַן אוֹמְרֵי יִגְדַּל שְׁמֶךָ, וְהֵם נַחֲלָתְךָ וְעַמֶּךָ
צְמֵאִים לְיֶשְׁעֲךָ כְּאֶרֶץ עֲיֵפָה לַמָּיִם.
לְתֹרַתְךָ לָמוֹ מְנוּחָה הוֹשַׁע נָא וְהוֹשִׁיעָה נָּא, אָבִינוּ אָתָּה.

HASHEM, SAVE US NOW,
BRING US SUCCESS NOW, AND FORGIVE US NOW.

Leader then congregation:

הוֹשַׁע נָא, אֵל נָא
אָנָּא הוֹשִׁיעָה נָּא.
הוֹשַׁע נָא, סְלַח נָא, וְהַצְלִיחָה נָא
וְהוֹשִׁיעֵנוּ אֵל מָעֻזֵּנוּ.

Hashem, answer those who call to You for water like You always have, and save Your Jewish people. We ask to be given the water we need like You have given all of our ancestors and leaders in the past.

Put down the Lulav and Etrog and pick up the Hoshanot.

תַּעֲנֶה אֱמוּנִים שׁוֹפְכִים לְךָ לֵב כַּמַּיִם וְהוֹשִׁיעָה נָּא.
לְמַעַן בָּא בָאֵשׁ וּבַמַּיִם וְהַצְלִיחָה נָא.
גָּזַר וְנָם יֻקַּח נָא מְעַט מַיִם וְהוֹשִׁיעֵנוּ אֵל מָעֻזֵּנוּ.

תַּעֲנֶה דְגָלִים גָּזוּ גִּזְרֵי מַיִם וְהוֹשִׁיעָה נָּא.
לְמַעַן הַנֶּעֱקַד בְּשַׁעַר הַשָּׁמַיִם וְהַצְלִיחָה נָא.
וְשָׁב וְחָפַר בְּאֵרוֹת מַיִם וְהוֹשִׁיעֵנוּ אֵל מָעֻזֵּנוּ.

תַּעֲנֶה זַכִּים חוֹנִים עֲלֵי מַיִם וְהוֹשִׁיעָה נָּא.
לְמַעַן חָלָק מְפַצֵּל מַקְלוֹת בְּשִׁקְתוֹת הַמַּיִם וְהַצְלִיחָה נָא.
טָעַן וְגָל אֶבֶן מִבְּאֵר מַיִם וְהוֹשִׁיעֵנוּ אֵל מָעֻזֵּנוּ.

תַּעֲנֶה יְדִידִים נוֹחֲלֵי דָת מְשׁוּלַת מַיִם וְהוֹשִׁיעָה נָּא.
לְמַעַן כָּרוּ בְּמִשְׁעֲנוֹתָם מַיִם וְהַצְלִיחָה נָא.
לְהָכִין לָמוֹ וּלְצֶאֱצָאֵימוֹ מַיִם וְהוֹשִׁיעֵנוּ אֵל מָעֻזֵּנוּ.

תַּעֲנֶה מִתְחַנְּנִים כְּבִישִׁימוֹן עֲלֵי מַיִם וְהוֹשִׁיעָה נָּא.
לְמַעַן נֶאֱמַן בַּיִת מַסְפִּיק לָעָם מַיִם וְהַצְלִיחָה נָא.
סֶלַע הָךְ וַיָּזוּבוּ מַיִם וְהוֹשִׁיעֵנוּ אֵל מָעֻזֵּנוּ.

תַּעֲנֶה עוֹנִים עֲלֵי בְאֵר מַיִם וְהוֹשִׁיעָה נָּא.
לְמַעַן פָּקַד בְּמֵי מְרִיבַת מַיִם וְהַצְלִיחָה נָא.
צְמֵאִים לְהַשְׁקוֹת מַיִם וְהוֹשִׁיעֵנוּ אֵל מָעֻזֵּנוּ.

תַּעֲנֶה קְדוֹשִׁים מְנַסְּכִים לְךָ מַיִם וְהוֹשִׁיעָה נָּא.
לְמַעַן רֹאשׁ מְשׁוֹרְרִים כְּתָאַב שְׁתוֹת מַיִם וְהַצְלִיחָה נָא.
שָׁב וְנָסַךְ לְךָ מַיִם וְהוֹשִׁיעֵנוּ אֵל מָעֻזֵּנוּ.

תַּעֲנֶה שׁוֹאֲלִים בִּרְבוּעַ אֶשְׁלֵי מַיִם וְהוֹשִׁיעָה נָּא.
לְמַעַן תֵּל תַּלְפִּיּוֹת מוֹצָא מַיִם וְהַצְלִיחָה נָא.
תִּפָּתַח אֶרֶץ וְתַרְעִיף שָׁמַיִם וְהוֹשִׁיעֵנוּ אֵל מָעֻזֵּנוּ.

HASHEM, PLEASE BE KIND TO YOUR JEWISH PEOPLE, FORGIVE OUR SINS, AND SAVE US. *When the Beit HaMikdash stood, the Jewish people used to pour water as an offering to Hashem to ask for the rain they needed. Now, even though the Beit HaMikdash no longer stands, we ask You, Hashem, to answer our calls for rain.*

Leader then congregation:

רַחֶם נָא קְהַל עֲדַת יְשׁוּרוּן, סְלַח וּמְחַל עֲוֹנָם וְהוֹשִׁיעֵנוּ אֱלֹהֵי יִשְׁעֵנוּ.

אָז כְּעֵינֵי עֲבָדִים אֶל יַד אֲדוֹנִים
בָּאנוּ לְפָנֶיךָ נְדוֹנִים. וְהוֹשִׁיעֵנוּ אֱלֹהֵי יִשְׁעֵנוּ.
גֵּאֶה אֲדוֹנֵי הָאֲדוֹנִים, נִתְגָּרוּ בָנוּ מְדָנִים
דְּשׁוּנוּ וּבְעָלוּנוּ זוּלָתְךָ אֲדוֹנִים. וְהוֹשִׁיעֵנוּ אֱלֹהֵי יִשְׁעֵנוּ.
הֵן גַּשְׁנוּ הַיּוֹם בְּתַחֲנוּן, עָדֶיךָ רַחוּם וְחַנּוּן
וְסִפַּרְנוּ נִפְלְאוֹתֶיךָ בְּשִׁנּוּן. וְהוֹשִׁיעֵנוּ אֱלֹהֵי יִשְׁעֵנוּ.
זָבַת חָלָב וּדְבָשׁ, נָא אַל תִּיבָשׁ
חֶשְׁרַת מַיִם כְּאֵבֶה תֶּחְבָּשׁ. וְהוֹשִׁיעֵנוּ אֱלֹהֵי יִשְׁעֵנוּ.
טְעֵנוּ בַשְּׁמֵנָה, בְּיַד שִׁבְעָה וּשְׁמוֹנָה
יָשָׁר צַדִּיק אֵל אֱמוּנָה. וְהוֹשִׁיעֵנוּ אֱלֹהֵי יִשְׁעֵנוּ.
כָּרַתָּ בְּרִית לָאָרֶץ, עוֹד כָּל יְמֵי הָאָרֶץ
לְבִלְתִּי פְּרָץ בָּהּ פֶּרֶץ. וְהוֹשִׁיעֵנוּ אֱלֹהֵי יִשְׁעֵנוּ.
מִתְחַנְּנִים עֲלֵי מַיִם, כַּעֲרָבִים עַל יִבְלֵי מַיִם
נָא זְכָר לָמוֹ נִסּוּךְ הַמַּיִם. וְהוֹשִׁיעֵנוּ אֱלֹהֵי יִשְׁעֵנוּ.
שִׂיחִים בְּדֶרֶךְ מַטְעָתָם, עוֹמְסִים בְּשַׁוְעָתָם
עֲנֵם בְּקוֹל פְּגִיעָתָם. וְהוֹשִׁיעֵנוּ אֱלֹהֵי יִשְׁעֵנוּ.

פּוֹעֵל יְשׁוּעוֹת, פְּנֵה לְפִלּוּלָם שְׁעוֹת
צַדִּיקִם אֵל לְמוֹשָׁעוֹת. וְהוֹשִׁיעֵנוּ אֱלֹהֵי יִשְׁעֵנוּ.
קוֹל רִגְשָׁם תִּשַׁע, תִּפְתַּח אֶרֶץ וְיִפְרוּ יֶשַׁע
רַב לְהוֹשִׁיעַ וְלֹא חָפֵץ רֶשַׁע. וְהוֹשִׁיעֵנוּ אֱלֹהֵי יִשְׁעֵנוּ.

OPEN THE GATES TO HEAVEN SO YOU CAN SHARE YOUR TREASURES WITH US. SAVE US, HASHEM, DO NOT LISTEN TO ANY BAD WORDS SAID ABOUT THE JEWISH PEOPLE.

Leader then congregation:

שַׁעֲרֵי שָׁמַיִם פְּתַח, וְאוֹצָרְךָ הַטּוֹב לָנוּ תִפְתַּח. תּוֹשִׁיעֵנוּ וְרִיב אַל תִּמְתַּח. וְהוֹשִׁיעֵנוּ אֱלֹהֵי יִשְׁעֵנוּ.

LET THE VOICE THAT WILL DECLARE MASHIACH HAS ARRIVED ANNOUNCE THIS NEWS! The voice which will declare Mashiach will come to lift up the Jewish people, put down our enemies, and save all.

Leader then congregation:

קוֹל מְבַשֵּׂר מְבַשֵּׂר וְאוֹמֵר.

אֹמֶן יִשְׁעֲךָ בָּא, קוֹל דּוֹדִי הִנֵּה זֶה בָּא. מְבַשֵּׂר וְאוֹמֵר.
בָּא בְּרִבְבוֹת כִּתִּים, לַעֲמֹד עַל הַר הַזֵּיתִים. מְבַשֵּׂר וְאוֹמֵר.
גִּשְׁתּוֹ בַּשּׁוֹפָר לִתְקֹעַ, תַּחְתָּיו הַר יִבָּקֵעַ. מְבַשֵּׂר וְאוֹמֵר.
דָּפַק וְהֵצִיץ וְזָרַח, וּמָשׁ חֲצִי הָהָר מִמִּזְרָח. מְבַשֵּׂר וְאוֹמֵר.
הֵקִים מִלּוּל נְאֻמוֹ, וּבָא הוּא וְכָל קְדוֹשָׁיו עִמּוֹ. מְבַשֵּׂר וְאוֹמֵר.
וּלְכָל בָּאֵי הָעוֹלָם, בַּת קוֹל יִשָּׁמַע בָּעוֹלָם. מְבַשֵּׂר וְאוֹמֵר.
זֶרַע עֲמוּסֵי רַחְמוֹ, נוֹלְדוּ כְּיֶלֶד מִמְּעֵי אִמּוֹ. מְבַשֵּׂר וְאוֹמֵר.
חָלָה וְיָלְדָה מִי זֹאת, מִי־שָׁמַע כָּזֹאת. מְבַשֵּׂר וְאוֹמֵר.
טָהוֹר פָּעַל כָּל אֵלֶּה, מִי רָאָה כָּאֵלֶּה. מְבַשֵּׂר וְאוֹמֵר.
יֶשַׁע וּזְמַן הוּחַד, הֲיוּחַל אֶרֶץ בְּיוֹם אֶחָד. מְבַשֵּׂר וְאוֹמֵר.
כַּבִּיר רוּם וָתַחַת, אִם־יִוָּלֵד גּוֹי פַּעַם אֶחָת. מְבַשֵּׂר וְאוֹמֵר.

לְעֵת יִגְאַל עַמּוֹ נָאוֹר, וְהָיָה לְעֶת־עֶרֶב יִהְיֶה־אוֹר. מְבַשֵּׂר וְאוֹמֵר.
מוֹשִׁיעִים יַעֲלוּ לְהַר צִיּוֹן, כִּי־חָלָה גַּם־יָלְדָה צִיּוֹן. מְבַשֵּׂר וְאוֹמֵר.
נִשְׁמַע בְּכָל גְּבוּלֵךְ, הַרְחִיבִי מְקוֹם אָהֳלֵךְ. מְבַשֵּׂר וְאוֹמֵר.
שִׂימִי עַד דַּמֶּשֶׂק מִשְׁכְּנוֹתַיִךְ, קַבְּלִי בָנַיִךְ וּבְנוֹתַיִךְ. מְבַשֵּׂר וְאוֹמֵר.
עִלְזִי חֲבַצֶּלֶת הַשָּׁרוֹן, כִּי קָמוּ יְשֵׁנֵי חֶבְרוֹן. מְבַשֵּׂר וְאוֹמֵר.
פְּנוּ אֵלַי וְהִוָּשְׁעוּ, הַיּוֹם אִם בְּקוֹלִי תִשְׁמָעוּ. מְבַשֵּׂר וְאוֹמֵר.
צָמַח אִישׁ צֶמַח שְׁמוֹ, הוּא דָוִד בְּעַצְמוֹ. מְבַשֵּׂר וְאוֹמֵר.
קוּמוּ כְּפוּשֵׁי עָפָר, הָקִיצוּ וְרַנְּנוּ שֹׁכְנֵי עָפָר. מְבַשֵּׂר וְאוֹמֵר.
רַבָּתִי עָם בְּהַמְלִיכוֹ, מִגְדּוֹל יְשׁוּעוֹת מַלְכּוֹ. מְבַשֵּׂר וְאוֹמֵר.
שֵׁם רְשָׁעִים לְהַאֲבִיד, עֹשֶׂה־חֶסֶד לִמְשִׁיחוֹ לְדָוִד. מְבַשֵּׂר וְאוֹמֵר.
תְּנָה יְשׁוּעוֹת לְעַם עוֹלָם, לְדָוִד וּלְזַרְעוֹ עַד־עוֹלָם. מְבַשֵּׂר וְאוֹמֵר.

Let the voice that will declare Mashiach has arrived announce this news!

Leader then congregation:

קוֹל מְבַשֵּׂר מְבַשֵּׂר וְאוֹמֵר. קוֹל מְבַשֵּׂר מְבַשֵּׂר וְאוֹמֵר.
קוֹל מְבַשֵּׂר מְבַשֵּׂר וְאוֹמֵר.

Hashem, save Your Jewish people. May the words of my prayers come close to You, Hashem, and may You provide for our needs every day. May the whole world know that Hashem is God and there are no other gods.

Beat the Hoshanot against a chair or the floor five times, then say the following:

הוֹשִׁיעָה אֶת־עַמֶּךָ, וּבָרֵךְ אֶת־נַחֲלָתֶךָ
וּרְעֵם וְנַשְּׂאֵם עַד־הָעוֹלָם:
וְיִהְיוּ דְבָרַי אֵלֶּה, אֲשֶׁר הִתְחַנַּנְתִּי לִפְנֵי יהוה
קְרֹבִים אֶל־יהוה אֱלֹהֵינוּ יוֹמָם וָלָיְלָה
לַעֲשׂוֹת מִשְׁפַּט עַבְדּוֹ וּמִשְׁפַּט עַמּוֹ יִשְׂרָאֵל, דְּבַר־יוֹם בְּיוֹמוֹ:
לְמַעַן דַּעַת כָּל־עַמֵּי הָאָרֶץ כִּי יהוה הוּא הָאֱלֹהִים, אֵין עוֹד:

Hashem, please accept our prayers and allow us to live for this coming year. May Your love for us be awakened so You can erase any punishment we should have received. May You forgive our sins and provide the rain we need for the year to come.

The Torah scrolls are returned to the Ark, which is then closed.

יְהִי רָצוֹן מִלְּפָנֶיךָ יהוה אֱלֹהֵינוּ וֵאלֹהֵי אֲבוֹתֵינוּ, הַבּוֹחֵר בִּנְבִיאִים טוֹבִים וּבְמִנְהֲגֵיהֶם הַטּוֹבִים, שֶׁתְּקַבֵּל בְּרַחֲמִים וּבְרָצוֹן אֶת תְּפִלָּתֵנוּ וְהַקָּפוֹתֵינוּ. וּזְכָר לָנוּ זְכוּת שִׁבְעַת תְּמִימֶיךָ, וְתָסִיר מְחִצַּת הַבַּרְזֶל הַמַּפְסֶקֶת בֵּינֵינוּ וּבֵינֶיךָ, וְתַאֲזִין שַׁוְעָתֵנוּ, וְתֵיטִיב לָנוּ הַחֲתִימָה, תּוֹלֶה אֶרֶץ עַל בְּלִימָה, וְחָתְמֵנוּ בְּסֵפֶר חַיִּים טוֹבִים.

וְהַיּוֹם הַזֶּה תִּתֵּן בִּשְׁכִינַת עֻזְּךָ חָמֵשׁ גְּבוּרוֹת מְמֻתָּקוֹת, עַל יְדֵי חֲבִיטַת עֲרָבָה מִנְהַג נְבִיאֶיךָ הַקְּדוֹשִׁים, וְתִתְעוֹרֵר הָאַהֲבָה בֵּינֵיהֶם. וְתִשָּׁקֵנוּ מִנְּשִׁיקוֹת פִּיךָ, מַמְתֶּקֶת כָּל הַגְּבוּרוֹת וְכָל הַדִּינִין. וְתָאִיר לִשְׁכִינַת עֻזְּךָ בְּשֵׁם יוּ״ד הֵ״א וָא״ו שֶׁהוּא טַל אוֹרוֹת טַלֶּךָ, וּמִשָּׁם תַּשְׁפִּיעַ שֶׁפַע לְעַבְדְּךָ הַמִּתְפַּלֵּל לְפָנֶיךָ, שֶׁתַּאֲרִיךְ יָמָיו וְתִמְחַל לוֹ חֲטָאָיו וַעֲוֹנוֹתָיו וּפְשָׁעָיו. וְתִפְשֹׁט יְמִינְךָ וְיָדְךָ לְקַבְּלוֹ בִּתְשׁוּבָה שְׁלֵמָה לְפָנֶיךָ. וְאוֹצָרְךָ הַטּוֹב תִּפְתַּח לְהַשְׂבִּיעַ מַיִם נֶפֶשׁ שׁוֹקֵקָה, כְּמוֹ שֶׁכָּתוּב: יִפְתַּח יהוה לְךָ אֶת־אוֹצָרוֹ הַטּוֹב אֶת־הַשָּׁמַיִם לָתֵת מְטַר־אַרְצְךָ בְּעִתּוֹ, וּלְבָרֵךְ אֵת כָּל־מַעֲשֵׂה יָדֶךָ: אָמֵן.

The Leader continues with Full Kaddish on page 187.

Seliḥot are said on Fast Days. On Tisha B'Av, Kinot are said instead.
On the Fast of Gedalya, the Seliḥot for the Ten Days of Repentance are said.

סליחות

On this sad day of Asara B'Tevet, Nevuchadnezzar, King of Bavel, surrounded the walls of Yerushalayim and did not allow people, food, or water to enter the city. This was the first stage in the destruction of the Beit HaMikdash and the Jews being asked to leave Israel.

סליחות לעשרה בטבת

סְלַח לָנוּ, אָבִינוּ, כִּי בְּרֹב אִוַּלְתֵּנוּ שָׁגִינוּ.
מְחַל לָנוּ, מַלְכֵּנוּ, כִּי רַבּוּ עֲוֹנֵינוּ.

After the sin of the Golden Calf, Moshe prayed to Hashem to forgive the Jewish people. In his prayer, Moshe listed the "thirteen middot of Hashem," the thirteen ways that Hashem shows mercy. Hashem told Moshe that if the Jewish people make a mistake in the future, they should use these words of prayer and they will not be ignored. When we remember the sad events of the past and think about the mistakes we make today, we say these words to ask Hashem for forgiveness, and feel confident that Hashem will listen to our prayers.

אֵל אֶרֶךְ אַפַּיִם אַתָּה, וּבַעַל הָרַחֲמִים נִקְרֵאתָ, וְדֶרֶךְ תְּשׁוּבָה הוֹרֵיתָ. גְּדֻלַּת רַחֲמֶיךָ וַחֲסָדֶיךָ, תִּזְכֹּר הַיּוֹם וּבְכָל יוֹם לְזֶרַע יְדִידֶיךָ. תֵּפֶן אֵלֵינוּ בְּרַחֲמִים, כִּי אַתָּה הוּא בַּעַל הָרַחֲמִים. בְּתַחֲנוּן וּבִתְפִלָּה פָּנֶיךָ נְקַדֵּם, כְּהוֹדַעְתָּ לֶעָנָו מִקֶּדֶם. מֵחֲרוֹן אַפְּךָ שׁוּב, כְּמוֹ בְּתוֹרָתְךָ כָּתוּב. וּבְצֵל כְּנָפֶיךָ נֶחֱסֶה וְנִתְלוֹנָן, כְּיוֹם וַיֵּרֶד יהוה בֶּעָנָן. ◂ תַּעֲבֹר עַל פֶּשַׁע וְתִמְחֶה אָשָׁם, כְּיוֹם וַיִּתְיַצֵּב עִמּוֹ שָׁם. תַּאֲזִין שַׁוְעָתֵנוּ וְתַקְשִׁיב מֶנּוּ מַאֲמָר, כְּיוֹם וַיִּקְרָא בְשֵׁם יהוה, וְשָׁם נֶאֱמַר

Congregation then Leader:

וַיַּעֲבֹר יהוה עַל־פָּנָיו וַיִּקְרָא

All say aloud:

יהוה, יהוה, אֵל רַחוּם וְחַנּוּן, אֶרֶךְ אַפַּיִם, וְרַב־חֶסֶד וֶאֱמֶת:
נֹצֵר חֶסֶד לָאֲלָפִים, נֹשֵׂא עָוֹן וָפֶשַׁע וְחַטָּאָה, וְנַקֵּה:

וְסָלַחְתָּ לַעֲוֺנֵנוּ וּלְחַטָּאתֵנוּ, וּנְחַלְתָּנוּ:

Continue:

סְלַח לָנוּ אָבִינוּ כִּי חָטָאנוּ, מְחַל לָנוּ מַלְכֵּנוּ כִּי פָשָׁעְנוּ. כִּי־אַתָּה אֲדֹנָי טוֹב וְסַלָּח, וְרַב־חֶסֶד לְכָל־קֹרְאֶיךָ:

כִּי־עִם־יהוה הַחֶסֶד, וְהַרְבֵּה עִמּוֹ פְדוּת: פְּדֵה אֱלֹהִים אֶת־יִשְׂרָאֵל מִכֹּל צָרוֹתָיו: וְהוּא יִפְדֶּה אֶת־יִשְׂרָאֵל מִכֹּל עֲוֺנוֹתָיו: פּוֹדֶה יהוה נֶפֶשׁ עֲבָדָיו, וְלֹא יֶאְשְׁמוּ כָּל־הַחֹסִים בּוֹ:

כְּרַחֵם אָב עַל בָּנִים, כֵּן תְּרַחֵם יהוה עָלֵינוּ.
לַיהוה הַיְשׁוּעָה, עַל־עַמְּךָ בִרְכָתֶךָ סֶּלָה:
יהוה צְבָאוֹת עִמָּנוּ, מִשְׂגָּב לָנוּ אֱלֹהֵי יַעֲקֹב סֶלָה:
יהוה צְבָאוֹת, אַשְׁרֵי אָדָם בֹּטֵחַ בָּךְ:
יהוה הוֹשִׁיעָה, הַמֶּלֶךְ יַעֲנֵנוּ בְיוֹם־קָרְאֵנוּ:

◂ סְלַח־נָא לַעֲוֺן הָעָם הַזֶּה כְּגֹדֶל חַסְדֶּךָ
וְכַאֲשֶׁר נָשָׂאתָה לָעָם הַזֶּה מִמִּצְרַיִם וְעַד־הֵנָּה:
וְשָׁם נֶאֱמַר

Congregation then Leader:

וַיֹּאמֶר יהוה, סָלַחְתִּי כִּדְבָרֶךָ:

Continue:

הַטֵּה אֱלֹהַי אָזְנְךָ וּשְׁמָע, פְּקַח עֵינֶיךָ וּרְאֵה שֹׁמְמֹתֵינוּ וְהָעִיר אֲשֶׁר־נִקְרָא שִׁמְךָ עָלֶיהָ, כִּי לֹא עַל־צִדְקֹתֵינוּ אֲנַחְנוּ מַפִּילִים תַּחֲנוּנֵינוּ לְפָנֶיךָ, כִּי עַל־רַחֲמֶיךָ הָרַבִּים: אֲדֹנָי שְׁמָעָה, אֲדֹנָי סְלָחָה, אֲדֹנָי הַקְשִׁיבָה וַעֲשֵׂה אַל־תְּאַחַר, לְמַעַנְךָ אֱלֹהַי, כִּי־שִׁמְךָ נִקְרָא עַל־עִירְךָ וְעַל־עַמֶּךָ:

This selicha focuses on the three sad events that happened around the day of Asara B'Tevet throughout Jewish history: (1) The walls of Yerushalayim were surrounded by our enemies. This led to the destruction of the Beit HaMikdash; (2) the death of Ezra HaSofer, the man who led the Jews back into Israel after we were forced to leave; and (3) the Torah was translated into Greek, causing people to misunderstand what the words of the Torah teach.

אֱלֹהֵינוּ וֵאלֹהֵי אֲבוֹתֵינוּ

אֶזְכְּרָה מָצוֹק אֲשֶׁר קְרָאַנִי. בְּשָׁלֹשׁ מַכּוֹת בַּחֹדֶשׁ הַזֶּה הִכַּנִי. גְּדָעַנִי הֱנִיאַנִי הִכְאַנִי. אַךְ־עַתָּה הֶלְאָנִי: דִּעֲכַנִי בִּשְׁמוֹנָה בוֹ שְׂמָאלִית וִימָנִית. הֲלֹא שְׁלָשְׁתָּן קָבַעְתִּי תַעֲנִית. וּמֶלֶךְ יָוָן אֲנָסַנִי לִכְתֹּב דָּת, יְוָנִית. עַל גַּבִּי חָרְשׁוּ חוֹרְשִׁים, הֶאֱרִיכוּ מַעֲנִית. וְעֵמְתִּי בִּתְשִׁעָה בוֹ בִּכְלִמָּה וְחֵפֶר. חָשַׁךְ מֵעָלַי מְעִיל הוֹד וָצֶפֶר. טָרֹף טֹרַף בּוֹ הַנּוֹתֵן אִמְרֵי שֶׁפֶר. הוּא עֶזְרָא הַסּוֹפֵר. יוֹם עֲשִׂירִי, צֻוָּה בֶן בּוּזִי הַחוֹזֶה. כְּתָב לְךָ בְּסֵפֶר הַמַּחֲזֶה. לְזִכָּרוֹן לְעַם נָמֵס וְנִבְזֶה. אֶת־עֶצֶם הַיּוֹם הַזֶּה: מִנְיַן סֵדֶר חֳדָשִׁים בַּעֲשָׂרָה בוֹ הֵעִיר. נְהִי וְיֵלֵל בְּמוֹ פִי אַפְעִיר. סֵדֶר פֻּרְעָנִיּוֹת בְּתוֹךְ לְבָבִי יַבְעִיר. בְּבֹא אֵלַי הַפָּלִיט לֵאמֹר הֻכְּתָה הָעִיר. עַל אֵלֶּה, עַל פְּנֵי אֲדָמָה זֵרִיתִי. פַּצְתִּי עַל אַרְבַּעְתָּן, לוּ חֵץ בִּלְבָבִי יָרִיתִי. צָרוֹת עַל אֵלֶּה, קֶבֶר לִי כָּרִיתִי. צַדִּיק הוּא יהוה, כִּי פִיהוּ מָרִיתִי: קָרָאתִי שִׁמְךָ, מִתְנַחֵם עַל רָעָתִי. רְאֵה עָנְיִי וּשְׁמַע קוֹל פְּגִיעָתִי. שְׁמַע תְּחִנָּתִי, חִישׁ נָא יְשׁוּעָתִי. אַל־תַּעְלֵם אָזְנְךָ לְרַוְחָתִי לְשַׁוְעָתִי: ◂ יֶרַח טֵבֵת, מְאֹד לָקִיתִי בוֹ. וְנִשְׁתַּנּוּ עָלַי סִדְרֵי נְתִיבוֹ. סָרַרְתִּי, פָּשַׁעְתִּי, יְגַלֶּה לִּי טוּבוֹ. הָאוֹמֵר לַיָּם עַד פֹּה תָבוֹא.

אֵל מֶלֶךְ יוֹשֵׁב עַל כִּסֵּא רַחֲמִים, מִתְנַהֵג בַּחֲסִידוּת. מוֹחֵל עֲוֹנוֹת עַמּוֹ, מַעֲבִיר רִאשׁוֹן רִאשׁוֹן. מַרְבֶּה מְחִילָה לְחַטָּאִים, וּסְלִיחָה

לְפוֹשְׁעִים. עֹשֶׂה צְדָקוֹת עִם כָּל בָּשָׂר וָרוּחַ, לֹא כְרָעָתָם תִּגְמֹל.
› אֵל, הוֹרֵיתָ לָּנוּ לוֹמַר שְׁלֹשׁ עֶשְׂרֵה, וּזְכָר לָנוּ הַיּוֹם בְּרִית שְׁלֹשׁ עֶשְׂרֵה, כְּמוֹ שֶׁהוֹדַעְתָּ לֶעָנָו מִקֶּדֶם, כְּמוֹ שֶׁכָּתוּב: וַיֵּרֶד יהוה בֶּעָנָן, וַיִּתְיַצֵּב עִמּוֹ שָׁם, וַיִּקְרָא בְשֵׁם, יהוה:

Congregation then Leader:

וַיַּעֲבֹר יהוה עַל־פָּנָיו וַיִּקְרָא

All say aloud:

יהוה, יהוה, אֵל רַחוּם וְחַנּוּן, אֶרֶךְ אַפַּיִם, וְרַב־חֶסֶד וֶאֱמֶת:
נֹצֵר חֶסֶד לָאֲלָפִים, נֹשֵׂא עָוֹן וָפֶשַׁע וְחַטָּאָה, וְנַקֵּה:
וְסָלַחְתָּ לַעֲוֹנֵנוּ וּלְחַטָּאתֵנוּ, וּנְחַלְתָּנוּ:

Continue:

סְלַח לָנוּ אָבִינוּ כִּי חָטָאנוּ, מְחַל לָנוּ מַלְכֵּנוּ כִּי פָשָׁעְנוּ. כִּי־אַתָּה אֲדֹנָי טוֹב וְסַלָּח, וְרַב־חֶסֶד לְכָל־קֹרְאֶיךָ:

אֱלֹהִים בָּאוּ גוֹיִם בְּנַחֲלָתֶךָ, טִמְּאוּ אֶת־הֵיכַל קָדְשֶׁךָ, שָׂמוּ אֶת־יְרוּשָׁלַםִ לְעִיִּים: אֱלֹהִים, זֵדִים קָמוּ עָלֵינוּ, וַעֲדַת עָרִיצִים בִּקְשׁוּ נַפְשֵׁנוּ, וְלֹא שָׂמוּךָ לְנֶגְדָּם.

כְּרַחֵם אָב עַל בָּנִים, כֵּן תְּרַחֵם יהוה עָלֵינוּ.
לַיהוה הַיְשׁוּעָה, עַל־עַמְּךָ בִרְכָתֶךָ סֶּלָה:
יהוה צְבָאוֹת עִמָּנוּ, מִשְׂגָּב לָנוּ אֱלֹהֵי יַעֲקֹב סֶלָה:
יהוה צְבָאוֹת, אַשְׁרֵי אָדָם בֹּטֵחַ בָּךְ:
יהוה הוֹשִׁיעָה, הַמֶּלֶךְ יַעֲנֵנוּ בְיוֹם־קָרְאֵנוּ:

This selicha focuses on the destruction of the Beit HaMikdash and the difficulties the Jewish people faced afterwards. The Jews were once like royalty to Hashem and are now unable to serve Hashem with korbanot. Other nations laugh at us as a result. We beg Hashem to forgive us and return us to our royal status.

אֱלֹהֵינוּ וֵאלֹהֵי אֲבוֹתֵינוּ

אֶבֶן הָרֹאשָׁה, לְעִיִּים וְלַחֲרִישָׁה, וְנוּחֲלֵי מוֹרָשָׁה, מְנוֹד רֹאשׁ בַּלְאֻמִּים. בְּקִרְבִּי לֵב נִכְאָב, נִדְוֶה וְנִדְאָב, נִשְׁאַרְנוּ כְּאֵין אָב, וְהָיִינוּ כִּיתוֹמִים. רַכָּה וַעֲנֻגָּה, בַּשּׁוֹשַׁנִּים סוּגָה, וְעַתָּה הִיא נוּגָה, מְסוּרָה בְּיַד קָמִים. הָיְתָה כְּאַלְמָנָה, קִרְיָה נֶאֱמָנָה, וְזֶרַע מִי מָנָה, נִמְכְּרוּ בְּלֹא דָמִים. מְעֻנָּגָה וְרַכָּה, צָלְחָה לִמְלוּכָה, וּמַעֲנִיתָהּ אָרְכָה, זֶה כַּמֶּה שָׁנִים וְיָמִים. בֵּית יַעֲקֹב לְבִזָּה, לְלַעַג וּלְעִזָּה, וְהָעִיר הָעַלִּיזָה, לְמַטְּעֵי כְרָמִים. רְוּוּיָה תַרְעֵלָה, בְּיַד בְּנֵי עַוְלָה, הָרְצוּיָה כְּעוֹלָה, וּכְקְטֹרֶת הַסַּמִּים. מָאֲסָה לִזְנֹחַ, תּוֹרַת אֲבִי זָנוֹחַ, וְלֹא מָצְאָה מָנוֹחַ, לֵילוֹת וְגַם יָמִים. נוֹרָא אֵל עֶלְיוֹן, מִמְּךָ יְהִי צִבְיוֹן, לְהָשִׁיב לְרִיב צִיּוֹן, שְׁנַת שִׁלּוּמִים. חַדֵּשׁ יָמֵינוּ כְּקֶדֶם, מְעוֹנָה אֱלֹהֵי קֶדֶם, וְלַבֵּן כְּצֶמֶר אֹדֶם, וְכַשֶּׁלֶג כְּתָמִים. ‹ חַזְּקֵנוּ בְּיִרְאָתֶךָ, וּבְקִיּוּם תּוֹרָתֶךָ, וּפָקְדֵנוּ בִּישׁוּעָתֶךָ, אֵל מָלֵא רַחֲמִים.

אֵל מֶלֶךְ יוֹשֵׁב עַל כִּסֵּא רַחֲמִים, מִתְנַהֵג בַּחֲסִידוּת. מוֹחֵל עֲוֹנוֹת עַמּוֹ, מַעֲבִיר רִאשׁוֹן רִאשׁוֹן. מַרְבֶּה מְחִילָה לְחַטָּאִים, וּסְלִיחָה לְפוֹשְׁעִים. עֹשֶׂה צְדָקוֹת עִם כָּל בָּשָׂר וָרוּחַ, לֹא כְרָעָתָם תִּגְמֹל. ‹ אֵל, הוֹרֵיתָ לָּנוּ לוֹמַר שְׁלֹשׁ עֶשְׂרֵה, וּזְכָר לָנוּ הַיּוֹם בְּרִית שְׁלֹשׁ עֶשְׂרֵה, כְּמוֹ שֶׁהוֹדַעְתָּ לֶעָנָו מִקֶּדֶם, כְּמוֹ שֶׁכָּתוּב: וַיֵּרֶד יהוה בֶּעָנָן, וַיִּתְיַצֵּב עִמּוֹ שָׁם, וַיִּקְרָא בְשֵׁם, יהוה:

Congregation then Leader:

וַיַּעֲבֹר יהוה עַל־פָּנָיו וַיִּקְרָא

All say aloud:

יהוה, יהוה, אֵל רַחוּם וְחַנּוּן, אֶרֶךְ אַפַּיִם, וְרַב־חֶסֶד וֶאֱמֶת: נֹצֵר חֶסֶד לָאֲלָפִים, נֹשֵׂא עָוֺן וָפֶשַׁע וְחַטָּאָה, וְנַקֵּה: וְסָלַחְתָּ לַעֲוֺנֵנוּ וּלְחַטָּאתֵנוּ, וּנְחַלְתָּנוּ:

Continue:

סְלַח לָנוּ אָבִינוּ כִּי חָטָאנוּ, מְחַל לָנוּ מַלְכֵּנוּ כִּי פָשָׁעְנוּ. כִּי־אַתָּה אֲדֹנָי טוֹב וְסַלָּח, וְרַב־חֶסֶד לְכָל־קֹרְאֶיךָ:

This selicha focuses on the pain and suffering the Jews felt when their enemies defeated them. The Beit HaMikdash, once beautiful, is now destroyed and we are filled with grief. We call out to Hashem to end our sadness and instead turn our fasting into joy.

The following is said responsively:

אֲבוֹתַי כִּי בָטְחוּ בְּשֵׁם אֱלֹהֵי צוּרִי
גָּדְלוּ וְהִצְלִיחוּ וְגַם עָשׂוּ פֶּרִי
וּמֵעֵת הֻדְּחוּ וְהָלְכוּ עִמּוֹ קֶרִי
הָיוּ הָלוֹךְ וְחָסוֹר עַד הַחֹדֶשׁ הָעֲשִׂירִי.

בָּעֲשִׂירִי לַחֹדֶשׁ סָמַךְ מֶלֶךְ בָּבֶל
וְצָר עַל עִיר הַקֹּדֶשׁ, וְנִקְרַב רַב הַחוֹבֵל
נִתַּתִּי הָדֵשׁ וְעֻנֵּיתִי בַּכֶּבֶל
וְהָיָה מִדֵּי חֹדֶשׁ לְאֵבֶל כִּנּוֹרִי.

רֵאשִׁית בִּכּוּרָה לְרֵאשִׁית הַחֵרֶם
שֵׂם אֲחֵרִים הִזְכִּירָה, וְהֶעָוֹן גּוֹרֵם
פְּנֵי אֵל לֹא הִכִּירָה, וְשֻׁטְּפָה בְּזֶרֶם
צָרָה כְּמַבְכִּירָה כָּעֵת בַּמָּרוֹם תַּמְרִיא.

הָאֱלֹהִים הֵבִיא יוֹם רָעָה וּמָצוֹר
צוָּה צָרַי סְבִיבַי עוֹלָלַי לְבַצּוֹר
יוֹם הֵרַךְ לְבָבִי וְאֵין כֹּחַ לַעְצוֹר
וְדִבֶּר אֶל נָבִיא, מְשֹׁל אֶל בֵּית הַמֶּרִי.

מִיּוֹשְׁבֵי שַׁעַר הֶעֱבִיר אַדֶּרֶת
חֲמָתוֹ כָּאֵשׁ בָּעַר, וְהֵרִים עֲטֶרֶת
וּמִלְּבָנוֹן יַעַר הִשְׁלִיךְ תִּפְאֶרֶת
וְרוּחַ סוֹעָה וָסַעַר תְּסַמֵּר שַׂעֲרַת בְּשָׂרִי.

יְפֵהפִיָּה נִמְשַׁלְתְּ, וְעַתָּה קְדוֹרַנִּית
בְּעָוֹן כִּי כָשַׁלְתְּ, וְלִבֵּךְ אֲחוֹרַנִּית
זִנְּבוּךְ וְנֶחֱשַׁלְתְּ רִאשׁוֹנָה וְשֵׁנִית
וְהִחְתֵּל לֹא חֻתַּלְתְּ מְעַט צֳרִי.

צַדִּיק הַצּוּר תָּם, נָשֹׂא עָוֹן נִלְאָה
מִכְּרוּב לְמִפְתָּן, לְפִנַּת גַּג דָּאָה
מֵעֲוֹן הַנִּכְתָּם, וְצַעֲקָתָם בָּאָה
רַבָּה רָעָתָם כְּעֵץ עֹשֶׂה פְּרִי.

חִזֵּק כָּל קָמַי, תּוֹכֵן הָעֲלִילוֹת
כִּי מָלְאוּ יָמַי בְּרֹעַ מִפְעָלוֹת
וּמְבַקֵּשׁ עֲלוּמַי שְׁכַחְתִּי גְמוּלוֹת
נוֹתֵן לַחְמִי וּמֵימַי, פִּשְׁתִּי וְצַמְרִי.

קָמַי פִּיהֶם פָּעֲרוּ וְנַחֲלָתִי בִּלְּעוּ
מְאֹד עָלַי גָּבְרוּ וְדָמִי שָׁתוּ וְלָעוּ
נָכְרִים עָלַי צָרוּ וְאֶת אַחַי הֵרֵעוּ
הָאוֹמְרִים עָרוּ עָרוּ, בְּנֵי שֵׂעִיר הַחֹרִי.

אָמְרוּ לְכוּ נְכַלֵּם, וְנַשְׁבִּיתָה זִכְרָם
אֵל קַנּוֹא וְנוֹקֵם, גְּמֹלֵם, יִשְׂאוּ אֶת שִׁבְרָם
כְּמַעֲשֵׂיהֶם שַׁלֵּם וְיֵבוֹשׁוּ מִשִּׂבְרָם
כְּאִישׁ חֲלוֹם חוֹלֵם שְׁלֹשָׁה סַלֵּי חֹרִי.

פְּצָעַי לֹא רֻכְּכָה וְחַבּוּרוֹתַי רֶצַח
וְעֵינַי הָכְהֳתָה, צוֹפָה לְדוֹדִי צַח
הַעוֹד לֹא שָׁכְכָה חֲמָתוֹ לָנֶצַח
עַל מֶה עָשָׂה כָּכָה וּמֶה חֳרִי.

רַחוּם זֶה אֵלִי, אַל לָעַד תִּזְנַח
אָרְכוּ יְמֵי אֶבְלִי וְעוֹד לִבִּי נֶאֱנָח
שׁוּבָה אֵל לְאָהֳלִי, מְקוֹמְךָ אַל תַּנַּח
שַׁלֵּם יְמֵי אֶבְלִי כִּי תָבוֹא עַל שְׂכָרִי.

יהוה מְנָת חֶלְקִי, חוּשָׁה לִי לְעֶזְרָה
וּפִתַּחְתָּ שַׂקִּי, שִׂמְחָה לִי לְאַזְרָה
וְתַגִּיהַּ אֶת חָשְׁכִּי בְּאוֹרְךָ לְהָאִירָה
אֶת נֶשֶׁף חִשְׁקִי, כִּי אַתָּה נֵרִי.

מִיָּגוֹן וַאֲנָחָה, פְּדֵה אֵל אֶת נַפְשִׁי
עֲשֵׂה לְעַמְּךָ הֲנָחָה, מַלְכִּי וּקְדוֹשִׁי
תַּהֲפוֹךְ לִרְוָחָה אֶת צוֹם הַחֲמִישִׁי
לְשָׂשׂוֹן וּלְשִׂמְחָה, צוֹם הָרְבִיעִי וְצוֹם הָעֲשִׂירִי.

Continue with אֵל מֶלֶךְ יוֹשֵׁב *on page 857.*

In the days of King Achashveirosh, he and his chief advisor, Haman, plotted to kill all the Jews. Letters were sent throughout the kingdom announcing the day that the Jews would be destroyed. Through the hand of Hashem, Esther, a Jew, was made queen by marrying Achashveirosh. She planned to risk her life by begging Achashveirosh to protect the Jewish people. In preparation, Esther and Mordechai asked all Jews to fast for three days so that Hashem would protect Esther. After the fasting, Esther went before Achashveirosh. Achashveirosh agreed to protect the Jews, and killed Haman instead. We fast on this day to remember the miraculous events that came about through fasting and praying to Hashem.

סליחות לתענית אסתר

סְלַח לָנוּ, אָבִינוּ, כִּי בְּרֹב אִוַּלְתֵּנוּ שָׁגִינוּ.
מְחַל לָנוּ, מַלְכֵּנוּ, כִּי רַבּוּ עֲוֹנֵינוּ.

After the sin of the Golden Calf, Moshe prayed to Hashem to forgive the Jewish people. In his prayer, Moshe listed the "thirteen middot of Hashem," the thirteen ways that Hashem shows mercy. Hashem told Moshe that if the Jewish people make a mistake in the future, they should use these words of prayer and they will not be ignored. When we remember the sad events of the past and think about the mistakes we make today, we say these words to ask Hashem for forgiveness, and feel confident that Hashem will listen to our prayers.

אֵל אֶרֶךְ אַפַּיִם אַתָּה, וּבַעַל הָרַחֲמִים נִקְרֵאתָ, וְדֶרֶךְ תְּשׁוּבָה הוֹרֵיתָ. גְּדֻלַּת רַחֲמֶיךָ וַחֲסָדֶיךָ, תִּזְכֹּר הַיּוֹם וּבְכָל יוֹם לְזֶרַע יְדִידֶיךָ. תֵּפֶן אֵלֵינוּ בְּרַחֲמִים, כִּי אַתָּה הוּא בַּעַל הָרַחֲמִים. בְּתַחֲנוּן וּבִתְפִלָּה פָּנֶיךָ נְקַדֵּם, כְּהוֹדַעְתָּ לֶעָנָו מִקֶּדֶם. מֵחֲרוֹן אַפְּךָ שׁוּב, כְּמוֹ בְּתוֹרָתְךָ כָּתוּב. וּבְצֵל כְּנָפֶיךָ נֶחֱסֶה וְנִתְלוֹנָן, כְּיוֹם וַיֵּרֶד יהוה בֶּעָנָן. ‹ תַּעֲבֹר עַל פֶּשַׁע וְתִמְחֶה אָשָׁם, כְּיוֹם וַיִּתְיַצֵּב עִמּוֹ שָׁם. תַּאֲזִין שַׁוְעָתֵנוּ וְתַקְשִׁיב מֶנּוּ מַאֲמָר, כְּיוֹם וַיִּקְרָא בְשֵׁם יהוה, וְשָׁם נֶאֱמַר

Congregation then Leader:

וַיַּעֲבֹר יהוה עַל־פָּנָיו וַיִּקְרָא

All say aloud:

יהוה, יהוה, אֵל רַחוּם וְחַנּוּן, אֶרֶךְ אַפַּיִם, וְרַב־חֶסֶד וֶאֱמֶת: נֹצֵר חֶסֶד לָאֲלָפִים, נֹשֵׂא עָוֹן וָפֶשַׁע וְחַטָּאָה, וְנַקֵּה:

וְסָלַחְתָּ לַעֲוֹנֵנוּ וּלְחַטָּאתֵנוּ, וּנְחַלְתָּנוּ:

Continue:

סְלַח לָנוּ אָבִינוּ כִּי חָטָאנוּ, מְחַל לָנוּ מַלְכֵּנוּ כִּי פָשָׁעְנוּ. כִּי־אַתָּה
אֲדֹנָי טוֹב וְסַלָּח, וְרַב־חֶסֶד לְכָל־קֹרְאֶיךָ:

קַוֵּה קִוִּינוּ יהוה, וַיֵּט אֵלֵינוּ וַיִּשְׁמַע שַׁוְעָתֵנוּ. אַף אֹרַח מִשְׁפָּטֶיךָ
יהוה קִוִּינוּךָ, לְשִׁמְךָ וּלְזִכְרְךָ תַּאֲוַת־נָפֶשׁ:

כְּרַחֵם אָב עַל בָּנִים, כֵּן תְּרַחֵם יהוה עָלֵינוּ.
לַיהוה הַיְשׁוּעָה, עַל־עַמְּךָ בִרְכָתֶךָ סֶּלָה:
יהוה צְבָאוֹת עִמָּנוּ, מִשְׂגָּב לָנוּ אֱלֹהֵי יַעֲקֹב סֶלָה:
יהוה צְבָאוֹת, אַשְׁרֵי אָדָם בֹּטֵחַ בָּךְ:
יהוה הוֹשִׁיעָה, הַמֶּלֶךְ יַעֲנֵנוּ בְיוֹם־קָרְאֵנוּ:

◂ סְלַח־נָא לַעֲוֹן הָעָם הַזֶּה כְּגֹדֶל חַסְדֶּךָ
וְכַאֲשֶׁר נָשָׂאתָה לָעָם הַזֶּה מִמִּצְרַיִם וְעַד־הֵנָּה:
וְשָׁם נֶאֱמַר

Congregation then Leader:

וַיֹּאמֶר יהוה, סָלַחְתִּי כִּדְבָרֶךָ:

Continue:

הַטֵּה אֱלֹהַי אָזְנְךָ וּשְׁמָע, פְּקַח עֵינֶיךָ וּרְאֵה שֹׁמְמֹתֵינוּ וְהָעִיר אֲשֶׁר־
נִקְרָא שִׁמְךָ עָלֶיהָ, כִּי לֹא עַל־צִדְקֹתֵינוּ אֲנַחְנוּ מַפִּילִים תַּחֲנוּנֵינוּ
לְפָנֶיךָ, כִּי עַל־רַחֲמֶיךָ הָרַבִּים: אֲדֹנָי שְׁמָעָה, אֲדֹנָי סְלָחָה, אֲדֹנָי
הַקְשִׁיבָה וַעֲשֵׂה אַל־תְּאַחַר, לְמַעַנְךָ אֱלֹהַי, כִּי־שִׁמְךָ נִקְרָא עַל־
עִירְךָ וְעַל־עַמֶּךָ:

This selicha focuses on the helpless feeling of the Jewish people when Haman made plans with King Achashveirosh to destroy the Jewish people. The Jews had no opportunity to defend themselves. Instead, the Jews cried out in prayer to Hashem and their prayers were heard. Hashem ripped up the evil plans of Haman and saved the Jewish people.

אֱלֹהֵינוּ וֵאלֹהֵי אֲבוֹתֵינוּ

אָדָם בְּקוּם עָלֵינוּ, חִיל אֲחָזָתְנוּ לִרְעֹד. בְּהִסְתַּפְּחוֹ לְמַלְכוּת חָנֵף, כִּמְעַט כָּשַׁלְנוּ לִמְעֹד. גָּמְרוּ לְמָכְרֵנוּ כְּתֵל וְחָרִיץ בְּלִי מִסְעוֹד. אָמְרוּ לְכוּ וְנַכְחִידֵם מִגּוֹי, וְלֹא־יִזָּכֵר שֵׁם־יִשְׂרָאֵל עוֹד: דַּלּוּ עֵינַי לַמָּרוֹם, קְרָאתִיךָ אוֹיְבַי לָקֹב. הַכְרֵת שֵׁם וּשְׁאָר, וּמְחֵה שֵׁם לִרְקֹב. וְצַר צוֹרְרַי בְּנִכְלֵיהֶם אֲשֶׁר נִכְּלוּ לַעֲקֹב. וַיֹּאמְרוּ, לֹא יִרְאֶה־יָּהּ, וְלֹא־יָבִין אֱלֹהֵי יַעֲקֹב: זְרוּיִים עֻנָּה וְיֻגָּה, וְלֹא מִלֵּב לְכַלּוֹתָם. חָבוּ לְפָנִים, וְרֻדּוּ בַּהֲסָרַת טַבַּעַת לְהַחֲלוֹתָם. טוּב דְּבָרוֹ הֵקִים לְעֵינֵי הַגּוֹיִם לְהַעֲלוֹתָם. בְּאֶרֶץ אֹיְבֵיהֶם לֹא־מְאַסְתִּים וְלֹא־גְעַלְתִּים לְכַלֹּתָם: יָדַע רֶמֶז הַקּוֹרוֹת לְעַם מֵעָפָר וּמְהֻדָּם. כְּתָב הַסְתֵּר אַסְתִּיר וּמָר דְּרוֹר מְפֹרְדָּם. לִשְׁבֹּת הָמָן מִמָּחֳרָת, הֲמִן הָעֵץ קִנְדָּס. תַּחַת הַנַּעֲצוּץ יַעֲלֶה בְרוֹשׁ וְתַחַת הַסִּרְפַּד יַעֲלֶה הֲדַס: מַקְשִׁיב דְּבַר שֶׁקֶר כְּתָב שִׂטְנָה וָעֶצֶב. נִתְעַטֵּף בְּבִגְדֵי שְׂרָד כִּטְעָה בְּמִנְיַן קֶצֶב. סִדֵּר לְהִשְׁתַּמֵּשׁ בְּשׁוֹנִים כְּלֵי הַמַּחְצֵב. וַיָּבוֹא גַם־הַשָּׂטָן בְּתֹכָם לְהִתְיַצֵּב: עַם הַנִּמְצְאִים בְּשׁוּשָׁן, בְּאָכְלָם מִזֶּבַח עוֹכְרָם. פָּעַר פִּיו לְהַשְׂטִינָם, וּלְהַסְגִּירָם בְּיַד נוֹתֵן מִכְרָם. צוּר הִסְכִּים לִכְתֹּב אִגֶּרֶת לְאַבֵּד שִׁבְרָם. אָמַרְתִּי אַפְאֵיהֶם, אַשְׁבִּיתָה מֵאֱנוֹשׁ זִכְרָם: קְדוֹשִׁים מַלְאֲכֵי שָׁלוֹם מַר יִבְכָּיוּן בִּצְעָקָה. רַחוּם הַבֵּט לַבְּרִית וְאַל תָּפֵר לְהַרְחִיקָהּ. שָׁמְעָה מוֹרָשָׁה, וַתִּלְבַּשׁ בִּגְדֵי אַלְמְנוּת וּמוּעָקָה. וַתָּשֶׂם יָדָהּ עַל־רֹאשָׁהּ, וַתֵּלֶךְ הָלוֹךְ וְזָעָקָה: תִּשְׁבִּי שָׂם אֵזוֹר שַׂק בְּמָתְנָיו תַּחְבֹּשֶׁת. מֵהֵר וְהוֹדִיעַ יְשֵׁנֵי מַכְפֵּל, אָבוֹת שְׁלֹשֶׁת. נָחַץ

לְרוֹעֶה, מַה לְּךָ נִרְדָּם לְהִתְעַשֵּׁת. קוּם קְרָא אֶל־אֱלֹהֶיךָ, אוּלַי יִתְעַשֵּׁת: חוֹתַם טִיט אֲשֶׁר נַעֲשָׂה, לְבִלְשָׁן סִפֵּר. מְנִינֻהָ לָמְדוּ לְאַחַר גְּזֵרָה כַּעַס לְהָפֵר. בֶּן קִישׁ הִקִּישׁ דַּלְתוֹת בֵּית הַסֵּפֶר. וַיְכַס שַׂק, וַיֵּשֶׁב עַל־הָאֵפֶר: רִבֵּץ תִּינוֹקוֹת לְפָנָיו יָמִים שְׁלֹשָׁה, צְמֵאִים וּמְכֻפָּנִים. בְּקוֹל יַעֲקֹב לַחֲלֹשׁ יְדֵי עַז פָּנִים. יָדָיו אֱמוּנָה לָאֵל, הַצִּילֵנִי נָא מֵעֶלְבּוֹנִים. פֶּן־יָבוֹא וְהִכַּנִי אֵם עַל־בָּנִים: מִזֶּה אֵלֶּה וּמִזֶּה אֵלֶּה, בְּנֵי אֵיתָנַי וְרַבָּנָי. כֻּלָּם צָעֲקוּ, וַתַּעַל שַׁוְעָתָם אֶל יהוה. יָהּ, לְקוֹל רִנּוּן כְּבוֹא, שָׁאַל לְפָנָי. וּמֶה קוֹל־הַצֹּאן הַזֶּה בְּאָזְנָי: רוֹעֶה הֱשִׁיבוֹ, הֵם קְטַנֵּי קֹדֶשׁ זֶרַע. יָהּ, הַצֵּל לְקוּחִים לַמָּוֶת מֵאוֹיֵב הָרָע. חַנּוּן נִכְמְרוּ רַחֲמָיו וַיְבַקֵּשׁ לִבְכּוֹת הַמְאֹרָע. וַיְהִי כִּקְרֹא מֶלֶךְ־יִשְׂרָאֵל אֶת־הַסֵּפֶר, וַיִּקְרַע: יְהוּדִי הוֹקִיעַ, יְלָדָיו לְמַטָּה וַאֲבִיהֶם לְמַעְלָה. אִישׁ אִישׁ בְּשָׁלֹשׁ אַמּוֹת, וְהָרְבִיעִית אֲוִיר מְגֻלָּה. מִשְׁנֶה נָקָם חָזָה, וְשָׂמַח וְשָׂח תְּהִלָּה. אֹתִי הֵשִׁיב עַל־כַּנִּי וְאֹתוֹ תָלָה: ‹ וַתִּכְתֹּב אֶסְתֵּר תֹּקֶף, לִקְרֹא כִּבְהַלֵּל מְהוֹדִים. מִלְמַעְלָה קִיְּמוּ מַה שֶּׁקִּבְּלוּ לְמַטָּה דוֹדִים. נֵס יְנוֹסֵס לְפַרְסֵם כְּאָז פִּלְאוֹ מַסְהִידִים. בָּעֵת הַזֹּאת רֶוַח וְהַצָּלָה יַעֲמוֹד לַיְּהוּדִים:

אֵל מֶלֶךְ יוֹשֵׁב עַל כִּסֵּא רַחֲמִים, מִתְנַהֵג בַּחֲסִידוּת. מוֹחֵל עֲוֹנוֹת עַמּוֹ, מַעֲבִיר רִאשׁוֹן רִאשׁוֹן. מַרְבֶּה מְחִילָה לְחַטָּאִים, וּסְלִיחָה לְפוֹשְׁעִים. עֹשֶׂה צְדָקוֹת עִם כָּל בָּשָׂר וָרוּחַ, לֹא כְרָעָתָם תִּגְמֹל. ‹ אֵל, הוֹרֵיתָ לָּנוּ לוֹמַר שְׁלֹשׁ עֶשְׂרֵה, וּזְכָר לָנוּ הַיּוֹם בְּרִית שְׁלֹשׁ עֶשְׂרֵה, כְּמוֹ שֶׁהוֹדַעְתָּ לֶעָנָו מִקֶּדֶם, כְּמוֹ שֶׁכָּתוּב: וַיֵּרֶד יהוה בֶּעָנָן, וַיִּתְיַצֵּב עִמּוֹ שָׁם, וַיִּקְרָא בְשֵׁם, יהוה:

Congregation then Leader:

וַיַּעֲבֹר יהוה עַל־פָּנָיו וַיִּקְרָא

All say aloud:

יהוה, יהוה, אֵל רַחוּם וְחַנּוּן, אֶרֶךְ אַפַּיִם, וְרַב־חֶסֶד וֶאֱמֶת: נֹצֵר חֶסֶד לָאֲלָפִים, נֹשֵׂא עָוֹן וָפֶשַׁע וְחַטָּאָה, וְנַקֵּה: וְסָלַחְתָּ לַעֲוֹנֵנוּ וּלְחַטָּאתֵנוּ, וּנְחַלְתָּנוּ:

Continue:

סְלַח לָנוּ אָבִינוּ כִּי חָטָאנוּ, מְחַל לָנוּ מַלְכֵּנוּ כִּי פָשָׁעְנוּ. כִּי־אַתָּה אֲדֹנָי טוֹב וְסַלָּח, וְרַב־חֶסֶד לְכָל־קֹרְאֶיךָ:

כִּי־עִמְּךָ מְקוֹר חַיִּים, בְּאוֹרְךָ נִרְאֶה־אוֹר: בְּקָרְאֵנוּ עֲנֵנוּ אֱלֹהֵי צִדְקֵנוּ, בַּצָּר הִרְחַבְתָּ לָנוּ, חָנֵּנוּ וּשְׁמַע תְּפִלָּתֵנוּ. וְעַתָּה יִגְדַּל־נָא כֹּחַ אֲדֹנָי, כַּאֲשֶׁר דִּבַּרְתָּ לֵאמֹר:

כְּרַחֵם אָב עַל בָּנִים, כֵּן תְּרַחֵם יהוה עָלֵינוּ.
לַיהוה הַיְשׁוּעָה, עַל־עַמְּךָ בִרְכָתֶךָ סֶּלָה:
יהוה צְבָאוֹת עִמָּנוּ, מִשְׂגָּב לָנוּ אֱלֹהֵי יַעֲקֹב סֶלָה:
יהוה צְבָאוֹת, אַשְׁרֵי אָדָם בֹּטֵחַ בָּךְ:
יהוה הוֹשִׁיעָה, הַמֶּלֶךְ יַעֲנֵנוּ בְיוֹם־קָרְאֵנוּ:

This selicha focuses on Hashem's might and involvement in guiding the Jewish people. Even when it appears that the Jewish people are weak and our enemies are overpowering us, Hashem overturns events to save us and punish our enemies. From the very beginning of the Purim story, Hashem allowed Mordechai and Esther to be placed in important positions in King Achashveirosh's palace to save the Jewish people from danger. We ask Hashem to continue to protect us and save us from danger today as He did for us in the time of Mordechai and Esther.

אֱלֹהֵינוּ וֵאלֹהֵי אֲבוֹתֵינוּ

אַתָּה הָאֵל עוֹשֵׂה פְלָאוֹת, בָּעַמִּים הוֹדַעְתָּ עֹז נוֹרָאוֹת, גָּאַלְתָּ בִּזְרוֹעַ עַמְּךָ מִתְּלָאוֹת, דִּכִּיתָ צָרֵיהֶם בְּמוֹתֵי תַחֲלוּאוֹת. הָאוֹיֵב בְּקוּמוֹ לְעוֹרֵר מְדָנִים, וְדִמָּה לְהַכְרִית פִּרְחֵי עֲדָנִים, זָמַם לִשְׁקֹל

לְגִנְזֵי אֲדוֹנִים, חֲלִיפֵי מְאַת כִּכְּרֵי אֲדָנִים. טְלָאֶיךָ הִזְהַרְתָּ שִׁקְלֵיהֶם לְהַקְדִּים, יָדַעְתָּ הָעֲתִידוֹת וְדָרַשְׁתָּ נִשְׁקָדִים, כִּבּוּי לְהַמְצִיא לְלַהַב יוֹקְדִים, לְקוּחִים לַמָּוֶת לְתַחְיֵי נִפְקָדִים. מַסֵּכָה צָרָה בְּעָבְדָם לְפָנִים, נִמְסְרוּ לְהָתֵז קְנוֹקְנוֹת וּגְפָנִים, סְבָבוּם מוֹקְשִׁים בְּכָל דְּפָנִים, עֵינֵיהֶם לְךָ תוֹלִים וּבְסִתְרְךָ נִצְפָּנִים. פּוּר נֶהְפַּךְ בְּאוֹיְבִים לִשְׁלֹט, צְלִיבָה הוּכַן אֲגָגִי לִקְלֹט, קָלַע וּבִלַּע פְּנֵי הַלּוֹט הַלּוֹט, רִיבֵי עַם בְּאַשְׁמַנִּים לַעֲלֹט. שָׁלוֹם וֶאֱמֶת נִכְתַּב מִכָּל צַד, תְּקֶף יֶשַׁע סֶלַע וּמְצָד, שׁוֹדֵד הֻשְׁדַּד וּבְרִשְׁתּוֹ נוּצַד, מִלָּשְׁנֵי נִסְחַף נִצְמַת וְנִרְצָד. עָשׂוּ שְׂמָחוֹת וְלַדּוֹרוֹת קְבָעוּם, וּמִקְרָאוֹת שִׁלְּשׁוּם וְלֹא רִבְּעוּם, נִסְכְּמוּ מִמַּעַל וּלְמַטָּה טְבָעוּם, בַּסֵּפֶר נֶחֱקַק עַל מָה קְבָעוּם. רָמָה יָדְךָ לִסְלֹחַ לַפּוֹשְׁעִים, יְהוּדִי וַהֲדַסָּה הֲקָמְתָּ מוֹשִׁיעִים, צִדְקָתָם עוֹמֶדֶת לָעַד לְשַׁעֲשׁוּעִים, חֵקֶר כְּבוֹדָם לְהִזָּכֵר לְנוֹשָׁעִים. קַנֵּא לִשְׁמְךָ נוֹרָא וְנִקְדָּשׁ, חֲזֵה כַּרְמְךָ נֶהֱרַס וְנִדָּשׁ, זְרוּיֵינוּ קַבֵּץ וְשִׁיר לְךָ יְחֻדָּשׁ, קַיְּמֵם וְהַחֲיֵם בְּבִנְיַן בֵּית הַמִּקְדָּשׁ. ◂ וְכַעֲשׂוֹתְךָ נוֹרָאוֹת בְּאוֹתָן הַיָּמִים, אִתָּנוּ הַפְלֵא תְּשׁוּעַת עוֹלָמִים, מְצוֹא לְפָנֶיךָ כֹּפֶר וְתַנְחוּמִים, אֵל מֶלֶךְ יוֹשֵׁב עַל כִּסֵּא רַחֲמִים.

אֵל מֶלֶךְ יוֹשֵׁב עַל כִּסֵּא רַחֲמִים, מִתְנַהֵג בַּחֲסִידוּת. מוֹחֵל עֲוֹנוֹת עַמּוֹ, מַעֲבִיר רִאשׁוֹן רִאשׁוֹן. מַרְבֶּה מְחִילָה לְחַטָּאִים, וּסְלִיחָה לְפוֹשְׁעִים. עֹשֶׂה צְדָקוֹת עִם כָּל בָּשָׂר וָרוּחַ, לֹא כְרָעָתָם תִּגְמֹל. ◂ אֵל, הוֹרֵיתָ לָּנוּ לוֹמַר שְׁלֹשׁ עֶשְׂרֵה, וּזְכָר לָנוּ הַיּוֹם בְּרִית שְׁלֹשׁ עֶשְׂרֵה, כְּמוֹ שֶׁהוֹדַעְתָּ לֶעָנָו מִקֶּדֶם, כְּמוֹ שֶׁכָּתוּב: וַיֵּרֶד יהוה בֶּעָנָן, וַיִּתְיַצֵּב עִמּוֹ שָׁם, וַיִּקְרָא בְשֵׁם, יהוה:

Congregation then Leader:

וַיַּעֲבֹר יהוה עַל־פָּנָיו וַיִּקְרָא

All say aloud:

יהוה, יהוה, אֵל רַחוּם וְחַנּוּן, אֶרֶךְ אַפַּיִם, וְרַב־חֶסֶד וֶאֱמֶת: נֹצֵר חֶסֶד לָאֲלָפִים, נֹשֵׂא עָוֹן וָפֶשַׁע וְחַטָּאָה, וְנַקֵּה:

וְסָלַחְתָּ לַעֲוֹנֵנוּ וּלְחַטָּאתֵנוּ, וּנְחַלְתָּנוּ:

Continue:

סְלַח לָנוּ אָבִינוּ כִּי חָטָאנוּ, מְחַל לָנוּ מַלְכֵּנוּ כִּי פָשָׁעְנוּ. כִּי־אַתָּה אֲדֹנָי טוֹב וְסַלָּח, וְרַב־חֶסֶד לְכָל־קֹרְאֶיךָ:

This selicha focuses on asking Hashem to save His people today as He did in the time of Mordechai and Esther. We are a small nation that wishes to be remembered as we beg Hashem to listen to our prayers, save us, and free us from our enemies.

The following is said responsively:

בְּמַתֵי מִסְפָּר חִלִּינוּ פָּנֶיךָ.
לְשַׁוְעַת נְכֵאִים אַל תַּעְלֵם אָזְנֶךָ.
הַקְשֵׁב תְּחִנָּתָם מִשְּׁמֵי מְעוֹנֶךָ.
כְּבִימֵי מֹר וַהֲדַס הוֹשַׁעְתָּ בָנֶיךָ.

תְּהִלּוֹת יִשְׂרָאֵל אַתָּה יוֹשֵׁב.
שַׁוְעָתָם מַאֲזִין וְרִנָּתָם קוֹשֵׁב.
רְפָאוֹת לְמַחַץ מַקְדִּים וּמְחַשֵּׁב.
קוֹנֶיךָ לְהֵיטִיב וְנֵויהֶם לְיַשֵּׁב.

צַר וְאוֹיֵב הִלְטִישׁ עֵינָיו.
פִּיהוּ פָּעַר לִשְׁאֹף עָנָו.
עֲשַׂת בְּשַׁלְוֹ לְהַשְׁמִיד קְהַל הֲמוֹנָיו.
סֶגֶל לְאַבֵּד חָרַת בְּנִשְׁתְּוָנָיו.

נוֹקֵם לְצָרִים וְנוֹטֵר לְאוֹיְבִים.
מְדַדְתָּ מִדָּתָם כְּזָדוּ לַאֲהוּבִים.
לוֹחֵם וְנִינָיו הֻתְלוּ מְצֻלָּבִים.
כְּבַחֲרוֹזֶת דָּגִים חֹרְזוּ תְחוּבִים.

יוֹם אֲשֶׁר שִׁבְּרוּ צוֹרְרִים.
טִבְחָה לָשִׁית בְּעַם נְצוּרִים.
חֻלְּפָה הַדָּת וְנָפְלוּ פְגָרִים.
זָלְעֲפוּ זוֹעֲמוּ מוּבָסִים מְגֻרִים.

וּבְכֵן יִתְעַלֶּה שִׁמְךָ וְיִתְנַשָּׂא.
הוֹדְךָ שְׁמֵי שָׁמַיִם כִּסָּה.
דַּכִּים בְּרוֹמִמְךָ נְתוּנִים לִמְשִׁסָּה.
גֵּיא וַאֲפָסֶיהָ תְּהִלָּתְךָ מְכַסָּה.

בִּינָה הֲגִיגֵנוּ עַתָּה, וּרְאֵה בַּצָּר.
בְּאַפְּךָ קוּמָה עַל צוֹרֵר הַצָּר.
אָדוֹן, קְרָאנוּךָ מִן הַמֵּצַר.
אָנָּא הוֹצִיאֵנוּ לַמֶּרְחָב וְחַלְּצֵנוּ מִצָּר.

מְאֹד תַּרְבֶּה לָנוּ מְחִילָה.
שְׁמַע תְּפִלָּה, וְהַעֲבֵר תִּפְלָה.
לוֹחֲצֵינוּ הַמְעֵד וּמַלְּאֵם חַלְחָלָה.
מִמֶּנּוּ רַחֲמֶיךָ לָעַד לֹא תִכְלָא.

Continue with אֵל מֶלֶךְ יוֹשֵׁב *on page 857.*

On this sad day, five major events took place in Jewish history, which will be listed in the first selicha. Most notably, our enemies broke through the walls that surrounded and protected Yerushalayim, which led to the destruction of the Beit HaMikdash. Many Jews were killed by our enemies. The remaining Jews were forced to leave Yerushalayim, as their homes and the Beit HaMikdash were taken by our enemies.

סליחות לשבעה עשר בתמוז

סְלַח לָנוּ, אָבִינוּ, כִּי בְּרֹב אִוַּלְתֵּנוּ שָׁגִינוּ.
מְחַל לָנוּ, מַלְכֵּנוּ, כִּי רַבּוּ עֲוֹנֵינוּ.

After the sin of the Golden Calf, Moshe prayed to Hashem to forgive the Jewish people. In his prayer, Moshe listed the "thirteen middot of Hashem," the thirteen ways that Hashem shows mercy. Hashem told Moshe that if the Jewish people make a mistake in the future, they should use these words of prayer and they will not be ignored. When we remember the sad events of the past and think about the mistakes we make today, we say these words to ask Hashem for forgiveness, and feel confident that Hashem will listen to our prayers.

אֵל אֶרֶךְ אַפַּיִם אַתָּה, וּבַעַל הָרַחֲמִים נִקְרֵאתָ, וְדֶרֶךְ תְּשׁוּבָה הוֹרֵיתָ. גְּדֻלַּת רַחֲמֶיךָ וַחֲסָדֶיךָ, תִּזְכֹּר הַיּוֹם וּבְכָל יוֹם לְזֶרַע יְדִידֶיךָ. תֵּפֶן אֵלֵינוּ בְּרַחֲמִים, כִּי אַתָּה הוּא בַּעַל הָרַחֲמִים. בְּתַחֲנוּן וּבִתְפִלָּה פָּנֶיךָ נְקַדֵּם, כְּהוֹדַעְתָּ לֶעָנָו מִקֶּדֶם. מֵחֲרוֹן אַפְּךָ שׁוּב, כְּמוֹ בְּתוֹרָתְךָ כָּתוּב. וּבְצֵל כְּנָפֶיךָ נֶחֱסֶה וְנִתְלוֹנָן, כְּיוֹם וַיֵּרֶד יהוה בֶּעָנָן. ◂ תַּעֲבֹר עַל פֶּשַׁע וְתִמְחֶה אָשָׁם, כְּיוֹם וַיִּתְיַצֵּב עִמּוֹ שָׁם. תַּאֲזִין שַׁוְעָתֵנוּ וְתַקְשִׁיב מֶנּוּ מַאֲמָר, כְּיוֹם וַיִּקְרָא בְשֵׁם יהוה, וְשָׁם נֶאֱמַר

Congregation then Leader:

וַיַּעֲבֹר יהוה עַל־פָּנָיו וַיִּקְרָא

All say aloud:

יהוה, יהוה, אֵל רַחוּם וְחַנּוּן, אֶרֶךְ אַפַּיִם, וְרַב־חֶסֶד וֶאֱמֶת:
נֹצֵר חֶסֶד לָאֲלָפִים, נֹשֵׂא עָוֹן וָפֶשַׁע וְחַטָּאָה, וְנַקֵּה:

וְסָלַחְתָּ לַעֲוֹנֵנוּ וּלְחַטָּאתֵנוּ, וּנְחַלְתָּנוּ:

Continue:

סְלַח לָנוּ אָבִינוּ כִּי חָטָאנוּ, מְחַל לָנוּ מַלְכֵּנוּ כִּי פָשָׁעְנוּ. כִּי־אַתָּה אֲדֹנָי טוֹב וְסַלָּח, וְרַב־חֶסֶד לְכָל־קֹרְאֶיךָ:

וְאַל־תִּתְּנוּ דֳמִי לוֹ, עַד־יְכוֹנֵן וְעַד־יָשִׂים אֶת־יְרוּשָׁלַםִ תְּהִלָּה בָּאָרֶץ: כִּי־עִמְּךָ מְקוֹר חַיִּים, בְּאוֹרְךָ נִרְאֶה־אוֹר: אֱלֹהֵינוּ, בֹּשְׁנוּ בְּמַעֲשֵׂינוּ וְנִכְלַמְנוּ בַּעֲוֹנֵינוּ.

כְּרַחֵם אָב עַל בָּנִים, כֵּן תְּרַחֵם יהוה עָלֵינוּ.
לַיהוה הַיְשׁוּעָה, עַל־עַמְּךָ בִרְכָתֶךָ סֶּלָה:
יהוה צְבָאוֹת עִמָּנוּ, מִשְׂגָּב לָנוּ אֱלֹהֵי יַעֲקֹב סֶלָה:
יהוה צְבָאוֹת, אַשְׁרֵי אָדָם בֹּטֵחַ בָּךְ:
יהוה הוֹשִׁיעָה, הַמֶּלֶךְ יַעֲנֵנוּ בְיוֹם־קָרְאֵנוּ:

◂ סְלַח־נָא לַעֲוֹן הָעָם הַזֶּה כְּגֹדֶל חַסְדֶּךָ
וְכַאֲשֶׁר נָשָׂאתָה לָעָם הַזֶּה מִמִּצְרַיִם וְעַד־הֵנָּה:
וְשָׁם נֶאֱמַר

Congregation then Leader:

וַיֹּאמֶר יהוה, סָלַחְתִּי כִּדְבָרֶךָ:

Continue:

הַטֵּה אֱלֹהַי אָזְנְךָ וּשֲׁמָע, פְּקַח עֵינֶיךָ וּרְאֵה שֹׁמְמֹתֵינוּ וְהָעִיר אֲשֶׁר־נִקְרָא שִׁמְךָ עָלֶיהָ, כִּי לֹא עַל־צִדְקֹתֵינוּ אֲנַחְנוּ מַפִּילִים תַּחֲנוּנֵינוּ לְפָנֶיךָ, כִּי עַל־רַחֲמֶיךָ הָרַבִּים: אֲדֹנָי שְׁמָעָה, אֲדֹנָי סְלָחָה, אֲדֹנָי הַקְשִׁיבָה וַעֲשֵׂה אַל־תְּאַחַר, לְמַעַנְךָ אֱלֹהַי, כִּי־שִׁמְךָ נִקְרָא עַל־עִירְךָ וְעַל־עַמֶּךָ:

This selicha focuses on the five sad events that took place on this day throughout Jewish history: (1) The Luchot were broken; (2) a Torah scroll was publicly burned by a Roman leader; (3) an idol was placed in the Beit HaMikdash; (4) our enemies, the Romans, broke through the protective walls of Yerushalayim; (5) we were no longer able to bring korbanot, sacrifices, in the Beit HaMikdash to serve Hashem. On this day many Jews lost hope in the Jewish future and therefore were punished. Today, we have hope and can therefore ask Hashem to turn the sadness we experienced on this day into joy and happiness.

אֱלֹהֵֽינוּ וֵאלֹהֵי אֲבוֹתֵֽינוּ

אָתָֽנוּ לְךָ יוֹצֵר רוּחוֹת, בְּרוֹב עֲוֹנֵֽינוּ כָּבְדוּ אֲנָחוֹת, גֵּֽזֵרוֹת עָצְמוּ וְרַבּוּ צְרִיחוֹת, כִּי בְּשִׁבְעָה עָשָׂר בְּתַמּוּז נִשְׁתַּבְּרוּ הַלֻּחוֹת. גָּלִֽינוּ מִבֵּית הַבְּחִירָה, דִּינֵֽנוּ נֶחְתַּם וְנִגְזְרָה גְּזֵרָה, וְחָשַׁךְ בַּעֲדֵֽנוּ אוֹרָה, כִּי בְּשִׁבְעָה עָשָׂר בְּתַמּוּז נִשְׂרְפָה הַתּוֹרָה. הָרְסוּ אוֹיְבֵֽינוּ הַהֵיכָל, וּבָרְחָה שְׁכִינָה מִזָּוִית הֵיכָל, וְנִמְסַֽרְנוּ בִּידֵי זֵדִים לְהִתְאַכָּל, כִּי בְּשִׁבְעָה עָשָׂר בְּתַמּוּז הָעֳמַד צֶֽלֶם בַּהֵיכָל. זֵֽרוּנוּ מֵעִיר אֶל עִיר, וְנִלְכַּד מִמֶּֽנּוּ רַב וְצָעִיר, חָֽרְבָה מְשׁוֹשֵֽׂנוּ וְאֵשׁ בָּהּ הִבְעִיר, כִּי בְּשִׁבְעָה עָשָׂר בְּתַמּוּז הָבְקְעָה הָעִיר. טָפַשׁ מִקְדָּשֵֽׁנוּ צַר הַמַּשְׁמִיד, וְנָטַל מֵחָתָן וְכַלָּה אֶצְעָדָה וְצָמִיד, יַֽעַן כִּעַסְנֽוּךָ נִתַּֽנּוּ לְהַשְׁמִיד, כִּי בְּשִׁבְעָה עָשָׂר בְּתַמּוּז בֻּטַּל הַתָּמִיד. כָּלָה מֶֽנּוּ כָּל הוֹד וָשֶֽׁבַח, חַרְבּוֹ שָׁלַף אוֹיֵב עָלֵֽינוּ לָאֶֽבַח, לִהְיוֹת עוֹלְלִים וְיוֹנְקִים מוּכָנִים לַטֶּֽבַח, כִּי בְּשִׁבְעָה עָשָׂר בְּתַמּוּז בָּטְלוּ עוֹלָה וָזֶֽבַח. מָרַֽדְנוּ לְשׁוֹכֵן מְעוֹנוֹת, לָכֵן נִתְפַּזַּֽרְנוּ בְּכָל פִּנּוֹת, נֶהְפַּךְ מְחוֹלֵֽנוּ לְקִינוֹת, כִּי בְּשִׁבְעָה עָשָׂר בְּתַמּוּז בָּטְלוּ קָרְבָּנוֹת. סָרַֽרְנוּ לְפָנֶֽיךָ מֵרִיב לְשׁוֹנוֹת, לָכֵן לָמְדָה לְשׁוֹנֵֽנוּ לוֹמַר קִינוֹת, עָזַֽבְנוּ בְּלִי לְהִמָּנוֹת, כִּי בְּשִׁבְעָה עָשָׂר בְּתַמּוּז גָּרְמוּ לָֽנוּ עֲוֹנוֹת. פֻּזַּֽרְנוּ בְּלִי מְצוֹא רְוָחָה, לָכֵן רָבְתָה בָּֽנוּ אֲנָחָה, צוּר רְאֵה נַפְשֵֽׁנוּ כִּי שָֽׁחָה, וְשִׁבְעָה עָשָׂר בְּתַמּוּז הֲפָךְ לָֽנוּ לְשָׂשׂוֹן וּלְשִׂמְחָה. קָשִֽׁינוּ עֹֽרֶף וְרָֽבְתָה בָּֽנוּ אָסוֹן, לָכֵן נִתַּֽנּוּ לִמְשִׁסָּה וְרִפְשׁוֹן, רְאֵה יהוה

וְחַלְּצֵנוּ מֵאָסוֹן, וְשִׁבְעָה עָשָׂר בְּתַמּוּז הֲפָךְ לָנוּ לְשִׂמְחָה וּלְשָׂשׂוֹן.
‹ שְׁעֵנוּ שׁוֹכֵן רוּמָה, וְקַבֵּץ נְפוּצוֹתֵינוּ מִקַּצְווֹת אֲדָמָה, תֹּאמַר לְצִיּוֹן קוּמָה, וְשִׁבְעָה עָשָׂר בְּתַמּוּז הֲפָךְ לָנוּ לְיוֹם יְשׁוּעָה וְנֶחָמָה.

אֵל מֶלֶךְ יוֹשֵׁב עַל כִּסֵּא רַחֲמִים, מִתְנַהֵג בַּחֲסִידוּת. מוֹחֵל עֲוֹנוֹת עַמּוֹ, מַעֲבִיר רִאשׁוֹן רִאשׁוֹן. מַרְבֶּה מְחִילָה לְחַטָּאִים, וּסְלִיחָה לְפוֹשְׁעִים. עֹשֶׂה צְדָקוֹת עִם כָּל בָּשָׂר וָרוּחַ, לֹא כְרָעָתָם תִּגְמֹל.
‹ אֵל, הוֹרֵיתָ לָּנוּ לוֹמַר שְׁלֹשׁ עֶשְׂרֵה, וּזְכָר לָנוּ הַיּוֹם בְּרִית שְׁלֹשׁ עֶשְׂרֵה, כְּמוֹ שֶׁהוֹדַעְתָּ לֶעָנָו מִקֶּדֶם, כְּמוֹ שֶׁכָּתוּב: וַיֵּרֶד יהוה בֶּעָנָן, וַיִּתְיַצֵּב עִמּוֹ שָׁם, וַיִּקְרָא בְשֵׁם, יהוה:

Congregation then Leader:

וַיַּעֲבֹר יהוה עַל־פָּנָיו וַיִּקְרָא

All say aloud:

יהוה, יהוה, אֵל רַחוּם וְחַנּוּן, אֶרֶךְ אַפַּיִם, וְרַב־חֶסֶד וֶאֱמֶת: נֹצֵר חֶסֶד לָאֲלָפִים, נֹשֵׂא עָוֹן וָפֶשַׁע וְחַטָּאָה, וְנַקֵּה: וְסָלַחְתָּ לַעֲוֹנֵנוּ וּלְחַטָּאתֵנוּ, וּנְחַלְתָּנוּ:

Continue:

סְלַח לָנוּ אָבִינוּ כִּי חָטָאנוּ, מְחַל לָנוּ מַלְכֵּנוּ כִּי פָשָׁעְנוּ. כִּי־אַתָּה אֲדֹנָי טוֹב וְסַלָּח, וְרַב־חֶסֶד לְכָל־קֹרְאֶיךָ:

אֱלֹהִים אַל־דֳּמִי־לָךְ, אַל־תֶּחֱרַשׁ וְאַל־תִּשְׁקֹט אֵל:
כִּי־הִנֵּה אוֹיְבֶיךָ יֶהֱמָיוּן, וּמְשַׂנְאֶיךָ נָשְׂאוּ רֹאשׁ:
אֵל־נְקָמוֹת יהוה, אֵל נְקָמוֹת הוֹפִיעַ:

כְּרַחֵם אָב עַל בָּנִים, כֵּן תְּרַחֵם יהוה עָלֵינוּ.
לַיהוה הַיְשׁוּעָה, עַל־עַמְּךָ בִרְכָתֶךָ סֶּלָה:

יהוה צְבָאוֹת עִמָּנוּ, מִשְׂגָּב לָנוּ אֱלֹהֵי יַעֲקֹב סֶלָה:
יהוה צְבָאוֹת, אַשְׁרֵי אָדָם בֹּטֵחַ בָּךְ:
יהוה הוֹשִׁיעָה, הַמֶּלֶךְ יַעֲנֵנוּ בְיוֹם־קָרְאֵנוּ:

This selicha focuses on the Jewish people's feelings of being defeated and lost on this day. Like a ship without a captain and a flock without a shepherd, the Jewish people felt as though their hope was gone with no chance of being saved. We ask Hashem that we never experience these types of events again and that these days of fasting and sadness be turned into days of celebration.

אֱלֹהֵינוּ וֵאלֹהֵי אֲבוֹתֵינוּ

אֲמָרֵר בְּבֶכִי מִפְּנֵי יָד שְׁלוּחָה בְּעִי. בְּנַאֲצִי בְּתוֹךְ בֵּיתוֹ בְּבִגְדִי וְקָבְעִי. גָּח וּבָרַח וְנָסַע עֶשֶׂר וְעָלָה לַשְּׁבִיעִי. דִּמַּנִי הֱצִיקַנִי הִשִּׂיקַנִי בַּחֹדֶשׁ הָרְבִיעִי. הֵבִיא מוֹעֵד בִּמְלֵאָתוֹ לִשְׁבֹּר בַּחוּרֵי גְמוּז. וְרִבָּה בוֹ פְּעָמִים בְּמִסְמוּס וּמִזְמוּז. זְבוּלוֹ כְּשָׂדָה שֶׁאֲנָנוֹת מְבַכּוֹת אֶת הַתַּמּוּז. חִיְּבַנִי וְאִיְּבַנִי אֲזַי בְּיֶרַח תַּמּוּז. טָמְנוּ פַּחִים חֲמִשָּׁה בְּמִקְרָא תְלָאוֹת מְשֻׁלָּחוֹת. יָכְלוּ לִי בְּשִׁבְעָה עָשָׂר בּוֹ בַּאֲלִיחוֹת. כִּי נוֹקַשְׁתִּי כְּכַלָּה עֲלוּבָה בְּחֻפַּת שַׁלְוָה וְהַצְלָחוֹת. לְרוֹעִי לֹא הִמְתַּנְתִּי שֵׁשׁ, וְנִשְׁתַּבְּרוּ הַלֻּחוֹת. מִיָּדוֹ עָדִיתִי חֲלִי כֶתֶם, אֶצְעָדָה וְצָמִיד. נִגָּרוּת בְּיוֹם אַפּוֹ, כְּשִׁחַתִּי דְּרָכַי לְהַשְׁמִיד. סֵדֶר עֲבוֹדָתוֹ וְקֵץ מִזְבְּחוֹ קִצַּתִּי לְהַעֲמִיד. עַל כֵּן מִלִּשְׁכַּת הַטְּלָאִים בָּטַל הַתָּמִיד. פּוֹר הִתְפּוֹרְרָה וְנִתְפַּזְּרָה סְעָרָה עֲנִיָּה. צִי נִמְשְׁלָה מִבְּלִי חוֹבֵל, וְנִטְרְפָה כָאֳנִיָּה. קַחְתָּה בְּחַטָּאתָהּ בְּרֹאשָׁהּ, וּבְכֶפֶל תַּאֲנִיָּה וַאֲנִיָּה. רִיבוּהָ צָרֶיהָ כְּהַיּוֹם, וְהָבְקְעָה הָעִיר בַּשְּׁנִיָּה. שֻׁלְּחָה כִּצְבִי מֻדָּח מֵאֵין דּוֹרֵשׁ לְהַסְתִּירָה. שְׁנָנוּ לְשׁוֹנָם וּנְתָנוּהָ כְּשֶׂה, צַמְרָהּ וַחֲלָבָהּ לְהַתִּירָה. תִּצְעַק עַל כְּלִי חֶמְדָּה שֶׁבּוֹ נִכְתָּרָה. תַּחְמוֹד עֵינֶיהָ נִצַּל כְּשָׂרַף אַפּוֹסְטְמוֹס הַתּוֹרָה. חֵרֵף עֲשׁוּקִים וּרְצוּצִים בַּעֲבוּר הַרְעִימָם סַכָּל.

יְרוּדִים בְּוֹהֶיָה לֶאֱכֹל וּבְהַסְתֵּר פָּנִים מִלְּהִסְתַּכֵּל. יַד הַשְּׁלִים מִכְּנַף שִׁקּוּצִים נֶאֱכָל. עֵת צָרָה כְּהִתְכַּנֵּס וְהָעֳמַד צֶלֶם בְּהֵיכָל. דְּוּוּיִם סְגוּפִים בָּנִים הָהָיוּ מִקֶּדֶם רִאשׁוֹנִים. סְמוּכוֹת צָרוֹתֵיהֶם זוֹ לְזוֹ כַּמָּה שָׁנִים. לוּקִים כַּאֲשֶׁר תַּעֲשֶׂינָה הַדְּבוֹרִים, וְהָעַקְרַבִּים שׁוֹנִים. הוֹגִים אָבַד שִׁבְרָם וּבָטֵל סִכּוּיָם בְּאִישׁוֹנִים. › אֵל קַנָּא, בְּהִתְאַפֵּק בִּמְקַנְאֶיךָ דְּשֵׁנִים וְטוּבִים. מְחַכִּים תָּקִים עוֹמְדִים לְעוֹלָמִים, כִּנְטִיעִים מְחֻטָּבִים בַּאֲהָבִים. הָאֱמֶת וְהַשָּׁלוֹם בְּצוֹמוֹת חֲטוּבִים. נֶצַח הֱיוֹתָם לְשִׂמְחָה וּלְשָׂשׂוֹן וּלְמוֹעֲדִים טוֹבִים.

אֵל מֶלֶךְ יוֹשֵׁב עַל כִּסֵּא רַחֲמִים, מִתְנַהֵג בַּחֲסִידוּת. מוֹחֵל עֲוֹנוֹת עַמּוֹ, מַעֲבִיר רִאשׁוֹן רִאשׁוֹן. מַרְבֶּה מְחִילָה לְחַטָּאִים, וּסְלִיחָה לְפוֹשְׁעִים. עֹשֶׂה צְדָקוֹת עִם כָּל בָּשָׂר וָרוּחַ, לֹא כְרָעָתָם תִּגְמֹל. › אֵל, הוֹרֵיתָ לָּנוּ לוֹמַר שְׁלֹשׁ עֶשְׂרֵה, וּזְכָר לָנוּ הַיּוֹם בְּרִית שְׁלֹשׁ עֶשְׂרֵה, כְּמוֹ שֶׁהוֹדַעְתָּ לֶעָנָו מִקֶּדֶם, כְּמוֹ שֶׁכָּתוּב: וַיֵּרֶד יהוה בֶּעָנָן, וַיִּתְיַצֵּב עִמּוֹ שָׁם, וַיִּקְרָא בְשֵׁם, יהוה:

Congregation then Leader:

וַיַּעֲבֹר יהוה עַל־פָּנָיו וַיִּקְרָא

All say aloud:

יהוה, יהוה, אֵל רַחוּם וְחַנּוּן, אֶרֶךְ אַפַּיִם, וְרַב־חֶסֶד וֶאֱמֶת:
נֹצֵר חֶסֶד לָאֲלָפִים, נֹשֵׂא עָוֹן וָפֶשַׁע וְחַטָּאָה, וְנַקֵּה:
וְסָלַחְתָּ לַעֲוֹנֵנוּ וּלְחַטָּאתֵנוּ, וּנְחַלְתָּנוּ:

Continue:

סְלַח לָנוּ אָבִינוּ כִּי חָטָאנוּ, מְחַל לָנוּ מַלְכֵּנוּ כִּי פָשָׁעְנוּ. כִּי־אַתָּה אֲדֹנָי טוֹב וְסַלָּח, וְרַב־חֶסֶד לְכָל־קֹרְאֶיךָ:

This selicha focuses on the deep pain that the Jewish people felt as they experienced the five sad events that took place on this day throughout Jewish history. On this day, our enemies were stronger and broke through the city walls of Yerushalayim. We ask Hashem that He punish our enemies, rebuild the Beit HaMikdash, and return us to our land, Israel.

The following is said responsively:

שְׁעֵה נֶאֱסַר, אֲשֶׁר נִמְסַר, בְּיַד בָּבֶל וְגַם שֵׂעִיר.
לְךָ יֶהֱמֶה, זֶה כַּמֶּה, וְיִתְחַנֵּן כְּבֶן צָעִיר.
יוֹם גָּבַר הָאוֹיֵב וַתִּבָּקַע הָעִיר.

לְזֹאת אֶבְכֶּה, וְאֶסְפֹּק כַּף, בְּיוֹם חֲמֵשׁ פְּזוּרוֹנִי.
וְעַל רֶגֶל הָעֵגֶל, הַלֻּחוֹת יְצָאוּנִי.
וְגַם הִשְׁמִיד הַתָּמִיד, וּבַסּוּגַר הֱבִיאָנִי.
וְהוּשַׂם אֱלִיל בְּהֵיכַל כְּלִיל, וּמֵעֲצָתוֹ כְּלָאָנִי.
וְהַמִּנְחָה הוּנָחָה, וְדָתְךָ, צָר בָּאֵשׁ הִבְעִיר.
יוֹם גָּבַר הָאוֹיֵב וַתִּבָּקַע הָעִיר.

מְאֹד אֶתְחַל, וְאֶתְחַלְחַל, בְּיוֹם שַׁדַּי דְּחָפָנִי.
וְהַשְּׁפִיפוֹן מִצָּפוֹן, כְּשִׁבֹּלֶת שְׁטָפָנִי.
מְאוֹר חָשַׁךְ, וְגַם שֵׁשַׁךְ, כְּמוֹ כַדּוּר צְנָפָנִי.
וְהַצַּיָּד שָׁלַח יָד, וְהַצָּפִיר וְהַשָּׂעִיר.
יוֹם גָּבַר הָאוֹיֵב וַתִּבָּקַע הָעִיר.

הוֹד לִבִּי וּמִשְׂגַּבִּי, הֲלָעַד אַפְּךָ יֶעְשַׁן.
הֲלֹא תִרְאֶה עַם נִלְאֶה, אֲשֶׁר הָשְׁחַר כְּמוֹ כִבְשָׁן.
גְּדֹר פִּרְצִי בְּבֶן פַּרְצִי, וּמֵחֱדֶק לְקֹט שׁוֹשָׁן.
בְּנֵה בֵּית זְבוּל, וְהָשֵׁב גְּבוּל הַכַּרְמֶל וְהַבָּשָׁן.
וְעַיִן פְּקַח, וְנָקָם קַח מֵאֶצֶר וּמִדִּישָׁן.
שְׁפֹט אִלֵּם, וְאָז יְשַׁלֵּם הַמַּבְעֶה וְהַמַּבְעִיר.
יוֹם גָּבַר הָאוֹיֵב וַתִּבָּקַע הָעִיר.

On all days continue:

אֵל מֶלֶךְ יוֹשֵׁב עַל כִּסֵּא רַחֲמִים, מִתְנַהֵג בַּחֲסִידוּת. מוֹחֵל עֲוֹנוֹת עַמּוֹ, מַעֲבִיר רִאשׁוֹן רִאשׁוֹן. מַרְבֶּה מְחִילָה לְחַטָּאִים, וּסְלִיחָה לְפוֹשְׁעִים. עֹשֶׂה צְדָקוֹת עִם כָּל בָּשָׂר וָרוּחַ, לֹא כְרָעָתָם תִּגְמֹל. › אֵל, הוֹרֵיתָ לָּנוּ לוֹמַר שְׁלֹשׁ עֶשְׂרֵה, וּזְכָר לָנוּ הַיּוֹם בְּרִית שְׁלֹשׁ עֶשְׂרֵה, כְּמוֹ שֶׁהוֹדַעְתָּ לֶעָנָו מִקֶּדֶם, כְּמוֹ שֶׁכָּתוּב: וַיֵּרֶד יהוה בֶּעָנָן, וַיִּתְיַצֵּב עִמּוֹ שָׁם, וַיִּקְרָא בְשֵׁם, יהוה:

Congregation then Leader:

וַיַּעֲבֹר יהוה עַל־פָּנָיו וַיִּקְרָא

All say aloud:

יהוה, יהוה, אֵל רַחוּם וְחַנּוּן, אֶרֶךְ אַפַּיִם, וְרַב־חֶסֶד וֶאֱמֶת: נֹצֵר חֶסֶד לָאֲלָפִים, נֹשֵׂא עָוֹן וָפֶשַׁע וְחַטָּאָה, וְנַקֵּה: וְסָלַחְתָּ לַעֲוֹנֵנוּ וּלְחַטָּאתֵנוּ, וּנְחַלְתָּנוּ:

Continue:

סְלַח לָנוּ אָבִינוּ כִּי חָטָאנוּ, מְחַל לָנוּ מַלְכֵּנוּ כִּי פָשָׁעְנוּ. כִּי־אַתָּה אֲדֹנָי טוֹב וְסַלָּח, וְרַב־חֶסֶד לְכָל־קֹרְאֶיךָ:

After saying the selichot, we ask Hashem to remember us, His Jewish people, and the promises He made to our ancestors. We ask Hashem to accept our apologies and allow us to return to Him so we can serve Him again in His house of prayer, the Beit HaMikdash.

זְכֹר־רַחֲמֶיךָ יהוה וַחֲסָדֶיךָ, כִּי מֵעוֹלָם הֵמָּה:
זָכְרֵנוּ יהוה בִּרְצוֹן עַמֶּךָ, פָּקְדֵנוּ בִּישׁוּעָתֶךָ.
זְכֹר עֲדָתְךָ קָנִיתָ קֶּדֶם, גָּאַלְתָּ שֵׁבֶט נַחֲלָתֶךָ
הַר־צִיּוֹן זֶה שָׁכַנְתָּ בּוֹ:
זְכֹר יהוה חִבַּת יְרוּשָׁלָיִם, אַהֲבַת צִיּוֹן אַל תִּשְׁכַּח לָנֶצַח.
אַתָּה תָקוּם תְּרַחֵם צִיּוֹן, כִּי־עֵת לְחֶנְנָהּ, כִּי־בָא מוֹעֵד:

זְכֹר יהוה לִבְנֵי אֱדוֹם אֵת יוֹם יְרוּשָׁלָםִ
הָאוֹמְרִים עָרוּ עָרוּ, עַד הַיְסוֹד בָּהּ:
זְכֹר לְאַבְרָהָם לְיִצְחָק וּלְיִשְׂרָאֵל עֲבָדֶיךָ
אֲשֶׁר נִשְׁבַּעְתָּ לָהֶם בָּךְ וַתְּדַבֵּר אֲלֵהֶם
אַרְבֶּה אֶת־זַרְעֲכֶם כְּכוֹכְבֵי הַשָּׁמָיִם
וְכָל־הָאָרֶץ הַזֹּאת אֲשֶׁר אָמַרְתִּי אֶתֵּן לְזַרְעֲכֶם, וְנָחֲלוּ לְעֹלָם:
זְכֹר לַעֲבָדֶיךָ לְאַבְרָהָם לְיִצְחָק וּלְיַעֲקֹב
אַל־תֵּפֶן אֶל־קְשִׁי הָעָם הַזֶּה וְאֶל־רִשְׁעוֹ וְאֶל־חַטָּאתוֹ:
זְכָר לָנוּ בְּרִית אָבוֹת כַּאֲשֶׁר אָמַרְתָּ:
וְזָכַרְתִּי אֶת־בְּרִיתִי יַעֲקוֹב
וְאַף אֶת־בְּרִיתִי יִצְחָק
וְאַף אֶת־בְּרִיתִי אַבְרָהָם אֶזְכֹּר
וְהָאָרֶץ אֶזְכֹּר:
זְכָר לָנוּ בְּרִית רִאשׁוֹנִים כַּאֲשֶׁר אָמַרְתָּ:
וְזָכַרְתִּי לָהֶם בְּרִית רִאשֹׁנִים
אֲשֶׁר הוֹצֵאתִי־אֹתָם מֵאֶרֶץ מִצְרַיִם לְעֵינֵי הַגּוֹיִם
לִהְיוֹת לָהֶם לֵאלֹהִים, אֲנִי יהוה:

עֲשֵׂה עִמָּנוּ כְּמָה שֶׁהִבְטַחְתָּנוּ: וְאַף גַּם־זֹאת בִּהְיוֹתָם בְּאֶרֶץ אֹיְבֵיהֶם, לֹא־מְאַסְתִּים וְלֹא־גְעַלְתִּים לְכַלֹּתָם, לְהָפֵר בְּרִיתִי אִתָּם, כִּי אֲנִי יהוה אֱלֹהֵיהֶם:

הָשֵׁב שְׁבוּתֵנוּ וְרַחֲמֵנוּ כְּמָה שֶׁכָּתוּב: וְשָׁב יהוה אֱלֹהֶיךָ אֶת־שְׁבוּתְךָ וְרִחֲמֶךָ, וְשָׁב וְקִבֶּצְךָ מִכָּל־הָעַמִּים אֲשֶׁר הֱפִיצְךָ יהוה אֱלֹהֶיךָ שָׁמָּה:

קַבֵּץ נִדָּחֵינוּ כְּמָה שֶׁכָּתוּב: אִם־יִהְיֶה נִדַּחֲךָ בִּקְצֵה הַשָּׁמָיִם, מִשָּׁם יְקַבֶּצְךָ יהוה אֱלֹהֶיךָ וּמִשָּׁם יִקָּחֶךָ:

מְחֵה פְשָׁעֵינוּ כָּעָב וְכֶעָנָן כְּמָה שֶׁכָּתוּב: מָחִיתִי כָעָב פְּשָׁעֶיךָ וְכֶעָנָן חַטֹּאותֶיךָ, שׁוּבָה אֵלַי כִּי גְאַלְתִּיךָ:

מְחֵה פְשָׁעֵינוּ לְמַעַנְךָ כַּאֲשֶׁר אָמַרְתָּ: אָנֹכִי אָנֹכִי הוּא מֹחֶה פְשָׁעֶיךָ לְמַעֲנִי, וְחַטֹּאתֶיךָ לֹא אֶזְכֹּר:

הַלְבֵּן חֲטָאֵינוּ כַּשֶּׁלֶג וְכַצֶּמֶר כְּמָה שֶׁכָּתוּב: לְכוּ־נָא וְנִוָּכְחָה יֹאמַר יהוה, אִם־יִהְיוּ חֲטָאֵיכֶם כַּשָּׁנִים כַּשֶּׁלֶג יַלְבִּינוּ, אִם־יַאְדִּימוּ כַתּוֹלָע כַּצֶּמֶר יִהְיוּ:

זְרֹק עָלֵינוּ מַיִם טְהוֹרִים וְטַהֲרֵנוּ כְּמָה שֶׁכָּתוּב: וְזָרַקְתִּי עֲלֵיכֶם מַיִם טְהוֹרִים וּטְהַרְתֶּם, מִכֹּל טֻמְאוֹתֵיכֶם וּמִכָּל־גִּלּוּלֵיכֶם אֲטַהֵר אֶתְכֶם:

רַחֵם עָלֵינוּ וְאַל תַּשְׁחִיתֵנוּ כְּמָה שֶׁכָּתוּב: כִּי אֵל רַחוּם יהוה אֱלֹהֶיךָ, לֹא יַרְפְּךָ וְלֹא יַשְׁחִיתֶךָ, וְלֹא יִשְׁכַּח אֶת־בְּרִית אֲבֹתֶיךָ אֲשֶׁר נִשְׁבַּע לָהֶם:

מ׳ל אֶת לְבָבֵנוּ לְאַהֲבָה אֶת שְׁמֶךָ כְּמָה שֶׁכָּתוּב: וּמָל יהוה ׳לֹהֶיךָ אֶת־לְבָבְךָ וְאֶת־לְבַב זַרְעֶךָ, לְאַהֲבָה אֶת־יהוה אֱלֹהֶיךָ בְּכ׳ ׳בָבְךָ וּבְכָל־נַפְשְׁךָ, לְמַעַן חַיֶּיךָ:

הַמָּצֵ׳ בְּבַקָּשָׁתֵנוּ כְּמָה שֶׁכָּתוּב: וּבִקַּשְׁתֶּם מִשָּׁם אֶת־יהוה אֱלֹהֶיךָ א׳ כִּי תִדְרְשֶׁנּוּ בְּכָל־לְבָבְךָ וּבְכָל־נַפְשֶׁךָ:

תְּבִיאֵנוּ ׳ךָ וְשַׂמְּחֵנוּ בְּבֵית תְּפִלָּתֶךָ כְּמָה שֶׁכָּתוּב: וַהֲבִיאוֹתִים ׳ וְשִׂמַּחְתִּים בְּבֵית תְּפִלָּתִי, עוֹלֹתֵיהֶם וְזִבְחֵיהֶם לְרָצוֹ׳ ׳י בֵּיתִי בֵּית־תְּפִלָּה יִקָּרֵא לְכָל־הָעַמִּים:

In this section, we ask Hashem to act kindly towards us, His Jewish people, and accept our prayers. If You, Hashem, are willing to accept us, we are excited to return closer to You, like our ancestors were.

The Ark is opened. The following until אַל תַּעַזְבֵנוּ *is said responsively, verse by verse:*

שְׁמַע קוֹלֵנוּ, יהוה אֱלֹהֵינוּ, חוּס וְרַחֵם עָלֵינוּ וְקַבֵּל בְּרַחֲמִים
וּבְרָצוֹן אֶת תְּפִלָּתֵנוּ.
הֲשִׁיבֵנוּ יהוה אֵלֶיךָ וְנָשׁוּבָה, חַדֵּשׁ יָמֵינוּ כְּקֶדֶם:
אַל תַּשְׁלִיכֵנוּ מִלְּפָנֶיךָ, וְרוּחַ קָדְשְׁךָ אַל תִּקַּח מִמֶּנּוּ.
אַל תַּשְׁלִיכֵנוּ לְעֵת זִקְנָה, כִּכְלוֹת כֹּחֵנוּ אַל תַּעַזְבֵנוּ.

אַל תַּעַזְבֵנוּ יהוה, אֱלֹהֵינוּ אַל תִּרְחַק מִמֶּנּוּ.
עֲשֵׂה עִמָּנוּ אוֹת לְטוֹבָה, וְיִרְאוּ שׂוֹנְאֵינוּ וְיֵבֹשׁוּ
כִּי אַתָּה יהוה עֲזַרְתָּנוּ וְנִחַמְתָּנוּ.
אֲמָרֵינוּ הַאֲזִינָה יהוה, בִּינָה הֲגִיגֵנוּ.
יִהְיוּ לְרָצוֹן אִמְרֵי פִינוּ וְהֶגְיוֹן לִבֵּנוּ לְפָנֶיךָ
יהוה צוּרֵנוּ וְגוֹאֲלֵנוּ.
כִּי לְךָ יהוה הוֹחָלְנוּ, אַתָּה תַעֲנֶה אֲדֹנָי אֱלֹהֵינוּ.

The Ark is closed.

וידוי

this section we think about any mistakes we may have made, admit acted incorrectly, and ask Hashem for forgiveness. We cannot hide ughts and actions from Hashem because He knows everything.

אֱלֹהֵינוּ וֵאלֹהֵי אֲבוֹתֵינוּ
תָּבֹא לְפָנֶיךָ תְּפִלָּתֵנוּ, וְאַל תִּתְעַלַּם מִתְּחִנָּתֵנ
שֶׁאֵין אָנוּ עַזֵּי פָנִים וּקְשֵׁי עֹרֶף לוֹמַר לְפָנֶי חָטָאנוּ.
יהוה אֱלֹהֵינוּ וֵאלֹהֵי אֲבוֹתֵינוּ, צַדִּיקִ
אֲבָל אֲנַחְנוּ וַאֲבוֹתֵינוּ חָטָאנוּ.

Strike the left side of the chest with the right fist while saying each of the sins in this paragraph.

אָשַׁמְנוּ, בָּגַדְנוּ, גָּזַלְנוּ, דִּבַּרְנוּ דֹפִי.
הֶעֱוִינוּ, וְהִרְשַׁעְנוּ, זַדְנוּ, חָמַסְנוּ, טָפַלְנוּ שֶׁקֶר.
יָעַצְנוּ רָע, כִּזַּבְנוּ, לַצְנוּ, מָרַדְנוּ, נִאַצְנוּ, סָרַרְנוּ, עָוִינוּ, פָּשַׁעְנוּ, צָרַרְנוּ, קִשִּׁינוּ עֹרֶף.
רָשַׁעְנוּ, שִׁחַתְנוּ, תִּעַבְנוּ, תָּעִינוּ, תִּעְתָּעְנוּ.

סַרְנוּ מִמִּצְוֹתֶיךָ וּמִמִּשְׁפָּטֶיךָ הַטּוֹבִים, וְלֹא שָׁוָה לָנוּ. וְאַתָּה צַדִּיק עַל כָּל־הַבָּא עָלֵינוּ, כִּי־אֱמֶת עָשִׂיתָ וַאֲנַחְנוּ הִרְשָׁעְנוּ.

הִרְשַׁעְנוּ וּפָשַׁעְנוּ, לָכֵן לֹא נוֹשָׁעְנוּ. וְתֵן בְּלִבֵּנוּ לַעֲזֹב דֶּרֶךְ רֶשַׁע, וְחִישׁ לָנוּ יֶשַׁע, כַּכָּתוּב עַל יַד נְבִיאֶךָ: יַעֲזֹב רָשָׁע דַּרְכּוֹ וְאִישׁ אָוֶן מַחְשְׁבֹתָיו, וְיָשֹׁב אֶל־יהוה וִירַחֲמֵהוּ וְאֶל־אֱלֹהֵינוּ כִּי־יַרְבֶּה לִסְלוֹחַ:

מְשִׁיחַ צִדְקֶךָ אָמַר לְפָנֶיךָ: שְׁגִיאוֹת מִי־יָבִין, מִנִּסְתָּרוֹת נַקֵּנִי: נַקֵּנוּ יהוה אֱלֹהֵינוּ מִכָּל פְּשָׁעֵינוּ וְטַהֲרֵנוּ מִכָּל טֻמְאוֹתֵינוּ וּזְרֹק עָלֵינוּ מַיִם טְהוֹרִים וְטַהֲרֵנוּ, כַּכָּתוּב עַל יַד נְבִיאֶךָ: וְזָרַקְתִּי עֲלֵיכֶם מַיִם טְהוֹרִים וּטְהַרְתֶּם, מִכֹּל טֻמְאוֹתֵיכֶם וּמִכָּל־גִּלּוּלֵיכֶם אֲטַהֵר אֶתְכֶם: עַמְּךָ וְנַחֲלָתְךָ רְעֵבֵי טוּבְךָ, צְמֵאֵי חַסְדְּךָ, תְּאֵבֵי יִשְׁעֶךָ. יַכִּירוּ וְיֵדְעוּ, כִּי לַיהוה אֱלֹהֵינוּ הָרַחֲמִים וְהַסְּלִיחוֹת.

אֵל רַחוּם שְׁמֶךָ. אֵל חַנּוּן שְׁמֶךָ. בָּנוּ נִקְרָא שְׁמֶךָ. יהוה עֲשֵׂה לְמַעַן שְׁמֶךָ. עֲשֵׂה לְמַעַן אֲמִתָּךְ. עֲשֵׂה לְמַעַן בְּרִיתָךְ. עֲשֵׂה לְמַעַן גָּדְלָךְ וְתִפְאַרְתָּךְ. עֲשֵׂה לְמַעַן דָּתָךְ. עֲשֵׂה לְמַעַן הוֹדָךְ. עֲשֵׂה לְמַעַן וִעוּדָךְ. עֲשֵׂה לְמַעַן זִכְרָךְ. עֲשֵׂה לְמַעַן חַסְדָּךְ. עֲשֵׂה לְמַעַן טוּבָךְ. עֲשֵׂה לְמַעַן יִחוּדָךְ. עֲשֵׂה לְמַעַן כְּבוֹדָךְ. עֲשֵׂה לְמַעַן לִמּוּדָךְ. עֲשֵׂה לְמַעַן מַלְכוּתָךְ. עֲשֵׂה לְמַעַן נִצְחָךְ. עֲשֵׂה לְמַעַן סוֹדָךְ. עֲשֵׂה לְמַעַן

עֻזָּךְ. עֲשֵׂה לְמַעַן פְּאֵרָךְ. עֲשֵׂה לְמַעַן צִדְקָתָךְ. עֲשֵׂה לְמַעַן קְדֻשָּׁתָךְ. עֲשֵׂה לְמַעַן רַחֲמֶיךָ הָרַבִּים. עֲשֵׂה לְמַעַן שְׁכִינָתָךְ. עֲשֵׂה לְמַעַן תְּהִלָּתָךְ. עֲשֵׂה לְמַעַן אוֹהֲבֶיךָ שׁוֹכְנֵי עָפָר. עֲשֵׂה לְמַעַן אַבְרָהָם יִצְחָק וְיַעֲקֹב. עֲשֵׂה לְמַעַן מֹשֶׁה וְאַהֲרֹן. עֲשֵׂה לְמַעַן דָּוִד וּשְׁלֹמֹה. עֲשֵׂה לְמַעַן יְרוּשָׁלַיִם עִיר קָדְשֶׁךָ. עֲשֵׂה לְמַעַן צִיּוֹן מִשְׁכַּן כְּבוֹדֶךָ. עֲשֵׂה לְמַעַן שִׁמְמוֹת הֵיכָלֶךָ. עֲשֵׂה לְמַעַן הֲרִיסוּת מִזְבְּחֶךָ. עֲשֵׂה לְמַעַן הֲרוּגִים עַל שֵׁם קָדְשֶׁךָ. עֲשֵׂה לְמַעַן טְבוּחִים עַל יִחוּדֶךָ. עֲשֵׂה לְמַעַן בָּאֵי בָאֵשׁ וּבַמַּיִם עַל קִדּוּשׁ שְׁמֶךָ. עֲשֵׂה לְמַעַן יוֹנְקֵי שָׁדַיִם שֶׁלֹּא חָטְאוּ. עֲשֵׂה לְמַעַן גְּמוּלֵי חָלָב שֶׁלֹּא פָשְׁעוּ. עֲשֵׂה לְמַעַן תִּינוֹקוֹת שֶׁל בֵּית רַבָּן. עֲשֵׂה לְמַעַנְךָ אִם לֹא לְמַעֲנֵנוּ. עֲשֵׂה לְמַעַנְךָ וְהוֹשִׁיעֵנוּ.

עֲנֵנוּ יהוה עֲנֵנוּ. עֲנֵנוּ אֱלֹהֵינוּ עֲנֵנוּ. עֲנֵנוּ אָבִינוּ עֲנֵנוּ. עֲנֵנוּ בּוֹרְאֵנוּ עֲנֵנוּ. עֲנֵנוּ גּוֹאֲלֵנוּ עֲנֵנוּ. עֲנֵנוּ דּוֹרְשֵׁנוּ עֲנֵנוּ. עֲנֵנוּ הָאֵל הַנֶּאֱמָן עֲנֵנוּ. עֲנֵנוּ וָתִיק וְחָסִיד עֲנֵנוּ. עֲנֵנוּ זַךְ וְיָשָׁר עֲנֵנוּ. עֲנֵנוּ חַי וְקַיָּם עֲנֵנוּ. עֲנֵנוּ טוֹב וּמֵטִיב עֲנֵנוּ. עֲנֵנוּ יוֹדֵעַ יֵצֶר עֲנֵנוּ. עֲנֵנוּ כּוֹבֵשׁ כְּעָסִים עֲנֵנוּ. עֲנֵנוּ לוֹבֵשׁ צְדָקוֹת עֲנֵנוּ. עֲנֵנוּ מֶלֶךְ מַלְכֵי הַמְּלָכִים עֲנֵנוּ. עֲנֵנוּ נוֹרָא וְנִשְׂגָּב עֲנֵנוּ. עֲנֵנוּ סוֹלֵחַ וּמוֹחֵל עֲנֵנוּ. עֲנֵנוּ עוֹנֶה בְּעֵת צָרָה עֲנֵנוּ. עֲנֵנוּ פּוֹדֶה וּמַצִּיל עֲנֵנוּ. עֲנֵנוּ צַדִּיק וְיָשָׁר עֲנֵנוּ. עֲנֵנוּ קָרוֹב לְקוֹרְאָיו עֲנֵנוּ. עֲנֵנוּ רַחוּם וְחַנּוּן עֲנֵנוּ. עֲנֵנוּ שׁוֹמֵעַ אֶל אֶבְיוֹנִים עֲנֵנוּ. עֲנֵנוּ תּוֹמֵךְ תְּמִימִים עֲנֵנוּ. עֲנֵנוּ אֱלֹהֵי אֲבוֹתֵינוּ עֲנֵנוּ. עֲנֵנוּ אֱלֹהֵי אַבְרָהָם עֲנֵנוּ. עֲנֵנוּ פַּחַד יִצְחָק עֲנֵנוּ. עֲנֵנוּ אֲבִיר יַעֲקֹב עֲנֵנוּ. עֲנֵנוּ עֶזְרַת הַשְּׁבָטִים עֲנֵנוּ. עֲנֵנוּ מִשְׂגַּב אִמָּהוֹת עֲנֵנוּ. עֲנֵנוּ קָשֶׁה לִכְעֹס עֲנֵנוּ. עֲנֵנוּ רַךְ לִרְצוֹת עֲנֵנוּ. עֲנֵנוּ עוֹנֶה בְּעֵת רָצוֹן עֲנֵנוּ. עֲנֵנוּ אֲבִי יְתוֹמִים עֲנֵנוּ. עֲנֵנוּ דַּיַּן אַלְמָנוֹת עֲנֵנוּ.

מִי שֶׁעָנָה לְאַבְרָהָם אָבִינוּ בְּהַר הַמּוֹרִיָּה, הוּא יַעֲנֵנוּ.
מִי שֶׁעָנָה לְיִצְחָק בְּנוֹ כְּשֶׁנֶּעֱקַד עַל גַּבֵּי הַמִּזְבֵּחַ, הוּא יַעֲנֵנוּ.
מִי שֶׁעָנָה לְיַעֲקֹב בְּבֵית אֵל, הוּא יַעֲנֵנוּ.
מִי שֶׁעָנָה לְיוֹסֵף בְּבֵית הָאֲסוּרִים, הוּא יַעֲנֵנוּ.
מִי שֶׁעָנָה לַאֲבוֹתֵינוּ עַל יַם סוּף, הוּא יַעֲנֵנוּ.
מִי שֶׁעָנָה לְמֹשֶׁה בְּחוֹרֵב, הוּא יַעֲנֵנוּ.
מִי שֶׁעָנָה לְאַהֲרֹן בַּמַּחְתָּה, הוּא יַעֲנֵנוּ.
מִי שֶׁעָנָה לְפִינְחָס בְּקוּמוֹ מִתּוֹךְ הָעֵדָה, הוּא יַעֲנֵנוּ.
מִי שֶׁעָנָה לִיהוֹשֻׁעַ בַּגִּלְגָּל, הוּא יַעֲנֵנוּ.
מִי שֶׁעָנָה לִשְׁמוּאֵל בַּמִּצְפָּה, הוּא יַעֲנֵנוּ.
מִי שֶׁעָנָה לְדָוִד וּשְׁלֹמֹה בְנוֹ בִּירוּשָׁלָיִם, הוּא יַעֲנֵנוּ.
מִי שֶׁעָנָה לְאֵלִיָּהוּ בְּהַר הַכַּרְמֶל, הוּא יַעֲנֵנוּ.
מִי שֶׁעָנָה לֶאֱלִישָׁע בִּירִיחוֹ, הוּא יַעֲנֵנוּ.
מִי שֶׁעָנָה לְיוֹנָה בִּמְעֵי הַדָּגָה, הוּא יַעֲנֵנוּ.
מִי שֶׁעָנָה לְחִזְקִיָּהוּ מֶלֶךְ יְהוּדָה בְּחָלְיוֹ, הוּא יַעֲנֵנוּ.
מִי שֶׁעָנָה לַחֲנַנְיָה מִישָׁאֵל וַעֲזַרְיָה בְּתוֹךְ כִּבְשַׁן הָאֵשׁ, הוּא יַעֲנֵנוּ.
מִי שֶׁעָנָה לְדָנִיֵּאל בְּגוֹב הָאֲרָיוֹת, הוּא יַעֲנֵנוּ.
מִי שֶׁעָנָה לְמָרְדְּכַי וְאֶסְתֵּר בְּשׁוּשַׁן הַבִּירָה, הוּא יַעֲנֵנוּ.
מִי שֶׁעָנָה לְעֶזְרָא בַּגּוֹלָה, הוּא יַעֲנֵנוּ.
מִי שֶׁעָנָה לְכָל הַצַּדִּיקִים וְהַחֲסִידִים וְהַתְּמִימִים וְהַיְשָׁרִים
הוּא יַעֲנֵנוּ.

רַחֲמָנָא דְּעָנֵי לַעֲנִיֵּי עֲנֵינָן. רַחֲמָנָא דְּעָנֵי לִתְבִירֵי לִבָּא עֲנֵינָן. רַחֲמָנָא דְּעָנֵי לְמַכִּיכֵי רוּחָא עֲנֵינָן. רַחֲמָנָא עֲנֵינָן. רַחֲמָנָא חוּס, רַחֲמָנָא פְּרֹק, רַחֲמָנָא שֵׁיזִב. רַחֲמָנָא רַחֵם עֲלָן, הַשְׁתָּא בַּעֲגָלָא וּבִזְמַן קָרִיב.

Continue with אבינו מלכנו *on page 147.*

[RA]BBIS' KADDISH

Mourner: Yitgadal ve-yitkadash shemeh raba. (*Congregation:* Amen)
Be-alema di vera chir'uteh, ve-yamlich malchuteh,
be-chayyeichon, uv-yomeichon,
uv-chayyei de-chol beit Yisrael,
ba-agala uvi-zman kariv,
ve-imru Amen. (*Congregation:* Amen)

Congregation: Yeheh shemeh raba mevarach le'alam ul-alemei alemaya.
Mourner: Yeheh shemeh raba mevarach le'alam ul-alemei alemaya.

Mourner: Yitbarach ve-yishtabach ve-yitpa'ar ve-yitromam
ve-yitnaseh ve-yit-hadar ve-yit'aleh ve-yit-hallal
shemeh dekudsha, berich hu. (*Congregation:* Berich hu)
Le-ela min kol birchata
/*Between Rosh HaShana & Yom Kippur:*
Le-ela le-ela mi-kol birchata/
ve-shirata, tushbechata ve-nechemata, da-amiran be-alema,
ve-imru, Amen. (*Congregation:* Amen)

Al Yisrael, ve-al rabanan, ve-al talmideihon,
ve-al kol talmidei talmideihon,
ve-al kol man de-asekin be-oraita
di be-atra ha-dein ve-di be-chol atar va-atar,
yeheh lehon ul-chon shelama raba,
china ve-chisda, ve-rachamei, ve-chayyei arichei, um-zonei
re-vichei, u-furkana min kodam avuhon di vish-maya,
ve-imru Amen. (*Congregation:* Amen)

Yeheh shelama raba min shemaya
ve-chayyim (tovim) aleinu ve-al kol Yisrael,
ve-imru Amen. (*Congregation:* Amen)

The mourner takes three steps back before saying this line, bows to the left when saying "May," bows to the right when saying "the One," bows to the middle when saying "make peace for us":

Oseh shalom/*Between Rosh HaShana & Yom Kippur:* ha-shalom/
bim-romav, hu ya'aseh ve-rachamav shalom aleinu,
ve-al kol Yisrael, ve-imru Amen. (*Congregation:* Amen)

YACHAD

קורן ירושלים

OUPRESS

MOURNER'S KADDISH

Mourner: Yitgadal ve-yitkadash shemeh raba. (*Congregation:* Amen)
Be-alema di vera chir'uteh, ve-yamlich malchuteh,
be-chayyeichon, uv-yomeichon,
uv-chayyei de-chol beit Yisrael,
ba-agala uvi-zman kariv,
ve-imru Amen. (*Congregation:* Amen)

Congregation: Yeheh shemeh raba mevarach le'alam ul-alemei alemaya.
Mourner: Yeheh shemeh raba mevarach le'alam ul-alemei alemaya.

Mourner: Yitbarach ve-yishtabach ve-yitpa'ar ve-yitromam ve-yitnaseh ve-yit-hadar ve-yit'aleh ve-yit-hallal
shemeh dekudsha, berich hu. (*Congregation:* Berich hu)
Le-ela min kol birchata
/*Between Rosh HaShana & Yom Kippur:*
Le-ela le-ela mi-kol birchata/
ve-shirata, tushbechata ve-nechemata,
da-amiran be-alema,
ve-imru, Amen. (*Congregation:* Amen)

Yeheh shelama raba min shemaya
ve-chayyim aleinu ve-al kol Yisrael,
ve-imru Amen. (*Congregation:* Amen)

The mourner takes three steps back before saying this line, bows to the left when saying "May," bows to the right when saying "the One," bows to the middle when saying "make peace for us":
Oseh shalom/*Between Rosh HaShana & Yom Kippur:* ha-shalom/
bim-romav, hu ya'aseh shalom aleinu, ve-al kol Yisrael,
ve-imru Amen. (*Congregation:* Amen)